A HISTORY OF THE AMERICAN PEOPLE

VOLUME TWO

SINCE 1865

VOLUME

II

SINCE 1865

NEW YORK: *ALFRED A. KNOPF*

1958

A HISTORY OF THE AMERICAN PEOPLE

BY

HARRY J. CARMAN

Columbia University

AND

HAROLD C. SYRETT

Columbia University

L. C. catalog card number: 52–5073

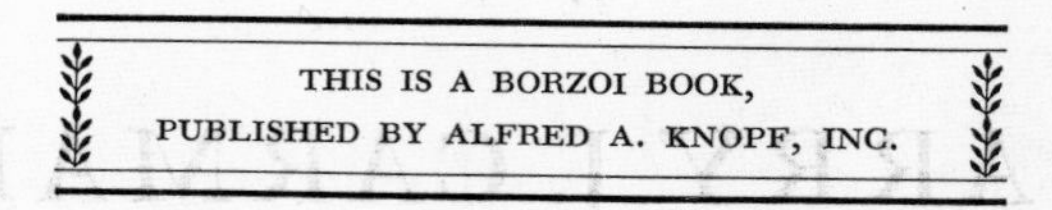

THIS IS A BORZOI BOOK,
PUBLISHED BY ALFRED A. KNOPF, INC.

Published 1952; second printing, 1953; third printing, 1955; fourth printing, 1956; fifth printing, 1957; sixth printing, 1958.

To M.M.C. & P.M.S.

To an Anxious Friend

You tell me that law is above freedom of utterance. And I reply that you can have no wise laws nor free enforcement of wise laws unless there is free expression of the wisdom of the people —and, alas, their folly with it. But if there is freedom, folly will die of its own poison, and the wisdom will survive. That is the history of the race. It is the proof of Man's kinship with God. You say that freedom of utterance is not for time of stress, and I reply with the sad truth that only in time of stress is freedom of utterance in danger. No one questions it in calm days, because it is not needed. And the reverse is true also; only when free utterance is suppressed is it needed and when it is needed, it is most vital to justice. Peace is good. But if you are interested in peace through force and without discussion, that is to say, free utterance decently and in order—your interest in justice is slight. And peace without justice is tyranny, no matter how you may sugar coat it with expediency. This state today is in more danger from suppression than from violence, because, in the end, suppression leads to violence. Violence, indeed, is the child of suppression. Whoever pleads for justice helps to keep the peace; and whoever tramples upon the plea for justice, temperately made in the name of peace, only outrages peace and kills something fine in the heart of man which God put there when we got our manhood. When that is killed, brute meets brute on each side of the line.

So, dear friend, put fear out of your heart. This nation will survive, this state will prosper, the orderly business of life will go forward if only men can speak in whatever way given them to utter what their hearts hold—by voice, by posted card, by letter or by press. Reason never has failed men. Only force and repression have made the wrecks in the world.

William Allen White
Emporia *Gazette*, July 27, 1922

P R E F A C E

J. B. BLACK in *The Art of History* contends that every age interprets "the record of the past in the light of its own ideas." We have preferred to take Black's words as a warning to historians rather than as a definition of written history, for we have made a conscious effort to judge the past in the light of the past and to avoid imposing the standards of our generation upon preceding generations. On the other hand, we have not renounced our right to interpret the past, for we have constantly tried to present the events of American history in meaningful patterns and to point out what we think is the significance of these events.

Our approach to history is eclectic. We do not think that the past should be studied from a single viewpoint or that it can be explained by one theory to the exclusion of all other theories. But, while rejecting any over-all thesis, we have not failed to take a stand on controversial issues. In each instance the nature of the issue has helped to determine our stand; and the fact that we have advanced a succession of different interpretations rather than used the same interpretations for a succession of events accurately reflects our conviction that every historical event is unique.

The organization of these volumes represents a compromise between the chronological and topical approaches to the material under consideration. We have divided American history into a number of comparatively large periods, and within each period we have dealt with a series of major topics. This method necessitates some repetition, but in a book that is designed for students repetition in our view is an asset rather than a defect. In addition, the organization makes it possible for the student at the instructor's discretion to omit certain chapters or sections without destroying the thread of the narrative. In the selection of topics, we have proceeded on the hypothesis that no part or period of American history is inherently more important than any other, and we have therefore sought to present fully the political, diplomatic, intellectual, social, economic, and religious history of the American people.

HARRY J. CARMAN
HAROLD C. SYRETT

ACKNOWLEDGMENTS

A History of the American People is an outgrowth of Professor Carman's *Economic and Social History of the United States.* We have used the earlier work, which covers the period from the first settlements in America to 1876, as a point of departure for our first volume. At some points we have expanded Professor Carman's material, and at others we have cut those portions of it that seemed unsuitable for a general textbook, but in every instance we have subjected it to extensive revisions. In addition, we have supplemented it with a full account of American diplomatic and political history.

Throughout the preparation of these two volumes we received considerable assistance from a number of friends and colleagues. Professors Herman Ausubel, Donald N. Bigelow, Henry F. Graff, and Chilton Williamson of Columbia University, Professors Michael Kraus and Oscar Zeichner of the College of the City of New York, Professor Oscar Handlin of Harvard University, Professors Frank Freidel and Fred A. Shannon of the University of Illinois, Professor James A. Barnes of Temple University, Professor Joe L. Norris of Wayne University, Professor R. J. Ferguson of the University of Pittsburgh, Professor Burke M. Hermann of Pennsylvania State College, and Mr. Thomas R. Hay furnished us with invaluable criticisms and suggestions. Lois Green Clark of Alfred A. Knopf, Inc. read the entire manuscript and showed unusual skill and knowledge in criticizing both its form and content. Mrs. Patricia Syrett typed most of the manuscript, and both Mrs. Syrett and Miss Margaret Carscadden performed a variety of generally unpleasant tasks associated with the work on this book. Both, moreover, treated its authors with remarkable tolerance and patience. Mr. James P. Shenton and Dr. Walter P. Metzger of Columbia University helped us in the preparation of the bibliography. We are also indebted to Professor Bigelow and Mr. Charles E. McCarthy for the assistance they gave us in checking the proof.

We are jointly responsible for whatever errors this book may contain.

Harry J. Carman
Harold C. Syrett

CONTENTS

ILLUSTRATIONS

IN THE TEXT

PLATES

MAPS AND CHARTS

[BY THEODORE R. MILLER]

A HISTORY OF THE AMERICAN PEOPLE

VOLUME TWO

SINCE 1865

CHAPTER I

THE LEGACY OF CIVIL WAR

THE CIVIL WAR, which was fought to preserve the Union, helped to undermine the economic and social foundations on which the antebellum Union had rested. After the war the South was reduced to the status of a conquered province and the North was transformed by a revolution that subordinated the farm to the factory and supplanted the standards of an agrarian society with the mores of an industrial civilization. By 1877, when the last Northern troops were withdrawn from the defeated South, it was clear that the North had won more than a military victory. Although farmers still comprised the single largest element in the population, the United States had—for good or ill—become an industrial nation.

1. THE VICTORIOUS NORTH

IN THE years immediately following the Civil War the North entered a period of unprecedented prosperity. Profits reached record levels, wages were higher than at any previous time in the nation's history, and farmers had little difficulty in disposing of their products at favorable prices. Turning their backs on the reforms that they had espoused before the war, Northerners plunged wholeheartedly into the more prosaic—but equally serious—business of making money. Few doubted that the end justified the means, and most agreed that the end was the accumulation of wealth.

The postwar boom was sustained by the rapid development of Northern industry. A friendly government, an expanding domestic market, and a seemingly limitless supply of natural resources combined to produce a spectacular growth in all forms of business activity. Capitalists who had accumulated wartime profits invested their surplus funds in new and old enterprises, and Europeans poured money into the American economy. The government, which before the war had devoted its energies to promoting the interests of the farmers, now aided industrialists by raising tariffs, encouraging the immigration of cheap labor, depriving Southern agrarians of a voice in national affairs, and turning over to private corporations extensive tracts of the public domain. Entrepreneurs were quick to take advantage of these opportunities, and for almost a decade after Appomattox the North steadily enlarged its manufacturing facilities, extended and improved its transportation system, and exploited its mineral resources.

Almost every branch of American industry grew with amazing rapidity during the war and postwar years. From 1860 to 1870 the number of factories in the United States increased by 80 per cent, railroad lines increased by 22,000 miles, oil refining developed into a major industry, and the United States became one of the world's leading producers of iron and steel. Comparable advances were made in the consumer goods industries. The output of shoes, for example, rose from 5,000,000 pairs in 1864 to 25,000,000 in 1870; the number of woolen mills increased from 1,559 in 1850 to 2,891 in 1870, the number of workers employed in the mills from 39,352 to 80,053, and the number of pounds of wool turned into cloth from 70,900,000 to 172,100,000. In many fields of manufacturing, moreover, there was a marked increase in the tempo of mechanization, in the subdivision of labor, in mass production, in industrial consolidation, and in the use of high pressure salesmanship to reach a national rather than local market.

The postwar boom presented speculators and freebooters with unexampled opportunities for quick profits. The inexperience of a large part of the investing public and the absence of restrictive regulations made it comparatively easy for economic adventurers to water stock, turn security exchanges into gambling casinos, and sell stock in any one of a variety of bogus enterprises. In an age that was perhaps the most corrupt in the nation's history, Daniel Drew, Jay Gould, and Jim Fisk earned well-merited reputations as practitioners of the art of fraudulent manipulation. One of their most notorious exploits was the "Erie War" waged against Cornelius Vanderbilt in 1867. When Vanderbilt, who was head of the New York Central, attempted to obtain control of the Erie from Drew, Gould and Fisk, they prevented him from securing a majority of the stock and crippled him financially at the same time by issuing $10,000,000 of worthless Erie securities which they dumped on the market at just the moment when Vanderbilt's heavy purchases had pushed the price to record levels. In the legal quarrels that followed, Gould and Fisk more than matched the bribes that Vanderbilt had paid to both judges and legislators. In the summer of 1868 they issued still more Erie stock, sold it to a gullible public, and put their profits in New York City's leading national banks. Because the National Banking Act of 1863 required every national bank in New York to maintain a reserve in greenbacks or other legal tender equal to 25 per cent of its indebtedness, Drew, Gould and Fisk were able to disrupt the money market by demanding that the banks repay them in greenbacks. To meet this demand the banks had to call in their loans, and the resulting money stringency produced a decline in both trade and security prices. The Erie triumvirate immediately capitalized on this situation by buying up large blocks of securities at a fraction of their former value. As gold had also fallen in price, they purchased it at bargain rates and pushed up its price to record figures by withdrawing it from the market. In the fall of 1869, after inducing President Grant to refrain from any move that might lower the price of gold, Gould and Fisk again cornered the country's gold supply. On September 24, 1869—or "Black Friday"—gold, which had been quoted at 132* on September 2, had reached 160; and the country was saved from financial ruin only after Grant had belatedly authorized the government to place $4,000,000 in gold on the market.

Drew, Gould, and Fisk were the most notorious—but not the only—examples of business corruption in the postwar decade. In an age in which misrepresentation was often synonymous with "good business," a premium was placed on results regardless of how they were achieved. Convinced that there was no greater crime than to die poor, many businessmen felt that they were forced by circumstances to be ruthless, predatory, and dishonest. Ethically it is difficult to distinguish between a railroad-wrecker like Daniel Drew and a professional desperado like Jesse James, and perhaps all that is left for the social historian to record is that the first died in his bed and that the second was killed by a bullet in the back of his head.

The corrupt practices of some of the nation's businessmen were matched by the fraudulent activities of numerous officials in the local, state and Federal governments. The success of many of the business

* This figure represents the price of gold in relation to greenbacks.

ventures undertaken in this period depended in part on some form of governmental assistance, and the politicians soon made it clear that they expected to be reimbursed for any aid that they provided. As a consequence, judicial decisions more than once went to the highest bidder, and legislators at every level of government were paid for subsidies, utility franchises, contracts for public works, monopolistic grants, and the assurance that the authorities would neither investigate nor regulate certain business practices. Because the politician had favors to sell and the entrepreneur had the money to purchase them, bribery became an accepted way of doing business. In Mark Twain's and Charles Dudley Warner's *The Gilded Age* (1873), one of the characters tells how to obtain a congressional appropriation for a "public improvement" company—a description that provides some indication (even after adequate allowance has been made for the satirist's right to exaggerate) of the techniques of political corruption.

Why the matter is simple enough. A Congressional appropriation costs money. Just reflect, for instance. A majority of the House committee, say $10,000 apiece—$40,000; a majority of the Senate committee, the same each—say $40,000; a little extra to one or two chairmen of one or two such committees, say $10,000 each—$20,000; and there's $100,000 of the money gone, to begin with. Then, seven male lobbyists, at $3,000 each—$21,000; one female lobbyist, $10,000; a high moral Congressman or Senator here and there—the high moral ones cost more . . . ten of these at $3,000 each, is $30,000; then a lot of small-fry country members, who won't vote for anything whatever without pay—say twenty at $500 apiece is $10,000; a lot of dinners to members—say $10,000 altogether; lot of jimcracks for Congressmen's wives and children—those go a long way—you can't spend too much . . . in that line—those . . . cost in a lump, say $10,000—along there somewhere;—and then comes your printed documents—your maps, your tinted engravings, your pamphlets, your illuminated show-cards, your advertisements in a hundred and fifty papers at ever so much a line—because you've got to keep the papers all right or you are gone up, you know. Oh, my dear sir, printing bills are destruction itself. Ours so far amount to—let me see—10; 52; 22; 13;—and then there's 11; 14; 33—well, never mind the details, the total in clean numbers foots up $118,254.42 thus far!

Although every major American city was looted by designing politicians during the postwar years, New York City enjoyed the dubious distinction of being the most corruptly governed municipality in the nation. A Tammany "ring," headed by William Marcy Tweed, a former chair-maker and volunteer fireman, robbed the city of millions of dollars annually. Under the direction of Boss Tweed, Mayor A. Oakey Hall, Peter B. Sweeny and "Slippery Dick" Connolly, New York increased its debt tenfold within a decade. A county courthouse, worth approximately $25,000, cost the taxpayers $8,000,000, and the building's furnishings added another $3,000,000 to the total. Paving contracts, public printing, sewers, parks, and hospitals all provided profits for members of the ring, which by 1871 had stolen more than $20,000,000. Tweed, who boasted that he would soon be as rich as Vanderbilt, moved to a large mansion on Fifth Avenue, kept his blooded horses in mahogany stables, and replied to his critics by asking: "What are you going to do about it?" And for a time it seemed as though nothing could be done. With the support of his henchmen in the state legislature and a subservient governor, he secured a revision of the city charter that placed New York completely at his mercy. At the same time a committee of prominent citizens, after investigating the city's finances, announced that they could discover no irregularities. Although Thomas Nast had waged a merciless campaign against Tweed in his cartoons in *Harper's,* it was not until an attempt was made to bribe both the *Times* and *Harper's* that public opinion turned against the boss. The chance installation of one of Tweed's enemies in the city comptroller's office led to a split in Tammany, a series of revelations, and the eventual prosecution of the machine leaders. Tweed, who was convicted of stealing $6,000,000, escaped to Spain; but he was subsequently extradited and returned to jail, where he died in 1878.

State governments were as corrupt as those of the nation's cities. Most New York state legislators—whether they were merchants, lawyers, up-state farmers or members of Tammany Hall—had their price; and at the height of the Erie War, one New York senator accepted $75,000 from Vanderbilt and $100,000 from Gould, and then voted for Gould. At Harrisburg, the capital of Pennsylvania, Simon Cameron and Matthew S. Quay saw to it that almost no bill of importance could be put through unpurchased. For years the Illinois legislature was run by the state's corporations, contractors, and land speculators. In Wisconsin a powerful railway lobby crushed unfriendly measures, while in Kansas, Missouri, and a number of other Western states the giving and taking of bribes was an accepted part of the legislative process.

Because the Federal government could offer businessmen particularly favorable prizes, its members were able to make enormous sums of money from graft and bribery. Politics was converted into a business, and, like any good businessman, the politician sold his wares and services to the highest bidder. Vernon L. Parrington, in describing what he called "the great barbecue," has written:

*Congress had rich gifts to bestow—in lands, tariffs, subsidies, favors of all sorts; and when influential citizens made their wishes known to the reigning statesmen, the sympathetic politicians were quick to turn the government into the fairy godmother the voters wanted it to be. A huge barbecue was spread to which all presumably were invited. Not quite all, to be sure; inconspicuous persons, those who were at home on the farm or at work in the mills and offices, were overlooked; a good many indeed out of the total number of the American people. But all the important persons, leading bankers and promoters and business men, received invitations. There wasn't room for everybody and these were presumed to represent the whole. It was a splendid feast. If the waiters saw to it that the choicest portions were served to favored guests, they were not unmindful of their numerous homespun constituency and they loudly proclaimed the fine democratic principle that what belongs to the people should be enjoyed by the people—not with petty bureaucratic restrictions, not as a social body, but as individuals, each free citizen using what came to hand for his own private ends, with no questions asked.**

In aiding the businessman, the government also accelerated the postwar cycle of boom and bust. By the end of the 1860's there was ample evidence of overexpansion in many areas of Northern business enterprise. The number of business firms in the United States jumped from 431,000 in 1870 to 609,904 in 1871. The annual increase in railroad mileage, which averaged about 1,300 miles in 1860–7, rose to about 5,000 in 1869, and to about 5,700 in 1870; and during the next two years 13,000 miles were built. But of 364 railroads in 1872, only 104 paid dividends, and 69 of these paid less than 10 per cent. At the same time American exports lagged behind imports, and in the early seventies the United States had to export $130,000,000 annually to cover its trade deficit and interest payments on the capital it had borrowed abroad. In addition, the nation's credit structure was top heavy, for in the period from 1868 to 1873 the volume of bank loans increased seven times as fast as bank deposits. Finally—and perhaps most dangerous—were the movements of capital from productive to speculative enterprises and the rise in the number of business failures from 2,915 in 1871 to 4,069 in 1872.

The crash came in 1873. On September 8, the New York Warehouse and Securities Company failed, to be followed within two weeks by Kenyon, Cox and Company and Jay Cooke and Company. On Septem-

* Vernon L. Parrington: *Main Currents in American Thought,* Vol. III, *The Beginnings of Critical Realism, 1860–1920* (New York: Harcourt, Brace & Company, Inc., 1930), p. 23. Copyright 1930 by, and reprinted with permission of, Harcourt, Brace & Company, Inc.

ber 20, the New York Stock Exchange closed for ten days "to save the entire Street from utter ruin"; but nothing could prevent the cumulative effect of the collapse. By the end of 1873 there had been more than 5,000 commercial failures with liabilities totaling $228,500,000, and 89 railroads had defaulted on their bonds. For the next five years there was little prospect of returning prosperity. In 1876–7, more than 18,000 business firms failed, at least half the nation's mills and factories closed, and unemployment steadily increased. It was not until 1878 that any signs of a business revival appeared, and it was not until 1880 that full recovery had been achieved.

2. THE DEFEATED SOUTH

AT THE end of the Civil War the South was bitter and exhausted. In five years the section's white population had declined from almost 5,500,000 to fewer than 5,000,000, and more than 250,000 Confederate soldiers had been killed during the war. To those who survived the present seemed intolerable and the future hopeless, for the war had destroyed not only a large part of the South's physical assets but also its way of life. With the Northern victory the Southerners were left with little to cherish but their memories.

Few parts of the South had escaped the effects of the war. From Harpers Ferry to Newmarket, Virginia—a distance of about eighty miles—barns, mills, haystacks, and houses had been burned to the ground. Livestock, fences, and bridges had been destroyed. The region between Washington and Richmond was a wasteland of gutted villages and farm buildings. In Georgia and the Carolinas, Sherman's army had left a path of destruction that was "heart-sickening," while large parts of Arkansas and northern Alabama presented scenes of appalling ruin. The valley of the Tennessee was so devastated that six years after the war Robert Somers, an English traveler, reported that

> *it consists for the most part of plantations in a state of semi-ruin, and plantations of which the ruin is for the present total and complete. . . . The trail of war is visible throughout the valley in burnt-up gin-houses, ruined bridges, mills and factories . . . and in large tracts of once cultivated land stripped of every vestige of fencing. The roads, long neglected, are in disorder, and having in many places become impassable, new tracks have been made through the woods and fields without much respect to boundaries.*

The towns and cities of the South were almost as desolate as the countryside. Richmond, largely destroyed by fire when it was evacuated by the Confederate troops, was a mass of charred ruins. In Columbia,

South Carolina, an area of eighty blocks containing 1,386 buildings had been converted into a dreary stretch of blackened chimneys and crumbling walls. Charleston, which had suffered from repeated bombardments and two disastrous fires, was described by a Northern visitor as a city "of ruins, of desolation, of vacant houses, of widowed women, of rotting wharves, of deserted warehouses, of weed-wild gardens, of miles of grass-grown streets, of acres of pitiful and voiceless barrenness." Masses of fire-smoked brick and mortar, burned timber, twisted scraps of tin roofing, and thousands of tons of débris were evidence that Sherman had passed through Atlanta. "Hell has laid her egg," said a Georgian viewing Atlanta, "and right here it hatched." In Mobile, nine blocks had been destroyed by an explosion; a large part of the wharves had been torn up and used for firewood; half the warehouses and shops were closed; and an atmosphere of decay enveloped the narrow, dirty streets in which wretched men loafed dispiritedly. Galveston, according to a reporter, was "a city of dogs and desolation . . . utterly insignificant and Godforsaken." Even in New Orleans, where there was little physical damage, the spirit of the people seemed broken, and business was virtually at a standstill.

The South was not only devastated, but its people were poverty-stricken. Their capital had disappeared in a sea of worthless Confederate stocks, bonds, and currency. Their banks and insurance companies were bankrupt. Their property in slaves, estimated at almost two billion dollars, had been wiped out by the Thirteenth Amendment to the Constitution. Farmers and planters lacked tools, stock, seeds, and money. Land values were incredibly low, and many plantations were heavily mortgaged. Mills, factories, and mines that had not been destroyed were closed. All coin had disappeared long before 1865, and stocks of merchandise were practically exhausted. Whitelaw Reid, a New York journalist who visited the South just after the war, wrote:

> *Everything has been mended, and generally in the rudest style. Window-glass has given way to thin boards in railway coaches and in the cities. Furniture is marred and broken, and none has been replaced for four years. Dishes are cemented in various styles and half the pitchers have tin handles. A complete set of crockery is never seen, and in very few families is there enough to set a table. . . . A set of forks with whole tines is a curiosity. Clocks and watches have nearly all stopped. . . . Hair brushes and tooth brushes have all worn out; combs are broken. . . . Pins, needles and thread, and a thousand such articles, which seem indispensable to housekeeping, are very scarce. Even in weaving on the looms, corn-cobs have been substituted for spindles. Few have pocket knives. In fact everything that has heretofore been an article of sale at the*

South is wanting now. At the tables of those who were once esteemed luxurious providers you will find neither tea, coffee, sugar, nor spices of any kind. Even candles, in some cases, have been replaced by a cup of grease in which a piece of cloth is plunged for a wick.

The South's economic problems were aggravated by the almost complete lack of transportation facilities. Horses, mules, wagons, and carriages were scarce; country roads had become practically impassable through neglect; and bridges that had not been burned or washed away were in need of repair. Most of the river steamboats had been captured or destroyed, while the few that were intact were worn out. With the exception of the railroads that had been used by the Federal government, Southern rail facilities were either destroyed or useless. Two thirds of the railroad companies in the section were bankrupt. Virtually all the Virginia lines were out of commission. Every mile of railway in Georgia and South Carolina that could be used by the Confederacy had been destroyed by Sherman. Alabama's eight hundred miles of railway were practically worthless, and the New Orleans, Jackson, and Great Northern—Mississippi's leading railroad before the war—was a scrapheap.

Southern commercial life was disrupted not only by the effects of the war but also by the breakdown of civil authority. With the defeat of the Confederate armies, the region's central, state, and local governments collapsed, and for some time there was little or no check placed on the more unruly elements in the population. Guerrilla and outlaw bands terrorized many parts of the South. In Texas alone more than five thousand men secured their livelihood by organized robbery and murder. Almost every neighborhood north of the Arkansas was pillaged by guerrillas, and in Alabama and Mississippi highwaymen made it practically impossible to carry on trade between towns.

Southern economic recovery was also impeded by the activities of Federal treasury agents who were paid a commission of approximately 25 per cent to discover and confiscate Confederate army stores. Left largely to their own devices, many of these agents seized and sold private property to which they had no legal claim. Horses, mules, wagons, tobacco, rice, sugar, and cotton were frequently taken in spite of the protests of their rightful owners. "I am sure I sent some honest cotton agents South," Secretary of the Treasury McCulloch wrote, "but it seems doubtful whether any of them remained honest very long." In his special report of 1866, McCulloch stated:

Contractors anxious for gain, were sometimes guilty of bad faith and peculation, and frequently took possession of cotton and delivered it under contracts as captured or abandoned, when in

> *fact it was not such, and they had no right to touch it. . . . Residents and others in the districts where these peculations were going on took advantage of the unsettled conditions of the country, and representing themselves as agents of this department, went about robbing under such pretended authority, and thus added to the difficulties of the situation by causing unjust opprobrium and suspicion to rest upon officers engaged in the faithful discharge of their duties. Agents . . . frequently received or collected property . . . which the law did not authorize them to take. . . . Lawless men, singly and in organized bands, engaged in general plunder; every species of intrigue and peculation and theft were resorted to.*

While these agents turned over about $34,000,000 to the United States, it is impossible even to guess how much money they kept for themselves. In subsequent years, 40,000 Southern claimants were indemnified for property that had been taken from them illegally. Many thousands of others, unable to prove that they had been defrauded, received nothing.

At the same time that the South was seeking to solve its economic problems, it was also forced to work out a new set of relationships between the region's white groups and the 3,500,000 newly-liberated Negroes. While some Negroes from the outset realized that freedom entailed responsibilities as well as privileges, the majority were at first too bewildered to appreciate the meaning of their new status. To some, freedom meant a change of name, a new job, and the right to go wherever they pleased. Many freedmen became migrants; some supported themselves by thievery; and still others died from hunger. Many, too, thought that freedom meant education, an opportunity to become the equals of the whites, and a gift from the government of "forty acres and a mule." A relatively large number of Negroes remained with their former masters until their rôle as freedmen had been clarified. Although freedom meant many different things to the Negroes, the white Southerners were almost unanimous in their agreement that it should not mean equality of the races.

The South was compelled to embark upon this critical period of readjustment without the political services of its former leaders, for the Federal government barred most members of the planter class from politics in the years following Appomattox. This policy, regardless of its merits, further antagonized a people who were already embittered by war and defeat. At the same time a large part of the control over Southern political affairs passed into the hands of Northern military and civilian officials. For the white Southerners the hatred engendered by the war was compounded by its aftermath, and in 1866 a Virginian patrician, in drawing up his will, wrote:

I have made several wills before when I had considerable property to give to my wife and children, but since the Yankees have stolen all my Negroes and robbed me of a great deal of my other personal property, pillaging my house, breaking open all the doors, and stealing all the clothing they wanted, I have very little to will. They stole a gold watch from me worth about three hundred dollars, which was a bridal present from me to my wife, when we were married half a century ago. They threatened to shoot me if I did not deliver the watch to them, and burn down my dwelling house, presenting their pistol at me frequently, and I, an old man of seventy-six that was too old and feeble to defend myself. I now, therefore, make this my last will and testament, in a manner and form following, viz: 1st, I give and bequeath to my children and grandchildren, and their descendants throughout all generations, that bitter hatred and everlasting malignity of my heart and soul against the Yankees, including all the people north of Mason and Dixon's line, and I do hereby exhort and entreat my children and grandchildren, if they have any love or veneration for me, to instill in the hearts of their children and grandchildren, and all their future descendants, from their childhood, this bitter hatred and these malignant feelings, against the aforesaid people and their descendants throughout all future time and generations.

To some Southerners, defeat and the prospect of Northern domination were so distasteful that they preferred emigration to remaining in the South. Scores of families left for France, England, and Latin America, while others moved to Northern cities. But most Southern leaders—including Robert E. Lee, Wade Hampton, and Jefferson Davis—felt that the South's difficulties were the very reason why its people should not abandon their homeland. Hampton urged his fellow citizens to "devote their whole energies to the restoration of law and order, the reestablishment of agriculture and commerce, the promotion of education and the rebuilding of our cities and dwellings which have been laid in ashes." And Lee, in arguing against emigration, maintained that all should "share in the fate of their respective states."

The thought of abandoning the country and all that must be left in it [he said] *is abhorrent to my feelings. . . . The South requires the aid of her sons now more than at any other period of her history. . . . All should unite in honest efforts to obliterate the effects of war, and to restore the blessings of peace. They should remain if possible in the country; promote harmony and good feeling; qualify themselves to vote; and elect to the state and general legislatures wise and patriotic men, who will devote their abilities to the interests of the country and the healing of all dissensions.*

For the mass of Southerners who remained in their section the most pressing problem was economic rehabilitation. Half a million farms and plantations, many of them bankrupt or on the verge of insolvency, had to be restored; gutted homes and a ruined transportation system had to be rebuilt; credit had to be re-established; and perhaps most important of all, some substitute had to be found for slave labor. Neither the whites nor the Negroes had had much experience with the wage system, and after the war a number of factors militated against its use. Because most farmers were penniless, they were unable to pay their hired help until they had marketed their crops. Moreover, many Southern whites were opposed on both social and economic grounds to employing free Negroes. Throughout these years, plans for transporting the freedmen to Africa or the West Indies and importing foreign white labor were seriously discussed in many parts of the South. But an impoverished South could offer few inducements to immigrants from the Old World, and few newcomers settled below Mason and Dixon's line. On the other hand, the Negro, who was reluctant to give up any part of his new freedom and was suspicious of white employers, showed no enthusiasm for hiring-out.

The wage system was tried in some parts of the rural South after the war, but in most instances it proved unworkable. The paralysis of Southern banking and the scarcity of money prevented all but a small number of planters and farmers from hiring help. Moreover, the Negroes generally objected to the terms on which they were employed. Frequently, they complained of low wages, and on numerous occasions —and often with much justification—they insisted that they were being cheated. As most freedmen soon refused to work for wages under these circumstances, Southern landowners increasingly turned to the share, or cropping, system. Under this arrangement, the planter provided the croppers with land, seed, draft animals, and implements and arranged credit facilities for them at the local store. The croppers, in turn, agreed to plant, cultivate, and harvest the crop in return for a portion of it that usually ranged from one third to one half. The store, which was owned by either the planter or a local merchant, provided the tenant with credit in return for a mortgage on his share in the season's crop. Although the so-called crop-lien system provided the agrarian South with much needed credit facilities, it was also largely responsible for the section's concentration on cotton—a cash crop—to the exclusion of most other products, the perpetuation of backward methods of farming in the region, and the creation of a class of virtual peons—both Negro and white—in the rural areas of the South.

The hard times following the war were responsible not only for the growth of share cropping and the crop-lien system but also for the break-up of most of the section's large plantations. Many planters were forced to dispose of their lands at a fraction of their prewar value, and the newspapers were filled with advertisements of plantations for sale at a "sacrifice." In 1865 it was possible to buy good land anywhere in the South at from three to five dollars an acre—or at a price that represented one fifth to one sixth of its value in 1860. With cotton prices high, poor men from all parts of the South took advantage of the unprecedented opportunity to acquire land.

> *Never perhaps* [wrote a Georgia editor] *was there a rural movement accomplished without revolution or exodus, that equalled in extent and swiftness the partition of the plantations of the ex-slaveholders into small farms. As remarkable as was the eagerness of the Negroes—who bought in Georgia alone 6,850 farms in three years—the earth-hunger of the poorer class of the whites, who had been unable under the slaveholding oligarchy to own land, was even more striking.*

Northerners also invested heavily in Southern land. A group of Ohioans, believing that they could revolutionize cotton production by introducing scientific methods of cultivation, settled in Noxubee and Lowndes counties, Mississippi; Whitelaw Reid moved to Louisiana; Colonel Henry Lee Higginson and others bought up large tracts of plantation land in Georgia; and John Hay put a considerable sum of money in Florida orange groves.

The break-up of the antebellum plantations transformed much of the South into a land of small farms. Tennessee, which in 1860 had only 82,368 farms, had 118,141 in 1870. In South Carolina the number increased from 33,000 to 52,000; in Mississippi from 43,000 to 68,000; and in Louisiana from 17,000 to 28,000. At the same time there was a corresponding decrease in the size of most Southern farms. The area of the average Louisiana farm decreased from 536 acres in 1860 to 247 acres ten years later; and even in North Carolina, which before the Civil War had had more small farms than most Southern states, the average farm fell from 316 acres to 212.

By 1875, Southern agriculture, although still relatively backward, had almost regained its prewar footing. Thousands of yeomen, who before the war had been forced out of the piedmont, had returned to the lowlands and acquired small holdings. Across the Mississippi pioneer farmers opened up extensive new cotton lands in Arkansas and Texas. From 1865 to 1875 the area under cotton cultivation averaged 8,810,000 acres annually. With the exception of 1866 and 1867, when the South suffered from severe droughts, yields rose steadily and good prices prevailed. By 1878 the crop equaled that of 1860. Not only were many farmers making money for the first time since the war, but the South was gradually lightening its heavy debt burden.

The reorganization of Southern agriculture was accompanied by fundamental changes in the section's mercantile system. Before the war the large planters had bought their supplies at wholesale rates in Mobile, Charleston, Richmond, New York, and other urban centers. In the postwar years the Southern farmer—both Negro and white—made his purchases at the village or crossroads store, which in turn obtained its goods from Northern merchants. In similar fashion, the individual farmer, instead of consigning his crop directly to commission jobbers as was the common practice before the war, sold it to a local dealer. As the character of the Southern economy altered, both towns and townspeople assumed a position of unprecedented importance in the South's economy. Many planters, who during the antebellum period had devoted their major efforts to the management of their plantations, turned to business enterprise. "The higher planting class," P. A. Bruce has written, "so far as it has survived at all, has been concentrated in the cities. . . . The talent, the energy, the ambition, that formerly sought expression in the management of great estates and the control of hosts of slaves, now seeks a field of action in trade, manufacturing enterprises; or in the general enterprises of development." While the South remained overwhelmingly agrarian, both the mores and economy of the section were increasingly shaped by a rising middle class—an influence that indicated that the North had won more than a military victory at Appomattox.

3. LINCOLN AND THE RADICALS

DURING the postwar years almost every aspect of Southern life was either directly or indirectly affected by the Reconstruction policies of the Federal government. The course of Reconstruction, in turn, was in large part determined by the outcome of the struggle between two Republican factions—Conservative and Radical—for the control of the nation's government. The Conservatives, who were led by Lincoln and probably composed the bulk of the party during the war, urged that the bitterness of the past be forgotten, that the Southern states be restored to their antebellum status as rapidly as possible, and that following the abolition of slavery no further moves be made to alter the social and economic structure of the South.

The Radicals were drawn from a number of diverse groups within the Republican party. Abolitionists, who had opposed slavery long before the war, demanded that the freedmen be granted political, social, and economic equality. The abolitionists, who distrusted both the Southern whites and the Northern Conservatives, had a powerful ally in the growing industrial class. For the preceding half-century, businessmen who had espoused the economic ideas of Hamilton, Clay, and Webster had been repeatedly outvoted by the nation's agrarians. But, when a large part of the opposition went down to ruin with the Confederacy, the way was clear for the industrialists to push their long-delayed schemes for transcontinental railroads, large-scale manufactures, high tariffs, and the exploitation of the nation's natural resources. Under the circumstances they had every reason to desire that the Republican party—champion of free homesteads, unrestricted immigration, internal improvements, protective tariffs, shipping subsidies, and a national banking system—retain its control over the national government. Finally, Republican politicians realized that by giving the Negro the vote and by withholding it from large numbers of white Southerners they could ensure the success of their party in the states of the former Confederacy. From these various elements within the Republican party came the Radicals who found a basis for co-operation in their common anxiety to break the power of the old white ruling class in the South.

During the postwar years the leading Radicals were Charles Sumner of Massachusetts, Thaddeus Stevens of Pennsylvania, Benjamin Butler of Massachusetts, Benjamin F. Wade of Ohio, Zachariah Chandler of Michigan, G. W. Julian of Indiana, Henry Wilson of Massachusetts, Richard Yates of Illinois, and James M. Ashley of Ohio. Of these, Stevens was pre-eminent in the House, while Sumner was perhaps the outstanding Radical in the Senate. Stevens, born in New England, spent most of his life practicing law in Pennsylvania. He had been a member of the Anti-Masonic party, a champion of free public schools, an abolitionist, and a member of the House of Representatives. From the end of the Civil War until his death in 1868, Stevens repeatedly demanded that the Southerners be deprived of their political rights, that they be compelled to pay the cost of the war, that their property be confiscated, and that the head of each Negro family in the South be given forty acres of land. Sumner was a Boston aristocrat and an intellectual who had opposed slavery all his life. A lawyer, scholar, politician, and reformer, he was one of the ablest opponents of Lincoln's and Johnson's lenient Reconstruction program. In Sumner's view the seceded states occupied the same status as territories, and the prerequisite for any Reconstruction plan had to be Negro suffrage. To their enemies, Stevens and Sumner were fanatics; to their supporters they were selfless crusaders. Both groups were right.

Both the Conservatives and the Radicals sought to re-enforce their respective positions with constitutional arguments. During the war, Northern officials had maintained that, since secession was illegal, the South in a constitutional sense had not withdrawn from the Union. It followed inevitably that there could be no question about readmitting the Southern states to a Union that they had never left. The problem, then, was to restore to the citizens of the South the rights which they had temporarily renounced but to which they were still entitled. While adopting this line of reasoning, the Conservatives did not think that constitutional questions should be emphasized at the expense of what they felt were practical considerations. On April 11, 1865, Lincoln spoke for many other Conservatives when he said:

> *We all agree that the seceded states, so-called, are out of their proper practical relation with the Union; and that the sole object of the government, civil and military, in regard to those States is to again get them into that proper practical relation. I believe it is not only possible, but in fact, easier to do this, without deciding, or even considering, whether these States have ever been out of the Union, than with it. Finding themselves safely at home, it would be utterly immaterial whether they had ever been abroad. Let us all join in doing the acts necessary to restoring the proper practical relations between these States and the Union; and each forever after, innocently indulge his own opinion whether, in doing the acts, he brought the States from without, into the Union, or only gave them proper assistance, they never having been out of it.*

In opposing the Conservative position, the Radicals, who formerly had argued that the Union was indissoluble, were compelled to take over the original Southern view of secession and maintain that the states of the Confederacy had actually withdrawn from the Union. By insisting that secession was a fact rather than an untenable constitutional theory, the Radicals could conclude that the inhabitants of the seceded states had forfeited the rights and privileges guaranteed by the Constitution. This interpretation of secession left the defeated South completely at the mercy of the victorious North. The inconsistency of the Radicals was matched by that of the Southerners. Having maintained during the war that their states were irrevocably out of the Union, they proceeded to ask at the end of the war that they be treated as though they had never left the Union.

In their conflicts with the Conservatives the Radicals were at first at a marked disadvantage, for Lincoln, as a wartime president, was able to put some Conservative policies into effect even before the final defeat of the Confederacy. Lincoln's program, which was known as the ten per cent plan, was first presented to the American people in December, 1863. According to its provisions, participation in the reconstructed state governments in the South was to be denied to military officers above the rank of colonel, naval officers above the rank of lieutenant, all civil diplomatic officers of the Confederacy, state governors, and all those who had left the United States army, navy, Congress, and judiciary to aid the rebellion. On the other hand, full pardon as well as restoration of property would be granted to any other Confederates who would take an oath to uphold the Constitution and comply with all executive proclamations and acts of Congress concerning slavery. In any state as soon as ten per cent of the population that had voted in 1860 had taken the oath, they could proceed to organize a new government loyal to the United States.

Even before the announcement of his ten per cent plan, Lincoln had taken steps to facilitate the reestablishment of Union governments in those Southern states that were controlled at least in part by Northern troops. In 1862 he had placed Tennessee, North Carolina, and Louisiana under the supervision of provisional military governors, and by 1864 Tennessee, Louisiana, and Arkansas had organized governments in accordance with the terms of the ten per cent plan. In addition, Lincoln recognized the loyal government that had been formed by the Unionists of western Virginia.

Although Lincoln had the authority to set up new governments in the Southern states, no state could be restored to the Union without congressional approval. Congress could not only refuse to recognize the validity of the Lincoln governments, but it also had the right to prevent the senators or representatives of any state from being seated. It was through Congress, therefore, that the Radicals sought to block the President's Reconstruction program. In opposing Lincoln's plan, the Radicals in Congress accurately reflected the widespread feeling in the North that the Southerners should be punished for both secession and the war. The Radicals also obtained considerable support from several moderate congressmen who felt that the President, in assuming the initiative in restoring the states of the South to the Union, had encroached on the province of the legislative branch of the government.

The Radicals made no attempt to conceal their hostility to the President's program. Largely because of Radical opposition, Congress refused to recognize the Lincoln governments; the representatives from the reorganized states were not seated; the Union—or Republican—platform of 1864 contained a plank calling for congressional control of Reconstruction; and the electoral votes of the states with Lincoln governments were not counted in the election of 1864. Most important of all, the Radicals spelled out their own Reconstruction plan in the Wade-Davis Bill, which was adopted by Congress in July, 1864. This measure, which was based explicitly upon the premise that the seceded states had actually left the Union, put readmission entirely in the hands of Congress and made complete subjugation the first prerequisite to reinstatement. As soon as the military conquest of a state had been completed, a census was to be taken of all adult white males. When a majority of these had taken the oath of allegiance, they would be permitted to elect delegates to a state constitutional convention. To secure a state's readmission into the Union, its convention had to abolish slavery, repudiate the debts of the Confederate state government, and disfranchise practically all citizens who had held high civilian and military offices under the Confederacy. When Lincoln prevented the adoption of this bill by a pocket veto, the Radicals replied with the Wade-Davis Manifesto warning the President to confine himself to his executive duties and to leave the problem of political reconstruction to Congress.

The Wade-Davis Bill and the manifesto that followed it revealed that there was a strong faction in each house of Congress that opposed both presidential control over Reconstruction and a lenient policy toward the defeated South. Although the exigencies of the military conflict prevented the Radicals from pressing their views during the war, they did secure the passage of a bill creating a Bureau of Refugees, Freedmen and Abandoned Lands in March, 1865. The Freedmen's Bureau, as the new agency was generally called, was set up to aid the Negroes in the South and to prevent any move to re-enslave them. Under the direction of General Oliver O. Howard, the bureau assigned "abandoned" and confiscated lands to the freedmen, distributed food and clothing, furnished medical aid, organized Negro schools, supervised Negro employment, and exercised certain judicial powers in cases involving freedmen. Beyond a doubt, the Freedmen's Bureau saved thousands of destitute freedmen from starvation; in three years it distributed nearly 21,000,000 rations, of which more than 15,000,000 went to freedmen.

The Freedmen's Bureau both antagonized the Southern whites and helped to make a reality of the Radical plans for the South. Within a short time the bureau had become little more than a branch of the Republican party, and much of its relief work had political as well as humanitarian objectives. In aiding the freedmen, the bureau in effect purchased their votes. Many of the bureau's officials, moreover, were corrupt and on several occasions they misappropriated the agency's funds. To most Southern whites the bureau was a symbol of all that they hated in Reconstruction; to the Radicals, on the other hand, it was a highly effective device for effecting a social and political revolution in the South.

4. JOHNSON AND THE RADICALS

MANY Radicals greeted Lincoln's assassination in April, 1865, with unconcealed rejoicing, for they believed that his successor, Andrew Johnson, favored a harsh policy for the South. Andrew Johnson, born in 1808 in North Carolina, was a self-made man and a Southern Democrat. Settling at an early age in Greeneville, Tennessee, he earned his living as a tailor and became a forthright spokesman for the more radical elements of the Democratic party in his state. For a decade after 1843 he was a member of the House of Representatives, and during the 1850's he served two terms as Governor of Tennessee. Elected to the Senate, he did not secede with his state, in spite of the fact that he had voted for Breckinridge in 1860. He was then named military Governor of Tennessee by Lincoln, and in this capacity he repeatedly demonstrated his courage and devotion to the Union cause. His nomination as the Republican vice-presidential candidate in 1864 was largely the result of the desire of the party's leaders to win the support of the War Democrats and to create the impression that the party stood for the Union regardless of partisan considerations.

Despite Johnson's record as an antisecessionist Democrat and a Union military governor of Tennessee, the new President soon revealed that he had little sympathy for either the Radical program or the plight of the South's former rulers. As a member of the South's so-called poor-white class, he was interested in neither the Southern aristocrat nor the Negro; his principal concern was the welfare of the section's poorer farmers. Moreover, as a Democrat of the Jeffersonian and Jacksonian persuasion, Johnson was not prepared to support the economic program that was being advanced by business groups within the Republican party. As a consequence, Johnson's Reconstruction policy was conservative in character and similar to the Lincoln program in its broad outlines. Under the Johnson plan, which went into effect soon after he took office, the President granted a general amnesty to all participants in the rebellion who took an oath of allegiance to the United States.* Southern states were to be readmitted to the Union as soon as their newly formed governments had repealed the ordinances of secession, abolished slavery by constitutional conventions and by legislative ratification of the Thirteenth Amendment, and had repudiated the debts incurred in the prosecution of the war. Although the Radicals denounced the Johnson program, they were powerless to prevent its immediate adoption; for when Johnson became President, Congress was not in session, and it did not reconvene until December, 1865. As a consequence, by the end of the year the seven Confederate states that had not been reconstructed under the Lincoln plan had established new governments in accordance with Johnson's proposals.

Following their reorganization under either the Lincoln or Johnson plans, the Southern states enacted the "Black Codes"—a series of laws that affected the status of the Negro in the South. This legislation

* The leaders of the rebellion and those owning property that was valued at more than $20,000 had to apply in person to Johnson for pardon.

granted the freedmen certain civil rights—to make contracts, to sue and be sued in regular state courts, to acquire and hold property (in most instances), and to be secure in person and estate. But at the same time the Black Codes imposed a number of restrictions on the freedom of the Southern Negro. They forbade intermarriage of the races; in some states they forbade Negroes to carry weapons without a license; in several states they did not permit Negroes to be witnesses in court against white persons; and in practically every state they severely circumscribed the freedman's right to work. The laws concerning vagrancy were discriminatory, and in many cases magistrates were given wide discretionary powers in ordering Negroes to be held as vagrants and in assigning them to the highest bidder to work out fines. The most drastic codes were enacted by Mississippi, Louisiana, and South Carolina—the states in which the Negroes outnumbered the whites. In Mississippi, for example, a freedman could not own or rent land except in incorporated towns and cities, while South Carolina forbade them to engage in any trade or business other than husbandry or domestic service except under a license requiring a substantial annual fee.

Northerners, almost without exception, condemned the Black Codes. Horace Greeley thought that they indicated that the South would not "stop short of the extermination of the black race," and the *Chicago Tribune* wrote "that the men of the North will convert the state of Mississippi into a frog-pond before they will allow any such laws to disgrace one foot of soil in which the bones of our soldiers sleep and over which the flag of freedom waves." Although the majority of Southern whites approved of the Black Codes, there were some who believed that they were both oppressive and politically inexpedient. The *Clarion*, one of the most influential papers in Mississippi, conceded that certain aspects of the Black Codes were "unfortunate," and the *Columbus Sentinel* stated that those responsible for the laws were a "shallow-headed majority more anxious to make capital at home than to propitiate the powers at Washington."

The Black Codes confirmed the worst fears of the Radicals concerning the South and the Lincoln-Johnson program; and when Congress convened in December, 1865, the Radicals were prepared to launch an all-out offensive against the President and his Reconstruction policies. Their first move was to have the House and Senate establish the Joint Committee of Fifteen on Reconstruction—which the Radicals dominated from the outset—to review Johnson's Reconstruction program and to pass on questions concerning the admission to Congress of members from the seceded states. Congress then approved a measure that extended the life and enlarged the powers of the Freedmen's Bureau. Johnson vetoed this measure in February, 1866, but in the following month the Radicals returned to the attack with a concurrent resolution stating that no senator or representative could be seated until Congress had granted representation to the state in question. At the same time Congress adopted over Johnson's veto the Civil Rights Bill, which forbade the states to discriminate against citizens because of their color or race and served as a warning to the Southern legislatures that their plan to set the Negro apart under the Black Codes would not be tolerated by the Federal government. If any doubt remained concerning either congressional or Radical supremacy, it was dispelled in July, 1866, when Radical majorities in the House and Senate passed—and then repassed over Johnson's veto—the Second Freedmen's Bureau Bill.

Because the Civil Rights Bill was subject to repeal by any succeeding Congress and because there was always the possibility that the Supreme Court might declare it unconstitutional, the Radicals decided to write it into the Constitution. Accordingly in April, 1866, the Joint Committee on Reconstruction submitted to Congress a proposal that eventually became the Fourteenth Amendment. Section 1 stated that the Negro was a citizen of the United States and of the state in which he resided, and that no state could deprive "any person of life, liberty, or property, without due process of law." Section 2 provided that representation among the several states should be apportioned on the basis of total population; but when the right to vote for national or state officials was denied by a state to any male inhabitants "being twenty-one years of age, and citizens . . . except for participation in rebellion or other crime," the state's basis of representation should be proportionately reduced. The third section disqualified for either state or Federal office all persons, "who, having previously taken an oath . . . to support the Constitution of the United States, shall have engaged in insurrection or rebellion against the same," until Congress by a two-thirds vote of each house removed such a disability. Section 4 confirmed the validity of the debt of the United States, outlawed the Confederate debt in all its forms, and denied the legality of all claims arising from the emancipation of the slaves.

The Fourteenth Amendment proved of inestimable aid to the Radicals. It not only enabled them to impose their program on the South, but it also provided them with another opportunity to discredit both Johnson and his Reconstruction policies. In submitting the amendment to the states for ratification, the President stated that he was opposed to its provisions and urged the Southern states to reject it. All but Tennessee, which was readmitted to the Union in July, 1866, followed his advice. In adopting this course both the President and the Southerners played into the hands of the Radicals, who now had little difficulty in convincing the voters that Johnson was allied with the former enemies of the North and that the people of the South had shown that they were not fit to govern themselves. In discussing the refusal of the

Southern states to ratify the Fourteenth Amendment, James A. Garfield of Ohio spoke for most of the Radicals when he said: "The last one of the sinful ten has at last with contempt and scorn flung back into our teeth the magnanimous offer of a generous nation. It is now our turn to act."

The conflict over the Fourteenth Amendment set the stage for the midterm elections of 1866. Instead of the traditional type of contest between the two major parties, the campaign quickly developed into a struggle between the President and the Radicals. At the "National Union Convention," held by Johnson's followers at Philadelphia in August, the Democrats overshadowed the Republicans, and during the entire campaign the President was handicapped by the fact that his program was more appealing to his one-time opponents than to the members of the party that had elected him. Johnson, moreover, was opposed not only by critics of his Reconstruction policies but also by numerous businessmen who feared that he would attempt to deprive Northern industry of the many favors that it had been granted by the Republicans. While the business class was still relatively small in numbers, it provided Radical campaigners with invaluable financial assistance.

Throughout the campaign of 1866, Radical newspapers and stump speakers attacked Johnson's character as well as his views on Reconstruction. On various occasions he was accused of being a drunkard, of maintaining a harem in the White House, and of having had a part in Lincoln's assassination. Although Administration spokesmen sought to refute these preposterous charges,* the accusations invariably received more publicity than the denials. At the same time the Radicals gave extensive publicity to reports of floggings and murders in the South, and the race riots in Memphis (May, 1866) and New Orleans (July, 1866) were pictured as the inevitable results of the President's Reconstruction program. In an effort to strike back at his detractors, Johnson made his famous—and, as it turned out, disastrous—"swing around the circle." A two-and-a-half-week (August 28 to September 15) speaking tour that took Johnson as far west as Chicago, the swing around the circle undoubtedly cost him more votes than he gained. At every stop organized heckling by Radical groups either drowned out his words or goaded him into making foolhardy and intemperate rejoinders. The effectiveness of such tactics was revealed by the outcome of the election, for the Radicals won overwhelming majorities in both houses of Congress.

* Johnson was drunk at his inauguration. Being sick and weak at the time, he thought that a drink or two might sustain him during the ceremonies; but he took too much and became intoxicated. He was not, however, a drunkard, and throughout his administration whatever drinking he did was in moderation.

Strengthened by their victory in the congressional elections of 1866, the Radicals forced through Congress the first Reconstruction Act of March 2, 1867. Under the terms of this act the South was placed under a comprehensive and rigorous military rule. The state governments set up under executive authority were abolished as illegal, and the entire region was divided into five districts each under the jurisdiction of "an officer of the army not below the rank of brigadier-general and . . . a sufficient military force to enable him to perform his duties and enforce his authority. . . ." To gain relief from military rule and to obtain representation in Congress, each state was required to call a convention consisting of delegates "elected by the male citizens . . . of whatever race, color or previous condition." This convention in turn was required to frame a new constitution giving Negroes the right to vote. When such a constitution had been ratified by the same electorate and approved by Congress and when the Fourteenth Amendment had been ratified, the state's congressional delegation could resume its seats in the Capitol. Supplementary Reconstruction Acts of March 23 and July 19, 1867 further perfected the administrative machinery for carrying out the objectives of the Radicals.

Although the Radicals had routed the Conservatives on every front, they were still not satisfied, for they also wished to impose drastic limitations on the constitutional powers of the executive branch of the government. To carry out this plan, they sponsored two measures, both of which were enacted on March 2, 1867. The first of these, the Tenure of Office Act, prohibited the President from removing officeholders except with the consent of the Senate. The second—a rider to the Army Appropriation Act—forbade the executive to issue orders to the army except through General Grant, to relieve Grant of command, or to assign him to any command away from Washington except at the General's own request or with the previous approval of the Senate. Violation of either of these acts was a misdemeanor punishable by imprisonment. The first measure was designed to prevent Johnson from removing Radical officeholders, and the second to prevent the President from exercising his constitutional command of the army.

Johnson soon played into the hands of the Radicals by removing Secretary of War Edwin Stanton from office. A member of Lincoln's cabinet, Stanton had remained in office in spite of his opposition to the President's Reconstruction program and his close association with most of the leading Radicals in Congress. After Stanton had refused to resign at the President's request in August, 1867, Johnson suspended him and named Grant as his temporary successor. When Congress convened in December, 1867, the Senate failed to approve the suspension of Stanton, and Grant—despite his earlier promise to stand by the President—withdrew and permitted Stanton to resume his duties as Secretary of War.

Johnson countered by dismissing Stanton, but the Secretary of War refused to give up his office. In removing Stanton without the consent of the Senate, Johnson violated the Tenure of Office Act.

Stanton's dismissal provided the Radicals with the opportunity for which they had been waiting, and under the leadership of Stevens the House on February 25, 1868, approved a resolution "That Andrew Johnson, President of the United States, be impeached of high crimes and misdemeanors in office." On March 2–3, the House adopted eleven charges against the President. The first nine charges were concerned with Johnson's violation of the Tenure of Office Act; the tenth charge accused him of attacking Congress with "inflammatory and scandalous harangues"; and the eleventh charge, or "omnibus article," summed up the earlier accusations and added a few more for good measure.

The trial before the Senate was presided over by Chief Justice Salmon P. Chase and lasted from March 5 to May 26, 1868. The prosecution, under the direction of Stevens and Benjamin F. Butler of Massachusetts, sought by the use of innuendo and unsubstantiated accusations to create the impression that Johnson was no "longer fit to retain the office of President." Johnson's lawyers emphasized that he had committed neither crimes nor misdemeanors, and that he had violated the Tenure of Office Act so that the courts would have an opportunity to decide on the constitutionality of a measure that he had considered unconstitutional from the outset.*

When the vote was taken in the Senate, Johnson was saved by seven Republican senators who put principle above party and voted with twelve Democrats to acquit the President. The final vote was 35 to 19, or one vote short of the two-thirds majority required by the Constitution.

With the failure of the impeachment proceedings, the Radicals turned their attention to the presidential campaign of 1868. At the Republican convention in Chicago every delegate voted for Grant on the first ballot, while Schuyler Colfax of Indiana, a Radical and Speaker of the House, was nominated for the vice-presidency. From the Republican standpoint Grant, who as far as can be ascertained had no previous party affiliations, was an ideal candidate. He had co-operated with the Radicals in the move to impeach Johnson, and his military career was a priceless asset in the North. The party's platform endorsed the Radical record in the South, advocated measures to encourage immigration, and reflected the Republican alliance with the business-creditor class by demanding a "hard" rather than "soft" currency.† The leading candidates

* Johnson had vetoed the Tenure of Office Act on the ground that it was unconstitutional, and Congress had repassed the act over his veto. In 1926 the Supreme Court in *Myers vs. U. S.* ruled that the Tenure of Office Act was unconstitutional.

† Debtors were inflationists because they wished to pay their debts with a cheaper currency than they had borrowed. Creditors were deflationists because they wished to be paid in a dearer currency than that which they had loaned.

for the Democratic nomination were Johnson and Chief Justice Salmon Chase, who after his failure to be selected by the Republicans indicated his willingness to lead their opponents. Although Johnson received sixty-five votes on the first ballot and Chase also had considerable support in the convention, the nomination eventually went to Horatio Seymour, a Union Democrat and former governor of New York. As his running mate, the Democrats chose Francis P. Blair, Jr. of Missouri, a former Republican who had become an outspoken opponent of Radical Reconstruction. The platform, while attacking Congressional Reconstruction for subjecting the South to "military despotism and Negro supremacy," had a "soft-money" plank calling for the payment of United States' bonds with greenbacks rather than with gold.

Throughout the campaign the Republicans enjoyed certain obvious advantages. Because of their monetary plank and the assistance which they had given industry in the past, they could count on liberal financial support from the nation's business groups. In addition, their control over the South assured them of a large bloc of votes in that area, while Grant's military record would make him the choice of practically every Civil War veteran in the North. Despite these facts, the Democrats, by constantly exposing and attacking Republican corruption in both Washington and the South, were able to make an unexpectedly strong showing. Although Grant received 214 electoral votes to 80 for Seymour, his popular majority was only 305,458 in a total vote of 5,724,684.

5. RADICAL RULE IN THE SOUTH

HAVING gained control of both the legislative and executive branches of the Federal government in Washington, the Radicals proceeded to carry out their Reconstruction program in the South. With the establishment of a military administration in the South in accordance with the terms of the Reconstruction Act of 1867, control of the section's political affairs passed from the hands of the upper class whites to groups that in the past had had little or no voice in the management of their states' governments. When the new registration of voters was completed under the direction of the district commanders in the South, there were 703,000 Negroes on the rolls and only 627,000 whites. In six of the ten unreconstructed states—Alabama, Louisiana, South Carolina, Florida, Mississippi and Georgia—there were Negro majorities. In every part of the South the white electorate was largely composed of Scalawags and Carpetbaggers. The Scalawags were native Southern whites who in most instances had opposed secession and were

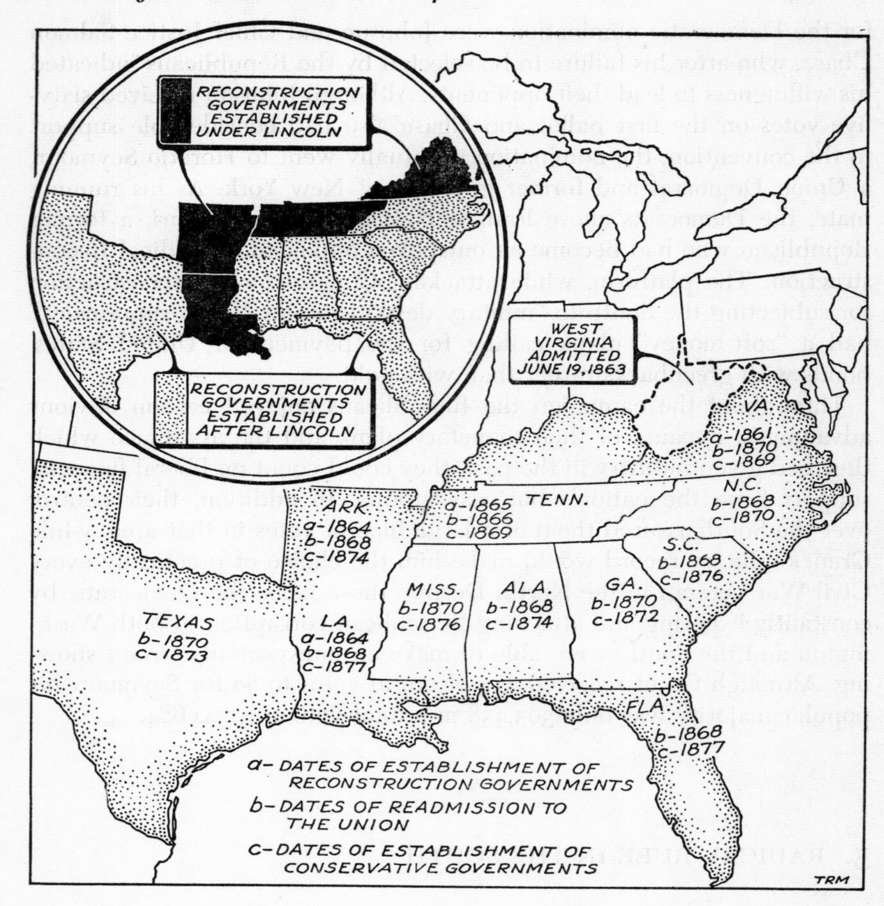

1. RECONSTRUCTION, 1861-77

now prepared to co-operate with the Radicals. The Carpetbaggers were drawn from every section and class of the North. At best they were humanitarians, and at worst they were adventurers. When the elected representatives of these groups met to draw up new state constitutions, they took as models the constitutions of the more progressive states of the North. Provision was accordingly made—on paper at least—for free public education, democratic local government, and complete civil and political equality regardless of race.

White Southerners, who at the close of the war had hoped that the freedmen would look to their former masters for leadership, were quickly disillusioned. The Negroes, who quite naturally attributed their changed status to the Republican party, saw no reason why they should now spurn their principal benefactors for an alliance with those who had fought to perpetuate slavery in the South. This view was reenforced by Radical spokesmen—including Northern soldiers, missionaries, school teachers and politicians—who traveled about the South denouncing the Democrats and praising the Republicans. At the same time the Freedmen's Bureau and the Union, or Loyal, Leagues, which had been organized during the war to promote the Northern cause, proved effective agencies for lining up the new Republican voters in the states of the ex-Confederacy.

Because of the undeviating loyalty of the Negroes to the Radical Republicans, the conservative whites of the South were unable to prevent the ratification of the new state constitutions. By the end of 1868, seven states—the two Carolinas, Georgia, Florida, Alabama, Louisiana, and Arkansas—had ratified the new instruments and had elected new governors and legislators. In 1870, when Mississippi, Texas, and Virginia took similar action, the Radicals were in control of all ten of the unreconstructed states. In every state but Georgia, they dominated every branch of the government. Ten of the fourteen United States senators and four of the seven Governors were Northerners who had moved to the South after the war, while Negroes and Scalawags filled most of the minor offices. Every one of the new legislatures contained a substantial number of freedmen, and in South Carolina the Negro members outnumbered the whites 88 to 67. Moreover, most of the new officials were men of little property. The members of the South Carolina legislature in 1868, for example, paid collectively less than $650 in taxes, and 91 of the 155 paid no taxes. In Alabama the total taxes paid by members of the legislature were estimated at less than $100. In the same period, New York and the five New England states were the only Northern states that permitted the Negro to vote, and four other Northern states—Minnesota, Michigan, Kansas, and Ohio—had recently voted down proposals to extend the franchise to the Negroes.

Corruption, incompetence, and extravagance frequently characterized the Carpetbagger-Scalawag-Negro administration of the state governments. In South Carolina, which was not altogether typical, more than $200,000 was spent for State House furniture that was actually worth less than $18,000. Bills were submitted for $750 mirrors, $60 chairs, $650 chandeliers, $600 timepieces, and $60 imported china spittoons. Under the heading "Legislative Supplies" appeared such items as Westphalia hams, imported mushrooms, a side of bacon, feather beds, extra-long stockings, garters, chemises, gold watches, corsets, perfumes, three gallons of whisky, and a metal coffin. A barroom with forty different kinds of beverages was maintained in the State House at government expense. On one occasion the legislature voted the Speaker of the House $1,000 to reimburse him for a lost bet on a horse race. Public printing, which from 1790 to 1863 had totaled $609,000, amounted in the years 1868–76 to $1,326,589. In Louisiana the legislative session of 1871 averaged $113.50 a day for "travelling and other expenses for each senator, representative, clerk, sergeant-at-arms, doorkeeper and page." In Arkansas the auditor's clerk hire, which was $4,000 in 1866, cost $92,000, or twenty-three times as much, in 1873.

Under Radical control, public indebtedness in the South mounted rapidly. In two years the public debt of North Carolina increased from $16,000,000 to $32,000,000; South Carolina's rose from $7,000,000 in 1865 to $29,000,000 in 1873. The debt of New Orleans multiplied twenty-five times and that of Vicksburg a thousandfold. As state debts mounted, taxes also increased. In 1870 Louisiana levied $21.85 on every $1000 worth of property compared with a rate of $7.47 in New York. Similarly, Mississippi's rate was $17.86 contrasted with $6.44 for Pennsylvania. At the same time property values declined sharply. The decrease in Alabama amounted to 65 per cent; in Florida 45 per cent; and in Louisiana from 50 to 75 per cent.

A number of circumstances help to explain, if not excuse, the behavior of the Radical state governments. While it is true that they were extravagant, it is also true that there was a pressing need for the expenditure of large sums of money in the postwar South. Not only did areas devastated during the war have to be rebuilt, but for years previous to the war the Southern states had neglected to provide their citizens with many essential services. To supply these deficiencies cost money; and, even though some legislatures spent funds on trifles and luxuries, they all provided the South with several much-needed improvements. Nor were the spending programs of the Radical governments necessarily opposed by all the members of the South's former ruling class. The states granted considerable subsidies to such projects as railroads, and the recipients of these grants found it easy to place their desire for profits ahead of their loyalty to their section. There is abundant evidence that Southern businessmen (regardless of what class they were drawn from) were as willing as those of the North to accept whatever assistance any government would give them.

Beyond a doubt the newly constituted Southern governments were often corrupt, but this fact does not mean that any particular locality or party had a monopoly on thieving politicians in the postwar period. While the Carpetbaggers, Scalawags, and freedmen were holding forth in the South, Boss Tweed, a Democrat, was robbing millions in New York City; the state legislatures at Harrisburg, Pennsylvania, and Albany, New York, were demonstrating that they could be as corrupt as any south of Mason and Dixon's line; and the Federal government in

Washington was being shaken by the revelation of unprecedented scandals. Corruption was a national rather than a sectional phenomenon and cannot be attributed exclusively to Radical misrule. Indeed, researches in recent years have revealed that some Radical governments were remarkably honest and efficient and that the Bourbon regimes that assumed power at the end of Reconstruction were often as corrupt as their predecessors had been. In Mississippi, for example, there were only three instances of official stealing under the Reconstruction government of the state. A Republican treasurer of a hospital stole $7,251; a Negro librarian took some books; and a native white Democratic treasurer stole $61,962. After the Southern Democrats had regained control of the state government, they elected an official who stole $315,612.

Care should also be exercised in judging the personnel of the Radical state governments. Although all the freedmen were inexperienced and most were illiterate, naïve, and susceptible to the influence of designing men, the fact remains that some of them compiled excellent records in public office. Nor were all Carpetbaggers rascals. Some went South to put into effect reforms that they had long advocated, others were undoubtedly motivated by a desire to make money—a desire that in other instances Americans have often been prone to commend rather than condemn. Most Scalawags, whom their fellow white Southerners branded turncoats and traitors to their section, in reality never shifted their allegiance. With a long record of opposition to slavery, planter rule, and secession, they revealed an understandable wish to participate in governments from which they had always been excluded.

Finally, any appraisal of the Radical state governments of the South should include some mention of their positive accomplishments. Although there was considerable variation from state to state, the Radical governments made a sustained—and sometimes successful effort—to provide educational facilities, revise tax laws on the basis of the ability to pay, reorganize voting districts so as to give adequate representation to the more populous but less wealthy regions, reform the judicial system, provide relief for the indigent, and build railroads, roads, schools, hospitals, orphan asylums, and insane asylums.

Of the various reforms advocated by the Radicals, those affecting education perhaps provide the best guide to the character of the Radical Reconstruction program within the Southern states. Before 1860 the South had only a semblance of a public-school system, and the war wiped out most of the hard-won gains of the antebellum years. Public and private educational institutions were forced to close; students and teachers were dispersed; many school buildings were burned or converted into hospitals, and public libraries practically disappeared. When the Radicals assumed control of the Southern state governments, they were faced with the task of restoring the shattered school-system and of furnishing the Negroes with adequate educational facilities. Although their actual accomplishments always fell short of their aspirations, the Radicals undoubtedly did more for Southern education in a few years than the Southerners had done in two centuries. By 1876 the constitution of nearly every Southern state contained provisions making tax-supported, free public-schools for both whites and Negroes mandatory. While lack of funds, racial animosity, and public indifference made it impossible to enforce these constitutional provisions rigidly, considerable progress was made in a relatively short time. In South Carolina, which has been repeatedly cited by opponents of Reconstruction as an outstanding example of Radical inefficiency and corruption, there were more than 50,000 white and 70,000 Negro children attending public schools in 1876. In 1860 the total figure had been 20,000.

In the eyes of most white Southerners, any accomplishments of the Radical state governments were largely, if not entirely, nullified by the means employed and by the grant to the freedmen of equal civil and political rights. Since they were unable to dislodge their opponents by the use of the ballot, many Southerners resorted to such extralegal agencies as the Ku-Klux Klan, Knights of the White Camelia, Society of the White Rose, '76 Association, and similar secret societies. Of these the Ku-Klux Klan was the most powerful. Organized at Pulaski, Tennessee, in 1865, the Klan spread rapidly over the entire South. Limited in membership to Southern whites, the Klan refused admission to Union veterans, Republicans, and Union Leaguers. Its members were pledged to oppose equality of the races, to work for the restoration of the "rights" of the Southern whites, and to "defend constitutional government." In 1867, just as the Reconstruction Acts were being put into operation, a grand convention in Nashville transformed the Klan into a sectional organization in which the former slave states, with the exception of Delaware, were erected into the "Invisible Empire." The administration of this empire was entrusted to a hierarchy of officials whose titles were calculated to frighten the ignorant and superstitious: Grand Wizard, Grand Dragons, Grand Titans, Grand Giants, and Grand Cyclops.

By nocturnal visits, warnings inscribed in blood, ghostly parades in white robes and weird-looking masks and other methods, the Klansmen terrified the freedmen. If "peaceful" intimidation failed, recourse was had to violence. The results achieved by the Klan and other similar orders were highly successful from the standpoint of the conservative whites. In addition to regulating the conduct of many Negroes, the vigilantes sharply scrutinized the activities and teachings of Northern preachers and teachers, dispersed gatherings of freedmen, and forced some Reconstruction officials to leave the South. Above all, by frightening large numbers of Negro voters away from the polls, they substantially reduced the electoral support of the Carpetbaggers.

The Radicals, who were determined to save the Negro vote, struck back at the Southern whites with the Fifteenth Amendment, which prohibited a state from denying any citizen the right to vote on account of race, color, or previous condition of servitude. Its ratification was required of those Southern states which had not at that time been readmitted to the Union, and the new amendment was proclaimed on March 30, 1870. It was immediately followed by the passage of an enforcement act imposing heavy penalties for infringement of either the Fourteenth or the Fifteenth Amendment. To circumvent the probability of loose interpretation in the South the framers of this bill placed jurisdiction over all cases arising under it in the hands of the Federal rather than the state courts. Democratic gains in the elections of 1870 stimulated the Radicals to push through another enforcement act (February, 1871) that extended rigorous Federal control over congressional elections in the South.* Less than two months later Congress passed the Ku-Klux Act, which gave the Federal courts jurisdiction over conspiracies against the freedmen and authorized the president to suspend the writ of *habeas corpus* and to declare martial law in any terrorized community. This measure was so effectively applied that by the fall of 1872 the South was largely at the mercy of the military.

6. GRANTISM

WHILE the Radicals were attempting to impose their program on the South, Grant was demonstrating in Washington how inadequately his triumphs on the field of battle had prepared him for the highest civilian office in the land. The Grant Administration was distinctive for the incompetence of most of its officials and the uninhibited fashion in which it turned over both the North and South to the country's special interests. Aside from Secretary of State Hamilton Fish, who held his position for the eight years that Grant served as President, the cabinet was a way station for incompetents and mediocrities.† During his two terms Grant made twenty-four appointments to his seven-man cabinet. Without any experience in politics, Grant turned over the management of most of the government's affairs to hacks or old army cronies. Instead of attempting to check corruption, he stood by dishonest officials on the ground that it was not right to abandon a friend

* This measure was designed not only to strengthen the Radicals in the South but to counteract the fraudulent and violent practices that prevailed in New York and other large Northern cities.

† Exceptions to this generalization were Attorney General E. Rockwood Hoar and Secretary of the Interior Jacob D. Cox, but both were forced out of the cabinet in 1870.

or subordinate in trouble. He had no interest in the reform of the tariff, currency or civil service; he lacked either the knowledge or inclination to espouse a program for the regulation of business; and he felt that Reconstruction could best be left in the hands of those who had controlled the South since 1866. The result was chaos; but it was a kind of chaos that permitted the politicians to get their graft, the businessmen to run the nation's economy with government aid rather than interference, and the Radicals to continue their domination of the South.

During Grant's administration, the Radical Republicans were able to continue their program of government assistance to the nation's businessmen. The railroads were granted huge tracts of the public domain; the Federal land laws were administered in such a way as to aid the speculator rather than the settler; and Congress conducted what amounted to a bargain basement for the sale of subsidies. Moreover, although Congress lowered the tariff in 1872 to aid the Republicans in the presidential campaign of that year, in 1875 the old rates were restored. Finally—and perhaps most important—the government gave the Northeastern businessmen-creditors the type of currency that they desired.

The first postwar conflict over the currency issue centered on the question of whether the government's war bonds should be redeemed in gold or in the unsecured Greenbacks that had been issued in accordance with the Currency Acts of 1862 and 1864. The inflationists and deflationists advanced the traditional arguments on both sides of the question, and the issue was further complicated by the fact that many of the bonds did not state specificially how they were to be redeemed. To the soft-money advocates this omission seemed to indicate that Greenbacks should be used. The hard-money groups, on the other hand, argued that, since Federal bonds had always been redeemed in gold in the past, the government had a moral obligation to abide by this precedent. The question was finally decided in favor of the deflationists. The Republican platform of 1868 included a gold-payment plank, and following the party's victory, Grant announced that the Republicans would observe their pledge. Accordingly, on March 18, 1870, Congress passed a law stating that the government would pay all its debts in "coin or its equivalent"—a phrase that Grant and his successors interpreted to mean gold. While it can be argued that the government was morally committed to this step, the fact remains that this policy resulted in a substantial —and unearned—profit for all those who had purchased bonds with depreciated paper money during the war.

The same groups that argued over the redemption of the war bonds were unable to agree on what policy should be adopted toward the Greenbacks. Issued during the war as part of the emergency financing program, the Greenbacks were legal tender notes whose value depended on government fiat rather than on their convertibility into specie. As soon as the war ended, creditors demanded that the government either destroy the Greenbacks or make them convertible into specie. Debtors were equally insistent in their opposition to the resumption of specie payments. The first victory, however, went to the hard money interests, for in 1866, Congress adopted a bill that provided for the gradual retirement of the Greenbacks. But in 1868, after $44,000,000 in Greenbacks had been withdrawn, Congress halted any further contraction of the currency.

While Congress was attempting to discover a satisfactory solution to the Greenback problem, the Supreme Court was seeking to determine whether or not the legal tender notes were constitutional. In 1869 in *Hepburn v. Griswold* the Court ruled that the Greenbacks were not legal tender. This case, however, concerned a debt that had been contracted before the Legal Tender Act of February 25, 1862, and therefore did not provide an adequate precedent; and in 1871 the Court in *Knox v. Lee* reversed its earlier decision. The majority opinion stated that "Congress has power to enact that the government's promises to pay money shall be, for the time being, equivalent in value to the representation of value determined by the coinage acts or to multiples thereof."

Although the Supreme Court's decision settled the legal status of the Greenbacks, it neither precluded nor insured the resumption of specie payments. The soft-money groups were as determined as ever in their opposition to any plans for the contraction of the currency; and when the Panic of 1873 created a money shortage, they seized on this development to urge the government to increase rather than reduce the supply of paper money. Responding to these demands, Congress in April, 1873, adopted a bill authorizing an expansion of the Greenbacks from $382,000,000 to $400,000,000. But Grant, to the chagrin of the nation's debtors, vetoed the bill. In his veto message the President said: "I am not a believer in any artificial method of making paper money equal to coin, when the coin is not owned or held ready to redeem the promises to pay, for paper money is nothing more than the promise to pay, and is valuable exactly in proportion to the amount of coin that it can be converted into."

The inflationists suffered their final defeat in the conflict over the Greenbacks in January, 1875, when Republican majorities in Congress passed the Resumption Act, which provided that specie payments were to be resumed on January 1, 1879. John Sherman, Secretary of the Treasury in President Hayes' cabinet, was the individual most responsible for the successful implementation of the Resumption Act. By selling bonds for gold he was able to build up an adequate specie reserve; and when the provisions of the Resumption Act went into effect, paper was quoted at par. Many students of this subject have commended the government for its adoption of a "sound" monetary policy; but it must be remembered that the Resumption Act took money from one group and gave it to another. Resumption was a deflationary measure that increased the value of a debtor's obligations while awarding a bonus to creditors.

Grant not only acceded to the demands of the businessmen and politicians, but he also refused to interfere with Radical plans for the control of the South. Although each of the ten unadmitted states had by 1870 established new governments in accordance with the terms of the Reconstruction Act, Federal interference in the South continued. Congressional committees repeatedly investigated the new state governments; Southern anti-Republicans were forced to relinquish offices to which they had been elected; and when the Radicals felt that the occasion warranted it, Federal troops were employed. Moreover, the Radicalism of the 1870's had lost most of the idealism that had been a distinguishing feature of the movement during the Civil War and in the years immediately after the conflict. The Radicals in Grant's administration paid less and less attention to the lot of the Negro, and they increasingly used Reconstruction as a device to conceal their attempts to promote the interests of Northern businessmen and the Republican party. Realizing that once the Southerners had regained their political rights, they might team up with their fellow agrarians in the West to repeal the government's favors to business and to vote the Republicans out of office, the Radicals used every conceivable means to prevent the participation of the South in national affairs. Many of the Radicals of the sixties had been reformers who wished to create a social revolution in the South; their successors, on the other hand, more often than not were spoils politicians who viewed Reconstruction simply as an instrument to aid themselves and their allies among the business classes. And this change in the attitude of the Radicals, in turn, accurately reflected the change in the character of the Republican party, which within less than two decades had been transformed from a militant crusading movement to a staunch defender of the *status quo*.

By 1872 a considerable number of Northern Republicans were openly opposed to the Administration's program in the South. Calling themselves Liberal Republicans, they maintained that the issues of the past were dead and that the government should concentrate on the many pressing problems of the present. As early as 1870 the Liberal Republicans in Missouri had split with the regular party and with the aid of the Democrats had elected B. Gratz Brown as Governor. The movement soon spread to other states, and in 1872 the Liberal cause was being supported by such outstanding Americans as Charles Francis Adams, who had been minister to England during the Civil War; Carl Schurz, a

German immigrant who represented Missouri in the Senate; Horace Greeley, editor of the New York *Tribune;* Chief Justice Salmon Chase and Justice David Davis of the Supreme Court; and Senator Lyman Trumbull of Illinois. While the Liberals placed their principal emphasis on their demand for the end of the Radical Reconstruction program, most of them also favored civil-service reform and tariff reduction.

When it became clear that the Radicals intended to renominate Grant despite opposition within the party, the Liberals held their own convention at Cincinnati in May, 1872. Their platform called for civil service reform and reconciliation with the South, but the delegates were unable to agree on a tariff plank, and the convention sidestepped the issue by referring "the discussion of the subject to the people in their Congressional Districts, and to the decision of Congress . . . , wholly free of Executive interference or dictation." The rift in the convention over the tariff question was further widened by the nomination of Greeley, who for years had advocated a high tariff in the columns of the *Tribune.* Despite Greeley's tariff views and his long association with the Republican party, the Democrats—more in desperation than from conviction—agreed at their convention to support both the platform and candidate of the Liberal Republicans. The combined parties, however, proved no match for the Republicans, and Grant, with 286 electoral votes to 66 for Greeley, carried every state but Georgia, Kentucky, Maryland, Missouri, Tennessee, and Texas. The Republican victory can be attributed to the party's ability to control a large part of the Southern electorate, Greeley's ineptitude as a candidate, the prosperous times that prevailed throughout the campaign, and the difficulties encountered by the Liberal Republicans in seeking low-tariff votes with a high-tariff candidate.

With the exception of the Resumption Act and the continued efforts of the Radicals to retain their control over the South, the most significant developments of Grant's second term were a series of revelations of widespread corruption in practically every branch of the government. As exposure followed exposure, the alliance between business and politics became increasingly clear. Moreover, it soon became apparent that politicians of every rank had participated in the "great barbecue." Robert Schenck used his post as Ambassador at the Court of St. James to foist bogus mining-stock on English investors; Senator James G. Blaine of Maine accepted a thinly disguised bribe in return for his efforts to secure a land grant for a Western railroad; General Daniel Butterfield, head of the New York subtreasury, helped Gould and Fisk corner the country's gold supply in 1869; and Secretary of the Treasury William A. Richardson had to resign when it was revealed that he had permitted one John A. Sanborn of Massachusetts to keep half of the $427,000 in back taxes that he had collected as a Federal agent. The internal revenue system was a center of corruption; taxes on tobacco, cigars, and above all, on distilled liquors, were openly evaded. A "Whisky Ring," composed in part of high government officials, defrauded the treasury of enormous sums. Even General O. E. Babcock, President Grant's private secretary, was involved, and Grant himself was the recipient of many presents from members of the ring. The government practice of rewarding those who gave information about tax evaders encouraged blackmailing, and "hush-money" running into millions of dollars went into the pockets of government agents as the price of silence. The administration of the customs was equally lax and corrupt. When Secretary of War William W. Belknap was accused of selling an appointment to a position in the trading post at Fort Sill, Oklahoma, he hurriedly sent his resignation to the President, who accepted it with "great regret." Nevertheless, the House of Representatives drew up and passed articles of impeachment on which Belknap was duly tried by the Senate. No question existed as to Belknap's guilt, and only the lack of technical jurisdiction saved him from conviction.

Most sensational of all the national scandals of this period was the Crédit Mobilier affair. Following the authorization of the Union Pacific Railway by Congress, a group of the controlling stockholders formed a construction company called the Crédit Mobilier, headed by Oakes Ames, Congressman from Massachusetts. In 1867 this concern obtained an award from the Union Pacific for building and equipping the railway. In payment the construction company received nearly all the stock of the Union Pacific at about one third its face value plus the proceeds from its bonds. To keep Congress in a friendly mood, Ames induced the Crédit Mobilier directors to transfer to him as trustee Crédit Mobilier stock that he sold to various members of the House and Senate at par value. Inasmuch as the stock was worth twice its par value, Ames found ready purchasers among his colleagues. Soon after the shares had been distributed where they would "do the most good," the Crédit Mobilier "cut a melon" of nearly $3,500 for every thousand dollars invested. All went well until 1872, when a Crédit Mobilier stockholder, Colonel H. S. McComb of Delaware, after a quarrel with Ames, turned over to the New York *Sun* a series of letters that at once led to a congressional investigation. Ames was found "guilty of selling to members of Congress shares of stock in the Crédit Mobilier . . . with intent . . . to influence the votes and decisions of such members . . ." and his expulsion from the House was recommended. Vice-President Schuyler Colfax, Senator Patterson of New Hampshire, Representatives James Brooks, James A. Garfield, and others were implicated with Ames in varying degree, although they stoutly maintained that they were not "guilty of any impropriety or even indelicacy."

Although Grant did not "cause" the corruption that flourished during his administration, he made no apparent move to prevent or expose it, and his naïve trust in a number of unscrupulous individuals undoubtedly helped to create an atmosphere in which official dishonesty seemed to be at least tacitly encouraged. To Grant the presidency was an honor that a grateful people had bestowed upon him for his outstanding record during the war. Under the circumstances, he usually preferred to stand by his friends—regardless of the crimes they committed—rather than to protect the honor of his administration or the interests of the taxpayers.

7. THE COMPROMISE OF 1877

THROUGHOUT Grant's two terms as President the Radicals steadily lost ground in the South, for neither constitutional amendments nor congressional "force acts" could hold the South for the Republicans, and the conservative Southern whites gradually reestablished their power. With the help of the Ku-Klux Klan the Republicans were ousted from control of Tennessee as early as 1869, and in Georgia, North Carolina, and Virginia in 1870. Four years later the conservatives carried Alabama and Arkansas. The following year Texas and Mississippi swung into the Democratic column. By 1875 only Florida, Louisiana, and South Carolina remained under Radical control, and in these states the ruling groups were torn by internal dissension. Attracted by new issues and new interests, the Northern electorate was manifesting a diminishing interest in the welfare of the freedmen. In the short session of the Forty-third Congress (1875) only one measure on the Radical program was adopted—the "Supplementary Civil Rights Bill," long urged by Sumner, which prohibited discrimination against Negroes in hotels, theaters, and public conveyances. When President Hayes withdrew the Federal troops from the states of Louisiana and South Carolina in 1877, the Radical governments in those states promptly collapsed. Political Reconstruction was practically at an end.

The final collapse of Radical rule in the South was the direct result of the disputed presidential election of 1876. The Republicans entered the campaign of 1876 with a number of serious handicaps. The Democrats had gained control of the House in 1874 and for two years a series of House committees had exposed Republican graft and corruption in the Federal government; the Radicals had been driven from all but three of the Southern states; and the country was still suffering from the depression precipitated by the Panic of 1873. Largely because of these considerations, the delegates to the Republican convention passed over a number of prominent men in the party who had been affiliated with the

Grant Administration and gave the nomination to Rutherford B. Hayes, an advocate of civil service reform and the Governor of Ohio for three terms. To oppose Hayes, the Democrats selected Samuel J. Tilden, a New York corporation lawyer who had taken a prominent part in the destruction of the Tweed Ring and had been elected governor of his state in 1874.

Hayes and Tilden had much in common, for both advocated hard money, the restoration of conservative rule in the South, and civil service reform. But the similarity of the two candidates' views did not detract from the bitterness with which both parties waged their campaigns. While Democratic stump speakers sought to make political capital out of the depression, corruption in high places, and the abuses of Radical Reconstruction, Republican orators warned the voters against entrusting the national government to a party that was still "the same in character and spirit as when it sympathized with treason." That Tilden received 4,300,590 popular votes to 4,036,298 for Hayes was due not only to the widespread disgust with the excesses of the Grant Administration, but also to the fact that the collapse of Radical rule in the South permitted a majority of the states in the region to return to the Democratic column.

Despite Tilden's popular majority, the Republicans were able to prevent his selection as President. On the day after the election, when the returns were still incomplete, it was clear that Tilden had 184 electoral votes—or one less than the necessary majority—and that the outcome of the contest would depend on the electoral votes of the three "unreconstructed" states of South Carolina, Florida, and Louisiana. Although the Republicans probably had a majority in South Carolina, the Democrats led in Florida and Louisiana. But in all three states the returning boards were controlled by the Republicans and in each instance they certified the Hayes rather than the Tilden electors. The Democrats, however, refused to accept this decision. The confusion was further confounded by the fact that one of the three Oregon electors (all of whom were Republicans) was declared ineligible. The Democrats insisted that the vacancy be filled by the elector with the next highest number of votes (that is, a Democrat), while the Republicans maintained that the two Republican electors had the right to name the third man on the slate.

Although both sides claimed the victory, it was apparent to all that the Federal government would have to settle the contest by ruling on the outcome of the election in the disputed states. No one, however, was quite sure which branch of the government should assume this responsibility. The Constitution stated that "The President of the Senate shall, in the presence of the Senate and House of Representatives, open all the certificates and the votes shall then be counted." But it did not state

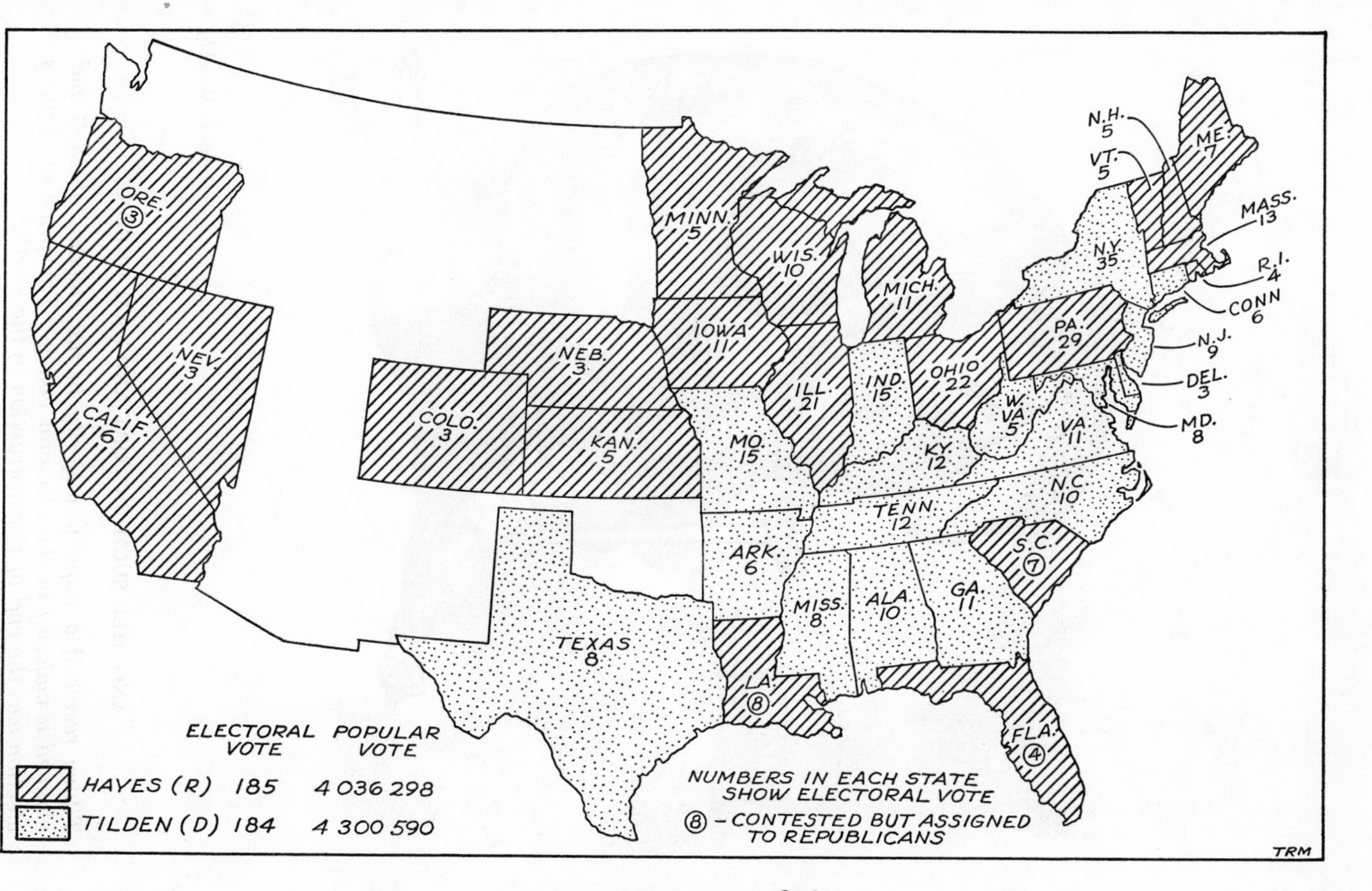

2. THE ELECTION OF 1876

Harper's Weekly

"ANOTHER SUCH VICTORY AND I AM UNDONE"

Tilden received a popular majority in the election of 1876 and claimed a majority in the electoral college. The price of Hayes's election was the end of Reconstruction in the South.

whether the votes should be counted by the President of the Senate, by the House and Senate voting separately, or by the House and Senate voting jointly. And this was the crucial question, for the President of the Senate was a Republican, the House was Democratic, the Senate was Republican, and the Democrats had a majority of the combined Senate and House membership. Under the circumstances, a decision on who was to count the vote (and thus rule on the disputed returns) was tantamount to a decision on who was to win the election.

After months of haggling and maneuvering the spokesmen for both parties in Congress decided to resolve the problem by the appointment of an electoral commission of five senators, five representatives, and five Supreme Court justices. The original plan for the commission called for the selection of seven Republicans and seven Democrats while the eighth member was to be Justice David Davis, an independent. Davis, however, became ineligible when he resigned from the Court to become a senator from Illinois. A Republican justice was appointed to fill his place on the commission which by a vote of 8 to 7 proceeded to uphold all the Republican claims. On March 2, 1877, the final count giving Hayes 185 electoral votes and Tilden 184 was approved by the Senate.

The Republican victory, which was achieved by depriving Tilden of electoral votes that were legitimately his, was made possible by Southern Democrats. In return for Republican promises of the withdrawal of the Federal troops from the South, of the appointment of at least one Southerner to the cabinet, and of generous appropriations for internal improvements in the South, the Southern Democrats agreed to join the Republicans in supporting the Electoral Commission's decision. Hayes, in turn, lived up to at least part of the bargain by making David M. Key of Tennessee Postmaster General and by withdrawing the last Federal soldiers from the South in April, 1877.

The compromise of 1877, which made possible Hayes' accession to the presidency, was in part the result of the activities of a lobby headed by Thomas A. Scott, president of the Pennsylvania Railroad, and by Grenville Dodge, who had served as chief engineer of the Union Pacific from 1866 to 1870. Both men were backers of the proposed Texas and Pacific railroad to the coast and they were able to convince many Southern congressmen, first, that such a line would aid the South, and, second, that its completion was dependent in turn on a Republican victory.

In a larger sense, the Southern support of Hayes in the disputed election of 1876-7 reflected the power of the business interests in the new South. Realizing that the expansion of the Southern economy depended in large measure on Federal grants, they backed the Republican party in the hope that it would be as generous to their section as it had been to the North since the end of the war. While these Southerners were Democratic in name, many were also ex-Whigs who did not find it

Harper's Weekly

"WE HAVE COME TO STAY"

Thomas Nast illustrates some Northern fears concerning the end of Reconstruction. A Southern congressman is unpacking Southern demands for pensions, reparations, and other favors from the Federal government.

difficult to support a party that espoused Henry Clay's program of internal improvements. In short, the only significant difference between the businessmen of the North and those of the South in 1877 was their party labels.

While the Radicals had failed to achieve their major objectives in the

South, they had been able to carry out their economic program in the rest of the nation. By 1877, industry was entrenched in the Northeast, and there seemed little or no likelihood that the Southern agrarians would ever again be powerful enough to thwart the country's businessmen. Moreover, the new Southern ruling class quickly revealed that it had little interest in challenging the reign of business. Known collectively as Bourbons, the Radicals' successors in the South consisted of remnants of the old planter-class and native whites who had been able to better their fortunes during the Reconstruction period. On the one hand the Bourbons proclaimed the uniqueness of their section, while on the other they sought to make it over in the image of the North. Under the Bourbons coal and iron mines were opened up in Alabama and Tennessee; textile factories were established in the Carolinas, Georgia and Alabama; New Orleans became the center of a growing sugar and molasses industry; and by the late seventies more than a hundred tobacco-manufacturing establishments were operating in North Carolina alone.

While seeking to create what they referred to as the New South, the Bourbons systematically eliminated the power of the Negro in their section's politics, largely by franchise provisions in the new constitutions that ingeniously sidestepped the Fifteenth Amendment. The most common were provisions that required literacy and educational tests, poll taxes, or property qualifications for voting. Most useful of all was the "grandfather clause," by which any man who could not meet the educational and property qualifications could nevertheless be admitted to the suffrage if he had voted before 1867 or was the son or grandson of a person who had. Obviously, this device strengthened the conservatives in two ways, since it not only acted to disfranchise the Negroes but gave the ballot to many "poor whites" who supported the conservative program.

By 1890 the last physical—if not emotional—traces of Reconstruction rule in the South had been removed, and Southern politics were dominated by native politicians whose interests were more sectional than national. But Southern problems were not solved by the ending of Reconstruction. The South's economy was controlled by Northern capital; many of its Negro and white farmers lived in abject poverty; and its social fabric was rent by interracial tensions and conflicts. Reconstruction now became a memory that, along with the Civil War, served as a psychological safety valve for those Southerners who preferred to think that their present difficulties could be attributed exclusively to their troubled past.

CHAPTER II

THE LAST FRONTIER

AMERICA'S last frontier stretched from the Middle Border to the settled regions of the Pacific coast. In 1860, this broad expanse, consisting of prairies, plains, deserts, and mountains, was occupied almost exclusively by Indians. Forty years later, the Indians had either been killed or forced onto reservations, much of the land had been taken up by Easterners and immigrants, and a large part of the area had been carved into states. As miners, cattlemen, and farmers moved into the region, an era in the nation's history ended, and only the folk image of the pioneer remained to remind twentieth century Americans of their forefathers' struggles with the wilderness.

8. THE WEST AND ITS RESOURCES

BECAUSE of its varied topography and climate, the West is not one, but several regions. Extending westward to approximately the ninety-eighth meridian—or roughly to west central Texas, Oklahoma, Kansas, Nebraska, and the Dakotas—are the level, treeless, prairie plains of the Illinois country and the gulf plains of the South.

Separated by the Ozark Mountains and plateaus, these two plains areas are of fluvial origin and barren of minerals. Sufficient rainfall, suitable temperatures, an absence of rocks and stones, and a rich soil make them ideally suited for agriculture. Eventually the southern part of this section became an extension of the cotton belt; the central part became the western half of the great corn- and winter-wheat region; and the northern part became the spring-wheat area.

West of the prairie and gulf plains are the semiarid High Plains. Embracing nearly all of western Texas, Oklahoma, Kansas, Nebraska and the Dakotas and extensive areas of eastern Montana, Wyoming, Colorado and New Mexico, this enormous tract was primarily a grassland region, where trees failed to develop because of unfavorable soil conditions, poor drainage and aeration, intense cold, high winds, deficiency of moisture, and repeated fires. The greater part of this territory was carpeted with a heavy, though not deep-rooted, sod and was the natural home of the short, or plains, grass. Nearer the slopes of the Rockies, where the climate was too dry to support continuous growth, the sod gave way to tuft or bunch grass and sage brush. The borderline between the short- and tuft-grass areas was governed by the seasons; in wet seasons the short grass encroached upon the bunch grass, while in dry seasons the reverse was true.

Beyond the high plains lie the stretches of plateau plains that are bounded on the east by the Rockies and on the west by the Pacific Mountain system. This region—which includes eastern California, southeastern Oregon, southern Idaho, and all of Arizona and Nevada—is in turn divided by a height of land into two parts. The lower, or southern, portion is composed of the southwestern plateaus and what is familiarly known as "The Great American Desert."* Because this desert area has a rainfall of less than ten inches a year, it is useless for farming unless irrigated. The northern plateau, with a heavier rainfall than the desert and a number of small rivers along its eastern and western margins, is capable of sustaining a pastoral economy. On the other hand, much of it is so dry that without irrigation it will support neither man nor beast. The climate of the northern plateau is very changeable; in summer, temperatures range from the blazing heat of a noonday sun to fifty degrees at night, and in winter, temperatures of twenty-five degrees below zero are common.

West of the Sierra Nevada Mountains and the Cascade range there is a wide diversity of both climate and topography. Central and southern California are subtropical, have virtually no rain in the summer, and

* The Great American Desert has many names. Northeast of Los Angeles it is called the Mohave Desert; northeast of Yuma, Arizona, the Colorado Desert; west of Yuma, the San Bernardino Desert; east of Yuma, the Arizona Desert; east of the Gulf of California, the Sonora Desert. Lower California is geographically part of this desert.

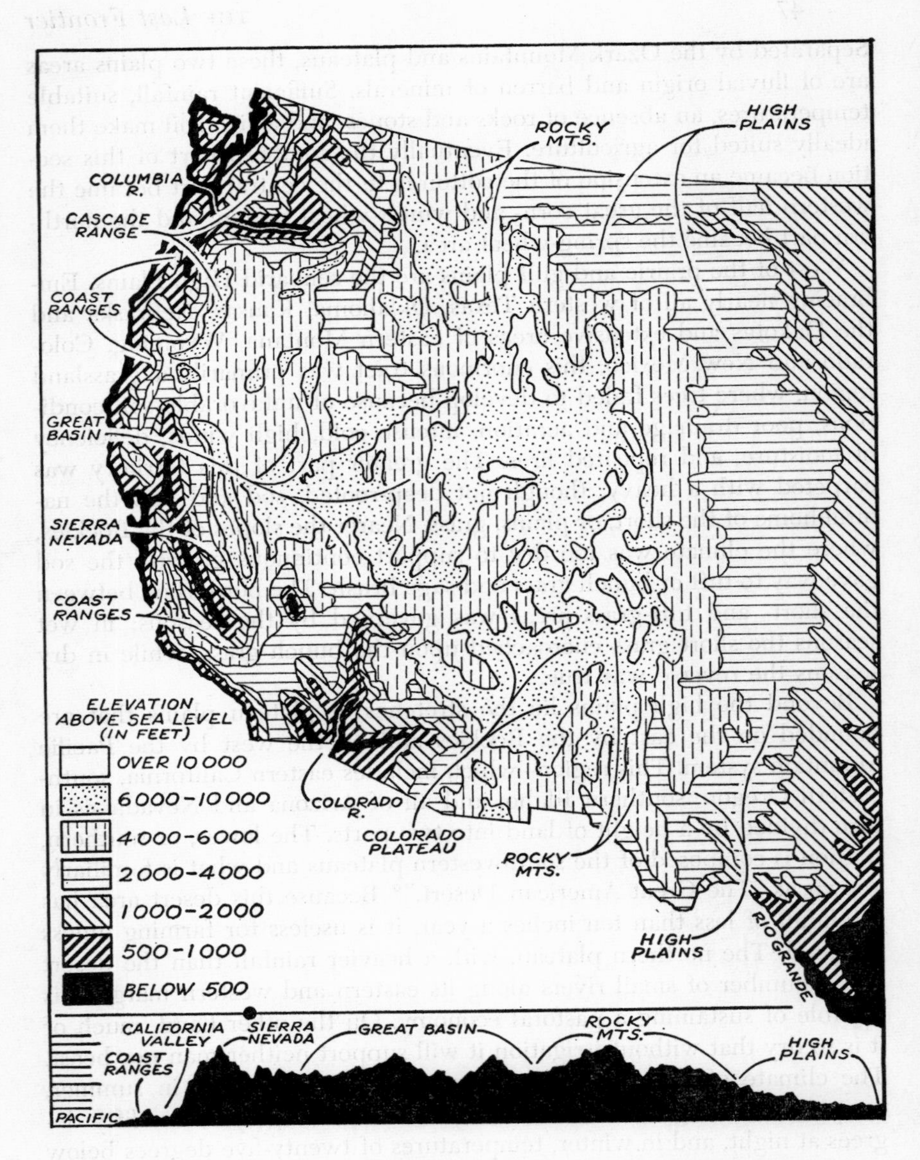

3. PHYSICAL CHARACTERISTICS OF THE LAST FRONTIER

possess stretches of some of the most fertile soil in the United States. Three hundred miles north of the great valley of California and separated from it by the Klamath Mountains is the long, fingerlike Willamette-Puget Sound Valley. Situated between the coastal range and the Cascades, this valley—with its rich soil, abundant rainfall, and favorable climate—attracted thousands of pioneer farmers during the 1840's and 1850's. North of the Columbia River the valley was heavily forested. Early settlers avoided this region, for clearing the land proved to be an arduous and expensive task, and the heavy rains had long ago washed away the potash and lime from the gravelly soil.

To the east of the Willamette-Puget Sound Valley and the Cascades is the Columbia River Basin. This plateau-basin of lava formation, which embraces the greater part of the central portions of the present states of Washington and Oregon, has a rich soil. Moreover, rainfall is so scanty that leaching—so ruinous to soils of a similar character—does not occur. At the mouth of the Snake River—the lower part of the basin—the rainfall averages only six inches, and over much of the remainder of the area it is less than ten. On the other hand, great storms blow in from the Pacific during the winter and spring months and prevent the region from becoming a desert. Despite these storms, much of the area does not get rain enough even for wheat, and unless irrigated it is fit only for grazing and dry farming.

Among the most valuable assets of the West were its mineral resources. In the mountainous and desert regions were vast stores of gold, silver, copper, iron, lead, quicksilver, zinc, nickel, salt, coal and petroleum. Rarer metals, although possessing a more limited value, were also plentiful and included platinum, osmium, iridium, arsenic, antimony, and bismuth. In what is now Colorado and in adjoining states were great stretches of oil-bearing shales capable of producing millions of barrels of oil, and practically all of the mountain ranges contained large quantities of granite, sienite, and marble. Limestones, slates, and sandstones of every shade were also plentiful.

Although a considerable portion of the trans-Mississippi West was treeless, certain parts of the region contained extremely valuable stands of timber. Minnesota had extensive forests of white pine and a scattering of harder woods. In the Northwest—western Montana, Idaho, Washington and Oregon—were forests of fir, spruce, cedar and pine. In northern California and on either side of the state's great central valley were unsurpassed forests of redwood, yellow pine, and Douglas spruce. The Osage Mountains, the plateau region of northwestern Arkansas and southwestern Missouri, and a narrow elongated strip in western Texas were the only important forest areas south of the Oregon Trail, and these produced hardwoods—oak of several species, hickory, black walnut, cherry, ash, yellow poplar, cypress, and sweet, sour, and black gum. The mountains of Utah, Arizona, Colorado, and New Mexico were also partially covered with pine and spruce.

Much of the West is either arid or semiarid, but some parts of it have ample supplies of water. Because of the heavy rainfall and deep snow fields of the Northwest, Oregon, Washington, and northern California possess water resources that are exceeded only by those of the Congo Basin in Africa. Without the water of the numerous streams of the Sierras, all southern California would be barren; and without the water supplied by the Colorado, the Gila, the Salt, the San Juan and the Green, all of the "Great American Desert" would be another Sahara. In similar fashion the Arkansas, the North and South Platte, the Yellowstone, and the Missouri can furnish enough water to make life possible on the semiarid plains east of the Rockies.

9. THE LAST STAND OF THE FIRST AMERICANS

ON THE EVE of the Civil War there were approximately 320,000 Indians in the United States. Of this number about 50,000 lived west of the Sierra Nevada and Cascade ranges, while from 225,000 to 240,000 inhabited either the plains or the intermountain valleys and plateaus between the Rockies and the Pacific-coast ranges. The northern Plains Indians, who numbered nearly 70,000, included four important nations: the Sioux, Crow, northern Cheyenne, and Arapaho. Of these the Crow alone were friendly to the whites. The 90,000 Indians who belonged to the southern Plains tribes were members of either the pacific and semicivilized Cherokees, Creeks, and Choctaws—all of whom had been removed from the East before the Civil War—or the militant Kiowas, Comanches, southern Cheyenne and southern Arapahoes. The most important tribes in the intermountain region were the Nez Percés, Utes, Bannocks, and Shoshones.

The Plains Indians—except for those transferred from the East—were nomadic, nonagricultural, and almost wholly dependent on the buffalo for their food, shelter, and clothing. Possession and complete mastery of the horse made them superior to all other Indians as hunters, warriors, and thieves. Their equipment for the hunt and the warpath consisted of a spear, knife, bow, and quiver of arrows. A shield made of smoked buffalo-hide hardened with glue from the hoofs afforded effective protection in battle. Horsemanship and dexterity in the use of weapons made the Plains Indians the most formidable warriors on the American continent.

The intermittent warfare that had characterized relations between the Plains tribesmen and the advancing whites in the decade before the Civil War was resumed in 1862, when 1,300 Sioux warriors went on the warpath. Led by Little Crow, they raided the outlying settlements in the Minnesota River region, killing more than 700 men, women, and children and destroying homes and other buildings. Meanwhile to the South, the central group of Arapaho and Cheyenne, who had been crowded onto a small, barren tract of land in southeastern Colorado, undertook a series of sporadic attacks on scattered farms, ranches, and stagecoaches. Encouraged by the lack of opposition, the Cheyenne launched a full-scale offensive in 1864. They swooped down on Ben Holladay's stage and freight line east of Denver and soon extended their operations from eastern Colorado to western Kansas and Nebraska. Within a short time every ranch but one along 370 miles of Holladay's route was deserted.

To the Westerners, the only solution to what they called the "Indian problem" was annihilation. In a proclamation to the citizens of Colorado, Governor John Evans stated that any man who killed a hostile Indian was a patriot; and the *Rocky Mountain News* undoubtedly spoke for most of its readers when it wrote that "a few months of active extermination against the red devils will bring quiet and nothing else will." These sentiments were shared by the military leaders conducting campaigns against the Indians. In November, 1864, Colonel J. M. Chivington, a preacher and a former missionary among the Indians, led nearly a thousand Colorado volunteers against 500 or 600 sleeping Cheyenne and Arapaho Indians who had encamped on Sand Creek under the impression that they were under the protection of the United States. The Indians, mostly women and children, were slaughtered with sickening barbarities. Easterners were shocked by the news of the Sand Creek massacre and demanded a congressional investigation. But in the West, Chivington was a hero.

Although there was a lull in hostilities after the Sand Creek massacre, warfare was soon resumed on an even more extensive scale. The Apache, Kiowa, Comanche, Arapaho, and Cheyenne, forced to give up their last bit of land in the Sand Creek reservation, spread terror over the region south of the Arkansas River. In the central and north Plains country the Indians went on the warpath. From Denver to the Missouri, they repeatedly raided the Platte route, cut telegraph lines, captured trains, and killed men and women. Hurried appeals to the Federal government for protection brought additional troops fresh from the Civil War, and by the end of 1865, 25,000 soldiers were in the field. They neglected no part of the frontier from Minnesota and Dakota to New Mexico and Arizona. They kept open the great central and southwestern routes, protected two thousand miles of the navigable Missouri above Kansas City, kept the overland telegraph from Omaha to Carson Valley uncut, and safeguarded the lives and property of the emigrants moving into the trans-Mississippi West.

The protection provided by the troops was obtained at a high price in both lives and money. James Harlan, Secretary of the Interior, estimated that every regiment used against the Plains Indians cost the Federal government $2,000,000 a year. Moreover, while soldiers demonstrated that they could kill Indians, they seemed altogether incapable of compelling the tribes to abandon the warpath. Largely because of these considerations, the government temporarily abandoned its policy of extermination for peaceful negotiation; but, although some agreements were concluded with a few tribes, no attempt was made to remove the causes of Indian hostility, and within a short time the tribes and the soldiers were again at war. For the next twenty years the Indians—under the direction of such illustrious warriors as Sitting Bull, Black Kettle, Red Cloud, and Crazy Horse—fought a courageous but losing campaign against American forces led by Generals Hancock, Miles, Custer, Sherman, and Sheridan. The duration of the conflict can be attributed not only to the tenacity of the Indians but also to the incompetence of some of those in command of the troops and to the friction that developed between the Departments of War and Interior. The Bureau of Indian Affairs, which had been placed under the War Department in 1832, was transferred to the Department of the Interior in 1849, and the two branches of the government were in constant conflict concerning their respective jurisdictions over the Indians. Officials of the Interior Department issued rifles and ammunition to Indians for hunting. But the weapons supplied to the tribesmen by the Department of the Interior after the Civil War were also used in fighting the armies of the War Department; and frequently the equipment given the Indians was superior to that used by the soldiers.

The Plains Indians were conquered not only by frontal assault but also by the destruction of the buffalo herds on which their tribal economy was almost wholly dependent. Buffalo meat, preserved by smoking, was the Indian's principal food. In addition, the buffalo provided him with material for his clothing, shoes, tents and blankets; its bones were fashioned into bows, knives, and hoes; its tendons supplied the Indians with thread and bow strings; and its intestines were made into sausages and its lungs into water bags. At the close of the Civil War there were at least fifteen million buffalo in the trans-Mississippi West. Their range originally lay between the Canadian plains to the north and the Gulf of Mexico on the south, but the building of the Union Pacific, which was begun in 1865, separated them into northern and southern herds.

As the demand for buffalo hides in the East increased, the Westerners undertook the systematic destruction of the herds; and the buffalo, with his slow gait, clumsy movements, and poor eyesight, fell an easy victim to the long rifles used by the professional hunters, teamsters, construction workers, trappers, guides, and soldiers. W. F. Cody (Buffalo Bill) killed 4,280 buffalo in eighteen months, and Colonel R. I. Dodge estimated that 5,500,000 were shot from 1872 to 1874. By 1875 the southern herd had been practically annihilated, and buffalo skins were a glut on the market. Although the northern herd was smaller and more isolated, the opening of the Northern Pacific Railroad made its destruction a matter of time. With the extinction of the buffalo, the Plains Indians, deprived of their means of subsistence, were no longer able to resist the advance of white settlers.

While the Plains Indians were being compelled to relinquish their hunting grounds to the white settlers, the Pacific coast and Rocky Mountain Indians were being confined to small, isolated reservations. Within a year of the discovery of gold at Sutter's Mill, Californians were demanding that the coastal tribes be moved to the eastern slopes of the Cascade Mountains. Although the California legislature was opposed to the granting of any lands to the Indians, the Federal government induced the tribes to emigrate to the interior. But the Indians found the region set aside for their use already occupied by miners and prospectors who refused to relinquish their claims. Treated at best as squatters on their own lands, thousands of Indians became mendicant hangers-on in the alleyways of a mushroom civilization. Penniless, abused, and infected with diseases they had never known before, the coastal tribes were all but wiped out by the end of the 1850's.

The Indians of the plateaus were treated in much the same fashion as those on the coast. Of the principal tribes—the Utes, Modocs, Shoshone, Klamath, Nez Percés, Yakima, and Bannocks—the Nez Percés were the most civilized. When settlers and miners entered Oregon in the decade before the Civil War, all these tribes were forced on to reservations. In 1855, in return for a promise of annuities and supplies, they moved to a reservation in northern Idaho. In the early 1860's miners entered this region and the Federal government demanded that the Nez Percés sign a treaty providing for a reduction in the size of their reservation. When Chief Joseph refused to approve the government plan, the Indians had no alternative but to wage a war of self-preservation. Although Joseph demonstrated that he was an extraordinarily able leader, superior numbers finally compelled him to yield. Eventually, he and his followers, who had dwindled to fewer than five hundred were moved first to Fort Leavenworth, Kansas, and then to the Indian Territory, where more than half of them were killed by disease.

In the southern plateau region the Apaches offered stubborn resistance to white encroachment. Under the leadership of Geronimo, the Apaches were resourceful fighters who repeatedly demonstrated their determination to die rather than give up their lands. But in 1886, Geronimo and his entire band were captured and deported to Florida as prisoners of war. Subsequently they were sent to Alabama and finally to Fort Sill, Oklahoma. With the exception of an uprising by the Sioux in 1891 and the warlike reprisals of a Chippewa band in Minnesota as late as 1898, the capture of Geronimo marked the end of the long series of Indian wars.

While the Indian was engaged in a day-to-day struggle to maintain his way of life, his fate was being decided in Washington. For years the Federal government had dealt with the tribes as independent nations, but in 1871, Congress abandoned this policy. Under the new program the Indians were made pensioners of the government and were forced on to reservations where they were permitted to lead a modified tribal life. By 1885 practically the entire Indian population of the United States was confined within the boundaries of 171 reservations. Although, all told, these reservations covered an area as large as Texas, they were scattered in twenty-one states and territories, most of which were west of the Mississippi.

Life on the reservation marked the final degradation of the Indian. Contagious diseases impaired his health; government handouts undermined his self-reliance; and unscrupulous traders and agents often deprived him of what he had been guaranteed by law. Although there were sporadic protests against government policies in the 1870's it was not until 1881, when Helen Hunt Jackson's *A Century of Dishonor* was published, that many Americans first realized the extent to which the Indian was being victimized. In the next year Eastern humanitarians organized the Indian Rights Association and in 1883 founded the Lake Mohonk Conference of Friends of the Indians. At the same time, memorials demanding an improvement in conditions on the reservations were sent to Congress by the legislatures of Maine, Connecticut, New York, Pennsylvania, Delaware and Michigan.

Many Americans believed that some reform was necessary, but there was little agreement on just what policy should be adopted. Some thought that the old tribal organization should be restored. Others, however, felt that an effort should be made to make the Indian a full-fledged member of American society. The most prominent spokesman of the latter group was Carl Schurz, who, after retiring from the Hayes cabinet, had become editor of the New York *Evening Post.* Arguing that the Indian question was a sociological rather than a military problem, he recommended that the reservations be abandoned and that the Indian be taught to adopt the white man's civilization. Schurz's program, which was also advocated by E. A. Hoyt, Indian Commissioner under President Hayes, called for giving individual Indians tracts of land to cultivate and eventually making them citizens. But the government, which showed little interest in these proposals, confined its efforts to providing minimal educational facilities for the Indians. By 1878 approximately four thousand Indian children were attending government reservation schools. An attempt was also made to give the Indians instruction in the use of domestic animals and farm implements. In 1879 a young army officer, R. H. Pratt, obtained permission to open an Indian boarding-school in the old army barracks at Carlisle, Pennsylvania, where he and his wife gave industrial training to Indian boys and girls and provided them with an opportunity to acquire the white man's technical standards.

It was not until the adoption in 1887 of the Dawes General Allotment Act that the government made an attempt to translate Schurz's proposals into law. This measure, which was sponsored by Henry L. Dawes, a senator from Massachusetts and a leading member of the Mohonk Conference, authorized the president to end the tribal government and parcel out the lands of any reservation to individual owners. Each head of a family was to receive 160 acres, each single adult or orphan 80 acres and each dependent 40 acres. The Indians who received land were to become American citizens, although they were denied the right to dispose of their holdings for twenty-five years. All reservation land not required for allotment to the Indians could be purchased by the government for sale to settlers. The money derived from these sales was to be held in a trust fund for educating the former tribesmen.

The division of lands under the Dawes Act added approximately four fifths of Indian territory to the public domain. Of the lands thus released for settlement the most popular was the territory that now comprises the state of Oklahoma. Even before this region was taken from the Indians, squatters had moved in and staked out their claims. Although these "sooners" or "boomers" were repeatedly driven off by army detachments, they invariably returned. In 1885—or two years before the passage of the Dawes Act—President Arthur issued a proclamation opening up 500,000 acres of Creek and Winnebago territory in western Oklahoma, but Cleveland sent troops to drive out the settlers. Not until 1889 was western Oklahoma opened to homesteaders. Homeseekers and speculators rushed into the region to pre-empt farms, town sites, and water sites, and in a matter of weeks the prairies of Oklahoma had been staked out and settled. In the following year Congress established the Territory of Oklahoma.

While the Dawes Act aided Western homesteaders, it provided few benefits for the Indians. Allotments were sometimes made before the Indians were capable of assuming the responsibility. On the other hand, the ambition of the more competent Indians was frequently blunted by the requirement that they could not sell for twenty-five years. In many instances the new citizens were victimized by unscrupulous politicians, cattlemen, and land speculators. Overindulgence in alcohol—for the Indian as a citizen had the right to buy and consume hard liquor—resulted in a marked increase in drunkenness, crime, and immorality. In 1906 the Burke Act was passed to remedy what were considered the major defects of the earlier legislation. Citizenship was deferred until the end of the probationary twenty-five years except for those individuals who could demonstrate ability and competence. But neither the Dawes nor

Burke Acts solved the Indian problem. While destroying the Indian's tribal institutions and industries the government had not provided him with adequate substitutes. Neither private property nor citizenship could compensate him for the loss of his former way of life.*

Some Americans looked on the final conquest of the Indians as the inevitable triumph of civilization over barbarism; others thought that it demonstrated nothing more than the ability of a powerful majority to destroy a weak minority. But regardless of how contemporaries regarded the passing of the Indian, two facts remain: a culture that had existed for centuries had been wiped out in three decades, and the last frontier had been opened up to settlers.

10. THE MINING FRONTIER

LONG before the final conquest of the Indians, the mining frontier had reached the Pacific coast and by 1880 more than 200,000 fortune seekers had invaded the trans-Mississippi West to exploit the section's mineral resources. As early as 1849 the California gold rush had established a pattern that was to be repeated on countless occasions throughout the mountainous regions of the Far West. With the announcement of each new discovery thousands of prospectors rushed into the locality, claims were hurriedly staked out, towns were thrown together out of whatever material was at hand, and gamblers and prostitutes seemed to appear from nowhere. When the supply of metal in the region was exhausted, the cycle was completed: the miners and hangers-on moved to other camps, and only a ghost town remained to mark the advance of the mining frontier.

Gold was discovered in Colorado in the same year as in California. In 1849 a party of Georgians who were bound for the California fields found gold near the junction of Cherry Creek and the Platte River, a short distance from the site of the present city of Denver. But no move was made to exploit the Colorado deposits until 1858, when gold was again discovered in the Pikes Peak district. News of the new field spread rapidly throughout the East and the Mississippi Valley, and within a short time fortune hunters on foot, on horseback, or in prairie schooners marked "Pikes Peak or Bust" moved across the plains toward Colorado. Approximately 100,000 people passed through Nebraska in 1859 on their way to the Colorado gold fields, and in April of that year,

* In 1933 with the advent of the F. D. Roosevelt Administration and the appointment of John Collier as Indian Commissioner, a reversal of policy was announced. Efforts to individualize the Indian were discontinued, and attention was directed to the fostering of tribal arts and handicrafts.

William Tecumseh Sherman, who was living at Leavenworth, Kansas, wrote:

> *At this moment we are in the midst of a rush to Pike's Peak. Steamboats arrive in twos and threes each day, loaded with people for the new gold region. The streets are full of people buying flour, bacon, and groceries, with wagons and outfits, and all around the town are little camps preparing to go West. . . . Strange to say, even yet, although probably 25,000 people have actually gone, we are without authentic advices of gold. Accounts are generally favorable as to words and descriptions, but no positive physical evidence comes in in the shape of gold, and I will be incredulous until I know some considerable quantity comes in in the way of trade.*

The Colorado mining boom ended almost before it began. While gold and other minerals were plentiful throughout the region, they were imbedded in quartz rock and required heavy machinery that could reach and reduce them. Individuals, unable to afford equipment for this type of mining, quickly became disillusioned. Some moved on to other camps; others settled on the fertile farming lands of the Platte Valley; and many returned home. As the would-be miners retraced their steps in wagons bearing the slogan "Busted by gosh" they met those on their way to the gold fields and quickly disabused them of their dreams of sudden wealth. The route far up the Platte to the Missouri was strewn with supplies that had been intended for use in the mining country, and it has been estimated that at least 50,000 prospective miners turned back before they reached Colorado. Before the Colorado fields could be exploited, new ways of working the refractory ore had to be discovered and sufficient corporate wealth had to be accumulated to make possible the large-scale investments that were needed. It was not until the mid-eighties, when the Guggenheim interests took over the Colorado mines, that the region was able to capitalize on its mineral resources. With the opening of the Cripple Creek district in the eighteen-nineties, Colorado became one of the nation's leading mining states.

Despite the early collapse of the mining boom in Colorado, several towns—including Oro City (now Leadville), Boulder, Golden, Black Hawk, Central City, Idaho, and Georgetown—were established to provide the new population with both living and recreational facilities. After four of the smaller villages—Auraria, Montana, Highland, and St. Charles—had been combined to form Denver, the new town became the principal entrepôt of the district. In 1860 it had a population of 5,000; five years later the figure was 8,000, and Denver was doing an annual business of $10,000,000. In August, 1859, delegates from the Colorado mining camps organized the territory of Jefferson and set up a provisional government of "Rocky Mountain growth and manufacture." Two years later the name "Colorado" was substituted for "Jefferson." Although the number of miners in the territory declined, its farm population increased steadily, and in 1876, Colorado was admitted to the Union.

Nevada's mineral wealth equaled or exceeded that of Colorado. Although a few miners had carried on placer operations in the Washoe district of Nevada throughout the 1850's, full-scale operations were not begun until the closing years of the decade. Of all the "finds" in the Washoe area, the Comstock Lode was the most famous and important. The lode was discovered by Ethan and Hosea Grosh and named after Henry Thomas Page Comstock, a visionary braggart known among his acquaintances as a "hell of a liar." As soon as news of the Comstock Lode reached the outer world, miners, gamblers, confidence men, and women of various degrees of morality converged on Nevada from all directions. By the fall of 1859 the mountain roads from California to the valley of the Carson were jammed with those bound for the Washoe. As during the California gold rush in 1849, people traveled in every way available—on horseback, by coach and wagon, and on foot; some trundled wheelbarrows before them; and one, Captain Richard Watkins, who had lost a leg in Nicaragua, went on crutches. More emigrants followed in 1860, and in a few months Washoe had more than twenty thousand people. Carson City, just off the California trail, and Virginia City, on the site of the Comstock Lode, became flourishing centers of the new mining operations.

Despite its underground wealth, the Washoe lacked all the resources that were needed for a self-sustaining economy. Everything — food, clothes, drink, and machines—had to come over the Sierras from California. Salt was hauled in from the marshes on the Walker River by camels. Wood for buildings, fuel, flumes, shafts, drifts, and winches also had to be freighted in from the outside; and the tree-lined shores of Lake Tahoe and the eastern slopes of the Sierras were quickly denuded. But these problems had little apparent effect on the region's prosperity; and Virginia City, a mining town in the district, probably holds the all-time record for conspicuous consumption. The members of its upper classes lived in mansions costing as much as a half-million dollars. Ornate furniture, brick mansions, high-stepping horses, silver-trimmed coaches and harness were the hallmarks of the community's *nouveaux riches;* and one aspiring citizen, in an effort to distinguish himself from his fellow millionaires, had his horses shod with silver shoes and his bed equipped with a specially designed headboard that extended from the floor to the fourteen foot ceiling of his bedroom. Like every self-respecting American community Virginia City had a school, church, and theater; like every mining town, it had its quota of iron-shuttered stores, hotels, restaurants, saloons, and gambling halls. Life in Virginia City was carried on in the midst of dense clouds of swirling smoke and alkali dust, while night and day a background of sound effects was provided by cursing teamsters, hissing steam, thundering machinery, and whining bullets.

The Nevada mines, like those of Colorado, required a large outlay of capital for their successful operation. Prospectors, lacking both the equipment and capital to develop their claims, were compelled to sell out to huge corporations. Comstock, for example, sold his claim in the lode that bears his name for $11,000, or a fraction of its actual value. The firms that took over Nevada's mines both spent and made large sums of money on their operations. Enormous profits were also made from speculations in mining stocks. The shares of the California Company, for example, rose from $37 in September, 1874, to $780 in January, 1875, and those of the Sierra Nevada went from $4 to $275 in eight months. The Federal Commissioner of Mining Statistics, in describing the security manipulations of the companies in the Washoe district, wrote: "It would confirm the mischievous feeling that mining is half grab and half gamble; that the only way to make money at it is to dig out what rich ore you can get and then find a fool to buy the property; or failing that to make a fool of that collective individual, the public, and to 'unload' yourself of your stock." But Washoe's mineral supplies were not inexhaustible, and by 1880 the bonanza days were only a memory. In that year Nevada's mining stocks, which had been valued at more than $393,000,000 in 1875, were worth less than $7,000,000.

Although Nevada attained statehood in 1864, it was in an economic sense little more than a colony of California throughout the early years of its history. Its mining population came from California, and Californians organized and controlled most of its companies, financed its corporations, manipulated the corporation stocks, and pocketed the profits. Topography, mineral resources, and proximity to California all combined to prevent Nevada from developing into a stable community with a diversified and expanding economy.

In the Pacific Northwest, as in Colorado and Nevada, the mining frontier conformed to the established pattern of discovery, boom, and bust. Following minor strikes in what is now northeastern Washington in 1855 and a major gold rush along the Fraser River in Canada two years later, extensive gold fields were opened up on the eve of the Civil War in the Clearwater Valley in the Snake River country. Additional deposits were found along the Salmon and Boise rivers, and both gold and silver were discovered in large amounts in the Owhyee River Valley. By 1863, when Congress organized the territory of Idaho, the Boise district had a population of 25,000 and the town of Boise had become an important stage junction and commercial center for the neighboring mine fields. When the gold-lead-silver mines were opened up in the Coeur d'Alene district twenty years later, Idaho experienced its second major mining boom within a single generation.

East of the Great Divide that separates Idaho from Montana, miners prospecting the headwaters of the Missouri discovered extensive ore deposits during the early sixties. By the close of the war large mining operations were being carried on around Bannack City, in the Alder Gulch and Virginia City region, and in Last Chance Gulch, where the principal community was Helena. Because communication facilities were inadequate, the territorial government of Idaho was unable to administer the Montana districts, and in 1864, Congress formed the territory of Montana. At the same time Wyoming was detached from Idaho and returned to Dakota. Four years later Wyoming was set up as a separate territory.

The early mining operations in Montana were limited to alluvial diggings. By 1876, placer mines in Montana had yielded $150,000,000 in gold, and as late as 1884 a contractor who was excavating for the foundation of the Montana National Bank in Helena was willing to accept the gold-bearing gravel that he dug out of the site as payment for his services. The region's richest deposits, however, were deeply imbedded in quartz veins, and eventually the placer diggings gave way to lode mining.

Gold was not the only valuable mineral in Montana; there were also rich deposits of silver, copper, antimony, arsenic, and manganese, and when the profits from placer mining began to decline in the mid-seventies, the first large-scale attempts were made to exploit the region's other mineral resources. Within a short time a few big corporations monopolized mining in Montana. Prominent in the development of these new ores were Marcus Daly and William A. Clark. Daly founded the Anaconda Copper Mining Company, owned valuable coal mines and extensive timber stands, organized banks, built power plants, started irrigation systems, and established Montana's leading newspaper. Clark controlled a number of mines in the vicinity of Butte and was the head of the Colorado and Montana Smelting Company.

The mines of New Mexico and Arizona, although not so valuable as some of those in other sections of the West, were among the oldest in the United States. Long before the Mexican cession in 1848, Indians were extracting gold, silver, and copper from the mines of this area. In the 1850's American prospectors first entered the region in large numbers. Operations, which were interrupted by the Civil War, were resumed in 1862, when old mines were reopened and new ones were discovered. A year later Arizona's population, which was composed almost exclusively of miners, was large enough to enable it to be separated from New Mexico and given territorial status. In subsequent years, as gold and silver production declined, copper mining became one of the section's leading industries. The mining camps of Arizona and New Mexico were as lawless as any in the United States. Raphael Pumpelly, who was the only one of five successive managers of a Tubac silver mine not to be killed by either Mexicans or Indians, wrote that in 1860

> *there was hardly a pretense at civil organization. Law was unknown and the nearest court was several hundred miles distant in New Mexico. Indeed, every man took the law into his own hands, and a man's life depended upon his own armed vigilance and prudence, and mainly on the fact that public opinion was the only code of laws, and a citizen's popularity the measure of his safety. In a society composed to a great extent of men guilty of murder and every other crime, popularity was not likely to attach to the better class of citizens. The immediate result of the condition of public opinion was to blunt ideas of right and wrong in the minds of newcomers, who, suddenly freed from the restraints of the East, soon learned to justify the taking of life on trifling pretexts, or even to destroy it for the sake of bravado. Murder was the order of the day; it was committed by Americans upon Americans, Mexicans and Indians; by Mexicans upon Americans; and the hand of the Apache was, not without reason, against both of the intruding races.*

The gold rush in the Black Hills of South Dakota, which began in the midseventies, differed little from those that had preceded it in other parts of the West. As in other areas, the individual miner soon gave way to the large corporation, and by 1880 the richest claims had been taken over by the Homestake Mining Company, a ten million dollar corporation that dominated the economic life of the region. The character of the population was also the same as that of the other mining camps, for only the names of the folk heroes—in this instance, Wild Bill Hickok and Calamity Jane—were different. Deadwood, the area's leading community—with its dance halls, saloons, barrooms, gambling joints, prostitutes, and gunmen—was in all essential respects a replica of Virginia City. Like its model, it was completely dependent on the outside world. Before the advent of the railroad, supplies were brought in by ox teams, and the output of the mines was sent out by stagecoach to either Cheyenne or Bismarck. The steel-lined, heavily guarded coach of Wells, Fargo and Company, which pulled out of Deadwood twice a month, transported sixty million dollars worth of gold without a loss, and it was not even in apparent danger until years later, when Buffalo Bill Cody made the attack on the Deadwood coach the most spectacular feature of his Wild West Show.

11. THE RISE OF THE CATTLE KINGDOM

THE Great Plains, extending from approximately the ninety-eighth meridian to the foothills of the Rockies, are treeless, semi-arid, and lacking in navigable rivers. The Plains were viewed by most Americans before the Civil War as a barren wasteland that could serve no other function than to provide a broad and level—although frequently hazardous—highway to the mining centers in the mountainous districts or the fertile and humid regions of the Pacific coast. As late as 1868, the Commissioner of the General Land Office wrote that "this belt of country is an obstacle to the progress of the nation's growth—or impediment to the prosperity of the new communities west of it, in not yielding that sustenance for increasing population." But the Plains, although offering few attractions to settlers, were ideally suited for grazing stock, and within a short time the entire area had been taken over by the cattle kingdom.

The cattle kingdom originated in southern Texas. Before the Texas revolution, Mexican rancheros maintained herds of Spanish stock, but when Texas gained its independence, the Mexicans were driven out, and Americans took over both the land and the stock. Because of inadequate transportation facilities, the Texans were unable to market the cattle, and in the ensuing years the stock ran wild and multiplied with amazing rapidity. From 1830 to 1860 the number of Texas longhorns increased 330 per cent and in the next decade it rose 1,070 per cent. In the same period, herds were being formed in the northern range country to satisfy the demands of emigrants, freighters, miners, soldiers, and railroad workers. Horace Greeley, on his way to Salt Lake City in 1859, found "several old mountaineers, who have large herds of cattle which they are rapidly increasing by a lucrative trade with the emigrants, who are compelled to exchange their tired, gaunt oxen and steers for fresh ones on almost any terms."

By 1876 the cattle kingdom had spread over western Texas, Oklahoma, Kansas, Nebraska, Montana, Wyoming, the Dakotas, Colorado, and parts of Utah, Nevada, and New Mexico. The rapid expansion of the Western cattle industry was made possible in large part by the extension of the nation's railroad system to the Great Plains. At the same time the growth of industry and urban concentration in the East had created an enormous demand for meat products at record prices. The Texans, who at the end of the Civil War, controlled the largest herds in America, were the first to take advantage of these developments. In 1866, they rounded up their long-neglected and semiwild stock and headed north. Crossing the Red River with approximately 260,000 head of cattle, they pushed on to Fort Worth and Denison and then proceeded either by way of Arkansas to Sedalia on the Missouri Pacific

Railroad or through the Indian Territory into southeastern Kansas. From the outset the Texans encountered a series of unexpected difficulties. Because much of the country through which they drove their cattle was rough and timbered, the stock frequently became unmanageable. Farmers along the route sought to prevent the passage of the herds across their lands and complained bitterly that the longhorns were damaging their crops and infecting their own cattle with Texas or Spanish fever. In the Indian Territory, both Indians and outlaws were a constant menace. A contemporary wrote:

> *The southwestern Missouri roads leading to Sedalia were the scenes of the worst of the work of these outlaws. . . . When outright murder was not resorted to as the readiest means of getting possession of a herd of cattle, drovers were flogged until they had promised to abandon their stock, mount their horses, and get out of the country as quick as they could. A . . . scheme of the milder-mannered of these scoundrels to plunder the cattlemen was that of stampeding a herd at night. This was easily done, and having been done the rogues next morning would collect as many of the scattered cattle as they could, secrete them in an out-of-way place,—much of the country being hilly and timbered—and then hunt up the owner and offer to help him, for an acceptable money consideration per head, in recovering his lost property. If the drover agreed to pay a price high enough to satisfy the pirates, they next day would return with many, if not all, of the missing cattle; but if not, the hold-ups would keep them, and later take them to the market and pocket the entire proceeds.*

Although only a small proportion of the cattle driven north in 1866 ever reached market, the Texans realized that they had solved their principal problem and that the only question remaining was the selection of a more suitable route. At this point the Texans were unexpectedly aided by J. G. McCoy, an Illinois live-stock dealer, who for some years had sought to find a convenient entrepôt for the buyers and the cattlemen. "The plan," McCoy later wrote, "was to establish at some accessible point a depot or market to which a Texan drover could bring his stock unmolested, and there, failing to find a buyer, he could go upon the public highways to any market in the country he wished. In short, it was to establish a market whereat the Southern drover and Northern buyer would meet upon an equal footing, and both be undisturbed by mobs or swindling thieves." McCoy took his proposals to a number of Western railroad executives, but they considered his plan impractical. Finally the general freight agent of the Hannibal and St. Joe agreed to grant favorable rates from the Missouri River to Chicago. McCoy then selected Abilene, a frontier settlement on the Kansas Pacific, as his base of operations and sent out word to the drovers that there was a market place for their cattle. The Texans did not have to be urged to drive their herds to Abilene, for it was an ideal cow-town. The surrounding country was unsettled, well watered, treeless, level, and covered with a rich growth of grass. Moreover, from Abilene cattle could be shipped directly to Chicago by the Kansas Pacific and Hannibal and St. Joe railroads.

The selection of Abilene as a market revolutionized the Western cattle industry. Crossing the Red River fifty miles to the west of the 1866 route, the Texans were able to drive their cattle without difficulty along the Chisholm Trail to Abilene. As farmers moved into Kansas, however, new trails to the West had to be developed. Of the other trails, the most important were the Dodge City route, which extended from the vicinity of Laredo, Texas, through Dodge City to Ogallala, a Nebraska town on the Union Pacific; and the Pecos, or Goodnight, Trail which ran from Central Texas to New Mexico and then on to Colorado and Wyoming. When east-west railroads—notably the Northern Pacific and the Cana-

MOVEMENT OF TEXAS CATTLE TO RAILROAD COW-TOWNS
1866–1880

To Sedalia, Missouri (partly diverted to other points)		
1866	260,000	260,000
To Abilene, Kansas		
1867	35,000	
1868	75,000	
1869	350,000	
1870	300,000	
1871	700,000	1,460,000
To Wichita and Ellsworth, Kansas		
1872	350,000	
1873	405,000	
1874	166,000	
1875	151,618	1,072,618
To Dodge City and Ellis, Kansas		
1876	322,000	
1877	201,159	
1878	265,646	
1879	257,927	1,046,732
To Dodge City, Caldwell, and Hunnewell, Kansas		
1880	384,147	384,147
TOTAL		4,223,497

dian Pacific—were built in the Northwest, the Western cattle trails were lengthened to Miles City and Glendive in Montana, and to Moosejaw in Sasketchewan. From 1860 to 1880 nearly 4,250,000 cattle went north over these trails to the meat-packing centers of the East and the upper range-country of the Great Plains. An even larger number went west to the ranges of New Mexico, Arizona, and other mountain states. Not all the cattle reaching the cow towns went promptly to the slaughter houses. Instead many were sold to Northern feeders who fattened them on the grasses of the public domain before shipping them to Omaha, Kansas City, or Chicago. As the cattle business developed, Texas growers found it to their advantage to give more attention to breeding. The more prolific females were sired with imported bulls; scrub bulls were weeded out; and eventually the rangy, muscular longhorn was supplanted by an improved meat animal.

Although cattle had been raised in America from the time of the first settlements on the Atlantic seaboard, it was not until the development of the cattle kingdom that the industry assumed its unique economic and social organization. Since the cattle were permitted to roam the Plains at will, grass and water were shared by all on a communal basis, and the brands* that served to identify the cattle's owners were the only evidence that the business was conducted on a private rather than cooperative basis. Each year, spring and autumn round-ups permitted the owners to reassert their property rights and to brand the calves that had been born during the preceding winter or summer. At the spring round-up, selections were made for the long drive to the north. Cowboys conducted every phase of these operations. Romanticized in song and fiction, they were in actuality skilled craftsmen who practiced an arduous and highly specialized trade. Most of their work was dull rather than colorful, and most of their tasks were monotonous rather than spectacular. The essential drabness of their lives is indicated by their desire to exchange their routine for the dance halls, saloons, and gambling casinos of the nearest cow-town. Like the mining camp, the cow town was distinguished by the exuberant life of its citizens and the number of them that met a violent death. In Dodge City, the "Cowboy's Capital," twenty-five men were killed in the first year of the town's existence. Outlaws were so well-known by nicknames that their real names were forgotten, and the town's citizens, who called their cemetery "Boot Hill," were the first people to use the word "stiff" as a noun.

Cattle raising, which was a highly speculative enterprise, was made even more hazardous by the many factors over which the cattlemen had relatively little control. In some areas large flocks of sheep destroyed the range grass and tainted the water. At the same time there was

* The practice of branding was not peculiar to the Great Plains, for it had been used in every frontier community where the stock grazed in common.

always the danger that Spanish or Mexican fever would infect the herds. Moreover, as the size of the herds increased and as homesteaders, or "nesters," moved on to the Great Plains, the ranchers found it increasingly difficult to maintain the open range. Finally, the herds were always menaced by cattle thieves. Many Indians and professional bad men—among whom were Sam Bass, Billy the Kid, Bullwhack Jones, and Scarface Ike—were proficient rustlers, and on numerous occasions cowboys stole from their employers.

Because neither Federal nor local governments were able to enforce law and order on the public domain, the cattlemen quickly realized that they would have to form their own quasi-official organizations to safeguard their interests. As early as 1868, small groups of Texas owners had established protective associations. In 1871 the Wyoming Stock Graziers' Association was organized. A year later two cattlemen's organizations were founded in Colorado, and the cattlemen along the North and South Platte formed the Laramie County Stock Growers' Association. Within a short time, individualism—regardless of how important a rôle it played in other frontier regions—had given way to co-operative effort in every part of the cattle kingdom. The purpose of the various associations, in the words of the president of the Montana organization, was

> *to establish a system that allows each individual stock grower to retain all the rights and privileges he now enjoys, and add to those privileges a system that will not only compel but encourage and even pay men to be honest; a system that protects our stock on any part of the Public Domain the same as on our home range; a system that will put a stop to animals being taken off the public range and advertised as estrays; a system that will not condemn our stock as estrays and offer them for sale, because they were driven or strayed from their home range; a system that protects in proportion to the stock owned and one that we all pay for in proportion to our protection; a system that will enable us to know the marks and brands and vent brands of every stock grower in the territory; a system that is more than democratic in its broadest sense, not only doing the greatest good to the greatest number but one that will result in great benefits to every stock grower; a system that will prevent our territory from becoming a paradise of thieves; a system that resolves stock growers into a protective force and pays them to look after the interests of one another, inasmuch as our interests are identical.*

The various stockmen's associations were able to produce a semblance of order in what was an essentially chaotic industry. They established range detective forces that put a careful watch on strangers—especially drifting cowboys—and cowboys with a bad record were blacklisted. They supervised round-ups and investigated complaints immediately.

They inspected brands at loading and marketing points, withheld cattle with altered brands from shipment, and returned them to their rightful owners. Those they accused of wrong-doing were prosecuted. The stockgrowers' associations were also responsible for legislation—both state and Federal—to protect cattle from disease, and the creation of the Bureau of Animal Husbandry in the Federal Department of Agriculture was the direct result of their agitation.

12. BOOM AND BUST IN THE CATTLE INDUSTRY

BECAUSE of its dependence on the Eastern market, the cattle kingdom was particularly sensitive to fluctuations in the business cycle. Even before the depression of the midseventies, the cattle industry on the Western plains began to fall off. The Texas drive of 1871, which was the greatest in history, coincided with a decline in the demand for meat products and a rise in rail rates. Many drovers were unable to find buyers, and approximately half the cattle brought from Texas had to be wintered at a loss on the Kansas plains. During 1872 the situation grew steadily worse, and the panic of the following year forced many cattlemen into bankruptcy. But on the Plains, as in the rest of the country, the depression eventually gave way to good times. By 1878 the worst was over and during the early eighties the cattle kingdom had its biggest—and last—boom. In 1883, steers on the Texas plains brought prices running from $35 to $50 a head, and beef cattle in the Chicago market sold for as high as $9.35 per hundred weight.

The boom of the early eighties was in part the result of the extension of the cattle kingdom to the northern ranges and the consequent increase in demand for new stock for these areas. From 1881 to 1885 the demand for cattle for the Northern ranges reached the limit of available supply, and the Texas producers could not fill the orders of the Northern ranchmen. Colorado, with its ranges already overcrowded, sent thousands of cattle into the vacated Indian lands along the Yellowstone and the Big Horn rivers. Additional thousands of breeding stock and young steers came from the farms of Illinois, Wisconsin, Michigan, Iowa, and Missouri. Finally, carload after carload of "pilgrims," "states" cattle, or "barnyard" stock was brought in from the Eastern states, and in 1882–4 as many cattle were shipped west as east. This influx of cattle transformed the Northern range country. Granville Stuart, in *Forty Years on the Frontier*, wrote:

> *It would be impossible to make people not present on the Montana cattle ranges realize the rapid changes that took place on*

> *those ranges in two years. In 1880 the country was practically uninhabited. One could travel for miles without seeing so much as a trapper's bivouac. Thousands of buffalo darkened the rolling plains. There were deer, elk, wolves, and coyotes on every hill and in every ravine and thicket. In the whole territory of Montana there were but 250,000 head of cattle, including dairy cattle and work oxen.*
>
> *In the fall of 1883 there was not a buffalo remaining on the range, and the antelope, elk, and deer were indeed scarce. In 1880 no one had heard tell of a cowboy in this "niche of the woods" and Charlie Russell had made no pictures of them; but in the fall of 1883 there were 600,000 head of cattle on the range. The cowboy . . . had become an institution.*

The rapid growth of the cattle industry in these years can also be attributed to the extension of the nation's railroad system to the west and southwest. By the 1880's Texas had been linked to the North and East by the Missouri, Kansas and Texas, commonly known as the "Katy." This line, which extended from Kansas City to Houston, joined the International and Great Northern, which in turn connected with Laredo on the Rio Grande. The St. Louis, Iron Mountain, and Southern, running south from St. Louis by way of Little Rock and Texarkana, served the eastern part of the state. Both roads made connections with the Texas Pacific, which extended entirely across the state to Fort Worth and El Paso. These lines made it possible to ship cattle direct from the Texas range to the great Mississippi Valley slaughtering and packing centers. And when in 1881 the Santa Fé, building southward from La Junta, made connections with the Southern Pacific and the Texas Pacific at Deming, New Mexico, Texas cattle could be sent to the Northern ranges through Denver and Cheyenne. The newly opened Northern Pacific as well as the Union Pacific were also feeders to the Northern range. In 1884 the Northern Pacific alone carried 98,219 head of Eastern stock westward to the plains country.

The cattle boom was sustained—if not caused by—the willingness of Easterners and Europeans to believe that the "boundless, gateless, fenceless pastures" of the Plains offered an easy and unexampled opportunity for quick wealth. The land was apparently free; the initial capital outlay was relatively small; and the chances for profits presumably limitless. These views, while having some basis in fact, were also the products of an extensive propaganda campaign to publicize the cow country. Territorial legislatures voted large sums for the preparation and distribution of pamphlets describing the grazing lands of the West. Newspapers in the East and in England and Scotland printed letters from stock growers, accounts of observers who had visited the cattle country, excerpts from the prospectuses of newly organized companies, and market reports on the movement, condition, and prices of range cattle. In the

Western press the cattle business was described exclusively in superlatives. The *Colorado Live Stock Record* wrote that cattle was "one of those investments which men cannot pay too much for, since, if left alone, they will multiply, replenish and grow out of a bad bargain"; and an exchange from the *Breeders' Gazette* of September, 1883 stated:

A good sized steer when it is fit for the butcher market will bring from $45 to $60. The same animal at its birth was worth but $5. He has run on the plains and cropped the grass from the public domain for four or five years and now, with scarcely any expense to his owner, is worth forty dollars more than when he started on his pilgrimage. A thousand of these animals are kept nearly as cheaply as a single one, so with a thousand as a starter and with an investment of but $5,000 in the start, in four years the stock raiser has made from $40,000 to $45,000. Allow $5,000 for his current expenses which he has been going on and he still has $35,000 and $40,000 for a net profit. That is all there is of the problem and that is why our cattlemen grow rich.

As tales of sudden riches on the Plains reached the East and Europe, capital flowed to the range country in unprecedented amounts. In 1883, twenty companies with a total capitalization of more than $12,000,000 were incorporated under the territorial laws of Wyoming. Many of these enterprises were backed by foreign capital; and in England, according to a contemporary observer, "drawing rooms buzzed with the stories of this last of bonanzas; staid old gentlemen, who scarcely knew the difference between a steer and a heifer, discussed it over their port and nuts." By 1882 there were almost a dozen English and Scotch cattle companies in the United States.

Newcomers from the East and Europe, who knew little or nothing about stock raising, flocked into the cattle country. Legitimate business gave way to speculation, and the cow towns were converted into miniature Wall Streets. Many companies were overcapitalized. Paper corporations with nothing but well-written prospectuses sold attractive stock certificates to gullible buyers at outrageous prices. In August, 1882, the *Laramie Boomerang* wrote:

Millions are talked of as lightly as nickels and all kinds of people are dabbling in steers. The chief justice of the Supreme Court has recently succumbed to the contagion and gone out to purchase a $40,000 herd. Large transactions are made every day in which the buyer does not see a hoof of his purchase and very likely does not use more than one-half of the purchase money in the trade before he has sold and made an enormous margin in the deal. . . . A Cheyenne man who don't pretend to know a maverick from a mandamus *has made a neat little margin of $15,000 this summer in small transactions and hasn't seen a cow yet that he has bought and sold.*

By the mideighties the boom had turned into a bust. The ranges were overcrowded, the market was glutted, and the inflated price structure of the cattle industry had collapsed; and before the cattlemen had a chance to recover from the depression, they were overwhelmed by a series of natural disasters. The winter of 1885–6 was unusually severe. Blizzards and low temperatures killed 85 per cent of the herds of western Kansas, Colorado, and the Texas Panhandle. A hot, dry summer, followed by a winter that was even more severe than that of 1885–6, completed the damage. In the spring of 1887 the coulees and aspen and cottonwood groves were filled with dead cattle, and all that was left of the great herds were some emaciated animals so weak that they were scarcely able to move.

The adverse weather conditions and the cycle of boom and bust marked the beginning of the end of the open range. From then on, pastures were fenced in, scrub stock was replaced with a better grade of beef cattle, ranchers began to grow hay and other forage crops, the cattle were fed during the winter, and wells and windmills were used to secure an adequate supply of water for the animals. By careful management and scientific methods, the Western cattle industry managed to survive—although on a considerably reduced scale—but the passing of the open range signalized the downfall of the cattle kingdom.

13. THE FARMERS' FRONTIER

THE WESTERN cattlemen had to contend not only with the vagaries of nature and of business cycles but also with the advancing agricultural frontier. Even before the boom of the eighties the homesteaders had driven most of the ranchers out of Kansas and staked out claims in many other parts of the cow country. To the cattleman, the farmer was an enemy. Relentlessly pushing on to land that the cattleman had come to look on as his own, the "nester" cut up the open range by fencing his land or by plowing a furrow around its margin. As the ranges became more crowded the cattlemen made every effort to drive out or exclude the homesteaders. Stock growers' associations issued manifestos and posted notices warning off newcomers. At the same time many cattlemen illegally enclosed great tracts of the public domain or acquired vast stretches of land through the use of dummy entrymen and false swearing. Many ranchers, moreover, resorted to force to preserve their grazing lands. But still the farmers came, and it was only a matter of time before the cattlemen were compelled to admit defeat.

In his conflict with the cattlemen, the farmer was for some years at a disadvantage because of his inability to find suitable fencing material. In the East the settler had used either stones or wood for fences, but on the Plains, where a homesteader's very livelihood depended on his ability to prevent the cattle from destroying his crops, both were lacking. Some farmers, thinking that the problem could be solved by importing wood from forested regions, soon found that the cost made this plan impractical. For a time it was believed that hedges would be a suitable substitute for fences, and throughout the West farmers experimented with them. But hedges in most instances were not strong enough to hold off the cattle, and it was not until the perfection of barbed wire in the midseventies that the farmers were provided with adequate fencing material. Barbed wire fences could not be broken down by cattle, did not shade the crops, and were relatively cheap to construct.

In 1874, Joseph F. Glidden, Jacob Haish, and I. L. Ellwood, three Illinois farmers, took out separate patents for barbed wire. Within a short time Glidden and Ellwood formed the Barb Fence Company, and in 1876 this concern was purchased by the Washburn and Moen Manufacturing Company of Worcester, Massachusetts. Although barbed wire was at first looked on with suspicion by both middlemen and farmers, its advantages were so obvious that it was soon selling as fast as it could be manufactured. By 1880, American factories were producing 40,000 tons of barbed wire annually; a decade later output had trebled and the cost to the consumer had dropped from $10 per 100 pounds to $3.45.

The introduction of barbed wire was accompanied by open warfare between the cattlemen and the farmer. The West was divided into "fence men" and "no-fence men." Ranchers cut the fences as quickly as the homesteaders built them, and on numerous occasions both sides tried to settle their differences with guns. But however much the cattlemen might wish that the "man who invented barbed wire had it all around him in a ball and the ball rolled into hell," they were fighting a losing battle. Barbed wire had come to stay, and its triumph marked the end of the open range. More than anything else, barbed wire was responsible for the successful advance of the farmer's frontier on the Great Plains. Some years after the cattlemen had gone down to their final defeat, an old trail driver wrote:

> *In those days* [the early seventies] *there was no fencing along the trails to the North, and we had lots of range to graze on. Now there is so much land taken up and fenced in that the trail for most of the way is little better than a crooked lane, and we had hard lines to find enough range to feed on. These fellows from Ohio, Indiana, and other northern and western states—the 'bone and sinew of the country,' as politicians call them—have made farms, enclosed pas-*

tures, and fenced in water holes until you can't rest; and I say D——n such bone and sinew! They are the ruin of the country, and have everlastingly, eternally, now and forever, destroyed the best grazing-land in the world.

In their efforts to settle in the Plains country, farmers were frequently impeded rather than assisted by the Federal government's land laws. The Pre-emption and Homestead Acts, both of which were designed to meet the needs of the pioneer in the forested and humid areas, proved altogether inadequate on the Last Frontier. The settler on the treeless level prairies found that the 160 acres granted him by the government were not sufficient to permit him to practice the large-scale agriculture for which the region was ideally suited, while the homesteader in the arid and semiarid sections was not even able to sustain life on the relatively small plot that he was allotted under the existing land laws. Irrigation might have made some of the arid lands productive, but in most instances the cost of irrigation was prohibitive. One authority on the history of public land policies has concluded that the "great weakness of the Homestead Act" was

*and is, its utter inadaptability to the parts of the country for which it was not designed. The idea of the farm small in acres within the semi-arid regions was tenacious but untenable. It was even vicious in its operation. Congress was converted to the homestead principle in the large, and instructed in detail, by the people on the Missouri River frontier, backed up by the experience of the whole country, not essentially different, between Ohio and the Missouri. The frontiersmen on the plains were too few in numbers, and too unlike the early frontiersmen to the East of them, to compel the working out of desirable modification of the land laws.**

Because of the Homestead Law's inadequacies, its provisions were frequently ignored by both cattlemen and farmers west of the ninety-eighth meridian. At the same time there were repeated requests that its provisions be altered. In response to these demands Congress in 1873 passed the Timber Culture Act. Under the terms of this act, any person receiving a homestead quarter-section could acquire an additional quarter-section by planting and maintaining forty acres of timber on it. The authors of the Timber Culture Act had assumed that if enough trees were planted, the arid West would have enough rainfall to permit its farmers to practice the same type of agriculture as in the humid sections of the country. But rain-making by legislative fiat proved farcical,

* Benjamin Horace Hibbard: *A History of the Public Land Policies* (New York: The Macmillan Company, 1924), p. 409. Copyright 1924 by, and reprinted with the permission of, The Macmillan Company.

and congressmen soon discovered that it was one thing to "enact" trees on the Plains and quite another to make them grow in regions lacking sufficient moisture. In 1891 the Timber Culture Act was repealed.

The Desert Land Act, passed by Congress in 1877, also failed to meet the needs of the Westerners. This act, which applied to the Dakotas, Montana, Idaho, Wyoming, Utah, Nevada, Arizona, New Mexico, and the arid parts of California, Oregon, and Washington, permitted an individual to acquire 160 acres of desert land. Instead of homesteading this tract, he had to buy it at $1.25 an acre. Moreover, to hold his land the purchaser had to spend at least $3 an acre on improvements and to irrigate at least one eighth of it within three years. The bill's provisions for cash expenditures destroyed whatever effectiveness it might have had. Few settlers could afford to buy these lands, and fewer still could afford to irrigate them. In addition, the sponsors of the measure overlooked the fact that there were large areas in the West where irrigation was impossible. Congress' effort to legislate the farmers westward was no more successful in 1877 that it had been in 1873.

The failure of Federal land legislation to meet the needs of Plains settlers can be attributed in large part to the fact that no attempt was made to take into account the difficulties inherent in farming in an arid or semiarid country. Cattlemen and farmers, both of whom had long recognized the problem, had sought to solve it by digging wells and erecting windmills. But water was so scarce and the obstacles so great that individuals could do little more than devise make-shift arrangements. Only a long-term plan, sponsored and executed by Federal authorities, could make the Plains habitable. Moreover, many parts of the West were so lacking in moisture that there was no known way of making them capable of supporting either human or animal life. The first public official to recommend a comprehensive and integrated program for the arid areas of the West was Major John W. Powell, a government geologist. In his *Report on the Lands of the Arid Region of the United States,* which was submitted to the Secretary of the Interior in 1878, Powell proposed that these lands be classified into mineral, timber, coal, irrigable, and pasture lands, that rectangular surveys be abandoned, and that the homestead system be modified to fit the new environment. Although Powell's recommendations were incorporated into two bills that were presented to Congress, no action was ever taken on either measure. In 1894, the Carey Act turned the problem of irrigation over to the individual states. This plan, however, proved altogether unworkable, and in 1902 with the adoption of the Newlands, or Reclamation, Act, the Federal government at last inaugurated a large-scale irrigation program.*

* By 1920 approximately 20,000,000 acres of land were under irrigation. This represented a very small fraction of the arid lands.

The Census Bureau in its report for 1890 announced that it was no longer possible to determine the frontier line of population in the West; but this fact did not signify the end of free land in the area. By June of 1890 only 372,659 homestead entries—or an area less than that of the state of Nebraska—had been perfected, and the amount of homestead land deeded after 1890 was four times the amount deeded before that date. Moreover, an enormous acreage of untenanted lands was still in the hands of the railroads and land companies. As late as 1890, Ohio alone had more improved farm land and approximately half as many farms as the entire Far West.

Yet the comparatively slow advance of the farmers' frontier beyond the Mississippi should not obscure the fact that the West at the turn of the century bore little resemblance to the same region on the eve of the Civil War. In 1889, North and South Dakota, Montana, and Washington were admitted to the Union; the next year Wyoming and Idaho became states; and within twenty years the territories of Utah, Oklahoma, Arizona, and New Mexico were transformed into states. Between 1860 and 1900 the West lost its most distinctive features. The Indians and buffalo were driven from the Plains; the miner and prospector gave way to the giant corporation; open-range cattle were supplanted by breeded stock that were confined to fenced-in pastures; and the struggling homesteader was followed by the large-scale producer of grains.* In the future, the West would be set off from the rest of the country, not so much by what it was, but by its memories of what it had been.

* See Chapter VI, pp. 191–3.

The Bettmann Archive

Homes for the Industrious!

IN THE

GARDEN STATE OF THE WEST.

THE ILLINOIS CENTRAL RAILROAD CO., HAVE FOR SALE

1,200,000 ACRES OF RICH FARMING LANDS,

In Tracts of Forty Acres and upward, on Long Credit and at Low Prices.

MECHANICS, FARMERS AND WORKING MEN.

THE attention of the enterprising and industrious portion of the community is directed to the following statements and liberal inducements offered them by the

ILLINOIS CENTRAL RAILROAD COMPANY.

which, as they will perceive, will enable them by proper energy, perseverance and industry, to provide comfortable homes for themselves and families, with, comparatively speaking, very little capital.

LANDS OF ILLINOIS.

No State in the Valley of the Mississippi offers so great an inducement as the State of Illinois. There is no portion of the world where all the conditions of climate and soil so admirably combine to produce those two great staples, CORN and WHEAT, as the Prairies of Illinois.

THE SOUTHERN PART

of the State lies within the zone of the cotton regions, while the soil is admirably adapted to the growth of tobacco and hemp; and the wheat is worth from fifteen to twenty cents more per bushel than that raised further north.

RICH ROLLING PRAIRIE LANDS.

The deep rich loam of the prairies is cultivated with such wonderful facility that the farmers of the Eastern and Middle States are moving to Illinois in great numbers. The area of Illinois is about equal to that of England, and the soil is so rich that it will support twenty millions of people.

EASTERN AND SOUTHERN MARKETS.

These lands are contiguous to a railroad 700 miles in length, which connects with other roads and navigable lakes and rivers, thus affording an unbroken communication with the Eastern and Southern markets.

APPLICATION OF CAPITAL.

Thus far, capital and labor have been applied to developing the soil; the great resources of the State in coal and iron are almost untouched. The invariable rule that the mechanical arts flourish best where food and fuel are cheapest, will follow at an early day in Illinois, and in the course of the next ten years the natural laws and necessities of the case warrant the belief that at least five hundred thousand people will be engaged in the State of Illinois in various manufacturing pursuits.

RAILROAD SYSTEM OF ILLINOIS.

Over $100,000,000 of private capital have been expended on the railways of Illinois. Inasmuch as part of the income from several these works, with a valuable public fund in lands, go to diminish the State expenses, the TAXES ARE LIGHT, and must consequently every day decrease.

THE STATE DEBT.

The State Debt is only $10,105,398, 14, and within the last three years has been reduced $2,959,746 80, and we may reasonably expect that in ten years it will become extinct.

PRESENT POPULATION.

The State is rapidly filling up with population; 868,025 persons having been added since 1850, making the present population 1,723,663, a ratio of 102 per cent. in ten years.

AGRICULTURAL PRODUCTS.

The Agricultural products of Illinois are greater than those of any other State. The products sent out during the past year exceeded 1,500,000 tons. The wheat crop of 1860 approaches 35,000,000 bushels, while the corn crop yields not less than 140,000,000 bushels.

FERTILITY OF THE SOIL.

Nowhere can the industrious farmer secure such immediate results for his labor as upon these prairie soils, they being composed of a deep rich loam, the fertility of which, is unsurpassed by any on the globe.

TO ACTUAL CULTIVATORS.

Since 1854, the company have sold 1,300,000 acres. They sell only to actual cultivators, and every contract contains an agreement to cultivate. The road has been constructed thro' these lands at an expense of $30,000,000. In 1850 the population of the forty-nine counties through which it passes was only 335,598; since which 479,293 have been added, making the whole population 814,891, a gain of 143 per cent.

EVIDENCES OF PROSPERITY.

As an evidence of the thrift of the people, it may be stated that 600,000 tons of freight, including 8,600,000 bushels of grain, and 250,000 barrels of flour, were forwarded over the line last year

EDUCATION.

Mechanics and workingmen will find the free school system encouraged by the State, and endowed with a large revenue for the support of schools. Their children can live in sight of the church and schoolhouse and grow with the prosperity of the leading State in the Great Western Empire.

PRICES AND TERMS OF PAYMENT.

The prices of these lands vary from $6 to $25 per acre according to location, quality, &c. First-class farming lands sell for about $10 or $12 per acre; and the relative expense of subduing prairie land as compared with wood lands is in the ratio of 1 to 10 in favor of the former. The terms of sale for the bulk of these lands will be

One Year's Interest in advance,

at six per ct. per annum, and six interest notes at six per ct. payable respectively in one, two, three, four, five and six years from date of sale; and four notes for principal, payable in four, five, six and seven years from date of sale; the contract stipulating that one-tenth of the tract purchased shall be fenced and cultivated, each and every year, for five years from date of sale, so that at the end of five years, one-half shall be fenced and under cultivation.

Twenty Per Cent. will be deducted

from the valuation for cash, except the same should be at six dollars per acre, when the cash price will be five dollars.

Pamphlets descriptive of the lands, soil, climate, productions, prices and terms of payment, can be had on application to

J. W. FOSTER, Land Commissioner, Chicago, Illinois.

For the names of the Towns, Villages and Cities situated upon the Illinois Central Railroad see pages 188, 189, 190, APPLETON'S RAILWAY GUIDE.

AN ILLINOIS CENTRAL LAND CIRCULAR, 1865

Despite the passage of the Homestead Act in 1862, settlers often had to buy land in the West from the railroads that had obtained large land grants from the Federal government.

The Bettmann Archive

THROUGH TO THE PACIFIC

Without through railroad transportation to the Pacific, the rapid settlement

CHAPTER III

THE DEVELOPMENT OF A NATIONAL RAIL SYSTEM

IN THE half-century after the Civil War the American people built the world's largest network of railroads. This expansion of the nation's transportation facilities, in turn, affected almost every phase of American civilization. The revolution in transportation helped to produce a realignment in political parties, contributed to the decline in provincialism, and fundamentally altered the government's relation to business enterprise. At the same time, the railroad made possible the rapid settlement of the trans-Mississippi West, the rise of great urban centers, the exploitation of mine, field, and forest, the regional concentration of agriculture and industry, and the distribution of the products of countless farms, mills, and factories to national and world markets. The construction of a country-wide transportation system was perhaps more responsible than any other development for the emergence of modern America.

14. THE GROWTH OF AMERICAN RAILROADS

IN THE decade before the Civil War the railroad mileage of the United States increased from 9,021 to 30,625 miles. The war temporarily interrupted the expansion of the nation's rail system, but construction was resumed after the peace; and between 1868 and the Panic of 1873, 28,000 miles of new track were laid in the United States. During the same years the consolidation of a number of existing roads provided passengers and shippers with through routes from the East to the Middle West. In 1869 the New York Central established continuous service between New York City and Chicago, and by 1874 the Pennsylvania, Erie, and Baltimore and Ohio had reached Chicago.

While the railroads of the Northeast were being consolidated into a few major systems, those of the South were being rebuilt and expanded. At the outset of the Civil War the South possessed 10,000 miles of railroad, most of which had either been destroyed by the conflict or had been rendered useless by constant use and neglect. During the period between the end of the war and the Panic of 1873, funds supplied by the Reconstruction governments, Northern capitalists and European investors enabled the section to rehabilitate its network of railroads and lay an additional 8,000 miles of track. Because of the South's geography most of the region's railroad mileage was confined to the sides of an imaginary triangle with its points at Atlanta, Richmond, and St. Louis. On the northern side of this triangle the Baltimore and Ohio vindicated its name in 1873 by completing its line to Cincinnati, while the Norfolk and Western penetrated the Appalachian Mountains of western Virginia and eastern Tennessee. On the eastern side the Richmond and Danville, which was controlled by the Pennsylvania Railroad, extended its lines to Atlanta. On the western side of the triangle the Louisville and Nashville connected Cincinnati and Louisville on the Ohio with the Gulf ports of Mobile and New Orleans. Farther to the West this line was paralleled by the Mobile and Ohio. By 1890 the South had more than 50,000 miles of railway.

Railway construction in the Middle West exceeded that of any other section in the years immediately following the Civil War. Even before the East-West roads had overcome the Appalachian barrier, railway lines were under construction that joined Cleveland, Sandusky, and Toledo on Lake Erie with Cincinnati and Portsmouth on the Ohio. Michigan had a road running from the Detroit River to the southeastern shore of Lake Michigan, and Indianapolis had rail connections with Louisville and other Ohio River ports. During the eight years after Appomattox new track was laid in every part of the Middle West. By 1873, Illinois led every other state in the region with approximately five thousand miles; Iowa had five great trunk lines; Wisconsin had more than doubled its railroad mileage; and eight states and territories—Colorado, Kansas, Minnesota, Nebraska, Nevada, the Dakotas, Oregon, and Utah—had been provided with rail facilities for the first time.

The completion of a series of railroads in the Middle West cut down on the freight carried on the Great Lakes and canals of the region. Shipment by rail was not only more direct, but transfer charges were largely eliminated, and commodities could be sent by train to all parts of the country. Equally important, the railroads made continuous hauls in all seasons, whereas water routes were useless in freezing weather. Despite the advantages of rail transportation, the waterways still carried enough freight to serve as a competitive check on the railroads. For example, all-rail rates in the Middle West for December, January, and February, 1872, were 44.4 per cent higher than average all-rail rates for June, July, and August of 1872. But the Lakes' freighters, in spite of a cut in rates, could not retain their one-time monopoly of the grain-carrying trade, and in 1872 approximately 70 per cent of the grain sent east was transported by trunk-line railroads. It was not until the midseventies, when the shipment of iron ore became a major business enterprise, that commerce on the Great Lakes began to revive.

The development of the nation's railway systems had an even more profound effect on the Mississippi's commerce than on that of the Lakes. Before the construction of the East-West railroads, the Mississippi was one of the nation's greatest commercial arteries. But by the early seventies its business was rapidly declining as railroads took over the shipment of the bulk of the region's grain crop. The railroads not only de-

GRAIN SHIPMENTS IN 1872.

	Bushels
Receipts of grain at Chicago and Milwaukee	111,478,245
Receipts of grain at St. Louis	28,365,945
SHIPPED EAST	
From Chicago and Milwaukee	102,695,975
From St. Louis	6,597,126
TOTAL SHIPPED EAST	109,293,191
SHIPPED SOUTH	
From Chicago and Milwaukee	738,665
From St. Louis	15,750,202
TOTAL SHIPPED SOUTH	16,488,867

prived the Mississippi of most of its traffic, but they also destroyed its distinctive way of life. In a characteristically vivid passage, Mark Twain described the change that occurred on the river:

Boat used to land . . . captain on hurricane roof . . . mighty stiff and straight . . . iron ramrod for a spine . . . kid gloves, plug tile, hair parted behind . . . man on shore takes off hat and says: "Got twenty-eight tons of wheat cap'n . . . be a great favor if you can take them." Captain says: "I'll take two of them . . ." and don't even condescend to look at him. But nowadays the captain takes off his old slouch, and smiles all the way around to the back of his ears, and gets off a bow which he hasn't got any ramrod to interfere with, and says: "Glad to see you, Smith, glad to see you—you're looking well—haven't seen you looking so well for years—what you got for us?" "Nuth'n," says Smith; and he keeps his hat on, and just turns his back and goes to talking with somebody else.

The fundamental changes produced by the development of a network of railroads in the East and Middle West were overshadowed by the extension of the nation's rail system to the Pacific coast. For almost two decades before the firing on Sumter, Americans in all sections of the nation had discussed both the desirability and feasibility of a transcontinental railroad. Throughout these years the project received its principal support from Asa Whitney, a New York merchant who had made a fortune in the China trade and had long been convinced that a railroad to the Pacific would enable American businessmen to regain their earlier ascendency in the Far East. Whitney sought to advance his program through lectures, pamphlets, addresses to state legislatures, and memorials to the Federal government. *Niles Weekly* thought him the "prince of all projectors," and *DeBow's Review* stated that he "perhaps more than any man in the country illustrated the importance of a connection to the Pacific." In 1845, five years before Senator Stephen Douglas and his associates obtained a land grant for the Illinois Central, Whitney asked Congress to grant a strip of the public domain sixty miles wide along the route of his proposed railway. Boards of trade and chambers of commerce, as well as sixteen state legislatures, sent resolutions to Congress in support of Whitney's plan.

Despite the efforts of Whitney and others, sectional rivalry blocked adoption of the bills, and it was not until after the South's secession that the project was approved. By an act of 1862 and an amendatory act of 1864, Congress created a Union Pacific Railroad Company and authorized it to build a line west from Omaha, Nebraska, through Wyoming, Utah, and Nevada to the eastern boundary of California. The Central Pacific, a California corporation organized by a group of Sacramento businessmen, headed by Leland Stanford, Collis P. Huntington, Mark Hopkins, and Charles Crocker, was to construct the western end of the line. Both companies received substantial aid from the Federal government. Congress donated a 400-foot right of way across the public domain, furnished the stone, timber, and earth needed for the undertaking, and awarded land grants of 12,800 acres in alternate sections for every mile of road constructed. In addition, both the Union Pacific and Central Pacific obtained a thirty-year government loan of $16,000 a mile for track laid through level country, $48,000 a mile for the mountainous regions, and $32,000 a mile for those portions constructed between the mountain ranges. This loan was secured by a second mortgage on the completed system, and the builders were permitted to issue first mortgage bonds equal in amount to the government lien.

The construction of the first transcontinental railway was attended by a series of problems that delayed, but did not prevent, the completion of the project. Because of the shortage of labor in the West, the Central Pacific had to import thousands of Chinese workers. Machinery and rolling stock, all of which came from the East, had to be shipped around Cape Horn or sent overland across the Isthmus of Panama. Iron, which sold for $62 a ton in New York, was worth $150 in San Francisco, and locomotives that cost $8000 in the East brought $32,500 in Sacramento. The difficulty of securing supplies was dwarfed by the magnitude of the engineering problem—mountains had to be scaled, tunnels bored, and snow that was often more than sixty feet deep had to be blasted out. Hundreds of workers lost their lives in snowslides and avalanches. Work was frequently interrupted by Indian raids. In spite of these handicaps the two lines met fifty-three miles west of Ogden, Utah, in the spring of 1869, the Central Pacific having received permission to build eastward beyond the California boundary. In May, when the last spike joining East and West was driven, Whitney's dream was at last realized, for the Chicago and Northwestern had already reached Omaha and made connection with the Union Pacific, and the Kansas Pacific had penetrated as far west as Denver and joined the Union Pacific at Cheyenne.

The completion of the first transcontinental railroad had immediate consequences. American manufacturers and merchants for the first time had an opportunity to distribute their goods to a nation-wide market. Businessmen interested in trade with the Orient and the Far West were placed in direct communication with both their customers and the sources of essential raw materials. At the same time Western miners and farmers were no longer priced out of the Eastern market by the high cost of transportation. Furthermore, the inauguration of transcontinental service was directly responsible for the construction of a number of parallel trunk lines. Before the Panic of 1873 temporarily checked the expansion of the nation's rail system to the Pacific coast, work was in progress on the Northern Pacific, Atlantic and Pacific, Texas and Pacific, and the Atchison, Topeka, and Santa Fé. Finally, the land-grant roads stimulated settlement west of the Mississippi. Built in advance of population and often heavily burdened with high construction costs and watered stock, many of the new trans-Mississippi railways found difficulty in obtaining sufficient receipts to meet current costs and dividends. Even the Union-Central Pacific, which at the outset enjoyed a regional monopoly, was soon in financial difficulties. As a consequence, they made every effort to people their wide holdings. They established land departments, subsidized advertising campaigns, sent recruiting agents to Eastern as well as European centers, and carried homeseekers at reduced fares.

The depression of the midseventies halted railroad construction in every section of the country; but the hard times proved only an interlude, and by the end of the decade the railroad boom was again in full swing. More than 40,000 miles of lines were built in the 1870's, and a

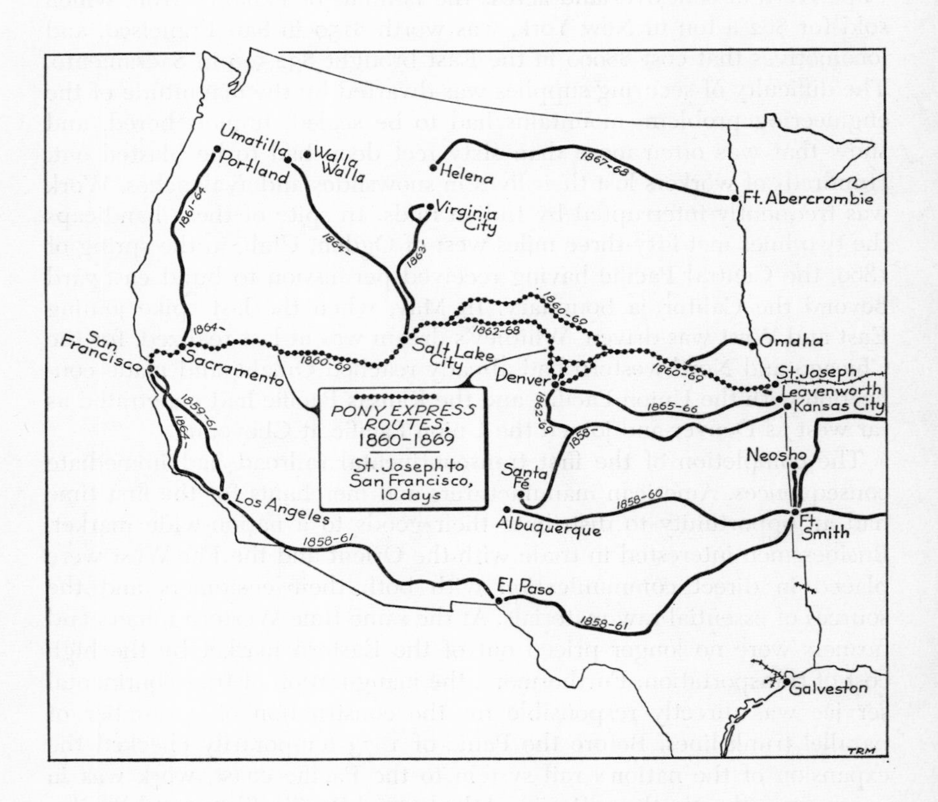

4. OVERLAND FROM THE MISSISSIPPI TO THE PACIFIC

These maps indicate the extent to which the main railroad lines, shown on the facing page, approximated the routes of the pony express and the overland stage, shown above.

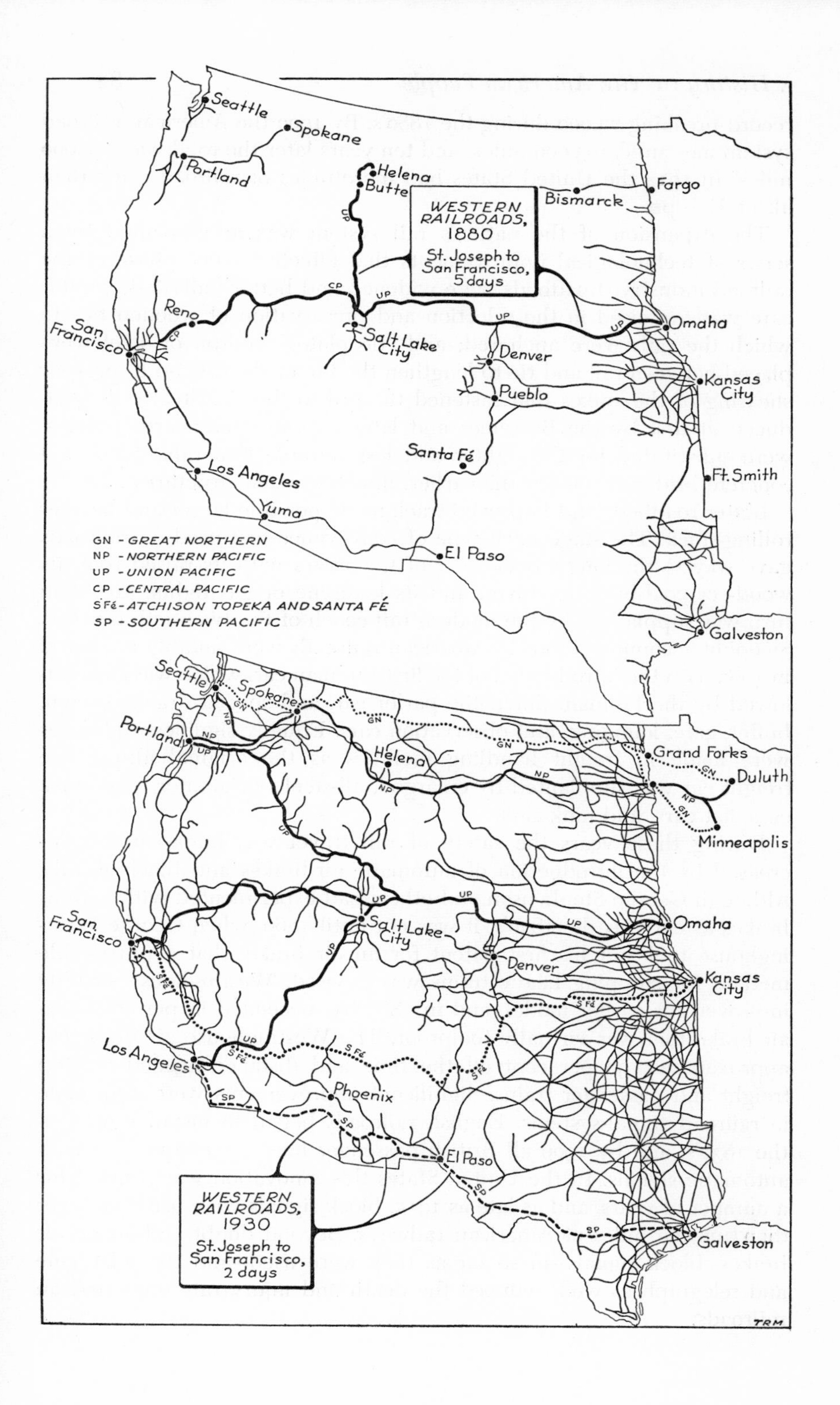
WESTERN RAILROADS, 1880
St. Joseph to San Francisco, 5 days
Seattle
Spokane
Portland
Helena
Butte
Fargo
Bismarck
Reno
San Francisco
Salt Lake City
Omaha
Denver
Kansas City
Pueblo
Santa Fé
Ft. Smith
Los Angeles
Yuma
El Paso
Galveston
GN - GREAT NORTHERN
NP - NORTHERN PACIFIC
UP - UNION PACIFIC
CP - CENTRAL PACIFIC
S Fé - ATCHISON TOPEKA AND SANTA FÉ
SP - SOUTHERN PACIFIC
Grand Forks
Duluth
Minneapolis
Phoenix
WESTERN RAILROADS, 1930
St. Joseph to San Francisco, 2 days
TRM

record-breaking 73,000 during the 1880's. By 1900 the American railroad system measured 193,000 miles; and ten years later the total was 240,000 miles. In 1914 the United States had more miles of railroad track than all of Europe.

The expansion of the nation's rail system was accompanied by a series of technological improvements that affected every phase of the railroad industry. Roadbeds were widened and better ballasted; greater care was exercised in the selection and preservation of wooden ties to which the rails were anchored; and "tie plates" of iron or steel were placed between rail and tie to lengthen the life of the tie and to prevent shearing of the spikes that fastened the rail to the tie. Steel rails, produced at first by the Bessemer and later by the open-hearth process, were substituted for the lighter and less durable iron rails. Steel and concrete bridges replaced the earlier, flimsy wooden structures.

Better roadbeds and improved track made possible larger and heavier rolling-stock. The stagecoach type of conveyance first used on railroads gave way to the long wooden car of the 1880's with its raised roof, its wood- or coal-burning stoves, and its kerosene or gas lights; and it in turn was supplanted by the modern rail coach of the twentieth century. Sleeping accommodations in American railroads were notably improved in 1865 with the introduction of the first Pullman car, which was soon followed by the Pullman diner, the parlor car, and special drawing-room, buffet, cafe, lounging, and observation cars. Equally significant changes were made in freight handling facilities as the original all-purpose freight car was supplanted by enlarged, all-steel refrigerator cars, stock cars, flat cars, and tank cars.

During these years the safety of rail travel was immeasurably increased by the introduction of automatic air-brakes and block signals. Although George Stephenson and others had experimented with various brakes as early as the 1830's, it was not until 1869, when George Westinghouse took out his first patent for an air brake, that a practicable method for stopping heavy trains was devised. Westinghouse steadily improved his earlier model, and in 1887 he succeeded in perfecting an air brake that was virtually foolproof. The Westinghouse air brake cut approximately 90 per cent off the time and distance needed to stop freight and passenger trains. Significant improvements were also made in railroad signal-systems. English railroads began to install signals in the 1830's, and by 1900 all British passenger lines were equipped with automatic signals. In the United States this innovation was resisted for a number of years, and as late as 1915, block signals were used on fewer than 100,000 miles of American railways. Beyond doubt, automatic air brakes, block signals—in so far as they were used—and the telephone and telegraph as well, reduced the death and injury rate on American railroads.

15. RAILROAD CONSOLIDATION IN THE EAST AND MIDDLE WEST

BEFORE the Civil War, railroad construction had been largely confined to relatively short, detached lines that supplemented water routes or connected nearby towns and cities. In the postwar years, many of these local roads were joined together to form more comprehensive units. The consolidation movement was in part the result of the desire of the railroad operators to provide their customers with continuous rail-travel over comparatively large distances. Even more important was the determination of many railroad executives to eliminate competition. The rate wars that developed among rival carriers demonstrated that unrestricted competition reduced the revenues of all lines. In an attempt to guarantee their profits the railroad operators organized pools. The rates fixed by the pools, however, could not be enforced, and so-called "gentlemen's agreements" were broken almost as soon as they were made. When voluntary measures failed to achieve the desired objectives, the more powerful roads bought up their weaker rivals. Through merger or purchase, competition was systematically eliminated, and by World War I a few gigantic systems dominated the American railroad industry.

The first major product of the consolidation movement was the New York Central system. As early as 1862, Cornelius Vanderbilt had started to piece together the links of an all-rail route between New York and Chicago. In 1869 he combined the New York Central and Hudson River railroads to establish a through route from New York City to Buffalo. In the following year, when he obtained control of the Lake Shore and Michigan Southern, the New York Central consisted of 965 miles of track connecting Chicago with the Atlantic seaboard. Agreements in 1870 with the Rock Island and the Chicago and Northwestern enabled him to provide uninterrupted service to as far west as Omaha. Before his death in 1877, he had secured the Michigan Central, which ran between Detroit and Chicago, and the Canadian Southern Railway, which linked Detroit and Toronto. A far-sighted railroad manager, Vanderbilt doubled-tracked the Central's lines with heavier rails, improved its roadbed, bridged streams and embankments with sturdier materials, bought new rolling stock, acquired the Grand Central Terminal in New York City, and shortened the running time for passenger service between New York and Chicago from fifty hours to twenty-four.

When Vanderbilt died, control of the New York Central passed to his son, William, and to the House of Morgan. But the change in administration did not prevent the road's continued expansion. By the turn of the century the New York Central had gained entrance into Boston and

Montreal, had penetrated the coal, iron and oil regions of central and western Pennsylvania, and had terminals in Wheeling, Cincinnati, Louisville, Cairo, Peoria, St. Louis, and in Mackinaw City at the upper extremity of the lower peninsula of Michigan. Both the mileage and the capitalization of the Vanderbilt system were further increased when the younger Vanderbilt was practically blackmailed into acquiring the New York, Chicago and St. Louis, and the West Shore lines. The first of these, known as the "Nickel Plate," paralleled the Lake Shore and Michigan Southern. Built by a group of railroad freebooters for no other purpose than to exact tribute from the owners of the New York Central, it was eventually purchased by Vanderbilt at a price so high that he is said to have thought the rails must be made of "nickel plate." The West Shore, extending up the west bank of the Hudson to Albany and then westward parallel to the original New York Central, was acquired under similar circumstances.

The New York Central's extensive facilities were rivaled by those of the Pennsylvania, which for a number of years had monopolized the traffic between Philadelphia and Pittsburgh. Under the direction of J. Edgar Thomson, the Pennsylvania reached Chicago almost as soon as the New York Central; and by buying the United Canal and Railroad Companies' lines across New Jersey it obtained an approach to New York City. During the seventies the Pennsylvania acquired through purchase a second line to Chicago and a direct route to St. Louis. By 1900 the Pennsylvania stretched westward to Keokuk and St. Louis, southward to Wilmington, Baltimore, Washington, and Richmond, and northeastward across New Jersey to the harbor of New York. Its lines connected most of the important industrial centers of the Middle and North Atlantic states, and it had feeders running south to the main Ohio River towns, and north to the principal Great Lakes ports. After A. J. Cassatt became president of the Pennsylvania in 1899, the company bored a double-track tunnel under the Hudson River, erected the Pennsylvania Terminal in New York City, made connections with the New Haven system, and acquired the Long Island Railroad. By 1914 the Pennsylvania was able to compete on even terms with the New York Central for the rail business of the greatest harbor in the world.

Because of its inability to gain direct access to New York City, the Baltimore and Ohio was always at a competitive disadvantage. Nevertheless, under the direction of John W. Garrett, who was president of the road from 1858 to 1884, the Baltimore and Ohio became one of the nation's major rail systems. It built branch lines, bridged the Ohio, extended its roads north to Lake Erie and west to Chicago, Cincinnati, and St. Louis, and constructed a new line between Baltimore and Philadelphia. It eliminated many dangerous and circuitous stretches, improved its roadbed and rolling stock, and made a beginning in double tracking the main line. Garrett also built or acquired steamboats, docks, resort hotels, and grain elevators; and in addition, he organized an express company, a telegraph company, and a sleeping-car company. After Garrett's death the Baltimore and Ohio became involved in a rate war with the Pennsylvania, its most formidable rival, and went into receivership. In subsequent years, it was controlled first by the Pennsylvania and then by the Union Pacific. Although during this period it acquired the Cincinnati, Hamilton, and Dayton Railroad, which tapped the coal districts of southern Ohio and linked Toledo and Detroit with Cincinnati, the Baltimore and Ohio failed to keep pace with its competitors. Not until Daniel Willard became its president in 1910 did the system again play a leading rôle in the history of American transportation.

The other major Eastern rail system to link the Northeast and Middle West was the Erie. More renowned for the stock manipulations of its directors than for the service it furnished its customers, the Erie in the postwar years was the most corruptly managed railroad in the land. It was not until the midseventies that the Erie was able to escape the clutches of Drew, Gould, and Fisk, and by then it was in bankruptcy. Following its reorganization in 1878, it resumed its policy of expansion until the Panic of 1893 forced it into the fourth receivership in its history. Reorganized once more—this time with the aid of the House of Morgan—the Erie's directors finally settled down to the mundane business of improving their line's facilities and of converting the road into one of the nation's most important carriers of anthracite and bituminous coal.

The principal railway systems of the South—the Southern Railway, the Atlantic Coast Line, and the Illinois Central—like the major railroads of the other sections of the country, were the products of a succession of mergers. The Richmond and West Point Terminal Railroad, the predecessor of the Southern Railway, was notable both for its financial manipulation and its consolidation activity in the postbellum transportation industry. By 1890, when it controlled approximately nine thousand miles of track, it had three important north-south lines and three east-west lines connecting the Mississippi Valley with the Atlantic coast. But the Richmond Terminal road was poorly built, badly co-ordinated, overcapitalized, and mismanaged. It was forced into receivership and in 1893 was reorganized by the House of Morgan; in the following year it emerged as the Southern Railway. Under Morgan domination it soon became the foremost railway system of the South. Stretching from Washington to New Orleans and extending up the valley of the Mississippi to Cincinnati and St. Louis, the Southern Railway eventually reached almost every city of importance in the territory bordering on both sides of the Appalachians.

The Atlantic Coast Line Railroad, the Southern Railway's chief rival, was the product of the consolidation of more than a hundred small independent railroads along the Atlantic Coast from Richmond, Virginia, to Fort Myers, Florida. This consolidation, which had been retarded by the Civil War, the Panic of 1873, and the use of different gauges, proceeded rapidly during the nineties, and in 1898 the Atlantic Coast Line Railroad of Virginia and the Atlantic Coast Line of South Carolina were organized. In 1900 these two companies were united by Northern financial interests to form the main route of the present Atlantic Coast Line. Farther south the Savannah, Florida, and Western, a combination of a large number of short lines, was purchased outright by the newly formed Atlantic Coast Line. Two years later John W. ("Bet-you-a-million") Gates bought control of the Louisville and Nashville, one of the most important north-south railroad arteries west of the Appalachians. The House of Morgan, fearing that Gates might use his newly acquired property to the detriment of the Southern Railway, fell into the speculative trap and paid Gates an enormous amount for his Louisville and Nashville holdings. Control over the Louisville and Nashville was then turned over to the Atlantic Coast Line.

The Illinois Central shared with the Southern the north-south rail traffic of the Mississippi Valley area. When the Illinois Central was completed in 1856, it consisted of 700 miles of track that roughly paralleled the state of Illinois' western border and a 250-mile branch line to Chicago. In subsequent years it increased its trackage to approximately 9000 miles by the acquisition of the Dubuque and Sioux City Railroad, the Chicago, St. Louis and New Orleans Railroad, the Yazoo and Mississippi Valley Railroad, and the Central of Georgia. These additions enabled the Illinois Central to cross the state of Iowa and reach New Orleans over a route closely paralleling the Mississippi, and to enter Savannah by way of Birmingham and Macon. Although the Illinois Central system hauled considerable quantities of cotton, grain, and fruit, approximately 50 per cent of its freight was composed of coal, iron, and other mineral products.

16. RAILROAD CONSOLIDATION IN THE TRANS-MISSISSIPPI WEST

TWELVE major rail systems were established in the region stretching from the Mississippi and Great Lakes to the Pacific Ocean. Six of these—the Union Pacific, Southern Pacific, Santa Fé, Northern Pacific, Great Northern, and the Chicago, Milwaukee, St. Paul, and Pacific—were transcontinentals that linked the Pacific ports of Los Angeles, San Francisco, Portland, Tacoma, and Seattle with the East. The tracks of five systems—the Chicago and Rock Island, the Chicago,

Burlington, and Quincy, the Chicago and North Western, the Missouri Pacific, and the St. Louis–San Francisco—were confined almost entirely to the valley, while the Western Pacific reached no farther east than Salt Lake City, where it made connections with the Denver and Rio Grande. Of the twelve trans-Mississippi systems, five had eastern termini in Chicago, two in St. Louis, two in St. Paul, one in Council Bluffs, and one in New Orleans.

The Western railroad industry attracted some of the nation's ablest business executives and some of America's most notorious freebooters. Among the latter was Jay Gould, who, after doing more than his share to wreck the Erie, purchased a controlling interest in a number of weak railroads in the trans-Mississippi West. Gould's acquisitions included the Kansas Pacific and the Denver Pacific, which together paralleled the Union Pacific as far as Cheyenne. By threatening to extend this line to Ogden and by cutting rates, he forced the Union Pacific to accept his terms for the consolidation of the three properties. Under this arrangement, Kansas Pacific and Denver Pacific stocks, quoted at 12, were exchanged for Union Pacific stock, quoted at 93. As a result of the bargain driven by Gould, the Union Pacific was saddled with two railroads that it did not need and was compelled to assume a burdensome financial responsibility. During the eighties the Union Pacific, faced by increasing competition and compelled by Gould to purchase from him lines that he had bought for relatively little, rapidly expanded its mileage. At the same time, the road, which from the outset had been hampered by its heavy indebtedness, was plunged into financial difficulties by Gould's manipulations. The Panic of 1893 drove it into receivership, and in the next four years it had to relinquish 5,800 miles of line. In 1897, following a foreclosure sale, the Union Pacific was taken over by E. H. Harriman.

Harriman had begun his business career in 1862 as a fourteen-year old office boy in Wall Street. Seven years later he owned a seat on the New York Stock Exchange, and in 1881 he entered the railroad industry with the purchase of a bankrupt railway that he immediately reorganized and sold at a profit to the Pennsylvania. After serving as a director of the Illinois Central, he turned his attention to the Union Pacific. Aware that the road, despite its financial difficulties, was potentially profitable, he participated in its reorganization in the mid-nineties, and became a member of its board in 1897, chairman of the board's executive committee in 1898, and president of the entire system in 1903. Soon after becoming chairman, Harriman spent $25,000,000 obtained from Kuhn, Loeb, and Company on improving the Union Pacific's roadbed, reducing grades, eliminating curves, purchasing new rolling-stock, and buying up other railroads. In 1900, he assured the Union Pacific of access to the Southwest by purchasing a half-interest in the San Pedro, Los Angeles, and Salt Lake. In the following year he acquired control of both the Southern Pacific and the Central Pacific. This transaction not only gave the Union Pacific direct connection with Sacramento and Oakland, but it also made Harriman the dominant railroad figure of the Southwest.

Before its acquisition by Harriman, the Southern Pacific was dominated by Leland Stanford, Collis P. Huntington, Mark Hopkins, and Charles Crocker. Setting out to monopolize California's railroads in 1872, these men had quickly learned that their economic objectives could be most readily attained by political means. They bought congressmen and state legislators and made the Southern Pacific offices in San Francisco the capital of the state in all but name. Despite the political power of its principal backers, the Southern Pacific was unable to exclude other lines from the Southwest, and throughout these years it was given serious competition by the Atchison, Topeka, and Santa Fé Railway. By 1884 the Santa Fé stretched from Atchison on the Missouri River to San Diego on the Pacific. Two years later it established connections with Chicago and Galveston on the Gulf of Mexico, and some years later, through purchase and construction it extended its tracks to San Francisco Bay.

Like the Southwest, the Pacific Northwest was provided with ample railroad facilities in the years after the Civil War. A branch line of the Union Pacific, four American transcontinental roads, and the Canadian Pacific all tapped this region. The first transcontinental line to serve the Northwest was the Northern Pacific. Although chartered by Congress in 1864 to build a railroad from some point on Lake Superior to Puget Sound, the company did not begin construction until 1870, when it secured the financial support of the banking house of Jay Cooke and Company. The crash of 1873 forced both Jay Cooke and Company and the Northern Pacific into bankruptcy; and not until the road was reorganized in 1875 was construction resumed. But before the Northern Pacific reached the Pacific coast, it was acquired by Henry Villard, who feared that the new line would jeopardize his extensive holdings in the Willamette and Columbia valleys. Soon after assuming the presidency of the Northern Pacific in 1881, Villard completed its route to Portland and then north to Tacoma on Puget Sound. In 1883 the ceremony of driving the last spike in the main line took place in the wilds of western Montana in the presence of such distinguished personages as President Arthur, General Grant, Viscount James Bryce, and a large number of lesser dignitaries, newspaper men, and soldiers. Pictures, stereopticon slides, and literature describing the event and advertising the Eden-like character of the Northwest found their way to all parts of the globe. Villard agents spread their dragnet throughout Europe in quest of immigrants who soon were settling in the Oregon country by the tens of thousands.

Villard's holdings in the Northwest were soon rivaled by those of James J. Hill, who in 1878 purchased the virtually bankrupt St. Paul and Pacific Railroad. Despite its name, this short Minnesota line, formerly a feeder of the Northern Pacific, was little more than a connecting link for the steamboat lines operating on the Mississippi and Red rivers. Hill promptly changed its name to the St. Paul, Minneapolis, and Manitoba Railroad and with the backing of Canadian and American capital pushed its rails westward and northward with a view to capturing Canadian as well as American business. By 1887 the road extended across the Dakotas to Great Falls, Montana, and in 1890 Hill created the Great Northern Railway Company. Three years later the Hill lines reached Seattle. Although the main routes of the Northern Pacific and the Great Northern paralleled each other they were in many respects markedly different. The Hill lines were built without government aid, were better located, and were more efficiently constructed. Routes with favorable grades were selected and sharp curves avoided. Overcapitalization was shunned, financial storms were weathered, and an uninterrupted dividend record maintained. Hill never lost sight of his dictum: "Intelligent management of railroads must be based on exact knowledge of facts. Guesswork will not do." As a railroad manager and financier, he was all that Jay Gould was not.

Like Villard, the creator of the Great Northern realized that the success of his transportation system rested almost wholly upon the development of the territory through which it ran. "Make it desirable," he said, "for people to come here, make it easy for them to carry on their business, and we will get the freight. We consider ourselves and the people along our line as co-partners in the prosperity of the country we both occupy; and the prosperity of the one should mean the prosperity of both; and their adversity will be quickly followed by ours." Not only did Hill carry on a continuous campaign to induce settlers to migrate to the territory served by his railways, but he also sought to make them prosperous customers after their arrival. He established banks, provided for the erection of schools and churches, ran agricultural demonstration trains over his lines, and distributed gratis to farmers of the Northwest blooded bulls imported from England. Throughout his career he never lost sight of the fact that his success as a railroader was intimately bound up with the economic welfare of those who had settled in his empire.

Hill, who received his main financial support from the House of Morgan, which in turn had obtained control over the Northern Pacific, was soon in conflict with Harriman. The immediate cause of their rivalry was the Chicago, Burlington, and Quincy. Because its main line extended from Chicago to Minneapolis, Kansas City, St. Louis, Omaha, Denver, and Billings in Montana, it would provide either Hill or Harriman with access to Chicago, a means of tapping the entire Mississippi Valley market, connections with the cotton carrying roads of the South, and a route that covered the principal lumber consuming states of the nation. When Harriman learned in 1901 that the Hill-Morgan interests had acquired the Chicago, Burlington, and Quincy for the Northern Pacific and Great Northern, he asked for permission to buy a one third interest in the Burlington. But Hill refused, and Harriman sought to obtain control of the Burlington by purchasing a majority of Northern Pacific stock in the open market. To forestall Harriman, the Hill-Morgan group also entered the market. Within a few days shares of Northern Pacific stock rose from $110 to $1000; and because many brokers sold short, 78,000 more shares of the stock were sold than actually existed. Harriman gained control of $78,000,000 out of a total capital stock of $155,000,000; but he still did not have control of the company, for he held only $37,000,000 of the $75,000,000 worth of common stock, whose owners could retire the preferred stock of which he now owned more than half. To avert what in all probability would have been a severe panic, both groups agreed to a truce. At Hill's suggestion they formed the Northern Securities Company with a capitalization of $400,000,000. The shares of this corporation, which was a holding company, were exchanged for all the stock of the jointly owned Northern Pacific and for the great majority of the stock of the Great Northern. Three of the fifteen directors of the Northern Securities Company were also directors of the Union Pacific. Three formerly independent roads—the Northern Pacific, the Great Northern, and the Chicago, Burlington and Quincy—were united, and Harriman shared in their control. Under this arrangement a small group of railroad operators and Wall Street financiers controlled practically all the major railroad lines west of the Mississippi.

17. FINANCING THE RAILROADS

ALL the postwar railway projects required large capital outlays. Money was needed for surveys, rights of way, grading, laying the rails, and the acquisition of rolling stock and other essential equipment. Railroad investments, moreover, were highly speculative, for many lines were built in advance of population, and there was no way of ascertaining their future earning power. Finally, because of the United States' limited financial resources, the supply of private capital was rarely equal to the demand. Despite these difficulties, the railroads were built; and to the funds supplied by American and European inves-

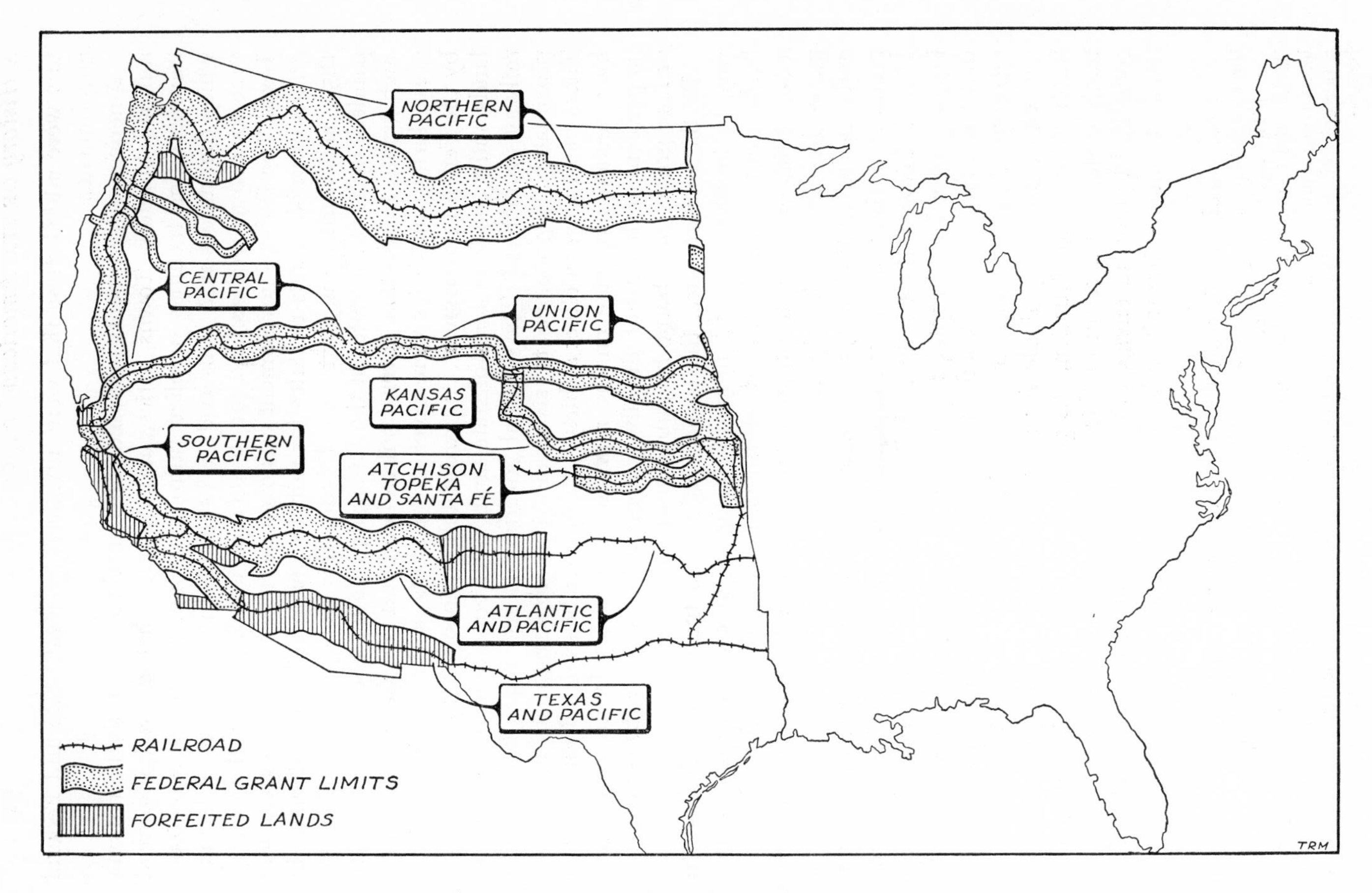

5. FEDERAL LAND GRANTS TO RAILROADS

tors were added those that were advanced by local, state and Federal governments.

American governments provided substantial assistance to the nation's railroad builders. Towns, cities, and counties that desired improved transportation facilities supplied railroad promoters with $300,000,000, while the states—at a conservative estimate—furnished an additional $228,000,000 as well as land grants totaling approximately the area of Texas. The Federal government was even more generous. Congressional grants of public lands to states for railway purposes were first made in 1850, and during the next two decades this policy was steadily expanded. By 1871 the states of the Mississippi Valley had received eighty such grants. In addition, several railroad corporations chartered by Congress during the sixties were given great tracts of the national domain by the Federal government. Approximately 131,000,000 acres of Federal lands and 55,000,000 acres of state lands were conditionally credited to railway promoters.* The Federal government also made loans of approximately $65,000,000 to six trans-Mississippi railroad companies. These loans were in effect a thirty-year interest bearing subsidy secured by a second mortgage on the railroad properties.† In all probability 40 per cent of the cost of all railway construction before 1870—exclusive of land grants—was borne by public authority.

By the midseventies, the earlier enthusiasm for railroads had given way to indifference and in many instances to open hostility. Labor leaders, antimonopolists, land reformers, homesteaders, and land speculators demanded that the policy of granting public lands to railroad companies be abandoned. Shippers, victimized by exorbitant rates, rebates, and other railroad abuses, also objected to government assistance to one group of businessmen at the expense of others. The activities of Drew, Fisk, and Gould, the Crédit Mobilier scandals, and the increasing number of railroad bankruptcies convinced Americans in all walks of life that the railroad promoters did not deserve the assistance that they had received. When the Supreme Court in 1872 ruled that counties, towns, and cities were fully liable for all debts that they had contracted to foster railroad construction, the program of public assistance was virtually ended. As a result of this decision taxpayers for many years to come had to pay out money to retire bonds that their governments had issued to finance the railroads. At the same time, there was no way to

* Because of failure to meet all the conditions under which this land was granted, the railroad companies were able to retain only about 116,000,000 acres.

† The leading railroad companies to which the loans were made were the Union Pacific, the Central Pacific, the Western Pacific, and the Kansas Pacific. Although the loans were made with the understanding that each year the railroads were to apply 5 per cent of their net earnings to the discharge of their debt to the government, it became necessary in the late 1890's for the government to threaten foreclosure in order to secure payment. In the settlements effected the government was a loser.

prevent the railroads from defaulting on their obligations. During the seventies, after the damage had been done, several states forbade the extension of public credit to private corporations. That government aid quickened the pace of railroad building is beyond doubt; that it encouraged the construction of roads before they were needed and induced investors to put their money into railroad projects of a highly speculative character is no less true.

Aside from government sources the railroads secured capital from private investors at home and abroad. In the initial stages of the American railroad industry, farmers, workers, and businessmen supplied a relatively large proportion of the funds needed to develop this new method of transportation. The depression of 1837 dried up many of the sources of venture capital in the United States, but by the 1850's and 1860's railroads were again regarded as sound investments. Men and women of small means continued to invest in railway stocks and bonds during these years, but much larger sums were supplied by individuals who had already acquired sizable fortunes from railroading, merchandising, or some other line of enterprise. John Murray Forbes of Boston, David A. Neal of Salem, John C. Green and the Griswolds of New York, all of whom helped to finance the railroads of the Middle West, had made fortunes in the China trade. Associated with them, among others, in their railroad enterprises were John W. Brooks of the Auburn and Rochester Railroad and Erastus Corning, an Albany hardware merchant and first president of the New York Central. The financial backers of the Illinois Central during its early years included Jonathan Sturges, one of the original promoters of the New York and New Haven Railroad; Morris Ketchum, member of the locomotive manufacturing firm of Rogers, Ketchum, and Grosvenor; Franklin Haven, president of the largest bank in New England; Robert Schuyler, president of five railroad companies and probably the most important railroad man of the antebellum period; and J. W. Alsop and T. W. Ludlow, organizers of the Panama Railroad and of the Pacific Mail Steamship Company. Josiah Perham who figured prominently in the early affairs of the Northern Pacific was a Maine merchant and manufacturer. Other investors in Northern Pacific were Governor J. G. Smith of Vermont, builder of the Vermont Central; Robert Bardell, president of the Erie Railway; William G. Fargo of the Wells Fargo Express; and a large Pennsylvania Railroad group headed by Thomas A. Scott and J. Edgar Thomson.

Because native capitalists—despite the growth of America's financial resources—were unable to satisfy the railroads' needs for funds, promoters were eventually forced to turn to Europe for additional money. Although Europeans had helped to finance some of America's earliest railroads, it was not until the 1850's that foreign capital began to play an important rôle in the American transportation industry. Large amounts of English capital, for example, went into the Erie, the Illinois Central, the Michigan Central, and other Midwestern roads. Dutch capitalists invested heavily in the Chicago and Northwestern and had two representatives on the line's board of directors. English and Dutch interests largely financed the Union Pacific; English and German investors had considerable money tied up in the Villard enterprises of the Pacific Northwest; and Europeans held three fourths of the Louisville and Nashville stock. The Northern Pacific seemed at times to be an exclusively German company. Although the excesses of Jay Gould and his followers and the Panic of 1873 sharply checked foreign investment in American railroads, foreign confidence soon revived and was not again seriously undermined until the depression of 1893. But the depression of the nineties, like that of the seventies, had only a temporary effect on the rate of European investment in the United States, and by the turn of the century Europeans owned $3,100,000,000 worth of American railroad securities. After 1900, this trend was reversed, and by 1920 domestic capitalists had taken over the ownership of most of the country's railroads.

DISTRIBUTION OF AMERICAN RAILROAD SECURITIES IN EUROPE

JANUARY 1, 1899*

England	$2,500,000,000
Holland	240,000,000
Germany	200,000,000
Switzerland	75,000,000
France	50,000,000
Rest of Europe	35,000,000
TOTAL	$3,100,000,000

18. EXPLOITING THE RAILROADS

MANY railroad promoters made their profits, not from the legitimate business of railroading, but from manipulation of the money provided them by public and private investors. Through watered stock, security speculation, dummy construction companies, padded costs, and a host of other questionable devices, they gutted the corporations that were unfortunate enough to fall under their control. As the money that they were pocketing had been supplied by either individuals or governments, the railroad executives were in effect robbing both the investor and the taxpayer.

* Reprinted with permission from William Z. Ripley: *Railroads, Finance, and Organization* (New York: Longmans, Green and Company, 1915), p. 6.

The postwar period is full of examples of fraudulent practices in the construction and operation of the railroads. Most of the nation's large rail systems were built by corrupt construction companies, of which the Crédit Mobilier, the Contract and Finance Company, and the South Improvement Company are merely the most notorious examples. Even those roads that were built with a minimum of fraud were frequently the victims of the dishonest—but highly profitable—manipulation of their securities. Railroad promoters, most of whom were speculators with little money of their own, enriched themselves by watering the stock of their companies, by selling bonds to the public while appropriating the stock as a bonus, and by speculating in their companies' securities. The *Banker's Magazine* estimated that in the five years following 1873, European investors in American enterprises—mostly railroads—had lost $600,000,000 by bankruptcy or fraud, and that this had been "going on for more than a generation."

Although the sixties and seventies have generally been thought to mark the high point of railroad corruption, an examination of the years immediately preceding the Panic of 1893 reveals that the railroad promoters had lost none of their earlier ability to dupe the public. With the first signs of hard times, the financial structure of the nation's railroad system began to disintegrate. By July, 1893, 126 companies had been consigned to receiverships, and a year later the number had risen to 192. From 1893 to 1898, approximately 67,000 miles, or about one third of the country's total mileage, underwent foreclosure. The first prominent road to go under was the Philadelphia and Reading. Within a short time, it was followed by the Erie, the Northern Pacific, the Union Pacific, and the Atchison, Topeka, and Santa Fé. A year or two later the Norfolk and Western collapsed, followed by the Baltimore and Ohio. Innumerable lesser lines were added to the wreckage.

Although many observers and railway officials attributed the plight of the railroads to the depression, the operators also had themselves to blame for their predicament. The failure of the Northern Pacific, which twice before had been in the hands of a receiver, was caused by overexpansion, overcapitalization, and a management that was guilty of both looting and inefficiency. The Erie, Santa Fé, and the Union Pacific went to the wall largely because of the mistakes and dishonest practices of past managements. The previous history of the Erie had been notorious. Organized in 1833 as the New York and Erie Railroad, it early met with financial difficulties and finally went into receivership in 1859. Reorganized as the Erie Railway it fell prey to the fraudulent ministrations of Daniel Drew, Jim Fisk, and Jay Gould, and in 1875 it was again in the receiver's hands. Three years later the New York, Lake Erie, and Western Railroad rose from the wreckage of the old Erie. The management of the new company was honest, far-sighted, and industrious; but the colossal overcapitalization that it had inherited from Drew, Fisk, and Gould, as well as a heavy floating debt, did not permit the road to regain enough strength to weather the financial storms of the 1890's.

Like the Erie, the Santa Fé could not escape its past. First opened in 1870, it expanded rapidly and by 1893 had more mileage than any other railroad in the world. But it had already experienced financial difficulties. From 1883 to 1886, as its mileage grew, its fixed charges increased, and its earnings declined. To add to its difficulties Jay Gould, who wanted to gain control of the road, did his best to force it into bankruptcy. In 1889 the company was reorganized, but conditions did not improve, and the Santa Fé had to go into receivership. A subsequent examination of its books disclosed irregularities, dishonest management, and manipulation of accounts.

The Union Pacific was no better off than the Erie or Santa Fé. With the exception of Charles Francis Adams, Jr., president during the eighties, the management from the first was inefficient, extravagant, and venal. Construction frauds saddled the Union Pacific and its subsidiaries with an enormous burden. Gould and his associates, notably Russell Sage and Sidney Dillon, pumped an unending stream of water into the company's stock and compelled the road to buy at exorbitant prices the Kansas Pacific and other lines owned or controlled by them. The depression of the midnineties merely completed the work of those who had already insured the road's insolvency. Gould and Sage did not confine their interests to the Union Pacific, for they employed much the same methods to loot the Toledo, Wabash and Western. Gould and Sage did not ruin every railroad that came under their control. For example, after acquiring the Missouri Pacific, they used it to enrich themselves by diverting freight to it at the expense of their other lines. But even in this instance they were unable to resist the opportunity to defraud investors; and when Missouri Pacific stock reached what they thought was a peak, they dumped it on the market, depressed its value, and then bought it back at a low figure.

The failure of the Philadelphia and Reading early in 1893—its third failure in fifteen years—also illustrates the laxity of American railroad management. Already badly overcapitalized, the Reading, by attempting to secure a partial monopoly of the anthracite coal business and to gain entrance into New England by buying up the stock of two New England roads on margin, ultimately found itself unable to borrow additional funds. Even before the road went into a receivership for the third time, the London *Economist* wrote:

> *The American railway world has afforded abundant scope in the past for all kinds of financial trickery and apparently the "smart" operators, who have reaped such a large harvest in the past, seem*

still disposed to look for further facilities for plunder in the future. The "crop of lambs" to be sheared, of course, varies from time to time, but, on the average, it would appear that the folly of investors may be regarded as a fixed quantity. That, at any rate, is the only conclusion we can draw from close observation of the policy which has been followed by the directors of the Philadelphia and Reading Railroad in the past three years. In this undertaking, which is now one of the most considerable in the United States, a very large amount of capital has been sunk by English investors, and yet their interests seem to count for nothing compared with those of the members of la haute finance, *who have temporarily a big speculative stake in the Reading securities. At least it is impossible on any other hypothesis to explain the action of the directors in regard to the payment of interest on the so-called Income Bonds. . . . To us it appears that there has been an utter lack of all principle in dealing with the right of the Income Bondholders, and their securities have been made to serve as first rate gambling counters for the benefit of the big financiers who are in a position either to pull the strings or to obtain all the inside information. Superficially, indeed, we see little difference between the methods pursued by the Reading directors and some of those which the late Jay Gould employed in his dealings with the Wabash and other similar victims.*

Unlike the Reading, whose management was never for any length of time endowed with a very scrupulous regard for the spirit of the law or for the niceties of business ethics, the Baltimore and Ohio was long regarded as one of the soundest and safest business enterprises in America. By 1887, however, the road, after three years of rapid expansion, needed financial assistance. A syndicate arranged by the House of Morgan and composed of the British banking firm of J. S. Morgan & Son, Baring Brothers & Co., and Brown, Shipley & Co., together with their American associates agreed to come to the relief of the embarrassed road on condition that the management of the company be placed in hands satisfactory to the syndicate. Although the road accepted these terms, the arrangement soon broke down, and debt piled up to such an extent that collapse was inevitable. An examination of the company's affairs during the period of receivership indicated that malpractices had been in large degree responsible for the concern's predicament. Once again the London *Economist* warned British investors to avoid American railway securities:

And when people here find that such malpractices as these have been carried on for a series of years, on what was believed to be one of the best-managed of the American railroads, and that, after they have been exposed, nobody seems to think of bringing those responsible for them to account, it cannot be wondered at if the small degree of confidence in American railroads that has been left them is still further impaired.

The last decade of the nineteenth century, which witnessed the reorganization of so many insolvent railways, also saw an enormous increase in banker financing and banker control of the American railway system. This development marked the culmination of a trend that had begun as early as the 1850's. In the initial stages of the revolution in transportation Eastern bankers like J. E. Thayer of Boston and Moses Taylor of New York and the Barings and Rothschilds of England had funds invested in American railroads. Jay Cooke and Company was closely associated with the Northern Pacific. The Farmers Loan and Trust Company of New York was financially interested in Villard's Northwest undertakings, and one of J. J. Hill's principal backers was George Stephen (afterward Lord Mount Stephen), president of the Bank of Montreal. By the 1890's the nation's major railroad corporations had passed to the control of a few of the largest banking concerns in the United States.

Banking firms like the House of Morgan, engaged primarily in investment banking, were practically compelled to become more interested in railroad finance and control. The railroad industry had become so chaotic because of overexpansion, cut-throat competition, litigation, speculation, blackmail, fraud, and the exploitation of railway-security holders that the elder Morgan and others began to fear for the safety of the investment business. Public confidence both at home and abroad had to be restored if the investment banker was to survive and flourish. As a consequence, banker penetration of the railroad field rapidly grew with the House of Morgan in the lead. To the motive of protection was soon added the desire for power and profits. Strategic stock-ownership, interlocking directorates, voting trusts, and the community of interests were the major devices employed to build up immense railway systems. By the end of the century a large share of the railroad mileage was concentrated in six dominant systems:

Harriman	20,245 miles
Vanderbilt	19,317 "
Morgan	19,073 "
Pennsylvania	18,220 "
Gould	16,074 "
Hill	10,373 "

Of these, only two—the Harriman and the Gould—were outside the complete or partial domination of the House of Morgan, and both of these were partially controlled by Kuhn, Loeb and Company.

19. STATE AND FEDERAL REGULATION

THE NATURE of railroading soon made it one of the nation's most competitive forms of business enterprise. With heavy fixed charges that continued regardless of the amount of freight carried, railroads were compelled to resort to almost any expedient to lure customers from rival lines. Soon after the Civil War some railroads began to offer rebates to large shippers in return for a monopoly of their transportation business. When this did not provide a sufficient attraction, favored customers were granted drawbacks, that is, a rebate on the freight charges paid by their competitors. On the other hand, most farmers and small businessmen, who had relatively little bargaining power, were frequently charged prohibitive rates. Towns and cities as well as individual shippers suffered from discriminatory railroad practices. Communities served by competing lines could count on minimum rail charges, whereas those with only one rail connection were charged all that the traffic would bear. Through the long- and short-haul freight clauses customers in some areas had to pay higher rates to ship goods a short haul than others who were more favorably located paid for a long haul. Thus, freight rates on the Pennsylvania Railroad from Pittsburgh to Philadelphia were higher than those on the same line from Cleveland to Philadelphia. Under the circumstances, the weight of goods and the number of miles they were carried frequently had little or no effect on the determination of freight rates.

The inability of the railroads to establish and maintain an equitable system of rate-making led many small shippers to demand that the government intervene to eliminate discriminatory railroad practices. Midwestern farmers, who were among the most helpless of the railroads' victims, took the lead in urging some form of governmental regulation. From 1870 to 1874, the Grange, a farmers' organization organized in 1867, was able to induce the legislatures of Illinois, Wisconsin, Minnesota, and Iowa to adopt laws fixing maximum and minimum rates for freight and passenger traffic and warehousing. The so-called Granger laws also provided for the abolition of passes and the establishment of state commissions to regulate rail transportation. Although the railroads sought to nullify the Granger laws through litigation, they met with little initial success. In 1876 in *Munn v. Illinois* the railroad lawyers maintained before the Supreme Court that a state's right to fix rates was a violation of that part of the Fourteenth Amendment which stipulated that a state could not deprive a person of property without due process of law. But the Court rejected this contention and ruled that "when . . . one devotes his property to a use in which the public has an interest, he, in effect, grants to the public an interest in that use, and must submit to be controlled by the public for the common good. . . . He may withdraw his grant by discontinuing the use; but, so long as he maintains the use, he must submit to the control." In the same year in *Peik v. Chicago and Northwestern Railroad,* the Court affirmed the right of a state to fix rail rates in interstate traffic. But ten years later this decision was reversed in the case of *Wabash, St. Louis, and Pacific Railway Company v. Illinois,* when a majority of the justices stated that the determination of rates for interstate shipments was outside the province of a state legislature. The Wabash decision made it clear that under the Constitution only the Federal government had the authority to regulate the nation's major rail systems.

As early as 1872, Congress had attempted a measure of railroad regulation with the adoption of an act that was designed to eliminate some of the abuses in the transportation of livestock. In the same year, President Grant in his annual message spoke of the need for "more certain and cheaper transportation, of the rapidly increasing western and southern products, to the Atlantic seaboard," and the Senate established a committee under William Windom to investigate railroad practices. The Windom Committee, which made its report in 1874, advocated numerous changes in the organization and administration of railroads, but placed its greatest emphasis on the desirability of a reduction in rail rates. Although the House responded to the Windom report with the enactment of a bill to lower rates, the Senate did not act on this measure. In subsequent years Congress shifted its attention from the problem of rate reduction to proposals for the prevention of discriminatory practices that were injurious to small shippers. Measures designed to prevent various forms of discrimination were repeatedly introduced into Congress, but it was not until the Wabash decision in 1886 that the need for this type of legislation became acute. Following the report of a committee headed by Senator Shelby Cullom of Illinois, Congress in 1887 adopted the Interstate Commerce Act.

The Interstate Commerce, or Cullom, Act stated that all charges for interstate "transportation of passengers, or property . . . , or for the receiving, delivering, storage, or handling of such property, shall be reasonable and just." Discriminatory practices such as rebates and drawbacks were declared unlawful, while the long- and short-haul abuse was made illegal under certain circumstances. Pooling agreements were specifically forbidden. Schedules of rates had to be published and filed with the government; and corporations and individuals who violated these provisions were subject to a fine of not more than $5,000.* The implementation of the regulatory provisions of the Cullom Act was entrusted to a five-man Interstate Commerce Commission, which was granted the "authority to inquire into the management of the business of all com-

* In 1889, provision was also made for imprisonment of individual violators.

mon carriers" in interstate trade and the right to "obtain from such common carriers full and complete information" concerning their business practices. After hearing complaints from shippers, the commission was empowered to direct railroads to alter their policies. If the railroad refused to obey the commission's order, provision was made for recourse to the courts.

The Interstate Commerce Act was, as Professor William Z. Ripley remarked, "a compromise, entirely satisfactory to no one."* Senator Nelson Aldrich of Rhode Island, who was opposed to any form of Federal regulation, thought the new law a "delusion and a sham . . . made to answer the clamor of the ignorant and the unreasoning." In the last analysis its effectiveness rested with the courts. The Interstate Commerce Act did not permit the commission to fix rates, and the judiciary alone had the power to determine the measure's scope and enforceability.

The effectiveness of the Interstate Commerce Act was impaired from the outset by the refusal of shippers, who feared retaliation from the railroads, to lodge complaints with the commission. During the first five years of its existence, the commission received only thirty-nine formal complaints. The commission soon learned that it was unable to compel witnesses to testify, and appeals to the courts produced interminable delays. Even those cases that eventually reached the Supreme Court generally resulted in decisions that upheld the railroad rather than the commission. From 1887 to 1905, the Supreme Court handed down sixteen decisions in cases appealed by the commission to the courts. In one of these the commission's ruling was partially reaffirmed; in the other fifteen its position was reversed. The most important effect of the Court's stand was to remove any remaining doubt concerning the inability of the commission to fix rates. In 1897 in the Maximum Freight Rate case, the Court ruled that "under the interstate commerce act the commission has no power to prescribe the tariff of rates which shall control in the future, and therefore cannot invoke a judgment in mandamus from the courts to enforce any such tariff by it prescribed." As Justice Harlan was to point out in a minority opinion a few months later, the Court's attitude meant that the commission had "been shorn, by judicial interpretation, of authority to do anything of an effective character." It was not until the advent of the Progressive movement that a successful effort was made to give the government adequate authority over railroad rates.

* William Z. Ripley: *Railroads; Rates and Regulations* (New York: Longmans, Green and Company, 1912), p. 453.

CHAPTER IV

INDUSTRIAL EVOLUTION AND REVOLUTION

THE FORCES that were responsible for the rapid development of American industry during the post-Civil War decades had been maturing for more than half a century before the outbreak of the conflict. The Civil War, contrary to popular belief, did not "cause" what is popularly known as the American Industrial Revolution; it did, however, speed up a process that had been evolving at a relatively slow rate during the antebellum period. Before the Civil War almost all the features of a modern industrial nation existed in isolated and embryonic form within the United States. After the war a period of unprecedented expansion placed the United States among the leading manufacturing nations of the world.

20. THE BACKGROUND OF INDUSTRIAL EXPANSION

BY 1860 the United States had a tradition of technological innovation, and "Yankee ingenuity" had already been applied to scores of industries. The sewing machine had revolutionized the men's clothing industry; the Hoe press had worked a similar transformation in the newspaper business; Colt revolvers were the best in the world; reapers had started their conquest of the prairies; vulcanized rubber was a commonplace; American iron manufacturers had experimented with the Bessemer process; New Englanders were turning out guns and watches on a mass production basis with standardized interchangeable parts; and Boston was the largest boot and shoe center in the world.

Some years before the first Southern cannon had been fired on Sumter, the New England textile industry—to mention only one example—had set the pattern for the future development of the American factory system. The application of machinery to the industrial process, division of labor, use of a landless proletariat as a laboring force, the corporate device for raising large amounts of capital on the basis of limited liability, trained clerical staffs, and a distinct managerial class were all characteristic features of many of the mill towns in the Merrimac and Connecticut valleys in the 1850's. Europe, too, provided many lessons from which the American factory owners profited. English industrialists, as pioneers, had been compelled to solve their technological and organizational problems on a trial and error basis. American manufacturers, entering ground which had already been cleared, were frequently able to avoid the mistakes of their European rivals and adopt only those techniques that had been proved effective.

American manufacturers in 1860 also possessed the advantage of living in a country generously endowed with the raw materials needed for industrial expansion. Timber stands, which had sustained successive generations of pioneer homebuilders, were still abundant. Coal and iron ore, the sinews of the nineteenth century Industrial Revolution, existed in apparently limitless quantities. The South produced more than enough cotton to supply New England's textile industry. There were vast deposits of oil to light the nation's lamps and in later years to drive its automobiles. Water power sites, which could eventually be used for generating electricity, dotted the American landscape from the Atlantic to the Pacific and from Canada to Mexico. On the mining frontier, which had been opened up in some sections of the West before the Civil War, there was found practically every metal—precious and base—that was known to man at the time. Not only did the United States own in abundance the natural resources for which the industrialists of other nations had to search the world over, but events were to demonstrate that in numerous instances these treasures belonged to a generous government that was willing to turn them over to railroad, mining, and manufacturing concerns for little or no money.

To plentiful natural resources was added a favorable market. When England had entered its period of rapid industrialization some fifty or more years earlier, its factory owners had had to dispose of the bulk of their goods abroad. Other European nations that turned to industry at a later date found the world market in large part pre-empted by the English. But the American manufacturer, situated in the midst of an expanding home market, could avoid international competition while he concentrated on fulfilling the needs of American consumers. The population of the United States which had stood at 23,191,876 in 1850 rose to 31,443,321 in 1860. Forty years later it totaled 75,994,575. It was not until the twentieth century that many American industrialists had to look abroad for the sale of their surplus products.

The American market, which in 1860 consisted largely of farmers in need of manufactured goods, was a vast free-trade area whose component parts were bound together by iron rails. More than twenty thousand miles of new railroad track were laid during the 1850's, and the period of greatest growth was still to come. Practically every phase of the economy was favorably affected by the railroad boom. Railroads brought manufacturers into contact with hitherto unavailable consumers and raw materials, provided work for numerous laborers, increased the demand for coal, iron, and timber, and extended the Western farmers' markets to world-wide proportions.

The marked increase in population after 1850 provided American industry with workers as well as customers. To the natural growth in the native population was added a growing stream of immigrants, many of whom proved to be ideal (from the industrialists' standpoint) human fodder for the nation's factory system. From 1860 to 1900 approximately fourteen million immigrants came to the United States. Unlike many of their predecessors of the antebellum period, they tended to settle in cities and become members of the industrial proletariat. Since few of these new Americans possessed any industrial skills, they were willing to toil long hours for little pay at menial and dangerous jobs. Labor leaders complained that the immigrant undermined standards built up by the native worker, but even they would not have denied that immigration was of major importance in the spectacular advance of American industry during the second half of the nineteenth century.

The supply of American capital to finance industrial expansion did not equal the nation's wealth in natural and human resources. Before 1850 the shortage of capital was perhaps the principal deterrent to the growth of manufacturing. Most investors preferred to put their money into foreign trade, western-land speculation, and internal improvements; and it was not until the 1850's that industry began to attract a sizable amount of capital.* Part of this money came from California's gold mines; part of it was drawn from the profits of trade; and a portion of it was supplied by European investors. After the Civil War, American

* The amount of capital invested in industry rose from $553,200,000 in 1850 to $1,009,000,000 in 1860.

industrialists continued to have difficulty in raising money for the promotion of new ventures and the expansion of existing facilities. But this was seldom an insuperable obstacle, for profits produced still more profits, and Europe poured unprecedented amounts of money into the American economy. It is impossible to estimate with any accuracy how much financial aid Europe gave to American industry, but no one doubts that it was considerable.

21. GOVERNMENT AID TO INDUSTRY

LONG-TERM changes in the European and American economies set the stage for the industrialization of the United States; but it was the Civil War that served as a catalytic agent and provided the impetus for the transformation of an evolutionary process into a full-scale revolution. In the 1850's, most Northern businessmen viewed the threat of sectional conflict with misgivings and foreboding. Secession would not only cut off the supply of such valuable staple products as cotton, but it would also reduce or eliminate the revenue derived from freight rates, loans, insurance, and commissions in the North-South trade. Events, however, soon demonstrated that the Northern businessman did not know his own best interests, for war-born prosperity more than compensated for the losses entailed in the severance of the economic ties that had bound the two sections. The government's war orders for clothing, food, munitions, building equipment, and rolling stock for the Union armies created a boom that affected every segment of the economy. The artificially stimulated prosperity of the war years provided Northern industrialists with both the incentive and funds to expand and mechanize their plants in an unprecedentedly short period of time.

As significant as the stimulus provided by the government's war expenditures was its willingness to adopt policies that would be of direct benefit to American industry and industrialists. Before 1861, the Federal government had been controlled by a loose alliance of Southern planters, Western farmers, and Northern commercial interests. Although these groups had frequently differed among themselves on a variety of issues, they had been in general agreement in their opposition to concessions to industry. With the election of 1860, however, there occurred a definite change in the attitude of the Federal government toward the development of American industry. This change cannot be attributed entirely to the exigencies of war, for the Republican party in its platform of 1860 had revealed its intention to aid business several months before the first Southern state had seceded.

The Republican party of 1860 was not a businessman's party, but a free-labor, free-farmer, free-soil party, which hoped to pick up some additional votes among the nation's businessmen. The Republican platform, therefore, contained planks promising businessmen a protective tariff, a national banking system, and improved transportation facilities. Although no adequate statistics are available, most evidence indicates that the majority of Northern businessmen in 1860 preferred the conservative Constitutional Union ticket to the Radical Republicans, whose victory might precipitate disunion. But when the Republicans repeatedly demonstrated during the war and postwar years that they planned to honor the promises that they had made in 1860, industrialists and financiers quickly joined the party and for all practical purposes took over its control.

The new Administration's attitude toward industry was made clear by its tariff policy. On March 2, 1861, two days before Abraham Lincoln's inauguration, Congress adopted the Morrill Act. This measure, which could not have been passed if seven Southern states had not already seceded, raised the tariff and proved a fitting prelude for wartime tariff policies. With the onset of war all taxes, including tariffs, were increased. A series of tariff bills, culminating in an act of 1864, placed the average rate at 47 per cent. Republican high-tariff advocates defended the increase in duties on the grounds that additional revenue was needed to finance the war and that manufacturers subjected to heavy internal revenue taxes could only be protected from foreign competition with a higher tariff barrier. When the war was over and government expenditures had declined, the excise taxes were drastically reduced. But the wartime tariffs remained, and protectionism became an established policy of the postwar Republican Administrations.

For more than half a century after Appomattox both parties continued the tariff policies that had been inaugurated during the Civil War. In 1867, Congress rejected a measure for tariff reduction; and in subsequent years it passed a number of special bills to provide greater protection for particular industries. Fear of political repercussions impelled the Grant Administration to enact a 10 per cent across-the-board reduction just prior to the election of 1872. But after a relatively short time these cuts were restored. In 1882 a commission appointed by President Arthur proposed a 20 per cent tariff cut, but Congress in a bill passed in 1883 reduced the general average by only 4 per cent. In ensuing years, the Republicans raised the tariff with the passage of the McKinley bill in 1890, the Dingley Tariff of 1897, and the Payne-Aldrich Act of 1909. Although the Democrats criticized Republican tariffs, they did not lower them substantially. Cleveland's appeal for tariff reduction in 1887 was checked by the Senate defeat of the Mills bill. The Wilson-Gorman Tariff, which became law without Cleveland's signature in 1894, carried only minor reductions in duties. It was not until 1913, with the passage

Puck

HISTORY REPEATS ITSELF—THE ROBBER BARONS OF THE MIDDLE AGES AND THE ROBBER BARONS OF TODAY

CORNELIUS VANDERBILT

ANDREW CARNEGIE

SAMUEL GOMPERS

JOHN PIERPONT MORGAN

GIANTS OF BUSINESS AND LABOR

of the Underwood-Simmons bill, that the Democrats under the leadership of Woodrow Wilson reversed the policy that had been established by the Morrill Tariff. In the fifty-two-year interval between these two measures, the consumers of the United States paid an enormous subsidy to American industry.

The financial policies of the Republican party that were inaugurated during the Civil War also redounded to the benefit of business groups. The banking acts of 1863 and 1864 provided a national banking system and a measure of financial stability after the unsettling effects of prewar wild-cat banking. Moreover, by increasing the reserve requirements for rural banks, this legislation accentuated the trend toward the concentration of financial control in the hands of larger bankers in the Northeastern cities. After the war, the government's financial policies continued to reflect the interests of these same groups. In 1869, Congress voted for the payment of all government obligations in gold, and in 1875 it provided for the resumption of specie payments. Both laws, aside from all other considerations, tended to benefit the business classes at the expense of other parts of the population.

Tariff and banking legislation during the war and postwar years was supplemented by government grants of land and some of America's most valuable resources to the nation's business leaders. Railroads were, of course, the principal beneficiaries of this generous policy. Counties, cities, and towns subscribed to railroad securities and awarded them terminal sites and rights of way. States turned over to railroads land that the Federal government had transferred to them for this purpose. Congress lent money to the Union Pacific and Central Pacific companies and gave great tracts of the public domain to the transcontinental lines. In addition to these direct land grants, which amounted to a cash subsidy, the railroads obtained huge amounts of land that had been reserved for the nation's farmers under the Homestead Act.

The government's land policies also permitted some of the nation's most valuable timber stands to pass into the hands of a relatively small number of acquisitive, but unscrupulous, entrepreneurs. Although the Homestead Act had been designed to apply only to farm areas, it was so loosely administered that this provision was frequently circumvented. In numerous instances employees of large lumber concerns took over timber lands under either the Pre-emption or Homestead Acts only to turn them over to the companies for which they were working.

The concentration of ownership of the nation's timber resources was facilitated not only by the Pre-emption and Homestead Acts, but also by laws which were enacted after the Civil War. The Timber Culture Act, which became law in 1873, stated that any individual who planted and protected forty acres of timber would be granted the quarter section of which the forty acres was a part. Although this law was designed to "encourage the growth of timber on the western prairies," it served mainly as a device to promote Western real-estate speculation. The Timber and Stone Act of 1878, which applied to land "unfit for cultivation," offered land for as little as $2.50 an acre—or at a price that has been estimated as less than the value of one log from one tree standing on this land. Because the government was either unable or unwilling to prevent land transfers under the Timber and Stone Act, this law permitted the monopolization of large amounts of valuable timber by a few wealthy individuals and corporations. In 1901, the Commissioner of the General Land Office stated:

> *Immense tracts of the most valuable timber land, which every consideration of public interest demanded should be preserved for public use, have become the property of a few individuals and corporations. In many instances whole townships have been entered under this law in the interest of one person or firm, to whom the lands have been conveyed as soon as receipts for the purchase price were issued.**

The government disposed of comparatively large amounts of the nation's mineral wealth in much the same fashion that it distributed timber stands. People taking up land under either the Pre-emption or Homestead Acts had to swear that their land did not contain valuable mineral deposits. But the government frequently was unable to check these statements, and the use of dummy settlers enabled a few individuals and concerns to acquire valuable minerals under both laws. Other legislation was circumvented with equal ease. A law in 1873 stipulated that government land containing iron ore could not be sold for less than $1.25 per acre. Since the minimum price tended to become the maximum price, an untold number of acres with iron-ore deposits was disposed of at this ridiculously low figure. Moreover, although the government did not intend to include iron-ore lands in its grants to railroads, it frequently did so. Finally, government lands containing minerals were distributed through grants made under the terms of the Timber and Stone Act.

Roy M. Robbins in his illuminating study of *Our Landed Heritage* has furnished some revealing examples of the effect of the government's land policy on the ownership of mineral deposits. The Minnesota Iron Company acquired 8,772 acres of iron-ore land through homestead and pre-emption entries. In 1882, at a public land sale at Duluth, O. T. Higgins, Frank W. Higgins, and the Higgins Land Company paid $14,000 for 11,000 acres. Fifty years later much of this land because of its mineral deposits was valued at $50,000 an acre. These and similar examples indicate that the American businessman was fortunate not only in his

* Quoted in Fred A. Shannon: *The Farmer's Last Frontier; Agriculture, 1860-1897* (New York, Farrar & Rinehart, Inc., 1945), p. 62.

country's unparalleled resources but also in a government that was willing to dispose of them for almost nothing.

As significant as what the government did for business enterprise during and after the Civil War was what it did not do. By refraining from thorough-going investigations of business practices, by not adopting legislation to protect labor, and by not establishing effective regulatory commissions, the Federal government gave immeasurable aid to business pioneers, who knew that they could move ahead as they wished without fear of either restriction or punishment. Most Americans, conditioned by successive frontier experiences and equipped with a set of values suitable for life in an economy composed of agrarian individualists, saw little or no reason before 1890 for the government's supervision of business activity. Although the Grangers advocated regulation of the railroads and some reformers crusaded against the trusts, the mass of people believed that the methods used to accumulate wealth were no concern of the government. Economic life, they insisted, was a race. The devil took the hindmost and the government had no right to deprive the winners of their prizes. This philosophy might result in waste, corruption, and injustice; but it also afforded American businessmen greater opportunities than those of any other land.

The assistance that the government extended to business enterprise after 1860 necessitates a revision in the traditional view of the American Industrial Revolution. Rapid industrial growth was more than a product of the ingenuity, drive, and resourcefulness of the nation's business leaders. It was also a government-supported project that was helped at least in part by high tariffs, land grants, favorable labor and financial policies, and the absence of public regulation. Without these various aids, the Industrial Revolution would have followed a course far different from the one it took after 1860.

22. GROWTH OF THE BASIC AMERICAN INDUSTRIES

IN THE United States from 1865 to 1914 there was a phenomenal increase in the production of durable and consumer goods; machinery was applied to virtually every part of the manufacturing process; and the factory system spread to the South and the West. By World War I, advances in technology, mass-production methods, and assembly-line techniques had combined with the natural advantages enjoyed by American industry to make the United States the world's leading manufacturing nation. During this period the index number of American industrial production rose from 13.3 in 1865 to 100 in 1899 and to 175.7 in 1914.

Coal was probably more responsible than any other natural resource for the transformation of the United States from an agrarian to an industrial economy. In addition to heat for industrial and domestic consumers and the coal gas that it furnished to the increasing number of American city dwellers, coal supplied most of the energy that drove the nation's railroad engines, turned the wheels in its factories, and made possible the spectacular development of the steel industry. American coal production rose from a yearly average of 20,538,000 short tons in 1861–5 to 269,700,000 in 1900 and 523,500,000 in 1914. Technological innovations were only a minor factor in the rapid growth of the coal industry, for it was not until after 1900 that some mines began to adopt automatic cutting tools and mechanical loaders. Anthracite coal production, which had exceeded bituminous output during the Civil War, steadily declined, and by 1915, bituminous coal was providing five times as much energy for the American economy as anthracite. Throughout these years Pennsylvania continued to mine the bulk of the nation's coal; but twenty-three other states, led by West Virginia, Illinois, and Ohio, also produced considerable amounts of coal before World War I.

The increase in coal production was accompanied by a corresponding development of the nation's iron and steel industry. Pig iron output in 1873 totaled more than 2,500,000 tons, or three times the output of 1865, and steel production increased from approximately 15,000 tons in 1865 to nearly 600,000 tons in 1876. But this growth was merely a beginning. By 1915 the production of pig iron and ferro-alloys had risen to 29,616,000 tons, and the manufacture of steel ingots and castings increased from 389,799 tons in 1875 to 42,773,680 tons in 1916. By World War I the United States was the leading steel and iron producing nation of the world.

The expansion of the iron and steel industry was facilitated by numerous technological improvements. Although the so-called Bessemer process for making steel had been invented in the 1850's simultaneously by the Englishman Henry Bessemer and the American William Kelly, this method was not used in the United States until the Civil War.* In 1864, Captain E. B. Ward, who had organized a company that had secured control of the Kelly patents, produced at Wyandotte, Michigan, the first Bessemer steel to be made in the United States. In the same year a concern at Troy, New York, headed by Alexander L. Holley,

* In the Bessemer process a blast of air is forced at high pressure through a great converter partly filled with molten iron. The air rushing through the incandescent liquid mass oxidizes the silicon and carbon. Inasmuch as some carbon is always required to produce steel, Bessemer intended to stop the process at the point where just enough carbon would be left for that purpose. This idea, however, proved impracticable. In 1856, another Englishman, Robert F. Muchet, remedied this difficulty by adding to the decarbonized and desiliconized white hot metal a compound (spiegeleisen) of iron, carbon, and manganese.

acquired Bessemer's American patents. Since neither firm could use the new process without infringing upon the legal prerogatives of the other, the two companies agreed in 1866 to merge their patent rights. Following this agreement the business of making Bessemer steel spread rapidly, and in the next ten years more than a dozen important Bessemer works were established. Another method of steel manufacture, the Siemens-Martin, or open-hearth, process,* was first introduced into this country in 1868 by Abram S. Hewitt, who, with his father-in-law, Peter Cooper, owned the New Jersey Steel and Iron Company at Trenton, New Jersey. While open-hearth steel was softer than Bessemer and therefore particularly suitable for locomotive boiler plates, it required more time and money to produce. The adoption of this method, therefore, advanced slowly at first, and only slightly over 8,000 tons were manufactured by 1875. The following year the output of open-hearth steel rose to more than 19,000 tons, and by 1908 its output had surpassed that of Bessemer steel.

Improvements in blast furnaces were paralleled by advances in rolling-mill techniques. Manual labor was almost entirely eliminated as the steel ingots were moved by huge cranes from the furnace to the rollers, where mechanical devices pushed them back and forth until they had been squeezed to the required size. The metal was then automatically cut into "blooms," which were transferred to other parts of the mill, where they were converted into rails, wire, structural steel, and a host of other products. By 1910 the output of rolled-steel products amounted to 21,621,000 tons—more than a four-fold increase over the figure for the 1880's.

The increase in steel production was made possible in part by the opening of new ore-fields that were adaptable to improved mining-techniques. The most important new deposits of iron ore were discovered in the Mesabi range in Minnesota, where large-scale operations were undertaken in the 1890's. By 1913 approximately 35,000,000 tons, or more than one half the nation's annual production of 62,000,000 tons, was being drawn from the Mesabi field. Since the Mesabi ore lay close to the surface and was of a fine texture, it could be mined by steam shovel and transported by cars that traveled on tracks laid in the open pits. Another source of iron ore, opened up soon after the Civil War and second only in importance to the Lake Superior district, was located in the area surrounding Birmingham, Alabama.

Western Pennsylvania and eastern Ohio comprised the leading steel-producing region of the United States. With abundant supplies of coal

* When first introduced in America the open-hearth method consisted in melting pig iron in a large dish-shaped vessel, or reverberatory furnace, and then decarbonizing it by adding wrought iron, steel scrap, or iron ore and spiegeleisen, or ferromanganese. The materials used were melted by the union of atmospheric air and combustible gases.

and limestone and with easy access by water to the Lake Superior ore fields, this region's superiority was never seriously challenged. The development of the Alabama steel industry, which also had ready access to coal and limestone, was retarded for a number of years by a grade of iron ore that could not be used in the Bessemer process and by the superior financial resources of its Northern competitors. Illinois, Indiana, and Michigan, which comprised the other outstanding center of the iron and steel industry, grew rapidly after the turn of the century.

The importance of steel production in the development of the new industrial order can scarcely be overestimated. Not only did it form the basis of many American fortunes, but it furnished employment to thousands of the country's fast-growing population. Transportation and structural engineering were to a very large extent revolutionized by the use of steel. The growth of the steel industry made possible the production of armor plate for the American navy, the construction of steel merchant ships, the building of bigger and stronger bridges, and the erection of skyscrapers, which were little more than steel skeletons covered with sheathings of masonry and windows. Steel also played a key rôle in the development of the American railroad system after the Civil War as iron rails were supplanted by the heavier and more durable steel product. This improvement in the quality of the tracks—in conjunction with scientific improvements in roadbed construction—enabled the railroad companies to use heavier rolling-stock and to move their trains at higher speeds. Finally, steel was used for a variety of other articles including locomotives, railway cars, farm machinery, castings, metal-working machinery, and tools of other kinds.

Copper, the most important of the nonferrous metals, was mined in only relatively small amounts until the 1880's, when annual production increased from 30,000 to 130,000 tons. By 1895 the United States was the world's leading copper producer, and fifteen years later American copper output totaled 540,080 tons. Copper, which had formerly been used almost exclusively for the manufacture of brass and sheathing, played an increasingly important part in the development of the electrical industry. After 1900 a large part of the American copper supply was employed in the manufacture of electric wires, transmission lines, and motors. Before 1880, Michigan was the nation's leading copper-producing state; but in the next two decades new fields were opened up in Montana and Arizona, and by World War I these two states accounted for more than half the nation's annual copper production.

Technological developments as well as ample natural resources were responsible for the growth of the copper industry. Because the Montana and Arizona fields contained only a small percentage of copper to the ton, steam shovels rather than hand drills were employed in mining. Oil flotation provided an effective and relatively simple method of separation. After the ore had been finely ground, it was placed in an oil and water mixture, from which the copper was drawn off after it had floated to the surface. Similar improvements were effected in refining. The adoption of the reverberatory furnace and the Bessemer process made possible savings in time, labor, and cost; and electrolysis produced a superior grade of copper and permitted the almost complete recovery of the copper in the crude ore.

As significant as the exploitation of the nation's mineral resources was the development of the petroleum industry. Petroleum had long been known to exist in the United States, and the journals of many of the early explorers of the valley of the Allegheny and its tributaries record the presence of thick oil on the surface of the springs and streams. By 1850, rock oil, as petroleum was usually called, was being sold all over the United States as a cure-all patent medicine; but the remarkable extent of its commercial possibilities was not realized until 1855, when Professor Benjamin Silliman of Yale, after an analysis of a quantity of the fluid, announced that it would furnish as good an illuminant as any the world knew, and that it would also yield gas, paraffin, lubricating oil, and other valuable products. Four years later, "Colonel" E. L. Drake, a former railway conductor, sank the first oil well near Titusville in western Pennsylvania. This well, not quite seventy feet in depth, began producing at the rate of five hundred barrels a month. The news of Drake's success spread rapidly, and western Pennsylvania was soon swarming with prospectors, speculators, and other adventurers. Land once considered worthless brought fabulous prices; towns came into being almost in a day; and millions of dollars were poured into dozens of hastily organized enterprises. By 1864 an area of more than 400 square miles about Titusville had been converted into a forest of derricks. Before half a dozen years had elapsed the Pennsylvania field expanded to cover approximately 2,000 square miles, and wells were being sunk from West Virginia to Missouri in the hope of finding new fields. By 1872 nearly 40,000,000 barrels of petroleum had been produced in the United States, and oil had climbed to fourth place among the country's exports.

Despite its rapid growth the industry faced many difficulties in its early, and most competitive, years. Large sums were invested in land, derricks, boring implements, and labor, and never yielded a cent in return. Adequate facilities for storing and transporting the crude product as it came from the ground were at first lacking, and the waste was enormous. The roads leading from the fields to the railroad terminals were quickly turned into quagmires of sticky mud by the weight of the loaded wagons dragged over ground soaked with rain and oil. Vehicles and teams were often ruined in a few days, but the freight rates were so high that teamsters seldom suffered loss. Much of the oil was floated to Pittsburgh in specially constructed barges that occasionally capsized or caught fire. But these difficulties were largely overcome by the introduction in the middle sixties of the pipe line and the tank car. By 1866 the heyday of the teamster was over, and soon thereafter the leaky and inflammable wooden tank-car gave way to the tubular iron cars. These improvements reduced the cost of oil transport by 60 per cent.

The oil-refining business proved to be even more profitable than production of the crude product. Before 1865, refineries, large and small, were widely scattered. With the introduction of the pipe line and the tank-car the refining of oil came to be chiefly concentrated in four inland centers: Oil City, Erie, Pittsburgh, and Cleveland. Some refineries were located on the seaboard in Boston, New York, Philadelphia, and Baltimore. Of the inland cities, Pittsburgh and Cleveland were the most important. Although two hundred miles from the oil region, Cleveland had taken the lead at the opening of the seventies. Not only did it command practically the entire Western market by rail and water, but it was closely linked with the East by railroad lines and by Lake Erie and the Erie Canal. Pittsburgh, on the other hand, was completely dependent on the Pennsylvania Railroad for the transportation of its product to the Eastern markets.

In the years that followed, rapid advances were made in every branch of the petroleum industry. Vast oil deposits discovered in the southern Plains states and California made a substantial contribution to the annual increase in petroleum production from 26,300,000 barrels in 1880 to 300,800,000 barrels in 1916. Devices were perfected for salvaging gasoline from the natural gas that had formerly been permitted to escape from the wells. A network of pipe lines was built across the country, and by 1900, more petroleum was transported by pipe line than by rail. The principal petroleum product before 1900 was kerosene, which was used for heat and illumination; but the development of electric lighting, the increasing demand for industrial lubricants, and the widespread adoption of the gasoline motor, especially in automobiles, revolutionized the petroleum industry during the first two decades of the twentieth century. Earlier methods of refining, designed primarily to produce kerosene by applying heat to petroleum, were supplemented by the "cracking process," which made possible the extraction of larger quantities of gasoline from petroleum than in the past. By 1918, American oil refineries were producing twice as much gas oil and fuel oils as kerosene.

The contributions of the extractive industries to the growth of the American economy were rivaled by the development of electricity as a source of light and power. Although Sir Humphry Davy had demonstrated an electric arc lamp powered by batteries to the Royal Society in London in 1807, it was not until seventy years later that Charles F. Brush of Cleveland perfected an arc lamp suitable for street illumination. Similar progress was made in the field of electromagnetic induction after Michael Faraday's pioneering discoveries in 1831, and by the 1870's the work of several scientists in a number of countries had made possible the construction of a dynamo that could generate a continuous supply of direct electric current. Arc lamps provided too glaring a light for use in either home or office, and it remained for Thomas A. Edison in 1879 to perfect a practicable carbon-filament lamp in his Menlo Park laboratory in New Jersey. Three years later Edison, who was as successful a businessman as he was an inventor, built a power station in New York to supply current to eighty-five buildings. Within six years the American people were using two million electric lights.

The Edison Electric Light Company, which had been formed in 1878, was merged with the Thomson-Houston Company in 1892 to form the General Electric Company. Its only important rival was the Westinghouse Electric and Manufacturing Company, which had been founded in 1886 by George Westinghouse, the inventor of the airbrake, to supply power for industry and transportation. The Edison firm relied on direct current, which could be transported only a relatively short distance, but Westinghouse was quick to realize the advantages of alternating current. Using transformers that had been developed by William Stanley in the 1880's and armed with the patent rights that he had purchased from Nikola Tesla, a Serbian immigrant, Westinghouse soon demonstrated that alternating current could be carried great distances at comparatively low costs. While the range of direct current was limited to little more than a mile, by the end of the 1890's alternating current was being transported as much as twenty miles.

Electric motors, which were first used in New England textile mills in the 1890's, were rapidly adopted in almost every other branch of American manufacturing. Because the electric motor was easily operated and controlled, could be stopped by a flick of a switch whenever necessary, and was readily adjustable to any floor plan or organization of the manufacturing process, it readily outstripped all rivals and became a commonplace in American industry. The electric power that provided current for illumination, drove motors in industry, and propelled street cars and electric trains was generated by either steam, water power, or internal combustion engines. In the years just preceding World War I, steam engines and steam turbines accounted for approximately two thirds of the electric power produced in the United States; but hydroelectric projects also were rapidly developed and expanded. The Niagara Falls power plant was in operation by the turn of the century, and in 1913 the giant Keokuk Dam on the Mississippi River began to produce electric power.

While basic industries such as iron, steel, and petroleum were developed with astounding rapidity after the Civil War and while new sources of power were applied to the manufacturing process, the consumer-goods industries increased their production by the widespread adoption of improved techniques. The canning of vegetables was a major industry as early as 1870, and by World War I every step in the canning process had been mechanized. The refrigerator car, whose practicality was demonstrated in the midseventies, revolutionized the meat industry and enabled the packers of Chicago to take on the task of feeding a large part of the nation. The growth of the shoe industry was to a considerable degree made possible by the invention of machines that eliminated a large amount of hand labor. These examples could be multiplied endlessly, for by 1914 there was scarcely a consumer-goods industry that had not expanded its output by substituting machines for hand labor. Many of the inventions that made this revolution possible were put into practical form by Americans, but in numerous instances they were based upon the earlier work of Europeans. Americans did not necessarily have a genius for invention; but they did have a genius for applying inventions to the industrial process.

American industrialists not only used machines more extensively than the manufacturers of any other country, but they were also the first to develop the techniques of mass production. The large-scale production of a standardized product with uniform, interchangeable parts had been carried to a high point of perfection by New England arms manufacturers in the decade before the Civil War. The Springfield arsenal, for example, took only eighty minutes to make a musket in a manufacturing operation that involved about three hundred different machines and five hundred separate mechanical processes. American pistols and guns, produced by such famous armsmakers as Colt, Whitney, Remington, and Sharpe had no superior throughout the world. Yankee gun-makers supplied not only the North during the Civil War, but also the European nations participating in the Crimean, Austro-Prussian, and Franco-German wars.

The growth of the firearms industry was accompanied by a corresponding development in the production of machine tools. Many pre-Civil War gun-makers not only made the machine tools for the production of arms but tools for the manufacture of other products as well. Machine shops occupied an essential position in American industry, for they turned out the basic machines that manufactured machines for the heavy-goods and consumer-goods industries. After the Civil War, machine shops grew in number and increased the variety and efficiency of their products. By 1900, automatic turret lathes, planers, gear-cutting machines, drills, and borers were being produced in large quantities. Machines were equipped with jigs that could be attached and removed according to need, and tremendous advances were made in both the speed and accuracy of operation of all machine tools. Although most

American machine tools had been originally patterned on English models, the Americans soon displayed their ingenuity at adapting these machines to a multiplicity of uses. In 1885 an Englishman wrote: "The tools and processes which we are inclined to consider unusual are the commonplaces of American shops, and the determination to do by hand nothing which can be done by machinery is the chief characteristic."

The mass production techniques made possible by the development of the machine tool industry were readily applied to the manufacture of such products as sewing machines, watches, clocks, and agricultural machinery. But it was the automobile manufacturer who pushed this system further than any other American industrialist. After the establishment of the industry in the 1890's, most automobiles were made of interchangeable parts, and during 1913–14, Henry Ford introduced the moving assembly line. Workers who had formerly moved around the plant to do their respective jobs now remained in one place while their job was brought to them. Each worker was assigned a simple, specific task, which he repeated on a never-ending series of cars-in-the-making that were dragged past him on a continuous belt. Mechanical conveyors had been used earlier in flour milling and meat processing, but to Ford and his imitators belongs the credit for developing this relatively simple device to an incredible degree of efficiency.

The increasing reliance of American manufacturers upon machine rather than manual labor put a new premium on technical knowledge, and graduates of the scientific schools that had been established after the Civil War found numerous jobs waiting for them in American industry. Large corporations began to hire scientists to devise new products and new machines or processes to manufacture them. As early as 1879 the American Telephone & Telegraph Company established its own laboratories manned by skilled technicians and experienced scientists. Other corporations followed suit, and by World War I the individual inventor laboring in his own improvised shop had become little more than a hallowed figure in the folklore of American industry. Inventions were now the result of the collective efforts of specialists who had no other job than to produce the inventions that were demanded by their corporation superiors. Science, like the machine, had been adapted by the American industrialist to fit the pattern of mass production.

A similar attempt was made to standardize the workers who tended the nation's machines. As early as the 1880's the American Society of Mechanical Engineers had begun to give its attention to increasing the productivity of labor as well as machinery. In 1895, Frederick W. Taylor, who was soon to become known as the "father of scientific management," addressed the society on "A Piece-Rate System." Taylor believed that the efficiency of factory workers could be increased by paying them according to their rate of production and by using time-and-motion studies to eliminate waste motions. Taylor's ideas received wide publicity and were adopted by a number of manufacturers. But to workers, "scientific management" was merely an old system under a new name. They preferred to call it the "speed-up."

23. INDUSTRIAL DEVELOPMENT IN THE WEST AND SOUTH

AS AMERICAN industry developed after the Civil War, there was a gradual shift of the nation's center of manufacturing to the West. The Northeast, which had been the leading American industrial section since colonial times, managed to maintain its supremacy until about 1880, but it then steadily lost ground. The development of industry in the Middle West was in part the result of the westward movement of population and the development of improved rail-facilities between the old and new sections; but it was also caused by the desire of manufacturers to be near essential raw materials that were not produced in quantity in the New England and Middle Atlantic states. Sometimes established Eastern industries emigrated from the East; for instance, the McCormick reaper works moved in successive stages from Virginia to Chicago by way of Cincinnati. In numerous other cases, Midwestern industries duplicated those of the East without supplanting them. Cincinnati, for example, was a center of the machine tool business in 1880 while this industry still flourished in New England. Finally, some industries, such as the manufacture of automobiles, were founded in the Middle West and never had any serious Eastern competitors.

As early as 1870 the pattern for the industrialization of the Middle West was beginning to take definite shape. According to the Federal census of that year, the number of the nation's manufacturing establishments had increased almost 80 per cent during the preceding decade. The gain was greatest in the states of the Old Northwest. Indiana, for instance, had twice as many establishments as in 1860, and Illinois three times as many. States in the upper Mississippi Valley, which on the eve of the war had been little more than agrarian frontier regions, now contained flourishing factory towns. Chicago was already internationally known for its stockyards, its Pullman cars, its clothing factories, and its agricultural machinery. Rockford, Peoria, Elgin, Joliet, Moline, and Quincy were other thriving Illinois industrial towns. The four Ohio cities of Akron, Canton, Cleveland, and Cincinnati, together with others less widely known, closely rivaled many of the industrial centers of the older mill zone. Even in Indianapolis, metropolis of an extensive and fertile agricultural region, nearly one fifth of the population of about 100,000 was employed in the city's furniture, starch, textile, vehicle, and farm-implement factories. Detroit was an important iron-manufacturing center, and its stoves had a country-wide reputation. Grand Rapids was well-known by 1873 for the production of popular-priced furniture. St. Louis and Milwaukee, with their large German population, had developed into famous brewing cities.

The meat-packing and flour-milling industries, both of which were closely related to agriculture, also established their capitals in the Middle West during these years. Boston, Providence, New Haven, New York, Baltimore, Philadelphia, Pittsburgh, and Buffalo had meat-packing establishments in 1860, but Cincinnati was, and had been for many years, the leading meat-packing center of America. During the next decade, however, Chicago dislodged Cincinnati.

This shift from Cincinnati to Chicago was made possible by the wholesale movement of cattle ranchers into the trans-Mississippi plains, the extension of the railroad systems into the cattle country, the development of the refrigerator car, and the appearance of men, such as Philip D. Armour, Nelson Morris, and Gustavus F. Swift, who ascertained the possibilities presented to the meat-packing industry by the growing ranching business of the West. Employing mass-production techniques and using the refrigerator car to obtain a national market, Armour, Morris, and Swift revolutionized the meat industry. Largely because of their efforts packing was increasingly concentrated in Chicago, and local butchers and slaughterhouses—particularly those in the East—found it exceedingly difficult to compete with the Chicago meat-barons. But the very developments that made Chicago the meat-packing capital of the United States eventually contributed to its comparative decline. Other cities further west were even closer to the source of the industry's raw material. The refrigerator car, which had made possible Chicago's final triumph over its Eastern rivals, enabled the meat-packing industry to resume its westward movement to the heart of the cattle country. Chicago never lost its prominence as an important meat-packing center, but by 1914 it had serious rivals in such states as Kansas, Nebraska, and Missouri.

Like the meat-packing business, the flour-milling industry took up the westward march but at a somewhat slower pace. In 1870, New York, Pennsylvania, and Illinois ranked in that order in quantity of flour output; and Richmond, Baltimore, Philadelphia, Newark, and Rochester were still the outstanding milling centers. But at the same time it was evident that a shift was underway from east to west in both the production and the milling of wheat. Minneapolis, destined shortly to become the greatest milling center in the world, had a monthly output approaching ninety thousand barrels. The millers, like the packers, had their aggressive and picturesque leaders. Among them were men like Cadwallader C. Washburn, Charles A. Pillsbury, and George M. Christian, who correctly judged the unusual advantages for flour milling possessed by Minneapolis, with its ample water-power facilities, its railways, and its proximity to the greatest spring-wheat section in America—the Red River Valley of Minnesota, the Dakotas, Manitoba, and Saskatchewan. Washburn and Pillsbury were New Englanders, and Christian, who became a partner in the Washburn establishment in 1869, came from Alabama. Washburn had been interested in water-power development around Minneapolis for some years before he erected his first flour mill in 1856. His business expanded rapidly, as did that of his competitors, especially after the adoption of two notable improvements, both of foreign origin. The first, known as the "middlings purifier," was a French invention, introduced in 1870 by Edmund La Croix of Minnesota. This process preserved much of the rich gluten previously lost with the bran. The other, the "gradual reduction," or roller process, was borrowed from Hungary. By this method wheat was gradually reduced to flour by slowly passing it under pressure through a series of iron rollers that were chilled to prevent the heating and discoloring of the flour. By the late seventies thousands of cars were needed annually to carry Minneapolis flour to the Atlantic seaboard, where much of it was transshipped to the markets of the Old World. Minneapolis eventually lost its supremacy as millers in other cities adopted more advanced milling techniques. In 1914 Minneapolis was still a leading flour-milling center, but so were several other cities.

Many other industries either emigrated to the Middle West or grew up in that region without the benefit of an Eastern background. The manufacturers of barbed wire moved from Worcester, Massachusetts, to Illinois in the 1890's to be closer to the prairie and Plains farmers. The iron and steel industry, which had centered around Philadelphia and Trenton in 1860, had shifted beyond the Alleghenies to the Pittsburgh-Youngstown region by 1890. Although this area remained the nation's most important steel-producing district, such Midwestern cities as Cleveland, Chicago, and Detroit also became important steel centers. The automobile industry was concentrated in Michigan not only because of the easy access to such products as steel but also because some of the industry's most notable pioneers happened to live in that state. In similar fashion, Akron, Ohio, became the leading tire-producing city of the United States largely by accident rather than by any inherent advantages that it enjoyed over other cities.

From the end of the Civil War to the outbreak of World War I the South was unable to compete in industrial growth with the Northern sections. The South had not only been devastated by war and racked by Reconstruction, but it also lacked adequate capital, large cities, a trained laboring force, experienced business executives, and an industrial tradition. Despite these drawbacks, many Southerners felt that the

South's salvation lay in the development of industry. During the Reconstruction period, the Southern railroad system was rebuilt and expanded, but little was done to promote manufacturing; and it was not until the 1880's that serious attempts were made to establish a textile industry in the South.

Most Southern cotton mills were built by enterprising members of the small Southern middle class, which had come to the fore during Reconstruction. Although the South possessed the necessary raw material and water-power sites for the manufacture of cotton textiles, it had neither the capital nor skilled workers required for this industry. But it did have a huge reservoir of unskilled labor. Textile factories, built with local savings or loans from the Northeast, attracted poor whites from miles around as soon as they were constructed. These people usually arrived at the site of the new factory with nothing but their clothing. Because they lacked both money and even the barest necessities of life, the mill owner had to furnish them with homes, churches, schools, and food. To pay for these the worker pledged his future labor; and the company town was born along with the Southern textile mill. This labor system, which had originated as a device for overcoming the Southern shortage of capital, quickly developed into a permanent scheme of exploitation that was characterized by low wages, long hours, and child labor. Workers who might otherwise have escaped were held in virtual bondage by the debts that they owed to the company store. But onerous as these policies may have been for the worker, they were principally responsible for the development of the Southern textile industry. During the last two decades of the nineteenth century, 240 cotton mills were built in the South, and the number of active spindles increased from 561,000 to 4,368,000.

The center of the Southern iron and steel industry was Birmingham, Alabama; and by 1892 the Tennessee-Alabama district was producing approximately 25 per cent of the country's total output of iron ore. The Tennessee Coal, Iron, and Railroad Company, which had been formed by Southerners with Southern capital, established a plant in Birmingham that soon became the South's largest steel producer. The company was continually beset by financial difficulties, however, and during the Panic of 1907 it was purchased by the United States Steel Corporation. The other large steel plant in the South before World War I was located at Sparrow's Point, Maryland, but it, too, fell under Northern control when it was acquired by the Bethlehem Steel Corporation in 1916.

Other leading industries of the South before World War I were lumbering, the manufacture of tobacco products, and the production of cottonseed oil. Because of the depletion of Northern forests, the South became the nation's foremost producer of lumber after 1900 and maintained its supremacy until 1930, when the Pacific Coast states took the

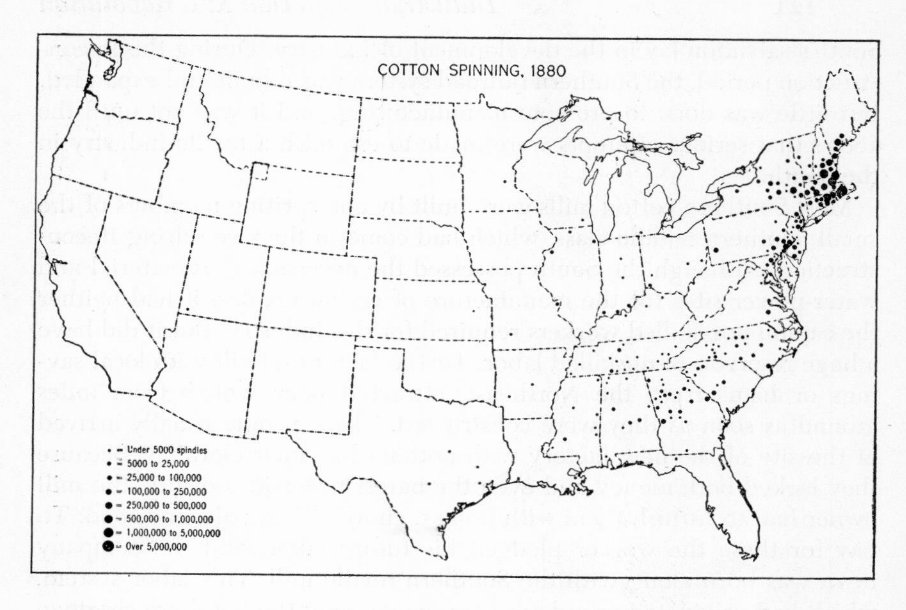

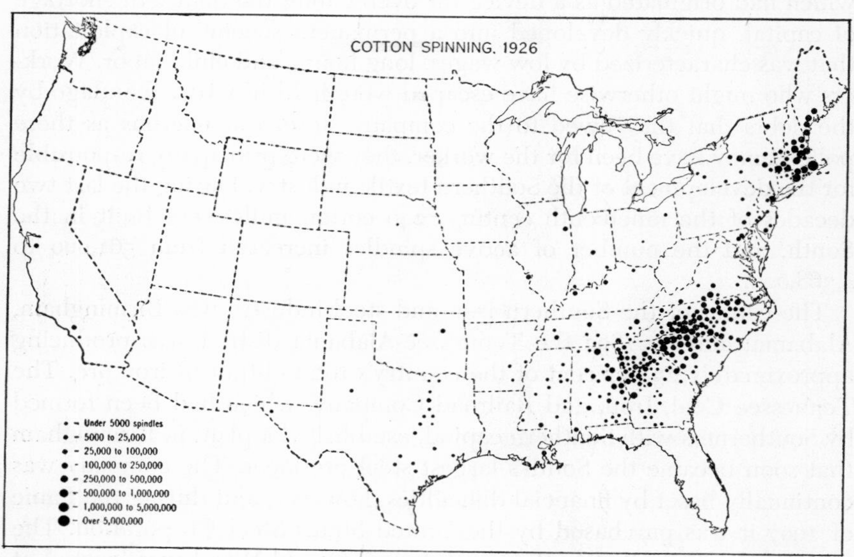

6. COTTON SPINNING, 1880 AND 1926

These maps indicate the comparatively rapid growth of cotton spinning in the South after 1880. [Reprinted with permission from Charles O. Paullin: Atlas of the Historical Geography of the United States *(Washington, D. C.: Carnegie Institution of Washington and the American Geographical Society of New York, 1932).]*

lead. The South also grew the bulk of the American tobacco crop, and Southern factories manufactured most of the cigarettes sold in the United States. Cottonseed, which had once been considered worthless, became the basis of a thriving industry soon after the Civil War. By the 1880's the cottonseed industry was producing annually $12,000,000 worth of fertilizer, cattle feed, and cooking oil.

The development of industry in the South and West contributed in large measure to the destruction of the economic sectionalism that had characterized the antebellum years. By 1914 every major section contained important manufacturing establishments, and no region dominated the rest of the nation industrially, as the Northeast had done before 1860. On the eve of World War I, Birmingham was a more important industrial center than any city in Massachusetts, and Chicago had long since outdistanced Philadelphia. The earlier pattern of the North-South and East-West economic sectionalism had given way to a regional division of labor in which every section of the nation concentrated on the production of its own manufactured specialties.

24. MITIGATING THE EFFECTS OF COMPETITION

THE RAPID expansion of American industry after the Civil War produced a corresponding increase in the extent and intensity of competition among businessmen. The spread of the railroad network tended to break down regional monopolies and bring all the producers within a single industry into direct competition with one another. Moreover, the prizes awarded the victors were greater than ever before. As unprecedented opportunities for profits were opened up by the discovery of new sources of raw materials, introduction of new manufacturing techniques, and sale of new products, each businessman made an all-out effort to outstrip his rivals in the race for the rich rewards made available by the growth of American industry.

As competition after the Civil War became more and more severe the businessman became more and more anxious to limit it. Theorists might view competition as the life of trade, but a growing number of business leaders came to look upon it as inefficient and wasteful and above all a threat to their profits. The threat was not an empty one, for in a number of instances price wars became so intense that all the members of an industry were compelled to operate at a loss. Even before the Civil War some industrialists had sought to check competition through combination; after the war the trend toward concentration was accelerated until by 1914 the control of large segments of American industry was in the hands of a relatively few individuals and corporations.

In their efforts to eliminate what came to be known as the "evils of competition," American businessmen resorted to a variety of devices. As one method to check competition proved either unworkable or illegal, another was employed until that too had to be either modified or abandoned. Although the businessmen's drive toward monopoly proceeded on a trial-and-error basis, the successive steps used by American businessmen fall into a rough pattern. Pools, which were used in many industries during the Civil War period, had generally been abandoned by the end of the 1880's as unworkable. After the formation of the Standard Oil trust in 1879, several corporations made use of the trust, but adverse court decisions soon led to the development of still other means to accomplish the same end. By 1900 most of the large semimonopolistic firms were organized as holding companies, and a few years later interlocking directorates were employed as a successful device for giving the appearance of competition to the reality of monopoly. Many firms used none of these techniques, but rose to positions of power within their respective industries by purchasing their less successful rivals.

Pools were designed essentially to limit competition in industries that contained a relatively large number of firms, none of which was strong enough either to eliminate or dominate its rivals. Pools—or "gentlemen's agreements," as they were frequently called—have been described as "partnerships of corporations" in which a number of concerns pledged themselves to observe regulations for production quotas, price fixing, division of markets, maintenance of minimum standards of quality, and pooling of patents. But from the businessman's standpoint pools had certain marked defects. Because pools were not sanctioned by law, unruly members could not be coerced through the courts. Although the success of a pool depended on the co-operation of all the firms within an industry, no company could be forced to join a pool, and a single member could destroy a pool's effectiveness by launching a price war. In short, the gentlemen's agreement was no stronger than the word or honor of its members—a fact that often gave it a very short life indeed.

The difficulties inherent in the pool as a mechanism for regulating competition were illustrated by the experiences of the Michigan Salt Association. In 1866, after overproduction had caused numerous failures among Michigan salt manufacturers, they combined to establish a common selling-agency to dispose of their output. Two years later they formed the Saginaw and Bay Salt Company, which lasted until in 1871 it was destroyed by dissension among its members. Declining prices again forced the member firms back into co-operation, and in 1876 they set up the Michigan Salt Association, which experienced a series of ups and downs for the next decade as it attempted to compel its members to abide by its regulations. Pools in other industries were usually even less successful, and in general they merely managed to postpone rather than eliminate price wars.

As pools repeatedly demonstrated that at best they could only provide the businessman with temporary relief from the effects of competition, a few far-seeing industrialists began to search for a more efficient means of regulating the policies of all the members within a single industry. Unlike the pool, the new device would have to include some method of coercion without violating established law. This problem was worthy of the talents of the man who did the most to solve it, for John D. Rockefeller was perhaps more generously endowed than any of his contemporaries with a combination of acquisitive instincts, leadership, ruthlessness, and organizing ability.

John D. Rockefeller received a thorough training in acquisitiveness from both his parents. His mother, a devout Baptist, taught him at an early age that it was his Christian duty to work hard, make as much money as possible, and give a tithe to the church. His father's approach to the problem of his son's education for life was somewhat more practical. On one occasion, he boasted to a friend: "I cheat my boys every time I get a chance. I want to make 'em sharp." As part of his program to keep his son sharp, the elder Rockefeller would lend him money and then before the note was due, appear and say: "I shall have to have that money." The younger Rockefeller always met this test. In his later life Rockefeller recalled with pride his father's labor policy:

> *He would hire men to work for him; after a time tell them with a smile, "I don't need you any longer"; then in a few days hire them over again. His "policy of firing and hiring over" he called it. It kept the men on tiptoe—no stagnation among them.*

Rockefeller, who in 1858 at the age of nineteen had entered the produce-commission business in Cleveland, came to the conclusion in the early sixties that the oil industry held out excellent prospects of financial gain. Accordingly, at the end of the war he sold his interest in the commission business and formed a company with Samuel Andrews, a Cleveland oil-refiner, to whom he had already lent money. At the outset Rockefeller realized that competition and small-scale production were unprofitable, and he determined to rid the refining industry of both. Rockefeller and Andrews enlarged their plant, took H. M. Flagler into partnership, established a New York office, and built a second refinery. Under Rockefeller's management the business of the firm expanded rapidly, and in 1870 the concern was transformed into the Standard Oil Company of Ohio with a capitalization of $1,000,000.

Powerful from the first, the Standard Oil Company proceeded methodically to eliminate its competitors. In 1872, Rockefeller joined with a group of Pittsburgh and Philadelphia refiners in forming the South Improvement Company—a combination of "insiders" designed to secure for its members control of the entire refining industry. This end was to be accomplished through a secret agreement between the new corporation and the Pennsylvania, Erie, and New York Central Railroads whereby the railroads, after considerably increasing freight rates on oil, were to grant rebates to the new syndicate not only on its own oil but on that of its competitors. For every barrel of oil, for example, shipped from the oil regions to New York at the published tariff of $2.56, the South Improvement Company was to receive a rebate of $1.06 not only on its own product but on that of its competitors. Although the Pennsylvania legislature was forced by the pressure of public opinion to annul the South Improvement Company's charter, Rockefeller's business was too important for the railroads to disregard, and he soon contrived to secure extensive private rebates for Standard Oil. One by one the independent refiners of Cleveland were forced to choose between selling out to Rockefeller or bankruptcy. In 1874, plants in Pittsburgh, Philadelphia, and New York were absorbed, and the following year the company's capital was increased to $3,000,000. By 1880, Standard produced more than 90 per cent of the nation's refined oil.

Rockefeller's hold on the nation's oil business was further strengthened by his control over the facilities for transporting petroleum. Despite the generous rebates that he received from the railroads, Rockefeller felt that his transportation costs were still too high, and in the mid-seventies Standard Oil undertook the construction of pipelines. By 1880 most of the pipe-lines in the Appalachian oil fields were controlled by the United Pipe-Line Company, a Standard subsidiary. In an effort to destroy this virtual monopoly, a group of independent producers formed the Tidewater Pipe-Line Company and built a pipe-line to one of the railroads that did not grant rebates to Standard. Rockefeller replied to this challenge by building more pipe-lines, by acquiring the refineries that did business with the Tidewater company, by spreading rumors that it was bankrupt, and by placing one of his men on its board of directors. In 1883, Tidewater gave up the unequal struggle, and an agreement was reached by which Standard's United Pipe-Line Company was to receive four fifths of the business while Tidewater was to have the remainder.

Rockefeller was also able to crush competition through a highly efficient and at times unscrupulous marketing-organization. The United States was divided into a number of sales districts over each of which presided a Standard executive. He, in turn, was assisted by corps of subordinates who not only sold Standard products but also made regular reports on the activities of Standard's competitors. If a rival firm undersold Standard, an agent would visit retailers in his territory and warn them of the dangers of doing business with Standard's competitors. If threats proved unavailing, Standard would launch a price war. There is no record of Rockefeller having lost such a conflict. Standard owned its own marketing system, did not have to pay middlemen, and with a nationwide business it could afford to sustain temporary losses in one district as long as it continued to make substantial profits in the rest of the country.

Standard Oil was not only able to destroy its leading competitors, but it was also the first company to discover a method for legalizing monopoly. By 1882, S. C. T. Dodd, a Standard lawyer, had worked out a plan for the use of the trust as a device for controlling Standard's properties. Under this arrangement, stockholders in seventy-seven companies transferred their stock certificates—that is, all their voting rights—to nine Standard trustees, who took over the management of the affairs of all the concerns. In return for their stock certificates, the stockholders received trust certificates that entitled their owners to dividends. As the earnings of all seventy-seven companies were placed in a single treasury, the holders of trust certificates were assured of dividend payments even if the particular company in which they had invested had lost money during the preceding year. The upshot of the trust agreement as it was developed by Standard Oil in the 1880's was that nine men (of whom Rockefeller was the most important) controlled virtually the entire petroleum business in the United States.

25. THE CONCENTRATION OF INDUSTRY

ONCE the feasibility of the trust had been proved, other industrialists—notably the whisky and sugar producers—employed it. But the trust enjoyed only a brief popularity, for it soon became apparent that it was vulnerable to attack from the courts. The sugar trust, which had been organized by H. O. Havemeyer in 1887 as the American Sugar Company, disbanded when New York State withdrew the charter of one of its member concerns. A temporary change in the structure of the trust proved unsatisfactory, and in 1891 the former participants in the trust established the American Sugar Refining Company in New Jersey as a fifty million dollar holding-company.* The effect of this change has been described by Ida Tarbell in *The Nationalizing of Business:*

> *Except for the change in legal structure, the business continued to be carried on as before. Under the new organization the man-*

* A holding company produced no goods. Instead, it bought up and held a controlling interest in a number of concerns, most of which were usually in the same industry.

agement was further unified, since there was now but one board of directors and one set of officers.

*Controlling about eighty-five per cent of the total sugar output, the American Sugar Refiining Company was able to raise prices at will. Representatives of the concern could offer no satisfactory reason why the price of sugar should rise in the face of economies claimed except that the company exercised a monopolistic control. From the beginning it adopted the policy of issuing no public statements. The only information it vouchsafed appeared in the annual reports required by the state of Massachusetts, and these were simply balance sheets which revealed little of its inside workings. According to H. O. Havemeyer, president of the company, even stockholders were not given information unless they demanded it as a body.**

Adverse court decisions also compelled Standard Oil to substitute the holding company for the trust. In March, 1892, the Supreme Court of Ohio ordered the dissolution of the Standard trust on the ground that it was designed to "establish a virtual monopoly" and was "contrary to the policy of our state." This decision, however, did not produce the desired results, for the nine Standard trustees, although they returned the stock to the stockholders, continued to manage the member concerns as "liquidating trustees," a stratagem that was not abandoned until Standard was charged with evasion of the court order five years later. In 1899 Standard's officials finally formed a holding company in New Jersey. Under the liberal incorporation laws of that state, the Standard Oil Company of New Jersey purchased the securities of the companies that had belonged to the trust, and Standard's control over the refining business was as complete as ever. In 1911, the Supreme Court ruled that Standard Oil of New Jersey had violated the Sherman Antitrust Act.† This decision, however, had little more effect than earlier state-court rulings on the management of Standard's affairs. While the Standard empire was broken up into its component parts, only the techniques of monopoly were altered. Through interlocking directorates and unwritten agreements, the officials of the legally separate Standard Oil companies in the various states continued to conduct their respective business with a remarkable degree of unanimity.

New Jersey's liberal incorporation laws, which were adopted as a means for increasing the state's revenue, provided the consolidationists with a convenient device for eliminating competition in their respective industries. Holding companies incorporated under New Jersey law had

* Ida Tarbell: *The Nationalizing of Business*, 1878–1898 (New York: The Macmillan Company, 1936), p. 206. Copyright 1936 by The Macmillan Company, and reprinted with their permission.

† See pp. 147–9.

no other function than to own a controlling share of the stock of other concerns regardless of where they were located or incorporated. In return for these privileges, the directors of a New Jersey corporation had to maintain a New Jersey office, which they generally used once a year when they went through the formalities of conducting their company's annual meeting. By 1901, the list of New Jersey corporations, which read like a Who's Who of American industry, included in addition to Standard Oil and the American Sugar Refining Company, Amalgamated Copper Company, American Smelting and Refining Company, Consolidated Tobacco Company, International Mercantile Marine Company, and United States Steel Corporation.

Most Americans referred to all large corporations as "trusts," a word that soon became synonymous in the public mind with monopoly. But in actuality only a few industrialists employed the trust form to attain concentration of control, and those who did were eventually forced to abandon it. Most monopolies of this period were achieved, not by the trust agreement, but through the merger of two or more companies or through the purchase of the weaker firms within an industry by their more powerful rivals. The National Cordage Company, for example, was the product of a merger of the four largest members of the industry. The American Tobacco Company, which was formed in 1890 by the five leading cigarette manufacturers under the leadership of James B. Duke, proceeded for another decade to purchase its leading competitors. In 1898 the Continental Tobacco Company was formed as a sister firm to take over the production of plug tobacco, and three years later the Consolidated Tobacco Company was established as a holding company to control the Continental and American Tobacco Companies. A somewhat similar policy of merger and acquisition was pursued by companies producing matches, lead, nails, barbed wire, meat, and a host of other commodities.

It was in the steel industry, however, that the merger reached its climax with the formation of the United States Steel Corporation in 1901. The consolidation movement in the steel industry was inaugurated by Andrew Carnegie in the 1870's. Born in Scotland of poor parents and brought to this country by his mother, Carnegie went to work as a bobbin boy in a cotton mill. At the age of fourteen he was a messenger for a Pittsburgh telegraph office. In 1853 he became private secretary to Thomas Scott of the Pennsylvania Railroad, who soon made him superintendent of the line's Pittsburgh division. During the Civil War, Carnegie invested his savings in iron making, and in 1865 he resigned from the Pennsylvania Railroad to devote his energies to the iron industry. In the early seventies he turned to steel production. After completing the Edgar Thomson Steel Works at Braddocks Field on the Monongahela River, Carnegie outdistanced all other steel producers in western Pennsylvania. Like the master consolidationist of the oil business, Carnegie obtained rebates from railroads and took advantage of the depression of the seventies to buy out his less fortunate competitors. In 1877 the Carnegie properties earned a profit of 42 per cent, and by 1880, Carnegie had become the undisputed leader of the Eastern steel industry. But he was still not satisfied, and in the ensuing years his company purchased more rivals, established its own fleet of ore boats on the Great Lakes, acquired a railroad, leased part of the Mesabi ore fields, and assured itself of an adequate supply of coke by merging with the Frick Coke Company. In 1892, with the organization of the Carnegie Steel Company, Carnegie retired from active business affairs and left the management of his steel empire to Henry Clay Frick. By 1900 the concern had a capital stock of $160,000,000.

While Carnegie was building up his steel industry in the Pittsburgh district, steel makers in other parts of the country were using similar methods to achieve comparable results. The major producer in the South was the Tennessee Coal, Iron, and Railroad Company. The Colorado Fuel and Iron Company was the largest single producer in the Rocky Mountain states. The Federal Steel Company, which was incorporated in 1898 and controlled the most important steel-producing facilities in the Middle West, had emulated Carnegie's policy of integration through its purchase of ore and coal fields, railroads, and ore ships on the Great Lakes. In 1901 a long step toward a national monopoly in the steel industry was taken with the formation of the United States Steel Corporation. Organized as a New Jersey holding company, the new steel corporation was a "combination of combinations," that included not only the Carnegie and Federal Steel companies, but ten other giant steel-concerns as well.

By the first decade of the twentieth century, there were few branches of American industry that had not been affected by the consolidation movement. In 1904, John Moody enumerated 318 industrial "trusts," which had a total capitalization of more than seven billion dollars and had been built up by a series of mergers involving more than fifty-two hundred separate plants. Of the ninety-two largest corporations in 1904, seventy-eight controlled 50 per cent or more of their respective industries; fifty-seven controlled 60 per cent or more; and twenty-six controlled 80 per cent or more. After 1905 the merger movement slackened perceptibly, for by then most of the major combinations had been formed. In the remaining years before World War I the nation's industrial trusts steadily strengthened their hold over the American economy.

Although the trust makers curbed or eliminated competition to assure their own profits, they always insisted that the growth of monopoly aided the general public. They maintained that they were substituting order and stability for the chaos that had characterized unlimited competition and that the concentration of industrial control reduced inefficiency, waste, and the duplication of effort and expense. To prove their point they cited the increase in American industrial output and the great variety of products that were manufactured by the trusts. As a last resort they often argued that the trend toward concentration was an inevitable development that neither they nor anyone else could obstruct.

Although monopoly may have been more efficient than competition and may have been responsible for the mass production of goods that might not otherwise have been manufactured, it had certain marked disadvantages for the American people. Under a competitive system a decline in demand brought about a corresponding decrease in prices. Monopolists, however, responded to a reduction in demand by cutting production rather than prices. Consequently, profits were frequently preserved at the expense of satisfying the wants of consumers. As a result, even in times of prosperity there was idle productive capacity at the very time that consumers were in need of countless products. As early as 1894, Henry Demarest Lloyd, in *Wealth Against Commonwealth,* pointed out the contradictions produced within the American economy by the growth of industrial concentration.

> *The world, enriched by thousands of generations of toilers and thinkers, has reached a fertility which can give every human being a plenty undreamed of even in the Utopias. But between this plenty . . . and the people hungering for it step the "cornerers," the syndicates, trusts, combinations, with the cry of "overproduction"—too much of everything. Holding back the riches of earth, sea, and sky from their fellows who famish and freeze in the dark, they declare to them that there is too much light and warmth and food. They assert the right, for their private profit, to regulate the consumption by the people of the necessaries of life, and to control production, not by the needs of humanity, but by the desires of a few for dividends. The coal syndicate thinks there is too much coal. There is too much iron, too much lumber, too much flour—for this or that syndicate.** *

Nor did industrial concentration produce the much advertised stability that had been predicted by its authors, for the business cycle turned as crazily as ever, despite the decline of competition. The economic revival that had followed the depression of the 1870's was interrupted by a slight recession in 1884. After recovering from this interlude, business boomed until it went into a full-scale depression in the midnineties.

* Henry Demarest Lloyd: *Wealth Against Commonwealth* (New York: Harper & Brothers, 1894), p. 1.

In 1893, 573 bank and loan companies were forced out of business, and there were 15,242 commercial failures. In the next three years, unemployment increased, industrial production declined, wages fell, and farm income decreased. It was not until 1897–8 that the worst was over and the business cycle began to resume its upward course. If the industrialists were prepared—and they were—to accept credit for the boom times of America's Iron Age, they also deserved much of the blame for the widespread economic distress that accompanied the depressions of the seventies and the nineties.

26. FROM INDUSTRIAL TO FINANCE CAPITALISM

THE INDUSTRIAL capitalists who after 1860 had played a major rôle in the development of American industry were eventually compelled to surrender some of their economic power to the nation's bankers. For twenty-five years after the Civil War, American big business was dominated by individuals like Rockefeller, Carnegie, Swift, and Havemeyer. These men, regardless of what critics might think of their methods, were producers who had grown up with their industries and were skilled industrial organizers. Industrial capitalists were doers. They may or may not have been crude, ruthless, and amoral; but they were all men of action who got things done. Their successors, the finance capitalists, were owners. They rose to power, not because they could contribute any special skills or knowledge to American industry, but because they controlled vast sums of money that could be used to purchase authority.

The triumph of finance capitalism was preceded by the rise and fall of the speculative capitalist. In the years immediately after the Civil War a large number of railroad and manufacturing concerns were established by enterprising individuals who frequently possessed more imagination than ready cash. To obtain sufficient capital for their grandiose schemes of industrial expansion and conquest, they issued securities which were sold to the general public. The clearing house for these transactions was the New York Stock Exchange, which then, as now, was the largest and most important security exchange in the United States. Because the stock market was unregulated, unscrupulous operators were in a position to take advantage of the ignorance and naïveté of investors. Nor were men lacking who were willing to capitalize on this situation, and for approximately twenty years after the Civil War, speculative capitalists like Drew, Fisk, and Gould dominated the activities of the New York Stock Exchange. In contrast to the industrial capitalists, the speculative capitalists made their profits by ruining corporations that had been built up by the skill, ingenuity, and hard work of others.

To speculative capitalists a corporation was akin to a carcass, and they were its bloodsuckers. They would draw off the blood, leaving only the skin and bones, and then pump in new blood so that it could be drawn off again. While other men produced goods for profits, the speculative capitalist obtained his profits from stock watering and stock manipulation. If Drew, Gould, and Fisk, for example, wanted additional funds, they merely printed more Erie stock and sold it to gullible investors. Their expenses stopped with the cost of printing, for new stock-issues were not accompanied by an addition to the railroad's physical assets. Furthermore, these stock jugglers could change the price of Erie stock whenever they wished. By dumping huge quantities of Erie stock on the market they would force down its value. When it had reached a suitable low point, they would buy it back, trade in it furiously among themselves to force up the price, sell it profitably when it could be pushed no higher, and then be ready to begin the process all over again.

The shift from speculative to finance capitalism was bridged in part by Jay Cooke, who obtained his wealth and fame by marketing the government's Civil War securities. Cooke was essentially a seller rather than a manipulator of stocks, and he was the first individual to introduce a semblance of order into a chaotic business. By combining shrewd appeals to patriotism with an over-all plan for the disposal of these issues, Cooke sold unprecedented amounts of bonds, and he was responsible for introducing into this country the system of underwriting securities. After the war, Cooke applied his techniques to the sale of corporate securities. When he marketed Northern Pacific stock, his firm employed a corps of trained salesmen and enlisted the support of local newspapers, postmasters, clergymen, lawyers, and shopkeepers.

When Jay Cooke's banking firm collapsed with the crash of 1873, his financial career was brought to an abrupt end. But before his failure, Cooke had set the pattern for the subsequent growth of investment banking under J. P. Morgan and the other finance capitalists of the next generation, and it was the development of investment banking that was largely responsible for the increasing influence of financiers over the direction and control of the American economy. Industrialists whose desire to launch new undertakings and enlarge their existing facilities was continually hampered by a shortage of available capital turned to the investment banker for the funds needed for such enterprises. In return for a commission, the investment banker marketed the industrialist's securities. Before long the investment banker began to insist that he be given a share in the management of the concerns in which his customers had invested their money. Industrialists, hard pressed for capital, were frequently not in a position to refuse such a request; and during the last two decades of the nineteenth century the names of prominent bankers appeared with increasing frequency on the directors' lists of some of the nation's most prominent railroad and manufacturing concerns.

The investment banker originally moved into the field of industrial capitalism to protect his clients' funds. Industrialists—especially railroad executives—had repeatedly demonstrated by their reckless and at times unscrupulous policies that some such form of guardianship was necessary. The bankers, however, were not long content to remain as mere watchdogs, and by the turn of the century numerous corporations had passed from the control of industrialists to that of bankers.

The leading American finance capitalist was J. P. Morgan, who after 1900 exerted more influence on the American economy than any other single individual. Unlike most of the industrial capitalists, Morgan had been born to wealth and had received a college education before entering business. As a young man he thought for a time of becoming a mathematics teacher, but he soon abandoned this idea and entered his father's banking house in London in 1856. Four lears later he opened a branch of the concern in New York. The Morgan firm was a typical private banking-establishment and concentrated on the sale of American securities abroad. In 1873 it had invaded Jay Cooke's special province when it marketed some government securities; but it was not until the 1880's, when it became involved in financing American railroads, that its impact on American industrial management and organization began to be felt.

J. P. Morgan's pre-eminence as an investment banker was the direct result of his ability to control the financial institutions that had ample supplies of capital for investment in the securities issued by railroad and manufacturing concerns. The leading commercial banks, trust companies, and insurance firms all had large sums of money available for investment, and any individual who could determine their policies would be in a position to dominate the nation's security market. Largely through a system of interlocking directorates the House of Morgan at the height of its power before World War I became the single most important influence in New York commercial banking. J. P. Morgan was a vice-president of the National Bank of Commerce; George F. Baker, a Morgan partner, was president of the First National Bank; and interlocking directorates and stock ownership gave the Morgan firm a powerful voice in the affairs of the Chase, Liberty, Hanover, and Astor National banks as well as several banks outside New York City. Morgan's influence over the management of the principal trust companies was equally pronounced. J. P. Morgan & Company organized the Bankers' Trust Company; it was associated with the Manhattan Trust Company through its control over the First National Bank; it took over the management of the Guaranty Trust Company in 1909; and it had representatives on the boards of the Union, Commercial, and Fidelity Trust Companies. Finally, Morgan's lines of power reached into some of the United States' richest insurance companies. George W. Perkins, a vice-president of the New York Life Insurance Company, was made a Morgan partner; and stock ownership gave the Morgan firm a powerful voice in the management of the Mutual Life Insurance Company and the Equitable Life Assurance Company.

Because of his firm's control over some of the wealthiest banks, trust companies, and insurance concerns in the land, Morgan had few rivals in the use of what Louis D. Brandeis called "other people's money." Consequently, industrialists who wished to raise money through security issues were frequently at his mercy. When Morgan marketed their securities, he demanded in addition to the usual commission a share in management. From 1890 to World War I the largest amounts of securities were issued by the United States government, railroads, and manufacturing companies. All three at one time or another came to Morgan, and all three accepted his terms.

By implication the Federal government acknowledged Morgan's control over a large part of the nation's financial resources during the struggle to maintain the gold standard in the midnineties. After two bond sales had failed to relieve the Treasury's gold shortage, Cleveland in 1895 was compelled to turn to the House of Morgan to market Federal securities in such a way as to increase the government's supply of gold. It was J. P. Morgan—rather than the United States government—who possessed the financial power to preserve the gold standard.

Morgan's ascendency over American railroading was consummated in 1889 at a meeting of rail executives over which he presided. At the conclusion of the conference, the following statement was released to the press by Morgan:

> *I am authorized to say, I think, on behalf of the banking houses represented here that if an organization can be formed practically upon the basis submitted by the committee, and with an executive committee able to enforce its provisions, upon which the bankers shall be represented, they are prepared to say that they will not negotiate, and will do everything in their power to prevent the negotiation of, any securities for the construction of parallel lines or the extension of lines not approved by that executive committee.*

Industrial capitalists had built the railroads, but they had been unable to solve the complex problems raised by unregulated competition. These problems held no terror for the bankers. In 1889, J. P. Morgan, as the nation's leading banker, informed the assembled railroad executives that an organization had been established to eliminate competition, and that he and his colleagues would run it. The finance capitalists were prepared to supply capital for railroad development, but as their price they asked for power to control the policies adopted by the railroads for which they had raised funds. Eventually J. P. Morgan & Company became the dominant force in the management of the Erie, the Chesapeake and Ohio, and most of the important railroad systems in the South and West. The House of Morgan did not confine its activities to railroading, for it also exerted considerable influence on a number of other branches of American industry. After 1900, the Morgan firm controlled the shipping, rubber, and electrical supply "trusts" in addition to its greatest industrial triumph, the steel "trust." At the time of its organization in 1901, the United States Steel Corporation included companies that produced approximately half the annual American supply of pig iron, coke, and steel rails, more than half of the output of structural steel, and virtually all the supply of barbed wire, wire nails, tin plate, and steel tubes. These companies also built nine tenths of the nation's bridges and owned a large proportion of the Lake Superior ore fields and the ore vessels on the Great Lakes. At the head of this huge corporation was J. P. Morgan, a banker who never knew and never made any pretense of knowing the first thing about the iron and steel industry.

After 1900, Morgan's control over the nation's financial and industrial life was rivaled, if not surpassed, by several Standard Oil officials who had invested their profits from the petroleum business in a wide variety of enterprises. The National City Bank, which had not fallen under Morgan's domination, was closely associated with Standard Oil and was known to Wall Street intimates as a "Rockefeller bank." Like the Morgan firm, the Rockefeller, or Standard Oil, group acquired control of valuable iron resources in the Lake Superior district and a number of large railroad corporations. This same small group formed powerful alliances with several public utilities and became dominant in the ice, smelting, and tobacco trusts. The Rockefeller and Morgan interests were not necessarily in competition, for they frequently had heavy investments in the same corporations and often had representatives on the same boards of directors.

An example of the effect of the rise of finance capitalism on the control of the American economy is furnished by Louis D. Brandeis in *Other People's Money,* a book that was largely based on the Pujo Committee's revelations concerning the money trust. Using the New Haven Railroad as an illustration, Brandeis pointed out that its "real managing directors were":

> *J. Pierpont Morgan, George F. Baker, and William Rockefeller. Mr. Morgan was, until his death in 1913, the head of perhaps the largest banking house in the world. Mr. Baker was, until 1909,*

*President and then Chairman of the Board of Directors of one of America's leading banks (the First National of New York), and Mr. Rockefeller was, until 1911, President of the Standard Oil Company. Each was well advanced in years. Yet each of these men, besides the duties of his own vast business, and important private interests, undertook to "guide, superintend, govern and manage," not only the New Haven but also the following other corporations, some of which were similarly complex: Mr. Morgan, 48 corporations including 40 railroad corporations with at least 100 subsidiary companies, and 16,000 miles of line; 3 banks and trust or insurance companies; 5 industrial and public-service companies. Mr. Baker, 48 corporations, including 15 railroad corporations, with at least 158 subsidiaries, and 37,400 miles of track; 18 banks, and trust or insurance companies; 15 public service corporations and industrial concerns. Mr. Rockefeller, 37 corporations, including 23 railroad corporations with at least 117 subsidiary companies, and 26,400 miles of line; 5 banks, trust or insurance companies; 9 public-service companies and industrial concerns.**

The triumph of finance capitalism produced a far greater degree of economic concentration within the United States than had existed at any previous time in American history. The industrial capitalists at most had been able to dominate a single industry, but finance capitalism cut across industries. Through interlocking directorates, community of interests, and stock purchases, investment firms like J. P. Morgan & Company, Kuhn, Loeb & Company, and Kidder, Peabody & Company could exercise a controlling influence over a host of unrelated industries. By 1912 the members of the House of Morgan and the directors of the banks and trust companies with which they were affiliated held 341 directorships in 112 corporations whose total assets were more than $22,000,000,000. After examining the ramifications of the Money Trust, the Pujo Investigating Committee concluded:

Far more dangerous than all that has happened to us in the past in the way of elimination of competition in industry is the control of credit through the domination of these [financial] *groups over our banks and industries. . . .*

. . . The acts of this inner group, as here described, have . . . been more destructive of competition than anything accomplished by the trusts, for they strike at the very vitals of potential competition in every industry that is under their protection, a condition which if

* Louis D. Brandeis: *Other People's Money; And How the Bankers Use It* (New York: Frederick A. Stokes Company, 1913), pp. 206–07. Copyright 1913 by Louis D. Brandeis and reprinted with the permission of his estate.

permitted to continue, will render impossible all attempts to restore normal competitive conditions in the industrial world.

Finance capitalists, who prided themselves on their conservative outlook, maintained that they had brought a much needed stability to the conduct of American business enterprise. The financiers argued that they had substituted the safe and sound banking practices for the exuberant recklessness of the industrial capitalists. Yet it was difficult to discern the fruits of this conservatism. Although the solemnity that characterized J. P. Morgan's conduct of his business bore no surface resemblance to the high jinks of a Gould, Drew, or Fisk, he was as fully versed in the dubious art of overcapitalization as the most flamboyant speculative capitalists. When the United States Steel Corporation was organized, it was capitalized at $1,400,000,000, or more than twice the value of its physical assets. Nor was this example an exception, for the water pumped into the stock of such enterprises as the New Haven Railroad revealed that even the speculative capitalists could have taken some lessons from the self-professed conservative bankers.

Despite the bankers' insistence that they represented sanity and stability in business life they were no more successful than the industrial capitalists had been in flattening out the curves in the business cycle. The policies of the finance capitalists were probably the influences most responsible for the depressions of 1903 and 1907. The overcapitalization of the numerous "trusts" that were created between 1898 and 1902 generated a stock boom that collapsed when the market became flooded with what James J. Hill called "indigestible securities." Recovery was well under way by the end of 1904, and business activity increased steadily until 1907, when the events of 1903 were repeated. In March, 1907, stock quotations fell sharply, but a general collapse was averted until the following October, when the failure of the Knickerbocker Trust Company precipitated a full-scale panic. Business did not revive until 1909; and minor recessions in 1910 and 1911 postponed full recovery until 1912–13. Depressions strengthened rather than weakened the hold of the leading finance capitalists on the American economy, for hard times gave them the opportunity to buy out their less fortunate rivals. During the Panic of 1907, the Morgan firm acquired Charles W. Morse's shipping combination; and the United States Steel Corporation, after receiving permission from President Roosevelt, purchased the Tennessee Coal, Iron, and Railroad Company.

Perhaps the outstanding effect of the growth of finance capitalism upon the development of American industry was the fashion in which it dulled, blunted, and thwarted initiative. The bankers supplanted a group of industrial pioneers who had built up industries by adopting daring innovations and by taking what often seemed to be needless chances. The finance capitalists, partly through ignorance of the nature of the industries that they controlled and partly through innate conservatism, devoted their efforts to keeping things as they were. Technological changes could be dangerous for they might make antiquated the existing machinery or patents in a particular industry. Other changes could threaten the much-advertised stability that the finance capitalists had proclaimed as their objective. In 1911 a memorial drawn up by the Investors' Guild stated:

> *It is a well-known fact that modern trade combinations tend strongly toward constancy of process and products, and by their very nature are opposed to new processes and new products originated by independent inventors, and hence tend to restrain competition in the development and sale of patents and patent rights; and consequently tend to discourage independent inventive thought, to the great detriment of the nation. . . .*

It was hardly an accident that the automobile industry, which developed faster than any other branch of American manufacturing in the years just preceding World War I, received little or no assistance from the nation's financiers. In explaining the attitude of the bankers toward the early automobile manufacturers, Henry B. Joy, president of the Packard Motor Car Company, said:

> *It is the observable facts of history, it is also my experience of thirty years as a business man, banker, etc., that first the seer conceives an opportunity. He has faith in his almost second sight. He believes he can do something—develop a business—construct an industry—build a railroad—or Niagara Falls Power Company,—and make it pay! . . .*
>
> *The motor-car business was the same.*
>
> *When a few gentlemen followed me in my vision of the possibilities of the business, the banks and older business men (who in the main were the banks) said, "fools and their money soon to be parted"—etc., etc.*
>
> *Private capital at first establishes an industry, backs it through its troubles, and, if possible, wins financial success when banks would not lend a dollar of aid.*
>
> *The business once having proved to be practicable and financially successful, then do the banks lend aid to its needs.*

Despite the waste, chaos, and questionable morality that characterized the development of American industry in the decades immediately following the Civil War, this age was filled with a lusty exuberance that is frequently associated with youth. During the first fifteen years of the twentieth century, signs of middle age, if not senility, became apparent as the "safe and sane" bankers took over the chairs around the directors' tables that had formerly been occupied by the last generation of industrialists that worked their way "up from the bottom." If nothing else, the arrival of the finance capitalists signified that the American economy had come of age.

27. THE DEFENSE OF BUSINESS

THE AMERICAN Industrial Revolution, like every successful revolution, produced a new ruling class. By 1875 most of the antebellum orators and statesmen had passed from the political scene, and the merchant princes and great landowning families had lost much of their ascendancy in economic affairs. For a short interregnum the United States was virtually leaderless; but after this period of transition the industrial capitalist—and later the finance capitalist—emerged as the dominant political, social, economic, and cultural force in American life.

"These modern potentates," as Charles Francis Adams called them, enjoyed power as supreme as that of any absolute monarch. They dictated terms to their workers, and, when the workers rebelled, used private or public armies to force compliance. They raised prices, and when consumers complained, joined with their competitors to raise them still higher. They bought legislatures, but when numerous scandals shocked the public into demanding reform, they abandoned such crass and costly methods to become political overlords in their own right. Above all, they lived as they pleased, spending their fortunes on entertainment, city palaces, country estates, grand tours, old art, and favorite churches or colleges.

Occasional complaints against their methods of acquiring and spending their wealth could be ignored or passed off with William Vanderbilt's famous dictum of the "public be damned." The people could object, but they must not interfere. Business leaders had nothing to hide, not because they were beyond reproach, but because they were beyond successful attack. H. O. Havemeyer boasted that he did not know enough about ethics to apply them to business; and J. P. Morgan did not hesitate to tell a reporter that he "owe[d] the public nothing." American business leadership, secure in the sense of its own raw strength, felt neither the need nor the desire to rationalize its position to its subjects.

Many successful businessmen adopted the views of Vanderbilt, Havemeyer, and Morgan, but others made an especial effort to win popular support for their policies. As early as 1878, Abram S. Hewitt in an address tc a meeting of the Church Congress on the "Mutual Relations of Capital and Labor" urged co-operation instead of conflict as a solution to the industrial disputes of the period; and in the 1880's Andrew Carnegie began to publish the first of his many articles in defense of the businessman. As opposition to business policies increased, numerous executives in a wide variety of industries came to the conclusion that they could no longer afford to ignore public opinion. In the language of the time, it was decided to "educate" the American people. In 1904, J. W. Van Cleave, president of the Buck Stove and Range Company, told the members of the Citizens' Industrial Association of America that is was their duty "as the employing classes of this country" to "crystallize public opinion." As there was nothing that could "resist the power of public opinion," Van Cleave concluded that there was "no reason why the employing classes, the intelligent classes, and the money classes, if you please, should not influence public opinion." Much the same advice was given a year later by Van Cleave's good friend, President David M. Parry of the National Association of Manufacturers.

During the first years of the new century several other business leaders recognized the necessity for channeling public opinion. In 1908, Colonel J. D. Powers, president of the American Bankers Association, urged the members of his organization to "begin a vigorous campaign of education." President Theodore Vail of the American Telephone and Telegraph Company ordered his corporation's officials to "educate the public." In a speech before the members of the American Electric Railway Association in 1916, Ivy Lee stated that "the greatest thing that could be done for . . . all the utilities of the United States, would be to do for them what Billy Sunday has done for religion."

In their attempts to explain the methods by which they had acquired wealth and power, businessmen usually appealed to some form of higher law that appeared in no statute book but was nevertheless considered immutable. In using this argument to rationalize their success, businessmen resorted to a technique that had been repeatedly employed by Americans in the years before 1860. The Puritans of the Massachusetts Bay Colony, the Revolutionists of 1776, the founding fathers of 1789, the expansionists of the 1840's, and the antagonists on both sides of the slavery conflict had all insisted that they were acting in conformity with a higher law that had been ordained by either God or nature and that took precedence over mere man-made laws. In similar fashion, the businessman after the Civil War frequently maintained that his exalted status in American economic society was the direct result of the workings of unalterable higher law.

Among the most popular of the higher laws espoused by the businessman was Darwin's law of evolution, which had been tailored by another Englishman, Herbert Spencer, to fit the needs of industrial capitalism.

Spencer in a number of articles, lectures, and books argued that Darwin's rules of natural selection applied not only to the beasts of the jungle but to individuals in economic society as well. Life was characterized by an unremitting struggle in which the weak fell by the wayside while the strong inevitably pushed forward. However unfortunate this process might appear to humanitarians, there was nothing that could be done to alter it, for it was a law of nature that only the fit survived. In short, only the rich were fit, and their wealth was a proof of their fitness.

The patness and easy generalizations of Spencer's theories naturally appealed to a generation of businessmen who at times must have themselves wondered why they, and not others, had been able to accumulate great fortunes in a few short years. Many businessmen soon became adept at handling the clichés of Social Darwinism, but Andrew Carnegie was the only American industrialist who attempted to master Spencer's philosophy in detail. To most businessmen, Spencer was valued as a man who had added a few valuable phrases to business' vocabulary of defense, but to Carnegie he was the man who had found the answer to all the world's mysteries. Carnegie knew Spencer intimately, visited him in England, was his host in America, and referred to him as "my teacher" and to himself as "one of his disciples." Carnegie's conversion to Social Darwinism was akin to St. Paul's experience on the road to Damascus. Going through the works of Darwin and Spencer, he came upon pages explaining "how man has absorbed such mental foods as were favorable to him, rejecting what was deleterious"; and then, wrote Carnegie "light came in as a flood and all was clear."

Social Darwinism was employed by Andrew Carnegie and numerous other American businessmen to defend their control of American capitalism. Like Spencer, they argued that economic society and life in the jungle were both characterized by a fierce, never-ending struggle for survival and supremacy. Those who were best equipped by nature for this battle invariably emerged as victors. Carnegie thought that the "degress of success" was in direct proportion to the "degree of ability," and most business leaders of his generation agreed with this view. Volney W. Foster, former president of the Western Paving and Supply Company, in 1902 attributed business success to a " 'divine ratio' between brains and capital, which if observed, brings rich rewards—violated it results in disaster." In the same year Russell Sage wrote: "So long as some men have more sense and more self-control than others just so long will some men be wealthy."

The corollary to the survival of the fittest was the failure and eventual destruction of the unfit. To a young man complaining that he had not had the "opportunity to prove his ability and to rise to partnership," Carnegie could quote Shakespeare:

The fault, dear Brutus, is not in our stars,
But in ourselves, that we are underlings.

In a similar vein, S. C. T. Dodd, who devised the trust form for the Standard Oil, told the students of Syracuse University in 1893 that there would "always be beggars on our streets, tramps on our roads, debauchery in our saloons, corruption in our politics, injustice and dishonesty in our business." Why was this so? "One reason is because nature or the devil has made some men weak and imbecile and others lazy and worthless, and neither man nor God can do much for one who will do nothing for himself." As long as some individuals "are content, or even consent, to work for barely sufficient to supply them with such barbarous needs, they will find the work and wages suited to their wants."

Carnegie conceded that nature's law at times seemed harsh, but he insisted that all progress depended on the elimination of the unfit. While admitting that the "price which society pays for the law of competition . . . is . . . great" and "may be hard on the individual," Carnegie concluded that it was "best for the race because it insures the survival of the fittest." Any attempt to circumvent the natural law by equalizing the rewards of the fit and unfit would defeat its own ends. "Abolish poverty," said Carnegie, "and what would become of the race? Progress, development would cease."

Despite Carnegie's admonition various attempts were made to abolish poverty. For example, workingmen, not content with the operation of natural laws, formed unions that presumably were designed to aid the unfit as well as the fit. Social Darwinists among businessmen repeatedly pointed out that such organizations were futile, for they rested on the false assumption that economic life was controlled by man instead of by natural law.

> *The workingmen* [wrote Henry Clews, a Wall Street broker] *are taken care of by the natural laws of trade far more perfectly than they can be by any artificial arrangement; and trade unions are simply an intrusion upon the domain of these laws, without the power to supplant or perfect their operation, and with a certainty of obstructing and preventing their tendency, with the inevitable result of mischief to all parties.*

Although it was true that "unions do occasionally get an advance in wages," it was certain, nevertheless, that the advance "would have come anyway by the natural laws of competition among the capitalists" and "without the loss of wages and suffering entailed by the strike." Under the circumstances, Clews concluded that "workmen would be safer in the end to wait for the natural advance."

The Social Darwinists also maintained that any governmental move to regulate or interfere with the economic order established by nature would be just as ineffectual as the attempts of organized labor to circumvent the natural law. Because business activity was controlled by a natural law that had been fixed for all time, man-made legislation could have no permanent effect on economic life. "Oh, these grand, immutable, all-wise laws of natural forces," exclaimed Carnegie in 1886, "how perfectly they work if human legislators would only let them alone! But no, they must be tinkering," and "so our governors, all over the world are at Sisyphus' work—ever rolling the stone uphill to see it roll back to its proper bed at the bottom."

In their efforts to justify their sudden rise to power and wealth, many American business leaders appealed not only to the law of nature but also to the teachings of Adam Smith and the other classical economists. The economic law that had been accepted as a fact by most Americans in the years before the Civil War presupposed a state of free competition that would automatically determine prices, direct the flow of capital, fix wages, and govern the quantity and quality of goods produced. If this system were permitted to operate without interference, its advocates asserted, it would inevitably lead to maximum production at minimum prices and maximum employment at maximum wages. If an entrepreneur raised prices above the level dictated by the condition of the market or if he produced inferior goods, capital furnished by another entrepreneur would appear to be used to manufacture superior goods at the market price. If wages and hours in any instance did not accurately reflect the available supply and demand of labor, the workers concerned would shift to employers who observed the economic law. As with the natural law, only the fit survived. If through inefficiency, a manufacturer or merchant could not meet the price standards of his competitors, he was forced out of business. This constant check on efficiency produced progress that was shared by all members of the population in the form of better goods at lower prices.

The watchdog of the economic law was the economic man. At all times he was supposed to know the available supply and demand of any given commodity, his competitor's costs and profits, and his own best interests. As a consumer he was clever enough to recognize shoddy goods when he saw them and to ascertain when prices had been artificially raised above the figure set by the supply-demand formula. As a worker, he was well enough informed to realize when his wages were below those fixed by a free labor-market, and he was mobile enough to shift and change employers at will. As a capitalist, he knew which forms of investment were the soundest, and his assets were so flexible that they could readily be transferred from one enterprise to another.

Although the growth of industrial concentration after the Civil War had helped to destroy the competitive conditions on which the operation of the economic law was dependent, leading American businessmen did not hesitate to use the language of the classical economists to defend their practices. The great advantage of the economic law to the nation's industrial and finance capitalists was that it enabled them to claim credit for all material progress while shirking any responsibility for economic adversity. Thus, depressions were usually pictured as resulting from violation of the economic law; in 1908, for example, the president of the American Bankers Association said that the panic of the preceding year had been beneficial, for it had punished those who had acted "so completely in contravention of the law of supply and demand." In similar fashion, the economic law rather than the businessman was held responsible for the depressed state of the workingman. "A laborer," said John D. Rockefeller from his retirement, "is worthy of his hire, no less, but no more. . . . You can't hold up conditions artificially, and you can't change the underlying laws of trade."

The economic law, like the natural law, left no room for government regulation of business. If prices, quality, wages, hours, interest rates, and rents were all automatically fixed by the economic law for the common welfare, no economic functions were left for the government. Businessmen argued that government interference in business affairs inevitably disrupted the operation of the economic law and injured the very people that it was designed to benefit. In 1900 the head of the sugar trust said: "Trade will always take care of itself. If it is left to pursue ordinary channels, A will see to it that B does not have any extraordinary advantages. It is only when the State interferes, that a situation is created of which advantage can be taken against the interest of the community."

Many businessmen maintained that moral considerations, as well as the natural and economic laws, determined the distribution of wealth in American economic society. The natural and economic laws were in theory at least derived from a study of man's past behavior; the moral law of the businessman emphasized what man should be. The exponents of the moral law argued that there was a direct correlation between morality and worldly success. Andrew Carnegie, for instance, once wrote: "A great business is seldom if ever built up except on lines of strictest integrity. A reputation for 'cuteness' and sharp dealing is fatal in great affairs." John D. Rockefeller stated that "there can be no permanent success without fair dealing"; and Judge Elbert Gary, the chairman of the board of the United States Steel Corporation, said: "Moral principles . . . [are] the base of all business success."

The moral law of the businessman was in some respects not unlike the teachings of Calvin, and considerable emphasis was placed on the Calvinistic doctrines of hard work, obedience, and thrift as means of acquiring wealth. "Most people who fail," wrote John Wanamaker, "only work half-time, take too many holidays, and are quitters." The businessman's philosophy of discipline was never more succinctly stated than when August Hecksher said: "You must learn to obey before you are fit to command." Finally, like Calvin's law of God, the businessman's moral law placed great emphasis on thrift. Solomon Guggenheim thought the "wage earner more extravagant in proportion to his earnings than the millionaire"; and his brother Daniel said that the rich were rich because "they have been thrifty," while the poor were "poor because they did not save."

Businessmen who appealed to the natural, economic, and moral laws to explain why they, and not others, had prospered experienced little apparent difficulty in convincing their contemporaries that they deserved their wealth. Farmers voiced occasional protests and workers at times resorted to violence; but most Americans envied rather than condemned successful businessmen. Clergymen, professors, and politicians generally agreed with business leaders that wealth came to those who deserved it. The mass of Americans, living in an age of rapid material growth, were certain that the businessman alone was responsible for the nation's phenomenal industrial progress. Although many Americans by 1890 believed that some business practices should be outlawed as "unfair," they were equally determined that the government should do nothing that would interfere with the right of the individual to "get ahead" in life.

28. THE GOVERNMENT AND INDUSTRIAL CONCENTRATION

THE AMERICAN antitrust movement, which emerged during the closing years of the nineteenth century and flourished during the heyday of the Progressive movement,* was an attempt to recapture the past. While European radicals were inclined to advocate government ownership of cartels, American critics of monopoly looked back wistfully to an earlier age of agrarian individualism. They did not want to turn the monopolists' wealth over to the proletariat, and they did not want to abolish private property; but they did want to prevent the monopolist from using his economic power to undermine the economic freedom of others. Although they lived in an age of bigness, they hoped to find some device for protecting the small producer. They had been nurtured on the American dream of rags to riches and log cabin to White House, which they now saw menaced by the trusts. They did not demand economic equality, but they did demand equality of economic opportunity.

* See Chapter XI, pp. 338–56.

Their creed was as old as their nation, for they believed that every one should be given the same chance to succeed.

The American opponents of monopoly feared an all-powerful government even more than they feared the trusts. Like Jefferson they viewed all governments with suspicion and as necessary evils that should be tolerated rather than encouraged. Although they thought that the government should be permitted to regulate business, they insisted that it confine its efforts to the restoration of competition. They viewed economic life as a race, and they looked on the government as a referee that would make sure that the contestants were given an equal opportunity to win. They believed that the race could be made fair for all if the government in its capacity as referee would revive and enforce the rules of economic individualism and competition that had been followed by the nation's artisans and farmers in the halycon day before the Industrial Revolution. Only the socialists, whose numbers were negligible, believed that the government should abolish the race.

By 1890, resentment against the "trusts" was general. Farmers and consumers complained of the high prices charged by trusts; workers objected to the labor policies of huge corporations; reformers pointed out the deleterious effects of industrial concentration on political democracy; and small entrepreneurs charged that they were being forced out of business by the "unfair" trade practices of monopolistic firms. Further impetus was given the antitrust movement by the facts turned up by Congressional investigations of railroad operations during the two years preceding the passage of the Interstate Commerce Act, by the revelations of other legislative committees, and by numerous newspaper accounts of the formation of trusts. Several states—particularly in the South and West—responded to these developments by adopting either laws or constitutional amendments that were designed to prevent any attempt to eliminate or restrict competition. By 1890 at least fifteen states had inserted antitrust provisions in their constitutions or had passed antitrust acts. These laws and amendments, which usually did little more than repeat the common law doctrines against monopoly and restraint of trade, failed to check the development of industrial concentration in the United States. Many trusts were more powerful than the state governments that attempted to regulate them; and as soon as one device for creating monopoly was declared unconstitutional by a state court, the trust makers merely resorted to another, equally effective technique. With the passage of the Sherman Antitrust Act on July 2, 1890, the Federal government belatedly recognized that no state or combination of states could adequately cope with what was essentially a national problem.

The Sherman Antitrust Act was brought forward by the Republicans as a device for satisfying the farmers and small businessmen in the party. The presidential campaign of 1888 had been fought largely over the tariff question. The Republicans were victorious, and they redeemed their campaign pledge with the enactment of the McKinley Tariff. This measure, which provided for a marked increase in most rates, was opposed by a substantial segment of the party's agrarian supporters in the Midwest. In an effort to appease these disgruntled farmers and any other groups opposed to monopoly, Congress went on record as favoring competition over industrial concentration. Apparently only a small number of congressmen thought that the new law would provide an effective means for destroying monopoly, and Senator Orville H. Platt undoubtedly spoke for many of his less frank colleagues when he said:

> *The conduct of the Senate for the past three days . . . has not been in the line of the honest preparation of a bill to prohibit and punish trusts. It has been in the line of getting some bill with that title that we might go to the country with. The question of whether the bill would be operative, of how it would operate, or whether it was within the power of Congress to enact it, have been whistled down the wind in this Senate as idle talk, and the whole effort has been to get some bill headed: "A Bill to Punish Trusts" with which to go to the country.*

The nature and scope of the Sherman Act, which was described in its preamble as "an act to protect trade and commerce against unlawful restraints and monopolies," was revealed by the first two sections of the law.

> *Sec. 1. Every contract, combination in the form of trust or otherwise, or conspiracy, in restraint of trade or commerce among the several States, or with foreign nations, is hereby declared to be illegal. Every person who shall make any such contract or engage in any such combination or conspiracy, shall be deemed guilty of a misdemeanor, and, on conviction thereof, shall be punished by fine not exceeding five thousand dollars, or by imprisonment not exceeding one year, or by both said punishments. . . .*
>
> *Sec. 2. Every person who shall monopolize, or attempt to monopolize, or combine or conspire to combine with any other person or persons, to monopolize any part of the trade or commerce among the several States, or with foreign nations, shall be deemed guilty of a misdemeanor. . . .*

Because of Congress' refusal to define with any degree of exactitude the terms employed in the Sherman Antitrust Act, it was left to the courts to determine the meaning of such words as "restraint" and "monopoly." Moreover, the law could not be enforced without the cooperation of the Attorney General, who was authorized to direct proceedings against alleged violators of the act. For more than a decade after the passage of the Sherman Act, neither Federal judges nor the Justice Department made any move that seriously jeopardized the development of industrial combinations in the United States. Richard Olney, Attorney General during the second Cleveland Administration, thought the Sherman law "no good," and the majority of opinions of the Supreme Court indicate that its members did not have a much higher opinion of the measure.

From 1890 to 1901 the Justice Department instituted only eighteen antitrust suits, four of which were directed against labor unions. Although the government obtained some convictions against industrial combinations, it failed in its efforts to force the dissolution of the powerful trusts that dominated the whisky, sugar, and cash-register industries. Soon after the passage of the Sherman Act, W. H. H. Miller, Harrison's Attorney General, started proceedings against the whisky trust. But when a district court ruled that the indictment against the whisky combine was "clearly insufficient according to the elementary rules of criminal pleading," the government abandoned the case and stopped similar proceedings against the cash-register trust. In 1895 the government's attempt to break up the sugar trust, which at the time controlled 98 per cent of the sugar refined and sold in the United States, was thwarted by the Supreme Court's decision in *United States v. E. C. Knight Co.* The majority of judges ruled that, although the sugar trust had a virtual monopoly over the manufacture of its product, the government had not been able to prove that the company had sought "to put a restraint upon trade or commerce." This decision, which was tantamount to a declaration that the Sherman Act was unenforceable, was considerably modified in 1899, when the Court in the Addystone Pipe case ruled that it was illegal for the members of a pool to enter into agreements for the sale and purchase of their product across state lines. The executive branch of the government, however, made little effort to take advantage of the Supreme Court's change of heart, and during McKinley's administration only three antitrust suits were instituted by the Attorney General. It was not until the presidency of Theodore Roosevelt and the advent of the Progressive movement that Federal government made a serious attempt to deal with the trusts.

CHAPTER V

THE INDUSTRIAL WORKER

THE growth of American industry was accompanied by a fundamental change in the social and economic status of the workingman. With the development of machine production, the former craftsman was transformed into an urban factory-worker who had little control over his wages and working conditions. His special skills no longer enabled him as an individual to bargain effectively with his employer, and the hostility of both the government and nonlaboring public to militant unionism made it difficult for him to improve his lot by joining with his fellow workers in any collective effort. From 1865 to 1914, American wage-earners at various times resorted to strikes, political action, and occasional violence, but in no instance did they win more than limited victories. Before World War I the weapons used by the workingman in industrial warfare never equalled in effectiveness those of the employer.

29. THE LABOR FORCE

BEFORE the widespread application of machinery to the manufacturing process, the typical American worker was a craftsman who held his job because of his skill. He usually owned his own tools, which along with his skills enabled him to approach the status of a creative artist. Frequently, he performed all the operations in the manufacture of a single product. Often he worked in his own home or in the cottage of a neighboring employer. He was not chained to his job, and he was neither a wage slave nor a landless proletarian. He was, in short, an individualist in an age that believed that economic opportunities for the individual were limitless.

When the growth of the factory system compelled a craftsman to become a machine tender he lost some of his most precious possessions. In place of his tools, which had been his servants rather than his master, was a machine that left little scope for individual initiative. He could no longer strive to turn out a superior product, for the machine always turned out the same product. His former skills, instead of being an asset, were frequently a liability in a job that required him to follow a rigid routine. In theory, the man ran the machine, but this was no more than a theory. In a craft society, tools had been subordinate to the creative instincts of their owner. In an industrial society, the machine tender was forced to subordinate his creative instincts to the relentless motions of the machine. More than any other single factor, the machine was responsible for changing the craftsman from an artist into an automaton.

The machine not only deprived the worker of his tools and his skills, but it also robbed him of his sense of security. As long as he had been a craftsman, the worker had possessed an undeniable asset when he bargained with his employer. Only he and those workers with similar skills and training could perform certain operations in the manufacturing process, and he had undoubtedly been as essential to his employer as his employer was to him. But a machine tender had comparatively little bargaining power as an individual. Almost any man of average intelligence who desired to work could be hired to supplant a machine tender who was dissatisfied with his job. And with frequent depressions and a steady flow of immigrants to the United States, there was always a backlog of potential factory-workers who were willing to accept jobs as machine tenders on terms laid down by the employer.

When the craftsman exchanged his own tools for a machine that belonged to his employer, he relinquished what little control he had once had over his working conditions. Wages, hours, and the physical environment of the factory were all determined by the employer. If a worker lost his job for any one of a variety of reasons, he knew that the possibility of finding another position depended more upon chance than upon any ability that he might possess. His ignorance concerning the current state of the labor market and his lack of mobility also prevented him from applying for jobs for which he might have been eligible. Moreover, there was always the possibility that he might become unfit for any type of manual labor. If he lost a foot or a hand in the machine that he was tending, he also lost his job and his ability to obtain other work. If he became too old to keep up with the pace set by the machine, he was turned out by his employer.

The marked increase in the size of individual manufacturing establishments after the Civil War, as well as the rapid mechanization of American industry, seriously affected both the status and the bargaining power of the individual worker. As corporations became larger, the former personal relationship between employer and employee disappeared. In the place of the owner of a small firm who had frequently worked along side his employees, had known their personal problems intimately, and had often helped them through sickness and other hardships were thousands of stockholders who were scattered throughout the United States —and even the world—and who neither knew nor cared about the fate of the workers employed by the corporations that they owned. Nor were the corporation's officials aware of the workers except as statistical abstractions that, taken collectively, were entered in the accounts as "labor costs." Directors, meeting in a downtown office building in New York, made decisions that affected the lives of thousands of workers to whom they usually felt neither financial nor moral obligations.

When the craftsman moved from a small shop to a large factory, he became a member of a working force that lacked both homogeneity and cohesiveness. After the Civil War the American laboring-class included women as well as men, children as well as adults, immigrants as well as native Americans, and Negroes as well as whites. Although the members of each of these groups had many points in common, most of them preferred to emphasize their differences. Men were opposed to women and children in industry; native workers looked with disdain on immigrants; and many white workers preferred to give up their jobs rather than work with a Negro. Thus, the exploitation of those workers who were the least able to defend themselves was made possible not only by the power possessed by the employers but also by the divisions within the laboring force.

From 1865 to 1914 the number of American women and children gainfully employed steadily increased. According to the census of 1870, nearly 750,000 children of both sexes between the ages of ten and fifteen worked to contribute to their own support or that of their families. By 1910, when every state but Nevada had adopted legislation either regulating or forbidding certain forms of child labor, nearly 2,000,000 children held jobs. During these same years more and more women became wage earners. In 1890, there were more than 3,700,000 women gainfully employed; by 1910 there were more than 8,000,000, and they comprised 21.2 per cent of all the gainfully employed in the nation. While many women worked as domestics (more than 2,400,000 in 1910), there were few jobs for which they were not eligible, and by 1910, women were represented in every industry group listed by the Federal census report of that year. Before the outbreak of World War I, women were employed in large numbers in paint factories, chemical works, rubber factories, cotton mills, shoe factories, munition plants, and clothing and hat factories. Many other women, as well as countless children, who were not listed as gainfully employed by the Federal census, worked long hours in tenements on a piece-work basis or in obscure sweatshops that made no report to the Federal authorities. As a rule, children in industry were paid less than women, who in turn earned less than men.

AVERAGE EARNINGS OF FACTORY WORKERS, FOR A YEAR OF 300 WORKING DAYS, 1904*

LOCATION	MEN	WOMEN	CHILDREN
Urban	$566	$307	$186
Rural	479	264	158

In the years immediately following the Civil War, most freed Negroes remained in the South and worked as farmers; and it was not until World War I that they migrated in comparatively large numbers from Southern farms to Northern cities to take jobs in industry. Many Southern Negroes who did not support themselves by farming were employed as domestics or longshoremen. Others worked in the so-called "Negro-job" industries, which included coal mining, railroading, lumbering, and the building trades. Although the South experienced a comparatively rapid industrial expansion after 1890, it had little effect on the Negro, for most of the new jobs were reserved for white workers. Male Negroes in 1910 comprised only a small percentage of the working class, but they were a disruptive force out of all proportion to their numbers. White workers considered Negroes a threat to their jobs and refused them admittance to their unions. That Negroes, who often could get no other type of work, served as strike breakers tended to confirm the hostility of the white workers and to re-enforce their traditional racial prejudice.

Immigrants comprised the largest and most important segment of the American labor force during most of the years between the Civil War and World War I. The foreign-born population of the United States increased from 4,138,697 in 1860 to 9,249,560 in 1890 and to 13,345,545 in 1910. Statistics compiled by the Immigration Commission in 1909 revealed that in most of the nation's leading industries immigrant workers outnumbered native Americans. In contrast to the majority of foreigners who migrated to the United States from northern and western Europe during the first half of the nineteenth century, most immigrants after the

* Isaac A. Hourwich: *Immigration and Labor; The Economic Aspects of European Immigration to the United States* (New York: G. P. Putnam's Sons, 1912), p. 298. Copyright 1912 by, and reprinted with the permission of, G. P. Putnam's Sons.

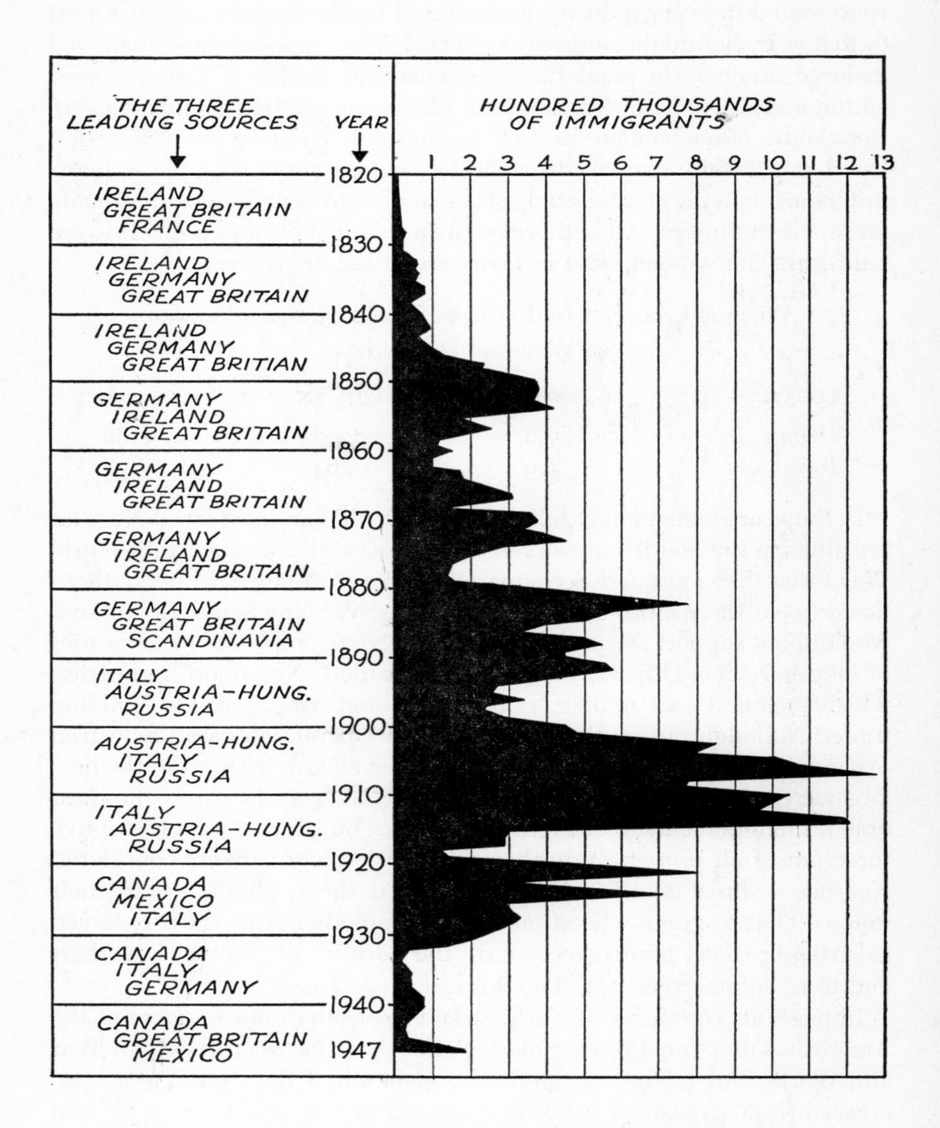

7. MIGRATION FROM THE OLD WORLD TO THE NEW

Sources of immigration shifted after 1890 from northern and central Europe to southern and eastern Europe. Sharp decreases in the movement of people to America were occasioned by war, hard times in the United States, and, after 1924, restrictive legislation.

Civil War came from countries in southern and eastern Europe. But this difference should not be overemphasized, for in reality the immigrant who reached the United States in the years after the Civil War had much in common with the immigrant who had preceded him to this country. Both were unskilled workers who had been farmers in their native lands. Both came to the United States largely for economic reasons. Both had had few educational opportunities. Both were eager to learn, and both were ripe for exploitation. It was not the immigrant who had changed, but the United States. The pre-Civil War immigrant arrived in a predominantly agrarian nation; his post-Civil War counterpart invaded an America that was on the way to becoming the most powerful industrial nation of the world.

Most immigrant workers who settled in the United States after 1865 lacked all the attributes necessary for success in American industrial society except a willingness to work. Without the skills and training needed for machine tending, they were compelled to accept menial jobs at low pay and poor working conditions. Because they frequently arrived with only a few cents in their pockets and the clothes on their back, they had to take whatever type of work was offered them at the wages and hours proposed. Their inability to understand English made them the easy victims of unscrupulous employers, and the strangeness of a new land made them too timid to protest when they were victimized. The combination of poverty and ignorance often drove the immigrant into the most hazardous jobs in American industry. Although inadequate statistics preclude any accurate estimate of the correlation between immigration and industrial accidents, all available evidence points to the conclusion that the two were closely linked. Many immigrants were attracted to such dangerous occupations as coal mining and steelmaking, in which their inability to read the warning signs prevented them from achieving even a minimum of physical security on the job.

In numerous construction and railroad camps in the South and West, the exploitation of the immigrant was a highly developed, extralegal system that was maintained by company guards with the tacit or overt support of the local authorities. With little knowledge of English and no conception of the labor standards of their adopted land, immigrants in these camps were forced to work twelve or more hours a day for little more than board and room in crude barracks. On and off the job they were guarded by armed bosses. If an immigrant worker left a construction camp, he was pursued by guards or by local officials who were usually willing to help the company "preserve law and order." If an immigrant refused to work, he was confined to his barracks or sent to the county jail until he had changed his mind.

The difficulties of the immigrant were enhanced by the prejudices of American laborers. Native workers usually viewed the immigrant with suspicion and derision because of his different customs and language. More important, they also looked on him as a threat to their security and refused him even a semblance of economic equality. Jobs that were thought beneath an American were considered good enough for an immigrant, and in many industries the poorest paying and the most hazardous forms of work were known as "foreign jobs." In some instances, different types of work within a single industry were assigned to separate nationalities, the most recent arrivals occupying the least desirable positions. With every new wave of immigration, each national group moved a step up the ladder of occupations. Thus, the Irish, who were disdained as "mick ditch diggers" before the Civil War, were supplanted in later years by new groups of foreigners whom the Irish-Americans referred to as "wops" and "hunkies."

After the Civil War, the Chinese, whose low standard of living enabled them to accept lower wages than most native workers, were the principal victims of the American opposition to immigrant laborers. In 1862, Congress had adopted legislation prohibiting the importation of Chinese contract labor, but this law was loosely enforced; and the Burlingame Treaty of 1868, which guaranteed the Chinese unrestricted immigration to the United States, did little to reassure American workers. In 1870 the hostility of organized labor was further aroused by the use of California Chinese as strikebreakers in Massachusetts. With the onset of the depression of the midseventies, native workers in California increasingly attributed their own difficulties to the influx of Chinese. Led by the demagogic Denis Kearney of San Francisco and not averse to resorting to mob action, California workers demanded that the state legislature impose severe restrictions on Chinese laborers. In 1879 this campaign bore its first fruits with the adoption of a new state constitution that prohibited California corporations from hiring Chinese workers. Two years later the national government, in response to pressure from labor groups and some businessmen who objected to competition from Chinese merchants in this country, concluded a new treaty with China that permitted the United States to regulate, restrict, or suspend Chinese immigration. In 1882, Congress implemented this treaty by suspending the immigration of Chinese laborers for ten years. This measure was reenacted for successive periods and was made permanent in 1904. A similar policy was adopted toward Japanese immigrants in 1907, when the Japanese government agreed not to issue visas to Japanese laborers who wished to emigrate to the United States.

Despite the numerous protests of organized labor, the Federal government made little attempt to check or regulate the flow of immigration from Europe. After the Civil War American employers imported gangs of workers as strikebreakers and manual laborers, and agents of American business firms toured southern and eastern Europe advertising the wonders of life in the New World. It was not until 1885 that Congress forbade the importation of contract labor to the United States, and it was not until 1891 that it enacted a law to prevent American employers from advertising for workers in foreign lands and steamship companies from serving as recruiting agents for American industry. Before the twentieth century the only other move to limit general immigration was made in 1882, when Congress excluded idiots, potential paupers, and criminals. The act of 1891 added immigrants with contagious diseases to the category of undesirables.

30. THE STANDARDS OF LABOR

ALTHOUGH there were numerous real and fancied differences among the various groups of American workers after the Civil War, they were all in essentially the same position. Regardless of age, sex, color, or nationality each wage earner was faced with the task of adjusting his life to fit the demands of modern industrial society. Working conditions varied from industry to industry and even from job to job within a single industry, but these were differences of degree rather than of kind. The wages of all workers were affected by fluctuations in the business cycle and other external forces over which they had little or no control. Some laborers had a shorter work-week than others, but all had to devote a large part of their waking hours to their jobs. Even those wage earners in relatively safe occupations were exposed to the possibility that they might be injured on the job; and no worker was free from the threat of unemployment.

During the half century that preceded the outbreak of World War I there was a marked increase in the money wages received by American workers. In 1860, artisans were paid approximately $12 a week. Twenty years later their average weekly wage had risen to $15, and in 1915 it was $24. Throughout this period, however, the wages of the common laborer in nonagricultural pursuits lagged far behind those of the artisan. The average weekly wages paid to a common laborer, approximately $6 a week in 1860, rose to only $7.50 in 1880 and to $12 in 1915. In the same fifty-five years the money wages received by male farm workers (who were paid in board as well as money) increased from $10 to $20 a month.

There was a general increase in real wages during this same period. As the cost of living declined and money wages rose after the Civil War, the index of real wages (1892 = 100) mounted from 49 in 1866 to 80 in 1873. Following the depression of the seventies, when real wages fell less than money wages, there was a steady increase in real wages until in

1892, on the eve of another depression, the index figure had reached 100, or more than double that for 1866. The sharp drop in prices in the depression of the 1890's sent real wages up to an index number of 110 in 1897, and during the next seventeen years it did not again fall below 100.

Despite the efforts of trade unions, the hours of labor in American industry remained relatively long until World War I. In 1860 some workers labored for as long as fourteen hours a day, and only a comparatively small number in the more skilled occupations had been able to achieve a ten-hour day. The standard work-week was six days, but in many industries wage earners were required to work every day of the week. Soon after the Civil War, organized labor established as its goal the eight-hour day, but throughout the nineteenth century this objective remained an ideal rather than a reality in most trades. Federal legislation that had been enacted in 1869, and amended in 1892 and 1912, established the eight-hour day for workers on government projects, and after 1900 numerous states passed laws regulating the hours of labor in industry. But a series of strikes in the mideighties, staged by organized workers in order to obtain the eight-hour day, were defeated in almost every instance by the superior force of the employers. By 1900, most American laborers still worked a ten-hour day and a six-day week.

Wages and hours, however, provide an inadequate guide to the status of the wage earner during the years after the Civil War, for on numerous occasions workers were unable to obtain any form of employment for protracted periods of time. The major depressions of the 1870's and 1890's threw uncounted thousands out of work, while the shorter panics and recessions of 1884, 1903, and 1907 also added to the ranks of the unemployed. In several industries seasonal unemployment drastically reduced the earnings of many wage earners in any given year. The introduction of new machinery and more efficient manufacturing processes reduced the size of the laboring force in a number of industries. Finally, changes in consuming habits frequently created unemployment; for example, the number of wage earners in the bicycle and motorcycle industries declined approximately 75 per cent from 1899 to 1909.

The lack of adequate statistics precludes a detailed study of the effect of increasing industrialization on the health of the worker. Beyond a doubt, however, the mental and physical well-being of numerous wage earners was adversely affected by long hours of monotonous labor in drafty, poorly illuminated, or dusty industrial establishments. Few statistics on industrial accidents were compiled during most of the years under consideration; but in 1913, Frederick L. Hoffman, a life insurance official who had made a close study of the available evidence, stated that the number of fatal industrial accidents "among American wage-earners, including both sexes, may be conservatively estimated at 25,000 for the year 1913, and the number of injuries involving a disability of more than four weeks . . . at approximately 700,000." Hoffman's study further revealed that the percentage of fatal industrial accidents was higher in mining than in any other single industry in the United States.

31. THE BEGINNING OF A NATIONAL LABOR MOVEMENT

MANY American workers were psychologically unprepared for the transition from a craft to an industrial economy. Brought up in a predominantly agrarian society that emphasized the opportunities for individual progress, native wage earners often clung to this pattern of thought long after the mechanization of industry had destroyed many of the premises on which it had been based. A similar view was held by many immigrants, who looked on America as a land of promise where their status would no longer be fixed by Old World traditions of caste and class. Although the growth of large manufacturing establishments, the subdivision of labor, the widespread use of machinery, and the heterogeneity of the working force all seemed to call for collective action, most workers nevertheless found it difficult to abandon their ideal of economic individualism. To many laborers, union membership was a badge of defeat that signified that they were no longer capable of fulfilling the American dream by rising above their class.

The reluctance of some workers to join unions was re-enforced by the views of Americans who were not wage earners. Farmers, businessmen, professional people, and white-collar workers generally looked on unions as alien devices for encouraging the lazy and penalizing the industrious. In conflicts between organized labor and organized capital before World War I the bulk of the nonlaboring public usually gave its moral support to the employers. The nation's newspapers seldom sympathized with striking workers, and on frequent occasions they described labor leaders as anarchists and dangerous radicals who sought to undermine the American way of life. The popular antipathy to unionism was shared by most public officials, who virtually never intervened to protect strikers, but frequently aided employers in the numerous industrial disputes of the period.

Despite widespread opposition to unions, numerous locals had been established in the United States during the first half of the nineteenth century. It was not, however, until the 1850's that any crafts were organized on a national basis. Before the spread of the railroad network, a worker's interest in his job was usually confined to his own plant or community. But as improved transportation facilities brought firms in widely separated parts of the country into competition with one another for the first time, the employees of these firms began to realize that working conditions were no longer an exclusively local concern. If the apprenticeship rules or the wage scale in one plant were lowered, it would not be long before competition would compel the managers of other plants to introduce similar changes. If a worker wished to maintain or improve the status of his craft, he had no alternative but to join a national union. The national trade-union was the wage earner's response to the increasing nation-wide competition of American industry.

Because artisans possessed considerably more bargaining power than common laborers, the national unions founded before the Civil War were confined almost exclusively to such skilled workers as typesetters, iron molders, hat finishers, and machinists. During the war new national unions were established and old ones strengthened as skilled workers sought to combat the rapid increase in prices and to take advantage of the labor shortage created by the army's drain on the supply of manpower. From 1861 to 1865 approximately twenty unions were founded in the Northern states, among them miners', railroad engineers', cigar makers', plasterers', carpenters', bricklayers', spinners', and shoe workers' unions. As in the preceding period, the mass of unskilled workers remained unorganized.

The trade unions of the Civil War era were designed primarily to prevent their members from becoming proletarians. Union leaders were more interested in restoring economic individualism for the workers than in developing class consciousness. Labor spokesmen, looking back longingly to a craft society in which each worker had a large measure of economic freedom, proposed legislation and programs that were designed, not to increase the laborer's wages, but to free him from the wage system. A. C. Cameron, editor of the *Workingman's Advocate,* urged the government to issue more Greenbacks as the only way of preventing the financier from destroying completely the independence of small worker-producers. Ira Steward, a member of the Machinists' and Blacksmiths' Union, advocated an eight-hour day for all workers, but insisted that this reform be achieved by legislation rather than by the use of the strike. Another reform demanded by virtually all the new national unions was the establishment of producers' co-operatives, through which, they believed, workers could escape the effects of the Industrial Revolution and return to the good old days when a skilled laborer was his own boss. In 1869, an official of the Knights of St. Crispin, the shoe workers' union, said: "The present demand of the Crispin is steady employment and fair wages, but his future is self-employment." But labor's faith in co-operatives was seldom rewarded. Although numerous unions formed producer co-operatives, in almost every instance these ventures were unable to compete successfully with established private firms.

The first attempt to gather the various trade unions into a single, nation-wide organization was made in 1866 with the formation of the

National Labor Union. Founded by a group of humanitarian reformers and union leaders, it was at first led by William H. Sylvis, the head of the iron molders' union. In its efforts to solve the labor problems posed by the growth of industry, the National Labor Union emphasized long-term reforms rather than militant trade-unionism. The use of the strike was minimized and its platforms called for eight-hour legislation, abolition of alien contract-labor, the establishment of a Federal department of labor, rights for women and Negroes equal to those of white men, land reform, and the elimination of monopoly. Because the wage earner was primarily concerned with more pay and improved working conditions, he quickly lost whatever interest he may have once had in the National Labor Union. As the workers withdrew, the leadership of the National Labor Union—in the words of Norman Ware—was taken over by "labor leaders without organizations, politicians without parties, women without husbands, and cranks, visionaries, and agitators without jobs."* In 1871 the National Labor Union entered politics and changed its name to the National Labor Party. After its poor showing in the election of 1872, it rapidly disintegrated. If it accomplished nothing else, the National Labor Union demonstrated that the reformers' demands for a new world held little appeal for the mass of wage earners in the post-war decade.

During the 1870's the strength and prestige of organized labor declined markedly under the impact of a series of major reverses. Numerous employers were determined to crush the union movement, and the depression so weakened the bargaining power of most unions that they were seldom able to hold their own. Moreover, the disclosure of the violent tactics employed by a group of Pennsylvania coal miners known as the Molly McGuires aroused still further hostility toward the entire labor union movement in the United States. The Molly McGuires, a secret organization among the members of the Ancient Order of Hibernians in the anthracite fields of Pennsylvania, committed a series of crimes, including murder, against the representatives of the coal operators. In 1876, the activities of the Mollies were made public by James McParlan, a Pinkerton detective, who had joined the group under an assumed name. As a result of McParlan's revelations, ten of the Molly McGuires were hanged and fourteen others received jail sentences. Although the activities of the Molly McGuires were an isolated phenomenon in the labor history of the period, many contemporary Americans considered them typical of the extremes to which workers as a class were willing to resort.

Organized labor suffered its severest defeat in the 1870's when the railroad strikes of 1877 were crushed by the superior force of the opera-

* Norman J. Ware: *The Labor Movement in the United States: 1860–1895* (New York: D. Appleton and Company, 1929), p. 11.

tors and the public authorities. Originating on July 17 on the Baltimore and Ohio lines as spontaneous walkouts in response to wage reductions and the use of the blacklist, the strike quickly spread to the important rail centers. State and Federal troops, which were used to oppose the strikers, were met with force by rail workers and groups of unemployed who joined in the struggle. Violence that flared up in Baltimore, Pittsburgh, Toledo, Chicago, St. Louis, and San Francisco resulted in millions of dollars worth of property damage. By August 3 the strikes on the leading lines had been broken. The willingness of the courts to grant injunctions to the operators, the aid provided by both state and Federal troops, the inadequate financial resources of the rail unions, and the refusal of the trainmen to go out with the engineers had all contributed in some measure to the ultimate failure of the workers to attain their objectives.

While national trade unions were enduring a succession of defeats in the 1870's, the Noble and Holy Order of the Knights of Labor was attempting to establish a workingman's organization that would cut across individual crafts and rest on such a broad foundation that it would be invulnerable to attacks from employers. Founded in 1869 as a secret benefit-society by nine Philadelphia garment cutters, the Knights of Labor under the leadership of Uriah Stephens expanded rapidly, and within four years eighty local assemblies had been established. The rapid growth of the Knights of Labor can be attributed in part to its secrecy, for workers who had been intimidated by the antilabor drives of the period welcomed an organization that would conceal the identity of its members from employers. A further appeal of the order lay in the elaborate ritual with which its meetings were conducted. In a world of increasing industrialization and declining individualism, the meetings of the Knights undoubtedly gave many workingmen a sense of importance and a feeling of release from the humdrum character of their jobs.

Membership in the Knights of Labor was open to "all who toiled." Stating that an "injury to one is an injury to all," the Knights accepted workers regardless of their sex, color, or degree of skill in their chosen trade. Unlike most trade unions, no provision was made for an apprenticeship for a craft, and the only "nontoilers" specifically excluded from the Knights were liquor dealers, lawyers, bankers, stockbrokers, and professional gamblers. The order gave little attention to organizing campaigns but welcomed all toilers who wished to join. The members were grouped in local and district assemblies that in some instances included the workers in a single trade and in other cases consisted of the wage earners in one locality regardless of their individual skills. The various forms of local organization employed by the order enabled it to absorb workers who wished to preserve their trade union affiliations as well as those who joined the movement without prior commitments.

Like the National Labor Union, the Knights of Labor espoused a series of reforms that were designed to restore the worker to the status of an individual producer. It opposed the use of the strike and announced that its objective was to make "every man his own master—every man his own employer." Its labor program included demands for the eight-hour day, compulsory arbitration of all labor disputes, equal pay for both sexes, abolition of child and prison labor, establishment of a bureau of labor statistics, and the formation of producer and consumer co-operatives by workers. But the Knights also urged many other changes that were only indirectly connected with the improvement of the status of the workingman; at various times in its history it advocated an income tax, abolition of national banks, paper money, public ownership of utilities, prohibition, and postal savings banks. Although the rank and file repeatedly resorted to the strike in attempts to attain higher wages and improved working-conditions, the officials of the organization gave them little encouragement. To the leaders of the movement, its principal task was to restore American economic society to the good old days when workers were economic individualists.

In 1878, the Knights of Labor established the General Assembly as the organization's ruling body; a year later Terrence Powderly was selected as Grand Master Workman supplanting Uriah Stephens as the Knights' executive officer; and in 1882, secrecy was abandoned. In the next four years both the numerical strength and bargaining power of the Knights of Labor increased measurably. During the depression of 1884–5, workers joined the Knights in large numbers and forced the leadership to adopt a somewhat more militant attitude than it had held in the past. Nevertheless, Powderly frequently refused to give either moral or financial support to striking members, and numerous unauthorized strikes were staged by the rank and file of the assemblies. The order achieved its greatest success in 1885–6 in strikes against the Gould railroad system when the workers not only attained their immediate objectives but also won recognition for their union from Gould. By January, 1886, the membership of the Knights of Labor approximated 700,000.

Despite the express prohibition of Powderly, many members of the Knights of Labor joined with other workers on May Day, 1886, in a nationwide demonstration for an eight-hour day. Although Chicago was considered the center of radical labor in the United States, the May Day celebrations in that city passed without incident. But two days later, when pickets and scabs clashed outside the McCormick reaper plant, the police intervened and killed four people. On the following night a protest meeting was held in Haymarket Square. When the police attempted to disperse the crowd, a bomb thrown into their ranks killed seven persons and injured several others. The Haymarket affair sent a wave of antilabor hysteria through the nation. Chicago officials arrested eight anarchists and charged them with inciting—but not actually committing—the crime. All were found guilty by the jury. Of the eight, four were hanged, one committed suicide, and the remaining three were sent to prison for life.*

Although the Knights of Labor had played little or no part in the events in Chicago that led up to the Haymarket bombing, the order was compelled to accept a large share of the onus for the incident. As the leading labor organization of the country, it was widely blamed for an event that many people considered a typical labor tactic. Moreover, many members of the order had participated in the eight-hour demonstrations that had preceded the Haymarket affair, and it was generally assumed that they had resorted to violence to attain their objectives after other methods had failed. Finally, Albert Parsons, one of the men hanged by the Chicago authorities for allegedly inciting the bombing, was a dues-paying member of the Knights of Labor. This combination of circumstances gave the Knights of Labor a setback from which it was never able to recover. An essentially conservative organization whose leaders had urged reform and condemned violence, it was the principal victim of the public outcry against a crime perpetrated by an individual whose identity to the present day remains unknown.

Although the Haymarket affair proved a turning point in the history of the Knights of Labor, the rapid decline in the numerical strength of the order after 1886 should not be attributed solely to this event. In part, the disintegration of the order was the result of its inability to achieve its announced objective of making every worker his own master. The Knights had great faith in co-operatives and at one time they were operating more than two hundred producer co-operatives, but eventually they all succumbed either to mismanagement or to the superior power exercised by private enterprises in the same industry. There was, moreover, a great discrepancy between the aims of the order's leadership and the demands of its members in the local and district assemblies. The long-range reforms proposed by Powderly and his associates had relatively little appeal for workers who wanted higher wages and a shorter working day. Nor did the attempt to organize all workers on the same basis regardless of their individual skills prove feasible. Because skilled laborers in times of industrial conflict ran the risk of blacklisting and other forms of employer retaliation that would prevent them from pursuing their chosen craft, they withdrew from the Knights in increasing numbers to join national trade unions that afforded them a greater measure of protection. The unskilled and semiskilled who remained in the order generally lacked the bargaining power needed to cope with militant employers who were backed by public opinion and government officials who were willing to use armed force and the courts to suppress "labor disturbances."

* In 1893, they were pardoned by Governor John Peter Altgeld of Illinois.

By 1890 the membership of the Knights of Labor had declined to approximately 100,000. After a political alliance with the farmers in the 1890's, the order ceased to play a rôle of any importance in the economic life of the nation. By the turn of the century, the assemblies were confined almost exclusively to small towns, where they served as fraternal societies for their comparatively few members.

32. BREAD AND BUTTER UNIONISM

THE KNIGHTS OF LABOR, whose principal appeal had been to the unskilled, had had comparatively little success in winning over the established craft unions to the desirability of one big union for all workers. The national trade unions that survived the disasters of the 1870's sought to build up a type of union organization that differed from that of the Knights in virtually every respect. Disdaining the Knights' program for reforming society as unrealistic and utopian, the trade unions rigorously confined their efforts to obtaining an increase in the pay checks and a reduction in the work week of their own members. To achieve these limited aims they relied on craft unions whose membership was restricted to the skilled members of a single trade. Through collective bargaining and use of the strike as a last resort they believed that they could compel employers to sign contracts that would guarantee union demands. The aims of the national trade unions appeared narrow when contrasted to those of the Knights; but they seemed capable of realization within the near future.

The trade-union philosophy of the 1870's was perhaps best exemplified by the International Cigar Makers' Union, which at the time consisted largely of highly skilled workers of foreign origin. Trained in the European tradition of unionism, they believed in a compact organization that would provide its members with concrete benefits. After an unsuccessful strike in 1877, the union was revived by Adolph Strasser and Samuel Gompers, both of whom had had experience in the labor movement in Europe. Through the regular collection of dues and by restricting membership to those with the same economic interests and demands, Strasser and Gompers were able to build a union that not only improved conditions within the industry but also furnished financial assistance to members suffering adversity. By 1880 the International Cigar Makers' Union had proved so effective that it was serving as a model for unions in several other industries.

In 1881, representatives of several craft unions met in Pittsburgh and formed the Federation of Organized Trade and Labor Unions of the United States of America and Canada. This organization consisted of trade unions that limited their membership to skilled workers. In 1886 the organization's name was changed to the American Federation of Labor, and Samuel Gompers was elected to the presidency, a position that he held every year but one until his death in 1924. When several national unions seceded from the Knights of Labor, the success of the federation was assured. Within a decade after Gompers had assumed office, the American Federation of Labor had become the most important labor organization in the United States.

The American Federation of Labor was a loose alliance of national trade unions each of which enjoyed a large measure of autonomy. The national unions were made up of locals with representation in city centrals and state federations, and federal unions were established as catchalls for groups of workers who were not eligible for membership in the established craft unions. Women, Negroes, and the unskilled were excluded by unions affiliated with the A. F. of L., and skilled workers were admitted only after they had served a long apprenticeship and paid a large initiation fee. The leaders shunned political and economic reforms and centered their attention almost exclusively upon attempts to raise the wages and shorten the work week of the comparatively small number of workers who belonged to member unions. They opposed third parties, although they paid lip service to the slogan that the ballot box should be used to reward labor's friends and punish its enemies.

The American Federation of Labor was essentially a conservative organization that was committed to few changes in the *status quo.* Although some socialists had played an important rôle in the federation during its formative years, they had been unable to convert either the leadership or the rank and file to their plans for the collectivization of the American economy. The A. F. of L. did not wish to alter the fundamentals of American economic society; but it did believe that, within that society, labor comprised a separate class and that it was the function of national trade unions to obtain a larger share of the fruits of American capitalism for the élite of the working class. The assumption that labor was a class by itself did not, however, lead to the conclusion that conflict between the laboring and employing classes was either inevitable or desirable. On the contrary, the A. F. of L. considered class co-operation essential to the welfare of the workingman. But if the employing classes refused to co-operate by signing collective-bargaining contracts that covered wages and hours, unions felt that they had no alternative but to strike to compel such co-operation from other classes. The strike was a class-conscious weapon, but it was only a means to an end, and the end was class co-operation.

The bread and butter philosophy of the American Federation of Labor made it more acceptable to American employers than almost any other type of workingman's organization. By restricting its membership to highly skilled workers and by organizing them according to their trades, it divided rather than united the nation's laboring classes. By confining its objectives to wages and hours, it sought to monopolize only the job, while permitting employers to continue to monopolize the management of the industrial economy. By refraining from active participation in politics and by opposing virtually every variety of radicalism, it lessened the possibility that American capitalism would be undermined through either legislation or reform. In short, the A. F. of L. demanded only the right to get more for its own members within the existing framework of American economic society.

In 1890 the unions belonging to the American Federation of Labor had a total membership of 550,000. A decade later the figure was 1,500,000 and in 1914 it was 2,000,000. Of the nation's major trade unions only the Railroad Brotherhoods remained unaffiliated with the federation. By 1914 a few A. F. of L. unions had won the eight-hour day for their dues payers, and others had established benefit programs to assist members who were unemployed. The National Civic Federation, which had been established to facilitate the peaceful settlement of industrial disputes, recognized the federation as the outstanding spokesman for the American worker and frequently provided it with a forum for presenting labor's side of a case. But the accomplishments of the A. F. of L. during its first two decades should not be exaggerated, for in reality it had little effect on the status of most American workingmen. The federation included only a small percentage of the total laboring force, and it was able to win only minor victories for even this limited and select group. Before the outbreak of World War I, militant employers supported by public officials were both better organized and more powerful than any labor union; and through the use of the blacklist, lockout, yellow dog contract, private and public troops, and injunctions they repeatedly thwarted the attempts of the worker to improve his economic position in American society.

33. THE THEORY AND PRACTICE OF CLASS CONSCIOUSNESS

BEFORE World War I the average American wage-earner often was as conservative in his economic outlook as was the American employer. Because he believed that his position as a worker was little more than a way station along the road to wealth and economic independence, he saw few reasons for changing the essential features of American capitalism. When he joined a union or went out on strike, he was not protesting against the profit system, but was merely demanding that a greater share of industrial profits be allotted to the workingman in the form of increased wages.

Despite the fundamental conservatism of most American workers, there were occasions on which they took the law in their own hands in their efforts to improve their economic status. The Molly McGuires employed murder as a weapon in their conflicts with the mine operators, and the railroad workers in the strike of 1877 destroyed millions of dollars worth of private property. In 1892, the striking workers at Andrew Carnegie's Homestead Steel plant in western Pennsylvania fired on and killed the strikebreakers who had been imported from the Pinkerton Detective Agency to take their jobs. Two years later in the Pullman strike, the workers again met force with force. Labor's use of violence in these and other instances arose, not out of a philosophy of class conflict, but out of a sense of desperation and hopelessness. It was only when every other means had failed or when he was attacked by armed thugs or government troops that the average American workingman employed extralegal methods to defend his job. He had no desire to overthrow the existing economic system; but if driven far enough, he would resort to force to protect what he considered his rights.

While few workers questioned the tenets of American *laissez faire* capitalism, some self-appointed labor leaders in the closing decades of the nineteenth century maintained that the lot of the workingman could not be improved within the framework of the existing economic system. Many of these left-wing labor theorists were immigrants who had been compelled to leave Europe because of their radical ideas. Basing their program largely on the teachings of Karl Marx, they sought to rouse the American working class to undertake a revolution that would overthrow American capitalism. Their failure stemmed directly from their hypotheses; for they were attempting to apply to an essentially fluid social order theories that presupposed a rigid class structure, and they were directing their appeal to workers who had little or no sense of class consciousness.

For approximately two and one-half decades after Appomattox, Chicago was the center of left-wing labor agitation in the United States. German, Austrian, and French immigrants who had been forced to cross the Atlantic partly because of their economic views settled in relatively large numbers in Chicago and attempted to develop a revolutionary spirit among the workers of their adopted land. Preaching either socialism or anarchy, they held secret meetings, printed pamphlets and papers, issued calls for all workingmen to "offer an armed resistance to the invasions by the capitalist class and capitalist legislatures," and urged wage earners to overthrow American capitalism by "energetic, relentless, revolutionary, and international action." There is no evidence that these appeals found a receptive audience among the masses of either native or foreign-born workers; and after the Haymarket bombing the Chicago radicals lost what little influence they had once possessed.

Among the leading critics of American capitalism in the years before World War I none was more outspoken and vitriolic than Daniel De Leon. Born on the island of Curaçao and educated in Germany, De Leon migrated in the midseventies to the United States, where he studied law and taught for a short time at Columbia College. De Leon soon abandoned both the law and teaching and devoted the remaining years of his life to propagating his version of socialism in the United States. Accepting without reservation the doctrines of Karl Marx, he outlined in numerous pamphlets and speeches his concept of socialism and his notions of how it could be achieved by American workers. He took a militant stand against traditional trade unions, whose leaders he termed "labor fakers," and urged all workingmen to join in an independent political movement that would win control of the government and establish a "socialist or co-operative commonwealth, whereby the instruments of production shall be made the property of the whole people." In 1892, De Leon joined the Socialist Labor party and in the following year he was selected as the party's candidate for governor of New York. Meanwhile as a member of the Knights of Labor he made an unsuccessful attempt to capture control of that organization. In 1895 he withdrew from the Knights to form the Socialist Trade and Labor Alliance, which devoted its principal efforts to attacking the conservative leadership of the American Federation of Labor and the wing of the Socialist party that lent its support to the existing structure of trade unionism in America. De Leon was both autocratic and doctrinaire, and he soon alienated all but a small coterie of his most loyal followers. Because the assumptions on which he based his doctrines were not shared by the mass of workers, he was unable either to destroy "Gomperism" in the American Federation of Labor or to build an effective socialist organization outside the established trade unions.

De Leon's failure was in contrast to the relative success of other socialists in formulating an anticapitalist creed that had its ideological roots in America rather than Europe. In 1897, Victor L. Berger and Eugene V. Debs, who had been converted to socialism during the prison term he received for contempt of court as leader in the Pullman strike, formed the Social Democratic party. Two years later they were joined by a splinter group from the De Leon forces, and in 1901 they founded the Socialist Party of America. Although the Socialist party also shared De Leon's distaste for Gompers' labor philosophy, its leaders were gradualists who believed that American economic society could be changed piecemeal by the democratic process. The long-term aim was the destruction of the capitalist system, but the immediate economic demands of the Socialist party often duplicated those of the Populists,* while its program of political reforms was essentially the same as that of the Pro-

* See Chapter VIII, pp. 267–72.

gressives.* By 1910 the Socialist party had a membership of approximately 125,000; it had elected Socialist mayors in Milwaukee, Schenectady, and a few other communities; and it had considerable influence in at least two national trade unions. Eugene Debs, who had served as the party's presidential candidate in every election from 1900 to the outbreak of World War I, polled 420,793 votes in 1908 and 900,672 votes in 1912.

While leaders like Debs and De Leon, working in the cities, were attempting to undermine capitalism with intellectual appeals to laborers, the mining frontier of the Rocky Mountain states was producing a class-conscious working-force that lived by violence and obtained its labor philosophy from actual experience on the job rather than from books. During the 1890's the Western silver and lead mines were the scene of a class warfare that included many of the more spectacular features of Billy the Kid's gun battles with the sheriff. As Selig Perlman and Philip Taft have pointed out, Western miners refused to

> *remain passive while their jobs were being given to strikebreakers. They defended their jobs with Winchester*[s] . . . . *Employers, Westerners like their employees, were even "quicker on the trigger." Armed guards and armed strikebreakers were mustered in as armies. Civil processes and "due process of law" were ignored and were replaced by "bull pens" and forcible deportations—the paraphernalia of dictatorship.*†

The opening guns in the class war of the mining frontier were fired in the Coeur d'Alene district of Idaho in the first years of the 1890's. When the operators, after a three-month lockout, reopened the mines, the workers refused to return to work at the wages offered. In the strike that followed, both sides relied exclusively on force to achieve their aims. Strikebreakers imported by the owners were driven from the mines by armed strikers. There were numerous battles between company guards and miners with casualties on both sides, and on one occasion the strikers blew up a mill with one hundred pounds of dynamite. The Governor of Idaho, after several futile attempts to restore order, appealed to the Secretary of War for assistance, and soon after the arrival of Federal troops the strike was completely crushed. Martial law was established. Union men, who were arrested and herded into bull pens, lost their jobs to strikebreakers as the army rigorously enforced the open shop. Thirty miners were accused of conspiracy and held for trial in the Federal courts, and eighty-five others were charged with

* See Chapter XI, pp. 338–56.

† Selig Perlman and Philip Taft: "Labor Movements," in John R. Commons (ed.): *History of Labor in the United States, 1896–1932* (New York: The Macmillan Company, 1935), Vol. IV, p. 169.

contempt of court. Those accused of conspiracy were eventually released, but twelve union men were found guilty of contempt and received sentences of from four to eight months.

The Coeur d'Alene strike led directly to the formation of the Western Federation of Miners. While serving their prison terms in the local county jail, the twelve men convicted of contempt discussed plans for the formation of a more effective metal miners' organization. Soon after their release from prison, arrangements were made for a miners' convention, and on May 15, 1893, delegates from Idaho, Montana, Colorado, and South Dakota gathered in Butte, Montana, to establish the Western Federation of Miners. Like most other American unions of the period, the Western Federation of Miners was originally conceived by its founders solely as a device for improving the wages and working conditions of its members, but the pressure of events quickly forced it into a more revolutionary position. In the decade after its organization the Western Federation of Miners waged a series of bitter and violent strikes in the mining camps of Cripple Creek and Telluride in Colorado and Coeur d'Alene in Idaho. In each of these struggles the essential features and tactics of the Coeur d'Alene strike of 1892 were repeated. To meet the force employed by the mine owners, the workers replied not only with arms but also with revolutionary doctrines that stemmed directly from the class war in which they were participating. Although the Western Federation of Miners had originally been affiliated with the American Federation of Labor, it withdrew in 1896, and along with Eastern socialists it became an outspoken foe of "Gomperism" in the labor movement. In 1902 the Western Federation of Miners' convention approved a resolution to "adopt socialism without equivocation," and within a short time a provision was inserted in the preamble of its constitution stating that

> *there is a class struggle in society and that this struggle is caused by economic conditions; . . . the producer . . . is exploited by the wealth which he produces, being allowed to retain barely sufficient for his elementary necessities; . . . that the class struggle will continue until the producer is recognized as the sole master of his product; . . . that the working class, and it alone, can and must achieve its own emancipation; . . . finally, that an industrial union and the concerted political action of all wage earners is the only method of attaining this end.*

In January, 1905, representatives of the Western Federation of Miners attended a secret conference in Chicago called by radical labor leaders and journalists. At this meeting plans were laid for a convention to organize "one great industrial union embracing all industries, . . . founded on the class struggle . . . and established as the economic organization of the working class, without affiliation with any political party." The convention, which met on June 27, 1905, was attended by two hundred radicals representing approximately forty different trades and occupations. The delegates, led by Eugene V. Debs, William (Big Bill) Haywood of the Western Federation of Miners, and Daniel De Leon, named the new organization the Industrial Workers of the World. Provision was made for the organization of workers into thirteen all-inclusive departments; numerous speakers attacked both the employers and the A.F. of L with equal vehemence; and the delegates approved a preamble, the first two clauses of which stated:

The working class and the employing class have nothing in common. There can be no peace so long as hunger and want are found among the millions of working people, and the few, who make up the employing class, have all the good things of life.
Between these two classes a struggle must go on until all the toilers come together on the political, as well as on the industrial field, and take and hold that which they produce by their labor, through an economic organization of the working class, without affiliation with any political party.

During the first three years of its existence the I.W.W. was torn by factional strife, and it was not until 1908 that these internal conflicts were resolved. At the 1906 convention an all-out struggle quickly developed between the so-called "radicals" and "conservatives," who thought that the creation of an effective organization should take precedence over the revolutionary demands of their opponents. The radicals, led by De Leon and supported by the rank and file of the poorer unions, easily routed the conservatives, who in almost any other labor organization would have been considered extreme left-wingers. Following the defeat of the conservatives the Western Federation of Miners and the members of the Socialist party withdrew from the I.W.W., and a new conflict arose between the more doctrinaire and moderate De Leonites and the representatives of the Western migratory and unskilled workers, who favored direct action rather than De Leon's theoretical approach. In the 1908 convention, De Leon and his followers were defeated and forced out of the I.W.W. The "Wobblies," as the members of the I.W.W. were called, were now firmly in control of the movement.

For more than a decade after the 1908 convention the I.W.W. stood for a down-to-earth radicalism that emphasized class struggle, one big industrial union, and revolution. While the ultimate aim of the movement was to "let the workers run the industries," its immediate objective, like that of most other labor organizations, was improved working conditions for its members. Drawing its support largely from the itinerant agricultural, lumber, and construction laborers in the West and from unskilled foreign-speaking workers in Eastern factories, the I.W.W. preached a rough-and-tumble creed of class conflict in which the bosses were always wrong, the "wage-slaves" and "working stiffs" always right, and all other unions were "nothing more than parasites upon workingmen."

Since it lacked both funds and public sympathy, the I.W.W. was frequently compelled to resort to unusual tactics to attain its objectives. When, for example, Spokane, Washington, in 1909 adopted an ordinance that deprived the Wobblies of the use of the city's streets for meetings and organization drives, the I.W.W. replied with a militant and spectacular "free speech" campaign that attracted nation-wide attention. As soon as one street orator was arrested by the Spokane police, another took his place. Within ten days, three hundred Wobblies had been arrested, the city jail was overflowing, taxpayers were complaining of the increased expense involved in feeding the prisoners and paying the salaries of the special police hired to enforce the ordinance, and each freight train that arrived in Spokane carried a fresh contingent of Wobblies, who were both ready and eager to mount a soap box and join their fellows in jail. Eventually the I.W.W. overwhelmed Spokane's officials and taxpayers by sheer numbers. The city and county jails were not large enough to hold all the offenders, and in March, 1910, the municipal authorities capitulated. I.W.W. speakers were granted the right to use the city streets, and arrangements were made for the release of the prisoners. Between 1909 and 1912 the I.W.W. repeated the techniques that they had perfected in Spokane to win free-speech fights in Fresno, California; Victoria, British Columbia; Kansas City, Missouri; Aberdeen, Washington; and San Diego, California.

I.W.W. activities were not confined to free-speech fights; the Wobblies also conducted a series of militant strikes among the itinerant workers of the West and the unskilled factory laborers of the East. An active organizing campaign among the lumber workers of Louisiana, Arkansas, and Texas culminated in 1912 in a seven-month strike in which the Wobblies were eventually defeated by state troops, company gunmen, the courts, and a Good Citizens' League. In 1913, the I.W.W. led twenty-eight hundred migratory workers, many of whom were women and children, in a strike against the Durst hop ranch in Wheatland, California. Once again, the employers were able to count on assistance from private armies and state and local authorities; but the publicity given to the strike led to some improvement in the management of the labor camps maintained by the large commercial farms in the state.

Although the I.W.W. had its largest following among the migratory laborers of the Middle and Far West, it directed several important strikes in Eastern industrial centers. In 1909, the I.W.W. took charge of a strike against the Pressed Steel Car Company of McKees Rocks,

Pennsylvania, and eventually compelled the employers to capitulate to the workers' demands. Three years later in Lawrence, Massachusetts, the Wobblies assumed the management of a strike of twenty-five thousand textile workers, most of whom were of foreign birth. They threw endless picket lines around the plants, established a relief system, and sent the children of many of the strikers to workers' homes outside of Lawrence for the duration of the strike. Despite the assistance that the employers received from local officials and fourteen hundred soldiers, the I.W.W. was able to fight the strike to a successful conclusion. In 1913 the I.W.W. led a strike of the textile workers in Paterson, New Jersey, where an attempt was made to repeat the tactics used at Lawrence, but after twenty-two weeks the strike ended in failure. A strike of the Akron, Ohio, rubber workers in the same year under the direction of the I.W.W. was equally unsuccessful.

In every strike conducted by the I.W.W. the employers were able to count on assistance from both the courts and the militia. Every I.W.W. leader who entered a strike area risked his freedom and even his life. Richard Ford and Herman Suhr were sentenced to life imprisonment for their part in the Wheatland strike. Big Bill Haywood, who directed numerous I.W.W. strikes, was arrested in Lawrence, Paterson, and Akron. Frank W. Little, an I.W.W. organizer, was lynched by vigilantes for his strike activities in Butte, Montana. Countless other Wobblies on numerous occasions were forced to flee for their lives, were herded into bull pens, or were beaten up by militiamen, police, company guards, or citizens' committees.

Although the Wobblies looked with scorn on the gradualist methods employed by such conservative organizations as the American Federation of Labor, they had little to show for their own militant tactics. Their repeated calls for direct action and their admitted radicalism antagonized the great majority of Americans, who were prepared to go to any extreme to crush the I.W.W. The result was that the American worker could expect little real assistance from any type of labor organization before World War I. The conservative unions were so conservative that they risked little for their members, while the radical unions like the I.W.W. were so radical that they frequently risked and lost all.

34. STATE AND FEDERAL LABOR LEGISLATION

BOTH radical and conservative unions generally relied on economic rather than political weapons to achieve their objectives; but it was in the state and national legislatures instead of on the picket lines that American labor won some of its most notable victories in the years before 1917. From the end of the Civil War until the turn of the century several states adopted measures designed to protect workingmen on the job. After 1900, state and Federal legislatures passed an amazing number and variety of labor statutes that provided certain minimum standards for men, women, and children in American industry. Organized labor frequently gave its support to these measures, but more often than not the principal sponsors of labor legislation were middle-class reformers who were determined to translate the ideals of the Progressive movement into law.

Labor laws enacted by the Federal government during the half century after Appomatox had a direct effect on only a small percentage of workers. The creation of a Bureau of Labor Statistics in 1884 and a Department of Labor in 1913 may have aided all workers, but other Federal measures in this period were limited in application either to government workers or to those employed by firms engaged in interstate trade. Congress passed an act for an eight-hour day for laborers on public works in 1868, and in 1892 it extended the eight-hour provision to all Federal workers. Under the La Follette Seamen's Act, which became law in 1915, seamen were guaranteed improved living conditions, a nine-hour day while in port, minimum standards of safety, and a measure of protection against tyrannical captains. In both 1916 and 1919, Congress passed bills designed to regulate the employment of children in interstate industries. Congress also succeeded in effecting numerous improvements in working conditions on the interstate rail-systems. In 1888, it set up a program for the arbitration of industrial disputes on interstate carriers; in 1908 it passed a statute that provided for employer's liability on railroads; and in 1916 it passed the Adamson Act, which established an eight-hour day for railroad employees.

The body of labor legislation enacted by Congress was negligible in comparison with the host of labor laws placed on the statute books of the various states during the same period. These measures covered almost every phase of working conditions in American industry. After 1900, and at the height of the Progressive movement, states vied with one another in their attempts to improve working conditions within their borders, and by the outbreak of World War I many American workers were protected by a series of state statutes that fifty years earlier would have been considered unthinkable violations of the principles of *laissez faire*.

After the Civil War, numerous states attempted to establish by statute minimum safety standards for various types of industrial workers. In 1877, Massachusetts, which pioneered in many fields of labor legislation, passed a bill requiring employers to set up protective devices to safeguard workers around elevators, machinery, and hoists. New York adopted somewhat similar legislation in 1887, and ten years later it provided for the enforcement of this measure by factory inspectors. By 1893, fourteen states and territories had adopted some form of safety legislation, and by 1917 most of the others had followed suit. Because of inadequate provisions and funds for enforcement, however, these factory laws benefited only a small percentage of American workers; and, in addition, the states were slow to establish systems for compensating disabled workers. In 1908, no state provided for compulsory compensation for workmen; but in 1909 Montana became the first state to pass such legislation, and by 1917, 32 states and three territories had adopted such legislation. On the other hand, there was little attempt to protect the laborer and others against the hazards of old age and unemployment. The first old-age pension law, which was adopted by Arizona in 1915, was declared unconstitutional; and no other state followed Arizona's lead until the 1920's. Before World War I no state made any attempt to assist its workers during periods of unemployment, and it was not until 1932 that Wisconsin became the first state to pass an unemployment-compensation bill.

In the years immediately preceding World War I, the legislatures of the various states probably devoted more attention to the problems of children in industry than to any other question raised by working conditions in American industry. In the first decade and a half of the twentieth century the majority of the states adopted laws that raised the minimum age of children in industry, excluded children from occupations that were hazardous to either their physical or moral well being, and limited their working hours. In 1900, twenty-four states and the District of Columbia had no minimum-age law for factory employees. Nine years later all but six states had adopted such legislation. From 1902 to 1907 forty-three states either passed new child-labor laws or strengthened existing statutes.

After 1900 several states also passed laws to safeguard women in industry. As late as 1896 only thirteen states had attempted to limit by statute the hours worked by women, and only three states had enacted laws that were capable of enforcement. One state established a weekly maximum of fifty-five hours for women; ten others provided a maximum of ten hours a day; the two remaining statutes, which called for an eight-hour day, could not be enforced. For some years, adverse court decisions retarded the adoption of further legislation, but after 1908, when the Supreme Court ruled favorably on an Oregon statute, progress was rapid and marked. From 1909 to 1917, nineteen states for the first time adopted legislation dealing with women in industry, and twenty states strengthened existing laws. Although these laws differed from state to state, the most progressive states generally limited a woman's work day to eight hours, forbade night work for women, and sought to protect all women in industry regardless of occupation.

State laws to limit the number of hours worked by men were far less numerous and effective than similar measures for women and children. By 1896, seventeen states had adopted hour laws for men in industry, but without exception, these statutes were limited in scope, and few attempts were made to enforce them. Although some states followed the lead taken by Congress in 1868 and passed eight-hour laws for laborers on state projects, in 1913 twenty-one states still lacked legislation regulating the length of the work day on public works. Despite the efforts of the American Federation of Labor and other workingmen's organizations for a general eight-hour law, the best that they could obtain from the state legislatures were eight-hour bills for particular industries such as railroading, mining, and street transportation.

Legislative attempts to establish a floor for wages had little effect on the workers' pay envelope in the years before the American entrance into World War I. In 1912, Massachusetts became the first state to adopt a minimum wage law. But this measure was enforceable only through publicity, and its rates were fixed according to the financial condition of the industries concerned as well as by the cost of living. In 1913 eight state legislatures passed minimum wage bills. Five of these statutes, unlike the Massachusetts law, provided for fines and imprisonment for employers who failed to abide by its provisions. From 1914 to 1917 three other states placed minimum wage bills on their statute books. The effectiveness of the minimum wage legislation of this period was, however, considerably reduced by adverse judicial decisions and the fact that, with the exception of Massachusetts, these laws had been adopted by states that had a comparatively small number of industrial establishments within their borders.

Although numerous states adopted a wide variety of labor laws, they

EXPENDITURES FOR LABOR LAW ADMINISTRATION IN ELEVEN STATES COMBINED, IN ACTUAL DOLLARS AND IN 1909 DOLLARS*

Year	Total expended in actual dollars	Total expended in 1909 dollars	Actual dollars expended per wage earner	1909 dollars expended per wage earner
1889	$202,549	$235,796	10.4 cents	12.1 cents
1899	405,790	481,364	16.9	20.1
1909	809,232	809,232	24.0	24.0

* Elizabeth Brandeis: "Labor Legislation," in John R. Commons (ed.): *History of Labor in the United States* (New York: The Macmillan Company, 1935), Vol. III, p. 636. Copyright 1935 by The Macmillan Company and used with their permission. The eleven states are: California, Connecticut, Illinois, Kansas, Massachusetts, Mississippi, Missouri, New Jersey, New York, Virginia, and Wisconsin.

seldom, if ever, made an adequate attempt to enforce these measures. In 1896, seventeen states provided for factory inspection, but there were only 117 factory inspectors in all. After 1900, several states sought to make the administration of their labor statutes more effective. Additional inspectors were hired; existing laws were amended in an effort to prevent evasions; and larger sums of money were allotted for the enforcement of the statutory labor standards. But the extent of these advances should not be exaggerated, for in 1912 there were still only 425 factory inspectors in the United States, and in no instance were the appropriations for the enforcement of state labor laws sufficient to meet even minimum needs.

35. ORGANIZED LABOR AND THE COURTS

ADVERSE court decisions as well as lax enforcement partially nullified the effect of numerous labor laws. Although the child-labor laws of 1916 and 1919 were the only important Federal labor bills declared unconstitutional by the judiciary in this period, state laws were repeatedly voided by the courts. Brought up in an age of unrestricted *laissez faire* and armed with the sweeping powers of the due-process clause of the Fourteenth Amendment, Federal and state judges did not hesitate to restrain the state legislatures from what they considered undue interference in the relations between employer and employee. In 1885 a New York court invalidated a state law forbidding the manufacture of cigars in tenement houses. An Illinois court in 1895 voided a law limiting the number of hours worked by women, although the Massachusetts Supreme Court had upheld a similar law almost twenty years earlier. In 1898 the Supreme Court upheld a Utah eight-hour law; but seven years later it invalidated a New York ten-hour law for bakers. Some years later this pattern was repeated by the Supreme Court when it approved an Oregon minimum wage bill in 1917, but reversed its decision when it was considering a similar bill for the District of Columbia in 1923.

Despite the opposition of many judges to various types of labor legislation, the courts were unable to check the passage of state labor laws. The pressure of public opinion frequently compelled the courts to reverse earlier antilabor decisions, and in general, judicial rulings succeeded at most in postponing rather than preventing the enactment of bills to provide essential safeguards for industrial workers. With a few notable exceptions, such as the invalidation of the Federal child-labor law, the courts by the end of the second decade of the twentieth century had approved the main body of labor reforms that had been written into the Federal and state statute books in the preceding half century.

Although the courts eventually sanctioned most of the laws designed to protect and benefit the worker, they seldom lent their support to organized labor in its conflicts with organized capital. The principal union weapons were the strike and the boycott, but on repeated occasions before World War I the judiciary ruled that both were illegal. The device most frequently used by the courts to restrict union activity was the injunction. Whenever an individual believed that any union policy was in any way destroying the value of his property, he was permitted to appeal to the courts for an order directing the union to abandon the policy in question. Since almost any attempt by a union to improve the lot of its members necessarily had an adverse effect on the property interests of someone, the courts were seldom at a loss to find a reason for issuing an injunction. Injunctions were used to restrain the workers in the railroad strikes of 1877, and in subsequent years there was hardly a major industrial conflict in which they were not employed to check unions. They proved to be such effective devices that many militant workers came to view them as little more than a thinly disguised legal device for strike breaking and boycott busting. Although the Clayton Act, which became law in 1914, specifically outlawed injunctions in labor disputes, judicial decisions largely nullified this provision in later years.

Judges who handed down antiunion decisions based their opinions on either the common law or the Federal statutes of the United States. Although as early as 1842, Judge Lemuel Shaw of Massachusetts in *Commonwealth v. Hunt* had exempted unions from some of the restrictions imposed by the common law, in later years the courts continued to rule on numerous occasions that certain forms of union activity were violations of the common law doctrines of unlawful conspiracy and illegal restraint of trade. Moreover, Congress in 1890 enacted the Sherman Antitrust Act, the first provision of which stated that "every contract, combination in the form of trust or otherwise, or conspiracy in restraint of trade or commerce among the several states, or with foreign nations, is hereby declared illegal." Although it has never been demonstrated that the authors of this measure intended it to apply to labor unions, members of the Federal bench frequently interpreted it in such a way that it could. Under the act the courts issued indictments, injunctions, and damage suits; and in the years after 1890 the Sherman Act was used more frequently against organized labor than against organized capital.

The Pullman strike of 1894 was the first major industrial dispute in which organized labor felt the full impact of the power of the courts.

When the American Railway union under the leadership of Eugene V. Debs supported a strike against the Pullman Car Company in Chicago, the Federal government requested an injunction under section 4 of the Sherman Act* to prevent the strikers from interfering with mail shipments on the railroads. In response to this demand, the court issued a preliminary order restraining any persons from

> *interfering with, hindering, obstructing, or stopping any mail train, express train or other trains, whether freight or passenger, engaged in interstate commerce . . . and from in any manner interfering with, injuring, or destroying any of the property of any of said railroads engaged in, or for the purpose of, or in connection with, interstate commerce, or the carriage of the mails of the United States; . . . and from using threats, intimidation, force or violence to induce employees to quit the service of the railroad, or to prevent persons from entering the employ of the railroads.*

When the workers ignored the court order, President Cleveland, despite the protests of Governor John Altgeld of Illinois, who insisted that he had the situation well in hand, dispatched Federal troops to Chicago, and after considerable violence the strike was crushed by superior force. Debs and other union leaders were arrested and charged with contempt of court for their refusal to observe the injunction. The presiding judge of the Circuit Court for the District of Chicago ruled that the injunction was authorized by both the Sherman Act and the common-law prohibition against unlawful conspiracy, and the defendants were sentenced to six months in prison. The case was then carried to the Supreme Court, which sustained the lower court's ruling. The Supreme Court refused to pass on the applicability of the Sherman Act, and based its decision on the grounds that the government had authority over the transportation of the mails and interstate commerce and that an injunction could be issued to prevent persons from jeopardizing this authority. In his opinion, Justice Brewer said:

> *Every government, entrusted by the very terms of its being with powers and duties to be exercised and discharged for the general welfare, has a right to apply to its courts for any proper assistance in the exercise of the one and the discharge of the other. . . . While it is not the province of the government to interfere in the mere*

* Section 4 of the Sherman Act read: "The several circuit courts of the United States are hereby invested with jurisdiction to prevent and restrain violations of this act. . . . Such proceedings may be by way of petition setting forth the case and praying that such violation shall be enjoined or otherwise prohibited . . .; and pending such petition and before final decrees the court may at any time make such temporary or restraining order or prohibition as shall be deemed just in the premises."

matter of private controversy between individuals, or to use its great powers to enforce the rights of one as against another, yet, whenever the wrongs complained of are such as affect the public at large, and are in respect to matters which by the constitution are entrusted to the care of the nation, and concerning which the nation owes the duty to all the citizens of securing to them their common rights, then the mere fact that the government has no pecuniary interest in the controversy is not sufficient to exclude it from the courts.

In every way the Debs case was an overwhelming defeat for organized labor. An unprecedentedly sweeping injunction had been issued to end a strike, and the judiciary had found a variety of reasons to substantiate its stand. The circuit court had stated that unions could be enjoined under both the common law and the Sherman Act. The Supreme Court had ruled that injunctions could be issued against any union that threatened the "general welfare." It is difficult to conceive of a strike that did not fall within at least one of these categories.

Judicial restrictions on the activities of organized labor extended to the boycott as well as the strike. When D. E. Loewe and Company of Danbury, Connecticut, refused to accede to the demand of the United Hatters of America, an A.F. of L. affiliate, that its plant be unionized, the American Federation of Labor retaliated by imposing a nation-wide boycott on all Loewe hats. The boycott was remarkably effective, and Loewe instituted a suit against the union in the circuit court in Hartford. The principal point at issue in what came to be known as the Danbury Hatters' case was whether or not the Sherman Act prohibited restraint of trade by a union. The circuit court answered this question in the affirmative, for it ruled: "The Act prohibits any combination whatever to secure action which essentially obstructs the flow of commerce between states, or restricts, in that regard, the liberty of a trader to engage in business." Because the union "aimed at compelling third parties and strangers involuntarily not to engage in the course of trade except on the conditions that the combination imposes," the court decided that the union's boycott was a violation of the Sherman Act. In 1908 the Supreme Court upheld the lower court's decision, and there no longer remained any doubt concerning the application of the Sherman Act to unions. The *American Federationist* wrote soon afterward: "Our industrial rights have been shorn from us and our liberties threatened."

Further evidence of the judiciary's conviction that the Sherman Act covered labor unions as well as trusts was furnished by the Buck Stove and Range case. Following the refusal of J. W. Van Cleave of the Buck Stove and Range Company to rehire striking workers, the American Federation of Labor instituted a boycott against his concern's products.

At Van Cleave's request a District of Columbia court issued both temporary and permanent injunctions that enjoined the members and officers of the American Federation of Labor from continuing the boycott. When Gompers and two other A.F. of L. officials ignored the injunction, the District court found them guilty of contempt of court and sentenced them to prison terms ranging from six months to a year. This decision was sustained by the Supreme Court, which ruled that the boycott violated both the common law and the provisions of the Sherman Act.*

The antiunion decisions of the Federal courts deprived organized labor of many of its most powerful weapons. Through the repeated use of the injunction and interpretations unfavorable to labor of the common law, the general-welfare clause, and the Sherman Act, the courts not only outlawed the boycott but almost every form of strike activity that unions needed if they were to attain their objectives. It was not until the passage of the Clayton Antitrust Act in 1914 that organized labor was provided with some measure of protection against the judiciary. Section 6 of the Clayton Act stated that the "labor of a human being is not a commodity or article of commerce. Nothing contained in the antitrust laws shall be construed to forbid the existence and operation of labor . . . organizations . . . nor shall such organizations or the members thereof, be held or construed to be illegal combinations or conspiracies in restraint of trade under the antitrust laws." Section 20 of the act restricted the issuing of injunctions in labor disputes. Samuel Gompers welcomed these two provisions as the Magna Carta of American labor, but his optimism proved premature, for the courts in subsequent years interpreted the labor sections in such a way that they were practically nullified. Unions had to wait until the adoption of the Norris-La Guardia Federal anti-injunction law in 1932 and the National Industrial Recovery Act in the following year before they received any substantial assistance or protection from the government.

Judicial curbs on the activities of organized labor were an accurate reflection of the basic antagonism toward unions on the part of a large segment of the American people. While most Americans agreed that the state or Federal governments should guarantee workers a certain measure of protection on the job, they were not prepared to endorse either the methods or the objectives of workingmen who banded together to present a united front to their employers. In general the public viewed with both suspicion and hostility such union techniques as the boycott, slowdown, picket line, and strike. On the other hand there appeared to be little concerted opposition outside union ranks to the use by employers of such devices as the lockout, yellow-dog contract, private or

* The Supreme Court, however, set aside the sentences imposed by the lower court on the A.F. of L. officials. *Gompers* v. *Buck Stove and Range Company*, 221 U. S. 418 (1907).

public armies, and strikebreakers. Most Americans, who had been taught since earliest childhood to accept and revere a theory of economic individualism that seemed amply substantiated by numerous evidences of material progress and by countless "rags-to-riches" stories, considered unions both a violation of the American creed and a threat to their ideals. As long as the American people clung to these views, unions could obtain only a few limited victories in their legal and economic struggles with the nation's employers.

CHAPTER VI

THE COMMERCIAL FARMER

DURING the fifty years between the Civil War and World War I, American agriculture was transformed by a series of developments that revolutionized both the methods of farm production and the position of the farmer in the national economy. The increasing use of machinery, the opening up of new agricultural areas, the changing character of the farmer's market, and the growth of specialization all combined to make agriculture a modern business enterprise. In the process the self-sustaining farm community was destroyed, and the commercial farmer become a businessman who bought what he consumed and sold what he produced. The farmer ceased to be an economic individualist whose livelihood was dependent on the outcome of his struggle with nature, for his profits now were determined not only by the elements but also by freight rates, world supply and demand, and the state of the money market.

36. THE GROWTH OF AMERICAN AGRICULTURE

DURING the second half of the nineteenth century there was a marked increase in the demand for American farm products. As western Europe—and particularly England—turned from agriculture to manufacturing, the American farmer began to assume the burden of feeding a sizable part of the Old World. In addition, the growth in the population of the United States and the rapid development of cities provided the farmer with a constantly expanding domestic market. At the same time, supply more than kept pace with demand, and from the Civil War to World War I, there was a spectacular rise in the number of American farms, the area of land under cultivation, the size of most of the major crops, and the application of machinery to agricultural production. Finally, the increase in both supply and demand was facilitated by a network of railroads that brought the farmer into contact with foreign as well as domestic consumers of his products.

From 1860 to 1910 the number of farms in the United States increased from approximately 2,000,000 to more than 6,000,000; the area of land under cultivation rose in round numbers from 163,000,000 to 347,000,000 acres; and the number of farm families rose by more than 1,500,000 to 6,123,610. Although every section of the country contributed to the expansion of American agriculture during these years, it was in the new lands in the Middle and Far West that the most significant advances occurred. Throughout most of these years the relatively cheap lands in the West attracted countless Easterners and immigrants, and between 1860 and 1900 the population of the West North Central states grew from 2,170,000 to 10,347,000; the West South Central states from 1,748,000 to 6,532,000; the Mountain states and territories from 175,000 to 1,675,000; and the Pacific states from 444,000 to 2,417,000. While some of the new inhabitants in these regions settled in towns and cities, the majority undoubtedly became farmers.

The farmers who occupied the new lands in the West were drawn from a variety of backgrounds. All the older sections were represented, but most of the new settlers came from the Old Northwest, and those who migrated from the Atlantic coast were comparatively few in number. Regardless of their place of origin, almost all the farmers in this region had an agricultural background. In addition, they possessed some means, for the cost of both the trip and the establishment of a new home prevented the poorest groups in the East from emigrating. Many immigrants also settled in the West. The post-Civil War immigrant generally settled in Eastern cities, but large numbers also became farmers in the West. The census of 1880 revealed that 73 per cent of Wisconsin's population was of foreign parentage, while in Minnesota the figure was 71 per cent, in the Dakotas, 66 per cent, in California, 59 per cent, and Nebraska, 44 per cent.

Only a relatively small percentage of the postbellum settlers in the West acquired their land under the terms of the Homestead Act. This law, which was enacted on May 20, 1862, awarded actual settlers in the public domain 160 acres of land. But it proved of little assistance to the Eastern laborer or tenant farmer who wished to take up land in the

West. No provision was made for the cost of the trip or for the credit that the potential settler needed to acquire draft animals and equipment. Moreover, in the arid and semiarid lands between the 100th meridian and the Pacific coast, where the great bulk of the area available for homesteading lay, the 160-acre unit was entirely too small for dry farming or grazing.

The Homestead Act encouraged rather than prevented land monopoly in the West. By making fraudulent entries or by taking advantage of the act's purchase and commutation clauses, foreign and domestic syndicates were able to purchase blocks of 100,000 acres or more. As a consequence, the greater part of the public domain first went to speculators, monopolists, and railroads and was then sold by these groups to actual settlers. Less than a sixth of the increase in agricultural acreage between 1860 and 1900 came as a result of direct gift from the government to homesteading farmers.

Although the best government lands had been pre-empted by the close of the century, scattered public lands of inferior quality still were available, and more land was homesteaded in the decades after 1890 than in the years 1862–90. To facilitate the settlement of these remaining lands Congress modified the Homestead Act. In 1904 the Kinkaid Act permitted the granting of 640-acre homesteads in western Nebraska, and in 1909 the Enlarged Homestead Act made it possible to acquire a 320-acre homestead in other states and territories. Finally, the Stock-Raising Homestead Act of 1916 authorized 640-acre homesteads in those areas classified as good only for grazing or forage.

Private rather than public enterprise was largely responsible for the movement of farmers into the West after the Civil War. Railroads and speculators, having acquired vast tracts of the public domain, made every effort to attract purchasers for their lands. Railroads and speculative groups like the National Land Company conducted extensive advertising campaigns and established immigration centers in New York and other Eastern cities. The same techniques were employed by Western state governments, land companies, and railroad and steamship concerns in Europe; and during the postwar years many foreigners were lured to the West by agents, publicity men, pamphlets, newspaper articles, and advertisements.

37. IMPROVED MACHINES AND TECHNIQUES

THE RAPID growth of American agriculture after the Civil War was due not only to the increase in the number of farmers and the amount of land under cultivation but also to the widespread use of machinery. Before 1850 the American farmer used simple, inexpensive tools, many of which were manufactured at home. His land was turned with heavy and clumsy plows drawn by horses and oxen raised on the farm. The seed was sown by hand and harrowed into the ground by homebuilt drags or even by bushes. The cotton was picked by hand,* and the grain was cut with a sickle or a cradle, bound by hand, and threshed on the barn floor with wooden flails. The grain was separated from the chaff by a manually operated fanning mill. If the farmer happened to be a producer of dairy products, he did all his work by hand; he milked the cows by hand, strained the milk by hand into pans, skimmed the cream by hand, and worked and churned the butter by hand. The tasks were endless, the hours of labor long, and the opportunity for profit limited. By 1900, however, many, though by no means all of the old ways had been abandoned, and mechanization had become an ideal, if not a reality, for all American farmers.

As early as 1860, patents had been granted in the United States for the basic principles of such modern farm machines as steel and chilled-iron plows, disc harrows, grain drills and planters, reapers, grain binders, threshing machines, and straddle row-cultivators. Although ignorance, lack of capital, and the weight of tradition often retarded the acceptance of these machines, farmers in every section eventually recognized the advantages of the new equipment. In 1860, the value of farm implements and machinery in the United States was $246,000,000; in 1900 the figure was $750,000,000, and a decade later it was $1,265,000,000.

The first agricultural implement to be significantly improved was the plow. As early as 1840, John Deere of Illinois began manufacturing steel-faced moldboard plows to which the soil would not readily stick. The Deere plow, though costly because of the high price of steel, sold widely. Meanwhile, others were attempting to manufacture cheap but efficient plows; and finally in 1868, James Oliver of Indiana fabricated a chilled-iron plow, and within a decade he had evolved the modern plow. The riding, or sulky, plow was also perfected in the years immediately preceding and during the Civil War. The first completely successful one was produced by F. S. Davenport and Robert Newton in 1864. Nine years later, sixteen different models were displayed at a St. Louis farming exhibition. The gang plow was also in production before the end of the century, especially in California. Inventions of other such soil-working implements as spring-tooth and disc harrows, seed planters, and an endless variety of cultivators followed closely on the heels of one another. The increased use of this new equipment not only facilitated the rapid exploitation of the virgin soils of the West but also helped to make the United States the granary of the world. In 1830, before the

* Until recently most of the cotton in the United States continued to be picked by hand.

invention of these implements, it took 32.8 minutes to prepare the soil for a bushel of wheat. In 1900, it took 2.2 minutes to perform the same operation.

Harvesting machines played as significant a role in the revolution in farm methods as the soil-working implements. The mowing machine and reaper had been invented long before the Civil War, and during the 1850's McCormick agents sold thousands of reapers in the Middle West. But these machines merely cut the grain and raked it off in unbound bundles. During the Civil War a harvester invented before 1860 was developed by the Marsh brothers of DeKalb, Illinois; it provided a platform on which men could ride and bind the grain as it came from the reel. In 1873, wire binders came into use. Although a great advance over the laborious task of binding by hand, the use of wire was not entirely satisfactory, and in 1878 the Deering Company acquired from John F. Appleby a twine knotter. McCormick soon had a similar device, and by 1880 the mechanical self-binder harvester was a complete success. Henceforth one man with a three-horse team or a tractor could accomplish as much as the toil and sweat of twenty men with sickle or cradle. Before the end of the century the giant combine—a machine that cut, threshed, and bagged the grain—was in use in California. The thresher, another pre-Civil War machine, was improved by the addition of feeders, weighers, and straw stackers. Corn-husking and corn-shelling machines, the corn binder, and ensilage and silo-filling machines revolutionized the handling of one of America's most important crops.

Machinery and mechanical processes also transformed the harvest of hay crops. The scythe gave way to the two-wheeled hinged-cutting bar-mowing machine; the horse-drawn wooden hay-rake of the first half of the nineteenth century was superseded first by the spring-tooth rake and then by the side-delivery rake; the pitchfork was partially displaced by the mechanical loader; and as early as the 1870's the tedder for shaking up the hay during the curing process was in use on many farms. Equally significant improvements were introduced in almost every other branch of agriculture. Machines for planting and spraying potatoes, for the grading and processing of fruits and vegetables, and for many of the operations in the dairying industry helped to expand the nation's agricultural output and to eliminate some of the backbreaking drudgery of farming. Even in the South, where hand labor persisted longer than in other sections, mechanization made some progress. The cotton gin was improved, and the cotton-seed planter, fertilizer distributor, and cotton-stalk cutter were introduced.

In the years between the Civil War and World War I relatively few changes were made in the power employed to operate the new machines. With the exception of the heavy steam tractors that were used in the wheat fields of California and the Northwest and on the sugar plantations of the South, horses, mules and oxen were the principal sources of power, and in 1910 not more than one thousand gasoline tractors were in operation on American farms.* But as the twentieth century progressed, electricity was increasingly used for farm power. Many farms, however, were not near power lines, and it was not until the New Deal that a concerted effort was undertaken to make rural electrification a reality. It has been only in recent years that any large number of farmers have been able to use electricity for the operation of household equipment and for such stationary barn-devices as milking machines, milk coolers, and water pumps.

It is difficult, if not impossible, to ascertain the exact effect of the application of machinery to agriculture, but reliable data indicate that it resulted in large savings in labor and money. Improved methods accounted for a saving of 48.1 per cent in the time needed for the production of the ten major crops listed in the accompanying table. With the exception of cotton and tobacco, the costs of machine labor were fractional in comparison with the costs of hand labor. In 1900, for example, 10 minutes of human labor was needed to produce a bushel of wheat from beginning to end whereas in 1830 the same process took 183 minutes. The savings in labor-power cost in 1900 over the same costs in 1830 totaled $523,000,000 in growing the nation's corn crop, $79,000,000 in growing the wheat crop, and $52,000,000 in growing the oat crop.

HOURS AND WAGES BY HAND AND BY MACHINE†

CROP	TIME WORKED				LABOR COST	
	Hand (1830)		Machine (1896)		Hand	Machine
	Hrs.	Minutes	Hrs.	Minutes	(1830)	(1896)
Wheat	61	5.0	3	19.2	$3.5542	$ .6605
Corn	38	45.0	15	7.8	3.6250	1.5130
Oats	66	15.0	7	5.8	3.7292	1.0732
Hay: loose	21	5.0	3	56.5	1.7501	.4230
Hay: baled	35	30.0	11	34.0	3.0606	1.2894
Potatoes	108	55.0	38	00.0	10.8916	3.8000
Cotton	167	48.0	78	42.0	7.8773	7.8700
Rice: rough	62	5.0	17	2.5	5.6440	1.0071
Sugar Cane	351	21.0	191	33.0	31.9409	11.3189
Tobacco	311	23.0	252	54.6	23.3538	25.1160
Total: ten crops	1194	12.0	619	15.4	95.4267	54.0711
Total: 27 different crops	9760	47.7	5107	52.6	$1037.7609	$598.1338

* In 1940, 1,600,000 gasoline-driven tractors were in use.

† Reprinted with permission from Fred A. Shannon: *The Farmer's Last Frontier; Agriculture, 1860–1897* (New York: Farrar & Rinehart, Inc., 1945), p. 143.

The social consequences of mechanization were equally significant. Not only was the backbreaking and spirit-deadening toil of American farmers reduced, but it became possible to feed and clothe the constantly growing urban population and accumulate surpluses for export in both peace and in war. The export of agricultural machinery brought similar relief to countless other persons in the rest of the world, and indeed, helped to check the foreign demand for the farm commodities of the United States. The introduction of expensive machinery also helped to make American agriculture more capitalistic. In the days of self-sufficiency, when agricultural implements were few and often homemade and when land was relatively cheap, it was not difficult financially to become a farmer. But the situation changed radically as the price of farm land advanced and costly machinery with which to work it had to be bought. The new machines not only required a large initial outlay, but they also absorbed considerable money in repairs, wore out more rapidly than the simple tools that they replaced, and often had to be discarded because they were outmoded by newer and improved models. Moreover, no farmer could completely escape the effect of machinery on American agriculture, for, as in industry, the price of any product was determined at least in part by the costs of the most efficient producers. The result was that many farmers who could not afford to purchase the new equipment had to give up their farms and work as machine tenders for their more prosperous colleagues. In this sense they were not unlike the craftsmen who were compelled by the rise of industry to take jobs in factories.

In addition to the application of machines to agriculture there were a number of other developments that enabled the farmer to increase his output. Fertilizers were more widely used than in the past, and from 1860 to 1910 the amount of commercial fertilizer used in the United States rose from 164,000 to 5,547,000 tons. Dry farming techniques and Federally sponsored irrigation projects, moreover, permitted many farmers to take up lands in arid regions that previously had not been suitable for cultivation. At the same time, the agricultural divisions of numerous state universities were emphasizing the need for scientific agriculture and were providing farmers with information that helped them to increase their crop yields. Even more important was the assistance furnished by the Federal government. In 1862 the United States Department of Agriculture was created and put under the direction of a commissioner, and in 1889 the head of the department was raised to cabinet rank. The department conducted countless experiments in every branch of agriculture, established bureaus that were concerned with almost every phase of farming, issued numerous pamphlets that contained practical information for farmers, gathered statistics on agriculture, and undertook a number of long-range programs that were designed to improve farming and aid farmers.

38. AGRICULTURAL SPECIALIZATION

THE introduction of machinery, the pressure of competition, regional differences in soil and climate, competition between soils and climate of different areas, and improvement in transportation facilities contributed increasingly after 1865 to crop specialization. Before the Civil War, specialized agriculture had been widely practiced in the South; and, although the war temporarily dethroned King Cotton, this change proved only an interlude rather than the reversal of a long-term trend. In 1866 the cotton crop was some two million bales, or less than half that of 1860; but five decades later, largely because of the increased use of fertilizers in the older cotton regions and the opening of new cotton-growing areas—especially in Texas and Oklahoma—it had risen to more than eleven million bales.

PRODUCTION OF COTTON IN LEADING COTTON-GROWING STATES IN BALES. ONE BALE EQUALS 500 POUNDS

STATES	1859	1879	1899	1919
Mississippi	962,000	963,000	1,286,000	957,000
Alabama	791,000	699,000	1,093,000	718,000
Louisiana	622,000	508,000	699,000	306,000
Georgia	561,000	814,000	1,232,000	1,681,000
Texas	345,000	805,000	2,584,000	2,971,000
Arkansas	293,000	608,000	705,000	869,000
Tennessee	237,000	330,000	235,000	306,000
South Carolina	282,000	522,000	843,000	1,476,000
North Carolina	116,000	389,000	433,000	858,000
Oklahoma			227,000	1,006,000

Tobacco was the South's other leading money-crop in the years between the Civil War and World War I. After 1865 the area of production shifted westward into Kentucky, western North Carolina, southern Ohio, and Missouri. Although Connecticut, Indiana, Pennsylvania, Ohio, and Wisconsin each produced some tobacco during these years, the South accounted for five sixths of the nation's crop. Rice, sugar, citrus fruits, peaches, peanuts, strawberries, potatoes, sweet potatoes, pecans, and garden truck were important minor crops produced in the region.

While cotton continued to dominate agriculture in the South, wheat and corn were conquering the Prairie states of the upper Mississippi

Valley. Conditions for such a conquest were almost ideal. Nature had blessed the area with a soil unsurpassed anywhere in the world. Its level character fitted it admirably for mechanized agriculture, and most of the more important types of farm machinery were the inventions of Prairie state people and were manufactured in Prairie state factories. No region of America, moreover, was so amply provided with transportation facilities. Here too there developed the great flour-milling and meat-packing centers that stimulated Prairie agriculture and in turn were nourished by it. On the other hand, the Prairie farmer at various times had to contend with such natural hazards as grass fires, blizzards, floods, droughts, and grasshopper plagues.

LEADING WHEAT PRODUCING STATES

(Figures in thousands of bushels)

1859		1879		1899	
Illinois	23,837	Illinois	51,110	Minnesota	95,278
Indiana	16,848	Indiana	47,284	North Dakota	59,884
Wisconsin	15,657	Ohio	46,014	Ohio	50,376
Ohio	15,119	Michigan	35,532	South Dakota	41,889
Virginia	13,130	Minnesota	34,601	Kansas	38,778
Pennsylvania	13,042	Iowa	31,154	California	36,534
New York	8,681	California	29,017	Indiana	34,986
Iowa	8,449	Missouri	24,966	Nebraska	24,924
Michigan	8,336	Wisconsin	24,884	Missouri	23,072
Kentucky	7,394	Pennsylvania	19,462	Iowa	22,769
Other States	42,611	Other States	105,159	Other States	226,940
Total	173,104		449,183		655,430

Wheat, a staple of all new lands in the North, had pushed forward with the advance of the frontier. In 1850 the center of wheat production was near Columbus, Ohio. Within another fifty years it had moved about 100 miles north and 680 miles west to the area beyond Des Moines in west central Iowa. For a short time after the Civil War the wheat growing areas east of the Mississippi held their own, but by the 1880's they tended increasingly to be outdistanced by the West North Central states. By the end of the century the East, though growing rapidly in population, was supplying a diminishing amount of wheat and other cereal breadstuffs. By World War I there were four rather distinct wheat producing areas in the United States: (1) The Eastern winter wheat belt stretching from Maryland and eastern Pennsylvania westward through Ohio, Indiana, and Illinois; (2) the hard red winter wheat region centering in Kansas, Nebraska, Central Oklahoma, and the panhandles of Oklahoma and Texas; (3) the hard red spring wheat area, which included the two Dakotas, the western border of Minnesota—especially the Red River Valley—northeastern and north central Montana, and Canada approximately as far north as Winnipeg on the east and Edmonton on the west; (4) the Far Western region, which included the Big Bend and Palouse districts of Washington and the adjoining portions of Oregon and northern Idaho. In all four of these regions a high degree of specialization prevailed.

Even more important than wheat in the nation's economy was corn. This crop, which exceeded in acreage and in production the combined quantities of wheat, oats, barley, rye, buckwheat, and rice, was in large measure consumed by hogs. Although corn was grown to some extent in every state in the Union, its production centered in the Corn Belt, the region of fertile prairie soils extending from Ohio westward and northward and embracing principally Indiana, Illinois, Iowa, Missouri, Minnesota, Kansas, Nebraska, and South Dakota. The total crop in 1860, to which the South contributed very considerably, was about 839,000,000 bushels. As more acreage in the trans-Mississippi North Central states was put into corn, production rose to unprecedented figures, the two-billion-bushel mark being exceeded five times during the last decade of the nineteenth century.

Although corn and wheat were the leading crops of the Prairie states, this region also produced large amounts of several other important agricultural commodities. At the close of the nineteenth century the twelve North Central states grew 77 per cent of the nation's oats, 57 per cent of its barley, 52 per cent of its rye, 58 per cent of its hay, and 53 per cent of its potatoes. They also had 44 per cent of the beef cattle, 52 per cent of the milk cows, 26 per cent of the sheep, 52 per cent of the horses, 23 per cent of the mules, and 61 per cent of the hogs.

The cattle and sheep raising industries were concentrated in the region west of the Mississippi River. In 1900 there were approximately 28,000,000 beef cattle in the United States. Of these 4,417,000 were in Kansas, Nebraska, and the Dakotas, 4,353,000 in Texas, and 1,395,000 in the Pacific states. The cattle industry was predominant on the Great Plains, but cattle were raised in every state in the Union, and those on general farms exceeded the number on ranches. In 1850 the center of the cattle industry was Lexington, Kentucky; seventy years later it was in the vicinity of Ellsworth, Kansas. Of the 61,500,000 sheep in the United States in 1900, more than 60 per cent were in the states stretching from North Dakota to Texas and westward to the Pacific coast. Within this region, in turn, most sheep were raised in the tier of states extending from Montana to New Mexico.

Commercial farming was not confined to the South and the Middle West, for specialization also increasingly characterized agriculture in the Northeast and on the Pacific coast. In the East, crop specialization was in large part the result of Western competition. New England and the Middle Atlantic states could no longer successfully compete with the Mississippi Valley in the production of cereals and livestock. In 1860, New England produced more than 1,000,000 bushels of wheat; in 1899, less than 137,000. During the same period, corn production in New England declined from 9,165,000 bushels to 6,615,000; beef cattle from 625,000 head to 474,000; and sheep from 1,780,000 to 585,000. The one marked increase was in dairy cattle, which rose from 680,000 head to 960,000 during these years. Topography, industrialization, urbanization, and nearness to market accounted in large measure for the growth of the dairy industry, which after 1900 became one of New England's foremost agricultural enterprises.

During the forty years after 1860 the Middle Atlantic states had a better agricultural record than did New England. Improved lands, for example, showed a 4,000,000 acre increase, whereas those in New England declined by approximately one third. As in New England, dairying was the mainstay of the region's agricultural economy, and in 1900, New York and Pennsylvania each had more than 1,000,000 dairy cows. Abandonment of farms in these states and the emigration of rural people to urban communities proceeded at a somewhat slower pace than in New England, but it proceeded nevertheless; and the following description of the farming situation in Connecticut in 1900 also applied to many parts of the Middle Atlantic states: "The most unobservant of travelers through the agricultural districts of the Nutmeg State cannot fail to note the brush-grown highways, the down-fallen walls, the decayed fences, dilapidated buildings and neglected fields which mark the decadence of the true agricultural spirit."

Although much of the land abandoned in the Northeast was wholly unfitted for farming, unsuitable topography and sterility of soil do not entirely account for the exodus. The possibility of a better job in a mill town at shorter hours and higher pay, the desire to find excitement and "to see the world," visions of fame and fortune, and the lure of more fertile and workable lands in the Prairie states were among the more important reasons why many went and few returned. With the continued growth of industry in the twentieth century and the advent of the automobile many of those who remained on the farm became part-time farmers who supplemented their income by obtaining employment in nearby factories and towns.

The Northeast did not have a monopoly on dairying, however. Even before 1900, farmers in the North Central states were turning in increas-

---

8. AGRICULTURAL REGIONS OF THE UNITED STATES

The agricultural regions that developed in the United States before World War I have remained relatively unchanged. [From the Bureau of Agricultural Economics, United States Department of Agriculture.]

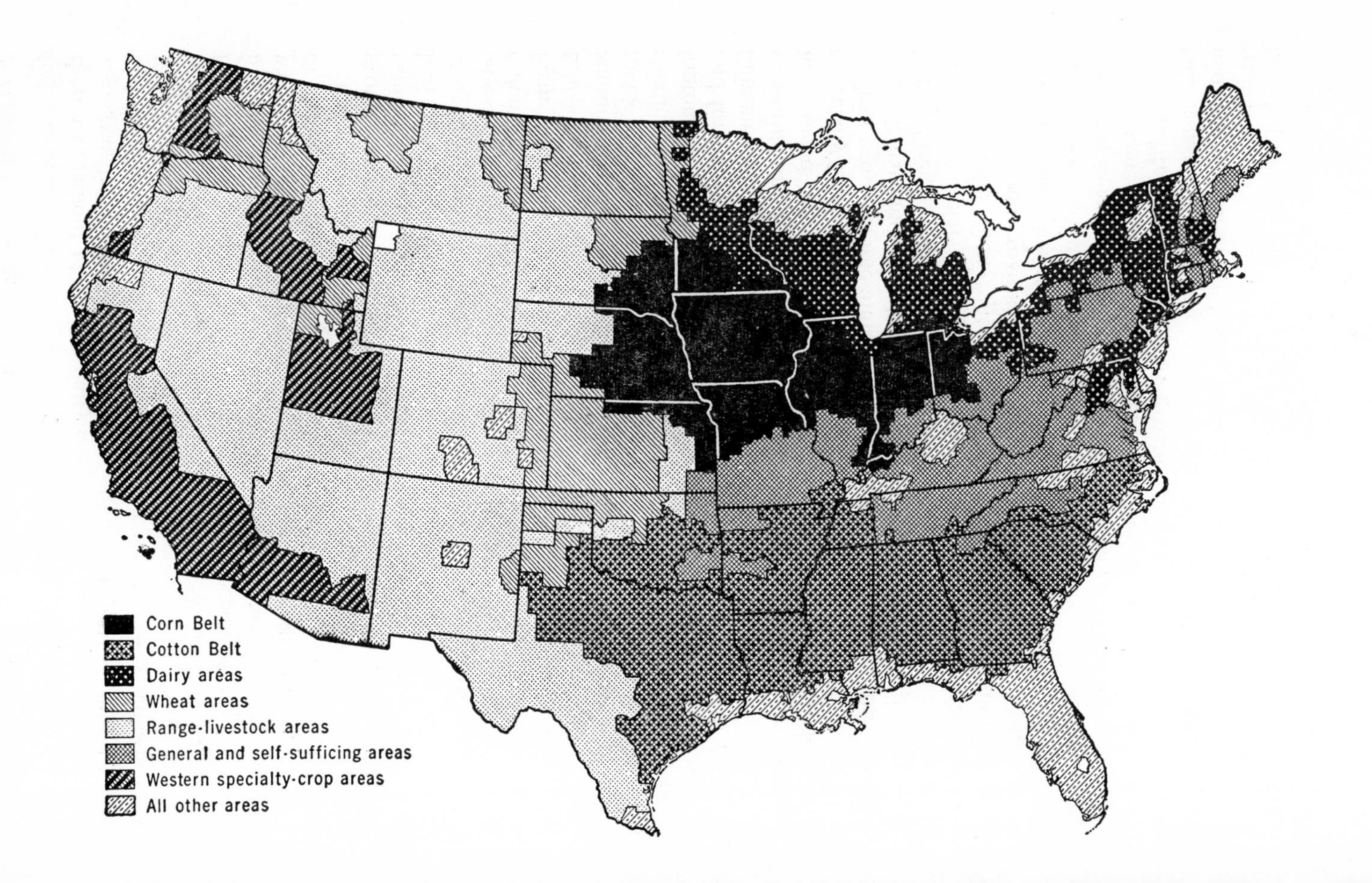
Corn Belt
Cotton Belt
Dairy areas
Wheat areas
Range-livestock areas
General and self-sufficing areas
Western specialty-crop areas
All other areas

ing numbers to the production of milk, butter, and cheese. By 1900 there were about 17,500,000 dairy cows in the United States. Iowa, with 1,500,000, led all other states and was followed by New York, Illinois, and Pennsylvania in that order. The next six states—Wisconsin, Ohio, Kansas, Nebraska, Missouri, Minnesota—were all in the prairie regions, and each had more than 500,000 dairy cows. By World War I the dairy industry had become one of the more highly specialized forms of farming in the United States. Although the dairy farmer might raise some wheat, potatoes, or a little garden truck, the production of milk, butter, or cheese had central place in his farm operations.

Truck farming, like the dairy industry, was intimately related to the growth in population, urbanization, improvements in refrigeration, and rapid transportation. By 1910 almost every village or city in America had in its immediate environs one or more truck gardens or farms. In most instances the variety of truck produced was much the same: radishes, lettuce, spinach, cucumbers, peas, beans, cabbage, beets, carrots, onions, eggplant, cauliflower, strawberries, celery, and potatoes. Some farms and even areas specialized in the production of one or two vegetables that required a special soil or climate. The midseason and late-summer crops of celery, for example, were concentrated mainly on the muck soils of New York, Michigan, New Jersey, and Pennsylvania with smaller acreages on the irrigated lands of Colorado, Oregon, and Washington. Many truck farms produced both for the fresh vegetable market and for the commercial canneries, which multiplied in number and in influence after the successful appearance in the 1870's of the tin can as a vegetable and fruit container. After 1900, Eastern truck farms increasingly faced the competition of the truck farmers of the Pacific Coast, especially California.

Fruit growing, like almost every other branch of agriculture, became a specialized industry during the fifty years after the Civil War. California, Oregon, and Washington went into the fruit-growing business on a commercial basis some years before World War I, and several Eastern states soon followed suit. Aside from Washington, northern California, and isolated areas in Idaho, Colorado, and northwestern Arkansas, the principal centers of apple production were south and east of large bodies of water—as in Michigan and New York—or east of mountain ranges—as in Virginia, Maryland, and North Carolina—which afforded some protection from severe cold. Because of high summer temperatures few apple trees were grown within two hundred miles of the Gulf coast. The North's monopoly in the production of apples was matched by that of the South and Southwest in the cultivation of citrus fruits. Oranges, grapefruit, lemons, limes, kumquats, dates, and figs came largely from Florida, California, Texas, and Arizona. A large part of the peach crop, three eighths of the plums, one third of the pears, nearly all the apricots, and the overwhelming tonnage of grapes were grown in California, while Oregon and Washington have in recent decades produced great quantities of apples and berries and other small fruit. California and Oregon were also the principal producers of the Persian, or so-called English, walnut.

39. THE FARMER'S MARKET

THE growth of specialized agriculture with its emphasis on cash crops made the post-Civil War farmer far more dependent on markets than he had been when he practiced diversified agriculture on a more or less subsistence basis. From 1860 to 1910 the constantly growing urban population of the United States furnished the American farmer with his principal domestic market. At the same time the growth of specialization compelled farmers who had formerly provided for many of their own needs to purchase a large variety of products from their fellow farmers. As a consequence, the rural market for farm products was expanded by farmers selling to farmers. During the last three decades of the nineteenth century, American farmers sold 82 per cent of the value of their output to consumers in the United States. The principal products in this domestic trade were cereals, meat, dairy products, cotton, wool, tobacco, fruit, and garden truck. Of these, cereals accounted for by far the largest volume of sales, and by 1900 they constituted almost half the total of all crops raised in this country.

The farmer's domestic market was supplemented by sales abroad. During the thirty years that preceded the Civil War, four fifths of American exports were farm products, consisting mostly of cotton, tobacco, cereals, and meat. In return for these commodities Europe sent to the United States tools, textiles, metals, glassware, earthenware, and other manufactured products. As industry grew in the United States, the American import of textiles and other finished goods declined, and in the decades after the Civil War this country's exports of manufactured articles mounted yearly. But the export trade in agricultural goods, although it declined in proportion to the total, still constituted an important part of American foreign trade. The European demand for American cereals, meat products, cotton, and tobacco seemed insatiable. For forty years after 1860 approximately 76 per cent of the United States' export trade was in agricultural products, and the value of American agricultural exports rose from about $277,000,000 in 1870 to more than $840,000,000 in 1900.

After 1900 there was a sharp decline in the volume of American agricultural goods sold abroad. Exports of fresh beef fell from 352,000,000 pounds in 1901 to 6,000,000 in 1914; wheat averaged only about 80,000,000 bushels annually from 1910 to 1912 as against 222,000,000 for the years 1900 to 1902. Similarly butter and cheese exports fell off from 79,000,000 pounds in 1898 to only 6,000,000 in 1913. Cotton, tobacco, and fruit were the only important farm products to improve their export status. Despite the growing competition of India and Egypt, cotton shipments abroad increased between 1905 and 1914. The bulk of the cotton exports continued to go to Europe, but during the years immediately before World War I, America also shipped large consignments to Japan in exchange for silk. Like cotton, exports of leaf tobacco rose from more than 300,000,000 pounds in 1899 to almost 450,000,000 in 1913. During these years the United States produced approximately one third of the world's tobacco crop. The principal importers of American tobacco were Great Britain, Germany, France, Italy, and China.

There were several reasons for the decline in the foreign market for American agricultural commodities. Among the most important was Europe's inability to continue to supply the United States with goods that could balance its own imports of American farm products. The United States was beginning to produce its own manufactures on a large scale, and the enactment of high protective tariffs helped keep out European goods. American imports of European manufactures dropped from more than 60 per cent of all imports in 1860 to about 30 per cent in 1900. In the same period, American imports of raw materials for manufactures trebled, but the source of these products was largely non-European. Because of its unfavorable balance of trade with the United States, Europe increasingly turned to Canada, Argentina, and Russia for grains, to Argentina for meat, to India and Egypt for cotton, and to Australia and New Zealand for sheep and dairy products. At the same time, European governments put higher tariffs on foreign farm products, and European farmers, through the use of more and better fertilizers and other improved techniques, were able to lessen their countries' dependence on imported agricultural commodities.

40. THE FARMER AS A BUSINESSMAN AND WORKER

IN THE YEARS after the Civil War the American farmer's increasing reliance on relatively expensive machines and his tendency to specialize in cash crops destroyed whatever economic independence he had once possessed. He had become a businessman and a capitalist; and his profit and loss ledger was now affected by forces over which he had no control. In an earlier America, a relatively small amount of money was required to become a farmer. But the post-Civil

War farmer needed money not only to acquire his land but also to buy the equipment needed to run a modern farm and to purchase the products that before the advent of specialization he had raised for his own and his family's consumption. The trend toward capitalistic farming during these years was further strengthened by rising land costs. Despite periodic depressions, land values rose steadily during the years after the Civil War, and in the decade of World War I they almost doubled.

It is virtually impossible to ascertain the effect of the transition from semi-self-sufficiency to capitalism on the economic status of the American farmer. Not only were there great variations among individual farmers, but the prosperity of each farmer depended among other things upon the location of his farm and the quality of its soil, his competence as a farmer, acts of nature beyond his control, domestic and world situations that affected the business cycle, credit facilities, land systems, competition, available avenues of communication and transportation, government policies, markets and marketing machinery, labor supply, and price structure. Nevertheless, certain major points can be emphasized. First, throughout the period under consideration the increase in the number of farmers in the United States did not keep pace with the increase in population. Although farm population increased, the percentage of farmers decreased from three fifths of the total population in 1860 to approximately one third at the end of World War I. If a longer-time span is considered, the proportionate decline in the popularity of agriculture becomes even more pronounced. As late as 1820, more than 90 per cent of the working population of the United States was engaged in agriculture. After that date and with the rise of factory production, there was a persistent decline; in 1920 the figure was 29.9 per cent and was growing smaller.

Although the absence of the necessary statistics preclude an accurate analysis of the farmer's economic position before World War I, it is possible to indicate in a general way his level of prosperity at any particular period. For eight years after the Civil War most farmers shared in the general prosperity that prevailed throughout the United States. During the depression of the midseventies, the farmer's market shrank, and the prices that he received for his commodities declined sharply. Moreover, during the boom that followed the depression the farmer did not regain the ground that he had lost, and the depression of the 1890's made a bad situation even worse. By the end of the century, however, most farmers had entered a period of prosperity caused in large part by an expansion of the home market that more than compensated for the decline in foreign sales. Moreover, many farmers began to experiment with other crops as sources of income. Sugar production was enlarged, the poultry and dairy industries were further developed, and new attention was given to the production of fruit and vegetables. From 1900 to 1914, agriculture was relatively prosperous, and the American farmer was better off than he had been at any time since the 1860's.

Perhaps the most accurate barometer of the effect of the commercialization of agriculture upon the farmer was the extent of his mortgaged indebtedness. In the period before the Civil War, when suitable farm lands were still relatively cheap, it was not necessary to go heavily into debt to become a farmer. But after the war the rising price of land and the need to acquire expensive machinery forced many farmers—particularly those taking up new lands in the West—to borrow large amounts of money at high interest rates. Moreover, the continuing agricultural distress during the last quarter of the nineteenth century generally prevented farmers from repaying the debts that they had contracted during the years of postwar expansion and prosperity. As a result, large numbers of farmers had difficulty in meeting even their interest payments, and many lost their farms through foreclosure.

For fifty years after the Civil War the equity of farm operators in farm property steadily declined. By 1910, farm mortgages totaled $3,207,863,000, and within the next decade this figure had more than doubled. The average farm mortgage was $1,224, in 1890, $1,715 in 1910, and $3,356 in 1920. It has been estimated that in 1890 there were as many mortgages as there were farms in Kansas, Nebraska, the Dakotas, and Minnesota. Although statistics are lacking on the mortgaged indebtedness of American farmers for the twenty-five years after the Civil War, the total undoubtedly represented a sizable percentage of the value of all farm property in the United States. Furthermore farmers were inclined to mortgage their property in periods of prosperity, when they needed funds for expansion; they therefore borrowed money when it was cheapest, but were often compelled to pay back the interest and principal during hard times, when money was dear.

Perhaps the most significant result of the commercialization of agriculture was the disappearance of a large number of middle-income farmers who owned and operated their own farms. After the Civil War this class, which had been idealized by Jefferson and had always served as the urban folk-image of the American farmer, was increasingly supplanted by a relatively small group of highly successful large-scale farmers on the one hand and a constantly expanding landless proletariat on the other. The extensive use of machinery, the reliance on cash crops,

---

9. THE GROWTH OF FARM TENANCY

These maps show the high percentage of farm tenancy in the South and in the rich agricultural states of the upper Mississippi Valley.

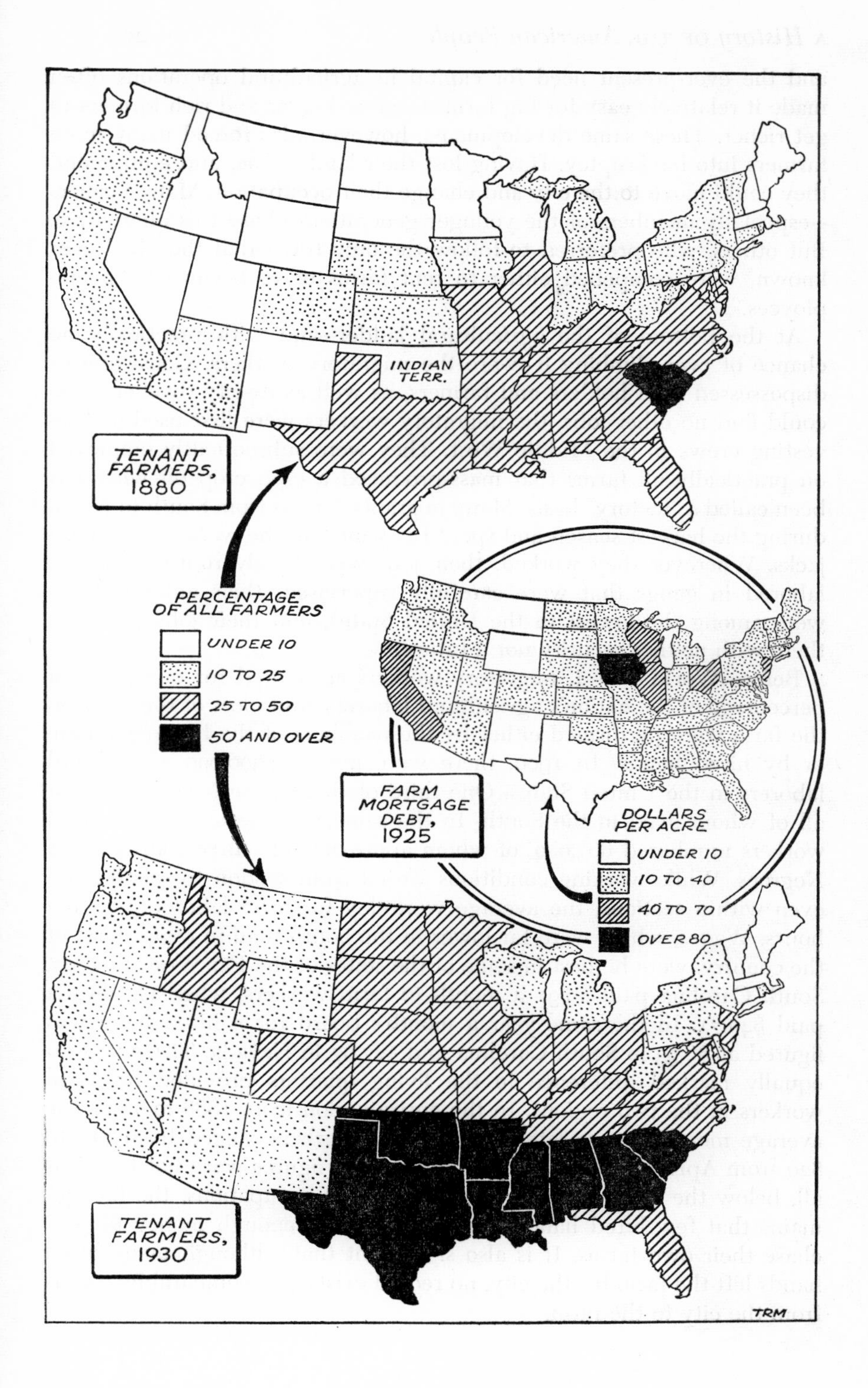
INDIAN TERR.
TENANT FARMERS, 1880
PERCENTAGE OF ALL FARMERS
UNDER 10
10 TO 25
25 TO 50
50 AND OVER
FARM MORTGAGE DEBT, 1925
DOLLARS PER ACRE
UNDER 10
10 TO 40
40 TO 70
OVER 80
TENANT FARMERS, 1930
TRM

and the ever-present need for capital in agricultural operations often made it relatively easy for big farms to grow bigger and rich farmers to get richer. These same developments, however, also forced many more farmers into bankruptcy. Having lost their land, home, and equipment, they could move to the city and change their occupation. Many farmers —especially members of the younger generation—chose this alternative. But others, who preferred to follow the only trade that they had ever known, were compelled either to rent farms or to become farm employees.

At the bottom of the agricultural ladder—and with practically no chance of ever climbing it—were the migratory workers. Consisting of dispossessed land holders and farmers, as well as ex-city dwellers who could find no other jobs, the migratory workers were first used as harvesting crews in the Middle West. They were subsequently employed on practically all farms that mass-produced a cash crop on what has been called a "factory" basis. Many migrants drifted from South to North during the harvest season and spent the winter in the woods as lumberjacks. Wherever they worked, their jobs were highly routinized, they labored in gangs that were carefully supervised, their annual wages were among the lowest in the United States, and their jobs provided them with neither security nor a future.

Before World War I, migratory workers accounted for only a small percentage of the nation's agricultural laborers, and most of the tasks on the farm were performed either by the members of the farmer's family or by hired hands. In 1900, there were nearly 4,500,000 agricultural laborers in the United States. One third of these were Negroes, almost all of whom lived in the South. In the same year, women agricultural workers numbered 663,000, of whom approximately three fourths were Negroes. While working conditions varied from section to section and even within sections, the average work-day for farm laborers was ten hours. Wages, which were far lower in the South than in other parts of the country, were highest in some of the states of the Far West. In 1895, South Carolina paid $9.91 a month to farm workers, whereas Nevada paid $40.71. In the same year a month's board for a hired hand was figured at $6.93 in South Carolina and $27.67 in Nevada. There was an equally marked difference in the living quarters provided for farm workers in the two regions. In the entire nation from 1866 to 1899, the average monthly wage-rate for male farm-workers ranged from $15 to $20 from April to December. Although these figures were not far, if at all, below the wage rates for many industrial occupations, the fact remains that few hired hands were able to save enough money to purchase their own farms. It is also significant that, although many hired hands left the farm for the city, no record exists of a comparable exodus from the city to the farm.

Many farmers, lacking the capital needed to become independent agricultural entrepreneurs, rented homes, land, and even the equipment either from absentee owners or from those in the immediate vicinity. By 1880, 25 per cent of all the farms in the United States were tilled by renters; twenty years later the proportion had risen to 35 per cent; and in 1910 it was 37 per cent. Some farmers who preferred to invest their capital in equipment and livestock rather than land became tenants by choice. But such farmers were the exception, and they constituted only a small fraction of the 2,354,676 tenant families in the United States in 1910. Although tenancy predominated in the South, it could be found in every section of the United States.

The tenant possessed a certain measure of economic independence, for he held a lease upon his land, he often had the right to select his own crops, and he paid a stipulated rent in either money or produce. The sharecropper, however, enjoyed none of these advantages. Sharecropping was a variation of tenancy that was developed in the post-Civil War years by Southern landlords who wished to devise a labor system that would require little capital and would compel the freedmen to resume the tasks that they had performed before the war. Sharecropping soon became the dominant labor system in many parts of the South. Under sharecropping the landlord supplied the land, cabin, mule, tools, seed, and food for the cropper and his family. At the end of the year the landlord took the entire crop and paid the cropper from a third to two thirds of the proceeds, depending upon his contribution. If the cropper contributed only his labor he received a third; if in addition, he furnished the draft animals, implements, seed, and fertilizer and was not otherwise in debt to the land owner, he received two thirds. In addition, the landlord could choose the crop to be planted by the tenant, and more often than not he chose cotton; for cotton was a cash crop and could not be eaten by the cropper or his family. Characterized by short-term leases, unwritten contracts, and the complete domination of the cropper by the planter, sharecropping exploited both Negroes and poor whites, retarded the diversification of Southern agriculture, sapped the initiative of its victims, perpetuated backward farming-techniques, and kept many Negroes in an economic and social position comparable to the one that they had occupied before the Civil War. Sharecropping degraded both the exploiters and the exploited.

Soon after its introduction in the South, sharecropping became intimately associated with the crop-lien system, under which the sharecropper, tenant, and sometimes the small land owner pledged his crop to the country merchant for groceries, seeds, implements, or even petty cash advanced during the growing season. The price of goods thus furnished ran from 10 to 200 per cent above prevailing prices, and interest rates were from 40 to 100 per cent above the average. Frequently, when the price of cotton was low and the cost of provisions and other supplies high—and they were always high—sharecroppers and tenants sank into a state of indebtedness that placed them wholly at the mercy of the merchants and forced them into what amounted to permanent bondage. When landlord and merchant were the same individual, the opportunities for human exploitation under the crop-lien system were almost unlimited.

In marked contrast to such depressed agricultural groups as the hired farm workers, tenants, and sharecroppers were a few large-scale farmers who ran their enterprises on a mass-production basis that was similar to that employed by Eastern industry. Not all such experiments worked well; cattle farms of more than 25,000 acres were established in Illinois after the Civil War, but rising land values made them impractical and by the 1880's most of them had been broken up into smaller units. The bonanza wheat farm, however, which in the meantime had appeared in the Dakotas and California, was sometimes highly profitable. The Northern Pacific established such a farm in the midseventies, and it soon became a model for others. The typical bonanza farm, which was often owned by Eastern capitalists, was between 75,000 and 100,000 acres. Most of the tasks were performed by machines operated by seasonal laborers whose economic functions were not unlike those of Eastern factory workers. One such farm of this period used 200 pairs of harrows, 125 seeders, 155 binders and 26 steam threshers. The administration of these farms was entrusted to managers, who were assisted by several superintendents, each of whom was responsible for the work on about 6,000 acres of land.

Such farms were few in number, and their only significance was in the extent to which they paralleled and reflected the major trends in American business enterprise. Like the Eastern factory, the bonanza farm was characterized by the widespread application of machinery, absentee ownership, mass production, specialization, and the employment of landless workers to perform routine jobs.

41. PATTERNS OF AGRARIAN PROTEST

WHILE the commercialization of agriculture made some farmers rich, it made many more poor. Machines and crop specialization had enabled the farmer to increase his production, but they had also placed him at the mercy of an economic system that was run by others. The farmer had become a businessman, but he possessed none of the powers that helped to make business leaders prosperous. Unable to eliminate competition, to control production, or to fix prices, he was victimized by those who could do all these things. The nub of the farmer's problem was competition, for it forced him to deal as an individual with monopolistic corporations whose strength lay in their proven ability to destroy individualism. Under the circumstances, the farmer was no match for the nation's organized business-groups. Farmers did not realize the seriousness of their plight during the post-Civil War boom, but during the period of agricultural distress that lasted from the early seventies until the end of the nineties they repeatedly complained that they were being defrauded by the railroad operators, middlemen, and bankers.

The farmer—particularly in the West—had originally been an enthusiastic advocate of railroad construction; but once the railroads were built, he became their implacable enemy. The railroads not only bribed public officials, granted favors to businessmen, and monopolized grain elevators, but they also charged farmers consistently higher rates than were paid by other shippers. Freight rates in the South and to the west of the Mississippi were invariably higher than in the Northeast, and the farmer was one of the principal sufferers from such railroad abuses as long- and short-haul discriminations, rebates, and pools. In some rural areas rates were so high that farmers on occasion destroyed their produce instead of shipping it; and there were times when freight charges approximated, or even equaled, the amount that the farmer received for the commodities he had sent by train. The farmer's transportation difficulties stemmed almost entirely from the monopolistic position of the railroads. Where there were no competing routes as alternatives, the farmer either had to pay the rates that were asked or not ship his goods.

The farmer was also at a marked disadvantage because of his inability to control the price that he received for his produce. The middlemen who purchased the farmer's commodities frequently combined to fix prices. Moreover, the middleman, because of his knowledge of market conditions and his possession of storage facilities, could buy when prices were low and sell when they were high. The farmer, on the other hand, possessed none of these advantages. He competed with his fellow farmers in both the United States and the rest of the world; he had no means for storing his crop until there was a rise in prices; and he had little or no knowledge concerning the state of the world-wide market for his goods. Wheat prices, for example, were determined by supply and demand in Chicago, New York, and Liverpool, but the farmer on the plains or prairies had no way of knowing of—let alone capitalizing on—the price changes that occurred in the wheat pits of distant cities.

The farmer was exploited by bankers as well as railroad operators and middlemen. Not only were many farmers compelled to mortgage their property, but they were in a position where they had to do it on the banker's terms or not at all. As a consequence, farmers assumed mortgages on which interest rates ranged from 8 to 24 per cent and in some instances were as high as 40 per cent. If they failed to meet these payments, they lost their property and their means of livelihood as well. At the same time the mortgage-ridden farmer could not fail to notice the difference between his way of life and that of the banker. While the farmer toiled from sun-up to sun-down only to end up in debt, the banker appeared to do nothing but sit behind a desk and watch the money accumulate. Throughout the agricultural regions of the West and South, bankers and loan sharks were viewed as hated symbols of all that the farmer was not.

To the other problems confronting the farmer was added his loss of political power. In the early years of the Republic the nation's agrarians had never lacked adequate and intelligent representation in either the state or Federal governments. But in the years after the Civil War, politicians increasingly responded to the demands of the businessman and largely ignored those of the farmer. The decline in agrarian political strength represented far more than a loss in prestige, for the government in aiding the businessman invariably injured the farmer. Repeated tariff increases not only raised the prices of goods that the farmer had to purchase but also tended to reduce the ability of foreign countries to pay for American farm products. The government's postwar monetary policy compelled agrarian debtors who had contracted debts in depreciated currency to repay them with money the purchasing power of which had increased from 15 to 20 per cent. The failure of either state or Federal government to carry out an effective program for the regulation of transportation, marketing, and finance left the farmer at the mercy of those he thought most responsible for his troubles.

Because the farmer was unable to solve his political and economic problems as an independent individual, he was more inclined than at any previous time in American history to co-operate with his fellow agrarians in an effort to improve his lot. The first important farmers' organization established after the Civil War was the National Grange of the Patrons of Husbandry. Formed in 1867 by Oliver Hudson Kelley and some other clerks in the Bureau of Agriculture, the Grange was conceived by its founders as primarily a social organization that would give its members a range of interests wider than that provided by the farm, that would offer members an opportunity to discuss their common problems, and that would furnish them with reliable information on improved agricultural methods. In a declaration in 1874 the Grange stated that its objectives were

to develop a better and higher manhood and womanhood among ourselves. To enhance the comforts and attractions of our homes,

> *and strengthen our attachments to our pursuits. To foster mutual understanding and co-operation. . . . To buy less and produce more, in order to make our farms self-sustaining. To diversify our crops, and crop no more than we can cultivate. . . . To discountenance the credit system, the mortgage system, the fashion system, and every other system tending to prodigality and bankruptcy.*

Women as well as men were admitted to the Patrons of Husbandry, and in addition to monthly meetings, local granges held picnics, sponsored discussion groups, and provided various forms of recreation for their members.

Since the Grange had been established at the height of the agricultural boom, it was not joined by many farmers during its early years. At the end of 1868 there were only ten granges in the United States, and six of these were located in Minnesota; two years later only nine states had granges. But in 1872, 1,105 granges were founded, and with the onset of the depression the number increased rapidly. By 1875 there were approximately 20,000 local granges with a total membership of more than 800,000. Most of the granges of this period were located in either the Middle West or the South.

The Grangers soon realized that many of their aims could be achieved only through political activity, and in the 1870's farmers in such states as Illinois, Minnesota, Kansas, Wisconsin, and Iowa ran and elected several candidates to state legislatures and courts. The principal result of this entrance of the Grangers into politics was the passage of the so-called Granger laws, which provided for the regulation of the railroads in some Midwestern states. The Grange also went into business. It established co-operative warehouses, grain elevators, and creameries, formed insurance companies, and set up factories to manufacture stoves, farm machines, and other necessities. All the Grangers' business ventures, however, proved short-lived. Farmers lacked the necessary experience for the management of such enterprises. Many of the co-operatives overexpanded, and others were unable to meet the competition of established firms in their respective fields.

By 1880 the Grange had little political influence, its attempts at business had failed, and its membership was down to 100,000. In subsequent years the Grange more than regained the ground that it had lost, but the new Grange was a social-welfare organization that entered neither business nor politics. As its political influence declined, however, other farm groups were organized within a number of Southern and Western states to agitate for measures that would give agrarians a larger share of the national income. By the end of the 1880's, most of these state organizations had been swallowed up by either the Northern or Southern Alliance; and in the early nineties the Alliances, in turn, gave way to the Populist party. Although the Populists reflected the widespread agrarian discontent in the United States, they were not able to dislodge the major parties, and William Jennings Bryan's defeat in 1896 marked a turning point in the history of the farmer's protest movement.* With the return of prosperity, farmers tended to forget their earlier grievances and to rejoin the established parties.

It was not until World War I that the farmer again resorted to political action to solve his economic problems. The Farmer's Non-Partisan League, which was organized in 1915 in North Dakota, within a short time attracted the support of farmers in a number of Midwestern states. The league achieved its principal success in North Dakota, where it put into effect most of the proposals that had been advocated by agrarian reformers since the Civil War. Under its direction, North Dakota's legislature adopted laws that provided for state ownership of flour mills and grain elevators, the establishment of a state-owned bank, and state loans to finance home construction and land purchases.

Although the various movements of agrarian protest undoubtedly helped some farmers, they did not solve the farm problem. By 1920 the American farmer was still at the mercy of the business cycle, his ultimate fate was still determined by world supply and demand, and he was still competing blindly with his fellow agrarians at home and abroad.

* See Chapter VIII, pp. 267–79.

CHAPTER VII

NEW AND OLD CULTURAL PATTERNS

DURING the half century that followed the Civil War, intellectual pursuits that had once been open only to the members of the upper classes were made available to an increasing number of individuals drawn from every walk of American life. At the same time the Northeast's one-time monopoly on intellectual activity was broken as creative talents of considerable stature appeared in every section of postwar America. While these developments at times led to vulgarity and commercialism in arts and letters, they also indicated that more and more Americans had both the time and inclination to develop artistic and intellectual interests.

42. THE EXPANSION OF EDUCATIONAL OPPORTUNITIES

DURING the years that followed the Civil War, American schools and colleges underwent a more radical transformation than in any other comparable period in the nation's history. With the multiplication of grammar and high schools and the establishment of state universities, the Jeffersonian dream of education for all at last seemed within realization. Equally significant was the abandonment of the rigid college curriculum of earlier years for a course of study that included not only some "practical" subjects but many fields of learning that the classicists had always insisted lay beyond the pale of formal education. These changes were accompanied by an increased emphasis on the training of specialists. Professional schools raised their standards and adopted newer techniques of instruction, while universities founded graduate schools on the German pattern to prepare their students for a life of scholarship.

Overshadowing all other developments in education was the expansion of public-school facilities. From 1870 to 1910 the number of pupils attending public schools increased from 6,871,522 to 17,813,852; the average number of days in the school session, from 132.2 to 157.5; and the annual per capita expenditure for education from $1.64 to $4.64. These figures reflected gains at more than the elementary level, for in the same years the number of high schools increased from 500 to more than 10,000. The number of kindergartens also increased rapidly. In 1873, St. Louis became the first American city to establish a kindergarten; a quarter of a century later there were approximately 3,000 kindergartens in the United States. During the same period a concerted effort was made to enforce school attendance, and by 1898 thirty-one states and territorial legislatures had adopted compulsory attendance statutes. Although these laws were loosely enforced, their success can be judged in part from the fact that the amount of formal education received by the average American rose from less than four years in 1880 to five years in 1900 and six years in 1914. Equally notable was the decline of national illiteracy from 17 per cent in 1880 to 11 per cent in 1900 and to 7.7 per cent in 1910.

Improvements in pedagogy, however, generally lagged far behind the expansion of school facilities. Corporal punishment, except in a few isolated instances, remained the standard method for enforcing classroom discipline. The curriculum in most elementary schools was limited to reading, writing, and arithmetic. Textbooks, which had to be purchased by the pupils, were generally the same as those that their grandparents had used. McGuffey's readers with their lessons in morality and exhortations to patriotism were an important part of many boys' and girls' grammar school training right down to the end of the century. A premium was placed on the pupil's ability to commit material to memory, and teachers were usually judged according to their success in maintaining classroom discipline and cramming the heads of their charges with an inordinate number of unrelated facts. Teachers were notoriously underpaid; the average annual salary was $189 in 1870 and only $325 in 1900. Under the circumstances few able women and an even smaller percentage of men were attracted to the teaching profession, and those who were, seldom elected to make it a lifetime career.

The traditional mold of public-school education was first broken in the 1880's with the adoption of improved textbooks and the expansion of the curriculum to include work in the sciences and such applied courses as drawing, manual training, cooking, sewing, and commercial subjects. Meanwhile a philosophy of education was emerging to supplant the widely accepted emphasis on "drill and review." Friedrich W. A. Froebel's ideas had already exerted a profound influence on kindergarten teaching, and after 1890, Johann Friedrich Herbart's insistence upon the need for arousing the student's interest attracted considerable attention among leading American educators.* The most important of the innovators, however, was John Dewey, who became head of the School of Education at the University of Chicago. Dewey, whose educational theories were to have a profound influence on the nation's public schools in subsequent years, believed that education was not only a preparation for life but a way of life that could develop the pupil both as a creative individual and an intelligent member of a democratic society. He proposed that the pupil learn by doing, rather than by rote. The classroom was to be an integral and related segment of the larger society.

Quantitative and qualitative gains in public school education were not shared equally by all sections of the country, for the Northeast led the West and South, and cities were everywhere in advance of rural districts. Kindergartens and high schools were concentrated in the cities, as were the better paid teachers, while sparsely settled regions generally had to be content with ungraded grammar schools and less well-trained teachers. Throughout the period under consideration the South lagged far behind other sections. During Reconstruction, Radical state governments provided for free tax-supported schools, and for the first time in its history the South was provided with an elementary school system comparable in organization to that of the North and West. Further impetus was provided to Southern education by such Northern philanthropists as George Peabody, who furnished $3,500,000 for the improvement of the Southern public schools. Building on the foundations erected during the Reconstruction period, the Southern school system advanced rapidly; enrollment doubled during the last quarter of the nineteenth century, and school revenues were steadily increased. On the other hand, as Arthur M. Schlesinger has pointed out in discussing the years 1878–98:

* Both Froebel and Herbart were leading German educators.

*The South throughout the period lagged behind the rest of the nation. Its chief energies were necessarily absorbed in the basic task of abolishing illiteracy, the curse of the white masses as well as of the colored race. In many rural districts schoolhouses were often mere log shacks without windows, desks, maps or blackboards. The school term averaged about a hundred days in 1890 as compared with one hundred and fifty in the Middle West and one hundred and seventy-four in the North Atlantic states. . . . At most, education was regarded in the South as an opportunity for the individual child and not as a civic obligation, for not one of the states of the former Confederacy applied the principle of compulsion to attendance.**

The interest of many adult Americans in their own as well as their children's education was demonstrated by the popular response to the Chautauqua movement. Organized in 1874 on the shores of Lake Chautauqua, New York, and soon imitated by numerous communities in other parts of the country, Chautauqua was in essence an informal summer school for adults. Visitors to Chautauqua had the opportunity to hear prominent speakers on a wide variety of subjects, participate in "Round Tables upon Milton, Temperance, Geology, the American Constitution, the Relations of Science and Religion, and the Doctrine of Rent," and attend the "Cooking School, the Prayer Meeting, the Concert, and the Gymnastic Drill." For those whose thirst for culture was not slaked during the summer months at Chautauqua, there were lectures and concerts throughout the winter in every town and city of consequence. Many cities also had evening schools to teach English to foreigners, and university extension divisions offered numerous courses covering all the important fields of learning. An incalculable but significant educational opportunity for individuals of all ages was provided by the increase in the nation's public library facilities. With funds supplied by the taxpayers and private benefactors, of whom Andrew Carnegie was by far the most generous, urban and rural communities established free circulating libraries that by the end of the century numbered more than nine thousand.

The expansion of facilities for education available to both children and adults was paralleled at the college level by the rise of the state university. With the assistance provided by the Morrill Act, the University of Wisconsin was reorganized in 1866, and new universities were established by Kansas in 1864 and Minnesota and California in 1868. The Morrill Act was also responsible for the founding of state agricultural colleges in Texas and Massachusetts; and the 960,000 acres

* A. M. Schlesinger: *The Rise of the City, 1878–1898* (New York: The Macmillan Company, 1933), pp. 165–6.

provided under its terms along with a gift of $500,000 from Ezra Cornell, made possible the opening of Cornell University in 1868. Although the new state universities conducted courses in the liberal arts, they sought to place their greatest initial emphasis on training in agriculture and engineering. The establishment of publicly supported institutions of higher learning provided new opportunities for women as well as men, for the state universities either admitted women from the outset or became coeducational soon after their founding.

Coeducational colleges never enjoyed the same popularity in other sections as in the West; but numerous women's colleges were established in the East during these years. Within a decade after Appomattox, Vassar, Smith, and Wellesley opened their doors to students, to be followed by Bryn Mawr and Mount Holyoke shortly thereafter. Meanwhile Harvard, Columbia, and Tulane—among others—had formed separate, but allied, women's colleges. By the end of the century, 80 per cent of the nation's universities and professional schools admitted female students.

43. UNIVERSITIES AND THE HIGHER LEARNING

THE LEAD in the movement to reorganize the liberal arts curriculum was taken by the privately endowed colleges of the Northeast. Reforms were long overdue. In 1865, most colleges were still ostensibly organized for the preparation of students for the ministry. Heavy emphasis was placed on instruction in mathematics, Greek, and Latin, while almost no work was given in modern languages, economics, politics, and government. Libraries and laboratory facilities were unbelievably inadequate; sectarian colleges refused to hire instructors of another denomination; and professors were compelled to teach courses in as many as four or five different fields of learning. Little attempt was made to stimulate intellectual curiosity, and academic attainment was too often confused with the student's ability to parrot masses of undigested information.

President Charles W. Eliot of Harvard deserves the principal credit for the renovation of collegiate instruction after the Civil War. Under his direction Harvard College raised its entrance requirements and abandoned its rigid program of required courses for an elective system that enabled the student to exercise considerable discretion in the determination of his course of study. Undergraduates, who were granted more personal freedom than had been customary in the past, were placed under the administration of a dean of students. Most important of all, the curriculum was expanded to include courses in physics, international law, political economy, fine arts, music, and advanced work in modern languages. Many of the changes introduced by Eliot at Harvard were soon adopted by other leading colleges under the direction of such able educators and executives as James McCosh of Princeton, James B. Angell of Michigan, Andrew D. White of Cornell, and Frederick A. P. Barnard of Columbia.

Through President Eliot's influence Harvard also became the first university to sponsor reforms in medical and legal education. In the past, graduates of Harvard's medical school, which was not inferior to others at that time, were sometimes appallingly ignorant and on occasion a menace to the lives of their patients. At Eliot's insistence, the academic year was lengthened, and students were required to concentrate on laboratory work and take written examinations, which had not been required in the past, because—in the words of the school's director—"a majority of the students cannot write well enough." In the law school the case system was substituted for the reading of the classic texts. Under the new method of instruction Harvard law students were compelled to learn the law by examining its actual operation rather than by memorizing accounts by authorities of how the law presumably operated. Within a short time Harvard's innovations had become commonplace in other leading medical and law schools.

Other forms of professional training kept pace with the advances in the medical and law schools. Technical institutes improved their offerings, and engineering education was broken down into its component parts. Normal schools increased in number, raised their requirements, and eventually developed into seedbeds of educational philosophy. Several universities established schools of architecture, and following the turn of the century, university business schools began to gain an academic respectability that they had not previously enjoyed. A noteworthy development in specialized education of a somewhat different character was the appearance in the South of several training schools for Negroes. Most prominent of these were the Hampton Normal and Agricultural Institute and the Tuskegee Institute, which was founded by Booker T. Washington, a graduate of Hampton. Both institutions provided the South with teachers, proficient farmers, and skilled craftsmen.

Although Harvard and Yale had reorganized their programs of graduate study in the early 1870's, Johns Hopkins, which was founded in 1876, soon became the most notable center of graduate studies in America. Daniel Coit Gilman, Johns Hopkins' first president, used the funds at his disposal, not to construct buildings and create a collegiate atmosphere shrouded in ivy, but to purchase books and assemble an outstanding faculty. Most of the members of the new staff had studied in Germany, and no attempt was made to conceal the fact that Johns Hopkins was patterned after German universities. Specialization was encouraged, and the "scientific" approach to research was held up as the ideal of scholarship. Within less than a decade, earnest young men —Woodrow Wilson among them—armed with Doctor of Philosophy degrees from Johns Hopkins, had gone forth to spread the new gospel among the other universities and colleges of the land. They were aided in this work by numerous other Americans who had done graduate work in Germany.* The impact upon American higher learning of the German approach to scholarship cannot be overemphasized. All the major universities soon accepted Johns Hopkins or such famed German institutions as Heidelberg, Berlin, Jena, and Leipzig as their models. There was little room left for the dilettante or the man of broad interests, for the pursuit of knowledge was judged so arduous a business that only the specialist could hope to master even a segment of his particular field.

German university standards were not the only significant European contribution to American thought after the Civil War, for the evolutionary theories of Charles Darwin were an even more potent force in shaping the course of American intellectual history during these years. Darwin's *The Origin of Species,* published in 1859, received little popular attention in America. But after 1865 John Fiske began to popularize Darwin's ideas in countless lectures and magazine articles, while the books of Herbert Spencer, one of Darwin's leading supporters in England, had a remarkably large sale in this country. In the decade following 1872, John Tyndall, Spencer, and Thomas Huxley visited America to expound the new theories. The clergy generally led the opposition, and university faculties soon split into two warring camps. The conflict lasted approximately two decades; but when the smoke of the battle finally lifted, it was found that the evolutionists had taken all but a few isolated and relatively unimportant academic outposts.

These new scientific theories, combined with the painstaking techniques taught by the German universities, were a great stimulus to American scientists. Americans contributed little to the world's knowledge of either chemistry or pure mathematics, but their accomplishments in astronomy, physics, and geology were notable. Edward C. Pickering of Harvard catalogued forty thousand stars and employed photography in unprecedented fashion to enlarge man's knowledge of the heavens. In physics no name ranked higher than that of J. Willard Gibbs of Yale, who made far-reaching discoveries in thermodynamics and was undoubtedly the outstanding American scientist of his day. Henry Adams thought Gibbs the "greatest of Americans," and modern scientists have made it clear that the relativity theory was made possible in part by his findings. Clarence King and Major J. W. Powell,

* In the 1880's there were more than two thousand American students enrolled in German universities.

who succeeded King as head of the United States geological survey, both won fame for their geological work in the West, while O. C. Marsh and E. D. Cope did important work in paleontology and T. C. Chamberlin made pioneer studies in the theory of glaciation.

The accomplishments of the natural scientists in their studies of the physical universe convinced many other scholars that the scientific method would prove equally fruitful in the study of man. In the past little attempt had been made to understand the workings of the human mind, and it was generally believed that the mind was a more or less static entity that distinguished human beings from other creatures. But under the influence of Darwinism, psychologists for the first time came to view the mind as a means by which the human organism adjusted to its environment. At the same time, as psychologists increasingly used laboratory techniques to test their hypotheses, psychology was transformed into a natural science. G. Stanley Hall, James M. Baldwin, Edward L. Thorndike, and William James all made notable contributions to the new science of psychology, and of these James was easily preeminent.

The new interest in science also led to a critical re-examination of the philosophical concepts of the antebellum period. Because Darwin's changing and evolving world stood in sharp contrast to the transcendentalists' world of absolutes and certainties, philosophers were forced either to reaffirm or to recast their theories. William T. Harris, who founded the St. Louis school of philosophy in 1867, avoided rather than solved the problem by rejecting Darwinism out of hand and remaining a Hegelian idealist. Others, while opposing idealism, sought to reconcile the "first and fundamental truths" of orthodox religion with the new science by relying on the "common-sense" approach of the Scottish realists. Still others—notably Charles Peirce, William James, and John Dewey—accepted the challenge posed by science and used it as a point of departure for the development of a philosophy of pragmatism.

For the moral idealism of the transcendentalists, the pragmatists substituted the concept of a world of evolving institutions and ideas. Life was viewed as an unending series of choices between alternatives, and the validity of each choice was measured by the consequences. Every general statement was a hypothesis that could be tested only by future experience, which in turn could only be corroborated by future experience. This was an infinite process that substituted the scientific method for the finality of either mysticism or authoritarianism. It required that man develop the "laboratory habit of mind," that he recognize that there is no "last analysis," and that he judge all ideas by their results.

Pragmatism was pluralistic, experimental, and individualistic. It gave the individual a method, but it did not give him a set of ready-made answers. Moreover, it warned him that no answer was final, for, as

James said: "What meets expediently all the experience in sight won't necessarily meet all farther experiences equally satisfactorily." Man did not know, he believed; and all his beliefs could be validated or invalidated only by their consequences.

> *True ideas* [William James wrote] *are those that we can assimilate, validate, corroborate, and verify. False ideas are those that we cannot.* . . . The truth of an idea is not a stagnant property inherent in it. Truth *happens* to an idea. It *becomes* true, is *made* true by events. Its verity *is* in fact an event, a process, the process namely of its verifying itself, its veri*fication.* Its validity is the process of its valid*ation.*

Pragmatism was not a doctrine of practical expediency, but a method for ascertaining truth by examining results instead of first causes. Peirce applied this method to the realm of ideas rather than to the world of every day affairs, and James once said that he advanced pragmatism as "a method of settling metaphysical disputes that might otherwise be interminable." But pragmatism could also be used as an instrument for reform, and under Dewey's influence it became a "method of understanding and rectifying specific social ills." Thus every institution became a means that could be judged by its ends; and if its ends failed to meet the needs of society, this fact could be recognized, and the institution could be altered accordingly. Using this approach, Dewey was able to employ pragmatism (or what he called instrumentalism) as the basis for fundamental reforms in education and in many other areas of human activity.

German scholarship and evolutionary theory, as advanced by Darwin and popularized by Spencer, had a profound effect on the social sciences. Historians such as James Ford Rhodes, J. B. McMaster, and Edward Channing turned out multivolume works that were crammed with "objective" facts, while graduate students dug deep to produce heavily documented monographs on a variety of specialized subjects. On the other hand, several scholars attempted to find laws for history as Darwin had done for natural science. Henry Adams sought to discover a universal law of history in the laws of thermodynamics; Frederick Jackson Turner sought the key to American history in the influence of the frontier; and Charles A. Beard looked for a similar key in the development of the American economy. Among the sociologists William Graham Sumner was an enthusiastic disciple of Darwin and Spencer. To Sumner all social developments could be explained by natural laws, and there were few social problems that could not be explained by the magic formula of the "survival of the fittest." Economists such as Thorstein Veblen, Wesley C. Mitchell, and John R. Commons, refusing to rehash the timeworn theories of the classical economists, directed their energies toward an analysis of the operation and evolution of the contemporary economic system. The political scientists also shifted their emphasis by concentrating more upon the actual workings of government and less on theories of how it should work.

Between the Civil War and World War I, America continued to be heavily influenced by European ideas and scholarship. But Americans had in turn influenced European thought and had made major contributions to the general store of knowledge; the United States was no longer an intellectual colony of Europe.

44. THE CHURCH IN RURAL AND URBAN AMERICA

FEW institutions found it more difficult to adjust their policies and principles to the sweeping economic and social changes of the post-Civil War period than the churches. The rise of industry and an industrial proletariat, the growth of cities, the widespread popularity of science, and the extent of material progress presented problems that in many respects were unprecedented in scope and complexity. Despite the fundamental nature of these developments, their effect was largely confined to urban areas, and there was little manifestation of their impact on religious life in the rural regions of the country. Many Americans continued to attend church as regularly as they had in the past. Many still believed in a literal interpretation of the Bible. But even in the backcountry sections of the South and Middle West, where traditional religious practices and beliefs were most strongly entrenched, some observers noted a diminution of the old-time zeal, and in the cities it was everywhere apparent that the position of the church was undergoing a radical transformation.

Among the better-educated groups in American religious circles nothing was more disruptive than the advent of the Darwinian theory of evolution. The immediate assumption of most religious leaders was that if Darwin was right the Bible had to be wrong. Consequently, during the early stages of what proved to be a prolonged debate, clergymen were almost unanimous in rejecting evolution out of hand as atheistic materialism. But Darwinism could not be talked out of existence, and an increasing number of clergymen thought it merited something beyond indignant condemnation. By the 1880's, they were making a genuine effort to come to terms with the once-despised theory. Some ministers maintained that science and religion were distinct, and that developments in one had no effect upon the other; others argued that evolution complemented rather than controverted the accepted religious belief in the development of man. By the end of the decade a workable thesis for reconciling the Bible and *The Origin of Species* had been made by such outstanding ministers as Henry Ward Beecher, Washington Gladden, and Lyman Abbott. Beecher told his Brooklyn congregation that evolution was the "deciphering of God's thought as revealed in the structure of the world;" Lyman Abbott wrote that "God is not merely a 'Great First Cause,' but the one Great Cause from whom all forms of nature and of life continuously proceed." In short, evolution, like everything else, provided evidence of the infinite wisdom of the Divinity.

As disturbing to many Americans as the question of the relation of Darwinism to religion were the problems raised by the development of what came to be known as higher criticism—an attempt, originally undertaken in Germany, to ascertain the historical validity of the Bible by subjecting it to scholarly examination. Students in Europe and America demonstrated that the Bible contained factual errors, and some of their discoveries were incorporated in a revised version of the King James Bible that appeared in 1881 and 1885 and was primarily designed to "adapt the King James version to the present state of the English language without changing the idiom and vocabulary." The higher criticism was vigorously opposed by fundamentalists of all varieties, and more than one denomination was torn by bitter controversy over the interpretation of the Bible as a whole or the exact meaning of specific passages within it. Despite the vehemence with which they defended their position, the upholders of the orthodox view were generally compelled to retreat as an increasing number of Americans—particularly in the urban centers—came to view Holy Writ less as an infallible record of a past era and more as a moral guide and literary masterpiece.

Economic as well as intellectual change had a profound effect upon American religion in the postwar years. During the Gilded Age some church members accumulated huge fortunes, and many of these either directly or indirectly shaped the policies and outlook of most of the nation's leading religious groups. Virtually every important industrialist of the period, with the exception of Andrew Carnegie, took an active part in church affairs; and even Carnegie, though presumably an agnostic, gave millions of dollars for the purchase of church organs. Successful businessmen not only donated large sums of money to religious institutions, but they increasingly occupied important lay positions within church organizations. As wealthy groups rose to prominence in church life, many ministers appeared to become more conservative in their outlook, church life grew more "respectable" than in the past, new and more costly church buildings were erected, and in the cities there was a steady emigration of church parishes from slum areas to middle- and upper-class neighborhoods. Of the major religious groups in the United States, the Roman Catholics alone remained relatively unaffected by these developments.

As churches gained in wealth and respectability, they frequently lost much of their former appeal for those Americans who had been accustomed to a more vigorous and emotional form of religious experience. To fill the needs of those who desired a somewhat more flamboyant religion than that provided by the wealthier denominations, there arose a number of new sects. They found their greatest following in the rural areas, where the tradition of the old-time religion remained strongest. Of these, the largest was probably the Church of the Nazarene, which was formed in 1894 with the union of eight smaller groups. In the cities, the new faiths were strongly tinged with mysticism. Typical of such creeds was Theosophy, which was founded in 1875 by Helena P. Blavatsky, a Russian noblewoman who had migrated to New York. Although Madame Blavatsky left the United States in 1878, a small band of Theosophists continued to preach her doctrine of the universal brotherhood of man and to examine the "hidden mysteries of nature."

Of the many new sects organized during this period, Christian Science, or Church of Christ, Scientist, was in many respects the most significant and unusual. Founded by Mrs. Mary Baker Eddy in the midseventies following treatments she received for a nervous disease from a mental healer, the Christian Science church taught that evil, sickness, sin, and death were products of the mind. Disease was a mental creation and would be eliminated as soon as the human mind was brought into harmony with the Eternal Mind. After incorporating her religious views in *Science and Health,* which appeared in 1875, Mrs. Eddy began the teaching of Christian Science to a small group of workers in Lynn, Massachusetts. When she met with only indifferent success, she transferred her activities to Boston in 1882. In the years that followed, the Christian Science Church grew rapidly, and by 1900 it had an estimated membership of 35,000. Its principal appeal was to the well-to-do among city dwellers. When Mrs. Eddy died in 1910, the Christian Scientists possessed numerous church buildings, an outstanding newspaper—the *Christian Science Monitor,* published in Boston—and a secure position among the diverse religious creeds of the United States.

Further evidence of the inability of the traditional churches to satisfy the spiritual needs of the masses was provided by the widespread popularity of evangelism during this period. Huge audiences flocked to hear the noted agnostic Robert Ingersoll attack organized religion; but far greater throngs were attracted by Dwight L. Moody's revivals. A man of commanding presence and considerable oratorical powers, Moody preached thunderous sermons that had an undoubted emotional impact upon his listeners. An additional feature of a Moody revival was the singing of Ira D. Sankey, who accompanied Moody on all his principal tours. Following the turn of the century, the leading evangelist was William A. ("Billy") Sunday, an ex-baseball player, who harangued his audiences with all the finesse of a circus barker at a sideshow. Moody and Sunday were merely the most famous of a large band of revivalists whose fiery sermons provided a high point in religious experience for countless Americans.

The increasing wealth of the established Protestant sects tended to alienate many workingmen who had formerly been church members. Not only did laborers often feel ill at ease in the rich surroundings of many of the more elaborate churches whose pews were filled with well dressed families from the upper and middle classes, but they also realized that more often than not Protestant clerics were inclined to side with employers rather than workers during industrial disputes. During the numerous strikes of the period, the workers found few defenders among the clergymen. Henry Ward Beecher probably spoke for many—though certainly not all—of his fellow ministers in 1877, when he said: "God has intended the great to be great and the little to be little. . . . I do not say that a dollar a day is enough to support a workingman. But it is enough to support a man! Not enough to support a man and five children if a man insists on smoking and drinking beer. . . . But the man who cannot live on bread and water is not fit to live."

Not all members of the clergy shared Beecher's views on current economic questions, however; an increasing number began to preach either the Social Gospel or Christian Socialism. Advocates of the Social Gospel, among whom Josiah Strong and Washington Gladden were outstanding, maintained that the problems created by the rise of industrial capitalism could only be solved by the universal application of the teachings of Jesus. Gladden in repeated volumes and sermons defended labor's right to organize and proposed that employer-employee strife be eliminated by an "industrial partnership" that would enable workingmen to receive "a fixed share" of industry's profits. In contrast to the reforms of the Social Gospel, the Christian Socialists proposed a collective society. Unlike the collectivists of Marxist persuasion, the Christian Socialists did not think that their ideal should be achieved by the class struggle, but rather by the observance of the law of love and the adoption of the precepts of Christ. The Christian Socialists elicited little support outside their own immediate circles; and Walter Rauschenbusch, who was one of the movement's staunchest supporters, later wrote: "We were few and we shouted in the wilderness."

The advocates of Social Christianity did not confine their activities to writing and talking, for in numerous instances they attempted to practice what they preached. As early as 1872, Jesse H. Jones, a Congregational minister in Massachusetts, organized the Christian Labor Union and agitated for both co-operatives and the eight-hour day. Washington Gladden sought to apply his labor theories as a strike mediator and entered local politics to combat municipal corruption. W. D. P. Bliss, an Episcopal clergyman of Boston, joined the Knights of Labor and became a candidate for lieutenant governor of Massachusetts on a labor ticket.

Although there is little evidence that their parishioners followed the examples set by such clergymen, the immense popularity of *In His Steps*, a novel by the Reverend Charles Sheldon, seems to indicate that a large number of people wished to hear their message. Published in 1897 and describing a community in which all church members agreed to live just as Jesus would presumably have done under similar circumstances, *In His Steps* became an immediate best seller, and by 1925, when it was still going strong, its sales in the United States and Great Britain had exceeded twenty million copies.

While advocates of Social Christianity sought to improve the lot of the poor by reforming the economic system, other church leaders in the cities attempted to aid the same groups through the development of institutional churches that offered educational opportunities, recreational facilities, and a measure of financial assistance to underprivileged city dwellers. The Grace Episcopal Church in New York in 1868 became the first church to provide such features. Four years later, the First Congregational Church of Elmira, New York, erected a building that contained a gymnasium, lecture rooms, and a library. In Philadelphia, Russell Conwell's Baptist Temple had social clubs, sewing classes, a gymnasium, reading rooms, and a night school that eventually became Temple University. Beyond question, the introduction of such facilities saved many urban churches from extinction during this period. The St. George's Episcopal Church of New York was an outstanding example. When it became an institutional church in 1882, it had seventy-five members; fifteen years later its membership exceeded four thousand.

Despite the manifold activities of the institutional churches, their accomplishments could not rival those of the Salvation Army. Some concept of the work of General Booth's organization in this period has been provided by Professor William W. Sweet:

> *In 1910 it was maintaining 896 corps with 2,875 officers and employees; it was conducting 75 workingmen's hotels, 4 women's hotels, 20 food depots, 107 industrial homes, 3 farm colonies, 20 employment bureaus, 107 second-hand stores, 4 children's homes, 4 day nurseries and 23 slum settlements. In that year 309,591 persons were given temporary relief, 3,972 mothers and 23,373 children were given summer outings, millions of pounds of ice and coal were distributed free among the poor, while employment was found for 65,124 men and 5,355 women.**

Of the major religious groups in the United States, only the Roman Catholics experienced comparatively little difficulty in meeting the problems created by the rise of industry and the city. Its long tradition

* William Warren Sweet: *The Story of Religion in America* (New York: Harper & Brothers, 1930), p. 526.

of religious work among the poor put the Catholic Church in an excellent position to take advantage of the very conditions that had proved so perplexing to many of the Protestant denominations. The Catholic Church, moreover, was fortunate during most of these years in that its leadership in America was entrusted to such an able and far-seeing religious leader as James Cardinal Gibbons. Gibbons was appointed Archbishop of Baltimore in 1877, and in 1886 he became the second American Cardinal. Thoroughly American in his outlook, he repeatedly urged the rapid assimilation of immigrants and upheld the separation of church and state. He was a life-long friend of labor and was instrumental in preventing papal condemnation of the Knights of Labor. A man of broad humanitarian instincts, he did all within his power to prevent the Catholic Church from "being represented as the friend of the powerful rich and the enemy of the helpless poor."

The membership of the Catholic Church in America increased rapidly throughout the entire period between the Civil War and World War I. The Catholic population of the United States, which was more than 6,000,000 in 1880, rose to approximately 12,000,000 in 1900 and to more than 16,000,000 in 1910. Almost half of this increase was accounted for by immigration; nearly 5,000,000 immigrants became members of Catholic parishes in the United States during the three decades following 1880. The mounting tide of Catholic immigration was largely responsible for the revival of antiforeign sentiment, which found expression in the organization of the American Protective Association. The A.P.A., founded in 1887 by H. F. Bowers, an Iowa lawyer, was blatantly anti-Catholic. It drew its chief support from the rural areas of the Middle West, where it appealed not only to anti-Catholic and antiforeign feeling but also to the traditional suspicion of the city. Gaining many of its adherents through the use of forged documents that purported to show the allegiance of American Catholics to Rome rather than Washington, it compelled all its members to swear to do whatever they could to "strike the shackles and chains of blind obedience to the Roman Catholic Church from the hampered and bound consciences of a priest-ridden and church-oppressed people." The A.P.A. entered politics and enjoyed some success in local and state elections. By 1894 it had approximately one million members. But it had reached the high point of its influence, and in the campaign of 1896 most Americans forgot their anti-Catholicism in the heated arguments over Bryan and free silver.

Organized opposition to Catholicism was not the only form of religious intolerance during this period, for members of almost every important Protestant group were at one time or another attacked for holding allegedly unorthodox views. In 1879 the Southern Baptist Seminary dismissed Professor C. H. Toy for his use of scientific methods in the study of the Old Testament, and three years later Dr. E. P. Gould, a

Baptist at the Newton Theological Institution in Massachusetts, was compelled to resign under somewhat similar circumstances. The Congregationalists at the Andover Theological Seminary in Massachusetts tried five faculty members for advanced ideas in 1886 and found one of them guilty, and the Episcopalians accused the Reverend R. Heber Newton of New York of heresy. Methodist opinion was responsible for the dismissal of the geologist Alexander Winchell from Vanderbilt University in 1878. During the 1890's, several prominent Presbyterians were also charged with unorthodoxy. Professors Charles A. Briggs and A. C. McGiffert, two distinguished members of the faculty of Union Theological Seminary, had to give up their positions because the Presbyterian General Assembly accused them of heresy. Similar action was taken by the General Assembly against Professor Henry Preserved Smith of Lane Theological Seminary, who was tried and found guilty.

Despite the bitterness displayed in these and similar cases, they generally represented the rear-guard actions of a type of orthodoxy that was frequently in full retreat. While some might complain that American religion had lost much of its one-time zeal, this fact had to be set against the growth of humanitarianism and a social conscience among the churches, the broadening of their interests, their partial acceptance of the scientific point of view, and the perceptible—although irregular—increase in religious toleration.

45. NEWSPAPERS FOR THE MASSES

DURING the last third of the nineteenth century there was a marked growth in the number of newspapers in the United States. New papers appeared with each new settlement in the West, and the economic and educational expansion of the South and Northeast provided the impetus for the founding of new journals and the expansion of old ones in the more settled regions. During the 1870's the number of papers doubled to reach almost seven thousand, and by 1890 there were more than twelve thousand newspapers in the United States. The multiplication and diffusion of newspapers were considerably facilitated by the press associations. The telegraphic reports of both the Associated Press and the United Press provided many of the smaller papers in the more remote sections of the country with almost as wide a range of news as that of the big city dailies.

The change in the character of the American press was as remarkable as its growth. By 1879, Horace Greeley, Henry J. Raymond, James Gordon Bennett, Samuel Bowles, and William Cullen Bryant were all dead, and the "personal" journalism of an earlier day had died with them. Their successors—notably, Charles A. Dana of the *Sun*, Whitelaw Reid of the *Tribune,* James Gordon Bennett, Jr. of the *Herald,* and Henry Watterson of the *Louisville Courier-Journal*—were in many respects as colorful and brilliant as the leading members of the preceding generation of journalists; but their papers were read more for their accurate and colorful news accounts rather than for the views of their editors. During the Civil War, an editor's opinion had become relatively unimportant when compared to the latest report from the front, and after the war the most successful papers were those that provided broad coverage of both the significant and insignificant news of the day. Equally important was the development of some degree of objectivity in the political reporting of some of the leading journals.

The appeal of the new journalism lay not only in its accurate and up-to-the-minute reporting but also in its attempts to amuse as well as inform the reader. A premium was placed on human-interest stories; as a city editor told a young reporter: "when a dog bites a man, that is not news; but when a man bites a dog that is news." Many papers contained humorous columns, and poetry and short stories were not uncommon features. A concerted effort was also made to brighten the appearance of papers. The New York *Evening Telegram* set the pattern for many others when in 1867 it began to use cartoons regularly. The development of stereotyped plates, which made possible the use of double-column cuts for news illustrations and advertisements, tended to break the monotony of page after page of single columns of print. Another technical advance was provided by the web-perfecting press, which printed both sides of the page as it was fed into the press on a continuous roll.

The relative decline in the importance of the editorial page was accompanied by a corresponding decrease in the amount of space which most papers allotted to national politics. After the war many editors announced that their journals would not continue to serve as the organs for a political party or any other special interest. Nevertheless, few papers ever bolted the party, and both politicians and advertisers frequently exerted considerable influence on a paper's policies. Professor Allan Nevins has written of the 1870's: "Tweed kept dozens of New York journalists on his payroll, and by his menaces awed even Bryant's *Evening Post;* the news columns of the very best papers could be purchased or colored by big advertisers; and the *Independent* . . . , for all its religious character, placed advertisements in its critical columns for a dollar a line and accepted a huge bribe from the firm of Jay Cooke for promoting the sale of Northern Pacific bonds by editorial puffs and special articles." *

Throughout the 1870's the most popular papers were those that were

* Allan Nevins: *The Emergence of Modern America, 1865–1878* (New York: The Macmillan Company, 1927), p. 242.

written in sprightly prose and that made a special point of reporting spectacular and unusual events. Typical was Charles Dana's New York *Sun,* which was ably and wittily written and devoted a considerable amount of space to murders, "society" news, and scandals. Even more enterprising was the *Herald,* which under the direction of the younger Bennett often made as well as reported the news. It was Stanley, a *Herald* reporter, who found Dr. Livingstone in darkest Africa, and on other occasions the *Herald* sponsored balloon flights, a Polar expedition, and archeological projects. In one of the most famous stunts of American journalism the *Herald* on November 9, 1875, covered its entire first page with an apochryphal account of the havoc and death caused by the wild animals that had escaped from the city zoo. It was only in the last paragraph that the reader learned that the "entire story given above is pure fabrication."

The new journalistic techniques that transformed the American press in the years following the Civil War reached their climax and fruition with the advent of Joseph Pulitzer and "yellow" journalism. Many other newspapermen had recognized the connection between sensationalism and circulation, but it remained for Pulitzer to realize that the growth of cities and the expansion of educational opportunities called for a new kind of newspaper. His appeal was to the semiliterate urban masses, for whom he provided a paper that was cheap, accurate, vivid, and simple.

Pulitzer, who was born in Hungary, migrated to the United States at the age of seventeen in time to serve nine months in the Union army during the Civil War. After the war he settled in St. Louis, where he obtained a job as a reporter on the German-language *Westliche Post.* He entered politics and obtained enough money in 1878 to purchase the *St. Louis Dispatch,* which he combined with the *Post.* Under his able direction the *Post-Dispatch* soon became St. Louis's leading evening paper. In 1883 he moved to New York and bought the moribund *World.* Under Pulitzer's management the *World* quickly became noted for its sensational, but honest reporting; its pictures, cartoons, and comic strips; and its editorial crusades, which were backed by exposures in its news columns. Its price was dropped to two cents, and in less than four years Pulitzer had built the *World* into a paper with a larger circulation than that of any other journal in the country. Pulitzer was responsible for two important innovations in American journalism—mass appeal and crusading zeal. To make sure that his paper would attract readers he filled it with woodcuts, placed enormous cartoons on the first page, gave extensive coverage to crime and murders with accompanying diagrams and an "X" to show where the body was found, and introduced the comic strip.

Pulitzer was never content with mere sensationalism; under his management the *World* espoused numerous reforms and quickly gained a well-deserved reputation as a crusading paper. When he took over the control of the *World,* he announced that it would be a paper that was "dedicated to the cause of the people rather than [to] that of purse-potentates" and that it would "expose all fraud and sham, fight all public evils and abuses" and "battle for the people with earnest sincerity." Pulitzer always strove to live up to this pledge, and the *World* at various times fought Tammany Hall, exposed railroad graft, took the lead in the attack against the trusts, opposed the machinations of the finance capitalists, and courageously supported countless other causes that its publisher considered worthwhile. Many of these crusades, it is true, were obviously undertaken to boost circulation; nevertheless, there were few major reforms of the period that did not have the unstinted support of the news and editorial columns of Pulitzer's *World.*

Pulitzer's formula proved so profitable that it soon had many imitators. Of these, none was more successful that William Randolph Hearst, who first applied Pulitzer's techniques to the San Francisco *Examiner.* In 1895, Hearst invaded Pulitzer's domain by purchasing the New York *Morning Journal.* He immediately began a circulation war with the *World* and cut the price of the *Journal* to one cent. By offering fabulous salaries to reporters, he was able to assemble one of the most brilliant staffs in American newspaper history. Stephen Crane worked for a time as a Hearst reporter, and Homer Davenport became the *Journal* cartoonist. Richard Harding Davis reported the coronation of the Tsar in Russia for the *Journal,* and Mark Twain kept its readers informed on Queen Victoria's golden jubilee in London. Beyond a doubt, Hearst, like Pulitzer, reached the masses; but, unlike his preceptor, Hearst soon gave up all but the pretense of being a crusading journalist.

The success of yellow journalism was revealed by the circulation figures of the *World* and the *Journal.* With the impetus provided by the approach of the Spanish-American War, the daily circulation of each paper exceeded 1,000,000, and during the war the *Journal* topped 1,500,000 with the *World* right behind it. Although these figures were far in excess of those for any other papers, many publishers nevertheless refused to employ the sensational techniques of either Hearst or Pulitzer. When Adolph Ochs took over the management of the *New York Times* in 1896, he pointedly announced that it would be a paper that would not soil the breakfast table. The *Christian Science Monitor,* founded by the Christian Science Church in 1908, shunned crime and disaster news and conscientiously avoided the methods of the yellow press. Equally opposed to the use of spectacular techniques in the dissemination of news were such papers as the New York *Evening Post* and the Boston *Transcript,* both of which refused to abandon their established ways in an effort to gain new readers among the masses.

As the circulation of the large urban dailies reached unprecedented figures, many of them became huge enterprises that in all essential features were similar to the large corporations of industry and transportation. Several papers were worth more than a million dollars, and at least one was valued at approximately ten million. Despite important exceptions, the increasing financial success of the larger papers often resulted in a corresponding growth of a conservative outlook in their editorial columns. This view was succinctly expressed by Arthur Brisbane, a Hearst employee: "Journalistic success brings money. The editor has become a money man. 'Where your treasure is, there your heart will be also.'" As journalism became more and more a big business, there was also a noticeable development toward standardization. The press services supplied the same news to all their customers, and syndicates furnished many papers with the same cartoons, comic strips, photographs, and feature stories. Equally striking evidence of the trend toward standardization was the formation of several newspaper chains that had papers in several cities under a single management. By 1912, Hearst, in addition to the San Francisco *Examiner* and the New York *Journal*, owned the Chicago *American*, Chicago *Examiner*, Boston *American*, Atlanta *Georgian*, and Los Angeles *Examiner*. In the same year Frank A. Munsey controlled papers in five Eastern cities, and by 1908 there were some twenty papers in the Scripps-McRae chain.

46. THE DEVELOPMENT OF THE POPULAR MAGAZINE

THE TRANSFORMATION of the American magazine proceeded at a more leisurely pace than did the nation's newspapers. In the decade and a half after Appomattox, the leading American monthlies were *Harper's*, the *Atlantic*, and *Scribner's Monthly* (which became the *Century* in 1881);* and the most influential weekly was the *Nation*, which was edited throughout these years by E. L. Godkin. The *Nation* concentrated on the discussion and interpretation of current events, and the *Independent* handled much the same material from a religious standpoint, but the monthly periodicals were essentially literary magazines. The *Atlantic*, *Harper's*, and *Scribner's* differed in several respects from the magazines of the antebellum period. They concentrated on American rather than English authors, and their contributors included writers from every section of the country. They supported various nonradical reforms such as civil service, tenement-house improvement, and the establishment of kindergartens. At the same time, under the leadership of *Scribner's* a successful effort was made to add

* In 1887 *Scribner's Magazine* began publication.

to the attractiveness of their appearance by the use of numerous illustrations, a finer grade of paper, and new type forms.

Despite innovations and improvements, these monthlies made little appeal to the general reading public. Their articles seldom dealt with subjects that were of immediate importance to the average American, and they made no effort to apply mass-production methods to the manufacture and distribution of their product. While the newspapers were altering both their policies and material to fit the tastes of an industrial, urbanized America, the editors of *Harper's*, *Scribner's*, and the *Atlantic* continued to publish magazines designed for a relatively small audience. Their circulation was confined to gentlemen-scholars and a small portion of the upper middle-class, and they made little or no attempt to reach a wider public.

The general indifference of the older monthlies to current events was partially responsible for the establishment after 1885 of a number of magazines that concentrated exclusively upon news. *Public Opinion* (1886), *Current Literature* (1888), and the *Literary Digest* (1890) sought to treat the news with a perspective that was missing in the daily press; the *Forum* (1886) and the *Arena* (1889) were crusading magazines that filled their pages with exposures and demands for reform. None of these magazines, however, reached the masses in any numbers, and it remained for Edward W. Bok, a Dutch immigrant, to apply some of the lessons of yellow journalism to periodical publishing. Bok became editor of the *Ladies' Home Journal* in 1889 and immediately set out to broaden its appeal. Like Pulitzer, he espoused various reforms, but for understandable reasons he placed his greatest emphasis on demands for women's rights. Much of the magazine's fiction was written by well-known authors. Nor did Bok overlook the use of sensational techniques; on one occasion he published an issue written entirely by the daughters of famous men. A special column provided advice to young girls in love, and considerable attention was always given to the everyday housekeeping problems encountered by women. By 1892, the *Ladies' Home Journal* had a monthly circulation of 700,000, and was far ahead of its nearest rival.*

Bok's methods were taken over and further developed by Frank A. Munsey, a businessman who also happened to be a newspaper and magazine publisher. He founded *Munsey's Weekly* in 1889 and shortly changed it to a monthly. From the outset Munsey employed the practices of big business to magazine publication. Like the industrial leaders, Munsey realized that the largest profits lay in mass production and a small return on each item sold. In 1893 he lowered the price of *Munsey's* to ten cents and before the end of the century the magazine's cir-

* In the same year the combined daily circulation of the New York *World* and *Evening World* was only 374,741.

culation had reached 650,000. The connection between Munsey's success and the advance of technology and industry are intimate. The invention of a photo-engraving process and the introduction of a type of glazed paper made from pulpwood rather than the more expensive rags made it possible for him to produce a magazine that was physically attractive to a wide range of people. The growth of industry and the concomitant growth of advertising made it possible for him to sell his magazine at a cost that the mass consumer could afford.

Samuel S. McClure was the first publisher to realize the possibility of using the mass-circulation magazine as an instrument for exposing the abuses of the day. *McClure's,* which was established in 1893, was distinguished by its excellent writing and well-known contributors. Although its profits derived from advertising rather than sales, it was unlike *Munsey's* in that it soon became the most famous crusading magazine of the period. After Ida Tarbell set the pattern in a series of articles on the Standard Oil corporation, muckraking accounts of political and corporate corruption appeared with increasing frequency in the pages of *McClure's.* Other magazines soon adopted the same formula and after the turn of the century *Everybody's, Cosmopolitan,* and *Collier's* provided their readers with a mixture of muckraking and advertising that proved highly profitable to their publishers.

In contrast to these magazines was the *Saturday Evening Post,* which never attempted to challenge the *status quo.* Crammed with profitable advertising, it had a circulation of close to two million by 1914 and was easily the most popular magazine of the age. Highly nationalistic, abounding in traditional morality, and pledged to keeping things as they were, the *Saturday Evening Post* was in many respects an accurate reflection of the attitudes of the large middle-class audience for which it was designed.

47. REGIONAL AND NATIONAL TRENDS IN LITERATURE

THE CIVIL WAR did not produce a sharp break in the history of American literature, for several prominent authors of the antebellum period continued to write during the postwar years. But with a few notable exceptions they belonged to the past, and they found it difficult to adapt their talents to the demands of an industrialized and expanding America. New forces were shaping American life, and a new literature appeared with the passing of the frontier, rise of the city, and growth of industry.

In the decades immediately preceding the Civil War the Northeast in general, and New England in particular, had had a virtual monopoly on American literature—a literature that despite Emerson's exhortation clearly revealed the influence of Europe and that, if the slavery issue is excepted, showed little concern with the problems that were agitating the mass of contemporary Americans. After the war, new and significant poets and novelists appeared in both the South and West. The colorful literary materials of the Far West were first exploited in verse by Joaquin Miller and in the short story by Bret Harte. Mark Twain, who joined the new school of Far Western writers with *Roughing It,* won more lasting fame both at home and abroad for his accounts of the Mississippi Valley in *Tom Sawyer, Huckleberry Finn,* and *Life on the Mississippi.* Other views of Middle Western society were provided by Edward Eggleston's *The Hoosier School-Master, The Circuit Rider,* and *Roxy;* Alice French's (Octave Thanet) fictional accounts of Arkansas and Iowa; John Hay's *Pike County Ballads;* and the novels of Constance Fenimore Woolson and Mary Hartwell Catherwood on the Great Lakes region. Meanwhile a new generation of Southern writers had appeared to present not only their section's problems but also the more picturesque features, which they felt set it apart from the rest of the nation. George W. Cable wrote of Creole customs in Louisiana; Thomas Nelson Page romanticized Virginia's crumbling aristocracy; Charles Egbert Craddock described life among the mountaineers in Tennessee; and in 1881, Joel Chandler Harris published his first book of Uncle Remus stories. In contrast to the Southerners who were inclined to romanticize the past and the Westerners who were captivated by the possibilities of the present and future, the writers of New England saw little but evidence of decay and decline. With extreme sensitivity gifted women like Sarah Orne Jewett, Rose Terry Cooke, and Mary E. Wilkins depicted the daily rounds of the descendants of a once-vigorous people who had been reduced to the crabbed and circumscribed existence of life in New England's stagnant seaports, isolated rural communities, and lonely hillside farms.

Depending on the observer's point of vantage the local colorists of the postwar years represented either an excessive provincialism or a healthy break with Europe. If they introduced no novel literary techniques, they usually selected uniquely American subjects and imparted to their writing what was considered a peculiarly American flavor. Their material was regional, but they wrote for a national audience, and the wide appeal of their books was an accurate reflection of the decline of localism and signs of an emerging national culture. Although they usually dealt with a particular problem or place in American society, they seldom subjected it to critical scrutiny. In general, they preferred to stay on the surface of their material and to concentrate upon the picturesque rather than upon the fundamental features of the segment of life that they were describing. Bret Harte is an extreme example of this tendency, for in stories like "The Outcasts of Poker Flat," and "The Luck of Roaring Camp," he wrapped the mining camps of the West in a blanket of romanticism that concealed their sordidness and converted their essentially brutal inhabitants into lovable and playful characters whose rough exteriors could never quite conceal their hearts of gold.

Mark Twain was the outstanding member of the postwar generation of regional writers; but he was, of course, much more than that. A skilled craftsman, unsurpassed as a storyteller, wit, and observer of American folkways, he was also a man whose life and writings in many respects reflected the cross-currents of the newly industrialized nation. Born in Missouri in 1835, Samuel Clemens spent a large part of his first thirty years in wanderings that took him thousands of miles from his native state and in a variety of jobs that included printing, journalism, piloting on the Mississippi (where he found his pen name in the boatman's cry for two fathoms), and prospecting in Nevada. He won his first large audience in 1869 with the publication of *The Innocents Abroad,* which ridiculed the American worship of Europe and appealed to the bumptious, boastful nationalism of the era. Within two years of the appearance of *The Innocents Abroad,* Mark Twain married and settled in Hartford, Connecticut. In his new rôle as a famous man of letters far from the scenes of his earlier adventures, he never quite made up his mind about his relation to the society in which he found himself. Although he lampooned the get-rich-quick mania in *The Gilded Age* (1873), he also hobnobbed with the *nouveaux riches,* and on occasion he sought wealth as avidly as any leader of the business world. In his most enduring books he glorified the simple pleasures of a small town in rural America; and both *Tom Sawyer* and *Huckleberry Finn* stand out not only as delightful reminders of an earlier way of life, but also as monuments to their author's insight, sense of humor, and sympathetic understanding of America and its people. Although he achieved an international reputation as a humorist, he did not enjoy being a professional funnyman, and he spent his declining years alternately searching for the meaning of life and condemning the "whole damned human race." But the contradictions in Mark Twain are relatively insignificant beside the superb creative talents that produced Huck, Colonel Sellers, Jim, Tom, the Duke, Injun Joe, and a host of others. He wrote for the masses, and his appeal was almost universal.

The inner conflicts that tortured Mark Twain throughout most of his adult years were shared to a greater or lesser degree by virtually every serious man of letters during the Gilded Age. To the creative mind the advent of big business, big money, and big cities posed a series of problems that seemed to defy solution. The author of the brilliant and at times elusive *The Education of Henry Adams* repeatedly showed the dilemma that confronted a sensitive intellectual in a world dedicated to material gain and dominated by the Grants, Vanderbilts, Fisks, and Tweeds. If he sought to participate in the economic and political life of his times, he was plagued by the conviction that every move he made represented a further compromise with his principles. On the other hand, if he withdrew from contemporary society, he knew that the very act of withdrawal helped to perpetuate the conditions that precluded his participation. Although Adams spent his life searching for the answers to these questions, he never found them. His disgust with the corrupt alliance between business and politics was announced in *Democracy,* a novel that he published anonymously in 1880. But he then withdrew from the fray to write a monumental history of the Jefferson and Madison Administrations, to seek a universal law of history, and finally in *Mont-Saint-Michel and Chartres* to immerse himself in a study of a society that gave its allegiance to spiritual rather than material values—or, as Adams put it, to the Virgin rather than the Dynamo.

Henry James, like Adams, was disgusted with what he considered the excesses of American democracy and plutocracy. Unlike Adams, he discovered a more congenial way of life, not in medieval France, but in a contemporary England, which had a less flamboyant democracy and a more polished plutocracy. Making frequent trips to the Continent and only occasional visits to America, he spent most of his life among people of gentility whose inherited fortunes permitted them to devote almost all their attention to the task of making a highly formalized ritual out of social intercourse. But as an artist he was able to view the world in which he moved with extraordinary objectivity and to use it as raw material for a series of novels and short stories that are distinguished by both their subtlety of approach and their penetrating analysis of human behavior. All his work reveals his concern with the clash between social conventions and human emotions, or between the form and the content of life. In his "international" novels (*The Ambassadors, The American,* and *The Portrait of a Lady* among others) he employs this theme to point up the contrasts between the European and the American civilizations, to show what he thinks each has to offer the other, and to examine the impact of Europe on people who had known only America.

Several authors indicated their dissatisfaction with the present by employing fiction to portray an idealized future. Of the Utopian novels, none enjoyed a wider popularity than Edward Bellamy's *Looking Backward, 2000–1887,* which within a decade of its publication in 1888 had been purchased by almost 400,000 Americans. The central character of *Looking Backward* awoke in the year 2000 in the midst of a completely socialist society the material well-being of whose members was matched by their spiritual serenity. Throughout the novel the advantages of a co-operative life in the future are set against the disadvantages of the competitive existence of the present. While other novels—William Dean Howells' *A Traveler from Altruria* among them—employed the same theme, none enjoyed a success comparable to that of *Looking Backward*, which led to the formation of clubs to hasten the new day and the establishment of a paper especially designed for readers who were interested in making a reality of Bellamy's blueprint of a socialist paradise.

While the Utopian novelists compensated for their dissatisfaction with the present by imagining a happier future, the bulk of the American reading public found its escape in a fiction that romanticized both the past and present. The popularity of any given novel often appeared to be in inverse ratio to its realism, and its sales mounted in almost direct proportion to the nobility of its hero, baseness of its villain, improbability of its plot, and triteness of its morality. Sticky love stories, historical romances, and adventure tales were usually without serious competitors, and at the end of the century the best seller lists included Charles Major's *When Knighthood Was in Flower*, S. Weir Mitchell's *Hugh Wynne*, Maurice Thompson's *Alice of Old Vincennes*, Paul Leicester Ford's *Janice Meredith*, Winston Churchill's *The Crisis* and *Richard Carvel*, George B. McCutcheon's *Graustark*, Owen Wister's *The Virginian*, John Fox's *The Little Shepherd of Kingdom Come*. Equally successful was the "by gosh" school of fiction, which gained both its distinction and popularity from the folksy and astute rural characters who filled the pages of such books as Edward Noyes Westcott's *David Harum* and Irving Bacheller's *Eben Holden*.

American children thrived on much the same type of literary fare as their parents. Horatio Alger, Jr. and William T. Adams, who wrote under the name of Oliver Optic, turned out what seemed to be a never ending stream of books that were all variations on the single theme of how a poor but noble boy overcame repeated buffetings to achieve worldly success. Girls, who liked their heroines pure in heart, could follow the trials and triumphs of Elsie Dinsmore in the *Elsie* books, ground out year after year by Martha F. Finley. Dime novels, which were read by countless children and semiliterate adults, were undoubtedly one of the most important single cultural influences of the age. Usually set against a Western background, they told tales of derring-do and made glamorous folk heroes of Indian fighters, rangers, cowboys, hunters, and prospectors. Crammed with exciting adventures strung together into a plot that hardly gave the reader—let alone the characters—a chance to catch his breath, the dime novel also abounded in the middle-class morality of the day. By the time that the posse had closed in on the cattle rustlers in the last chapter, the reader had learned that hard work rather than crime paid dividends; that justice always triumphed; that idleness and evilness were synonymous; that the home and mother were sacred; and that fortitude could surmount any adversity.

In contrast to authors who patched together romantic stories of some never-never land were the many serious novelists who sought to illuminate rather than escape the social and economic problems of the Gilded Age. The increasing importance of the workingman in an industrialized America was reflected by a number of attempts to deal with labor problems in fiction. The case for the factory worker was presented by Elizabeth Stuart Phelps in 1871 in *The Silent Partner*, and Thomas Bailey Aldrich in 1880 attacked unions in *The Stillwater Tragedy*. Four years later, Henry Adams' friend John Hay published *The Bread-Winners*, a novel that was as critical of organized labor as Adams' *Democracy* had been of organized politics. No novelist worthy of the task rose to the defense of labor in these years, and it was not until the appearance of Jack London's proletarian novels in the first decades of the new century that the workingman received a thoroughly sympathetic treatment in American fiction. Meanwhile rural America was subjected to a searching scrutiny that bore little resemblance to the sentimental effusions of James Whitcomb Riley. In *Main-Travelled Roads* Hamlin Garland broke with the "frost is on the pumpkin" school of literature to describe the depressing effects of mud, monotony, sweat, manure, and isolation upon farm life in the Middle West. Equally notable was E. W. Howe's *The Story of a Country Town*, an account of the narrowing and stultifying influences of a small rural community.

The rural studies of Garland and Howe were matched by novels that dealt realistically with the impact of industry upon urban social life. In *The Rise of Silas Lapham*, William Dean Howells portrayed with sympathetic understanding the difficulties encountered by a self-made businessman who attempted to cope with the complexities of Boston's established society, while in *A Hazard of New Fortunes* he covered the whole range of New York's social classes. Edith Wharton, like Howells, was fascinated by the psychological stresses and strains that the invasion of the old urban aristocracy by the *nouveaux riches* produced, and in novels such as *The House of Mirth* (1905) she wrote with remarkable insight and skill of the rôle of wealth in the determination of social standing. *Ethan Frome*, which was Mrs. Wharton's outstanding book and defies comparison with her other novels or those of any other writer, was a moving and horrifying account of personal tragedy on a bleak and isolated New England farm. The plight of the city's poorer classes, on the other hand, was described with unprecedented frankness by Stephen Crane's *Maggie: A Girl of the Streets*. Although the characters are wooden and Crane all but hits the reader over the head to make his point, *Maggie* stands as a monument to the author's determination to record the effect of urban poverty on slum dwellers. Crane's *The Red Badge of Courage,* which was far more successful as a work of art, was equally perceptive in its analysis of the reactions of a rookie Union soldier to his first battle. Much has been made of the fact Crane had never seen a battle when he wrote this book; the book, however, gains its effect, not from Crane's knowledge of war, but from his ability to bring out the emotions of an individual in a crisis that was not of his own making.

The rise of realism in the last two decades of the nineteenth century resulted in a new regional literature that was both more subtle and more genuinely representative than was the work of the local colorists immediately after the Civil War. Howells and Mrs. Wharton largely concentrated on subjects dealing with the Northeast. Hamlin Garland dealt with the Middle Border, and Booth Tarkington skillfully mixed realism and romanticism in his books on the middle class in the towns and cities of the Middle West. In Ellen Glasgow, who began to write at the end of the century, the South at last produced a novelist who could look at its institutions and its people without the aid of rose-colored glasses. Writing of Virginia in the Civil War period and of urban and rural life in the Old Dominion after the war, she refused either to sentimentalize the South's past or to withhold her irony from those who refused to recognize the passing of the section's older traditions and culture.

The trend toward a fiction that would expose rather than conceal the main currents of contemporary American life reached its climax before World War I in the naturalistic novels of Frank Norris and Theodore Dreiser. Both men were convinced that the individual was a plaything of irresistible impersonal forces and that moral influences were of no importance in a world governed by chance. Summing up his philosophy of naturalism at the end of *The Octopus,* Norris wrote: "Nature was, then, a gigantic engine, a vast cyclopean power, huge, terrible, a leviathan with a heart of steel, knowing no compunction, no forgiveness, no tolerance; crushing out the human atom standing in its way, with nirvanic calm, the agony of destruction sending never a jar, never the faintest tremour through all that prodigious mechanism of wheels and cogs." In *The Octopus* and *The Pit,* Norris made men puppets of an all powerful nature that was represented by the "vast Titanic flood" of wheat "along its predetermined courses from East to West."

Theodore Dreiser, who first attracted attention through his frank discussion of sex in *Sister Carrie* (1900), was fully as much of a determinist as Norris. In *The Titan* and *The Financier,* he described in awkward but always powerful prose the career of a traction magnate who was pictured, without moral condemnation, as a prisoner of his environment. Dreiser had a passion for accuracy and made little effort to conceal the fact that the central character of both books was modeled after Charles

T. Yerkes, who had gained notoriety and wealth from the street railway business. Similarly, *An American Tragedy* (1925), in which Dreiser sought to demonstrate that society rather than the individual executed by society was responsible for a murder, was based on the newspaper reports of a murder trial that had taken place in 1907.

Social commentary was not confined to serious fiction, for the nation's leading humorists were frequently its most perspicacious critics. Artemus Ward, Josh Billings, and Petroleum V. Nasby of the Civil War era, and Finley Peter Dunne at the end of the century, all poked fun at the foibles of the American people and the contradictions of American life. But beneath their flippancy and wit was a strong undercurrent of cynicism that revealed the temper of the times far more effectively than their jokes. Artemus Ward spoke for the whole postwar generation when he said: "You scratch my back & Ile scratch your back;" and Finley Peter Dunne at the time of the anthracite coal strike in 1902 had his Mr. Dooley say: "The rich can burn with indignation, thinkin' iv th' wrongs inflicted on capital, th' middle or middlin' class will be marchin' with th' milishy, an' th' poor can fight among thimsilves an' burn th' babies." These men, who wrote for a nationwide audience, made their audience laugh, but more often than not it was laughing at itself.

48. THE ARTS IN A BUSINESS AGE

THE development of American art and architecture reflected both the growing wealth of the United States and the cultural dependence of the New World on the Old. The new millionaires who comprised the aristocracy of pork, oil, steel, railroads, and coke were quick to emulate the upper classes of Europe by becoming patrons of the arts. With little or no training in artistic appreciation, they sought to corner the world's supply of culture in much the same fashion that they had monopolized their chosen industries. Pictures, statues, tapestries, and even homes were valued more for their price tags than for any intrinsic merit. These men could afford the best; and they hired professional collectors to buy up Europe's art treasures regardless of cost and commissioned architects to build them sumptuous town houses and country castles that in so far as possible duplicated the homes of the titled nobility of England and the Continent. Although the obsession of many of the well-to-do with European art provided little work or encouragement for American artists, it was either directly or indirectly responsible for the establishment of most of the nation's important art museums. In 1865 there was not a single American art gallery comparable to those in Europe. Within thirty-five years every large city possessed at least one important museum of fine arts. In almost every instance American museums were made possible by private gifts of money and art treasures. The establishment of the Corcoran Art Gallery in Washington in 1869, the Boston Museum of Fine Arts in 1870, and Metropolitan Museum of Art in New York City in 1879 were all products of both the interest and generosity of a few rich individuals. In subsequent years most of the great collections amassed by the postwar generation of millionaires were turned over to museums and thus made available to the public.

While men of wealth invested their surplus funds in Europe's past, the mass of Americans were largely indifferent to art and architecture. To countless Americans, painting and drawing were synonymous with illustration. Pictures were usually judged by the ability of the artist to duplicate the accuracy of a photographer. At the same time architecture more often than not was either disdained as unnecessary in a nation where individuals for generations had built their own homes or was viewed as a device for concealing the true functions of buildings beneath masses of decorative and extraneous material. Moreover, those who dedicated their lives to the arts were looked upon with considerable suspicion. To a people subjected to successive frontier experiences and brought up on the doctrine of hard work, the man of the studio often seemed a capricious idler who flouted custom and was willing to live on the gifts of others rather than to earn his own bread.

Americans during the Gilded Age—as in most other ages—liked to think of themselves as a practical people. Although they disdained the aesthete and had little patience with the artist who insisted on being "arty," they approved of "sensible" art. Specifically, they approved of pictures which were "pretty," painted a moral, or told a story that they could understand. This widely held attitude may have militated against the growth of a native school of art, but it proved a boon to American illustrators. The rapid expansion of the magazine and book-publishing industries, moreover, provided an expanding market for a number of proficient illustrators during the postwar decades. Howard Pyle, Edwin A. Abbey, and Joseph Pennell won the most enduring reputations as illustrators, but there were many others of marked ability. By the turn of the century countless Americans were familiar with M. A. Woolf's pictures of immigrants, the rural scenes of A. B. Frost, Frederic Remington's Indian and cowboy paintings, and E. W. Kemble's studies of Negroes.

Lacking both a receptive audience at home and an established national tradition of their own, many American painters turned to Europe for both their inspiration and training. Although several Americans studied at either Munich or Düsseldorf, the focal point of American artists abroad remained France, where they either enrolled at the conservative *École des Beaux Arts* or joined the ranks of the rebels. The traditionalists, however, always outnumbered the innovators, and the *Beaux Arts* was responsible for a whole generation of American artists who reflected the dominant trends in French painting. Among the outstanding traditional painters were Benjamin R. Fitz, Walter Shirlaw, Wyatt Eaton, and Elihu Vedder, all of whom employed the techniques that they had learned abroad to portray the nude against an idealized background and in the neoclassical style of the academy. Despite the prestige of the *École des Beaux Arts,* several Americans rejected it for France's Barbizon school of landscape painting, which emphasized the creation of a mood rather than exactness of detail and stressed the use of color rather than precision of line. To these Barbizon painters, nature did not provide scenes to be copied, but stimuli to which the sensitive artist could react as a creative individual.

Of the many American painters who fell under the influence of the Barbizon school special mention should be made of William Morris Hunt, George Inness, and Homer Martin. Hunt, who studied at Rome, Düsseldorf, and Paris before spending three years at Barbizon, returned to the United States in 1855 to take the lead in the revolt against the academics. He was a remarkably influential teacher and a painter whose versatility enabled him to produce not only outstanding landscapes but murals and portraits as well. Inness, probably the ablest American landscape painter of his day, defies rigid categorization. In addition to unusual technical ability, Inness' canvasses reveal both a variety of approach and an emotional power that had largely been lacking in the work of earlier American landscape artists. Martin, who like Inness never ceased to experiment, eventually became a convert to Impressionism, and in his later years he was an ardent disciple—although never a mere imitator—of Corot. Alexander Wyant, the other notable landscape artist of the period, owed more to the Englishman Constable than to the Barbizon school; and his paintings, while suffering from a certain monotony of approach, are distinguished by the delicacy of their execution.

As an increasing number of artists returned from abroad with new and exciting ideas, there developed a sharp cleavage between the younger and older generations of American painters. When the progressives were rebuffed by the National Academy of Design, they formed the Society of American Artists in 1877. Championing the cause of the younger men and serving as the first president of the Society of American Artists was John La Farge, who was considerably older than most of the insurgents. With a multiplicity of interests, dynamic personality, and broad background in a number of diverse fields of learning, La Farge was both the most versatile and eclectic of the American artists of the period. Painting landscapes as well as portraits, he was also this country's first authentic muralist, and through his pioneer work in opalescence he made a major contribution to the art of designing stained-glass windows. Although he was well versed in Japanese art, the Old Masters, and the Pre-Raphaelites, his fascination with the effect of light on color put him in the advance guard of Impressionism. Although he encouraged the new generation of painters who had been trained in France, he himself belonged to no school, and in 1877 he wrote: "I should mistrust the French ambitions anyhow. It is by nobody's taste you must go, unless you find a mind just at sympathy with yours, and unless they can give you reasons, and the reasons should always be big ones."

The careers of Thomas Eakins and Winslow Homer provided additional evidence that American painting was not wholly dependent on European influences. Both men approached their work as realists; both found their subjects in the everyday scenes and life of their fellow Americans; and both, as Homer Saint-Gaudens has pointed out,

> *gave no thought to French influence or German influence. They detested hypocrisy. Art patter appealed to them not at all. They had a holy horror of bores. They painted with the American sense of fact developed to a high degree. They looked at nature, not at other men's canvasses. The only thing that counted in their work was what that which was set before them had to say to them, not details of trivial significance, but what was dramatic, epic, and of broad humanity.**

Eakins, who undertook a one-man crusade against respectability in art, had a monumental scorn for pictures that were merely pretty. In such studies as the "Clinic of Dr. Gross" and "The Thinker," he portrayed his subjects with an integrity of purpose and a precise—even harsh—objectivity that precluded even a hint of flattery. Homer, whose range was considerably broader than that of Eakins, infused his paintings and sketches with a vitality, vigor, and ruggedness that made him the most truly American artist of his generation. Trained as a lithographer, Homer served as an artist-correspondent for *Harper's Weekly* during the Civil War. When he turned to painting he won immediate recognition with his "Prisoners from the Front," which was shown by the New York Academy of Design in 1866. During the next forty years Homer with almost fanatical intensity and singleness of purpose devoted his energies to the production of powerful and forthright studies of scenes in the Caribbean, Adirondacks, and along the coast of his native Maine.

In contrast to such essentially American painters as La Farge, Eakins,

* Homer Saint-Gaudens: *The American Artist and His Times* (New York: Dodd, Mead & Company, 1941), p. 177.

and Homer was a group of brilliant expatriates that included Mary Cassatt, John Singer Sargent, and James McNeill Whistler. Miss Cassatt, after extensive study in America and Europe, settled in Paris where she became one of the acknowledged leaders of the Impressionist school.* Sargent, whose studio was in London, won renown on both sides of the Atlantic for his highly stylized, and sometimes idealized portraits of wealthy leaders of English and American society. Whistler, after being expelled from West Point and serving a short term in the employ of the Coast and Geodetic Survey, studied in Paris for a number of years, and then spent the remainder of his years in England. Egotistical, belligerent, and unconventional in manner and dress, he relentlessly battled the Philistines and championed art-for-art's-sake. Always more interested in achieving a total effect than in creating a likeness, he sought to do to color what the musician did to sound. On one occasion he wrote that it was the function of the artist to view nature, "not with the enlarging lens, that he may gather facts for the botanist, but with the light of the one who sees in her choice . . . of brilliant tones and delicate tints, suggestion of future harmonies." Equally at home with oil, watercolor, etching, or lithography, he turned out a prodigious amount of work between fights with critics and lawsuits against detractors. Best known for the "Portrait of the Artist's Mother," he was equally effective in the "Little Rose of Lyme Regis," "Thomas Carlyle," "Miss Alexander," and his innumerable "Harmonies," "Symphonies," and "Arrangements."

Despite the versatility and skill of individual artists, American painting as a whole lacked the vitality and originality of European painting during the closing decades of the nineteenth century. No significant school of painting had emerged in the United States, and the bulk of the American work seemed trite and pedestrian when compared to the exciting developments in France. But in the midst of apparent indifference and complacency, new forces were shaping the rising generation of American painters. After 1900 a group of young New Yorkers turned their backs on both Europe and their own national past to produce a series of starkly realistic studies of contemporary urban life. Depicting elevated railroads, hall bedrooms, saloons, dance halls, prize fights, bums and floozies, men like George Bellows, Robert Henri, John Sloan, George Luks, and William Glackens shocked the complacent by their determination to paint what they saw as they saw it. As fully important a development as the advent of the hardboiled school was the opening in 1913 of the New York Armory Show. Concentrating largely on the work of contemporary French painters, it provided America with its first real taste of Post-Impressionism, Modernism, and Cubism. Its impact was immediate and pronounced. Conservatives rushed to the defense of the

* Degas, on viewing Miss Cassatt's work, remarked: "I won't admit that a woman can draw like that."

old ways and thereby publicized the new; the radicals replied in kind; and painting became front-page news. The Armory Show was a turning point in the history of modern American painting, for it marked the beginning of the end of the long years of provincialism of the American painter and his public.

The history of American sculpture roughly paralleled that of painting. Sculptors as well as painters were dependent upon European training and were confronted by problems arising from public indifference and the necessity for adjusting their creative faculties to the requirements of an industrialized and urbanized America. But in sculpture as in painting, innumerable obstacles proved only temporary barriers to progress, and the notable achievements of a few gifted individuals eventually overshadowed the earlier years of mediocrity.

In the decade that followed the Civil War, American sculpture was characterized by a degree of banality and triteness that has seldom, if ever, been equaled in the history of American art. The nationalism engendered by the war and its aftermath was reflected in such a plethora of statues of military heroes that it was said that the foundries were turning them out on a mass-production basis. Middle-class homes were cluttered with highly romanticized plaster versions of figures from antiquity and the American past. Iron deer were considered the last word in lawn decoration, and few cities possessed a public monument of artistic merit. Of foreign influences, the Italian was most important, and the neoclassical school of sculpture had no serious rival. Typical of the period was the work of William Wetmore Story, who had a prediliction for mournful females and noble males, all of whom he clad in the flowing robes of Greece and Rome.

The impetus for the break with the Italian tradition was provided by the Centennial Exposition of 1876, which furnished many Americans with their first view of the work of the leading French sculptors of the day. In the ensuing years Paris supplanted Rome as the mecca of American sculptors, and the neoclassicists steadily lost ground to a group of artists who had received most of their training in France. With their emphasis on naturalism, skillful use of broken surfaces, undoubted technical ability, and originality of approach, these younger men gave American sculpture a distinct character that, although it revealed foreign influences, was nevertheless unmistakably American. Of the new generation of sculptors, none won a more lasting or merited fame than Augustus Saint-Gaudens. Born in Ireland, brought to New York as a young child, trained in France as well as Italy, Saint-Gaudens became an artist whose individuality and power of expression put him in a class by himself. The Farragut and Sherman monuments in New York, the Lincoln statue in Chicago, and the profoundly moving nameless figure that marks the grave of Mrs. Henry Adams in Washington—to mention only the most noted examples of his work—are all distinguished by their vitality, depth of feeling, and subtle mixture of realism and symbolism.

Although Saint-Gaudens' pre-eminence makes the work of all of his contemporaries suffer by comparison, many other sculptors of the same period were nevertheless creative artists of considerable ability. John Quincy Adams Ward, who never studied abroad, led the revolt against neoclassicism with his statues of Garfield in Washington, D. C., and Henry Ward Beecher in Brooklyn. Ward, who continued to practice his art well into the twentieth century, stands out as one of the freshest and most invigorating forces in the history of American sculpture. George Grey Barnard, a student of Rodin in Paris, produced a series of massive figures that were remarkably successful in conveying a sense of raw strength, while F. W. MacMonnies, who studied under Saint-Gaudens and was a painter as well as sculptor, gained his principal distinction from his ability to give his work a sense of movement. Daniel Chester French, one of the most prolific sculptors, produced a number of noteworthy statues of prominent Americans including his "Lincoln" at Lincoln, Nebraska, his "Washington" at Paris, and his "Grant" at Philadelphia.

49. FORM AND FUNCTION IN AMERICAN ARCHITECTURE

ARCHITECTURE, far more than either painting or sculpture, reflected the vulgarity and materialism that typified so much of American life during the Gilded Age. In an era of ostentation and social flux, architecture offered an opportunity for conspicuous consumption that few were able to resist. With an apparent determination to make every building look like a wedding cake, American architects developed a Victorian Gothic style that managed to conceal any hint of functionalism beneath a myriad of scrolls, brackets, railings, cupolas, balconies, gables, and turrets. Gaudy rather than utilitarian and at best a corruption of the traditional Gothic, Victorian Gothic was used not only in churches, but in banks, homes, art museums, college halls, and government buildings. Despite its enormous popularity, Victorian Gothic did not have the field to itself, and Fiske Kimball, in describing what he termed the "Battle of Styles," mentioned "Italian villas," "chalets," "Moorish cottages," and a number of public buildings that revealed the French influence of the Second Empire. In the Northeast, meanwhile, there was a Colonial revival, and in Florida there was an attempt to return to the earlier architecture of Spanish America. The half-timbered Queen Anne house topped by bunched chimneys gained an increasing vogue among middle- and upper-class home-owners, while the Fifth Avenue mansions and country palaces designed by Richard Morris Hunt furnished unbelievably luxurious settings in the European tradition for the aristocracy of American industrial and finance capitalism.

The first indication that American architecture was beginning to emerge from the depths to which it had sunk after the war was provided by the work of Henry Hobson Richardson, who was the leading member of a new group of younger architects who had received their training at the *École des Beaux Arts* in Paris. Richardson, who, as Lewis Mumford has pointed out, was "not a decorator, but a builder," quickly rejected the Victorian Gothic for the more forthright Romanesque of southern France and Spain. His outstanding buildings were all distinguished by their heavy stonework, broad arches, squat pillars, and an over-all air of massed—even ponderous—strength that induced one critic to suggest that they were defensible only in a military sense. Although Richardson's name is usually associated with church architecture and his first notable building was Trinity Church in Boston, he was equally successful in his designs of railroad stations, town halls, jails, libraries, and college buildings. Until his death in 1886, Richardson had no serious rivals among American architects, and his buildings continue to stand as monuments to the skill and integrity of their creator. Essentially a romantic, who in the midst of an age of shifting values sought stability in an alien and vanishing tradition, Richardson founded no schools and his art died with him.

Richardson was a craftsman who wished to improve old techniques rather than devise new ones, but several of his contemporaries realized that the Industrial Revolution had presented them with both the need and opportunity for a novel and indigenous form of architectural expression. Feeling that the architectural forms that had been developed to meet the demands of ancient and medieval Europe were ludicrous when applied to a factory or commercial structure, they sought to perfect a type of building that would satisfy without sham the requirements of modern American economic life. Steel and glass were their distinctive materials. As early as 1851 the Crystal Palace in London had demonstrated the possibilities inherent in the use of broad areas of glass; for years engineers had shown in bridge construction that first iron and then steel had tremendous structural potentialities. It was in every way fitting that the Brooklyn Bridge, which was completed in 1883, was the age's finest example of the daring but simple fashion in which the matter-of-fact employment of new materials could solve problems of design as well as of engineering.

Modern architecture—as it was called to distinguish it from the traditional styles—centered from the outset in Chicago, where convention seemed somewhat less oppressive than in the East and the fire of 1876 had presented builders with a clean slate. Although at first influenced by Richardson, Western architects soon evolved a style of their own that quickly became identified with the multistoried, steel-framed office building. The elevator, which had been perfected in the seventies, had little effect on commercial architecture as long as a building's height was limited by the masonry of its supporting walls; but when the elevator was hung in a steel frame, restrictions on upward growth were removed. As early as 1883, William Le Baron Jenney's design for the Home Insurance Building in Chicago had called for the use of iron uprights and cross beams to serve as supports for the structure's walls and floors, and a few years later the same device was employed in the Tacoma Building. It was only a matter of time before steel was substituted for iron and the modern office building emerged as a continuous steel frame sheathed in masonry that was broken at regular intervals by strips of windows. The leading exponents of the new style were Daniel Burnham, John Root, and Louis Sullivan; and of the three, Sullivan was easily pre-eminent. An artist as well as a builder, Sullivan brought to his work crusading zeal, a thorough mastery of his craft, and a philosophy of functionalism that emphasized the harmony between art and nature. Sullivan was at his best in the Wainwright Building in St. Louis, which more clearly than any other structure revealed his deep-seated conviction that: "whether it be the sweeping eagle in his flight, or the open apple-blossom, the toiling work-horse, the blithe swan, the branching oak, the winding stream at its base, the drifting clouds over all the coursing sun, form ever follows function, and this is law."

Sullivan's work received little immediate recognition in the East, where a classical revival was reaching its high point in the numerous buildings of the New York architectural firm of McKim, Mead, and White. Emphasizing form rather than function and employing the classical façade, McKim, Mead, and White raised an ancient tradition to new summits of perfection. But their technical proficiency could not obscure the sterility of the mode of expression that they had adopted. The architectural forms of Greece, Rome, and the Renaissance could not meet the needs of a nation of farmers, factory hands, and office workers, and the firm's most noteworthy buildings gave little indication of the age in which they had been built. The classical revival achieved its greatest triumph at the Chicago World's Fair of 1893. Although Sullivan designed the fair's Transportation Building and other Western architects were also represented, the over-all theme was an uncompromising classicism. Although much has been made of the architectural splendor of the World's Fair, the fact remains that its outstanding feature was its almost complete absence of originality.

Despite the triumph of the traditionalists at the World's Fair, they were soon forced to give ground. As urban concentration increased, ground rents rose proportionately. Under the circumstances, the lesson seemed obvious: the taller the building, the greater the profits. Thus, economic rather than aesthetic considerations forced the adoption of the steel-framed office-building, for it alone could be pushed skyward beyond the seven or eight stories that all-masonry walls could sustain. Because of the extraordinary pressure of population and the limits imposed on horizontal growth by its island location, Manhattan was destined to provide the setting for the nation's first modern skyscrapers. The Flatiron Building, which was designed by Daniel Burnham and reached twenty stories at its completion in 1902, was followed within a decade by the much taller Metropolitan Tower, Municipal Building, and Singer and Woolworth buildings. These early New York skyscrapers and their counterparts in other cities generally represented an unhappy compromise between the old and new, for their towering steel frames were covered with a mass of decorative material that tended to obscure the clean and essentially beautiful upward sweep of their lines. Not until the next generation did architects come to realize that the attractiveness of the skyscraper was enhanced by emphasizing rather than concealing the fundamental simplicity of its design.

The skyscraper was neither derivative nor imitative, but uniquely American, and no other product of American artistic development so accurately reflected the age and land that created it. City planners could complain that it robbed its neighbors of sunlight and that it increased the problems arising from the density of urban population, but to millions of people throughout the United States and the rest of the world the skyscraper stood as a symbol of American aspirations, ingenuity, and wealth.

CHAPTER VIII

THE POLITICS OF CONFORMITY AND REVOLT

IN PRE-SUMTER America the politician and clergyman had been the leading spokesmen of the American people, but in the postwar years both were relegated to a relatively subordinate position. With the rapid growth of industry and the increasing public esteem accorded to businessmen, politics declined in prestige, and party strife appeared—on the surface at least—to be little more than a game. But, still, it was a game in which the stakes could be high, for it often involved the awarding of lucrative contracts, grants of large tracts of Western land, or increases in tariff schedules for certain favored industries. To the players the game presented an opportunity for an all-out struggle for the spoils of office; to the businessman the game's outcome was largely irrelevant, for regardless of the results of any election the structure of the American economy remained virtually unchanged. Republicans and Democrats waged a relentless war that they fought with all the weapons at their command; but one party's defeat and another's victory had no appreciable effect on the course of American civilization. Both parties existed to keep things as they were, and the advent of a new administration in Washington signalized little beyond the appearance of a new set of office-holders.

50. THE POLITICS OF DEAD CENTER

IN THE YEARS following Grant's two terms as President of the United States, American politics were characterized not by exceptional corruption or marked inefficiency, but by the mediocrity of many of those who held important government positions. Rutherford B. Hayes, James A. Garfield, Chester A. Arthur, Grover Cleveland, and Benjamin Harrison were essentially colorless men who believed that the President was an executive agent rather than the initiator or formulator of policies. They displayed little interest in reform. Even their most ardent supporters hesitated to picture them as crusaders, and few historians would label any one of them a statesman. Honest, plodding, dull, unimaginative, they kept the rigging on the ship of state in adequate repair, but they seldom displayed any desire to venture into uncharted waters. While farmers complained of declining income, workers conducted militant strikes, and industrial leaders amassed huge fortunes, Presidents performed the routine duties of their office and did little to disturb the *status quo.* From 1877 to 1893, American politics were in dead center, not because there were no issues, but because the politicians refused to recognize and act on the issues.

The postwar Republican party, like every major political party in American history, was a loose alliance of diverse groups that presumably had little in common. Geographically the Republican party represented an axis that extended from the Northeast to the upper Middle West. At one pole were most American businessmen, who had been attracted to the party during and after the Civil War by its tariff policies, banking and monetary programs, and the fashion in which it had distributed war contracts. At the other end of the axis was the bulk of America's grain growers. They and their forefathers had helped to found the party in the 1850's, and during the war they had been rewarded with the Homestead Act. In addition to these two major groups, several others adhered to the Republican party. Negroes supported it because it had given them their freedom. Northern war veterans viewed it as the party that had fought and won the war and that had continued to provide them with generous pensions. Countless other Americans consistently voted the Republican ticket because of the memory of Lincoln, the party's intimate association with the anti-slavery crusade and the preservation of the Union, and their belief that Republicanism was as much of a crusading doctrine as it had been in the antebellum years.

Because the groups supporting the Republican party usually comprised a majority of the voters, the party was able to retain its control over the machinery of the Federal government throughout most of the postwar years. From James Buchanan to Woodrow Wilson (1861–1913), Grover Cleveland was the only Democrat to occupy the White House. While the Republicans at times lost one branch—and occasionally both branches—of Congress to the opposition, they were able to dominate the judiciary during the entire period. Still another measure of Republican success was the fashion in which the party repeatedly broke up into factions that contended for the fruits of repeated victories. As early as the midseventies the party was split into the Half-Breeds, led by James G. Blaine of Maine, and the Stalwarts, led by Roscoe Conkling of New York. Although the members of one faction hated those of the other as much as, if not more than, they hated the opposition, they did not disagree on policy. Their major differences arose over the party's division of the spoils. The Half-Breeds believed that all Federal jobs should be occupied by Half-Breeds, whereas the Stalwarts contended that Stalwarts alone should staff the government.

In addition to the Half-Breeds and Stalwarts, the Republican party contained a rather sizable reform wing. In 1872, representatives of this branch of the party, calling themselves Liberal Republicans, sought to revive the crusading spirit that had once characterized Republicanism. The Liberal Republicans, whose principal strength was in the Middle West, advocated a more moderate Reconstruction policy, a reversal of the trend toward the centralization of government, and a reduction in the tariff. This program was similar to that of the Democrats, with whom the Liberal Republicans allied in 1872 in an attempt to elect Horace Greeley to the presidency. But Greeley proved an inept candidate, and in the election he was easily defeated by Grant. In 1880 the reform elements within the party successfully blocked the nomination of Grant, and four years later they sought to prevent the selection of Blaine as the party's standard bearer. When, despite their protests, Blaine received the nomination, they bolted the party and under the name of Mugwumps cast their votes for Cleveland.

In contrast to the Republicans, the Democrats could seldom afford the luxury of factionalism, and, as the minority party, they were only infrequently troubled by the problems involved in the distribution of Federal patronage. The Democratic party had two principal sources of support—the Solid South and most of the big-city machines of the Northeast. Following Reconstruction the South became a one-party section, and every Democratic presidential candidate began his campaign with the assurance that he would receive all the electoral votes of the states that had once comprised the Confederacy. Because the West was generally Republican and the South always Democratic, it was the Northeast that decided most national elections. While the Democratic machines of the Northeast provided the party with consistent urban majorities, they usually lacked sufficient strength to prevent the Republicans in the rural areas from controlling the political machinery and electoral vote of their respective states. Furthermore, the Democrats had trouble in finding leaders to take the place once occupied by the antebellum planters. Neither Northern city bosses nor Southern politicians proved capable of the task, and from 1865 to 1896 the party's principal national spokesmen consisted of a small group of merchants and international bankers who were opposed to Republican high-tariff policies. But these businessmen, unlike those in the Republican party, could not furnish an effective leadership for a party that drew its support from Southern agrarians and the urban underprivileged.

From 1876 to 1892, few issues of any importance divided the Democrats and Republicans. Although the tariff provided a never-ending subject of debate, it nevertheless was not basically altered by either party. Currency questions—particularly the relation of silver to gold—frequently agitated the voters, but each party contained inflationist and deflationist wings. Neither party ever put forward a program for the control of business, and the Interstate Commerce Act of 1887 and the Sherman Antitrust Act of 1890 were passed by bipartisan majorities. When Congress voted on economic issues party lines tended to blur as the agrarian forces of the South and West combined to oppose the business interests of the Northeast. The politicians of both parties always feared that a clear-cut stand on any major issue would reduce their chances of success by alienating substantial blocs of voters. Politics had become a big business in its own right, and no party leader was prepared to adopt a policy that might jeopardize his own and his followers' chances of obtaining and holding public office. The party in power did not wish to alter a system that had proved so profitable. The politicians of the minority party, looking forward to the day when they would take over the government, had no desire to destroy a system that would be fully as profitable to them as it had been to their opponents.

51. HAYES, GARFIELD, AND ARTHUR

THE ATTITUDE of both parties made it virtually impossible for either the executive or legislative branches of the government to carry out constructive policies, as the record of the Hayes Administration clearly demonstrated. When Hayes became President on March

4, 1877, many of his supporters confidently expected that he would soon make the voters forget the excesses of "Grantism." Born and brought up in Ohio, Hayes had served as a volunteer officer with the Union Army during the Civil War and had made a notable record as the governor of his state. Throughout the campaign of 1876 he had repeatedly emphasized the need for reform, and his cabinet contained several men of undoubted ability and integrity. Despite these facts, his Administration was largely devoid of accomplishment.

Hayes' mediocre record as President was in part the result of his obvious lack of political acumen and in part the result of circumstances over which he had no control. During the first two years of his term, the Democrats controlled the House, and during the last two years, the opposition had majorities in both branches of Congress. Nor did Hayes' program win the support of either the people or the politicians. While his decision to end Reconstruction pleased the Southerners, it did not make them Republicans, and it antagonized many Northerners who were still unwilling to forgive and forget. His announcement, upon assuming office, that he did not plan to run for re-election made it difficult for him to deal with Republican politicians who knew that within four years they would no longer be under obligation to him. His hard-money policies alienated the inflationist wing of the party in the West, but it did not prevent Congress in 1878 from repassing over his veto the Bland-Allison Act for government silver purchases.* Although he made no move to regulate industry, commerce or finance, he did not hesitate to call out the Federal troops to oppose the railroad strikers in 1877. Finally, and most important of all, his handling of the patronage widened rather than narrowed the cleavage in the party between the Stalwarts and the Half-Breeds.

For more than a decade before Hayes became President, sporadic efforts had been made to eliminate the more glaring evils of the spoils system. As early as 1864, Charles Sumner had proposed a plan for civil-service reform, and four years later Congress had considered and rejected a bill that provided for competitive examinations for applicants for certain government posts. Meanwhile an educational campaign for civil-service reform was being conducted by such men as Senator Carl Schurz of Missouri, G. W. Curtis of *Harper's Weekly,* and E. L. Godkin of the *Nation.* In 1871, Grant responded to this pressure by appointing a civil-service commission with Curtis as its chairman; but three years later the commission's funds were cut off by Congress. Soon after Hayes assumed office, Carl Schurz, who was Secretary of the Interior, attempted to introduce a merit system in his department. At the same time Secretary of the Treasury John Sherman sought to remove some of the most glaring abuses of the patronage system in the New York custom

* See p. 263.

house. By making this move, Sherman openly defied Senator Roscoe Conkling, the party's leading Stalwart and the boss of the Republican machine in New York. Conkling not only wished to retain control over the most important source of patronage in his state, but he was also prepared to defend the spoils system as a positive good that alone made possible the existence of American political parties. To Conkling, parties were "not built up by deportment, or by ladies' magazines, or gush!" but by jobs for faithful political workers.

The struggle between the Administration and Conkling was precipitated by the report of a commission that stated that the workers in the New York custom house accepted bribes and were compelled to make regular contributions to the Republican party in order to hold their jobs. Hayes in an executive order of June 22, 1877, prohibited political activity among government employees, and Sherman ordered Chester A. Arthur, Collector of the Port of New York, and Alonzo Cornell, the port's Naval Officer, to clear up the mess in the custom house. But both men were Conkling's lieutenants, and they refused to follow the instructions of the Secretary of the Treasury. Conkling, for his part, lashed out at the Administration; and when Hayes in October, 1877, named Theodore Roosevelt, Sr., and L. B. Prince to succeed Arthur and Cornell respectively, Conkling was able to win the support of enough senators to prevent the confirmation of the President's nominees. Hayes countered by making two new appointments following Congress' adjournment in July, 1878. When Congress reassembled, Conkling returned to the offensive; but he was so vitriolic in his attacks on the President that he alienated many Republicans, and in February, 1879, Hayes' appointees were finally confirmed by the Senate.

Conkling carried his fight with the Administration to the Republican convention of 1880, where he hoped to defeat the Half-Breeds by securing Grant's nomination for a third term. The two other leading candidates were Sherman and Blaine; George F. Edmunds of Vermont, and Elihu Washburn of Illinois, also had some support. Although Grant led all the other contenders for more than thirty ballots, he could not secure a majority, and the delegates finally settled upon James A. Garfield of Ohio as a compromise candidate. A Union veteran and senator who had also served in the House for a number of years, Garfield was a Half-Breed. To "balance" the ticket and to appease the Stalwarts, the Republicans therefore gave the vice-presidential nomination to Chester A. Arthur. The Democrats nominated General Winfield S. Hancock of Pennsylvania and William H. English of Indiana. Hancock, who had played a relatively important part in the Union victory at Gettysburg, had won the approval of the South by his conduct as military Governor of Louisiana. English was a nonentity who had supported the Buchanan Administration's pro-Southern policies before the war. In the ensuing campaign both parties were careful to avoid the issues, and much was made of the military records of the two candidates. In reality, neither Hancock nor Garfield stood for much of anything except a desire to be president, and Garfield's victory can perhaps most accurately be attributed to the fact that his party controlled the national patronage and that it was only slightly less bankrupt politically than the Democratic party.

With Garfield's accession to the presidency the intraparty squabble over the patronage was resumed. The new President left no doubt concerning his attitude by making Blaine Secretary of State, by refusing to appoint any Stalwarts to important positions in the Administration, and by giving the juiciest patronage plums in New York to the Half-Breeds. Conkling continued to fight back,* but the whole sorry spectacle was soon climaxed by a national tragedy. On July 2, 1881, Charles J. Guiteau, a Stalwart and a disappointed officeseeker, shot and mortally wounded Garfield. As he stood over the President's body, Guiteau said: "I am a Stalwart and Arthur is President now."

Garfield died on September 19, 1881, and Chester A. Arthur, after a career as a spoils politician, became President. A former teacher and lawyer, he had worked his way up through the Republican organization and had earned the dubious distinction of being widely known as the "Gentleman Boss." As head of the New York custom house he had made the customs service synonymous with political graft and corruption. "For twenty years," Matthew Josephson has written, "he had devoted himself to gathering and awarding the spoils of office; one saw him in smoky hotel rooms, where brandy and cigars were dispensed freely, . . . negotiating with committees, chairmen, [and] agents."† But on becoming President, Arthur turned on his past and provided the people of the United States with a constructive, although not outstanding, administration. If anything, Arthur's long experience with professional politicians admirably prepared him for a position in which he had to be constantly on guard against the pressures of the special interests. On taking office he refrained from dismissing many of the Half-Breeds that had been appointed by Garfield, and throughout his term he repeatedly showed that he could not be controlled by either a faction or a party.

The most notable achievement of Arthur's Administration was the adoption of a law that was designed to mitigate the worst evils of the spoils system. Garfield's assassination had shocked the people into de-

* In a dramatic gesture that was designed to prove that he had his state's support in his campaign against Garfield, Conkling resigned from the Senate. Then, he and Senator Thomas Platt of New York, who had also resigned, asked the New York state legislature to give them a vote of confidence by re-electing them to the Senate. But the plan backfired, when the legislature refused to do their bidding. Vice-President Arthur lowered his own prestige and that of his office by going to Albany to lobby for the re-election of Conkling and Platt.

† Matthew Josephson: *The Politicos; 1865–1896* (New York: Harcourt, Brace and Company, Inc., 1938), p. 323.

manding some type of reform and revelations before his death concerning the corruption attending the award by the Post Office of contracts for "star routes"* had provided additional evidence of the need for ridding the government service of political appointees. In his first message to Congress, Arthur proposed that "appointments should be based upon ascertained fitness," and in January, 1883, Congress passed the Pendleton Act. A Democratic bill that had been sponsored by Senator George H. Pendleton of Ohio, the Pendleton Act was passed by bipartisan majorities in the House and Senate. This measure provided for the creation of the Civil Service Commission, the establishment of a classified service among certain groups of postal and custom-house workers, and competitive examinations for the positions that fell within the law. Although only 14,000 government employees in a force of more than 100,000 were placed under the jurisdiction of the law, the President was given the authority to extend the classified lists in the executive branch of the government. Dorman B. Eaton, the Secretary of the Civil Service Reform Association, was appointed the first chairman of the commission, and Arthur scrupulously observed both the spirit and the letter of the law during the remainder of his term as President.

Although Arthur could claim little personal credit for the adoption of civil-service reform, there were a number of instances in which he clearly revealed his political independence. Despite the fact that the leading figures in the "star route" frauds were important members of the Republican national machine, he vigorously backed their prosecution. In 1882, he pleased the taxpayers, if not their representatives, by vetoing a river and harbors bill. This was a pork-barrel measure that Congress soon repassed over the President's veto. Arthur also vetoed an act of 1882 that excluded the entry of Chinese into the United States for twenty years. His opponents in Congress could not muster the necessary two-thirds majority to override his veto, and eventually a compromise measure that reduced the period of exclusion to ten years was approved by both President and Congress. In his tariff policy, Arthur received little co-operation from his colleagues in the legislature. Although Congress accepted his proposal for a tariff commission, it staffed the new board exclusively with protectionists. When the commission, to virtually everyone's surprise, recommended a tariff reduction, Congress ignored this proposal and adopted a bill that called for an increase in some rates and small cuts in others.

* The "star routes" were those routes on which mail was carried by either riders or stages. They received their name because the Post Office used a star to identify them on its lists. In the star-route frauds the principal culprits were Second Assistant Postmaster General Thomas J. Brady, who acted in collusion with star-route contractors, and Stephen W. Dorsey, who was grossly overpaid for the star routes that he operated. Dorsey was an ex-senator from Arkansas and the secretary of the Republican National Committee.

52. CLEVELAND AND HARRISON

ARTHUR'S record as an independent alienated many of the party's regulars, while at the same time it failed to make the reformers forget his earlier activities as a spoils politician. The result was that the Republican convention of 1884 passed over Arthur and gave the nomination to James G. Blaine of Maine. Largely because Blaine was the first Republican nominee since the Civil War without a military record, the party named John A. Logan of Illinois, a Union veteran, to the second place on the ticket. In a famous speech at the Republican convention of 1876, Robert Ingersoll in a moment of aberration had referred to Blaine as a "plumed knight." In reality, the Republican candidate was a veteran politician with a particularly tarnished reputation. One of the most unsavory episodes in his long career had occurred when he had helped the Little Rock and Fort Smith Railroad save a land grant and then sold the company's stock on a commission basis to his fellow congressmen. The details of this exploit were contained in the so-called Mulligan Letters, which throughout the campaign were widely publicized by the Democrats.

The reformers, or Mugwumps, in the Republican party had opposed Blaine at the convention; and after they failed to block his nomination, they made it clear to the Democrats that they would support Grover Cleveland if he received the Democratic nomination. Because the Democrats, who had to attract independent votes to win, were in no position to argue, Cleveland was duly nominated. For vice-president the Democrats selected Thomas A. Hendricks of Indiana. As assistant district attorney and sheriff of Erie County, New York, Mayor of Buffalo, and Governor of New York, Cleveland had been an aggressive, uncorruptible Democrat who had antagonized the leaders of Tammany Hall and the other machine groups in the party while winning a nation-wide reputation as a reformer. In most essential respects, he was all that Blaine was not.

The campaign of 1884 was one of personalities and vituperation. While the Democrats rehashed the contents of the Mulligan Letters, the Republicans charged—and Cleveland made no attempt to hide the fact—that the Democratic candidate was the father of an illegitimate son. As election day approached, observers felt that New York, where the parties seemed evenly divided, held the key to the outcome of the contest and that the Irish voters in New York City probably held the balance of power in the state. In the closing days of the campaign the Reverend Dr. Samuel Burchard, in a speech at the Fifth Avenue Hotel in New York, said the Democrats were the party of "Rum, Romanism, and Rebellion." The Irish, who needed no further instructions, voted for the Democrats; Cleveland carried New York; and New York's

Harper's Weekly

THE PLUMED KNIGHT

Senator James G. Blaine of Maine, leader of the Half-Breeds and inveterate candidate for the presidency, finally won the nomination in 1884. This attack on him was made by a spokesman for the liberal branch of the Republican party in 1880, just before the nominating convention of that year. Robert Ingersoll, in the convention of 1876, had called Blaine a "plumed knight"; Thomas Nast indicates his notions of what the plumes were made of.

electoral votes provided him with a sufficient majority to insure victory. But Cleveland's plurality over Blaine was only 23,000, and the electoral vote was 219 to 182.

Despite the fact that Cleveland was the first Democrat—if Johnson is excepted—to occupy the White House since 1861, his accession to office produced no major changes in the government policies. Preferring to follow rather than lead, Cleveland devoted the major energies of his first term to administrative reforms. The Navy Department eliminated a number of irregularities while continuing the expansion program that had been inaugurated under Garfield and Arthur. In the Department of the Interior a concerted move was made to check the government's policy of giving large areas of land away to private corporations. Cleveland also tried to reverse the Republicans' generous pension policy. He vetoed not only a number of special pension measures but also the Blair Dependent Pensions Act, which would have provided governmental assistance for any Civil War veteran who had served three or more months and was at present disabled. In addition, Cleveland attempted to continue the civil-service program that had been established under the Pendleton Act; but at the end of his administration most government jobs were occupied by loyal Democrats.

Only once during his first term did Cleveland take the initiative; in 1887 he urged Congress to reduce the tariff. The House responded with the Mills Bill, which included most of the President's suggestions. In the Senate, however, the Republicans introduced a protectionist measure. When it proved impossible to work out a satisfactory compromise bill, the movement for tariff reduction ended with nothing accomplished.

Many historians have praised Cleveland for his courage, devotion to principle, and his refusal to let his first Administration become the victim of special interests. Although Cleveland was obviously a man of integrity, his accomplishments were nevertheless largely negative. None of the sweeping changes that were transforming the American economy was reflected in his acts and statements as President; nor did he ever indicate that he was aware of the widespread protests of the nation's farmers and workers. Aside from his tariff message, he operated on the assumption that politics and economics belonged in separate and airtight compartments. And even in his campaign for tariff reduction he failed to attain his objectives. While it is possible to commend Cleveland's intentions, it is impossible to credit him with any major achievements. In this sense he failed as a presidential leader. He also failed as a party politician, for in 1889 the Democrats were compelled to relinquish control of the government to the Republicans.

For the presidential campaign of 1888 the Democrats again nominated Cleveland for the presidency and made Allen G. Thurman their vice-presidential candidate. Although many Republicans thought that Blaine should be given another chance, the party's convention on the eighth ballot gave the necessary number of votes to Benjamin Harrison of Indiana, and chose Levi Morton, a New York banker, as his running mate. Harrison, who was the grandson of William Henry Harrison, was a rather colorless individual who had served one term in the Senate but had never been identified with any particular cause or measure. In contrast to 1884, personalities were largely ignored during the campaign, for the Democrats sought to make the tariff the sole issue, and the Republicans gladly accepted the challenge. But once again the Irish played a dramatic rôle. When Sir Lionel Sackville-West, the British minister to the United States, received a letter asking him how he thought a naturalized American should vote, he replied that Cleveland's election would best serve the interests of Great Britain. Matthew Quay, Pennsylvania's Republican boss and chairman of the party's campaign committee, had Sackville-West's reply published. Although there is no way of knowing, it seems likely that many Irish-Americans, upon learning that Cleveland was a friend of Ireland's enemy, decided to vote for Harrison.

The election of 1888 was probably the most corrupt in the nation's history. The Republican campaign chest was filled to overflowing with contributions from manufacturers who opposed the Democratic tariff plank, and much of the money was used to purchase votes in doubtful states. The election was very close, and it appears reasonable to conclude that the Republicans' fraudulent practices were one of the more important factors responsible for Harrison's victory. Although Cleveland polled approximately 100,000 more votes than Harrison, the Republicans won in the electoral college by a vote of 233 to 168. When Harrison learned of the outcome of the election, he said: "Providence has given us the victory." Matt Quay, who had borne the glad tidings, was so aghast at this interpretation of the election that he is reported to have said: "Think of the man. He ought to know that Providence hadn't a damn thing to do with it. . . . [Harrison will] never know how close a number of men were compelled to approach the gates of the penitentiary to make him President."*

Cleveland had sought to keep the government aloof from the conflicts that raged between various special interests, but Harrison went to the other extreme and in effect turned the government over to the most powerful pressure groups in the land. When Harrison became President, veterans wanted more pensions, Republican spoilsmen wanted jobs, manufacturers wanted higher tariffs, and Westerners wanted more favorable silver legislation. Within a short time all these groups had been satisfied. The Democrats were cleaned out of government office, and John Wanamaker, the Postmaster General, practically ignored civil

* Quoted in Josephson: *Politicos,* 433.

service regulations. The tariff presented a somewhat more difficult problem, for the government had a surplus that presumably would have been augmented by an increase in duties. But this was not an insuperable problem, for it was always possible to spend money on pensions and silver purchases. When Corporal James Tanner was appointed head of the Pension Bureau by Harrison, he said: "God help the surplus"; and within a short time he was busily engaged in obtaining an appropriation "for every old comrade who needs it." Furthermore, Harrison approved the Dependent Pensions Act, which had been vetoed by Cleveland. Any remaining doubts about the problem of a surplus were removed by the passage of the Sherman Silver Purchase Act. With the way thus cleared for an increase in the tariff, Congress adopted the McKinley Tariff, which represented a new high in American protectionism.

The McKinley Tariff, which became law on October 1, 1890, was introduced into Congress by William McKinley, a representative from Ohio and chairman of the House Ways and Means Committee. McKinley had devoted his political career to extolling protectionism, and the

The Bettmann Archive

THE PASSAGE OF THE TARIFF BILL

The McKinley Tariff of 1890 was higher than any previous tariff in the history of the United States and reflected the extent of the businessman's power in the government.

tariff measure that bore his name accurately reflected his views. In some instances rates on certain manufactured goods were so high that they were prohibitory, and in others provision was made for the imposition of duties on products that were not even manufactured in the United States. Although American agriculture was not generally threatened by foreign competition, the McKinley Tariff placed duties upon such commodities as butter, eggs, potatoes, and wheat. Another unusual feature of the new tariff was the intricate method that it employed to take care of every segment of the sugar industry. To aid and protect the American refining industry—most of which was controlled by the Havemeyer Sugar Trust—the duty was removed from raw sugar while a tariff of one-half cent a pound was placed on refined sugar. To safeguard the interests of native sugar-growers, the act called for the payment of a bounty of two cents a pound on all raw sugar produced in the United States. Finally, provision was made for a type of reciprocity that was designed to further Secretary of State James G. Blaine's plans for the increase of United States exports to Latin America. A number of Latin American products consumed in the United States were placed on the free list with the stipulation that the President could put duties on them if the countries of their origin failed to reduce the rates on certain American exports before January 1, 1892.

The McKinley Tariff was just one more piece of evidence indicating that the businessman had become the most powerful man in American politics. Whether he worked behind the scenes or openly participated in party affairs, he had ample reason to believe that his wishes would not be ignored. Regulatory measures such as the Interstate Commerce and Sherman Antitrust Acts did not disturb him unduly, for he knew that there was little prospect of their being rigidly enforced. If all else failed, there was always the Supreme Court, which throughout these years gave the businessman virtually free rein by interpreting the laws in an industrial economy of large-scale producers in accordance with the mores of a vanished agrarian society of small producers. At times the businessman had his way because of the prevailing belief that business expansion represented a desirable form of progress. At other times he was compelled to resort to extralegal or illegal devices to achieve his objectives in politics. But regardless of the methods he employed, he could count on the fact that the government would do relatively little to threaten his control over the American economy.

53. THE CURRENCY ISSUE

DESPITE the desire of Democratic and Republican politicians to prevent the rise to prominence of any question that might threaten their continued control over the government, they were unable to keep the currency issue out of American politics. Debates, and even armed conflicts, over the nation's currency had played an important part in American political history since colonial times, and in the years after the Civil War the battles between the inflationists and deflationists were fought with especial intensity. As in the past, the creditors demanded deflation, while the debtors were outspoken advocates of inflation. The business groups of the Northeast were proponents of "hard" money, whereas the mortgage-ridden farmers of the West and South asked for an expansion of the currency. Although the Republican party was thought by many contemporaries to be the champion of "sound" money and the Democrats were usually identified with "soft" money, neither party pursued a consistent currency policy during the last third of the nineteenth century. Both parties contained inflationist and deflationist blocs, and in congressional votes on the currency issue, party lines were frequently obliterated by sectional and economic interests.

The Republican party, despite its strength among agrarian debtors in the West, had adopted a postwar currency policy designed to meet the needs of its Eastern members; and although the Democrats generally opposed the Republicans' deflationary program, they were either unable or unwilling to prevent its adoption. In the circumstances, the inflationists were virtually compelled to turn to third-party movements to advance the cause of what came to be known as Greenbackism. Both the National Labor Union and the National Labor party had demanded currency inflation, and in 1874 the Independent party—or Greenback party, as it was usually called by contemporaries—was organized to work for an expansion of the currency. Consisting of a comparatively small number of labor leaders, farmers, and small businessmen, the Greenback party in 1876 nominated Peter Cooper for the presidency on a platform calling for the repeal of the Resumption Act. After the party's poor showing in the election of 1876—Cooper received less than 1 per cent of the total vote cast—the party was reorganized, and in 1878 it ran congressional candidates under the name of the Greenback-Labor party. With labor as well as currency planks, it was was able to poll approximately 1,000,000 votes, or more than ten times as many as Cooper had obtained two years earlier. But 1878 marked the high tide of Greenbackism, for its strength in the ensuing years rapidly declined, and in 1880, James B. Weaver, the party's presidential candidate, received only 308,578 votes. The decline of the Greenback party can be attributed to the return of prosperity following the depression of the midseventies, to the fact that the resumption of specie payments in 1879 failed to produce the hard times that the inflationists had repeatedly predicted, and to the growing prominence of the silver issue.

Although the place of silver in the nation's monetary system was eventually to become one of the most controversial issues in the entire history of American politics, it attracted comparatively little attention in the decade that immediately followed the Civil War. During these years silver was not coined extensively, silver dollars were bulky and therefore little used, and because silver was undervalued at the mint, only relatively small amounts of it were sold to the government. In 1873, when the silver dollar was dropped from the list of government coins, there was no concerted opposition to the move, and the Senate unanimously adopted a bill that authorized the abandonment of the silver dollar. In later years the silver interests were to refer to this step as the "Crime of '73," but there is no evidence that it was so viewed by contemporaries.

The Bettmann Archive

THE TWO-HEADED DEMOCRATIC TIGER

In 1876 the Democrats attempted to straddle the currency issue by counterbalancing the hard-money Samuel J. Tilden of the East with the soft-money Thomas A. Hendricks, supported by the West. For the next twenty-five years this issue continued to divide the Democratic party.

Because of a series of unforeseen developments in both Europe and the United States, the coinage of silver became a controversial issue at the very time that the government was refusing to inflate the currency with paper money. The money stringency caused by the Panic of 1873 produced demands for silver coinage as well as paper inflation; and when Grant blocked a paper expansion of the currency, the addition of silver was viewed by many proponents of soft money as the only logical alternative. At the same time a decline in the demand for silver in the world market placed the nation's silver-mining interests in a precarious position. In 1871, Germany demonetized silver, and three years later the countries of the Latin Union suspended the minting of silver coins. In the same period, the opening up of new silver deposits in Nevada led to a sharp increase in American silver supplies. The consequent drop in silver prices induced the silver interests to turn to the government for assistance, and Congress, in 1878 responded to this pressure with the adoption of the Bland-Allison Act. Enacted by a bipartisan coalition that drew its principal support from the mining states of the West and the farm states of the West and South, the Bland-Allison Act was repassed over President Hayes' veto. This measure required that the Secretary of the Treasury "purchase . . . silver bullion, at the market price thereof, not less than two million dollars worth per month, nor more than four million dollars per month, and cause the same to be coined monthly, as fast as so purchased," into silver dollars at the current ratio to gold.

Although many deflationists predicted that the Bland-Allison Act would drive gold from circulation, such forecasts were not borne out by the events of the years immediately following the bill's adoption. The silver dollars proved as unpopular as they had before their demonetization in 1873, and they formed a relatively insignificant part of the country's monetary system. Furthermore, the government always purchased the minimum rather than maximum amount of silver called for by the Bland-Allison Act. Finally, the revival of the American export market after the depression of the 1870's caused an influx of gold and increased the nation's gold supply to such an extent that there seemed little likelihood that gold would be driven from circulation by silver. Despite these developments, both Republican and Democratic Treasury officials were disturbed by what they considered the potential dangers of the Bland-Allison Act. In 1884, Hugh McCulloch, Arthur's Secretary of the Treasury, declared that the continued coinage of silver would eventually force the government to abandon gold payments. In the following year, Daniel Manning, Secretary of the Treasury under Cleveland, demanded the repeal of the Bland-Allison Act on the grounds that gold was being hoarded* and that the business community was losing confidence in the nation's currency system.

The Treasury Department's concern over the future of its reserves of gold was not shared by a comparatively large group of congressmen who were determined to expand rather than contract the currency. Representatives and senators from the Western mining states formed an interparty alliance known as the "silver bloc." Pledged "to do some-

* This statement was in accordance with the economic dictum known as "Gresham's law." According to this "law," "bad," or cheap, money drives "good," or dear, money out of circulation.

thing for silver," they could count on the co-operation of several farm-state congressmen whose constituents were demanding that inflationary measures be taken to lighten the burden of agrarian debt. To the farmer, silver seemed to offer the only solution to a problem that he thought could be largely explained in terms of supply and demand. While the production of gold had declined from $129,614,000 in 1866 to $118,848,700 in 1890, the population of the United States had steadily increased. There was, as the farmer saw it, simply not enough money for all. But as the output of gold decreased, that of silver rose from $11,000,000 in 1865 to $57,000,000 in 1890. The farmer felt that the obvious solution was the coinage of silver.

In a bid for the votes of both the mining and farm states the Republicans in the campaign of 1888 promised to aid the silver interests. And with the adoption in 1890 of the Sherman Silver Purchase Act they redeemed their campaign promise. The Sherman Act was made possible by a deal that called for Western Republican votes for the McKinley Tariff Act in return for Eastern Republican votes for silver; it was generally opposed by the Democratic inflationists, most of whom felt that it did not go far enough.

The Sherman Silver Purchase Act directed the Secretary of the Treasury to buy 4,500,000 ounces of silver each month and to pay for these purchases with treasury notes. The act further stated that it was the "established policy of the United States to maintain the two metals [silver and gold] on a parity with each other upon the present legal ratio"; and the Secretary of the Treasury was authorized to redeem the treasury notes "in gold or silver coin, at his discretion."*

54. CHECKING THE DRAIN ON GOLD

WHEN the Sherman Silver Purchase Act was adopted, the United States treasury had a surplus; but within four years the surplus was converted into a deficit by the Harrison Administration's generous pension program, a drop in tariff receipts under the McKinley Tariff, and the silver purchases required by the law of 1890. As the surplus declined, the pressure on gold increased. Individuals, fearing the effect of the silver purchase program on the nation's monetary system, hastened to convert their assets into gold. At the same time the flow of gold from the United States to Europe was accelerated by the decline of American exports in 1892.

* As long as the Sherman Silver Purchase Act was in effect, the Treasury Department interpreted this provision to mean that the "notes shall always be redeemed in gold or its equivalent."

Although the currency question was the most important issue facing the voters in 1892, it was largely ignored by both major parties, and only the Populists, a newly formed agrarian party, came out for the free coinage of silver. The Democrats, hoping to capitalize on the widespread dissatisfaction with the McKinley Tariff, again nominated Cleveland and ran him on a low-tariff platform. The Republicans, who had been overwhelmingly defeated in the midterm elections of 1890, once more chose Harrison, and the Populists nominated James B. Weaver of Iowa. The outcome of the election was an accurate indication of the voters' disgust with Harrison's submission to the pressure groups that had played such an important rôle under his administration. The Democrats gained control of both houses of Congress, and Cleveland received 227 electoral votes to 145 for Harrison and 22 for Weaver.

Cleveland not only inherited the financial problems that had confronted Harrison, but he was also forced to contend with the Panic of 1893. The hard times that followed were attended by numerous business failures, widespread unemployment, severe personal hardship, and a deterioration in the government's financial position. Federal revenue fell off sharply, and many people, fearing that their gold and silver certificates would not continue to be redeemable in gold, hastened to present them to the treasury before it was too late. As a consequence, the net gold reserve declined from $190,232,405 in 1890 to $114,342,367 in 1892 and $64,873,025 in 1894. Under the circumstances, it seemed to be only a matter of time before the United States would be forced to abandon gold payments.

Despite the strength of the silver interests in the Democratic party, Cleveland was determined to maintain the gold reserves, and soon after taking office in 1893 he demanded the repeal of the Sherman Silver Purchase Act. Congress, however, was reluctant to take this step, and it was only after Cleveland had used the patronage to win over a number of doubtful representatives and senators that the bill for the repeal was adopted. This measure ended silver purchases by the government, but it did not fundamentally alter the government's problem, for gold was still flowing from the treasury at an alarming rate. The basic difficulty was that the government had to pay out gold to those individuals who presented either silver or gold certificates to the treasury; but it was also compelled by law to put these notes back into circulation as currency; and they could then be resubmitted to the treasury for more gold. This "endless chain," as it was called, could only be broken by convincing the people that the country was not about to be forced to end gold payments. In short, if individuals were confident that the government had an adequate supply of gold, they would no longer seek to redeem their notes.

By 1894 the government's gold stocks were so low that the Cleveland Administration decided that they could only be replenished by the sale of bonds for gold. But this expedient did not immediately produce the desired results, for the first two bond issues in January and November, 1894, which were subscribed to by banking syndicates, were purchased by gold that had been obtained from the treasury in exchange for notes. Because this operation left the government's gold supply in no better shape than before the bonds had been issued, Cleveland was forced to turn to a syndicate led by J. P. Morgan. In February, 1895, Morgan agreed to buy bonds with gold, half of which would be obtained from Europe and none of which would be drawn from the treasury of the United States. Morgan further agreed to use his influence to check the flow of American gold to Europe. Although Morgan received the bonds at 104½, they subsequently rose to 119. Historians have consumed considerable quantities of paper and printer's ink in debates over whether or not Morgan's terms were extortionate; most think that they were, but the Cleveland Administration nevertheless attained its objective. Morgan fulfilled his part of the bargain, confidence in the nation's monetary system was restored, and payments in gold were continued. Contemporaries —particularly representatives of the farm and silver groups—complained that Cleveland had subordinated the welfare of the nation to the interests of the money power, but such charges could not change the fact that the arrangement with Morgan was so successful that in 1896 the government was able to by-pass the bankers and offer its fourth bond issue of $100,000,000 directly to the public.

The split in the Democratic party created by the repeal of the Sherman Silver Purchase Act made it practically impossible for the Administration to carry out its program of tariff reduction. The advocates of inflation in the Western wing of the party were no longer prepared to recognize Cleveland as their leader, and Eastern Democrats proved as willing to co-operate with the Republicans on the tariff as they had on the currency question. As a result Cleveland's plans for tariff reform were blocked by party factionalism and the pressure of the special interests. Although the Wilson Bill, which was introduced by Representative William L. Wilson of West Virginia and adopted by the House, was a low tariff measure that resembled the Mills Bill, its character was completely altered by the more than six hundred increases that were added to it by Senate amendments. The sugar bounty was ended, but duties were imposed on raw as well as refined sugar. In addition, provision was made for an income tax, but in 1895 the Supreme Court ruled it unconstitutional. While generally lower than the McKinley Tariff, the Wilson Tariff, which was approved by the House and Senate in 1894, was blatantly protectionist, and Cleveland allowed it to become law without his signature.

By the end of his second administration Cleveland had alienated

The Bettmann Archive

'HRESHING BY STEAM IN THE GREAT WHEAT FIELDS OF THE DAKOTAS, 1878

:ONSEQUENCE OF LARGE-SCALE FARMING—THE MIGRANT WORKER OF TODAY

Courtesy U.S.D.A., photograph by Ackerman

THE LEAKY CONNECTION

According to this cartoonist, the farmer's profits were siphoned off into the pockets of middlemen through the leaks in the joints of the monopoly pipeline.

large blocs of voters. His tariff policy had satisfied no one completely; his use of Federal troops in the Pullman strike had antagonized the workers; and his stand on the silver question had convinced the farmers and Western miners that the Democrats as well as the Republicans were controlled by Wall Street. His one positive accomplishment was to continue gold payments; but in doing so, he had also split his party into two irreconcilable groups and had provided the United States with its most controversial issue since the Reconstruction period. Most important of all, he had provided the farmers with the final bit of evidence that they needed to prove to themselves that the government of the United States was owned and run by the moneyed interests of the seaboard cities. Convinced that only expansion of the currency by the free coinage of silver could solve their major economic problems, the farmers of the West and South resolved to join forces with the Western silver miners to wrest control of the government from the "bloated bondholders" of the East.

55. THE AGRARIAN PROTEST

SOME years before Cleveland's successful defense of the gold reserves, large numbers of American farmers had reached the conclusion that they could achieve their major objectives only by resorting to political action. They had played a dominant rôle in the nation's economic, social and political life before the Civil War, and they found it difficult to accept the subordinate position to which they had been relegated in the postwar decades. The farmer's principal grievances were economic, and they were caused in large part by his inability to control the conditions upon which his profits depended. With much justification the farmer complained that he had little or no voice in the determination of the prices of the products that he bought and sold, the terms on which he obtained credit, the value of his currency, and the rates on which he was charged to ship his produce to market. To be sure, the prewar farmer had no more control than the postwar farmer over the prices at which he sold his commodities; but he had not been at the mercy of railroads in a position to charge exorbitant rates, and his representatives in the government had been able to prevent the enactment of tariff, credit, and currency laws detrimental to his interests. Thus to the farmers their lack of economic power was merely a manifestation of their loss of political power. Reasoning that those who controlled the government were using it to further their own interests, they concluded that they could improve their lot only by voting the businessmen and their representatives out of office and by then converting the nation's political machinery into an instrument that would benefit the country's farmers. This struggle was as old as the American nation; and, in launching their campaign, the farmers of the 1890's were refighting the battles that Jefferson and his agrarian allies had fought and won in the 1790's.

In the 1870's the Grange won a number of notable political victories in several Midwestern farm states. But once it had obtained the type of railroad regulation that it desired, the Grange tended to lose interest in politics. The decline in political power, however, was paralleled by the rise of other farm organizations in the agricultural regions of the South and West. As early as 1878 a Grand State Alliance was formed in Texas, and within a decade it had combined with the Farmers' Union of Louisiana to organize the National Farmers' Alliance and Co-operative Union of America. By 1887, the Alliance had extended its membership to nine Southern states. In the same years, the Agricultural Wheel, which had been founded in Arkansas in 1882, soon attracted the support of many Southern farmers. In 1888 the two organizations joined forces to form the Farmers' and Laborers' Union of America. Although the union had a number of political planks in its platform, its principal objectives were social, and its economic program placed emphasis on agricultural improvement through the use of more efficient farm techniques and the establishment of co-operatives.

The growth of a Southern agricultural organization was paralleled by a somewhat similar development in the rural sections of the Northwest. The National Farmers' Alliance—or Northwest Alliance, as it was more generally known—was first established in Illinois, and in 1880 it established itself as a national organization. Although the Northwest Alliance encouraged the formation of co-operatives, it also gave considerably more attention to political action than did the Southern farm groups. In its platform of 1887, the Northwest Alliance demanded the free coinage of silver, paper-money issues, the direct election of senators, and the nationalization of the railroad and telegraph systems. Although the alliance made no attempt to form a third party, it proposed that "farmers throughout the country . . . aid in the work of immediate organization, that we may act in concert for our own and the common good." In December, 1889, both the Northwest Alliance and the Farmers' and Laborers' Union—which was renamed the National Farmers' Alliance and Industrial Union—held their conventions in St. Louis. Although representatives of both groups sought to devise a formula on which they could unite, the negotiations broke down, and the two organizations continued to go their separate ways.

Despite the reluctance of both Alliances to form a third party, the platforms that they adopted at St. Louis contained numerous demands that could be obtained only by political action. The Southern Alliance—

as the National Farmers' Alliance and Industrial Union was generally called—advocated the free coinage of silver, abolition of national banks, government ownership of the railroads and telegraph, and the prevention of trading in grain futures. To these demands was added a proposal for a system of commodity credit that would be financed and administered by the Federal government. Under this plan the government would set up a series of subtreasury offices and grain elevators in which a farmer could deposit his nonperishable staples. In return for his crops the farmer would receive a certificate of deposit that could be used to obtain a loan that was worth 80 per cent of the current price of the commodities stored. Produce that was not reclaimed at the end of the year was to be sold at auction. While the Northwest Alliance did not adopt the subtreasury plan, its platform in all other essentials was similar to that of the Southern Alliance.

The refusal of either the Democratic or Republican parties to accept the program of the Alliances forced the agrarians to enter their own candidates in the election campaigns of 1890. In the Southern states the Alliance sought to gain control of the Democratic party machinery. In the West the farmers drew up their own tickets and formed third parties—which were variously named People's, or Independent, or Industrial parties—to challenge the dominant Republicans. Despite the lack of a national political organization, the farmers won a number of notable victories. In the South, they gained majorities in five state legislatures and elected three Governors, one senator, and forty-four representatives. In the West the farmers made their most impressive showing in Kansas, where the People's party secured control of the lower house of the legislature and elected five congressmen and one senator. In Nebraska they obtained a majority in the legislature, while the Independent candidate won the senatorial race in South Dakota.

The outcome of the election of 1890 was all the evidence needed by the farmers to convince them of the wisdom of forming a national party. In May, 1891, representatives of various farm groups met at Cincinnati with delegates from the Knights of Labor in a convention that voted overwhelmingly for the organization of a third party. More than a year later—in July, 1892—the Populists held their first national convention in Omaha. After stating that "wealth belongs to him who creates it," the party's first platform demanded "free and unlimited coinage of silver and gold at the present legal ratio of sixteen to one"; a graduated income tax; the nationalization of railroads, telephones and telegraphs; a reform of the nation's land system; and the establishment of postal savings banks. The Populists also made an attempt to appeal to a wider electorate than that of the farm sections. The currency plank was designed to attract not only farmers but also the voters in the silver mining states. Labor's interests were revealed in planks calling for immigration restriction, abolition of detective—that is to say, strikebreaking—agencies, and the enforcement of the eight-hour day in all Federal projects. War veterans were promised pensions; and the support of political reformers was sought with demands for a single term for the President of the United States, the direct election of senators, and the initiative, referendum, and recall. For their candidates the Populists nominated General James B. Weaver, a Union veteran, for president and General James G. Field, a Confederate veteran, for vice-president.

In the election of 1892, Weaver and Field polled 1,041,600 popular votes and 22 electoral votes. In the West, the Populists carried North Dakota, Colorado, Idaho, Kansas, and Nevada, and showed considerable strength in both Oregon and Nebraska. The Southern Populists, while less successful than those of the West, for the first time since the end of the Reconstruction weakened, if they did not break, the Democratic party's monopoly in the South's political affairs. Two years later, in the midterm elections of 1894, the Populists polled 1,471,600 votes and elected six senators and seven representatives.

Although in the campaigns of 1892 and 1894 the Populists received the support of the silver miners—and to a lesser extent, that of the workers and reformers—the party was essentially agrarian in make-up and outlook. In down-to-earth language the party's spokesmen preached a type of agrarian radicalism that shocked and appalled "respectable" groups in the East. They urged their supporters to "rob the plutocrat who puts chains and shackles upon your limbs," and in attacks on their opponents they frequently displayed a remarkable command of invective. Pitchfork Ben Tillman, while campaigning nominally as a Democrat, denounced Cleveland's candidacy as "a prostitution of the principles of the Democracy . . . and a surrender of the rights of the people to the financial kings of the country." In Kansas, "Sockless" Jerry Simpson, referring to his opponent as "Prince Hal," ridiculed him for wearing silk stockings. Mrs. Mary Lease, another Kansan, took the stump to urge the farmers of the state to "raise less corn and more hell." In a speech that was typical of her own, as well as many other Populists', campaign oratory, Mrs. Lease said:

Wall Street owns the country. It is no longer a government of the people, by the people and for the the people, but a government of Wall Street, by Wall Street and for Wall Street. The great common people of this country are slaves, and monopoly is the master. The West and South are bound and prostrate before the manufacturing East. Money rules, and our Vice President is a London banker. Our laws are the output of a system which clothes rascals in robes and honesty in rags. The parties lie to us and the political speakers mis-

lead us. . . . The common people are robbed to enrich their masters. . . . There are thirty men in the United States whose aggregate wealth is over one and one-half billion dollars. There are a half a million looking for work. . . . We want money, land and transportation. We want the abolition of the National Banks, and we want the power to make loans direct from the government. We want the accursed foreclosure system wiped out. . . . We will stand by our homes and stay by our firesides by force if necessary, and we will not pay our debts to the loan-shark companies until the government pays its debts to us. The people are at bay, let the bloodhounds of money who have dogged us thus far beware.

Despite the wide range of issues covered by the Populists' platforms, the party after 1892 was increasingly forced to subordinate all other questions to that of silver. Not only did the demand for the free coinage of silver have the greatest appeal to dissatisfied groups both within and outside the ranks of the farmers, but it was also an issue on which the Democratic and Republican parties appeared unwilling to compromise. In 1895 a Populist party manifesto stated:

As early as 1865–66 a conspiracy was entered into between the gold gamblers of Europe and America . . . [for] the following purposes: to fasten upon the people of the United States the burdens of perpetual debt; to destroy the greenbacks which had safely brought us through the perils of war; to strike down silver as a money metal; to deny to the people the use of Federal paper and silver—the two independent sources of money guaranteed by the Constitution; to fasten upon the country the single gold standard of Britain, and to delegate to thousands of banking corporations, organized for private gain, the sovereign control, for all time, over the issue and volume of all supplemental paper currency.

By 1894 the Populists were convinced that the future of their party rested with the silver issue. Party speakers subordinated other planks in the Populist platform to silver; rural papers carried countless editorials on the advantages of the free coinage of silver; and books and pamphlets on the subject became best sellers. Of all the literature dealing with the "money question," none was as influential or as popular as W. H. Harvey's *Coin's Financial School.* Issued in 1894, this book described how a "Professor Coin" won over a number of widely known advocates of the gold standard to silver by the clarity of his exposition and the skill with which he refuted their arguments. It has been estimated that *Coin's Financial School* was read by a half million Americans, many of whom undoubtedly agreed with Harvey that silver was the "money of the people, and gold the money of the rich." The year after the appearance of *Coin's Financial School,* Ignatius Donnelley, a Minnesota Populist, published *The American People's Money,* in which a farmer repeatedly scored in an argument with a businessman. Although less popular than *Coin's Financial School,* Donnelley's book, by going beyond the demand for silver to other planks of the Populist program, provided a more reliable explanation of the period's agrarian discontent.

56. THE CAMPAIGN OF 1896 AND ITS AFTERMATH

THE POPULISTS based their hopes for success in the election of 1896 on the conviction that both the Democrats and Republicans would refuse to advocate the free coinage of silver. With the gold vote thus split between the two major parties, the Populists were confident that they could capture both the executive and legislative branches of the government. The Republicans did not disappoint the Populists, for their convention was dominated at all times by Mark Hanna and his supporters from the gold wing of the party. Hanna, who did not hesitate to proclaim that "no man in public life owes the public anything," was the archetype of the businessman in politics. Having gained control of the Republican party in Cleveland and then in Ohio, he was now ready to take over the party's national organization. Hanna's plans called for the nomination of his fellow-Ohioan, William McKinley, whose assets as a candidate were undeniable. A handsome man of commanding appearance, he looked like an artist's stereotype of a "statesman"; and William Allen White has written that he "walked among men [like] a bronze statue . . . determinedly looking for his pedestal."* Despite an extensive career in state and national politics, he had seldom taken a clear-cut stand on any controversial issue. Eastern businessmen knew and approved of him as the author of the tariff act that bore his name, while Westerners were reminded that he had voted for the Bland-Allison Act and that he favored some form—precisely what form was never made clear—of bimetallism. To the voters of every section he was announced by Hanna as "Bill McKinley, the advance agent of prosperity."

In the months preceding the Republican convention, Hanna had secured the support of almost all the Southern and Western delegates for McKinley. Easterners, who were worried about McKinley's vague re-

* William Allen White: *Masks in a Pageant* (New York: The Macmillan Company, 1928), p. 155.

The Bettmann Archive

TAKING THE GOLD CURE

Mark Hanna, who controlled the Republican party machinery and was responsible for McKinley's nomination, is represented as forcing the gold standard upon his candidate.

marks on bimetallism* and who resented Hanna's plans to seize control of the party, were faced by a *fait accompli.* McKinley was nominated on the first ballot, and the party's currency plank opposed the free coinage of silver (except by international agreement) and "every measure calculated to debase our currency." Following the adoption of the gold-standard plank, thirty-four delegates, led by Senator Teller of Colorado, withdrew from the convention amidst cries from the majority of "Go!

* Hanna, who favored the gold standard as much as the Eastern Republicans, refused to commit himself until the last moment. When Hanry Cabot Lodge told Hanna that he would have to put a gold plank in the platform, the following exchange took place:

Hanna: "Who in hell are you?"

Lodge: "Senator Henry Cabot Lodge, of Massachusetts."

Hanna: "Well, Senator Henry Cabot Lodge, of Massachusetts, you can go plumb to hell. You have nothing to say about it."

Go! . . . Go to Chicago [the site of the Democratic convention]! Take the Democratic train!"

The Democratic convention differed in all essential respects from that of the Republicans. From the outset the party's rebels were in the ascendancy, and rebellion and silver were synonymous. The platform, which was an itemized repudiation of the Cleveland Administration, demanded not only the "free and unlimited coinage of both silver and gold at the present legal ratio of 16 to 1," but it also advocated Federal regulation of the trusts and railroads and condemned the government's sale of the bonds to the banks and the use of the injunction in labor disputes. But it was silver—and silver alone—that brought the delegates to the point of hysteria and provided William Jennings Bryan with an opportunity that has seldom been granted to any other American politician. As the final speaker representing the silver faction in the debate over the platform, Bryan found an overwhelmingly sympathetic audience that did not need to be convinced but asked only to be aroused. And Bryan did not disappoint his listeners. Opening his speech in a seemingly moderate and even conciliatory tone, he gradually developed a simple but vivid thesis, which he presented with mounting fervor. Drawing a line between the "struggling masses" and the "idle hoarders of idle capital," he hammered away at the single theme that the producing classes had been made prisoners of a system from which they could be released only by the free coinage of silver. As he developed the agrarian indictment of the financial classes, he identified himself and his party with the sons of the soil, who had made possible America's growth and success but who were now forced to fight in "defense of our homes, our families, and posterity." Once more, the Jeffersonians were asked to overthrow the New Federalism, right the balance between city and country, and return the country and its economy to their rightful rulers. The issues were clear and the time for action had arrived. In his concluding passages, Bryan contrasted the contending forces and called on his supporters to launch a crusade:

> [The advocates of gold] *come to us and tell us that the great cities are in favor of the gold standard; we reply that the great cities rest upon our broad and fertile prairies. Burn down your cities and leave our farms, and your cities will spring up again as if by magic; but destroy our farms and the grass will grow in the streets of every city in the country.*
>
> . . . *If they* [the gold interests] *dare to come out in the open field and defend the gold standard as a good thing, we will fight them to the uttermost. Having behind us the producing masses of this nation and the world, supported by the commercial interests, the laboring interests and the toilers everywhere, we will answer their*

demand for a gold standard by saying to them: You shall not press down upon the brow of labor this crown of thorns, you shall not crucify mankind upon a cross of gold.

Bryan's speech, which had been repeatedly interrupted by bursts of sustained applause, was followed by an hour-long ovation. The convention had found both its issue and its leader; and on the following day Bryan was nominated on the fifth ballot and Arthur Sewall of Maine was chosen as his running mate. To Eastern business groups, the Democratic convention was a "political debauch" and Bryan was a class-conscious radical demanding a revolution. But if Bryan's opponents had taken the trouble to read carefully the speech of this hitherto obscure Nebraskan politician, they would have discovered that he was asking only for a return to an America of an earlier day. He was not urging the proletariat on to the barricades, but asking only that the nation's small producers—whether in factory, shop, or farm—be restored to the place that they had once occupied in the American economy. In a significant section of his speech that was addressed to the convention's gold delegates he said:

When you come before us and tell us that we are about to disturb your business interests, we reply that you have disturbed our business interests by your course.

We say to you that you have made the definition of a business man too limited in its application. The man who is employed for wages is as much a business man as his employer; the attorney in a country town is as much a business man as the corporation counsel in a great metropolis; the merchant at the cross-roads store is as much a business man as the merchant of New York; the farmer who goes forth in the morning and toils all day, who begins in the spring and toils all summer, and who by the application of brain and muscle to the natural resources of the country creates wealth, is as much a business man as the man who goes upon the Board of Trade and bets upon the price of grain; the miners who go down a thousand feet into the earth, or climb two thousand feet upon the cliffs, and bring forth from their hiding places the precious metals to be poured into the channels of trade are as much business men as the few financial magnates who, in a back room, corner the money of the world. We come to speak of this broader class of business men.

The Democratic party's stand on the currency question upset the plans of the Populist leaders and forced them into a position where they could do little but choose between the lesser of two evils. If they nominated their own candidates, they would split the silver vote and give the election to the Republicans. If, on the other hand, they supported

Bryan, they would be signing their own party's death warrant. Meeting three weeks after the Democrats, the delegates to the Populist convention finally concluded that the pressure of events compelled them to abandon Populism for silver and Bryan. In nominating Bryan they staked everything on a panacea rather than a program; and Henry Demarest Lloyd, a Chicago reformer who had sympathized with the Populists' social and economic reforms, wrote:

> *The Free Silver movement is a fake. Free Silver is a cow-bird of the Reform movement. It waited until the nest had been built by sacrifices and labour of others, and then it laid its eggs in it. . . . The People's party has been betrayed.*

While the Populists were willing—however reluctantly—to vote for Bryan, they could not accept Sewall, who was a banker, railroad director, and shipbuilder. Moreover, the Southern delegates, bitterly opposed to a coalition with the Democrats, demanded that the party make at least a show of independence. It was with these considerations in mind that the convention selected Tom Watson, a veteran agrarian leader in Georgia, as the party's candidate for vice-president.

Although the Gold Democrats nominated their own ticket, they played a relatively insignificant rôle in the campaign of 1896, for to most voters the choice was between Bryan and silver on the one hand and McKinley and gold on the other. The Democratic-Populist candidate conducted a strenuous campaign in which he concentrated on the silver issue, and he traveled 18,000 miles and made countless speeches. (John Hay said that Bryan made only one speech, but that he made it twice a day.) The Republicans under Mark Hanna's direction kept their candidate at home, where he waged a decorous "front-porch" campaign. Almost daily, large crowds of loyal Republicans visited McKinley at what the silver groups nicknamed the "shrine of the golden calf." McKinley's statements, which were carried in the nation's leading newspapers, harped on the single theme that the Republicans alone were capable of providing the country with prosperity and stability. As the campaign drew to a close the Republicans revealed both their fear of the election's outcome and their determination to win the contest. Many businessmen, drawing up contracts, inserted in them a clause making their validity contingent on Bryan's defeat; workingmen's pay envelopes frequently contained notices warning that a Democratic victory would cost them their jobs; and some farmers were threatened with foreclosure if the silver interests carried the election.

Although McKinley's majority in the electoral college was unexpectedly large—271 to 176—, it did not reflect the closeness of the election. The popular vote for Bryan totaled 6,502,925 to McKinley's 7,104,-779; but the Democrats and Populists had been able to carry only the

10. THE ELECTION OF 1896

South and the Far West. The Republican victory can be attributed in large part to the efficient organization that Hanna had created for the campaign, the party's almost inexhaustible supply of funds, and the support that McKinley received from representatives of the most influential classes in the population. While Democratic-Populist campaign expenditures were only $300,000, the Republicans in the last weeks of the contest spent $25,000 a day and during the entire campaign they probably spent more than $7,000,000. At the same time the repeated warnings of college presidents, clergymen, business leaders, and newspaper editors that a vote for Bryan was a vote for anarchy and revolution presumably affected the decisions of many undecided voters. Finally, the outcome of the election seems to indicate that most members of the nonagrarian middle class and labor groups considered Bryan a threat to their property, savings, and income; and without the support of this large but unorganized segment of the population, no party could win a national election.

The election of 1896 marked a turning point in American history. As a struggle between agrarian poverty and business wealth, its outcome placed the political stamp of approval upon the transformation of the United States into an industrial nation. Silver was a symbol—and, from the standpoint of the Populists, an unfortunate one—rather than a cause of the deep-seated cleavage in American society. The farmers had based their appeal on class and sectional issues only to discover that this was a weapon that the businessman had long ago learned to wield with devastating effectiveness. The Populists were accused by their opponents of being radical revolutionaries, but they were nothing more than political realists who knew that those who controlled the government were its principal beneficiaries. They wished not to overthrow the government, but to capture it so that it could be made to work for the agrarians rather than the businessmen. They had gambled everything on the election of 1896, and they had lost. A hundred years after the inception of the struggle between Jefferson and Hamilton, the agrarians went down to their final defeat.

The Populists lost the argument as well as the election, for their predictions concerning the effect of the gold policies on the nation's economy were not substantiated by the events of the years immediately after 1896. The upswing of the business cycle following the depression of the midnineties benefited the farmer as well as other occupational groups within the nation. European crop failures in 1897 and increasing industrial production in the United States expanded the farmer's market both at home and abroad. At the same time the opening up of the Rand gold fields and the introduction of the cyanide process for refining gold combined to disprove the farmers' contention that there could never be an adequate supply of gold.

On assuming office, one of McKinley's first acts was to call Congress into special session to consider an upward revision of the tariff. The resultant Dingley Tariff, which was introduced by Representative Nelson Dingley, Jr. of Maine and adopted by Congress in 1897, marked a new high in American protectionism. Duties were placed on raw wool, hides, and other products that had been on the free list since 1890; the McKinley Tariff rates on metals, which had been removed by the Wilson Tariff, were restored; especial care was again taken to safeguard the interests of sugar refiners; and the reciprocity provisions of the McKinley Tariff were revived. Rates were so high under the Dingley Tariff that imports declined despite returning prosperity; and during the first year that the tariff was in operation, the revenue collected from it was $27,000,000 less than that produced by the Wilson Tariff during a similar period. If there remained any doubt in contemporary minds concerning the significance of the election of 1896, it was removed by the Dingley Tariff.

Because of the large number of Western inflationists in his party, McKinley approached the currency issue with far more caution than he had the tariff. A month after his inauguration, he appointed a three-man commission to investigate the status of international bimetallism in Europe. But when Great Britain made it clear that it had no interest in silver coinage in any form, the President was able to tell the "soft money" groups in his party that the Administration's only alternative was the gold standard. At the same time the upswing in the business cycle and the marked increase in world gold production deprived the inflationists of their two most effective points. Accordingly, in March, 1900, the Currency Act which legalized the gold standard, was adopted. Under this measure, a gold dollar of 25.8 grains nine tenths fine was made the unit of value; all other forms of the currency were to be kept at parity with the gold dollar; and parity was to be maintained through a special gold fund of $150,000,000.

The Currency Act of 1900 stands as an epitaph to the agrarian protest movement. Mark Hanna had promised the voters prosperity; and the cyclical movement of American business activity—if not the Republicans—had fulfilled this promise. Good times blunted the old reform impulses, and farmers tended to forget their earlier grievances, return to the traditional parties, and take their stand with the defenders of the *status quo.*

CHAPTER IX

OVERSEAS EXPANSION

FROM its inception the United States was expansionist. Between 1789 and 1861 Americans pushed steadily into the unsettled lands of the North American continent, and their government made the acquisition of more territory a fundamental tenet of American foreign policy. The purchase of Louisiana, the acquisition of Florida, the annexation of Texas, the conquest of New Mexico and California, and the division of Oregon all testified to the willingness of political leaders to satisfy the land hunger of an overwhelmingly agrarian nation. Although certain commercial groups looked with avidity on such overseas outposts as Samoa and Hawaii and the slave interests clamored for Cuba, the government held steadfast to a policy of continental expansion.

In the years between Appomattox and Versailles the United States became an industrial nation and a world power. This double transformation diverted American imperialism into new channels, and the old lure of continental expansion gave way in the American mind to the new magic of expansion overseas into Hawaii, Samoa, Guam, Midway, Wake, Puerto Rico, and the Philippines. Expansionism was not dead, but its character and direction had changed with the transition of the United States from an agrarian to an industrial economy.

57. IMPERIALISTS WITHOUT A MANDATE

IN THE YEARS that immediately followed the Civil War, the American people temporarily abandoned their traditional interest in the territorial expansion of the United States. Worn out by almost half a decade of internecine conflict, they were inclined to shun any foreign adventures that might lead to further bloodletting and misery. The principal issues of the day were, not the acquisition of weak neighbors or distant islands, but the reconstruction of the South, the subjugation of the last frontier, and the development of industry.

Nevertheless, a few imperialists maintained that the United States should resume the policy of territorial expansion that had been interrupted by sectional rivalries. These postbellum imperialists were both a reflection of the past and a portent of the future. Although they continued to urge the continental expansion of the United States, they argued even more strongly that America's destiny lay on the high seas. The shifting currents of American expansionism were most clearly revealed by the policies of William H. Seward, who served as Secretary of State under Presidents Lincoln and Johnson and in many ways bridged the pre-Civil War spirit of Manifest Destiny and the spread-eagle Americanism of the 1890's. Seward's expansionist policies were based on his convictions that American continental domination and American sea power were intimately related, and that the increased strength with which the United States had emerged from the Civil War could permit it to assume a more important rôle in world power-politics. To the earlier interests of the United States in the Atlantic Ocean and on the North American continent Seward planned to add interests in the Caribbean, the Pacific, and eastern Asia.

In Seward's mind, the purchase of Alaska in 1867 was an integral part of a larger program for the extension of American political and economic control across the Pacific; and as early as 1860 he had predicted that the Alaskan "outposts of St. Petersburg" would eventually "become outposts of my own country—monuments of the civilization of the United States in the Northwest." Despite Seward's interest in the acquisition of Alaska, the impetus for its transfer originated in Russia rather than the United States. During the Crimean War, Russia had considered disposing of its North American possession as a strategic liability, and in 1860, Baron de Stoeckl, the Russian minister to the United States, discussed the possibility of an American purchase of Alaska with Senator William Gwin of California and Assistant Secretary of State John Appleton. By the conclusion of the Civil War the Russian plans for the disposal of Alaska had crystalized, and in December, 1866, the Tsar directed Stoeckl to offer Alaska to the United States for not less than $5,000,000. There were numerous considerations behind the Tsar's decision. The Russian American Company in Alaska was close to bankruptcy, and the Tsarist government was not disposed to subsidize it. Moreover, numerous Russian officials were convinced that Alaska should be abandoned so that the government could concentrate its energies on the economic development of the Amur region in Siberia. Finally, it was thought that the sale of Alaska would improve relations between the United States and Russia, while at the same time Russia would rid itself of a region that was considered a potential source of conflict.

In March, 1867, Baron Stoeckl made his offer to the American Secretary of State. Seward referred the matter to the President and cabinet, and the purchase of Alaska for $7,200,000 was approved. As soon as these terms were accepted by the Tsar's government, a treaty embodying them was drawn up and signed on March 30, 1867. The American people, who had not been informed of these negotiations until they were completed, greeted the treaty with surprised approval. Although few Americans, aside from some fishermen and traders on the Pacific coast, had displayed any previous concern with Alaska, most of them were delighted with what they considered a good bargain. Seward's principal problem was, not the American people, but the United States Senate. To overcome the opposition of many senators who viewed with suspicion any project emanating from the unpopular Johnson Administration, Seward launched a campaign of education. Reports concerning Alaska's salubrious climate and limitless resources were given to the press; letters of prominent Americans favoring annexation appeared in leading newspapers; senators were wined and dined; and the need for promoting Russian-American friendship was emphasized to such an extent that opposition to the treaty became tantamount to an expression of hostility toward a generous and friendly Tsar. Most important of all, Seward was able to elicit the support of Charles Sumner, the expansionist senator from Massachusetts and the chairman of the Senate Foreign Relations Committee. The turning point in the Senate debate was a three-hour speech by Sumner, who urged the acquisition of Alaska on the grounds that it would cement Russo-American friendship, insure American fishing and hunting privileges, prevent England from extending its domain in North America, increase United States trade with the Orient, and spread American institutions by removing "one more monarch from this continent." On April 9, the Senate ratified the treaty by a vote of thirty-seven to two. The House showed some reluctance to approve the appropriation for the purchase and did not act until July, 1868. But the Administration had made it almost impossible for the House to do otherwise than pay, for the United States had formally taken possession of Alaska in October, 1867, and a subsequent withdrawal would have been interpreted as a rebuke to Russia. As a further inducement, Stoeckl promised some of the recalcitrant representatives part of the purchase price as a reward for an affirmative vote. On July 14, 1868, the appropriation was approved by a vote of 113 to 43.

The American people were inclined to look on the purchase of Alaska as an accident, but Seward considered it just one part of a much larger program for strengthening and expanding the American position in the Pacific. In 1867 he proposed that the United States co-operate with the French in a punitive expedition against Korea, and in the same year he annexed the Midway Islands. Meanwhile he continued to urge that the United States acquire the Hawaiian Islands. Nor was Seward alone in his interest in the Pacific. During the 1870's American traders and naval officers were casting covetous eyes on the Hawaiian Islands and Samoa. A commercial treaty brought the Hawaiian Islands within the American sphere of influence in 1875, and an agreement was reached with Samoa three years later. Imperialists of Seward's school would have liked a more aggressive policy in the Pacific, but they had to be content with these limited advances.

The growth of American interests in the Pacific was paralleled by demands that the United States extend its sovereignty over all of North America. Canada, squeezed between the United States and an American Alaska, was considered by Seward and his fellow imperialists to be a ripening fruit that would eventually fall into the hands of a patient United States. On the other hand, the expansionists were not averse to speeding up nature's process. Bellicose politicians warned Britain that it could only atone for its assistance to the Confederacy during the Civil War by ceding Canada to the United States. Aggressive Americans also welcomed the notorious but ineffective Fenian raids. Irish nationalists in the United States gathered at a few points along the Canadian border from 1866 to 1871 with the avowed purpose of attacking Canada. Although American imperialists gave the Fenians their blessing and the United States government made little attempt to interfere with their plans, inadequate numbers and resources turned the projected invasions of Canada into a fiasco.

The widespread belief that Canada would eventually become a part of the United States took into consideration every factor but the Canadian people. The very ardor of the American imperialists so stimulated Canadian nationalism that the maintenance of an autonomous Canada became one of the cardinal points of its government's foreign policy; and by the end of the 1890's, when American expansionism had reached flood tide, Canadian patriotism (as well as the American determination to build an island empire) had removed Canada from the timetable of American imperialism.

The unfulfilled dreams of the post-Civil War expansionists included the Caribbean as well as Canada and the Pacific. Seward, anxious to extend American influence to this region, sought to promote American canal interests in Nicaragua, negotiated a treaty that was never ratified for the purchase of the Danish West Indies, and attempted to secure an American toehold in Santo Domingo. On a cruise of the Caribbean in 1866, Seward was impressed by the desirability of Samaná Bay in the republic of Santo Domingo as a naval base. A year later his son Frederick was sent to Santo Domingo to secure a leasehold or cession of Samaná Bay, but the mission proved a failure.

Seward's interest in Santo Domingo had been based on strategic considerations, but there were some speculators who were agitating for American intervention as a device for promoting their own fortunes. William L. Cazneau and Joseph Warren Fabens were two New England adventurers who had concocted a host of dubious ventures in Dominican minerals, cotton, banking, harbor improvements, a steamship line to New York, and a fantastic arrangement that permitted them and their associates to obtain one fifth of the republic's land in return for what was called a geological survey. They were joined in these enterprises by politicans like Ben Butler, industrialists like Cyrus McCormick, old cronies of President Grant like Ben Holliday, and financial firms like the New York investment house of Spofford, Tileston & Company. Because the value of their varied projects would be vastly enhanced by the American annexation of Santo Domingo, the speculators appealed to President Grant, who was easily convinced of the necessity for obtaining a naval base on Samaná Bay. In 1869, Orville Babcock, the President's secretary, was sent to Santo Domingo, where he was conducted through the maze of Dominican politics by a representative of the speculators. According to the terms of the agreement that Babcock reached with the local officials, the United States was given the right to purchase Samaná Bay for $2,000,000 or to acquire all of Santo Domingo by assuming its public debt of $1,500,000. As evidence of American sincerity, President Grant advanced $150,000 to the island government, and American warships soon appeared in Dominican waters. When a treaty of annexation was presented to the Senate in 1870, Grant did not overlook a single argument in urging its ratification. He said:

> *The people of San[to] Domingo are not capable of maintaining themselves in their present condition, and must look for outside support. They yearn for the protection of our free institutions . . . , our progress and civilization. Shall we refuse them? The acquisition of San[to] Domingo is desirable because of its geographical position. . . . The acquisition of San[to] Domingo is an adherence to the "Monroe doctrine;" it is a measure of national protection; it is asserting our just claim to an influence over the great commercial traffic soon to flow from west to east by way of the Isthmus of Darien; it is to build up our merchant marine; it is to furnish new markets for the*

products of our farms, shops and manufactories; . . . it is to settle the unhappy condition of Cuba and end an exterminating conflict; it is to provide honest means of paying our honest debts without overtaxing the people; it is to furnish our citizens with the necessaries of everyday life at cheaper rates than ever before; and it is, in fine, a rapid stride toward that greatness which the intelligence, industry and enterprise of the citizens of the United States entitle this country to assume among nations.

Grant's message stands as an impressive summary of the rationale of American imperialism. Within thirty years the American people would employ each and every one of Grant's arguments as valid reasons for overseas expansion, but in 1870 they held little or no appeal, and the Senate rejected the treaty.

Nor were the American people willing to intervene in Cuba during these years, although there were numerous pretexts that could have been used by a nation committed to expansion. The rebellion that broke out in Cuba in 1868 and ended a decade later with a Spanish victory elicited the sympathies of many Americans, but not their active support. Emerging from the Civil War as the undisputed leader of the Western hemisphere, the United States was admirably situated to take advantage of Spain's distress. But despite traditional appeals to American humanitarianism, the American people were able to restrain their emotions, and Secretary of State Hamilton Fish steered the United States along the course of strict neutrality.

From 1865 to 1880, the United States possessed all the prerequisites of expansionism but one. It had the power, the arguments with which imperialists always rationalize their moves, and a few key figures in American economic and political life who were willing to lead their country into overseas adventures. Only a popular mandate was lacking.

58. THE WILL TO EXPAND

THE WILLINGNESS of the American people in the 1890's to sanction a type of imperialism that they had rejected in the 1870's can be attributed to the changing character of the United States. In the interval between the Civil and Spanish American wars the United States had become a world power with vital interests in two oceans. While the Mexican War and the Oregon settlement had extended the territory of the United States to the Pacific Ocean, it was not until after 1865 that the Far West was linked with the East by rail, and it was not until 1890 that the major portion of the territory acquired before the war was settled by the American people. The march of American civilization to the Pacific coast compelled the formulators of American foreign policy to devote as much attention to developments in the Pacific as they formerly had to those in the Atlantic. But a Pacific policy could not be conducted in a vacuum, for its ultimate success was predicated on the expansion of the American navy, the construction of an Isthmus canal, and the acquisition of Caribbean bases to guard its approaches. The conduct of American foreign policy was also profoundly affected by economic developments within the nation. As the American economy shifted from agriculture to industry, the demands for the acquisition of overseas bases to protect and stimulate American commerce exercised a proportionately greater influence upon the direction of American foreign policy.

The effect upon foreign policy of the altered strategic and economic position of the United States was in part revealed by the vigorous diplomacy of James G. Blaine, who served as Secretary of State under Presidents Garfield and Harrison. In many respects Blaine's objectives were similar to those of Seward, and the principal difference between the two men lay in their times rather than their aims. Aside from Alaska, Seward's program of expansion had elicited little popular response. Blaine's aggressive moves in the Pacific and Latin America ushered in a new era in United States relations with the rest of the world.

James G. Blaine's foreign policy was the product of his determination to find a market for the surplus goods of American industry and of his desire to insure his country against foreign attack. In his attempts to carry out this policy, Blaine directed his attention toward most of the areas that had been coveted by the leading American imperialists of the past. He was convinced that economic and strategic considerations rendered necessary the annexation of Hawaii by the United States. He thought that Canada also fell within the American sphere of influence, and in 1891 he predicted that Canada would "ultimately . . . seek admission to the union." He sought unsuccessfully to obtain naval bases in Haiti and Santo Domingo and worked assiduously to reserve for the United States the exclusive right to build a canal across the Central American isthmus.

Blaine's preoccupation with American overseas commerce was most clearly revealed in his Latin American policy. Because he believed that Latin America would never be a profitable market for American goods until it was freed from war and strife, he set out to establish the United States as the arbiter of all disputes among the nations south of the Rio Grande. On various occasions during his two terms as Secretary of State, Blaine attempted to settle differences arising between Mexico and Guatemala, Costa Rica and Colombia, British Guiana and Venezuela, and Chile and Peru. This type of intervention, however, not only had no appreciable effect upon the volume of American exports to Central and South America, but it resolved none of the disputes in question and increased the traditional antagonism of the Latin Americans for the gringos to the north. Equally unsuccessful were Blaine's efforts to increase hemispheric trade through conferences called to effect tariff reductions. His proposal for a Pan-American conference in 1881 was abandoned when he was forced to resign after Garfield's death, but eight years later he was able to preside over the first Pan-American Conference, which convened in Washington during Harrison's administration. Despite Blaine's prestige as the representative of the conference's most powerful member nation, the Latin American delegates had no desire to give up their highly profitable economic relations with Europe for what were at best dubious commercial ties with the United States, and they rejected Blaine's plans for either a customs union or tariff reciprocity.

Although Blaine had little to show for his aggressive foreign policy, his ideas were gaining an increasing popularity among the American people. Moreover, numerous other politicians began to proclaim their belief in what came to be known as a "large policy." As early as 1886, Theodore Roosevelt was anticipating the "day when not a foot of American soil will be held by any European power." Roosevelt's good friend, Senator Henry Cabot Lodge of Massachusetts, thought that "from the Rio Grande to the Arctic Ocean there should be but one flag and one country" and that the United States should control the Hawaiian Islands, Samoa, an Isthmus canal, and Cuba. Even the anti-imperialist Cleveland at the time of the Venezuelan crisis of 1895 was to employ the language of the new nationalism with such vigor that the United States and Great Britain were to be brought closer to war than at any time since 1815.

The politicians' demands for a glorious foreign policy were reenforced by the writings of numerous authors who argued that Charles Darwin's evolutionary theories applied to nations as well as to animate beings. According to these apostles of the new imperialism, no nation could be static, and the stronger nations were destined by a higher law to assimilate their weaker and less fortunate neighbors. The survival of the fittest was a slogan that applied to international society as well as to the jungle. Among the most ardent advocates of international Darwinism was Alfred Thayer Mahan, a Navy captain, whose book *The Influence of Sea Power upon History* was first published in 1890. In this and subsequent articles and books, Mahan maintained that, since international relations were "dog-eat-dog," it behooved the United States to be the eater rather than the eaten. By referring to history, Mahan was able to prove to himself that a nation's ability to survive was determined by its seapower, a broad concept that referred not only to fighting ships and coastal defenses, but to overseas bases, a merchant marine, and coaling stations. Seapower and commercial supremacy were inseparable, and both could be promoted by a large navy, an extensive merchant marine, and a far-flung colonial system. Specifically, Mahan insisted that the American people construct a canal across the Isthmus and seize commercial and military outposts among the islands of both the Pacific and the Caribbean.

Other followers of Darwin maintained that the "racial superiority" of the American people had already rendered inevitable the expansion of the United States over large portions of the globe. John Fiske, one of Darwin's earliest and most ardent disciples in the United States, argued in 1885 in a magazine article entitled "Manifest Destiny" that the English race was destined to take over the whole world. In the same year, Josiah Strong, a Congregational clergyman, published a book entitled *Our Country: Its Possible Future and Its Present Crisis*. Strong wrote that the Anglo-Saxon was "divinely commissioned to be in a peculiar sense his brother's keeper" and that the United States was to "become the home of this race, the principal seat of his power, the great center of his influence." Strong concluded that the racial superiority of the American people ordained that there could be no limit to the territorial expansion of the United States. In similar vein, Senator Albert J. Beveridge stated that overseas conquests were inevitable, for the "American Republic is part of the movement of a race,—the most masterful race of history,—and race movements are not to be stayed by the hand of man."

It is impossible to measure the effect of these advocates of imperialism on the thoughts of the American people, but that they had an effect there can be no doubt. Their articles were published in popular magazines; their lecture tours included most of the major cities and many smaller towns; and their avenues of access to those in power were many and varied. Moreover, many politicians with delusions of imperialistic grandeur occupied strategic positions in the government. James G. Blaine was Secretary of State in 1881 and 1889–92; Theodore Roosevelt was the Assistant Secretary of Navy who planned Dewey's attack on Manila; and Lodge and Beveridge were both influential members of the Senate for several years. On more than one occasion these and other similarly minded politicians were able to employ their official positions to make a reality of their dream of the United States' destiny to become a world power. From 1880 to 1900 the United States developed into an intensely nationalistic nation, and the preachers of expansionism—whether they were admirals, clergymen, politicians, or professors—more than any other individuals both promoted and reflected the growth of American imperialism.

The shifting strategic and economic bases of American foreign policy and the emergence of a vigorous nationalism were also revealed in the changed attitude of the American people toward their navy. Although the Union government had been quick to employ steam and armor plate on its warships during the Civil War, during the years that followed the conflict the American navy fell far behind those of the European powers. Concentration upon domestic problems forced naval considerations into the background, and by 1880 the United States Navy consisted of 140 ships, most of which were wooden and almost all of which were unfit for service.

With the inauguration of James A. Garfield, conditions were ripe for rebuilding the American navy. Reconstruction as a political issue had been liquidated, and the depression of the seventies had passed. With a surplus in the treasury and no pressing domestic concerns, the United States was free to concentrate on a program to build its naval strength up to a point commensurate with its status as a rising world power. It soon became clear that it was pointless to plan for an Isthmus canal and island bases in two oceans while the United States remained the naval inferior of several South American countries.

The turning point in the post-Civil War navy was signalized in 1881 with the creation by Congress of the Naval Advisory Board, whose principal function was to make incessant requests for larger and ever larger naval appropriations. The big-navy enthusiasts were now provided with an official lobby that was financed by the taxpayers of the United States. This system soon bore results, and in 1883, Congress authorized the Secretary of Navy to have built four steel ships that would be equipped with steam as well as sails. The strategic and economic implications of the new naval policy did not become clear until after 1890, when a Navy Policy Board that had been created by Secretary of the Navy Benjamin Tracy made a report that reflected the changed position of the United States as a world power. While the board conceded that the United States had "no colonies nor any apparent desire to acquire them," that its overseas trade was largely "carried in foreign vessels," that its manufactured products were competing "with those of other nations in but few markets," and that the United States was not threatened by any foreign power, it nevertheless requested Congress to authorize the construction of more than two hundred warships of all classes. The board's recommendation was based on the assumption that the United States would soon find itself in commerical rivalry with the major powers of the world and that it also would need more ships to protect the proposed Isthmus canal.

The Naval Act of 1890, which came as a direct result of this report did not go as far as the policy board had recommended, but it did mark the beginnings of the change from the concept of the navy as a defensive force to that of a navy designed to meet a potential enemy on the high seas. The strategic implications of this legislation were also indicated by the report of the House Naval Affairs Committee, which visualized the bill as a measure for establishing battleship fleets in the western Atlantic, the Caribbean, and the Pacific. Despite the depression of the 1890's the new naval policy was consistently pushed by both Democratic and Republican Administrations, and under the impetus of the new nationalism the United States moved from twelfth to third place among the world's naval powers during the last two decades of the nineteenth century.

59. INTERVENTION IN SAMOA

THIRTY years after the Senate had rejected President Grant's comprehensive list of arguments for expansion, the United States was fully prepared to embark on a course of overseas imperialism. An industrial nation with strategic and commercial interests in both the Atlantic and Pacific, it also possessed both the seapower and aggressive nationalism essential to any people who wished to take over the control of less powerful island dwellers.

The relations of the United States with Samoa clearly illustrated this change. Samoa occupies an important niche in the history of American imperialism. The peaceful invasion of the Samoan Islands by the United States after the Civil War was one of the earliest examples of the effect of new economic and strategic interests upon the nation's foreign policy. The ease with which a comparatively small and unrepresentative group of Americans involved the United States with Samoa revealed the key rôle of the naval and commercial groups in the development of American expansionism. The rivalry among the American, German, and British interests in these islands was a specific illustration of the way that the extension of American influence into the Pacific brought the United States into conflict with the major powers of Europe.

Before the Civil War, New Englanders had engaged in the China trade and the United States Navy had displayed some interest in Samoa. The completion of the first transcontinental railroad in 1869 again focused the attention of some commercial groups on the Pacific trade. A New York shipbuilder drew up plans for a steamship line between San Francisco, New Zealand, and Australia with way stations at Hawaii and Samoa, and a group of San Francisco businessmen formed the Polynesian Land Company to speculate in Samoan real estate. Because the success of these ventures was largely dependent on the extension of American political control to Samoa, their authors urged that the United

States establish a naval base at Pago Pago, Samoa's principal harbor, and take over control of the island government. As a direct result of the agitation of these businessmen, Commander Richard W. Meade visited Samoa on an American warship in 1872 and negotiated a treaty that granted naval rights in the islands to the United States. The Senate, reflecting the popular aversion of the time to foreign adventures, never acted on the treaty.

The Senate's failure to ratify the Samoan treaty delayed rather than halted the American advance into the Pacific. In 1873, President Grant selected as his special agent in Samoa Colonel A. B. Steinberger, a former employee of one of the leading San Francisco speculators in Samoan land. Steinberger, who is one of the most unusual figures in the diplomatic history of the United States or any other country, treated the natives with so much consideration and understanding that they permitted him to reorganize their government and selected him as their premier. The same policies that made Steinberger attractive to the natives rendered him unpopular with the British and German traders in the islands, and in 1875 he was deported on a British man-of-war. But the memory of his enlightened regime remained in the islands after his departure. In 1877, La Mamea, a Samoan prince, was escorted by a United States vice-consul to Washington, where he proposed an American protectorate over Samoa. In the following year a treaty between the United States and Samoa was ratified by the United States Senate. The American people were irrevocably committed to a major rôle in Samoa.

The Samoan treaty of 1878 granted the United States the right to establish a naval base at Pago Pago and provided that if "any differences should have arisen, or shall hereafter arise, between the Samoan government and any other government in amity with the United States, the government of the latter will employ its good offices for the purpose of adjusting these differences upon a satisfactory . . . foundation." Although this provision did not convert Samoa into an American protectorate, it was sufficient to embroil the United States in the island's politics for more than two decades. When Samoa in 1879 signed treaties with Britain and Germany awarding them commercial privileges, the United States found itself in conflict with two of the world's most powerful nations. Samoa became the center of an imperialistic free-for-all in which the diplomatic, commercial and military representatives of the three rival nations maneuvered, threatened, and intrigued with the natives. An attempt by Secretary of State Thomas Bayard in 1887 to reach a *modus vivendi* with the British and German ministers in Washington ended in a stalemate that was followed by an intensification of the struggle for power in Samoa. The Germans, making an undisguised bid for control, deposed the native King, replaced him with one of their own supporters, and waged an undeclared war against bands of Samoan guerrillas. When British, American, and German warships appeared in the Samoan harbor of Apia, the possibility of open conflict was only averted by a hurricane that disabled all but one of the vessels.

The United States' efforts to hold its own against the European imperialists in Samoa brought to the surface the latent nationalism of the American people. Congress voted funds for the protection of American lives and property in Samoa, and the press criticized the aggressive policy of the Germans. The American people were determined to uphold what they considered their country's national honor in the face of Germany's high-handed behavior. The popular support of the government's policy in Samoa did not arise from a desire to acquire some remote tropical islands, but was based on the conviction that the United States could not retreat in Samoa without loss of national honor. The United States wished to become a major power, and its citizens demanded that it behave like one when its interests came into conflict with those of the imperialist nations of Europe.

Because Bismarck was unwilling to permit a possible conflict in the Pacific to upset the delicately balanced system of alliances that he was constructing in Europe, he invited Britain and the United States to send delegates to Berlin to settle these differences in Samoa. The agreement that emerged from the Berlin conference of 1889 provided for a tripartite protectorate over Samoa—a plan that changed the form rather than the substance of the earlier arrangement. The old pattern of deceit, distrust, recrimination, and open warfare was resumed to the mounting disgust of the American people. The more moderate Samoan policy pursued by the anti-imperialist Cleveland Administration in the midnineties served only as an interlude. In 1899, the Americans, having overrun Cuba, Puerto Rico, and the Philippines, could see no reason for refusing to add Samoa to the list; the largest share of the islands was ceded to Germany, but the United States acquired Tutuila, which included the harbor of Pago Pago.

The history of American intervention in Samoa illustrates the transformation of the American attitude toward overseas expansion during a period of approximately thirty years and the way in which the Americans entered into the task of empire building through the back door and almost accidentally. A few traders accompanied by some naval officers involved the United States government in the politics of islands that were also coveted by Germany and Great Britain. German and American nationalism did the rest. Although the American people originally had no apparent desire to acquire any part of Samoa, they soon discovered that the question had become much bigger than the problem of controlling a few islands in the South Pacific. It was a matter of national honor in which the prestige of the United States was pitted against that of two of the most powerful nations of the Old World.

60. THE ANNEXATION OF HAWAII

INTERVENTION in Samoa was not an isolated incident in the history of American foreign policy, for many of the same circumstances that brought it under partial American control operated with equal force in Hawaii. In both instances, the desire of naval and commercial groups for a Pacific base furnished the original impetus for American intervention. The attempt to check Germany in Samoa was paralleled by a similar wish to prevent Hawaii from falling under the control of either England or Japan. As in Samoa, Grover Cleveland temporarily checked the tide of American expansionism in the Hawaiian Islands only to see them engulfed by the wave of imperialism that accompanied the Spanish American War. There were, however, elements in the American penetration of Hawaii that had not been present in that of Samoa. American missionaries played an important rôle in stimulating an early American interest in Hawaii; the growth of the native sugar-industry conditioned the moves and attitudes that culminated in American annexation; and the State Department generally employed a more aggressive diplomacy in Hawaii than in Samoa.

New England missionaries had reached Hawaii in 1819, and during the first half of the nineteenth century, American traders in China and whalers had employed it as a base for their operations in the Pacific. The Whigs, responding to the demands of their commercial constituents, on more than one occasion had insisted that Hawaii belonged within the American sphere of interest. Even the predominantly agrarian Democrats, swept along by the heightened spirit of Manifest Destiny in the 1850's, made a futile attempt to annex Hawaii in 1854. Every rumor that Hawaii might be taken over by some rival power only added to the general American conviction that the islands should either remain independent or be acquired by the United States.

The American missionaries, traders, and sugar planters who by 1850 dominated Hawaii's political and economic life believed that increased trade with the United States would promote Hawaiian prosperity without threatening its sovereignty. Commercial treaties negotiated with the United States in 1855 and 1867 were rejected by American senators who wished to protect the Louisiana sugar growers and feared that Hawaiian prosperity would lessen rather than promote the chances for eventual American annexation of the islands. It was not until 1875 that these objections were overcome and a reciprocity treaty with Hawaii ratified by the United States Senate. By permitting Hawaiian sugar to enter the United States duty free, the treaty of 1875 produced unprecedented prosperity for Hawaii's largest industry and bound its economy firmly to that of the United States. During the first ten years of the treaty's operation, Hawaii's annual sugar exports to the United States increased from 17,909,000 to 169,653,000 pounds.

The treaty of 1875 was more than a commercial agreement, for exclusive American control over Hawaii was insured by a provision that forbade the native ruler to "lease or otherwise dispose of or create a lien upon any port, harbor, or other territory in his dominions, or grant any special privilege or rights or use therein to any Power, State or Government, . . . [or] make any treaty by which any other nation should obtain the same privileges relative to the admission of articles free of duty, thereby secured to the United States." Hawaii's bonds with the United States were further strengthened in 1887, when the United States was granted the right to construct a naval base at Pearl Harbor.

The treaty of 1875 redounded almost exclusively to the benefit of a comparatively small group of Hawaiian sugar producers. With a large share of Hawaiian wealth in their hands, an expanding market for their sugar in the United States, a docile native government, and a guarantee against foreign intervention, they considered their position ideal in every respect. But the economic and political power of the islands' white oligarchs, while extensive, was based entirely on outside forces over which they had little or no control, and the events of the opening years of the 1890's clearly revealed their vulnerability. The McKinley Tariff, which was adopted by Congress in 1890, removed the duty on foreign raw sugar and gave a bounty of two cents a pound to the producers within the United States. Deprived of their privileged position in the American market and confronted by economic ruin, the Hawaiian sugar interests were easily converted to the belief that their only salvation lay in annexation to the United States. Although a few of the islands' largest growers opposed annexation for a time on the ground that United States' laws prohibiting the import of contract labor would deprive them of their supply of cheap Oriental workers, the effects of the McKinley Tariff eventually convinced all but a few that there was no alternative to union with their erstwhile benefactor.

Political as well as economic considerations increased the desire of the American minority in Hawaii for annexation after 1890. The pronounced antiforeign views of Queen Liliuokalani, who ascended the Hawaiian throne in 1891, indicated that it would only be a matter of time before the white oligarchy lost its hold over the native government. When the Queen in 1893 made good her boast of "Hawaii for the Hawaiians" by transferring the political power formerly held by the sugar growers to her own hands, the Americans in the islands decided that it was time to act. They hastily organized a revolution and asked the United States to intervene to protect the lives and property of its nationals in Hawaii. This appeal did not go unheeded. John L. Stevens, the American minister to Hawaii, in his dispatches to the State Department had repeatedly advocated that the United States take a more active rôle in Hawaiian affairs. On numerous occasions he predicted a revolt against the Queen and warned his home government that it would have to act with dispatch if it wished to anticipate British intervention or prevent the islands' native population from being swamped in the mounting wave of Oriental immigration. There is no reason to believe that Stevens' attitude toward Hawaii was not an accurate reflection of the views of his friend and superior, Secretary of State James G. Blaine.

The revolution engineered by the small but powerful group of American annexationists on January 16, 1893, received the moral and physical support of the United States government. Although Stevens was absent from Honolulu during the ten days that preceded the *coup d'état*, he returned in time to insure the revolution's success by landing 160 marines from an American warship in the harbor. The temporary government set up by the revolutionists was granted immediate American recognition by Stevens, and a delegation was hastily bundled off to the United States to negotiate a treaty of annexation. On February 1, Stevens announced an American protectorate over Hawaii and cabled the State Department: "The Hawaiian pear is now fully ripe, and this is the golden hour for the United States to pluck it."

Despite the dispatch with which the annexationists had acted, they had not moved fast enough to prevent Grover Cleveland from balking their plans. He withdrew the treaty of annexation, which had been submitted to the Senate on February 15, soon after his inauguration on March 4. James H. Blount, who shared the President's anti-imperialist views, was sent to Hawaii as Cleveland's special representative. After a comprehensive but hardly impartial study of recent developments in the islands, Blount reported that the Hawaiian people were opposed to annexation and that the revolt would have collapsed if Stevens had not employed the power and prestige of the United States. Although Cleveland withdrew American support from the new government, he was not able to effect the restoration of Queen Liliuokalani, and the white oligarchy continued to rule the islands until Dewey's victory at Manila helped to convince the American people that they had a date with destiny in Hawaii as well as in the Philippines.

Cleveland was praised as a man of principle by his supporters and accused of pig-headedness by his opponents. In any event he never permitted the popular will to interfere with his own concept of right and wrong. McKinley, who had fashioned a successful political career out of changing with the shifting temper of the times, was not burdened with Cleveland's scruples concerning Hawaii. Soon after McKinley assumed office in 1897, a new treaty of annexation was submitted to the Senate. When it appeared that the annexationists would not be able to command the necessary two-thirds vote, the treaty was supplanted by a joint resolution for annexation which required only a simple majority in both houses.

Annexationists both in and out of Congress who urged the acceptance of the joint resolution employed the traditional arguments that have been used by imperialists in perhaps every age and nation. Appealing to history—that bargain basement of all special pleaders—they cited the long list of prominent Americans who had advocated the acquisition of Hawaii in the past. Hawaii was pictured by the annexationists as a strategic necessity for the navy, a source of inestimable wealth to American economic interests, a moral obligation upon the American people, and an obvious opportunity for the nation to fulfill its manifest destiny. Each of these arguments was re-enforced by the imperialist insistence that if the United States did not take Hawaii, some other nation would. England had already announced its intentions with the request for a cable station in Hawaii, and a Senate committee warned against the "silent but rapid invasion of the pagan races from Asia."

The anti-imperialists, who found their principal strength among the Democrats, sought to refute each of the annexationists' points. They too could appeal to history by stating that there was no American precedent for overseas expansion. They predicted that the acquisition of Hawaii was only the first of many projected steps toward the creation of an American empire that would undermine the country's democracy at home. To the promise of commercial prosperity, they replied that annexation was a plot contrived by and for the islands' few powerful sugar-growers. Talk of moral obligation was ridiculed, and Champ Clark termed Manifest Destiny the "specious plea of every robber and freebooter since the world began." The anti-imperialists may have won the argument, but they lost the vote, and on July 7, 1898, Hawaii became a territory of the United States.

Events in both Samoa and Hawaii indicate the pattern of American imperialism during the last quarter of the nineteenth century. In both instances a few individuals—whether traders, naval officers, whalers, sugar planters, diplomats, or missionaries—committed the American people to a policy that they had not specifically endorsed. These individuals with special interests then only had to wait for events to take their course. By sitting tight, they were able to see their aims achieved as successive diplomatic incidents and fundamental changes in the American economy and strategic position combined to convince the mass of Americans that it was both their duty and destiny to acquire these islands.

61. THE MARTIAL SPIRIT

A LARGE part of the territory that the United States acquired before the Civil War consisted of the remnants of Spain's crumbling American empire. Louisiana, Florida, Texas, New Mexico, and California had all at one time or another belonged to the King of Spain. Although these territories comprised an area many times the size of the original states of the Union, they had been obtained at what were considered bargain prices in American money and blood.

Although the antebellum United States appeared particularly well suited to serve as the receiver of Spain's bankrupt North American empire, it was unable to extend its control to Spain's most valuable Caribbean possession. Nor did this failure occur for want of trying, for throughout these years the potential value of Cuba to the United States was widely recognized. Its location gave it the strategic key to the Caribbean, and from 1820 to 1860, American trade with Cuba was exceeded only by that with the United Kingdom and France. On numerous occasions before the Civil War, prominent American expansionists displayed a marked interest in Cuba's future. Thomas Jefferson and John Quincy Adams stated that Cuba was destined eventually to become a part of the United States, and in response to the demands of their Southern supporters, who wanted additional slave territory, Presidents Polk and Pierce made unsuccessful attempts to wrest the island from Spain. The failure of the United States to acquire Cuba before 1860 revealed, not a fear of Spain or a lack of expansionist enthusiasm, but the North's aversion to the extension of the South's peculiar institution and the general conviction that Cuba posed no threat to American security as long as it remained in such weak hands.

In the decade following the Civil War the United States had both the opportunity and power to intervene in Cuba. The Ten Years' War, as the revolution that broke out in Cuba in 1868 was called, was replete with instances of Spanish cruelty and oppression. But the American people, despite a tradition of sympathy for those fighting for their freedom against European oppression, made no overt move to take advantage of Spain's distress. The *Virginius* affair, in which fifty-three passengers and crew members were taken from a ship flying the American flag and executed by the Spanish, was a more provocative incident than any that had preceded the Mexican War, but the United States was willing to accept apologies and an indemnity from the Spanish government and to remain at peace.

Although Spain was able to end the Cuban rebellion in 1878, it had learned little from a decade of bloodletting. The Spanish government was reimposed with no abatement in the corruption and favoritism that had characterized the administration before the rebellion. Forced into the straitjacket of Spanish mercantilism, the Cubans were again subjected to an inequitable tax system and a tariff that compelled them to obtain most of their imports from Spain while sending approximately 75 per cent of their exports to the United States. After 1890 the United States as well as Spain contributed to Cuba's misfortunes. A large part of Cuba's sugar crop, which represented four fifths of the island's wealth, had been sold in the United States through a preferential tariff agreement; but the Wilson-Gorman Tariff of 1894 deprived the Cubans of this free market by imposing a duty on their sugar. By 1895 the Cuban people had had enough, and once again they revolted against their Spanish rulers.

At the outset of the Cuban revolt, General Martínez Campos, who had induced the rebels to lay down their arms in 1878, was placed in charge of Spanish forces in Cuba. When his policy of "conciliation backed by the sword" produced neither victories nor any diminution in the revolutionary ardor of the Cubans, he was supplanted by the more aggressive General Valeriano Weyler. Nicknamed the "Butcher" by the American press, Weyler proclaimed martial law, systematically destroyed whatever property which might be of value to the rebels, and herded the island's noncombatants into concentration camps, or *reconcentrados,* where they died by the thousands. Weyler's policies were duplicated by those of the insurgent leader, Máximo Gómez. Realizing that his forces were no match for the Spanish troops, Gómez set out to wreck Cuba's productive capacity so thoroughly that the Spanish would have no alternative but to evacuate the island. Although American sympathies were overwhelmingly on the side of the rebels and American sensibilities were shocked by Weyler's (and not Gómez's) tactics, there was little difference in the conduct of the two belligerents. The Cubans, determined that this revolt would not be a repetition of their earlier failure, were willing to resort to almost any device to rid the island of its hated rulers. For their part, the Spanish were equally insistent that the rebellious spirit of their Cuban subjects be crushed once and for all.

The mounting enthusiasm of the American people for the Cuban cause was equaled by President Cleveland's determination to prevent the United States from being drawn into the conflict. In the face of a steady stream of atrocity stories, a flood of releases from the propaganda mills of the Cuban "junta" in this country, and frequent demands for a firmer attitude toward Spain, the Cleveland Administration refused to intervene. A congressional resolution urging American recognition of Cuban belligerency was ignored by the President. The American navy and revenue service made valiant, if not always successful, efforts to intercept filibustering expeditions to Cuba, and American diplomacy was employed to protect American lives and property in Cuba, rather than to promote the cause of the insurgents. Cleveland would make only one

Judge

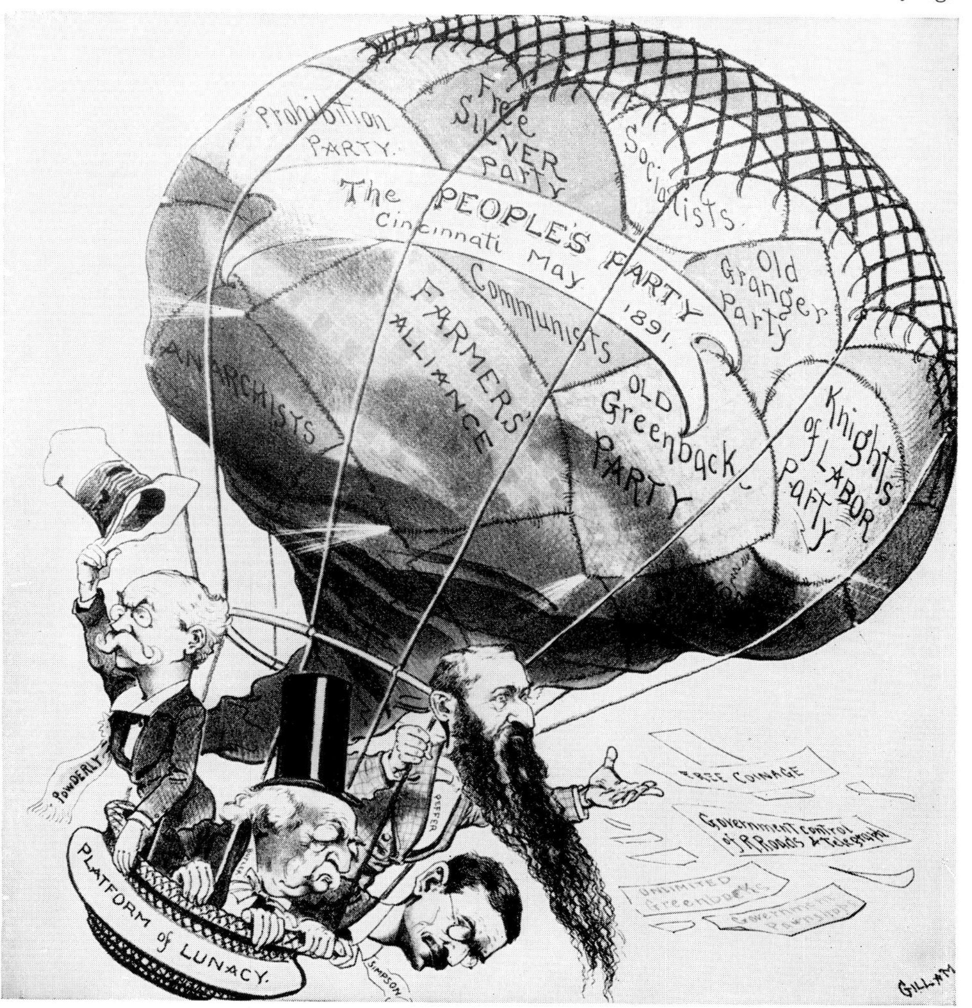

A PARTY OF PATCHES

Judge *comments on the formation of the People's party in 1891.*

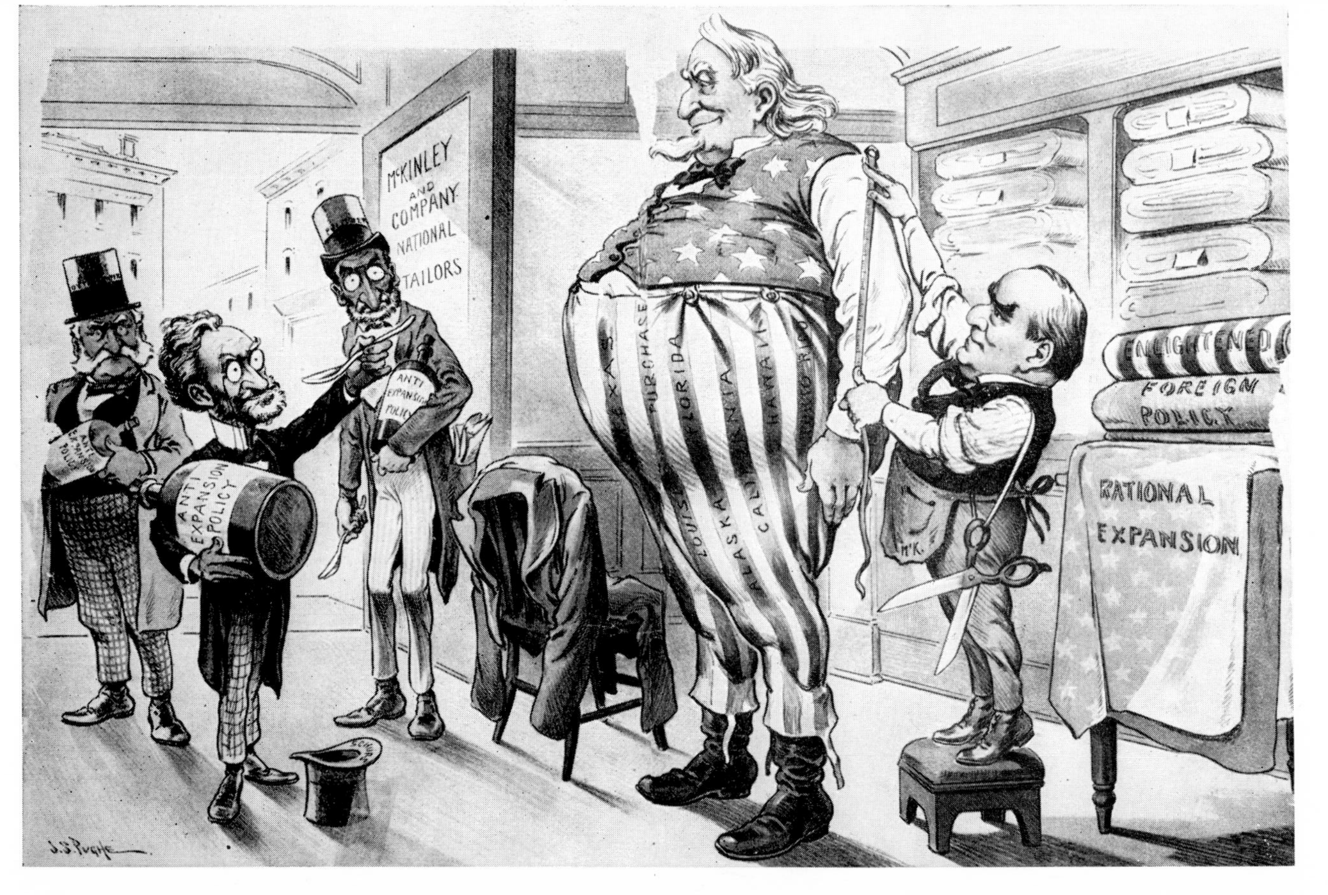

UNCLE SAM'S EXPANSION SUIT

McKinley measures Uncle Sam for his new suit. The cartoonist provides the following dialogue: "The Antis.—Here, take a dose of this . . . and get thin again!

concession to the interventionists. In April, 1896, his Administration made an offer of American mediation, only to have the proposal promptly rejected by the government in Madrid. There was little immediate change in American policy when McKinley succeeded Cleveland to the presidency. The earlier attempts to prevent filibustering and to protect American lives and property in Cuba were continued, and McKinley's offer of American mediation in September, 1897, was refused, as Cleveland's had been in the previous year.

The United States went to war against Spain in 1898, not because of the aggressive character of the McKinley Administration, but because the American people were overwhelmingly in favor of war. Seldom, if ever in American history, has there been a more genuinely popular war. In no instance was the American desire for war more clearly revealed than in the nation's press. Most American papers became megaphones for Cuban independence, but only a few were able to approach the extremes of jingoism attained by New York's yellow journals—Joseph Pulitzer's *World* and William Randolph Hearst's *Journal.* Both papers colored the news in favor of the insurgents, announced the most trivial anti-Spanish incidents in spectacular and provocative headlines, and on occasion fabricated stories that would appeal to their readers' sympathies for the Cubans. Examples of Spanish cruelty, which the *Journal* compared to the "Spanish inquisition of the sixteenth century," were described in purple prose and lurid pictures. Running through every Cuban news report, editorial, and illustration in the *World* and *Journal* was the theme that the American people should come to the assistance of their oppressed and stricken neighbors.

To ascertain the motives of the newspaper publishers who played up the bloody and spectacular aspects of the war in Cuba, it is not necessary to go any further than their desire for profits. Aside from their private views on the Cuban Revolution, Hearst and Pulitzer knew that murder sold papers, and the conflict in Cuba could be reported as mass murder. Moreover, their papers' descriptions of the suffering endured by the Cubans played on the traditional American sympathy for the underdog fighting for his liberty against European despotism. The economic advantage of appealing to the average American's interest in blood and ideals was demonstrated by the increase in the *Journal's* circulation from 416,885 to 1,025,624 during the excitement over the destruction of the *Maine.* The effect upon readers of the yellow journals' treatment of the revolt in Cuba is more difficult to ascertain than the motives of the publishers. Certainly the press did not create American opinion, for most Americans had favored the Cuban cause from the first day of the rebellion, but beyond a doubt the strictures of the more bellicose papers went far toward crystallizing and re-enforcing the views already held by their readers.

Hearst and Pulitzer were not the only individuals who urged the United States on toward war, for the martial spirit also received widespread support from American clergymen. In the months that preceded the intervention of the United States in Cuba, many Protestant ministers argued that the United States was impelled by moral and religious duty to aid the long suffering Cubans. A Methodist paper stated that American participation would be "just" and that in the event of war "Methodism will be ready to do its full duty," and "every Methodist preacher will be a recruiting officer." Other Protestant groups, with the exception of the Quakers and Unitarians, were equally bellicose. A Presbyterian journal asked: "Shall thousands of starving and dying Cubans appeal to the humane people of this republic in vain?" An Episcopal bishop said that the only way to implement President McKinley's "humane and righteous determination was by force of arms; and that means war." The Catholics, however, saw no religious justification for a war to free Catholic Cuba; and one Catholic paper suggested that the warlike intentions of Protestant clergymen be satisfied by organizing them into a regiment and shipping them off to Cuba in a body.

The warlike ardor of the American people, as exemplified by the popularity of the yellow press and the enthusiasm of their clergymen, was endorsed by many professional politicians who were looking for a popular issue. After the fright that they had received from William Jennings Bryan in 1896, they were more than receptive to a glorious foreign adventure with which to divert their constituents from the troublesome silver question and the other issues that arose out of agrarian discontent. In addition to the party hacks who were looking for a safe issue, there were several other key political figures who had long advocated that the United States undertake overseas expansion and who welcomed the rising tide of nationalism. A few weeks after the outbreak of the revolt in Cuba, Senator Shelby M. Cullom stated that "we certainly ought to have that island in order to round out our possessions as they should be, and if we cannot buy it, I for one should like to have an opportunity to acquire it by conquest." Theodore Roosevelt made no attempt to hide his desire for war, and his friend John Hay asserted that a war would be "as necessary as it was righteous." Not only did these men whip up the popular enthusiasm for intervention, but their positions of power at times enabled them to take specific steps that hastened the advent of the war that they so heartily desired.

In February, 1898, the demands of the American interventionists were given a seeming validity by two "incidents"—the word applied in the language of diplomacy to those minor crises that precede and frequently lead to the major crisis of war. On February 9, 1898, William Randolph Hearst's New York *Journal* published a letter written to a friend in Cuba by Enrique Dupuy deLôme, the Spanish minister to the United States.

In addition to suggesting the desirability of establishing a lobby to influence the United States Senate, deLôme criticized President McKinley's annual message of the previous December for its "ingrained and inevitable coarseness" and described the President as "weak and a bidder for the admiration of the crowd, besides being a common politician who tries to leave a door open behind himself while keeping on good terms with the jingoes of his party." DeLôme's immediate resignation on the publication of the offending letter did nothing to lessen the enthusiasm of the American people for a war that they now considered inevitable. The jingoism engendered by the publication of the deLôme letter was only exceeded by the popular outcry that greeted the announcement of the sinking of the *Maine* after an explosion in Havana harbor on February 15, 1898. The question of who sank the *Maine*—a question that has remained unanswered—was no mystery to the American people in 1898. "Remember the *Maine*" became the national war whoop as most Americans shouted their agreement with Theodore Roosevelt's announcement that the "*Maine* was sunk by an act of dirty treachery on the part of the Spaniards."

The only significant check upon the popular demand for war after the sinking of the *Maine* came from the nation's business groups. In 1895, American trade with Cuba was valued at $65,000,000, and American capital invested in the island totaled $50,000,000. These figures, however, represented only a small segment of American economic activity, and the vast majority of American businessmen, who had no financial stake in a war to drive Spain out of Cuba, looked on the possibility of armed conflict with considerable trepidation and hostility. After suffering from the depression of the midnineties, American business leaders were convinced that the signs of returning prosperity would quickly be dispersed by a war against Spain. Throughout the winter of 1897–8, every threat of war was accompanied by antiwar editorials in the financial press and sharp declines in stock prices. Theodore Roosevelt became so incensed at the attitude of the business groups that he said: "We will have this war for the freedom of Cuba in spite of the timidity of the commercial interests."

The aversion of America's business leaders to war was shared by President McKinley. A gentle man with kindly impulses, he had no desire to lead his country into war; and as a businessman's President, he had no wish to offend his strongest allies. But McKinley was also a politician who was not willing to run the risk of defying public opinion indefinitely. On March 27, McKinley asked Spain to abolish its concentration camps in Cuba and to announce a six-months armistice. Spain's immediate refusal to consider McKinley's proposals was reversed under pressure from the Vatican, and by April 9, the Madrid government had signified its willingness to comply with both of the American President's demands. Spain was too late, however, for two days later McKinley sent his war message to Congress. After reviewing the course of the revolution in Cuba and the attempts of the United States to terminate it, he gave the reasons for his fateful decision:

> *In the name of humanity, in the name of civilization, in behalf of endangered American interests which give us the right and the duty to speak and to act, the war in Cuba must stop. In view of these . . . considerations, I ask Congress to authorize and empower the President to take measures to secure a full and final termination of hostilities between the government of Spain and the people of Cuba, and to secure in the island the establishment of a stable government, . . . and to use the military and naval forces of the United States as may be necessary for these purposes.*

Spain's capitulation to McKinley's ultimatum of March 27 was mentioned by the President in a single sentence on the last of the nine closely printed pages that made up his war message. But Congress, which knew a mandate when it saw one, had abandoned all thought of further negotiation with Spain. A joint resolution, which was passed on April 19, authorized the President to use force to drive Spain from Cuba and to insure the island's freedom. The Teller Amendment, which was adopted on the same day, renounced American claims to Cuba. The Teller Amendment has been variously interpreted as an indication of American altruism and as a device employed by the American sugar interests for denying their Cuban competitors free access to the American market.

62. LIQUIDATING THE SPANISH EMPIRE

THE AMERICANS at last had their war. For most of them, it appeared as the natural outcome of their moral indignation over what they considered an intolerable situation in Cuba. Their feeling of revulsion had been to a certain degree spontaneous, but it had also been nurtured by the yellow press, which wanted a larger circulation; by professional imperialists who thought that the United States should undertake a "large policy"; by clergymen who were moved by humanitarian considerations; and by politicians who wished to bury the issues of 1896.

Although most Americans approved of Congress' decision to free Cuba, neither they nor their leaders had bothered to prepare for the war that they entered with such enthusiasm. The army consisted of only 28,183 regulars whose military experience had been largely confined to

Indian fighting in the West and patrol work in Alaska. Even in the navy there appeared to be some doubt as to just how the war should be fought. Admiral Mahan, who was the acknowledged authority on such matters, had taught that seapower should be employed, primarily, in maintaining a blockade, and for a short time a naval blockade of Cuba was contemplated. But the American people wanted a shooting war, and Congress was willing to give it to them. On April 22, the President was empowered to call on the states for volunteers. The next day, McKinley asked for 125,000 men.

The almost inconceivable confusion that attended the American war effort revealed the wisdom or good fortune of the United States in selecting a weak and decadent Spain as the guinea pig on which to try out its hypernationalism. The Administration managed to repeat all the mistakes of the Civil War while applying none of its lessons. State governments, rather than the national government, were responsible for recruiting. Political appointments to military posts were insured by permitting governors to select all lower officers. Tampa, despite its inadequate rail facilities, was made the port of embarkation and gained the dubious distinction of being the center of some of the government's more spectacular blunders. Only the resourcefulness of a Theodore Roosevelt was equal to the problems posed by the confusion in Tampa in the early summer of 1898. When Roosevelt, on arriving in Tampa, discovered that two other regiments were about to board the transport that had been assigned to his Rough Riders, he acted with characteristic dispatch.

> *I ran at full speed* [wrote Roosevelt] *to our train; and leaving a strong guard with the baggage I double-quicked the rest of the regiment up to the boat to board her as she came into the quay and then to hold her against the 2d . . . and the 71st, who had arrived a little late, being a shade less ready than we in the matter of individual initiative. There was a good deal of expostulation, but we had possession.*

In attempting to supply the troops, the War Department broke down completely. On June 4, Major-General Miles wrote from Tampa: "Several of the volunteer regiments came here without uniforms; several came without arms, and some without blankets, tents or camp equipage." Winter uniforms were issued for a summer campaign in the tropics. Because of the shortage of modern rifles, the volunteers had to use old fashioned Springfields, and the Rough Riders, whose Lieutenant-Colonel had friends in Washington, were the only volunteer regiment with smokeless powder. Medical supplies remained inadequate throughout the war. The food was wretched, and the soldiers with considerable justification referred to the canned meat as "embalmed beef."

Those Americans who could fight the Spanish American War in their front porch rockers instead of in the swamps and jungles of Cuba were willing to overlook the lapses of the War Department. To them, as to John Hay, it was a "splendid little war." It was a short war, as all wars should be. It was a colorful war, supplying in two and a half months as many slogans and heroes as subsequent wars would produce in five years. Most important of all it was a glorious war, for the American victories were unrelieved by a single piece of bad news from the front. Dewey's destruction of the Spanish fleet at Manila was matched by the annihilation of its counterpart at Santiago Bay. The land fighting, which consisted of three minor engagements in Cuba, also followed a most acceptable pattern. The battles were not struggles of attrition between huge conglomerates of nameless automatons, but more intimate conflicts that permitted cavalry charges and deeds of individual heroism.

After ten weeks without a single success, the Spanish on August 12 accepted an armistice that granted Cuba its freedom and the United States Puerto Rico and any island that it might select in the Ladrones. The fighting was over in Cuba, but it had just begun in the Philippines. On the day after the signing of the armistice, eleven thousand American soldiers entered the city of Manila as occupiers rather than liberators. The Filipinos, who had been led by the American commander to believe that they would share in the city's occupation, interpreted the American move as a breach of faith. Filipino insurgents had been fighting for their independence rather than to exchange one set of rulers for another. As soon as they realized that the American troops had no intention of withdrawing, they turned on their new conquerors. The Philippine rebellion, which was ably led by Emilio Aguinaldo, was to last more than two years. Before it was finally suppressed, Americans in the Philippines found themselves resorting to much the same tactics—even the once despised concentration camps—that they had found so revolting in Cuba.

While the rebellion in the Philippines was still raging, the delegates convened in Paris on October 1, 1898, for the peace conference. The preliminary problems were handled with dispatch. The United States had already selected Guam in the Ladrone Islands, and Spain reluctantly agreed to assume Cuba's debt of approximately $400,000,000. Only the fate of the Philippine Islands remained to be settled. They could be returned to Spain, granted their independence, or retained in whole or part by the United States. Although the average American before the Spanish-American War was as little acquainted with the Philippines as his counterpart before World War II was with the Marshalls, there was little doubt in his mind that it was both the duty and the destiny of the United States to acquire the Philippines. The appearance of a powerful German fleet in Manila Bay soon after Dewey's victory seemed sufficient evidence that a Spanish-controlled or independent Philippine government would immediately fall prey to one of Europe's imperialist powers. On the other hand, under American control, the expansionists argued, the Philippines would give the United States a strategic and economic base in the Far East. Businessmen who had opposed American intervention in Cuba had been converted to expansionism by the easy successes of the Spanish-American War and were now convinced that the Philippines would give American producers access to the Oriental market. Humanitarians also joined the chorus, insisting that the United States had an obligation to uplift the benighted but obstinate Filipinos. Finally, many Americans wanted the Philippines because their acquisition seemed a fitting climax to the glorious adventure of war.

The anti-imperialists, while in a definite minority, made up for their lack of numbers by their industry. Bound together by the Anti-Imperialist League, they included Democratic and Republican politicians like Grover Cleveland, William Jennings Bryan, Carl Schurz, and George F. Hoar; philanthropists like Andrew Carnegie; editors like E. L. Godkin of the *Nation* and Samuel Bowles of the Springfield *Republican;* clergymen like Bishop Henry Codman Potter, Henry Van Dyke, and Charles Parkhurst; college professors like William James, Felix Adler, and William Graham Sumner; and a notable group of literary figures among whom were Mark Twain, William Dean Howells, William Vaughn Moody, and Thomas Bailey Aldrich. The anti-imperialists devoted some attention to refuting the economic, strategic, and humanitarian claims of their opponents, but the central theme of their argument was their insistence that the acquisition of the Philippines would be a complete denial of the fundamental American concept that all government rested on the consent of the governed. Despite the luster of their leaders' names and the logic of their arguments, the anti-imperialists were fighting a losing battle. The American people had already made up their minds. So, too, had McKinley, and after some soul searching he ordered the American commissioners in Paris to take all of the Philippine Islands. On a later occasion, McKinley told a group of clergymen that it had not been an easy decision:

> *I walked the floor of the White House night after night until midnight; and I am not ashamed to tell you, gentlemen, that I went down on my knees and prayed Almighty God for light and guidance more than one night. And one night late it came to me this way—I don't know how it was but it came: (1) that we could not give them back to Spain—that would be cowardly and dishonorable; (2) that we could not turn them over to France or Germany—our commercial rivals in the Orient—that would be bad business and*

discreditable; (3) that we could not leave them to themselves—they were unfit for self-government—and they would soon have anarchy and misrule over there worse than Spain's was; and (4) that there was nothing left for us to do but to take them all, and to educate the Filipinos, and uplift and civilize and Christianize them, and by God's grace do the very best we could by them, as our fellow-men for whom Christ also died. And then I went to bed, and went to sleep and slept soundly.

When Spain displayed an understandable reluctance to part with the Philippines, the United States agreed to pay $20,000,000. The Treaty of Paris was signed on December 10, 1898, and ratified by the United States Senate two months later.

Although there is no accurate way of ascertaining the public reaction to America's overseas imperialism, all the available evidence suggests that the mass of people approved of the acquisition of overseas possessions. Imperialism was one of the major issues of the election of 1900, and the Republican advocates of expansion gained a decisive victory. McKinley was renominated by the Republicans, and Theodore Roosevelt was selected as his running mate. The Democrats again chose Bryan, while Adlai E. Stevenson of Illinois, who had served as Vice-President under Cleveland from 1893 to 1897, was given second place on the ticket. Bryan insisted that imperialism was the "paramount issue," but Democratic campaign speakers also repeated their earlier demands for free silver and a reduction in the tariff. The Republicans campaigned on their party's record. While defending expansion abroad, they pointed with pride to prosperity at home. The depression had given way to a boom, and Republican orators and editorial writers did their best to convince the voters that "the full dinner pail" could be attributed to McKinley, the gold standard, and the Dingley Tariff. In winning the election, McKinley had a larger majority than in 1896, and he carried every state outside the South except Missouri and Kentucky and the silver states of Colorado, Idaho, Montana, and Nevada. The popular vote was 7,207,923 to 6,358,133, and the electoral vote, 292 to 155.

The last two years of the nineteenth century were a major turning point in American history. In a matter of months the United States had acquired Hawaii by legislative act, secured a part of Samoa through negotiation, obtained Puerto Rico, Guam, and the Philippine Islands by conquest, and taken possession of Wake (in 1899). Before 1898 many Americans had believed that the United States was a world power. In 1900 they knew it. What they did not realize was that empire building entailed responsibilities as well as glory.

CHAPTER X

THE AMERICAN EMPIRE

THE ACQUISITION of islands in the Caribbean and Pacific forced the United States to devise a colonial policy and to revise its foreign policy. Both tasks proved more complex and onerous than the imperialists had anticipated. Not only was it difficult—and at times impossible—to reconcile the interests of colony and mother country, but the people of the United States repeatedly indicated that they were unwilling to make the sacrifices needed to defend their newly won interests in two hemispheres. In 1898 many Americans had looked on imperialism as a glorious adventure, but in subsequent years they were to learn that the maintenance of an overseas empire involved burdens as well as prestige and expenditures as well as profits. It was a hard lesson, and the Americans learned it the hard way.

63. PROBLEMS OF ADMINISTRATION

ALTHOUGH the American people appeared to forget in the Philippines many of the ideals for which they had professedly fought in Cuba, they revived them as soon as their empire had been secured. As if tormented by a national guilt-complex for their violations of the creed of their fathers, they set to work to furnish the inhabitants of the newly acquired islands with schools, hospitals, roads, pseudo-democracy, and the miracle of American plumbing. Whenever possible and profitable, the American dollar marched side by side with humanitarianism into the farthest reaches of the new American empire.

Although an uneasy conscience—or perhaps, as some contemporaries preferred to put it, a sense of justice—drove the American people to "uplift" the "backward peoples" who had come under their control, they did not feel equally obliged to extend to their new subjects all the blessings of American liberty. In the first years of the new century the Supreme Court in a series of controversial and confusing rulings known as the Insular Decisions announced that all the provisions of the Constitution did not necessarily apply to those Americans who lived under the flag, but beyond the continental borders, of the United States. It made a distinction between incorporated and unincorporated territories. Residents of the unincorporated territories were denied the "fundamental" rights of the Constitution and were excluded from the American tariff system unless Congress specifically ruled otherwise. Stripped of their legal verbiage, the Insular Decisions were the Supreme Court's statement that the executive and legislative branches of the government could do whatever they wished with the new American colonies.

A preview of American colonial policy was furnished by the accomplishments of the American occupation forces in Cuba before their withdrawal in 1902. Under the leadership of General Leonard Wood, the Americans sought to impose a new way of life upon the Cuban masses. The island's administrative machinery was overhauled, and its financial system was reorganized. Schools were set up on the American model. The moribund University of Havana was revived, modernized, and given a new faculty. Physical rehabilitation was undertaken with the construction of roads, railroads, bridges, schools, and hospitals. All these activities were overshadowed, however, by the conquest of Cuba's most dreaded disease, yellow fever. Under the direction of Dr. Walter Reed, a group of American doctors proceeded on the then novel assumption that yellow fever was carried by the stegomyia mosquito rather than produced by filthy living conditions. They permitted themselves to be bitten and infected, and within a relatively short period, they were able to substantiate this hypothesis. Once the source of the disease had been ascertained, the army cleaned up the breeding grounds of the mosquitoes, and by the conclusion of the occupation, American military forces had won a battle of more lasting glory than any of the victories over the Spanish a few years earlier.

Cuba's nominal independence was preserved while its continued subservience to the United States was insured by the Platt Amendment, which was passed as a rider to an army appropriation bill in 1901. The island's independence was guaranteed against outside interference other than that of the United States; a limit was set on the Cuban debt; and Cuba was compelled to grant the United States land for coaling stations and the right to intervene for the maintenance of Cuban independence and domestic tranquillity. For almost three decades the Platt Amendment served as a pretense for the protection of American strategic and economic interests in Cuba. Changes in political conditions in the United States had little effect upon its Cuban policy, for Presidents Theodore Roosevelt (1901–09), William Howard Taft (1909–13), and Woodrow Wilson (1913–21) all sent troops to occupy the island. Although Americans insisted that they were intervening to insure the stability of government in Cuba, in each instance the presence of American troops served only to perpetuate reactionary and autocratic native regimes. Without the chance to change their government by ballots, the Cuban masses also had to forego bullets as their larger neighbor used force to maintain a stability that was designed to preserve the economic and strategic *status quo*. It was not until 1934 and the advent of the New Deal's Good Neighbor policy that the Platt Amendment was abrogated.

Cuba's experience as an independent nation revealed that economic imperialism did not necessarily have to be preceded by territorial acquisition. After the withdrawal of American troops from Cuba in 1902 and the lapse of the Foraker Amendment, which prohibited the award of economic concessions to Americans during the occupation, American economic interests steadily penetrated the island. American investments in Cuba, which in 1898 approximated fifty million dollars, were estimated by the United States Department of Commerce at more than one billion dollars in 1924. Some of this capital went into Cuban railroads, tobacco plantations, public utilities, government securities, and mineral resources, but the bulk of American funds in Cuba was in sugar production. Before 1910, the ownership of the island's sugar industry was divided almost equally among European, American, and Cuban capitalists; by 1920, however, American-owned mills were producing almost half the Cuban sugar supply, and eight years later American mills accounted for nearly two thirds of the total. Cuba's economy was bound to that of the United States by commercial ties as well as capital outlay. In 1921, Cuban exports to the United States amounted to about $230,000,000 out of a total of about $278,000,000. In the same year American products accounted for about $264,000,000 of Cuba's total import bill of more than $354,000,000. Nominally independent Cuba was the United States' most successful experiment in economic imperialism.

Although Cuba was never formally incorporated into the American colonial system, in most other respects it served as a model for the treatment of the various parts of the United States' newly acquired empire. The details might vary from possession to possession, but in every instance humanitarianism and a measure of self-government were paralleled by policies that were designed to promote the strategic interests of the United States and American economic expansion. The results of the program were far from uniform. The Philippines turned out to be an economic liability and failed the only strategic tests to which they were submitted under American rule. Hawaii, on the other hand, developed into an asset of immeasurable strategic and economic value. Puerto Rico, although it never played a major rôle in American power politics, became a major asset to small but powerful groups of American businessmen.

The Philippine Islands were to be viewed by many Americans as a showcase of a new and enlightened type of imperialism. The United States expended large amounts of money on physical improvements, health and educational programs, administrative reforms, and the purchase of land owned by the Catholic orders in the islands. Moreover, it promised the Filipinos their independence as soon as they had successfully completed a probationary period. In 1900, William Howard Taft headed a commission to establish a civil government in the islands. A year later Taft became the first civil Governor of the Philippines. The other members of the commission also stayed in the islands and with the assistance of three Filipinos served as the legislative branch of the government. After 1907 the Filipinos were permitted to elect their own assembly, while the United States continued to retain its control over the upper house and the executive. Taft and the four Governors who followed him from 1903 to 1913 instituted public-works programs, improved educational facilities and strengthened the government's finances. The mass of Filipinos approved of good roads and public schools, but they were not satisfied; they demanded independence rather than paternalism. It was with this object in mind that Woodrow Wilson named Francis Burton Harrison as Governor in 1913. Under Harrison's administration, Filipinos were given a larger share in the government, and native business enterprise and agriculture were encouraged. Furthermore, Congress, with the support of the Wilson Administration, in 1916 passed the Jones Act which substituted an elective senate for the commission and promised the Filipinos independence as soon as they had established a "stable government." Both Wilson and Harrison assumed that the latter requirement had been fulfilled, but when the Republicans returned to power in 1921, they ruled otherwise. New commissions were sent out to investigate the islands and Harrison's major policies were reversed by Governor Leonard Wood and his successors. It was not until 1932 that the Hawes Act, passed over President Hoover's veto, provided for Philippine independence by the end of a decade. Although the Filipinos rejected this offer, they accepted a somewhat similar one when it was proffered through the Tydings-

McDuffie Act of 1934. On July 4, 1946, the Filipinos proclaimed their independence—almost a half century after Admiral Dewey had sailed into Manila Bay.

Although American financial and commercial interests exercised a predominant influence over the Philippine economy, these islands never produced the tangible rewards that had been visualized by the imperialists at the turn of the century. The $166,245,000 that represented the total American investment in the Philippines in 1930 and the $78,183,000 in American exports to the Philippines in the same year accounted for only a small fraction of the sum that the United States expended annually on the administration and defense of the islands. On the other hand, the United States annually imported approximately 99 per cent of the Philippines' total sugar exports, 96 per cent of its coconut oil exports, and 62 per cent of its cordage exports. These and several other commodities entered the United States duty free to the obvious economic disadvantage of the American producers of the same or comparable products. Despite the extent of American control, the Philippine Islands were an outstanding failure as a venture in economic imperialism.

Puerto Rico was handled in somewhat the same fashion as the Philippines, but with less fortunate results from the standpoint of the Puerto Ricans. In April, 1900, the end of the military occupation of Puerto Rico was signalized by the passage of the Foraker Act, which provided for a government that consisted of an executive council and a governor, both of which were to be selected by the President of the United States, and a house of delegates to be elected by the Puerto Ricans. In 1917 the Jones Act made Puerto Ricans citizens of the United States and abolished the executive council for an elective upper house of the legislature. American political control, however, was assured: the President of the United States was to appoint the governor, and he had the right to veto the acts of the Puerto Rican legislature. No other important changes were made in the administration of Puerto Rico until 1946, when Jesus T. Piñero became the island's first native Governor. In 1947 the United States Congress adopted a bill that provided for the popular election of the governor, and in 1948, Luis Muñoz Marin, the leader of the Popular Democratic party, was elected Governor for a four year term.

The Puerto Rican economy was never able to provide the masses with an adequate standard of living. A large percentage of the population had hookworm, malaria, tuberculosis, and other diseases; unemployment was a constant problem; and most of the rural families suffered from chronic undernourishment. Puerto Rico's economic difficulties stemmed in large part from a lack of resources to support a population that expanded from 953,243 in 1899 to 2,113,058 in 1947. In addition, sugar cultivation so overshadowed other forms of economic activity that the island was unable to produce most of the necessities required by its inhabitants. Because Puerto Rico was within the American tariff wall, most of its sugar was exported to the United States, and approximately half of its output of sugar was produced by American-owned mills in the island.

For the past half century the United States has tried in various ways to improve social and economic conditions in Puerto Rico. Attempts have been made to expand educational facilities, and the Federal government has financed a number of internal improvements. During the depression of the thirties Federal relief and land-reform programs were introduced, and during Rexford Tugwell's term as Governor (1941–6), the Puerto Rican government took over the operation of some public utilities. In recent years, Puerto Rico has sought to attract industry by offers of tax exemption and assurances of cheap labor. Despite the very real improvements effected by the United States and island governments, Puerto Rico has remained a "stricken land."

The Virgin Islands, which were purchased from Denmark by the United States in 1917, proved to be the least profitable of the American colonies. They were placed at once under the administration of a governor appointed by the president. In 1927 the inhabitants of the Virgin Islands were made citizens of the United States, and in 1936 the islands' two municipal councils were authorized to meet jointly as the "Legislative Assembly of the Virgin Islands." Although the islands enjoyed free trade with the United States, they produced little that could be exported to the mainland. At the same time, the islands' economy was unable to provide for the needs of the inhabitants. As a result the Virgin Islands —as Herbert Hoover said in 1931—were an "effective poorhouse" that was maintained by the United States. Since 1917, Federal expenditures for internal improvements, economic rehabilitation, and relief programs in the Virgin Islands have been a constant drain on the United States Treasury. The United States, however, has not been able to solve the islands' basic economic problems, and at no time have a majority of the inhabitants been able to attain more than a bare subsistence.

From an economic standpoint Hawaii and Alaska proved to be the United States' most successful ventures in empire building. Hawaii, which was brought within the American free-trade area, developed an economy that closely integrated with that of the United States. Concentrating on the production of sugar and pineapples, it sent almost all of its output to the United States, while more than 90 per cent of its imports came from the mainland. In 1939, Hawaii's imports from the United States were valued at $101,817,000, while its exports to the United States totaled $113,207,000. Alaska was also a valuable economic asset to the United States. By 1937 its mines had produced minerals worth $750,000,000, and in the year ending June 30, 1947 its exports of fish, furs, gold, and other products to the United States were valued at more than $80,000,000. Even more important were the territory's undeveloped assets, for its unexploited mineral deposits, timber stands, and hydroelectric sites made it potentially the richest of all the American possessions.

The administrative systems that were devised for Hawaii and Alaska had many points in common. Under the terms of an act of 1884, provision was made for the appointment of a governor and judicial officials for Alaska, and in 1912 the territory was granted the right to have a bicameral legislature. Since 1900, Hawaii's government has consisted of a governor appointed by the president, an elective legislature of two houses, and a judicial system whose top officials have been Federal appointees. In recent years both Hawaii and Alaska have sought admission to the Union as states, a demand that was supported by President Truman, the Interior Department, and the two major parties in their 1948 platforms. Although the House of Representatives in 1950 adopted statehood bills for Alaska and Hawaii, no action was taken on either measure by the Senate.

64. POWER POLITICS IN THE FAR EAST

THE CREATION of an American empire in the Pacific marked the end of an era in American diplomacy. For more than a century the relations of the United States with Europe had centered on American efforts to prevent the leading nations of the Old World from extending their influence to the Western hemisphere. With the acquisition of such distant possessions as the Philippines, however, continental domination as exemplified by the Monroe Doctrine was no longer enough. If American diplomats wished to protect their newly won outpost in the Pacific, they would have to take an active rôle in Far Eastern power politics.

When the United States entered the Philippines, international relations in the Far East were in flux. China appeared to be on the verge of disintegration, and the world's major nations were closing in for the kill. Following its easy victory in the Sino-Japanese War of 1894–5, Japan moved into Formosa and strengthened its hold over Korea. Japan's lead was quickly followed by several European powers as England, France, Germany, and Russia began a frantic scramble in China for spheres of influence, leaseholds, and railroad concessions. The United States, which for more than half a century had enjoyed the same commercial privileges in China as other nations, saw its new economic and strategic base in the Far East threatened even before it was firmly established. England was equally disturbed by developments in the Orient during the 1890's. While France, Russia, and Germany arranged and rearranged alliances, England's diplomatic isolation weakened its chances in any war that might grow out of imperialistic rivalries in the Far East. As the nation with the largest commercial stake in China, it would be the greatest loser if Chinese independence were destroyed. In an effort to rebuild its fences in the Far East, England turned to the United States. In 1898, Sir Julian Pauncefote, the British ambassador in Washington, suggested to Secretary of State John Sherman that England and the United States undertake a joint Far Eastern policy to guarantee equality of commercial opportunity for all foreign nations in China. The British proposal was rejected by Sherman; but within two years it had become the cornerstone of American Far Eastern policy under John Hay.

When John Hay became Secretary of State in September, 1898, he selected as his principal adviser on the Far East W. W. Rockhill, who had spent many years in China and had formed a lasting friendship there with Alfred Hippisley, another old China hand and a British subject. In 1899, Hippisley outlined a course of action for the United States in China and sent it to Rockhill in the form of a written memorandum. Rockhill submitted Hippisley's proposals to Hay, who, after making some minor revisions, dispatched them as a circular note to Germany, Japan, Italy, Russia, France, and England. What came to be known as the Open Door Note asked each nation to pledge itself not to interfere with the commercial rights of other nationals in its leaseholds or spheres of influence. Although most of the powers in replying to the Open Door Note employed language that was ambiguous enough to be meaningless, Hay announced that the principle of commercial equality had been accepted by all the nations with interests in China.

Within a year after its promulgation, the Open Door policy was seriously threatened by the Boxer Rebellion, an armed antiforeign protest that was suppressed by the combined military forces of all the powers, including the United States, that had received concessions from China. Hay, fearful that the foreign troops in China might be employed to shut the Open Door, on July 3, 1900, sent another circular note to the powers, which stated that the United States intended to "preserve Chinese territorial integrity and administrative entity." China escaped dismemberment after the Boxer Rebellion, but not because of the American note. Each nation with a stake in China was so afraid that any overt move would precipitate a general world war for which it was not prepared that it was willing to settle, however reluctantly, for the maintenance of the uneasy balance of power in the Far East. There is no reason to believe that John Hay's efforts had any effect upon either the economic or territorial situation in the Far East.

The Open Door policy was the product of American commercial aspirations and strategic necessity. American trade with the Far East represented only 2 per cent of the United States' total foreign trade, but several American politicians and businessmen thought that the acquisition of the Philippines had provided the United States with an ideal opportunity for increasing its commerce with the Orient. John Hay's notes were designed to prevent this potential market from being pre-empted by the European powers. As important as these economic considerations was the strategic problem posed by the Philippine Islands. The American people, with a one-ocean navy and little inclination to sacrifice their lives in the defense of the Philippines, nevertheless insisted that the United States hold the islands against all comers. As force was out, only diplomacy remained. John Hay based his policy on the hypothesis that the Philippines could only be saved from foreign aggression by the maintenance of the balance of power in the Far East and that this in turn could be achieved by preserving Chinese territorial integrity. Hay's successors never challenged this analysis, and Presidents Theodore Roosevelt (1901–09), William Howard Taft (1909–13), and Woodrow Wilson (1913–21) all made an independent China the keystone of their Far Eastern policy.

John Hay tried to save China and the Philippines by writing notes; Theodore Roosevelt sought the same ends by pursuing a spirited and often spectacular diplomacy—a technique that he once somewhat inaccurately described by saying that he preferred to "speak softly and carry a big stick." In one respect Roosevelt's problem differed from Hay's, for before the conclusion of his administration Japan had emerged as a major power in the Orient. Therefore, while Hay's policy of necessity had been directed primarily toward checking the advances of the European nations in China, Roosevelt had to concentrate upon curbing the expansion of Japan.

Roosevelt's Far Eastern policies were first revealed by his part in the Russo-Japanese War. At the outset of the war, Roosevelt and most other Americans gave their moral support to what they considered a weak Japan struggling against a mighty, autocratic, reactionary enemy. Russia, however, proved to be a hollow shell. Nevertheless, Japanese leaders feared that the drain of successive victories on the meager resources of Japan would result in ultimate defeat if the conflict turned into a war of attrition. With this in mind they requested the American President to intervene as peacemaker in the Far East. Roosevelt, well aware of the dangers involved in such a rôle, was at first reluctant to accept, but the logic of the American position in the Orient eventually convinced him that he could not afford to refuse. A clear-cut victory for either Russia or Japan would have threatened the territorial integrity of China and jeopardized the American position in the Philippines. Like John Hay

Theodore Roosevelt assumed that an independent China was the keystone of American Far Eastern policy.

The treaty of peace, which concluded the Russo-Japanese War and was sponsored by Theodore Roosevelt at Portsmouth, New Hampshire, in 1905, represented a victory for the Japanese, who obtained the southern half of the island of Sakhalin, the Liaotung leasehold in Manchuria, the South Manchurian Railway, and further recognition of their power over Korea. Despite these advantageous terms, the treaty fell short of Japan's war aims, for Roosevelt refused to accede to the Japanese demand for a huge indemnity from Russia. While this tactic successfully maintained the precarious balance of power in the Far East, it also produced considerable anti-American feeling among the Japanese masses, who had looked on the indemnity as a device for relieving them of the high taxes made necessary by the attempt to maintain a wartime economy with inadequate resources.

The aftermath of the Russo-Japanese war was also attended by a marked increase in anti-Japanese sentiment in California. This attitude was only in small measure a reaction to the Japanese military successes in the recent war; it was largely the product of such diverse forces as racial prejudice, fear of the effect of cheap Oriental labor upon California's standard of living, and an irresponsible press led by William Randolph Hearst's San Francisco *Examiner* with its repeated warnings against the "yellow peril." The San Francisco school board in October, 1906, ruled that the ninety-three Japanese children in the city would have to attend a separate school, and the Japanese government objected strenuously. Although Theodore Roosevelt had no jurisdiction over San Francisco's educational system, he sent a special deputy and numerous threats to San Francisco in an attempt to prevent a few municipal officials from involving the United States in an international incident. When bluster failed to move the members of the school board, Roosevelt reversed his tactics and invited them to Washington, where they speedily succumbed to the famous Roosevelt personality. The school board's rule was rescinded, and Roosevelt in 1907–08 reassured the jittery Californians by negotiating the Gentlemen's Agreement by which Japan promised to prohibit the emigration of Japanese workers to the United States. Roosevelt had been able to settle a disagreeable dispute through tact, ingenuity, and genuine statesmanship, but he was afraid that the Japanese would assume that he had been truckling to them. To convince Japan that the United States had acted out of generosity rather than timidity, he sent the United States' fleet on a round-the-world trip that included a long and impressive visit to Japan. Since the American people were unwilling to die for the Philippines, Theodore Roosevelt would save them by bluff and bravado.

Theodore Roosevelt also sought to maintain the American position in the Orient by exacting pledges from Japan to support the *status quo* in the Far East. In an executive agreement negotiated by Secretary of War Taft in 1905, American recognition of Japanese control over Korea was balanced by Japan's acceptance of the American position in the Philippines. Three years later in the Root-Takahira Agreement both countries pledged themselves to uphold the existing territorial settlements in the Far East, the Open Door, and Chinese territorial integrity. Both agreements were based on the same hypothesis. Although Theodore Roosevelt could not stop the advance of Japan in the Far East, he could blunt it and demand a *quid pro quo*—the continued inviolability of the Philippines. He would have preferred to have had it otherwise, but there was no alternative. While Roosevelt's Far Eastern policy undoubtedly represented a retreat from the position taken by Hay, his active diplomacy at all times prevented it from developing into a rout.

William Howard Taft, who became President in 1909, changed the techniques, but not the objectives, of his predecessors' Far Eastern foreign policy. For John Hay's note writing and Theodore Roosevelt's big stick Taft substituted what was popularly known as dollar diplomacy. The origins of dollar diplomacy in the Far East go back to Willard Straight, who had served in the American consular service in the Far East and convinced Secretary of State Philander Knox that there were limitless opportunities for the investment of American capital in China. Dollar diplomacy, as conceived and promulgated by the Taft Administration, was designed not only to promote American business activity abroad but also to enlist the support of the nation's leading financiers in the government's struggle to maintain the balance of power in the Orient. As in the past, the American stake in the Far East would be preserved by saving China from foreign aggressors. Just how the dollar would buttress diplomacy was explained by a State Department memorandum of 1909:

The nations that finance the great Chinese railways and other enterprises will be foremost in the affairs of China and the participation of American capital in these investments will give the voice of the U. S. more authority in political controversies in that country which will go far toward guaranteeing the preservation of the administrative entity of China. . . . So long as the U. S. holds the Philippines, the domination of China by other nations to our exclusion would be fraught with danger and it is unthinkable that this country should be squeezed out of any combination exercising an influence at Peking. The balancing of power in China is essential to peace in the Orient. . . . Our interests in Asiatic waters require the preven-

tion of the establishment of predominant interests and influences at Peking on the part of other powers and that American prestige in China be undiminished.

In 1909 the State Department induced some of the leading financiers of the United States to join a consortium of British, German, and French bankers who planned to construct the Hukuang Railroad in the provinces of Hupeh, Kwangtung, and Szechuan. The British were opposed to American participation in the project, but China was prevailed upon to withhold permission for the undertaking until the American capitalists had been included in the consortium. There is little reason, however, to believe that American investment in the Hukuang Railroad had any appreciable effect upon the attainment of the United States' long term objectives in the Orient. Even more unfortunate was Taft's attempt to apply dollar diplomacy in Manchuria. On the assumption that continued Russian and Japanese control of Manchuria's two principal rail systems represented a threat to the Open Door, Knox suggested that China borrow enough money from private investors abroad to purchase the two rail systems. Neither Russia nor Japan wished to relinquish their hold over Manchuria, and they rejected the American proposal.

Many Americans believed that the election of Woodrow Wilson to the presidency in 1912 had marked the advent of a new era in the United States' Far Eastern relations. Wilson was the first Democrat to occupy the White House since Cleveland's administration in the midnineties. He was a professed idealist, while Roosevelt and Taft had posed as practical men in foreign affairs. Most important of all, he had campaigned as an opponent of unregulated business, and there seemed no reason to believe that he would encourage American business excesses abroad while he curbed them at home. On the other hand, the situation in the Far East during Wilson's administration was in many respects similar to that under Taft and Roosevelt. This fact more than Wilson's personal wishes in the long run forced him to adopt much the same course that his predecessors had followed in the Orient from 1899 to 1912.

For a short time Woodrow Wilson was able to substitute his brand of idealism for dollar diplomacy in the conduct of Far Eastern policy. Before Wilson became President, Taft and Knox had urged the participation of American bankers in a six-power loan to China. One of the new President's first moves was to announce that his Administration was withdrawing the government's support from a project that it considered a threat to the continued independence of China. Wilson was also able to apply his ideals to the problem created by the resurgence of anti-Japanese feeling in California. When the California legislature announced that it intended to pass a law forbidding the ownership of land by Japanese in California, Wilson exerted considerable moral pressure to block this legislation and dispatched Secretary of State Bryan to the scene of the controversy. Although the California lawmakers eventually had their way, the law that they enacted was milder than had been originally anticipated.

But these minor steps in Wilson's Far Eastern policy do not indicate the extent to which he carried on the program of his predecessors. Like Roosevelt, Wilson was soon made to realize that American policy in the Far East depended upon Japan's moves rather than upon the ideals worked out by a college president in the confines of his study. In 1914, Japan in accordance with a treaty of alliance signed with Great Britain in 1902, declared war on Germany. Under her status as a belligerent, she then seized several German islands in the Pacific and assumed the German economic and political rights in the Shantung peninsula. A year later she made her boldest bid for Asiatic domination with the presentation to China of the famous Twenty-One Demands. China was asked to give Japan full control over Shantung, to agree to an increase in Japanese power in Manchuria, and to grant Japan special economic privileges in China proper and a predominant rôle in the Chinese government. Although the United States objected vigorously to this new manifestation of Japanese imperialism, it could not prevent continued Japanese expansion. Under diplomatic pressure Japan modified, but did not renounce, her claims in China. Moreover, the United States soon sanctioned the new Japanese position on the mainland. The Lansing-Ishii agreement of 1917, while reiterating both nations' earlier pledges to uphold the Open Door and the territorial integrity of China, also contained a formal American recognition of Japan's "special interests in China."

Soon after the conclusion of the Lansing-Ishii agreement, the Wilson Administration took more forceful measures to check Japanese expansion. The first of the American countermoves revealed a sharp clash between Wilsonian ideals and the facts of the Far Eastern situation, for in 1918 Wilson insisted that American bankers participate in a new loan to the Chinese government. The wheel had turned full circle and the realities of Far Eastern politics had forced Wilson to resort to the same dollar diplomacy that he had so heartily condemned in Taft. But Wilson was to go much further than either of his immediate predecessors, for he dispatched soldiers as well as dollars to the Orient. In 1918, the Allied nations, including the United States, sent troops to various parts of Russia, which under its new Bolshevik government had concluded a separate peace with Germany. Nine thousand American soldiers arrived in Siberia in August, 1918, and remained until April, 1920. Although Wilson's military moves prevented the Japanese from acquiring any territory in Russia's Asiatic domain, at the Versailles peace conference he was compelled to agree to Japan's control over the former German islands in the Pacific and the Shantung peninsula.

By the conclusion of his second term in the White House, it was clear that Wilson, like Theodore Roosevelt and Taft before him, had lost ground in the Far East. All three men had sought to preserve the existing balance of power by curbing Japan. Moreover, despite Wilson's protestations to the contrary, he had employed his predecessors' methods. Following Japan's Twenty-One Demands, he had resorted to Theodore Roosevelt's technique of recognizing the inevitable, and in 1918 he had championed Taft's much maligned dollar diplomacy. And to these steps, he had added a third—armed intervention. Despite all these efforts, the United States during Wilson's administration had retreated in the Far East; for Japan had advanced.

65. THE STRUGGLE FOR THE PANAMA CANAL

AMERICAN imperialism after 1895 was not confined to the acquisition of islands. In its relations with Latin America the United States repeatedly demonstrated that it was capable of extending its political and economic influence over vast areas without the formality of taking title to them. Diplomatic maneuvers, military occupation, and economic pressure were all employed at various times to exact compliance from the Latin Americans to the will of the United States while permitting them to maintain the fiction of political independence. Whenever American leaders felt the need to justify these tactics to themselves or to the world they could always resort to the Monroe Doctrine. In his annual message of 1823, Monroe had stated that the United States would look with hostility on European interference in the internal affairs of any nation in this hemisphere. After 1900, American officials redefined Monroe's words to say that European intervention could only be prevented by the intervention of the United States.

Although numerous American capitalists profited from the aggressive Latin American policy of the United States from 1890 to 1920, its primary motivation was not economic. The government officials who conducted American foreign relations in the first two decades of the twentieth century viewed their country's moves in Latin America as a means of protecting the United States rather than as devices for enriching American investors, manufacturers, and merchants. In still another sense, the determination of the United States to dominate Central and South America was just one more manifestation of the nationalism that was both a cause and an effect of the United States' emergence as a world power at the beginning of the twentieth century.

At the center of the strategic problem raised by the relations of Latin America to the United States was an Isthmus canal. Until Americans had obtained such a canal, their efforts were directed toward that end. After the canal had been secured, American foreign policy south of the Rio Grande was oriented around attempts to protect it. As early as 1846 the United States had negotiated a treaty with New Granada (later Colombia) that granted the United States the right of transit across Panama in return for an American guarantee of New Granada's sovereignty over the Isthmus. Four years later, the extensive British interests in Central America were recognized by the United States in the Clayton-Bulwer Treaty. Both nations agreed that any future canal would be a joint undertaking and would remain unfortified. The Clayton-Bulwer Treaty did not eliminate Anglo-American rivalry in Central America, and throughout the 1850's there was a growing feeling in the United States that an Isthmus canal should be an exclusively American project. The outbreak of the Civil War, however, put a temporary end to plans of the American canal enthusiasts.

Canal diplomacy in the years following the Civil War was complicated by financial obstacles as well as international rivalries. As the only possible canal routes lay through Nicaragua or Colombia, and as neither of these countries possessed adequate financial resources for such a large undertaking, capital would have to be obtained from outside sources. In 1878, a French company under Ferdinand de Lesseps, the builder of the Suez Canal, received a concession from Colombia to build a canal across the Isthmus of Panama. The possibility that an important commercial route and a vital naval link might come under the control of a foreign power convinced many Americans of the necessity for the construction and ownership of such a canal by the United States. Reflecting this sentiment, Secretary of State James G. Blaine in 1881 protested to the British that the Garfield Administration considered the Clayton-Bulwer Treaty a violation of the Monroe Doctrine and a threat to American supremacy in the Western hemisphere. Britain, however, had no intention of altering its policies in Central America to suit the whim of the American Secretary of State, and the British foreign minister informed Blaine that the canal "question had already been settled by the engagements of the Clayton-Bulwer Treaty and that Her Majesty's government relied with confidence upon the observation of all the obligations of that treaty." Blaine's failure was followed by a more devious, if not more subtle, American attempt to nullify the effect of the treaty. In 1884, Frederick Frelinghuysen, President Arthur's Secretary of State, concluded a treaty with Nicaragua that provided for the joint ownership of a Nicaraguan canal and a United States' guarantee of protection to Nicaragua against outside aggression. The Frelinghuysen-Zavala Treaty failed of the necessary votes for ratification during

Arthur's administration, however, and was withdrawn from the Senate by Grover Cleveland soon after he became President in 1885.

During the years between Frelinghuysen's unsuccessful attempt to circumvent the Clayton-Bulwer Treaty and the outbreak of the Spanish-American War, the American people displayed little interest in an Isthmus canal. By 1889 the French threat had been removed by the failure of the De Lesseps company after an expenditure of approximately $300,000,000. In similar fashion the Maritime Canal Company, an American corporation with a concession in Nicaragua, had abandoned its efforts in 1893 after three years of preliminary work. It was not until 1898 that the United States again turned its attention toward such a canal. The U.S.S. *Oregon's* race from Puget Sound around the tip of South America to beat the Spanish fleet to Cuba pointed an obvious strategic lesson. Equally important was the transformation of the United States into a two-ocean power with a one-ocean navy. To protect its new acquisitions in the Caribbean and the Pacific, a means of transit across the Isthmus seemed essential. Admiral Mahan had urged the United States to obtain Caribbean and Pacific bases to safeguard a future canal. Now that they had the bases, Americans turned the argument around and maintained that they needed a canal to protect the bases. Added to these strategic considerations was the renewed demand of the commercial interests for a shorter route between the United States' Atlantic and Pacific ports. Moreover by the end of the 1890's England was ready to reverse its earlier stand on the Clayton-Bulwer Treaty. Harassed by the vexatious problems of the Boer War and alarmed by the system of alliances being built up by its European rivals, England considered a retreat in Central America a small price to pay for the continued friendship of the most powerful nation in the Western hemisphere. In 1899, Sir Julian Pauncefote and John Hay negotiated a treaty that was rejected by the Senate because it did not allow the United States to fortify the proposed canal. Two years later the second Hay-Pauncefote Treaty, which permitted the United States to construct and maintain a fortified canal was ratified by the Senate by a vote of 72 to 6.

With the elimination of the Clayton-Bulwer Treaty, the principal question remaining was the location of the future canal. Theodore Roosevelt, who became President in September, 1901, apparently favored Nicaragua, and a group of engineers known as the Walker Commission reported that construction costs would be cheaper in Nicaragua than in Panama. It was, however, a matter that could not be settled on its merits alone, for it soon became hopelessly complicated by the machinations of backers of the French canal company, known as the Universal Inter-Oceanic Canal Company, which had gone bankrupt in 1889, only to be reorganized five years later as the New Panama Canal Company. All pretense of canal building had been abandoned, and the only reason for the new concern's existence was its desire to sell its concession to the United States. Any doubt concerning the objectives of the French company was removed when it reduced the price of its concession to the United States from $109,141,500 to $40,000,000 (and thus made the Panama route no more expensive than its rival) as soon as the Walker Commission indicated its preference for the Nicaraguan route. The company took particular care to point out to America's leading politicians the advantages of Panama over Nicaragua, and it chose William N. Cromwell, a prominent New York attorney, as its Washington lobbyist. Cromwell, who was later to charge his employers $800,000 for services rendered, induced the Republicans to drop the word "Nicaragua" from the canal plank of their 1900 platform and contributed $60,000 of his client's money to the Republican National Committee. His activities were equalled or surpassed by those of Philippe Bunau-Varilla, an engineer in the original company, who arrived in the United States to point out the dangers of Nicaragua's volcanos to such influential politicians as McKinley, Roosevelt, and Mark Hanna.

It is impossible to measure the effect of the tactics of the New Panama Canal Company upon the American decision to build a canal in Panama instead of Nicaragua; but in June, 1902, Congress passed the Spooner Act, which authorized the president to secure a right of way across the Isthmus of Panama. If Colombia were to prove recalcitrant or unreasonable, the president was to undertake negotiations with Nicaragua. By constantly threatening to turn to Nicaragua, the United States was able to exact favorable terms from Herrán, the Colombian representative in Washington. The Hay-Herrán Treaty, which was signed in 1903, granted the United States a six-mile-wide canal zone across the Isthmus of Panama for $10,000,000 and annual payments of $250,000. Although the treaty was speedily accepted by the United States Senate, it was rejected by Colombia, which wanted a higher price, part of the fee promised to the French company, and a guarantee against a possible American infringement of its sovereignty.

Colombia's refusal to accept the American offer infuriated Roosevelt, who wrote to Mark Hanna on October 5, 1903, that the United States was "certainly justified in morals, and therefore . . . in law . . . in interfering summarily [in Panama] and saying that the canal is to be built and that they must not stop it." The supporters of the canal project were determined that if Colombia was not amenable to diplomatic reason, they would resort to force. Reassured by his conviction that Roosevelt would look with favor on a popular uprising in Panama, Bunau-Varilla set to work to plan a Panamanian revolution. From his headquarters in a New York hotel room, which he described as the "cradle of the Panama Republic," Bunau-Varilla supplied the "revolutionaries" in

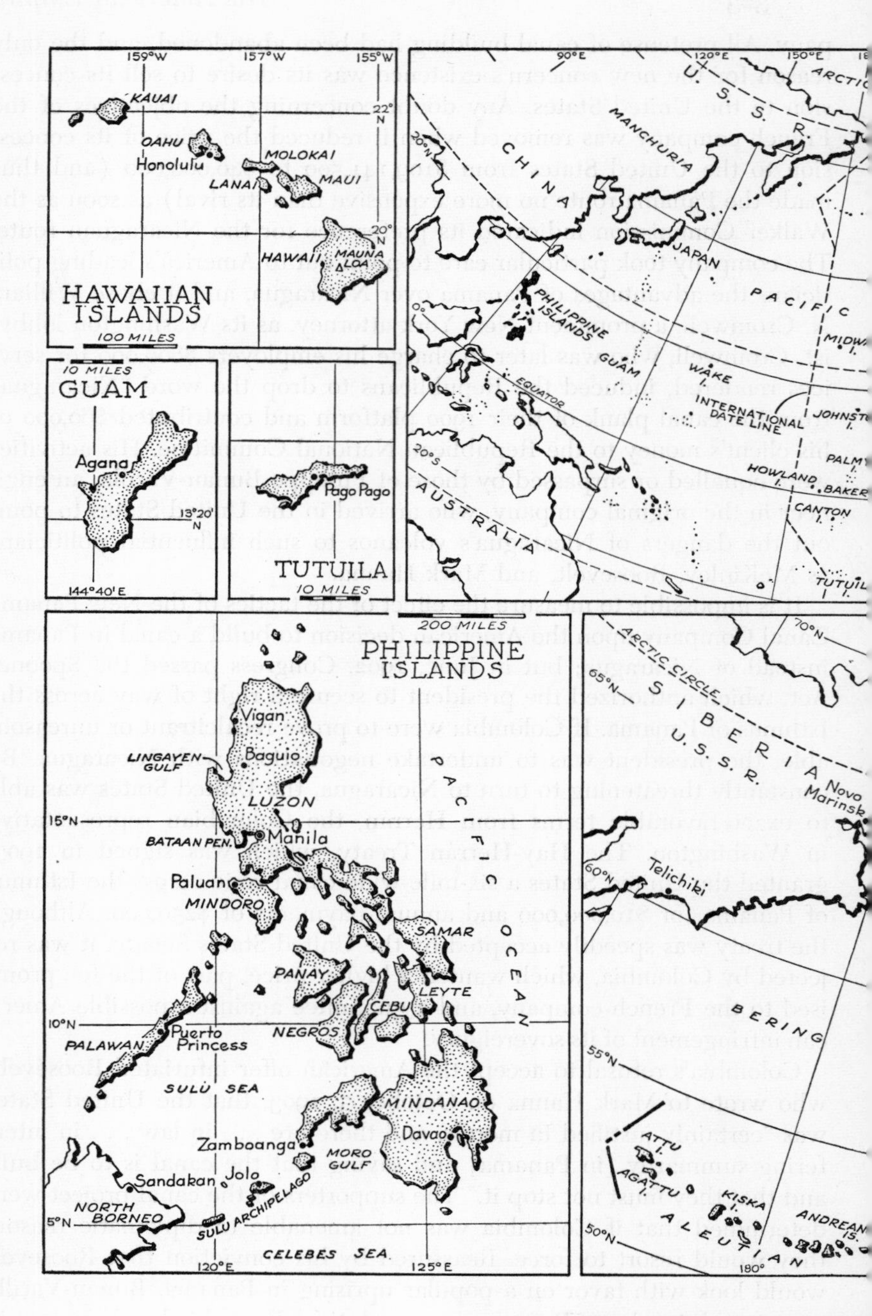

11. THE TERRITORIAL POSSESSIONS

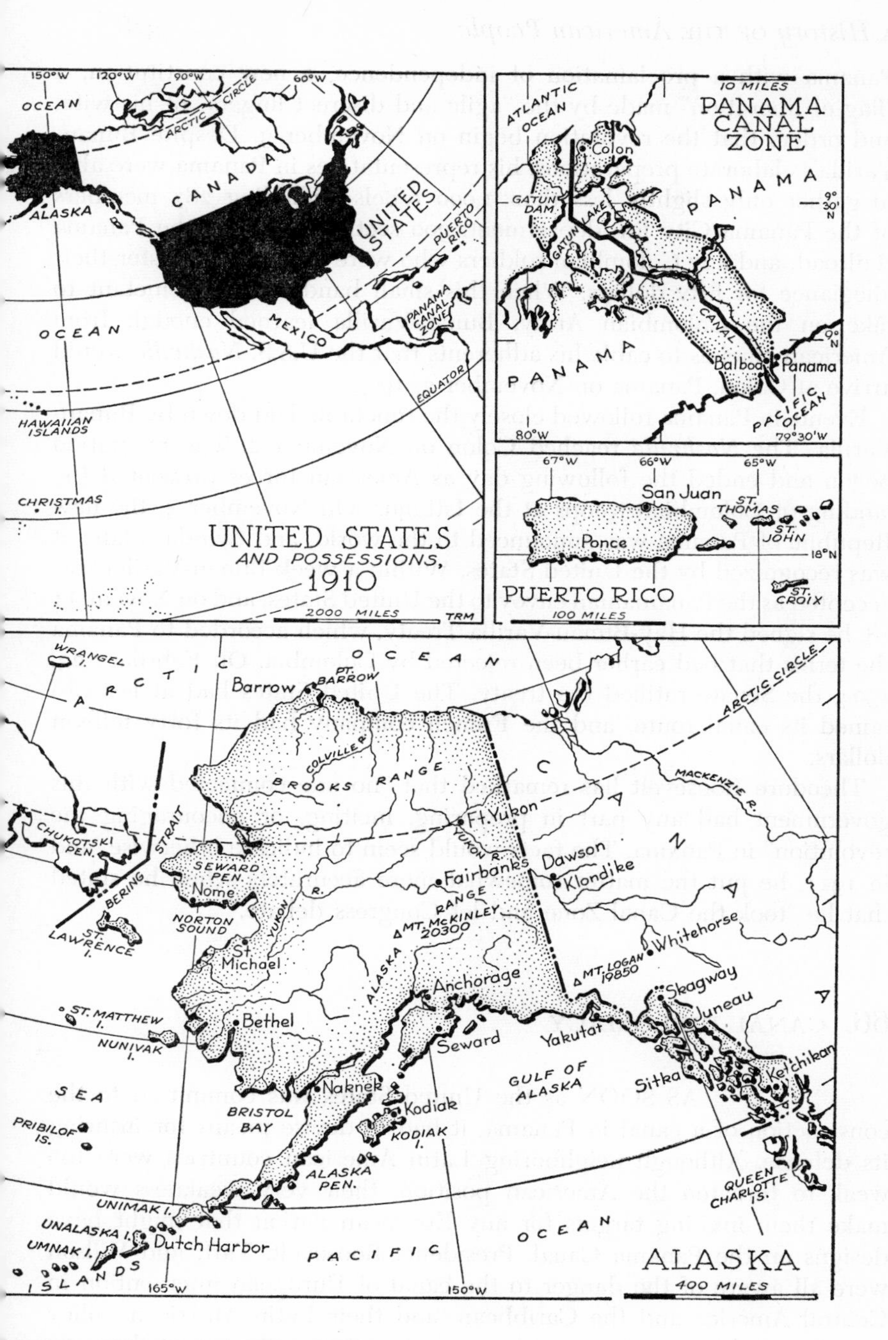

OF THE UNITED STATES IN 1910

Panama with a proclamation of independence, a new constitution, a "flag of liberation" made by the "agile and discreet fingers" of his wife, and orders that the revolution begin on November 3. Despite Bunau-Varilla's elaborate preparations, his representatives in Panama were able to gather only slightly less than 1,000 rebels—including 287 members of the Panama City fire department, 300 section hands of the Panama Railroad, and any Colombian soldiers who were willing to transfer their allegiance for fifty dollars. When this small band seemed reluctant to take on the Colombian Army, Bunau-Varilla learned enough from American officials to cable his adherents that the U.S.S. *Nashville* would arrive at Colon, Panama on November 2, 1903.

Events in Panama followed closely the timetable laid down by Bunau-Varilla. The *Nashville* reached Colon on November 2. The revolution began and ended the following day as American forces prevented the landing of Colombian troops at the Isthmus. On November 4, the new Republic of Panama was announced to the world, and two days later it was recognized by the United States. Within a week Bunau-Varilla was accepted as the Panamanian envoy to the United States, and on November 18, he signed the Hay-Bunau-Varilla Treaty, which accorded to Panama the terms that had earlier been rejected by Colombia. On February 23, 1904, the Senate ratified the treaty. The United States had at last obtained its canal route, and the French company had its forty million dollars.

Theodore Roosevelt has remarked that "no one connected with this government had any part in preparing, inciting, or encouraging the revolution" in Panama. The facts would seem to indicate otherwise, and in 1911, he put the matter somewhat more accurately when he stated that he "took the Canal Zone and let Congress debate."

66. CANAL DIPLOMACY

AS SOON as the United States was committed to the construction of a canal in Panama, it had to devise means for insuring its defense. Although neighboring Latin American countries were too weak to threaten the American position, their very weakness would make them inviting targets for any European nation that might have designs on the Panama Canal. Presidents Roosevelt, Taft, and Wilson were all aware of the danger to the canal of European intervention in Central America and the Caribbean, and their Latin American policy was designed to maintain and increase American influence in these regions. From 1903 to 1921, the United States added to its holdings in the Caribbean, pumped American capital into shaky regimes in Latin

America, employed the Monroe Doctrine in a fashion that had never been anticipated by its author, and on several occasions sent American troops to those countries that appeared to lack "stability."

The first challenge to the United States' canal diplomacy occurred before the consummation of the Panama Revolution. In 1902, Great Britain, Germany, and Italy decided to employ force to collect the debts that Venezuela owed their nationals. When they had blockaded Venezuela and bombarded one of its towns, Roosevelt indicated his disapproval of such vigorous measures and warned against any violations of the Monroe Doctrine. The possibility of armed intervention in Venezuela was removed when the blockading powers agreed to submit their claims to the Hague Tribunal. A by-product of the Venezuelan debt question was the Drago Doctrine. In December, 1902, Luis M. Drago, the Argentine foreign minister, proposed in a note to the United States "that the public debt can not occasion armed intervention nor even actual occupation of the territory of American nations" by European powers. Five years later the Drago Doctrine was incorporated into international law by the Hague Conference.

Roosevelt's casual attitude toward the blockade of Venezuela gave no indication of the determination with which he was to seek to prevent European intervention in the Dominican Republic. By 1904, Santo Domingo was bankrupt and owed eighteen million dollars to its foreign creditors. During the Venezuelan dispute, Roosevelt had written: "If any South American country misbehaves toward any European country, let the European country spank it." But by 1904, Roosevelt had decided that the United States had better do the spanking and in his annual message he described the United States' new duties as a stern parent under the Roosevelt Corollary to the Monroe Doctrine:

> *Chronic wrong-doing, or an impotence which results in a general loosening of the ties of civilized society, may in America, as elsewhere, ultimately require intervention by some civilized nation, and in the Western Hemisphere the adherence of the United States to the Monroe Doctrine may force the United States, however reluctantly, in flagrant cases of such wrong-doing or impotence, to the exercise of an international police power.*

Although Roosevelt's statement was couched in moral terms, he was not interested in improving the character of the Dominican people. Nor did the Roosevelt Corollary represent either economic or territorial aggression. If a potentially hostile power were situated at the gateway to the future canal, the United States' most vital interests would be in continual jeopardy. In Roosevelt's mind it was therefore necessary to anticipate the moves of any European rival. The strategic implications of the Roosevelt Corollary to the Monroe Doctrine were clear enough to most

Americans; to Latin Americans, who necessarily viewed the corollary from another perspective, it was a policy that forced them to arrange their lives according to the dictates of the United States.

Secure in his sense of the righteousness of his new doctrine, Roosevelt in 1905 concluded an agreement with the Dominican Republic that placed the Dominican customs system under the jurisdiction of an American citizen who would impound 55 per cent of its revenues to be applied to the European debts. When the Senate refused to accept this agreement, Roosevelt induced the Dominicans, who knew that he had superior force on his side, to appoint an unofficial American collector. Under his administration, customs receipts were doubled, the European creditors accepted an almost 50 per cent reduction in the debts, and the accounts were settled.

In 1912 the scope of the Monroe Doctrine was again expanded with the announcement of the so-called Lodge Corollary. In 1911 a Japanese fishing company had attempted to lease a large tract of land from Mexico in Magdalena Bay. When the State Department indicated its disapproval of the project, the Japanese concern had abandoned its plans. A year later a resolution introduced by Henry Cabot Lodge and adopted by the Senate revealed the continuing concern of the United States with its canal defenses. According to the Lodge Resolution, the United States would view with "grave concern" the acquisition by a foreign corporation of "any harbor or other place in the American continents . . . so situated that the occupation thereof for naval or military purposes might threaten the communications or the safety of the United States."

The policies exemplified by the Roosevelt and Lodge Corollaries were pursued by the Taft Administration under the name of dollar diplomacy. Although the methods might differ, the objectives remained fixed. The heart of the United States' Latin American policy was still the defense of the Panama Canal. To prevent rival imperialist nations from intervening in the neighborhood of the canal, Taft proposed to supplant European investments in this strategic area with American private capital. If the Caribbean and Central American republics had to rely on American rather than European financial resources, all pretext for European intervention in this area would be removed, and the continued safety of the canal would be assured.

On numerous occasions President Taft and Secretary of State Knox attempted to apply their formula of dollar diplomacy to financially weak regimes in the area that the United States considered its own private preserve. In 1909, when British bondholders began to move for the collection of their debts in Honduras, the Administration requested American financiers to assume the country's debt. A year later, a group of New York bankers were induced to take over the assets of the National

Bank of Haiti. When a revolution occurred in Nicaragua, Taft refused to accord diplomatic recognition to the new regime until it accepted large credits from American bankers for the liquidation of its debts to the British. Nicaraguan opposition to the plan was overcome by a visit from an American warship, and in 1911 a United States citizen took over the control of the country's customs revenues. In practice, dollar diplomacy proved to be the big stick with only minor variations of detail in application. If the country in question was not amenable to economic pressure, force could always be employed.

Shortly after Woodrow Wilson became President of the United States, he delivered a speech at Mobile, Alabama, in which he stated that the United States' Latin American policy would no longer be concerned with the "pursuit of material interest," but would be devoted to the promotion of "human rights" and "national integrity." Although Wilson's words may have heartened the anti-imperialists in the United States, Latin Americans were to find little evidence that his words meant any fundamental change in American foreign policy. The marines did not leave Nicaragua, and the Bryan-Chamorro Treaty provided for exclusive American canal rights in Nicaragua, the leasing of the Great Corn and Little Corn Islands and the Gulf of Fonseca to the United States, and a new American loan to Nicaragua. A revolution in Haiti in 1915 brought the American marines as quickly as in similar circumstances under either Taft or Roosevelt.

In defense of Wilson's diplomacy of force in Latin America, it should be pointed out that he was confronted by a strategic problem more pressing and more difficult than the problems faced by either of his immediate predecessors. During World War I, Germany's designs upon the Caribbean were a reality that could not be conjured away by expressions of Wilsonian idealism. More than ever before, the United States had to look to its canal defenses. Nor was force the only method employed to counteract the possibility of European intervention in the Caribbean; in 1917 the United States strengthened its hold over that region with the purchase of the Danish West Indies for twenty-five million dollars.*

Whenever the security of the United States was not at stake, Wilson's Latin American policy was more likely to accord with his ideals. When the question of the United States' responsibility for the revolution in Panama was reopened, the Wilson Administration agreed to a treaty that provided for an apology to Colombia and the payment of twenty-five million dollars in indemnity. At the time Theodore Roosevelt stated: "An administration that will conclude such a treaty as this treaty for

* During Grant's administration a treaty of annexation had not been acted on by the Senate, and in 1902, Denmark refused an American offer to purchase the islands for $5,000,000.

the payment of blackmail to Colombia has forfeited all right to the respect of the people of the United States." Apparently more than one third of the Senate agreed with this estimate; although the treaty was submitted to the Senate in June, 1914, it was not ratified until seven years later, when Harding was President—and then only after the deletion of the apology from the treaty and the discovery of valuable petroleum deposits in Colombia.

Woodrow Wilson's Mexican policy also stands as an attempt to elevate principles over material benefits in the conduct of American foreign affairs. Shortly before Wilson became President, Francisco Madero, President of Mexico, was deposed and subsequently murdered by his successor, Victoriano Huerta. In the normal course of events, the United States would have recognized the Huerta regime as soon as it had demonstrated its ability to maintain its control over the Mexican government and people. This policy was in accordance with the precedent established by Thomas Jefferson as Secretary of State in 1793, when he extended American recognition to the revolutionary regime in France. But Wilson, deciding to break a tradition that went back to the beginning of the American Republic, announced that he would not recognize a government that rested upon force rather than the popular will. If the Mexican people wished to enter into diplomatic relations with the United States, they would have to supplant the Huerta dictatorship with a constitutional democracy. On the other hand, the United States pledged itself not to intervene in Mexico's domestic affairs. Wilson was determined to stick to his policy of "watchful waiting" despite the continued loss of American life in Mexico, the jibes of his Republican opponents, the alacrity with which the European nations recognized the Huerta government, and the laments of American investors in Mexican oil, land, and railroads.

Although Wilson's Mexican policy may have represented a triumph of ideals over *Realpolitik,* it also revealed considerable confusion in its author's mind. In the first place, Wilson's policy can hardly be characterized as one of waiting, for diplomatic pressure was being put upon Huerta to resign, and after February, 1914, the United States permitted the export of arms to Venustiano Carranza and Pancho Villa, Huerta's principal rivals in Mexico. Moreover, Wilson's Mexican policy was in conflict with itself. He opposed American intervention in Mexico, while at the same time he demanded that the Mexicans change their form of government; but Mexico could not be transformed into a constitutional democracy without pressure from the United States. Finally, Wilson's criticism of Huerta strengthened rather than weakened the latter's popularity among the numerous Mexicans who were inclined to look on the United States with distaste and suspicion.

The deadlock between Mexico and the United States was broken by the events that followed the arrest of some American sailors by the Mexican authorities in Tampico on April 9, 1914. Although the men were immediately released and the Mexican officer responsible for the arrest apologized, Admiral Mayo, the commander of the American fleet, demanded a twenty-one gun salute to the American flag and a "formal disavowal of and apology for the act, together with . . . assurance that the officer responsible for it will receive severe punishment." Although Wilson thought the terms of Mayo's ultimatum too harsh, it was virtually

McCutcheon in the Chicago Tribune

INVOKING THE MONROE DOCTRINE

This cartoon shows a Midwestern conception of the ineffectiveness of the Monroe Doctrine during the dispute with Mexico in Wilson's administration.

impossible for him to repudiate the American commander, for a refusal by Wilson to support Mayo's stand would have been interpreted as an American retreat by the Mexicans and a sacrifice of national honor by the Americans. Huerta, well aware of Wilson's dilemma, resolutely refused to order the salute to the American flag. By April 20, Wilson's patience was exhausted, and he asked Congress for authority to intervene by force in a move that —as he carefuly pointed out—would be directed against the Mexican ruler rather than the Mexican people. The following day American naval forces shelled and captured the Mexican city of Vera Cruz. A full scale war between Mexico and the United States was averted, however, by a timely offer of mediation on the part of Argentina, Brazil, and Chile. Under the terms of the settlement worked out by the A.B.C. powers in June, 1914, the United States waived an indemnity and recognized a provisional Mexican government. Huerta fled Mexico in July; Carranza took over the presidency; and a disappointed Pancho Villa went on the warpath and attacked *Carranzistas* and American citizens indiscriminately. When Villa raided towns in Texas and New Mexico, American troops under General John Pershing invaded Mexico in a futile attempt to capture the rebel leader. The American forces were not withdrawn from Mexico until February, 1917; then, as the American people directed their energies toward the much larger conflict in Europe, the Mexicans settled down to the task of working out their revolution in their own way.

Woodrow Wilson's attempt to substitute ideals for force in Latin America produced only meager results. He had to resort to the tactics of his predecessors to maintain the position of the United States in the Caribbean, and his sympathy for the plight of the Mexican masses did not prevent the bombardment of Vera Cruz and the occupation of Mexican soil by American troops. Wilson's recourse to the accepted techniques of twentieth-century imperialism in Latin America, as in the Far East, revealed that the United States' foreign policy was determined, not by the high moral purpose of its President, but by geography, economics, "national honor," and the moves of its rivals. When the noble sentiments of Wilson's state papers and the details of execution are removed from Wilson's Latin American policy, little remains to differentiate it from the hardboiled programs of Roosevelt and Taft.

67. BUSINESS AND IMPERIALISM

IT IS impossible to dissociate economic pressures from the development of American foreign policy in the years between the Civil War and World War I. Before 1860, the agrarian demand for more land and the desire of commercial interests to protect and widen their overseas markets had left their imprint on the relations of the United States with the other nations of the world. After the Civil War the transformation of the United States into a leading industrial nation necessarily had an effect on the economic relations of the United States with the other countries of the world.

Before the Civil War the primary foreign economic interest of the United States was in foreign outlets for the surplus products of the American soil. Southern cotton and Western grains made up the bulk of American exports in the two decades before 1860, and they found their principal buyers in England and on the European continent. After the Civil War the United States continued to ship large amounts of agricultural goods abroad, but to these established exports there were soon added some of the products of the expanding industrial system. After 1900 the United States' economic relations with the rest of the world entered into a third stage. Foreign trade continued to increase, but for the first time relatively large amounts of capital began to seek places of investment beyond the borders of the United States. America's foreign economic interests were still essentially commercial before 1914, but the years between the Spanish-American War and World War I were the transitional stage in the shift of the United States' foreign economic stake from commerce to investment.

The outstanding change in the United States' world economic position in the half century that followed the Civil War was the increase in foreign trade. The yearly average value of American exports from 1866 to 1870 amounted to less than $400,000,000; from 1896 to 1900 it was well over $1,000,000,000; and between 1911 and 1915 it was more than $2,500,000,000. Imports increased in a comparable fashion.

As significant as the volume of this trade was its changing character. The impact of American industrial development upon foreign trade was revealed by the relative decline in the export of agricultural products and raw materials from a yearly average of about 80 per cent of the total exports between 1866 and 1870, to about 70 per cent between 1896 and 1900, to about 54 per cent from 1911 to 1915. The percentage of manufactured exports remained almost constant at about 20 per cent of total exports from 1865 to 1900, but when American industry began to saturate the home market in the first decade of the twentieth century, the volume of manufactured exports rose precipitously, and between 1910 and 1915 they amounted to about 46 per cent of the total American exports. Despite these figures, most American industrial firms were not competing in the world market, and a considerable proportion of the increase in manufactured exports was represented by the foreign activities of a few highly concentrated industries. For example, the United States Steel Corporation in 1913 had 268 selling agencies in sixty different countries and exported 1,800,000 tons of steel annually. Standard

Oil, the first large-scale trust, was also one of the first American industrial firms to make a concerted effort to dominate the foreign market. It purchased petroleum fields in the Middle East and Latin America; its salesmen invaded Europe and Asia; and eventually it worked out a cartel arrangement with its English and Dutch rivals for the division of the world market. Standard Oil's pattern of foreign expansion was duplicated by James B. Duke's American Tobacco Company, which had important sales outlets in Asia and Germany and an agreement with the Imperial Tobacco Company for the apportionment of the British and American markets. The overseas activities of these companies were, however, the exception rather than the rule in American industry before 1914.

Imports as well as exports were affected by the growth of American industrial enterprise. During the thirty years that followed the Civil War, American manufacturers strengthened their hold upon the home market, and imports of manufactured goods declined somewhat. Imports of raw materials for American industry increased, however, from a yearly average of about 12 per cent of the total goods imported each year between 1866 and 1870 to about 35 per cent of the goods imported yearly between 1911 and 1915.

A further indication of the new position of the United States in the world economy is provided by an examination of the channels of American commerce from 1871 to 1921. The sources of the United States' imports remained relatively constant during these years, but there were several significant changes in the destination of American exports. While exports to Europe declined from about 80 per cent of the total between 1871 and 1875 to about 60 per cent between 1911 and 1915, those to Canada and Nova Scotia rose from about 6 per cent to about 14 per cent during the same period. On the other hand, there was little change in the proportion of American products shipped to South America, and American exports to Asia between 1911 and 1915 still accounted for less than 6 per cent of the total.

The marked increase in American foreign trade was not accompanied by a comparable development in the country's merchant marine. In 1860, American ships in foreign trade totaled nearly 2,400,000 tons and 66 per cent of the nation's water-borne foreign commerce was carried in American vessels. During the Civil War many American ships were destroyed, however, and approximately 1,000,000 tons were transferred to foreign registry. In the ensuing years, no effort was made to revive the American merchant fleet, and by 1910 it had shrunk to less than 800,000 tons and less than 9 per cent of American water-borne foreign commerce was carried in American bottoms. It was only after the outbreak of World War I that the United States regained its place as a leading maritime nation.

After 1900, American capital as well as agricultural and manufactured goods became an exportable commodity. In the years that followed the Civil War, American industrial development and the extension of the country's railroad system had been financed in part by foreign capital. With the advent of the twentieth century, the trend began to be reversed. In 1900, the direct investments of the United States abroad amounted to $455,000,000, and twelve years later the total was $1,740,000,000. The bulk of this increase was represented by the accelerated flow of capital to Canada, Mexico, Central America, and the Caribbean Islands. Despite the increase in foreign investments, however, foreign capital in the United States still exceeded the sum of American investments abroad before World War I. In 1914, American investments abroad approximated $2,500,000,000, whereas foreign capital in the United States ranged between $4,500,000,000 and $5,000,000,000.

Although a rising industrial nation, the United States differed from other industrial nations in ways that profoundly influenced the conduct of American foreign policy before World War I. First of all it was still a debtor nation; and as long as it had no large investments abroad, its government could devote its energies toward ends other than the protection of the foreign investments of its nationals. Its debtor status, however, did not produce a feeling of subservience in the United States to the world's powerful creditor nations. A firmly established government, a continent with apparently limitless resources, and a tradition of political isolation combined to convince the average American that his country was neither the master nor the servant of the great powers of the world. Secondly, before 1914 the American economy had not yet reached the stage where its continued prosperity was dependent upon either foreign raw materials or foreign markets for its manufactured goods. Coal and iron—the sinews of the nineteenth-century Industrial Revolution—existed in lavish amounts in the United States, and ample quantities of practically every other kind of natural resource needed for the development of manufacturing could be found within the country's borders. Although the United States was never in a position to practice economic isolation, it was more generously endowed with essential raw materials than any other industrial capitalist nation in the world. Thirdly, the manufactured goods produced in the United States were consumed almost entirely at home. The Midwestern grain grower had to export to live, but the American industrialist still made the bulk of his sales in an expanding home market. Finally, the United States was unique among the industrial capitalist nations of the world in that it did not have to concern itself with the problem of supporting surplus population.

Thus the American Republic was not under pressure to undertake a program of what some historians have described as investment imperialism—that is, the export of capital and manufactured goods to the so-called backward regions of the world, the establishment of exclusive control over foreign supplies of essential raw materials, and the construction abroad with exported capital of railroads and factories, all with the aim of development to the highest point possible the industries of the nation sponsoring this program. Instead, it could devote most of its energies to developing what can be termed commercial or trading imperialism—that is, the expansion of foreign trade rather than the exploitation of the "backward" areas of the world.

There was nothing novel about commercial imperialism in American history. It had played its part in the participation of certain mercantile groups in the American Revolution, and in subsequent years it had been endorsed by the Federalists under Alexander Hamilton and by such prominent Whigs as Daniel Webster and Henry Clay. When the agrarian followers of either Jefferson or Jackson were in power, commercial imperialism was renounced in theory, if not in practice; but such economic foreign policy as the United States had was designed primarily to expand American foreign trade. Only small amounts of capital were sent abroad, and these were usually invested in raw materials and agriculture, rather than industrial enterprises. With the advent of the Republican party to power in 1861, there was an increasing emphasis upon commercial imperialism. During the Civil War, the United States on two occasions employed war ships to bombard the Japanese, who were reluctant to enter into commercial intercourse with this country, and in 1871, the same tactics were employed unsuccessfully against Korea. James G. Blaine's Latin American policies and John Hay's Open Door notes are further indications of the Republican party's preoccupation with foreign trade. Even dollar diplomacy, which was concerned with the investment of American capital abroad, was, according to President Taft, "an effort frankly directed to the increase of American trade."

The increased flow abroad of American capital after 1900 did not fundamentally alter the predominantly commercial character of the United States foreign policy before World War I. American investments did not necessarily mean American political control. The growth of the American economic stake in Canada was at no time a threat to that country's sovereignty or self-rule. The funds that were pumped into Latin America and the Far East under Taft's program of dollar diplomacy to a considerable extent represented the government's attempt to enlist private economic assistance to secure political ends rather than the traditional picture of a government protecting the foreign interests of its grasping capitalists. On the other hand, there were a few instances of American economic penetration abroad that in all essentials were identical with the more highly developed economic imperialism of the European powers. As early as the 1880's, United States' consular agents were actively engaged in the promotion of the sales of Standard Oil's products in China; and the extent of American economic control over Cuba had rendered that island an economic vassal of the United States by 1920. Moreover, although the United States' willingness to resort to armed intervention in the Caribbean and Central America may have been motivated by strategic considerations, it nevertheless served as a guarantee to American investors that their foreign investments would not be jeopardized by internal upheavals. Finally, the combination of adventurous American capitalists and an interventionist United States government produced a private colonial empire in Central America that rivaled or surpassed the imperialistic accomplishments of the older European nations. As early as 1900 the United Fruit Company, which had extensive holdings in both Cuba and the so-called banana republics, owned more than 250,000 acres of plantation, 112 miles of railroad, and investments of approximately $17,000,000. Twenty-eight years later its possessions in the Caribbean area were valued at $111,300,000 and included nearly 2,500,000 acres of land, more than 1600 miles of railways, and about 700 miles of tramways.

Despite the numerous examples of American economic imperialism between 1865 and 1914, American foreign policy never became the plaything or puppet of the nation's businessmen. While government officials may have been extraordinarily receptive to the wishes of the merchant, manufacturer, and financier in domestic affairs, in foreign policy they were inclined to subordinate economic interests to what they viewed as the greater glory of their country and to what they considered necessary to protect their nation in an international society that was as amoral and anarchistic as that of cannibal tribes.

CHAPTER XI

THE PROGRESSIVE MOVEMENT

THE PROGRESSIVE movement was a many-sided attack upon the various abuses that had become glaring in the decades following the Civil War. Although the Progressives never established a national organization to direct and co-ordinate their numerous campaigns, they nevertheless were bound together by a contagious enthusiasm for reform and an all-pervading optimism that at times approached naiveté. Working through local, state, and national legislatures and moving in and out of the established national parties as the occasion demanded, they were able to make their influence felt upon virtually every part of American life from the end of the century until the outbreak of World War I. The activities of the Progressives ranged over the entire spectrum of reform, but all their reforms had a common objective. The growth of industrial and finance capitalism had disrupted the American civilization of an earlier day, and the Progressives were bent on restoring the ideals of the past without sacrificing the material gains of the present.

68. THE PROGRESSIVE SPIRIT

THE PROGRESSIVE movement was a middle-class attempt to recapture an earlier age when the individual rather than the group had been the mainspring of American political and economic life.

Far from being revolutionaries, the Progressives wished to conserve the traditional American values, which they felt were being undermined by recent tendencies in business and government. They believed in political democracy, individual initiative, competitive capitalism, and property rights. Although many of their reforms called for an extension of government control, they were enemies rather than proponents of socialism. In their minds, a moderate increase in the power of the government provided the only means for preserving individual freedom and preventing the growth of those abuses that might eventually induce the masses to turn to socialism as a last resort. To the Progressives the growth of governmental authority was a means to an end and never an end in itself.

Like the reformers of the pre-Civil War era, the Progressives were convinced that man was a rational creature who knew his own best interests. If given all pertinent information concerning any problem, he was capable of weighing the facts, arriving at the correct conclusion, and pursuing a course of action that would benefit not only himself but society. Man, in short, was inherently progressive. It was true that certain barriers to progress had appeared in recent years, but these were man-made obstacles that man could remove. The Progressives, of course, were not alone in their belief in the inevitability of both individual and collective improvement. What set them off from other Americans was their enthusiastic determination to speed up the process of improvement.

The Progressives' faith in the judgment of the individual led them to a reaffirmation of the principles of political democracy. Every man was thought capable of governing himself, and the alleged defects of democratic government were considered corruptions rather than inherent weaknesses of the democratic process. If representative government had broken down, the Progressives reasoned, its collapse was due to its failure to be genuinely representative. Because of their confidence in the ability of the individual to vote in his own best interest, the Progressives urged that all be permitted to participate directly in government and that the gap that separated the rulers and the ruled be eliminated so that the two groups could be essentially the same. Specifically, they recommended such reforms as the direct election of senators, and the initiative, referendum, and recall. Through these and similar devices the Progressives believed that they would be able to insure a popular government in which the influence of either wealth or political machines would be reduced to a minimum. There was nothing novel in the political philosophy of the Progressives, for their principal tenets—if not their methods—had been advocated by Thomas Jefferson at least a century earlier.

In economics as in politics the Progressives' principal concern was with the welfare of the individual. They wished, not to destroy competitive capitalism, but to revive it by checking the growth of monopoly and promoting equality of opportunity. The Progressives viewed economic life as a race in which some contestants had gained such pronounced advantages that many of the less favored runners stood little or no chance of winning. Unlike the socialists, they did not wish to abolish the race, but to make certain that everyone began at roughly the same starting line and that all the competitors observed certain elementary rules of fairness. The government would be called on to serve as referee to enforce the rules and punish the violators. No attempt would be made to make every person run as fast as every other person, but each individual would be assured of the chance to run as fast as he possibly could. The Progressives were always among the strongest advocates of competition; it was only "unfair" competition to which they were opposed.

The Progressives could lay little or no claim to originality, for most of their general principles and specific proposals had been advanced earlier by reform groups during the Gilded Age. The Greenback-Labor party, aside from its demands for cheap paper-money, had advocated a program that in many respects was similar to that put forward by the Progressives a quarter of a century later. Several farm and labor organizations, as well as many small businessmen, had sought to curb the power of the trusts. Numerous local groups had been formed in the cities to combat corruption in municipal government and to improve the lot of the urban poor through humanitarian reforms. Finally, the Populists, in addition to their advocacy of free silver, had adopted a series of platforms, many of whose planks were taken over by the Progressives with little or no change.

The Progressives were also indebted to a number of individuals who during the last quarter of the nineteenth century repeatedly voiced their opposition to many of the practices that had attended the growth of American industrial capitalism. Of the many precursors of the Progressive movement, special mention should be made of Henry George and Henry Demarest Lloyd. Henry George, when living in California in the sixties, had been struck by the fashion in which the movement of population into an area forced up property values and provided land speculators with an unearned profit; and during a visit to New York City in 1869 he had been further impressed by the contrast between the city's astonishing material progress on the one hand and the poverty in its slum sections on the other. After extensive reading and research he concluded that the explanation for this paradox lay in the nation's land system, and in 1879 he published a fully developed version of this theory in *Progress and Poverty.* Although the manuscript of *Progress and Poverty* aroused no enthusiasm among commercial publishers and had to be privately printed, it soon reached a remarkably wide audience. George's theories on rent, which made up an important part of *Progress and Poverty,* were generally similar to those of the classical economist Ricardo. But the book, which revealed a characteristic faith in the ability of man to progress, was much more than an economic treatise in the classical tradition; it also contained an exceedingly able analysis of the American economy. According to George, it was the expropriation of land by a few wealthy individuals and groups that had created the gross inequities of nineteenth-century America. His cure was the Single Tax—a tax upon the unearned profit obtained from land through the rise in its value, which he believed was caused, not by its improvement, but by the increased demand for it as population increased. Such a tax, which George thought would yield enough to pay all the costs of government and thus make a tax on land improvements unnecessary, would cause speculators to sell their lands at reasonable prices and would eliminate land monopoly and with it the main obstacles to individual progress—all without eliminating the essential features of the capitalist system. Although few Progressives supported the Single Tax as a solution, many of them were either directly or indirectly influenced by George's analysis of why wealth was unequally distributed in the United States.

Henry Demarest Lloyd, like George, set the pattern for many of the Progressives of the next generation. A newspaperman assigned to the Chicago financial district, Lloyd soon became critical of many of the business practices that he was reporting. As early as 1881 he wrote an exposé of Standard Oil for the *Atlantic Monthly.* Entitled "The Story of a Great Monopoly," this article provided Lloyd with the formula that he used in 1894 in *Wealth Against Commonwealth.* In contrast to *Progress and Poverty, Wealth Against Commonwealth* offered no panaceas. Instead, it contained a mass of facts dealing with the growth, techniques, and effects of monopoly in the United States. Gathering his information from court records and legislative reports, Lloyd supplied his readers with names, dates, statistics, and countless examples to substantiate the thesis of its title. His book was to be the model for most of the muckraking exposés of the Progressive era.

Henry George and Henry Demarest Lloyd were probably the most influential precursors of the Progressives, but there were many others who helped to prepare the way for the general upsurge in reform after 1900. The importance of these forerunners of Progressivism should not, however, be overemphasized. While the Progressives borrowed heavily, they were more than mere imitators. In contrast to many of their predecessors they were able to make reform an exciting—and even a fashionable—adventure. They were able, moreover, to generate a nation-wide demand for change that bore little resemblance to the special pleading of a particular group.

69. THE MUCKRAKERS

IT WAS the good fortune of the Progressives that they put forward their reform program at a time when the American people were both willing and able to listen to their message. The depression of the nineties had raised doubts in the minds of many concerning the unmitigated blessings of industrial and finance capitalism, while the cynicism that often accompanied the get-rich-quick mania of the Gilded Age had begun to wear thin even before the appearance of the Progressives. At the same time recent developments in education and publishing had made it possible for the Progressives to disseminate their ideas to a nation-wide audience. Because of the rapid expansion of the school system, more Americans than at any other time in the past were capable of assimilating the proposals advanced by the Progressives, and the existence of several popular magazines and newspapers provided the reformers with effective vehicles for reaching the masses. Finally, there were a number of able writers who took advantage of these opportunities to dramatize the Progressives' complaints against the *status quo*. The "muckrakers,"* as they were called, devoted their talents to exposing what they thought were the outstanding evils of American political and economic life.

Although Henry Demarest Lloyd and others had written exposés as early as the 1880's, it was not until the end of the century that the muckraking technique was fully developed. S. S. McClure, the first publisher to see the possibilities of the muckraking article, in 1893 sent a writer to the Chicago World's Fair to gather material on the Armour Institute of Technology. When the reporter included some information on the meat-packing industry, McClure was struck by the potential appeal to American readers of factual surveys of the practices of the nation's leading business firms. In the ensuing years McClure mulled over this idea, and in 1897 he asked Ida Tarbell to prepare a study of the Standard Oil Corporation. After extensive and painstaking research Miss Tarbell published the first of a series of articles on Standard Oil in *McClure's* in November, 1902. Miss Tarbell's reports were notable both for their sensational revelations and for their high standards of scholarship. That McClure had not misjudged his audience was soon revealed by the sharp increase in the circulation of his magazine after the publication of the first installments of the Standard Oil series.

Ida M. Tarbell's "History of the Standard Oil," which ran in *McClure's* during 1902–04, quickly became a model for several other contributors to the same magazine. Lincoln Steffens studied municipal corrup-

* They received this name from Theodore Roosevelt, who compared them to the character in *Pilgrim's Progress* "who could look no way but downward with the muckrake in his hands."

tion in a series of articles that later appeared in book form as *The Shame of the Cities.* Ray Stannard Baker uncovered the malpractices of the railroads, and Burton J. Hendrick used the facts obtained by Charles Evans Hughes' investigation for an exposé of the life insurance companies. These and the many other muckraking articles that appeared in *McClure's* had a number of notable features. They were based on thorough and time-consuming research. A premium was placed on objectivity, and an attempt was always made to eliminate, or at least subordinate, editorial comment. Although the articles were serious, the startling nature of their material and their lively prose made them interesting to the average reader.

McClure's success with muckraking prompted other magazine publishers to follow his lead. By 1905, *Munsey's, Everybody's,* the *Cosmopolitan, Hampton's, Pearson's, Collier's,* and the *American* were all carrying accounts of political and economic malfeasance and double-dealing. Thomas W. Lawson's "Frenzied Finance" was largely responsible for increasing *Everybody's* circulation from 197,000 to 735,000, while other notable muckraking jobs included such articles as David Graham Phillips' "Treason of the Senate" in the *Cosmopolitan,* Samuel Hopkins Adams' studies of dishonest advertising and the patent-medicine business in *Collier's,* Ray Stannard Baker's examination of the position of the Negro in American society in the *American,* Upton Sinclair's exposés of the meat-packing industry in *Collier's* and *Everybody's,* and Charles Edward Russell's description of the "beef trust" in *Everybody's.* Despite the high standards set by many of these reporters, muckraking became increasingly sensational, and by 1910 it had lost much of its former objectivity. As readers tired of the constant stream of exposures, some publishers sought to hold their attention with articles that emphasized the spectacular while ignoring those features of the muckraking study that had made it unique.

The muckrakers were always more adept at calling attention to abuses than at explaining them. There was a strong moral overtone to much of their work, for they generally attributed corruption or wrongdoing to the presence of "bad" men in positions of power. This approach tended to convert reform into little more than a matter of individual differences. If some men were "bad," the problem was not insoluble, for it was always possible to replace them with "good" men. Only a few muckrakers went beyond this point to ask why such men had gained important offices in business and government in the first place. None of the muckrakers was more fascinated by this question than Lincoln Steffens. When he first began to investigate municipal administration, he assumed that "bad" men made "bad" governments. But on numerous occasions he observed that when reformers "drove the rascals out of office," such a change had little or no effect on government. When "good" men assumed office, they somehow became "bad." Steffens believed that the system rather than the individual was at fault; the officeholder—whether good or bad—had favors (such as street railway franchises) to bestow, and the businessman had money with which to purchase these favors. As a consequence, the system made both bad government and bad men inevitable. When a clergyman asked Steffens if he thought Adam was to blame, Steffens replied: "No, it was the apple."

Muckraking was not confined to the pages of the nation's periodicals, for many authors applied much the same technique to fiction. The muckraking, or reform, novel followed a pattern as rigid as that of the dime novel. In each case, an individual was pitted against a corrupt and powerful system of political or economic control. Despite seemingly hopeless odds, the hero battled on until the last chapter, when his efforts were rewarded with the collapse of the forces of evil. By the final page the "bad" man, who represented the system and who might be a machine politician or the head of a trust, had been routed, and the reader knew that the "good" man, who had done the routing, would live happily ever after. Of the many novelists who employed this formula, none adhered to it more closely than Winston Churchill. After achieving considerable success with historical fiction, Churchill turned to accounts of New Hampshire politics with the publication of *Coniston* and *Mr. Crewe's Career*. In both novels, the characters were essentially symbols, and the corrupt bosses in the long run were always defeated by the virtuous reformers. A somewhat similar approach was used by David Graham Phillips in *The Plum Tree* and *Light-Fingered Gentry*, Booth Tarkington in *The Gentleman from Indiana*, and virtually every other author who used fiction to promote reform.

When the muckraking novel was employed to describe economic abuses, it frequently became a device for extolling a particular social or economic system. The numerous novels written by Upton Sinclair during the Progressive era were all little more than tracts. In *The Jungle*, which was Sinclair's best-known book, the central character after suffering almost indescribable hardships in the Chicago meat-packing industry, eventually—that is, in the last chapter—solved his problems by becoming a socialist. While Sinclair wrote *The Jungle* to promote socialism, the book's effect was quite different. Because of its vivid accounts of the unsanitary methods used in the preparation of meat, it became one of the principal factors responsible for demands for the enactment of pure food legislation. Other novelists, such as Jack London, converted the muckraking novel into a propaganda vehicle for Marxism. By his mixture of communist theory, criticism of capitalism, and undiluted adventure, London won a large audience of readers, most of whom had little or no interest in his economic theories.

Scholarship, as well as literature, was influenced by the muckraking spirit. Many historians assumed a critical—and at times, even hostile—attitude toward the American past, and students of sociology, economics, and government tended to place their greatest emphasis on what they considered the defects of American society. Gustavus Myers' *History of Tammany Hall* (1901) and *History of the Great American Fortunes* (1909–10) applied the muckraking technique to both political and economic history. Van Wyck Brooks in *The Wine of the Puritans* (1909) employed a similar approach to social and intellectual history in an effort to demonstrate his thesis that the Puritan tradition was largely responsible for the defects in contemporary American culture. In *The Spirit of American Government,* which appeared in 1907, J. Allen Smith shocked conservatives by attacking the Constitution as a reactionary and antidemocratic document. Six years later Charles A. Beard's *An Economic Interpretation of the Constitution of the United States* reconsidered the Constitution in the light of the economic interests of its authors. Louis Brandeis muckraked finance capitalism in *Other People's Money* (1914), and Thorstein Veblen's numerous articles and books pointed out the contrasts between the existing economic practices of monopoly and the accepted economic theories of competition.

Scholarly accounts of the flaws of America's present and past reached only a relatively small audience, but there were also books designed to provide the general reader with both a summary of current abuses and a blueprint for a brighter future. In *The Promise of American Life* (1909) Herbert Croly outlined a reform program that was a curious mixture of twentieth-century Progressivism and eighteenth-century Federalism. Croly agreed with Hamilton that the government should be granted extensive authority over the lives of its citizens, but he thought that such authority should be used to assist the masses rather than the upper classes. Walter Weyl, who, like Croly, wished to draw up a guide for a better America, preferred Jefferson to Hamilton. In *The New Democracy* (1912), Weyl argued that economic democracy was a prerequisite of an effective political democracy. Much the same material appeared in Walter Lippmann's *Preface to Politics* (1913), which repeatedly emphasized the intimate connection between economics and government. To provide a continuing forum for the point of view represented in these books, Croly founded the *New Republic* in 1914. Although its circulation was always insignificant when compared to that of the "slick" magazines, the *New Republic* continued as a muckraking magazine long after the collapse of the Progressive movement.

By 1914 the muckraking era had ended. Readers had had a surfeit of sensational exposures. Moreover, some evidence exists that the pressure of advertisers, on whom the muckraking periodicals were dependent, was partially responsible for halting magazine attacks on business. Finally, with the advent of World War I both the muckrakers and their audience shifted their attention from abuses at home to problems abroad. During the ten or more years in which they had flourished, the muckrakers had poked into almost every corner of American life. Although frequently negative in their approach, they played an essentially constructive rôle in American life. Even though they limited their attention to abuses, they were often responsible for setting in motion campaigns to eliminate the abuses. Nor should their popularity with American readers be overlooked. If self-criticism is one of the measures of the health of a democracy, the success of the muckraking magazines indicates that American democracy was flourishing.

70. THE STRUGGLE AGAINST BOSS RULE

PROGRESSIVISM was to a considerable extent an urban counterpart of Populism, and many of the earliest Progressive reforms were directed against abuses that had attended the growth of cities. Although the rapid rise of industry had produced dislocations virtually everywhere in America, it was the city rather than the country that suffered from extremes of progress and poverty, degrading living conditions, and corrupt political machines. In their efforts to meet the manifold problems created by the rapid urbanization of the United States, the Progressives were seldom doctrinaire; they were always more interested in results than in the methods by which they sought to attain their objectives.

Although numerous municipal reformers had battled the professional politicians during the seventies and eighties, it was not until the end of the century that a concerted effort was made to overhaul the government of American cities. By 1900 every major city contained at least one reform group that was attempting to find a formula for destroying the corrupt alliance between wealth and politics. The task was never an easy one, for the success of the local political bosses rested on what appeared to be an unbeatable system. In return for the votes of the poor the machine distributed favors that ranged from an occasional bag of coal to an annual outing in the country, while it obtained its funds from selling street railway and lighting franchises, building contracts, police protection, and countless other privileges to businessmen who were both willing and able to pay the price. Despite the strength of the opposition, however, the Progressives attacked the machine politicians on many fronts, and in a number of instances they won some noteworthy, if limited, victories.

While local differences precluded the formation of an effective national organization for municipal reform, many of the Progressive mayors had a common bond in their mutual indebtedness to Henry George. The author of *Progress and Poverty* had not been particularly concerned with city administration, but he had presented those who were with a lucid analysis of the central problem of American civilization in the Gilded Age. Typical of the so-called Henry George mayors was Samuel Jones, who served as mayor of Toledo, Ohio, from 1897 to 1904. Known as Golden Rule Jones, because of his repeated attempts to apply the Golden Rule to public life, he fought the professional politicians and their allies among the business groups throughout his administration. When the Republican organization turned against him, he campaigned successfully for re-election without funds or formal party endorsement. When the utilities objected to his methods for awarding franchises, he came out for municipal ownership of the street railway and lighting facilities. When he antagonized the former rulers of Toledo, he went directly to the people and won them over to his idea that municipal government should be conducted on a nonpartisan basis. Following no apparent system and often giving the impression of extreme naïveté, Jones in reality understood the workings of the alliance between politics and business as well as those who had profited from this arrangement.

Golden Rule Jones was only one of the many outstanding municipal reformers of the Progressive era. Brand Whitlock, who succeeded Jones as chief executive of Toledo, was in many respects as successful a reform mayor as Jones. Tom Johnson, who became a Single Taxer after reading one of Henry George's books during a train trip, abandoned a successful business career to enter municipal politics. As mayor of Cleveland from 1901 to 1909, he won a national reputation for his campaign for home rule, the municipal ownership of utilities, and the Single Tax. Much the same pattern was repeated in several other cities. Mayor Hazen S. Pingree attacked the street railways in Detroit; reformers smashed the political rings that had formerly ruled St. Louis and Minneapolis; Emil Seidel, a socialist, became mayor of Milwaukee in 1910; and New York City voters elected John Purroy Mitchel as mayor on a reform ticket in 1913.

No generalizations can adequately cover the accomplishments of the municipal reformers during the Progressive period. Many of their victories were short-lived, but they were also responsible for several important changes in both the structure and spirit of local government. In several instances they were able to gain an increased measure of home rule, although most state legislatures still exerted a remarkable degree of control over the city governments. As a result of Progressive agitation, many cities experimented with the commission form of government, which had been first tried by Galveston in 1900 after a disastrous tidal wave. The city-manager plan, which turned the government of a city over to a paid manager, also attracted wide attention after it had been successfully adopted by Dayton, Ohio, in 1914. Several cities sought to increase the power of their elective officials by decreasing their number. An attempt was also made to achieve greater efficiency in administration through up-to-date bookkeeping systems, executive budgets, the public purchase of supplies, expansion of the civil-service system, and training schools for firemen, policemen, and teachers.

The Progressives were repeatedly thwarted in their attempts to reform municipal politics by the superior strength and resources of their opponents. In many instances, the utilities that the Progressives wished to regulate were parts of powerful economic empires covering several states and exerting widespread political and financial influence. Moreover, lack of home rule frequently made city officials little more than puppets of the state legislatures. In several instances municipal reformers sought to overcome these obstacles by transferring their attention to state politics. Tom Johnson, for example, campaigned unsuccessfully for the governorship of Ohio; Hazen S. Pingree's opposition to Detroit's utilities was at least partially responsible for his election to the governorship of Michigan; and Joseph Folk became Governor of Missouri in 1904 after smashing the political "ring" in St. Louis.

Of the many Progressives active in state politics few, if any, won a wider or more deserving fame than Robert M. La Follette. Born and educated in Wisconsin, he began his political career as a regular Republican. When he was defeated for election to a fourth term in the House of Representatives, he returned to Wisconsin and campaigned against the state Republican machine and its allies among the lumber and railroad interests. Despite the opposition of the regular organization, he was elected Governor in 1900 and re-elected in 1902 and 1904. By 1906, when La Follette entered the United States Senate, he had helped to place on the Wisconsin statute books every important feature of what had become known as the "Wisconsin Idea." While La Follette was Governor, Wisconsin adopted the direct primary, passed laws to conserve the state's natural resources, developed an equitable tax system, and passed a body of labor legislation that included safety regulations, a workman's compensation act, and a child-labor law. Equally notable were several innovations in administration. Women were appointed to numerous positions; professors from the University of Wisconsin served in various divisions of the state government in an advisory capacity; and nonpartisan commissions were established to regulate various economic activities. As significant as any of La Follette's specific reforms was the impetus that his accomplishments gave to the Progressive movement throughout the nation. Wisconsin, which had been one of the most boss-ridden, interest-dominated states in the Union, within a few short years had been converted by La Follette into both a symbol and model for Progressives throughout the nation.

While no other Progressive working to reform the state government achieved either the prominence or success of La Follette, many other individuals made notable contributions to the movement. William S. U'Ren, although he only once held office, was largely responsible for Oregon's adoption of the Australian, or secret, ballot, direct primary, initiative, referendum, and recall. In New Jersey, Republicans Everett Colby and George L. Record first proposed many of the reforms that were later put into effect by Woodrow Wilson and the Democrats after 1910. Every section of the Union produced a number of remarkable reform Governors. Albert B. Cummins served as a Progressive Governor of Iowa from 1902 to 1908; Charles Evans Hughes was elected as a reform Governor of New York in 1906; Hiram S. Johnson won the governorship of California in 1910 following his repeated assertions that "the Southern Pacific Railroad must be kicked out of state politics"; and Charles B. Aycock, Napoleon B. Broward, William Goebel, and Braxton B. Comer were among the leading reform Governors in the South. Despite differences in approach and personality, the state Progressives had certain features in common. Without exception they sought to destroy the alliance between organized big business and organized politics.

Throughout the Progressive era the political reformers within the states advanced a number of plans for destroying machine rule by increasing both the power and opportunities of the voter. Thus, to enable the people rather than the bosses to select candidates, the Progressives espoused the direct primary. In 1903, Wisconsin became the first state to adopt the direct primary for all nominations. Two years later Oregon adopted a similar reform, and by 1915 some form of the direct primary was in use in approximately two thirds of the states. Yet, despite the enthusiasm with which the Progressives backed the direct primary, it failed to weaken appreciably the power of the professional politicians, for frequently the machine was able to control the direct primary just as effectively as it had controlled the convention. Far more effective than the direct primary as a device for strengthening popular rule was the substitution of the direct election of senators for their selection by the state legislatures. Instead of waiting for a constitutional amendment, several states introduced a system of preferential ballot that compelled the members of the state legislature to choose the senatorial candidate desired by a majority of the voters. By 1912 twenty-nine states had provided some method to permit the voters to exercise considerable control over the selection of senators, and in the next year the Seventeenth Amendment, which provided for the popular choice of senators, became part of the Constitution.

In their efforts to promote popular government within the states, the Progressives placed heavy reliance on the initiative, referendum, and recall. Through the initiative a small percentage of voters could compel the legislature to consider a measure, the referendum permitted the people to vote on a bill that was before the legislature. South Dakota introduced the initiative and referendum in 1898, and Utah followed in 1900 and Oregon in 1902. By 1918 twenty-one states from every section of the country had provided for the use of both the initiative and referendum. The recall, which enabled the voters to pass on the fitness of an official or his policies in a special election, was first adopted by the cities of Los

Harper's Weekly

FATHERS STAY IN THE NURSERY WHILE MOTHERS GO OUT INTO PUBLIC LIFE—A CARTOON AGAINST WOMEN'S SUFFRAGE

Angeles and Seattle. After Oregon approved the recall in 1908, ten other states followed suit within the next six years. The recall aroused greatest interest where it was applied to the judiciary. When Arizona in 1911 applied for statehood with a constitution containing a clause calling for the recall of judges, President Taft vetoed the resolution granting admission. Arizona deleted the offending clause, gained admission to the Union in 1912, and readopted the recall the following year.

The movement for women's suffrage, which had had a long and hectic history throughout the nineteenth century, was given a marked impetus by the spirit of reform generated during the Progressive era. By 1900 only Wyoming, Colorado, Utah, and Idaho had given women full voting rights. During the next decade women's rights made little progress but between 1910 and 1912 five states amended their constitutions to include provisions for women suffrage. By 1914 women enjoyed the same political rights as men in eleven states. Progress, however, seemed disappointingly slow to the suffragettes, and such leaders as Mrs. Carrie Chapman Catt and Dr. Anna Howard Shaw decided to direct their energies toward the adoption of a constitutional amendment. Through petitions, mass demonstrations, parades, pamphlets, and picketing, women's organizations aroused widespread interest in the demand for an amendment and compelled the Wilson Administration to come out in favor of women suffrage in 1917. When the United States entered World War I and many women began to fill jobs formerly occupied only by men, the suffragettes were able to add one more argument to an already imposing list. In June, 1919, Congress approved an amendment that stated: "The right of citizens of the United States to vote shall not be denied or abridged by the United States or by any states on account of sex." By August, 1920, it had been ratified by the required number of states and became the Nineteenth Amendment to the Constitution.

When the Progressive era drew to a close after the outbreak of World War I, the reformers could point to a long list of impressive accomplishments in municipal and state politics. Many Progressives thought that they had routed the bosses once and for all. When subsequent events demonstrated that they had won a battle instead of a war, critics charged that the Progressive approach to politics had been both naive and superficial. But this judgment was not altogether fair. The Progressives had supplied the American voter with the machinery for self-government. If future generations did not wish to avail themselves of the privileges won by Progressivism, they, and not the Progressives, were to blame.

71. AID FOR THE UNDERPRIVILEGED

THE PROGRESSIVES were responsible for a number of important contributions to the cause of democratic government, but they did not limit their activity to political reform. Realizing that many of the most distressing features of American life could be attributed to poverty in the midst of plenty, the Progressives advanced a broad program of reform that was humanitarian in outlook and pragmatic in approach. Convinced of both the sanctity of private property and the right of the individual to manage his own affairs, they asked only that the poor be given a helping hand. They did not wish to revolutionize the pattern of American life, but they insisted that the weak be afforded some protection against the strong, that the state assume a measure of responsibility for the care of those who were unable to care for themselves, and that the poor be provided with at least minimum living standards and recreational facilities.

To mitigate some of the harsher aspects of industrialism the Progressives within the states sponsored a variety of laws to protect men, women, and children at work. Largely because of the agitation of the Progressives several states adopted workmen's compensation statutes, safety and health codes, prohibitions against child labor, minimum wage and maximum hour provisions, and laws designed to safeguard women in industry. Moreover, toward the end of the Progressive era a few states undertook to furnish assistance to those individuals who were unable to earn their own living. Arizona in 1914 became the first state to enact an old-age pension law. This measure was, however, invalidated by the state's supreme court, and it was not until the end of the 1920's that an appreciable number of states paid pensions to the aged.* Programs to aid mothers with dependent children were inaugurated by Illinois and Missouri in 1911 with the adoption of legislation providing for regular payments to women who for whatever reason received no other assistance in the support of their children. The pioneering efforts of the Progressives to obtain the passage of social security legislation were limited in scope and few in number, but they established a pattern that was to be widely emulated by the next generation of reformers in both the state and national governments.

In their efforts to lighten, if not eliminate, the burden of poverty, the Progressives devoted especial attention to the problems arising from the rapid urbanization of the United States. Of these, none seemed more pressing than the wretched housing facilities available to the poor in the largest cities. Although Jacob Riis and many others had waged a valiant campaign against the slums before 1900, they had met with little success and not until the new century was any noticeable progress made in the battle against the slums. It was in New York City, where the living conditions of the poor were as deplorable as those of any other American city, that the first significant efforts to improve them were undertaken. In 1898 the Charity Organization of New York proposed legislation that would outlaw the most blatant abuses, and two years later the competition that it sponsored for the design of a model tenement attracted widespread attention. The state legislature in 1900 conducted a survey of New York City's slums, and in the following year it adopted a law regulating housing facilities in cities of more than 250,000. Under the provisions of this statute, all rooms and halls had to be ventilated, and certain minimum safety and health requirements were made mandatory. But the new law produced little immediate effects, and it was another decade before there was any marked improvement in the tenements of New York City.

Other states were quick to adopt legislation similar to that of New York. In 1905, New Jersey passed a tenement-house law that applied to

* By 1931, thirteen states had passed old-age pension laws.

every city of the state, and somewhat similar measures were approved by the legislatures of Connecticut in 1905 and Pennsylvania in 1907. Most of the larger cities also raised their minimum housing requirements through the revision of their building codes. By 1908, Baltimore, Boston, Chicago, Cleveland, and San Francisco, as well as New York City, had tightened up the regulations governing the construction of tenements. But new laws did not necessarily mean improved living conditions, for the Progressives were always far more successful at getting laws enacted than in getting them enforced. Even in those cities in which the letter of the law was observed, overcrowding, filth, and disease remained the principal features of life in the tenements. A trip through the slum areas of any American city at the conclusion of the Progressive period provided ample proof of the extent to which the reformers had failed. The Progressives, as in so many other instances, had called attention to the problem, but they had not been able to solve it.

The Progressives attempted not only to improve the living conditions of slum dwellers but also to provide them with opportunities for recreation and self-improvement. No single institution played a more important rôle in this effort than the settlement house. In 1886, Dr. Stanton Coit established the nation's first settlement house with the founding of the Neighborhood Guild in New York City. In succeeding years the American settlement-house movement, which was profoundly influenced by the work done at Toynbee Hall in London, developed with remarkable rapidity. In 1889, Hull House, probably the best known American settlement house, was opened in Chicago by Jane Addams and Ellen G. Starr; and about the same time the Henry Street Settlement in New York and the South End House in Boston were founded. By 1895 there were approximately fifty settlement houses in the United States, and within the next five years this number doubled. Situated in slum and factory areas, settlement houses offered a wide variety of constructive activities to children and adults who possessed virtually no other means of escape from the stultifying and frustrating influences of their environment. Behind the projects, classes, games, and entertainments conducted by the settlement houses was a philosophy of reform that was admirably summarized by Jane Addams when she wrote:

> *The Settlement, then, is an experimental effort to aid in the solution of the social and industrial problems which are engendered by the modern conditions of life in a great city. It insists that these problems are not confined to any one portion of a city. It is an attempt to relieve, at the same time, the overaccumulation at one end of society and the destitution at the other; but it assumes that this overaccumulation and destitution is most sorely felt in the things that pertain to social and educational advantages. From its very nature*

it can stand for no political or social propaganda. It must, in a sense, give the warm welcome of an inn to all such propaganda, if perchance one of them be found an angel. The one thing to be dreaded in the Settlement is that it lose its flexibility, its power of quick adaptation, its readiness to change its methods as its environment may demand. It must be open to conviction and have a deep and abiding sense of tolerance. It must be hospitable and ready for experiment. It should demand from its residents a scientific patience in the accumulation of facts and the steady holding of their sympathies as one of the best instruments for that accumulation. It must be grounded in a philosophy whose foundation is on the solidarity of the human race, a philosophy which will not waver when the race happens to be represented by a drunken woman or an idiot boy.[*]

The growing concern over the need for adequate recreational facilities for city children was further revealed by the rapid increase in the number of municipally owned and operated playgrounds in the United States. With urban real estate at a premium this problem of city living had long been neglected. As early as 1885 a group of philanthropic Bostonians had provided sand gardens for children, but not until 1899, when New York City opened thirty-one playgrounds, was the problem squarely faced by other cities. By 1915, when 432 cities were maintaining 3,294 play areas, the playground had become a commonplace feature of the American urban scene. With adequate facilities and supervision, playgrounds offered city children not only enjoyment but also lessons in group activity that were largely unavailable in other sectors of city life. The increasing number of fresh air camps enabled a few city youngsters a brief chance at life in the country, while the Boy Scouts of America, organized in 1910, gave boys from town and country alike experience in camping and woodcraft. The establishment in 1912 of both the Girl Scouts and Campfire Girls opened up similar opportunities to young girls.

While additional recreational facilities in congested urban areas undoubtedly helped to reduce juvenile delinquency, an equally significant contribution to the campaign to check criminal activity among the young was made by the juvenile courts. Recognizing that the judicial process used for adult lawbreakers was in many respects unsuitable for children, Illinois in 1899 became the first state to establish special courts for youthful offenders. By 1910 every major American city had followed Illinois' example. The juvenile court emphasized rehabilitation rather than retribution, and every effort was made to convert potential criminals into useful citizens. Although many selfless individuals devoted their lives

[*] Jane Addams: *Twenty Years at Hull-House* (New York: The Macmillan Company, 1910), pp. 125–6. Copyright 1910 by The Macmillan Company, and reprinted with their permission.

to work among juvenile delinquents, few did as much as Judge Ben Lindsey of Denver. In addition to conducting a model children's court that won a justly earned national reputation, Judge Lindsey lectured and wrote widely on the most advanced methods for handling young people who had run afoul of the law.

The Progressive assault against the evils that arise from poverty included an extensive health program for the underprivileged. At the turn of the century a few cities undertook the medical and dental inspection of all school children, and within a decade and a half the city without such a service was the exception rather than the rule. Most major cities adopted milk codes to enforce pasteurization and prevent dilution, and milk stations in many urban centers distributed milk at cost to the poor. Baby clinics and visiting nurses assured infants of expert medical supervision, and provided mothers with instructions on the most advanced methods in the care of their children. Many cities also established day nurseries that assumed responsibility during the day for the children of working mothers. While most of these benefits were enjoyed almost exclusively by urban dwellers, the establishment by the Federal government of the Public Health Service in 1912 and the organization of such private institutions as the Rockefeller Foundation in 1913 indicated an increasing awareness that ill-health was a national rather than a local problem.

During the Progressive era, as in earlier reform periods in American history, there was a marked upsurge in the apparently endless crusade against alcoholic beverages. Although a militant prohibition movement had existed in the United States throughout most of the nineteenth century, it had little to show for its efforts, and by 1900 only five states—Kansas, Maine, North Dakota, New Hampshire, and Vermont—were legally dry. But the long years of failure and frustration were almost over for the prohibitionists. The enthusiasm for all manner of reform generated by the Progressives provided the foes of the "demon rum" with a more receptive audience than in any other age in American history. Prohibitionism continued to be most popular among religious groups in rural sections, but the determination of the Progressives to root out every variety of evil won the movement many new adherents who had previously displayed little or no interest in the problem of strong drink. Another important element of support was furnished by employers, many of whom were willing to back any movement that seemed capable of enforcing sobriety among their workers.

The spearheads of the prohibitionist campaign were the Anti-Saloon League, which was loosely affiliated with a number of Protestant sects; the Women's Christian Temperance Union; and the Temperance Society of the Methodist Episcopal Church. All three organizations carried on an extensive propaganda designed to convince the voters of the need for outlawing the liquor trade. Under the leadership of Wayne B. Wheeler and William H. Anderson, the prohibitionists soon demonstrated their skill at pressure politics. They established lobbies at the state capitals and at Washington; they organized drives for funds, and they injected prohibition into virtually every major political dispute. The success of these tactics was soon apparent. In the South, where it was thought that the use of alcoholic beverages contributed to racial tensions, seven states went dry in the years between 1907 and 1915, and four others in the Middle and Far West quickly followed suit. By April, 1917, when the United States entered World War I, twenty-six states had adopted prohibition laws.

Despite repeated victories in rural America, the Prohibitionists were unable to rout the "wets" in the large cities.* Eventually it became apparent to the leaders of the movement that only an amendment to the Federal Constitution could topple these last strongholds of the opposition. The United States' participation in World War I, moreover, provided the prohibitionists with one of their most telling arguments. If Americans had to conserve food to win the war, the use of grains for the manufacture of alcoholic beverages was a drag on the war effort that could not be tolerated by patriotic citizens. Before the end of the war, Congress prohibited the manufacture or sale of intoxicants, and in 1917 both the House and Senate approved the Eighteenth Amendment, which forbade the "manufacture, sale, or transportation of intoxicating liquors." Ratification by the states followed speedily. By January, 1919, thirty-six state legislatures had acted favorably, and the Eighteenth Amendment went into effect a year later. The Volstead Act, providing the machinery for the enforcement of national prohibition, was adopted by Congress over President Wilson's veto in October, 1919, and the United States entered the "dry decade."

Although few leading Progressives played a prominent rôle in the prohibition crusade, the two movements had many points in common. The members of both groups were moral in their approach, eclectic in their methods, adept at dramatizing evil, and convinced that their own version of "do-goodism" held the answer to whatever problem they attacked. Nor were these their only points of similarity, for the Progressives as well as prohibitionists more often than not were willing to settle for a law that would control the manifestations rather than root out the origins of the principal flaws in American society.

* In 1914, Chicago had more saloons than the entire South.

CHAPTER XII

T. R., TAFT, AND WILSON

72. THE STRENUOUS LIFE
73. THEODORE ROOSEVELT AND THE TRUSTS
74. SAFEGUARDING THE PEOPLE'S INTERESTS
75. THE TAFT ADMINISTRATION
76. THE SCHOLAR IN POLITICS
77. THE NEW FREEDOM

THE ADVENT of Progressivism as a significant force in national affairs was signalized, but not caused, by the accession of Theodore Roosevelt to the presidency in 1901. Although most of Roosevelt's domestic policies had been advanced by William Jennings Bryan in the nineties, and although his record as a reformer never equaled that of such men as Robert La Follette in the Senate and George W. Norris in the House, the fact remains that to great numbers of Americans, Theodore Roosevelt and Progressivism were synonymous. Moreover, when he left the White House in 1909, he was succeeded by William Howard Taft, who, despite his willingness to co-operate with the conservatives on numerous occasions, carried forward many parts of the program that had been inaugurated by Roosevelt. Finally, in Woodrow Wilson's first administration (1913–17) several additional planks in the Progressive platform were translated into law. While Roosevelt, Taft, and Wilson employed different methods to achieve their objectives, they all shared a similar belief in both the efficacy and desirability of reform.

72. THE STRENUOUS LIFE

THEODORE ROOSEVELT was born in 1858 of well-to-do parents in New York City. A sickly boy, he had a sheltered childhood and was educated by tutors until his family sent him to boarding school. After graduating from Harvard in 1880, he served for three years as a Republican assemblyman in the New York state legislature; and as a member of the New York delegation to the Republican convention of 1884, he opposed Blaine's nomination. For the next two years he abandoned the East and politics for life as a rancher in the Dakotas, but in 1886 he was back in New York where he waged an unsuccessful campaign as the Republican candidate for mayor. As a reward for his work in the Harrison campaign in 1888, he was made a member of the Civil Service Commission, and in 1895 he was appointed to the presidency of the New York City police board. Two years later he became the Assistant Secretary of the Navy in the McKinley Administration.

Although Roosevelt was a nationally known figure before 1898, it was his spectacular rôle in the Spanish-American War that first gave him a unique place in American politics. When he returned home from Cuba a conquering hero, he was elected Governor of New York. Although his administration was a popular one, Roosevelt's independence satisfied neither the New York Republican machine nor its boss, Tom Platt. As a consequence, Platt in 1900 decided to kick Roosevelt upstairs into the vice-presidency. Although Roosevelt at first announced that "under no circumstances" would he accept the nomination, and although Mark Hanna warned that Roosevelt's selection would mean that there was "only one life between this madman and the White House," the former Rough Rider was offered and accepted second place on the McKinley ticket. His nomination was due not only to Platt's desire to rid New York of its unruly Governor, but also to Roosevelt's tremendous popularity among the rank and file. In addition, his candidacy was backed by Boise Penrose and Matthew Quay, the Republican bosses of Pennsylvania. Although they had no use for Roosevelt's political views, their objections to Mark Hanna's control of the party made them willing to support any candidate that was opposed by the Republican national leader. Six months after McKinley's second inauguration, Roosevelt was President. On September 6, 1901, McKinley was shot by an anarchist in Buffalo, New York, and eight days later he died. Mark Hanna's worst fears were realized, and at McKinley's funeral he said to a friend: "Now . . . that damned cowboy is President."

Although during Roosevelt's administration more reform bills were adopted than had been in any other administration since the Civil War, it was the President's personality rather than his program that most impressed the American people. The most versatile President since Jefferson, he was among other things an explorer, naturalist, politician, soldier, big-game hunter, historian, literary critic, naval administrator, and athlete. While his critics often accused him of superficiality, he was at home with specialists in many fields. Soon after graduating from Harvard he published *The Naval War of 1812* (1882), which for years was the outstanding work on the subject. In subsequent years, he wrote *Hunting Trips of a Ranchman* (1885), *Thomas Hart Benton* (1886), *Gouverneur Morris* (1888), *Ranch Life and the Hunting Trail* (1888), and the four-volumed *The Winning of the West* (1889–96) as well as numerous articles, reviews, and editorials. A further indication of Roosevelt's many-sidedness was provided by the diversity of his friends and acquaintances. During his lifetime he was on good terms with kings, politicians, cowboys, scholars, professional prize fighters, soldiers, and diplomats.

Roosevelt's versatility was matched by his spirited dedication to what he called the strenuous life. A man who often confused action with accomplishment, he frequently gave the impression that the ideal society was one in which all its members were in constant motion. He was not above exhorting the American people to "hit the line and hit it hard," and he made a conscious effort to live up to his theories. He killed a Spanish soldier in Cuba; he took his friends and associates on hikes that exhausted them; and a special messenger had to climb a mountain to inform him of McKinley's death. One critic thought Roosevelt "pure act," and an Englishman called him "an interesting combination of St. Vitus and St. Paul." While it is impossible to doubt his physical fortitude, he demonstrated on repeated occasions that he lacked the type of courage that would have required him to stick by a principle that had proved overwhelmingly unpopular.

Among Roosevelt's outstanding characteristics was a highly developed sense of self-righteousness and a penchant for preaching to the people of the United States and the rest of the world. Confident of his own rectitude, he delivered innumerable sermons on any subject that happened to take his fancy. On a tour of Europe in 1910 he urged the French to have larger families, told a London audience how Great Britain should manage its affairs in Egypt, and informed the Germans that "one of the prime dangers of civilization" was "the loss of the virile fighting virtues, of the fighting edge." In America he frequently lectured to audiences of one or more on the evils of being a dilettante, responsibilities of wealth, fruits of hard work, joys of family life, advantages of "strenuosity," disadvantages of cynicism, and the need for spelling reform.

Like most aggressive and imaginative people Roosevelt enjoyed attention and acclaim. When he went west for the first time, he dressed in chaps and a ten-gallon hat for the ferryboat ride across the Hudson to his train. As New York police commissioner, he prowled the city streets at night to catch policemen derelict in their duty. In 1912, after being shot by a fanatic he insisted on making a scheduled speech in which he said: "I am going to ask you to be very quiet and please excuse me from making a long speech. I'll do the best I can, but there is a bullet in my body. It is nothing." His writing seldom left any doubt concerning the author's identity, and Harry Thurston Peck, a Columbia professor of classics, said: "In writing one of his . . . books he used . . . 'I' so frequently that his publishers were compelled to order from a typefoundry a fresh supply of that particular letter."

Roosevelt's enthusiastic and impetuous approach to almost any problem that came to his attention frequently involved him in embarrassing scrapes while he was President. In 1906, for example, he became so convinced of the advantages of simplified spelling that he ordered the government printer to adopt it. But when the public refused to take the project seriously and Congress objected to the proposed changes, Roosevelt dropped the whole idea On another occasion he joined with John Burroughs, the naturalist, in attacking the "nature fakers," which was the name Roosevelt gave to the authors of children's books whose descriptions of animals were more fanciful than accurate. This campaign also backfired. William J. Long, a Congregational minister who had been singled out by the President as "perhaps the worst of the offenders," challenged his critic's qualifications as an authority on wild life and maintained that Roosevelt's knowledge of animals was largely limited to the methods of killing them. While such incidents were trivial and tended to amuse rather than annoy most Americans, there were other times when the President's impetuosity produced unfortunate, or even tragic, results. For example, he ordered the dishonorable discharge of all the members of three companies of Negro troops stationed in Brownsville, Texas, after some of them had been accused—unjustly, as it later developed—of murder. This was the same Roosevelt, who in October, 1901, had shattered precedents by inviting Booker T. Washington, the outstanding Negro educator, to have dinner with him at the White House.*

Whatever the defects of Roosevelt's character—and it is easy for the historian to overemphasize them—many of his contemporaries considered him the greatest man of his own or any other age. Lord Morley thought that the two "great wonders of nature" in the United States were Niagara Falls and Roosevelt. Rudyard Kipling, who had known Roosevelt in Washington when both were young men, wrote that when Roosevelt talked, "I curled up on the seat opposite and listened and wondered until the universe seemed to be spinning around and Theodore was the spinner." To countless others, Theodore was the spinner, for most people who came in contact with him—as well as many who knew him only through the newspapers—were completely captivated by his vibrant personality.

Roosevelt's critics have pointed out that he often preferred words to

* White Southerners bitterly criticized Roosevelt for this action, and he did not do it again while he was President.

acts and that he was not above subordinating his principles to the main chance. Such charges, however, cannot detract from Roosevelt's contribution to Progressivism. With a flair for dramatizing the issues of the day, an apparently inexhaustible supply of energy, and an almost boyish enthusiasm for every manner of project, Roosevelt became a symbol of the Progressive spirit to millions of Americans. He was not an original thinker; he possessed at best only a rudimentary knowledge of economics; and the lessons in morality that he delighted in expounding were commonplace. But these were irrelevancies. To countless reformers struggling against seemingly hopeless odds, Roosevelt made Progressivism a noble and exhilarating adventure. Frances Perkins, in recalling her early experiences in the Progressive movement, has written:

> *. . . It was the era of Theodore Roosevelt, and we were all . . . under his spell. . . .*
>
> *Like many young people, I was an ardent admirer of Theodore Roosevelt. He had been a vigorous and educative President. He had recommended to the people Jacob Riis's book* How the Other Half Lives. *I had read it, and Theodore Roosevelt's inaugural address of 1905, and had straightaway felt that the pursuit of social justice would be my vocation.**

73. THEODORE ROOSEVELT AND THE TRUSTS

WHEN Roosevelt became President in 1901 he was distrusted by many Old Guard Republicans who viewed him as an erratic young man uncontrollable by the party's leaders. Roosevelt recognized this opposition and immediately moved to overcome it. On taking office he not only retained all of McKinley's cabinet,† but he also announced that he intended "to continue, absolutely unbroken," his predecessor's policies. Behind Roosevelt's conciliatory attitude were two considerations. First, he realized that because an accident rather than the people had made him President he would have to proceed with considerable

* Frances Perkins: *The Roosevelt I Knew* (New York: The Viking Press, 1946), pp. 9–10.

† The cabinet that Roosevelt inherited from McKinley consisted of the following: John Hay, Secretary of State; Lyman L. Gage, Secretary of the Treasury; Elihu Root, Secretary of War; John D. Long, Secretary of the Navy; E. A. Hitchcock, Secretary of the Interior; Charles E. Smith, Postmaster General; Philander C. Knox, Attorney General; James Wilson, Secretary of Agriculture. There were several cabinet shifts during Roosevelt's two terms; the most important occurred in 1904, when William Howard Taft succeeded Root as Secretary of War, and in 1905, when Root succeeded Hay as Secretary of State. In 1903, George B. Cortelyou became the first Secretary of Commerce and Labor.

caution until the next presidential election. Secondly, he was a consummate politician who always knew that his ultimate success in office depended on the strength of his party. Under the circumstances he could not afford to offend those who had to be his most powerful allies. Throughout his administration he repeatedly employed the tactics that he had used right after McKinley's death, and he soon showed that his political genius lay in his ability to retain the backing of those that he presumably opposed. Even though on numerous occasions he castigated the "interests," the Republicans never lost the support of the business classes during his presidency. He posed as an enemy of the conservatives and the professional politicians; but both groups stood by him as long as he was in the White House. Frequently he gave the impression of being an extremist, but in reality he never strayed far from the middle of the road, and in discussions of public questions he was usually careful to balance his "on-the-one-hands" with an equal number of "on-the-other-hands."

Roosevelt's ability to steer a middle course was illustrated by the fashion in which he handled the coal strike that occurred during his first term. In May, 1902, 150,000 anthracite coal miners went on strike and under the leadership of John Mitchell of the United Mine Workers demanded a 20 per cent increase in wages, a nine-hour day, and union recognition. The operators, however, refused to make any concessions. After the strike had dragged on for five months and the approach of winter made a resumption of coal production imperative, Roosevelt called a meeting in Washington of representatives of both the employers and employees. When the operators refused to give any ground, Roosevelt announced that he planned to appoint an investigating commission, and indicated that he might use the army to run the mines. At the same time Secretary of War Elihu Root impressed on J. P. Morgan the seriousness of the situation. Morgan, in turn, induced the operators to agree to arbitration, and on October 13 they requested the President to name a commission. The miners then returned to work, and in March of the following year the commission's report led to the establishment of a nine-hour day, the creation of arbitration machinery for the settlement of disputes in the industry, and a 10 per cent wage increase. The settlement of the dispute was a notable triumph for Roosevelt. Without permitting himself to be identified in the public mind with either management or labor, he had convinced the mass of Americans that he was working in their interests and that the government would see that they had coal regardless of who won the strike.

Roosevelt's middle-of-the-road policy—as well as his determination to move with caution during his first term—was also revealed by his attitude toward the trusts. By 1901 the trusts had few defenders in the United States, and the question in most people's minds was not whether monopoly should be curbed, but just how the government should attempt to curb it. Although Mark Hanna and a few others still believed that the growth of monopoly was no concern of the government, the vast majority of Americans felt that something should be done to preserve *laissez faire* and to compel businessmen to observe the rules of what had come to be known as "fair competition." Muckraking articles and state and Federal investigations of big business had convinced all but a small segment of the population that the trusts used "unfair" business practices, raised prices to artificial levels, and crushed the small businessman. Theodore Roosevelt, who was not inclined to ignore a popular mandate, quickly put himself in the forefront of the antitrust movement and enshrined himself in the public mind as "Teddy, the Trustbuster."

To Roosevelt, monopoly presented a problem that he thought could only be solved by distinguishing between "good" and "bad" trusts,* for he believed that industrial concentration was an accomplished fact that would have to be accepted even by its opponents. He therefore demanded the regulation rather than the extermination of trusts. Although he frequently gave the impression of impetuosity, he did not think that governmental action against the trusts should be precipitate or drastic; but he did think that certain minimum standards of business behavior should be enforced by the government. At times it was difficult to tell just where Roosevelt did stand on the trusts, a fact that was admirably expressed by Finley Peter Dunne's Mr. Dooley when he said:

> *"Th' thrusts" says he* [Roosevelt], *"are heejous monsthers built up by th' inlightened intherprise iv th' men that have done so much to advance progress in our beloved counthry," he says. "On wan hand I wud stamp thim undher fut; on th' other hand not so fast. What I want more thin th' bustin' iv th' thrusts is to see me fellow counthrymen happy an' continted. I wudden't have thim hate th' thrusts. Th' haggard face, th' droopin' eye, th' pallid complexion that marks th' inimy iv thrusts is not to me taste. Lave us be merry about it an' jovial an' affectionate. Lave us laugh an' sing th' octopus out iv ixistence."*

In 1903, Congress, at Roosevelt's suggestion, established the Bureau of Corporations under the Department of Commerce and Labor. The bureau did little regulatory work, but it gathered and disseminated information concerning corporate practices that it considered unfair. Through the use of what James R. Garfield, the bureau's first head, called "efficient publicity," it provided the Justice Department with the material needed for the prosecution of "bad" trusts, and it was able to arouse public opinion sufficiently to induce some corporations to alter

* Roosevelt never made clear the difference between a good and a bad trust.

their methods of conducting their businesses. Most of the bureau's accomplishments, however, occurred during Roosevelt's second term. George B. Cortelyou, who was head of the Department of Commerce and Labor, was also Republican national chairman, and beyond a doubt he did not favor any disclosures that might cause industrialists to refuse to contribute to Roosevelt's 1904 campaign chest. A month before the election, Joseph Pulitzer in a signed editorial in the *World* charged that the Bureau of Corporations had done nothing during the 583 days that it had been in existence. He then added:

> *Supposing, Mr. President, even at this late day, you were to give the country a little of that real publicity you once favored by telling it— 1, how much has the beef trust contributed to Mr. Cortelyou? 2, how much has the paper trust contributed to Mr. Cortelyou? 3, how much has the coal trust contributed to Mr. Cortelyou? 4, how much has the sugar trust contributed to Mr. Cortelyou? 5, how much has the oil trust contributed to Mr. Cortelyou? 6, how much has the tobacco trust contributed to Mr. Cortelyou? 7, how much has the steel trust contributed to Mr. Cortelyou? 8, how much have the national banks contributed to Mr. Cortelyou? 9, how much has the insurance trust contributed to Mr. Cortelyou? 10, how much have the . . . railroads contributed to Mr. Cortelyou?*

For those "bad" trusts that could not be reformed by publicity Roosevelt resorted to court proceedings under the Sherman Act. His first and greatest success in his antitrust campaign came in 1904 when the Supreme Court ordered the dissolution of the Northern Securities Company, the holding company that controlled the Hill, Morgan, and Harriman railway systems. In a five to four decision the Court ruled:

> *It is manifest that if the Anti-Trust Act is held not to embrace a case such as is now before us, the . . . intention of the legislative branch of the Government will be defeated. If Congress has not, by the words used in the act, described this and like cases, it would, we apprehend, be impossible to find words that would describe them.*

Although the Northern Securities decision was almost universally condemned by members of the business community, it had little apparent effect upon their willingness to support Roosevelt for a second term in 1904. Although some members of the party favored Hanna's candidacy, he died before the convention met, and Roosevelt received the nomination by acclamation. The Democrats, hoping to appeal to the business vote, nominated Alton B. Parker, a conservative New York judge who favored the gold standard. This strategy failed completely, however, and as election day approached, one prominent businessman after another urged Roosevelt's election. When the final returns were in, it was learned that Roosevelt had won by 336 electoral votes to 140 for Parker and a popular vote of 7,623,486 to Parker's 5,077,911. In a post-election statement that he was later to regret, Roosevelt announced that "under no circumstances" would he be a "candidate for or accept another nomination" for the presidency. But his real interest was in the present rather than the future, and he knew that the election meant that he was now President in his "own right." For the first time he felt free to carry out what he liked to call "my policies" and to give the people of the United States a "square deal."

Following his election in 1904, Roosevelt pushed his antitrust program with renewed vigor. Suits were instituted against the beef, oil, powder, and tobacco trusts, among others, and attempts were also made to break up such railroad combinations as the Reading Company, the Union Pacific Railroad Company, and the New York, New Haven, and Hartford Railroad Company. While Roosevelt was President, the Department of Justice obtained twenty-five antitrust indictments. Roosevelt's accomplishments as a trustbuster, however, were more apparent than real, for only a few trusts were busted and those that were soon reappeared in another guise with their control over their particular segments of the American economy unimpaired. If nothing else, the Roosevelt Administration revealed that a government armed with nothing more powerful than the Sherman Act could not destroy monopoly as fast as the monopolists were able to destroy competition.

On at least one occasion Roosevelt, who undoubtedly enjoyed denouncing the "malefactors of great wealth," was forced to acknowledge —and even sanction—the control of the trustmakers over the American economy. At the height of the Panic of 1907, Henry Clay Frick and Elbert Gary made an early morning call at the White House as emissaries of J. P. Morgan. Informing the President that the complete collapse of the stock market could only be averted by permitting Morgan to buy Tennessee Coal, Iron, and Railroad Company securities from a brokerage company that was about to fail, they demanded assurances that such a purchase would not lead to the government's prosecution of the Morgan-dominated United States Steel Corporation as a trust. Roosevelt could not put off his decision, for Gary and Frick insisted that they had to have an answer before the stock exchange opened for the day. Roosevelt gave his assent, word was relayed to Morgan in New York, and the market was saved. Roosevelt later said of his interview with Gary and Frick: "I answered that, while of course I could not advise them to take the action proposed, I felt it no public duty of mine to interpose any objections."

Numerous factors were responsible for the failure of Roosevelt and his successors to check the growth of industrial concentration in the

United States. Many trusts were old, respected, and powerful corporations with widely distributed securities. While the American people enjoyed hearing their Presidents denounce the "interests," few were prepared to face the economic chaos that would have followed any wholesale and thoroughgoing application of the Sherman Act. Moreover, many trusts appeared to enjoy their advantageous position because of patent rights, and it was generally thought that patent monopolies did not fall within the jurisdiction of the law. Finally, the courts showed no disposition to employ the Sherman Act as a device for either preserving or restoring competition. The Supreme Court was not inclined to consider mere size a violation of the antitrust legislation. Nor were defendants held guilty for past violations of the law if they had abandoned illegal practices before being brought to trial. In a number of decisions the Court indicated that its rulings were based on the methods rather than the extent of concentration. In general, the Justices appeared willing to accept the elimination of competition if the monopolists refrained from using methods that were blatantly predatory. This view, which came to be known as the "rule of reason," was advanced by Justice White in 1911 in the opinion he wrote for the Standard Oil case; the authors of the Sherman Act, he stated, intended that "the standard of reason [should] . . . be the measure used for the purpose of determining whether in a given case a particular act had or had not brought about the wrong against which the statute provided." The rule of reason, which was closely akin to Roosevelt's distinction between good and bad trusts, set up a subjective standard that permitted the Court to pursue whatever course it desired in subsequent antitrust suits.

74. SAFEGUARDING THE PEOPLE'S INTERESTS

CLOSELY related to Roosevelt's antitrust campaigns were his efforts to stamp out the discriminatory rail practices that aided and abetted the growth of monopoly. The failure of the Interstate Commerce Act to check even the most flagrant abuses of the railroads had resulted in an increasing demand that greater authority over carriers be vested in the Interstate Commerce Commission. Despite repeated protests, the act was not amended until 1903, when Congress responded to the pressure of the railroads rather than the public for changes in the law. Many rail executives whose lines had suffered severe losses because of rebating and other forms of rate cutting demanded that the government grant them further protection against cutthroat competition. Congress responded to these requests with the passage of the Elkins Act, which was designed to make the railroads adhere to their published rates. The Elkins Act, which was not concerned with the reasonableness of the rates charged by the railroads, consisted of little more than a list of penalties that could be imposed upon those rail corporations that did not play the competitive game according to established rules.

Roosevelt had little or nothing to do with the adoption of the Elkins Act, and no concerted effort was made to carry out its provisions until after the election of 1904. Between October, 1905, and March, 1907, the beef packers, the tin-plate combination, and the American Sugar Refining Company were convicted of accepting rebates. The American Sugar Refining Company's infractions resulted in a $300,000 fine, while a lower court decision that was subsequently reversed imposed a $29,240,000 fine on the Standard Oil Company. In these and many other cases there was ample evidence of the widespread use of the hidden, or "smokeless," rebate. In an attempt to conceal their evasion of the law, carriers granted shippers rebates in the form of rental for a spur track, an allowance for fictitious damage in transit, a "refund of terminal charges," and "lighterage demurrage." Through these and similar devices, many railroads continued to violate the Elkins Act, and most students of the subject are inclined to agree with the commission's statement in 1908 that "many shippers still enjoy[ed] illegal advantages."

The Elkins Act, which was passed by Congress to prevent competing lines from destroying each other, left unanswered the problem of protecting shippers against excessive rate changes. Although bills that were introduced into Congress in 1894, 1899, and 1902 provided for increased authority for the commission, they all failed of enactment. In 1904, at President Roosevelt's urging, the House passed the Esch-Townsend Bill, but the Senate, dominated by Nelson Aldrich and the Old Guard of the Republican party, refused to approve it. In the following year, after the President had renewed his demands, the House enacted the Hepburn Bill, and the Senate followed suit in 1906. The Hepburn Act broadened the powers of the Interstate Commerce Commission by granting it authority over pipe lines, express and sleeping car companies, and "all services in connection with the receipt, delivery, elevation, and transfer in transit, ventilation, refrigeration or icing, storage, and handling of property transported." On complaint of shippers, the commission was empowered to establish maximum rates, but these could be either altered or suspended by the courts.

Although Roosevelt had repeatedly urged greater Federal control over the railroads, his stand during the debates on the Hepburn Bill disappointed many Progressives. Following the bill's adoption in the House, it went to the Senate, where it was opposed by Nelson Aldrich and soon became bogged down in a controversy concerning the extent of judicial authority over the regulation of the railroads. The Progressives favored a "narrow judical review" in which the courts would merely decide the jurisdiction of the law. Conservatives advocated a "broad review," which would give the courts an opportunity to pass on the reasonableness of rates. Senator Benjamin ("Pitchfork Ben") Tillman, who was in charge of the bill in the Senate, introduced an amendment calling for the "narrow review" after learning that Roosevelt was prepared to back such a proposal. But when it appeared that the amendment would lose by one vote, Roosevelt withdrew his support, and the "narrow review" was defeated. Roosevelt, who did not wish to split the Republicans by defying the Old Guard, had surrendered to the conservatives in the party; and Progressives such as Robert La Follette never forgave him for what they felt was an act of pure expediency.

The immediate result of the Hepburn Act was to increase the number of complaints filed with the Interstate Commerce Commission. From July, 1906, to August, 1908, more than 1,500 formal complaints were lodged with the commission in contrast to the 878 complaints filed in the eighteen years preceding the enactment of the new law. The increase in the commission's business did not, however, indicate a corresponding increase in its effectiveness. The Hepburn Act did not permit the commission to pass on the reasonableness of new rate schedules; its authority was limited to the regulation of rates against which individual shippers had complained. As a result, the railroads were still able to raise rates at will. Moreover, the judiciary continued to block any attempt to transform the commission into a genuine rate-making body.

Roosevelt's efforts to curb the trusts and railroads were paralleled by the first Federal attempts to regulate the food and drug industries. For some years, Dr. Harvey W. Wiley, who had been chief chemist of the Department of Agriculture, had been conducting studies on the effects of adulterated foods and drugs, and as early as 1902, Congress had considered a bill calling for accurate labels on drugs and commercially prepared foods. In 1905, Roosevelt recommended the passage of a pure-food law, and Senator Albert Beveridge of Indiana urged the government to set up a system for the inspection of meats. Meanwhile patent medicines had been muckraked in both *Collier's* and the *Ladies' Home Journal;* and Upton Sinclair's *Jungle* had made countless Americans aware of the revolting conditions in Chicago's packing houses. All of these developments were responsible in some degree for the adoption of the Pure Food and Drug Act (June 23, 1906) and the Meat Inspection Act (July 1, 1906). The first of these measures eliminated some of the most glaring abuses in the processed-food and patent-medicine industries; the second provided for the Federal inspection of all meat in interstate commerce.

Throughout his administration, Roosevelt demonstrated greater concern over the lot of the workingman than had any of his predecessors in the White House. His rôle in the coal strike in 1902 made him the first President to view Federal intervention in a labor dispute as a device that was not designed exclusively to aid the employers. In 1905 he recommended an investigation of child labor and the adoption of an employers' liability law; a year later he warned against the "grave abuses" caused by the use of the injunction in strikes; and in his message of January 31, 1908, he not only reviewed the points that he had made on earlier occasions but also urged Congress to adopt a workmen's compensation law for government employees. Congress responded to the President's demands in 1906 by enacting an employers' liability act that covered accidents on common carriers, and when the Supreme Court declared this law unconstitutional, Congress passed a new law in 1908 that overcame the Court's objections. In the same year Congress adopted a bill regulating the hours worked by trainmen and telegraph operators on interstate railroads.

Roosevelt's pioneering work in the conservation of natural resources was his most enduring contribution. In 1902 with his support Congress adopted the Newlands Act, which provided that the money obtained from the sale of public lands was to be used to reclaim through irrigation the arid regions of the West. Under this measure approximately three million acres were irrigated within four years. Roosevelt also deserves a large share of the credit for checking the destruction of American forests by the lumber interests. While he was President, the national forests were increased from 43 to 194 million acres; reforestation was undertaken; publicity was given to the need for saving the country's timber resources; and the United States Forest Service was established to co-ordinate and direct the government's varied conservation activities. All of these accomplishments were made possible in large part by the invaluable assistance given to Roosevelt by Gifford Pinchot, the director of the United States Forest Service. Equally important was the way in which Roosevelt publicized the need for preserving America's natural resources. He sponsored a number of conferences that aroused the interest of many local, state, and territorial officials in co-ordinating all conservation activities, protecting valuable mineral resources and water power sites, improving navigable streams, and making an inventory of the nation's physical resources. Even Roosevelt's most vehement detractors have found little to criticize in his work as a conservationist.

Some months before the election of 1908, Roosevelt had picked Secretary of War William Howard Taft of Ohio as his successor. The Republican convention, meeting at Chicago in June, duly nominated Taft on the first ballot and Representative James S. Sherman of New York was selected for the vice-presidency. The Republican platform called for the continuation of Roosevelt's policies, tariff revision, and increased Federal control over the trusts and railroads. The attempt by a group of Western delegates led by La Follette to make the convention adopt a

Harper's Weekly

"FORWARD MARCH"

This Republican attack on Bryan in 1908 pictures him as taking the radical path while his party follows the road to conservatism.

more radical program was overwhelmingly rejected and branded as "socialistic and Democratic." When the Democrats convened at Denver on July 7, they nominated Bryan on the first ballot and chose John W. Kern of Indiana as his running mate. In addition to a strong antitrust plank, the Democratic platform included demands for an income tax and the prohibition of the use of injunction in labor disputes. Taft, with 7,678,908 votes to 6,409,104 for Bryan, carried all the states outside the South except Nebraska, Colorado, Nevada, Kentucky, Maryland, and Oklahoma. The electoral vote was 321 for Taft and 162 for Bryan. The programs advanced by the two candidates were very similar, and the election was in reality an endorsement of Roosevelt and his policies.

Having completed both his term as President and his task as President-maker, Roosevelt sailed for Africa to hunt big game. President Taft wrote ex-President Roosevelt: "I can never forget that the power I now exercise was voluntarily transferred from you to me, and that I am under obligation to you to see that your judgment in selecting me as your successor and bringing about the succession shall be vindicated according to the standards which you and I . . . have always formulated." J. P. Morgan, on learning of Roosevelt's trip, is reported to have said: "Let every lion do his duty."

75. THE TAFT ADMINISTRATION

WILLIAM HOWARD TAFT had been born in Ohio, had been educated at Yale, and had studied law at Cincinnati. Throughout most of his adult life he had held public office. Before becoming President he had been Solicitor General under Harrison, a circuit court judge, civil Governor of the Philippines, administrator of the Canal Zone, and Secretary of War. A genial, well-meaning man, he lacked both the political skill and the limitless energy of his predecessor. Inherently conservative, he nevertheless believed in "progress," but he thought that it should be achieved in easy stages and by constitutional methods. Unlike the man who had done the most to make him President, he did not think that there was any occasion upon which the end justified the means.

Taft as a president was very different from Roosevelt. Roosevelt felt that as the executive he had an obligation to lead Congress; but Taft believed that the legislature and executive were separate, though equal, branches of the government. In his view, Congress made the laws, and he carried them out. Beyond making recommendations to Congress, he showed little interest in developing the presidential powers as Andrew Jackson, Abraham Lincoln, and Theodore Roosevelt had before him. An ex-judge, who hoped that some day he would be a member of the Supreme Court, Taft was always painfully aware of the limitations that the Constitution imposed on his office; Roosevelt, on the other hand, had assumed an almost cavalier attitude toward the Constitution. Finally—and perhaps most important of all—Taft lacked Roosevelt's ability to arouse the enthusiasm of the American people. To Roosevelt they were his friends and confidants; he knew their likes and dislikes, and he knew how to share his ideas with them. Taft was never able to establish the same kind of an alliance with the voters, although his personal correspondence reveals that he frequently shared the views of the majority.

When Taft became President the Progressive bloc in the Republican party was more powerful than it had been at any time during Roosevelt's administration. Roosevelt, despite displays of independence, had co-operated with such Old Guard Republicans as Nelson Aldrich in the Senate and Speaker Joe Cannon in the House. By 1909, however, the Republican Progressives in Congress were prepared to take over the control of the party, and under the leadership of Robert La Follette in the Senate and George Norris in the House they were making plans to overthrow both Aldrich and Cannon. Taft was in a position where he had to take sides, and he soon made it clear that he stood with the Old Guard. Roosevelt, although he had adopted a similar policy when the issue was not as clearly drawn, was nevertheless considered the nation's outstanding Progressive by a large number of his contemporaries; but Taft, by following the pattern set by his mentor, was branded a conservative. The Progressives were also disturbed by the make-up of Taft's cabinet;* for, although it contained three holdovers from the Roosevelt regime, it was also heavily weighted with corporation lawyers.

At the very outset of Taft's administration, the battle over the Payne-Aldrich Tariff revealed both the cleavage in the Republican party and the strength of the Old Guard in Congress. Roosevelt had managed to avoid the tariff issue, but for years the party's Western agrarians, who looked on the tariff as a device for taxing the consumer to benefit the manufacturer, had been demanding a cut in the rates that had been established under the Dingley Act of 1897. The Republican platform of 1908 had advocated a revision of the tariff, and during the campaign Taft made it clear that he interpreted revision to mean reduction. On March 15, 1909, the President called a special session of Congress to consider a new tariff bill. Within a short time the House had adopted

* The Taft cabinet consisted of Philander C. Knox, Secretary of State; Franklin MacVeagh, Secretary of the Treasury; Jacob M. Dickinson, Secretary of War; George von L. Meyer, Secretary of the Navy; Richard A. Ballinger, Secretary of the Interior; Frank H. Hitchcock, Postmaster General; George W. Wickersham, Attorney General; James Wilson, Secretary of Agriculture; Charles Nagel, Secretary of Commerce and Labor. In 1911, Henry L. Stimson succeeded Dickinson as Secretary of War and Walter L. Fisher succeeded Ballinger as Secretary of the Interior.

the Payne bill, which provided for moderate, but not drastic, reduction of the duties on a number of articles; but in the Senate, the Committee on Finance, of which Aldrich was chairman, substituted increases for most of the decreases and killed the House plan for an inheritance tax. In its final form the Payne-Aldrich Tariff Act established a higher level of rates than the Dingley Act. Many of its schedules showed the influence of the various "interests" over Congress; it contained a number of "jokers" (such as providing protection for an industry in which there was only one firm); and the only duties that it lowered were those affecting industries that could not conceivably be threatened by foreign competition. It was an Eastern bill that had been fashioned by Old Guard Republicans to satisfy the party's industrialists.

During the debate in the Senate over the Payne-Aldrich bill a group of Midwestern Progressives—among whom were Robert La Follette of Wisconsin, Jonathan Dolliver and Albert Cummins of Iowa, Moses Clapp of Minnesota, and Albert Beveridge of Indiana—repeatedly criticized those features of the measure that they felt aided the few at the expense of the many and that ignored the interests of the nation's agrarians. Aldrich refused even to reply to these charges; and, although his opponents won the argument by default, he won the fight, for both the Senate and House approved the bill. Throughout the controversy Taft made no move to aid the opponents of the tariff, and when he signed the Payne-Aldrich Act on August 5, 1909, he was bitterly denounced by agrarian spokesmen for both the Republican West and the Democratic South. Nor did a series of speeches that Taft made in the West in September repair the damage. When he spoke of carrying out Roosevelt's policies, he seemed a hypocrite to Westerners, and in a speech at Winona, Minnesota, when he referred to the Payne-Aldrich Act as the best tariff act in the history of the Republican party, he convinced them that he neither understood nor cared about their problems. The result of the Payne-Aldrich Act and Taft's support of it was an East-West split in the Republican party; but this division was more than geographical, for among the bill's opponents in the West were some of the party's outstanding Progressives, while its Eastern supporters included many leading conservatives.

To the Western opponents of Taft were soon added the critics of Secretary of the Interior R. A. Ballinger's conservation policies. A Seattle lawyer who frequently appeared more interested in the niceties of law than the preservation of the nation's natural resources, Ballinger was condemned by conservationists for permitting private groups to take over Federal water-power sites in Montana and Wyoming and for supporting the Guggenheim claims to valuable coal lands in Alaska. When Gifford Pinchot, the chief of the Forest Service, and Louis Glavis, the head of the Field Division of the Interior Department, attacked Ballinger's policies in print and public statements, both men were dismissed by Taft. However justified their removal—and by attempting to discredit their superior in public they gave the President no alternative—it shocked conservationists and convinced countless followers of Roosevelt that Taft was deliberately sabotaging his predecessor's program. Pinchot, for his part, hurried abroad to report to Roosevelt, who, after his trip to Africa, was making a triumphant tour of Europe's capitols.

The cleavage within the Republican party was further widened by the attempt of a group of Republican insurgents in the House to curb the extensive powers of Speaker Joe Cannon. Because the Speaker had the right to appoint all committees, he was in a position to name his allies to the most important posts in the House, while his rôle as the leading member of the Ways and Means Committee enabled him to determine in large part which bills should be considered by the lower branch of the legislature. Cannon, by using his authority to advance the cause of conservatism in the House, had turned his office into a symbol not only of Old Guard rule but also of autocracy. In 1909, twelve Republican representatives indicated their objections to Cannon's rule by voting against his re-election as Speaker. A year later a coalition of Democrats and insurgent Republicans, led by George Norris of Nebraska, was successful in pushing through an amendment to the House rules that weakened the power of the Speaker by giving the House the power to elect the Rules Committee. In the following session the same groups were able to strip the Speaker of much of his remaining authority. Under the new rules all committees were made elective, and the Speaker's power was limited to that of a presiding officer.

By 1910, Taft had alienated all the major factions in the Republican party except the Eastern conservatives, and the midterm elections resulted in an overwhelming victory for the Democrats. The new House contained 229 Democrats to 161 Republicans, and the small Republican majority in the Senate was largely nullified by the tendency of the insurgents to join forces with the Democrats. Roosevelt had bequeathed to Taft one of the most successful political organizations in the nation's history; but in two years Taft had reduced it to a shambles. Rightly or wrongly the voters were convinced that Taft had turned his back on Progressivism and surrendered to the Conservatives.

Despite the Progressives' dissatisfaction with Taft, during his administration several reforms that they endorsed were adopted. Roosevelt won fame as a trustbuster, but Taft attacked more powerful monopolies than had his predecessor, won more convictions, and collected larger fines. Under the direction of George W. Wickersham, Taft's Attorney General, antitrust proceedings were instituted against the United States Steel Corporation, the American Sugar Refining Company, the International Harvester Company, the General Electric Company, and the National

Cash Register Company. Moreover, during Taft's four years in office the Department of Justice prosecuted twice as many cases as it had during the seven years that Roosevelt had served as President. Other Progressive victories during Taft's administration included the passage of the Mann-Elkins Act for the regulation of railroads, the division of the Department of Labor and Commerce into two departments, the establishment of the Children's Bureau, the adoption of a parcel post law and a postal savings law, the creation of a tariff commission, and the enactment of legislation providing for publicity for campaign expenditures. In addition, during Taft's tenure of the presidency, the Sixteenth and Seventeenth Amendments, both dear to the hearts of the Progressives, were first proposed. Moreover, as a conservationist, Taft became the first President to withdraw oil lands from public sale, created a Bureau of Mines, purchased a vast area of forest land in the Appalachians, and promoted legislation that permitted the government to conserve mineral as well as surface resources.

A review of the record of the Taft Administration, however, does not necessarily provide an accurate index of the President's progressivism. While he continued—and even expanded—Roosevelt's antitrust and conservation programs, there were other fields in which he actively opposed the Progressives' objectives. For example, the bill that he proposed for the control of the railroads and that was introduced into Congress by Stephen B. Elkins actually deprived the government of some of its existing regulatory powers over the railroads. But the Progressive bloc virtually amended the original Elkins bill out of existence and the Mann-Elkins Act, which became law on June 18, 1910 bore little resemblance to the measure that had been advocated by Taft. The Mann-Elkins Act gave the Interstate Commerce Commission the authority to suspend new rates until they had been examined for their reasonableness; it outlawed unequivocably the long-and-short-haul abuse; and it established a Commerce Court to review the commission's decisions.* Like previous legislation the Mann-Elkins Act fell short of the expectations of its authors, and its effective operation was soon impeded by the advent of war. On the other hand, it marked an important victory for the advocates of Federal regulation. After a long and bitter struggle, the government had won the undisputed right to fix the rates charged by the carriers.

Regardless of Taft's status as a Progressive—and historians are generally inclined to view him as more of a Progressive than did his contemporaries—the fact remains that his effectiveness as a reformer was largely nullified by his ineptitude as a politician. Instead of attempting to appease dissident groups within his party, he often gave the impression that he was going out of his way to antagonize them. Thus in 1911, when he returned to the tariff problem with a plan for reciprocity with

* The Commerce Court was abolished in 1913.

Canada, he advocated a measure that once again was objectionable to the party's Western agrarians. The Taft program called for free trade in many agricultural commodities on the one hand and imposed identical rates in both countries upon a number of manufactured articles on the other. To the Western farmer this arrangement seemed grossly unfair, for it provided for a type of reciprocity that exposed him to Canadian competition while it assured industrialists of adequate protection. Despite Western opposition, Taft, with the aid of the Democrats, was able to get Congress to adopt his measure. Meanwhile in Canada the Liberals, who had endorsed reciprocity, had fallen from power, and the Conservatives rejected the proposal on the ground that it was a threat to Canadian independence. The upshot of the whole affair was that once more Taft had not only failed to achieve his objective, but he had also aroused the hostility of a powerful wing of the Republican party.

Although Taft lacked all the attributes that had made Roosevelt popular with the electorate, it was his policies rather than his personality that caused the steady decline in his prestige during his administration. His friendship with the leading conservatives in the House and Senate displeased Progressives in both parties. His sponsorship of the Payne-Aldrich Act and the reciprocity program with Canada antagonized Republican farmers in the West. His record as an antiunion judge during his years on the bench had deprived him of the backing of organized labor even before his accession to the presidency. And his willingness to advocate legislation favorable to the railroads seemed to offer convincing proof that he was not a genuine Progressive. Taft, in short, was satisfactory to no one but the party's Old Guard, and by 1911 a large number of Republicans were openly opposed to his nomination for a second term. In January of that year some of the party's insurgents organized the National Progressive Republican League to work for the nomination of a Progressive at the next Republican national convention. Its choice to lead the Republican party in 1912 was Robert La Follette. In December, 1911, La Follette began his campaign for the Republican nomination with a series of speeches in which he called for an effective antitrust program, the establishment of a Federal commission to regulate business, the reduction of the tariff by a nonpartisan board, and the direct primary, initiative, referendum, and recall. But on February 12, 1912, after a savage attack against the "money trust" in a speech at Philadelphia, La Follette suffered a nervous and physical breakdown that forced him to withdraw from the campaign.

La Follette's collapse cleared the way for Roosevelt, who soon showed that he was not averse to capitalizing on the enthusiasm that the Wisconsin senator had aroused for the progressivism within the Republican party. Roosevelt's decision to seek the Repubican nomination in 1912 can be attributed to a number of diverse circumstances. One considera-

Harper's Weekly

THE LATEST ARRIVAL AT THE POLITICAL ZOO

Roosevelt's decision to run on a third-party ticket in 1912 was regarded by many of his former supporters as evidence of all consuming hunger for political office.

tion was his undoubted disgust with Taft's record. Even before Taft's inauguration, there had been rumors that he had misgivings about his successor; and when Roosevelt returned from his trip to Africa and Europe in the spring of 1910, he informed some of his friends that he was dissatisfied with Taft's conduct of the government. Taft's refusal to reappoint several officials that had served under Roosevelt, his stand in the Ballinger-Pinchot controversy, and his decision to prosecute the United States Steel Corporation despite Roosevelt's promise to the Morgan firm, all contributed to the former President's willingness first to suspect and then to oppose his one-time protégé. Nor should Roosevelt's temperament be overlooked. He was, as always, ambitious; he had greatly enjoyed his years in the White House; and he had presumably learned to his distress that the life of an ex-President was little more than a series of anticlimaxes. Finally, Roosevelt was aware that his candidacy would be backed not only by many of the party's rank and file but also by several prominent business leaders. Among the latter were George Perkins, a former Morgan partner; Frank Munsey, a millionaire newspaper publisher; H. H. Wilkinson, president of Crucible Steel; T. Coleman Du Pont of the Powder Trust; and Alexander T. Cochran, who had made a fortune in the carpet business. All these men were political realists who, knowing that Taft could not win in 1912, supported Roosevelt because of his popularity rather than because of his program.

After seven Progressive Governors—acting with Roosevelt's knowledge—requested him to be a candidate, he announced on February 24, 1912, that his hat was "in the ring." The Roosevelt supporters based their hopes on their ability to capture the Republican convention when it met in Chicago in June; but this plan was forestalled by the party's regulars, who through the use of the patronage were able to control the convention's proceedings. The struggle between the two groups centered on a number of contested seats, and in almost every instance the Taft rather than Roosevelt delegates were seated. As a consequence, Taft was nominated on the first ballot, and James S. Sherman of New York, who had served as Taft's vice-president, was again given second place on the ticket.

After an all-night session in the traditional smoke-filled hotel room, the Roosevelt high command decided to bolt the party and run an independent ticket. The convention of the Progressive, or Bull Moose,* party was held in Chicago on August 5 and was attended by reformers, social workers, professors, members of what Roosevelt on other occasions had called the "lunatic fringe," businessmen, and some Republican politicians who recognized the hopelessness of Taft's candidacy. It was

* The name was used because of Roosevelt's frequent use of the term and his statement that he felt as "strong as a bull moose."

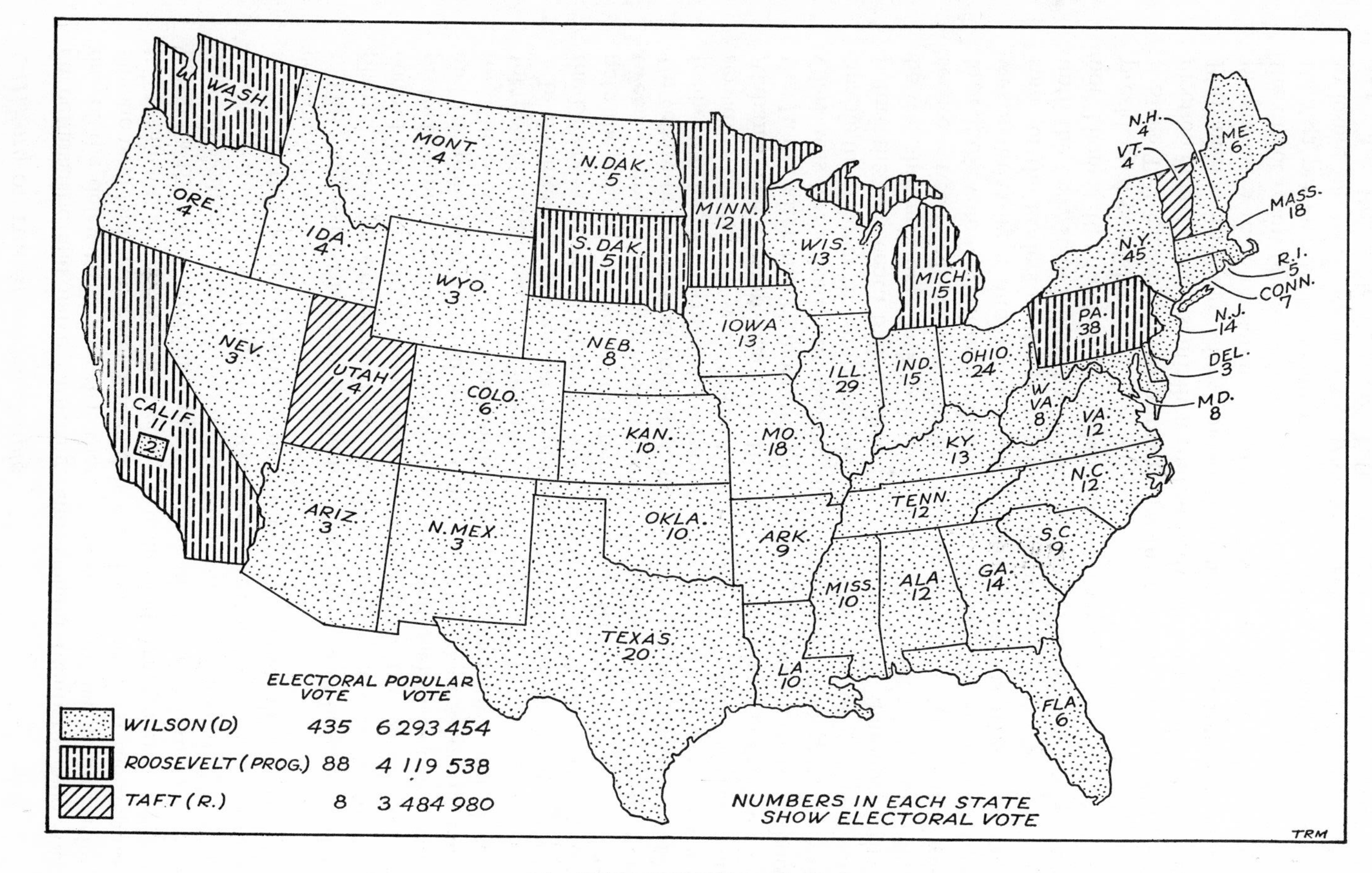

12. THE ELECTION OF 1912

an enthusiastic and naïve gathering, and Donald Richberg, who was one of the delegates, wrote that there "was room on that platform for anyone who had seen Peter Pan and believed in fairies." At the Republican convention Roosevelt had said: "We stand at Armageddon and we battle for the Lord," and his supporters took him at his word. The New York delegation entered the convention hall singing "Onward, Christian Soldiers," and throughout the proceedings most of the delegates acted as though they were attending a revival meeting rather than a political convention.

The Progressive platform, in addition to antitrust and tariff-reduction planks, called for women suffrage, the direct primary, increased Federal control over railroads, governmental aid to agriculture, legislation to protect women in industry, minimum-wage and maximum-hour laws, and the prevention of child labor. Following the adoption of the platform, Roosevelt was duly and enthusiastically nominated, and Hiram Johnson of California was chosen as his running mate.

In the interval between the Republican and Progressive conventions, the Democrats met at Baltimore. Many thought that Bryan would dominate the convention, but it soon became clear that the contest was between several conservatives and Woodrow Wilson, a former Princeton University professor and president, who had won a reputation as a reformer during his term as Governor of New Jersey. The leading conservative candidates were Oscar W. Underwood, a congressman from Alabama, and Champ Clark of Missouri, who had become Speaker of the House after the Democratic victory in 1910. On the early ballots Clark was in the lead; but, despite the efforts of his managers, he was unable to win over the supporters of either Underwood or Wilson. Even before the fourteenth ballot, when Bryan dramatically announced that he was shifting from Clark to Wilson, it was clear that Clark could not secure a two-thirds majority in the convention. In the ballots that followed, the vote for Wilson gradually increased, and his ultimate victory was assured by a number of deals negotiated by his managers with some of the leaders of the party's state machines. It was not, however, until the forty-sixth ballot that Wilson obtained the nomination. Governor Thomas R. Marshall of Indiana was selected as the party's vice-presidential candidate.

Since Taft was supported primarily by the nation's conservatives, the election of 1912 was essentially a contest between Roosevelt and Wilson. Both men were Progressives, and both men advanced roughly similar programs in their numerous campaign speeches. Wilson's victory was the direct result of the split in the Republican party, for he polled less than 42 per cent of the popular vote, or less than Bryan had obtained in losing the elections of 1896, 1900, and 1908. Wilson received 6,293,-454 votes, Roosevelt 4,119,538, Taft 3,484,980, and Eugene Debs, the

Socialist candidate, 900,672. The electoral vote was 435 for Wilson, 88 for Roosevelt, and 8 for Taft. The Democrats also carried the House of Representatives by 290 to 145 and the Senate by 51 to 45. The election of 1912 was a clear-cut defeat for the Old Guard and its policies, for the Progressives, voting for either Wilson or Roosevelt, had overwhelmed those who had stood by Taft and the *status quo.* Wilson's victory ushered in the final stage of the Progressive movement.

76. THE SCHOLAR IN POLITICS

WOODROW WILSON was a skillful politician, a remarkably effective public speaker, an acknowledged authority on American government, and a moralist whose belief in his own righteousness sometimes resembled that of a Calvinist divine. On repeated occasions, he was able to beat the professional politicians at their own game. His public addresses were both models of clarity and moving appeals to the emotions of his listeners. He had spent most of his mature years studying the theory and practice of American government, and his books on this subject included *Congressional Government* (1885) and *Constitutional Government in the United States* (1908). He possessed a deep-seated sense of right and wrong that seemed particularly appropriate in a president who had assumed office at the height of the Progressive movement. Wilson was both the product and the maker of his times, and during his first administration the Progressives won their most noteworthy—as well as their last—victories in national politics.

Born in 1856 in Virginia, Wilson received his education at Princeton and Johns Hopkins. After dabbling in the law, he turned to college teaching and served on the faculties of Bryn Mawr, Wesleyan, and Princeton. In 1902 he became president of Princeton, where he introduced a number of notable reforms, but was unable to work effectively with a majority of the university's trustees and alumni. When his position at Princeton became untenable, he entered politics and in 1910 was elected Governor of New Jersey. Although he had been a life-long conservative and his candidacy had been sponsored by several influential business leaders and the New Jersey Democratic machine, he repudiated his former ideas and supporters soon after taking office. As New Jersey's chief executive, Wilson pushed through the state legislature a series of political and economic reforms that won him a national reputation as an outstanding Progressive. During the 1912 campaign he put forward in numerous speeches a program that outlined the principal features of what he called the New Freedom.

Wilson's conversion to progressivism had come comparatively late in life. A Southern Democrat whose position as president of Princeton had brought him into contact with wealthy trustees and alumni, he had shared most of the political and economic opinions of his associates. While still at Princeton he had criticized trustbusting on the ground that it destroyed "individual liberty" and had announced his opposition to the "hostile" program of the "radical" Roosevelt. In 1908 he had stated that Bryan's ideas should be "knocked once and for all into a cocked hat" and that the Democratic party should again stand for the "conservative principles which it once represented." These views had made Wilson acceptable to George Harvey, the head of the publishing concern of Harper and Brothers, an associate of Morgan, and a wealthy man in his own right. As early as 1906, Harvey had begun to call Wilson to the attention of Democratic party leaders, and he had become the Princeton president's first political mentor. It was Harvey, moreover, who had been most responsible for convincing James Smith, the Democratic boss of New Jersey, that Wilson should be given the party's gubernatorial nomination in 1910. Smith, who had once referred to Wilson as a "Presbyterian priest," soon had had reason to regret his decision. The new Governor had not only turned his back on the machine that had help to elect him, but he had also deposed its boss in a victory that was so complete that he could write: "I pitied Smith at the last." Harvey, too, had soon been jettisoned. Upon entering political life Wilson had abandoned his conservative views, and within a short time he had placed himself at the forefront of the Progressive movement. Under the circumstances, Harvey's outspoken support had become a liability, and on December 7, 1911, Wilson had told him as much. For the rest of his life, Harvey remained Wilson's implacable enemy.

When Wilson entered the White House he had a definite attitude toward the presidency. He wanted to be a "strong" President who would provide the country with leadership, but he did not want to assume the rôle of an autocrat in his dealings with Congress. A close student of the English ministerial system, he considered it superior to the American plan of checks and balances. In Wilson's mind the principal defect of the United States form of government was the separation of powers and the consequent rivalry between president and Congress. To prevent such a rivalry from developing in his own administration he sought to work in close harmony with such Democratic congressmen as Carter Glass, Oscar Underwood, and Champ Clark. These men, as well as most of the other Democratic leaders in Congress, were Southern conservatives and professional politicians. This fact, however, did not prevent them from pushing Wilson's reform program through Congress. In part, they supported him because a large part of his program was similar to the one that the Southerners had been demanding for years, and in part because he made no effort to interfere with the "bread and butter" side of the party. Throughout his administration Wilson gave little attention to the distribution of the patronage, and the task of rewarding loyal Democrats with jobs was left to Colonel Edward House, Wilson's close friend and adviser, Postmaster General Albert S. Burleson,* and Joseph Tumulty, the President's private secretary.

During his first administration Wilson repeatedly demonstrated his skill as a politician and his ability as a presidential leader. By becoming the first President since John Adams to deliver his messages in person to Congress, he both symbolized and dramatized his concept of the unity between the executive and legislative branches of the government. When it appeared that the Federal Reserve bill might become bogged down in Congress because of disagreements among Secretary of the Treasury William G. McAdoo, Representative Carter Glass, and Senator Robert L. Owen, Wilson was able to effect a compromise that was satisfactory to all three men. On still another occasion, when the Underwood tariff bill was jeopardized by pressure from various special interests, he successfully exposed the lobbyists in a public statement that referred to "great bodies of astute men [who] seek to create an artificial opinion . . . for their private profit."

77. THE NEW FREEDOM

WILSON'S views on social and economic questions were neither radical nor novel, and many parts of the New Freedom were as old as the United States. Some of Wilson's ideas went back at least to Jefferson, and his economic ideas were not unlike those of a nineteenth-century liberal. He believed that competition was the life of trade and that it was the function of the government not only to enforce competition but also to see to it that competitors observed certain elementary rules of fairness. It was Wilson's conviction that a free capitalism was inherently beneficial but that within recent years its development had been obstructed by the special privileges that had been won by the few at the expense of the many. This situation could only be rectified by the restoration of freedom where it had been circumscribed by such devices as high tariffs, industrial and financial

* In addition to Burleson, Wilson's cabinet consisted of William Jennings Bryan, Secretary of State; William Gibbs McAdoo, Secretary of the Treasury; Lindley M. Garrison, Secretary of War; Josephus Daniels, Secretary of the Navy; Franklin K. Lane, Secretary of the Interior; James C. McReynolds, Attorney General; W. C. Redfield, Secretary of Commerce; David F. Houston, Secretary of Agriculture; William B. Wilson, Secretary of Labor. There were comparatively few changes in the Wilson cabinet during his two terms. The most significant shifts were in 1915, when Robert Lansing succeeded Bryan as Secretary of State, and in 1916, when Newton D. Baker succeeded Garrison as Secretary of War.

monopolies, and the almost unlimited power of the employer over his employees. Even though any attempt to remove these drags on a free economy would necessarily entail a considerable degree of government intervention, Wilson believed that only in this fashion could the "unnatural" restraints on freedom of competition and equality of opportunity be eliminated. The system was essentially sound; it should not be destroyed, but reformed. To achieve this objective, he successfully sponsored legislation that reduced the tariff, regulated credit and banking facilities, and curbed the trusts.

The Underwood Tariff, which was adopted by Congress in 1913, was the first part of the Wilson program to be placed on the statute books. Although Wilson was not a free trader, he believed that the tariff should be designed for revenue only. Like the other members of his party—particularly those from the agrarian South—he opposed the existing tariff schedules on the grounds that they promoted the growth of trusts and enabled favored businessmen to gain an unfair advantage over their foreign competitors at the expense of the American consumer. The Underwood Tariff lowered duties on more than nine hundred articles and provided for only eighty-six increases. *Ad valorem* duties were substituted for specific rates; numerous raw materials were placed on the free list; and the duties on most manufactured goods were reduced. Provision was also made for a graduated income tax. Regardless of the merits of the Underwood Tariff, it never received a fair test. The outbreak of World War I soon disrupted international trade, and after the war the Republicans lost little time in returning to their party's traditional high-tariff policy.

The second major plank of the New Freedom was translated into law with the adoption by Congress in December, 1913, of the Federal Reserve Act. The report of the Pujo Committee in February of the same year had revealed the existence of a "money trust" that controlled a number of the nation's leading industries. There were, moreover, two inherent defects in the national banking system, which had long been recognized by reformers and businessmen alike. It provided the country with an inelastic currency that did not expand and contract in accordance with the needs of the business community, and it contained no method by which healthy banks could come to the assistance of hard-pressed institutions during a financial panic. In 1908, Congress attempted to insure against a repetition of the events of the Panic of 1907 with the passage of the Aldrich-Vreeland Act, which permitted banks during a financial crisis to issue bank notes against government securities and some types of commercial paper. This measure, however, was admittedly only a palliative, and the bill also called for the creation of a commission to recommend reforms in the banking system. The commission's report, which appeared in 1912, recommended a plan that would have placed the sole control of American banking in the hands of the nation's bankers. In rejecting the suggestions of the commission Wilson proposed the establishment of a banking system that would provide an elastic currency based on commercial and agricultural assets rather than government bonds, decentralized public control, and some means for the rapid mobilization of bank reserves during a period of crisis. All Wilson's suggestions were incorporated in the Federal Reserve Act, which became law in December, 1913. This measure provided for the establishment of from eight to twelve Federal Reserve banks, which would serve as central banks in their respective districts. The policies of the Reserve banks were to be formulated and supervised by the Federal Reserve Board. Membership in the system was to include all national banks as well as those state banks and trust companies that met certain specified requirements. The regional Reserve banks were authorized to hold deposits for member banks, clear their checks, discount the paper of member banks and fix discount rates, and issue Federal Reserve notes and bank notes. Under the new system the country was provided with a more elastic currency, a more equitable distribution of the nation's financial resources, an added curb on speculation, and a form of Federal administration that was characterized by a skillful blend of centralized and regional control.

In asking Congress for antitrust legislation Wilson repeated his belief in competition and stated that the government had an obligation to "make men in a small way of business as free to succeed as men in a big way." Unlike Roosevelt, Wilson did not differentiate between good and bad trusts, for he considered any form of industrial concentration an obnoxious deviation from the desired norm of competition. Wilson always believed that the only way to handle the trust problem was "to kill monopoly in the seed." On the other hand, he was not opposed to mere size, and on one occasion he said: "I am for big business and I am against the trusts. Any man who can survive by his brains, any man who can put the others out of business by making the thing cheaper to the consumer at the same time that he is increasing its intrinsic value and quality, I take my hat off to."

To make possible the type of competitive economy envisioned by Wilson, Congress in 1914 adopted the Federal Trade Commission Act and the Clayton Antitrust Act. The Federal Trade Commission Act provided for a five-man commission to be appointed by the president and approved by the Senate. The commission, which supplanted the Bureau of Corporations, was empowered to "gather and compile information concerning . . . the organization, business, conduct, practices, and management of any corporation engaged in commerce" and to "prevent persons, partnerships, or corporations . . . from using unfair methods of competition." To enforce its decisions, the commission was authorized to issue "cease and desist" orders. Corporations engaged in interstate commerce were required to "file with the commission . . . annual or special [reports] . . . or answers in writing to specific questions, furnishing to the commission such information as it may require as to the organization, business, conduct, practices, management, and relation to other corporations, partnerships, and individuals of the respective corporations filing such reports."

The Clayton Antitrust Act, apart from its sections dealing exclusively with labor, was an attempt to avoid the generalizations of the Sherman Act by providing an itemized list of those corporate activities that constituted restraint of trade. Among the practices forbidden by the act were price discrimination among purchasers, exclusive or tying clauses in contracts, intercorporate stockholdings, and interlocking directorates. These practices, however, were not entirely proscribed, for the Clayton Act specifically stated that they were to be considered illegal only when they tended to eliminate competition. In an effort to increase the possibility of enforcing the antitrust laws the act further provided that whenever a corporation violated an antitrust statute, its responsible officers were to be punished by a fine of not more than $5,000 or by imprisonment for not more than one year, or by both.

The Federal Trade Commission and Clayton Acts did not live up to the expectations of their authors. Soon after their enactment the Wilson Administration, confronted by the task of preparing for war, realized that the success of industrial mobilization was dependent in large part upon the same monopolies that it had once hoped to destroy, and no attempt was made to enforce the antitrust laws during the war years. After the war, successive Republican administrations showed no disposition to revive the antitrust crusade. The Federal Trade Commission, which was originally conceived as a government watchdog that would ferret out and eliminate specific instances of the restriction or destruction of competition, soon developed into a routine investigating agency. Moreover, the commission, like so many other government bureaus set up to regulate business, soon assumed many of the same patterns of thought as the very groups it was seeking to regulate. The Clayton Act quickly proved to be no more effective than the Sherman Act. Judges, who were given wide discretion in determining whether corporate practices listed in the measure actually lessened competition, handed down a series of decisions during the 1920's that in effect nullified most of its provisions.

The failure of the Federal government to eliminate monopoly was in large measure the result of a dilemma that the American people could not resolve. Most Americans in the decades preceding World War I opposed big business, but they were even more hostile to big government. Monopoly could have been destroyed by an all-powerful state, but the cure was feared more than the disease. As a consequence, no course remained open for the government but to make solemn gestures toward the restoration of competition, while at the same time it made no move to alter the structure of American industrial capitalism in any of its fundamentals. Like pronouncements against sin, the government's antitrust campaign appealed to the popular conscience without having any appreciable effect upon the object under attack.

While the tariff, banking, and antitrust laws were the cornerstones of the New Freedom, they comprised only a partial list of the reform measures that Wilson sponsored. Particularly notable were numerous measures adopted to safeguard and strengthen the position in the American economy of workingmen and farmers. In addition to the labor provisions in the Clayton Act, Wilson demonstrated in numerous other ways his friendly attitude toward the workers. As his Secretary of Labor, he selected William B. Wilson, a member of the United Mine Workers who had been proposed for the post by the American Federation of Labor. Moreover, during his first term, Congress adopted the Adamson Act (1916), which established an eight-hour day for workers on interstate railways; a Workmen's Compensation Act that covered Federal employees; the Keating-Owen Child Labor Act (1916),* which prohibited the employment of children under fourteen years of age in industries that produced goods for interstate trade; and the La Follette Seamen's Act (1915), which marked the first attempt by Congress to establish minimum standards for the working conditions of seamen in the merchant marine.

The Wilson Administration was also notable for the assistance that it provided the farmers. To furnish farmers with credit facilities comparable to those enjoyed by businessmen, Congress in 1916 approved the Federal Farm Loan Act. Under this measure, twelve Federal land banks were established to make loans at easy rates to individual farmers. The farmers were also assisted by the Grain Standards and Bonded Warehouse Acts; the Smith-Lever Act of 1914, which made possible farm demonstration work in rural communities; and the Smith-Hughes Act of 1917, which provided further funds for agricultural education.

Woodrow Wilson's Administration marked the culmination of the Progressive movement. With a remarkable singleness of purpose, he had transformed the often nebulous aspirations of the Progressives into a national program of reform that had been adopted by Congress with only minor changes. Never a radical, he had not sought to change the pattern of American political or economic life in any of its fundamentals. Many businessmen looked on him as almost a revolutionary, but in reality he had done little that threatened either their income or

* This measure was subsequently declared unconstitutional by the Supreme Court.

power. What he had done was to show some concern for the hitherto forgotten men of the American economy. The small entrepreneur, importer, worker, and farmer for the first time since the Civil War had received some benefits from a government that had formerly bestowed its principal favors on big business.

In 1912, Wilson had campaigned for the New Freedom; four years later his party's slogan was: "He Kept Us Out of War." The election of 1916 signalized the end of one of the most notable reform eras in American history, for it revealed that the New Freedom was dead and that progressivism had been buried with it. Perhaps the American people had grown tired of reform; certainly the war left little time for domestic concerns. In any event, by 1916, Wilson had completed his program, and progressivism had run its course. To complain, as many critics have, that the Progressives left much work still to be done ignores their major accomplishments. Neither doctrinaires nor utopians, they had attacked the outstanding abuses of contemporary society with a vigor and enthusiasm that had enabled them to revitalize American democracy and to drive a few rather sizable wedges into the ranks of the nation's privileged. One measure of their success is gained by a comparison of the administrations of Harrison and McKinley with those of Roosevelt, Taft, and Wilson.

CHAPTER XIII

WORLD WAR I

NINETEENTH-CENTURY Americans were inclined to view the Atlantic Ocean as both a barrier and a highway. While it would prevent Europe from exporting its wars to the Western hemisphere, it would also serve as a means for facilitating the exchange of goods between the Old World and the New. American isolationism, based on the concept of the Atlantic as a defensive wall and a commercial highway, was upset during the Napoleonic Wars. The Atlantic trade was disrupted, and Europe's war spread to North America. But this was only an interlude, and between the Treaty of Ghent and World War I, isolation as practiced by the United States proved to be a highly effective policy. For a hundred years Americans were able to keep out of Europe's conflicts, while their overseas trade increased. It was not until 1917 that the American people were again forced to the conclusions of 1812. Once more the Atlantic had become a military as well as an economic highway. With the return of peace the United States Senate ignored the lessons of 1917 in a futile attempt to apply a nineteenth-century policy in a twentieth-century world.

78. THE UNITED STATES, ENGLAND, AND GERMANY, 1870-1914

THE WAR that was precipitated by the assassination of the Austrian Archduke at Sarajevo on June 28, 1914, was the culmination of decades of economic rivalry, armament races, balance-of-power politics, heightened nationalism, and chaos resulting from the absence of either international law or morality. Just how responsible any particular country was for the collapse of international society in 1914 it is impossible to ascertain. Germany hoped that a system of alliances and an aggressive foreign policy would enable it to obtain colonies and hold on to the gains of the Franco-German War; Russia was prepared to counter any threat to its domination of the Slavic world; France was seeking Alsace-Lorraine and revenge for the defeat of 1870–71; England, the world's greatest "have" nation, was determined to maintain the *status quo;* Italy was ready to embark on any adventure that might transform it from a minor to a major power. For more than half a century these ambitions had canceled each other off as the European balance of power managed to survive a series of nerve-wracking crises. But in 1914 the delicate equilibrium produced by mutual stresses and strains broke down completely, and for the first time since the end of the struggle against Napoleon in 1815, a local conflict developed into a general European war.

Although the mass of Americans displayed little or no interest in the rivalries of the European nations during the half century that preceded the outbreak of war in 1914, American diplomats in the same period became increasingly aware that their country could no longer afford to play the rôle of an aloof bystander in the struggle among the world's leading powers. Imperialism and diplomatic isolation were not always compatible, for the American advance across the Pacific had brought the United States into direct contact with the most powerful nations of Europe. A decision on the future of Samoa, for example, was not an exclusively American problem, but merely one segment of a much larger problem, which involved the world-wide interests of both Germany and England. If the United States was to attempt to play the part of a world power, it could no longer afford to ignore the policies of its fellow powers. Despite traditional American attitudes, the United States was compelled by its policy of overseas imperialism to join in balance-of-power politics. Since the whole system was maintained by pitting one group of nations against another, there could be no such thing as a lone wolf. Once the United States left its continental borders, it had to take sides; and the available evidence suggests that American diplomats had selected England as their country's partner some years before World War I.

The retreat from isolationism did not come easily for the United States government, and before 1900, England, rather than the United States, took the initiative in the development of an Anglo-American rapprochement. The first indication that England was willing to revise its traditional policy toward the United States occurred during the Civil War. At the outset of the war, the Union government established a blockade of the Confederacy's ports. England, as the South's largest customer and the world's leading naval power, had both the motive and wherewithal to challenge the North's blockade. But, unlike the United States during the Napoleonic Wars, England not only scrupulously observed the blockade regulations but co-operated with the United States in their enforcement. For the first time in the history of either nation, England indicated that it might be ready to treat the United States as an equal.

Further evidence of England's new attitude toward the United States was its willingness to accept the Treaty of Washington in 1871. During the Civil War, the English had outfitted some Southern commerce raiders—the most notable being the *Alabama*—which had preyed on Northern shipping with remarkable success. Following the war any attempt to reach an understanding with England was rendered more difficult by the activities of the Fenians and the American Anglophobes who were determined to use the *Alabama* claims as a pretense for humiliating England and expanding the territory of the United States. Charles Sumner, the chairman of the Senate Foreign Relations Committee, estimated that English aid to the Confederacy had cost the United States $2,125,000,000, while other American jingoists urged that England atone for its lack of neutrality by relinquishing its North American possessions. The controversy over the *Alabama* claims was further complicated by the inability of the two countries to agree on the location of the Canadian-American boundary in the San Juan Islands in Puget Sound and the extent of American fishing privileges in Canadian waters.

The success with which the Washington conference overcame the numerous obstacles to Anglo-American friendship was testimony to far-seeing statesmanship on both sides of the Atlantic. Hamilton Fish, the American Secretary of State, had no sympathy with Sumner's preposterous demands and was willing to deal with England on a realistic basis. The English, for their part, were so convinced of the need for peaceful co-operation with the United States that they were willing to place it ahead of Canada's demands for reparations for the Fenian raids, for more stringent control over Americans fishing in Canadian waters, and for commercial reciprocity with the United States. The Treaty of

Washington selected the German Emperor as arbitrator for the San Juan boundary dispute, expanded American fishing privileges in Canadian waters, and referred the *Alabama* claims to a five-man commission that was to be guided in its decision by a set of rules that insured in advance a victory for the American claims. Meeting in Geneva in 1872, the commissioners, after lengthy debate and bitter opposition from the English representative, awarded the United States $15,500,000 for the *Alabama* claims. In the same year the Kaiser decided in favor of the United States in the San Juan boundary dispute.

The Treaty of Washington is a landmark in Anglo-American relations, for it demonstrated that both countries could settle even their most vexatious disputes peacefully. It revealed England's recognition of the increasing power of the United States and the realization of both countries that they had much to gain and little to lose by co-operation. On the other hand, it did not preclude future controversies between England and the United States. There was a long legacy of hatred and suspicion between the two countries that could not be dispelled by a single treaty, and the robust tradition of Anglophobia in the United States persisted well into the period after the Civil War. The Irish vote was an especially formidable obstacle to friendlier relations, for the almost even balance between the Republican and Democratic parties made it far more influential in American politics than its actual numerical strength would indicate.

The desire of numerous American politicians to make political capital out of the anti-English sentiment in the United States prevented any genuine understanding between the two countries during the quarter century that followed the Treaty of Washington. Both Blaine and Frelinghuysen needlessly antagonized the British by their stand on the Clayton-Bulwer Treaty, and the fisheries question continued to plague the diplomats of both nations. When the United States in 1885 terminated the fisheries clauses in the Treaty of Washington, Canada replied by seizing American ships in Canadian waters. In 1888, Secretary of State Thomas F. Bayard and Joseph Chamberlain headed a commission that worked out a compromise plan providing for substantial concessions by both countries. But 1888 was an election year, and the Republican-controlled Senate in a bid for the Irish vote rejected the treaty in August. Similar difficulties were encountered in the attempt to resolve the dispute that arose from the American protest over pelagic sealing by Canadian schooners off the Pribiloff Islands in the Bering Sea. The Cleveland Administration, ignoring the traditional American policy of freedom of the seas, began to seize Canadian ships on the ground that the Bering Sea was a *mare clausum.* When Harrison succeeded Cleveland as President, Blaine had to retreat from this untenable position, and in 1892 he agreed to submit the question to arbitration. A year later an international tribunal in Paris ruled against the American claims and made the United States liable for $473,000 for past seizures.

The climax of anti-British sentiment in the United States was reached in 1895 with Secretary of State Olney's belligerent note to England concerning Venezuela. For more than half a century Britain and Venezuela had engaged in a desultory dispute over the location of the boundary line of British Guiana. When the British landed troops in Venezuela in 1895, American jingoists professed to see a British plot in Latin America and the Cleveland Administration concluded that the United States would have to save Venezuela from British imperialism. On July 20, 1895, Olney wrote to the British government requesting that it observe the Monroe Doctrine and submit its boundary dispute with Venezuela to arbitration.

> *Today* [wrote Olney] *the United States is practically sovereign on this continent, and its fiat is law upon the subjects to which it confines its interposition. Why? It is not because of the pure friendship or good will felt for it. It is not simply by reason of its high character as a civilized state, nor because . . . justice and equity are the invariable characteristics of the dealings of the United States. It is because, in addition to all other grounds, its infinite resources combined with its isolated position render it master of the situation, and practically invulnerable as against any or all other powers.*

Although the British had indicated on numerous occasions that they were ready to go more than half way to secure American friendship and co-operation, they were not prepared to be bullied into joining a partnership as the junior member. Lord Salisbury waited four months before he replied to what Cleveland called Olney's "twenty-inch gun"; and, when he did reply, he announced:

> *The disputed frontier of Venezuela has nothing to do with any of the questions dealt with by President Monroe. It is not a question of the colonization by a European Power of any portion of America. It is not a question of the imposition upon the communities of South America of any system of government devised in Europe. It is simply the determination of the frontier of a British possession which belonged to the Throne of England long before the Republic of Venezuela came into existence.*

Salisbury's blunt refusal to tolerate what he obviously considered American meddling made Cleveland "mad clear through," and on December 17, 1895, he requested Congress to appoint a commission to determine the boundary and to be prepared to authorize the use of force to uphold the commission's decision. Although the United States was in no position to take on the British fleet, Cleveland's message produced a war scare. But at the height of the crisis, English public opinion asserted itself, and numerous organizations and organs representing various strata of English life made it clear that they were opposed to a war with the United States. After a frenzy of uninhibited jingoism, the American people also awoke to the realization that armed conflict with England would be unthinkable. Responding to these unexpected displays of friendly sentiment in both countries, British and American diplomats were able to reach a face-saving compromise. England agreed to accept the good offices of the United States through an arbitration treaty that assured it in advance of its principal contentions. In 1899 a tribunal established under the terms of the treaty of arbitration upheld most of the British claims but gave Venezuela continued control of the mouth of the Orinoco River.

The peaceful settlement of the Venezuela dispute marked another important advance along the road to Anglo-American friendship. In rejecting war as an instrument for settling their differences, both countries had been motivated by considerations of national interest. Great Britain, diplomatically isolated and disturbed by the rising power of Germany, could not afford to alienate a potential ally. The United States, on the threshold of its overseas adventures, also needed powerful friends if it was going to hold its own in the free-for-all of imperialist competition.

When the United States embarked on a career of imperialism at the end of the 1890's, the foreign policies of both countries were closely coordinated. The British government gave moral support to the United States during the Spanish-American War and bestowed its unofficial blessing on the American acquisition of bases in the Pacific and Caribbean. After the establishment of the American colonial empire the two nations frequently co-operated in those parts of the world where they had joint interests. The Open Door notes, for instance, were an American policy with an English author. In 1901 the British gave way on the canal question and five years later the British fleet was withdrawn from the Caribbean. For its part, the United States, with new responsibilities in the Pacific and the Caribbean, was more than willing to entrust the Atlantic to British naval power. Furthermore, during Wilson's administration the United States demonstrated that it could grant as well as demand concessions. In 1912, Congress exempted American coastal shipping from the payment of Panama Canal tolls. When Great Britain protested that the act violated the terms of the Hay-Pauncefote Treaty, Woodrow Wilson, who had previously supported the measure, reversed his stand and by exerting pressure on Congress was able to effect its repeal.

To some extent the growing diplomatic co-operation between the United States and Great Britain was achieved at the expense of Canada, for Great Britain demonstrated that it was willing to sacrifice the im-

The Bettmann Archive

TIME TABLE OF THE

DEAD RIVER GRAND TRUNK RAILWAY

GREAT CENTRAL THROUGH ROUTE.

BROAD GAUGE--QUICKEST TIME.

S. U. R. E. DEATH, President. **RUM POLICY, Secretary.**

Accidents by COLLISIONS are entirely avoided, as no UP-TRAINS are run over the road.

Trains Move by the following Progressive Time Table.

LEAVE	
briety,	5 00
amsellerville,	5 15
ppington,	5 25
ippleton,	6 00
apersville,	6 13
oafersburg,	6 30
owdyville,	6 45
uarrelsville,	7 00
iarsville,	7 10
ightington,	7 15
ardington,	7 33
uzzler's Junct'n,	7 35
runkard's Curve,	8 00
ebauch Slough,	
oter's Hollow,	
ason Crossing,	
hieves' Gully,	
ambler's Causeway,	
ill-conscience Cut,	
risonton,	
eggarstown,	
auper Desert,	

EXPRESS.

Reformationburg,
Robberstown,
Delirium Falls,
Demonland,
Hornetsnest Thicket,
Snakesburg,
Screech Owl Forest,
Dismal Swamp,
Hobgoblin Woods,
Rattlesnake Ledge,
Dark Tunnel,
Whirlwind Crossing,
Thunderland,
Poison Switch,
Bloody Chasm,
Maniac Marsh,
Misery Thicket,
Desperation,
Suicide Cave,
Murderer's Gulch,
Hangman's Hollow,
DEAD RIVER, or PERDITION.

LIGHTNING EXPRESS.

☞ All trains will stop at *Reformationburg* passengers desire to leave at that station. But all persons so stopping will forfeit their through ticket to *Perdition*.

☞ Tickets are sold by all Sample Rooms and Rum Holes, they being our only authorized agents.

☞ Daily Patrons of the Road, above *Tippleton*, supplied with Through Tickets at reduced rates.

☞ From *Drunkard's Curve* the train is an Express—all *taking in* being done above that station, and principally of respectable people. Passengers for all places *beyond* are *thrown out* without stopping the train, except at *Reformationburg*.

☞ Persons desiring to leave the train, will find the Stages of the TEMPERANCE ALLIANCE at *Drunkard's Curve*, ready to convey them free to any of the villages upon COLD STREAM RIVER.

☞ Passengers not allowed to stand on the platform, or to put their heads out of the windows below *Debauch Slough*—the corporation not wishing to alarm persons who are not patrons of the Road.

☞ Sleeping cars are provided for through passengers, who will be awakened frequently, that an opportunity for alcoholic refreshments may be given.

☞ Persons living in the vicinity of this Road must "look out for the engine," as no bell is rung or brakesmen employed below *Drunkard's Curve*, and the Company disclaim all responsibility for damages.

☞ All Baggage at the risk of the owners. Widows and Orphans in pursuit of baggage lost by friends on this Road, are informed that the Corporation will adhere strictly to the usages of the Road, and positively will not restore lost baggage.

☞ The Conductor of the morning Jersey Lightning Express is *T. H. E. Devil, Esq.*, well known to the traveling public who patronize our line, and popular at the principal stations on the Dead River Line.

☞ Being the Ruler of Perdition, he spares no pains in securing the through tickets, or rendering other services to passengers bound for his kingdom.

☞ Passengers in the sleeping cars, especially Stockholders, will be *waked up at Screech Owl Forest, Thunderland,* and at the *end of the* Road.

☞ Stages from *Tobaccoland* connect with all Trains.

☞ Special Trains will be dispatched at any time, on application made to the Superintendent, for political conventions, picnic parties, and all associations owning allegiance to *King Gambrinus* or *King Alcohol.*

NOTICE.—At the request of Superintendent Alcohol, there will be a Business Meeting, by and by, of the Stockholders and Conductors of the Road, to hear a Report concerning

Liabilities under the Higher Law!

READER, will you assist in diffusing information about the above Road, so that multitudes who are invited to excursions upon it may be informed of the country through which it passes, and where it terminates. This advertisement will be sent free to any address, on application to

R. H. McDONALD & CO.,
532 Washington St., New York City.

A PROHIBITION POSTER

The Temperance movement continued to grow after the Civil War. This "timetable" shows the stations along the drunkard's road: Loafersburg, Quarrelsville, Thieves' Gully, and so on to Dead River of Perdition. At Drunkard's Curve the train becomes an express, but passengers who alight here can take the Temperance Alliance Stage.

ILLUSTRATIONS FROM *The Bettmann Archive*

BOOKER T. WASHINGTON

HENRY GEORGE

JANE ADDAMS

EUGENE V. DEBS

MELIORIST REFORMERS OF DIFFERING VIEWS

mediate interests of its North American possessions for the continued friendship of the United States. In 1903 a commission of three Americans, two Canadians, and one Englishman was appointed to settle a Canadian-Alaskan boundary dispute. After some not so subtle threats by Theodore Roosevelt, the English representative on the commission joined the three Americans to outvote the Canadians on practically every point under consideration. Canadians, enraged at what they considered the mother country's perfidy, were not solaced by the realization that their country was little more than a pawn in an Anglo-American chess game that included the Atlantic, Pacific, Caribbean, and Far East as well as North America. A new world power had appeared and Great Britain was determined to readjust its policies to take advantage of this development. Nor was Canada always the loser under this arrangement, for the Anglo-American understanding was accompanied by a corresponding shift in Canadian-American relations. The United States was at last ready to acknowledge that Canada was here to stay and was prepared to treat it as a fellow nation rather than as a future American colony. In 1909, Canada and the United States ratified the Boundary Waters Treaty, which governed the use of the waters of the rivers and lakes shared by the two countries, and three years later the vexatious fisheries dispute was finally liquidated when a decision handed down by the Hague Court was confirmed by the Anglo-American Convention of July 20, 1912. Canada, in turn, revelled in its new status, and in 1911 it rejected President Taft's proposal for reciprocity on the ground that it threatened Canadian independence.

At the outbreak of World War I, Anglophobia was still a popular pastime for some Americans, and there were still congressmen who had gained office by twisting the British lion's tail for their constituents; but these facts had little or no effect upon the conduct of Anglo-American diplomacy. During the past half century the numerous disputes between the two nations had always been settled amicably and each succeeding crisis served only to accentuate their essential solidarity. Great Britain, with interests in every corner of the globe, had encouraged the friendship of its fellow Atlantic power. The United States, with a new overseas empire to defend, had turned, however reluctantly, toward the nation with the world's strongest navy. As satiated powers, both countries had a stake in the maintenance of the international *status quo* and were inclined to look with distrust and hostility upon any nation that threatened to upset the precarious balance of power.

The development of an informal Anglo-American entente during the half century that preceded World War I was paralleled by a growing American suspicion of Germany. To numerous Americans, Germany was synonymous with ruthlessness, arrogance, and militarism—a combination of attributes that was frequently summed up by Americans with the single word "Prussianism." The Kaiser was thought by many Americans to be a typical Prussian, and occasionally the German ruler seemed to go out of his way to substantiate this conclusion. When German troops were departing for China in 1900, the Kaiser was reported to have ordered them to "give no quarter, spare nobody, make no prisoners. Use your weapons so that for a thousand years hence no Chinaman will dare look askance at any German. . . . Be terrible as Attila's Huns."

In the American mind Germany was more than a land of unpleasant people; it was also a potential menace to the security of the United States. Although the German navy was considerably smaller than its British counterpart, Americans were generally convinced that it represented the single greatest threat to the Monroe Doctrine. Presidents Grant and Theodore Roosevelt and Secretaries of State Fish, Bayard, Hay, and Root all intimated or openly expressed their fear of the effect of Germany's foreign policy upon the United States. Behind the American distrust of Germany lay the fact that similar stages of national development had made the two countries rivals in many fields. Both nations were intent on the development of their own industrial systems, and both were determined to obtain overseas possessions. Great Britain could afford to take a lenient view toward American imperialism, for it had its empire; but Germany and the United States, as late comers to the imperialistic scramble, knew that this was their last chance to obtain colonies; and because only the crumbs of the imperialist banquet were left, both countries struggled with particular intensity to get their share of the remaining scraps.

On numerous occasions German and American expansionism clashed in the Caribbean and the Pacific. When the Grant Administration attempted to obtain all or part of Santo Domingo, both official and unofficial American observers stated that Germany was also determined to annex the island. It was Germany, rather than Great Britain, that aroused the hostility of the United States in Samoa. During the Spanish-American War, German friendship for Spain was as pronounced as that of Great Britain for the United States, and the appearance of a German fleet in Manila Bay after Dewey's victory seemed additional proof to many Americans that Germany was attempting to thwart American colonial ambitions. The German bombardment of Fort San Carlos in Venezuela in January, 1903, was considered by many Americans a characteristic display of German militarism. When the Danish Landsthing refused to ratify a treaty for the purchase of the Danish West Indies by the United States, Americans (incorrectly) attributed the defeat of the treaty to pressure from Germany. Finally, the only instance of American intervention in a European dispute resulted in a triumph for France and a setback for Germany. In the Moroccan crisis of 1905,

Theodore Roosevelt was the individual most responsible for the calling of the Algeciras Conference (1906), which, while preserving peace, checked Germany in North Africa.

The Kaiser, although aware of the anti-German sentiment in the United States, made only ineffectual attempts to counteract it. A statue of Frederick the Great that the Kaiser presented to the United States re-enforced the belief of many Americans that the donor was bent on following the military career of his illustrious predecessor. In 1901 he conferred a medal upon Theodore Roosevelt. A year later Prince Henry was sent to the United States on a goodwill mission and Alice Roosevelt was asked to christen the yacht that was being built for the Kaiser in the United States. When she asked her father for assistance in the preparation of a speech for the occasion, the "only motto sufficiently epigrammatic," that came to the President's mind "was 'Damn the Dutch.' "*

At the outbreak of World War I few Americans were prepared to fight Germany or die for England. On the other hand, many American diplomats had come to believe that a German victory and an English defeat would constitute a major disaster for the United States.

79. THE WAR OF WORDS

ALTHOUGH Europe had been on the brink of war for more than a decade, when the conflict began, most Americans were psychologically unprepared for it. The initial reaction of the American people to the news of war was shock and revulsion; and Senator John Sharp Williams of Mississippi undoubtedly expressed the general American disgust when he stated that he was "mad all over, down to the very bottom of my shoes, and somewhat sick and irritable, too," at this "outbreak of senseless war, setting all Europe aflame." Americans could not help feeling that it was altogether unreasonable of Europeans to start killing one another at a time so inconvenient to the United States.

At the start of the war the United States government proclaimed its neutrality, and two weeks later President Wilson asked his countrymen to be "impartial in thought as well as in action." Although the American people were united in their determination to prevent the United States from being drawn into the war, they found it difficult, if not impossible, to refrain from giving their moral support to one or the other set of belligerents. Some Americans for a short time made a sincere but futile effort to comply with the President's request; others refused even to go

* Henry F. Pringle: *Theodore Roosevelt; A Biography* (New York: Harcourt, Brace and Company, Inc., 1931), p. 282.

through the motions of pretending that they were neutral in thought. From the very first day of hostilities Americans were divided into two camps, and those who favored the Allies far outnumbered the friends of Germany. Few newspapers managed to maintain even a semblance of neutrality and a large segment of the American press announced the outbreak of the war by attributing it to the Central Powers in general and the Kaiser in particular.

The pro-Allied sentiment that dominated American public opinion from 1914 to 1917 was determined in part by the American reaction to the events of the first weeks of the war. American sympathy for Belgium was easily converted into hostility for Belgium's invaders. France's valiant and successful resistance to an unexpected attack elicited the respect and support of many Americans. The stories of German atrocities in Belgium and the accounts of the German destruction of some of Europe's most famous cathedrals and centers of learning seemed to substantiate the Allied contention that Germany was waging a war against Western civilization. In some instances, anti-German sentiment in the United States was also based on considerations of national and personal interest. Those Americans who recognized the importance of Anglo-American understanding to their country's security thought that an Allied defeat would leave the United States an island of democracy in a hostile and militaristic world. Other Americans, who had developed close economic ties with England, saw their prosperity threatened by a German victory. Regardless of motives, Americans supporting the Allies had one feature in common. They all agreed that the United States would be better off in a world dominated by the Anglo-French Entente than by Germany.

Those Americans who did not sympathize with the Allies were drawn from diverse walks in American life. Many, but not all, German-Americans were convinced of the righteousness of Germany's cause. Some people of Jewish faith, remembering the persecution of their coreligionists by the Tsarist government, hoped that Russia's enemy would be victorious. The Irish-Americans, with a long legacy of hatred for the English, were overwhelmingly on the side of the nations that were fighting Ireland's oppressors. In addition, there were Americans who were equally opposed to both belligerants. In certain parts of the Midwest where isolationism was particularly strong, many people tried to ignore the war on the assumption that its outcome did not concern the United States. Socialists and members of the I.W.W. considered the struggle in Europe an imperialist war and predicted that a victory for either side would be a defeat for the workingmen of the world. Pacifists refused to take sides as a matter of principle. Throughout the war both the friends of Germany and the advocates of neutrality of thought remained a minority. Rightly or wrongly, most Americans believed that the Allies were fighting on the side of democracy and humanity.

American views on both sides were re-enforced by the one-sided accounts of the events in Europe that were exported by the belligerents to the United States from 1914 to 1917. Germany and Great Britain were especially assiduous in their efforts to cultivate American public opinion, and soon after the start of the war they launched large scale propaganda campaigns in the United States. Despite the expenditure of a considerable amount of money and the employment of practically every conceivable publicity technique, it is doubtful if either German or British propaganda induced many Americans to change their minds about the war in Europe. In most instances propaganda served to substantiate opinions that were already held, rather than to formulate new ones. Americans did not have to be told what to think about the various belligerents in Europe, but they did enjoy having their conclusions corroborated by either British or German spokesmen.

Like all successful propagandists, the British permitted no neutral colors to soften the black and white picture that they painted for their American audience. According to British propaganda, the Prussian military clique that ruled Germany had been preparing for war since 1870. The Sarajevo crisis was not an historical accident but the pretext employed by the German leaders to inaugurate their program of world conquest. France, Russia, and Great Britain had devoted all their efforts to the preservation of peace, but they at last had been forced into a position where they had no alternative but to resort to arms to save themselves and civilization. British propagandists not only made Germany solely responsible for the war but described German soldiers as little better than brutal automatons who were prepared to resort to any cruelty to further their country's program for enslaving the world. Some Americans might question the validity of some of the charges against Germany, but they could not disprove them; and Germany's invasion of Belgium, her use of poison gas, and her destruction of innocent lives at sea convinced some of the most dubious that the British had not understated their case.

English propaganda techniques in the United States were subtle and persuaded many Americans that they were convincing themselves of the worth of the Allied cause. Only established channels of news dissemination were used, and whenever possible, Americans were knowingly or unknowingly employed to spread the British version of the war among their fellow Americans. A year after the United States had entered the war Sir Gilbert Parker, a Canadian novelist in charge of British propaganda in the United States, revealed the scope and methods of his organization:

> *Among other things, we supplied three hundred and sixty newspapers in the smaller States of the United States with an English newspaper, which gives a weekly review and comment of the affairs of the war. We established connection with the man in the street through cinema pictures of the Army and Navy, as well as through interviews, articles, pamphlets, etc.; and by letters in reply to individual American critics, which were printed in the chief newspaper of the State in which they lived, and were copied in newspapers of other and neighboring States. We advised and stimulated many* [individuals] . . . *to write articles; we utilized the services and assistance of confidential friends; we had reports from important Americans constantly, and established association, by personal correspondence, with influential and eminent people of every profession in the United States, beginning with university and college presidents, professors and scientific men and running through all the ranges of the population. We asked our friends and correspondents to arrange for speeches, debates, and lectures by American citizens, but we did not encourage Britishers to go to America and preach the doctrine of entrance into the war. Besides an immense private correspondence with individuals, we had our documents and literature sent to great numbers of public libraries, Y.M.C.A. societies, universities, colleges, historical societies, clubs, and newspapers.*

Despite the expenditure of considerable amounts of money and time, the German propagandists were no match for the British. German press releases were distributed to American newspapers, speakers were sent on lecture tours across the country, and on August 10, 1914, George Sylvester Viereck established *The Fatherland,* a newspaper that presented the German version of the war. While the English made their appeal to American emotions, the Germans sought to convince the Americans by learned, but often obtuse, legal arguments. But it was more than faulty techniques that defeated the German propagandists, for all the advantages lay with the British. With control over the Atlantic cables and the chance to censor all the war news emanating from Europe, the British had an easier access to the American public than the Germans. An even greater asset enjoyed by the British but denied to the Germans was the assurance of an overwhelmingly receptive audience in the United States. Prominent Americans willingly co-operated with the British publicists in the United States, and from 1914 to 1917 well-known English authors like H. G. Wells, G. K. Chesterton, and Rudyard Kipling were as popular as propagandists with the Americans as they had been as writers before the war. Finally, the Germans lost the war of words in America because their government repeatedly played into the hands of the British propagandists. While it is possible that some Americans were deceived by the Allied description of the extent of Germany's war guilt, no foreign spokesmen had to tell them the significance of the invasion of Belgium. Here was a fact: a neutral, inoffensive country had been invaded by an aggressor nation whose foreign minister referred to the treaty guaranteeing Belgium's neutrality as a "scrap of paper." From the German standpoint the invasion of Belgium may have been a military necessity; but to Americans it was an inexcusable breech of international law, and David Starr Jordan spoke for many Americans when he stated that "the invasion of Belgium changed the whole face of affairs. As by a lightning-flash the issue was made plain: the issue of the sacredness of law; the rule of the soldier or the rule of the citizen; the rule of fear or the rule of law."

After the invasion of Belgium many Americans were prepared to believe anything concerning the Germans. Count Bernstorff, the German ambassador in Washington, said that the "Belgian question was the one which interested Americans most and which was most effective in working up American opinion against us," and the readiness with which Americans accepted reports of German rape, plunder, and oppression in Belgium seem to substantiate Bernstorff's impression. Despite the fact that a group of American journalists who were permitted to visit Belgium reported that in their opinion the so-called atrocity stories were groundless, most Americans preferred to think otherwise. Even some of the more skeptical were converted in May, 1915, by the publication of Lord Bryce's *Report of the Committee on the Alleged German Atrocities,* which corroborated many of the earlier reports concerning the behavior of German troops in Belgium.

If the Americans were taken in by the atrocity stories, they did not have to be told by the British what to think about other aspects of Germany's conduct of the war. Submarine warfare was a reality and not a rumor; and neither German explanations nor apologies could convince most Americans that Germany was justified in killing their fellow citizens on the high seas. The destruction of Louvain and bombardment of the cathedral of Rheims may have been a by-product of war, but to the average American it represented a wanton disregard for two of the greatest cultural landmarks of western Europe. And even if Americans were willing to make allowances for Germany's conduct of the war, they found it difficult to exonerate its representatives in the United States From 1914 to 1917 agents of the Central Powers fomented strikes in American munition plants and along the waterfront, took a leading part in the American peace movement, and destroyed with explosives American factories, bridges, and cargoes bound for the Allies.

There is little reason to believe that German or British propaganda caused many Americans to shift their allegiance from one belligerent to another. Germany made few converts among those Americans who were not pro-German in 1914. The Allies were probably more successful, but the principal accomplishment of the Allied propagandists was not in winning Americans over to their side, but in strengthening the convictions of those who had already declared their support for the enemies of Germany. Much more significant than the success of British propaganda were the factors that made possible this success. One of these was Germany's conduct of the war. Another was the combination of circumstances that before 1914 had combined to convince many Americans that their interests lay with England rather than Germany. No amount of German propaganda could have induced the United States to fight on the side of the Central Powers. German propagandists, well aware of this fact, hoped to secure nothing more than the maintenance of American neutrality. On the other hand, the British propagandists, assured of a friendly reception, set their sights on American intervention as their maximum aim. Most important of all, from the first day of the war the British had one advantage that was never shared by the Germans—they could tell the mass of Americans what they wanted to be told.

80. WAR TRADE AND LOANS

THROUGHOUT the period of American neutrality the Allies received material as well as moral support from the United States. Following the failure of Germany's bid for a quick victory, the war became a struggle of attrition. As the troops of both sides dug into their trenches, questions of strategy and tactics often had to be subordinated to the problem of how to obtain adequate supplies for the armies at the front. Because the European neutrals had imposed embargoes on the export of war matériel, only the United States remained to make up the deficiencies of the Allies. Germany, too, would have liked to have drawn on American resources; but the effectiveness of the British blockade prevented all but a trickle of American goods from reaching the Central Powers.

American trade with the Allies soon reached enormous proportions.* But there was considerable American opposition to the continued export of this war matériel. Pacifists complained that it prolonged the war; pro-German groups considered it unfair to the Central Powers; and

* Exports to England, France, Italy, and Russia rose from $824,860,237 in 1914 to $3,214,480,547 in 1916, while direct exports to Germany and Austria-Hungary declined from $169,289,775 to $1,159,653 in the same years. The bulk of the American war trade with the Allies consisted of foodstuffs and war matériel. From 1913–14 to 1916–17, American grain exports to Europe increased from 112,503,000 to 333,127,000 bushels and the value of munitions of war shipped from the United States to the Allies from August, 1914, to March, 1917, totaled $2,187,948,779.

isolationists thought that it jeopardized American neutrality. Numerous resolutions condemning the war shipments were introduced into Congress; but none was ever adopted and the Wilson Administration never made any move to prevent the trade. In October, 1914, the State Department announced that "a citizen of the United States can sell to a belligerent government or its agent any article of commerce which he chooses." Under accepted international law, Americans were permitted to ship war supplies to the belligerents, and on December 15, 1914, Count von Bernstorff, the German ambassador to the United States, wrote to Secretary of State Bryan:

> *Under the general principles of international law no exception can be taken to neutral states letting war material go to Germany's enemies from or through their territory. This is in accordance with Article 7 of the Hague Convention of October 18, 1907, concerning the rights and duties of neutrals in naval and land war. . . . According to the principles of international law above cited, a neutral state need not prevent furnishing supplies of this character. . . . Our enemies draw from the United States contraband of war, especially arms. . . . This in itself they are authorized to do.*

The fact that Germany recognized the legality of the American export of war matériel to the Allies did not make this practice any more acceptable in German eyes. The Germans could not escape the conclusion that many of their soldiers were being killed by American bullets, and in 1917 a German author complained:

> *Germany finds herself in the position of a warrior, hemmed in on all sides, whose enemies are aiming at his heart. Every time this warrior succeeds in disarming the foe most harmful to him, every time the warrior strikes the sword from the hand of the enemy, a so-called neutral comes running from behind and places a new weapon in the hand of the defeated foe.*

To repeated requests from the Central Powers that it place an embargo on arms shipments, the United States government always replied that any restriction on this trade would violate an established American policy and undermine its principle of strict neutrality. The official American position on the munitions trade was given by Secretary of State Robert Lansing in a note to Austria in August, 1915. As all the belligerents had known that international law permitted the export of war matériel by a neutral country, and as some of them had presumably entered the war with that fact in mind, Lansing concluded that it would be unjust for the United States to change the rules governing the conduct of neutrals after the war had started. Lansing further stated that the United States wished to establish a precedent, for with a small peacetime military establishment, the United States would be unable to "repel invasion by a well-equipped and powerful enemy" unless it could receive the same type of assistance that it was now giving to the Allies.

Lansing, who thought that American interests would be threatened by a German victory, refused to take any step that might weaken the Allied war effort. But he was not alone in his opposition to an arms embargo. The United States did not stop the trade in contraband of war, because the American people did not want to stop it. In August, 1914, the United States was in the midst of a depression that was only partially alleviated by the Allied war orders placed with American manufacturers in the winter of 1914–15; but by the following summer the corner had been turned, and within a few months the war trade had converted the depression into a boom. Few Americans wished to exchange this prosperity for an economic neutrality that would benefit only the Central Powers. Practically every American business firm derived a direct or indirect benefit from the war trade with Europe, and those concerned with supplying war equipment to the Allies made unprecedented profits. The earnings of American steel and iron companies increased from $203,153,879 in 1915 to $1,034,892,465 in 1917; the wartime profits of E. I. du Pont de Nemours, which supplied an estimated 40 per cent of all the ammunition used by the Allies, amounted to $266,000,000; and J. P. Morgan & Company, which served as the American commercial agent for the French and British, collected commissions exceeding $30,000,000 for the purchases it made for both governments in the United States. Nor was this prosperity confined to businessmen. Workers and farmers, sharing in the good times engendered by the exports to the Allies, were no more disposed to cut off the source of their new wealth than were the nation's industrial and financial executives. To those Americans who were hoping for an Allied victory, the export of arms, ammunition, and foodstuffs proved a double boon, for it both satisfied their consciences and lined their pockets. Finally, political conditions favored the continuation of American shipments to the Allies. The Wilson Administration, with its overwhelming sympathy for the Allied cause, was more than willing to make its official stand on the war trade conform to the popular mandate.

From the standpoint of many Americans the most disturbing feature of the shift from depression to a war-born prosperity was the prospect that their European customers would run out of money. This difficulty was not, however, insuperable; for if the government's permission could be secured, American bankers were prepared to finance the Allies. During the first week of hostilities J. P. Morgan & Company had asked the Wilson Administration's approval of a loan to France. Although no law forbade the extension of financial assistance by individual Americans to the belligerents, Secretary of State Bryan rejected the Morgan proposal on the ground that "loans by American bankers to any foreign nation which is at war are inconsistent with the true spirit of neutrality." Bryan, as a pacifist, thought that a refusal to lend money to either side would shorten the war. Moreover, he believed that American neutrality required that any loans to the Allies be matched by loans to Germany. But if American citizens and banks acquired a direct economic stake in the outcome of the war, Bryan feared that the American people would be divided along the lines of their economic interests and that the nation's most powerful financial institutions would exert tremendous pressure on the government in an attempt to influence the conduct of American foreign policy.

In the latter part of October, 1914, the Administration partially amended the earlier stand taken by Bryan. Although the government did not state that it would sanction war loans, it did indicate that it was powerless to prevent them and that it would not object to short-term credits to the belligerents. The individual most responsible for the change in policy was Robert Lansing, who at the time was counselor for the State Department. When the National City Bank asked for permission to grant short-term credits to the Allies, Lansing submitted the bank's request with minor revisions as a memorandum to the President. Wilson was convinced by the bankers' arguments that there was a "decided difference between an issue of government bonds which are sold in open market to investors" and "credits which will avoid the clumsy and impracticable method of cash payments." After being informed of the President's consent, the National City Bank on November 4 announced the completion of the arrangements for a $10,000,000 special credit to the French government.

Credits were at best a stopgap, for they postponed rather than solved the problem of the Allies' inability to pay for their purchases in the United States. By August, 1915, leading American bankers were insisting that the government would have to permit long-term loans if it wished to save the Allies and maintain American war trade. The fears of the bankers were shared by some of the most important officials in the Wilson Administration. Lansing, who had succeeded Bryan as Secretary of State, wrote to Wilson that the Administration should not permit its earlier opposition to loans to "stand in the way of our national interests which seem to be seriously threatened." Secretary of the Treasury McAdoo favored "anything that would help to finance export trade" and stated that if Americans did not "finance it," it would "stop and that would be disastrous." Wilson, however reluctantly, was won over by his advisers to the need for a loan and on September 25, 1915, a group of American bankers completed negotiations for a loan of $500,000,000 to the French and British governments. The Anglo-French loan was the first of many to the Allies, and by April, 1917, American investors had purchased $2,300,000,000 of bonds from the enemies of Germany.

Although the war trade and war loans certainly strengthened the economic ties between the United States and the Allies, it is impossible to "prove" that they were responsible for the eventual American participation in the war in Europe. The insistence of the isolationists of the twenties and thirties that the United States went to war to save the bankers' loans is without foundation in fact. As all but the first loan were backed by collateral deposited in the United States, the American investors stood to lose nothing by an Allied defeat. Moreover, some businessmen who were deriving the largest benefits from their trade with the Allies were worried by the economic implications of American intervention. While an American declaration of war would undoubtedly mean larger war orders, many businessmen were convinced that it would also mean higher taxes and increased government regulation. There is no evidence to indicate that businessmen as a class were any more desirous of war in 1917 than were the members of any other economic group.

81. THE DIPLOMACY OF NEUTRALITY

THE ECONOMIC and sentimental ties that bound the United States to the Allies did not weaken the determination of most Americans to stay out of the war in Europe. Although many Americans felt free to criticize the belligerents and to extract profits from Europe's distress, they were unalterably opposed to American intervention in the conflict. From 1914 to 1917 the United States government accurately reflected the wishes of the majority of its citizens by adhering to a policy of neutrality while demonstrating by overt acts that its sympathies lay with the Allies.

Wilson's conduct of American foreign policy during the period of American neutrality was a compromise between two extremes of American opinion; and as the war progressed, it was bitterly attacked by pacifists and extreme isolationists on the one hand and the advocates of American intervention on the Allied side on the other. William Jennings Bryan, as the leading spokesman of the former group and with strong support in the rural regions of the West and South, thought that the United States should have nothing to do with the war except to offer its services as a mediator. To Bryan and his followers, there was little or no difference between the belligerents, and the Wilson Administration's obvious friendship for the Allies was a violation of American neutrality that would lead to war. Directly opposed to Bryan was a group of Americans—largely drawn from the Northeast—who believed that the United States had a vital stake in the outcome of the war. Maintaining that a Germany victory would threaten world democracy and American security, they urged intervention and criticized Wilson's devotion to neutrality as evidence of shortsightedness and even cowardice. Those who viewed the war in this light, while in a distinct minority, included several prominent Americans. Theodore Roosevelt, Charles W. Eliot, former president of Harvard, and the New York publisher George H. Putnam, among others, predicted that an Allied defeat would be followed by a German attack on the United States. Between the extremes represented by Bryan and the interventionists were the masses of Americans, who recognized a certain validity in the arguments of both groups but preferred to take their stand on a middle ground that permitted them to endorse neutrality while at the same time recognizing the possibility that they might eventually be compelled to abandon it.

Woodrow Wilson, like most other Americans, was at various times receptive to the views of both the interventionists and the spokesmen for the extreme pacific-isolationist school of American neutrality. On numerous occasions before he became President, Wilson had condemned war as an ineffective and immoral device for settling international disputes. During his first months in office he gave his wholehearted support to Bryan's cooling-off treaties, and after the sinking of the *Lusitania* he asserted that there was "such a thing as a man being too proud to fight" and "such a thing as a nation being so right that it does not need to convince others by force that it is right." But there was another side to Wilson. In 1911 in a speech that foreshadowed his stand in April, 1917, he stated that there were "times in the history of nations when they must take up the crude instruments of bloodshed in order to vindicate spiritual conceptions" and that "when men take up arms to set other men free, there is something sacred and holy in the warfare." Wilson's view of American neutrality was also colored by his lifelong study and admiration of British politics and literature, for he had come to believe that there was an essential unity among the "English-speaking peoples" and that it should be encouraged on the diplomatic level. For his commencement address at Princeton in 1878, Wilson had chosen the subject "Our Kinship With England." Twenty-two years later, while a professor at the same institution, he had referred to "our happy alliance of sentiment and purpose with Great Britain." The war strengthened rather than weakened Wilson's sympathies for England, and in the first days of 1915 he told his secretary that "England was fighting our fight."

The difficulties that beset the conduct of American foreign policy from 1914 to 1917 were in part the result of the efforts of the American people and government to reconcile their desire to remain at peace with the ever present danger that peace for the United States might mean victory for Germany. American neutrality was at best a tentative neutrality, for it was always based on the hypothesis that Germany would be defeated. Moreover, the American attempt to steer a neutral course

McCutcheon in the Chicago Tribune

FINE BALANCE REQUIRED TO AVOID TROUBLE

was always complicated by the lack of any accepted standards governing the conduct of nonbelligerents during a war. In 1909 an effort had been made to arrive at a series of rules for neutrals through the Declaration of London, which forbade paper blockades, denied the continuous voyage, and stated that only war materials could be seized as contraband by the belligerents. From the standpoint of international law as expressed by the Declaration of London, the United States was as free to trade in noncontraband with the Central Powers as with the Allies.

But the British government had never ratified the Declaration of London, and during the war it revealed that it had no intention of living up to its provisions. England, fighting for its very existence, was determined that its seapower would not be weakened by any theoretical considerations of how it should employ its strongest weapon.

Throughout the period of American neutrality the British interfered with American trade to such a point that freedom of the seas became little more than a meaningless slogan. At the start of the war England established a long-range blockade that enabled it to intercept neutral vessels on the high seas, and by a series of Orders in Council it then widened the blockade's scope until it covered virtually all neutral commerce with the Continent. The contraband list was extended to include goods that had not previously been considered war matériel; the doctrine of continuous voyage was invoked to permit the seizure of goods bound for neutral countries that traded with Germany; and the North Sea was declared a military area, so that every neutral ship entering it was first funneled through an English port. To these measures were added others that convinced many Americans that England was as interested in destroying American commerce as in defeating Germany. The inspection of mail between the United States and Europe was interpreted by many American businessmen as a device employed by their English competitors for learning their trade secrets. American ships bound for neutral countries were detained in England for months, while English trade with the Continent increased. The publication of the British blacklist of American firms and individuals suspected of trading with Germany antagonized even the strongest pro-Allied supporters in the United States and moved Woodrow Wilson to state that it was the "last straw" and that he had almost reached the end of "his patience with Great Britain and the Allies."

Wilson never reached the end of his patience with Great Britain and the Allies; but his Administration, impelled by the need to uphold American rights and under terrific pressure from outraged American citizens, protested repeatedly to the British about violations of American neutrality. The British met the American protests with delay, long and involved legal arguments, the inference that Germany's behavior on the high seas was even more objectionable—and no change in policy. England had no other alternative but to hope that the United States would not resort to force to uphold its position; or, as Sir Edward Grey, the British Foreign Minister, later expressed it: "British action preceded British argument; the risk was that action might follow the American argument." Action never did follow American argument, for Wilson and his advisers, with the exception of Bryan, did not want to take any steps that might lessen the Allied chances of victory. Such men as Colonel E. M. House, Robert Lansing, and Walter Hines Page, the American ambassador in London, subordinated practically every other consideration to their desire for an Allied victory. House, as Wilson's personal representative, became an intimate of the leaders of France and England and shared their views on Germany and the war. Lansing from the first days of the war believed that it would only be a matter of time before the United States would have to join the Allies to insure Germany's defeat. Page was a wholehearted supporter of the English cause and some of his critics complained that he had become more English than American.

Although American officials made frequent protests to the British government for its violations of American neutrality, they never even suggested that the United States planned to take any drastic steps to uphold its position. Typical of the American attitude was a note sent to England in December, 1914, which asked the English not to interfere with American trade "unless such interference is manifestly an imperative necessity to protect their national safety, and then only to the extent that it is a necessity." Moreover, Page and House were willing to assist English officials in replying to the American notes. After the war Sir Edward Grey wrote that Page's advice and suggestions "were of the greatest value in warning us when to be careful or encouraging us when we could safely be firm." American diplomatic protests were frequently designed for home consumption rather than to bring England to an accounting. After the war Lansing wrote that the notes that were

> *sent were long and exhaustive treatises which opened up new subjects of discussion rather than closing those in controversy. Short and emphatic notes were dangerous. Everything was submerged in verbosity. It was done with deliberate purpose. It insured continuance of the controversies and left the questions unsettled.*

The Wilson Administration overlooked British violations of American neutral rights, but it insisted that Germany scrupulously observe the letter of international law. German-American relations were marked by a comparative absence of controversy until February 4, 1915, when Germany announced that all the waters "surrounding Great Britain and Ireland including the whole English Channel are hereby declared to be comprised within the seat of war and that all enemy merchant vessels found in those waters after the eighteenth instant will be destroyed." Six days later the United States government stated that Germany would be held to "strict accountability" for any injury to American lives or property; for the American government contended that its protection extended to American citizens traveling on belligerent ships in a war zone and insisted that the Germans conform to the rules that covered surface raiders by refraining from sinking any merchant ship until they had searched it and provided for the safety of its passengers and crew. The Germans, however, realizing that their acceptance of the American arguments would destroy the effectiveness of the U-boat, refused to alter their original plan beyond assuring the United States that it was "very far indeed from the intention of the German Government . . . to destroy neutral lives and neutral property."

The refusal of either the American or German governments to retreat from their original stands on the question of submarine warfare soon produced a series of incidents that brought relations between the two countries to the breaking point. On March 28, 1915, Leon C. Thrasher, an American citizen, lost his life when the British ship *Falaba* was torpedoed. On April 28 the *Cushing*, an American ship, was attacked by a German seaplane, and on May 1 the American tanker *Gulflight* was torpedoed with the loss of its captain and two of its crew members. The American people had hardly had time to recover from the shock of these events when news was received that on May 7 the British liner *Lusitania* had been torpedoed off the Irish coast and that the 1,198 drowned included 128 Americans. German protests that the ship was carrying munitions and that German advertisements in the press had warned Americans not to travel on the *Lusitania* could not obscure the fact that Germany had committed a colossal blunder. The American people were horrified at the ruthlessness of the German attack, and American papers referred to the disaster as "slaughter," "wholesale murder," and "piracy." Colonel House predicted that the United States would be "at war with Germany within a month," and Walter Hines Page wrote from London: "We live in hope that America will come in. . . ." Bryan alone among prominent government officials protested that England was "using our citizens to protect her ammunition."

With the sinking of the *Lusitania* the Wilson Administration was confronted by the problem of deciding whether to follow a course of impartial neutrality as advocated by Bryan or to accept Lansing's view that there should be one kind of neutrality for the Allies and another for Germany. Wilson was not prepared to lead the country into war against Germany in May, 1915, but there was no doubt in his mind that Lansing was right and Bryan wrong; and in his protest to the German government, he stated that American citizens had the right to travel "on lawful errands as passengers on merchant ships of belligerent nationality," and that submarine attacks on passenger ships violated all the accepted principles of humanity. Bryan, certain that the President's policy would lead to war, argued that the United States should either put off the day of reckoning with Germany as it had already done with England or remove the cause of the controversy by refusing to accept responsibility for Americans traveling on belligerent ships. When Wilson rejected both these alternatives, Bryan resigned from the cabinet to work outside the government for his concept of American neutrality.

Wilson's decision to accept Lansing's rather than Bryan's views on submarine warfare was the turning point in the history of American neutrality. Wilson, basing his stand on principle, insisted that the United States could not stand by while Germany violated the laws of civilization by murdering innocent American citizens. But Bryan, too, relied on principles and stated that Wilson's policy endangered American lives and neutrality. To Wilson's insistence that Germany was destroying American rights, Bryan replied that England was doing the same. There were, however, certain problems that Bryan refused to face. While it was true that Great Britain interfered with American commerce, it was also true that British policies never resulted in the loss of a single American life. Bryan could argue that Britain was merely in a more fortunate position than Germany in this respect, but the fact remained that the Germans killed Americans and the British did not. Bryan also refused to recognize the importance of strategic considerations in the conduct of the American policy of neutrality. Bryan's solution of the submarine problem would have aided Germany and jeopardized the Allied chances of success. Bryan was willing to ignore this result, but Wilson was not, for he felt that a German victory represented a threat not only to democracy but to the future security and independence of the United States. Lansing, who convinced Wilson, was himself convinced that an Allied defeat would expose the United States to attack and possible destruction. To Wilson and his principal advisers from the time of Bryan's resignation in June, 1915, until the American declaration of war in April, 1917, the possibility of a German victory was all important in determining the United States' policy toward the war in Europe. To Bryan it was an irrelevancy.

In the months following the sinking of the *Lusitania,* Wilson refused to retreat from his original stand on the question of submarine warfare. On August 19, the British liner *Arabic* was torpedoed and sunk by a German submarine. Two Americans went down with the *Arabic* and a complete diplomatic break between the United States and Germany was averted only when Bernstorff exceeded his instructions to inform the State Department that "liners will not be sunk by our submarines without warning and without safety of the lives of noncombatants, provided that the liners do not try to escape or offer resistance." After reprimanding Bernstorff for his unauthorized statement, the German government realized that it would have to support him, and on October 5 it assured the United States that the "orders issued by His Majesty the Emperor to the commanders of the German submarines . . . have been made so stringent that the recurrence of incidents similar to the *Arabic* case is considered out of the question." Despite the unequivocal language of these guarantees, German submarines continued to attack passenger vessels. On November 7, 1915, several Americans lost their lives when the Italian liner *Anconia* was sent to the bottom of the Mediterranean by an Austrian submarine, and on March 24, the *Sussex*, a French Channel steamer, was torpedoed and some of its American passengers were injured. The attack on the *Sussex*, which was a violation of the German government's assurances to the United States and its orders to its own submarine commanders, produced a diplomatic crisis comparable to the one that had followed the sinking of the *Lusitania*. On April 18, Lansing warned Germany that unless it abandoned its "relentless and indiscriminate warfare against vessels of commerce by the use of submarines," the United States could "have no choice but to sever diplomatic relations." Germany, which was not yet prepared to convert the United States into an enemy, on May 4, 1916, gave in to American pressure and announced that merchant vessels would "not be sunk without warning and without saving human lives" if the "United States will now demand and insist that the British Government shall forthwith observe the rules of international law." Although there was no noticeable change in Anglo-American diplomatic relations after May, 1916, Germany lived up to what came to be known as the *Sussex* pledge until the inauguration of its campaign of unrestricted submarine warfare in February of the following year.

Although Wilson had rejected Bryan's demand for strict neutrality and had adopted Lansing's firm policy toward Germany, he continued to share with his former Secretary of State the belief that it was the duty of the United States to attempt to end the war by peaceful mediation. In 1915 and again in the early part of 1916 he sent Colonel House on a peace mission, but House's efforts did little more than indicate the unwillingness of either set of belligerents to end the war on the other's terms. Wilson, however, still clung to the idea that peace without victory was as possible as it was desirable, and in December, 1916, he asked the belligerents to state the conditions on which they would conclude peace. The replies to Wilson's request demonstrated again that each nation put victory ahead of peace, for both the Allies and Germany made it clear that they did not plan to end the war until they had won it.

82. THE END OF NEUTRALITY

WILSON'S neutrality policy played a major part in the campaign of 1916, for the Democrats maintained that his proven ability to keep the United States out of war made it imperative that he be elected to a second term. To oppose Wilson, the Republicans selected

Charles Evans Hughes, an Associate Justice of the Supreme Court and a former Governor of New York. Since Roosevelt was back in the fold and Hughes was acceptable to both the party's conservative and liberal factions, the Republicans at first appeared capable of winning the election. But as the campaign progressed, Hughes' position became increasingly difficult, for criticisms of American foreign policy were liable to be interpreted as disloyalty, while little could be gained by attacking a reform program similar to the one that progressive Republicans had long urged. Wilson, on the other hand, could stand on his record in both domestic and foreign affairs. The election was exceedingly close, and until the final returns were in, it was thought that Hughes had won. But Wilson made an unexpectedly strong showing west of the Mississippi and was re-elected by a popular vote of 9,129,606 to 8,538,221 and an electoral vote of 277 to 254. The Democrats also retained their control over both branches of Congress.

While Wilson was campaigning for peace, he did not ignore the possibility that a prolongation of the conflict might eventually lead to American participation, and with considerable fanfare he launched his preparedness campaign in the summer of 1916. Despite marked opposition from the South and West, Congress passed bills providing for an increase in the size of the army and navy, an expansion of the merchant marine, and the establishment of a skeletal organization for the mobilization of American industry. Preparedness was a natural by-product of the Administration's neutrality policy, for after the attack on the *Sussex* the question of whether the United States would remain at peace or go to war was now left to the Germans rather than to the Americans. By his firm stand on German submarine warfare against merchant shipping, Wilson had placed the United States in a position where it could not avoid war if the Central Powers decided to break the rules he had laid down.

As early as August, 1916, the German high command had concluded that unrestricted submarine warfare alone could prevent Germany from being defeated by the British blockade. Although German officials realized that a violation of the *Sussex* pledge would inevitably lead to war with the United States, they were confident that their submarines would defeat England before the United States could give effective military assistance to the Allies. By 1917, Germany had completed its arrangements for a knockout blow, and on January 31, 1917, the German government informed the United States that its submarines would attack all merchant vessels within prescribed zones in the Atlantic and the Mediterranean.

The German announcement of unrestricted submarine warfare left Wilson with no choice, and on February 3 he announced to a cheering Congress that the United States had severed diplomatic relations with

Germany. Hoping that war could still be averted and that the United States might be able to ride out the crisis with a policy of armed neutrality, Wilson on February 26, 1917, asked Congress for the power to arm American merchant ships. When a Senate filibuster killed the bill, Wilson decided to act without congressional authorization. But neither Wilson nor any other American could now guide the course of American foreign policy, for after January, 1917, the German government alone could determine if and when the United States would go to war. And Germany soon left little doubt as to how the issue would be resolved. On March 1, 1917, the American press carried the news that the British had intercepted the so-called Zimmermann note, in which the German foreign minister had urged Mexico to take advantage of an American declaration of war by joining with Japan in an attack on the United States in order to recover the territory lost in the Mexican War of 1848. The American people at last were being forced to the conclusion that had been held by the interventionists since the outbreak of the war—that Germany was determined to destroy American independence. Only an incident was now needed to drive the United States into war, and during March it was supplied five times over as five American merchant vessels were torpedoed by German submarines. Wilson, concluding that Germany was waging an undeclared war against the United States, delivered his war message to Congress on April 2. Four days later, after overwhelming congressional approval, the United States was at war with Germany.

To the very last, Wilson had hoped that circumstances would not force him to lead the American people into war. But by March, 1917, circumstances were beyond his control. The only alternatives were peace and national degradation on the one hand, and war on the other. It was not an easy choice for a man of conscience, but Wilson consoled himself with the thought that the United States was joining the forces of democracy and humanity against those of evil and autocracy. The United States was not only fighting for its rights, but for the rights of all mankind, and in his address to Congress on April 2 he closed with an appeal for an armed crusade for

> *democracy, for the right of those who submit to authority to have a voice in their own Governments, for the rights and liberties of small nations, for a universal dominion of right by such a concert of free peoples as shall bring peace and safety to all nations and make the world itself at last free. To such a task we can dedicate our lives and our fortunes, everything that we are and everything that we have, with the pride of those who know that the day has come when America is privileged to spend her blood and her might for the principles that gave her birth and happiness and the peace which she has treasured. God helping her, she can do no other.*

Many Americans entered World War I sharing their President's conviction that they were fighting for justice and democracy. When the war was over, many of these Americans felt cheated. The condition of the world seemed worse than before they had attempted to reform it, and upon looking back to the spring of 1917, they were even able to convince themselves that they had been swept up by an emotional nationalism that had made them exaggerate the importance of the German attacks on their country. Only a few Americans were able to escape this postwar disillusion, for they alone had gone to war with their eyes open. Long before 1917 they had looked upon American participation in the conflict as a necessary move to preserve the security of the United States by maintaining the supremacy of the Anglo-French Entente in the world balance of power. Whether they were right or wrong in their analysis remains one of history's imponderables, but no one can assert that they failed to obtain their objective. American participation in World War I removed, if only temporarily, the German threat to the security of the United States.

83. THE WAR FRONT

THE AMERICAN people went to war in April, 1917, buoyed up by a patriotic fervor that permitted them to ignore the scope and difficulties of the task before them. But if the Americans were naive, they learned fast, and by the end of the war they had raised, equipped, and transported a modern army, paid higher taxes than ever before, and accepted a degree of control over industry, agriculture, and labor that a few years earlier they would have branded as socialistic. On the other hand, although American democracy was able to survive the new stresses and strains to which it was subjected during the war, the number of political prisoners in American jails in 1918 revealed that victory abroad had been attained by a retreat, if not a defeat, at home.

For a short time after April 6, 1917, many Americans still thought that belligerency would prove no more burdensome than friendly neutrality. These dreams of a soft war were dispelled by the early arrival in Washington of the Allied War Missions with the news that without immediate and unprecedented American aid their countries would be defeated. Most disturbing of all was the Allied insistence that the United States send an army as well as supplies to Europe. General Joffre, the French representative, announced that he had come to the United States to "discuss the sending of an American expeditionary force to France" and urged that "the American soldier come now." The suggestion that they might have to fight and die for victory came as a distinct shock to those Americans who had planned to contribute their country's resources rather than their lives to the Allied cause. The National Defense Act of June, 1916, had provided for a regular army of only 175,000, and the government, in contrast to the American people, had realized even before the arrival of the Allied Missions that the United States would have to resort to a draft to build an effective fighting force. When the Administration's conscription bill was introduced into Congress, opponents of the measure protested that it was unrealistic, for the United States did not have the ships to transport an army to France even if it could raise one. Others argued that compulsory military service was un-American. Champ Clark complained that his constituents in Missouri could see "precious little difference between a conscript and a convict," and Theodore Roosevelt, while supporting a draft for others, thought that he should be permitted to raise a volunteer unit as he had done in 1898. But this was no war for cavalry charges and adventurous amateurs, and on May 18, 1917, the Selective Service Act became law. By the end of the war, 2,810,296 of the 24,234,021 men between the ages of 18 and 45 who had registered at their local draft boards had been inducted into service; and through the draft and enlistments the United States was able to increase the combined strength of its army, navy, and the National Guard from 378,619 on April 2, 1917 to 4,791,127 on November 11, 1918. The draft met with little popular resistance. Only 3,989 inductees claimed exemption as conscientious objectors, and of this number only 450 preferred jail to "some form of service satisfactory to the Government."

By the end of the war the United States had shipped 2,079,880 men—not all of whom were fighting men—and more than 5,000,000 tons of supplies to Europe. The ships that transported these goods and men were organized in convoys and sailed under the protection of the United States Navy. The success of the convoy system, which was directed by Admiral Albert Gleaves, is revealed by the fact that German submarines did not sink a single American troopship on the eastward passage. Furthermore, by November, 1918, the American navy had approximately 300 ships manned by 75,000 men in European waters, all under the command of Admiral William S. Sims, whose headquarters were at London. The work of the fleet was supplemented by about 500 navy planes stationed in Europe. In addition to its convoy duties, the navy helped the British fleet maintain the blockade and played an important rôle in the relentless warfare against German U-boats. American warships, among other things, laid antisubmarine mines, attacked submarines with depth charges, engaged in mine sweeping, and participated in assaults on submarine bases. It was, moreover, largely because of the insistent demands of the United States that a mine barrage was laid across the northern outlet of the North Sea. The Navy's air arm provided assistance to convoys, took an active part in the antisubmarine campaign, and joined the army air force in raids on Germany.

General John J. Pershing, who was made commander in chief of the American Expeditionary Force, reached Paris in June, 1917. Active American participation in the European fighting first occurred in October, 1917, when a small detachment of United States troops took up positions in the vicinity of Toul at the southern end of the Western Front. Five months later (March 21, 1918), when the Germans launched the first of their spring offensives that were designed to win the war, there were approximately 300,000 American soldiers in France. In the next four months, the Germans undertook five major assaults, each one of which seriously imperiled the Allied armies. The American force, at Foch's insistence, was split up and used piecemeal to help stem the German attack. As a consequence, Americans saw action at Aisne (May 27-June 5), Noyon-Montdidier (June 9–15), and Champagne-Marne (July 15–18). In the last of these engagements American troops made a notable contribution to the ultimate defeat of Germany. In checking the German advance at the Marne, they prevented the enemy from taking Paris, and at Château-Thierry they successfully resisted one of the heaviest German assaults of the entire war. General Walther Reinhardt, German chief of staff, attributed his army's repulse at the Marne to "the unexpectedly stubborn and active resistance of fresh American troops."

Largely because of the fighting qualities that the Americans displayed on this occasion, Marshall Foch, who was in supreme command of the Allied armies, consented to the demand that Pershing had made from the outset—that an independent American command be created. Foch had been determined to have the relatively untrained American troops used as reserves and replacements for the British and French; but Pershing had felt that Foch's plan would undermine the morale of the American troops and produce an adverse effect on the war effort at home. Finally, in August, 1918, the First American Army was formed and assumed the responsibility for holding part of the Allied line; and by the end of the war, the Americans were occupying about one fourth of the front, or more than the British. Pershing had to rely on the Allies for much of his matériel, however. The procurement of adequate supplies for his troops was always one of Pershing's most pressing problems, and throughout the war the Americans were hampered by the comparative lack of tanks, airplanes, and artillery.

Following the German defeat at Champagne-Marne, the Allies began a series of co-ordinated counterattacks that were to last until the end of the war. The first assignment given the American army in the Allied offensive was the reduction of the St. Mihiel salient, a sixteen-mile-wide wedge that extended across the Meuse River southeast of Verdun and that had been held by the Germans for four years. On September 12, 500,000 Americans, assisted by French and British planes and using French artillery, began their attack. Within four days, they had—with the help of some French colonial troops—driven back the German forces and straightened out the front in the sector. Pershing now prepared to push forward and conquer Metz, but this project was vetoed by Foch, who had other plans for the American army. During the battle the Americans suffered 7,000 casualties, captured more than 400 guns, and took 16,000 prisoners.

After its victory at St. Mihiel, the American army was shifted to the west and began an advance down the Meuse River and through the Argonne Forest with Sedan as its ultimate objective. The Meuse-Argonne campaign, which began on September 26, was part of the general Allied attack that included the Somme offensive (August 8–November 11), the Oise-Aisne offensive (August 18–November 11), and the Ypres-Lys offensive (August 19–November 11). The American and French forces that participated in the forty-day Meuse-Argonne battle captured more than 25,000 prisoners, 874 cannon, and 3,000 machine guns. Of the 1,200,000 Americans engaged in the fighting, 117,000 became casualties. Although the war ended before the capture of Sedan, the American forces advanced steadily throughout the campaign, and the progress of the Meuse-Argonne attack along with the successful offensives on the other sectors of the front led directly to the German decision to ask for an armistice.

The major American military effort was confined to France, but an American regiment was dispatched to Italy in July, 1918, and two American divisions fought with the French in Belgium during the last month of the war. In addition, after the Russian Revolution and Lenin's *coup d'état*, a limited number of American troops joined the European Allies in widely separated attacks on Soviet Russia. Five thousand American soldiers fought in the Archangel-Murmansk campaign in 1918–19, and 9,000 Americans participated in the attacks on Vladivostock and eastern Siberia. It was not until April 1, 1920, that the last American troops were withdrawn from Russia's eastern-most possessions.

During World War I, 1,400,000 American soldiers were on overseas duty. In the course of the fighting, the Americans had captured 1,400 guns, taken 44,000 prisoners, and destroyed 755 enemy airplanes. At the same time, 48,909 Americans were killed in battle, 237,135 were wounded, 2,913 were reported missing in action, 4,434 were captured, and 56,991 died of disease.*

* Russian battle deaths were 1,700,000; German, 1,600,000; French, 1,385,000; British, 900,000; Austro-Hungarian, 800,000.

84. THE HOME FRONT

ALTHOUGH only a comparatively small percentage of the American population had to fight in the war, every American had to help pay for it. The Department of the Treasury put the direct cost of the war to the United States up to October, 1919, at $32,830,000,000. Of this amount approximately one third was contributed by American taxpayers, while $21,326,777,000 was raised by four Liberty Loans in 1917–18 and a Victory Loan in 1919. Profiting from the experiences of the European belligerents earlier in the war and Jay Cooke's spectacular success in the Civil War, the Administration decided to sell its bonds directly to the individual buyer and to attempt to reach small as well as large investors. All five bond sales, each of which was oversubscribed, were put across by the traditional sales methods of American business enterprise. States were assigned quotas and encouraged to compete with one another; volunteers of all kinds, from Wall Street bankers to Boy Scouts, aided in the work; rallies were held in public squares; captured war matériel was exhibited with appropriate slogans; full page advertisements were inserted in the press; ministers preached "Liberty loan sermons"; stage stars sold bonds to their audiences; prominent Americans toured the country urging greater contributions; and the manufacture and distribution of "Liberty loan posters" became a major industry. Those who otherwise might not have bought bonds frequently did so under the impact of social pressure. A German-sounding name, a guilty conscience about a draft exemption, or a desire to keep up with the Joneses were probably as effective methods of bond selling as all the stratagems of the American advertising industry.

The difference between the total cost of the war and the proceeds from the bond sales was made up by taxation. New duties were imposed on every form of luxury from chewing gum to Pullman berths, but the bulk of the additional revenue during the war was produced by increased taxes on incomes and business profits. When the United States entered the war the basic income-tax rate was 2 per cent and the maximum surtax 13 per cent. Under the War Revenue Act of October, 1917, the basic rate was raised to 4 per cent and the maximum surtax to 50 per cent. Provision was also made for a 6 per cent tax on corporations and an excess profits tax of 20 to 60 per cent on the business earnings of individuals and corporations. Increased expenditures during the second year of American participation in the war necessitated a further upward revision; and in September, 1918, the basic income tax was raised to 12 per cent, the highest surtax to 65 per cent, and the excess profits tax to a range of 35 to 70 per cent. Of the more than $32,000,000,000 raised by the government for the prosecution of the war, $10,338,000,000 were advanced to the Allies as loans, and the remainder was employed to meet the costs of the American war effort.

When the United States entered the war, the task of organizing the American economy for victory was undertaken by the Council of National Defense, which had been established by Congress in 1916 as part of the preparedness campaign. In the months that followed the American declaration of war, the council, which consisted of six cabinet members and advisers from labor and industry, assigned the management of the American war economy to a series of especially created agencies, such as the War Industries Board, the Food Administration, the War Trade Board, the Railroad Administration, the War Shipping Administration, and a host of others that covered practically every phase of American wartime life. As the war progressed, it became increasingly apparent that the efficiency of the Council of National Defense and its subordinate agencies was being impaired by the failure to provide for the centralization of both authority and responsibility. By the spring of 1918, when the war in Europe was approaching its climax, the hodgepodge of conflicting wartime bureaus was seriously threatening the ability of the United States to supply its troops at the front, and the government was forced to recognize that it would have to overhaul its entire wartime organization. On March 18, 1918, the War Industries Board was made an autonomous agency with almost limitless authority over American industrial life and was placed under the chairmanship of Bernard Baruch, who was responsible only to the president. Two months later, Congress passed the Overman Act, which granted the president the power to abolish old agencies and create new ones, to use money for whatever purposes he thought necessary and "to utilize, co-ordinate, or consolidate any executive or administrative commissions, bureaus, agencies, offices, or officers now existing by law."

The reorganization of the War Industries Board converted Bernard Baruch into a virtual tsar over American industrial enterprise. For the duration of the war no part of the American economy escaped Baruch's influence, and under his direction the War Industries Board fixed the prices of military and civilian goods, standardized industrial products, granted priorities to some firms and withheld them from others, compelled "nonessential" industries to convert to war production, assumed charge of all the government's purchases, and undertook a program for the conservation of the country's resources. While these measures often proved strong medicine to a people bred on economic individualism, critics could be silenced by an appeal to their patriotism. Moreover, the efficacy of a planned economy was soon demonstrated by the results, for during the last months of the war American factories poured forth an uninterrupted stream of goods for the armies of the United States and its allies.

To insure the continued production of American industry the government also had to take unprecedented steps to conserve and allocate the American fuel supply. Soon after the United States entered the war, increased demand for coal, a shortage of freight cars, and the flow of miners to the armed services and higher paying jobs combined to produce a serious fuel shortage. To meet the crisis the President in August, 1917, established the Fuel Administration, which, under the chairmanship of President Harry A. Garfield of Williams College, assumed responsibility for the production and distribution of coal and petroleum products. Fuel consumption was reduced by the inauguration of daylight saving time, the temporary closing of nonessential industrial plants, and an informal but effective rationing system that included "fuelless Mondays" and "gasless Sundays" for the nation's automobile users. Under the supervision of the Fuel Administration drastic methods were also employed to increase coal production during the war. Submarginal mines were brought into operation; more efficient mining methods were introduced; and the relations between miners and mine owners were placed under government supervision.

Although the government's control over industrial production was largely confined to regulatory measures, the need for haste in the delivery of American soldiers and goods to Europe compelled it to take over entirely the operation of the country's transportation and communication facilities. Five days after the American declaration of war, railroad officials representing 631 lines set up the Railroads' War Board as a voluntary association for the elimination of competition for the duration of the war; but within eight months the administration of American railroads had become so chaotic that the Atlantic ports were receiving practically no shipments from the west, the railroad executives were begging the government for assistance, and a member of the Interstate Commerce Commission was complaining that the "element of self-interest . . . is a persistent factor in postponing and resisting measures that seek . . . to secure transportation results as a whole." By the end of 1917 the situation was menacing the entire American war effort, and Woodrow Wilson announced—to the joy of the owners, who had been losing money despite the tremendous increase in traffic—that the government would take over the nation's railroads. Under the direction of Secretary of the Treasury McAdoo, the railroads were operated as a unified system, were compensated on the basis of their earnings for the three years preceding June 30, 1917, and were far more efficiently administered than they had been under private enterprise. Before the end of the war, the Treasury Department also assumed responsibility for the management of express companies and inland water transportation, while the telephone, telegraph and cable services became adjuncts of the Post Office Department.

Overseas as well as domestic transportation facilities were taken over and managed by the government during the war. The control of American exports was placed under a single agency with the creation in October, 1917, of the War Trade Board; but a far more difficult problem than the regulation of American overseas trade was the task of finding additional ships to carry it. Although Woodrow Wilson had recommended as early as 1914 that the government build and operate its own fleet of merchant vessels, Congress had refused to act despite the proven ability of the German submarines to sink ships faster than the Allies could build them. It was not until September 7, 1916, that Congress established the United States Shipping Board with an appropriation of fifty million dollars for the purchase or construction of merchant ships. Following the American entry into the war, the Shipping Board set up an Emergency Fleet Corporation to build, buy, and commandeer an American merchant marine. Under the successive administrations of General George W. Goethals and Charles M. Schwab, the Emergency Fleet Corporation seized enemy vessels in American ports, bought neutral vessels, took over the operation of American private shipping, and built four enormous shipyards with ninety-four ways for the construction of new ships. By September 1, 1918, the Shipping Board controlled 8,693,579 tons of merchant shipping—a figure, however, that testified to the Fleet Corporation's ability to lay its hands on practically everything that would float rather than to the speed with which it built ships. A month before the end of the war only 465,454 tons of shipping had been completed under the direction of the Fleet Corporation, and the fabulous Hog Island shipyard with its eighty miles of railroad and 250 buildings did not deliver its first ship to the government until three weeks after the armistice had been signed.

Although the government exercised what amounted to the power of life and death over American business enterprise during the war, few business firms suffered because of the government's policies, and under government control most of them enjoyed the most prosperous years of their existence. Despite the increase in taxes and the government's attempts at price fixing, several corporations made unprecedented profits during the war. In 1918, ten steel companies had profits ranging from 30 to 319 per cent of their investments. The profits of the four leading meat-packing concerns rose from an average of $19,000,000 during 1912–14 to $68,000,000 after the United States entered the war. In 1917, twenty-one copper companies earned 24 per cent on their investment, while in the same year the profits after taxes of forty-eight lumber companies were 17 per cent and those of 106 refining companies 21 per cent.

In part the increased earnings of American business enterprise were due to the buyers' market that prevailed during the war years, but in other instances they were the direct result of official laxity. Several key positions in the wartime organization for the control of the American economy were held by dollar-a-year men, who served the government for virtually nothing while continuing to receive large salaries from private corporations for which they formerly had worked and with which they frequently had to deal as government representatives. On occasion some dollar-a-year men revealed that their loyalties were with their private employers rather than the taxpayers, and in at least one instance—that of aircraft production—the American war effort was seriously impeded by the maladministration of a dollar-a-year man. The government also facilitated war profiteering by the device it employed for letting contracts. Because the War Industries Board did not want production delayed by prolonged negotiations over terms with contractors, it abandoned the traditional practice of competitive bidding for the cost-plus contract, which guaranteed the firm in question a flat profit ranging from 2½ to 15 per cent of the cost of production. By padding their costs, several contractors were able to obtain proportionately larger profits. There is little doubt that businessmen as a class were as patriotic as any other group of Americans, but this point cannot obscure the fact that some of them were willing to put a price on their patriotism.

An integral part of the government's plan of industrial mobilization was its program for the elimination of management-labor strife during the war. Although the Wilson Administration had won the support of a large segment of organized labor with the passage of the Clayton and Adamson Acts, American workers were far from satisfied with their lot during the period of American neutrality. Wages in 1916 were 6 per cent higher than in 1913, but prices had risen approximately 50 per cent during the same period. Moreover, the huge wartime profits of American industry convinced many workers that they deserved a larger share in the national income and that they should use the strategic position given them by war conditions to gain advantages that had been denied them in peace. Finally, left-wing or direct-action labor organizations such as the Industrial Workers of the World, which condemned the war as an imperialist struggle fought for the benefit of the nation's financiers and industrialists, refused on more than one occasion to give the government their support.

On March 9, 1917, Samuel Gompers, as the spokesman for conservative labor in the United States, announced that the American workingman was ready to stand behind his government in a war against Germany. But Gompers, who was an advisory member of the Council of National Defense, did not give the Wilson Administration a blank check, for he demanded that the government in return for labor's co-operation curb war profiteering among businessmen, prevent employers from crushing the labor movement under the guise of patriotism, and set up some machinery that would enable the workers to preserve their rights without recourse to strikes. In the formulation of its wartime labor program, the government made an effort to fulfill these conditions. In March, 1918, the War Labor Conference Board, which had been set up as an advisory body by the Secretary of Labor two months earlier, drew up a set of principles that guided the Administration for the remainder of the war. In return for a no-strike pledge, labor was assured of the right to "organize in trade-unions and to bargain collectively through chosen representatives"; the maintenance of existing standards in union shops; "safeguards and regulations for the protection of the health and safety of workers"; "the basic eight hour day in all cases in which existing law requires it"; and in all other cases the settlement of the question of hours "with due regard to governmental necessities and the welfare, health, and proper comfort of the workers"; and a "living wage" with "minimum rates of pay . . . to insure the subsistence of the worker and his family in health and comfort." A National War Labor Board was established under the chairmanship of former President Taft and Frank P. Walsh to "settle by mediation and conciliation controversies arising between employers and workers," while "questions involving the distribution of labor, wages, hours, and working conditions" were handled by a War Labor Policies Board headed by Professor Felix Frankfurter of Harvard University.

Through the government's wartime labor program the mass of American workingmen made greater gains than in any previous period in American history. By the end of the war, wages were 30 per cent above the 1913 level, and real wages approximated those of 1916. The length of the working day was also whittled down during the war, and by 1918, 48.6 per cent of all American workers were employed on a forty-eight-hour week. Finally, the American Federation of Labor with the support of the government increased its membership from 1,996,004 in 1913 to 2,726,478 in 1918. Radical labor, on the other hand, suffered a severe setback during the war. In June, 1917, 1,186 striking members of the I.W.W. at the Bisbie, Arizona, copper mines were deported by the owners to Columbus, New Mexico, where they were interned; and for the remainder of the war the union's leaders were hounded and thrown into jail by the Department of Justice. Even conservative labor's advances proved to be only an interlude made possible by a friendly government. Few of its wartime gains had come as a result of its own efforts, superior organization, or class solidarity; and when the Wilson Administration was followed by one that was hostile to organized labor, right-wing labor, with few resources of its own, fell an easy prey to militant employers who were bent on destroying the American labor movement.

Farmers and housewives, as well as workers and businessmen, were mobilized for victory by the government, for the need to increase agricultural production and reduce domestic food consumption soon became one of the most pressing problems of the war. Since Russian food supplies were shut off and a large part of the most fertile regions of France were devastated, unprecedented demands were placed on the United States for foodstuffs for the Allies and the American armed forces. Under the slogan "Food Will Win the War" the government set to work to increase the output of the nation's farms and to cut down the consumption of those essentials that were most needed abroad. As early as May, 1917, Herbert Hoover, who had been widely acclaimed for his work as chairman of the Commission for Belgian Relief, was named Food Administrator, and three months later he was given as much authority over the production and distribution of American agricultural products as was eventually exercised by Bernard Baruch over industry. By the end of the war the Food Administrator had assumed control over the shipments of all American foodstuffs, taken over and resold the supply of imported raw sugar, licensed approximately a quarter million food distributors, and established a Grain Corporation that purchased the entire wheat crops of 1917 and 1918 at fixed prices.

The American farmer did not have to be urged to increase production, for the assurance of high prices and the demands of patriotism provided him with all the incentive that was necessary. During the war years American agricultural production increased 24 per cent, while the annual wheat crop rose from 636,655,000 to 967,790,000 bushels from 1917 to 1919, and wheat acreage increased from 45,000,000 to 75,000,000 acres. This phenomenal rise in production was obtained, however, at a considerable price to the farmers, for in the postwar years they were to discover that they had mortgaged their future for wartime prosperity. With the easy credit facilities provided by the government, many staple producers expanded their holdings and assumed an inflated debt burden that they were unable to carry after the European demand fell off. Moreover, the war, by hastening the trend toward one-crop specialization, lessened the farmer's flexibility and made it that much more difficult for him to meet the needs of a changing peacetime market. Finally, by ploughing up millions of acres of the Great Plains, the farmer prepared the way for a harvest of dust a few years later. By the 1920's, when the European market had collapsed, the American farmer, who had boasted during the war that he had fed the Allies, frequently found it difficult to feed himself.

In his program for the reduction of the domestic consumption of food, Hoover preferred to rely on exhortation rather than compulsion. European rationing systems were rejected for "wheatless Mondays," "meatless Tuesdays," and a propaganda campaign that preached the "gospel of the clean plate" and urged Americans to eat "whales, porpoises, and dolphins" and "less wheat, meat, milk, fats, sugar." Consumers were also asked to increase the supply of foodstuffs, and with government encouragement suburbanites planted war gardens, and women volunteered

ILLUSTRATIONS FROM *Wide World Photos*

WOODROW WILSON

HENRY CABOT LODGE

ELIHU ROOT

CHARLES EVANS HUGHES

AMERICAN FIGURES IN WORLD POLITICS

Life

"SAY, WHERE D'YA WANT THIS?"

Harding indicates the attic, Cox the living room.

The Bettmann Archive

WONDER IF IT'S STORMPROOF?

The San Francisco Chronicle *worries about the seams in the League umbrella.*

Life

BARGAIN DAY IN WASHINGTON—THE HARDING ADMINISTRATION

for a land army to relieve the farmers' labor shortage. The mass of Americans willingly supported the whole of the government's program for food administration, and the steady increase in the number and size of American food shipments to Europe testified to the effectiveness of supplementing close government supervision over some details of the program with appeals for voluntary co-operation.

The government not only attempted to regulate the American economy during the war, but it also sought to direct and channel American thinking along those lines that it considered most conducive to American victory. On April 14, 1917, eight days after the American declaration of war, the Committee of Public Information was established with George Creel, a former newspaperman, as its chairman. Creel always maintained that his committee was in "no degree . . . an agency of censorship, a machinery of concealment or repression," but that it was waging a battle of words in a "fight for the *minds* of men, for 'the conquest of their convictions' " and that the "battle-line ran through every home in the country." Creel's audience was not, however, confined to the United States, for "every conceivable means was used to reach the foreign mind with America's message"; and in 1920, Creel stated that "before this flood of publicity the German misrepresentations were swept away in Switzerland, the Scandinavian countries, Italy, Spain, the Far East, Mexico, and Central and South America."

To present the government's interpretation of the United States' rôle in the war, Creel enlisted the support of businessmen, politicians, professors, college presidents, poets, novelists, artists, photographers, essayists, and numerous others who defy classification. Nor was Creel's assertion that there was "no medium of appeal that we did not employ" an exaggeration. The committee published more than fifty pamphlets in English and other languages and distributed them to more than 75,000,000 people in the United States; issued the *Official Bulletin of the United States,* a daily newspaper for government employees, with a circulation of 100,000; distributed "news" to more than 1,600 newspapers including the foreign-language press; organized the Four Minute Men with 75,000 speakers who made 755,190 speeches, "every one having the carry of shrapnel"; used 1,438 different drawings in its campaign of "pictorial publicity"; established the Division of Women's War Work, which "prepared and issued the information of peculiar interest to the women of the United States"; distributed movies bearing titles such as "Pershing's Crusaders" and "America's Answer"; and issued more than 200,000 stereopticon slides. Creel always insisted that he was interested only in publicizing the truth; but the line between education and indoctrination was a thin one, and Creel's office was responsible for more than one fabrication. Furthermore, the tendency of the Committee on Information, like all propaganda agencies, to attribute nothing but evil to the enemy and nothing but good to its own cause heightened the feelings of hate and distrust that permeated American society during the war years.

In its efforts to shape the American mind, the government did not limit itself to arguments, for many of those who refused to agree with the official stand on American policy were persecuted and in several instances sent to jail. In short, many of those that the government could not convince it arrested. While every nation at war must take certain precautions to insure its internal security, there is no evidence that the government's program of wartime thought control contributed in any appreciable measure to the safety of the United States. On the other hand, there can be no doubt that it put a premium on conformity, destroyed the civil rights of many of its citizens, and created a mass hysteria that was as serious a threat to American democracy as Germany's military forces. While President Wilson urged freedom for the world, his own government systematically hacked away at the very bases of freedom in the United States.

The government's campaign to persecute and prosecute those who refused to accept its views was carried out under two statutes enacted during the war. The Espionage Act of June 15, 1917, provided:

> *Whoever, when the United States is at war, shall . . . convey false reports or false statements with intent to interfere with the operation or success of the military or naval forces of the United States, or to promote the success of its enemies, or . . . cause . . . insubordination, disloyalty, mutiny, or refusal of duty, in the military or naval forces of the United States or shall willfully obstruct . . . the recruiting or enlistment service of the United States . . . shall be punished by a fine of not more than $10,000 or imprisonment for not more than twenty years, or both.*

Under the terms of the Sedition Act, which became law on May 16, 1918, Americans were forbidden to "willfully utter, print, write, or publish any disloyal, profane, scurrilous or abusive language about the form of government of the United States, or the military or naval forces of the United States, or the uniform of the Army or Navy of the United States"; or to "urge, incite or advocate any curtailment of production in this country of any thing or things, product or products, necessary or essential to the prosecution of the war."

Armed with the sweeping powers provided by national and state legislation, Federal and local officials undertook to purge the country of its disloyal elements. The Post Office Department banned from the mails the *Masses,* the socialist *Milwaukee Leader,* Thorstein Veblen's *Imperial Germany and the Industrial Revolution,* the *Nation,* and a magazine that quoted Jefferson on Irish independence. The Justice Department, however, outdid every other branch of the government in its determination to rid the country of what it considered subversive and traitorous elements. Its Bureau of Investigation made illegal arrests, confiscated private papers, raided newspaper offices, destroyed private property, and held prisoners without bail. People were sent to jail, not for overt acts, but for opinions uttered "in the heat of private altercation, on a railroad train, in a hotel lobby, or at that battle ground of disputation, a boarding-house table."* Men and women were imprisoned for saying that the war should be financed by higher taxes instead of bond sales and for criticising the Red Cross or Y.M.C.A. One woman was sentenced to ten years in jail for stating: "I am for the people, and the government is for the profiteers." A movie producer received a similar sentence for releasing a film that depicted English soldiers killing women and children in the American Revolution. The Justice Department also enlisted the support of "hundreds of thousands" of Americans in a hunt for German spies. John Lord O'Brian, assistant to the Attorney General during the war, stated in 1919 that these amateur spy chasers did little but add to the "war hysteria and war excitement" and that "no other cause contributed so much to the oppression of innocent men as the systematic and indiscriminate agitation against what was claimed to be an all-pervasive system of German espionage."

During the war and the years immediately following it, left-wing labor groups and other radicals were the principal targets of the government's loyalty program. On September 5, 1917, agents of the Department of Justice made simultaneous raids on I.W.W. headquarters throughout the nation. In the trials that followed, one hundred Wobblies, including Big Bill Haywood, were given prison sentences that ranged from one to twenty years and were fined a total of $2,300,000. By February, 1918, Haywood estimated that there were 2,000 members of the I.W.W. in jail. The Socialists fared little if any better as Eugene V. Debs, Victor Berger, and several others were sent to prison because of their refusal to give the war their moral support. If no other evidence were available, the number of men and women who lost their freedom because of the unpopularity of their ideas was sufficient proof that the New Freedom was dead and that the war had killed it.

Although the American war effort was not without blemishes, the fact remains that it achieved its immediate objective. Within sixteen months a peace-loving, heterogeneous people had raised, shipped, and supplied an army that proved the decisive factor in the final German defeat. This success, however, represented only one half of the task that the United States had undertaken, and within a short time the American people were to learn that winning the peace could be even more difficult than winning the war.

* Zechariah Chafee, Jr.: *Free Speech in the United States* (Cambridge, Mass. Harvard University Press, 1941), p. 53.

85. THE FIGHT FOR A JUST PEACE

THROUGHOUT the war Wilson never permitted the peoples of the world to forget the ideals for which he thought the United States and its allies were fighting. In numerous speeches, which George Creel's Committee on Public Information distributed to Allied and neutral countries and even behind the enemy's lines, the American President proclaimed that the United States was waging war against the German government rather than the German people and that peace would mean neither annexations by the victors nor the payment of reparations by the losers. But Wilson went beyond the immediate question of the fate of the Central Powers, for he insisted that following the war, international anarchy would have to give way to international order and that the nations of the world would have to set up and join an organization to maintain peace. While Wilson's peace proposals proved an invaluable Allied military weapon in that they doubtless lessened the will of the German masses to continue the war, they were not an accurate summary of Allied war aims.

Even before the American entrance into the war, Wilson in a speech to the Senate on January 22, 1917, announced his opposition to a "peace forced upon the loser, a victor's terms imposed upon the vanquished," for it "would be accepted in humiliation, under duress, at an intolerable sacrifice, and would leave a sting, a resentment, a bitter memory upon which terms of peace would rest, not permanently, but only as upon quicksand." For a punitive peace Wilson would substitute a "peace without victory" and "a peace between equals." Approximately a year later Wilson was ready to fill in the details of his proposals for an enduring peace, and on January 8, 1918, he announced his Fourteen Points:

I. *Open covenants of peace, openly arrived at. . . .*

II. *Absolute freedom of . . . the seas . . . in peace and in war. . . .*

III. *The removal, so far as possible, of all economic barriers and the establishment of an equality of trade conditions among all the nations consenting to the peace and associating themselves for its maintenance.*

IV. *Adequate guarantees given and taken that national armaments will be reduced to the lowest point consistent with domestic safety.*

V. *A free, open-minded, and absolutely impartial adjustment of all colonial claims, based upon a strict observance of the principle that in determining all such questions of sovereignty the interests of the populations concerned must have equal weight with the equitable claims of the government whose title is to be determined.*

VI. *The evacuation of all Russian territory. . . .*

VII. *Belgium . . . must be evacuated and restored, without any attempt to limit the sovereignty which she enjoys in common with all other free nations.*

VIII. *All French territory should be freed and the invaded portions restored, and the wrong done to France by Prussia in 1871 in the matter of Alsace-Lorraine . . . should be righted. . . .*

IX. *A readjustment of the frontiers of Italy should be effected along clearly recognizable lines of nationality.*

X. *The peoples of Austria-Hungary, whose place among the nations we wish to see safeguarded and assured, should be accorded the freest opportunity of autonomous development.*

XI. *Rumania, Serbia, and Montenegro should be evacuated; occupied territories restored; . . . and the relations of the several Balkan states to one another determined by friendly counsel along lines of allegiance and nationality. . . .*

XII. *The Turkish portions of the present Ottoman Empire should be assured a secure sovereignty, but the other nationalities which are now under Turkish rule should be assured an undoubted security of life and an absolutely unmolested opportunity of autonomous development, and the Dardanelles should be permanently opened as a free passage to the ships and commerce of all nations under international guarantees.*

XIII. *An independent Polish state should be erected which should include the territories inhabited by indisputably Polish populations, which should be assured a free and secure access to the sea. . . .*

XIV. *A general association of nations must be formed under specific covenants for the purpose of affording mutual guarantees of political independence and territorial integrity to great and small states alike.*

Wilson and many of his supporters in both Europe and the United States assumed that in his pronouncements on the settlements that would follow the war he was speaking for both the Allied governments and the American people; but Wilson, although his prestige was enormous during the last stages of the war, had neither an Allied nor an American mandate as a peacemaker, and if his peace plans were to succeed, he had to win the Allied leaders over to his program and to convince the voters of his own country that his proposals would not jeopardize what many considered the national interests of the United States. Both tasks proved far more arduous than Wilson had anticipated.

The struggle over Wilson's proposals at the Paris Peace Conference has frequently been described as a clash of personalities. According to this view, Wilson, a noble idealist, was pitted against the wily, pragmatic Clemenceau, while Lloyd George played the part of the clever politician, and Orlando went home in a huff. In reality the contest at Paris was as much a conflict of national aspirations as an argument among four high-spirited men. Italy entered the war for loot, and as soon as it became apparent that all its demands would not be met, the Italian representatives withdrew from the conference. Clemenceau and Lloyd George were the spokesmen of democracies, and the electorates of both countries had clearly indicated that they favored a harsh peace. The French and English people had been through more than four years of death, misery, and destruction, while Germany had emerged from the war physically intact. Although the French and English masses could admire Wilson's peace aims in the abstract, they could not accept them as a substitute for the punishment of the enemy and a guarantee against future German aggression. Wilson offered them world order and international good will; they demanded revenge and security. Lloyd George had received the overwhelming support of England's voters when he promised to hang the Kaiser, and Clemenceau was undoubtedly speaking for most Frenchmen when he demanded that Germany be divested of the Rhineland and forced to pay reparations.

Prior commitments, as well as the wishes of their countrymen, accounted for the opposition of the Allied leaders to the Fourteen Points. During the first years of the war, England, France, Italy, Rumania, and Japan had negotiated a series of secret treaties that provided for the partition of the German and Austrian empires. Although Wilson undoubtedly knew of the existence of these secret treaties, he had made no effort to induce the Allies to renounce them when the United States entered the war. And when the war was over, neither the Allied statesmen nor their constituents were prepared to abandon these territorial gains for the American President's version of a peace without victory.

Wilson was placed at a further disadvantage in his negotiations with the Allied leaders because he arrived in Paris without the full support of the American voters. Wilson, who had proved himself a master politician when he pushed his domestic reform program through Congress, failed to keep his political fences in repair after the United States entered the war. Overcome with a sense of his own moral superiority and convinced of the advantages of his own peace proposals, he preferred to ignore rather than recognize any domestic opposition. On the surface, at least, his task should not have been impossible. During the early years of the war in Europe, Republican leaders had apparently favored some form of world organization. The League to Enforce Peace, which had been founded in 1915 and had soon become the most prominent of private societies established to promote peace through international co-operation and control, had received strong Republican support.

William Howard Taft served as its president, and in 1916, Henry Cabot Lodge had publicly endorsed its objectives. But in 1918, the chances of a Republican victory in the midterm elections took precedence over the demand for international planning, and the party's high command decided to capitalize on the traditional isolationism of its Midwestern agrarian supporters and the general war weariness of all voters by attacking the President's foreign policy. Wilson replied on October 24, 1918, by requesting the election of a Democratic Congress as proof of American loyalty. The Republicans, quick to recognize the extent of Wilson's blunder, pointed out that they as well as the Democrats had demonstrated their loyalty with their lives and their money, and on election day enough American voters ignored the President's request to give the Republicans control of both the House and Senate. Despite the success of these tactics, Wilson made no move to blunt or deflect the Republican offensive. He called on no prominent Republicans for assistance in the formulation of America's peace proposals, took no leading Republican politicians with him to Paris, and invited no member of the Senate to join the American delegation to the peace conference.

The Paris Peace Conference, which convened on January 18, 1919, fell far short of the ideal envisioned by Wilson. The legacy of centuries of hypernationalism, imperialism, and balance-of-power politics could not be uprooted by appeals to reason, and in the end the very forces in international society that Wilson had hoped to destroy wrecked his plans for a just peace. Moreover, the threat of both national and international chaos in many parts of the world put such a premium on speed that complex problems which had perplexed statesmen for generations had to be resolved in a matter of days or hours. Sometimes the extraordinary size of the conference militated against its efficiency and made it so unwieldy that there seemed no alternative but to substitute secret for open diplomacy. Long before the Germans were called in to sign the completed treaty on June 28, 1919, the plenary conference of the twenty-seven Allied and Associated Powers had become little more than a rubber stamp for decisions reached in advance by France, Great Britain, the United States, and Italy in either the Council of Ten or the Council of Four. Finally, the fear of communism conditioned many of the conference's most important decisions. Russia, in addition to the Central Powers, had been excluded from the deliberations at Paris, and in the minds of many delegates the need to thwart Soviet plans for a world revolution took precedence over any desire to draw up a program for lasting peace.

Despite the obstacles that confronted him at Paris, Wilson was able to have some of his ideas for the reorganization of world society incorporated into the peace treaty. Germany's former colonies were not annexed by the Allied powers, but held as mandates under the general supervision of the League of Nations. An attempt was made to apply the principle of self-determination to the formation of the new states in eastern Europe. While Wilson could not prevent the territorial aggrandisement of the victors, he did succeed in forestalling the Italian annexation of Fiume and the Japanese acquisition of the Shantung peninsula; and Clemenceau abandoned French claims to the Rhineland in return for Wilson's promise of a treaty that stated that the United States would "come immediately" to the aid of France if there were "an unprovoked movement of aggression" by Germany. Most important of all, Wilson won the approval of the other delegates for the League of Nations and the inclusion of the League Covenant in the Treaty of Versailles.

The Covenant of the League of Nations, the first draft of which was drawn up in ten days by the League Commission under the chairmanship of Woodrow Wilson and presented to the peace conference on February 14, 1919, provided for a permanent Secretariat, Assembly, Council, Permanent Court of International Justice, and International Labor Office. The Assembly, which was to consist of representatives of all the member nations, was to be largely a deliberative and an advisory body. The Council, which was to be made up of delegates from the United States, Great Britain, France, Italy, Japan, and four other nations to be selected by the Assembly, was to be empowered to mediate disputes involving member states, act as a clearing house for the League's mandates, propose ways to prevent aggression, and formulate and implement plans for the "reduction of national armaments to the lowest point consistent with national safety." The Council was also to be authorized to establish a Permanent Court of International Justice, which would "hear and determine any dispute of an international character which parties thereto submit to it" and "give an advisory opinion upon any dispute or question referred to it by the Council or by the Assembly." Practically all decisions of the Council would require the unanimous approval of its members. The International Labor Office was to "endeavor to secure and maintain fair and humane conditions of labour for men, women, and children" and to have "general supervision over the execution of agreements with regard to the traffic in women and children, the traffic in opium and other dangerous drugs," and the "trade in arms and ammunition."

The Covenant contained numerous sections on the prevention and limitation of war. Aggression was specifically outlawed by Article X, which stated that the "members of the League [would] undertake to respect and preserve as against external aggression the territorial integrity and existing political independence of all Members of the League" and that if there were either threatened or actual aggression, the Council would "advise upon the means by which this obligation shall be fulfilled." Member states, moreover, pledged themselves to submit "any dispute likely to lead to a rupture" to the Council or to the Permanent Court of Arbitration. If a member of the League resorted to war in violation of the Covenant, all other League members were obliged to "subject it to the severance of all trade or financial relations, the prohibition of all intercourse between their nationals and the nationals of the covenant-breaking State, and the prevention of all financial, commercial, or personal intercourse between the nationals of the covenant-breaking State and the nationals of any other state, whether a Member of the League or not." The Council was also directed to recommend to the "several Governments concerned what effective military, naval or air force the Members of the League shall severally contribute to the armed forces to be used to protect the covenants of the League." Although the Covenant called for the abrogation of all international "obligations or understandings" that were inconsistent with its terms, it also contained a provision that sanctioned "treaties of arbitration or regional understandings like the Monroe Doctrine."

Although the Covenant of the League of Nations was made an integral part of the Treaty of Versailles, the settlements reached at Paris remained in almost all other respects a victors' peace. Germany was compelled to accept full responsibility for the war, pay reparations to the victors, abolish its fleet and army, relinquish its colonies, transfer Alsace-Lorraine to France and part of Silesia and Posen to Poland, consent to the French occupation of the Saar until 1935, and turn over the control of a large portion of its economy to the Allies. Germany's losses were the Allies' gains, for the provisions of the secret treaties that divided the spoils of war were in many instances incorporated into the Treaty of Versailles.

86. THE LOST PEACE

THE CONCESSIONS that were wrung from Wilson in return for support for the League produced a peace settlement that bore little resemblance to the program outlined in the Fourteen Points. The treaty contained a section on reparations that heightened rather than reduced international tensions and rivalries. It did not solve the problem of national boundaries in eastern Europe, and self-determination created as many minority problems as it solved. The League was designed to preserve world peace, but the Covenant furnished no workable formula for the reduction of national armaments. Although political peace depended on economic co-operation, no provision was made at Paris for the removal of trade barriers that separated the nations of the world. Despite the defects of the treaty, it remained the best that Wilson could obtain under existing circumstances, and many of his critics in the United States objected to the agreements reached at Paris for far less statesmanlike reasons.

The opposition that developed within the United States to the Treaty of Versailles included various groups of Americans who had few, if any, other points in common. Friends of Germany and many liberals thought the terms of the treaty too harsh. Irish-Americans feared that the Covenant would insure Ireland's continued subservience to England. Italian-Americans complained that the treaty deprived Italy of the fruits of victory. Some Republicans disliked a peace framed by Democrats. Many isolationists thought that the League would destroy American sovereignty by creating a world superstate.

Within the Senate there were four distinct groups that participated in the struggle over the ratification of the agreements reached at Paris. Many, but not all, Democratic senators thought that the Treaty and Covenant should be adopted without either major or minor changes. At the other extreme were a few "bitter enders" who were led by Senators William E. Borah of Idaho and Hiram Johnson of California and who were unalterably opposed to any kind of American participation in a world organization. Several Republicans, who joined Henry Cabot Lodge as strict reservationists, although unable to accept Borah's and Johnson's isolationist views, were equally determined to defeat any peace proposals presented to the Senate by Woodrow Wilson. A larger number of Republicans and a few Democrats, who became known as the mild reservationists, supported the Covenant in principle but favored certain changes that they believed necessary to insure the rights of the United States.

In most accounts of the defeat of the League of Nations in the Senate, Henry Cabot Lodge has been cast as the villain of the piece—a rôle that he may or may not deserve, but that does not necessarily explain all the events of the drama enacted in Washington during 1919–20. Although Lodge beyond a doubt loathed Woodrow Wilson with all the malevolence that some other Republicans were to reserve for the next Democratic occupant of the White House and although he was determined to use the League as a lever for partisan advantage, his approach was not altogether negative. Lodge was an ultranationalist who in general advocated the same kind of punitive peace that had been advanced by Clemenceau at Paris. He supported an American alliance with France, thought that the League and the Treaty should be considered separately, and approved of German reparations. Both Wilson and Lodge wished to prevent another war. While Wilson insisted that the way to preserve peace was to eliminate the causes of war, Lodge maintained that the threat of war could be removed only by making the victors so strong and the defeated so weak that Germany would neither dare nor be able to become an aggressor nation in the future. Both men could agree that Germany should never be permitted to start another war and that the United States should support a system of collective security, but they could not agree on the means for attaining these objectives. Wilson was an internationalist, Lodge, an interventionist; neither was an isolationist.

Since Borah, Johnson, and the other "bitter enders" were opposed to any type of American participation in European affairs, they were outside the main struggle in the Senate, and the real contest lay between the Wilson Democrats and the Lodge Republicans. Neither side was willing to compromise, and Lodge was prepared to resort to any tactics to block Senate approval of the League of Nations. He therefore joined forces with the bitter enders, who, although opposed to Lodge's interventionism, considered it a less immediate threat to American isolation than Wilson's internationalism. He directed a propaganda campaign against the President's foreign policy with funds supplied by Henry Clay Frick and Andrew Mellon, two Republican millionaires from Pennsylvania who were so hostile to Wilson's domestic reforms that they welcomed the opportunity to finance the plans for his downfall. Finally, Lodge skillfully employed parliamentary tactics to defeat the League with a flanking movement rather than a frontal attack.

Throughout the summer of 1919 the Senate Foreign Relations Committee, which had fallen under the control of the strict reservationists after the congressional elections of the preceding autumn, aroused considerable hostility to the President's peace program by conducting hearings that emphasized the divisive forces within the United States and erroneously created the impression of overwhelming American opposition to the League. In early September, Wilson, after urging the Senate to act on the treaty, undertook a speaking tour of the West in a final attempt to rally public opinion. On September 25, 1919, after a speech at Pueblo, Colorado, he suffered a stroke and returned to Washington a crippled and helpless man. He was confined to his room in the White House, where he was guarded and held incommunicado by his wife and physician. The United States was virtually without a chief executive; Wilson lost contact with the Democratic leadership in the Senate, and Henry Cabot Lodge put the finishing touches on his plans for defeating the Versailles Treaty by indirection.

The balance of power in the conflict between the Administration Senators and the strict reservationists lay with the mild reservationists, who were led by such prominent Republicans as Frank B. Kellogg, Knute Nelson of Minnesota, and C. L. McNary of Oregon. As the Administration Democrats and the mild reservationists between them had enough votes to ratify the treaty, Lodge's strategy was designed to prevent the two factions from joining forces. Lodge's original plan had been to mutilate the Covenant beyond recognition, but the forty-five amendments that he proposed were easily defeated by a coalition of the Democratic supporters of Wilson and the moderate Republicans. When this stratagem failed, Lodge abandoned the amendments, which would have changed the actual content of the treaty and required the approval of the other signatory powers, for fourteen reservations that were American interpretations of the Covenant. Since the fourteen reservations were acceptable to the mild reservationists, the success of Lodge's policy rested on his assumption that Wilson would not permit his Democratic followers to accept a treaty that included any reservations.

The famous fourteen reservations, which soon became the focal point of the struggle over the treaty in the Senate, did not change the meaning of the Covenant nor relieve the United States of any of its fundamental obligations to the League of Nations. They were, however, phrased in such a way as to create the impression that the United States would never give more than reluctant co-operation to the League. The reservations concerning the Monroe Doctrine and the American right to withdraw from the League merely repeated provisions in the Covenant. The reservation for Article X—a reservation responsible for more controversy than any other—stated that the United States would refuse to come to the aid of a League member attacked by another nation "unless in any particular case the Congress, which, under the Constitution, has the sole power to declare war . . . shall, in the exercise of full liberty of action, by act or joint resolution so provide." This reservation proved especially obnoxious to Wilson, but it was a simple statement of fact; for under the Constitution, Congress alone had the right to declare war.

The Lodge reservations were acceptable to all but the bitter enders, who were opposed to the League with or without changes, and the Wilson Democrats. The mild reservationists did not consider the reservations a threat to American participation in the League. Several prominent Republicans outside the Senate held a similar view, and the League to Enforce Peace endorsed the reservations. Before the Senate's final rejection of the treaty even the British government let it be known that it did not consider the reservations detrimental to the League. But Woodrow Wilson, as Lodge had anticipated, thought differently. He looked on the reservations as a denial of all that the League represented and a challenge to his own moral superiority. Sick and politically isolated, he ordered the Democratic senators to vote against the reservations. Party regularity did the rest, for by taking this stand Wilson ruled out compromise, missed his last chance for an alliance with the mild reservationists, and gave the victory to his archantagonist. To the very end Wilson persisted in believing that the choice lay between the treaty as he had presented it to the Senate and a treaty with the Lodge reservations. The votes in the Senate revealed the extent of Wilson's miscalculations. The alternatives were the treaty with reservations or no treaty at all.

On November 19, 1919, the Senate failed to ratify the treaty with the fourteen reservations by a vote of 39 to 55. The fifty-five Senators who voted in the negative comprised the Administration Democrats and the bitter enders. (Although Borah and Johnson had helped Lodge draft the fourteen reservations, they had also informed him that they planned to vote against them.) The thirty-nine Senators who voted in favor of the treaty with reservations consisted of the mild reservationists and the Lodge group. In a second vote on the same day on the treaty without reservations thirty-eight Democrats were defeated by a combination of the mild reservationists, the strict reservationists, and the bitter enders.

The public's response to the debacle of November 19 was immediate and pronounced. The American people had expected some form of peace settlement to be approved by the Senate; and church groups, civic organizations, labor unions, and such prominent Republicans as Elihu Root, William Howard Taft, and Herbert Hoover all urged the Senate to reconsider its decision. On March 19, 1920, the Senate yielded to this pressure and voted for the last time on the Versailles Treaty with reservations. Once again Woodrow Wilson played the rôle that Lodge had assigned him, for he stated that the reservations destroyed the meaning of the original peace settlement and inferred that he would veto a resolution of ratification of the treaty with reservations. Despite Wilson's warning, twenty-one Administration Democrats from the Northern states strayed from the preserve to join twenty-eight Republicans in voting for ratification. But twenty-three Democrats, mostly from the South, combined with twelve Republicans to vote against it. Of the eighty-four Senators present, only forty-nine—seven less than the two-thirds majority needed—had voted for the treaty with reservations. It was not until the summer of 1921 that a joint resolution in Congress officially ended the war between the United States and Germany.

Henry Cabot Lodge, as has been so frequently stated, may have murdered the peace treaty and the Covenant; but this accusation cannot obscure the assistance that he received from both willing and unwilling accomplices. Nor can the clash of two dominant personalities overshadow the deeper forces behind the League's defeat in the United States. In 1917 the United States had forsaken isolation to join in a program of collective security to curb an aggressor nation. Two years later the United States was asked to participate in a peacetime program of collective security. But this break with the past was too sharp for most Americans, and they reverted to the isolationist policy that they had honored and cherished for more than a century before 1917.

Even after the vote of March 19, Wilson refused to accept defeat.

Once again he decided to appeal to the people, and he proclaimed that the election of 1920 would be a solemn referendum on the League. But there were several reasons why the election of 1920 was neither solemn nor a referendum. Warren G. Harding, who made a farce of the campaign, either knowingly or unknowingly confused the League issue, while at the same time one group of prominent Republicans proclaimed that a vote for Harding was a vote for the League, and another announced that it was a vote for American isolation. Moreover, the American people were voting on many other issues beside the League. Most important of all, they were voting for reaction, or, as Harding preferred to put it, a "return to normalcy." The Americans in 1920, after two decades of uplift, striving, and noble aspirations both at home and abroad, were tired of reform as represented by either the Progressive movement or a crusade to make the world safe for democracy. In 1920, Americans did not vote against the League; they voted for a return to the days of President McKinley.

CHAPTER XIV

THE GOLDEN AGE OF AMERICAN BUSINESS

87. FROM DEPRESSION TO PROSPERITY
88. AMERICAN INDUSTRY DURING THE BOOM
89. CONTROL OF BUSINESS
90. EXPORTING AMERICAN CAPITAL
91. EXPORTING AMERICAN GOODS
92. THE CULT OF BUSINESS

THROUGHOUT the 1920's the mass of Americans devoted themselves with unexampled vigor to the accumulation of wealth. For a decade after the Armistice the American heritage of humanitarian reform, which had achieved concrete expression in Wilsonian progressivism, was pushed into the background as most Americans, swept along on a wave of prosperity, turned wholeheartedly to the equally American tradition of Yankeeism with its emphasis on new gadgets, sharp bargaining, and getting ahead. Relatively full employment, a stream of new products, and a cynicism born of disillusionment all combined to convert the pursuit of the dollar into an almost universal national pastime in the postwar years. Only a few heretics questioned the wisdom of elevating the morality of the counting house into a national religion; and only a few Cassandras predicted that what Charles and Mary Beard have referred to as the "golden glow" would inevitably be followed by the gloom of a depression that would be as pronounced as the prosperity that had preceded it.

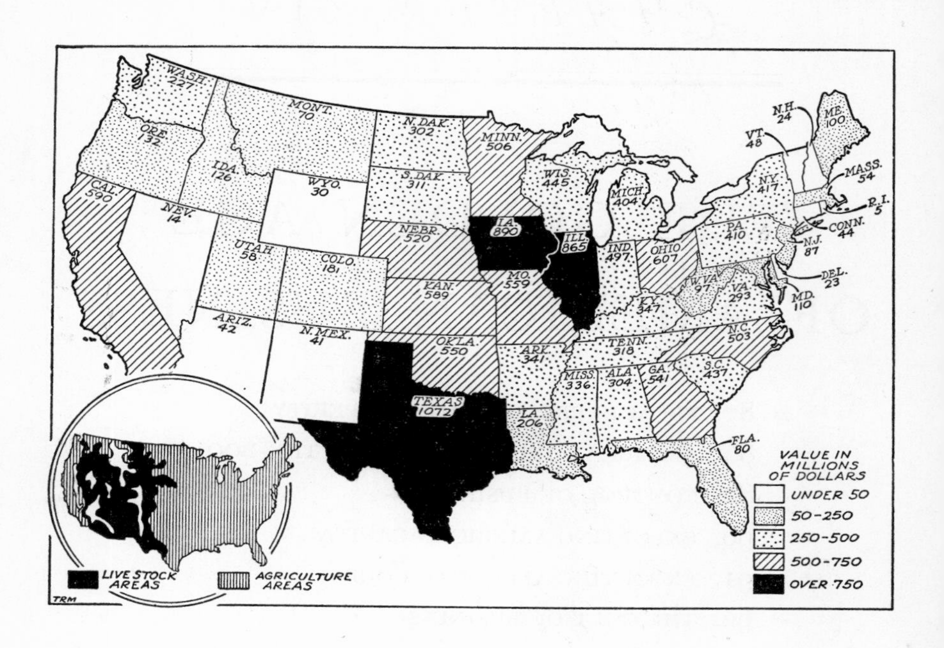
WASH. 227
MONT. 70
N.DAK. 302
MINN. 506
N.H. 24
ME. 100
VT. 48
ORE. 132
IDA. 126
S.DAK. 311
WIS. 445
MICH. 404
N.Y. 417
MASS. 54
CAL. 590
WYO. 30
NEV. 14
IA. 890
R.I. 5
CONN. 44
ILL. 865
PA. 410
UTAH 58
NEBR. 520
IND. 497
OHIO 607
N.J. 87
COLO. 181
MO. 559
W.VA. 97
VA. 293
DEL. 23
KAN. 589
KY. 347
MD. 110
ARIZ. 42
N.MEX. 41
OKLA. 550
TENN. 318
N.C. 503
ARK. 341
MISS. 336
ALA. 304
GA. 541
S.C. 437
TEXAS 1072
LA. 206
FLA. 80
VALUE IN MILLIONS OF DOLLARS
UNDER 50
50-250
250-500
500-750
OVER 750
LIVE STOCK AREAS
AGRICULTURE AREAS
TRM

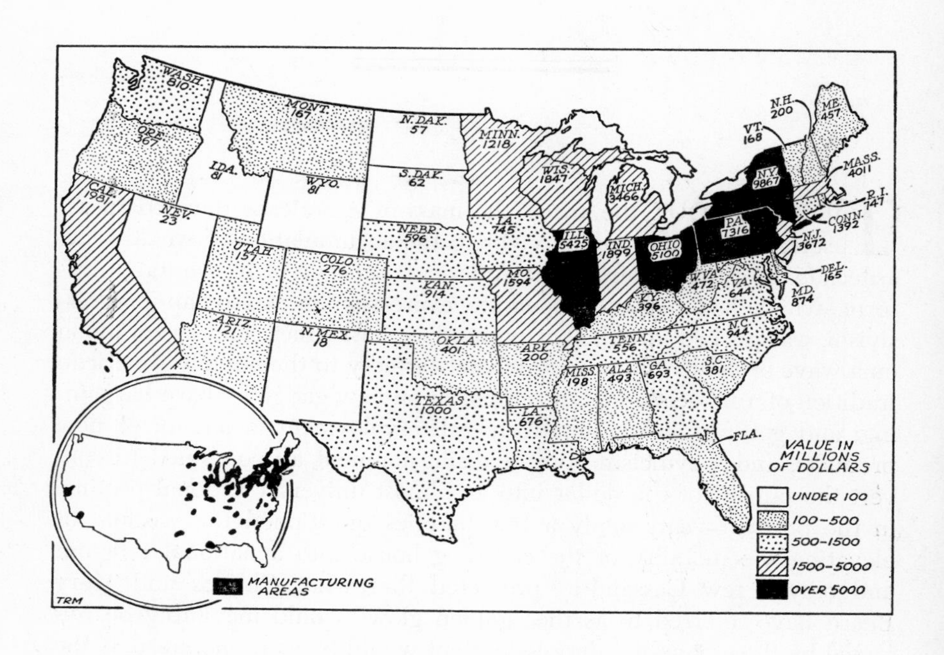
WASH. 810
MONT. 167
N.DAK. 57
MINN. 1218
N.H. 200
ME. 457
VT. 168
ORE. 367
IDA. 81
S.DAK. 62
WIS. 1847
MICH. 3466
N.Y. 9867
MASS. 4011
CAL. 1981
WYO. 81
NEV. 23
R.I. 747
CONN. 1392
IA. 745
ILL. 5425
PA. 7316
N.J. 3672
UTAH 157
NEBR. 596
COLO. 276
IND. 1899
OHIO 5100
DEL. 165
MO. 1594
W.VA. 472
VA. 644
KAN. 914
KY. 396
MD. 874
ARIZ. 121
N.MEX. 18
OKLA. 401
TENN. 556
N.C. 944
ARK. 200
S.C. 381
MISS. 198
ALA. 493
GA. 693
TEXAS 1000
LA. 676
FLA.
VALUE IN MILLIONS OF DOLLARS
UNDER 100
100-500
500-1500
1500-5000
OVER 5000
MANUFACTURING AREAS
TRM

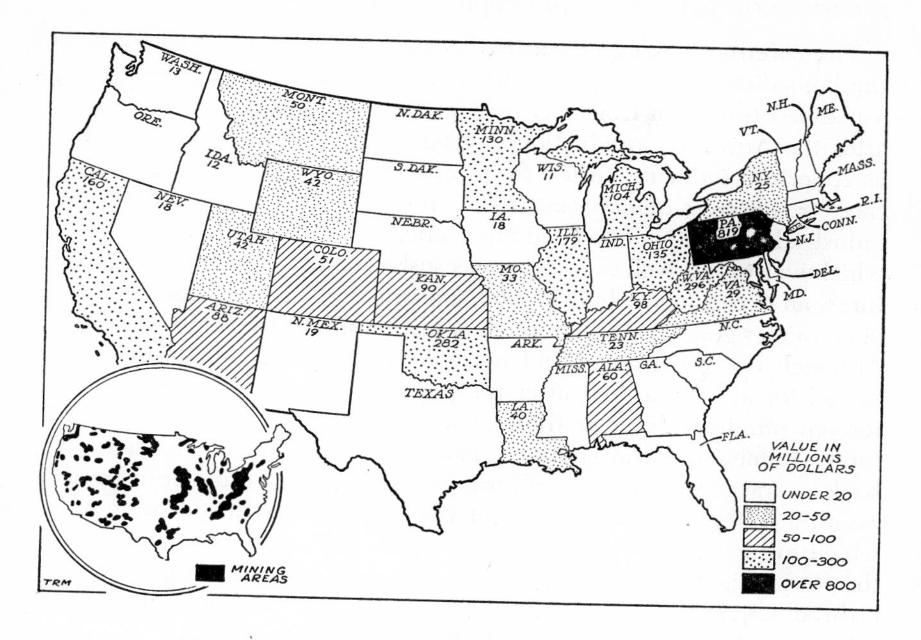

13. AMERICAN PRODUCTIVE CAPACITY, 1920

Although in 1920 the United States was one of the great agricultural nations of the world, the value of its industrial output was four times that of its farm produce. The other major source of its wealth was its mines, which contained almost all the metals known to man. The inset maps show areas of concentration in farming, manufacturing, and mining in 1935.

87. FROM DEPRESSION TO PROSPERITY

MOST Americans were as unprepared for the economic problems of peace in the fall of 1918 as they had been for those of war in the spring of 1917. While numerous officials recognized the need for a gradual relaxation of the government's wartime controls over the economy, they were powerless before the popular demand for an immediate return to private enterprise; and the announcement of the Armistice set off a hectic scramble for what Warren G. Harding was later to call "normalcy." Pleas for an orderly demobilization of the armed forces and a public-works program to bridge the gap between war and peace were ignored as the troops were rushed back from Europe, war contracts were canceled, priorities were abandoned, and the business-men-bureaucrats hurried home from Washington to their corporations.

The carefree junking of wartime economic controls did not produce the immediate depression that had been predicted by the advocates of a planned transition from war to peace. For approximately six months after the Armistice, production declined and unemployment increased as American industry shifted from military to civilian production; but these trends were quickly reversed, and by the opening months of 1920, industrial production exceeded the average for 1918. The postwar boom, which was to last well into 1920, was sustained by government expenditures, an expansion of both public and private credit facilities, the sale of consumer goods, and the foreign demand for American farm products. Although the government had relaxed its wartime regulations, it continued for at least a year after the peace to create both domestic and foreign purchasing power through its post-Armistice military expenditures, payments on war contracts, loans to Europe that found their way back to American producers of farm products, the retention of its control over the railroads until 1920, and the Emergency Fleet Corporation, which turned out more ships after November, 1918, than it had during the war. In addition to the government's unplanned pump-priming, increased activity in such private enterprises as the building and automobile industries and the easy credit facilities available throughout most of 1919 contributed to the postwar boom. Since the Federal Reserve System kept its rediscount rate low to facilitate government borrowing and businessmen were eager to purchase supplies that could be sold on a rising market, bank loans to private borrowers reached new highs, and the postwar prosperity was quickly converted into a speculative boom. As funds that otherwise would have been employed for productive uses were diverted into security and commodity speculation, prices, relieved of their wartime controls, shot to dizzying peaks; and by 1921 the boom had turned into a bust.*

The depression of 1920–1 was in large part caused by a reversal of the forces that had produced the preceding period of prosperity. Because the government abandoned its war and postwar spending policy in the winter of 1919–20, domestic purchasing power that had been partially financed by Federal expenditures was drastically reduced. The foreign demand for American farm products also fell off when the government ended its loans to Europe. At the same time, credit facilities were tightened up as the Federal Reserve Board increased the rediscount rate to 4¾ per cent at the end of 1919 and to 7 per cent on June 1, 1920. Private bankers, taking their cue from the government, curtailed their

* From 1920 to 1921 the wholesale price index (1926 = 100) dropped from 154.4 to 97.6; the number of unemployed grew from 1,305,000 to 4,225,000; commercial failures increased from 8,881 to 19,652; and the index of farm prices (1910–14 = 100) fell from 205 to 116.

loans. As interest rates rose, the businessmen who were dependent on easy credit facilities were forced to dispose of their products at a loss. Every move by businessmen to readjust their policies to meet the new situation only accentuated the deflationary trends that they were attempting to prevent, and by the middle of 1920 the downward spiral of prices was in full swing.

The depression of 1920–1 affected the various economic groups within the United States in different ways. Although many workers lost their jobs and others were compelled to accept a shorter work week, prices fell more rapidly than wages, and those who held their jobs probably benefited from the depression. Some manufacturers and merchants were forced into bankruptcy, but those who remained in business were often able to cushion the effects of the depression by reducing output instead of prices. Moreover, many large corporations had accumulated such enormous reserves during the war years that they were able to continue to pay dividends throughout the depression. Unlike the worker and businessman, however, the farmer could discern no silver lining in the cloud of depression. His crops brought lower prices; mortgages on his property were foreclosed; and manufactured goods that he needed continued at relatively high prices. The volume of American agricultural exports to Europe did not decline to any extent in 1920–1, but the ability of Europeans to pay for these products did. American manufacturers could meet this problem by reducing exports to Europe, but the farmer, who had expanded his acreage during the war years and who knew of no over-all plan for curtailing production and exports, continued to ship his agricultural surpluses abroad, but for drastically reduced prices.

The United States emerged from the postwar depression without the assistance of either government spending or a revival of the European market; the changes that produced an upswing in the business cycle in 1922 occurred within the American economy. Inventories that had been accumulated at inflated prices during the boom were reduced by either bankruptcy or sales at lowered prices; but the purchasing power of the American people did not undergo a corresponding decline. Consequently, when inventories approached the vanishing point, the continued demands of American consumers could only be met by an increase in production. As soon as industry expanded its output, unemployment decreased, purchasing power increased, and the downward spiral was checked as the cycle of depression gave way to one of prosperity. The tempo of these developments was accelerated by an expansion of the building industry. Since material costs were low, rents were high and housing was short, conditions were propitious for a building boom, and in 1922, Americans spent approximately twice as much money on residential construction as they had in 1919.

After the depression of 1920–1, American industry, except for minor recessions in 1924 and 1927, expanded steadily until the stock market crash of October, 1929. The prosperity that prevailed during most of the 1920's was characterized by a relatively constant price level, a marked increase in the production and sale of consumer and durable goods, and a steady—and toward the end of the decade, a spectacular—rise in investments. From 1921 to 1929 the national income mounted from 50.7 to 81.1 billion dollars, and the index of industrial production (1899 = 100) went up from 177.9 in 1921 to 319.4 in 1929. This expanding industrial production was accompanied by a corresponding increase in capital accumulations, and from 1922 to 1929, corporate capital funds rose from $184,000,000,000 to $228,000,000,000.

88. AMERICAN INDUSTRY DURING THE BOOM

THE TREMENDOUS increase in industrial output, which was one of the principal features of the American economy in the 1920's, was in part the result of the employment of more effective means of production and a consequent increase in the productivity of the individual worker. In 1929, 51 workers in manufacturing, for example, could produce as much as 64 workers in 1922 and 84 in 1919. The productivity of the agricultural worker also increased, and in 1929, 67 farm laborers could do the work of 84 in 1919. Since the cost-of-living index remained almost constant during this period, the effects of increased individual productivity were reflected in the growth of consumption, salaries, wages, and profits.

This increased productivity was the result of the use of more machinery, the adoption of more efficient machinery, improved methods of machine tending, and the employment on a wider scale of comparatively new sources of power. Because of the increase in the wage level and the relatively large supply of money available for investment throughout the twenties, capitalists were more than ever inclined to invest their surplus funds in plant equipment that would cut the costs of labor. It worked both ways. Technological advance increased wages and a rising wage-scale stimulated the demand for a wider and more intensive application of machine techniques. The shutting off of immigration and the consequent decline in additions to the skilled labor force also accelerated mechanization.

With a few major exceptions, the technological advance of the twenties represented little in the way of innovation but constituted an improvement, extension, and rationalization of the changes that had been earlier introduced on a smaller scale. Standardization of products, the assembly line, and internal combustion engine—to mention only a few notable examples—were accepted parts of the American industrial scene before 1919; but it was in the 1920's that their application and development were accelerated. The same was true of the use of electric motive power. In 1914, 30 per cent of American industry was powered by electricity; in 1929, the figure was approximately 70 per cent.

AMERICAN PROSPERITY, 1922–9*

	1922	1929
Employee compensation	$37,003,000,000	$52,214,000,000
Cost of Living Index	97.7	100.
Consumers' Outlay	$56,100,000,000	$77,200,000,000
Property Income	$11,925,000,000	$16,822,000,000
Dividends	$2,962,000,000	$6,117,000,000

The widespread use of electric power not only increased the productivity of American factories, but it also made possible changes in their location and design. Since electric power could be carried hundreds of miles from its point of origin, factories could be situated close to the market or to raw materials, rather than near sources of power. Furthermore, the use of electricity permitted the abandonment of the old belt-and-shaft organization of the industrial process and the construction of long one- or two-storied factories that could carry through every step of the manufacturing process under a rational plan. And as factories began to be built out instead of up, high real-estate costs drove many manufacturing firms from the city to suburban or rural districts.

Few industries played a more important rôle in the prosperity of the 1920's than the building business. Because of restrictions placed on new construction during the war, the United States entered the post-Armistice decade with a pent-up demand for new homes, factories, and commercial buildings. The total value of all construction (including public works), which in 1919 had amounted to about $6,000,000,000, never fell below $10,000,000,000 in the years from 1924 through 1929. Some indication of the effect of the building boom upon the American economy can be ascertained from the fact that the construction industry during the twenties accounted for 4.4 per cent of the nation's employees,

* From George Soule, *Prosperity Decade: From War to Depression, 1917–1929,* p. 122, published by Rhinehart & Company, Inc., 1947; based on figures in Simon Kuznets, *National Income and Its Composition.*

paid 7.5 per cent of the nation's wage and salary bill, and afforded a major market for such diverse products as steel, glass, bricks, cement, lumber, electrical equipment, and plumbing supplies.

As important as the building industry was the growth of the automobile business. By 1929, Americans owned and operated approximately 23,000,000 passenger cars, or one car for every five or six people in the country. The mass manufacture and sale of automobiles were made possible by the adoption of improved methods of production, ample supplies of capital for investment, and an expanding market. The vertical integration of the industry was carried to new extremes; the assembly line reached a greater degree of efficiency than had ever been known in the past; and the labor hours per unit of product declined approximately 7.4 per cent each year from 1919 to 1929. As the automobile manufacturers increased their efficiency and productivity, their number declined. Although approximately 200 firms had been established to manufacture automobiles, only 44 were in existence in 1927, and of that number Ford and General Motors did the bulk of the business. For a number of years Ford's profits were about 100 per cent, and those of General Motors exceeded $200,000,000 a year from 1927 through 1929.

Throughout the 1920's the profits of the automobile manufacturers were sustained by a nation of gadgeteers who were convinced that the automobile was the supreme gadget. For customers without cash there was installment buying; for car owners there were trade-ins; and for everyone there were enticing advertisements. To many Americans, if they bothered to think about them, these inducements seemed superfluous. By the middle of the 1920's, automobile worship had become an American cult, as countless thousands in speakeasies, drugstores, Pullman cars, front porches, and apartments argued with almost religious zeal over the relative merits of the different "makes" and speculated on the appearance of "next year's models." In certain circles the man or boy who could not distinguish between a Maxwell and a Franklin was a person apart and an object of mild suspicion. There was little opportunity, however, to select cars on the basis of price. Automobile models were bunched as to size and cylinders, and within the various groupings there was little price competition among the nation's automobile manufacturers.

The impact of the automobile industry on the economy was apparent in many ways. In 1929, automobile manufacturers accounted for 12.7 per cent of American industrial production, employed 7.1 per cent of factory wage earners, paid 8.7 per cent of manufacturing wages, consumed 15 per cent of the nation's steel production and a comparatively large percentage of the output of the rubber, plate glass, nickel, and lead industries. Without the automobile, the roadbuilding program that necessitated the use of large supplies of cement, macadam, and an enormous labor force would not have been necessary. The automobile industry also made possible hot-dog stands, billboards, gasoline stations, and garages.

The spectacular effects of the automobile industry in the postwar years were rivaled, but not surpassed, by developments in the radio and motion picture businesses. In 1923, 190,000 radio receiving sets were manufactured. In 1929 almost 5,000,000 sets were produced, or a gain of 2,500 per cent in six years. Equally significant was the growth of the movies, which had progressed from infancy to a major industry during the first three decades of the twentieth century. By 1930 there were more than 22,000 motion picture theaters, which catered to approximately 100,000,000 customers each week of the year. At the end of the 1920's the motion picture industry employed 325,000 people and represented an investment of $2,000,000,000.

The prosperity of the postwar decade was also sustained by the expansion of the electrical appliance and chemical industries. The electrical appliance industry, the total production of which was valued in 1899 at $92,000,000, produced products whose value amounted to $1,637,307,035 in 1927. The chemical industry, which had experienced a forced growth of tremendous proportions during the war years, by 1929 was producing products with a total value of $3,750,000,000 and the Du Pont corporation alone was turning out more than a thousand different products.

The industrial expansion of the 1920's was accompanied by a corresponding growth in American advertising. If industry was to escape what manufacturers preferred to call "overproduction," consumers had to be educated to the uses and advantages of the products that were placed on the market by American manufacturers. Installment buying was considered a partial solution to this problem, but an even greater reliance was placed on advertising. Although statistics on the advertising industry are inadequate, it has been estimated that $1,782,000,000 was spent on advertising in 1929. The bulk of this money was used for campaigns to make individuals feel inadequate in the eyes of their neighbors. Dissatisfaction or a sense of personal inferiority was created, and sales were increased by warnings that social prestige depended on the purchase of the latest gadgets. To sustain the spirit of competitive consumption induced by the advertisers, producers of consumer goods continually changed the styles of their products so that the American people were readily able to ascertain which of their fellow citizens had been able to purchase the latest—and therefore the best—of any particular commodity. While the increased advertising of the twenties undoubtedly facilitated the introduction into the American economy of certain new products on a mass scale, it also made possible the sale of countless gewgaws and doodads that had no other social function than to make life more complicated and to serve as badges of gradation in the American social hierarchy.

All industries did not share equally in the prosperity of the twenties. As consumer tastes changed, so did the production schedules and profits of individual industries. With increased competition from other forms of transportation, the annual return on railroad investments rose from 4.4 per cent in 1923 to only 4.7 per cent in 1927. The net income of the bituminous coal industry declined from 1.7 per cent of the national income to .73 per cent in 1929. The textile industry also suffered during these years.

Nor was the prosperity of the twenties distributed equally among the various sections of the nation. In some rural regions, prosperity was little more than a word that described life in other parts of the United States but that had no connection with agrarian reality. Moreover, American industrial enterprise, following earlier trends, continued to move from its earlier home in the Northeast, especially from New England, to other parts of the nation, especially the South.

In the 1920's many New England textile mills—the most important industry of the section—moved to other regions to find cheaper operating costs. Similar migrations occurred in the Massachusetts shoe industry and in the Maine paper business. Most of the textile factories went South—particularly to North Carolina, Georgia, and Virginia—where labor costs were from 25 to 60 per cent lower than in New England. Paper manufacturing also shifted its center southward. Shoe manufacturers, out of a desire to get in closer contact with their market, more than any hope of finding cheaper labor, migrated in large numbers to the West—especially to St. Louis—and from 1919 to 1925 the number of wage earners employed in Massachusetts shoe factories declined from 80,000 to 57,000.

In many instances the shifting geographic bases of American industrial enterprise were caused by the introduction of new industries or the expansion of old ones, rather than through industrial migration. The rapid expansion of the automobile and rubber industries during the twenties transformed Detroit and Akron into major industrial centers. The development of the canning industry gave considerable impetus to the expansion of California's economy. The increase in the production of Southern steel mills also added considerably to the industrial potential of that region. By the end of the twenties, industrial sectionalism had broken down considerably, and manufactured products were turned out by states in every one of the country's major sections.

Although there were marked changes in the physical location of American industry during the 1920's, these were not necessarily accompanied by shifts in the centers of control of American business endeavor.

New factories might be built in the South, but the directors who controlled these enterprises still held their annual meetings in Boston, New York, and Wilmington, Delaware. Industrial facilities may have been geographically decentralized, but the control of American economic life became increasingly centralized during the years between the advent of normalcy and the Great Depression.

89. CONTROL OF BUSINESS

WORLD WAR I accelerated earlier trends toward the concentration of control over American industry and finance. During the last months of the war, economic competition within the United States virtually ceased as the government assumed responsibility for the regulation of the quantity, quality, prices, and distribution of many goods. Although some businessmen objected to the extent of government control, they did not object to the profits that were provided by the wartime planned economy; and during the postwar decade they turned with renewed determination to the prevention of what many of them termed the "evils of competition."

The methods employed to achieve concentration of economic power during the 1920's were in many instances those that had been found effective during the previous half century. From the Armistice to the stock market crash of 1929, competition was hedged in, restricted, and even eliminated by such traditional devices as the merger, holding company, interlocking directorate, community of interest, trade association, patent monopoly, and gentlemen's agreement. There were, however, some striking ways in which the postwar movement to eliminate competition differed from that of the earlier age. Prewar steps toward industrial concentration had been designed primarily to destroy rivals. After 1919 an attempt was made to devise some plan to curb competition in such a way that all the members of a particular industry would be assured of their profits. The new consolidationists could achieve this objective by stabilizing prices, allocating production, and sharing markets. Moreover, most of the earlier efforts to restrict competition had centered on efforts to corner supplies of raw materials and to gain ascendency over the production of heavy goods. The combinations of the twenties dealt primarily with consumer goods. The shift in emphasis can be put another way. Before World War I, businessmen fought each other; after the war they combined to present a united front against consumers.

One of the most successful devices for the reduction of competition in the postwar decade was the merger, which could be achieved by the union of two or more firms or the purchase of one company by another. From 1919 to 1930 more than 8,000 separate manufacturing and mining concerns and approximately 1,800 banking firms were liquidated by merger, and from 1919 to 1928 the independence of 4,329 public utilities was destroyed in the same fashion. There was a parallel development in the field of merchandising and in 1929 chain stores accounted for one fifth of total retail sales.

PERCENTAGES OF TOTAL SALES BY CHAIN STORES IN 1929*

KIND OF BUSINESS	PERCENTAGE OF TOTAL SALES BY CHAINS
Department stores	16.7
Variety stores	89.2
Men's stores	21.2
Family clothing stores	27.3
Women's apparel stores	22.7
Shoe stores	41.7
Furniture stores	14.2
Radio stores	19.1
Grocery stores (no meat)	45.7
Combinations (groceries—meats)	32.2
Restaurants, etc.	13.6
Cigar stores and stands	25.1
Filling stations	33.8
Drugstores	18.5
Jewelry stores	6.4
All stores	20.0

The holding company, a variation of the merger, was also widely used in the postwar decade as a device for achieving concentration of control within a particular industry. A holding company was designed neither to produce nor distribute goods, but rather to control through stock ownership a cluster of corporations that performed those functions. In general it was not necessary for a holding company to acquire a majority of the securities of the firm that it wished to control; for the stock of the company in question was usually held in relatively small amounts by numerous investors scattered over the United States and even the world, and a minority bloc of stock thus could enable the holding-company directors to maintain their grip on a subordinate firm. The holding company enjoyed its greatest popularity in the public utilities, and by 1930, ten groups of such companies controlled 72 per cent of the nation's electric business. The power of the holding company over its member

* Reprinted with permission from Alfred I. Bernheim (ed.): *Big Business: Its Growth and Its Place* (New York: Twentieth Century Fund, Inc., 1937), p. 49.

firms was for all practical purposes absolute. Throughout the 1920's the directors of the largest holding companies issued watered stock, transferred the assets of one subsidiary to another, circumvented tax regulations, victimized investors, and in general employed their positions of power not only to restrict competition but also to enhance their own wealth by involved and often illegal forms of stock manipulation.

Concentration of control within the American economy was further facilitated by patent rights held by certain business firms. Under the patent laws of the United States, inventors were granted the exclusive right for seventeen years to employ their inventions in whatever fashion they saw fit. Firms that acquired patent rights were therefore often able to establish partial monopolies in their respective industries. A patent pool enabled a group of vacuum cleaner manufacturers to raise prices repeatedly in the five years after 1919, while a similar arrangement permitted the leading manufacturers of washing machines to control approximately 85 per cent of their industry's output. Until 1925, new patents were pooled by the National Automobile Chamber of Commerce, which included all the members of the industry except Ford.

Throughout the 1920's, the radio industry was also operated according to the dictates of a group of firms that owned the principal patents and rights necessary for the manufacture of radio equipment. In 1919 the Radio Corporation of America was established by General Electric, and arrangements for pooling patents were soon reached with the American Telephone & Telegraph Company, the International Radio Company, and Westinghouse. Under these and similar agreements, the Radio Corporation gained control of approximately 3,500 patents. By 1930 the corporation, which was now controlled by General Electric and Westinghouse, not only held the essential patents for the manufacture of radio equipment, but owned the National Broadcasting Company and had substantial interests in the movie industry and the gramophone business. In 1929, according to the Department of Justice, "practically 95 per cent in value of all radio apparatus manufactured, used and sold in interstate commerce" was produced under patents owned and licensed by the Radio Corporation of America.

Control of patent rights, moreover, played an important part in the participation of American corporations with European firms in cartel agreements for the limitation of competition on a worldwide basis. The Radio Corporation of America pooled its patent rights and divided the world market under an agreement with the British Marconi Company. Dye patents formed the basis of a cartel to which I. G. Farben of Germany and Du Pont of America belonged; and under an understanding reached by General Electric and the German firm of Krupp the price and sale of tungsten carbide were placed under the rigid control of a cartel. American businessmen also joined cartels that regulated the sale and price of such products as matches, zinc, copper, glass, lead, titanium, and electric lamps.

In some instances businessmen who wished to preserve the façade of competition while destroying its substance entered into either formal or unwritten agreements for the restriction of competition to sales methods. Through this arrangement, rival firms turned out practically identical products at identical prices. The consumer, unable to select the goods that he wished to purchase according to standards of style, quality, or price, was compelled to make his decision on the basis of his reaction to the rival companies' advertisements and sales talks. Although businessmen maintained that this type of competition produced a stable economy, the fact remained that the elimination of price and quality competition redounded almost exclusively to the benefit of the producer-seller while providing no comparable advantages for the consumer. Moreover, the Panic of 1929 and the ensuing depression revealed that the much publicized stability of the preceding decade might have been more realistically described as rigidity.

Throughout the 1920's, the elimination of price and quality competition was achieved by such varied devices as the trade association, bellwether pricing, and unwritten agreements among a few large corporations within a single industry. Although trade associations had flourished for many years before 1917, it was not until the war and postwar years that they became effective instruments for regulating competition. By 1925 there were approximately one thousand American trade associations, many of which attempted to insure the profits of their members through price agreements, standardization of products, and restriction of output. It is impossible to determine with any degree of accuracy just how much trade associations restricted competition during the twenties, but many such associations openly acknowledged in their published codes that the elimination of competitive strife was one of the principal reasons for their existence.

In some industries that were dominated by a single large corporation the prices were fixed by directives issued by representatives of the industry's leading firm. This system—known as price leadership—prevailed in the steel industry for many years, during which the United States Steel Corporation served as the industry's bellwether. Throughout the 1920's none of the smaller firms possessed either the courage or strength to challenge the leadership of the United States Steel Corporation, which, with the support of the American Iron and Steel Institute, pegged the price of steel rails at $43 a ton from 1922 to 1929.

When an industry consisted of only a few giant firms, neither the trade association nor a bellwether was needed to insure the elimination of price competition. Because each of the few major companies realized that a reduction in the price of its commodity would lead to a relentless price war, there was a tacit but none the less real understanding that no company would cut prices. Competition among the few large firms in the industry was confined to sales and advertising campaigns, and each firm produced practically identical products at virtually identical prices. In the 1920's, the automobile manufacturers, with the exception of Ford, worked on this general principle. An even more striking example was afforded by the cigarette industry, which was dominated by six major concerns that turned out cigarettes indistinguishable in shape, size, and price. Competition in the cigarette industry of necessity was restricted to the war that these firms waged on billboards and advertising pages of newspapers and magazines.

A further indication of the increasing concentration of control over American economic life during the postwar decade was provided by the comparatively small number of men who held key positions as directors on the boards of the largest industrial and financial corporations; for, as in the days of the money trust, the same names appeared with monotonous regularity on the directors' lists of the country's leading firms. The practice of allowing a few men to serve simultaneously on the boards of several corporations produced a concentration of control that is revealed by the following list* of names and the number of boards on which each served:

Samuel Insull: more than 80
Richard B. Mellon: nearly 50
William L. Mellon: 38
P. A. Rockefeller: 68
Oris P. Van Sweringen: 32
Sidney Z. Mitchell: 35
Patrick E. Crowley: 70
Charles E. Mitchell: 32

Interlocking directorates were not confined to a single industry, for numerous business executives occupied key positions on the boards of companies in unrelated fields of economic endeavor. The Du Ponts, for example, had family representatives on the boards of General Motors and numerous banks and chemical concerns. Thomas W. Lamont served on the boards of several railroads, the Guaranty Trust Company, International Harvester, the Lehigh Valley Coal Company, and the Crowell Publishing Company, among others. Albert H. Wiggin, who was chairman of the board of the Chase National Bank, was also a director of almost fifty public-utility, manufacturing, and financial corporations.

There was practically no way in which the mass of American security holders could determine the policies that were pursued by the directors

* See Harry W. Laidler: *Concentration of Control in American Industry* (New York: Thomas Y. Crowell Company, 1931), pp. 441–2.

of the corporations in which they owned stock, for by the end of the 1920's the separation of corporate ownership and management was virtually complete. The existence of huge corporations with stock held by thousands of individuals scattered over the entire world transformed the earlier concept of private property into a fiction; for, whatever the theory, most stockholders possessed, in fact, no power over their property other than that of disposing of their securities at the market price. As the stockholder's ability to manage his property declined, the economic power of what can accurately be termed the managerial class increased by default. The annual meetings of such a corporation became a farce, for the security owners, who might be numbered in the tens of thousands and who were widely dispersed, had no effective way of making their influence felt. The directors, in short, were able to manage many of America's largest corporate enterprises without interference. This situation, for instance, prevailed in the American Telephone and Telegraph Company; in 1929 the largest amount of stock held by any one of this corporation's 469,801 stockholders amounted to only .60 per cent of the total. Although this company represented the most extreme example of the separation of ownership and management through the dispersion of stock ownership, its position was not unique, for the same type of management control characterized such corporations as the Pennsylvania, New York Central, Southern Pacific, Union Pacific, Baltimore & Ohio, and Northern Pacific railroads, as well as the Western Union Telegraph Company, Consolidated Gas Company of New York, General Electric, and the United States Steel Corporation.

In other instances control of a corporation by one or a few individuals was achieved by more obvious stratagems. If a single person owned as little as 10 to 20 per cent of the stock of a corporation in which all the other shares were widely held in small amounts, it was comparatively simple for him to determine the concern's policy. Since the other stockholders, though they formed a majority, could not unite to oppose him because of geographic obstacles, lack of interest, and inadequate knowledge, he could determine the corporation's policy by voting his stock as a bloc. In other instances, control was kept in a few hands by issuing "A" and "B" stock. Only the "A" stock carried voting rights, and it was retained by a small group, while the nonvoting "B" stock was sold on the open market to the security-buying public.

Through the separation of ownership and management, the control of a minority bloc of stock, and the issuing of nonvoting stock, the management and direction—but not the ownership—of the country's largest corporations fell under the control of a handful of men. Moreover, these corporations through interlocking directorates and numerous other ties were often bound to one another. The result was that a tiny proportion of the total population dominated a large part of the economic life of a nation that included more than 120,000,000 human beings. In 1930, A. A. Berle and Gardiner C. Means in *The Modern Corporation and Private Property* revealed that one half the nation's economic activity was controlled by 200 giant nonbanking corporations and that the almost exclusive control of these corporations was vested in the hands of less than 2,000 men. Most Americans had little conception of how closely this concentration of economic control impinged on their daily living, but Berle and Means in a significant passage on the dependence of the average individual on these 200 corporations and their 2,000 directors conclusively demonstrated that "these great companies form the very framework of American industry" and the "individual must come in contact with them almost constantly."*

90. EXPORTING AMERICAN CAPITAL

WORLD WAR I transformed the United States into a creditor nation, and for ten years after the signing of the peace treaty American investments abroad increased, and the value and volume of American exports remained at relatively high levels. Because the United States had both capital and goods that the domestic economy could not absorb, American business and governmental leaders sought to dispose of these surpluses in foreign countries. It was not until after the crash of 1929 that many Americans realized for the first time that the prosperity of the United States and the prosperity of the world were indivisible and that it was no longer possible to view international economic relations as a one-way street along which profits always traveled to rather than from the United States.

During the war the United States' status in the world economy was fundamentally altered. Because of the Allied demand for American products, exports mounted precipitously, and foreign investments in the United States were liquidated to pay for American goods. American exports, which had been valued at $2,364,579,000 in 1914, had risen to $7,920,426,000 by 1919. The United States' international balance sheet in 1914 had shown a deficit of $3,686,000,000. At the end of 1919 it showed a credit of $12,562,000,000.

Throughout the 1920's the United States strengthened its creditor position in the world economy. Because many American corporations had made unprecedented profits during the war and because American productive capacity could not be expanded indefinitely, there was a comparatively large supply of capital available for investment abroad

* Adolph A. Berle and Gardiner C. Means: *The Modern Corporation and Private Property* (New York: Commerce Clearing House, Inc., 1932), p. 24.

during the postwar decade. Nor was there any lack of foreign demand for American funds. Large segments of the European economy that had been destroyed during the war could be rebuilt only with outside financial assistance. Canada and the Latin American nations, as relatively undeveloped regions, also needed funds for the exploitation of large-scale industrial, mineral, and agricultural enterprises. American capitalists were quick to take advantage of these opportunities, and in 1929 the balance of American private investments abroad was $8,078,-000,000. Ten years earlier the balance had been $2,971,000,000.

Part of this increase in American private investments abroad during the 1920's was accounted for by direct investments or by the transfer of capital to other countries for the establishment of American business enterprises outside the United States.* Before World War I, American direct investments abroad had generally been used for the acquisition and exploitation of foreign natural resources. American capitalists had put their money in Latin American and Canadian mines, South American meat products, Central American fruit plantations, and the Cuban sugar industry, but they had shown little interest in direct investments in foreign manufacturing. Before 1898 Americans had made fewer than thirty direct manufacturing investments in Europe and Canada and virtually none in the other countries of the world. Between 1898 and 1915, 227 additional direct manufacturing investments were made in Europe and Canada.

Although Americans after the war continued to make direct investments in foreign agricultural and mineral resources, they sent considerably more money abroad than in the preceding period for the establishment of foreign factories. By the end of the twenties American-owned

AMERICAN DIRECT INVESTMENTS, BY GEOGRAPHIC AREAS†
(IN MILLIONS OF DOLLARS)

AREAS	1919	1929
Europe	693.5	1,340.3
Canada and Newfoundland	814.3	1,675.4
Cuba and other West Indies	567.3	1,025.5
Mexico	643.6	709.2
Central America	112.5	250.9
South America	664.6	1,719.7
Africa	31.0	117.0
Asia	174.7	446.5
Oceania	53.0	116.8

* A Ford factory in Germany or a Central American banana plantation owned by the United Fruit Company are examples of direct investments abroad.

† Reprinted with permission from Cleona Lewis: *America's Stake in International Investments* (Washington, D. C.: The Brookings Institution, 1938), p. 606.

factories abroad were turning out almost all of the same kinds of products that were manufactured in the United States. In 1929, such private investments abroad totaled $7,553,300,000, as opposed to $634,500,000 in 1897 and $2,652,300,000 in 1914.

The largest share of American direct investments abroad was located in Canada, and by the end of the twenties Americans owned approximately one third of all the capital in Canadian industry. As the accompanying table indicates, the so-called backward regions held little appeal for American capitalists, for the moderately and highly developed national economies accounted for the bulk of such investments.

During the twenties American capital was also shipped abroad in large amounts for the purchase of foreign securities—an item that appeared on the international balance sheet under the heading of portfolio investments. In 1929, American portfolio investments amounted to $7,339,800,000 as contrasted to $2,324,100,000 in 1919. A large percentage of these totals was in either foreign government or industrial securities. Like direct investments, American portfolio investments were usually located in the more economically advanced nations, where the opportunity for profits seemed greater and relatively stable economic and political conditions reduced the chances of loss on the investment.

AMERICAN PRIVATE PORTFOLIO INVESTMENTS, BY GEOGRAPHIC AREAS*
(IN MILLIONS OF DOLLARS)

AREA	1919	1929
Europe	1,293.3	3,260.2
Canada and Newfoundland	728.5	2,002.8
Cuba and other West Indies	38.9	128.4
Mexico and Central America	265.3	266.0
Central America	2.3	35.4
South America	111.6	1,294.1
Africa	0.2	2.2
Asia	134.8	593.9
Oceania	1.2	241.2

Before World War I, most investment bankers in the United States had been content to sit in their offices and wait for foreign business to come to them. After the war, banks sent their representatives all over the world to hunt for borrowers. Since some American bankers were more interested in commissions than in the nature of the securities that they were offering to the American public, many foreign stock issues floated in the United States proved to be of little or no value. Cleona Lewis in *America's Stake in International Investments* gives some indication of the types of securities sold to American investors and the lengths to

* Compiled from Lewis: *America's Stake in International Investments*, p. 606.

which American banking firms were willing to go to find foreign outlets for American surplus capital in the 1920's:

> *Whereas in the middle decades of the nineteenth century American promoters had scoured Europe in search of foreign lenders, in 1925–29 they were searching the world over for foreign borrowers. At one time, according to testimony before the Senate Committee on Finance investigating the sale of foreign securities in the United States, there were 29 representatives of American financial houses in Colombia alone trying to negotiate loans for the national government, for the departments, and for other possible borrowers. Some 36 houses, most of them American, competed for a city of Budapest loan and 14 for a loan to the city of Belgrade. A Bavarian hamlet, discovered by American agents to be in need of about $125,000, was urged and finally persuaded to borrow 3 million dollars in the American market. In Peru, a group of successful American promoters included one Peruvian, the son of the President of that Republic, who was afterward tried by the courts of his country and convicted of "illegal enrichment." In Cuba the son-in-law of the President was given a well-paid position in the Cuban branch of an American bank during most of the time the bank was successfully competing against other American banks for the privilege of financing the Cuban government.**

The third major entry on the credit side of the American international balance sheet represented the loans that the United States government had made to European nations during the war and immediate postwar years. These so-called war debts (although some of them had been contracted for purposes of postwar reconstruction rather than war) amounted to $9,982,000,000 in 1919 and $11,685,000,000 in 1929.

Although the United States did not demand reparations, the American position in the world economy was necessarily affected by the efforts of the other Allied nations to exact regular reparations payments from Germany. In May, 1921, the Reparations Commissions, which had been established by the Paris Peace Conference, put Germany's total reparations bill at thirty-three billion dollars. When Germany defaulted on its reparation transfers within a year after the commission had drawn up its schedule, the French occupied the Ruhr, and the Allies stopped payment on their war debts to the United States, despite the American insistence that there was no connection between reparations and war debts. As a result, the United States on more than one occasion was compelled to take a leading part in revising the postwar international debt structure. In the years after 1923 the United States negotiated a

* Lewis: *America's Stake in International Investments*, 377–8. Copyright 1938 by, and reprinted with the permission of, The Brookings Institution.

AMERICA'S INTERNATIONAL BALANCE SHEET*
(IN MILLIONS OF DOLLARS)

Items	1919	1929
Assets (private account):		
Securities or portfolio investments	2,576	7,839
Direct investments	3,880	7,553
Short-term credits	500	1,617
TOTAL	6,956	17,009
Liabilities:		
Securities or portfolio investments	1,623	4,304
Direct investments	900	1,400
Sequestered properties	662	150
Short-term credits	800	3,077
TOTAL	3,985	8,931
Net assets (private account)	2,971	8,078
Intergovernment debts:		
To the United States government	9,982	11,685
By the United States government	391	...
Net assets, on government account	9,591	11,685
TOTAL NET ASSETS ON PRIVATE AND GOVERNMENT ACCOUNT	12,562	19,763

series of agreements with the debtor nations for the funding of the war debts on a basis that would eventually reduce their total by approximately 50 per cent. Moreover, the Dawes and Young plans, both of which were prepared by commissions headed by Americans, furnished conclusive evidence that the United States as the world's greatest lending nation could not afford to ignore the financial relations of Germany and its principal creditors.

The Dawes Plan, which went into effect in 1924, called for the reduction in annual—but not the total—German reparations, a loan to sustain the German currency, and the French evacuation of the Ruhr. Under the Dawes Plan, Germany resumed its payments to the Allies, who in turn resumed their payments to the United States. As the German reparations transfers were in large part financed by American loans and as the Allied debt payments were taken out of German reparations, the whole operation amounted to a series of maneuvers by which money exported from the United States traveled through Germany to the European Allies and then back to the United States.

When American private investments abroad began to decline in 1928–9, Germany again defaulted. The Young Plan, which was inaugu-

* Reprinted from Lewis: *America's Stake in International Investments,* p. 450. Copyright 1938 by, and reprinted with the permission of, The Brookings Institution.

rated in 1929 to meet this development, reduced Germany's total reparations to $26,800,000,000 to be paid in fifty-nine annual installments. At the same time the connection between war debts and reparations was recognized by a provision stating that any reduction in war debts would be accompanied by a proportionate cut in Germany's reparations bill. In 1931, under the impact of the world economic collapse, the Young Plan went the way of its predecessor. Germany abandoned even the pretense of meeting its obligations, and the other European nations except Finland either stopped their payments or made only insignificant payments on their war debts. By 1933, when Hitler came to power, Germany had paid approximately $4,500,000,000 in reparations and had borrowed almost $2,500,000,000 from the United States. The Allies, who had always insisted that reparations and war debts were intimately related, had paid only slightly more than $2,500,000,000 to the United States.

91. EXPORTING AMERICAN GOODS

DURING the years between the Armistice and the Great Depression the United States sought foreign outlets for its surplus goods as well as for its excess capital. During the 1920's American producers of such staples as tobacco, cotton, and cereals were as dependent upon the foreign market for their prosperity as they had been in the years before the war. Moreover, many American businessmen who before 1914 had limited their sales to the domestic market were compelled after 1918 to look abroad for customers for the additional products that could be turned out by factories expanded during the war. Conditions in the rest of the world also favored an increase in American exports. The war had not only destroyed part of the productive capacity of some of America's principal economic rivals, but it had weakened their ability to compete in the world market. Germany had lost its colonies, some of its European resources, and its military power. The European Allies in their efforts to defeat the Central Powers had of necessity neglected foreign markets, which frequently went by default to American capitalists. On the other hand, certain developments tended to limit the opportunities open to American exporters. Throughout the twenties most of the world outside the United States was in a state of economic depression. At the same time the United States high-tariff policies, by cutting down on American imports, deprived foreigners of the exchange needed to purchase American goods.

The increasing importance of industry in American economic life was revealed in part by the changing nature of the goods transferred in

EXPORTS AND IMPORTS OF MERCHANDISE, 1917–29
(IN THOUSANDS OF DOLLARS)

YEAR	EXPORTS	IMPORTS	EXCESS OF EXPORTS OVER IMPORTS
1917	6,233,513	2,952,468	3,281,045
1918	6,149,088	3,031,213	3,117,875
1919	7,920,426	3,904,365	4,016,061
1920	8,228,016	5,278,481	2,949,535
1921	4,485,031	2,509,148	1,975,883
1922	3,831,777	3,112,747	719,030
1923	4,167,493	3,792,066	375,427
1924	4,590,984	3,609,963	981,021
1925	4,909,848	4,226,589	683,258
1926	4,808,660	4,430,888	377,772
1927	4,865,375	4,184,742	680,633
1928	5,128,356	4,091,444	1,036,912
1929	5,240,995	4,399,361	841,634

American foreign trade. Finished manufactured products, which had comprised only 24 per cent of the total of American exports in 1900, accounted for 50 per cent of the nation's total export bill in 1929. Changes in American imports were less pronounced and the ratio of manufactured to crude materials in American imports remained relatively fixed during these years. As in the prewar period, Europe was the United States' best customer, and the principal source of its imports, while Canada continued to buy more American goods and sell more to the United States than any other single nation.

The United States' favorable balance of trade with the nations of Europe during the 1920's was sustained in large part by American loans. Because the United States refused—or was unable—to increase its imports from Europe, Europe could only finance its purchases in the United States with dollars supplied by American capitalists. In 1928, however, the stream of American capital flowing abroad showed signs that it had reached and passed its crest. A year later this trend was confirmed by the October crash, which marked the beginning of a sharp decline in American purchases of foreign goods and supplies. However difficult the lesson may have been, American businessmen were at last forced to the conclusion that the United States, as the world's leading creditor nation, could not go on indefinitely selling more than it purchased from the other nations of the world.

The economic foreign policy of the United States during the 1920's was not dependent upon territorial acquisitions for its success. Nor did the colonies that the United States had acquired before the war play a major rôle in American overseas trade and investments. Unlike the prewar imperialists, American investors and industrialists were contending, not for small tropical islands containing a few natives and palm fronds, but for raw materials for American factories, markets for finished goods, and outlets for surplus capital. This was a bloodless war, which American business leaders waged with their rivals in other nations and whose outcome was seldom in doubt. By the end of the decade it was apparent that the United States had won the conflict by a wide margin. The price of both the war and victory, however, was a high one, for the United States was soon compelled to serve as receiver for a world economy in bankruptcy.

92. THE CULT OF BUSINESS

AS BUSINESSMEN continued to pile up profits both at home and abroad, many Americans began to look on business enterprise—and particularly business success—as the *summum bonum* of American civilization. By the midtwenties the popular devotion to business standards and ideals as guides to daily living had approached the proportions of a national religion. Like most other religions, business worship had its clergy, and until the advent of the depression few Americans challenged the right of businessmen to serve as the high priests of the nation's largest cult.

Business worship rested upon the widely held belief that unregulated business enterprise was the principal source of the remarkable material progress of the postwar decade. Intellectuals and radicals who questioned the values of America's business civilization were viewed by their contemporaries as frustrated critics who had not been able to "make good" on their own and were taking out their disappointment by attacking the system that had revealed their inadequacies. Moreover, skeptics or heretics could always be refuted by referring to such tangible evidence of the beneficent effects of business enterprise as new cars, radios, refrigerators, and a host of other products. In short, business represented the ideal way of life because business was booming; and to the average American, business prosperity and progress had become interchangeable and synonymous terms.

To most Americans, businessmen were authorities not only on business matters but on practically every other subject. Henry Ford's remark that history was "bunk" gained wider currency than any comment by a contemporary historian. *The Man Nobody Knows,* which was written by a prosperous advertising executive to demonstrate that Christ was the world's most successful businessman, had a larger circulation than any book by a contemporary clergyman. The estimate of Mussolini's fascist regime in Italy was fixed in many American minds by the statements of businessmen who visited Italy and returned to the United States to report that the trains ran on time.

The elevated rank enjoyed by the businessman during the postwar decade was not altogether accidental, for during these years organized business groups made a concerted effort to demonstrate to the rest of the population that their members deserved positions of power and prestige. Employing every medium of communication, businessmen's associations and individual industrialists and financiers sought to sell their ideas as well as their products to the American consumer. The propaganda mills of the United States Chamber of Commerce, the National Association of Manufacturers, and individual trade associations ground out an endless stream of releases; many teachers, politicians, authors, and clergymen either volunteered or were enlisted as defenders of American business enterprise; and once a week small businessmen in towns throughout the land gathered at luncheon as Rotarians, Lions, or Kiwanis to sing songs about serving their fellowman and to hear a speaker give a "booster" talk.

Like many of his products, the businessman's message was standardized. It extolled the "American Way" of unrestricted business enterprise and branded as un-American those who wished to redefine or regulate the freedom of the nation's financiers and industrialists. In the businessman's catalogue of un-Americans were militant trade unionists; "radicals," a term broad enough to include liberals, Socialists, and Communists; and anyone else who advocated the extension of the government's regulatory power over business practices. On the positive side the businessman's creed stressed that business' principal function was to serve the people; that only the able and industrious gained wealth and authority in the business world; and that unhampered business enterprise had made the United States the richest, freest, and most powerful nation in the world. Business leaders with ample funds for disseminating their propaganda and with their own records of success to use as illustrations had little trouble in convincing the mass of Americans that the businessman's philosophy was indeed the American philosophy.

CHAPTER XV

FROM NORMALCY TO DEPRESSION

WHILE businessmen were expanding their power and increasing their profits, politicians were playing a relatively minor rôle in American life. The Republicans, who controlled the Federal government from 1921 to 1933, were dedicated to the preservation of the *status quo,* and they refrained from taking any steps that might have jeopardized American prosperity. Throughout the postwar decade the government aided and encouraged business, left the workers to shift for themselves, and refused to come to the assistance of the majority of the farmers who were not sharing in the nation's prosperity. The Democrats did not seriously challenge this program during the boom, and it was not until the advent of the depression that they succeeded in making an effective appeal to American voters.

93. THE ADVENT OF NORMALCY

THE POLITICAL climate of postwar America was fully revealed in the presidential campaign of 1920. When the Republican delegates gathered at Chicago in June, 1920, the conservatives were in control of the party's machinery, and the convention's proceedings were in large measure dominated by a Senate cabal headed by Henry Cabot Lodge. The platform adopted by the Republicans not only failed to advocate any program of social legislation but called for a reduction in income taxes, a cut in the public debt, "constitutional government," the repeal of the excess profits tax, and an increase in the tariff. On the critical question of the League the platform was suitably vague, and the party was pledged to "such agreement with other nations as shall meet the full duty of America to civilization and humanity in accordance with American ideals and without surrendering the right of the American people to exercise its judgment and its power in favor of justice and peace." Some months before the convention, it was clear that General Leonard Wood, Governor Frank O. Lowden of Illinois, and Senator Hiram Johnson of California were the leading candidates for the Republican presidential nomination. But in the opening ballots none of these could obtain a majority, and at the end of the sixth ballot the convention recessed to give the party's leaders a chance to arrange for a compromise choice; those in control of the convention then made it clear that they favored the selection of Senator Warren Gamaliel Harding of Ohio; and with the tenth ballot he was nominated. Governor Calvin Coolidge of Massachusetts was named as his running mate.

When the Democrats convened at San Francisco at the end of June, their party was disorganized and without adequate leadership. Wilson was too sick to take an active part in party affairs, and Bryan, although he attended the convention, had nothing to say about its management. Few of the delegates gave any indication that they retained any of the crusading fervor that had characterized the first Wilson Administration. The liberals were disgusted with the Administration's suppression of civil liberties during the war and postwar years, and the representatives of the Solid South and the Northern city machines had little to offer in the way of a constructive program. As a result, the Democratic platform indicated little interest in domestic reform and was hardly more constructive than that of the Republicans. Concerning foreign policy, however, the Democrats took a clear-cut stand. Their platform endorsed Wilson's policy in Mexico, advocated independence for Puerto Rico and the Philippines, and stood firmly behind the League of Nations. In its League plank, the party went on record as favoring "the League as the surest, if not the only, practicable means of maintaining the permanent peace of the world and terminating the insufferable burden of great military and naval establishments." Although they advocated "the immediate ratification of the Treaty without reservations which would impair its essential integrity," the Democrats did "not oppose the acceptance of any reservations making clearer or more specific any of the obligations of the United States to the League associates."

The three leading contenders for the Democratic nomination were William Gibbs McAdoo, who had served as Secretary of the Treasury until 1919 and who was Wilson's son-in-law, Attorney General A. Mitchell Palmer of Pennsylvania, and Governor James M. Cox of Ohio. In the opening rounds the contest appeared to be between McAdoo and Palmer, but Cox moved forward steadily at Palmer's expense. It was not, however, until the forty-fourth ballot that Cox received the necessary two-thirds majority. Franklin D. Roosevelt, who had served as Assistant Secretary of the Navy during both Wilson Administrations, was nominated for the vice-presidency. In addition to the major party candidates, Eugene V. Debs headed the Socialist ticket, and Parley P. Christensen of Utah that of the Farmer-Labor party.

While Cox waged a vigorous campaign that took him to every section of the country, Harding remained at his home in Marion, Ohio, and made only a few formal speeches. Those that he did make were extraordinarily vague, and McAdoo did not overly exaggerate when he said that Harding's speeches left "the impression of an army of pompous phrases moving over the landscape in search of an idea; sometimes these meandering words would actually capture a straggling thought and bear it triumphantly, a prisoner in their midst, until it died of servitude and overwork." Cox placed his greatest emphasis on his party's demand for American participation in the League of Nations. The Republicans, who had done the most to prevent the acceptance of Wilson's proposals for a postwar settlement, hedged on the League issue. Harding talked on every side of the question; Republican isolationists told isolationist audiences that Harding was unalterably opposed to the League; and a group of the party's internationalists announced that a vote for Harding was a vote for the League.

Wilson had asked that the election be made a "solemn referendum" on the League, but the outcome of the contest revealed that Harding more accurately reflected most voters' views when he demanded a return to "normalcy." Harding carried 37 states and received 16,152,220 votes to 9,147,353 for Cox. The electoral vote was 404 to 127, and the Republicans also won impressive majorities in both the Senate and the House. The Republican victory—Joseph Tumulty, Wilson's former secretary, called it an "earthquake"—can be attributed, not to the Republicans' stand on either foreign or domestic policy, but to the desire of a majority of the voters to turn their backs on reform both at home and abroad.

Warren G. Harding was a small town politician and newspaperman, who—as some of his contemporaries liked to remark—"looked like a President." Born in 1865 in Ohio, he had attended the Ohio Central College, taught school for a term, read a little law, tried the insurance business and finally had become the proprietor of the Marion (Ohio) *Star*. Under Harding's direction the *Star* had been an uninspired, staunchly Republican paper; but it had provided its owner with a position of prestige in his town and county and had enabled him to enter Ohio politics. Always a Republican regular, Harding had become one of Senator Joseph B. Foraker's henchmen and a relatively prominent political figure in the state. He had served in the state senate from 1900 to 1904, had been Lieutenant Governor from 1904 to 1906, had been defeated for the governorship in 1910, and had been elected to the United States Senate in 1914. During his term in the Senate, Harding had never been associated with an important bill, had been frequently absent, and had always voted as the party leaders dictated. A jovial, easy-going, shallow man, who found his principal friends in the Capitol's poker-playing set, Harding brought to the White House the moral code of the hangers-on around a rural county courthouse.

With a few exceptions, Harding's cabinet consisted of either mediocrities or incompetents. Secretary of State Charles Evans Hughes, Secretary of Commerce Herbert Hoover, and Secretary of Agriculture Henry C. Wallace were perhaps the best qualified of Harding's appointees. Hughes was a former Governor of New York State, an Associate Justice of the Supreme Court, and the Republican party's unsuccessful presidential candidate in 1916; Hoover was a former mining engineer who had served as Food Administrator during the war and had administered American relief in Europe; Henry C. Wallace was the publisher of an Iowa farm journal and had a first-hand knowledge of the problems of the Western farmer. For Secretary of the Treasury, Harding chose Andrew W. Mellon of Pittsburgh, who was head of the aluminum trust and one of the wealthiest men in America; for Postmaster General he named Will H. Hays of Indiana, the chairman of the Republican National Committee; for Secretary of the Interior he chose Albert B. Fall, of New Mexico, a friend of Harding in the Senate and an outspoken opponent of conservation; and for Attorney General he selected Harry M. Daugherty, an Ohio political hack who had inaugurated the Harding boom for president. The remaining cabinet posts were filled by Edwin Denby of Michigan (Secretary of the Navy), James J. ("Puddler Jim") Davis of Pennsylvania (Secretary of Labor), and John W. Weeks of Massachusetts (Secretary of War).

Harding made practically no attempt to provide the country with constructive leadership during his term as President. Congress was permitted to go its own way, the heads of the various departments were practically autonomous, and Harding took care of the loyal party workers and his cronies from Ohio. The results of this laissez-faire attitude were on the one hand a Washington conference for naval reduction under the direction of Secretary of State Hughes, and on the other, scandals in the Justice, Navy, and Interior departments. Because there were only a few men of Hughes' ability and integrity in the Harding official family, the scandals outweighed any achievements that might have benefited the voters. After his death in 1923, scandal and Harding became virtually synonymous in many people's minds, and William Allen White wrote that "the story of Babylon is a Sunday school story compared with the story of Washington from June, 1920, until July, 1923."

The first evidence of corruption in the Harding Administration occurred in March, 1923, when it was found that Charles R. Forbes, the director of the Veterans' Bureau, had misappropriated his agency's funds. Through collusion with contractors and with those who sold supplies to the bureau Forbes had squandered or stolen approximately $200,000,000. When it became clear that the graft and fraud in the Veterans' Bureau could no longer be concealed, Forbes in February, 1923, fled to Europe and resigned his office. A month later a Senate subcommittee began an investigation that eventually led to the indictment and trial of Forbes and a contractor named John W. Thompson. In 1925 both men were found guilty of conspiracy to defraud the United States government. Each was fined $10,000 and sentenced to two years in prison. Thompson died before his sentence began, but Forbes served a term of one year and nine months in the Federal penitentiary at Leavenworth. Charles F. Cramer, the legal adviser to the Veterans' Bureau and a close friend of Forbes, committed suicide soon after the Senate committee began its investigation.

The corruption in the Veterans' Bureau was matched, and perhaps even exceeded, by that in the Justice Department. Attorney General Daugherty, who was Harding's most intimate political associate, was accused by a Senate investigating committee of permitting the withdrawal of alcohol from government warehouses. When Daugherty, who had earned an illegal profit from these transactions, refused to co-operate with the Senate committee's investigation of his department, he was forced out of office by President Coolidge in 1924. Also implicated in the charges against Daugherty was Jess Smith, another member of the "Ohio gang." Smith committed suicide before the expiration of Harding's term, and it was later discovered that he had accepted $50,000 to obtain a favorable decision in a case before Alien Property Custodian Thomas W. Miller. Miller, in 1927, was found guilty of conspiring to defraud the government and was sentenced to eighteen months' imprisonment and the payment of a fine of $5,000; but Daugherty, who was brought to trial on the same charge, escaped because the jury disagreed.

The series of scandals in the Harding Administration was climaxed by the revelations concerning Secretary of the Interior Fall's handling of the oil reserves. After persuading Secretary of the Navy Denby to transfer the government oil reserves at Elks Hill, California, and Teapot Dome, Wyoming, to the Interior Department, Fall then leased the first of these to E. M. Doheny and the second to Harry F. Sinclair. Both leases were made without competitive bidding, and in both instances Fall received large bribes in return for facilitating the transfers. In October, 1923, a Senate investigation conducted by Thomas Walsh, a Montana Democrat, showed that Doheny had paid Fall $100,000, and that Sinclair had paid him $223,000 in Liberty Bonds and $85,000 in cash. Following these revelations, Fall and Denby were forced to resign from the cabinet, and in 1927 the government was able to recover its oil reserves. Fall was convicted in 1929 of accepting a bribe and was sentenced to a year's imprisonment and the payment of a $100,000 fine. Doheny and Sinclair, however, were acquitted of charges of conspiracy.*

94. COOLIDGE AND HOOVER

WHEN Harding died at San Francisco on August 2, 1923, after a trip to Alaska, comparatively little was known about the corruption of many of the officials in his Administration. Harding's death marked the end of the "Ohio gang's" rule in Washington and ushered in the era of "Coolidge prosperity." Despite repeated revelations of graft in the Harding regime during the next five years, most Americans appeared willing to forget the sordid features of the "return to normalcy" and to concentrate on the opportunities for profits provided by the boom. Coolidge had not been even remotely connected with any of the illegal activities of the Harding Administration, and his honesty was beyond question. To many Americans he symbolized everything that Harding was not. When he was sworn in as President of the United States in a Vermont farmhouse that belonged to his father and was lighted by oil lamps, he seemed to the American people the archetype of the frugal, simple—but not simple minded—New England Yankee. It was an appealing picture—and also an incongruous one—of a man who was to head the government of the most powerful industrial nation of the world during a period of flamboyant prosperity and extravagance.

From his birth in Vermont in 1872 until his accession to the presidency in 1923, Calvin Coolidge had given little indication that he possessed any of the qualifications needed by the President of the United States. After graduating from Amherst College and studying law, he had begun practice in Northampton, Massachusetts, in 1897. In the course of the next twenty years he had served successively as a councilman, city solicitor, clerk of courts, a member of the Massachusetts legislature, mayor of Northampton, member of the state senate, and Lieutenant Governor. Throughout this period he had demonstrated little beyond the fact that he was a staunch Republican and a firm believer in the

* Sinclair went to jail for three months and paid a $1,000 fine for contempt of the Senate. Later, during his trial for conspiracy, he was found guilty of having the jury followed by detectives, and he was given a six-months' jail term.

theory that the government should aid business but should not otherwise concern itself with the economic life of the nation. In 1919, however, Coolidge became Governor of Massachusetts, and within a short time the Boston police strike had made him a national figure.

On September 9, 1919, the Boston police went on strike after the police commissioners refused to recognize the union that they had organized under the auspices of the American Federation of Labor and had dismissed some of the force for union activity. Following outbreaks of disorder in many parts of the city, the mayor transferred some state militia companies in the city to police duty. Within two days order had been restored; but on the afternoon of September 11, when the situation was well in hand and after Coolidge had refused to respond to earlier demands of the municipal officials for assistance, he ordered the state militia to Boston and wired President Gompers of the American Federation of Labor: "There is no right to strike against the public safety by anybody, anywhere, any time." Coolidge's stand—and few outside Boston knew how tardily he had acted—caught the public imagination and was directly responsible for his selection as the Republican party's vice-presidential candidate in 1920.

Perhaps Coolidge's most remarkable achievement as President was his ability to make the voters forget the excesses of his predecessor's Administration. Although he took over the Harding cabinet, he gradually forced the corrupt out of office. At the same time, his own honesty was so unquestioned that it was widely felt that his assumption of office represented a clean break with the immediate past. The willingness of a large part of the public to pass over the graft and corruption that had characterized the Harding term can also be attributed in part to the fashion in which a large portion of the press handled the disclosures of malfeasance in Washington. As Frederick Lewis Allen has written:

> *The harshest condemnation on the part of the press and the public was reserved, not for those who had defrauded the government, but for those who insisted on bringing the facts to light. Senator Walsh, who led the investigation of the oil scandals, and Senator Wheeler, who investigated the Department of Justice, were called by the* New York Tribune *"the Montana scandal-mongers."* The New York Evening Post *called them "mud-gunners."* The New York Times, *despite its Democratic leanings, called them "assassins of character." In these and other papers throughout the country one read of the "Democratic lynching-bee" and "poison-tongued partisanship, pure malice, and twittering hysteria," and the inquiries were called "in plain words, contemptible and disgusting."**

* Frederick Lewis Allen: *Only Yesterday; An Informal History of the Nineteen-Twenties* (New York: Harper & Brothers, 1931), pp. 154–5. Copyright 1931 by, and reprinted with the permission of, Harper & Brothers.

When the Republican convention met at Cleveland on June 10, 1924, Coolidge had been in office less than a year. Since becoming President, he had initiated no policies, and in Congress his party's program had been blocked by a combination of Democrats and a small group of Midwestern Republican insurgents, who were led by such Senators as Robert La Follette and George Norris. Nevertheless, Coolidge was the inevitable Republican choice. He had become identified in the popular mind with the business boom—an impression that was assiduously fostered by Republican politicians—and many Americans found his simple ways, his taciturnity, and his unassuming appearance and manner a refreshing change from the almost austere idealism of a Wilson or the surface slickness and lax morality of a Harding. Coolidge was nominated on the first ballot, and Charles G. Dawes, a Chicago banker, received the vice-presidential nomination. The party's platform differed little in essentials from that of 1920. The Republicans still opposed American participation in the League (although they advocated American membership in the World Court), and they still favored high tariffs and low taxes.

When the Democrats gathered for their convention on June 24 in New York, their party was divided into two diametrically opposed factions. On the one hand, there was the Solid South, and on the other, the big city machines of the North. In the past these two factions had usually been able to maintain an uneasy, but none the less effective, alliance, but in 1924 they were split by both the prohibition and Ku Klux Klan issues. The South, like most of the nation's rural regions, was militantly dry, whereas the Northern urban wing of the party was overwhelmingly wet. At the same time, the Klan had been revived after the war as an anti-Negro, antiforeign, antisemitic, anti-Catholic organization. Such nativist doctrines held a strong appeal for many Southerners; but in the North many of the Democratic party's rank and file as well as its leaders were drawn from some of the very groups that were opposed by the Klan. At the outset of the convention any possibility of party harmony was destroyed by the introduction of a resolution that specifically denounced the Klan. But this resolution was defeated by 4.3 votes, and in its place the convention adopted a plank that read: "We insist at all times upon obedience to the orderly processes of the law and deplore and condemn any effort to arouse religious or racial dissension." In other planks the Democrats advocated lower taxes, a scientific approach to the tariff, a child labor amendment, Philippine independence, and a referendum on the League question.

The sectional split in the Democratic party was carried over to the contest for the presidential nomination. McAdoo was the candidate of the South, while the Northerners gave their votes to Alfred E. Smith, who was a native of New York City, a wet, a Catholic, a member of Tammany

Hall, and an outstanding reform Governor of New York State. These two men were so evenly matched that for 102 ballots neither could obtain a two-thirds majority. Finally, on July 8, the deadlock was broken with the nomination of John W. Davis of West Virginia and New York. On the one hundred and third ballot Davis was nominated. Because he was a corporation lawyer—one of his clients was the House of Morgan—the Democrats sought to balance their ticket with Charles W. Bryan of Nebraska, whose only claim to recognition was that he was William Jennings Bryan's brother. When the convention finally broke up on July 10, the Democrats were even more divided than when they had met.

The campaign of 1924 was marked by the appearance of a powerful third-party movement that reflected the dissatisfaction of many workers, farmers, and liberals with the policies of the two major parties. The origins of the new party went back to 1922, when the Railroad Brotherhoods had called a Conference for Progressive Political Action. In the next two years the C.P.P.A. sought to win the support of the American Federation of Labor, the Socialist party, and dissatisfied agrarians, and by 1924 it had the nucleus of a genuine farmer-labor party. At its first nominating convention in July, 1924, the C.P.P.A. selected Robert La Follette as its candidate and authorized him to pick his own running mate and draw up his own platform. La Follette chose Senator Burton K. Wheeler, a Democrat from Montana, for second place on the ticket and wrote a platform that blended socialism with Midwestern progressivism. La Follette's program called for a reduction in taxes on small incomes and an increase in the levies on well-to-do individuals and corporations, public ownership of the railroads and of a number of the nation's natural resources, a lowering of the tariff, the abolition of judicial review, the popular election of Federal judges, Federal protection of the rights of labor, and Federal aid for distressed farmers. Although La Follette's candidacy was subsequently endorsed by both the Socialist party and the American Federation of Labor, he was handicapped throughout the campaign by the lack of a national political organization and of even a minimum amount of money.

In winning the election of 1924, Coolidge received 54.1 per cent of the popular vote compared to the 61.02 per cent obtained by Harding in 1920. Still, Coolidge won an overwhelming victory. With 15,725,016 votes to 8,386,503 for Davis and 4,822,856 for La Follette, Coolidge had a plurality of more than 7,000,000 and a majority of 2,500,000. Coolidge carried all but the Solid South and Oklahoma (which voted for Davis) and Wisconsin (which voted for La Follette). The electoral vote was Coolidge 382, Davis 136, and La Follette 13. The Republicans also won large majorities in both the House and Senate. Few conclusions can be drawn from the outcome of the election of 1924 aside from the fact that a majority of the electorate had voted for prosperity.

Coolidge had a modest view of the duties of his office and the functions of the government. He never gave any evidence that he thought that the President should initiate legislation or provide the country with aggressive and constructive leadership. He made no attempt to impose a program on Congress, and there is reason to believe that he felt that a recess in law making would have been a good thing for everyone concerned. He had no comprehension of the problems of either the farmers or the workers, and on two occasions he vetoed the McNary-Haugen Bill for farm relief without offering any alternative to this measure. As long as he was President, he was generally satisfied to sit by and watch the wheels of governmental machinery turn, but he did not favor the addition of any new wheels, and he did not want the tempo of the old ones altered. Coolidge's theory of government was a simple one. He thought that the government should maintain law and order, aid business, refrain from any other form of intervention in the nation's economic life, and practice economy. Beyond these functions, he thought that the government should do nothing.

Coolidge's policy of thrift fitted in admirably with the temper of the times, for as long as business boomed, there were large numbers of Americans who preferred to have the government play a relatively passive rôle. As a result, Coolidge was widely credited with aiding, if not causing, prosperity, and there were millions of Americans who felt that the country was safe as long as he was in the White House. But Coolidge did not press his luck, and on August 2, 1927, while on a vacation in the Black Hills of the Dakotas, he surprised almost everyone by announcing: "I do not choose to run for President in 1928." Although his supporters argued that his statement did not exclude him from running if he was drafted, no draft developed; and on the eve of the convention it was a foregone conclusion that Secretary of Commerce Herbert Hoover would be the party's choice. Hoover was nominated on the first ballot, and in an attempt to appease the dissatisfied agrarians in the party, Senator Charles Curtis of Kansas was named for the vice-presidency. The Democrats convened at Houston and selected Alfred E. Smith on the first ballot. Their vice-presidential nomination went to Senator Joseph T. Robinson of Arkansas, who was a dry and a Protestant. Both parties shunned reform proposals in their platforms. The Republicans praised the Coolidge Administration, and the Democrats condemned it; but on most essential points the two parties seemed in essential agreement. The Democrats even abandoned their traditional low-tariff position to advocate rates that would equal the "actual difference between the cost of production at home and abroad."

Smith and Hoover had little in common aside from their humble origins. Hoover, who had been born of Quaker parents in 1874 in Iowa, had been left an orphan at an early age. After graduating with an

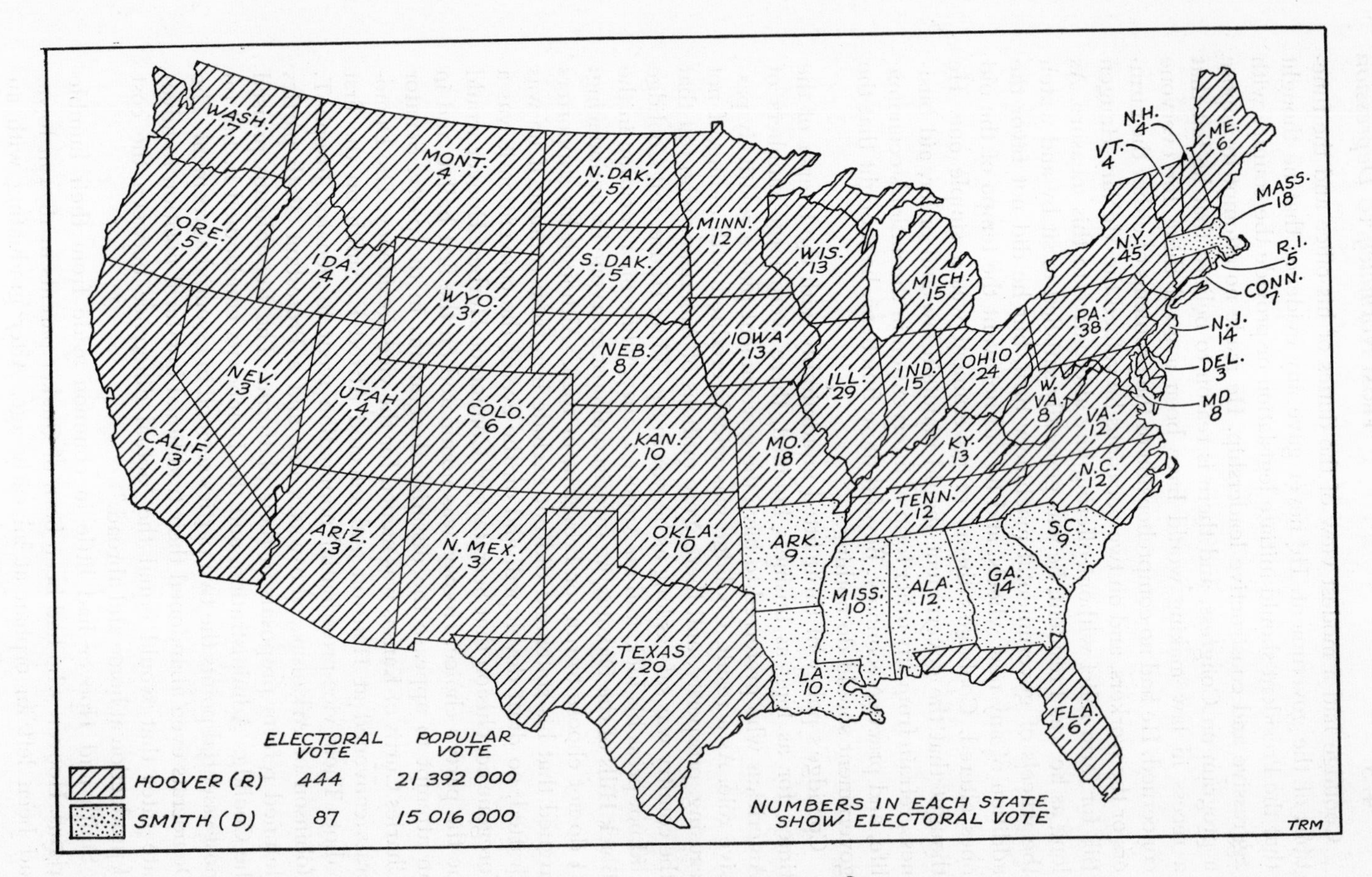

14. THE ELECTION OF 1928

engineering degree from Leland Stanford University he acquired a fortune as a mining promoter in Asia, Europe, and North America. Following his service as head of Belgian Relief, he had become Food Administrator during the war, chairman of the American Relief Administration in the period right after the war, and Secretary of Commerce under Harding and Coolidge. Smith had been born in the slums of the East Side of New York in 1873. He had attended parochial school, had tried a variety of manual jobs, and at an early age had become a member of Tammany Hall. Working up through the ranks of the machine, he had eventually been elected Governor of New York, and in all he had served four terms in Albany. As Governor he had compiled an outstanding record as a reformer, a vote getter, and a practical politician.

Throughout the campaign, Smith labored under numerous difficulties. A wet, a Catholic and a Tammanyite, he seemed to be all that the voters in the rural sections of the South and West suspected and abhorred. At the same time a vicious whispering campaign was responsible for rumors that if Smith won, the Catholic Church would take over the control of the government of the United States. Finally, like Davis before him, the Democratic candidate had to campaign against Republican prosperity. These obstacles were too much for Smith, and he was the first Democrat since Reconstruction not to obtain all the electoral votes of the Deep South. He lost Florida, North Carolina, Tennessee, Texas, and Virginia; and aside from the remaining states in the South he carried only Massachusetts and Rhode Island, each of which had a large Catholic vote. The electoral vote was 444 to 87, and the popular vote was 21,391,381 to 15,016,443. Once again the Republicans gained sizable majorities in both branches of Congress.

The presidency of the United States was the first elective office held by Herbert Hoover, and his work both as a mining engineer and as Secretary of Commerce had done little to prepare him for his new post. An efficient administrator and able organizer, he had had no experience in the give-and-take of American politics. While he possessed many of the qualifications needed by a successful President, he had none of the attributes of a party leader. He was a rigid man who was unable to improvise; he lacked the human touch that is the hallmark of effective political leaders, whether they serve as ward leaders or as Presidents; he often gave the impression—rightly or wrongly—that he thought that programs and plans were more important than individuals; and finally, he was a theorist who was reluctant to abandon his theories when day-to-day events tended to disprove them. In short, Herbert Hoover was not a politician. Like Harding and Coolidge, Hoover believed that the government should aid, but not regulate, business; but unlike his predecessors, he thought that this should be done on a scientific, rather than on a catch-as-catch-can, basis. He was convinced that if the government followed such a policy, the boom could be maintained indefinitely.

The announcement of Hoover's cabinet proved a shock and a disappointment to those who thought that the new President would utilize the talents of specialists to man the government departments. Secretary of State Henry L. Stimson was an acknowledged authority on American foreign policy, and both Secretary of the Treasury Mellon and Secretary of Labor Davis had served under Harding and Coolidge, but the remaining cabinet posts were filled by virtual unknowns. The make-up of Hoover's cabinet marked the President's first defeat at the hands of the politicians. Instead of being able to surround himself by experts as he had wished, he was forced to appoint men whose only discernible qualification was their loyalty and service to the Republican party.

From the outset Hoover had difficulty in carrying out his policies and in working harmoniously with Congress. The Senate objected to many of his appointments. It refused to confirm John J. Parker's nomination to the Supreme Court, and Charles E. Hughes' selection as Chief Justice of the Court was approved over the objections of many Senators. Moreover, there were many conflicts between the executive and legislative branches of the government over specific measures. Hoover objected vigorously to congressional plans for the development of the Tennessee Valley; he had to stand by helplessly while his own party drew up a tariff measure of which he disapproved; and, although he prevailed upon Congress to adopt his proposal for farm relief, the measure failed to achieve its objectives.

Hoover's misfortunes were climaxed by the Panic of 1929 and the ensuing depression. As a man who had entered office as the advertised guardian of prosperity, he was lamentably unprepared to cope with the most severe depression in the history of the nation. In the 1930 elections, the Democrats obtained a clear-cut majority of the House, and two years later they gained control of the presidency and both branches of the legislature.

95. THE GOVERNMENT AND BUSINESS ENTERPRISE

FOR TWELVE years after the inauguration of Warren G. Harding on March 4, 1921, the United States government strengthened rather than circumscribed the economic power of the country's business executives. The mass of Americans and their Republican officials believed that the government's primary function was to encourage and assist—but not to regulate—American business enterprise; and government leaders made a concerted effort to translate the philosophy of Alexander Hamilton into a twentieth-century reality. Harding's plea for a return to what he chose to call "normalcy" was no more than a slogan to cover the removal of governmental restraints that had been placed on business during the Progressive era and the war. Calvin Coolidge put the same thought in somewhat different words when he stated that the "business of the United States is business." Herbert Hoover, as third in the trinity of Republican Presidents of the twenties, thought that unrestricted business enterprise, with the aid of a benevolent government, had brought the United States "nearer to the final triumph over poverty than ever before in the history of any land."

Because each of the three Republican Presidents of this period believed in government aid to business, the policies that they pursued bore only superficial differences. Following Harding's death in 1923, flamboyant corruption was abandoned for government assistance to business under the guise of rock-ribbed, homey practicality. With President Coolidge as a symbol of Yankee shrewdness, the government continued to pass out favors to the businessman, while the mass of people felt safe as long as "Silent Cal" was in office. When Coolidge was succeeded by Hoover in March, 1929, the symbol—but not the technique—was changed. After Coolidge's homespun humor and common sense, the American people entrusted the preservation of prosperity to a man who was enshrined in the public mind as the stereotype of the coldly efficient engineer who would employ scientific methods to promote the glories and productivity of American finance and industrial capitalism. Despite the change of actors, the script remained the same. Harding spoke not only for himself but his two successors when he asked for "less government in business and more business in government."

In some respects government aid to business after World War I represented an extension of methods that had been employed in the past but were carried to new extremes during the 1920's. The high-tariff policy, which had been a cornerstone of the Republican program since the Civil War, was revived by the party after 1920 to rectify what the party's leaders considered to be the mistakes of the Underwood-Simmons Tariff of 1913. Their Midwestern agrarian supporters were crying for relief and their business constituents were voicing their perennial demand for more protection; and Republican leaders concluded that a new tariff would not only implement their traditional program but would also prove a boon and a sop to the party's two largest groups of supporters.

On May 27, 1921, less than three months after Harding's inauguration, a special session of Congress passed an "emergency" tariff bill that placed duties on wool, sugar, meat, wheat, and corn. In 1922 the Emergency Tariff was superseded by the Fordney-McCumber Act, which in general either restored or raised the rates that had prevailed during the Taft Administration. Critics of the bill were assured that it furnished a scientific approach to protectionism, for it established a tariff commission that

Knott in the Dallas News

IT WORKS BOTH WAYS

According to this cartoonist, the extraordinarily high tariffs of 1922 and 1930 were as harmful to the trade of the United States as to that of other countries.

was to recommend revisions to the president when necessary—a provision that would both eliminate needless increases in duties and prevent American wage standards from being undermined by cheap European competition. The president was empowered to make rate changes that did not deviate more than 50 per cent from those of the Fordney-McCumber Act. In practice this system produced 32 increases in specific tariff rates and reductions in the duties on mill feed, bobwhite quail, paintbrush handles, cresylic acid, and phenol.

Since the lot of the farmer showed no noticeable improvement under the Fordney-McCumber Act and large segments of the business community were demanding even more protection, the Republicans in 1928 decided that a further increase in tariff schedules was desirable. With the announcement of Republican tariff plans, lobbyists representing every conceivable economic group descended upon Washington to tell receptive House and Senate committees why their particular tariff schedules should be raised. The resultant Hawley-Smoot Tariff, which was passed in 1930, provided for even higher rates than those of the Fordney-McCumber Act. Although the Fordney-McCumber and Hawley-Smoot tariffs were described by the Republican party as measures that benefited the entire nation, they were in substance little more than a government-enforced subsidy that every American consumer had to pay to American business enterprise. Moreover, both acts made it clear that the United States was committed to a policy of economic nationalism.

During the twenties the tax system was also revised to fit the desires of businessmen—particularly the richest. Andrew Mellon, who had made a fortune in banking and aluminum and had served as Secretary of the Treasury under the three Republican Presidents, repeatedly stated that high taxes on personal and corporation incomes were detrimental to business development. By draining off surplus capital into the nonproductive government, steep taxes, in Mellon's view, forestalled the use of funds for the establishment of new industries and the expansion of old ones. In response to his demands, Congress in 1921 repealed the excess profits tax and within the next five years it reduced the rates on income taxes. Moreover, the Treasury Department made no attempt to check the evasion of taxes by individuals and corporations in the upper brackets. During the twelve years of the Republican reign, tax returns were never made public, and the Treasury Department looked the other way as millionaires cut down on their tax bills by illegal transfers of their securities and the formation of somewhat fictitious nonprofit (and hence nontaxable) institutions.

Governmental policy not only increased the opportunities for profits of American businessmen but also lent its support to the businessman's drive to eliminate competition. Under Herbert Hoover, who served as Secretary of Commerce during the Harding and Coolidge administrations, the Department of Commerce urged industries to adopt self-imposed "codes of fair practice," to standardize products, and to promote the exchange of information among competitors. The Federal Trade Commission, which had been created at the high tide of the New Freedom to ferret out violations of the antitrust laws, had passed under the control of the Republican friends of big business by the midtwenties. Instead of seeking to preserve competition, the new commissioners frequently gave the impression that they were attempting to minimize it. Comparatively few cease-and-desist orders were issued, charges of unfair business practices were kept secret, and the members of various industries were given governmental sanction and support when they made informal attempts to regulate competition.

The Supreme Court, as well as the executive branch of the government, endorsed the moves made by trade associations to reduce competition. In 1921, it is true, the Court ruled against a trade association of hardwood-lumber producers who had followed the advice of one of their officers to "curtail production and to wait for higher prices." In its decision the Court stated that the "united action of this large and influential membership of dealers contributed greatly to the extraordinary price increase" in the industry. But four years later the court reversed itself when it stated in essence that trade associations could limit competition if they were careful to disguise their real intentions. The Court also sanctioned the consolidation movement. Particularly significant in this respect was the Court's decision in the antitrust suit against the United States Steel Corporation (1920), where it ruled that neither size nor the possession of unused power to restrain competition provided sufficient grounds for ordering the dissolution of the corporation or for requiring it to give up any of its subsidiaries.

Throughout the 1920's the government granted special privileges to a number of different industries. The billions that national and local governments spent on highway construction from 1920 through 1930 amounted to an indirect subsidy to the automobile industry. During the same period the airlines received direct financial assistance from the government in the form of mail contracts that were the equivalent of outright subsidies. But the government did not stop there, for the air mail routes were awarded in such a way as to strengthen the large concerns, and during the Hoover Administration Postmaster General Brown contributed to the elimination of competition among the airlines by forcing the smaller companies to join forces with their more powerful rivals.

The merchant marine, like the airlines, received special consideration from the government. During and immediately after the war the government had become the largest shipowner and shipbuilder in the world. The backlog of government-owned shipping was viewed as both a menace and an opportunity by the owners of America's private shipping lines. Ship operators demanded that the government either junk or turn over to them the usable part of its merchant fleet at a small percentage of its original cost. In addition, they asked that the government give them financial assistance through mail contracts and credits for expansion. The government, in general, met these demands. Under the Merchant Marine (or Jones) Act, which was passed by a Republican Congress in 1920, the Merchant Fleet Corporation was to continue to operate some ships until they could be disposed of to private buyers; after 1921 the Shipping Board sold the government-owned ships to private shipowners at approximately 14 per cent of their original cost. Because American operators were still unable to compete successfully with foreign shipping interests, Congress passed the Merchant Marine Act (or Jones-White Act) of 1928. This measure provided for a $250,000,000 loan to private companies for new construction and a thinly disguised subsidy in the form of mail-carrying contracts. The government's policy insured profits to the operators, but imposed increased burdens on the American taxpayer.

Among industries that were directly affected by governmental policy during the 1920's, few, if any, were more important than the railroads. The war was scarcely over before President Wilson raised the question of the future control of the railroads, and during the next twelve months the subject was extensively debated both in and out of Congress. One proposal called for the continuation of the wartime arrangement for five years so that the government could rehabilitate the roads and the public could evaluate the government's management of the lines in peacetime. A second proposal, the Plumb Plan, had been drawn up by Glenn R. Plumb, counsel for the four Railroad Brotherhoods, and had the support of both the American Federation of Labor and several intellectuals. This plan provided for the government ownership of the railroads and their management by representatives of the government, operators, and employees. Finally, the return of the roads to private ownership and operation was advocated by the Association of Railway Executives, the National Association of Owners of Railway Securities, and the United States Chamber of Commerce. Although the Plumb Plan was energetically pushed and the suggestion for continued government operation had many backers, public sentiment seemed overwhelmingly in favor of a return to private operation. As a consequence, President Wilson on December 24, 1919, announced that on March 1, 1920, the railroads would be returned to private management.

The terms under which the railroads were restored to their owners were incorporated in the Transportation Act of 1920 (or the Esch-Cummins Act). This measure gave the Interstate Commerce Commission extensive authority over all railroads, rail-and-water links, telephone, telegraph, and wireless systems, and pipelines within the United States. Provision was also made for Federal sponsorship of a reduction of competition in the railroad industry. Pooling, which had been outlawed for more than thirty years, was made permissible when in the opinion of the commission it would "be in the interest of better service to the public, or economy of operation, and will not unduly restrain competition." At the same time the commission was empowered to prepare a tentative plan for the consolidation of the railroads into a relatively small number of competing systems that would "employ uniform rates," "earn substantially the same rate of return," and be exempt from antitrust legislation. The Transportation Act's sections on rates and earnings revealed the government's desire to guarantee the railroads an adequate return on their investment. The commission was authorized to "initiate, modify, establish or adjust . . . rates so that carriers as a whole . . . will, under honest, efficient and economical management and reasonable expenditures . . ., earn an aggregate annual net railway operating income equal, as nearly as may be, to a fair return upon the aggregate value of the railway property of such carriers." As a means of equalizing the returns of the various lines, the act called for the recapture of all earnings in excess of 6 per cent of the railroad property. One half of this surplus was to be retained in a reserve fund out of which dividends, interest, and rentals could be paid in lean years when any carrier failed to earn 6 per cent on the value of its property; the other half was to go into a revolving fund that would be used for loans to needy roads for capital expenditures or for refunding maturing securities. Finally, the Transportation Act provided for the establishment of a Railway Labor Board to mediate industrial disputes on interstate lines.

From the standpoint of the railroads the most important result of the Transportation Act was the increase in the earnings of Class 1 lines from 3.44 per cent in 1921 to 5.80 per cent in 1929. On the other hand, the commission's attempts to decide what constituted a "fair rate of return" and to devise some method for determining the "value of railroad property" posed problems that were never satisfactorily solved. The commission, moreover, was unable to put the recapture clause into effect; and the provisions dealing with consolidation produced endless bickering but few tangible results. Yet despite the government's inability to implement its plans for the integration of the railroads into a few major competitive systems, individual railroad corporations experienced little apparent difficulty in the execution of their own programs for the elimination of competition. Thus, the same interests that controlled the Pennsylvania Railroad Company were able by means of two holding companies—the Pennroad Corporation and the Pennsylvania Company—to secure control of the Detroit, Toledo and Ironton, the Canton Railroad, the Pittsburgh and West Virginia, the Raritan River, the Wabash, the Ann Arbor, the Lehigh Valley, and the Norfolk and Western, and to obtain a voice in the management of the Boston and Maine, the New York, New Haven, and Hartford, and the Seaboard Air Line. The far-flung Van Sweringen system was made possible by such holding companies as the Vaness Company, the General Securities Corporation, the Allegheny Corporation, the Chesapeake Corporation, and the Virginia Transportation Corporation. The Transportation Act of 1920, which had been drawn up as a device for regulating the railroads, failed in almost every respect to live up to the expectations of its authors.

As significant as the specific favors that the government granted to business was the negative assistance that it provided by refusing to take any steps to curtail the power of business leadership. An indication of the effects of this policy is furnished by the relations between the government and the public utilities. The Federal Power Commission, which was established by the Federal Water Power Act of 1920 and consisted of the Secretaries of War, Agriculture and Interior, was authorized to grant licenses to power corporations on public lands and navigable rivers and to regulate the rates that the licensed companies charged consumers. Between 1920 and 1930 the Federal Power Commission issued 449 licenses, but it proved altogether incapable of regulating the American power industry. Although a governmental investigation in 1928 revealed that the National Electric Light Association was distributing propaganda to schools and colleges, bribing professors and newspaper editors, and seeking to prevent adequate utility regulation by employing—as one of its officials remarked—every publicity technique except skywriting, the government made no move to prevent these practices. Nor did the government compel the utilities to pump the water out of their stock, reduce their rates, or eliminate the numerous abuses that characterized the holding company of the 1920's. When Congress under the liberal leadership of George Norris sought to attack the problem from another direction by enacting legislation for the conversion of the Muscle Shoals facilities into government-owned and -operated nitrate and power plants, the plan was vetoed by Presidents Coolidge and Hoover. In his veto message, Hoover said:

> *For the Federal Government deliberately to go out to build up and expand such an occasion to the . . . purpose of a power and manufacturing business is to break down the initiative and enterprise of the American people; it is destruction of equality of opportunity of our people; . . . it is the negation of the ideals upon which our civilization has been based.*

The government's philosophy of aid to business was based on the premise that the businessman knew what was best for business. The farmer and worker, however, were placed in a different category. Not knowing their own best interests—or so the theory went—they had to take what the government was willing to give to them in the way of Federal assistance.

96. THE GOVERNMENT AND THE FARMER

AMERICAN farmers benefited less from the business boom of the 1920's than any other major occupational group in the United States. For almost two years after the Armistice, American agricultural prosperity was sustained by full employment at home and the continuing demand for American food products abroad. But in 1921, farm profits declined under the impact of depression. Unlike businessmen, for whom deflation was only an interlude, many farmers remained depressed members of American economic society until a second world war placed even greater demands upon their productive capacity.

Throughout the 1920's, most American farmers were unable to recover the ground lost during the postwar depression. Annual farm income decreased, the total value of farm properties fell, and fixed agricultural charges mounted steadily. Many farmers, caught between rising costs and declining income, considered themselves fortunate when a year's labor did not add to their already considerable debts.

The chronic agricultural depression of the 1920's was caused primarily by the decline in European demand for American farm products. In some instances the farmer lost part of his foreign market to Europeans who resumed production after the war and to the staple producers of such countries as Canada and Australia where labor costs were less than those in the United States. The European consumption of American farm products was also curbed by the frenzy of postwar nationalism, which created a desire for self-sufficiency and high tariff-barriers—a brand of twentieth century mercantilism to which the United States contributed its share with the Fordney-McCumber and Hawley-Smoot tariffs. As a result of these developments, American agricultural exports dropped from an index number of 134 in 1919–20 (1909–1913 average = 100) to 117 in 1928–9, while the value of American agricultural exports, which had stood at $3,861,000,000 in 1919–20, fell to $1,915,000,000 in 1921–2 and remained at a somewhat lower figure for most of the remaining years of the decade.

The decline in the value of the American farmer's exportable surplus could not be met by a corresponding increase in domestic consumption. Because of changes in dietary habits, per capita food consumption in the United States was slightly less in the 1920's than during the prewar years, and immigration restriction and a falling birth rate reduced the number of the farmer's potential customers within the United States. At the same time there was little increase in the consumption of nonedible crops produced by the farmer. During the postwar decade, wool, cotton, and tobacco sales within the United States either declined slightly or just managed to hold their own.

The decline in the effective demand for American agricultural products proved the first step in what in many instances was to become a vicious circle. A shrinking market reduced the prices of American farm commodities; lower prices induced the farmer to increase production in the hope that he could balance his losses with greater sales; and increased production, by widening the spread between supply and demand, tended to force prices down still further. Although the farm population declined by approximately 1,200,000 from 1920 to 1930, the index of agricultural production (1923–5 = 100) rose from 96.4 in 1920 to 108.2 in 1928; for the use of machinery and adoption of improved agricultural techniques had increased productivity per worker 25 per cent and productivity per acre 16 per cent during the years from 1919 to 1932. As the twenties progressed, farm prices regained some of the ground lost during the depression year of 1921, but they did not again reach the levels that they had attained during the war and post-war booms. Nor did they increase as rapidly as prices paid by farmers. The index of the purchasing power of farm products rose from 100 in 1913 to 118 in 1917, fell to 75 in 1921 and increased to only 89 in 1929.

INDEX OF FARM PRICES AND PURCHASING POWER OF FARM PRODUCTS, 1913–29*

YEAR	FARM PRICES	PRICES PAID BY FARMERS	PURCHASING POWER OF FARM PRODUCTS
1913	100	100	100
1917	176	150	118
1920	205	206	99
1921	116	156	75
1922	124	152	81
1929	138	155	89

Because he was one of the few remaining economic individualists in American society, the farmer was poorly equipped to meet changing conditions in the domestic and world markets. Unlike most other producers he had little or no control over the terms at which he disposed of his commodities. The manufacturer was able to maintain prices in the home market by hiding behind the tariff wall, by combining with other industrialists to fix prices, or by gearing production to changes in demand. But the farmer, who was competing in a world market in which prices were affected by such whims of nature as droughts in Canada or floods in India and by such whims of man as war or economic nationalism, was unable to control farm prices either at home or abroad. As a result, in the twenties the American farmer was helpless as world demand fell off while his fixed charges remained at or above their wartime highs.

The agricultural depression of the twenties tended to intensify rather than to lessen existing class differences within the farm population. In 1929, 11 per cent of all the farmers received approximately 50 per cent of the total farm income. In the same year half the farm families each produced less than $1,000 worth of products a year, and there were 750,000 farm families—two thirds of them in the South—each of which

* Reprinted with permission from Frederick C. Mills: *Economic Tendencies in the United States; Aspects of Pre-War and Post-War Changes* (New York: The National Bureau of Economic Research, Inc., 1932), p. 348.

produced annual crops worth less than $400. Furthermore, farm tenancy continued to increase. By 1930, 42.4 per cent of American farms were operated by tenants. While farm tenancy enabled some poor but ambitious farmers to improve their economic status, the average tenant—whether his contract called for cash or crop payments—remained throughout his life a debt-ridden, undernourished, rural slum-dweller, who had no interest in maintaining or improving the owners' buildings and land.

Although many farmers found agriculture unprofitable during the twenties, some managed to prosper. In 1929 approximately 25,000 farms, which accounted for 9.7 per cent of total agricultural production, had gross annual incomes of $20,000 or more. Those farmers who could afford to adopt the most advanced labor saving devices were frequently able to make not only an adequate, but an excellent, living; and there were several large commercial farms that covered vast areas of land, employed an extensive labor force, organized production along the same lines as a factory, and made both substantial and regular profits. Moreover, those farmers who grew crops that did not have to be exported generally found agriculture a prosperous enterprise during this period. Throughout the 1920's the dairy farmers of the upper Northeast and Middle West, the fruit growers of Florida and California, and the truck farmers of the Northeast and Pacific coast were able to maintain a standard of living superior to that of the mass of American farmers. Finally, many farmers were able to increase their incomes through cooperatives, which sold farm products and purchased supplies for their members.

In the twenties, as in earlier periods of agricultural distress, the farmer looked to the national government for assistance and relief. After the failure of the Populist movement in the 1890's, farm leaders concluded that they could obtain their demands only by working within the framework of the two established parties. In the nineties the farmers had attempted to capture control of the government from the businessman. In the twenties, farmers sought through a bipartisan alliance in Congress to exact concessions from a businessman's government. The farm bloc, which consisted largely of Southern Democrats and Midwestern Republicans, exercised influence out of all proportion to its size, for it frequently held a balance of power that permitted it to block any piece of legislation in either the House or the Senate.

In waging his political battles in the postwar era, the farmer benefited from certain political and cultural institutions. Farmers were overrepresented in the Senate to which relatively sparsely settled agrarian states sent the same number of senators as the thickly populated states of the Northeast. A somewhat similar situation prevailed in the House, for despite the great increase in urbanization, there had been no redistribution of congressional seats since 1910. Political spokesmen for farmers also had the advantage of representing the interests of a group that occupied a high place in the scale of traditional American values. To the average American, the farmer seemed the most typical and American of all Americans. According to American folklore, city dwellers were to be viewed with suspicion, if not hostility, while farmers were looked upon as pioneers and individualists who were the last remaining repositories of those simple and homely virtues that had made America great. An indication of the strength of this myth can be found in the advantage enjoyed by a candidate for office who was announced to the voters as a son of the soil. Even city newspapers, while often objecting in the strongest terms to the political demands and techniques of the agrarians, seldom, if ever, accused farmers (as they did big business or labor lobbyists) of being un-American.

To prod farm senators and representatives (who seldom needed prodding) farmers supported a variety of organizations that maintained lobbies in the nation's capital. Throughout the twenties the three most important farm pressure groups were the Farm Bureau Federation, the National Grange, and the Farmers' Educational and Co-operative Union, which was generally known as the Farmers' Union. The Farm Bureau Federation had grown out of the Federal and state agricultural-extension program of World War I and in general represented the largest, most prosperous, and conservative farmers. The Grange, which had stemmed from the agrarian discontent in the decade after the Civil War, had forsaken its radical past to espouse the cause of conservative commercial agrarianism. Only the Farmers' Union professed to speak for the small farmer, and, unlike the other two farm pressure groups, it advocated inflation, government price fixing, and co-operation with the less radical labor organizations of the day. In addition to the big three were several other farm organizations, which represented either special localities or the producers of particular crops. Despite his power in Congress, however, the farmer had little to show for his political strength. Although numerous laws were enacted to assist the farmer in the fourteen years after the Armistice, there is no evidence that the mass of farmers benefited from these measures.

The crux of the farmer's plight was that he had an exportable surplus that not only sold at a low price in the world market but forced down the price of his products within the United States. As soon as the problem was recognized for what it was, the farm politicans cast about for some device for eliminating this effect of the exportable surplus upon domestic farm prices. One of the most popular legislative devices for separating the domestic and foreign markets was contained in the McNary-Haugen Bill, which was passed with the support of the Farm Bureau in 1927 and 1928 and was on both occasions vetoed by President

Coolidge on the ground that it provided for "unsound" price fixing. Under the McNary-Haugen Bill, the government was to purchase the leading agricultural staples at a price that would assure the farmer a profit. The government would then dispose of the surplus in the world market at the world price. The difference between the domestic price and the world price was to be made up by an equalization fee that would be levied on the farmer for every unit of his product that he sold. The farmer, therefore, would receive from the government the fixed price minus the equalization fee. If the surplus increased, so did the equalization fee, and the farmer's returns decreased proportionately.

The export-debenture plan, which was backed by the Grange and had the same objectives as the McNary-Haugen Bill, was never approved by Congress. This proposal called for pegging domestic prices through the payment by the government of export bounties on cattle, corn, cotton, rice, swine, tobacco, and wheat. The bounty was to be one half of the tariff duties on the specified farm products and was to take the form of debentures that would be negotiable instruments and would be acceptable to the government for the payment of import duties. In effect, this plan provided that the increase in domestic prices over world prices would be financed by part of the government customs receipts.

The Farm Union in the same period advocated the domestic allotment plan, which did not receive legislative sanction until after the advent of the New Deal. Under this proposal the domestic consumption of each major crop was to be estimated in advance of planting and each farmer was then to be allotted his share of the crop—*i.e.* his domestic allotment. Any amount produced in excess of the quota was to be sold in the foreign market at the world price. This plan, like the others, was designed to establish a double price standard—one for domestic consumers and another for foreign buyers.

Part of the reason for the legislative failure of the programs to relieve the plight of the farmer was the inability of the three most powerful farm organizations to agree on any single proposal. By dissipating their strength in rivalry, the organized farmers were unable to rectify the inequities of a tariff that redounded to the benefit of the industrial producers. An even more fundamental reason for the failure of these measures was that they did not receive the support of the Republican leadership. Because the farm problem was so desperate, however, the Administration, while rejecting other bills, had for political rather than economic reasons to advance a program of its own. The Republican party's plan for the relief of the farmer was incorporated in the Agricultural Marketing Act, which became law in June, 1929.

The Agricultural Marketing Act was designed to give the farmer government assistance in developing farm co-operatives that would enable him to merchandise his crops efficiently—and hence profitably. To implement this program a Federal Farm Board was established and furnished with a revolving fund of $500,000,000 that was employed to establish nation-wide farm co-operatives for each major agricultural product. In addition, the board advanced the co-operatives money that could be lent to their farmer members, who would use their crops as security for these credits. The co-operatives, in turn, were empowered to hold their products off the market until prices had reached a favorable level.

From the outset the operation of the Agricultural Marketing Act was rendered unworkable by the depression. It did the co-operatives no good to withhold crops for higher prices while farm prices steadily declined. As a result, in more than one instance prices fell below the loan rates that the co-operatives offered to their members. While the loan rate on wheat was $1.25 a bushel, its market price was $1.10. In cotton the two prices were 16 cents and 14.5 cents. The difference between the market and co-operatives' prices enabled speculators to buy up crops on the open market and sell them to the co-operatives at the higher price. To forestall this trade and save the co-operatives from bankruptcy, the government established "stabilization corporations" for wheat and cotton. The grain corporation took over the supplies held by the co-operatives at the loan prices and bought wheat in the open market during 1930 and 1931. But as soon as the government guaranteed grain prices, production increased, and the original problem was aggravated rather than solved. In the summer of 1931 the board, which had purchased 250,000,000 bushels of wheat, admitted defeat and abandoned the market. Prices fell precipitously, and a bushel of wheat that had sold for $1.30 in July, 1929, brought only $.53 three years later, while the price of cotton declined from $.179 a pound in August, 1929, to $.065 in August, 1932.

The Farm Board failed to improve the economic status of the farmer because of its inability to control production. Regulated prices and unrestricted production in a period of depression inevitably combined to produce farm surpluses—the very thing which the Farm Board had attempted to eliminate. The Farm Board was well aware of its inability to help the farmers by price fixing alone, and it is significant in the light of subsequent New Deal policy that in August, 1931, the board proposed that every third row of cotton be "plowed under" and that Congress pass legislation permitting the government to control farm output.

Although the Agricultural Marketing Act was undoubtedly the outstanding piece of farm legislation enacted in the twenties, it was not the only law passed to assist the farmer. The Packers and Stockyards Act of 1921 was designed to aid cattle raisers by forbidding combinations and price-fixing agreements among packers. The Capper-Volstead Co-operative Act of 1922 exempted agricultural co-operatives from the jurisdiction of the Sherman Antitrust Law. The Federal Intermediate Credit Act of 1923 provided for the establishment of banks that would deal only in loans to farmers. In addition to these specific measures, there were numerous other ways in which the government continued to assist the farmer. Among other things the government in the twenties aided the farmer through land grant agricultural schools, experiment stations, model farms, extension education in agriculture, home demonstrations for farm women, government sponsored clubs for boys and girls, free information services on agricultural methods and market conditions, grading services, market regulations, easy credit facilities, and a host of other services too numerous to enumerate.

Although no other economic group received so many different kinds of aid from the government as the farmer, agriculture remained the most depressed industry throughout the twenties. While the farmer won many battles in Congress, he never won the war. One explanation of this apparent paradox was that the government was also aiding other groups—business, for example—during this same period. But there were more fundamental reasons for the continuing plight of the farmer. If he had to depend on an exportable surplus for his profits, he could achieve a permanent and solidly based prosperity only in an expanding world economy. But the problem also could have been solved in other ways, although less satisfactorily. If industrial production had expanded enough to offset the decline of agriculture as an income-producing occupation, the marginal and surplus farming population could have been absorbed in manufacturing and distribution industries. But no such industrial expansion occurred, for industrial employment did not increase rapidly enough to take up the slack. The crux of the American farm problem during the 1920's lay in the fact that there was unemployment in the city as well as poverty on the farm.

97. THE DECLINE OF ORGANIZED LABOR

THROUGHOUT the 1920's the majority of American workers enjoyed a higher standard of living than at any other previous time in American history. For a decade after 1919, real wages increased while the length of the average work week declined. But despite these advances, labor's position was far from ideal. After 1921, job insecurity became an increasingly serious problem for many workers, and in some industries wages and hours remained at their prewar levels. At the same time a large segment of the organized labor movement was reduced to virtual impotence. Subjected to a series of attacks by aggressive employers and softened by years of prosperity, the nation's unions declined in both militancy and numbers.

Despite fluctuations in the business cycle, the purchasing power of the average American worker increased during the post-Armistice decade. While the index of the worker's money earnings rose from 218 in 1920 to only 224 in 1928, the index of his real earnings mounted from 106 to 132 in the same years. During the depression year of 1921, money wages declined, but prices fell more rapidly, and real wages more than held their own. Labor's principal financial gains occurred from 1920 to 1923, when real wages rose 13 per cent, and from 1926 to 1928, when they rose 11 per cent. During the first period the worker profited from declining prices. During the second there was an increase in money earnings while prices were relatively stable.

EARNINGS OF WORKERS, 1919–28*

YEAR	AVERAGE ANNUAL EARNINGS IN DOLLARS	MONEY EARNINGS INDEX (1914 = 100)	REAL EARNINGS INDEX (1914 = 100)
1919	1,144	187	105
1920	1,337	218	106
1921	1,171	191	108
1922	1,144	187	113
1923	1,228	200	119
1924	1,225	200	118
1925	1,255	205	119
1926	1,375	219	126
1927	1,375	219	128
1928	1,405	224	132

The increase in the worker's earnings was accompanied by a slight decline in the length of the work week. In 1914 the average number of hours worked per week in American manufacturing industries was 51.5. By 1920 the figure was 48.7, and it fell to 45.5 in 1921. With the passing of the postwar depression, however, the length of the average work week increased, and by 1925–6 it was 48.2 hours.

Statistics on average wages and hours provide only a partial, and at times distorted, picture of working conditions during the postwar decade, for many laborers remained submarginal members of American society. The Southern textile industry continued to maintain company towns, pay weekly wages of about ten dollars, and enforce a work week of more than sixty hours. Somewhat similar conditions prevailed in

* By permission from *Recent Social Trends; Report of the President's Research Committee on Social Trends,* Vol. II, p. 820. Copyright 1933. McGraw-Hill Book Company, Inc.

many Southern coal-mining districts, and by 1928, blast-furnace workers were still employed on a sixty-hour week. Despite the protests of reformers, child labor had not been eliminated, and as late as 1930 two states permitted children to work in factories for sixty hours a week, and five other states allowed them to work a fifty-four-hour week.

Furthermore, unemployment undermined the status of the working class during the twenties. Full employment, which had characterized the war and postwar years, vanished during the depression of 1920–1, and throughout the remaining years of the decade there was always a backlog of unemployed. Although estimates on the number of unemployed vary, most students of the subject agree that at any given time from 1922 to 1929 there were at least 1,000,000 individuals who were unable to find work. Economists have been unable to decide whether or not the paradox of unemployment in the midst of prosperity should be ascribed to technological innovation; but there is little doubt concerning some of the other effects of the machine upon the worker during this period. Machine tending often dulled his creative spirit, made the task of earning a living more monotonous, produced a mounting tension among the more imaginative, and cut down on the job opportunities for older men.

Few gains achieved by individual workingmen in the 1920's came as a result of union activity, for after a splurge of strikes during the years immediately following the Armistice, organized labor became increasingly timid. The American labor movement had emerged from World War I with unprecedented strength. Virtually full employment, a comparatively high level of real wages, the largest union membership in American history, and governmental support of such traditional labor aims as minimum wages, maximum hours, and collective bargaining combined to make organized labor's position appear impregnable. This imposing list of advantages was, however, more than counterbalanced by certain inherent weaknesses in the American labor movement. Despite the marked increase in union membership during the war, the heavy goods industries remained relatively unorganized; and many war workers had been converted to unionism in name rather than fact. In addition, the Armistice canceled some of organized labor's most impressive wartime gains. Union members who had been employed in war industries lost their jobs and frequently whatever enthusiasm they may have had for the labor movement. An even more serious blow was the loss of government backing. During the war the Wilson Administration had harassed the left-wing unions but had endorsed conservative labor's demand for union recognition. After the war the government continued its attacks on the radical labor movement but withdrew its support from the right-wing unions, which were left to shift for themselves. Thrown on their own resources for the first time since 1917, American unions soon revealed that they were no match for the employing classes.

In the period immediately following the war the government staged a nation-wide drive against representatives of left-wing organizations that professed to speak for the nation's workingmen. From 1919 until March, 1921, Attorney General A. Mitchell Palmer, with the assistance of numerous state and local officials, waged a relentless campaign against those individuals whose ideas were to the left of the norm established by the government during the war years. In January, 1920, 2,500 assorted radicals were arrested in a series of government raids. Deportation warrants were issued for approximately 5,000 aliens whose views the government looked on with suspicion. New York State imprisoned the officials of both the Communist and Communist Labor parties, and in 1920 the legislature at Albany expelled five of its members because they were Socialists. The wave of postwar reaction also washed away the International Workers of the World, for the government arrested I.W.W. leaders until the organization was practically arrested out of existence.

The conservative unions were at most only indirectly affected by the government's antiradical campaign; and at the end of the war the lines were drawn for a vindictive struggle between right-wing organized labor and organized management. Many employers who had been compelled by the government to shorten the work week, raise wages, and recognize unions as collective bargaining agencies, were determined to restore working conditions to the *status quo ante bellum.* Union leaders and members, on the other hand, who had adopted—although they had not always abided by—a no-strike pledge during the war years, were equally determined to take advantage of the removal of government controls.

As the cost of living mounted steadily and employers gave no indication that they planned to grant wage increases, unions in widely separated occupations launched a series of postwar strikes. In 1919 there were 3,630 strikes, in which 4,160,348 workers participated. The members of the men's clothing industry conducted a successful strike in New York City for a forty-four-hour week. The New England telephone and textile workers went on strike. In Seattle the workers in all trades conducted a five-day general strike. Actors and actresses, who had formed Equity in 1913, struck successfully for recognition of their organization as their bargaining agency. In 1920 both the railroad switchmen and workers in the printing trades conducted nationwide strikes. Although the workers won a considerable number of their conflicts with management in 1919–20, their over-all record was not so impressive as many contempories imagined. Moreover, organized labor's postwar victories were outweighed by setbacks in the steel and coal industries.

American steel companies had thwarted all attempts to organize their workers before World War I. But in August, 1918, a National Committee for the Organizing of the Iron and Steel Industry succeeded where others before it had failed. Although the companies acknowledged the success of the committee's campaign by granting a basic eight-hour day, discharging union members, and prohibiting meetings of their employes, neither concessions nor repressive measures had any appreciable effect on the growth of the new movement. The companies, however, steadfastly refused to recognize the unions as bargaining agencies, and their policy of dismissing workers for union membership forced the committee to try a general strike. After Judge Elbert Gary, as head of the United States Steel Corporation, had repeatedly stated that he would not deal with the union leaders, the strike was called; and on September 22, 1919, more than 300,000 steel workers—under the leadership of William Z. Foster, a former syndicalist (and a future communist)—left their jobs. The employers fought the strike with private guards, strikebreakers, state and Federal troops, martial law, and a vigorous propaganda campaign that emphasized Foster's racial views. Despite considerable assistance, however, from other unions and some nonlaboring groups, the strikers lacked the weapons to overcome the advantages enjoyed by the employers. In November and December many workers began to return to their jobs, and on January 8, 1920, the union leaders announced the end of the strike. Twenty men—eighteen of them strikers—lost their lives in the conflict. The steel workers had to wait until 1937, the C.I.O., and the New Deal before they could win the struggle that they had lost in 1919–20.

The coal miners' attempts to win concessions from the operators were little more successful than those of the steel workers. On November 1, 1919, the miners in the bituminous fields struck for higher wages and a shorter work week. When a Federal District judge in Indiana, on the motion of Attorney General A. Mitchell Palmer, issued an injunction against the striking miners, the union leaders capitulated, and John L. Lewis announced: "We cannot fight the government." But the strikers refused to return to work, and the strike dragged on until a Federal commission granted the miners part of their wage demands, but refused to make any change in basic hours. In 1922 both the anthracite and bituminous miners struck in protest against the operators' proposal to reduce wages and circumscribe the union's control over its members. Lewis was unable to obtain more than a temporary agreement that reimposed the previous scale. As the decade progressed the United Mine Workers steadily lost ground in their successive struggles with the employers, and by 1929 the union's membership had dwindled away to a fraction of its former strength.

After its initial outburst of postwar militancy, organized labor lapsed into relative quiescence for the remainder of the 1920's. Most labor leaders appeared more interested in maintaining their hold on their respective organizations than in increasing union membership, agitating for labor legislation, or employing the strike to obtain improved working conditions. The total of American trade unionists dropped from 5,110,800 in 1920 to 4,330,000 in 1929. The unions, moreover, were limited to a few industries, and by the end of the decade workers in the building, printing, public service, transportation, and entertainment industries accounted for 70 per cent of the total union membership in the United States. The annual number of strikes declined even more markedly during these years, and in 1929 there were only 921 strikes involving fewer than 300,000 workers.

NUMBER OF STRIKES AND NUMBER OF WORKERS INVOLVED IN STRIKES, 1919–29*

YEAR	NUMBER OF STRIKES	WORKERS STRIKING (IN THOUSANDS)
1919	3,630	4,160
1920	3,411	1,463
1921	2,385	1,099
1922	1,112	1,613
1923	1,553	757
1924	1,249	655
1925	1,301	428
1926	1,035	330
1927	707	330
1928	604	314
1929	921	289

The declining strength and vitality of American unionism during the postwar decade was in part the direct product of the boom. With a relatively fixed standard of living, a shorter work week, and increased wages, many workers felt that unions had little or nothing to offer them. Equally important, the unions were weakened by the frontal and flank attacks of numerous employers, who carried out their anti-union campaigns with either the tacit or real support of the Federal, state, and local governments. Although the government's wartime administration had compelled many businessmen to change their labor policies, it had not compelled them to change their minds; and with the return of peace numerous employers in widely separated industries banded together to destroy the labor movement in the United States.

The inauguration of the employers' anti-union drive coincided with the advent of the postwar depression. Under the name of the open-shop

* Reprinted with permission from John Ignatius Griffin: *Strikes; A Study in Quantitative Economics* (New York: Columbia University Press, 1939), pp. 38, 44.

movement, such traditional opponents of organized labor as the National Metal Trades Association, the National Founders Association, and the National Association of Manufacturers sought to eliminate not only the closed shop but unions themselves. By the autumn of 1920 there were approximately 250 open-shop associations in the United States and more than 50 in New York State alone. The leaders of the open-shop drive emphasized that they were interested in protecting such traditional American values as individualism and the inalienable right of every American to work where he pleased. As unions interfered with this right, the organized employers branded them "Un-American" and announced that the open-shop program was the "American Plan." The advocates of the "American Plan" did not confine their efforts to propaganda, for they also sought to attain their objectives with such traditional anti-union weapons as the yellow-dog contract, injunction, and lockout, and the use of strikebreakers, labor spies, and armed thugs.

Although the open-shop drive destroyed some of the war-born unions and checked the growth of the labor movement as a whole, it did not succeed in its campaign to eliminate the established craft-unions. When manufacturers attempted to smash the old-line unions in the printing, clothing, and building trades with lockouts and boycotts of firms using union help, they won only limited and temporary victories, for these craft organizations had monopolized the job as effectively as any businessman had monopolized his industry. Nevertheless, when the open-shop drive was over, virtually all that remained of the American labor movement was a small group of craft unions in the American Federation of Labor and Railroad Brotherhoods, while the great mass of workers who could not crash labor's elite remained unorganized.

Employers resorted to paternalism as well as force in their attempts to deprive unions of effective control over the American worker. "Welfare capitalism," as the program was called by its authors, was designed among other things to sap the strength of the organized labor movement by granting the worker demands that the union leader asserted could be attained only through organization. In addition to such traditional union goals as increased wages and the eight-hour day, welfare capitalism provided for concessions ranging from bonuses in company stock, pension plans, and unemployment insurance to clean rest-rooms, recreational facilities, and an annual outing or picnic. To curb any latent enthusiasm for unionism among their employees, several advocates of welfare capitalism established company unions, which were confined to a single plant or company. Such unions symbolized management's determination to atomize the labor movement, and had few functions other than to serve as a rubber stamp for the employer's policies. Although numerous workers undoubtedly benefited from some policies of welfare capitalism, the fact remained that its primary objective was to promote the employers' rather than the workers' interests. Not until the Great Depression did the mass of workers learn that what the company had given it could also take away.

The government, in contrast to its attitude toward businessmen and farmers, made little or no attempt to improve the status of the workingman; and in disputes between capital and labor it frequently sided with management. Federal and state troops were employed on more than one occasion either to intimidate or coerce strikers. Attorney General Palmer continued the government's wartime campaign against radical unionism until the end of the Wilson Administration. The courts issued numerous injunctions against various forms of union activity and handed down a number of rulings that organized labor considered detrimental to its interests. In 1919 a Federal district court imposed triple damages under the Sherman Act upon a union for calling a strike, and the Supreme Court in a series of significant cases upheld the validity of the yellow-dog contract, ruled that a union boycott was illegal, virtually outlawed peaceful picketing, and invalidated a District of Columbia minimum-wage law for women.

In the railroad industry, where the government was assigned a specific rôle in labor-management relations, it repeatedly re-enforced the operators' position with both its prestige and power. The Railroad Labor Board, which was established under the Transportation Act of 1920 and consisted of nine members with equal representation from the public, management, and labor, was empowered to recommend but not enforce decisions in disputes between the rail unions and operators. In April, 1921, the board approved a reduction in wages for the railroad workers. When the board in July, 1922, authorized another wage reduction, 400,000 workers in the railroad shops went on strike. Presidential attempts at mediation failed when the operators refused to restore seniority rights to the strikers, and on September 1, 1922, Attorney General Daugherty obtained one of the most sweeping injunctions in American labor history. Although few strikers observed the court's order to return to work, several roads involving 225,000 workers settled with the unions, while the remaining 175,000 had to accept total defeat at the hands of obdurate railroad executives who had received both the sympathy and support of the Harding Administration.

Some states sought to protect the worker and his organizations with minimum-wage and maximum-hour regulations and laws that exempted unions from antitrust legislation, but others sought to check the development of the labor movement. Twenty-one states enacted anti-syndicalist laws directed primarily against the Industrial Workers of the World and Communists, rather than against regular unions. In 1920, Kansas adopted legislation that provided for compulsory arbitration before an "Industrial Court," prohibition of the check-off, and penalties for interference in the production and transportation of necessities of life. Several other states passed laws that prohibited picketing, boycotts, and union interference with the operation of mines and railroads.

Without government support, union leaders were unable to compete with employers who either intimidated workers with superior force or dulled their aggressiveness with paternalism, and by 1929, organized labor had been relegated to a relatively minor rôle in American economic society. Confined to only a small minority of the working class and lacking popular support, an over-all philosophy, and an aggressive leadership, the American labor movement was totally unprepared to meet the cataclysm of depression.

98. FROM BOOM TO BUST

AS THE 1920's progressed, politicians and businessmen vied with one another in asserting that the United States had found the key to eternal prosperity. Magnus W. Alexander, president of the National Industrial Conference Board, stated in 1927 that there was "no reason why there should be any more panics," and a year later a New York business executive announced that the United States was "only at the beginning of a period that will go down in history as the golden age." These statements, which were typical rather than isolated examples of business opinion, were echoed by men prominent in public life. In 1928, ex-Secretary of State Charles Evans Hughes saw little cause for alarm in the economic situation, for "prosperity feeds upon itself"; and Secretary of the Treasury Andrew Mellon assured the American people that the "high tide of prosperity will continue." In the presidential campaign of 1928, Herbert Hoover said: "The poor-house is vanishing from among us. We have not yet reached the goal, but given a chance to go forward with the policies of the last eight years, and we shall soon with the help of God be in sight of the day when poverty will be banished from this nation." The American people elected Mr. Hoover, and within eight months after his inauguration the United States had entered upon the worst depression in its history.

Despite the optimism of the nation's leaders, evidence of an approaching depression was not lacking. There were increasingly numerous indications that the nation's ability to produce was outrunning its ability to consume. Wages and salaries rose steadily during the post-Armistice decade, but they did not mount rapidly enough to keep abreast of the increase in profits, rents, and dividends. Individuals who derived their income from the mere fact of ownership rather than from labor could only dispose of their surplus capital by reinvesting it in productive enterprises. Instead of solving the problem, this practice aggravated it, for the flow of these additional funds into industry served only to increase the nation's productive capacity.

The inability of consumption to keep pace with production would not have presented an insoluble problem if the American economic system had been flexible enough to adapt itself to changing conditions. The postwar decade produced numerous technological innovations that made necessary rapid readjustments in all segments of the economy. As production increased, some device had to be found to supply consumers with the additional funds which would enable them to satisfy their desire for a higher standard of living. As new techniques created new industries and eliminated old ones, both capital and labor had to be sufficiently mobile to shift from industry to industry and even from firm to firm within a single industry. Workers who had lost their jobs through technological unemployment had to be assured of new opportunities in other fields of endeavor, and investors had to be prevented from putting their capital into those enterprises that were already turning out more products than the market could absorb.

Because of the decline in competition in the postwar years, prices tended to become less responsive to changes in supply and demand than at any other previous peacetime period in American history. In the past, Americans had always assumed that prices served as the governor, or regulator, of the entire economy; that is, that any difference between the supply and demand of a particular product would be removed by a rise or decline in its price. But as price competition—particularly in the heavy goods industries—was either circumscribed or eliminated, prices frequently bore little relation to the supply-demand equation. Price rigidity in many industries made it difficult for a manufacturer to ascertain when his market was approaching the saturation point and made it highly improbable that prices would fall in response to a decline in demand.

Price rigidity in several instances created profits that under a system of pure competition would have been reduced by price cuts but that in the twenties were retained and plowed back into industry to increase productive capacity. As a result, the gap between supply and demand was frequently widened rather than narrowed by the price policies of the more prosperous corporations. Price maintenance was accompanied by a similar stickiness in wages. Although industrial wages rose during the 1920's, the earnings of the mass of consumers did not increase enough to permit them to purchase all the products that were turned out by American industry. The increasing imbalance between supply and demand could have been righted only through drastic price reductions or marked increases in salaries and wages. But neither policy was adopted by any considerable number of American entrepreneurs during the 1920's.

The tendency of effective demand to lag behind the available supply was aggravated by the depressed condition of American agriculture. Many farmers had been marginal members of American economic society since 1921. Sharecroppers, tenant farmers, agricultural laborers, and independent farmers in backward areas had not been able to consume any sizable part of the output of American factories during the postwar decade. Moreover, there was no immediate prospect that these poorer farmers would be able to improve their status and thus increase the total American capacity to consume. If American industrialists wished to dispose of any additional products, they had to look to other places than the farm market.

The dependence of American farmers and industrialists on the foreign market for the disposal of their surplus products made the continuation of prosperity partially dependent on conditions over which the United States had relatively little control. Since sales abroad were in large measure financed by American loans, the foreign market was bound to collapse as soon as Americans curtailed their foreign investments. When the speculative boom of the late twenties began to attract to the stock market funds that might otherwise have been sent abroad, the foreign demand for American goods showed signs of declining. Because industry as well as agriculture had come to rely on foreign sales for part of its profits, any shrinkage in the foreign market inevitably necessitated drastic readjustments within the United States.

Continued American prosperity was further imperiled after 1927 by a decline in the rate of growth of both the automobile and building industries. The number of new registrations for passenger cars totaled almost two million in 1924, declined to less than half that figure in 1927, and increased to only slightly more than one million in 1928. The American market for automobiles was evidently approaching the saturation point. The record of the housing industry followed a generally similar trend. For each successive year from 1921 through 1926, more dwellings had been constructed than in the preceding year. But with 1927 the trend was reversed. Since both the automobile and housing industries had made major contributions to the boom of the midtwenties, their relative decline was bound to have an adverse effect on the entire economy.

The final development that set the stage for the collapse of American prosperity in 1929 was the speculative boom that developed with increasing intensity in the years after 1927. As more investors put their money into securities in the hope of making a quick profit on a speculative rise in stocks, the character of the New York Stock Exchange was fundamentally altered. Instead of serving primarily as a device for the accumulation of capital for industrial enterprises, the exchange became a betting ring where people gambled on stocks in much the same fashion that gamblers wagered on roulette or horse races. Security prices were forced up by competitive bidding rather than by any fundamental improvement in American corporate enterprise, and there was little correlation between actual conditions in American industry and stock-market quotations.

Part of the capital that flowed to the New York Stock Exchange in the last two years of the 1920's was supplied by corporations with unexpended and apparently unexpendable cash reserves. Plagued by the fear of overproduction—or more accurately, underconsumption—corporate officials could think of no other way of employing their firms' surplus funds than by placing them at the disposal of the investment market. The traditional function of the stock market was thus reversed. Instead of being used as a device for gathering funds for corporate expansion, it was transformed into a receptacle for the profits of corporations that were threatened by overexpansion.

Speculation in the security market was encouraged by some of the leading financial institutions. Investment banks resorted to the practices of soap and cigarette companies to dispose of new security issues. High-pressure sales techniques, nation-wide advertising campaigns, and specially trained security salesmen recruited from the graduating classes of large Eastern universities were all used to attract additional funds to the stock market. As an inducement to individuals of limited means, investment trusts were set up for co-operative stock purchases under banker direction, and liberal margin requirements permitted the investor to enter the market on a shoestring. By buying on margin, the investor had to pay only a fraction of the quoted price of any particular security. The additional money needed to cover the purchase was supplied by the broker, who obtained these funds from a bank with which he had deposited his customer's stock as collateral. The margin buyer was particularly vulnerable to even a small decline in stock quotations. With any decrease in security values he would have to pay the broker additional money to cover the corresponding decrease in his collateral. If he should be unable to supply this money—and usually he could not—the broker would be compelled to sell the stock to protect himself at the bank. Once this process had started there was always the danger that it could not be stopped. If brokers were to dispose of their customers' holdings and investors were to sell part of their securities to meet the emergency, prices would be further depressed, and more margin buyers would be compelled to dump more stocks on the market. The circle would then be complete, for there was no apparent way of checking this downward spiral after it had been set in motion.

As the stock-market boom was financed in large part by money obtained at low interest rates, the Federal Reserve Board might have been able to retard speculation by raising its rediscount rate. But in 1927 the board, at the request of foreign bankers who wished to check the flow of gold from Europe to the United States, lowered its rediscount rate. As the supply of cheap money made available by this move could not all be absorbed by industry, some of it was used for speculation. A year later, when the board proposed an increase in the rediscount rate, this step was successfully opposed by American bankers. In March, 1929, the board asked the bankers to reduce their loans to brokers; but once again the nation's financiers refused to comply with the board's request. It is, however, unlikely that any change in policy at such a late date would have had any appreciable effect on the course of events. With corporations pouring their surplus funds into the stock market, there was little that the Federal Reserve Board could do by 1929 to check the speculative rise in stocks. Nevertheless, in August, 1929, the board belatedly increased the rediscount rate from 5 to 6 per cent.

In the summer of 1929 some observers began to predict that any decline in security prices would inevitably pave the way for a full-scale crash. During the last two weeks of October these fears were confirmed. On October 19, stocks took their first serious tumble. After a brief rally they went down again on October 24, when almost thirteen million shares were traded. A group of bankers tried to check the collapse by entering the market to purchase securities at a point above their quoted prices. Once more there was a short rally, but it was followed by a complete collapse, and on October 29, the bottom dropped out of the stock market. Approximately sixteen and a half million shares were traded, and some stocks dropped as much as 80 per cent. The crash had come, and the great boom was on its way to becoming the greatest depression in American history.

Many contemporaries failed to realize that the stock-market crash marked the end of American prosperity, for it was rather generally believed that the sharp decline in security prices was a healthy development in that it had checked speculation while leaving American productive capacity intact. On October 26, 1929, *The Wall Street Journal* undoubtedly spoke for many Americans when it stated that "suggestions that the wiping out of paper profits will reduce the country's real purchasing power seem far-fetched." During November, Julius Rosenwald, the head of Sears Roebuck & Co., announced that "comparatively few people are reached by this crash"; and President Herbert Hoover stated that "any lack of confidence in the economic future or the basic strength of the business of the United States is foolish." These optimistic views were all based on the belief that the stock-market crash had not destroyed any real wealth—an idea expressed by Charles M. Schwab in December when he said:

> *This great speculative era in Wall Street, in which stocks have crashed, means nothing in the welfare of business. The same factories have the same wheels turning. Values are unchanged. Wealth is beyond the quotations of Wall Street. Wealth is founded in the industries of the nation, and while they are sound, stocks may go up and stocks may go down, but the nation will prosper.*

Although the stock-market crash may have destroyed only paper wealth, the fact remained that many Americans felt considerably poorer in November, 1929, than they had in September of the same year. They began to limit their purchases, and business leaders who were not sure of what was coming next also started to retrench. The heavy-goods industries, which had played such an important rôle in the boom, were the first to feel the effects of the changed attitude, for only a small percentage of the population was compelled to cut down on the purchase of consumer goods. As confidence in the general economic situation weakened, orders were canceled, new investments dried up, and the very thing that businessmen feared most was promoted by their fear. The boom was over, and the downward spiral gained momentum as business fears and business stagnation complemented one another to accelerate the descent into depression. The decline in the production of both capital goods and durable consumer goods forced these industries to lay off workers, reduce wages, and shorten the work week. Increasing unemployment and a falling wage-scale were accompanied by a corresponding decrease in purchasing power.

The course of the American economy was steadily downward until the first months of 1931, when there was a slight revival of business activity. But this proved only a flurry, for the earlier downward trends quickly re-asserted themselves. Another partial recovery in the early autumn of 1932 was equally deceptive, and the depression reached its all-time low in March, 1933. The national income, which had been $83,326,000,000 in 1929, decreased to $39,963,000,000 in 1932; and the number of unemployed in the first months of 1933 was in the neighborhood of 12,000,000. Between 1929 and 1932 the index number (1935–9 average = 100) of the physical volume of industrial production declined from 110 to 58; the industrial wage bill declined from $10,909,000,000 to $4,608,000,000; farm income declined from $12,791,000,000 to $5,562,000,000; the Dow-Jones average of stock prices declined from $125.43 to $26.82; and the wholesale-price index (1926 = 100) declined from 95.3 to 68.3.

99. THE GOVERNMENT AND THE DEPRESSION

IN EVERY depression before 1929, forces at work within the economy—or else a war—had eventually checked the deflationary spiral and cleared the way for a new cycle of prosperity. Through price and wage slashes, foreclosures, bankruptcies, and the exhaustion of inventories, the economy had been forced down to a bedrock base from which it could once again begin the long, hard climb toward prosperity. But from 1929 to 1933 the American economy seemed bottomless, and many of the tendencies that had produced the boom of the 1920's militated against an automatic recovery.

In the years after the stock-market crash, for example, many industrialists who had been able to fix prices during prosperity continued to keep them at artificially high levels during the depression. Price rigidity in the midst of deflation was particularly pronounced in the heavy-goods industries, many of which reduced production and payrolls while maintaining prices. Throughout the depression, nickel remained at 35 cents a pound, sulphur at $18 a ton, and aluminum dropped from 24 cents a pound in 1929 only to 23 cents in 1932. Aside from the railroads, most big corporations showed profits—although not as large as in the twenties—during the depression. On the other hand, in agriculture and in many consumer-goods industries, competition forced producers to adopt just the opposite policy. Prices were slashed, and production was increased.

Price maintenance, although frequently of direct advantage to those who practiced it, aggravated the severity of the depression by delaying the resumption of large-scale production and by adding to the number of unemployed. Moreover, the price policies of the durable-goods industries placed an additional burden on the manufacturer of consumer goods, who had to pay abnormally high prices for everything he bought while forced to sell his own products at the prevailing low prices. By keeping prices at fixed levels, instead of permitting them to fall with the decline in demand, the directors of many of the nation's basic industries prolonged the depression and virtually eliminated any possibility of a self-generating recovery within the economy.

The depression was intensified not only by price rigidity but also by the decline in the European demand for American products, the depressed condition of the United States' farm population, and the large debt burden that had to be carried during a period of deflation. American exports declined in value from $5,241,000,000 in 1929 to $1,611,000,000 in 1932. Since American foreign trade had been largely financed by loans abroad, there was little chance that this trade could be revived in the near future. Nor could the farmer, for whom the depression in many instances had merely meant a transition from bad to worse, supply industry with the needed purchasing power to check the deflationary trends that had been set in motion by the Panic of 1929. Finally, private debts that had been contracted during the boom had become an almost intolerable burden. As individuals and business firms defaulted on their obligations, the number of foreclosures and bankruptcies mounted until they threatened to drag the entire economy down with them into chaos and ruin.

At the outset of the depression, Herbert Hoover, along with most other Americans, assumed that government intervention would not be needed to prevent human suffering and check the deflationary spiral. When it became evident that the depression was more than a temporary phenomenon, Hoover sought by reassuring statements to convince the American people that their economic problems were mainly psychological and that a return of confidence would be accompanied by a return of prosperity. But the President's repeated pleas for a change of attitude had no appreciable effect on the course of the depression. To the homeless, unemployed, and hungry, Hoover's analysis of the causes of their plight seemed not only naive but heartless. The resident of a Hooverville—as the makeshift shanty towns that were occupied by jobless wanderers were called—knew that the government would have to do more than change his outlook to change his status.

Hoover was criticized by many contemporaries for attempting to end the depression with words, but it should not be assumed that the government relied only on reassuring statements as a device for restoring prosperity. In the winter following the crash, the Federal Reserve Board attempted to expand credit by lowering the rediscount rate, and the Farm Board made an heroic, but unsuccessful, effort to sustain agricultural prices by preventing farm surpluses from glutting the market. Hoover also sought the voluntary co-operation of the business community for a program to sustain purchasing power. In 1930, Colonel Arthur Woods was selected by Hoover to head a committee to collect money for relief. At the same time, at a series of conferences sponsored by the government, leading businessmen assured the President that they would not cut wages. Nevertheless, although businessmen in general observed this pledge until the middle of 1931, they did not hesitate to reduce their working force.

Despite numerous requests that the government take more vigorous steps to relieve suffering and hardship, President Hoover held firm to his belief that the American people would have to rely on their own efforts to pull themselves out of the depression. When some congressmen urged direct relief for victims of the Arkansas drought in 1931, the President insisted that the congressional appropriation be advanced to the farmers as a loan rather than as direct relief. He was equally adamant a year later, when he was confronted by the demands of World

War I veterans for the payment in full of their bonuses. The "bonus army," some fifteen thousand veterans asking for the immediate payment of their bonuses, descended on Washington in the summer of 1932. When they refused to leave, Hoover, in response to an appeal of the District of Columbia Commissioners, called on the army, led by General Douglas MacArthur, to drive them from the capital.

Because Hoover, with much justification, believed that American recovery was being retarded by developments abroad and that the depression was a world-wide rather than an American phenomenon, he made a valiant attempt to shore up the European economy. On June 21, 1931, he proposed a moratorium on intergovernmental debts. France, which interpreted the American President's suggestion as a pro-German move, withheld its approval until July 23. But by then it was too late, for the German and Austrian economies had already collapsed, with disastrous effects upon all the central European nations. As the repercussions of the European debacle began to be felt in the United States, the government concluded that decisive action was necessary. In December, 1931, the National Credit Corporation was established as a device to enable large banks to use their combined funds to save small banks from failure. In January, 1932, Congress set up the Reconstruction Finance Corporation and provided it with $2,000,000,000 to be lent to banks, railroads, and mortgage companies that were threatened by bankruptcy. A month later the Glass-Steagall Act made possible an even more liberal rediscount rate for the Federal Reserve System. Although most of these measures were designed to rescue big business, the government pumped some money into the bottom as well as the top of the economy. The Federal Land Banks lent approximately $125,000,000 to help save some farm mortgages; the income tax was raised; expenditures on public works were increased; and the Federal Home Loan Bank Act was passed by Congress in July, 1932, to aid home owners who were in danger of losing their property through foreclosure.

In the three years after the stock-market crash of 1929, Herbert Hoover had moved a long way from his original position on the nature of the depression and the rôle of the government in the American economy. But as unemployment mounted, business failures increased, banks closed their doors, farmers lost their property, and workers lost their jobs, the American people demanded that the government go even further in its efforts to relieve distress and end the depression. But Hoover would go no further, and, rightly or wrongly, he was held responsible for the hard times. Still, the Republican's only alternative seemed to be to nominate him for a second term, and at the party's convention on June 14, 1932, both Hoover and Curtis were again chosen as the party's standard bearers. The Republican platform reaffirmed the Hoover Administration's policies. When the Democrats met in Chicago

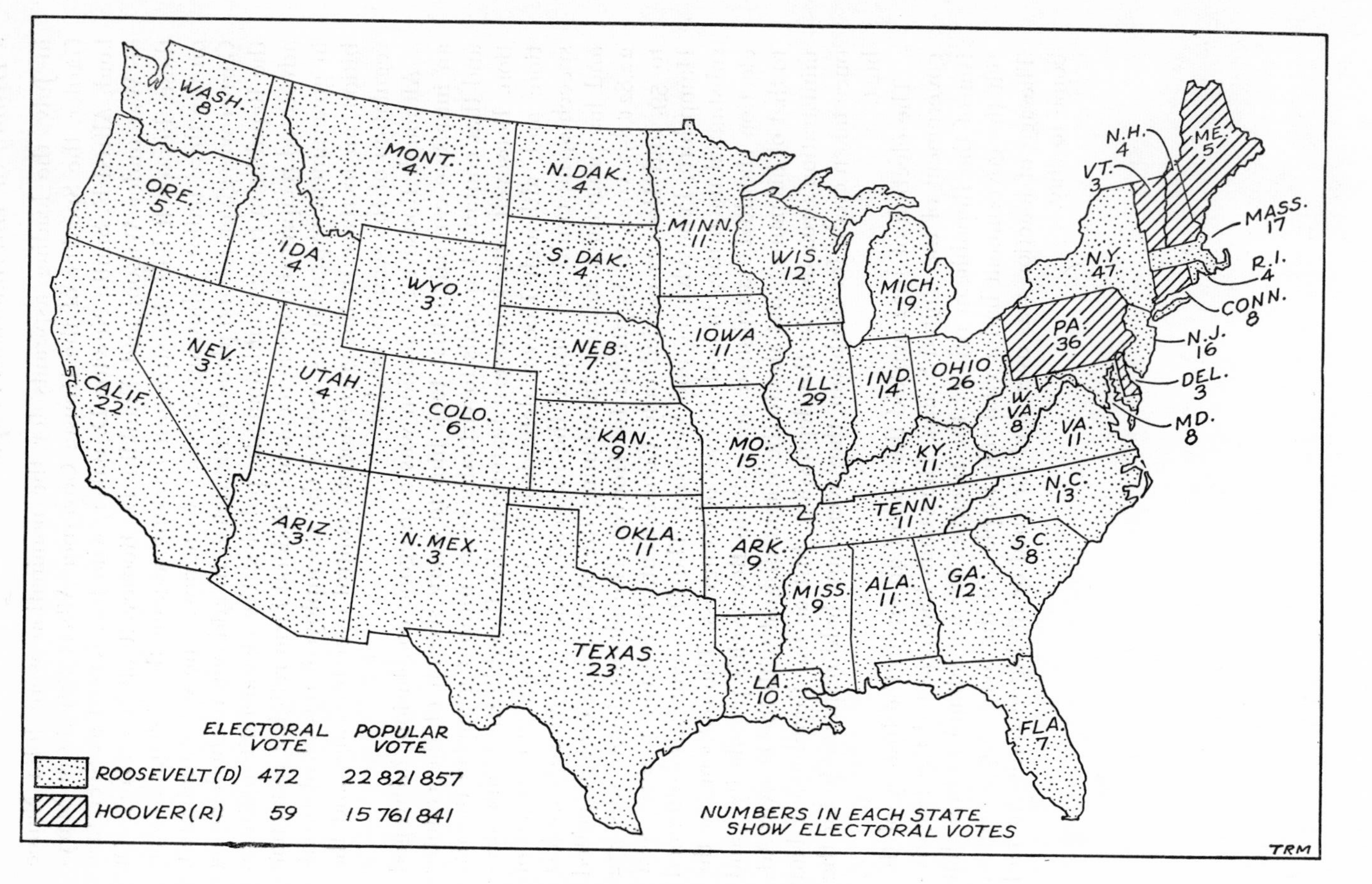

15. THE ELECTION OF 1932

in July, the leading aspirants for the nomination were John Nance Garner, the Speaker of the House; Governor Albert Ritchie of Maryland; Alfred E. Smith; Newton D. Baker, who had served as Secretary of War under Wilson; and Franklin D. Roosevelt of New York. Of these, Roosevelt had the strongest backing among the delegates; and on the third ballot, following Garner's withdrawal, he was nominated. Garner was given second place on the ticket. In addition to condemning the Republican foreign and domestic policies, the Democratic platform advocated reciprocal trade agreements, Federal farm relief, a reduction in government expenditures, aid for the unemployed, repeal of prohibition, an increase in the government's control over banking, and the regulation of the security market.

Although Roosevelt's election was a foregone conclusion, he waged an intensive campaign that took him to every section of the country and that contained appeals to virtually every interest group in the nation. Roosevelt attacked every feature of the Republican Administration; and, although Hoover defended his record with a number of speeches, he could not dispell the impression that his cause was lost and his program a failure. In winning the election, Roosevelt polled 22,821,857 votes to 15,761,841 for Hoover. The electoral vote was 472 to 59, and Hoover carried only Connecticut, Delaware, Maine, New Hampshire, Pennsylvania, and Vermont. The Democrats also obtained substantial majorities in both houses of Congress. The outcome of the election should be attributed not only to Roosevelt's popularity (and to that of his name), but also to the voters' disgust with the Hoover Administration's reaction to the depression. Just as the Republicans had once taken credit for the boom, they were now held responsible for the bust.

The election of 1932 marked the end of an era in the history of the government of the United States. The voters had rejected the negativism of the Republican rule of the twenties for an Administration that felt the government had a vital rôle to play in the lives of the people. The age of inaction was over, and for good or ill, big government had come to stay.

CHAPTER XVI

THE NEW DEAL AND AMERICAN CAPITALISM

DURING its life the New Deal was all things to all men. Depending on the viewpoint of the observer the New Deal was either capitalistic or socialistic, progressive or reactionary, ruthless or humanitarian. Nor was there any agreement about its leadership. To some the New Dealers were a gang of hard-headed, opportunistic politicians; to others they were starry-eyed, impractical professors; and to still others they were reformers and selfless idealists. In truth, the New Deal and the New Dealers were none of these and all of them, for there was not one, but many New Deals.

100. THE NATURE OF THE NEW DEAL

FRANKLIN DELANO ROOSEVELT was born in 1882 to wealth and prestige at his family's estate in Hyde Park, New York. Educated at the Groton School, Harvard College, and Columbia Law

School, he was equipped by both birth and training to assume the rôle of a country squire or successful businessman. Although he entered a New York law firm, he soon showed an aptitude for politics. In 1910 he became a member of the New York State Senate, where he compiled a reform record and impressed a social worker named Frances Perkins as a rather snobbish young aristocrat with an annoying habit of looking down his nose at people with whom he was talking. Despite his cousin Theodore's party affiliations, he was a Democrat and one of the early boarders of the Wilson bandwagon. When Wilson entered the White House, Roosevelt became Assistant Secretary of Navy, and during the war years he played a leading part in planning and administering the expansion of the American navy. Selected as the Democrats' vice-presidential candidate in 1920, he stumped the country for the League of Nations and was retired to what seemed political obscurity by the Harding landslide.

In 1921, Roosevelt was stricken with infantile paralysis, and he spent the next seven years waging a battle successful enough to permit him—though still pitifully crippled in both legs—to re-enter politics. Al Smith, the Democratic presidential nominee in 1928, prevailed on Roosevelt to run for the governorship of New York. Despite Smith's defeat in the nation and in his own state, Roosevelt was victorious, and in 1930 he was re-elected by a plurality of 725,000. As Governor of New York, Roosevelt pushed to completion some of the reform programs inaugurated by Smith, furnished direct relief for the state's needy, advocated the public development of power resources and the regulation of utilities, urged repeal of the Eighteenth Amendment, supported organized labor's traditional demands, and maintained an uneasy alliance with Tammany Hall. As a result of his gubernatorial record, the careful spadework done by Louis Howe and James A. Farley, and the alignment of the various factions within the Democratic party, Roosevelt was chosen the party's standard bearer in 1932. Roosevelt received 22,821,857 popular votes to Hoover's 15,761,841. The electoral vote was 472 to 59.

With the exception of Abraham Lincoln, no other American president has assumed office at a time of graver crisis than Franklin Roosevelt. The banking system had ceased to operate; factories were producing at a fraction of capacity; idle workers numbered in the millions; and once-docile farmers were prepared to take the law in their own hands to save their homes and fields. Even more threatening than the state of the economy was the state of people's minds. A sense of hopelessness mingled with an undercurrent of panic, and signs were not lacking of a mass hysteria that could sweep the country into chaos and ruin. On March 4, 1933, the American people were beaten, confused, and frightened.

Franklin Roosevelt's inaugural address was an earnest of his leadership, for he demonstrated that he had the ability to rise to the occasion, no matter how awful that occasion might be. In solemn but buoyant words, he gave new hope to the American people:

> *This great Nation will endure as it has endured, will revive and will prosper. So . . . let me assert my firm belief that the only thing we have to fear is fear itself—nameless, unreasoning, unjustified terror which paralyzes needed efforts to convert retreat into advance. In every dark hour of our national life a leadership of frankness and vigor has met with that understanding and support of the people themselves which is essential to victory. I am convinced that you will again give that support to leadership in these critical days. . . .*
>
> *We face the arduous days that lie before us in the warm courage of national unity; with the clear consciousness of seeking old and precious moral values; with the clean satisfaction that comes from the stern performance of duty by old and young alike. We aim at the assurance of a rounded and permanent national life.*
>
> *We do not distrust the future of essential democracy. The people of the United States have not failed. In their need they have registered a mandate that they want direct, vigorous action. They have asked for discipline and direction under leadership. They have made me the present instrument of their wishes. In the spirit of the gift I take it.*

The New Deal lived up to the promise of the inaugural, for Roosevelt soon provided both leadership and action. The New Deal has justly been accused of inefficiency. It undoubtedly made countless mistakes, and it lacked consistency; but it never stood still. In this fact lay its strength with the American people, for rightly or wrongly the masses were convinced that the national government was employing its resources and power to solve their desperate economic problems. The New Deal was a crisis government that lived from one domestic crisis to another until it was finally swallowed up in the world-shattering crisis of war. Its long tenure was due, not so much to its ability to solve the problems that arose out of successive crises, but to its ability to convince the American people that they and their government could solve them. The lasting contribution of the New Deal to American life was not its bridges, roads, buildings, or dams, but its transformation of a bankrupt democratic spirit into an exciting, exhilarating, hope-giving, meaningful, every-day experience.

The New Deal came into being because of a major depression, and it did not escape the shadow of this crisis until the outbreak of war in Europe and Asia. Although the methods might change and the emphasis might shift, the restoration of prosperity always remained the end-all and be-all of the New Deal throughout its history. At times frankly stop-gap methods were employed to check the hard tide of disaster, and at other times what were conceived of as long-term reforms were introduced. But reform measures that were designed to improve the lot of the masses also had as their objective the ending of the current depression and the prevention of future ones. No amount of emphasis on other aspects of the New Deal can obscure the fact that its primary purpose was not to change American society, American government, or the economic system, but to change the course of the business cycle, and to reverse the train of events that had been set in motion by the stock-market crash of October, 1929.

In their efforts to end the depression the New Dealers were careful to refrain from any moves that would alter the basic character of the American economic system. The New Deal's opponents frequently accused it of socialism and even communism, but in reality it aspired only to preserve and reinvigorate American capitalism. Although the Roosevelt Administration advocated an increase in government control over business, it did not propose that the government take over and operate the national economy. Businessmen were asked to observe certain rules that they had not observed in the past, but businessmen were never compelled to conduct their businesses as servants of an all-powerful state. Even when the government became an entrepreneur, as in the Tennessee Valley Authority, its avowed and achieved purpose was to stimulate private enterprise. When Franklin Roosevelt was asked by a reporter if he was a Communist, he was dumbfounded and replied: "I am a Christian and a Democrat—that's all."

In its attitude toward business enterprise, the New Deal was in the tradition of both Jacksonian democracy and Woodrow Wilson's New Freedom. On the assumption that certain practices militated against the efficient operation of capitalism and cut down the chances of economic advancement for all elements of the population, the New Deal set about to restore an equilibrium between the various branches of the economy. It attempted reform, not revolution; its policies were designed to achieve equality of economic opportunity rather than economic equality. It believed that only in this way could the economy be revived and saved. Businessmen objected to the New Deal's methods and accused it of socialism; yet the New Deal was determined to save capitalism in spite of the capitalists whose practices during the 1920's had almost destroyed it.

The New Deal's approach to the economic problems of the 1930's was not doctrinaire. No technique or limited objective was considered sacroscant, and whenever one method failed to produce the desired results, it was hastily abandoned for another that seemed at the time to hold more promise. Roosevelt graphically explained his willingness to vary the means for attaining a fixed goal when he resorted to the language of the athletic field to describe the shifting policies of his Administration:

> *It is a little bit like a football team that has a general plan of game against the other side. Now, the captain and the quarterback of that team know pretty well what the next play is going to be and they know the general strategy of the team; but they cannot tell you what the play after the next play is going to be until the next play is run off. If the play makes ten yards, the succeeding play will be different from what it would have been if they had been thrown for a loss. I think that is the easiest way to explain it.*

101. THE POLITICS OF THE NEW DEAL

THE NEW DEAL was a political organization as well as a crisis government. Like every major American political movement, the Democratic party of the 1930's was a hodgepodge of conflicting interests and groups. The core of party strength was supplied by the alliance that Jefferson had established between Southern agrarians and Northern city machines. Despite the allegedly radical policies of the New Deal, the Solid South remained loyal to the Democratic party through the four successive presidential elections won by Roosevelt; and the voters in the cities, whether controlled by machines, as in Chicago, or influenced by loosely organized reform movements, as in New York, gave the New Deal consistently large majorities in every election from 1932 through 1944.

The political genius of the New Deal's leaders lay in their ability to attract additional blocs of voters to the Democratic party. Before 1932 the American labor movement had dissipated its political strength by refusing to identify its interests with any party. After 1933 the average workingman was an ardent and steadfast New Dealer. While a few labor leaders (notably John L. Lewis after 1940) turned against the Roosevelt Administration, the majority of workers remained enthusiastically loyal to a government that had done more for them in a few years than all previous governments had been willing or able to accomplish in almost one and a half centuries.

Another major political triumph of the New Deal was its successful appeal to Negro voters in the Northern states. Since the Civil War the Negro had looked on the party of Lincoln as his liberator and staunchest political ally. But Republicans had come to take the Negro vote for granted and had made no move to improve the lot of this underprivileged minority for more than fifty years. Republican negligence proved to be the Democrats' opportunity. New Dealers permitted the Negro (if he did not live below the Mason-Dixon Line) to share equally with his fellow-white citizens in most of the government's social and economic programs. Moreover, the Roosevelt Administration gave its support to labor organizations that opposed and forbade racial restrictions in their membership. Finally, under the impact of war, the government established the Fair Employment Practices Committee in an attempt to guarantee the Negro as well as other minority groups equality of economic opportunity. Northern Negroes repaid the New Deal with their votes.

The New Deal also gained many votes in the traditionally Republican states of the grain-growing Midwest. In 1932 and 1936 none of these states gave their electoral votes to the Republicans. This success can be attributed to the hard times that prevailed in the region, the voters' disgust with the demonstrated inability of the Republicans to relieve the farmers' plight, and the New Deal's obvious willingness to spend time and money on attempts to better the farmer's economic status. As conditions improved, however, Democratic strength in the agrarian Midwest declined. In 1940 the Republicans recaptured North and South Dakota, Nebraska, Kansas, Colorado, Iowa, and Indiana. Four years later, ten of the twelve states carried by the Republicans were located in the Middle West.

One important group of New Deal supporters defies classification by occupation, class, or race. In general these were middle-class reformers and progressives, who belonged to the tradition of Theodore Roosevelt's New Nationalism, Woodrow Wilson's New Freedom, and Robert La Follette's Progressive party of the twenties. Sometimes they were young people who had been swept up by the idealism that characterized much New Deal activity. Often they were professors who saw for the first time some of the lessons that they had taught in the classroom being applied to the nation. Sometimes they were clergymen and social workers who were attracted by the social reforms of the New Deal. Finally, a few were members of the same upper-class aristocracy of landed and mercantile wealth that had produced Franklin D. Roosevelt and that still looked with suspicion upon the works of the new aristocracy of industry and finance.

With the exception of the Negro and to a lesser extent the worker, all groups that supported the New Deal had representatives in important positions in the hierarchy of New Deal officialdom. Secretary of the Treasury Henry Morgenthau, Jr., was a friend and neighbor of the President at Hyde Park. Secretary of Agriculture Henry Wallace, whose father had held the same position in the Harding and Coolidge cabinets, represented the dissatisfied Republican farmers of the Middle West. Postmaster General James Farley was the spokesman of Northern city machines; Secretary of State Cordell Hull was an old-line Wilsonian Southern Democrat; Secretary of the Interior Harold Ickes and Secretary of Labor Frances Perkins, the first woman to hold a cabinet position, had both been stalwart Progressives when the first Roosevelt was in the White House; Secretary of Commerce Harry Hopkins had spent his years before the New Deal as a social worker. Professors were to be found in virtually every branch of the government except the cabinet. They comprised almost all of the Brain Trust, as the President's early circle of advisers was called. One of them eventually became a member of the Supreme Court, and former college and university teachers were liberally sprinkled throughout most of the famous alphabetical agencies.

Despite the complexity and many-sidedness of the New Deal, its history followed a general pattern whose outlines are discernible, if not clear-cut. In the first weeks of its existence, the New Deal devoted its energy to shocking and jolting the American people out of their lethargy and defeatism. The country demanded action, and the Administration provided a type of leadership that soon revived the confidence of the people in their own and their nation's destiny. By closing the banks, passing the Emergency Bank Act, juggling the currency, establishing the Civilian Conservation Corps, and other such moves, the Administration with the aid of a docile Congress fulfilled its first objective—that of convincing most Americans that the government was capable of meeting the emergency.

As soon as the crisis had passed, the New Deal launched its first major program to restore prosperity. There is little that a government of a capitalistic country can do to end a depression except to pump money into the economy. If the money is pumped into the top of the economy, the assumption is that it will trickle down (like water that is poured into a drip coffee pot) to people in the lower income brackets. If money is pumped into the bottom of the economy, it is assumed it will (like water in the bottom of a coffee percolator) percolate up through the entire economy in the form of increased purchasing power. While the New Deal never employed either method to the exclusion of the other, during the first two years of its existence it devoted most of its efforts to the drip method* and pumped huge sums of money into the economy at its top. It also put into effect a program espoused by many businessmen since World War I and advanced by Herbert Hoover as Secretary of Commerce: under the National Industrial Recovery Act, which became law in June, 1933, trade associations with the support of

* This strategy had been employed on a smaller scale by Herbert Hoover, and Roosevelt preserved and expanded Hoover's Reconstruction Finance Corporation.

the government took over the management of a large part of the American economy. The early New Deal thus conferred more substantial favors upon the businessman than upon any other group.

Despite these favors, many businessmen quickly lost their initial enthusiasm for the New Deal. It was not long before they realized that the government could regulate as well as aid business. Banks were placed under closer supervision; Federal control over the security market was increased; and the government invaded the Tennessee Valley. Moreover, the New Deal distributed favors to groups other than the businessman. Labor was granted certain rights; the unemployed were given relief payments; and the farmer was paid to restrict production under the first Agricultural Adjustment Act. By 1934 many businessmen had concluded that the advantages of government aid were outweighed by the disadvantages of government regulation.

The Roosevelt Administration responded to business opposition by altering its over-all approach to the problem of restoring prosperity. With the invalidation of the N.I.R.A. by the Supreme Court in 1935, the government abandoned even the pretense of co-operation with the business community. In 1933, Roosevelt had asked "our industry" for a "great spontaneous co-operation." Three years later he referred to some businessmen as "economic royalists." The change in the President's attitude was reflected in the shifting course of the stream of government money. After 1934 the government pumped the bulk of its funds into the bottom rather than the top of the economy; for with the establishment of the Works Progress Administration in April, 1935, the New Deal set about in earnest to build prosperity from the bottom up. It curtailed aid to business but continued to support the farmer with a crop allotment program and the worker with the enactment in July, 1935, of the National Labor Relations Act.

The New Deal's early policies were endorsed by the nation's voters in 1934 and again in 1936. In the midterm elections the Democrats obtained large majorities in both the House and Senate, and in 1936 their candidates were once more Roosevelt and Garner. The party's platform was an unqualified endorsement of the Roosevelt policies. When the Republicans convened in June, 1936, at Cleveland, they were hampered by the lack of a clear-cut program or a ready-made candidate. They knew what they were against, but they did not seem sure of what they would like to put in its place. In an effort to resolve this problem they promised to attain the New Deal's objectives without using its methods. Like the Democrats, they planned to end unemployment, restore prosperity, and aid the needy; but they also assured the voters that in carrying out this program they would preserve states' rights, uphold the Constitution, and safeguard the "American system of free enterprise." For their candidates, the Republicans chose Governor Alfred M. Landon of Kansas and Frank Knox, the owner-publisher of the Chicago *Daily News.*

Throughout the campaign of 1936 the Republicans maintained that the New Deal was destroying the American way of life and depriving individuals of their freedom. This theme was repeatedly emphasized by an overwhelming majority of newspapers and by the American Liberty League, which had been formed in 1934 by Republican business groups and was joined by such well-known Democrats as Alfred E. Smith, ex-Governor Joseph B. Ely of Massachusetts, and former Secretary of State Bainbridge Colby. The Republicans also took care to present Landon to the voters as a man who understood the problems of both the businessman and the farmer. On the one hand, he was pictured as a hard-headed executive who had had a successful career in the oil business; on the other he was put forward as a typical Kansan who knew at first hand the needs and aspirations of the farmers.

The Democrats campaigned on their record and asked for a mandate to carry their program to completion. Making no effort to attract support from the business community, the New Dealers sought votes among the workers, farmers, and people on relief. Although these groups comprised a majority that clearly approved of Roosevelt's policies, the *Literary Digest* on the basis of a straw poll predicted a Republican victory. Democratic campaign manager James A. Farley, however, declared that Roosevelt would carry all states but Maine and Vermont, and the election returns proved him right. Roosevelt had 523 electoral votes to 8 for Landon, and the popular vote was 27,751,579 to 16,679,583. In the new House there were 328 Democrats to 107 Republicans, and in the Senate, 77 Democrats to 19 Republicans. Further evidence of Democratic strength was to be seen in the relatively small vote for any third party candidates. The combined vote polled by William Lemke (Union Party), Norman Thomas (Socialist), and Earl Browder (Communist) was only a little more than a million.

After this electoral triumph, President Roosevelt felt strong enough to overcome the judicial barrier to the progress of the New Deal. The Supreme Court, to which he had had no opportunity to make a single appointment during his first four years in office, had declared unconstitutional a long series of New Deal measures that included the N.I.R.A., A.A.A., the Railroad Pensions Act, the Bituminous Coal Act, the Municipal Bankruptcy Act, and the Frazier-Lemke Farm Bankruptcy Act. Faced by judicial opposition such as had plagued and stumped other strong Presidents, Roosevelt resolved on a bold course, and on February 5, 1937, he announced to Congress a plan for what his enemies called "packing" and his supporters termed "democratizing" the Supreme Court.

The Court bill introduced into Congress provided that Supreme

Court justices be permitted to retire at the age of seventy; that the president be allowed to appoint an additional justice for each one who at seventy refused to retire; and put the Court's maximum size at fifteen rather than nine justices. Aside from the merits of this bill (and many students of constitutional law thought that its merits were considerable), its immediate effect was to disrupt the loosely organized alliance of groups that had endorsed Democratic policies in the 1936 election. Republicans took new hope, and with the aid of newspaper editors and columnists, radio commentators, and many lawyers, they launched propaganda that pictured the bill as a threat to the fundamental rights of every American citizen. Most Southern Democrats, whose conservatism had been shocked by New Deal "radicalism," joined forces with the Republican opponents of the President's Court plan. Some liberal Democrats (led by Burton K. Wheeler of Montana) who had formerly given their allegiance to the Administration's domestic measures also fought the reorganization. Although Congress eventually rejected his proposals, the President nevertheless achieved his immediate objective. Even before the end of Congressional debate on judicial reform, the Court handed down several pro-New Deal decisions, and a series of retirements soon permitted the President to fill the Court with a liberal majority that generally endorsed the New Deal program. But the extent of the President's victory could not obscure the fact that he had seriously impaired the political strength of the Democratic party.

Opposition to the Court program convinced the President and his closest advisers that the objectives of the New Deal could not be attained until the Democratic party had been rid of its more conservative elements. As Basil Rauch put it in *The History of the New Deal,* President Roosevelt hoped to produce an "adjustment of party lines which would make party labels correspond with political philosophies" by "making his own party an organization exclusively of liberals, and the Republican party one exclusively of conservatives."* In the 1938 primaries Roosevelt singled out as conservatives several Democratic candidates for Congress (all but one of whom came from the South), and asked the voters to defeat them. Only one of the candidates (the non-Southerner) on what the President's opponents called his "purge list" was rejected by the voters. After the election the party was no closer to unity than before, and the Republicans had gained new seats in Congress for the first time since 1928.

The New Deal, slowed down by the fight over the Court and the President's intervention in the 1938 campaign, was brought to a full halt by events abroad. Confronted by a divided party at home and a world about to go to war, Roosevelt in the winter of 1938–9 abandoned

* Basil Rauch: *The History of the New Deal* (New York: Creative Age Press, 1939), p. 317.

his domestic program and tried to prepare both his party and the na tion for a war that he had come to believe inevitable. Southern conservatives, who a short time before had been threatened with expulsion from the party, received the Administration's blessing as they gave their wholehearted support to its foreign policy. Midwestern liberals from both parties, who had backed the government's domestic reforms, more often than not turned against the New Deal when the President abandoned his plans for social betterment at home to concentrate on events in Europe and the Far East. Only the New Dealers in the Northern and Far Western cities remained loyal to the Roosevelt Administration from beginning to end, for they alone approved of both its domestic and foreign policies.

The New Deal as a reform movement was dead by 1939. As such it had lived a comparatively short life. It had not come into existence until 1934–5, when it had turned from what was essentially a businessman's program to reform. It had reached its high-water mark with the election of 1936, after which it had disintegrated rapidly under successive political setbacks. By 1939, only the wishful thinkers among the most loyal continued to believe that the New Deal of the midthirties would be revived. The New Deal was dead, although its formal interment did not take place until a press conference on December 28, 1943, when the President recognized the fact:

> *The net of it is this—how did the New Deal come into existence? It was because there was an awfully sick patient called the United States of America, and it was suffering from a grave internal disorder—awfully sick—all kinds of things had happened to this patient, all internal things. And they sent for the doctor. And it was a long, long process—took several years before those ills, in that particular illness of ten years ago were remedied. But after a while they were remedied. And on all those ills of 1933, things had to be done to cure the patient internally. And it was done; it took a number of years.*
>
> *And there were certain specific remedies that the old doctor gave the patient. . . .* [The patient is] *all right now—it's all right internally now—if they just leave him alone.*
>
> *But since then, two years ago, the patient had a very bad accident —not an internal trouble. Two years ago, on the seventh of December, he was in a pretty bad smashup—broke his hip, broke his leg in two or three places, broke a wrist and an arm, and some ribs; and they didn't think he would live, for a while. And then he began to "come to"; and he has been in charge of a partner of the old doctor. Old Dr. New Deal didn't know "nothing" about legs and arms. He knew a great deal about internal medicine, but nothing about surgery. So he got his partner, who was an orthopedic surgeon, Dr.*

Win-the-War, to take care of this fellow who had been in this bad accident. And the result is that the patient is back on his feet. He has given up his crutches. He isn't wholly well yet, and he won't be until he wins the war.

For all its varied activities, the large sums of money it spent, and its willingness to resort to almost any technique, the New Deal did not succeed in attaining its long-term objective. The war, not the New Deal, restored American prosperity. The fact that the New Deal failed to end the depression should not, however, obscure its major accomplishments. It saved American capitalism, and in doing so it preserved many other valuable national assets. It saved untold lives—and—perhaps equally important—it saved the self-respect of countless American citizens. It added to the nation's physical assets, and it broadened the cultural opportunities of many Americans who hitherto had displayed little interest in music, painting, drama, literature, and a host of other activities that ranged from basket weaving to folk dancing. Finally, it awakened the American people to a new interest in their government and their way of life. The lasting contribution of the New Deal to its age and to posterity was this revitalizing of American democracy at a time when the democratic way of life around the world was at its nadir.

102. BANKING AND SECURITIES LEGISLATION

THE UNITED STATES, which had been the world's banker during the post-Armistice decade, was unable to shore up international finance after the Panic of 1929. President Hoover made a valiant attempt to save the world through international co-operation, but he was overwhelmed by forces beyond his control. When the financial structure of central Europe collapsed in 1931, it dragged down the rest of the Continent with it. A general abandonment of the gold standard signalized the shift in control of world finance from bankers, who had been guided by the profit motive, to politicians, who viewed financial power as an instrument of national policy.

American banks were totally unprepared to meet the cataclysm at home and abroad in the years after the stock-market crash. Although total deposits in the nation's banks had increased between 1920 and 1929, there had also been an alarming increase in bank failures during these years. From 1921 through 1929, more than 5,700 banks closed their doors. Thereafter the number of bank failures mounted precipitously. In 1930, 1,352 banks with deposits of $853,363,000 were forced out of business; in 1931, 2,294 banks with deposits of $1,690,699,000 failed, and in 1932, 1,456 banks with deposits of $715,626,000 closed their doors.

The disintegration of the American banking system developed into a full-scale panic during the early months of 1933. Gold was being drained from banks into private hoards or to Europe, while distraught depositors tried to rescue what was left of their savings. As soon as one bank was forced to suspend, depositors with money in other banks rushed to withdraw it before their bank suspended too. Every bank failure produced others until even the relatively sound banks were hard pressed to meet their obligations. A run on one bank bred others as rumors based on fact and fancy convinced the American people that their entire banking system was about to pass into oblivion. During the last week of the Hoover Administration almost every bank in the country was either closed or besieged by a line of frightened but determined depositors.

Several Governors responded to the emergency by suspending all banking activity within their states. Nevada's Governor took the lead in October, 1932, and the Governor of Michigan followed his example in February, 1933; by March 3, twenty-three states had declared bank holidays. On the morning of the new President's inauguration, most of the remaining state governments, under pressure from the incoming Administration, also ordered bank holidays.

On March 6, President Roosevelt issued a proclamation that suspended all banking operations and transactions in gold for four days. The following day Secretary of the Treasury Woodin ordered member banks to turn over their gold and gold certificates to the Federal Reserve banks in exchange for some other form of currency. Congress, which convened in special session on March 9, passed within four hours of its introduction the Emergency Banking Act, which validated the President's earlier moves and provided for the reopening of banks in sound financial condition. On March 12 the President delivered his first "fireside chat" to American radio listeners. After explaining what had been "done in the last few days, why it was done, and what the next steps are going to be," he assured the American people:

It was the government's job to straighten out this situation and do it as quickly as possible. And the job is being performed.

I do not promise you that every bank will be reopened or that individual losses will not be suffered, but there will be no losses that possibly could be avoided; and that there would have been more and greater losses had we continued to drift. I can even promise you salvation for some at least of the sorely pressed banks. We shall be engaged not merely in reopening sound banks but in the creation of sound banks through reorganization.

Authorized by the Emergency Banking Act the President took control of all transactions in gold and foreign exchange; the Reconstruction Finance Corporation advanced funds to banks in distress; additional currency was created by the issuance of Federal Reserve bank notes under more liberal terms than in the past; and normal banking operations were speedily resumed in most sections of the country. Three days after the banking holiday, 76 per cent of the member banks of the Federal Reserve System had been reopened, and within two months more than 12,000 banks, with 90 per cent of the nation's bank deposits, were again in business. By a combination of shrewd psychological maneuvers and bold executive moves, Roosevelt had led the American people through the banking crisis.

When the New Deal turned from stop-gap measures to a long-range banking program, it was faced by two alternatives. It could nationalize the banking system or return it to the private bankers who, before March, 1933, had controlled it under the Federal Reserve System. The New Deal took the second course, despite the recent evidence of the bankers' ineptitude and despite the fact that their loose banking practices had contributed to the cycle of boom and bust. If the government had taken over the banks during the weeks immediately following the inauguration, it probably would have encountered little opposition. Bankers as a class were thoroughly discredited in the minds of the American people, and enough depositors had lost their savings to provide support for governmental operation of the banks. But President Roosevelt, who was soon to earn the undying hatred of the bankers, rejected all suggestions for socializing the American banking system. In his first inaugural, he criticized the money changers who "have fled from their high seats in the temple of our civilization," but he made no move to deprive them of their seats. He merely asked them to move over.

New Deal plans for the reform of American private banking were incorporated in the Banking Act of June, 1933. Provision was made for the insurance of bank deposits, and the Federal Deposit Insurance Corporation was established to administer the program. Commercial banks were compelled to give up their investment affiliates so that they could no longer use depositors' funds to purchase securities that were sold by their investment branches. National banks were allowed to engage in statewide branch banking. A number of changes were also made in the regulations that governed the Federal Reserve System. Morris Plan banks and savings banks were declared eligible for admission to the system; member banks were forbidden to pay interest on demand deposits; and the Federal Reserve Board was given full authority over the open-market activities of member banks.

A more thorough overhauling of the Federal Reserve System was undertaken in the Banking Act of 1935. The Federal Reserve Board was then reorganized under the name of the Board of Governors and was made more directly responsible to the president. The Board of Governors was empowered to fix reserve requirements for member banks and was given the deciding voice in an Open Market Committee, which controlled the credit operations of reserve banks. The Banking Acts of 1933 and 1935 were both designed to increase the authority of the government over money and banking by transforming the Federal Reserve System from an appendage of private enterprise into a branch of the government. Equipped with such additional powers, Administration leaders believed that they could end the current depression and avert future economic crises.

In its efforts to reshape the institutions that had been at least partially responsible for the 1929 crash and the depression, the New Deal also extended and tightened up government control of the security markets. Speculation in stocks had not only contributed to the economic collapse but had also been attended by numerous malpractices that were brought to light by the Senate Committee on Banking and Currency during the thirties. Among other things, the committee condemned liberal margin requirements, manipulation of security prices through pools, the lack of accurate information available to security purchasers, the sale of securities at less than market price to favored individuals, and the use of investment trusts to enhance the wealth of trustees at the expense of investors. With the committee's findings as a guide, Congress enacted a series of laws that provided for increased government control over stock exchanges, holding companies, investment trusts, and bankruptcy proceedings.

Under the Securities Act of 1933 and the Securities Exchange Act of 1934, the issue and marketing of securities were placed under the supervision of a five-man Securities and Exchange Commission selected by the president. The principal functions of the commission were to furnish the public with accurate information of security offerings and to prevent the reappearance of those abuses that had characterized the stock exchanges of the twenties. All listed stocks had to be registered with the commission, and pertinent facts concerning securities and the corporations issuing them had to be made available to the commission and to potential investors. The commission could compel individuals and corporations to alter or cease certain practices that violated the laws of 1933 and 1934 or its own administrative rulings. Stock exchanges had to be licensed by the commission, had to give full publicity to their practices, and had to conduct their business according to certain prescribed rules.

The powers of the Securities and Exchange Commission and the protection afforded the security-buying public were further increased by a series of statutes enacted between 1935 and 1940. The Public Utility Holding Company Act of 1935 placed virtually the complete management of holding companies under the supervision of the commission. Although the measure disappointed many liberals, who had demanded the abolition of holding companies, it included the famous "death sentence," which provided for the dissolution of any holding company that failed to demonstrate its usefulness within a period of five years. Chapter X of the National Bankruptcy Act authorized the commission to represent investors in court proceedings that dealt with corporate reorganization. Finally, in 1939–40 another series of laws broadened the commission's authority over investment trusts.

These laws gave adequate protection to the American investor for the first time. Whether they have also reduced the possibility of violent fluctuations in the business cycle remains to be demonstrated. It is worth pointing out, however, that increased government control was accompanied by a marked decrease in the buying and selling of stocks. One hundred and twenty million shares were traded on the New York Stock Exchange in July, 1933, but only seven million or so during the same month in 1940. Those who suffered most from these changes were those who had profited most under the old regime; and they, although bitterly critical of the New Deal for its innovations, had no alternative to offer but a return to the practices of the past.

103. MONEY AND ITS CONTROL

NEW DEAL banking and security laws were generally conceived by their authors as moves to reform American capitalism; but the Administration's manipulation of the currency was an undisguised attempt to restore prosperity by a government-generated inflation. During the first months of the New Deal, President Roosevelt accepted the monetary theories of Professors George F. Warren and Frank A. Pearson, who argued that if the price of gold was increased through government purchase, the value of the dollar would decline and prices would correspondingly rise. The government was soon committed to such dealings in gold. When this policy failed, an attempt to achieve the same result by changing the gold content of the dollar proved equally disappointing.

To carry out its program for stimulating recovery by depreciating the dollar, the executive branch of the government, through a series of congressional enactments and special executive orders, took control of all gold in the United States. In April of 1933 the President, acting on the powers granted him by the Emergency Banking Act, ordered that all gold be turned over to the Federal Reserve banks. An executive order imposed an embargo on gold exports, and a joint resolution adopted by

Congress in the first week of June nullified the gold clause in public and private contracts. Authority over gold was now firmly in government hands, and any obstacles that might have checked the Administration's plans for inflation had already been removed by the Thomas Amendment to the Agricultural Adjustment Act in May, 1933. This catch-all provision permitted a government-inspired inflation under a number of alternative devices that included the purchase of government securities in the open market by Federal Reserve banks, an issue of paper money or silver certificates, bimetallism, a reduction in the gold content of the dollar, and a change in the reserve requirements of member banks in the Federal Reserve System.

The Administration's attempt to restore prosperity by currency manipulation brought it into direct conflict with the nations at the London Economic Conference, which were seeking an international solution to world-wide economic problems. This conference, sponsored by the League of Nations, had been called to consider such questions as the reduction of trade barriers, the establishment of sound currencies, and monetary stabilization. Hoover had accepted the League's invitation to the United States before the expiration of his term of office, and Roosevelt had appointed a delegation headed by Secretary of State Hull. Soon after the conference convened in June, the delegates of other countries asked the United States to join them in a plan for international currency stabilization; but the President—in what Broadus Mitchell has called "probably the most momentous decision that Franklin Roosevelt made"—rejected this proposal. His decision not only disrupted a conference that from the outset had little or no chance of success, but it also made clear the fact that he placed American recovery ahead of world recovery and that the United States was going to substitute economic nationalism for international co-operation. In his message to the conference on July 3, Roosevelt said:

> *I would regard it as a catastrophe amounting to a world tragedy if the great Conference of Nations, called to bring about a more real and permanent financial stability and a greater prosperity to the masses of all Nations, should, in advance of any serious effort to consider these broader problems, allow itself to be diverted by the proposal of a purely artificial and temporary experiment affecting the monetary exchange of a few Nations only. . . .*
> *The sound internal economic system of a Nation is a greater factor in its well-being than the price of its currency in changing terms of the currencies of other nations.*

Pursuing the proposals of Professors Warren and Pearson, the government started its gold-buying program in October, 1933, with purchases by the Reconstruction Finance Corporation. The government's price for gold, which then stood at $20.67 an ounce in contrast to the world price of $29.80, was raised to $34.45 by the end of the next January, when the policy was abandoned. This gold-buying program aroused the hostility of the business community but had no noticeable effect upon the general price level. In January, 1934, the Administration changed its tactics (but not its objective) with the passage of the Gold Reserve Act. Among other things, this measure permitted the president to alter the gold content of the dollar by as much as 60 per cent, withdrew all gold from circulation, and forbade the redemption of currency in gold. Two billion dollars of the "profit" that would accrue to the government as a result of devaluation was assigned to an Exchange Stabilization Fund, which was to be employed by the treasury to prevent fluctuations in foreign exchange rates. The Gold Reserve Act was, in effect, the final step taken to remove the United States from the gold standard. At the same time an attempt was made to maintain the illusion that the country still operated on a gold standard. In theory the currency was backed by gold; but in fact, no one could turn his currency into gold, there were no gold coins, and private individuals were not permitted to trade in gold. For good or ill, the Gold Reserve Act substituted a managed currency for the gold standard—a shift that forty years earlier would have been considered earthshaking, but one that was reaffirmed by the Supreme Court in 1935 with its decisions in the so-called gold cases.

Following the passage of the Gold Reserve Act, the President revalued the dollar at 59.06 cents, and the treasury, which had been granted sole authority over gold purchases, fixed the price of gold at $35.00 an ounce. There is little reason to believe that either action had any more effect upon the general price level than the program that they superseded. These New Deal gold policies produced one notable result, however: they undoubtedly accelerated the flow of the world's gold supply to the United States. By July, 1940, the Federal government controlled approximately 80 per cent of the monetary gold in the world. This vast hoard was buried in Fort Knox, Kentucky, where it was guarded by the army and served as an expensive monument to a type of economic society that had been vanquished by the Great Depression.

The failure of gold purchases to increase prices generally did not prevent the government from undertaking a similar program in silver. Through silver purchases, the Administration hoped not only to promote domestic inflation but also to subsidize the Western silver producers. The Thomas Amendment to the Agricultural Adjustment Act empowered the president to introduce the free coinage of silver at any ratio to gold on which he might decide; and at the London Conference the United States, along with the other silver-producing countries, agreed to buy thirty-five million ounces of silver annually from 1934 through 1937. In June, 1934, Congress passed the Silver Purchase Act, which authorized the Secretary of the Treasury to purchase silver until it comprised 25 per cent of the value of government monetary stocks or until the price of silver reached $1.29 an ounce. This act further provided that silver certificates be issued against all silver purchased by the government and permitted the president to nationalize silver whenever he saw fit. On August 9, President Roosevelt nationalized silver.

The New Deal initiated its silver-purchase program in December, 1933, and during the succeeding six and one-half years, the treasury purchased well over two billion ounces of silver and issued over one billion dollars in silver certificates and silver dollars. This program, however, fell short of both the stated objectives of the Silver Purchase Act of 1934. By June, 1940, the price of silver, instead of being at the stipulated $1.29 an ounce, was lower than the price that had prevailed before the government began its silver purchases. Nor did the government succeed in bringing its supply of silver up to one fourth of its total metallic monetary stocks; for, while the treasury acquired silver, it also acquired gold. As a result in June, 1940, the government was further away from its aim of one silver dollar for every three of gold than it had been in 1934. The silver-purchase program was equally disappointing as a device for raising prices. It is impossible to disassociate the effects of the silver policy from those of other inflationary schemes of the day, but it has been generally conceded that the price level did not change appreciably as a result of the government's acquisition of silver. Government silver-purchases chiefly provided the nation's silver producers with a handsome subsidy.

The international results of this silver policy were just the opposite of those intended. Instead of strengthening the silver-standard countries, the high prices offered by the United States frequently disrupted their economies. Both China and Mexico profited from selling silver to this country, but they were both compelled to overhaul their currency systems because of the concentration of the world's silver supply in the United States. On the other hand, the countries that exchanged their silver for American dollars did not use their dollars to increase their purchases of American products.

After 1934 the New Deal abandoned its attempts to promote inflation by manipulating the currency and adopted other devices to achieve the same end. In an effort to revive business activity, the Administration continued to employ the powers over bank credit granted by Congress and to increase its loans to private enterprise. While these policies provided the nation's banks with additional funds, they did not succeed in expanding bank credit, for few business executives were inclined in those years to assume new financial obligations. In the second half of the thirties, the New Deal also attempted to force up prices through heavy government expenditures.

Throughout the 1920's successive Republican Administrations had curbed government expenditures in order to retire war debts. Despite a sharp decrease in tax revenues, the national debt was reduced by one third between 1919 and 1929, but after 1930, plans for continued debt reduction were abandoned as the Hoover Administration made a desperate effort to balance the budget (that is, to have government income equal government expenditures during the fiscal year). For some time after the stock-market crash, Hoover was able to keep the budget in balance, but when the government began to aid business with funds to prevent the complete breakdown of the economy, Federal expenditures began to exceed receipts. On June 30, 1932, the government had a deficit of nearly $3,000,000,000.

President Roosevelt, who had criticized Hoover's "extravagance" during the 1932 campaign, entered office pledged to balance the budget, and in March, 1933, Congress at his request passed the Economy Act. The effect of this measure, which reduced Federal salaries, benefits, and pension payments, was soon washed away, however, by the flood tide of New Deal spending. At first New Dealers viewed government spending as an unpleasant necessity. Accordingly, Reconstruction Finance Corporation funds were used to bail out business firms in distress, and other money was employed to provide the needy with either direct relief or employment. But what had been originally conceived of as an emergency policy soon became a permanent program and was developed into an established theory for ending the depression. Taking over the ideas of John Maynard Keynes, the prominent English economist, New Dealers came to believe that idle savings were responsible for business stagnation. They therefore proposed to free these savings and place them in the hands of consumers, whose purchases would simulate industrial output. This course involved "deficit financing," which was an anathema to the orthodox, but the New Dealers argued that the cure was less painful than the malady and that the government would abandon its spending program as soon as the patient was restored to health. In his 1940 budget message the President explained the theory on which much New Deal spending rested:

> *Following 1933 the fiscal policy of the Government was more realistically adapted to the needs of the people. All about were idle men, idle factories, and idle funds, and yet the people were in desperate need of more goods than they had the purchasing power to acquire. The Government deliberately set itself to correct these conditions by borrowing idle funds to put idle men and idle factories to work.*

Throughout its history the New Deal failed to balance the budget, and from the fiscal year of 1932 to 1940 the national debt increased from $19,487,010,000 to $42,967,000,000.

Although the New Deal obtained the bulk of the funds for its spending program by borrowing (that is, by increasing the national debt), it also had recourse to the issue of more currency and to an increase in taxation.* Businessmen objected to heavier taxes and warned of the dangers of unrelieved heavy spending. Partly as a result of this criticism and partly because of increasing signs of a business revival, the govern-

* The amount of money in circulation rose from $5,720,000,000 in 1933 to more than $8,000,000,000 in 1940; and the annual internal revenue of the Federal government in the same period went up from $1,619,839,000 to $5,340,452,000.

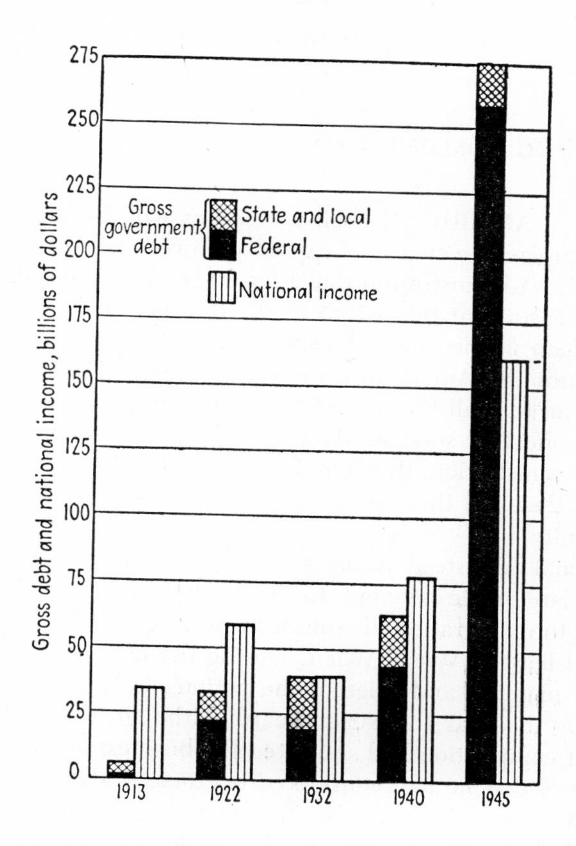

16. GROSS GOVERNMENT DEBT AND NATIONAL INCOME

[Reprinted with permission from J. Frederic Dewhurst and associates: America's Needs and Resources *(New York: Twentieth Century Fund, 1947).]*

ment reduced its expenditures in 1937; a depression followed (the Administration called it a "recession") and lasted until the government resumed its spending program in the middle of 1938.

The developments of 1937–8 seem to indicate that there was a close connection between government fiscal policies and the course of the business cycle during the 1930's; but even if this point is conceded, the fact remains that the Administration was still no closer to a solution of its problem. On the one hand, it was granted by even the most ardent New Dealers that continued deficit financing would eventually produce a runaway inflation and economic chaos worse than depression. On the other hand, a reduction in government expenditures was accompanied by a descent still further into the depths of depression. This was the dilemma that was raised by New Deal spending—and it was a dilemma that the war rather than the New Deal resolved.

104. CURBING COMPETITION

AMERICAN business leaders who looked on the New Deal as the implacable enemy of capitalism owed their survival in large measure to the Administration that they so freely criticized. By adopting drastic measures at the height of the banking crisis, the New Deal saved American finance—and American capitalism as well. By pumping money into the American economy, the New Deal sustained the very capitalism that all businessmen agreed was essential to their individual and collective success. By establishing the National Industrial Recovery Administration, the New Deal introduced a plan of economic organization that had the initial support of practically the entire business community.

The National Industrial Recovery Act, which represented the New Deal's first large-scale attempt to revive industry, was essentially a program for the integration of American business enterprise. Its origins went back at least to World War I. During the last months of the war, the quality, quantity, and price of the nation's industrial products had been fixed by the War Industries Board. Although this system for the restriction of competition had subjected the businessman to a degree of outside control that he had considered onerous, it also had guaranteed his profits. After the war some businessmen were reluctant to abandon what one of them referred to as a "sensible and advantageous . . . method of compulsory standardization." The War Industries Board had relied heavily on trade associations for the regulation of industry, and during the Administrations of Harding and Coolidge, Herbert Hoover in his capacity as Secretary of Commerce lent his department's support to trade association attempts to dull the edge of competition in a number of industries.

Throughout the 1920's, the general prosperity that characterized the decade pushed into the background earlier demands for the creation of a single authoritative agency to co-ordinate the activities of different industries. As long as business boomed, there seemed little need to inaugurate an all-encompassing plan for the control of prices and production; but the depression revived earlier demands for over-all planning. In 1930, Bernard Baruch demanded "industrial self-government under governmental sanction"; the next year Gerard Swope, president of General Electric, proposed a detailed program to mitigate or eliminate competition; the United States Chamber of Commerce approved a report calling for the relaxation of the antitrust laws and the creation of a "National Economic Council" to deal with the "tendency of productive capacity to outrun the ability to buy"; and the National Association of Manufacturers took a similar stand.

The National Industrial Recovery Act, which became law in June, 1933, incorporated many of these proposals. Industries were permitted to ignore the antitrust laws and to draw up codes of fair practice that would be enforceable by law. In return for these concessions, business was compelled to make others. The government could reject a code, and labor was guaranteed the right of collective bargaining and provisions for maximum hours and minimum wages. The National Recovery Administration, established to supervise and enforce the provisions of the law, was headed by a chief administrator assisted by advisory boards for industry, labor, and agriculture.

The National Industrial Recovery Act was a comprehensive attempt to save American industrial capitalism from self-destruction. To achieve this purpose its authors assumed that collective action was superior to competition and that members of the American business community were capable of co-operation. They also assumed that business could best be organized under the control of businessmen willing to accept government regulation in return for government support. The specific object of the act was to raise prices to the 1926 level; its general aim was to revive business enterprise and end unemployment by reducing competition and creating a government-enforced balance between employer and employee, seller and buyer, big business and small business. Businessmen were asked to put aside their selfish interests, and the government accepted the fact that the American economy had already attained a high degree of integration. The N.I.R.A. sought, not to destroy these collectivist features, but to preserve, harness, and control them for what it considered the good of the entire nation. It represented, in short, a long step toward a planned economy. It did not, however, make a sharp break with the past, for businessmen were to do much of the planning. In many respects the game was unchanged; but now the rules were out in the open for all to see. The government would enforce these rules and serve as referee, but business would still furnish the players.

Under the operation of the National Recovery Administration each industry submitted a tentative code that was first checked by government specialists and then submitted to a public hearing conducted by a deputy administrator for the industry. After conflicting views had been reconciled either by compromise or by administrative ruling, the completed code was referred to the President, whose approval turned it into law for the industry. Firms observing N.R.A.* regulations were permitted to display posters bearing the Blue Eagle, which was the official symbol of the Recovery Administration. Each of the 746 basic and supplementary codes that were eventually approved contained the labor guarantees required in the act, and rules of "fair competition," which usually included provisions for minimum prices; standardization of products, services, and business practices; price filing; and regulation of the industry's capacity to produce. Among the practices outlawed by many codes as "unfair competition" were false advertising and branding, breach of contract, price discrimination, tie-in sales, attacks upon the reputation of competitors, combinations to fix prices, and the pirating of a competitor's employees.

The inauguration of the National Recovery Administration under General Hugh S. Johnson as Administrator was accompanied by fanfares of government publicity and a fervid scramble for privileges among the representatives of virtually every vested-interest group in the United States. Code making, which had been conceived of as a co-operative effort among government, business, labor, and consumer, more often than not developed into an enterprise in which business—and in most cases, big business—played the leading rôle. In almost every instance labor leaders fought for enlarged rights for their members, and the government sought to serve as mediator; but the consumer, despite provisions for his protection, was left out in the cold Some codes were no more than a simple statement of objectives; others covered countless details and provided for practically every contingency that might arise. Moreover, all codes were drawn up and approved so hastily that they contained numerous inequities, contradictions, and violations of the spirit and even the letter of the law. A number of codes included provisions for limiting production, allocating quotas, and fixing prices at abnormally high levels. Instead of paving the way for recovery, these regulations often maintained the rigidity that had been one of the principal factors in prolonging the depression.

* N.R.A. refers to the National Recovery Administration. N.I.R.A. refers to the National Industrial Recovery Act.

Most businessmen quickly lost their initial enthusiasm for the N.I.R.A. Many employers objected specifically to its labor provisions and in more general terms to the extent of government "interference" permitted by the act. At the same time, signs of returning prosperity convinced some businessmen that they could dispense with government assistance. Late in 1934, Henry I. Harriman, president of the United States Chamber of Commerce, saying that "we are no longer pressed by the tide of disaster," suggested that the N.I.R.A. be supplanted by legislation that would "place upon industry the sole responsibility for formulating codes of unfair competition." The government would "have no authority to impose or modify codes of unfair competition"; but if it did "not approve of a code which . . . [had] been presented by industry, it . . . [might] of course, state the modification it . . . [desired] and industry . . . [would] then determine whether it . . . [would] accept the changes requested or go on without a code."

Even more serious than growing business opposition to the N.I.R.A. was evidence that the program was failing to achieve its objectives. Selfish interests had not been subordinated to the general welfare. Prices in several industries were so high that they reduced consumption. Some industrialists made inordinate profits, and others who would have been forced out of business in a competitive economy remained in operation. Instead of freeing small business from the domination of big business, most codes accentuated the trend toward concentration of power within a single industry. Finally, the Administration was unable to prevent code violations, despite its repeated announcements that it was going to "crack down" on those who broke the law. Swamped with protests over alleged violations, uncertain as to the extent of their authority, and not desiring to antagonize those upon whom the success of the program depended, N.R.A. officials were both unable and unwilling to take drastic action against recalcitrant businessmen. Moreover, their rulings over interstate business could only be enforced by the courts, whose lengthy processes were no substitute for the immediate decisions required; and they were unable to coerce companies in intrastate business except by forbidding them to display the Blue Eagle posters.

On May 27, 1935, the Supreme Court in a unanimous decision invalidated the N.I.R.A. on the grounds that Congress could not enact laws regulating the business practices of firms in intrastate trade and that the National Industrial Recovery Act represented an attempt on the part of Congress to delegate its legislative functions to the president.* Although the Supreme Court's decision received wide publicity and seemed to close forever any possibility of a revival of the N.I.R.A., in one sense it was an anticlimax. By the spring of 1935, the act had so little popular support, was so loosely enforced, and so flagrantly violated

* *Schechter Poultry Corp.* v. *United States,* 295 U.S. 495.

that it was already in its death throes. The Court merely applied the *coup de grâce.*

The New Deal never attempted to resurrect the N.R.A., but it sought to perpetuate its principal features in the coal industry. The Guffey-Snyder Bituminous Coal Stabilization Act of August 30, 1935, included practically all the provisions of the defunct Bituminous Coal Code. As a hedge against an adverse court decision, observance of the code was made theoretically voluntary, but the refund of nine tenths of a 15 per cent tax on the market value of coal to those producers who abided by the code was a strong inducement to co-operate. In the spring of 1936, however, the Guffey-Snyder Act went the way of the N.R.A. when the Supreme Court ruled that it was unconstitutional.

The National Recovery Administration, which had been hastily conceived and haphazardly organized, had placed the government squarely behind industry's drive toward monopoly. Furthermore, it had bred conflict and confusion rather than the co-operation and order at which its authors had aimed. Yet its positive accomplishments should not be overlooked. It furnished industry with the leadership that private enterprise was unable to supply, and it provided business with the shot-in-the-arm that was needed to lift it out of the economic doldrums.

105. CURBING MONOPOLY

AFTER the invalidation of the N.I.R.A. by the Supreme Court, the New Deal confined its attempts at regulating business practices to labor legislation and to the supervision of specific industries in which the public interest seemed to require Federal control. Numerous commissions, modeled on the Interstate Commerce Commission rather than the code authorities of the N.R.A., were established to supervise rather than revive certain industries. The Federal Communications Commission, formed as a result of the Communications Act of June 19, 1934, was given powers over the radio, telegraph, and cable industries comparable to the powers of the Interstate Commerce Commission. In similar fashion the Motor Carrier and Air Mail Acts of August, 1935, extended the authority of the Interstate Commerce Commission over interstate bus, truck, and airplane companies; and in 1938 the Civil Aeronautics Authority was set up to regulate the nation's airlines.

Although the New Deal in its early stages gave greater support to the integration of business enterprise than any other single Administration in American history, by the last years of the 1930's it had become a stalwart champion of economic competition. The shift in New Deal emphasis from a planned to a competitive economy grew out of the belief that the recession of 1937–8 had been caused by the high prices established by monopolists. In April, 1938, Roosevelt delivered a message to Congress in which he assailed the development of monopoly; and in June, Congress set up the Temporary National Economic Committee to "make a full and complete study and investigation with respect to the concentration of economic power in, and financial control over, production and distribution of goods and services." Manned by experts from governmental agencies and by congressmen, the T.N.E.C. through a series of hearings and research projects sought to demonstrate that concentration (or the absence of competition) was responsible for many of the economic ills of contemporary American society. Publishing its findings in thirty-seven volumes of testimony, forty-three monographs, and a *Final Report and Recommendations,* the T.N.E.C. presented a comprehensive and documented history of the decline of competition in the United States. In industry after industry, the committee gave facts, dates, and figures on such traditional devices for circumscribing competition as price fixing, patent monopolies, holding companies, trade associations, interlocking directorates, and international cartels.

In 1938 the New Deal also launched a large-scale trust-busting program reminiscent of the brave, dead days of an earlier Roosevelt. Thurman Arnold, a Yale professor of law, who in 1937 had written a book in which he referred to antitrust laws as "the great myth," was made Assistant Attorney General in charge of the Justice Department's antitrust division. Arnold sharpened up his spear, saddled his snow-white charger, hired bright young law-school graduates as fellow warriors, and set out to defeat an enemy that had lost many battles but never a war.

Under Thurman Arnold's energetic direction, the Justice Department prosecuted entire industries, as well as individual firms, and labor unions, as well as corporations. The basic test was whether or not prices had been held at an artificial level through collusion, and those groups that showed a willingness to abandon such practices escaped penalty. Suits were filed against both unions and contractors in the building industry. The motion-picture industry was also prosecuted. In 1939, General Motors was convicted of a violation of the Sherman Act and fined twenty thousand dollars, and in the next year twelve oil companies were found guilty of conspiracy.

There is no reason to believe that the New Deal, despite its efforts, succeeded in restoring competition. As in the past, economic concentration seemed to proceed at a steady rate regardless of the program pursued by the government. In 1942, in industries that accounted for one third the value of all American manufactured products, the four largest producers in each industry turned out more than three quarters of the industry's product.* In contrast to earlier periods, the increased concentration in American industry during the 1930's was the result, in general, not of mergers but of an increase in the size and power of existing concerns.

Although the New Deal swung from support for collective action to advocacy of competition, it never relaxed its efforts to stimulate American business enterprise. The New Dealers repeatedly attacked business leadership, but they always recognized that the restoration of American prosperity depended upon the revival of American commerce and industry. Liberal critics of the Hoover Administration had complained that it had subsidized business, but the New Deal continued and expanded the Hoover program for aid to corporate enterprise. The scope and extent of the Reconstruction Finance Corporation's activities were greatly enlarged under the New Deal; and from the agency's inception in 1932 until December 31, 1941, its loans and other authorizations totaled more than $9,000,000,000. While a large proportion of these funds was employed to aid agriculture, banks, and governmental agencies, the R.F.C. also extended credit to industrial enterprises. From 1932 to 1939, it lent more than $400,000,000 to American industry. A similar policy was pursued by the Federal Reserve banks, and from 1934 to 1939 they made loans to industry to the amount of about $123,000,000. New Deal expenditures in other sectors of the economy provided equally valuable—although less direct aid—to American industrialists, wholesalers, and retailers. In so far as Federal funds expended on relief programs, public works, and social security payments increased the effective purchasing power of the nation's consumers, they all helped to sustain business enterprise. Many businessmen took delight in condemning the New Deal for its heavy expenditures, but it is difficult to see how the average businessman could have lived without them.

The New Deal also undertook to stimulate business activity through a revival of foreign markets. Monetary manipulation was, among other things, an unsuccessful attempt to maintain American foreign trade by offsetting the effect of the depreciation in value of the currencies of other countries. The two Export-Import banks, established in 1934 and combined in 1936, promoted American commerce by extending loans to customers of the United States abroad. The Roosevelt Administration's recognition of the Soviet Union in November, 1933, was prompted

* In 1926, 316 corporations controlled 35 per cent of the nation's working capital. In 1938, they controlled 47 per cent. Two hundred and five manufacturing corporations, each of which in 1942 had more than $50,000,000 in assets, owned 37 per cent of the nation's manufacturing assets in 1934 and 49 per cent in 1942. In 1942 the manufacturing corporations that received annual net incomes of $5,000,000 or more had slightly more than half of the total manufacturing income as compared with 46 per cent in 1929. On the other hand, manufacturing corporations with incomes of less than $250,000, which had received 19.1 per cent of the total income in 1929, had only 11.6 per cent in 1942.

in part by a desire to increase American exports; and in 1935 the two countries signed a trade pact in which Russia agreed to purchase thirty million dollars worth of American goods annually. Finally, the New Deal through its reciprocal trade program sought not only to mitigate the acknowledged evils of economic nationalism but also to widen the opportunities open to American exporters.

The Trade Agreements Act, passed by Congress in 1934 and repassed at three-year intervals during the remainder of the New Deal's tenure, rejected both the straight-line reductions of the Wilson Administration and the high-tariff policies of the Republicans. Tariff making was removed from the control of congressional committees and of pressure groups and placed in the hands of the executive, who was empowered to make changes in rates up to 50 per cent, although not to alter the free list. Under the operation of the act, tariff schedules were proposed to the Secretary of State by committees after they had held hearings for interested business groups. The Secretary of State then proceeded to negotiate treaties with foreign governments for a mutual (but not necessarily identical) reduction in tariff barriers.

Between 1934 and the United States' entrance into World War II, Secretary of State Cordell Hull negotiated twenty-six reciprocal trade agreements with nations that accounted for approximately two thirds of American foreign trade. The effect of these treaties upon the domestic economy cannot be discovered with any degree of exactitude, for the recession of 1937–8 and the defense boom that developed soon after make it impossible to test results that would be difficult to ascertain under any circumstances. It is interesting, nevertheless, that from 1934 to 1940 the increase in American exports to treaty countries was almost twice as great as the increase in exports to nontreaty countries. American manufacturers, although they conceded that the program aided exporters, complained that it deprived them of the protection that they had been afforded by the Republican high-tariff policies. This view was not, however, borne out by the facts. From 1934 to 1940 imports from treaty countries rose by 35 per cent while those from nontreaty countries mounted by 37 per cent. Whatever success was achieved by the reciprocal trade program was due in large measure to the efforts of Cordell Hull, who gave the program his whole-hearted support from 1934 to 1945, when he resigned as Secretary of State.

Businessmen opposed to the New Deal frequently cited its invasions of the sacred precincts of free enterprise as evidence in support of their contention that the Roosevelt Administration had an anticapitalist bias; but the New Deal, although it entered many fields that had formerly been restricted to private business, endeavored, not to socialize the nation's economy, but to invigorate American capitalism or to assume those tasks that businessmen had refused to undertake. The Reconstruction Finance Corporation and other government lending agencies were employed by the New Deal, not to drive bankers out of business, but to furnish the American economy with credit that could not be provided by private financial institutions. The New Deal's slum-clearance and housing program, which aided the producers of building materials, was undertaken only after it was clear that the construction industry was either unwilling or unable to do as much. The Rural Electrification Administration was established because the power industry had failed to cater to this potential market, and the Administration's success was demonstrated by the increased sales of electric power. And the Tennessee Valley Authority, which marked the most significant New Deal departure from the traditional concept of the government's rôle in the American economy, was intended not only to promote reforestation, flood control, the national defense, and agriculture but also to "provide for the . . . industrial development of said valley." There can be little doubt that this last objective was fulfilled. In 1944, David Lilienthal, who at the time was chairman of T.V.A., wrote:

> *What of business in the industrial sense? That too is developing, and at a rapid rate. Even before the war the valley saw the addition or expansion of several large industries devoted to the basic materials of modern industry, such as aluminum, ferro-silicon, heavy chemicals; these included two of the largest phosphatic chemical works in the country. . . .*
>
> *At least as important as these heavy industries is the rise of new light industries and the expansion of plants that existed before 1933. The industries added since 1933 range from those for the processing of frozen foods and the production of cheese to the manufacture of aircraft and mattresses, bottle washers, stoves, flour, inlaid wood, barrel heads and staves, electric water heaters, furniture, hats and shoes, pencils, carbon electrodes, boats, horse collars, oxygen, ground mica, and acetylene, metal dies, ax handles, and barites.**

Thus, the New Deal at various times in its career both supported and attacked business consolidation and collective action, subsidized industry, financed purchasing power, regulated certain key industries, aided exporters, and undertook economic enterprises that in the past had been reserved for private individuals or companies. But it did not succeed in achieving the aim that underlay these diverse and often conflicting policies: it was not able to lift American business enterprise to the levels that it had attained in the 1920's. Instead of regaining prosperity, business experienced a series of cyclical movements within the larger framework of depression. Soon after Roosevelt had entered office, there was a

* David E. Lilienthal: *TVA; Democracy on the March* (New York: Harper & Brothers, 1944), p. 35.

minor boom that lasted into the fall of 1933. Although the tempo of this upsurge was not sustained, it was followed by a gradual but steady recovery that lasted until August, 1937, when the recession began. With the resumption of government spending, the recession was halted, and business once again began to climb slowly and unsteadily upward until the demands of war succeeded in producing a boom that no amount of New Deal ingenuity had been able to promote.

Before the outbreak of World War II business activity, as measured by *The New York Times's* weekly index, did not once equal (although it almost did on two occasions) the high point reached in June, 1929; and it was not until mid-1940 that the earlier mark was surpassed. The national income, which had been $83,326,000,000 in 1929, fell to $39,-963,000,000 in 1932, rose to $71,513,000,000 in 1937, dropped to $64,-200,000,000 in 1938, and reached $70,829,000,000 in 1939. The index number for the physical volume of industrial production (1935–9 average = 100) ranged from 110 in 1929 to 58 in 1932, 113 in 1937, and 88 in 1938. Capital issues, which had totaled $11,592,200,000 in 1929, did not exceed $6,254,300,000 during any single year of the 1930's. Corporate dividends, which had been $9,809,000,000 in 1929, fell to $3,229,000,000 in 1932, and were only $5,098,000,000 in 1938 and $5,837,000,000 in 1939. The value of American exports declined from $5,240,995,000 in 1929 to $1,611,016,000 in 1932 and had mounted to only $3,177,-176,000 by 1939. Imports followed a somewhat similar trend, dropping from $4,399,361,000 in 1929 to $1,322,000,000 in 1932 and rising to $2,-318,081,000 in 1939. These statistics, if they reveal nothing else, demonstrate that the New Deal did not end the depression.

Without the crutch supplied by the New Deal, American industrial capitalism might well have perished; but no amount of New Deal ministration could make the cripple a healthy man. Only war was capable of effecting such a miraculous cure.

CHAPTER XVII

RELIEF AND REHABILITATION UNDER THE NEW DEAL

WHILE the New Deal attempted both to revive and to regulate American business enterprise, it also sought to assist those groups that in the past had in large part been ignored by the government. It encouraged workers to organize and assured them of certain minimum standards; it subsidized farmers; and it gave the unemployed either relief grants or jobs on projects financed by the government. Critics of the New Deal frequently complained that aid to the worker, farmer, and unemployed was a political device for purchasing the votes of the masses. Whether or not this charge was fair (and the New Dealers vehemently denied that it was), the fact remained that the government was not only helping those most in need of assistance but was also attempting to end the depression by increasing purchasing power.

106. LABOR LEGISLATION

AS THE prosperity of the twenties gave way to the depression of the thirties, many American workers learned for the first time that they lacked both the ideological resources and the economic weapons for life in twentieth-century America. Lay-offs, wage cuts, and bread lines made the average worker frightened rather than angry, disheartened rather than militant. In March, 1933, he wanted neither charity nor revolution; but he did want hope, leadership, and an adequate standard of living. Soon after taking office, the Roosevelt Administration sought to fulfill these demands.

The New Deal's labor program may have arisen, as many of its friends have contended, from the humanitarian impulses of its authors, but it was also based on a desire to restore American prosperity and to enhance the strength of the Democratic party. By raising wages and ending unemployment the Administration leaders thought that they could create a mass purchasing-power that would stimulate industrial activity and prevent the reappearance of the disparity between wages and profits that had helped to destroy the prosperity of the twenties. And Democratic leaders realized that the industrialization of the United States had created a large industrial labor force that would probably vote in a bloc if it received suitable favors from the party in power. Organized labor's overwhelming support of Franklin Roosevelt in successive presidential elections provided conclusive proof of the validity of this second theory.

To achieve the political and economic objectives of its labor policy the New Deal employed three methods: (1) It supported collective bargaining by giving both moral and tangible aid to workers who wanted to unionize their industries. (2) It provided relief for those who for whatever reason could not work. Direct relief and jobs on public works and in make-work programs were furnished to the unemployed as emergency measures. Social security and unemployment compensation were advanced as long-term solutions. (3) Finally, the New Deal sought to impose and enforce certain minimum standards for workers who were employed.

Aside from relief and social-security measures, which gave help to many others besides industrial workers, there were only three major New Deal labor laws. The N.I.R.A. secured to labor certain guarantees that lasted until the act was invalidated by the Supreme Court in 1935. In that year Congress passed the National Labor Relations Act, and three years later the Fair Labor Standards Act became law. Precedents were not lacking for these laws, for similar measures had been adopted by several states during the Progressive era and the 1920's, by the Federal government during World War I, and by most of the industrial nations of Europe during the preceding half century.

Soon after Roosevelt entered office, he was forced by the pressure of events to take a stand on the question of government aid to labor. On April 6, 1933, the Senate passed the Black Bill, which provided for a thirty-hour week in factories. At the same time the House was considering a similar bill, introduced by William P. Connery, chairman of the House Committee on Labor. Leading industrialists quickly made known their opposition to the Black-Connery Bill in speeches, chamber of commerce resolutions, and their testimony before the House Labor Committee. The Administration, responding to this pressure, withdrew its tentative support from the measure and offered instead the National Industrial Recovery Act as an alternative program that would meet the needs of both industry and labor.

To tide labor over in the interval between the enactment of the National Industrial Recovery Act and the completion of codes for the various industries, Roosevelt on July 27, 1933, asked all employers to sign the President's Re-employment Agreement. More than 2,000,000 employers responded to his request and agreed not to employ anyone under 16 years of age; to establish a maximum work week of 40 hours for clerical help and 35 hours for factory workers; to pay minimum wages that ranged from $12 to $15 a week for clerical workers and from 30 to 40 cents an hour for factory employees; to maintain existing wages that were above these minimum rates; and to refrain from unnecessary price increases. Approximately 16,300,000 employees were covered by the President's Re-employment Agreement, and it has been estimated that it had provided jobs for about 2,462,000 workers by the end of October, 1933, when N.R.A. codes began to go into effect.

The N.R.A. was essentially a program to enable business—especially big business—to regain what it called stability and its critics called profits. There were, however, important economic and political reasons why the plan had to include provisions for improving the status of labor. Price increases could only be maintained if they were accompanied by wage increases that would help to sustain mass purchasing-power. Moreover, the Administration was not in a position to antagonize the labor vote by aiding industrialists while it ignored workers. As a result, the Roosevelt Administration offered labor through the N.I.R.A. certain basic guarantees that were covered in the famous Section 7A of the act:

> *Sec. 7. (a) Every code of fair competition, agreement, and license approved, prescribed, or issued under this title shall contain the following conditions: (1) That employees shall have the right to organize and bargain collectively through representatives of their own choosing, and shall be free from the interference, restraint, or coercion of employers of labor, or their agents, in the designation of such representatives or in self-organization or in other concerted activities for the purpose of collective bargaining or other mutual aid or protection; (2) that no employee and no one seeking employment shall be required as a condition of employment to join any*

company union or to refrain from joining, organizing, or assisting a labor organization of his own choosing; and (3) that employers shall comply with the maximum hours of labor, minimum rates of pay, and other conditions of employment approved or prescribed by the President.

The establishment of the N.R.A. was accompanied by marked advances in the status of the American worker. From October, 1933, to May, 1935, the index of industrial employment (1923–5 = 100) rose from 84.6 to 90, and the index of manufacturing payrolls (1923–5 = 100) increased from 61.1 to 61.7. The average hourly earnings of industrial workers mounted from an average of 44 cents in 1933 to 52 cents in May, 1935; while the length of the average work week fell from 42 to 36 hours. Furthermore, Section 7A strengthened—although it is impossible to say how much—the organized labor movement in the United States. By 1935, the American Federation of Labor was claiming (undoubtedly it exaggerated) 4,500,000 members, and at the same time the independent-union membership totaled at least 300,000. On the other hand, the N.R.A. failed to achieve many of the goals that had been set for labor by the Administration. The wage and hour provisions of many codes frequently duplicated existing standards and brought improvements only to those workers employed in the less advanced firms in an industry. Section 7A was bitterly attacked and openly evaded by many employers, who either refused to recognize unions or established company unions in evident violation of the law. Nor did the N.R.A. produce the expected co-operation between capital and labor, for the number of strikes increased from 841 in 1932 to 1,856 in 1934.

When the Supreme Court on May 27, 1935, ruled that the National Industrial Recovery Act was unconstitutional, the Administration was compelled to resort to other means to implement its labor program. In an attempt to fill part of the void created by the Court's decision, Congress in July, 1935, passed the National Labor Relations Act. The Wagner Act, as it was more commonly called, stated that "employees shall have the right of self-organization, to form, join, or assist labor organizations, to bargain collectively through representatives of their own choosing, and to engage in concerted activities, for the purpose of collective bargaining or other mutual aid or protection." Employers were forbidden to interfere with the rights thus granted to workers or to maintain or support company unions. The administration of the act was entrusted to a three-man National Labor Relations Board, which was empowered to summon employers to appear before it, issue cease and desist orders, hold elections to determine what collective-bargaining agency a particular group of workers wanted, and hear complaints from workers concerning violations of the law. Workers who appealed to the board were guaranteed against retaliation by their employers, and the board's rulings were enforceable through the courts.

Employers, who were assured by some of the most prominent lawyers in the United States that the Wagner Act was unconstitutional, ignored it and sought to hamper its effectiveness by tying it up in court proceedings. The Supreme Court, however, upset the predictions of the "experts" by a series of decisions in 1937–8 that upheld the validity of every feature of the act. Despite the opposition that it aroused among employers, the National Labor Relations Board proved to be one of the most efficient and effective of all New Deal agencies. From 1935 through 1940, the board handled approximately 30,000 cases, most of which were settled by agreement. It prevented nearly 900 strikes, settled more than 2,100 strikes that had already been called, and reinstated more than 21,000 workers dismissed for union activities.

The New Deal sought not only to protect and support the organized-labor movement but also to raise wages and reduce the work week through congressional legislation. The Walsh-Healey Government Contracts Act, passed in 1936, required corporations operating under contracts with the Federal government to pay the prevailing wages for their industry, maintain a maximum eight-hour day and forty-hour week, and employ no one under sixteen years of age. The Fair Labor Standards Act of 1938 established maximum hours and minimum wages for all workers in industries in interstate commerce. Minimum wages were set at twenty-five cents an hour with the provision that this figure would be increased to forty cents within the next seven years. Maximum hours, limited to forty-four, were to be reduced to forty within two years. Wage committees were empowered to fix minimum wages for specific industries with due consideration for regional differences in the costs of production and transportation. Goods produced by child labor (except in agriculture) could not be shipped in interstate trade. Employers who violated the law were liable to a fine of ten thousand dollars and a jail sentence of six months.

Despite the efforts of the New Deal to aid the worker through legislation, it was never able to devise a law for ending unemployment, for the number of individuals seeking, but unable to find, work was never less than seven million from 1933 to 1940. Nor did the New Deal aid all elements of the laboring population equally. Domestic servants, many white-collar workers, and those not employed in industries in interstate trade fell outside the jurisdiction of both the Wagner and Fair Labor Standards Acts. Nevertheless, in spite of these deficiencies in its labor policy, the New Deal did more for American labor than had any previous Administration. It raised the wages and improved the working conditions of a large share of American workers. Equally important, it set off the greatest organizing drive in the history of American unionism.

107. THE GROWTH OF INDUSTRIAL UNIONISM

THE RAPID development of industrial unionism under the direction of what eventually came to be known as the Congress (originally, Committee) of Industrial Organization grew out of the opportunities presented by the National Industrial Recovery Act. To the N.R.A. advisory board the President appointed John L. Lewis of the United Mine Workers, Sidney Hillman of the Amalgamated Clothing Workers, George L. Berry of the Printing Pressmen, and President William F. Green of the American Federation of Labor. Both Lewis and Hillman believed that the labor movement should take advantage of the labor provisions in the National Industrial Recovery Act by launching a campaign to organize the relatively unskilled workers in the mass-production industries. Green, while giving lip service to this proposal, made few moves to implement it, for he feared that a flood of new members would destroy the exclusive character of the A. F. of L. From June to October, 1933, the A. F. of L. organized fewer than half a million workers outside the clothing and textile industries, both of which were committed to the new type of unionism. Moreover, the A. F. of L. placed these workers in special unions that were confined to individual plants and served only as way-stations for new members until they could be transferred to the federation's established craft-unions.

The allegiance of the A. F. of L.'s hierarchy to craft unionism and its lukewarm attitude toward new members were in sharp contrast to the policies pursued by the leaders of the coal and clothing unions. Throughout the summer of 1933, the United Mine Workers carried on an intensive organizing drive, and Lewis conducted a series of successful strikes in the unorganized coal fields in several Southern states. When the N.R.A. coal code went into effect, the miners were almost completely organized. Similar campaigns were waged by Hillman in the men's clothing industry and by David Dubinsky, president of the International Ladies Garment Workers, in the women's clothing industry. Workers in widely varied fields responded to the efforts of industrial-union organizers with alacrity and enthusiasm. Between 1933 and 1935, the membership of industrial and semi-industrial unions increased by 132 per cent, whereas there was only a 13 per cent increase in the membership of craft unions. The growth of industrial unionism was accompanied by increasing labor militancy as the number of strikes rose from 2,288 involving 849,002 workers from

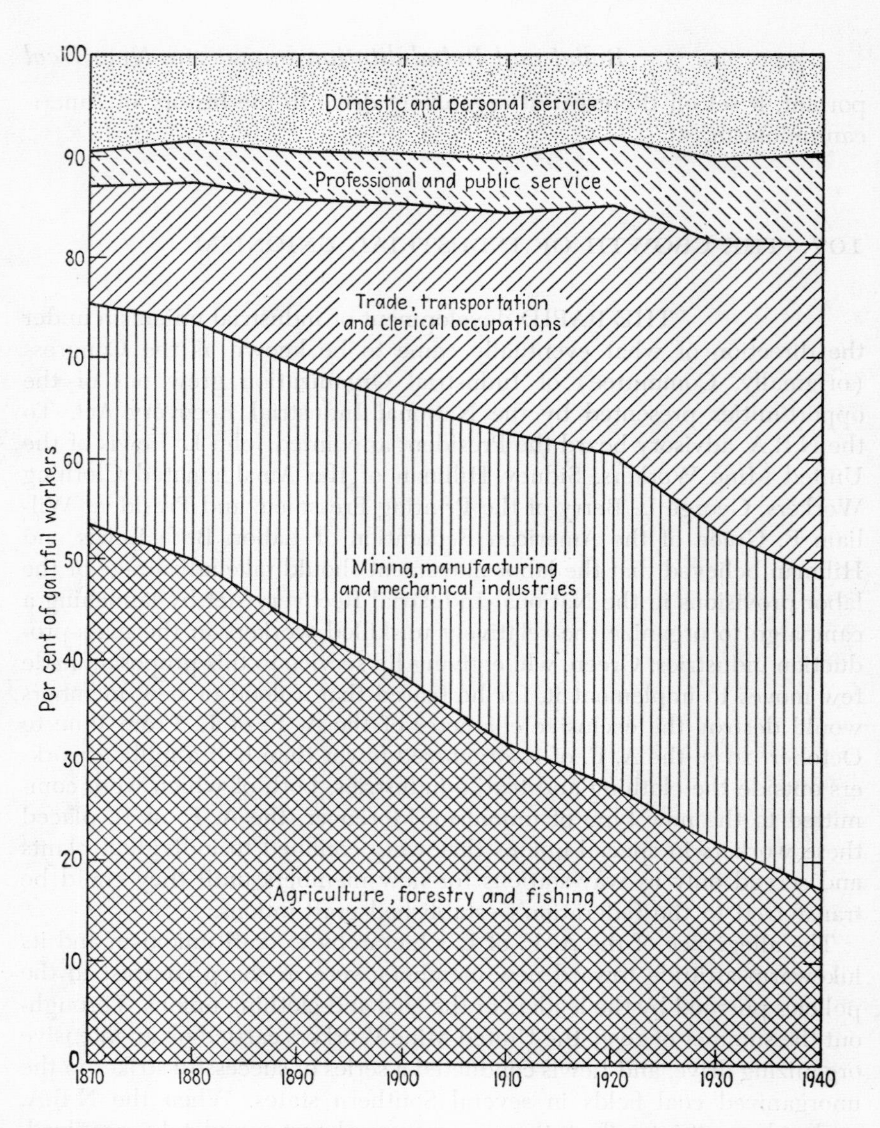

17. THE CHANGING COMPOSITION OF THE AMERICAN LABOR FORCE

The great shift of workers from agriculture into other occupations was in large measure the result of the introduction of labor-saving devices into farming. Note that the proportion of those working at clerical jobs or in the distributive functions such as trade and transportation shows the greatest increase. The development of more efficient machinery has kept industry's share of the labor force comparatively static in spite of enormous industrial expansion. [Reprinted with permission from J. Frederic Dewhurst and associates: America's Needs and Resources *(New York: Twentieth Century Fund, 1947).]*

1930 to 1932 to 5,565 strikes involving 3,752,180 workers from 1933 to 1935. In 1934 the workers of San Francisco conducted a general strike; textile workers went out on a nation-wide strike; and only presidential intervention averted an automobile strike.

Those A. F. of L. leaders who had advocated a drive to organize workers in the mass-production industries brought their demands out into the open at the Federation's 1934 convention in San Francisco. The old guard, firmly in control of the convention machinery, was determined to maintain the A. F. of L.'s traditional allegiance to craft unionism. Proposals for industrial unionism made from the floor of the convention were referred to the resolutions committee, which, in the words of Benjamin Stolberg, "for over half a century had served as a lethal chamber for all opposition."* But largely as a result of the efforts of John L. Lewis within the committee, this tactic failed, and the convention adopted a compromise resolution that called for an organizing campaign in the iron and steel industry and the granting of provisional charters to the automobile, cement, and aluminum industries. When the A. F. of L. convened in 1935 at Atlantic City, it was clear to all that the old guard had refused to carry out the resolution that had been adopted the preceding year. Lewis was bitter over what he considered a betrayal and told the assembled delegates: "At San Francisco they [the A. F. of L. old guard] seduced me with fair words. Now, of course, having learned that I was seduced, I am enraged and I am ready to rend my seducers limb from limb."

But Lewis' colorful oratory did not sway the delegates, who voted almost two to one for the Executive Council and craft unionism. Feeling became so bitter that Bill Hutcheson, boss of the carpenters' union, called Lewis an unprintable name, and Lewis replied by slugging him in the jaw. Three weeks after this convention the Committee on Industrial Organization was formed by John L. Lewis and other A. F. of L. supporters of industrial unionism; and on November 23, 1935, Lewis wrote William Green: "Dear Sir and Brother: Effective this date I resign as vice-president of the American Federation of Labor."

The break between the two organizations became irrevocable on August 4, 1936, when the Executive Council of the American Federation of Labor voted to suspend the C.I.O. unions unless they disbanded within a month. By this act the A. F. of L. deprived itself of approximately one third of its membership and practically all of its militant leadership.

At its inception the C.I.O. consisted of almost a million members drawn largely from the United Mine Workers, Amalgamated Clothing Workers, and International Ladies Garment Workers. It won its first major victory when it organized the steel industry, which had long been

* Benjamin Stolberg: *The Story of the C.I.O.* (The Viking Press: New York, 1938), p. 19.

considered the citadel of antiunionism in American industry. On June 3, 1936, the C.I.O. set up the Steel Workers' Organizing Committee with Philip Murray at its head and $500,000 in its war chest. The S.W.O.C. had little trouble in inducing the numerous company unions in the steel industry to come over to the C.I.O., and on March 2, 1937, it achieved what most observers had considered the impossible by concluding a contract with the United States Steel Corporation for an eight-hour day, forty-hour week, increased wages, and vacations with pay. The fall of "Big Steel" was the signal for others to follow suit, and within two months the S.W.O.C. had negotiated similar contracts with more than 250 independent steel companies and U. S. Steel subsidiaries. Only "Little Steel" (the name applied collectively to Republic, Bethlehem, Inland, and Youngstown Sheet and Tube steel companies) held out; and the Little Steel strike, which began in May, 1937, was eventually smashed by the energetic and often ruthless tactics of the company executives under the leadership of Tom Girdler, president of the Republic Steel Corporation. It was not until 1941 that the Little Steel companies were compelled by the N.L.R.B. to recognize the S.W.O.C. as the collective-bargaining agency in its plants.

The C.I.O.'s success in steel was equaled or surpassed by its triumphs in the automobile industry. Like the steel firms, the automobile makers had resisted for a number of years any attempts to unionize their plants. With the advent of the N.R.A. the workers in several Detroit automobile factories had formed independent unions. The American Federation of Labor, alarmed by both the prospect of an independent labor movement and the admission to its membership of a mass of unskilled workers, sought to resolve this problem by the formation of "federal local unions" for automobile workers. By the end of 1934 these federal locals had more than 100,000 members, and in August, 1935, the A. F. of L. reluctantly permitted them to combine in the United Automobile Workers of America. But after the A. F. of L. leadership demonstrated that it planned to sabotage rather than promote industrial unionism in the automobile industry, the rank and file rebelled. In 1936, the U.A.W. made Homer Martin its president, and joined the C.I.O.

Although C.I.O. officials did not want to challenge the automobile firms until they had organized the steel industry, their hand was forced by several U.A.W. locals that called unauthorized strikes late in 1936. In these "sitdown" strikes they introduced a successful technique by which workers refused either to work or leave the plants where they were employed. By the middle of January a full-scale strike was in progress against General Motors. The workers resorted to the sitdown strike, and the company replied with propaganda and violence. Largely because of the intervention of Governor Frank Murphy of Michigan, General Motors capitulated on February 11. The company recognized the union and signed a union contract; and the U. A. W. won all its demands except the closed shop. Within a month workers at the Chrysler plants had struck, and on April 6, Walter Chrysler agreed to a contract similar to the General Motors agreement. After these initial victories the C.I.O. moved against Ford in a long drawn-out struggle that was complicated by the factionalism of the automobile workers, which was only partially removed when R. J. Thomas succeeded Homer Martin as president of the U.A.W. It was not until 1940 that Ford—after N.L.R.B. intervention, numerous outbreaks of violence on both sides, and a strike—capitulated in a contract that granted the union virtually all its demands. By 1941- five years after its affiliation with the C.I.O., the U.A.W. had 392,000 members.

Outside the steel and automobile industries, the C.I.O. made its principal gains among the rubber, textile, and maritime workers. At the end of 1940 the C.I.O. had a membership of approximately 4,000,000 and had exerted a profound influence upon the course of the American labor movement. It had not only improved the standard of living for its own members but for countless other workers as well. Numerous employers undoubtedly raised wages, reduced the work week, and granted other concessions to their employees in an attempt to forestall an anticipated invasion of the C.I.O. The C.I.O., moreover, aroused the A. F. of L. from its lethargy. Goaded into action by the gains of its rival, the Federation increased its membership from approximately 3,500,000 in 1935 to 4,247,-443 in 1941. Finally, the C.I.O. stimulated political interest and activity among the workers. Labor's Non-Partisan League, formed by the C.I.O. in 1936, worked for Roosevelt's re-election in that year and a similar group did the same in 1940.* The American Labor party, organized in New York by the C.I.O. and independent liberals, supported the New Deal in national affairs and progressive candidates in both city and state contests. Similar policies were pursued by the C.I.O.'s Non-Partisan Leagues in Michigan and Pennsylvania.

Many employers responded to the growth of organized labor during the 1930's with the same tactics that had been used by American industrialists a half century earlier. The extent to which corporate executives relied on force, brutality, and deception to combat unionism was laid bare by the La Follette civil liberties subcommittee, which was established after the passage of the Wagner Act to investigate "violations of the rights of free speech and assembly and undue interference with the right of labor to organize and bargain collectively." The La Follette Committee hearings revealed the existence of an antiunion vigilanteism that made

* The United Mine Workers contributed $500,000 to the 1936 campaign, but in 1940, John L. Lewis, convinced that the President had not repaid the C.I.O. for its support four years earlier, turned against Roosevelt and asked the workers to repudiate him. After Roosevelt's re-election in 1940, Lewis withdrew from the C.I.O. and Philip Murray succeeded him as president.

Seibel in the Richmond Times Despatch

WHO CAUGHT IT?

After the establishment of the C.I.O. there were frequent conflicts between the two big labor organizations over which one had the right to unionize particular groups.

the original Ku Klux Klan seem by comparison as vicious as a sewing circle. At the first threat of a strike, employers with the assistance of "leading citizens" and local patriots would form a "citizens' association" to "preserve law and order." The preservation of law and order entailed breaking both the strike and the offending union through newspaper and radio propaganda, threats to workers and their families, and on occasion the use of armed thugs and the National Guard to coerce strikers. Some industrialists viewed conflict with their employees as warfare, and they armed themselves accordingly. Corporations spent large sums of money to purchase military equipment, and companies existed for no other purpose than to market these supplies. American industry, according to the La Follette Committee, bought more than $450,000 worth of tear gas from 1933 to 1936, and in two months during 1937, steel companies expended almost $500,000 for gas and munitions. During the Little Steel strike the Republic Steel Corporation, in the words of the committee, "owned 552 revolvers, 64 rifles, and 245 shotguns, with over 83,000 rounds of ball and shot ammunition."

Many large industrial corporations also hired private detectives as strikebreakers and labor spies. Frequently, detectives, some with criminal records, were sworn in as local law officers during a strike. As labor spies, they reported employee attitudes, sabotaged existing unions, and on occasion had themselves elected to important union positions. Corporations using detectives as either strikebreakers or spies included Montgomery Ward, Goodrich Rubber, General Motors, United States Steel, The Pennsylvania Railroad, The Aluminum Company of America, Radio Corporation of America, Borden Milk, and Campbell Soup. Ford, which did not appear on this list, refused to rely on outside detective agencies. Ford's antiunion work was handled by Ford service men, a group of some eight hundred thugs who had no job other than to intimidate and, if necessary, beat up workers suspected of union activity. With this organization at its command, the Ford empire was akin to a police state where the crimes ranged from talking on the job to joining a union.

The C.I.O.'s ability to overcome the formidable obstacles placed in its path by employers was due not only to the support that it received from the government but also to its willingness to break with traditional union practices. The C.I.O. made its appeals to workers who had previously been ignored; it introduced new techniques in organization and strikes; and most of its leaders were young, militant liberals who had not been discouraged by labor's past failures. As significant as any of these innovations was a change in ideology, for the success of the C.I.O. revealed a growing class consciousness among American workers. The increase in the number of strikes from 1,856 in 1934 to 4,740 in 1937, the use of the sitdown strike, and the attempt to attract the middle class through the organization of white-collar workers all indicated in some measure the development of a sense of class feeling in the laboring population.

Although many workers became relatively more class conscious, few became revolutionists. The new union members and their leaders did not want to overthrow either the government or the existing economic system. Like the A. F. of L., the C.I.O. demanded above all more money and less work for its members. Furthermore, the C.I.O. agreed with the A. F. of L. that these goals could best be attained through the strike and collective bargaining. The difference was a matter of emphasis. The C.I.O. believed that no worker could attain these ends without the cooperation of all workers. Unlike the A. F. of L., the C.I.O. worked for labor as a class, rather than for its elite.

108. SUBSIDIZING THE COMMERCIAL FARMER

AMERICAN farmers, who had enjoyed few of the blessings of prosperity during the twenties, felt the full impact of the depression in the early thirties. Between 1929 and 1932, farm income shrank from $12,791,000,000 to $5,562,000,000; the index of prices received by farmers (1910–14 =100) fell from 147 to 65; and the total value of American farm property declined disastrously. Confused, discouraged, and without adequate leadership, farmers increased production to compensate for the decline in prices, thus forcing prices even lower. As farm income decreased, bankruptcies and foreclosures mounted. From 1930 to 1933 the number of farms that changed ownership as a result of forced sales and related defaults more than doubled. Rather than lose their homes, otherwise conservative farmers resorted to force. Potential bidders at sheriffs' sales were frightened into silence by armed farmers as owners bought back their farms at a fraction of their value. Iowa farmers went on strike, dumped milk on the roadside, and prevented a judge from proceeding with foreclosures by dragging him from the bench and threatening to hang him. Overwhelmed by forces that they neither controlled nor understood, many American farmers abandoned their traditional air of resignation and gave way to blind, unreasoning anger.

The New Deal checked the rising panic among farmers with bold action. Although in the long run the New Deal probably came no closer to a solution of the so-called farm problem than had its Republican predecessors, it nevertheless succeeded in restoring the farmer's confidence in himself and in his way of life. Like many of its other policies the New Deal's farm programs were often hastily conceived, inefficiently administered, and poorly co-ordinated; but no one—including the farmer—ever accused the New Deal of indifference. The key to its farm program can be found, not in what it did for the farmer, but in the fact that it always did something.

The New Deal's attempts to aid the farmer fell into four major categories: (1) financial aid to farmers threatened by bankruptcy; (2) attempts to reduce farm surpluses; (3) assistance to marginal and submarginal farmers; and (4) the conservation of the nation's agricultural resources.

When Franklin Roosevelt entered office on March 4, 1933, he was at once confronted with an epidemic of farm foreclosures. On March 27, by executive order he established the Farm Credit Administration and placed all existing farm-credit agencies under its control. Congress passed the Emergency Farm Mortgage Act of 1933 in May and the Farm Credit Act in June. These measures authorized land banks to use $2,000,000,000—which they were to raise through bond issues—to pay off farm creditors and take over farm mortgages. Congress appropriated an

The Bettmann Archive

BIRTHPLACE OF THE FORD CAR, 1893—A RECONSTRUCTION

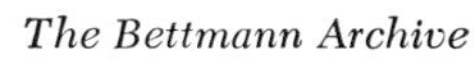

The Bettmann Archive

AN AERIAL VIEW OF THE RIVER ROUGE PLANT, FORD MOTOR COMPANY, 1946

Wide World Photos

SLUMS ON NEW YORK'S LOWER EAST SIDE

The New York Public Library

A NEW YORK HOUSING AUTHORITY PROJECT

additional $200,000,000 for special loans (called Land Bank Commissioner loans) of not more than $5,000 each to farmers whose credit rating was so low that they could not obtain Land Bank Funds. But the Farm Credit Administration, immediately swamped with applications, could not keep pace with the rate of foreclosures, and it asked farmers faced with immediate loss of their property to wire the President "collect" for help.

These emergency measures saved a large part of the farm population from bankruptcy.* In addition, in response to pressure for a national moratorium, Congress passed the Frazier-Lemke Farm Bankruptcy Act in the spring of 1934. Farmers threatened by foreclosure were granted a five-year moratorium on mortgage payments and the right to buy back their farms from creditors at a price set by a Federal district court. When this measure was invalidated by the Supreme Court, it was replaced by a second Frazier-Lemke Act in 1935; this law, somewhat less generous to farmers in debt, was upheld by the Court. These Federal farm-relief measures were paralleled by mortgage moratoriums put into effect by a number of state governments.

In addition to its emergency aid to rural debtors, the Federal government took responsibility for supplying farmers with credit for their normal operations. The Farm Credit Act of 1933 had provided for the creation of the Production-Credit Corporations, which lent money to farmers for financing a crop. The act also established the Central Bank for Co-operatives in order to extend credit to both marketing and purchasing co-operatives. Finally, Congress authorized, as it had done in the past, special loans to farmers who suffered from droughts, floods, or other natural disasters. By the end of the 1930's the government was providing the farmer with a large share of the loans that had formerly been advanced by private bankers.

The New Deal's emergency and long-term farm-credit policies comprised only a minor, although essential, part of its farm program; from 1933 until the outbreak of war in Europe the government's major efforts to aid the farmer centered on plans for raising farm prices by reducing agricultural surpluses. Government control over surplus agricultural production was not a new proposal. It had been advocated by some Populists in the 1890's, and the Federal Farm Board had urged farmers to curtail production during the Hoover Administration. But the board could not enforce its recommendations, and American farmers answered its requests with bumper crops. New Dealers, while accepting the Federal Farm Board's objectives, concluded that they could only be attained

* From May through December, 1934, the Farm Credit Administration granted loans to 550,000 applicants and assumed mortgages amounting to $1,500,000,000, or approximately one fifth of the nation's total farm mortgage debt of $8,000,000,000. During the same period the F.C.A., through voluntary debt adjustment committees, helped more than 40,000 farmers to reduce their debts by approximately $75,000,000.

if the government were armed with authority to compel farmers to curtail output. Many critics of the New Deal justly protested that this policy would only lead to scarcity in a time of want. More often than not, however, they failed to realize that American industry had long ago adopted the same policy and that the government had endorsed it in the National Industrial Recovery Act.

The first Agricultural Adjustment Act, which was passed on May 12, 1933, was designed to "re-establish prices to farmers at a level that will give agricultural commodities a purchasing power with respect to articles that farmers buy, equivalent to the purchasing power of agricultural commodities in the base period, . . . August, 1909–July, 1914."* To attain what came to be known as "parity prices," the Secretary of Agriculture was empowered to make cash "benefit payments" to farmers who signed contracts to reduce the acreage that they had formerly allotted to certain "basic crops." The land taken out of production through these agreements was to be left idle or used for soil-conserving crops and kitchen gardens. The original list of "basic crops," which included cotton, wheat, field corn, hogs, tobacco, rice, and dairy products, was later expanded by the addition of barley, rye, flax, grain, sorghums, cattle, peanuts, sugar beets, sugar cane, and potatoes. Funds to finance this program were to be raised by an excise tax on food processors. The Agricultural Adjustment Administration was set up within the Department of Agriculture to manage general policy, but the day-to-day supervision of the program was placed in the hands of county associations consisting of local producers who had signed A.A.A. agreements.

Because the Agricultural Adjustment Act went into effect after most farmers had finished their spring planting in 1933, crop destruction in some instances had to be substituted for acreage restriction. Overproduction in cotton and hogs, especially, threatened to have a ruinous effect upon prices, and the A.A.A. offered cash payments to farmers who would destroy a portion of these commodities. In 1933, cotton planters ploughed under approximately one fourth of the potential cotton crop, and the government paid farmers $9,000,000 for the slaughter of more than 6,000,000 pigs. Although these drastic measures raised prices somewhat, cotton farmers and corn-hog producers clamored for further assistance. As a result, the Administration established the Commodity Credit Corporation in the fall of 1933 to make loans to any corn and cotton growers who deposited their crops as collateral and agreed to sign A.A.A. restriction contracts for 1934 and 1935. Under this arrangement the farmer could not lose. If the market price of his crop fell below the government's loan rate, he could cancel his debt by letting the government take over his crop. If the market price went above the loan rate, he could redeem

* This base period represented a peacetime high in the purchasing power of American farm products.

his crop and sell it at the higher figure prevailing in the open market. In short, the Commodity Credit Corporation put a floor under cotton and corn prices (originally $.10 a pound for cotton and $.45 a bushel for corn) beneath which they could not fall. In later years a similar arrangement covered other commodities as well.

Since the Agricultural Adjustment Act could be partially circumvented by more intensive cultivation of the restricted acreage and by increased production on farms outside the program, Congress in 1934 enacted laws to curtail all production of certain crops. The Bankhead Cotton Control Act set production quotas for cotton growers and imposed taxes on farmers who exceeded their quotas. The Kerr-Smith Act imposed a tax upon the sale of all tobacco produced by farmers who had not signed A.A.A. contracts. A similar law passed in 1935 for the restriction of the potato crop never went into effect. Since no farmer could afford to pay the taxes imposed by the Bankhead and Kerr-Smith Acts, co-operation was now virtually mandatory. The farmer, an economic individualist to the last, refused to change his old ways until the New Deal, however reluctantly, resorted to coercion.

It is difficult to judge the effects of the Agricultural Adjustment Act upon American agriculture. More than 30,000,000 acres were withdrawn from production in both 1934 and 1935 and government payments to farmers from 1933 through 1935 totaled $1,151,000,000, but the program did not always achieve its stated objectives. Drought rather than A.A.A. contracts was responsible for the drastic reduction in the corn and wheat crops; the 1935 peanut crop was larger than that of any preceding year; and curtailment of cotton and tobacco production was largely due to the tax provisions in the Bankhead and Kerr-Smith Acts. On the other hand, evidence is not lacking that the economic status of the farmer improved considerably during this period. The total cash income received by farmers rose by about one half between 1932 and 1935; and the index of prices received by farmers (August, 1909–July, 1914 = 100) increased from 65 in 1932 to 114 in 1936. Whether these gains should be largely attributed to the A.A.A., to the New Deal's other inflationary schemes, or to the effects of drought cannot, of course, be determined with any accuracy.

On January 6, 1936, the Supreme Court in the Hoosac Mills case ruled that the A.A.A.'s methods for the control of production were unconstitutional because they invaded the powers reserved to the states. Other features of the act were not questioned in this case, and they were continued as in the past. The Administration, however, had no intention of permitting unregulated surpluses, and in February, 1936, Congress passed the Soil Conservation and Domestic Allotment Act, which despite its title, was essentially another device for crop restriction. It was advanced as a plan for increasing soil fertility and conserving soil resources, but it also had as one of its stated objectives the re-establishment of "the ratio between the purchasing power of the net income per person on farms and that of the income per person not on farms, that prevailed during the five year period August, 1909–July, 1914." Under this law, the Agricultural Adjustment Administration was authorized to pay farmers for adopting such soil-conserving measures as contour plowing and terracing, for reducing acreage devoted to soil-depleting crops, and for increasing the area planted in soil-building crops. Since the principal cash crops (such as corn, wheat, cotton, and tobacco) were also the principal soil-depleting crops, the government once again was in a position to reduce surpluses by subsidizing farmers who curtailed their production of staple agricultural commodities. This program, however, was to be financed by congressional appropriations rather than by processing taxes.

The Soil Conservation Act enabled the government to pump cash into the farm economy, but it proved to be an inadequate solution to the problem of farm surpluses. A serious drought cut farm output in 1936, and farmers responded to the price rise that followed with record plantings and more intensive cultivation in 1937. The inevitable occurred. The 1937 crops were the largest since World War I; farm prices declined, and in 1938, gross farm income fell for the first time since 1933.

The failure of the Soil Conservation Act to check surplus agricultural production led to the passage of a second Agricultural Adjustment Act on February 16, 1938. This law, like its predecessors, was intended to establish for farmers "parity prices" and "parity of income," and it put into effect Secretary of Agriculture Wallace's concept of the ever-normal granary. It provided for the continuation of the soil-conservation program, but its chief emphasis was on devices to insure the Administration's control over farm output through cash payments to farmers. The government was empowered to make national acreage allotments for certain staple crops (cotton, wheat, tobacco, corn, and rice), to be based on estimates of the "normal" domestic and foreign demand and of the reserve necessary for use in times of shortage. Farmers who did not exceed their allotments were to receive soil-conservation payments. Loans were to be extended to farmers who produced more than their allotments and stored their surpluses for sale in subsequent years of less abundance. With the approval of two thirds of the producers of any of the five staples covered by the act, the government was authorized to impose a marketing quota and to tax all sales in excess of this quota. If the price of any of the five commodities fell below parity, the government could make up part or all of the difference with "parity payments" to farmers. Finally, the Federal Crop Insurance Corporation was created to safeguard wheat farmers against crop failures.

Despite its elaborate provisions and the extensive authority that it gave the government, there is little to indicate that the second A.A.A. was any more successful that the first. Government payments to farmers amounted to $807,000,000 in 1939 and $766,000,000 in 1940, but the farmer's cash income mounted only slightly during these years. It was not until 1941 with purchases under Lend-Lease that American agriculture entered upon its first boom in two decades.

The New Deal's major farm policies were devoted to efforts to raise farm income by crop and acreage restrictions, but the Roosevelt Administration resorted to many other tactics in its all-out war on surpluses and low farm prices. For example, the first Agricultural Adjustment Act (1933) had permitted marketing agreements among farmers' associations and middlemen and the Secretary of Agriculture. Processors and distributors who co-operated in this program agreed to pay higher prices, while the government granted them immunity from antitrust laws and set up machinery for curtailing the production of the farm products in question. In addition, repeated attempts were made to dispose abroad America's excess agricultural commodities. Reciprocal trade treaties provided a foreign market for some surplus farm-products. Export subsidies were also employed on occasion to stimulate agricultural exports, but they were always used sparingly for fear of foreign reprisals.

In a further effort to raise farm prices (as well as to aid the needy), the government disposed of large amounts of surplus agricultural goods among the poor. In August, 1933, the Federal Surplus Relief Corporation was established to buy excess farm commodities and to distribute them as direct relief.* In the last years of the New Deal, this program was supplemented—at least on an experimental basis—by the food stamp plan, inaugurated in 1939 and soon in use in 132 cities. People on relief could buy orange-colored stamps that were exchangeable for all grocery products; and they were given blue stamps, exchangeable for any commodity on the government's current surplus-list. School lunches were distributed to undernourished children, and by-products such as peanut oil were disposed of as surplus commodities.

109. AIDING THE MARGINAL FARMER

DESPITE the New Deal's efforts to co-ordinate its farm and relief programs, it was repeatedly—and justly—criticized for subsidizing scarcity during a time of unprecedented economic distress. Although President Roosevelt complained that at least one third of the

* Later this became the Federal Surplus Commodities Corporation and still later the Surplus Marketing Administration.

nation was ill-clothed and ill-fed, his Administration was directly responsible for destroying products that could have been used to alleviate this condition. Furthermore, this program of scarcity redounded almost exclusively to the benefit of commercial farmers. Sharecroppers, tenant farmers, and hired farm-laborers received little or no assistance from the two A.A.A. programs, for any improvement in their economic status depended upon expanding rather than contracting American agriculture. Lacking powerful lobbies and congressmen responsive to their demands, the underprivileged rural groups found it difficult to obtain political redress for their economic grievances.

Nevertheless, the Administration expended time, energy, and money on programs to aid the poorer farm groups. In the midthirties there were at least five million underprivileged rural dwellers—tenant farmers, sharecroppers, farmers on poor land, agricultural laborers, and farmers whose holdings were too small to provide them with an adequate standard of living. Some of these farmers had been made poor by the depression, but many others had known nothing but poverty all their lives. To them hardship was not a temporary phenomenon, but an accepted part of their permanent status.

Like the rest of the population, farmers were eligible for Federal relief benefits supplied by the Federal Emergency Relief and Public Works Administrations. The first agency provided them with cash and the second gave them jobs on government construction projects. Approximately 3,500,000 rural families were aided by these two New Deal programs. But the New Deal's assistance to the marginal farmer went beyond relief. In 1934 it gave away tools and seeds as well as cash. These gifts were of little use, however, to farmers who lived on such barren soil that no improvement in their agricultural techniques and equipment could make their land productive.

Since it was obvious that aid to submarginal farmers on submarginal land offered no long-term solution to the problem of rural poverty, the Administration decided to undertake a resettlement program. Accordingly, in 1934 the purchase of submarginal lands began on a limited scale and the occupants, who were granted loans, were transferred to productive regions.* At the same time a few agricultural communities were established near cities to enable urban workers to increase their income by part-time farming. The progress of these communities was continually impeded, however, by administrative difficulties and lack of sufficient government support. In a move to co-ordinate these diverse plans, President Roosevelt in April, 1935, created the Resettlement Administration and gave it jurisdiction over the whole problem of rural rehabilitation.

From the outset the Resettlement Administration was confronted by

* A project of both the A.A.A. and the F.E.R.A.

a variety of almost insurmountable obstacles. Its executive officer, Rexford G. Tugwell, was accused (unjustly) of being an ultraradical collectivist, and a suspicious Congress never provided the agency with adequate funds. Marginal farmers sometimes refused to be resettled. Surveys revealed that only a comparatively small amount of land was both suitable and available for resettlement. Finally, many occupants of submarginal lands were incapable of being transformed into self-supporting farmers; they were farmers only in the sense that they lived on the land—they did not live off it. Few had had even the rudiments of formal education, and many were so old that there was little chance that they would ever again be self-supporting or gainfully employed.

Despite these difficulties, the Resettlement Administration made marked advances in its struggle against rural poverty. Under its direction nine million acres of submarginal land were removed from cultivation, new communities were erected in resettled areas, loans were extended to farmers unable to obtain credit elsewhere, and some of the most backward farmers were instructed in the basic techniques of scientific agriculture. Whenever possible, the agency took a co-operative approach to its problems. Loans were extended to groups of farmers to enable them to buy and share supplies, machinery, and other equipment that they could not have afforded as individuals.

The Resettlement Administration's program for aid to the depressed part of America's rural population convinced Roosevelt that an even broader approach to the problem of rural poverty was necessary. In 1936, he appointed a special committee to study farm tenancy. The committee went beyond its original instructions and in its final report discussed not only farm tenancy but almost every problem that affected the plight of depressed groups in rural America. Largely as a result of these findings Congress in 1937 passed the Farm Tenancy Act, which provided for loans to tenant farmers, sharecroppers, and farm laborers to assist them in the purchase of farms, livestock, equipment, and supplies. It reorganized the Resettlement Administration as the Farm Security Administration and gave the new agency all the functions of its predecessor except the purchase of submarginal lands, which was turned over to the Soil Conservation Service.

The Farm Security Administration continued the program of loans and information on up-to-date agricultural methods.* The program was applied on a limited scale, but it was undoubtedly beneficial to those it reached. The diet and health of the rural poor improved; education was

* By June, 1940, 1,400,000 families had received some form of financial assistance from the F.S.A., and 120,000 loans had already been paid back. Of 360,000 families that participated in the program in 1939, the net income per family had increased 43 per cent since receiving F.S.A. loans.

made available to their children; and their mortgaged indebtedness decreased. In addition, the agency established a series of camps for migratory rural workers. Although these camps received widespread publicity because one of them figured prominently in John Steinbeck's widely-read novel *The Grapes of Wrath,* they were actually few in number. By June, 1940, there were only fifty-three camps, all located in California, Florida, and Texas. These camps, which afforded "Okies" and other migrants some living quarters and sanitation, were violently opposed by residents of nearby communities because they attracted "undesirable" citizens who put an additional burden on local relief agencies.

The Federal Security Administration also inaugurated a frankly experimental program to enable the rural dispossessed to become independent farmers. It advanced loans to about 13,000 tenants, sharecroppers, and farm laborers. Each borrower was charged 3 per cent interest on a loan of about $5,500, which was to run for 40 years; in return he had to manage his farm in accordance with rules stipulated by the F.S.A. Of an equally experimental nature was the program for co-operative and subsistence homesteads. In all, the agency established 164 experimental communities. Some of these followed the lines laid down in the earlier plans for rural homes for urban workers and were known to the public as Greenbelt towns. Others were genuinely co-operative agricultural communities in which farming was practiced on a communal basis.

The New Deal's farm program included plans for saving physical as well as human resources. The A.A.A. made soil conservation a means for restricting production; but other New Deal agencies viewed soil depletion as a problem in its own right. The Soil Erosion Service (later the Soil Conservation Service), established in 1933, conducted a nation-wide survey of land resources, set up experimental stations to study various types of soil depletion, and created demonstration areas in which farmers were shown the most advanced methods for combatting erosion. Furthermore, a conservation program was conducted jointly by the Federal and state governments. The Soil Conservation Act of 1935 stipulated that states participating in the national program could receive Federal benefits. At the request of twenty-five or more farmers, state boards formed soil conservation districts that adopted erosion control regulations enforceable by law.* Further national and local co-operation was achieved in 1938 through an agreement for the establishment by the Department of Agriculture and the state agricultural universities of land-use planning committees. These committees, made up of government experts and local farmers, analyzed existing land condi-

* By 1940, 359 soil conservation districts had been organized in 34 states.

tions and worked out solutions to the problems encountered. Finally, several divisions of the Federal government that were only incidentally concerned with the problem of soil waste made important contributions to the preservation of agricultural resources. The reforestation work of the Civilian Conservation Corps reduced, however slightly, the menace of floods. The T.V.A. conducted a remarkably successful conservation program among the farmers in the Tennessee Valley. Both the Resettlement and Farm Security Administrations furnished their clients with information on soil-building methods. And the government undertook to plant a hundred-mile-wide band of trees on the Great Plains from Canada to Mexico to break the force of the winds that blew across the "dust bowl." By mid-1940 approximately 190,000,000 trees had been planted on about 210,000 acres of "shelter belt."

Between 1933 and the United States' entrance into World War II the New Deal did more for the farmer than for any other single group in the population. It extended him credit, paid him not to produce, taught him how to be more productive, and instructed him in the most advanced methods of soil conservation. But it went even further, for in aiding the farmer it injured others. By forcing up the prices of farm products during a period of widespread want, it imposed a heavy burden on American consumers when they were least able to afford it. The New Deal saved American agriculture, but in doing so it made the farmer a privileged member of American economic society.

To be entirely successful, a farm program for the thirties had to insure high prices both for agricultural commodities that were consumed within the United States and for the farmer's exportable surplus. The New Deal could not supply both these *desiderata,* however, for parity prices and a healthy export market were (and are) incompatible. Farmers could not export their surplus products unless other nations lowered their tariffs—a step that they refused to take unless the United States did the same. But the American farmer was opposed to a reduction in the duties on agricultural goods. If this step had been taken, he would have lost his domestic market to foreign competitors. He needed both parity and the foreign market to prosper, but he could not increase his exports without losing parity.

Confronted by what appeared to be an insoluble problem, the New Deal abandoned the foreign market (if an exception is made of its reciprocity program) and concentrated on the domestic. Nevertheless, the status of the American farmer was still an international rather than a national problem—a problem that could be solved temporarily by periods of war and postwar scarcity, or permanently by such unlikely developments as the end of economic nationalism and an expanding world economy.

110. RELIEF GRANTS AND JOBS FOR THE UNEMPLOYED

THE NEW DEAL exerted a more direct effect upon the lives of the American poor than had any other Administration in the history of the United States. Assuming office at a time of national crisis, when the unemployed numbered in the millions and countless individuals were unable to obtain adequate food, clothing, or shelter, the New Deal took unprecedented steps to aid those suffering from economic adversity. In 1929 most Americans believed that the national government was a necessary evil and that it had no right to help the needy. Ten years later all but a few die-hards agreed that it was the function of the Federal government to come to the assistance of those who were unable to support themselves. The New Deal may not have revolutionized the American economy, but it helped to revolutionize the American attitude toward poverty. In the 1920's a man without a job was considered lazy; under the New Deal he was considered a victim of economic forces over which he had no control.

Although the number of unemployed workers never fell below one million during the boom of the golden twenties, the Federal government made no move to provide the jobless with either work or relief. Americans generally thought that anyone could find a job if he tried and that those who were out of work had only themselves to blame for their predicament. The dole, used in England at the time, was considered an un-American device that would sap the initiative of those who came to rely on it. At most, unemployed Americans in the 1920's could expect help from private charities or municipal relief agencies. The widely held belief that it was wrong for the Federal government to aid the unemployed conditioned the Hoover Administration's attitude toward the depression for almost two years after the stock-market crash of 1929.

Herbert Hoover, who had gained a world-wide reputation for his administration of Belgian relief during World War I, was opposed to Federal relief for the unemployed on the grounds that it would make them dependent on an all-powerful government, that it would put a needless drain on the public treasury, and that it would alter the fundamental character of the United States government. In October, 1930, when the unemployed numbered almost five million, Hoover announced that the "sense of voluntary organization and community service . . . has been strong enough to cope with the problem [of unemployment] for the past year." But reassuring statements, governmental committees, "spread the work" campaigns, pleas by public officials, and re-employment drives conducted by civic organizations were all equally unavailing, and by 1931 the unemployed numbered approximately nine million. Private relief agencies, despite heroic efforts, lacked both the coordination and the resources to cope with the extraordinary demands placed upon their facilities.

In March, 1932, the Federal government made its first move to give direct aid to the needy when Congress voted for the transfer of surplus farm products to the Red Cross for distribution among the unemployed. In July of the same year Congress passed, and Hoover approved, the Emergency Relief and Construction Act, which appropriated funds for a Federal construction program and authorized loans to state and local governments for public works and relief. In the same month, at the President's urging, Congress adopted the Home Loan Bank Act, which provided for Federal loans to building and loan companies, savings banks, and insurance concerns. Proposals both in and out of Congress that the Federal government expand its public-works program and provide direct relief for the unemployed were steadfastly rejected by President Hoover, who alternately branded them as "inflationary" plans, "pork-barrel" bills, and pleas for "a cold and distant charity" at variance with the American tradition. But by 1932, as the outcome of the presidential election indicated, a majority of the American people no longer accepted Hoover's estimate of the government's rôle in a period of national emergency.

During the first two Roosevelt Administrations, the government conducted a many-sided attack upon unemployment and poverty. No single theory can explain these policies, for they were the products of a complex mixture of political, economic, and humanitarian considerations. The New Dealers did not intend to let people starve, but they also believed that Federal expenditures to aid the needy were an integral part of their program to stimulate industrial recovery. Nor was any particular method considered sacrosanct; relief was furnished through cash payments, loans, food and clothing allotments, make-work projects, and public works. Some relief policies followed patterns established by the preceding Administration, but in every instance they were so expanded that they bore slight resemblance to the measures that had been reluctantly approved by Hoover.

Roosevelt indicated the broad outlines of his unemployment program in an address to Congress in March, 1933. He suggested "three types of legislation":

> *The first is the enrollment of workers now by the Federal government for such public employment as can be quickly started and will not interfere with the demand for or the proper standards of normal employment.*
>
> *The second is grants to States for relief work.*
>
> *The third extends to a broad public works labor-creating program.*

Congress acted quickly. On March 31, it approved "an Act for the relief of unemployment through the performance of useful public works and other purposes"; and five days later the President established the Civilian Conservation Corps in accordance with the terms of this bill. In mid-May, Congress created the Federal Emergency Relief Administration, which was authorized to distribute aid to the needy through state and municipal agencies; and in mid-June, Congress set up the Public Works Administration, which established a program of public works.

The Civilian Conservation Corps was designed to furnish work and healthy living conditions to young men who had come of age during the depression years. Members of the corps were stationed in camps throughout the country and were paid a monthly wage of $30, of which $22 was sent to their parents. "C.C.C. boys," the majority of whom were drawn from cities, worked on reforestation and fire-prevention projects, and constructed roads, recreational facilities, woodland trails, and bridges. Although the camps were built by the War Department, the supervision and spirit of the program was predominantly civilian. By 1935, C.C.C. camps had a capacity of more than 500,000, and by the end of 1941, 2,750,000 young men had been on the C.C.C. rolls.

Although the C.C.C. provided work for only a relatively small part of the population, its effects were nevertheless significant. Not only did it build up and conserve the country's natural resources, but it also gave productive work, new interests, and a lift in morale to boys who had formerly known discouragement and defeat. It was undoubtedly the most popular of the New Deal relief agencies and by the end of the 1930's most Americans agreed that President Roosevelt had not overstated the case for the C.C.C. when he said to Congress in March, 1933:

> *It will conserve our precious natural resources. It will pay dividends to the present and future generations. It will make improvements in national and state domains which have been largely forgotten in the past few years of industrial development.*
>
> *More important, however, than the material gains will be the moral and spiritual value of such work. . . . We can take a vast army of these unemployed out into healthful surroundings. We can eliminate to some extent at least the threat that enforced idleness brings to spiritual and moral stability.*

The Federal Emergency Relief Administration, Congress's response to the President's request for "grants to States for relief work," was directed by Harry Hopkins, a former social worker, who had supervised New York state relief while Roosevelt was Governor. This part of the relief program was similar in some respects to Hoover's policy of state-aid, but it provided for outright grants rather than loans to affiliated agencies. Hopkins soon realized that cash payments, or a dole, were at best a short-term solution for a long-term problem, and as early as the summer of 1933 the agency began to experiment with work-relief projects. By 1935, when it was disbanded, almost half the people receiving its aid were on work relief. Unskilled workers on these jobs were paid a minimum of thirty cents an hour, and efforts were made to furnish workers with jobs that suited their skills. During its lifetime the F.E.R.A. conducted rural-aid programs, assisted students, provided home relief, and subsidized co-operative relief projects. It spent approximately four billion dollars, 71 per cent of which was contributed by the Federal government and the remainder by states and municipalities. The number of people receiving its assistance was never constant; but the agency's high point was reached in February, 1934, when almost eight million families were "on relief."

Because the scope and flexibility of the F.E.R.A. was limited by the provision that it work through local agencies, in November of 1933 the President established the Civil Works Administration, which was administered directly from Washington. During the few months of its life, the C.W.A. started 180,000 projects on which considerably more than 4,000,000 individuals were employed. Conservative opponents of the New Deal criticized this program as wasting the taxpayers' money by paying people to rake leaves and pick up papers. But most of the funds were used for such utilitarian projects as road repairs; the improvements of schools, parks, and playgrounds; and erosion control. Moreover, the C.W.A. did what its critics could not do: it provided work for those who did not have it. When the agency was disbanded in the spring of 1934, most of its projects were taken over by the F.E.R.A.

The Public Works Administration, established in the summer of 1933 and placed under the direction of Secretary of the Interior Harold L. Ickes, was viewed by New Dealers as essentially a pump-priming device. Its funds were used primarily to stimulate private enterprise and only incidentally to hire workers from the pool of unemployed.* Ickes insisted that all its projects be "useful" and in the national interest, and contracts were made with private companies. The agency either financed its own projects or made loans or grants to states and cities to cover in part the cost of undertakings that it had approved. Its methods were frequently criticized by opponents of economic planning, but no one could justly accuse it of "boondoggling."† Projects included bridges, dams, sewage systems, school and college buildings, recreational facilities, airports, low-income housing, roads, hospitals, and reclamation work.

The New Deal relief and public-works programs were launched at a time of national emergency with little opportunity for long-term planning or a study of over-all objectives. Agencies frequently worked at cross-purposes or duplicated each other's efforts; methods for distributing

* However, it employed about 500,000 men during 1934.

† The term applied by critics of New Deal relief policies to government-made work that had no other apparent value than to furnish the unemployed with jobs.

relief were changed with confusing frequency; and no attempt was made to distinguish between relief clients who had been forced out of work by the depression and the "unemployables" who could not have found jobs even in prosperous times. By the end of 1934, President Roosevelt and his advisers were forced to conclude that the government's entire relief program would have to be overhauled. In January, 1935, the President proposed a new policy: Federal aid was to be restricted to "employables," and the care of "unemployables" was to be turned over entirely to state and local agencies. Any semblance of a Federal dole would then be removed, for Federal assistance would be confined to work relief.

Under the Emergency Relief Act of May, 1935, the new program was put into effect. No move was made to alter the methods or organization of the C.C.C. or the P.W.A.; but by executive order, the President entrusted all other work relief to the Works Progress Administration (later the Works Projects Administration). The new agency, headed by Harry Hopkins until he became Secretary of Commerce in 1939,* planned and maintained its own projects, and did not work through state and municipal intermediaries. Care was taken to select projects that were useful to the general public, that did not compete with private enterprise, and that permitted the expenditure of money on wages rather than materials.†

The W.P.A. quickly became the largest single employer in the United States.‡ Because of the revival of private-business activity and mounting criticism of the spending and relief programs, the government cut work-relief rolls in 1937. But the decrease in government expenditures was accompanied by business recession and a consequent increase in unemployment; and the policy of retraction was reversed.¶ The work-relief projects affected almost every phase of American life. During its lifetime the agency constructed airports, bridges, parks, schools, post-office buildings, public golf courses, roads, auditoriums, hospitals, libraries, sewers, levees, and drainage ditches. It conducted classes in sewing, art, vocational training, and naturalization; it distributed free lunches to school children, renovated clothing and books, taught illiterates to read, staged plays and symphonies, constructed and maintained conservation projects, gave inoculations against contagious diseases, inspected teeth, killed rats, and stuffed birds. In short, there was little that the W.P.A. did not do. Furthermore, it attempted to place the unemployed in those jobs for

* In the same year the relief administration was again reorganized and both the W.P.A. and P.W.A. were placed under the Federal Works Agency.

† W.P.A. wages varied in accordance with the individual worker's skills and the region in which he was employed. In 1935, wages ranged from $19 to $94 a month; the minimum, however, was gradually increased until it reached $31.20 in 1939.

‡ By December, 1935, 2,600,000 workers were on W.P.A. jobs.

¶ By November, 1938, 3,271,000 people were on W.P.A. rolls. Between 1935 and July, 1941, the W.P.A. spent $11,365,000,000 on more than 250,000 projects and provided employment for more than 8,000,000 different individuals.

which their past training best suited them. The W.P.A. building at the New York World's Fair bore the following inscription:

> *WPA seeks to employ at their own skills: accountants, architects, bricklayers, biologists, carpenters, chemists, dentists, draftsmen, dietitians, electricians and engravers, foresters and firemen, geologists and gardeners, hoisting engineers and housekeepers, instrument men and iron workers, inspectors, jackhammer operators and janitors, kettlemen and kitchen maids, librarians and linotypers, locksmiths and lumbermen, millwrights and machinists, musicians, nurses and nutritionists, oilers and opticians, painters and plasterers, plumbers and pattern makers, photographers and printers, physicians, quarry men and quilters, riveters and roofers, roadmakers and riggers, sculptors and seamstresses, stonemasons and stenographers, statisticians, teamsters and truck drivers, teachers and tabulators, upholsterers and ushers, veterinarians, welders and woodchoppers, waiters and watchmen, X-ray technicians.*

A striking feature of the W.P.A. was the fashion in which it subsidized cultural pursuits through its relief programs. Musicians, artists, actors, and writers, who had lost their jobs and were ill-equipped to take work in other occupations, were given the opportunity to pursue their chosen careers. In July, 1935, the agency established the Federal Music Project, which conducted music classes and hired unemployed musicians to give orchestra, band, and choral concerts. A similar program was undertaken by the Federal Art Project for painters and sculptors, who were employed to decorate public buildings, conduct free art classes, and operate community art centers. The Federal Theater Project, under the energetic and enthusiastic direction of Hallie Flanagan, gave jobs to actors, stage hands, and scene painters, produced numerous plays of social significance on a commercial basis, staged marionette shows for children, and sent touring companies into regions that had hitherto been ignored by the legitimate theater. The Federal Writers Project gave employment to more than six thousand novelists, poets, journalists, and others, who prepared guidebooks, volumes of folklore, regional studies, and pamphlets. Finally, the Historical Records Survey gathered from both obvious and obscure sources vast amounts of valuable data on the American past. The W.P.A. was severely criticized for its cultural programs, but the fact remains that the New Deal was the first Administration in American history to recognize that the creative arts as well as agriculture, manufacturing, and transportation deserved the sympathy and support of the national government.

The W.P.A.'s work-relief program was supplemented by that of the National Youth Administration, which gave assistance to young men and women between the ages of sixteen and twenty-five. The N.Y.A., authorized by the Emergency Relief Appropriation Act of 1935, aided boys and girls who had left school, and it furnished part-time employment to students in high schools, colleges, and universities. Its "out-of-school" projects were generally similar to those maintained by the W.P.A. The student program provided clerical work in academic laboratories, libraries, and administrative offices to young people who needed financial assistance to continue their studies. The N.Y.A. never received the popular support accorded the C.C.C., however, and it was continually hampered by inadequate funds and inept local administrators.

Opponents of the New Deal repeatedly charged that these various relief agencies spent too much money on essentially nonproductive projects; but these critics failed to mention that the New Deal bureaus refrained from setting up productive enterprises largely because of the pressure of businessmen who feared government competition. Moreover, as more than one student of the New Deal has pointed out, business leaders generally ceased to criticize government spending when in the 1940's the Roosevelt Administration stopped feeding the poor of America and began to manufacture weapons of war.

111. SOCIAL SECURITY AND HOUSING PROGRAMS

DURING the first years of the New Deal, Federal relief agencies made little attempt to differentiate between people who had been thrown out of work by the depression and those whose economic distress could be attributed to other causes. But when in 1935, with the inauguration of the W.P.A., the government limited its relief activities to victims of the depression, it set up a long-range social security program for the care of dependent children, the aged, the handicapped, and the temporarily unemployed. This move was long overdue. Most of the nations of western Europe had had social security acts on their statute books for a number of years, but only a few American states had passed similar laws—all of which were inadequate—and the Federal government had done nothing. With the advent of the depression this situation had become a disaster for countless Americans, and the void created by the government's inactivity had been quickly filled by panaceas, some harmless, but some dangerous. Upton Sinclair had attracted slightly less than a majority of California's voters in the state's 1934 gubernatorial election with his promise to "End Poverty in California"; Senator Huey Long, dictator of Louisiana and self-styled "Kingfish," had promised to make "every man a king"; Dr. F. G. Townsend had assured his aged followers that his plan would give them $200 a month; and demagogues like Father Coughlin and Gerald L. K. Smith had outlined programs that were startlingly similar to those of Nazi Germany and Fascist Italy. The popularity of these and similar proposals among the poor, as well as humanitarian considerations, convinced Roosevelt that the national government could no longer put off the adoption of social security legislation.

The Social Security Act, which became law in August, 1935, provided for either direct or indirect assistance to the aged, the infirm, widows, dependent children, and the unemployed. Most of the aged were eligible for either annuities or pensions. Annuities ranging from $10 to $85 a month were paid to workers who retired at the age of 65 and who had participated in the program before their retirement. Funds to finance these benefits were raised by a payroll tax that was shared equally by employer and employee. By 1940, more than 50,000,000 workers had social security cards; but casual laborers, merchant seamen, civil servants, and the employees of nonprofit institutions were not covered. To provide for the aged in these groups and for workers who were older than 65 at the time that the law was passed, the government helped the individual states to finance pensions for the elderly poor.* A similar pension program was established to aid the blind, the crippled, and dependent children.

The Social Security Act provided for unemployment compensation through a plan of collaboration between national and state governments. Benefits to unemployed workers ranged between $5 and $15 a week and lasted in most states for approximately 15 weeks. Workers in firms with fewer than 8 employees and the same groups that were ineligible for social security annuities, however, were excluded from participation in the unemployment insurance program. Money to maintain the various state systems was furnished by a 3 per cent payroll tax on employers. By June, 1940, more than 28,000,000 workers were covered by unemployment insurance.

An integral part of the New Deal's relief and security programs was the attempt to assist families threatened with the loss of their homes and to furnish better living facilities for the underprivileged. The Home Owners Loan Corporation, established in 1933, assumed the mortgages of impoverished homeowners who would otherwise have been deprived of their property through foreclosure proceedings.† By consolidating homeowners' mortgaged indebtedness, reducing the principal, lowering the interest rate, and extending the period for repayment, it prevented countless American families from being forced out of their homes by their creditors. These lending activities were largely confined to urban dwellers, but similar aid was given to many distressed farm owners under

* About 2,000,000 people received this form of aid in 1940, but average pension payments were only $20 a month, and in some Southern states the figure was much lower.

† Between 1933 and 1936 this agency lent more than $3,000,000,000 to more than 1,000,000 homeowners.

the agricultural relief programs. Householders were further aided by the Federal Housing Authority, created in June, 1934, to lend money at low rates of interest to owners who wished to repair, enlarge, or renovate their homes.

To provide adequate housing facilities for at least some tenement dwellers, the New Deal undertook a program of slum clearance and public housing. In June, 1933, the P.W.A. established an Emergency Housing Division to plan and finance low-cost urban housing projects to be constructed by private contractors. By 1937, when it was terminated, the P.W.A. Housing Division had subsidized more than 50 public-housing developments; but the average rent per dwelling unit was $26 per month, a figure beyond the means of many American slum dwellers.

In 1937 the Administration's low-cost housing program was reorganized with the adoption of the Wagner-Steagall Act. The United States Housing Authority was created and was authorized to take over the P.W.A.'s housing projects and to lend or grant money to local housing authorities for slum clearance and Federal-planned public housing. By 1941 the U.S.H.A. had eliminated more than 78,000 unsafe and unsanitary residential buildings and had provided new dwellings for almost 200,000 families. Rentals in these projects averaged $12.64 a month, and the average annual income of families occupying them (late in 1941) was $837. The accomplishments of the U.S.H.A. were impressive, however, only when compared to past efforts to house the poor; and when the agency was liquidated because of the war, slums were still a most noticeable and disheartening feature of every large American city.

Although the New Deal conducted a war on many fronts against poverty throughout the entire nation, it won its most significant victories in the Tennessee Valley. National relief, security, and housing programs were often conceived in haste, diluted by political expediency, and hampered by an inefficient bureaucracy and administrative confusion. The plan for the rehabilitation of the Tennessee Valley, on the other hand, was a long-term project in which recovery, industrial growth, the conservation of human and natural resources, and the revival of agriculture were all viewed as interrelated parts of a common regional problem.

A number of circumstances, in addition to the New Deal's determination to alleviate the human distress caused by the depression, lay behind congressional approval of the Tennessee Valley Act of 1933. The Tennessee River, which with its tributaries flows through seven states, was subject to repeated and devastating floods. On its shores at Muscle Shoals, Alabama, the government in 1918 had constructed a dam and two nitrate plants that had produced vast quantities of explosives during the last months of World War I. After the war the government had attempted to sell its facilities at Muscle Shoals, but potential buyers had offered to pay only a fraction of the plant's original cost. As a result, the installations, which were capable of producing fertilizer and electric power for peacetime uses, remained idle, while congressional moves for government operation were blocked by Presidents Coolidge and Hoover. But soon after Roosevelt entered office, Senator George W. Norris, with Administration support, revived his earlier proposals for a government program for the Tennessee Valley; and in the spring of 1933, Congress established the Tennessee Valley Authority to produce cheap power, promote conservation, improve navigation, and advance the "economic and social well-being of the people."

The Tennessee Valley Authority was created as an independent Federal agency and given considerable latitude in the making and executing of policy in the area under its control. Despite their extensive powers, its officials preferred to help people to help themselves rather than to impose from above programs that had little popular support or understanding. Whenever possible, "demonstration units" were used to convince residents of the valley of the advantages of new techniques in farming and conservation. Individuals were urged to co-operate in solving their common problems, while the T.V.A. stood ready to furnish them with the necessary information, guidance, and encouragement. A close alliance was developed between the Authority and state and local governments, state universities, and business and civic organizations in the valley; and virtually every T.V.A. program was conceived as a joint undertaking to which the support of such groups was essential. The Authority also relied heavily on experts and specialists who were drawn from practically every field of endeavor to provide the facts that could be used to develop a better way of life for all people in the valley.

During its early years the T.V.A. was vigorously opposed by local power concerns and by conservative critics of the New Deal throughout the nation. In their campaign the private power companies were led by Wendell Willkie of Commonwealth and Southern, which eventually sold its interests in the valley to the government at a high price. Other private utilities followed Commonwealth and Southern's example. By the end of the 1930's the accomplishments of the T.V.A. had made it generally popular throughout the United States and, indeed, famous all over the world. It found its staunchest supporters, however, among the people who lived in the region it served. Under its guidance the residents of the valley acquired cheap power, protection against floods, instruction in soil conservation and improved farming techniques, a connected series of navigable rivers and lakes, fertilizer, new conveniences for their homes, libraries, jobs, medical assistance, adult-education classes, and recreational facilities. These, and many other benefits, were not bestowed on a subservient people by an all-powerful, paternalistic ruler, but were

18. TENNESSEE VALLEY AUTHORITY

the direct products of intelligent planning, genuine co-operation between the citizen and his government, a regional approach to regional problems, and a reawakened democratic spirit that was both a cause and an effect of the progress achieved under the T.V.A.

New Deal relief and security measures, which were often criticized by conservatives for going too far and by radicals for not going far enough, provided more assistance to the poor of the United States than had been furnished by all previous Administrations combined. In his second inaugural address President Roosevelt referred to "one third of a nation ill-housed, ill-clad, ill-nourished." While even the stoutest advocates of the New Deal could never claim that Roosevelt had completely remedied this situation, its severest critics would have to concede its major accomplishments. The New Deal failed to find a solution to the problems of unemployment and of poverty; but it fed the hungry, gave jobs to the jobless, and provided a measure of security for the insecure. Most important of all, it aroused hope, faith, and courage in people who had thought they had lost everything.

CHAPTER XVIII

AMERICAN CULTURE IN A MACHINE AGE

DURING the years that followed World War I, the machine exerted a more profound influence on the pattern of American culture than at any other previous time in history. The machine placed a premium on conformity, and its application to practically every phase of life was the single most important factor in undermining American individualism. The great mass of Americans accepted without question the uniform modes of thought and behavior imposed on them by a machine civilization; but a small minority of intellectuals protested that the United States was being transformed into a nation of automatons. Disgusted by what they considered the standards of an alien world, serious writers and artists complained that there was no place for creative individuals in a society in which men were ants and the ant hill was more important than those who had made it. Thus the United States had two cultures; both were undeniably American, but they had little else in common.

112. THE STANDARDIZATION OF AMERICAN LIFE

THE POST-VERSAILLES decades, which saw new triumphs in the standardization of American products, were characterized by an equally significant trend toward the standardization of the

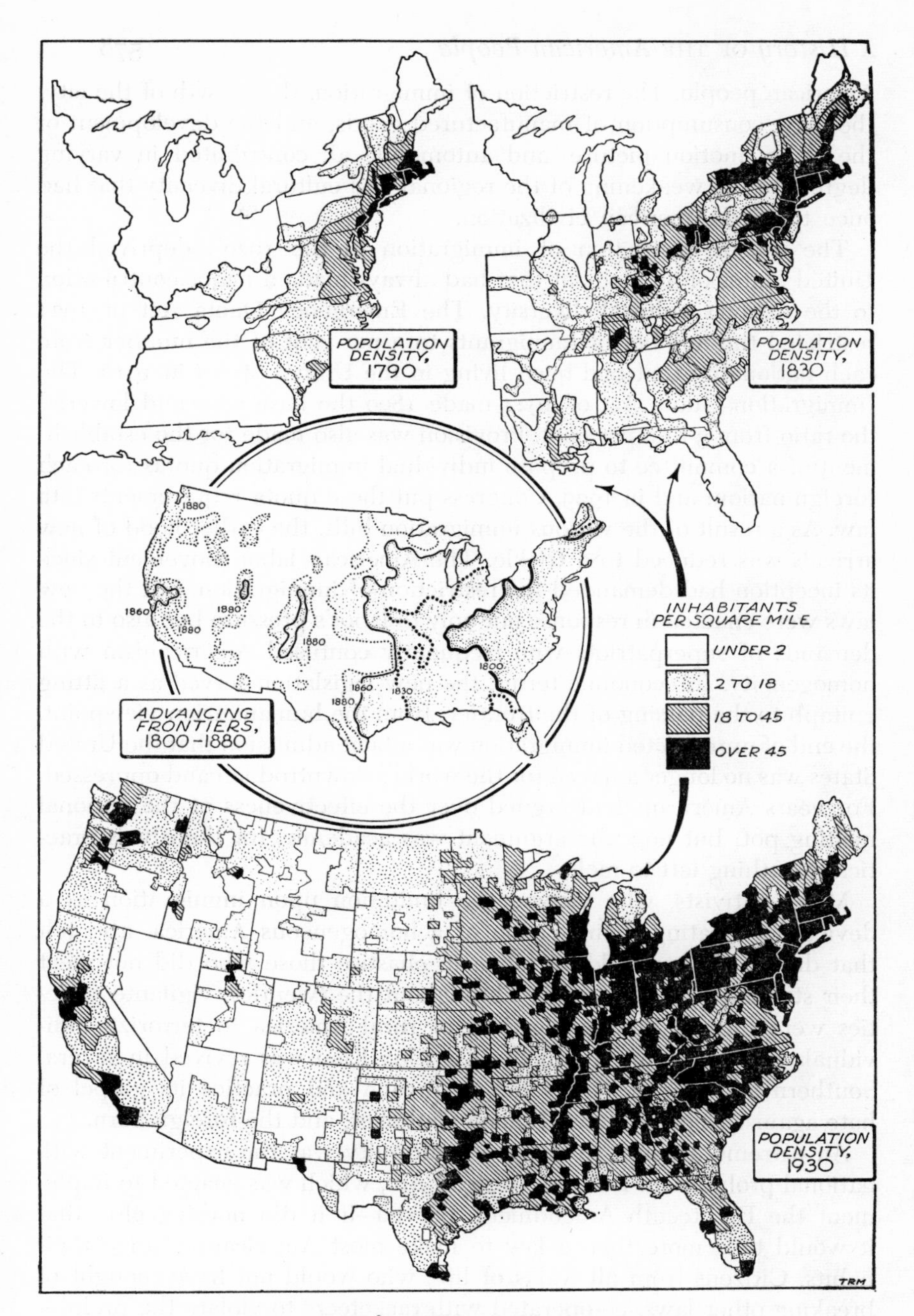

19. AMERICA'S EXPANDING POPULATION

By 1930 the frontier was only a memory, and the growing density of population was reflected in both the spread and popularity of urban mores.

American people. The restriction of immigration, the growth of the city, the mass consumption of manufactured goods, and the development of the radio, motion picture, and automobile all contributed in varying degrees to the weakening of the regional and cultural diversity that had once typified American civilization.

The drastic restriction of immigration in the 1920's deprived the United States of an element that had always made a major contribution to the nation's cultural diversity. The Emergency Quota Act of 1921 restricted the number of immigrants to 3 per cent of the number from each nationality that had been living in the United States in 1910. The Immigration Quota Act of 1924 made 1890 the base year and lowered the ratio from 3 to 2 per cent. Provision was also made for the establishment of a committee to propose individual immigration quotas for each foreign nation; and in 1929, Congress put these quota requirements into law. As a result of the various immigration bills, the earlier flood of new arrivals was reduced to a trickle. The American labor movement since its inception had demanded the restriction of immigration, but the new laws were enacted in response not only to labor's pressure but also to the demands of superpatriots who frequently confused Americanism with homogeneity. In economic terms, the new legislation served as a fitting epitaph to the passing of the frontier; from the humanitarian viewpoint, the end of unrestricted immigration was a tacit admission that the United States was no longer a haven for the world's downtrodden and oppressed. For years Americans had argued over the effectiveness of the national melting pot; but now the argument was academic, for there was practically nothing left to melt.

Many nativists, who viewed the limitation upon immigration as a device for creating their version of a homogeneous America, also felt that drastic steps should be taken to chastise those who did not meet their standards of uniformity. Throughout the twenties, vigilante societies were formed in some sections of rural America to terrorize individuals into conformity; and the Ku Klux Klan was revived in several Southern and Midwestern states to preach and practice its gospel of hate against Negroes, Jews, Roman Catholics, and the foreign-born.

An extreme attempt to enforce conformity was the experiment with national prohibition. But the Volstead Act, which was enacted to implement the Eighteenth Amendment, proved—if it did nothing else—that it would take more than a law to make most Americans change their habits. Citizens from all walks of life, who would not have thought of breaking other laws, co-operated with racketeers to violate the prohibition statute. The Volstead Act changed the nation's drinking habits, opened up new areas of criminal activity, and gave to the American language such words as "bootlegger" and "speakeasy"; but it is difficult to demonstrate that it reduced appreciably the amount of alcoholic beverages consumed in the United States.

Although the attempt to make Americans conform to prohibition failed, there is no evidence that most of them objected to the pressures exerted by business enterprise to standardize their lives. Mass production required mass consumption, and large-scale manufacturers were compelled to attract every American consumer that they could. As increasing numbers of Americans came to buy the same or similar products, distinctive regional mores began to give way to a national norm, and the differences between urban and rural ways of living diminished. Although the people of one section often retained their traditional attitudes and prejudices, their daily rounds of work and play were usually the same in all essentials as those of the residents of every other section of the country. Whether or not the members of a family listened to the radio, kept their food in an electric refrigerator, cleaned their rugs with a vacuum cleaner, went to the movies, and wore clothes of the latest style no longer depended on where they lived, but on their ability to pay for such things.

The standardization of consuming habits affected almost all of American life, but its impact was particularly apparent in the food that Americans ate and the clothes that American women wore. With the factory production of breadstuffs and the commercial canning of fruits, vegetables, and meat products, Americans in every locality and in every walk of life tended to eat the same kinds of food. Rich and poor bought much the same products, and often their diets differed only in the amount they ate. As a result of these developments, regional dishes lost much of their one-time popularity, for there were few American women who did not prefer the easily prepared brand-name products in the corner grocery to the time-consuming recipes that had been the pride of their grandmothers. Similar considerations were responsible for the standardization of women's clothes. In an earlier day, a woman's background and place in the social hierarchy could often be ascertained by her dress, but with the mass production of dresses at relatively low prices the old correlation between style and rank disappeared. Expensive designers still set the mode, but their fashions were easily imitated by manufacturers who sold to a national market. As a result, the shop girl, stenographer, or farmer's daughter often wore clothes that to the untutored, masculine eye were the same as those imported from Paris for women of wealth and leisure.

The national advertising campaigns that helped to make possible the mass distribution of manufactured products contributed to the standardization of customs and attitudes, as well as of consuming habits. Although individual advertisements might differ, the people in them usually shared the same aspirations and bore the same general appearance. More often than not, the men and women in advertisements wore their good looks like uniforms, were interested in things rather than ideas, and were devoted to improving their social and economic status. In the world created by advertisers, the form rather than content of life was emphasized, and readers and radio listeners were told that they too would both look and be like the smiling, well-scrubbed, handsome models if they made a small down payment, hurried to their nearest department store, or filled out the enclosed blank. As the advertiser wished all Americans to buy the goods that he was seeking to sell, it was necessary to tell them how to resemble the stereotypes that had been created by the account executives, copywriters, and commercial artists of the advertising agencies. Through billboards, radios, magazines, newspapers, and the mails, the advertisers outlined a pattern of behavior for practically every conceivable situation. While advertising performed an obvious economic function, by its very nature it was compelled to accentuate uniformity rather than individual differences.

In the years between the two world wars the nation's newspapers and popular magazines both reflected and promoted the standardization of American culture. Because newspapers were responsive to the same forces that had produced concentration in other fields of economic endeavor, the number of papers steadily declined, and there were few large cities that did not have at least one paper with a hyphenated title as a memorial to the decline of competition. The trend toward concentration—as well as toward uniformity—was also manifested by the increasing number of newspaper chains, which were formed on the supposition that news, like groceries, could be distributed by A & P methods. With the development of the newspaper chain, a single publisher was able to formulate the editorial policy of numerous papers throughout the country. Columnists, who expressed opinions on a variety of subjects, often had their material syndicated in as many as one hundred different papers. Similarly, press associations distributed news and what were accurately called "canned editorials" to papers read by such diverse readers as Southern sharecroppers, Dakota wheat farmers, and New York tenement dwellers. While every important newspaper had some feature that set it off from other journals, this fact could not obscure the similarity of the content and presentation of many of the nation's papers.

The transformation of the American newspaper was paralleled by somewhat similar developments in magazine publishing. Older periodicals such as *Harper's* and the *Atlantic Monthly* had only a small percentage of the total magazine circulation of the postwar decades, while the muckraking magazines that had enjoyed an enormous vogue in the Progressive era had given way to the so-called slicks. Magazines like the

Saturday Evening Post, Ladies' Home Journal and *Collier's* were read by millions, represented tremendous capital investments, and frequently were only one of several magazines published by a single firm. It was almost impossible to distinguish one of these magazines from the others by its contents. They were all crammed with the same advertisements, the same human-interest articles, and the same love, adventure, and success stories. It is significant that the *Nation* and the *New Republic*—to mention only two examples—used an altogether different formula and were such unsuccessful publishing ventures that they had to be maintained by subsidies. Magazines, like automobiles, were most popular when they were turned out as standard models on a mass-production basis.

The most notable innovation among mass-circulation papers and magazines was the appearance of journals especially designed to fit the needs of people living at the accelerated tempo set by an industrial civilization. The tabloid paper, an urban phenomenon, was small enough to be handled by passengers on crowded subway trains and simple enough in format and content to be understood by people who had to suffer countless distractions while they read. Tabloids were aimed at the masses, but weekly news-magazines such as *Time* were directed at upper- and middle-class readers who were in a hurry. Businessmen who were so absorbed in their work or recreation that they had neither time nor inclination to keep abreast of current events were provided with weekly summaries of recent developments in politics, business, medicine, science, education, and foreign affairs. A somewhat similar need was met by the *Reader's Digest,* a monthly that compressed articles that had first appeared in national magazines. The enormous popularity of this magazine resulted in the establishment of similar digests that published monthly condensations of articles on practically every subject known to man. In the 1930's, with the advent of picture magazines, the movement to simplify reading matter had apparently reached its logical conclusion. *Life, Look,* and countless imitations made few demands on what they called their readers; and if the past is a guide to the future, Americans can conceivably look forward to the day when their magazines will be entirely free of the printed word.

The radio and motion picture, like the newspaper and popular magazines, provided their audiences with standardized material distributed on a national scale. The same movies were exhibited in every community of any size throughout the land, and radio programs on national networks were carried simultaneously by chains of stations that were strung across the nation. Movie stars provided models of behavior, dress, and mannerisms for countless Americans, while the all-pervading, standardized speech of the radio announcer threatened to drive regional dialects and modes of speech into oblivion. Although a few radio stations devoted a large portion of their time on the air to classical music and although some motion-picture producers recognized both the educational and artistic potentialities of their medium, most movie and radio scripts were devoted to boy-meets-girl themes, adventure stories, and a type of humor that often seemed to be directed at the lowest level of intelligence in the audience. If a student of American civilization in the decades between the two world wars were compelled to confine his research to movie and radio programs, he might well conclude that all Americans except criminals lived and worked in pleasant surroundings and were primarily interested in making love, earning money, and killing Indians and gangsters.

Both the movies and radio were responsible for a significant change in American recreational habits. At one time most Americans sought relaxation and amusement through formal or informal social intercourse with their friends and neighbors. Recreation was viewed as a co-operative affair, and there was a tacit understanding that each participant was expected to contribute to the enjoyment of all. But the radio and the movie made no demands on the members of their audience except that they remain quiet. Recreation was transformed into a passive experience for the people and a business enterprise for its promoters. Entertainment was sold in much the same manner as any other product. As a result, the line between business and pleasure frequently became blurred. Americans, for example, saw nothing paradoxical in equating amusement with the "entertainment industry," while at the same time they called the advertising business the "advertising game."

The impact of the automobiles on American life was equally revolutionary. People, whose experiences had often been limited to one locality, were given a new mobility that weakened traditional ties to both their homes and their communities. A provincialism that had been in part the result of the enormous distances that separated the different regions of the nation, tended to disappear as growing numbers of Americans took to the road to see how their fellow countrymen lived. The automobile put a large number of the American people on wheels. It was responsible for the ritual of the "Sunday drive"; it provided adolescents and their parents with one more point on which they could disagree; it helped to make hijacking effective and prohibition a mockery; it changed the methods of criminals who wished to make a getaway and policemen who wished to catch them; it permitted cities to extend their borders and suburbs to enjoy building booms; it took customers away from trolleys, subways, and railroads; it lifted love-making out of the horse and buggy stage, and gave Americans greater opportunity for what they unashamedly and accurately called necking. If any mechanical contrivance dominated America between the two world wars, it was the automobile.

The increasing urbanization of the United States also contributed to the establishment of uniform standards of behavior and thought for the American people. In its simplest terms the influence of the city is indicated by the growth in urban population. According to the census of 1900, more than 60 per cent of the population lived in rural areas, and not until 1920 did city dwellers outnumber rural inhabitants. Of the 106,000,000 or so people in the United States in 1920, more than 54,000,000 lived in cities. By 1930 almost 70,000,000 people in a population of more than 123,000,000 were city dwellers. The census, however, does not provide an altogether adequate index of urbanization, for it fails to include in its statistics on urban population many who live in the suburbs and are city people in all but name. Working in the city, reading city newspapers, and obtaining their recreation either in or not far from the city, the suburbanite resembles the inhabitant of the city in all but the small patch of grass that surrounds his home.

The growth of cities can be attributed not only to the opportunities that they provided for the acquisition of wealth but also to the excitement and freedom that has been traditionally associated with urban living. Many moved to the city to get or hold a job; but others went because they felt that they were misunderstood by their parents, because they had fought with their friends, or because they thought that their intellectual and social attainments were being wasted in a small town. The city, in its turn, was able to assimilate the ever-increasing flood of new arrivals because of the numerous technological devices that had been perfected after the Civil War. The expansion of the railroad system, the refrigeration of meat, and canning of fruits and vegetables made it possible to crowd together in a relatively small area vast numbers of people who were not able to produce their own foods. The elevator and the use of structural steel permitted cities to grow skyward, while the subway, elevated railroad, trolley, and automobile enabled them to expand horizontally. Each of these developments had been introduced to relieve urban congestion, but each in turn aggravated rather than eliminated the problem that it was designed to solve. Every effort to make the life of the city dweller more bearable made it possible for the city to handle more people. Urbanization is the history of congestion, and the modern city has demonstrated beyond all doubt that congestion feeds on congestion.

The constant pressure of population on urban areas made it difficult, if not impossible, to find adequate space in which the inhabitants of cities could work, sleep, and play. Skyscrapers built in the city's most congested portion provided additional office space, but they contributed to the congestion that had made them necessary. Since industrial production could not be organized along the vertical lines of the skyscrapers, most factories were located on the cheaper land in the city's outskirts. Sites that had not been pre-empted by either factory or office structures went by default to the city's residents. The poor lived in slums in buildings that had been abandoned fifty or more years before by the well-to-do. Crowded together, lacking adequate sanitary facilities, and an easy prey to disease, the poor were living examples of the disastrous results of urban congestion. By the 1920's most of the urban middle- and upper-classes had abandoned private houses for apartments. Less crowded, cleaner, costlier, and better equipped than slum dwellings, the apartments of the rich had no other features that distinguished them from the tenements of the poor. Rich and poor alike lived in cells; the rich merely occupied bigger and better cells. After business firms and their employees had been housed, little room was left in cities for recreational facilities. Parks and playgrounds, most needed in congested areas, could seldom be placed there because overcrowding had made the cost of land so high. Some cities refused to face this problem, and others sought to solve it by establishing a large play area such as New York City's Central Park, but no city was able to provide all its residents with enough space to ensure them a healthy existence.

The remarkable growth of urban population was both the cause and result of the expansion of the city's functions in the national economy. The pre-Civil War city had been essentially a market place where goods from the immediate hinterland and abroad had been bought and sold. After the war the city became the home of the factory, and through the development of the railroad it was transformed into a market place for the goods of the entire nation as well as for those of the surrounding countryside. By the 1920's the city had assumed still another function, for it had become the financial center for much of the economy. With the last development the city's economic power was made virtually absolute. All lines of economic authority emanated from the city to the rest of the country, and decisions reached by relatively small groups of businessmen in New York, Chicago, Los Angeles, and other cities affected the lives of countless Americans in every part of the United States.

The city's control over the economy was in large part responsible for its control over much else in American life. Although many Americans might live in suburbs, small towns, or isolated farms, the way they lived was more often than not determined by those who occupied the seats of power in the cities. The radio, motion picture, newspaper, and magazine industries in the 1920's were urban methods of communication that were used to disseminate urban values throughout the nation. The books that Americans read and the advertisements that helped to shape their habits of consumption were urban products that were distributed to a national audience. Between one third and one half of the American people lived in rural areas, but no American was able to escape the city's influence. In the words of one student of modern urban development, "America is the city."

113. WRITERS OF THE LOST GENERATION

IMMEDIATELY after World War I, American literature was distinguished by a vigor, diversity, and originality of approach and subject matter that made these years unique in the history of American writing. Following the war there appeared in rapid succession a number of young authors who combined unusual literary talents with a deep-seated antagonism toward contemporary conventions. Some emphasized the sordid and ugly, others were fascinated by themes of violence, and still others sought refuge in obscurantism; but all were iconoclastic. In the twenties, disillusion and cynicism provided the dominant themes. With the onset of the depression, literature often served as a vehicle for social protest, and it was not until the approach of World War II that authors sought to rediscover traditional American values.

The serious writing produced by the postwar generation was by and large a literature of revolt. Bitter over the war and disquieted by what they considered the excessive materialism and essential vulgarity of American life, many authors of the twenties proclaimed themselves a "lost generation" that had little use for earlier canons of taste and literary expression. Although they did not comprise a definite school, much of their work was distinguished by a hard-boiled, fast-paced realism. No subject was taboo, and their frank handling of sex shocked many American traditionalists. Above all, they were readable. With a knack for making the trivial appear significant they could turn such incidents as the lighting of a cigarette or the purchase of a newspaper into acts that seemed important and momentous in themselves.

With the publication in 1920 of *This Side of Paradise,* F. Scott Fitzgerald became the first important spokesman for the lost generation. Writing of playboys, the idle rich, Eastern college girls and boys, he filled his books with accounts of weekends in New York, parties on Long Island, and "proms" at Princeton. His gilded youths and rich tycoons searched unremittingly for diversions and happiness that always seemed to elude them. Wealth did not aid their quest, for money could not help them in a world in which all the old values were gone and "all faiths in man shaken." Seeking pleasure, they never found it, whether they were the bloodless expatriates of *Tender Is The Night* (1934) spinning out their days on the Riviera, self-made men like *The Great Gatsby* (1925), or movie moguls like *The Last Tycoon* (1941). Fitzgerald was something of a snob who believed that "the rich are not as we are,"* but he was also a master craftsman.

Fitzgerald's novels on the mores of the Eastern plutocracy were paralleled by Ernest Hemingway's fictional studies of nihilism and disillusion

* To which Ernest Hemingway had one of his characters reply: "Yes. They have more money."

among the members of the war generation. Following war service as an ambulance driver on the Italian front, Hemingway moved to Paris, where, under the influence of Gertrude Stein,* he labored to create a style that, while deceivingly simple in appearance, was eminently suited to evoking a mood or conveying the feel, look, and smell of a particular locality. No writer of the period exerted a more marked influence on the style of his fellow authors or on the tastes of the American reading public. After experimenting with the short story, he turned to the novel and won immediate acclaim with *A Farewell to Arms* (1929). No other book written by an American so completely caught the sense of helplessness felt by the individual caught up and swept along willy-nilly by twentieth-century warfare. Hemingway's characters did not act; they were acted upon. To Hemingway and the other young men of his generation, war—indeed, all experience—seemed to have no other meaning. *The Sun Also Rises,* which appeared in 1926, is peopled by footloose expatriates who are cut off from the past, dissatisfied with the present, and have no hope for the future. Always fascinated by violence, Hemingway was attracted to bull fighting, which he studied assiduously and described authoritatively in *Death in the Afternoon* (1932). In his world all life was reduced to action, for among life's uncertainties there seemed little else that either mattered or could be measured.

While Fitzgerald and Hemingway criticized America through implication by discussing those who rejected its standards, Sinclair Lewis in his novels of the middle class satirized those who made the standards. In *Main Street* and *Babbitt,* Lewis described the daily rounds of work and pleasure of Midwestern small-town businessmen who belonged to the country club, attended chamber of commerce meetings, and believed in "good fellowship." These inveterate "boosters" and "go-getters," who worshipped worldly success and accepted without question the standards of a business civilization, were all that the lost generation was not. Many thought Lewis's pictures caricatures, but his views were largely substantiated by the findings of Robert and Helen Lynd in *Middletown,* a sociological study of Muncie, Indiana. Once Lewis had mastered his formula, he applied it to novels dealings with doctors *(Arrowsmith),* ambitious women *(Dodsworth),* and clergymen *(Elmer Gantry).* In all but the last, which is a savage and unconvincing attack on the clergy, Lewis's satire is comparatively gentle, and the discerning reader often carries away the impression that the author was genuinely fond of the people he seemed to be ridiculing.

* One of the outstanding creative figures of modern American literature—and also an expatriate—Gertrude Stein is difficult to classify. She carried experiment with language the farthest of anyone, using automatic writing techniques that she learned as a graduate student under William James. Her influence on other writers has been important, but otherwise her work, by its nature, finds few readers.

Wide World Photos

HARRY HOPKINS

Wide World Photos

JOHN L. LEWIS

Wide World Photos

BERNARD BARUCH

Wide World Photos

GENERAL GEORGE C. MARSHALL

FORCES IN RECENT HISTORY

Wide World Photo

FRANKLIN D. ROOSEVELT, AUGUST 21, 1944

Like Lewis, Sherwood Anderson felt that America's business civilization had blighted man's spirit; but unlike Lewis, he was interested in understanding and explaining the emotional problems of an individual rather than in satirizing individual types. In such novels and collections of short stories as *Winesburg, Ohio; Poor White; The Triumph of the Egg; Horses and Men;* and *Dark Laughter,* he analyzed—even psychoanalyzed—frustrated men and women whose emotions had been scarred by the pressures of convention and standardization in the small town. All his work appears to show the influence of Freud, yet his earliest and best known work, *Winesburg, Ohio,* was apparently written before he had heard of Freud.

During the twenties poetry as well as fiction was distinguished by the contributions of a number of new writers who possessed unusual talent and whose work represented a sharp break with the past. After the publication of Whitman's most notable works there had been little poetry of importance published in America aside from Edward Arlington Robinson's internal monologues and bitter portraits of New England life and Emily Dickinson's lyrics (all but two of which were published after her death in 1886). But just before the war there was a sudden flowering of American poetry. Between 1908 (when Ezra Pound's first works appeared) and 1914, many of the poets of the twenties published their first poems. In 1912, Harriet Munro founded *Poetry,* which began at once to print the work of such poets as T. S. Eliot, Robert Frost, Amy Lowell, Carl Sandburg, and Robinson Jeffers, and in 1913 Vachel Lindsay published *General William Booth Enters into Heaven and Other Poems.*

Of the new generation of poets, Ezra Pound and T. S. Eliot were undoubtedly the most significant, and both men provide ample evidence of what F. O. Mathiessen has referred to as the "cleavage between . . . mass civilization and minority culture."* Pound, who left the United States because "there was no one in America whose work was of the slightest interest for a serious artist," lived first in England, then in France, and finally in Italy, where he eventually became an outspoken supporter of Mussolini. His eccentricities, the extreme difficulty of his later poetry, and his defense of Fascism have made him the subject of severe attack; but his great influence upon and extraordinary generosity toward other poets—especially Eliot—in whose work he believed cannot be ignored. Eliot, who himself settled in England, embraced the Anglican faith, and became a staunch defender of the right of aristocrats to remain aristocrats, once said of Pound: "I must confess that I am seldom interested in what he is saying, but only in the way he says it." In his

* Robert E. Spiller, Willard Thorp, Thomas H. Johnson, Henry Seidel Canby (eds.): *Literary History of the United States* (New York: The Macmillan Company, 1948), Vol. II, p. 1335.

own poetry Eliot displayed a horror of the emptiness of contemporary existence, a wide background in mythology and literature, and extraordinary ability as a lyrical poet. Eliot, Pound, and the less skillful practitioners of what came to be known as the "new poetry" were in essence writing for themselves and their relatively small coterie of disciples. Most Americans did not know that they existed.

During the twenties there emerged a group of playwrights who contributed more to the development of the American drama in a decade than their predecessors had in over a century. In the past playwrights had tended to avoid contemporary problems and had attempted to amuse or divert audiences with characters that were stereotypes and with plots that were melodramatic or sentimental. But during and immediately after World War I there appeared a number of playwrights who were interested in social satire and realism, who often wrote "problem plays," and who frequently used the drama as a vehicle for protesting against what they felt was the excessive materialism of the times. Among such playwrights were Eugene O'Neill, Elmer Rice, Maxwell Anderson, and Robert E. Sherwood. Of these O'Neill was clearly outstanding. Catholic in taste, and receptive to both new ideas and dramatic techniques, O'Neill at various stages in his career could be described as a Freudian, a mystic, a nihilist, an advocate of social and economic change, a romanticist, and a realist. Nevertheless, he wrote neither to instruct, entertain, nor reform, but to explain, often brilliantly, the nature of those questions that have confronted every individual of every generation—whether his plays were set in the jungle *(The Emperor Jones)*, the sea *(Bound East for Cardiff)*, nineteenth-century New England *(Desire Under the Elms)*, or America in the Civil War era *(Mourning Becomes Electra)*.

Critics as well as creative writers proclaimed their disdain for an American civilization in which precedence was given to pecuniary rather than intellectual values and in which middle-class mores determined the standards of culture. H. L. Mencken, as editor of the *American Mercury*, poked vicious fun at what he considered the foibles of democracy (which he called "boobocracy"), boosterism, and fundamentalism. Professors Paul Elmer More and Irving Babbitt, spokesmen for the "new humanism," criticized the crassness of American life and demanded an aristocracy of the intellect. Somewhat similar was the approach of the "Twelve Southerners," who in 1930 wrote *I'll Take My Stand*. Protesting the fate of the arts in a sea of materialism, they outlined a program of feudal agrarianism in which the masses would till the fields while the elite remained in their studies and followed the pursuits of gentleman scholars. The conservative attack on middle-class values was matched by that of such "literary radicals" as Randolph Bourne, Lewis Mumford, and Van Wyck Brooks, who denounced the philistines, and deplored a culture that insisted on keeping life and literature in separate compartments and that forced the intellectual to live and work outside the mainstream of American life.

Students of the past also found little to commend in America. Biographers directed their efforts to "debunking" the outstanding figures of a younger America. Many historians used the economic interpretation of history to reduce such events as the American Revolution and the Civil War to mere clashes between conflicting profit systems; others viewed history as nothing more than a chronological account of backstairs gossip. Of the major historians of the day, only Vernon L. Parrington found in the American past an enduring and ennobling tradition. In his *Main Currents of American Thought* he treated the ideas of the nation's leading thinkers from Colonial times to the present as a never-ending struggle between Jeffersonian democratic liberalism and Hamiltonian aristocratic conservatism. Parrington left no doubt in his readers' minds that his point of view was "liberal rather than conservative, Jeffersonian rather than Federalistic," and that Americans in search of a creed had to look no further than their own nation's past.

114. LITERATURE OF PROTEST AND AFFIRMATION

THE 1929 stock-market crash and the Great Depression affected many of the writers of the thirties as profoundly as war and boom had influenced those of the preceding decade. While the authors of the twenties had been quick to criticize American institutions, they had usually written as interpreters of contemporary life rather than as reformers. They had seldom advanced any specific program, and few were doctrinaire in approach. As the depression deepened, however, an increasing number of writers wished to correct as well as point out abuses. Several novelists hewed to the Communist line, and many others employed their work to espouse a particular reform. Even those who preferred to "let the facts speak for themselves" tended to emphasize the inequalities and inadequacies of American society in more vigorous and bolder fashion than in the past.

During the thirties there appeared a number of novels whose Marxist slant was apparent. Authors like Michael Gold, Albert Halper, Meyer Levin, and Albert Maltz produced a series of proletarian novels in which adherence to communism usually overshadowed considerations of literary craftsmanship. At the same time, a number of non-Marxist novelists also employed fiction as a device for attacking what they thought were the abuses and defects of contemporary society. Often realistic in approach and frequently emphasizing brutality, sordidness, and ignorance, they found a receptive audience among American readers during the depression years.

One of the most sweeping indictments of American society was provided by John Dos Passos's triology *U.S.A.*, in which Wobblies, high-pressure salesmen, bums, chorus girls, executives, and a host of others move in and out of a plot that gains its form from its apparent formlessness. Through short biographies of prominent Americans and recurrent chapters labeled "Camera Eye" and "Newsreel," Dos Passos employed newspaper headlines, snatches of popular songs, and stream of consciousness to convey to the reader the infinite variety of the American scene. Despite their different interests and backgrounds, the characters in *U.S.A.* ultimately are defeated, and Dos Passos makes it clear that in his opinion each defeat can be attributed to the American economic system. His final chapter, entitled "Vag," describes a homeless boy bumming rides on a highway:

> *The young man waits at the edge of the concrete, with one hand he grips a rubbed suitcase of phony leather, the other hand almost making a fist, thumb up*
>
> *that moves in ever so slight an arc when a car slithers past, a truck roars clatters; the wind of cars passing ruffles his hair, slaps grit in his face.*
>
> *Head swims, hunger has twisted belly tight, . . .*
>
> *Eyes black with want seek out the eyes of the drivers, a hitch, a hundred miles down the road.*
>
> *Overhead in the blue a plane drones. Eyes follow the silver Douglas that flashes once in the sun and bores its smooth way out of sight into the blue.*
>
> *(The transcontinental passengers sit pretty, big men with bank-accounts, highlypaid jobs; . . . telephone girls say goodmorning to them. . . .*
>
> *The transcontinental passenger thinks contracts, profits, vacation-trips, mighty continent between Atlantic and Pacific, power, wires humming dollars, cities jammed, hills empty, the indiantrail leading into the wagonroad, the macadamed pike, the concrete skyway; trains, planes: history the billion dollar speedup. . . .)*
>
> *The young man waits on the side of the road; the plane has gone; thumb moves in a small arc when a car tears hissing past. Eyes seek the driver's eyes. . . .*
>
> *went to school, books said opportunity, ads promised speed, own your home, shine bigger than your neighbor, the radiocrooner whispered girls, ghosts of platinum girls coaxed from the screen, millions in winnings were chalked up on the boards in the offices,*

paychecks were for hands willing to work, the cleared desk of an executive with three telephones on it;

waits with swimming head, needs knot the belly, idle hands numb, beside the speeding traffic.

*A hundred miles down the road.**

While all writers of the period did not necessarily accept Dos Passos's economic interpretation, they often shared his sense of futility. Like Dos Passos they stripped their characters of conventional restraints, made them victims rather than masters of their surroundings, and then turned them loose to fight, make love, suffer, and die. William Faulkner wrote in detail of the Negroes, poor whites, planters, and businessmen in an imaginary county of his native state of Mississippi. As addicted to violence as the members of the hardboiled school of fiction and employing an extraordinarily involuted style, Faulkner dealt with the deleterious effects on the South of its uneasy transition from a plantation to commercial society. Thomas Wolfe, like Faulkner a Southerner, found his best subject in himself. In *Look Homeward, Angel; Of Time and the River;* and *The Web and the Rock* he wrote thinly disguised autobiographies, which are glutted with much extraneous material and distinguished by some of the most powerful descriptive passages in the entire range of American literature. James Farrell, who followed in the naturalist tradition of Theodore Dreiser, spared no details in his novels of Chicago's Irish-Americans, and his *Studs Lonigan* trilogy contains all relevant—and perhaps some irrelevant—sociological data on the manner in which environment shaped and eventually destroyed the book's central character. The almost inconceivable hardships and degradation experienced by Southern poor whites was told in an often ribald and salty fashion by Erskine Caldwell in such novels as *God's Little Acre* and *Tobacco Road.* John Steinbeck's *Grapes of Wrath* chronicled the trials and tribulations of the Okies on their long and heart-rending migration to California. With a compassion for his characters that distinguished him from most other novelists of the age, Steinbeck in the *Grapes of Wrath* produced one of the decade's most moving and widely-read novels.

Although much of the literature of the twenties and thirties indicates clearly that its creators were at war with the present and the past, there were several gifted writers who did not view their work as an instrument of either social or individual protest. Throughout these years, Robert Frost in his poems on the New England hill country and its people turned his back on the "new poetry" to demonstrate that the themes of an earlier age still had meaning to a skillful and perceptive artist. Among the novelists Ellen Glasgow and Willa Cather deserve special mention

* John Dos Passos: *The Big Money* (New York: Harcourt, Brace and Company, Inc., 1933), pp. 559–61. Reprinted with the permission of John Dos Passos.

for their ability to impart to their work a universality that lifted them above the cross-currents of their own age. From World War I until her death in the 1940's, Ellen Glasgow continued to reveal her ability as both a literary craftsman and an ironical observer of human nature. Willa Cather, in *O Pioneers!, Death Comes For the Archbishop, My Ántonia,* and *Sapphira and the Slave Girl,* demonstrated that she was without a peer in her ability to create what she once described as the "inexplicable presence of the thing not named, of the overtone divined by the ear but not heard by it, the verbal mood, the emotional aura of the fact or the thing or the deed, that gives high quality to the novel or the drama, as well as to poetry itself."

In the years after 1935 the disdain of many writers for contemporary American society was gradually forced into the background by the compulsion of events in Europe and Asia. As the Fascist leaders intensified their attacks on the ideals and aspirations that had been traditionally revered by the American people, a growing number of authors began to extol those parts of the national culture that they had previously ignored or scorned. Poets, essayists, and novelists, warning of the threat from abroad, urged their countrymen to undertake a program of moral rearmament and to look to a glorious past for both strength and inspiration in the present crisis. Carl Sandburg in 1928 had written of those "who died hungry and crying," and in 1936 in *The People, Yes* he condemned the "tycoons, big shots and dictators" and praised the masses that "go back to the nourishing earth for rootholds." Three years later he completed a multivolumed Lincoln biography that left the Civil War President even more of a folk hero than before Sandburg had undertaken his task. Van Wyck Brooks, who in 1916 had scorned America's intellectual history as a "universe of talent and thwarted personality evaporating in stale culture," in the thirties glorified New England's literary past in *The Flowering of New England* and *New England Indian Summer.* In 1940 in *The Irresponsibles,* Archibald MacLeish, a one-time exponent of the "new poetry," castigated intellectuals for their withdrawal from the life about them and their failure to defend the "rule of moral law, the rule of spiritual authority, the rule of intellectual truth" against the Fascist "revolution of gangs."

Among the novelists there was a marked trend away from earlier attitudes and toward a literature of exhortation and affirmation. Sinclair Lewis abandoned satire to warn against the dangers of native fascism in *It Can't Happen Here.* John Dos Passos in *The Ground We Stand On* turned from fiction and angry denunciation to a sustained eulogy of an American tradition, which he thought the "grandest and most nearly realized . . . pictures in all history." Equally significant was Ernest Hemingway's transformation from nihilism to faith in democracy. *For Whom the Bell Tolls,* which was published in 1940, reveals Hemingway's old obsession with the man of action; but, unlike Hemingway's earlier heroes, Robert Jordan as a member of the Loyalist forces in Spain knew why he was fighting.

115. THE ARTS

IN THE postwar decade the arts, like literature, often reflected the wide gulf between the nation's creative minority and the mass of Americans. Although many artists continued to produce more or less prosaic work that was wholly acceptable to the conventional-minded, others adopted techniques and forms of expression that made their art largely incomprehensible to all but a handful of professionals. Modern American painters, sculptors, and musicians liked to believe that their approach to their subject matter was highly individualistic, but in reality they borrowed much from abroad, and the center of new artistic cults and schools remained in Europe.

There was no lack of traditional art in America in the 1920's. Portraits were painted in the flattering style that their subjects had always demanded and to which artists had often been forced to conform. Murals in public buildings exalted the American past; those on the walls of business establishments glorified the exploits of industry, commerce, and finance. Popular art remained almost exclusively descriptive. Illustrations in advertisements and the slick magazines and on calendars and posters depicted American individuals and scenes in idealized and unimaginative fashion. In sculpture, military and patriotic studies provided major themes. World War I, like earlier American wars, produced its quota of military monuments, and within a few years after Versailles every American community of any size could boast of at least one statue of a determined-looking doughboy advancing into battle. Nor did the sculptors ignore the glories of the past. Daniel C. French's figure of the Great Emancipator in the Lincoln Memorial in Washington and Gutzon Borglum's enormous heads of Washington, Jefferson, Lincoln, and Theodore Roosevelt, hacked out of the stone of a mountain side in the Black Hills of the Dakotas, were merely the most famous examples of the continued popularity of the heroic and grandiose in American sculpture in the postwar years.

Many modern sculptors and painters, finding little to admire in the taste of their countrymen, sought refuge and appreciation among small cliques of fellow artists in America and Europe. Expatriates in spirit and often in fact, they were ill at ease in their native land, and their disdain for American culture was matched by their respect for the more advanced art movements abroad. Rejecting pictorial art, they employed novel techniques and new materials to gain unusual effects. Much of their work, moreover, was characterized by a degree of distortion that made their subjects all but unrecognizable to the layman. Whether surrealists, cubists, or abstractionists, the modernists were united in their belief in the necessity of finding means that would best enable them to express their highly individualized reactions and emotions. To the modern artist, his work was not a method of communication but a form of self-revelation. As such it could only be introspective. When the modernists were accused of insanity, degeneracy, or fraud by contemporaries, this was neither more nor less than they expected from those they termed philistines.

During the 1930's the depression and the New Deal's art program both broadened and redirected the main currents of American artistic expression. Under the impact of hard times and the reformatory spirit that they induced, many artists, who in the boom years had ignored the masses, now sought to depict their plight. The Federal Arts Project not only provided sculptors and painters with work and encouragement, but it also gave them a degree of freedom that had not always been possible under a system of private patronage. Murals, etchings, water colors, and statues of the depression decade recorded America's failures as well as its achievements and the aspirations of the poor as well as the accomplishments of the well-to-do. The dust bowl and the picket line were considered suitable subjects for the serious artist, and the tribulations of the sharecropper, wage earner, and unemployed received much of the attention that had once been accorded the triumphs of industrialist, politician, and soldier.

From the standpoint of the social historian, one of the most notable features of the history of art in the 1920's was the growing preoccupation of American painters and sculptors with native themes that had formerly been slighted. Little known figures from the American past were resurrected, and the Indian, Negro, and immigrant, instead of being romanticized or stripped of their dignity, were treated with an understanding that made them both individuals and Americans in their own right. At the same time such painters as Thomas Hart Benton, John S. Curry, and Grant Wood found in their native Midwest scenes and people that they felt were typically American. Employing a realistic approach that was tempered by a sympathy for their subjects, they sought to have their canvasses demonstrate Benton's dictum that "no American art can come to those who do not live an American life, who do not have an American psychology, and who cannot find in America justification of their lives." This shift of emphasis was reflected in the patronage of art as well as in its creation. Private collectors displayed an increasing interest in the work of American artists; folk art and primitivism achieved a considerable vogue; and in 1930 the Whitney Museum in New York became the first institution to purchase and show only native art.

The painters and sculptors who sought to emphasize their Americanism through their choice and treatment of subjects did not have the field to themselves, for throughout these years there was a noticeable narrowing of the chasm that had formerly separated the modernists and their potential audience. It became increasingly fashionable for wealthy patrons to collect modern works rather than old masters. The Whitney Museum placed its greatest emphasis on contemporary art, and the Museum of Modern Art, founded in New York in 1929, consistently lived up to its name. As Oliver W. Larkin in *Art and Life in America* has written:

> *At the Museum of Modern Art in 1936 one could see . . . the nervous patterns and insistent flat colors of Miro's* Person Throwing a Stone at a Bird, *the alarmingly empty spaces of Tanguy's* Mama, Papa is Wounded! *the paradoxical objects which Pierre Roy assembled in* Daylight Saving Time . . . ; *a woman by Max Ernst whose head became a fan and through whose perforated torso one saw a distant shoreline; Masson's* Battle of Fishes *with scribbled shapes of brush and pencil on canvas and sandpaper; the flaccid watches of Dali with bugs swarming over them in* The Persistence of Memory.*

Modern architects, dependent on a mass market for their livelihood, were furnished with little opportunity for experimentation, and in their efforts to redesign the American home they met almost universal opposition. Believing that form should follow function, they were thwarted not only by the more conventional views of most of their contemporaries but also by the high cost that their individualistic approach to architecture entailed. For the average American a house was a major investment, and few prospective home owners had either the courage or inclination to sink their savings in a house that defied tradition. While the ability and prestige of a Frank Lloyd Wright enabled him to obtain a commission for such a masterpiece as his "Falling Water" house, his work represented an exception to the rule, rather than a trend.

During the construction boom of the twenties, home architects were largely supplanted by building contractors who erected from a single set of plans houses that were indistinguishable from one another in all but a few external features. Arranged row on row in real-estate developments, builders' houses were generally occupied by manual and clerical workers of moderate income. For the more well-to-do, Tudor, Colonial, Spanish, and French models were preferred. Aside from their mechan-

* Oliver W. Larkin: *Art and Life in America* (New York: Rinehart & Company, Inc., 1949), p. 410.

ical gadgets, the homes of the rich, like those of the poor, provided few indications that they had been built to meet the needs of twentieth-century American life.

Industrial rather than home architecture provided the modernists with their greatest opportunity, for businessmen were quick to perceive the economic advantages of functionalism. Rationally planned factories and office buildings with maximum light and air for workers were good business as well as good architecture. Once again it was Frank Lloyd Wright who showed the way to his less imaginative colleagues. His pioneering designs for the Johnson Wax Company and the Larkin buildings demonstrated that modern architecture in the hands of a dedicated genius could be both profitable and aesthetically pleasing.

Throughout these years the Federal government provided many architects with employment, but offered few of them a chance to use their creative talents. The large number of government buildings erected in Washington during the twenties and thirties were all of traditional design. Lewis Mumford thought they comprised

> *a monument of irregional and irrational planning. Closed courts that trap the summer sun without taking advantage of summer breezes, window area sacrificed to classic massiveness, grotesque waste of money on tedious stone columns that further diminish light and air. Nowhere a clear indication of the purpose of the building or the location of departments. This unified building project might have set a masterly precedent for rational building in every city: unfortunately, it was organized esthetically for an obsolete baroque picture, characteristic of a despotic order.**

While the public-housing projects instituted by the New Deal represented a significant departure in urban housing, the need to hold down costs and the emphasis on uniformity left little room for the introduction of architectual innovation. Some impetus was given to community planning with the government's establishment of Greenbelt towns, but this type of planning never got beyond the experimental stage. Despite the models provided by Radburn, New Jersey, and the numerous planned communities in Europe, town planning remained an art that serious modern architects enjoyed discussing but were unable to practice.

American music, more than any other form of creative endeavor, has suffered from the comparative lack of a native tradition. After World War I, more Americans than ever before became interested in concert and operatic music, but it was Europe's classics rather than contemporary American pieces that attracted the largest audiences. Although the radio and the Federal Arts Project gave countless Americans their

* Lewis Mumford: *The Culture of Cities* (New York: Harcourt, Brace and Company, Inc., 1938), p. 357.

first opportunity to listen to serious music, the works they heard were more often than not foreign rather than native compositions. Following World War II, President Truman urged Americans to patronize native composers, and in January, 1947, Douglas Moore wrote in *The Saturday Review of Literature:*

> *American music is played and sung of course but more often than not as a gesture thought to involve sacrifice on the part of the artist, the manager, and the audience. . . . Even in New York, where there is a small public for new music and programs are somewhat more venturesome, a survey of . . . concerts given . . . at Carnegie, Town Hall, and New York Times Hall shows that, of seventy-three programs presented, fifty contained not a single American item. Of 739 compositions, forty-five (less than seven percent) were by American composers of this age or any other.*

Perhaps the most significant development in postwar American music was the emergence of a group of young composers whose work was frankly experimental. Feeling that any attempt to imitate the techniques and forms of an earlier age was an evasion of their artistic responsibility and integrity, such modern composers as Roy Harris, Aaron Copland, and Virgil Thompson among others sought a new "musical language" that would "speak to the men and women of the artist's own time with a directness and immediacy of communicative power that no previous art expression [could] give." Although the modernists frequently dealt with American themes, few Americans either appreciated or enjoyed the new music. To the traditionalists, who had long associated "good music" with such names as Bach, Mozart, Beethoven, and Chopin, modern composers seemed capable of producing only what Copland has called "cacophonous harmonies, . . . tuneless melodies, . . . headsplitting sonorities . . . , confusing rhythms and cerebral forms." Thus, in music, as in sculpture, painting, and poetry, a relatively small number of thoughtful and talented artists were shut off from a large potential audience by a barrier that neither group seemed capable of removing.

In contrast to serious American music, jazz was an indigenous product that was unaffected by developments outside the United States. Although few experts have been able to agree on a definition of jazz, H. O. Osgood probably reached the only satisfactory conclusion when he wrote that it was the "spirit of the music, not the mechanics of its frame . . . that determines whether or not it is jazz." Originating in the early years of the twentieth century among Negro musicians extemporizing in honky-tonks in and around New Orleans, jazz moved on to Chicago and then to the rest of the nation. By the 1920's it had become both big business and an integral part of the country's culture. Jazz might be "sweet," "hot," "swing," "blues," or any one of a number of other variations; but whatever it was called, it was immensely popular. George Gershwin, Irving Berlin, Jerome Kern, Louis Armstrong, and a host of others wrote for the masses, and there was never any problem about their being able to communicate with their audience. Americans might not know it, but "St. Louis Blues," "Rhapsody in Blue," "Night and Day," and "Star Dust" were examples of an American folk music that put Europe in this country's debt. In the words of Marion Bauer, "Jazz was another American shot that was heard around the world! And it has beaten its insidious rhythms into every corner of the globe."*

116. SCIENCE, RELIGION, AND EDUCATION

SINCE the first English settlements in the New World, it had been an integral part of the American creed that religion, education, and material progress could cure all the ills of mankind. In the 1920's and 1930's, although the creed was modified, it contained many of its original elements. Religion no longer seemed as important as it once had, but education and material progress under the guise of scientific achievement retained their earlier hold on the American imagination.

In the years between the two world wars many Americans were inclined to believe that natural science provided mankind with the possibility of unlimited material progress. To most Americans the scientist was an inventor who discovered new products and devised new machines that made life easier for all; and everywhere they looked Americans could see the beneficent results of the scientist's labors. Plastics, improved means of communication and transportation, "wonder" drugs, and energy-giving vitamins were only a few of the many developments that served to convince the masses that science was capable of eliminating all the world's misery and hardship. Many people—particularly in the depression years—attributed unemployment to the increasing application of science to industry, but few were prepared to reject science's practical achievements. The popular view of the rôle of science in American life was re-enforced by newspapers that publicized applied rather than pure science, by industrial firms that spent millions annually on research programs, and by universities that expended larger sums on scientific research than on other forms of scholarly activity.

Americans respected scientists not only because of their practical achievements but also because of the precision and certainty with which they appeared to work. In an age of shifting values, repeated crises, and numerous social upheavals, both applied and pure science were regarded

* Marion Bauer: *Twentieth Century Music* (New York: G. P. Putnam's Sons, 1947), p. 317.

as the only fields of learning in which absolute truth was either known or ascertainable. The distinction that most people made between the "exact" and the "social" sciences was ample proof of the popular faith in the natural scientist. But, while laymen revered the scientist for his accuracy and even his omnipotence, scientists themselves had become increasingly aware of the tentative nature of their findings and conclusions. Because all scientific observations and measurements were made by men, they were as fallible as men. Moreover, the popularization of Einstein's relativity theory seemed to pull the last remaining support from beneath the nineteenth-century world of scientific absolutes. If everything was relative to time and space, concepts of determinism and causality became meaningless, and the one certainty was uncertainty. In the words of Merle Curti: "The principle of indeterminism, of uncertainty . . . appeared to be the only principle anyone could be certain of, if indeed he could be certain even of that."*

Despite a growing awareness of the limitations of their discipline, scientists throughout the 1920's and thirties steadily expanded the area of knowledge in a wide variety of fields. Robert A. Millikan, H. Victor Neher, and Arthur H. Compton conducted pioneer studies of cosmic rays. Harold Urey's discovery of heavy water and the atom-smashing projects of Ernest O. Lawrence, Carl D. Anderson, and Enrico Fermi paved the way for the development of the atom bomb in the war years. American astronomers, employing the world's most powerful telescopes, charted hitherto unknown portions of the universe and supplied some of the evidence that tended to substantiate Einstein's theory. In genetics Thomas Morgan's experiments with the vinegar fly and Hermann J. Muller's studies of fruit flies produced new evidence on the rôle of mutation in evolution. Anthropologists like Franz Boas, Margaret Mead, and Ruth Benedict employed science to undermine the myth of racial superiority; psychiatrists continued to apply and revise the lessons taught by Freud; and psychologists turned increasingly to the laboratory to test their hypotheses. There was no brand of scientific learning to which Americans had not made notable contributions and in many fields they were pre-eminent.

The almost universal respect accorded science and scientists had little apparent effect, however, on the place of traditional religion in American life. Throughout most of the period between the two wars church membership increased at practically the same rate as the population.† Although the depression seriously impaired church finances and cut down

* Merle Curti: *The Growth of American Thought* (New York: Harper & Brothers, 1951), p. 723.

† The number of church members rose from 41,926,854 in 1916 to 54,624,976 a decade later. In 1926 the value of all church property was estimated at $7,000,000,000 in contrast to the $4,677,000,000, which represented the total value of property used for public school purposes.

on the rate of growth in membership, there was a marked revival of church strength and influence during the war years. By the early 1940's the number of church members thirteen years of age and over approximated 60,000,000, while total membership exceeded 70,000,000. In 1944, the Roman Catholic Church reported 23,419,701 members, and the membership of Protestant churches was approximately 42,000,000.

Despite the growth in church membership, the influence of organized religion declined perceptibly in the years that followed World War I. Many Protestants were no longer concerned with the strict observance of the Sabbath; Sunday movies, despite the opposition of some church groups, had become commonplace; and ministers repeatedly complained from their pulpits that the automobile and the golf course provided Sunday diversions that were more attractive to many parishioners than church. Since the battle between science and religion had been settled to the satisfaction of the vast majority, religious controversies occurred less frequently and were conducted with less vehemence than in former years. Agnosticism was common enough to go largely unnoticed, while even those Americans who attended church regularly seemed to lack much of the enthusiasm and intensity that had once been considered an essential ingredient of religious experience.

In an effort to check the declining influence of the churches, many religious leaders made special efforts to appeal to the more mundane tastes of church members. Practically all urban—as well as many rural—churches had ambitious social and recreational programs that covered almost every range of activity. Some churches provided their members with psychiatric assistance, others conducted classes in subjects that ranged from dancing to manual training, and still others conducted extensive athletic programs. C. Luther Fry, writing in *Recent Social Trends* in 1933, said:

> *Church social life has been greatly elaborated. . . . Cultural activities incidental to educational aims have taken such new forms as dramatics and forums for discussions of public questions. . . .*
>
> *Organized athletics as a . . . form of normal church expression, in contrast with its employment in occasional institutional churches, show a marked increase during the last generation. Recently over one third of a representative sample of Protestant city churches reported this element in their programs. The vogue of athletics has brought about changes in church plant and staff. Increasingly the modern church includes a gymnasium, baths and game room, while athletic directors and recreational specialists have appeared with increasing frequency among the church's paid workers.**

* *Recent Social Trends in the United States; Report of the President's Research Committee on Social Trends* (New York: McGraw-Hill Book Company, 1933), Vol. II, p. 1058.

Although the church seemed less important to Americans than it once had, there is ample evidence that there was still widespread interest in religious matters. Throughout the postwar years books on religious subjects enjoyed considerable popularity. In the 1920's Lewis Browne's *This Believing World* and Bruce Barton's *The Man Nobody Knows* and *The Book Nobody Knows* were bestsellers, while in the next decade Lloyd Douglas's *Magnificent Obsession* and *Green Light* and Henry C. Link's *The Return to Religion* attracted numbers of readers. Some indication of the inadequate appeal of the established churches to many groups of Americans was also provided by the number of new sects and cults that were formed in these years. The Oxford Group, which made its greatest appeal to the young, preached "moral rearmament" and pacifism. Jehovah's Witnesses warned against the impending Last Judgment. George Baker, who was called Father Divine, adopted as his slogan: "Peace, it's wonderful!" and won numerous adherents in New York's Harlem and in the Negro sections of other cities. The American people generally may have lost much of their one-time religious zeal during the period of boom and bust, but there were many who refused to recognize this fact.

That all did not approve of the increasing secularization of American life was also revealed by the diminished, but still powerful, fundamentalist spirit that pervaded many rural areas. Fundamentalists comprised the shock troops of the Prohibition movement, and they formed the last remaining stronghold of opposition to Darwinism. In the South, where fundamentalism remained particularly strong, some states in response to pressure from religious groups adopted laws that forbade the teaching of evolution in the public schools. In 1925, John T. Scopes, a young school teacher in Dayton, Tennessee, was brought to trial for violating the state law. William Jennings Bryan served as the leading prosecuting attorney and argued for a literal interpretation of the Bible; Clarence Darrow, an acknowledged agnostic and one of the country's outstanding criminal lawyers, defended Scopes. The so-called monkey trial attracted national—and even world-wide—attention and interest. Every important paper and press association had correspondents in Dayton, and approximately two million words of telegraphic copy were filed on the trial within ten days. Scopes was found guilty, but the decision was reversed on technical grounds by the state's supreme court. To his fellow-Fundamentalists Bryan, who died at the conclusion of the trial, had gloriously waged the good fight for the Lord. To millions of other Americans, who thought that the conflict between religion and science had long since been resolved, Bryan's part in the trial seemed a pathetic reminder of an earlier and less sophisticated America.

Although organized religion appeared to have lost much of its one-time vitality, education continued to rank high in the hierachy of American values. The almost universal respect for education was reflected in increased school and college enrollments, new buildings, and expanded curricula. The number of pupils enrolled in public schools increased from 21,578,316 in 1920 to 25,433,542 in 1940, while the number of teachers rose from 679,533 to 875,477 in the same period. The average annual salary per teacher which was $871 in 1920 was $1,441 twenty years later. During the same two decades the total annual expenditure for education increased from $1,036,151,000 to $2,344,049,000. The postwar boom enabled many towns and cities to build new schools. In the depression the construction program was continued with the aid of Federal funds. By 1940 almost every community of any appreciable size had added to its school plant during the previous twenty years.

Institutions of higher learning expanded even more rapidly than elementary and secondary schools. During the prosperous twenties, when a college degree was often viewed as a badge of social distinction and a passport to business success, large numbers of boys and girls who in earlier years would have been satisfied with a high school diploma decided that their formal education would not be complete without a bachelor's degree. In the depression, when it was often impossible to obtain a job, many young people preferred four years of college to the harsh realities of the business world. Because of these considerations college enrollments steadily increased. Meanwhile annual expenditures for higher education in 1940 were almost three times as large as those in 1920.

As significant as the growth of educational facilities was the expansion of the average school's curriculum. The first eight grades of public schools, which had at one time taught little beyond the three "R's," enlarged their curricula to such an extent that by 1930 the typical elementary school offering included as many as thirty different subjects. There was a corresponding multiplication of courses in the high schools. Since large numbers of the children were drawn from every background and represented different degrees of intelligence, considerable emphasis was placed on practical subjects. Boys were taught machine-shop practices and woodworking; girls attended classes in sewing and cooking; all could study typewriting, stenography, and bookkeeping. Traditionalists complained that the schools were teaching children how to earn a living rather than how to think and that no amount of vocational training was an adequate substitute for a thorough grounding in the accepted academic subjects.

Curriculum changes were sometimes accompanied by new teaching methods sponsored by the advocates of progressive education. Learning by rote and complete reliance on textbooks gave way to an emphasis upon individual differences among students and an attempt to make learning an exciting experience rather than a series of dreary tasks. Severe classroom discipline was abandoned for a more informal attitude based on the assumption that interested pupils seldom present behavior problems. Efforts were also made to integrate subjects, and frequent use was made of available library resources. Tests were used to determine individual capacities and interests; slow learners were given special assistance; and children of unusual ability were permitted to progress at a much more rapid rate than others. Traditional schools were characterized by their rigidity; progressive schools were distinguished by their willingness to experiment and their flexibility.

Colleges, like public schools, had to revise their programs to fit the needs of a larger and more diversified student body. Two-year junior colleges were founded by private and public agencies for those high school graduates who did not wish to spend four years on a liberal arts program, or who desired to acquire the necessary prerequisites for entrance into a professional school in the shortest possible time. The popularity of such institutions is revealed by the fact that the number of junior colleges increased from 52 in 1920 to 456 in 1940. Meanwhile many colleges and universities added so many new subjects to their curricula that they resembled educational cafeterias where the customer could purchase whatever suited his fancy. The annual catalogues of some institutions listed classes in ceramics, fly-casting, hotel management, millinery, salesmanship, ice-cream manufacture, and a host of other "applied" subjects. At the same time increasing attention was given to the arts, as new courses were instituted in painting, sculpture, music, drama, and the dance. Finally, several colleges expanded their already extensive athletic programs. Stadiums and field houses became important parts of the academic landscape; intramural sports provided students with unprecedented recreational facilities; and football games between major college teams that were more often than not manned by players with "athletic scholarships" attracted huge throngs of spectators and were accompanied by the same type of ballyhoo that attended any other large commercial undertaking in the twentieth-century America. Some of those who could remember an earlier and simpler type of college wondered if it were possible to broaden higher education without also debasing it.

As in the past, the nation's educational system was largely controlled by those in the upper brackets of American economic society, and many schools were dominated by men drawn from the ranks of business and the professional classes. While such individuals respected education and more often than not were devoted to their tasks, they were frequently of a conservative turn of mind. Commenting on this situation in *Are American Teachers Free?*, Howard K. Beale has written:

*Perhaps the most dangerous, because the most general and most subtle, control over teachers is that exercised by business. . . . Business men . . . dominate most boards of school trustees whether private or public. Their influence gives them power, too, over superintendents. This power comes partly from the fact that their gifts finance private schools and their taxes pay for public ones. It arises in part from the respect that schoolmen, in a society in which values are adjudged by practical and material standards, feel for the man of affairs who has been most successful in accumulating wealth. . . . This power of business is used to see that schools "teach" ideas that will give the next generation the same uncritical awe of financial success, however unscrupulous, that this generation has had. Business's chief interest in the schools is the indoctrination of pupils and teachers with concepts that will silence criticism of business and its methods and insure large profits for the future. Reforms, which might limit its profits, must never be discussed in the schools. . . . Business men would not state their purpose in just these terms. They always translate their economic desires into terms of "the public good," "Americanism," "rugged individualism," or even "patriotism." After all, don't large business profits mean prosperity for all—or at least for all who count? "Prosperity trickles down to the masses" is the doctrine business taught this generation when it was in school. Men are so used to confusing their own desires with fine principles that most men seeking to control the schools in order to protect their business probably have really convinced themselves that this is an act of pure public service.***

Businessmen were also able to exert some influence on colleges and universities. Although privately supported institutions were directly dependent on the successful businessman for a major portion of their funds, business control of the collegiate purse strings seldom produced an easily discernible academic subservience. On the other hand, few colleges pursued policies which were openly at variance with the ideals of their principal benefactors. Furthermore, college and university presidents, who were primarily concerned with raising endowment funds, frequently shared the economic and social views of their business-dominated boards of trustees. The indirect effect of business domination of higher education was revealed in part by the popularity of business schools in the large universities and the growing number of "practical," or "service," courses offered by various institutions. Business occupied a particularly strong position in many college science departments, for numerous industrial firms began to contribute money to various educa-

* Howard K. Beale: *Are American Teachers Free?* (New York: Charles Scribner's Sons, 1936), pp. 545–6. Copyright 1936 by, and reprinted with the permission of, Charles Scribner's Sons.

tional institutions for scientific research. These business-financed projects were, however, usually confined to experiments that would produce practical results, and the professor of physics or chemistry interested in pure science occasionally found himself without adequate research funds, while his more practical colleague was supplied with ample money by a large industrial corporation.

Professors teaching at public institutions were subjected to many of the same pressures as their colleagues in the endowed colleges and universities. The legislatures that voted the appropriations for the state universities were usually no more amenable to unorthodox economic and social theories than were the business-benefactors of private institutions. Furthermore, in many states, teachers of every rank were compelled to sign loyalty oaths, which on the surface asked for allegiance to traditional American ideals, but which in reality were demands that the teacher refrain from challenging any aspect of the *status quo*. It is, of course, impossible to measure the effect of business on American secondary and higher education. Although it is obviously inaccurate to state categorically that the businessman controlled education, it is equally inaccurate to maintain that he exercised no influence upon it.

Schools and colleges, like virtually every other institution in the interwar decades, revealed the inability of Americans to resolve the problems posed by two contrasting—and often conflicting—patterns of culture. On the one hand, there was the machine civilization with its relentless pressure toward conformity and standardization. On the other hand, there was a comparatively small minority of Americans who protested that the United States had confused uniformity with progress. The prize for which each side was contending was the American individual; for, while the machine could provide him with many more social and material advantages than had ever been available to man in the past, it also was capable of destroying his individualism.

CHAPTER XIX

FROM ISOLATION TO INTERVENTION

IN 1917 the United States embarked on what many Americans believed was a crusade to make the world safe for democracy. Three years later most Americans were convinced that the rest of the world was beyond saving and that the United States would do well to ignore it. During the next two decades the occasional efforts of either Republican or Democratic officials to promote international co-operation and collective security were largely nullified by the overwhelmingly isolationist spirit of the American people, and it was only in Latin American affairs that the government was able to abandon traditional foreign policy.

After 1939 the American people were compelled to learn again the lessons of 1812 and 1917. Once more they were forced step by step to the realization that isolation had made them the victims rather than the masters of events. Once more the American people debated while the rest of the world fought. The Japanese ended this debate at Pearl Harbor, and the ensuing war and its aftermath put the citizens of the United States in a position of responsibility from which they could not retreat even if they had desired to do so.

117. PEACE AT BARGAIN RATES

FOLLOWING the United States' rejection of the League of Nations most Americans turned with a sense of relief from the cares of an unhappy world to the opportunities for profits presented by the boom of the golden twenties. Convinced that the peace settlements were a failure and that the American decision to participate in the war had been a mistake, they seemed intent on forgetting their recent part in world events. They overlooked their enthusiasm for war in 1917 and soon convinced themselves that they had been tricked into fighting by the skill of English propagandists, the machinations of wily Continental diplomats, the naïveté of their own officials, the desire of the bankers to "save their loans," and the greed of the munition makers, or "merchants of death." In the popular view the peace conference demonstrated beyond doubt the folly of the decision of 1917, for it was generally believed that the meetings in Paris had shown that a noble, disinterested America would always be duped when it tried to reform the decadent, corrupt Old World.

The American people emerged from World War I with an overwhelming desire to avoid future wars regardless of consequences. Having refused to join the League of Nations, they were equally opposed to the participation of the United States in any plans for collective security that might eventually have to be implemented by a resort to force. They had crossed the Atlantic once to prevent Europe from destroying itself, and they were now determined that neither they nor their children would ever recross it on a similar mission. As the current expression had it, Europe could "stew in its own juice." To the average American of the 1920's war could be avoided by the United States if it refused to fight and if it refused to participate in any diplomatic intercourse that might eventually lead to war. In most people's minds the maintenance of peace was a matter of will power. War, like alcohol, was strong stuff; but Americans could swear off it if they possessed sufficient resolution.

Despite the attitude of the American people, the United States government during the postwar years was never in a position to ignore developments in the outside world. American businessmen had interests in every corner of the globe, and the State Department repeatedly demonstrated its belief that it had an obligation to protect the American dollar in foreign lands. The hope of collecting war debts owed the United States by several nations necessitated constant attention to the complexities of European economics and politics. American possessions in the Caribbean and Pacific could be safeguarded only by an active diplomacy. As a result of these considerations any attempt to pursue a policy of outright isolation was out of the question. While the American people had repudiated Wilsonian internationalism and Theodore Roosevelt's interventionism, their officials frequently had to resort to both techniques in their efforts to maintain the traditional position of the United States in world affairs. But regardless of what policy the government followed, its conduct of foreign affairs was always hampered by the refusal of the mass of Americans to make any sacrifices for the peace and security that they so ardently desired. They refused to give up even a modicum of national sovereignty to promote plans for international co-operation. They also refused to limit American freedom of action by permitting their nation to join a system of hard-and-fast alliances to check aggressors. Finally, they refused to accept the penalty of isolation: they neither abandoned their overseas economic interests nor spent money for the defense of an isolated United States. Americans, in short, wanted a cheap peace—a peace that could be obtained at little or no sacrifice in money or in individual and national responsibility.

Despite the campaign of confusion waged by the Republicans on the League issue in 1920, President Harding soon made it clear that his Administration had no intention of taking the United States into the League of Nations. Yet Harding and Secretary of State Hughes were quickly forced to the conclusion that it was impossible for them to conduct American foreign policy on the assumption that the League did not exist. As early as 1922 the United States sent unofficial observers to League of Nations meetings on the opium and white slave trade, and within a short time similar American representatives were attending conferences dealing with the trade in arms and munitions. By 1931, two hundred and twelve Americans had served as United States delegates to League conferences, and five Americans were stationed permanently at Geneva to look out for United States' interests in the League. These cautious moves on the part of the United States toward co-operation with the League should not, however, be emphasized too much, for during the 1920's the United States assumed no responsibility for making or implementing League policy, and no responsible American official ever proposed that the United States take the next logical step and join the League.

The opposition of successive Republican Administrations to any form of effective co-operation with the League did not extend to the World Court, which had been established in 1922 in accordance with Article XIV of the League Covenant. In 1923, President Harding advocated that the United States join the World Court, and in the following year similar recommendations were made by both the Republican and Democratic parties in their platforms. The Senate, however, waited until 1926 before adopting a resolution that favored American participation in the Court. Moreover, the Senate made its approval contingent upon the acceptance by the League of five reservations, one of which provided that the Court would not hear any disputes that involved the interests of the United States without first obtaining American consent. Although the members of the League in 1929 agreed to the conditions laid down by the United States, the Senate refused to act until 1935, when it blocked American participation in the Court in a vote that fell seven short of the two-thirds majority needed for ratification. If nothing else, the outcome in the Senate revealed that even when extraordinary precautions were taken to safeguard the sovereignty of the United States, the representatives of the American people hesitated to approve any step that might be interpreted as a return to Wilsonian internationalism.*

Although the United States refused to support the League, it took some steps to preserve peace through a program of international co-operation that by-passed the League. Because many Americans in the years that immediately followed World War I believed that one of the principal causes of the war had been the armament races that had preceded the conflict, there was a widespread demand that the United States take the lead in planning to reduce the size of the world's navies. When Senator William E. Borah introduced in February, 1921, a resolution that advocated a disarmament conference, it was almost universally approved by the American people. The Harding Administration, accordingly, on August 11, 1921, extended invitations for such a conference to Great Britain, France, Japan, Italy, Belgium, Portugal, Holland, and China. At the first plenary session of the Washington Naval Conference in November, 1921, Secretary of State Hughes not only proposed disarmament as a vague principle to be achieved in some distant day but specifically recommended a ratio of 5–5–3 for the navies of the United States, Great Britain, and Japan respectively. As Hughes pointed out, this program meant that the United States would be compelled to scrap 30 capital ships "with an aggregate tonnage (including that of ships in construction, if completed) of 845,740 tons," and that the three powers together would have to destroy a total of 1,878,043 tons.

Three important treaties were adopted by the nations attending the Washington Conference. The Four-Power and Nine-Power treaties provided for the maintenance of the *status quo* in the Pacific and in eastern Asia; they represented an effort to support international co-operation in the Far East. The Washington Treaty established a ratio, of 5, 5, 3, 1.75, 1.75 for the capital ships of the navies of the United States, Great Britain, Japan, France, and Italy respectively. Further provision was made for the destruction of ships in excess of the stipulated quotas, and the five nations concerned agreed to a ten-year moratorium on the construction of new naval craft.

* Even though the United States never joined the World Court, four Americans became World Court judges.

Because the provisions of the Washington Treaty affected only capital ships, repeated attempts were made to extend its provisions to auxiliary vessels. The Geneva Disarmament Conference, called in 1927 at the instigation of the United States, failed to reach an agreement largely because of the lobbying activities of American shipbuilders. Three years later a conference in London adopted some restrictions on the construction of smaller ships, provided a more liberal quota for the Japanese navy, and extended the ban on the construction of new ships to 1936. In 1934, Japan announced that it would not be bound by restrictive naval agreements after 1936, and in that year all naval powers of the world openly resumed the competition for supremacy that they had in part renounced in 1922.

Despite high American hopes, the agreements reached at the Washington and London conferences contributed little to the elimination of the factors that jeopardized the peace of the world. Because the Four-Power and Nine-Power pacts included no machinery for enforcing the *status quo* in the Pacific, they remained little more than declarations of a policy to which the United States agreed in principle rather than in fact. Through the Washington and London disarmament programs Americans reduced the size of their fleet, but they did not reduce the dangers of war. Instead of promoting peace, this type of disarmament promoted nothing but the welfare of the American taxpayer, who was no longer required to support a large naval establishment; and while making concessions to the taxpayer, the American authors of naval disarmament weakened the ability of the United States to defend itself and its possessions in the event of war.

Thus, having refused to join the only existing international organization to preserve the peace, the United States then refused to accept the responsibilities of isolation by preparing for any eventuality through an extensive armament program. Military preparedness cost money and the American people preferred a kind of disarmament that not only benefited their pocketbooks but also salved their consciences by leading them to believe that they had made a genuine—although painless—contribution to world peace.

Further evidence of the United States' desire to prevent war without making the necessary commitments to preserve peace was revealed by the Pact of Paris. To many Americans, who thought that wars were caused by unscrupulous and irresponsible politicians, peace could be achieved by inducing the leaders of the nations of the world to renounce war as an instrument of national policy. In response to this widespread belief Secretary of State Kellogg in 1928 negotiated an agreement outlawing war with Aristide Briand, the French foreign minister. The Kellogg-Briand Pact, or Pact of Paris, was eventually ratified by some sixty other nations, but it contained no provisions for either removing the economic and political causes of war or for curbing aggressor nations, and most of the participating nations insisted on a series of qualifications that largely destroyed whatever effectiveness the pact might have had. For its own part, the Senate, in ratifying the document in August, 1928, stipulated that the Pact of Paris in no way interfered with the Monroe Doctrine, with any measures needed for the defense of the United States, or with the right of the United States to refuse to take any steps to curb an aggressor nation.* The principal value of the Pact of Paris to the American people was not that it reduced the possibility of their going to war, but that it persuaded them that they had made a major contribution to the cause of peace without any risk or cost to themselves.

The painless form of international co-operation espoused by the United States at the Washington and London conferences and in the Pact of Paris was duplicated during the 1920's in the nation's economic foreign-policy. The United States soon became entangled in the reparations question through its desire to collect its war debts, and the Dawes and Young plans may be viewed as an American attempt to resolve Europe's postwar economic problems; but neither proposed that the United States accept any responsibility for a long-term program for the economic reconstruction of Europe, and both were soon swept away by the forces that they were designed to control. After 1929, President Hoover thought that the United States should take the lead in a world-wide move to combat the depression, but his efforts were thwarted by circumstances beyond his control. In all other respects, the economic foreign-policy of the United States during the postwar years was narrowly nationalistic. The United States had emerged from World War I the world's largest creditor nation, but its businessmen continued to seek new markets abroad for their surplus goods, while at the same time the American government repeatedly raised tariff barriers to prevent the entrance of foreign goods into the United States.

The Democratic victory at the polls in 1932 had no appreciable effect upon the conduct of American foreign policy. Throughout the 1930's most Americans were so engrossed in their own economic troubles that they were not inclined to consider the troubles of the rest of the world. But as the decade progressed, and while the various dictator nations grew stronger, the American people—however reluctantly—were driven to the conclusion that their choice no longer lay between isolation and international co-operation but between isolation and war.

* Probably the only tangible effect of the Peace of Paris upon international conduct was that after its ratification several nations avoided being branded as aggressors in violation of the pact's terms by going to war without bothering to issue a formal declaration of war.

118. MARINE DIPLOMACY

DURING the first two decades of the twentieth century the United States pursued an interventionist policy in Latin America in an attempt to safeguard the Canal Zone and to protect American investments in countries south of the Rio Grande. During the Administrations of Harding and Coolidge there was no fundamental change in either the objectives or methods of the Latin American diplomacy of the United States. The Caribbean remained an American lake, and the Big Stick was used whenever the interests of the United States seemed to require its use. But with the accession of Herbert Hoover to the presidency, these tactics were largely abandoned, and the United States undertook a program of hemispheric co-operation that provided the groundwork for Franklin D. Roosevelt's Good Neighbor Policy.

In a speech at Rio de Janeiro in 1922, Secretary of State Charles Evans Hughes declared that the United States desired the "independence, the unimpaired sovereignty and political integrity, and the constantly increasing prosperity of the peoples of Latin America." Despite the disinterested tone of this statement, the United States during the Harding and Coolidge Administrations made it abundantly clear that this country still retained the right to determine how the Latin American countries should attain these objectives. In 1921 the United States sent a battleship to Panama to hasten the cession of the disputed Toco territory to Costa Rica. The Washington Conference of 1922–3 on Central American Affairs, attended by the five republics of Central America, was called by the United States to devise a formula to prevent wars or revolutionary upheavals that might threaten American strategic interests in the Canal Zone. American troops, stationed in the Dominican Republic when Harding took office, were not withdrawn until 1924. When a revolution broke out in Honduras in 1923, the United States landed marines and took the lead in setting up a provisional government. During the dispute between Chile and Peru over the ownership of Tacna-Arica, President Coolidge ordered both countries to resolve the issue with a plebiscite. By the midtwenties the United States was either employing financial pressure or sending in marines to influence the policies of some ten Latin American nations.

The determination of the United States to resort to "marine diplomacy" to protect its economic and strategic stake in Latin America was fully revealed by American policy in Nicaragua. The withdrawal of American troops from Nicaragua in 1925 was followed by a revolution, and in the next year American forces reoccupied the country. By 1927, when five thousand American marines were in Nicaragua, President Coolidge stated: "There is no question that if the revolution continues, American investments and . . . interests in Nicaragua will be very seriously affected, if not destroyed. . . . American as well as foreign bondholders will undoubtedly look to the United States for the protection of their interests." Nor did Coolidge feel that the United States should be condemned for protecting its interests in Nicaragua. In the President's opinion, Americans had a "moral responsibility" in this country, and were "not making war on Nicaragua any more than a policeman on the street is making war on passersby."

To restore order in Nicaragua, the United States granted recognition to the regime of Adolfo Díaz and permitted it to obtain arms from American arsenals. At the same time an embargo was imposed on arms shipments to Díaz's rival, Sacasa, who had been recognized as Nicaragua's President by Mexico. In 1927, Henry L. Stimson, President Coolidge's special envoy to Nicaragua, induced the contending factions to accept a truce that provided for disarming the rebels, supervising new elections, and reorganizing the police force, all under American supervision. The Nicaraguan elections of 1928 and 1932 were managed to the apparent satisfaction of the country's different factions except for General Sandino, who took to the hills and waged a guerrilla campaign until he was assassinated in 1934.

The only evidence that the Coolidge Administration preferred diplomatic negotiation to intervention in Latin America was provided by American relations with Mexico. The Mexican Constitution of 1917, which provided for the nationalization of her oil and mineral deposits, had aroused the fears of American investors and been largely responsible for the refusal of the United States to recognize President Obregón until 1923, when he exempted from nationalization any property acquired before the adoption of this constitution. In 1924, however, he was succeeded by President Calles, who thought the nationalization clause was retroactive. A diplomatic crisis soon developed. Some American newspapers, supported by Roman Catholics opposed to Calles' anticlerical program, and by Americans with oil interests in Mexico, editorialized on the possibility of war. But President Coolidge sent Dwight W. Morrow, a Morgan partner, as ambassador to Mexico in 1927, telling him: "My only instructions are to keep us out of war with Mexico." Through a display of genuine friendship for the Mexican people, Morrow was able to win enormous popularity for himself and to reduce markedly the widespread suspicion of American motives. Through skillful and informal diplomacy, he was able to resolve—for the time being, at least—the vexatious dispute over nationalization. Mexico agreed to leave undisturbed the American oil rights obtained before 1917, and the Mexican Supreme Court reversed the government's earlier stand on this matter.

119. THE GOOD NEIGHBOR POLICY

DWIGHT MORROW'S successful mission to Mexico foreshadowed a fundamental shift in American relations with Latin America. Latin American opposition to the domination of the United States came out into the open at the Havana Inter-American Conference in January, 1928. In an unaccustomed display of courage, some Latin American delegates criticized the interventionist policies of the United States and supported a resolution that no nation had the right to "intervene in the affairs of another." Secretary of State Hughes, who protested that any government—meaning the United States—was "fully justified in taking action . . . for the purpose of protecting the lives and property of its nationals" in any country in which they were threatened, was able to block this resolution. His victory was in reality little more than a delaying action, for the larger problem of formulating a mutually satisfactory hemispheric policy remained to be solved. Latin Americans were making it increasingly clear that if this country continued to intervene in their affairs, it would have to rely on force and could no longer disguise its moves by posing as a benevolent but stern parent disciplining children for their own good. Moreover, "marine diplomacy" in Latin America was bound eventually to weaken the position of the United States in other areas of the world, for few nations would take seriously its protests against aggression in Europe and Asia while it repeatedly invoked the Monroe Doctrine in an aggressive manner in Central America. In the face of these considerations, the Hoover Administration saw no alternative but to rely on hemispheric co-operation rather than the Big Stick.

The first indication that the United States was prepared to abandon its traditional resort to intervention in Latin America was furnished by the Washington Conference on Conciliation and Arbitration, which met in December, 1928, in accordance with a resolution adopted at the earlier Havana Conference. The Washington Conference drew up treaties of conciliation and arbitration, signed by the United States, which provided for the compulsory arbitration of legal disputes among the signatories and for the conciliatory settlement of all disputes not submitted to arbitration. Evidence that the United States would support decisions reached at the Washington Conference was offered by the publication in 1930 of a detailed revision of its traditional interpretation of the Monroe Doctrine. Composed by J. Reuben Clark in December, 1928, the *Memorandum on the Monroe Doctrine* stated that the Theodore Roosevelt Corollary was not "justified by the terms of the Monroe Doctrine":

> *So far as Latin America is concerned, the doctrine is now, and always has been, not an instrument of violence and oppression, but an unbought, freely bestowed and wholly effective guarantee of their*

freedom, independence and territorial integrity against the imperialistic designs of Europe.

In the interval between his election and his inauguration Herbert Hoover took a good-will tour in Latin America, and while in Argentina he stated that the "fear of some persons concerning supposed intervention is . . . unfounded." During his administration Hoover sought to make a reality of this pronouncement, and in numerous instances he and his advisers were able to dispel some of the accumulated suspicion of the United States in the Central and South American republics. Following the supervision of the 1932 elections in Nicaragua, the United States withdrew its troops. American forces remained in Haiti throughout Hoover's term of office, but his Administration abandoned Wilson's policy of nonrecognition by accepting without question new governments in the Dominican Republic, Panama, and six other nations. Moreover, when El Salvador in 1932 defaulted on a bond issue, the United States reversed its earlier policy by refusing to employ its prestige and power to assist American bankers in the recovery of their losses. Finally, American opposition to intervention by the League of Nations in Latin American affairs was partially abandoned when Secretary of State Stimson in February, 1933, announced his approval of the League's proposed settlement of the dispute between Peru and Colombia over the territory of Leticia.*

The Latin American policies inaugurated by Herbert Hoover were continued by Franklin D. Roosevelt, who broadened their application and made them an integral part of his conduct of foreign relations. Upon taking office March 4, 1933, the President stated that he planned to "dedicate this Nation to the policy of the good neighbor—the neighbor who resolutely respects himself and, because he does so, respects the rights of others—the neighbor who respects his obligations and respects the sanctity of his agreements in . . . a world of neighbors." Although these words seemed to refer to the United States' relations with all the nations of the world, President Roosevelt made it clear that they had particular relevance for the Latin American republics.

The Good Neighbor Policy was incorporated into a larger program of hemispheric co-operation in a series of inter-American conferences at which the United States formally abandoned the last vestiges of interventionism. In 1933, Secretary of State Hull joined with the other delegates at the Montevideo Conference of American States in approving a pact, one part of which stated that "no state has the right to intervene in the internal or external affairs of another." Three years later at the Buenos Aires Inter-American Conference the United States' delegation

* On the other hand, the Hoover Administration displayed little enthusiasm for the League's attempts to end the Chaco War between Bolivia and Paraguay.

accepted a proposal stipulating that the participating nations would refrain from intervening "directly or indirectly, and for whatever reason, in the internal or external affairs of any of the other parties."

The Good Neighbor Policy received its first test in Cuba, and at first it appeared that dollar diplomacy would prevail. When the reactionary regime of President Machado was overthrown in 1933, the United States refused to recognize his successor, Ramón Grau San Martín, on the ground that because American property in Cuba was jeopardized he was not able to preserve order. President Roosevelt ordered warships to Cuban waters and withheld recognition from the new government until Carlos Mendieta, an avowed conservative acceptable to American business interests and the Cuban army, assumed the presidency in January, 1934. These tactics proved to be only temporary expedients, however, and they were soon supplanted by a program of political and economic co-operation. In May, 1934, the Senate ratified a treaty that abrogated the American right to intervene in Cuba under the Platt Amendment. In the following year the reciprocity treaty of 1902 was altered to permit lower duties on goods in Cuban-American trade, and the Jones-Costigan Act made possible increased imports of Cuban sugar.

On repeated occasions the United States demonstrated that it was prepared to implement the Good Neighbor Policy by abandoning its traditional tactics. The recognition in 1934 of the Martinez regime, which had come into power in El Salvador through a *coup d'état,* indicated that the United States was at last prepared to accept Latin American governments regardless of how they gained office. In the same year the American occupation of Haiti was terminated with the withdrawal of the marines and the sale of the National City Bank's interests to the Haitian government. Under the terms of an agreement signed in 1936 and ratified in 1939, the United States gave up its right to intervene in Panama, renounced its unilateral guarantee of Panama's independence, and increased its annual payments for canal rights from $250,000 to $430,000.

In its diplomatic relations with Mexico the Roosevelt Administration more than once repudiated dollar diplomacy. The Mexican government refused to compensate foreign owners of expropriated lands, and in 1938, President Cardenas decreed the seizure of all foreign-owned properties in petroleum. Although the Mexican government put the value of these holdings at a fraction of their true worth, the United States never even hinted that it planned to intervene to uphold the economic interests of its nationals. After protracted negotiations, the two countries reached a settlement on November 19, 1941. The amount of compensation for expropriated oil properties was to be fixed by a commission composed of representatives of Mexico and the United States, and Mexico agreed to satisfy all other property claims with the payment of $40,000,000 over a period of seventeen years. In the following year the two-man commission put the value of American-owned petroleum holdings in Mexico at $23,995,999.*

The Good Neighbor Policy was not confined to a renunciation of the right of intervention, for an attempt was also made to supplant economic nationalism with a program of economic co-operation. Trade between the United States and other nations of the hemisphere was promoted by the reciprocity treaties that Secretary of State Hull negotiated with fifteen different Latin American states before 1943. The export of United States capital to the Central and South American countries, which before the New Deal had been largely restricted to private investments, was increasingly taken over by the Federal government. By December 31, 1941, the Export-Import Bank had authorized over $300,000,000 in gov-

* In 1938, the United States Department of Commerce estimated that the direct investments of United States nationals in the Mexican petroleum industry totaled $69,000,000.

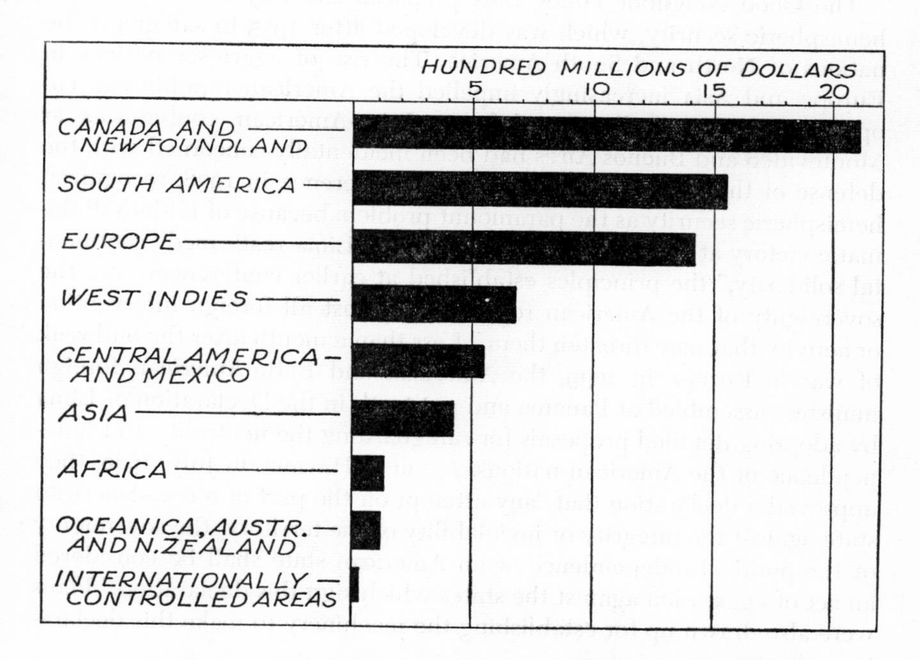

20. AMERICAN INVESTMENTS ABROAD, 1940

The attempts of the United States to promote political co-operation in the Western hemisphere were accompanied by large economic investments in Canada and South America.

ernment loans to Latin America, and the United States Treasury had made available large sums of money for the use of the governments of Mexico, Brazil, and Argentina. Unlike private investors, whose desire for profits overshadowed other considerations, the Federal government sought to place its loans in such a way that they might prove mutually beneficial to the United States and the borrowing nations.

The New Deal facilitated the exchange of ideas as well as of capital and goods among the American republics. In 1938, the State Department created a Division of Cultural Relations "to establish the conditions of a friendly co-operation and peaceful existence in the Western hemisphere." As the extent of Axis propaganda in Latin America became apparent, the United States enlarged its cultural program to include the exchange of musicians, painters, writers, teachers, and students, and the use of such media as the motion picture, radio, and printed word. Within a short time countless Latin Americans had been exposed to some form of Yankee culture, while within the United States interest in things Latin American approached the proportions of a fad.

The Good Neighbor Policy thus prepared the way for a system of hemispheric security, which was developed after 1935 to safeguard the nations of North and South America. The rise of aggressor nations in Europe and Asia increasingly impelled the American republics to co-operate for their collective defense. Inter-American conferences at Montevideo and Buenos Aires had been incidentally concerned with the defense of the Americas; but the Lima Conference in 1938, recognized hemispheric security as the paramount problem because of Hitler's diplomatic victory at Munich. The Declaration of Lima reaffirmed "continental solidarity," the principles established at earlier conferences, and the sovereignty of the American republics "against all foreign intervention or activity that may threaten them." Less than a month after the outbreak of war in Europe in 1939, the American and Latin-American foreign ministers assembled at Panama and put teeth in the Declaration of Lima by adopting detailed proposals for safeguarding the neutrality and independence of the American nations. Again at Havana, in July, 1940, they approved a declaration that "any attempt on the part of a non-American state against the integrity or inviolability of the territory, the sovereignty or the political independence of an American state shall be considered an act of aggression against the states which sign this declaration." Plans were also drawn up for establishing the machinery to make this declaration effective.

When the Japanese attacked Pearl Harbor on December 7, 1941, the United States enjoyed unprecedented prestige among the nations of Latin America; and knew that its southern neighbors would stand as coequal partners in a common enterprise to safeguard the future of the Western hemisphere.

120. RETREAT IN THE FAR EAST

FOLLOWING American acquisition of the Philippines, the Far Eastern policy of the United States was directed to the maintenance of the *status quo* in Asia and the islands of the Pacific. Because Japan had greater opportunity than any other nation to upset existing territorial arrangements in the Orient, American diplomacy in the Far East became essentially anti-Japanese. To check Japan, the United States sought to shore up China, which American officials regarded as the keystone in the shaky arch of Far Eastern relations.

Although the American people endorsed their government's objectives in the Far East, they were not prepared to use force to achieve them; and for the first two decades of the twentieth century Japan steadily extended its influence beyond the borders of its home islands. After years of peaceful penetration, Japan formally annexed Korea in 1910. In World War I, when the attention of other major powers was concentrated on Europe, Japan extorted a number of far-reaching concessions from China. Finally, in accordance with the postwar settlements of 1919–20, she retained her economic interests in Shantung and obtained mandates over the former German islands in the Carolines, Marshalls, and Marianas. Although Japan under the terms of the League Covenant was not allowed to fortify her mandated islands, no machinery existed to enforce this provision. By 1921, Japan had become the most powerful nation in the Far East and was in a position to threaten not only the independence of China but even American interests in the Philippines.

President Harding, like Roosevelt, Taft, and Wilson before him, was faced with the task of devising some formula short of war to prevent Japan from adding to its already extensive conquests in the Far East. In the past, dollar diplomacy, occasional flourishes of the Big Stick, and solemn pronouncements unsupported by force had all failed to provide more than a temporary check to the Japanese advance. The United States had attempted to maintain the *status quo* in the Far East by balance-of-power politics only to learn after repeated setbacks that there was no nation in the Orient strong enough to serve as a counterbalance to Japan. To President Harding and Secretary of State Hughes, both of whom had turned their backs on the League of Nations, a system of collective security in the Far East seemed to be the only alternative for the United States.

The Harding Administration's collective-security program for the Far East was inaugurated at the Washington Conference of 1922 with the adoption of the Four-Power and Nine-Power treaties. In the Four-Power Treaty, the United States, Great Britain, France and Japan agreed to respect one another's rights in the Pacific, and to discuss any conflicts in a joint conference. If their rights were threatened by the aggression of any other power, each was to communicate with the others before taking action.

The Nine-Power Treaty, signed by all the nations attending the conference, was designed to make more effective the "principles of the Open Door or equality of opportunity in China" and to preserve China's independence. The powers agreed to respect China's "sovereignty, independence, and . . . territorial and administrative integrity," and to maintain "the principle of equal opportunity for the commerce . . . of all nations" throughout China. All were to refrain from seeking special privileges in China that might interfere with the existing rights of subjects of friendly states.

American adherence to the Four-Power and Nine-Power pacts imposed no obligations on the United States and did not alter its foreign policy in the Far East in any fundamental respect. Neither agreement contained any provision for enforcing its terms. Nor was an attempt made to erect an effective balance-of-power system to hold Japan in check. Russia was the only nation with interests in the Far East that could have served as a counterpoise to Japan in such a balance, but the widespread fear of communism among the nations attending the Washington Conference kept the Soviet Union outside any system of collective security. When the conference adjourned, Japan was still the most powerful nation in the Far East, and no effective steps had been taken to prevent its continued advance. In the language of power politics the Four-Power and Nine-Power pacts were "scraps of paper."

For almost a decade after 1922, Japan sought to achieve what it considered its legitimate objectives in the Far East by ostensible co-operation and friendship with the United States. But when these tactics failed to produce the desired results, the Japanese authorities embarked on a program of undisguised aggression in Manchuria. For some years Japanese privileges there had included jurisdiction over all her nationals and the right to maintain troops along the South Manchurian Railway. In 1931, Japan seized upon an incident along this railway as a pretext for a full-scale invasion of Manchuria. Since no nation was able or willing to stop the Japanese armies, they quickly overran the entire province, and reduced it in 1932 to the puppet state of Manchukuo.

The Japanese invasion of Manchuria was a flagrant violation of both the Kellogg-Briand Pact and the Nine-Power Treaty. At the outset of the conflict Secretary of State Stimson informed the Japanese that they were not living up to their treaty obligations. When his protest produced no visible effect, Stimson sent an American representative to the League Council as an "observer and auditor" during its sessions on the Manchurian crisis. The League Council invoked the Kellogg-Briand Pact against the Japanese in October, 1931, and appointed a commission under the chairmanship of Lord Lytton to investigate the situation in Manchuria. The Japanese, however, continued their advance. The United States, Secretary Stimson concluded, could "not condone the tearing up of the treaties, and if it would not take any military or economic action to defend them," it must refuse to recognize the Japanese conquests. Accordingly, on January 7, 1932, Stimson stated in a note to China and Japan that

> *in view of the present situation and of its own rights and obligations therein, the American government deems it to be its duty to notify both the Imperial Japanese Government and the Government of the Chinese Republic that it cannot admit the legality of any situation* de facto *nor does it intend to recognize any treaty or agreement entered into between those Governments, or agents thereof, which may impair the treaty rights of the United States or its citizens in China, including those which relate to the sovereignty, the independence, or the territorial and administrative integrity of the Republic of China, or to the international policy relative to China, commonly known as the open door policy; and that it does not intend to recognize any situation, treaty or agreement which may be brought about by means contrary to the covenants and obligations of the Pact of Paris of August 27, 1928, to which Treaty both China and Japan, as well as the United States, are parties.*

When Stimson announced this policy of nonrecognition, he realized that it was nothing more than "a moral weapon, a moral sanction." Japan could be stopped only by force, and the American people had no intention of fighting or even of threatening to fight Japan in order to free Manchuria. Overwhelmed by problems arising out of the depression and opposed to intervention in a remote and little known corner of the globe, most Americans viewed Stimson's stand with either suspicion or hostility. The effectiveness of his note to Japan was further reduced by the refusal of any other major power to adopt a similar policy. Stimson had hoped for British co-operation, but it was announced that "His Majesty's Government have not considered it necessary to address any formal note to the Japanese Government on the lines of the American Government's note." Nor was the League of any assistance, for the Lytton Commission's report, though critical of the Japanese attack, led to no action.

When the Chinese protested the invasion of Manchuria by boycotting Japanese goods, Japan in January, 1932, attacked Shanghai. Stimson, unable to win the major powers over to a protest against Japan's violation of the Nine-Power Treaty, was again the only important statesman to condemn Japanese aggression. He did not send another formal note to the Japanese, but in a widely publicized letter to Senator Borah, he reiterated the United States government's opposition to Japanese aggression.

The Japanese conquest of Manchuria and the attack on Shanghai brought out into the open the deficiencies of the collective security system fashioned by the United States at the Washington Naval Conference. No nation with interests in the Far East was either willing or able to resort to force to stop the Japanese advance. The United States, which took the firmest stand in 1931–2, was no more prepared than any other country to take positive steps to check Japanese expansion. Protests unsupported by force were a language that the officials of Japan could both understand and ignore. Japan's invasion of Manchuria posed a problem for the United States that could not be postponed indefinitely. Eventually the American people would be forced to decide whether they wished to abandon their traditional objectives in the Far East or to uphold them by force of arms.

121. THE QUEST FOR NEUTRALITY

NEITHER the advent of the Great Depression nor the transition from a Republican to a Democratic Administration had any appreciable effect upon the isolationist spirit of the United States. If anything, these developments re-enforced the widely held view that the United States should concentrate on its own problems and ignore those beyond its borders. Events abroad seemed to most Americans to demonstrate that the rest of the world was no longer worth saving. Japan's victory in Manchuria, Mussolini's blatant nationalism, and the rise to power of the Nazis in Germany all contributed to the American conviction that the United States had better—as the current expression went—"put its own house in order" without wasting its energy on attempts to support an international order that was obviously collapsing.

The belief that the United States should refuse to assume even a limited responsibility for the fate of the rest of the world was held by some liberal supporters of Franklin Roosevelt's New Deal, as well as by many of the Administration's conservative critics. A few years earlier many of these same New Dealers had been among the most enthusiastic supporters of Woodrow Wilson's plans for the League. By 1933, however, they were arguing that international co-operation was no longer feasible. In their minds, the rest of the world was lost, and only America was capable of salvation. Committed to the idea that governmental planning could restore American prosperity, they thought that international planning for peace was incompatible with domestic programs for recovery. With the conversion of these liberals to isolationism, all but a handful of Americans abandoned the view that the United States had any obligations to the other nations of the world.

Roosevelt himself was, at first, in sympathy with the views of the liberal isolationists. In the preconvention contest for the Democratic nomination, Franklin D. Roosevelt, who had campaigned for the League as the Democratic vice-presidential candidate in 1920, made it clear that he did not intend to revive the issue. Before the New York State Grange in 1932, he stated his new position:

> *The fact remains that we did not join the League. The League has not developed through these years along the course contemplated by its founder* [Woodrow Wilson], *nor have the principal members shown a disposition to divert the huge sums spent on armament into the channels of legitimate trade, balanced budgets, and the payment of obligations. American participation in the League would not serve the highest purpose of the prevention of war and a settlement of international difficulties in accordance with fundamental American ideals. Because of these facts, therefore, I do not favor American participation.*
>
> *What the world needs most today is a national policy which will make us an example of national honor to other nations.*

Once in power, like the Republicans before them, the New Dealers often wavered without any apparent pattern between isolationist and internationalist policies. In 1934 the United States joined the International Labor Office of the League of Nations, and in the following year the Administration made a futile effort to induce the Senate to ratify a proposal for American adherence to the World Court. Recognition of the Soviet Union by the United States in 1933 reflected the desire of the Administration to increase American overseas trade and the awareness of the American people that the Communist dictatorship was not going to be overthrown by the Russian people. These tentative moves toward a greater measure of international co-operation were more than offset, however, by the economic policies of the New Deal. Soon after taking office President Roosevelt withdrew American support from the London Economic Conference. Unlike Hoover, Roosevelt was apparently convinced that domestic recovery took precedence over world recovery, and throughout most of the depression years the United States was committed to a form of economic nationalism that was only slightly mitigated by the Hull reciprocal trade treaties. The same spirit of economic nationalism was revealed in Congress with the passage of the Johnson Act in 1934, outlawing private American loans to nations that had not paid their so-called "war debts."

The isolationism of the early 1930's was predicated in large part on the assumption that the United States could remain at peace by simply refusing to fight. This approach to international relations was strengthened by the prevailing belief that business and political leaders were responsible for wars in general and for the last war in particular. Several popular books appeared in the decade and a half after Versailles to claim either implicitly or explicitly that the United States had gone to war in 1917 through the machinations of its bankers and munitions-makers, the gullibility of its public officials, and the ease with which its citizens had been taken in by Allied propaganda. Many Americans found their prejudices about the rôle of businessmen in war confirmed by the Nye Committee hearings in 1934, which revealed that many Americans had made a great deal of money during World War I, although it did not prove that businessmen were responsible for American participation in the conflict.

The general feeling that a nation's leaders rather than its people were responsible for war led directly to the adoption by Congress of measures designed to prevent American officials from placing the country in a position where its only alternative was a resort to arms. By the midthirties the American people felt that events in Europe had amply demonstrated the need for such legislation. In 1935, Italy invaded Ethiopia, Hitler began to rearm in violation of the Versailles Treaty, and Japan abandoned any pretense of abiding by the agreed ratios for naval limitation. In the following year, Germany remilitarized the Rhineland, civil war divided Spain into two armed camps, and Hitler and Mussolini announced the formation of the Rome-Berlin Axis. In 1937, Japan began its undeclared war against China. Fearful that these events in Europe, Asia, and Africa would involve the United States in war, Congress sought to keep the United States at peace by neutrality acts forbidding any economic or political commitments to belligerent nations. Beyond a doubt most Americans at the time approved of this effort to maintain peace by statute.

The Neutrality Act of 1935 was adopted in response to the crisis precipitated by Mussolini's attack on Ethiopia. Congress imposed an embargo upon the export of implements of war to belligerents and directed the president to deny protection to American citizens traveling on ships of nations at war. Following Italy's invasion of Ethiopia, the President, in accordance with the provisions of the Neutrality Act, announced an embargo on arms shipments to Italy, and two days later the League Council agreed to apply sanctions against Italy. The United States government was under no obligation to abide by League policy; nevertheless, it requested American exporters to halt shipments to Italy of any materials that could be used in war. But when Mussolini made it clear to Britain and France that sanctions might mean war, the League program broke down, and the Roosevelt Administration was left in the embarrassing position of asking Americans to uphold voluntarily a program that had been rejected by its authors.

The events of 1935 convinced many Americans that the United States

Doyle in the Philadelphia Record

GALLEY SLAVES

During the 1930's many Americans believed that munitions makers and profiteers had been responsible for involving the United States in World War I.

should exercise even greater vigilance in the maintenance of its neutrality, and in February, 1936, the original act was expanded to prohibit loans to belligerents. Because the existing laws did not apply to civil wars, Congress in January, 1937, adopted a joint resolution forbidding the export of munitions "for the use of either of the opposing forces in Spain." Finally, in May, 1937, Congress passed still another neutrality act. This measure not only included essential features of the earlier bills, but also provided that no belligerent nation could obtain raw materials from the United States unless it paid for them on delivery and imported them in its own vessels. The so-called "cash-and-carry" clause of the Neutrality Act of 1937 indicated that Americans wished to stay out of war, but not to renounce the profits of war.

122. ISOLATIONISTS AND INTERVENTIONISTS

ALTHOUGH the neutrality legislation imposed certain restrictions on the nation's officials, it did not—and could not—curb people's emotions. The dilemma that confronted the American people was clearly revealed by their attitude toward the Spanish Civil War. Soon after the revolting Nationalists—led by General Francisco Franco and supported by large segments of the Spanish clergy, army, and aristocracy—started the war, Americans found that it was almost impossible not to take sides. The intensity of the conflict in Spain and its effect upon American public opinion were heightened by the brutality displayed by the contending forces, the aid that Communist Russia dispatched to the Loyalists, or Republicans, and the military assistance—including troops—that Fascist Italy and Nazi Germany sent to the Nationalists. Many American liberals, who a short time before had been outspoken isolationists, began to demand that the United States provide some form of active support for the Loyalists. Joined by American Communists and Communist sympathizers, these groups formed numerous organizations to aid the Loyalists, and by the end of the Spanish Civil War, millions of American dollars and approximately three thousand American men had crossed the Atlantic to aid the enemies of Franco. At the same time, many—but not all—American Catholics, who believed that Russian intervention in Spain had converted the war into an unholy crusade against Roman Catholic Christianity, were equally determined in their support of the Nationalists.

Although Americans could congratulate themselves on their success in maintaining strict neutrality, many of them were aghast at the results of this policy. When Guernica was razed by Fascist bombs in 1937, prominent Americans condemned this display of brutality; even Senator William E. Borah, who for years had been considered one of the nation's leading isolationists, said:

> *So long as men and women may be interested in searching out from the pages of history outstanding acts of cruelty and instances of needless destruction of human life they will linger longest and with the greatest horror over the . . . story of the fascist war in Spain. . . . Guernica was not a single instance; it was merely the culmination of a long line of unspeakable atrocities.*

Events in Germany, like those in Spain, horrified many. They were alarmed by Hitler's imperialistic rantings and revolted by the Nazi persecution of the Jews, the repeated pronouncements of Nordic supremacy, and the systematic destruction of German democracy and trade unionism. Equally disturbing was the fashion in which the German-American Bund and demagogues like Father Coughlin, a Michigan priest, accepted and preached the Nazi doctrines. In response to these developments some Americans who presumably believed in neutrality acted in a thoroughly unneutral manner. When demonstrators were arrested in 1935 for ripping down the Nazi flag from the German liner Bremen in New York harbor, the judge hearing the case denounced the Nazis in such violent terms that the German government lodged an official protest in Washington. In 1937, Mayor Fiorello La Guardia of New York proposed the erection of a chamber of horrors at the city's World's Fair for "that brown-shirted fanatic who is now menacing the peace of the world."*

The outbreak of war between Japan and China in 1937 produced further confusion among Americans. They felt moral indignation, but it did not preclude them from leaving China in the lurch. Newspapers and public speakers condemned the Japanese, but the United States did little to assist China or to check Japan.

As the dictator nations accelerated their tempo of aggression, the Roosevelt Administration began a cautious, but none the less real, attempt to abandon economic nationalism and political isolation for a positive program of strengthening America's moral and military defenses. The President made no move to have the Neutrality Acts repealed, but he indicated that he thought that American security was imperiled by developments abroad. On October 5, 1937, in what came to be known as the "quarantine" speech, Roosevelt said:

> *It seems to be unfortunately true that the epidemic of world lawlessness is spreading.*
>
> *When an epidemic of physical disease starts to spread, the community . . . joins in a quarantine of the patients in order to protect the health of the community against the spread of the disease. . . .*
>
> *War is a contagion, whether it be declared or undeclared. It can engulf states and peoples remote from the original scene of hostilities. We are determined to keep out of war, yet we cannot insure ourselves against the disastrous effects of war and the dangers of involvement. We are adopting such measures as will minimize our risk of involvement, but we cannot have complete protection in a world of disorder in which confidence and security have broken down. . . .*

* New York had a large Italian vote, and it was perhaps for this reason that La Guardia did not similarly denounce Mussolini as a "black-shirted" fanatic.

> *Most important of all, the will for peace on the part of peace-loving nations must express itself to the end that nations that may be tempted to violate their agreements and the rights of others will desist from such a course.*

In the following year, on October 18, 1938, the President assured a Canadian audience at Kingston, Ontario, that the "United States will not stand idly by if Canada . . . [ever] is threatened by any other nation." Roosevelt was determined to support his words with acts, and as early as January, 1938, he asked Congress to appropriate a billion dollars for the construction of a two-ocean navy. Twelve months later, when it was decided to re-establish a permanent Atlantic squadron, the United States was fully committed to the concept, if not the reality, of a two-ocean navy.

Every attempt by the President either to clarify the issues that were dividing the world or to safeguard America against attack was greeted by vehement protests and cries of "war mongering" from the isolationists. No amount of isolationist arguments, however, could change the course of events in Europe. In 1936 Hitler announced the remilitarization of the Rhineland; and in March, 1938, Austria was incorporated into the Third Reich. Prime Minister Neville Chamberlain, on returning to England in 1938 from Munich where he and Premier Daladier of France had permitted Hitler to acquire the Sudetenland, announced that he had achieved "peace in our time." Eight months later Germany occupied all of Czechoslovakia. The capstone in Hitler's preparations for world conquest was put in place with the signing of the Russian-German Pact in August, 1939. Two weeks later, on September 1, Hitler's armies marched into Poland. England and France declared war on Germany. World War II had begun.

The outbreak of war in Europe widened rather than narrowed the split in American public opinion over the nation's foreign policy. To President Roosevelt and his advisers, the war demonstrated the need for strengthening American defenses, for asserting the moral leadership of the United States, and for aiding the enemies of the Axis countries. To opponents of the President's program, the war offered further proof of the necessity for isolating America from the conflicts in Europe and Asia. After September, 1939, the isolationists included many Midwesterners who still adhered to a once respected tradition, some native Fascists, the members of the German-American Bund, conservatives who feared Russia more than Germany, and the remnants of the American pacifist movement. They were in many ways a motley crew, for within their ranks could be found rabble rousers like Gerald L. K. Smith, publishers like Robert McCormick of the Chicago *Tribune,* businessmen like Robert E. Wood of Sears, Roebuck, German-Americans like Fritz Kuhn of the Bund, politicians like Senator Burton K. Wheeler of Montana and Representative Hamilton Fish of New York, and an indeterminate number of sincere idealists whose aversion to war overrode all other considerations. American communists were enthusiastic isolationists as long as the Soviet-German Pact lasted. As soon as Germany invaded Russia, they became equally enthusiastic interventionists.

Many of the isolationist groups in the United States eventually joined forces in the America First Committee. The functions of the committee were twofold: it sought through speeches, pamphlets, and articles to win a majority of the American people over to isolationism, and as a pressure group it attempted to prevent Congress from adopting measures that might jeopardize the peace of the United States. Charles A. Lindbergh, who had won fame because of his solo flight across the Atlantic in 1927 and whose father, as a member of the House of Representatives, had voted against war in 1917, was the committee's most famous member and one of its principal spokesmen. From September, 1939, until the Japanese attack on Pearl Harbor the isolationists labored incessantly to reconcile the irreconcilable. Maintaining that the Axis powers could not be beaten, they concluded that the United States should come to terms with the dictators. But at the same time they saw no inconsistency in stating that the United States was capable of defending itself without allies against a hostile world. To the isolationist the Atlantic and Pacific oceans remained barriers as formidable to a potential aggressor as they had been in the days of the sailing ship. On the one hand, they thought air power had made Germany invincible. On the other, they apparently did not consider air power a threat to the security of the United States.

More damaging to the isolationists than their arguments were the inferences that could be drawn from these arguments. The more isolationists talked about American interests, the more they seemed to be defending Germany's interests. Although most America Firsters were not Nazi sympathizers, they were wholeheartedly supported by the native Nazis, and on more than one occasion isolationist congressmen permitted the German-American Bund to use their franking privilege for the distribution of pro-Nazi propaganda free of charge throughout the United States.

The most convincing answer to isolationist arguments was supplied by events in Europe. Following six months of inaction in the "phony war," Hitler's armies in the spring of 1940 overran Denmark, Norway, Belgium, Holland, and then France. To Americans who did not subscribe to the doctrines of the America First Committee the fall of France was an overwhelming catastrophe that marked the end of an era in Western civilization. The disaster was only partly mitigated by the evacuation of the British Expeditionary Force from Dunkirk. In subsequent months, when Britain stood alone, freedom-loving people took heart from the valiant defense put up by the R.A.F. against the Nazi bombers, and admired the courage of the English people, who refused to be terrorized into submission. Only extreme isolationists seemed unmoved by the struggle. They had always been inclined to blame "perfidious Albion" for many of America's ills, and they now believed that England was certain to fall and that the United States must stand alone.

The isolationists preferred to ignore the implications of the Nazi victories, but the Roosevelt Administration viewed the German advance as further—and conclusive—evidence of the need for bold and forthright action by the United States. In the months that followed the President did not make even a pretense of being neutral in thought or action. On June 10, 1940, when Italy invaded southern France after the Germans had overpowered the French armies, Roosevelt in a memorable speech at the University of Virginia said that the "hand that held the dagger has struck it into the back of its neighbor," and he added:

> *In our American unity we will pursue two obvious and simultaneous courses; we will extend to the opponents of force the material resources of this nation, and, at the same time, we will harness and speed up the use of those resources in order that we ourselves in the Americas may have equipment and training equal to the task of any emergency and every defense.*

President Roosevelt was supported in his program to strengthen the defenses of both Britain and the United States by a large proportion of the city dwellers on the Atlantic and Pacific coasts, and by most of the Southern members of his party. In addition, the Committee to Defend America by Aiding the Allies, led by William Allen White and endorsed by prominent Americans from every walk of life, undertook a full-scale—and generally successful—campaign to educate their fellow citizens to the necessity for rushing supplies to beleaguered Britain. Moreover, in the presidential campaign of 1940 the Republican candidate joined Roosevelt in urging all aid short of war for Britain.

By 1940, Roosevelt and most of his supporters had reached the conclusion that the world situation made it imperative that he break the two-term tradition for presidents. Accordingly, at a Democratic convention that was completely dominated by Administration forces, Roosevelt was nominated for a third term, and largely because of Roosevelt's insistence, Secretary of Agriculture Henry Wallace was given second place on the ticket. The party's platform reaffirmed the Administration's domestic and foreign policies. When the Republicans met at Philadelphia, their leading candidates were Senator Arthur Vandenberg of Michigan, Senator Robert Taft of Ohio, and District Attorney Thomas Dewey of New York. All three were more isolationist than interventionist, and all were more acceptable to the party's politicians than to its rank and file. At the grass-roots level of the party, Wendell Willkie, a former Democrat and president of the utility company Commonwealth and Southern, was easily the most popular candidate. Although Dewey led on the first three ballots, Willkie was ahead on the fourth, and two ballots later he was nominated. The Republican platform criticized, but did not repudiate, virtually all of the New Deal's domestic program, and on the crucial foreign issue of the day it stated: "We favor the extension to all peoples fighting for liberty, or whose liberty is threatened, of such aid as shall not be in violation of international law or inconsistent with the requirements of our own national defense."

Roosevelt made only a few campaign speeches, but Willkie traveled extensively, spoke often, and discussed the major questions before the voters in a forthright fashion. A firm believer in the need for American preparedness and assistance to the Allies, he refused to make foreign policy a campaign issue. At the same time his approval (despite certain qualifications) of most of the New Deal's social and economic objectives left him in a position where he could do little more than promise to carry out the Democratic program more efficiently than the Democrats had done. In going down to defeat (by a popular vote of 22,305,198 to 27,244,160 and an electoral vote of 449 to 82), Willkie at least had the satisfaction of knowing that he had conducted his campaign on a high level and that he had helped to demonstrate that American democracy had retained its vitality in a period of crisis and in a world at war.

123. MEASURES SHORT OF WAR

SOON after the outbreak of war in Europe, Congress at the President's request repealed the provisions for an arms embargo in the neutrality legislation. Not, however, until the fall of France did the government undertake a broad program that would both promote national security and provide assistance to the enemies of Hitler. Following the President's request on May 16, 1940, for "at least 50,000 planes a year," Congress passed a series of appropriation bills that provided for a spectacular increase in American military expenditures. Meanwhile plans for placing the fleet in the Atlantic on a par with that in the Pacific were accelerated. In the summer of 1940, furthermore, the National Guard was made a part of the regular army, and the United States adopted its first peacetime conscription act. Of these measures, only the last was opposed by the critics of the President's foreign policy. Although the isolationists were unable to prevent the passage of the conscription act, they limited its effectiveness through an amendment that prohibited drafted men from being sent outside the United States and its possessions.

The Roosevelt Administration found it comparatively easy to obtain support for its defense measures, but it ran head on into the isolationists when it sought to find ways and means to assist Britain. Nevertheless, through a variety of devices the President and his advisers succeeded in giving the English substantial assistance in the period between the fall of France and American entry into the war. In June, 1940, the United States made available to England a large supply of guns and ammunition that had been manufactured during World War I. Two months later the President concluded an agreement providing for the transfer to the British of more than fifty "over-age" destroyers (which had been used in World War I) in exchange for a ninety-nine-year rent-free lease on sites for naval bases in the British West Indies, British Guiana, Bermuda, and Newfoundland. Having drawn up the bargain in secrecy, the President presented it to Congress as a *fait accompli.* Although the isolationists were bitter in their denunciation of both the agreement and Roosevelt's methods of obtaining it, Congress in essence ratified the arrangement by appropriating the funds needed to implement its provisions.* In the months that followed the announcement of the destroyer-bases agreement, the United States transferred bombing planes and revenue cutters to the British, and American factories in increasing numbers began to turn to the production of war matériel for both the United States and England.

Despite the extraordinary measures taken by the President to convert the United States into what he called an "arsenal of democracy," it soon became apparent that any large-scale program of assistance would be thwarted by England's inability to continue to pay for the war goods produced by American industry. The same problem had been solved in 1914–17 through private loans; but Roosevelt proposed a far more sweeping and statesmanlike solution. In his annual message to Congress on January 6, 1941, the President said:

> *I . . . ask this Congress for authority and . . . funds sufficient to manufacture additional munitions and war supplies of many kinds, to be turned over to those nations which are now in actual war with aggressor nations.*
>
> *Our most useful and immediate rôle is to act as an arsenal for them as well as for ourselves. They do not need man power. They do need billions of dollars worth of the weapons of defense.*

* The chain of American bases was further extended in the spring of 1941 with the occupation of Greenland and Iceland by the United States. At the same time preparations were made for the establishment of an American base in Northern Ireland.

The time is near when they will not be able to pay for them in ready cash. We cannot, and will not, tell them they must surrender, merely because of present inability to pay for the weapons which we know they must have.

I do not recommend that we make them a loan of dollars with which to pay for these weapons—a loan to be repaid in dollars.

I recommend that we make it possible for those nations to continue to obtain war materials in the United States, fitting their orders into our own program. . . .

For what we send abroad, we shall be repaid, within a reasonable time following the close of hostilities, in similar materials, or at our option, in other goods of many kinds which they can produce and which we need.

The Lend-Lease bill, which was introduced into Congress in January, 1941, authorized the executive branch of the United States government to manufacture through government facilities or to purchase from private producers any "defense article" or "any other commodity or article for defense." Such articles could be sold, exchanged, or leased by the President to any anti-Axis country in return for "payment in kind or property, or any other direct or indirect benefit which the President deems satisfactory." After extended debate and over the objections of the isolationists the Lend-Lease bill was adopted on March 11, 1941, and Congress made an initial appropriation of seven billion dollars to carry out its provisions. It is impossible to overestimate the significance of Lend-Lease. It not only provided an effective means for the transfer of military goods with maximum flexibility and a minimum of red tape, but it also signalized to the world that the United States was prepared to use its physical—if not its military—resources to check the advance of the dictators. Although the bulk of the early shipments under Lend-Lease went to the British Isles, the Soviet Union after its invasion by Germany in June, 1941, received an increasingly large supply of such goods. By September, 1942, thirty-five countries, as well as the British Commonwealth of Nations, had obtained assistance from the United States under the terms of the Lend-Lease Act.

The Roosevelt Administration, which saw no point in manufacturing goods for the anti-Axis coalition only to have them sunk by German submarines, soon recognized the need for American intervention in the war in the North Atlantic. The Soviet Union was not equipped to wage this type of warfare and the British were unable to spare additional planes and ships for work in the Atlantic. Under the circumstances the President concluded that American aid to the Allies could be effectively rendered only if the United States increased its merchant tonnage and used its warships to assist the British and Canadians in convoy work; but because participation in convoying would obviously move the United States closer to full-scale participation in the war, the American people were reluctant to sanction such a drastic departure from the traditional concept of neutrality. The President, for his part, was never altogether frank in his public discussions of the rôle of the United States Navy in the early stages of the war in the North Atlantic.

In April, 1941, American troops established a base in Greenland, and three months later American troops began to replace the British forces in Ireland. At the same time American planes and war vessels were used to guard shipments across the Atlantic. The President originally stated that the American navy was being used for patrol duty in the North Atlantic, but neither the Germans nor the mass of Americans were able to discover the difference between patrol and convoy duties. In May, 1941, in proclaiming an unlimited national emergency, the President told the American people that the Atlantic patrol was "helping . . . to insure the delivery of needed supplies to Britain" and that "all additional measures necessary to deliver the goods will be taken." Roosevelt justified his acts by an appeal to the traditional doctrine of "freedom of the seas," but a more accurate appraisal of events would have emphasized strategic necessity. If the control of the Atlantic were to pass into the hands of a hostile power, the security of the United States would be jeopardized.

As the Americans extended their naval arm over the Atlantic and the Germans pushed the war zone closer to the United States, incidents were inevitable. In May, 1941, an American merchantman, the *Robin Moor,* was sunk by a German submarine, which left the ship's crew and passengers to their own devices in small boats on the open sea. Some four months later the President announced that the American destroyer *Greer* had been "attacked" while on "patrol" by a German submarine. With the torpedoing of the *U.S.S. Kearny* on October 17 and the sinking of the *U.S.S. Reuben James* two weeks later, all pretense of patrol was abandoned. On October 27 the President said: "We Americans have cleared our decks and taken our battle stations." The line between all aid short of war and a shooting war was becoming thinner every day. Congress, despite the protests and delaying tactics of the isolationists, made the law conform to the reality by repealing on November 13 the remainder of the neutrality legislation.

While seeking to re-enforce the enemies of Hitler, President Roosevelt also sought to impress on the world the extent of American hostility toward the Axis countries. He repeatedly denounced the rulers of Germany, and he repeatedly made clear his conviction that Britain (and after June, 1941, Russia) was fighting American battles. On May 27, 1941, he pointed out what he considered the inevitable consequences of a German victory to the American people:

Your Government knows what terms Hitler, if victorious, would impose. They are, indeed, the only terms on which he would accept a so-called "negotiated" peace.

And, under those terms Germany would literally parcel out the world—hoisting the swastika itself over vast territories and populations, and setting up puppet governments of its own choosing, wholly subject to the will and policy of a conqueror. . . .

No, I am not speculating about this. I merely repeat what is already in the Nazi book of world conquest. They plan to treat the Latin American nations as they are now treating the Balkans. They plan to strangle the United States of America and the Dominion of Canada.

The unity of the United States and Britain and their determination to retain control over the Atlantic was symbolized by the conference between President Roosevelt and Prime Minister Churchill that was held in the North Atlantic in August, 1941. From this meeting there emerged the Atlantic Charter. In eight sections the Atlantic Charter stated the two leaders' objectives and aspirations in a world at war:

First, their countries seek no aggrandizement, territorial or other;

Second, they desire to see no territorial changes that do not accord with the freely expressed wishes of the people concerned;

Third, they respect the right of all peoples to choose the form of government under which they will live; and they wish to see sovereign rights and self-government restored to those who have been forcibly deprived of them;

Fourth, they will endeavor . . . to further the enjoyment by all states . . . of access, on equal terms, to the trade and to the raw materials of the world . . . ;

Fifth, they desire to bring about the fullest collaboration between all Nations in the economic field with the object of securing, for all, improved labor standards, economic advancement, and social security;

Sixth, after the final destruction of the Nazi tyranny, they hope to see established a peace which will afford to all Nations the means of dwelling in safety within their own boundaries, and which will afford assurance that all the men in all the lands may live out their lives in freedom from fear and want;

Seventh, such a peace should enable all men to traverse the high seas and oceans without hindrance;

Eighth, they believe that all of the Nations of the world . . . must come to the abandonment of the use of force. . . . They believe, pending the establishment of a wider and permanent system of general security, that the disarmament of . . . [aggressor] *nations is essential. They will likewise aid and encourage all other practicable measures which will lighten for peace-loving peoples the crushing burden of armaments.*

124. PEARL HARBOR

THE ATTENTION that the Roosevelt Administration devoted to the war in Europe and the North Atlantic did not blind it to the Japanese threat to American security in the Far East and the Pacific. As early as 1934, Joseph C. Grew, United States ambassador to Japan, had forecast in a cable to his superiors in Washington that Japan planned to

obtain trade control and eventually predominant political influence in China, the Philippines, the Straits Settlements, Siam and the Dutch East Indies, the Maritime Provinces and Vladivostock, one step at a time, as in Korea and Manchuria, pausing intermittently to consolidate and then continuing as soon as the intervening obstacles can be overcome by diplomacy or force.

If any doubt remained concerning Japan's expansionist policies, it was removed by the "China incident." After fighting broke out between Japanese and Chinese troops near Peiping in July, 1937, Japan launched a full-scale war against China. Japan's attack on China was denounced by a conference of nineteen nations meeting at Brussels (November 3–24, 1937), but the Japanese ignored world opinion and continued their offensive. Meanwhile, American citizens in China were killed or injured as a result of the war, and reports of Japanese atrocities appeared in the American press. When the *Panay*, an American gunboat on the Yangtze River, was bombed and sunk by Japanese planes on December 12, 1937, some alarmists thought war unavoidable; but most Americans had no desire to fight a war in China, and the incident was passed over after Japan had apologized and paid reparations to the United States.

Following the outbreak of hostilities in Asia, the President did not invoke the Neutrality Act on the technical ground that, since Japan had not declared war on China, a state of war did not exist. In reality, the President probably did not wish to take any step that might preclude assistance to China. Regardless of the reasons for his policy, however, its result was to increase the effectiveness of the Japanese military machine. It has been estimated that in 1938 the United States supplied Japan with 90 per cent of its scrap iron and steel, 91 per cent of its copper, 66 per cent of its oil, 45 per cent of its lead, and 67 per cent of its metal-working machinery. In the same period, American aid to China was negligible.

By the end of the decade, Japan was prepared to establish what its leaders called the "Co-Prosperity Sphere of Greater East Asia" or the "New Order in East Asia." In the spring of 1940, Japanese officials, who were presumably seeking to divert public opinion at home from the stalemate in China, made it clear that they were contemplating an attack on French Indo-China and the Netherlands East Indies. In September of the same year, the Japanese forced the French government to grant them bases in northern Indo-China. In the same month representatives of Japan, Germany, and Italy met in Berlin and concluded a treaty which provided that the three nations would "assist one another with all political, economic, and military means when one of the powers was attacked by a power not then involved in the European war or in the Chinese-Japanese conflict." Because the Soviet Union was exempted by name from the Berlin Treaty's provisions, there could be no doubt that the pact was aimed at the United States. With the signing of a Russo-Japanese treaty of neutrality on April 13, 1941, Japan had completed its diplomatic offensive and was prepared to launch its assault against southern Asia. Moreover, as early as January, 1941, the Japanese high command had drawn plans for a surprise attack on Pearl Harbor, and in May the Japanese navy began its preparations for the attack

Americans officials could—and did—issue formal protests condemning Japanese aggression, but Japan had long ago demonstrated that it understood no language but force. The United States, however, was singularly unprepared to use force in the Far East, for there was presumably no way of converting a one-ocean navy into a weapon that could both aid Britain and check Japan. Under the circumstances the Roosevelt Administration could only apply economic pressure to Japan while it sought to build up its naval strength. In July, 1940, the President prohibited the export of oil and scrap metal without license and restricted the sale of aviation gasoline to the Western hemisphere. Two months later the United States granted the Chinese government a loan of $25,000,000 and placed an embargo on scrap iron and steel shipments to all countries except Great Britain and the nations of North and South America. In December of the same year, the United States provided China with $50,000,000 for the stabilization of its currency.

By the summer of 1941, both nations had taken positions from which they could not retreat without a serious loss of national prestige. Japan was determined to carry out its program of expansion, and the United States was convinced that it could not stand by while the Japanese completed its plans for the conquest of southern Asia. On July 23, 1941, when Japan compelled France to grant it strategic bases in southern Indo-China, the Roosevelt Administration re-enforced its diplomatic protests by announcing that it was freezing all Japanese assets in the United States. Japan countered immediately by freezing American assets in Japan.

Throughout the spring and summer of 1941, Kichisaburo Nomura, the Japanese ambassador to the United States, made repeated suggestions to Secretary of State Hull for a settlement of the two countries' differences in the Far East. But as all the Japanese proposals provided in effect for American approval of Japan's expansionist program, they were rejected by the United States. The American proposals were equally unacceptable to Japan, for they called for the end of Japanese aggression and the withdrawal of Japanese forces from China. Although relations between the two countries remained in uneasy equilibrium throughout the remainder of the summer, a crisis developed soon after General Hideki Tojo took control of the Japanese cabinet on October 16.

Because of the United States' opposition to further Japanese aggression, Japan had been forced into a position where it had either to negotiate or fight. Before the end of the year it had done both. In early November, Saburo Kurusu arrived in Washington as a special envoy to assist Nomura in discussions with Secretary of State Hull. On November 20, the Japanese representatives presented the following proposals to Hull:

> 1. *Both the Governments of Japan and the United States undertake not to make any armed advancement into any of the regions in the Southeastern Asia and the Southern Pacific area excepting the part of French Indo-China where the Japanese troops are stationed at present.*
> 2. *The Japanese Government undertakes to withdraw its troops now stationed in French Indo-China upon either the restoration of peace between Japan and China or the establishment of an equitable peace in the Pacific area. . . .*
> 3. *The Government of Japan and the United States shall co-operate with a view to securing the acquisition of those goods and commodities which the two countries need in Netherlands East Indies.*
> 4. *The Governments of Japan and the United States mutually undertake to restore their commercial relations to those prevailing prior to the freezing of the assets.*
>
> *The Government of the United States shall supply Japan a required quantity of oil.*
>
> 5. *The Government of the United States undertakes to refrain from such measures and actions as will be prejudicial to the restoration of general peace between Japan and China.*

Because the Japanese note was tantamount to a request for American assistance in—and approval of—Japan's conquests in Asia, it was rejected by the United States, which on November 26 made a series of counter-proposals. After calling for international political and economic co-operation, the American note proposed: (1) a multilateral nonaggression pact among the nations with interests in the Far East; (2) a treaty that would guarantee the territorial integrity of French Indo-China; (3) the withdrawal of all Japanese forces from China and Indo-China; (4) Japanese support of the National Government of the Republic of China; and (5) the ending of American and Japanese extraterritorial rights in China. If Japan was willing to accept this program the United States was prepared to negotiate a trade treaty with Japan, to have the freezing restrictions in both countries removed, and to agree upon a plan for the stabilization of the dollar-yen rate.

The American proposals were as unacceptable to the Japanese as those of Japan had been to the United States. Each nation, in effect, had served the other with an ultimatum. Japan, having rejected the American note of November 26, kept the discussions open long enough to carry out the plans that its military leaders had perfected months earlier. For the next ten days Kurusu and Nomura continued to play their appointed rôles as negotiators while the Japanese task force advanced across the Pacific toward Hawaii. On December 7, 1941, both the negotiations and American neutrality were ended by the Japanese attack on Pearl Harbor. Striking at dawn with submarines and ship-based planes, the Japanese completely surprised the American defenders and inflicted heavy damage on the warships based at Pearl Harbor.

The Japanese attack ended almost a decade of debate on American foreign policy. Congress signalized the end of the debate on December 8, 1941, when a resolution recognizing a state of war with Japan was unanimously approved by the Senate and received the votes of all but one member of the House. Three days later, after Germany and Italy had declared war on the United States, both branches of Congress unanimously approved resolutions that recognized the existence of a state of war between the United States and the European members of the Axis. The United States had entered its second world war within a quarter of a century.

CHAPTER XX

WORLD WAR II AND ITS AFTERMATH

WORLD WAR II made unprecedented demands upon the American people. Before the final defeat of the enemy on two widely separated fronts, the United States had raised and equipped fighting forces that numbered in the millions, had placed its entire economy on a wartime footing, had joined a world-wide coalition, had provided its allies with large amounts of military equipment, and had taken a leading part in planning for a postwar international organization. These and many other tasks were willingly assumed by most Americans for the duration of the war. After victory, however, Americans discovered that the problems of peace could be fully as complex as those of war. Within a year after the defeat of the Axis, powerful special-interest groups had resumed their struggle for the control of the American economy, and the Soviet-American friendship of the war years had given way to mutual suspicion and hostility.

125. GLOBAL WAR

AMERICAN global strategy during World War II was always based on the conviction of the Roosevelt Administration that Germany was a more formidable enemy than Japan and that war in

Europe should take precedence over the conflict in the Pacific and Asia. This policy proved unpopular with many Americans who wished to obtain immediate revenge for the attack on Pearl Harbor and were appalled by the ease with which Japan enlarged its empire in the weeks following America's entry into the war. In rapid succession the Japanese occupied the Aleutian Islands, and conquered Malaya, the city of Singapore, the Dutch East Indies, Burma, New Guinea, and New Britain. These victories enabled the Japanese to menace both India and Australia, to cut the Burma Road, on which China depended for its supplies from the Allies, and to gain almost complete control over the sea lanes of the western and southern Pacific. But to Americans the most stunning Japanese victory occurred in the Philippines, where some 15,000 American and 40,000 Filipino troops under the command of General Douglas MacArthur waged a valiant but losing struggle against 200,000 Japanese. Cut off from supplies and re-enforcements and compelled to retreat to the Bataan Peninsula on the island of Luzon, the American and Filipino forces found their position hopeless. On May 6, 1942, after MacArthur had been transferred to Australia, the small group of defenders on the island fortress of Corregidor surrendered to the Japanese.

Although the Allies in the months that followed Pearl Harbor were unable to stem Japanese expansion in the Far East, the United States was soon in a position to undertake limited, but effective, counterattacks. In May, 1942, American vessels inflicted heavy damage on an enemy flotilla in the Coral Sea, and a month later American planes scattered and repulsed a formation of advancing Japanese warships off Midway Island. At the same time American submarines and planes undertook what proved to be an increasingly successful campaign of attrition against Japanese sea and air power. American ground forces launched their first offensive in the Pacific war on August 7, when marines landed on Florida Island in the Solomons and then moved on to Guadalcanal. In the subsequent months of bitter struggle the Japanese proved themselves resourceful jungle fighters who preferred death to surrender. While the fighting continued on Guadalcanal, Australian and American troops under MacArthur's command launched a campaign to drive the Japanese out of New Guinea.

The year 1943 marked the turning point of the war in the Pacific. By September the United States had regained control over all the Aleutians, and in November American marines and soldiers began a bloody but successful invasion of the Gilbert Islands in the mid-Pacific. The neighboring Marshalls were the next American objective, and Kwajalein was captured in the opening months of 1944. Within six months the United States had taken Saipan in the Marianas and Guam and Tinian as well, and for the first time it was in a position to begin systematic air attacks on the enemy's home islands. Meanwhile MacArthur's troops had landed on Leyte in the Philippines on October 20, 1944. When the Japanese fleet attempted to isolate the American invaders from their bases of support, it was decisively defeated in the Philippine Sea. Within three months the Americans were on Luzon, and on February 3, 1945, they entered Manila. American forces in the Pacific still had a long road to travel to reach Tokyo, but no one doubted that they were on their way.

The progress of the war in Asia was in marked contrast to Allied successes in the Pacific. Logistic problems and the determination of the Allies to concentrate their major efforts on the war in Europe precluded any large-scale material or military assistance to the hopelessly outclassed Chinese. Brigadier General Claire Chennault's "Flying Tigers," a small American air group stationed in China, achieved a series of spectacular victories against enormous odds, but they were always hampered by a shortage of equipment and personnel. For a time it was thought that British and American troops in India under Lord Louis Mountbatten would drive back the Japanese. But Mountbatten's Burma campaign in 1944 made little headway against a stubborn enemy army that was superbly trained in the techniques of jungle warfare.

The completion of the war in the Orient had to wait on Allied victory in Europe. Both Britain and the Soviet Union, having borne the full brunt of the Nazi attack, considered Germany rather than Japan the principal enemy, and President Roosevelt readily accepted this view. For some months after Pearl Harbor, the United States could only assist its European allies with supplies, but throughout this period American troops and equipment were shipped in increasing numbers to bases in Northern Ireland, and American planes soon joined the British in raids on the Continent. It was in the Mediterranean, however, rather than in northern Europe that the United States struck its first major blow against Hitler's empire. For two years British troops had been fighting a seesaw battle with the Germans and Italians for the control of North Africa. Then, on November 7, 1942, after General Bernard Montgomery's Eighth Army had routed the Axis troops at El Alamein, American and British soldiers under the command of General Dwight D. Eisenhower landed in French Morocco and Algeria. Although this region was controlled by Marshal Henri Pétain's pro-Axis government, the success of the invasion was assured with an armistice arranged by Vichy's Admiral François Darlan. Despite the saving in lives and bloodshed, the so-called Darlan deal was in some ways unfortunate. American liberals bitterly resented an agreement with a high official of the Vichy regime. Moreover, when Darlan was assassinated on December 24, the appointment of General Henri Giraud to succeed him further confused the already complex French political situation. General Charles de Gaulle, as the leader of the Free French, objected vehemently to Giraud's selection. But the United

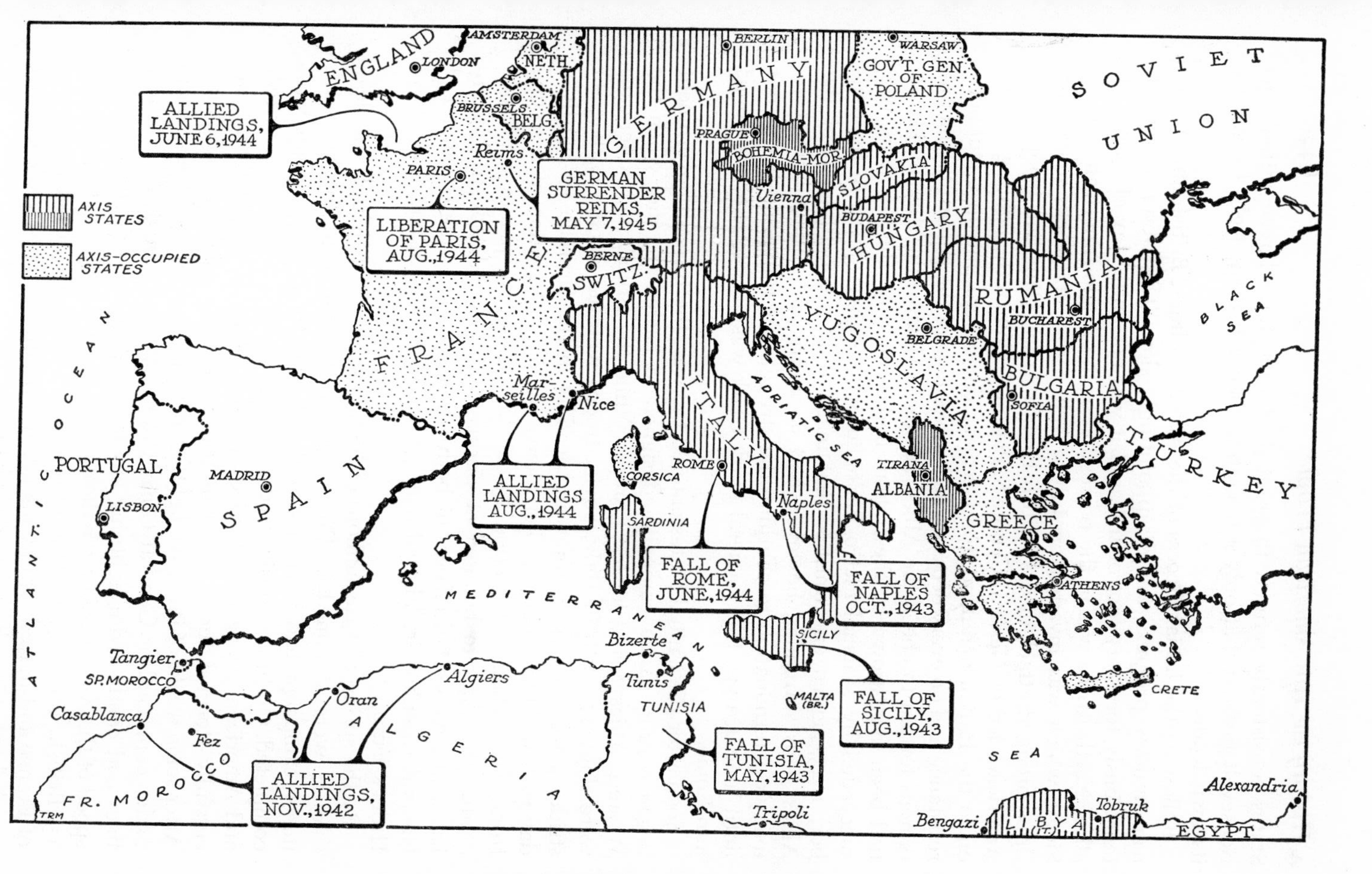

21. WESTERN FRONTS, 1942-5

[Reprinted from C. E. Black and E. C. Helmreich: Twentieth Century Europe: A History *(New York: Alfred A. Knopf, Inc., 1950).]*

States consistently refused to grant de Gaulle formal recognition, for Roosevelt insisted that only a liberated France had the right to choose its own leaders.

Following the initial success of the Allied landings, British and American military progress was disappointingly slow. The Germans fought tenaciously for every foot of soil, and it was not until May of 1943 that all of North Africa was in the possession of the Anglo-American armies. Sicily, which was invaded on July 9, fell within six weeks under the three-pronged attack of the British Eighth Army, Canadian troops, and Americans led by General George S. Patton, Jr. When the fighting moved on to the Italian mainland, the Germans once more put up a stubborn resistance and on every occasion took advantage of the peninsula's mountainous terrain to check the Allied advance. Meanwhile Mussolini, who had been overthrown by the Italians and rescued by the Germans, was succeeded by Marshal Pietro Badoglio, whose government in September, 1943, signed an armistice that made Italy a cobelligerent of the Allies. This surrender, however, had no appreciable effect upon Germany's determination to continue the struggle for Italy, and it was not until June 4, 1944, that General Mark Clark was able to lead his troops into Rome.

Soon after the United States entered the war, the Russian government began a propaganda campaign designed to hasten the day when the Western Allies would invade Europe. While the British and Americans were slogging north in Italy, Soviet troops were advancing with giant strides across eastern Europe, and leaders in the Kremlin let hardly a day pass without renewing their demands for the creation of a second front. Throughout this period British and American planes continued around the clock to hammer at German military and industrial establishments, while staff officers of both countries, under the command of General Eisenhower, labored over plans for the impending invasion of Hitler's Europe.

By the spring of 1944 millions of highly trained British and American soldiers were stationed in England; enough equipment for the war's major campaign had been accumulated; and the invasion plans were completed. On June 6, designated as "D" Day, the first Canadian, British, and American troops were ferried across the English Channel and successfully stormed the Nazi fortifications on the beaches of Normandy. After some weeks of intensive fighting at St. Lô and Caen, the Americans under command of General Omar Bradley broke through the German lines and conducted a lightning advance that equaled or surpassed the speed of the Nazi *blitzkrieg* in the opening months of the war. On August 15, British, French, and American armies landed on the southern coast of France and moved rapidly inland, and Bradley's troops made their triumphal entry into Paris ten days later.

In the autumn of 1944, when the Western Allies were fighting on German soil and the Russians were advancing rapidly from the East, it was often thought that Germany would fall before the end of the year. But the Germans dug in, and in December, General Karl von Rundstedt launched a surprise counteroffensive that opened a wide gap in the Allied lines in the Ardennes area. In the Battle of the Bulge the American troops first checked and then drove back the German advance, but it was not until February that the Allies were ready for their final assault against Hitler's Germany. By March, British and American soldiers were across the Rhine, the Russians had taken Poland and were well into eastern Germany, and the Anglo-American army in Italy was driving the Nazi troops up the Po Valley. In the following weeks, German resistance on all fronts disintegrated before the blows of the Allied forces. On May 2, three days after Mussolini had been executed by Italian partisans, hostilities in Italy ended. When the Russians entered Berlin at the end of April, Hitler committed suicide, and Admiral Karl Doenitz, his successor, sued for peace. On May 7, Allied leaders met with General Alfred Jodl at Rheims and accepted Germany's unconditional surrender.

Following the defeat of Germany the Allies were free for the first time to concentrate on the war in the Far East. The Japanese, although forced on the defensive by successive defeats in the Pacific in 1943–4, gave every indication that they were prepared to fight to the last man before capitulating. As the Americans drew nearer to the enemy's homeland, moreover, they found that each island was more heavily fortified and more tenaciously defended. Iwo Jima, a 3- by 5-mile island 750 miles from Tokyo, was assaulted by American troops on February 19, 1945, but it took a month to capture and cost the Americans 20,000 men in casualties. On April 1, Americans landed on Okinawa in the Ryukyus, and once again the enemy made them pay dearly for every foot of ground they gained. Before the Japanese surrendered all of Okinawa in June, they had killed more than 11,000 Americans and wounded some 33,000. Throughout the battle Japanese suicide pilots in *Kamikaze* planes had inflicted severe damage on the United States' supporting fleet.

Although the fighting on Iwo Jima and Okinawa seemed to indicate that the Japanese were in no mood to end the war on American terms, President Truman on July 26, 1945, announced that Japan could only avoid total destruction by an immediate and unconditional surrender. No mention of the newly perfected, but still secret, atom bomb was made in the President's announcement; and when the Japanese ignored the ultimatum, an atom bomb was dropped on Hiroshima on August 5. The bomb left the city a shambles and either killed or injured almost every one of its 343,000 inhabitants. When this event produced no response from the Japanese government, a second atom bomb was dropped four days later on the city of Nagasaki. On August 9, Russia entered the

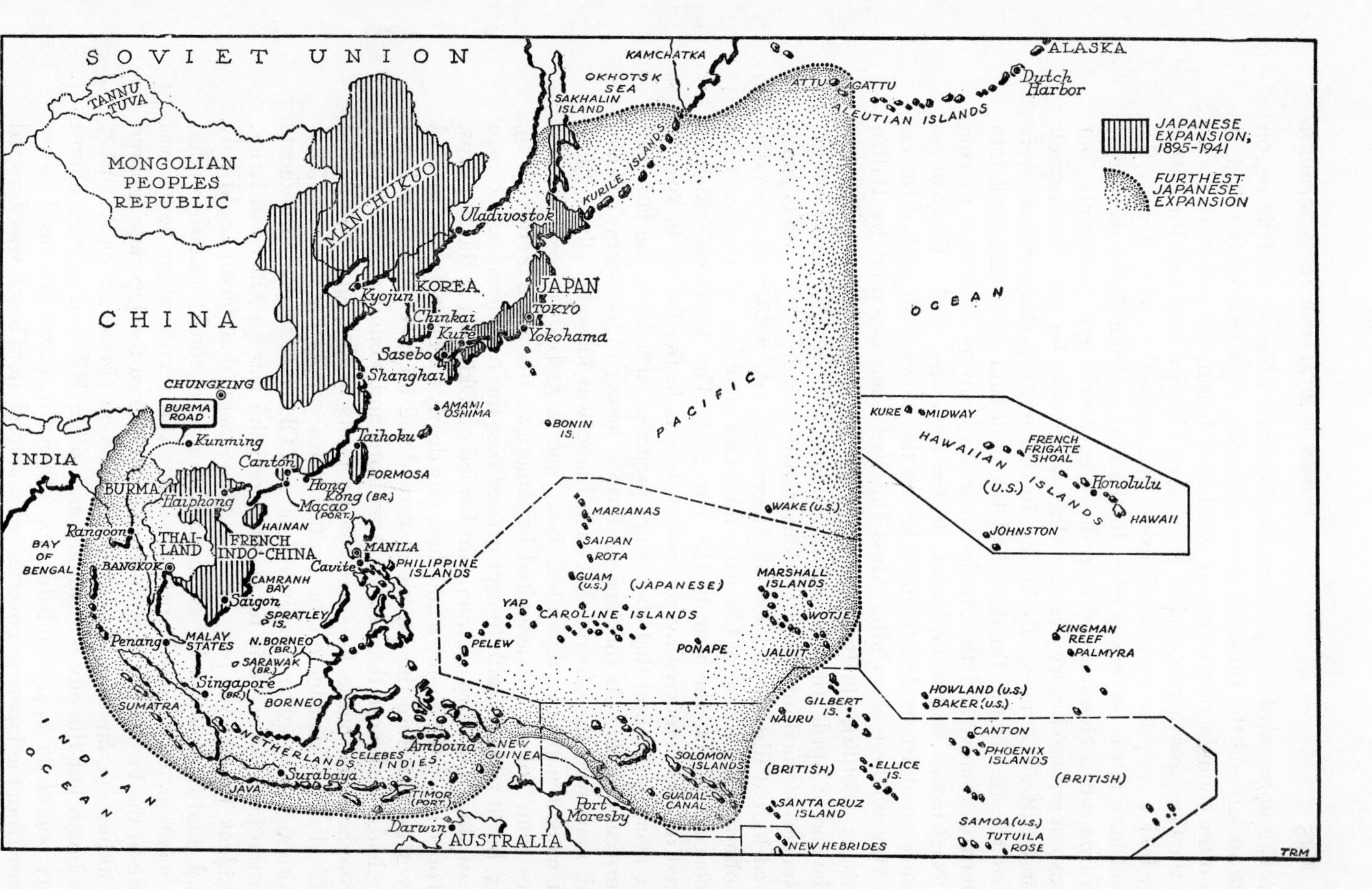

22. PACIFIC THEATER, 1941-5

[Reprinted from C. E. Black and E. C. Helmreich: Twentieth Century Europe: A History *(New York: Alfred A. Knopf, Inc., 1950).]*

war against Japan and began a rapid advance in Korea and Manchuria. Within a week the Allies had the unconditional surrender of Japan. The war in the Pacific was officially terminated on September 1, when Japan's war leaders signed the terms of surrender on the battleship *Missouri* in Tokyo Bay.

American jubilation over the end of the war was tempered by a realization of how the final victory had been achieved. The atom bomb, which had been developed during the war by American, British, and Canadian scientists at a cost of approximately two billion dollars, was acclaimed on all sides as a marvel of scientific achievement. But no amount of pride over the accomplishments of Allied scientists could obscure the fact that the atom bomb had already demonstrated that it was the most destructive weapon ever invented by man. While Americans talked hopefully of the use of atomic energy in peacetime pursuits, all knew that its use in another war could lead to the annihilation of mankind.

The victories achieved by American fighting forces in both the Pacific and European theaters of war were made possible in part by a relentless diplomatic offensive. The United States not only had to anticipate and counter the diplomatic moves of the enemy, but also as one member of a gigantic coalition it was at all times compelled to maintain the closest possible liaison with the leaders of its allies. Nor could the problems of war exclude those of peace, and during the conflict representatives of what came to be known as the United Nations repeatedly discussed their countries' plans for the postwar world. The ultimate responsibility for the conduct of wartime diplomacy rested with President Roosevelt, but the implementation of various policies was often entrusted to Secretary of State Cordell Hull, Harry Hopkins, the President's close friend and adviser, and a host of other loyal, but often unsung, civil servants.

Throughout the war a particular effort was made to maintain amicable relations with neutral nations in vital war areas and to ensure the co-operation of the other governments of this hemisphere. Contacts were maintained with the Vichy government as long as it could affect the course of the war, and then it was abandoned to its well-merited fate. Sweden's and Eire's neutrality was always scrupulously respected, while diplomatic pressure was directed against Spain to prevent it from throwing in its lot with Germany. Although many Americans objected to a policy of ostensible friendship with Franco's Fascist regime, the Roosevelt Administration refused to make any move that might have driven Spain into the camp of the enemy. In this hemisphere the Good Neighbor Policy of the preceding decade provided an excellent foundation on which to erect a program of wartime co-operation. Relations with Canada were cordial during the entire war, while the ties that bound the United States to all the Latin American nations except Argentina were consistently strengthened. At the conference of foreign ministers at Rio de Janeiro in 1942, plans were developed for economic assistance to the Latin American countries and for the elimination of Axis agents below the Rio Grande. For the remainder of the war the United States bolstered the economies of its Latin-American neighbors, and they in turn supplied the United States with raw materials and various types of military equipment.

On the economic front co-operation among the United Nations was an integral part of the joint war effort. Throughout the war Lend-Lease provided the principal means by which the United States gave its allies material assistance. Lend-Lease exports increased from some $740,000,000 in 1941 to $11,297,500,000 in 1944. In 1944, which was in many respects a typical year, slightly less than one half of the Lend-Lease exports was sent to the United Kingdom, and more than one third was shipped to the Soviet Union. Machinery and vehicles constituted the largest single category of Lend-Lease exports, and foodstuffs the second largest. President Roosevelt repeatedly pointed out that Lend-Lease was a two-way street, but the fact remains that reverse Lend-Lease, or the transfer of goods to the United States by its allies, never even approximated the flow of products in the other direction.*

In striking contrast to the conduct of inter-Allied diplomacy in 1914–18, World War II was characterized by a marked degree of co-operation and interchange of views among the leaders of the United Nations. Soon after the attack on Pearl Harbor, Prime Minister Winston Churchill visited President Roosevelt in Washington, and until the latter's death the two men remained in almost daily contact through radio-telephone or trusted intermediaries. Despite differing social and economic views, each understood and appreciated the other's ability; both placed victory above all other considerations; and both shared a strong belief in the essential unity of the Anglo-American peoples. British and American relations with the Soviet Union were conducted on a less personal basis, but the Western democracies always made the greatest effort to maintain cordial and intimate contacts with the Russian rulers. In August, 1942, Churchill visited Stalin in Moscow, and the American ambassador to the Soviet Union represented the United States at the talks that took place. In October of the following year foreign ministers of the Big Three,† meeting in Moscow, arrived at an understanding on the second front, and after they had been joined by the Chinese foreign minister, they drafted tentative proposals for a postwar organization to preserve peace. Meanwhile Churchill and Roosevelt had conferred at Casablanca

* From the inception of the Lend-Lease program in March, 1941, until its termination in August, 1945, the value of all reverse Lend-Lease shipments was $7,800,000,000.

† Britain, the Soviet Union, and the United States.

in January, 1943, and had announced to the world that the Axis powers could obtain peace only through "unconditional surrender." In November of the same year the President, Churchill, and Generalissimo Chiang Kai-shek of China agreed on the dismemberment of the Japanese Empire following the war's successful conclusion, while a subsequent conference attended by Roosevelt, Churchill, and Stalin at Teheran resolved the principal problems concerning the prosecution of the war in Europe. No further meeting proved necessary until January, 1945, when the leaders of the Big Three met at Yalta, where problems of the impending peace overshadowed military discussions.

As the war progressed, the various inter-Allied conferences of necessity had to devote an increasing amount of time and attention to postwar planning. The Moscow Declaration, promulgated by the foreign ministers of the Big Four* in 1943, had pledged their countries to the formation of a "general international organization" to prevent war. On November 5, the Connally Resolution expressed the Senate's overwhelming approval of the Moscow Declaration.

126. THE CIVILIAN AND THE WAR

THE WAR, which in Europe and Asia brought intolerable suffering and misery to millions of noncombatants, was at most a source of inconvenience to American civilians. While the exigencies of global warfare required a large degree of government control over the activities of the individual, at no time was life in the United States regimented as in other belligerent nations. Most Americans, who enjoyed unprecedented prosperity and who knew their country's stake in the outcome of the war, did not permit their traditional distaste for government restrictions on personal freedom to interfere with their determination to supply the armed forces with the equipment on which ultimate victory depended.

The fact that nearly every American had at least one relative in military or naval service provided the civilian population with its most immediate contact with the war. From 1941 to 1943 the size of the armed forces increased from fewer than 2,000,000 to almost 9,000,000 men, and in 1944–5 the total was considerably more than 11,000,000. The army alone enrolled 10,800,000 men during the war. Every branch of the service permitted women to enlist for noncombatant work, and in 1945 the Army's Wacs, the Navy's Waves, the Coast Guard's Spars, and the Marines' Women's Auxiliary totaled 258,000. At the same time Americans in every community throughout the land served as volunteer

* Great Britain, the United States, the Soviet Union, and China.

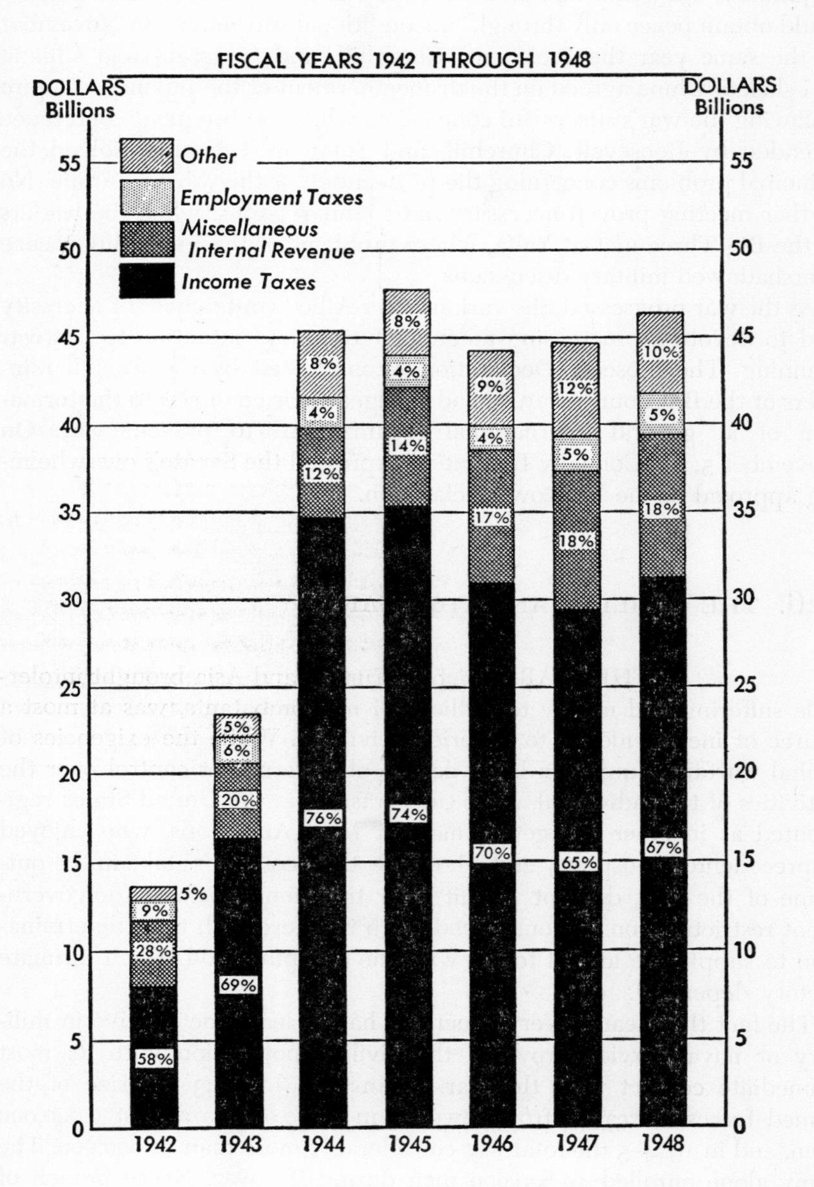

23. FEDERAL RECEIPTS, 1942–8

[From the United States Department of the Treasury.]

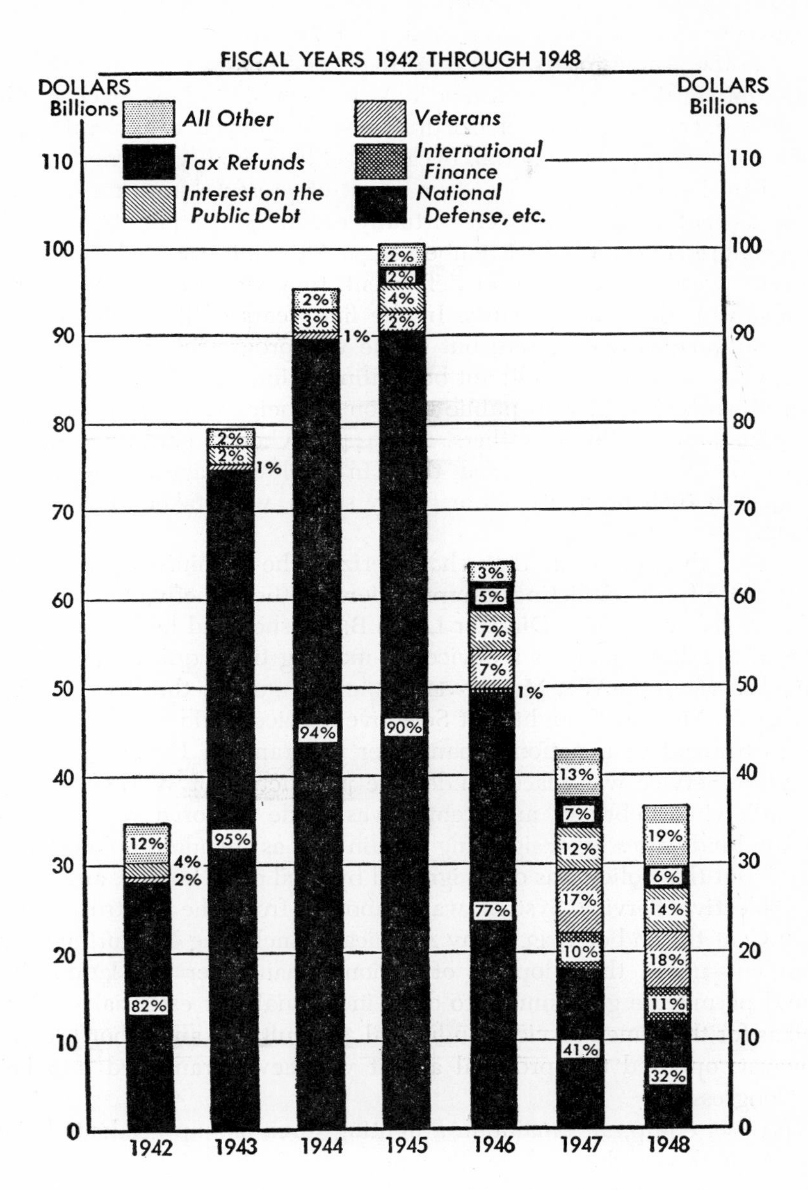

24. FEDERAL EXPENDITURES, 1942–8

[From the United States Department of the Treasury.]

air-raid wardens under the direction of the Office of Civilian Defense.

No clear-cut basis was ever established for the selection of men to serve in the armed forces. The rules that governed exemptions changed with the shifting political winds in Washington. Because each of the nation's sixty-five hundred local draft-boards enjoyed considerable autonomy, they were on numerous occasions able to modify or ignore orders issued by Federal authorities. As a result of pressure from farm politicians, agricultural workers were virtually exempted from military service by a congressional act of November, 1942. Although essential workers in industry were also eligible for deferment, they were called up in large numbers by their local boards. In the first years of the draft, fathers were automatically deferred; but as the war progressed, it became apparent that this policy could not be continued indefinitely. Nevertheless, many boards, sensitive to public opinion in their communities, refused to order the induction of fathers. By 1944–5, when the army was insisting on the need for young men, those in the lowest age categories, regardless of their occupational or family status, were taken ahead of all others.

Part of the confusion that characterized the administration of the draft arose from conflicting interpretations of the Selective Service Act. While Selective Service Director Lewis B. Hershey and his subordinates viewed the draft solely as a device for meeting the requirements of the armed services, the War Manpower Commission under the chairmanship of Paul V. McNutt thought that Selective Service could also be used as the instrument of a national manpower program. In December, 1942, Selective Service was placed under the jurisdiction of W.M.C., and in the following February an attempt was made to force workers into essential industries by designating certain jobs as "nondeferable occupations." But this policy was often ignored by local draft boards; and when the Selective Service System was removed from the control of the W.M.C. at the end of 1943, many Americans—including McNutt and the President—urged the adoption of national manpower legislation that would permit the government to draft individuals for essential work as well as for the armed services. Industrial, agricultural, and labor leaders, however, opposed this proposal and it was never translated into law by Congress.

To raise, equip, and maintain a fighting force of unprecedented size put extraordinary demands on the government's financial resources. By the summer of 1943 the government was spending $8,000,000,000 per month, and from 1941 to 1945 the national debt rose from less than $48,000,000,000 to $247,000,000,000. To obtain funds for prosecuting the war, the Treasury Department resorted to mass borrowing, and Congress resorted to new and higher taxes. An attempt was made to sell bonds to rich and poor alike, and all Americans were urged by press, radio, movie, sound trucks, and door-to-door canvasses to put their savings into war bonds. Many workers bought bonds regularly through payroll deduction plans. In addition to round-the-year advertising campaigns, the government conducted eight special drives to increase bond sales. From May, 1941 through 1946, government bond sales amounted to more than $61,000,000,000.

Taxation provided funds enough to cover approximately two fifths of the cost of the war to the United States. During the war years government receipts from taxation mounted from a little less than $7,000,000,000 in 1941, to more than $42,000,000,000 in 1945. Only single persons with incomes under $500 and married couples with less than $1,200 were not compelled to file income-tax returns. A new schedule of surtaxes went as high as 98 per cent. Additional revenue also came from stepped-up corporate taxes, excess profit taxes on corporate income, and an expanded schedule of excise taxes that covered the sale of a wide variety of products. After July 1, 1943, taxes on the income of salaried workers and wage earners were collected by employers at the source under a withholding plan that was devised to facilitate payments and assure the government of its revenues.

Much of the money expended by the government during the war was used to purchase products of American industry. Although some industries were converted to war production soon after the outbreak of the conflict in Europe, not until well into 1942 were the nation's factories devoting practically all their facilities to the manufacture of military equipment. Early in 1941, eleven months before the attack on Pearl Harbor, the President had established the Office of Production Management, with William S. Knudsen as director, to accelerate and co-ordinate the output of war goods. But the O.P.M.'s authority was never clearly defined, and shortly after the United States went to war it was supplanted by the War Production Board. Donald Nelson, who was made Chairman of the W.P.B., had general authority over the "war procurement and production program." In addition to the W.P.B., a number of other government agencies were set up to handle special problems of war production. Among these were the Office of Rubber Director, Production Urgency Committee, Smaller War Plants Corporation, and the Petroleum Administrator for War.

Although the government was frequently accused of impeding the production program with bureaucratic controls and administrative inefficiency, the fact remains that American factories broke all previous records for industrial output in the war years.* From 1940 to 1944 the index

* By the middle of 1945 the United States had produced 297,000 airplanes, 6,500 naval vessels (as well as 64,500 landing vessels), more than 17,000,000 rifles, and 5,400 cargo ships, 315,000 pieces of field artillery, 4,200,000 tons of artillery shells, and 41,400,000,000 rounds of ammunition.

of industrial production (1935–9 = 100) rose from 125 to 235. Concentration on the manufacture of war materials necessarily had an adverse effect on civilian industries, some of which had to suspend operation. Nevertheless, there is abundant evidence that American industry as a whole earned enormous profits during the war. The net income of American corporations rose from $17,000,000,000 in 1940 to $28,000,000,000 in 1943.

The rapid expansion of American industry produced a corresponding increase in the nation's labor force. The 1940 census reported approximately 8,000,000 unemployed workers in a total labor force of more than 55,000,000. Shortly after the United States had entered the war, unemployment all but disappeared. Women joined the labor force in increasing numbers and often took jobs that had formerly been held almost exclusively by men. The scarcity of labor also made it possible for many boys of high school age, men over sixty-five, and individuals who were physically handicapped to obtain employment. The growth of the labor force was paralleled by increases in wages and the length of the work week. The average weekly earnings of all workers in manufacturing industries rose from $25.20 in 1940 to $46.08 in 1944. In the same period, the length of the average work-week increased from 38.1 to 45.2 hours.

Although both the C.I.O. and A. F. of L. made a no-strike pledge soon after the Japanese attack on Pearl Harbor, many unions resorted to the strike to obtain wage increases that would match the rise in prices. In response to public demands for a check on wartime strikes,* Congress in June, 1943, passed the Smith-Connally Act over the President's veto. This measure empowered the President to seize any plant or firm that was threatened by a strike, and provided penalties for leaders or instigators of strikes against companies working on government contracts. When John L. Lewis's United Mine Workers threatened to strike in November, 1943, Secretary of the Interior Ickes, at the President's direction, took control of the mines. A month later the railroads, under similar circumstances, were seized by the government and placed under the army's authority. While strikes and the menace of strikes received a great deal of unfavorable publicity in the nation's press, a review of the record reveals that work stoppages had comparatively little effect on wartime industrial production.

Meanwhile the National War Labor Board, which had been established in January, 1942, was attempting—but with little success—to stabilize wages. The first major break in the wage line occurred in the

* Strikes, 1941 to 1944:

	1941	1942	1943	1944
Number of strikes	4,288	2,968	3,752	4,956
Number of workers involved	2,362,620	839,961	1,981,279	2,115,637
Number of man-days idle	23,047,556	4,182,557	13,500,529	8,721,079

summer of 1942, when the board approved a 15 per cent increase for the members of the C.I.O. United Steel Workers in the nation's smaller steel plants. What came to be known as the Little Steel Formula was soon extended to cover workers in other industries.

During the war years the farmer's income, like that of the worker and industrialist, steadily increased. Although farmers would understandably have preferred to have had prices fixed by supply and demand, the government imposed price ceilings on most food products and guaranteed agricultural profits through an expanded program of parity payments. Because parity prices applied to only a few basic crops, however, they did not provide an adequate method for inducing farmers to grow other crops that were needed by the war economy. As a result, and despite the creation of a War Food Administration, the government had little control over agricultural production in the war years.

The high wartime level of industrial wages and of farm income and a concurrent shortage of consumer goods produced an increase in the cost of living that threatened to jeopardize the successful prosecution of the war. Although it was hoped that heavier taxation and bond sales would siphon off some surplus purchasing power, the principal effort to check the inflationary spiral was made by the Office of Price Administration under the chairmanship of Leon Henderson. Price ceilings were imposed on many consumer goods in short supply, and a rationing system was set up to insure equitable distribution of scarce, essential commodities. In view of the difficult task that confronted it, the O.P.A. achieved considerable success. The index (1935–9 = 100) of consumers' prices rose from 105.2 in 1941 to 116.5 in 1942, 123.6 in 1943, and leveled off at 125.5 in 1944. Rents, which were frozen in 1942, did not vary appreciably for the remainder of the war.

World War II gave rise to little of the hysteria that had blemished the war record of the United States in 1917–18. The Roosevelt Administration made a concerted effort to prevent the war from being used as an excuse for fomenting suspicion, intolerance, and hatred on the home front. The Department of Justice methodically and without fanfare checked on people of questionable loyalty and invoked the law against those suspected of supporting the enemy. Pro-Fascist organizations such as the German-American Bund and the Silver Shirts were disbanded; enemy-owned businesses in the United States were confiscated; and more than three thousand enemy aliens were interned—a remarkably small number, for the Alien Registration Act of 1940 had revealed that there were some 5,000,000 aliens in the country. The Justice Department's most spectacular coup was the capture of eight German agents who had been landed on the East coast by submarine. Following a military trial, six were put to death and two sentenced to life imprisonment. An otherwise laudable record on civil rights in wartime was marred, however, by the treatment of 110,000 West-coast Japanese-Americans, the majority of whom had been born in the United States. Taken from their homes by the army, they were "relocated" at some distance from the West coast in camps where living conditions were far from ideal. Not until the end of the war were they permitted to return to their former homes.

The war was attended by a marked increase in racial tension. Negroes found the armed services' policy of segregation especially distasteful in a war that was being fought against an enemy that had made a national religion of the myth of racial supremacy. On the other hand, white Southerners, who had moved out of their section to take jobs in industry, resented the economic and social position of the Negro in the North. There was, moreover, widespread hostility among many Southern whites toward the Fair Practices Employment Committee, which had been appointed by the President in 1941 to prevent racial discrimination in employment. These stresses and strains, aggravated by agitators, produced a number of anti-Negro riots, the most serious of which occurred in Detroit in June, 1943. The battle that raged in Detroit's streets did not end until Federal troops had intervened and more than forty Negroes and whites had lost their lives. Although Negroes were the principal victims of racial prejudice during the war, other minority groups were on occasion subjected to abuse, indignities, and even assault. In 1943 a mob of young men attacked Mexican boys in Los Angeles, and in the same year there were demonstrations of anti-Semitism in both Boston and New York.

The government's attempt to control public opinion was designed to promote the successful prosecution of the war rather than to police the American mind. A system of voluntary press and radio censorship, instituted in the winter of 1941–2, was placed under the supervision of Byron Price, who, as Director of Censorship, was also authorized to censor all information that passed in or out of the United States. But no attempt was made to conduct domestic propaganda on a scale comparable to that undertaken by George Creel in World War I, for each branch of the government released its own information. After June, 1942, the information programs of these government agencies were co-ordinated by the Office of War Information, headed by Elmer Davis. The O.W.I. through a series of overseas broadcasts also conducted a campaign of psychological warfare that was designed to undermine enemy morale.

Politics was one of the few forms of traditional American life that the war did not seriously modify. The Republicans, as the minority party, often found it difficult to criticize the conduct of the war without also seeming to criticize the United States' war objectives. On the other hand, they were quick to accuse the Roosevelt Administration of inefficiency and to complain of restrictions on civilian activity, and in the 1942 congressional elections they captured thirty-four additional seats in the House and eight in the Senate. By 1944 the Republican chances of victory appeared better than at any time since the advent of the New Deal. The Republican convention recognized Governor Thomas E. Dewey of New York as the party's standard bearer, and he was nominated on the first ballot. At the Democratic convention, where Roosevelt's renomination was assured, a contest developed over the selection of a vice-presidential candidate. Although Henry Wallace entered the convention with strong hopes that he would again be given second place on the Democratic ticket, he was defeated by the city machines and Southern delegates. The convention finally settled upon Senator Harry S. Truman of Missouri, a former stalwart of Kansas City's Pendergast machine, who had attracted favorable attention by his conduct of a Senate committee that investigated war production.

The 1944 campaign revealed the dilemma of the Republicans, for Dewey in most of his public statements felt compelled to accept much of the New Deal's foreign and domestic policies. He struck repeatedly at the confusion and conflicts within the Administration, but he could promise the voters little more than that the Republicans would carry out the Democratic program more effectively than the Democrats themselves had been able to do. In meeting the Republican challenge, Roosevelt attacked the G.O.P.'s isolationist record, pointed to his party's achievements during the war, and promised Americans an "economic bill of rights." Since both candidates favored the establishment of an international organization to preserve peace, this issue played a minor part in the campaign.

On election day the voters endorsed the Roosevelt Administration for the fourth successive time. With 432 votes to 99 for Dewey, Roosevelt won a smashing victory in the electoral college, but his popular majority of only 3,260,000 was less than that received by any successful presidential candidate since World War I. The Democrats also won a majority of the gubernatorial contests, held their own in the Senate, and picked up twenty-one seats in the House. Among other notable features of the election were the defeat of several prominent isolationists, the all-out campaign conducted for Roosevelt by the C.I.O.'s Political Action Committee, and the continued strength of the Democrats in urban areas.

Within six months of his re-election to a fourth term as President, Roosevelt was dead. Possessed of an exuberant personality that had seemed capable of carrying him through any crisis, he had thrived on conflict and had thoroughly enjoyed his job. But more than twelve years of unprecedented responsibility had inevitably undermined his physical stamina. When he returned from the Yalta Conference early in 1945 he was badly run-down, and he had not fully recovered when he went to Warm Springs, Georgia, to recuperate. There he died from a cerebral

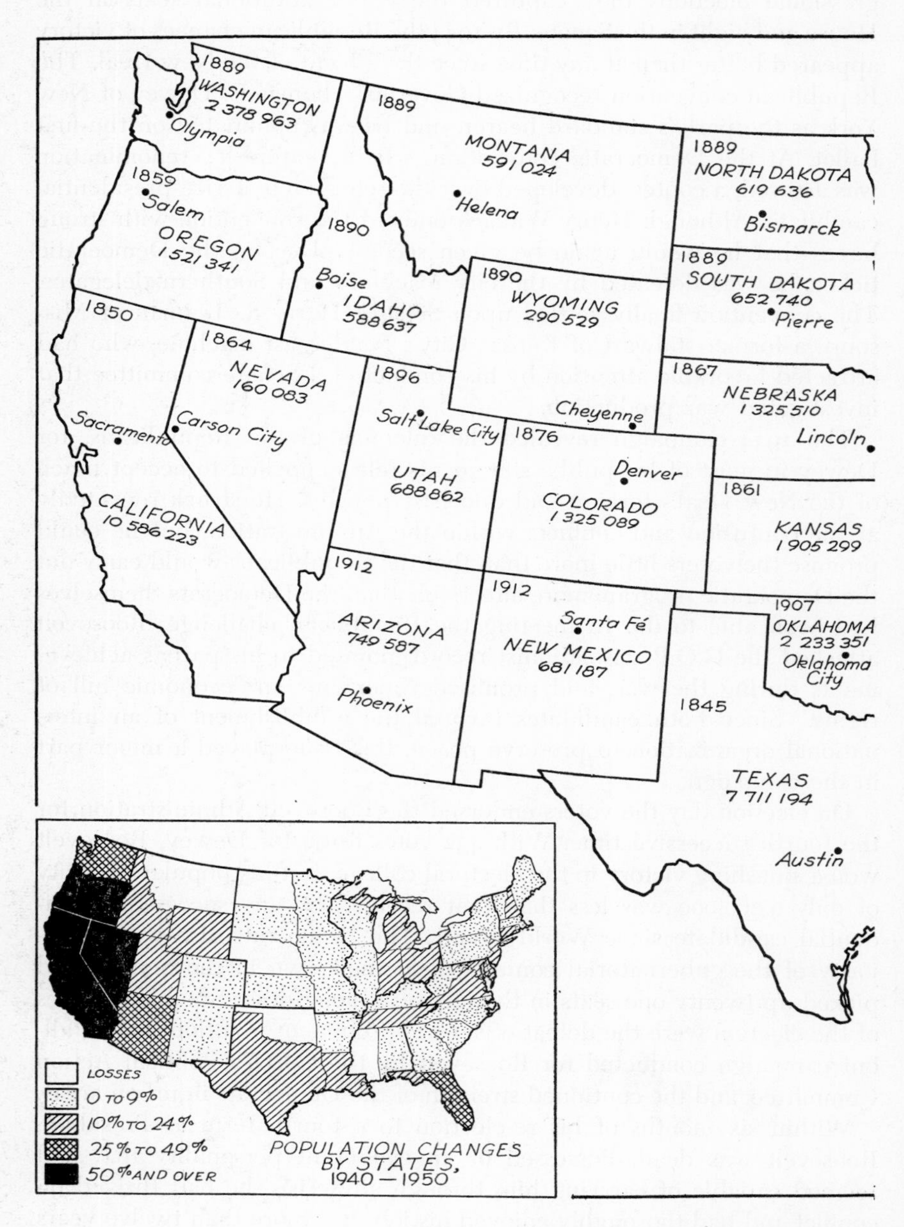
1889
WASHINGTON
2 378 963
Olympia
1889
MONTANA
591 024
Helena
1889
NORTH DAKOTA
619 636
Bismarck
1859
Salem
OREGON
1 521 341
1890
Boise
IDAHO
588 637
1890
WYOMING
290 529
1889
SOUTH DAKOTA
652 740
Pierre
1850
1864
NEVADA
160 083
1896
1867
NEBRASKA
1 325 510
Cheyenne
Lincoln
Sacramento
Carson City
Salt Lake City
1876
UTAH
688 862
Denver
COLORADO
1 325 089
1861
KANSAS
1 905 299
CALIFORNIA
10 586 223
1912
1912
1907
OKLAHOMA
2 233 351
Oklahoma City
Santa Fé
ARIZONA
749 587
NEW MEXICO
681 187
Phoenix
1845
TEXAS
7 711 194
Austin
LOSSES
0 TO 9%
10% TO 24%
25% TO 49%
50% AND OVER
POPULATION CHANGES BY STATES, 1940 — 1950

25. CONTINENTAL UNITED STATES

UNITED STATES, 1950
MAP SHOWS STATES, CAPITALS, DATES OF ADMISSION AND 1950 POPULATION TOTALS
1858
MINNESOTA
2 982 483
St. Paul
1848
WISCONSIN
3 434 575
Madison
1837
MICHIGAN
6 371 766
Lansing
1846
IOWA
2 621 073
Des Moines
1818
ILLINOIS
8 712 176
Spring-field
1816
INDIANA
3 934 224
Indian-apolis
1803
OHIO
7 946 627
Columbus
1821
Jefferson City
MISSOURI
3 954 653
Topeka
1792
Frankfort
KENTUCKY
2 944 806
1863
W. VA.
2 005 552
Charles-ton
1788
Richmond
VIRGINIA
3 318 680
1796
Nashville
TENNESSEE
3 291 718
1836
ARKANSAS
1 909 511
Little Rock
1817
MISS-ISSIPPI
2 178 914
Jackson
1819
ALABAMA
3 061 743
Montgomery
1788
Atlanta
GEORGIA
3 444 578
1812
LOUISIANA
2 683 516
Baton Rouge
1845
Tallahassee
FLORIDA
2 771 305
1789
Raleigh
NORTH CAROLINA
4 061 929
1788
Columbia
SOUTH CAROLINA
2 117 027
1787
PENNSYLVANIA
10 498 012
Harrisburg
Trenton
1788
NEW YORK
14 830 192
Albany
NEW HAMPSHIRE
533 242
VERMONT
377 747
1791
Montpelier
Concord
1788
1820
MAINE
913 774
Augusta
MASS.
4 690 514
Boston
1788
Hartford
1788
R.I., 1790
791 896
Providence
1787
CONNECTICUT,
2 007 280
NEW JERSEY,
4 835 329
Dover
1787
DELAWARE,
318 085
1788
MARYLAND,
2 343 001
Annapolis
Washington, D.C.
802 178
500 MILES
TRM

IN THE MIDTWENTIETH CENTURY

hemorrhage on April 12, 1945. On the same day, Harry S. Truman was sworn in as the thirty-third President of the United States.

127. POSTWAR DOMESTIC PROBLEMS

AMERICANS in all walks of life viewed the end of the war abroad as a signal for the immediate restoration of a peacetime economy at home. For almost four years they had dreamed of the fruits of peace, and they were now determined to enjoy them. Servicemen wished to be discharged; businessmen and farmers wanted prices raised and taxes lowered; workers felt that they deserved wage increases; landlords demanded the removal of ceilings on rents; and consumers clamored for new automobiles, homes, and the countless gadgets that had been denied them during the war. In and out of the government were those who warned that a speedy and unplanned return to a peacetime economy would create more problems than it would solve; but they were helpless before the unrelenting pressure of practically every special-interest group in the country. Despite the pleas of the Truman Administration for an orderly and gradual transition from war to peace, the American people had their way, and within a year after the Japanese surrender, most of the government's wartime restrictions and controls had been removed.

Because of pressure on the government by servicemen and their families, demobilization proceeded at a rate much more rapid than either military or civilian leaders thought advisable. By January, 1947, the armed forces, which at their peak in 1944–5 had numbered over 11,000,000, had declined to about 1,000,000 men, of whom half were stationed abroad in American armies of occupation. Officials responsible for national defense, who deplored this policy of wholesale discharges, urged the establishment of universal military training. But Congress, despite mounting tension between the Soviet Union and the United States, balked at this proposal and in its stead voted to continue the draft. The peacetime selective-service law imposed drastic limitations on the maximum size of the nation's armed services and provided for the exemption of fathers, eighteen-year-olds, and most veterans of World War II.

Although during the war there were frequent predictions that it would be exceedingly difficult for returning servicemen to adjust themselves to civilian life, the great majority of veterans made the transition with little or no trouble. As veterans, moreover, they were granted a number of special privileges in postwar America. Under the "G. I. Bill of Rights," which became law in June, 1944, they were assured educational opportunities and certain forms of economic assistance that were not available to civilians. Unemployed veterans were entitled to draw twenty dollars a week for not more than a year, and veterans who wished to purchase a house or start a small business were granted liberal credit facilities. The government, in addition, paid for the tuition and books of veterans in colleges and vocational institutions and made monthly subsistence payments to veterans who were students. Finally, through the Veterans' Administration, which was almost a government within the government, many veterans received special medical services, disability pensions, and vocational rehabilitation.

The comparative ease with which most veterans resumed civilian life was made possible in part by a boom that eliminated all threats of widespread postwar unemployment. The backlog of consumer demand that had been built up during the war created a sellers' market in which buyers seldom bothered to quibble over either price or quality. Moreover, heavy government expenditures on both European recovery and the largest peacetime military establishment in the nation's history also contributed either directly or indirectly to the prosperity of American businessmen, workers, and farmers. By 1947, when industry had completed its reconversion to peacetime production, the number of employed reached a record 60,000,000, and the annual value of goods and services produced amounted to the unprecedented total of $225,000,000,000.

The boom was accompanied by a rapid and spectacular increase in prices, and throughout the postwar years inflation remained a constant threat to continued American prosperity. In the months that followed the Japanese surrender, farmers and businessmen, anxious to take full advantage of the great demand for their products, conducted extensive propaganda for the immediate removal of all government restrictions on prices. The National Association of Manufacturers, which was the principal spokesman for the advocates of decontrol, maintained that in a free market, production would increase, and prices would of their own accord reach an equitable level for all concerned. On the other hand, the Truman Administration urged that price ceilings and rationing be continued until supply had had an opportunity to catch up with demand. Congress, however, proved more susceptible to the importunities of the inflationists than to the logic of the President, and in June, 1946, it merely extended the life of the O.P.A. with little promise of effectively checking the upward spiral of prices. When Truman vetoed this measure, Congress responded with an almost identical bill. As the only alternative to runaway inflation, the President reluctantly accepted it. By autumn, when prices under the new law had risen precipitously and the government was being condemned both for permitting inflation and retaining controls, Truman decided to abandon the struggle. On October 14, he announced the removal of all controls except those on rents. Although the President lost the battle over prices, he won the argument, for by December, 1946, prices were almost 32 per cent higher than in the preceding year.

Workers, as well as farmers and businessmen, were responsible for the postwar inflationary spiral. Labor leaders opposed the lifting of price ceilings, but they did not hesitate to call a series of strikes to obtain wage increases, which in turn pushed prices still higher. In their efforts to have income keep pace with the mounting cost of living, workers succeeded only in aggravating the problem that they were attempting to solve. In the winter of 1945–6, there were strikes in the automobile, steel, and electrical industries. In April, 1946, the United Mine Workers went on strike and were joined by the railroad employees a month later; but when President Truman threatened to turn the roads over to the army to operate, the strikers returned to work. The first round of postwar strikes resulted in wage increases of approximately $.18 an hour. Subsequent strikes added still more to the nation's wage bill, and from 1945 to 1948 average hourly wage rates rose from $1.02 to $1.33. But labor, like Alice in Wonderland, no matter how hard it ran, seemed to stay in the same place, for in the same period the cost of living index (1935–9 = 100) increased from 128.4 to 171.1.

The most far-reaching labor crisis of the postwar years was set off by a strike of John L. Lewis' United Mine Workers on April 1, 1946. The President seized the mines; and when the operators refused to accept a contract that had been negotiated by Federal authorities, the government retained its control over the industry. In November of the same year, Lewis issued a second strike call, and the government replied with injunction proceedings. When Lewis ignored the injunction, he was ruled in contempt of court by a Federal district judge, who fined him $10,000 and the United Mine Workers $3,500,000. On March 6, 1947, the lower court's decision was sustained by the Supreme Court, although the union's fine was subsequently reduced to $700,000. Three months after the Supreme Court's decision, a Republican-controlled Congress adopted over the President's veto the Taft-Hartley Act. This law, which its authors asserted was designed to redress the Wagner Act's alleged wrongs to employers, permitted management to sue unions that did not abide by their contracts, outlawed the closed shop, restricted the union shop, forbade campaign contributions by unions, gave employers the right to refuse to institute the check-off, required union leaders to sign a non-Communist affidavit, and made a sixty-day "cooling-off" period prerequisite to all strikes. Labor leaders unable to agree on almost anything else were all but unanimous in condemning what they called the "Taft-Hartley slave labor law."

The postwar political scene was in many respects as confused as the nation's economy. In the months that followed Japan's surrender, the Truman Administration was held accountable for most of the domestic problems that it had consistently—if unsuccessfully—attempted to avoid. High prices, black markets, the housing shortage, and strikes were all indiscriminately attributed to the party in power, and in the 1946 congressional elections the Republicans gained control of both the Senate and House for the first time since the advent of the New Deal. Confident of victory in 1948, the Republican majorities in the eightieth Congress not only adopted the Taft-Hartley Act, but also consistently refused to heed the President's repeated demands for an expanded New Deal program of social and economic legislation.

The Republican convention, which was held in Philadelphia in June, 1948, nominated Governor Thomas E. Dewey of New York a second time for the presidency and Governor Earl Warren of California for the vice-presidency. Less than a month later the Democrats convened in the same city to make the appropriate gestures in what most observers agreed was a lost cause. Many delegates hoped that they could induce either General Dwight D. Eisenhower or Supreme Court Justice William O. Douglas to accept the nomination; but when both announced that they were not candidates, Truman's selection was assured. As his running mate, the Democrats chose Senator Alben Barkley of Kentucky. Many Southern Democrats, objecting to their party's strong stand in favor of civil-rights legislation, formed the States' Rights, or Dixiecrat, party. The Dixiecrats nominated Governor J. Strom Thurmond of South Carolina and Governor Fielding Wright of Mississippi and adopted a platform that placed its greatest emphasis upon white supremacy. At the other end of the political spectrum was the Progressive party, whose standard bearers were Henry Wallace, who had broken with the Truman Administration over foreign policy, and Senator Glenn Taylor of Idaho. Advocating co-operation with the Soviet Union and championing—but not defining—the "common man," the Progressives attempted to convince voters that Henry Wallace had inherited the mantle of Franklin D. Roosevelt.

Throughout the campaign the so-called—and often self-styled—experts, the newspapers, and the professional poll-takers were unanimous in their predictions of a sweeping Republican victory. Dewey, convinced that he was riding an irresistible wave of popular sentiment, made cautious and sedate speeches in which he buried the issues beneath generalizations about the need for national unity. President Truman, who alone refused to concede his own defeat, waged an aggressive campaign. In countless speeches, prepared and off-the-cuff, which he delivered before huge urban audiences and at every whistle stop, he charged that the eightieth or "do-nothing"—as he called it—Congress had consistently ignored the wishes of the people. Advocating civil-rights legislation, an expansion of public power facilities, continued aid to agriculture, a firm policy toward the Soviet Union, and an increase in social-security benefits, the President made clear to the voters exactly where he stood on every major issue in the campaign.

On the day after the election Truman almost alone could take credit for engineering the most stunning upset in the history of American presidential elections. With 49.5 per cent of the popular vote, Truman had won 303 electoral votes, Dewey 189, Thurmond 39, and Wallace none. The Democrats also regained control of both branches of the Congress and won impressive victories in state gubernatorial contests. Since both major parties had been in substantial agreement on foreign policy, the Democratic victory represented a reaffirmation by the voters of the domestic policies that had first been espoused by the New Deal. The Republicans, as in the past, had gone down to defeat before a farmer-labor alliance. While it was generally conceded before the election that the Democrats would receive labor's vote, their remarkably strong showing in the agricultural Midwest surprised almost everyone but President Truman.

Despite the extent of the Democratic victory, Truman found the eighty-first Congress almost as obdurate as its predecessor, and two years after the election there was little indication that Congress was prepared to accept his "Fair Deal" program. Through filibusters in the Senate, Southerners were able to prevent the enactment of civil-rights legislation, while a coalition of Republicans and Southern Democrats blocked most of the Administration's social and economic measures. Republicans meanwhile charged that the government harbored Communists and Communist-sympathizers, and the Democrats insisted that they were as anti-Communist as their opponents. Loyalty checks were instituted to weed Communists out of government service; the House Committee on Un-American Activities publicized the testimony of ex-Communists; the Attorney General's office published a list of subversive organizations; and in 1949 ten leaders of the Communist party were found guilty by a Federal district court in New York of plotting to overthrow the United States government. While all responsible and patriotic Americans recognized the need for exposing those whose first loyalty was to a foreign government, many complained of the methods used in the campaign against Communists. On numerous occasions, anti-Communists accused whoever had views left of center of sympathizing with the Soviet Union. There was always the danger that anti-Communism might be converted into a full-scale crusade to control the thinking of loyal Americans who were not Communists.

128. THE UNITED STATES AND THE UNITED NATIONS

DURING the war, Allied leaders had devoted an increasing amount of time and energy to postwar planning. The failure of the League of Nations served as a constant reminder of the need for action, and they were determined to work out plans for a postwar association of nations while the spirit of unity engendered by war still prevailed. The problem first arose among Allied spokesmen at the conference of foreign ministers at Moscow in 1944. Although no attempt was then made to devise a detailed plan, the Moscow Declaration pledged the Soviet Union, China, the United States, and Great Britain to establish a "general international organization" to preserve peace. On November 5, the Connally Resolution voiced the Senate's overwhelming approval of the Moscow Declaration. More tangible evidence of Allied willingness to co-operate on nonmilitary problems was furnished by the creation in November, 1944, of the United Nations Relief and Rehabilitation Administration. Consisting of more than forty nations under the leadership of the Big Four and with Herbert H. Lehman as Director General, U.N.R.R.A. was designed to help feed, clothe, and shelter the millions who had lost their homes and means of support because of the war. Equally significant was the formation of the International Bank for Reconstruction and Development and the International Monetary Fund. Both were established to promote international economic co-operation and stability, and both were set up in July, 1944, by the delegates to a conference held at Bretton Woods in New Hampshire.

In June, 1944, President Roosevelt made public his Administration's plans for a post-war organization to preserve the peace. Making it clear that he did not favor a world superstate, he said: "We are seeking effective agreement and arrangements through which the Nations would maintain, according to their capacities, adequate forces to meet the needs of preventing war and of making impossible deliberate preparation for war, and to have such forces available for joint action when necessary." Two months later representatives of the Big Four attended the Dumbarton Oaks Conference to work out preliminary plans for the United Nations. The delegates agreed that the new organization should consist of a security council, to be controlled by the major powers with authority to determine and implement United Nations' policies; a general assembly, in which every state was to be represented, but with only advisory functions; a court of justice; and an economic and social council.

Before any action had been taken on these proposals, Roosevelt, Stalin, and Churchill met at Yalta, in the Crimea, in February, 1945. The Yalta discussions covered a wide variety of topics, and revealed a potentially serious cleavage of views between the Soviet Union and the Western Allies. Roosevelt went to the Yalta Conference determined to win Russian backing for a postwar international organization. Stalin, for his part, was preoccupied with increasing Soviet power and assuring Russian security. At Stalin's insistence, Churchill and Roosevelt agreed that Byelorussia and the Ukraine, both member republics of the U.S.S.R., would be granted separate representation in the United Nations; that each member of the United Nations Security Council would have the right to veto decisions of the other members; that the Soviet Union could annex the eastern portion of Poland, which in turn would be compensated with a comparable amount of German territory; and that southern Sakhalin and the Kuriles as well as a preferential position in Manchuria should be granted to the Soviet Union. In return, Stalin pledged that Russia would support the United Nations, work for the establishment of democratic governments in Poland and Yugoslavia, and join in the war against Japan after Germany's defeat. The problem of the postwar occupation of Germany was resolved by a decision to divide it into four zones, which would be assigned to Great Britain, France, the Soviet Union, and the United States, respectively.

Four months after the Yalta meeting, the preliminary plans for a postwar international organization were transformed into the United Nations Charter at the San Francisco Conference. Attended by some fifty nations that had declared war against the Axis, the conference in general ratified the Dumbarton Oaks proposals and the decisions reached at Yalta. The Charter was drawn up on the hypothesis that the strongest nations were best suited to serve as guardians of world peace. Final authority was vested in the Security Council, which in turn was dominated by its permanent members—China, France, the Soviet Union, Great Britain, and the United States. The Charter provided for the election by the Assembly of six other members for two-year terms, but this was hardly more than a gesture, for each of the Big Five possessed the right of veto, and all Security Council decisions required a majority of seven votes. Representatives of the smaller nations at San Francisco, who had seen the major powers fight two world wars within twenty-five years, felt that they had reason to ask who was going to police the policemen. Since they had no choice in the matter, most preferred to accept the Charter in the hope that the Big Five* would be able to evolve an effective method for reconciling their differences. In the United States there was practically no organized opposition to the Charter, and it was ratified by the Senate on July 28, 1945.

The United Nations began to function with the first meeting of the General Assembly in January, 1946. In the same month the Security Council convened, and within a short time Trygve H. Lie of Norway was selected as the first Secretary-General of the United Nations. In

* Great Britain, the United States, the Soviet Union, China, and France.

26. THE ORGANIZATION OF THE UNITED NATIONS

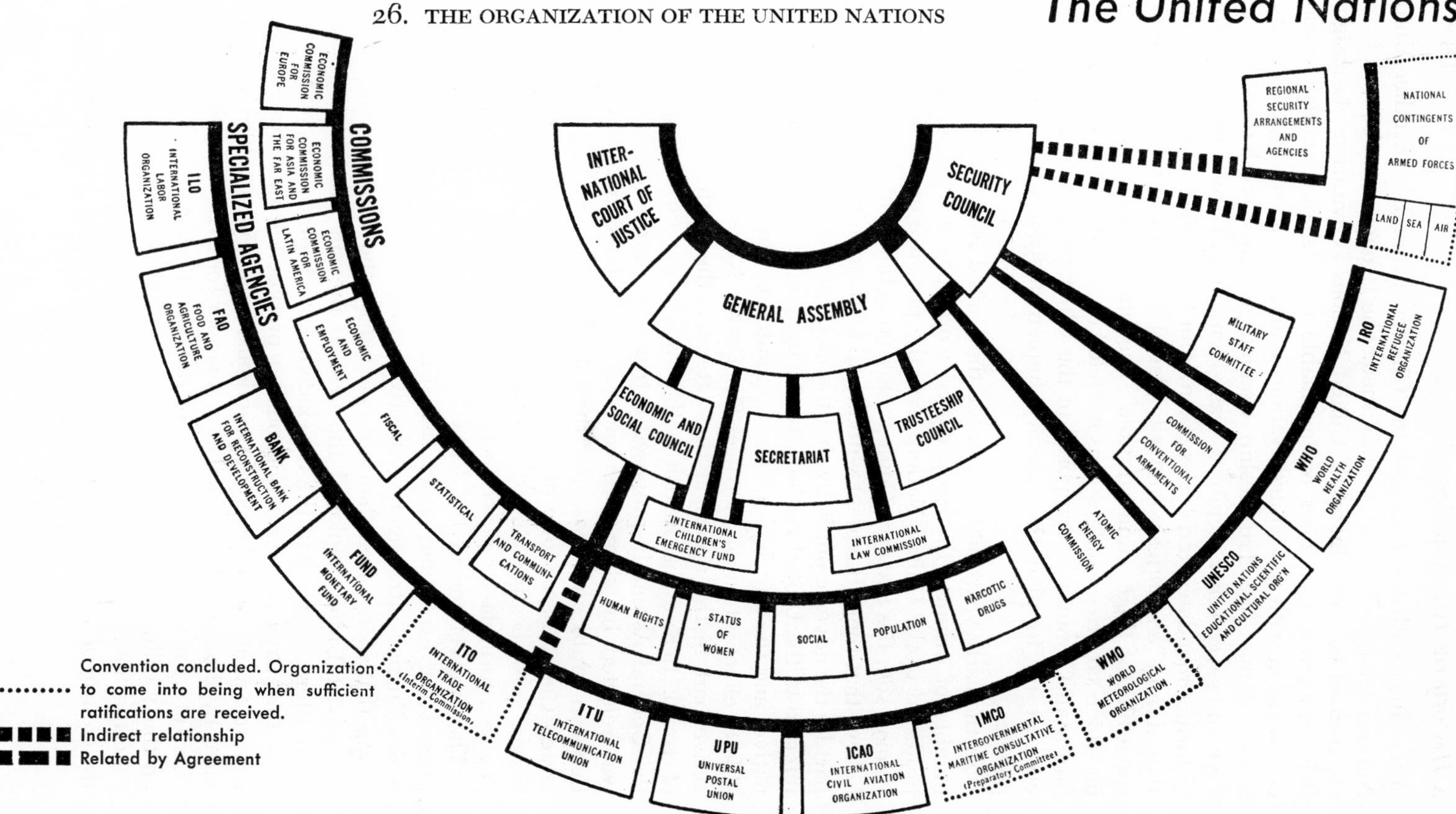

accordance with the terms of the Charter, a number of other United Nations agencies were also established. The Economic and Social Council, formed to co-ordinate all United Nations activities in its assigned field, prepared a number of invaluable reports and worked in close co-operation with the United Nations education, scientific, and cultural organizations. The Trusteeship Council, which consisted of the Big Five and seven other members, was given authority over the disposition of former mandates, territories taken from the defeated enemy in World War II, and "territories voluntarily placed under the system by states responsible for their administration." The International Court of Justice, on which sat fifteen judges, was modeled on the World Court. The Military Staff Committee, composed of the Chiefs of Staff of the Big Five, was set up to plan the military implementation of United Nations policies.

In the early years of its existence the United Nations intervened in a number of disputes that jeopardized world peace. In 1946, when Iran protested to the United Nations over the presence of Russian troops on Iranian soil, the Security Council took no action; but there is reason to believe that the subsequent withdrawal of Russian troops was caused in part by the adverse publicity that the incident received after it had been referred to the United Nations. In the fighting in Indonesia between the natives and the Dutch, a mission appointed by the Security Council was able to effect a temporary truce. The United Nations took a much more active part in the upheaval that attended the birth of the new state of Israel. Before the British withdrawal a commission appointed by the General Assembly proposed a tripartite partition of Palestine that was rejected by all parties concerned. In the fighting that followed between Arabs and Jews after the establishment of the government of Israel, Count Bernadotte of Sweden and Ralph Bunche of the United States, as successive United Nations mediators in Palestine, helped to devise a formula for peace in the Holy Land.

The intervention of the United Nations in Indonesia and Palestine proved the exception rather than the rule, for on virtually all other issues Russian intransigence effectively thwarted the will of a majority group that more often than not was led by the United States. In 1947 the Soviet Union employed the veto to prevent the Security Council from attempting to halt the Greek civil war. Another Russian veto overrode the majority's resolution on the proposed United Nations policy toward Spain, and Russian obstructionism made impossible the appointment by the Security Council of a governor for Trieste. In the first three years of its existence, a majority of the Security Council was overridden on thirty different occasions by Russia's resort to the veto. At the same time the Soviet Union and the United States were unable to agree on the control of atomic energy. The United States had proposed the establishment of an International Atomic Energy Commission with complete authority over the manufacture and use of atomic energy in every nation. The Russians countered with a plan calling for every nation to renounce atomic warfare. Since both countries refused to give way, there the matter stood. When President Truman announced on September 23, 1949, that the Russians had exploded an atom bomb, Americans realized that they were in the most deadly armament race in the history of mankind.

129. THE UNITED STATES AND A DIVIDED WORLD

THE CONTEST in the United Nations between the United States and the Soviet Union reflected a larger conflict between these countries around the globe. Using every means short of war to attain their objectives, each continually ran the risk of provoking the other to war. Under pressure of this remorseless struggle, the entire world was divided into two hostile camps, and each constantly sought to outmaneuver the other.

The "cold war" between the Soviet Union and the United States developed in Europe soon after the surrender of Germany. In July, 1945, the leaders of the Big Three had met for the last time at Potsdam to discuss the policies that they would adopt toward Germany and her allies. Although all were agreed on the desirability of concluding peace treaties with Bulgaria, Finland, Hungary, Italy, and Rumania as soon as possible, the completion of these pacts proved a long and arduous task. Successive meetings of foreign ministers or their deputies in Moscow, London, New York, and Paris were repeatedly disrupted and delayed by the obstructionist tactics of the Soviet representatives; and it was not until February, 1947, that their work was finally completed. The treaties deprived Germany's wartime satellites of their power to make war and levied on them heavy reparations. Provision was also made for a number of territorial changes. Italy was forced to relinquish land to Albania, France, Greece, and Yugoslavia and to place its colonies under the joint control of France, Great Britain, the Soviet Union, and the United States. Trieste was made a free city, and its administration was turned over to a governor to be selected by the United Nations Security Council.

The cleavage that had developed between the Soviet Union and the Western democracies not only delayed the peace settlements with Germany's satellites, but it postponed indefinitely any final agreement about the future of either Austria or Germany. Both countries were divided into four zones of occupation, but in Austria the administrative difficulties inherent in such a system were mitigated by the fact that the Austrians were permitted to have their own government. In Germany, where the stakes were higher and the method of control more complex, the opportunities for confusion and conflict were correspondingly greater. Each occupying nation had complete authority over its own zone, but any policy that affected all of Germany required unanimous approval of the American, British, French, and Russian commanders in Germany, who collectively comprised the Allied Control Council. The area of possible disagreement was further broadened by placing the city of Berlin, which was in the center of the Russian zone, under four-power control.

At the outset the Allies were in complete agreement about the need for punishing Germany and destroying its war potential. Drastic restrictions were placed on heavy industry, and each power was permitted to obtain its reparations from Germany in the form of industrial equipment needed to rebuild its own war-torn areas. The victors were also free to use German prisoners of war in their reconstruction programs. The leading Nazis were placed on trial at Nuremburg in November, 1945, before a four-power tribunal. Of more than twenty defendants, three were acquitted, eight were sentenced to prison, and ten were hanged.* Meanwhile the "smaller fish" were turned over to "denazification" courts, which undertook the almost impossible task of attempting to determine which Germans had actively supported the Hitler regime.

Although the Western Allies and the Soviet Union were fully agreed that the war guilt was Germany's, there was little else on which they could reach a common understanding. Reparations provided an endless source of conflict, and there were constant and interminable disputes between the British, French, and American commanders on the one hand and the Russian authorities on the other. As the Western powers became convinced that the Soviet Union was aiming at the control of all Germany, they tended to submerge their own differences and seek methods for uniting their respective zones. In December, 1946, the British and American zones were joined in an economic union to which the French zone was soon added.

The conflict between East and West in Germany became especially dangerous in 1948. In the spring the Soviet Union withdrew from the Allied Control Council; and Great Britain, France, and the United States made tentative plans for the political union of their zones. When the Western Allies in the summer of 1948 announced a new currency for use in their zones and in the portion of Berlin under their control, the Russians imposed a blockade upon all Western rail and water shipments into the German capital. Rather than evacuate Berlin, the Allies used British and American planes to fly supplies into the beleaguered city.

* Göring, who was sentenced to be hanged, committed suicide.

Within a few weeks the "air-lift" was operating around the clock and supplying western Berlin with enough food, fuel, and raw materials to keep its economy functioning. For several months neither side would give way; the Russians set up a separate police force and civil government for their sector of Berlin and the Allies established a counterblockade to prevent shipments from the western to the eastern sectors of Germany. Finally, in the spring of 1949 the Russians let it be known that they were willing to end their blockade if the Western powers would end theirs, and in May both blockades were lifted.

The Russian blockade of Berlin increased the determination of the Allies to establish a separate German government that would give the residents of their zones a measure of self-rule. Elections were accordingly held for delegates to a constituent assembly. Although ultimate authority was still in the hands of the occupying powers, the new government of the "Federal Republic of Germany" went into effect in May, 1949, and Konrad Adenauer was the first Prime Minister. The Russians meanwhile had strengthened their hold over the economic and political life of their zone, and the prospects of a united Germany seemed more remote than at any time since the war.

The "cold war" between the Soviet Union and the West quickly spread beyond Germany to the rest of Europe. Russian troops had occupied countries along the Soviet border and with the aid of native Communists they converted Hungary, Poland, Yugoslavia, Bulgaria, and Rumania* into Russian satellites whose rulers maintained close contact with the leaders in the Kremlin. At the same time Communist minorities in Italy and France resorted to sabotage and obstructionism in their efforts to gain economic and political power. The Western powers were unable to prevent any of these developments; but when the withdrawal of British troops from Greece seemed to leave the way open for the Communists to overthrow the Greek government, the United States assumed the diplomatic offensive. On March 12, 1947, President Truman asked Congress for $300,000,000 to aid Greece and an additional $100,-000,000 for Turkey, which alone stood between the Soviet Union and the Dardanelles. What soon became known as the Truman Doctrine was approved in Congress by a coalition of Democrats and Republicans who espoused a bipartisan foreign policy to check further Russian expansion.

The Truman Doctrine was at best a stop-gap arrangement that was devised to do no more than meet a specific emergency. It soon became apparent, however, that a long-range program of assistance was needed both to revive the European economy and to prevent the Communists from adding to their gains. U.N.R.R.A., to which the United States contributed much the largest share of money and supplies, had no way of

* Czechoslovakia was added to this list in 1948 following a successful Communist coup.

preventing the Communist rulers in eastern Europe from using its relief shipments for political purposes, while the 1945 loan to Great Britain had proved a palliative rather than a cure. The first responsible official to propose a constructive and over-all solution to Europe's economic problems was Secretary of State George C. Marshall. In an address at Harvard University in June, 1947, he suggested that if Europe's leaders would ascertain what their countries could achieve through economic co-operation and what their principal needs were, the United States would be prepared to provide them with the necessary financial assistance. Marshall's proposal met with an overwhelmingly favorable response in western Europe, and in September, 1947, the representatives of sixteen European nations, including those from the combined British and American zones in Germany, met in Paris to work out the details of the program. Because Russia considered the Marshall Plan an instrument of American imperialism, none of the Soviet Union's satellite nations was permitted to attend the conference. When the delegates had completed the laborious task of drawing up a balance sheet for western Europe's economy, it was decided that $21,780,000,000 in loans and credits would be needed through 1951. After reviewing the conference's findings, the United States agreed to underwrite Europe's recovery with $17,000,000,000 for a four-year period.

Despite repeated demands in and out of Congress for a reduction in government expenditures, the Marshall Plan—or European Recovery Program—met with little opposition in the United States, for most Americans were convinced that it provided the only feasible method for preventing the hard times and chaos on which communism flourished. Congress in December, 1947, made a stop-gap E.R.P. appropriation of $597,000,000, and in the following April it voted an appropriation of $5,300,000,000 to cover the first year of the plan's operation. To administer the foreign-aid program, the Economic Cooperation Administration was established, and Paul G. Hoffman was made its director.

The effects of E.R.P. upon western Europe were almost immediately apparent. It not only made possible a marked improvement in the European economy, but it also enabled democratic political leaders to adopt a stronger line toward the Communist opposition within their countries. Equally significant was a growing trend toward international economic co-operation. By 1949 the Benelux states (Belgium, the Netherlands, and Luxemburg) had worked out a plan for a customs union, and in the following year Foreign Minister Robert Schuman of France proposed the internationalization of the Ruhr's steel industry. But by far the most conclusive evidence of the effectiveness of E.R.P. was provided by the Soviet Union's determination to speed up its diplomatic offensive. In September, 1947, while the Marshall Plan delegates were conferring in Paris, the Soviet Union and its satellites formed the Cominform to chastise

Marshall Tito of Yugoslavia for his alleged "deviationism" and to reaffirm a single propaganda line for Communist parties throughout the world. Most Western observers were convinced that the Cominform was merely the Comintern under another name and that Moscow had once again become the capital of the world revolutionary movement. The creation of the Cominform was followed in February, 1948, by the Communist coup in Czechoslovakia, and in the summer of the same year the Russians imposed their blockade upon Berlin.

By 1948 the aggressive character of Russian foreign policy had convinced the Western powers that military as well as economic unity was needed to insure their security. When Great Britain and the countries of northwestern Europe began to confer about mutual defense, they received the active encouragement of the United States, which soon became a full partner in the discussions. In March, 1949, ten European nations as well as Canada and the United States signed the North Atlantic Treaty. Under the terms of this pact each nation agreed to come to the assistance of any of the others that might be attacked. By 1950 the United States was shipping arms to its European allies, and the military staffs of the various signatory countries were discussing the rôle of each in the event of war.

Throughout the postwar years the problems that confronted the United States in the Far East were fully as serious and complex as those in Europe, and it was only in Japan that American policy proceeded more or less according to plan. Unlike the occupation of Germany, that of Japan was almost exclusively under the control of the United States. Although a Far Eastern Commission, consisting of eleven Pacific powers, had been established in Washington and although there was an Allied Control Commission in Tokyo made up of the United States, the Soviet Union, China, and the British Commonwealth, these bodies had little effect on day-to-day policies in Japan. General Douglas MacArthur, as commander of the American occupying forces, exercised practically dictatorial powers over the Japanese, who for their part docilely obeyed his orders. As in Germany, care was taken to destroy the war potential. Drastic curbs were imposed upon all forms of heavy industry, and of the twenty-eight Japanese leaders placed on trial for war crimes, seven were executed. The Japanese masses, meanwhile, seemed as intent on pleasing the Americans as they once had been on killing them.

MacArthur's policies resulted in a number of sweeping changes, at least on the surface of Japanese life. To break the economic power of the old ruling class and to improve the lot of the masses, large estates were broken up, and the major industrial and financial monopolies were dissolved. Although the Emperor was retained in order to facilitate the occupation, he was divested of both his power and his claim to divinity. Under a new constitution that went into effect in 1946, provision was made for a democratically elected legislature of two houses, and all Japanese were guaranteed certain basic civil rights. Women were given the right to vote; labor was encouraged to develop a trade-union program; and children were provided with a school system that emphasized democracy rather than militarism.

The Philippine Islands, as well as Japan, played an important rôle in American Far Eastern policy in the postwar years. The islands, which were granted their independence by the United States on July 4, 1946, were unable either to defend themselves against potential aggressors or to rebuild their war-torn economy without outside assistance. At the same time strategic considerations and a sense of moral obligation prevented the United States from withdrawing completely. It was therefore to the advantage of both countries that the United States take an active interests in Philippine affairs. Through the Military Assistance Act the United States agreed to aid the new country in the establishment of an effective military force, while the Philippines in return granted the Americans the right to maintain naval and military bases in the islands. The Philippine Trade Act of 1946 provided for free trade between the islands and the United States for eight years, and the Philippine Rehabilitation Act appropriated $720,000,000 to repay Filipinos for property damage incurred during the war.

It was on the Asiatic mainland that American diplomacy suffered its most far-reaching reverses in the years after the war. In China the Communists swept all before them. The civil war, which had been interrupted by the Japanese invasion, was resumed by the Chinese Communists and Chiang Kai-shek's Nationalist forces soon after Japan's defeat. General George C. Marshall, as President Truman's special representative, was able to arrange a truce in January, 1946. Within a few months, however, the Communists, who had been granted control over Manchuria by the Russian forces that were occupying it, broke the truce, and with the aid of Soviet arms they began a steady advance against relatively weak Nationalist opposition. Neither Marshall nor any other American could devise any effective policy toward China. On the one hand, the Chinese Communists were openly hostile to America; on the other, there seemed no possibility that Chiang Kai-shek's Nationalists would provide China with either an honest or efficient government. As a consequence, the United States had to stand by while the Communists overran China, and Chiang Kai-shek was forced to transfer what remained of his government to the island of Formosa. Although some Americans, during the earlier stages of the civil war had believed that the Chinese Communists were merely agrarian reformers without Russian ties, this illusion was completely shattered in 1950, when Mao Tse-tung, the Chinese Communist leader, paid a state visit to Moscow that both symbolized and reaffirmed the unity of the two countries' revolutionary movements.

In Korea the conflict between the Communist and democratic worlds was waged by soldiers as well as diplomats. Although promised eventual independence by the Cairo Conference, Korea was occupied at the end of the war by both the Soviet Union and the United States, with the 38th parallel dividing the Russian zone in the north from the American zone in the south. Under the Russian administration the land in the northern zone was redistributed among the peasants, and a "Democratic People's Republic," patterned on the Soviet model, was established early in 1948. American occupation officials, while making few changes in the organization of the Korean economy, set up a provisional government that was viewed as the first step toward the creation of a united, democratic Korea. But when the United Nations General Assembly authorized an election for the establishment of a single government in Korea, the Soviet Union refused to allow the Koreans in its zone to vote and blocked the Security Council's intervention in Korean affairs by its use of the veto.

Despite constant friction and numerous incidents, the two zones maintained an uneasy peace until June 25, 1950, when North Korean troops launched a full-scale invasion of the southern half of the country. The South Koreans were no match for the invaders, who had been trained and equipped by the Soviet Union, and in the initial stages of the fighting the North Koreans captured the capital city of Seoul and continued to push southward.

Within twenty-four hours of the outbreak of fighting, the Security Council—in a meeting that was not attended by the Soviet Union—accused the North Korean Communists of a "breach of the peace" and demanded that they withdraw from the territory south of the 38th parallel. In addition, the nations belonging to the United Nations were asked to do all within their power to restore the *status quo ante bellum*. On June 27, President Truman announced that American military forces would be used to assist the South Koreans, and on the same day the Security Council requested the members of the United Nations to "repel the armed attack in Korea." Within a short time Americans comprised the largest element in the U.N. army on the peninsula,* and General Douglas MacArthur was made commander in chief of the U.N. forces.

During the first month of the war the U.N. armies were repeatedly defeated by the numerically superior North Koreans, and by the first week in August they held only a beachhead (approximately the size of

* By February, 1951, twelve other countries had sent ground troops to Korea and ten had contributed either air or naval units.

Connecticut) located in the southeast corner of the Korean peninsula. Here, despite repeated attacks, the Americans and South Koreans were able to hold their ground, and on September 15 they took the offensive. While ground troops drove north from the beachhead, an amphibious landing at Inchon on the west coast of Korea enabled the U.N. forces to outflank a large part of the invading army. Within two weeks U.N. troops had fought their way across the 38th parallel and on November 21, advance units reached the Yalu River. The war seemed practically over, and MacArthur informed his soldiers that they would be home for Christmas. But on November 26, more than 200,000 Chinese Communists joined the North Koreans in a full-scale counterattack against the U.N. armies. Taken by surprise and overwhelmed by superior numbers, the U.N. forces retreated on every sector of the front, and it was not until mid-January that they were able to stabilize their lines some seventy-five miles south of the 38th parallel. In the following months the U.N. troops advanced some miles beyond the parallel in the west.

During the first nine months of the war in Korea, General MacArthur and the Truman Administration had repeatedly disagreed over the conduct of American foreign policy. The U.N. commander in chief believed that the China coast should be completely blockaded, that the United States should give all possible assistance to Chiang Kai-shek on Formosa, and that planes should be permitted to bomb enemy bases in what he referred to as the "privileged sanctuary" of Manchuria. President Truman opposed all these moves on the ground that they might convert the local war in Korea into a global war. After MacArthur issued repeated public statements that both implicitly and explicitly criticized the Administration policy in the Far East, President Truman in April, 1951, dismissed him for insubordination. Lieutenant General Matthew B. Ridgway, former commander of operations in the field, took over MacArthur's duties in both Japan and Korea. MacArthur, who received a hero's welcome on his return to the United States, defended his record and his program in an address to a joint session of Congress. While large numbers of Americans thought that MacArthur had been shabbily treated, others, who agreed with the President, maintained that civilian rather than military authority should determine American foreign policy and that the United States should do all within its power to prevent a third world war.

The ability of the U.N. forces to check the Communist advance in Korea was in all probability responsible for a Russian proposal in June, 1951, that "discussions be started between the belligerents for a cease fire." Both sides welcomed the chance to end the war without apparent loss of face, but in the ensuing truce talks the Communist and U.N. representatives had difficulty in finding any area of substantial agreement. Because neither was in a position to dictate terms to the other, the negotiations were reduced to a form of diplomatic chess in which constructive efforts to reach a settlement were necessarily subordinated to the desire to anticipate and check the other side's moves. During the prolonged stalemate at the conference table, fighting continued sporadically under what reporters described as a tacit agreement to "ease" rather than "cease" fire.

The intervention of the United States in Korea served as a constant reminder to all Americans of their country's rôle in world affairs. Not only were Americans fighting and dying for a system of collective security, but the United States had also taken the lead in rebuilding the defenses of western Europe and in employing economic, diplomatic, and military power to shape the course of events in every part of the globe that was not ruled by a Communist dictatorship. In a world that had become two worlds, the United States was the undisputed leader of the democracies, and once again Americans could say with Jefferson that "the last hope of human liberty in this world rests on us."

APPENDIX

I. THE CONSTITUTION OF THE UNITED STATES

II. ADMISSION OF STATES TO THE UNION

III. PRESIDENTIAL ELECTIONS, 1864–1948

IV. PRESIDENTS AND THEIR CABINETS, 1865–1950

V. JUSTICES OF THE SUPREME COURT, 1860–1950

VI. STATISTICAL TABLES

I

*THE CONSTITUTION OF THE UNITED STATES OF AMERICA**

WE THE PEOPLE of the United States, in Order to form a more perfect Union, establish Justice, insure domestic Tranquility, provide for the common defence, promote the general Welfare, and secure the Blessings of Liberty to ourselves and our Posterity, do ordain and establish this CONSTITUTION for the United States of America.

ARTICLE I.

SECTION 1. All legislative Powers herein granted shall be vested in a Congress of the United States, which shall consist of a Senate and House of Representatives.

SECTION 2. The House of Representatives shall be composed of Members chosen every second Year by the People of the several States, and the Electors in each State shall have the Qualifications requisite for Electors of the most numerous Branch of the State Legislature.

No Person shall be a Representative who shall not have attained to the Age of twenty-five Years, and been seven Years a Citizen of the United States, and who shall not, when elected, be an Inhabitant of that State in which he shall be chosen.

[Representatives and direct Taxes † shall be apportioned among the several States which may be included within this Union, according to their respective Numbers, which shall be determined by adding to the whole Number of free Persons, including those bound to Service for a Term of Years, and excluding Indians not taxed, three fifths of all other Persons.] ‡ The actual Enumeration shall be made within three Years after the first Meeting of the Congress of the United States, and within every subsequent Term of ten Years, in such Manner as they shall by Law direct. The Number of Representatives shall not exceed one for every thirty Thousand, but each State shall have at Least one Representative; and until such enumeration shall be made, the State of New Hampshire shall be entitled to chuse three, Massachusetts eight, Rhode-Island and

* This version of the Constitution is that published by the Office of Education, United States Department of the Interior, 1935, and follows the original document in spelling and capitalization.

† Modified as to income taxes by the 16th Amendment.

‡ Replaced by the 14th Amendment.

Providence Plantations one, Connecticut five, New-York six, New Jersey four, Pennsylvania eight, Delaware one, Maryland six, Virginia ten, North Carolina five, South Carolina five, and Georgia three.

When vacancies happen in the Representation from any State, the Executive Authority thereof shall issue Writs of Election to fill such Vacancies.

The House of Representatives shall chuse their Speaker and other Officers; and shall have the sole Power of Impeachment.

SECTION 3. [The Senate of the United States shall be composed of two Senators from each State, chosen by the Legislature thereof, for six Years; and each Senator shall have one Vote.] *

Immediately after they shall be assembled in Consequence of the first Election, they shall be divided as equally as may be into three Classes. The Seats of the Senators of the first Class shall be vacated at the Expiration of the second Year, of the second Class at the Expiration of the fourth Year, and of the third Class at the Expiration of the sixth Year, so that one-third may be chosen every second Year; [and if Vacancies happen by Resignation, or otherwise, during the Recess of the Legislature of any State, the Executive thereof may make temporary Appointments until the next Meeting of the Legislature, which shall then fill such Vacancies.] †

No Person shall be a Senator who shall not have attained to the Age of thirty Years, and been nine Years a Citizen of the United States, and who shall not, when elected, be an Inhabitant of that State for which he shall be chosen.

The Vice President of the United States shall be President of the Senate, but shall have no vote, unless they be equally divided.

The Senate shall chuse their other Officers, and also a President pro tempore, in the absence of the Vice President, or when he shall exercise the Office of President of the United States.

The Senate shall have the sole Power to try all Impeachments. When sitting for that purpose, they shall be on Oath or Affirmation. When the President of the United States is tried, the Chief Justice shall preside: And no person shall be convicted without the Concurrence of two thirds of the Members present.

Judgment in Cases of Impeachment shall not extend further than to removal from Office, and disqualification to hold and enjoy any Office of honor, Trust, or Profit under the United States: but the Party convicted shall nevertheless be liable and subject to Indictment, Trial, Judgment, and Punishment, according to Law.

SECTION 4. The Times, Places and Manner of holding Elections for Senators and Representatives, shall be prescribed in each State by the Legislature thereof; but the Congress may at any time by Law make or alter such Regulations, except as to the Places of Chusing Senators.

[The Congress shall assemble at least once in every Year, and such Meeting shall be on the first Monday in December, unless they shall by Law appoint a different Day.] ‡

SECTION 5. Each House shall be the Judge of the Elections, Returns and

* Superseded by the 17th Amendment.
† Modified by the 17th Amendment.
‡ Superseded by the 20th Amendment.

Qualifications of its own Members, and a Majority of each shall constitute a Quorum to do Business; but a smaller number may adjourn from day to day, and may be authorized to compel the Attendance of absent Members, in such Manner, and under such Penalties, as each House may provide.

Each House may determine the Rules of its Proceedings, punish its Members for disorderly Behavior, and, with the Concurrence of two thirds, expel a Member.

Each House shall keep a Journal of its Proceedings, and from time to time publish the same, excepting such Parts as may in their Judgment require Secrecy; and the Yeas and Nays of the Members of either House on any question shall, at the Desire of one fifth of those Present, be entered on the Journal.

Neither House, during the Session of Congress, shall, without the Consent of the other, adjourn for more than three days, nor to any other Place than that in which the two Houses shall be sitting.

SECTION 6. The Senators and Representatives shall receive a Compensation for their Services, to be ascertained by Law, and paid out of the Treasury of the United States. They shall in all Cases, except Treason, Felony, and Breach of the Peace, be privileged from Arrest during their Attendance at the Session of their respective Houses, and in going to and returning from the same; and for any Speech or Debate in either House, they shall not be questioned in any other Place.

No Senator or Representative shall, during the Time for which he was elected, be appointed to any civil Office under the Authority of the United States, which shall have been created, or the Emoluments whereof shall have been increased, during such time; and no Person holding any Office under the United States shall be a Member of either House during his continuance in Office.

SECTION 7. All Bills for raising Revenue shall originate in the House of Representatives; but the Senate may propose or concur with Amendments as on other bills.

Every Bill which shall have passed the House of Representatives and the Senate, shall, before it become a Law, be presented to the President of the United States; If he approve he shall sign it, but if not he shall return it, with his Objections, to that House in which it shall have originated, who shall enter the Objections at large on their Journal, and proceed to reconsider it. If after such Reconsideration two thirds of that House shall agree to pass the bill, it shall be sent, together with the objections, to the other House, by which it shall likewise be reconsidered, and if approved by two thirds of that House, it shall become a Law. But in all such Cases the Votes of both Houses shall be determined by Yeas and Nays, and the Names of the Persons voting for and against the Bill shall be entered on the Journal of each House respectively. If any Bill shall not be returned by the President within ten Days (Sundays excepted) after it shall have been presented to him, the Same shall be a Law, in like Manner as if he had signed it, unless the Congress by their Adjournment prevent its Return, in which Case it shall not be a Law.

Every Order, Resolution, or Vote to which the Concurrence of the Senate and House of Representatives may be necessary (except on a question of Adjournment) shall be presented to the President of the United States; and before the Same shall take Effect, shall be approved by him, or being disapproved by him, shall be repassed by two thirds of the Senate and House of Representatives, according to the Rules and Limitations prescribed in the Case of a Bill.

SECTION 8. The Congress shall have Power To lay and collect Taxes, Duties, Imposts and Excises, to pay the Debts and provide for the common Defence and general Welfare of the United States; but all Duties, Imposts and Excises shall be uniform throughout the United States;

To borrow money on the credit of the United States;

To regulate Commerce with foreign Nations, and among the several States, and with the Indian Tribes;

To establish an uniform Rule of Naturalization, and uniform Laws on the subject of Bankruptcies throughout the United States;

To coin Money, regulate the Value thereof, and of foreign Coin, and fix the Standard of Weights and Measures;

To provide for the Punishment of counterfeiting the Securities and current Coin of the United States;

To establish Post Offices and post Roads;

To promote the Progress of Science and useful Arts, by securing for limited Times to Authors and Inventors the exclusive Right to their respective Writings and Discoveries;

To constitute Tribunals inferior to the Supreme Court;

To define and punish Piracies and Felonies committed on the high Seas, and Offenses against the Law of Nations;

To declare War, grant Letters of Marque and Reprisal, and make Rules concerning Captures on Land and Water;

To raise and support Armies, but no Appropriation of Money to that Use shall be for a longer Term than two Years;

To provide and maintain a Navy;

To make Rules for the Government and Regulation of the land and naval forces;

To provide for calling forth the Militia to execute the Laws of the Union, suppress Insurrections and repel Invasions;

To provide for organizing, arming, and disciplining the Militia, and for governing such Part of them as may be employed in the Service of the United States, reserving to the States respectively, the Appointment of the Officers, and the Authority of training the Militia according to the discipline prescribed by Congress;

To exercise exclusive Legislation in all Cases whatsoever, over such District (not exceeding ten Miles square) as may, by Cession of particular States, and the acceptance of Congress, become the Seat of the Government of the United States, and to exercise like Authority over all Places purchased by the Consent of the Legislature of the State in which the Same shall be, for the Erection of Forts, Magazines, Arsenals, dock-Yards, and other needful Buildings;—And

To make all Laws which shall be necessary and proper for carrying into Execution the foregoing Powers, and all other Powers vested by this Constitution in the Government of the United States, or in any Department or Officer thereof.

SECTION 9. The Migration or Importation of such Persons as any of the States now existing shall think proper to admit, shall not be prohibited by the Congress prior to the Year one thousand eight hundred and eight, but a tax or duty may be imposed on such Importation, not exceeding ten dollars for each Person.

The privilege of the Writ of Habeas Corpus shall not be suspended, unless when in Cases of Rebellion or Invasion the public Safety may require it.

No Bill of Attainder or ex post facto Law shall be passed.

No capitation, or other direct, Tax shall be laid unless in Proportion to the Census or Enumeration herein before directed to be taken.

No Tax or Duty shall be laid on Articles exported from any State.

No Preference shall be given by any Regulation of Commerce or Revenue to the Ports of one State over those of another: nor shall Vessels bound to, or from, one State, be obliged to enter, clear, or pay Duties in another.

No Money shall be drawn from the Treasury, but in Consequence of Appropriations made by Law; and a regular Statement and Account of the Receipts and Expenditures of all public Money shall be published from time to time.

No Title of Nobility shall be granted by the United States: And no Person holding any Office of Profit or Trust under them, shall, without the Consent of the Congress, accept of any present, Emolument, Office, or Title, of any kind whatever, from any King, Prince, or foreign State.

SECTION 10. No State shall enter into any Treaty, Alliance, or Confederation; grant Letters of Marque and Reprisal; coin Money; emit Bills of Credit; make any Thing but gold and silver Coin a Tender in Payment of Debts; pass any Bill of Attainder, ex post facto Law, or Law impairing the Obligation of Contracts, or grant any Title of Nobility.

No State shall, without the Consent of the Congress, lay any Imposts or Duties on Imports or Exports, except what may be absolutely necessary for executing its inspection Laws: and the net Produce of all Duties and Imposts, laid by any State on Imports or Exports, shall be for the Use of the Treasury of the United States; and all such Laws shall be subject to the Revision and Control of the Congress.

No State shall, without the Consent of Congress, lay any duty of Tonnage, keep Troops, or Ships of War in time of Peace, enter into any Agreement or Compact with another State, or with a foreign Power, or engage in War, unless actually invaded, or in such imminent Danger as will not admit of delay.

ARTICLE II.

SECTION 1. The executive Power shall be vested in a President of the United States of America. He shall hold his Office during the Term of four years, and, together with the Vice-President, chosen for the same Term, be elected, as follows:

Each State shall appoint, in such Manner as the Legislature thereof may direct, a Number of Electors, equal to the whole Number of Senators and Representatives to which the State may be entitled in the Congress: but no Senator or Representative, or Person holding an Office of Trust or Profit under the United States, shall be appointed an Elector.

[The Electors shall meet in their respective States, and vote by Ballot for two persons, of whom one at least shall not be an Inhabitant of the same State with themselves. And they shall make a List of all the Persons voted for, and of the Number of Votes for each; which List they shall sign and certify, and transmit sealed to the Seat of the Government of the United States, directed to the President of the Senate. The President of the Senate shall, in the Presence of the Senate and House of Representatives, open all the Certificates, and the Votes shall then be counted. The Person having the greatest Number of Votes shall be the President, if such Number be a Majority of the whole Number of Electors appointed; and if there be more than one who have such Majority, and have an equal Number of Votes, then the House of Representatives shall immediately chuse by Ballot one of them for President; and if no Person have a Majority, then from the five highest on the List the said House shall in like Manner chuse the President. But in chusing the President, the Votes shall be taken by States, the Representation from each State having one Vote; a quorum for this Purpose shall consist of a Member or Members from two-thirds of the States, and a Majority of all the States shall be necessary to a Choice. In every Case, after the Choice of the President, the Person having the greatest Number of Votes of the Electors shall be the Vice President. But if there should remain two or more who have equal votes, the Senate shall chuse from them by Ballot the Vice-President.] *

The Congress may determine the Time of chusing the Electors, and the Day on which they shall give their Votes; which Day shall be the same throughout the United States.

No person except a natural-born Citizen, or a Citizen of the United States, at the time of the Adoption of this Constitution, shall be eligible to the Office of President; neither shall any Person be eligible to that Office who shall not have attained to the Age of thirty-five years, and been fourteen Years a Resident within the United States.

In Case of the Removal of the President from Office, or of his Death, Resignation, or Inability to discharge the Powers and Duties of the said Office, the same shall devolve on the Vice President, and the Congress may by Law provide for the Case of Removal, Death, Resignation, or Inability, both of the President and Vice President, declaring what Officer shall then act as President, and such Officer shall act accordingly, until the disability be removed, or a President shall be elected.

The President shall, at stated Times, receive for his Services a Compensation, which shall neither be increased nor diminished during the Period for which he shall have been elected, and he shall not receive within that Period any other Emolument from the United States, or any of them.

Before he enter on the execution of his Office, he shall take the following Oath or Affirmation:—"I do solemnly swear (or affirm) that I will faithfully execute the Office of President of the United States, and will, to the best of my Ability, preserve, protect, and defend the Constitution of the United States."

SECTION 2. The President shall be Commander in Chief of the Army and Navy of the United States, and of the Militia of the several States, when called

* Superseded by 12th Amendment.

into the actual Service of the United States; he may require the Opinion, in writing, of the principal Officer in each of the executive Departments, upon any subject relating to the Duties of their respective Offices, and he shall have Power to Grant Reprieves and Pardons for Offenses against the United States, except in Cases of Impeachment.

He shall have Power, by and with the Advice and Consent of the Senate, to make Treaties, provided two thirds of the Senators present concur; and he shall nominate, and by and with the Advice and Consent of the Senate, shall appoint Ambassadors, other public Ministers and Consuls, Judges of the supreme Court, and all other Officers of the United States, whose Appointments are not herein otherwise provided for, and which shall be established by Law: but the Congress may by Law vest the Appointment of such inferior Officers, as they think proper, in the President alone, in the Courts of Law, or in the Heads of Departments.

The President shall have Power to fill up all Vacancies that may happen during the Recess of the Senate, by granting Commissions which shall expire at the End of their next Session.

SECTION 3. He shall from time to time give to the Congress Information of the State of the Union, and recommend to their Consideration such Measures as he shall judge necessary and expedient; he may, on extraordinary occasions, convene both Houses, or either of them, and in Case of Disagreement between them, with respect to the Time of Adjournment, he may adjourn them to such Time as he shall think proper; he shall receive Ambassadors and other public Ministers; he shall take Care that the Laws be faithfully executed, and shall Commission all the Officers of the United States.

SECTION 4. The President, Vice President and all civil Officers of the United States, shall be removed from Office on Impeachment for, and Conviction of, Treason, Bribery, or other high Crimes and Misdemeanors.

ARTICLE III.

SECTION 1. The judicial Power of the United States, shall be vested in one supreme Court, and in such inferior Courts as the Congress may from time to time ordain and establish. The Judges, both of the supreme and inferior Courts, shall hold their Offices during good Behaviour, and shall, at stated Times, receive for their Services, a Compensation, which shall not be diminished during their Continuance in Office.

SECTION 2. The judicial Power shall extend to all Cases, in Law and Equity, arising under this Constitution, the Laws of the United States, and Treaties made, or which shall be made, under their Authority;—to all Cases affecting ambassadors, other public ministers and consuls;—to all cases of admiralty and maritime Jurisdiction;—to Controversies to which the United States shall be a Party;—to Controversies between two or more States;—between a State and Citizens of another State; *—between Citizens of different States,—between Citizens of the same State claiming Lands under Grants of different States, and between a State, or the Citizens thereof, and foreign States, Citizens or Subjects.

In all Cases affecting Ambassadors, other public Ministers and Consuls, and

* Restricted by the 11th Amendment.

those in which a State shall be Party, the supreme Court shall have original Jurisdiction. In all the other Cases before mentioned, the supreme Court shall have appellate Jurisdiction, both as to Law and Fact, with such Exceptions, and under such Regulations as the Congress shall make.

The trial of all Crimes, except in Cases of Impeachment, shall be by Jury; and such Trial shall be held in the State where the said Crimes shall have been committed; but when not committed within any State, the Trial shall be at such Place or Places as the Congress may by Law have directed.

SECTION 3. Treason against the United States, shall consist only in levying War against them, or in adhering to their Enemies, giving them Aid and Comfort. No Person shall be convicted of Treason unless on the Testimony of two Witnesses to the same overt Act, or on Confession in open Court.

The Congress shall have power to declare the Punishment of Treason, but no Attainder of Treason shall work Corruption of Blood, or Forfeiture except during the Life of the Person attainted.

ARTICLE IV.

SECTION 1. Full Faith and Credit shall be given in each State to the public Acts, Records, and judicial Proceedings of every other State. And the Congress may by general Laws prescribe the Manner in which such Acts, Records and Proceedings shall be proved, and the Effect thereof.

SECTION 2. The Citizens of each State shall be entitled to all Privileges and Immunities of Citizens in the several States.

A Person charged in any State with Treason, Felony, or other Crime, who shall flee from Justice, and be found in another State, shall on demand of the executive Authority of the State from which he fled, be delivered up, to be removed to the State having Jurisdiction of the crime.

No Person held to Service or Labour in one State, under the Laws thereof, escaping into another, shall, in Consequence of any Law or Regulation therein, be discharged from such Service or Labour, but shall be delivered up on Claim of the Party to whom such Service or Labour may be due.

SECTION 3. New States may be admitted by the Congress into this Union; but no new State shall be formed or erected within the Jurisdiction of any other State; nor any State be formed by the Junction of two or more States, or parts of States, without the Consent of the Legislatures of the States concerned as well as of the Congress.

The Congress shall have Power to dispose of and make all needful Rules and Regulations respecting the Territory or other Property belonging to the United States; and nothing in this Constitution shall be so construed as to Prejudice any Claims of the United States, or of any particular State.

SECTION 4. The United States shall guarantee to every State in this Union a Republican Form of Government, and shall protect each of them against Invasion; and on Application of the Legislature, or of the Executive (when the Legislature cannot be convened) against domestic Violence.

ARTICLE V.

The Congress, whenever two-thirds of both Houses shall deem it necessary, shall propose Amendments to this Constitution, or, on the Application of the

Legislatures of two-thirds of the several States, shall call a Convention for proposing Amendments, which, in either Case, shall be valid to all Intents and Purposes, as part of this Constitution, when ratified by the Legislatures of three-fourths of the several States, or by Conventions in three-fourths thereof, as the one or the other Mode of Ratification may be proposed by the Congress; Provided that no Amendment which may be made prior to the Year One thousand eight hundred and eight shall in any Manner affect the first and fourth Clauses in the Ninth Section of the first Article; and that no State, without its Consent, shall be deprived of its equal Suffrage in the Senate.

ARTICLE VI.

All Debts contracted and Engagements entered into, before the Adoption of this Constitution, shall be as valid against the United States under this Constitution, as under the Confederation.

This Constitution, and the Laws of the United States which shall be made in Pursuance thereof; and all Treaties made, or which shall be made, under the Authority of the United States, shall be the supreme Law of the Land; and the Judges in every State shall be bound thereby, any Thing in the Constitution or Laws of any State to the Contrary notwithstanding.

The Senators and Representatives before mentioned, and the Members of the several State Legislatures, and all executive and judicial Officers, both of the United States and of the several States, shall be bound by Oath or Affirmation to support this Constitution; but no religious Test shall ever be required as a qualification to any Office or public Trust under the United States.

ARTICLE VII.

The Ratification of the Conventions of nine States shall be sufficient for the Establishment of this Constitution between the States so ratifying the same.

Done in Convention by the Unanimous Consent of the States present the Seventeenth Day of September in the Year of our Lord one thousand seven hundred and Eighty seven, and of the Independence of the United States of America the Twelfth. In Witness whereof We have hereunto subscribed our Names.*

GEORGE WASHINGTON
President and deputy from Virginia

NEW HAMPSHIRE
John Langdon
Nicholas Gilman

MASSACHUSETTS
Nathaniel Gorham
Rufus King

CONNECTICUT
William Samuel Johnson
Roger Sherman

NEW YORK
Alexander Hamilton

NEW JERSEY
William Livingston
David Brearley
William Paterson
Jonathan Dayton

* The full names of the signers follow, not the signatures as they appear on the document.

PENNSYLVANIA
Benjamin Franklin
Thomas Mifflin
Robert Morris
George Clymer
Thomas FitzSimons
Jared Ingersoll
James Wilson
Gouverneur Morris

DELAWARE
George Read
Gunning Bedford, Jr.
John Dickinson
Richard Bassett
Jacob Broom

MARYLAND
James McHenry
Daniel of St. Thomas Jenifer
Daniel Carroll

VIRGINIA
John Blair
James Madison, Jr.

NORTH CAROLINA
William Blount
Richard Dobbs Spaight
Hugh Williamson

SOUTH CAROLINA
John Rutledge
Charles Cotesworth Pinckney
Charles Pinckney
Pierce Butler

GEORGIA
William Few
Abraham Baldwin

ARTICLES IN ADDITION TO, AND AMENDMENT OF, THE CONSTITUTION OF THE UNITED STATES OF AMERICA, PROPOSED BY CONGRESS, AND RATIFIED BY THE LEGISLATURES OF THE SEVERAL STATES, PURSUANT TO THE FIFTH ARTICLE OF THE ORIGINAL CONSTITUTION *

[ARTICLE I.] †

Congress shall make no law respecting an establishment of religion, or prohibiting the free exercise thereof; or abridging the freedom of speech, or of the press; or the right of the people peaceably to assemble, and to petition the Government for a redress of grievances.

[ARTICLE II.]

A well regulated Militia, being necessary to the security of a free State, the right of the people to keep and bear Arms shall not be infringed.

[ARTICLE III.]

No Soldier shall, in time of peace, be quartered in any house, without the consent of the Owner, nor in time of war, but in a manner to be prescribed by law.

[ARTICLE IV.]

The right of the people to be secure in their persons, houses, papers, and effects, against unreasonable searches and seizures, shall not be violated, and

* This heading appears only in the joint resolution submitting the first ten amendments.

† In the original manuscripts the first twelve amendments have no numbers.

no Warrants shall issue, but upon probable cause, supported by Oath or affirmation, and particularly describing the place to be searched, and the persons or things to be seized.

[ARTICLE V.]

No person shall be held to answer for a capital or otherwise infamous crime, unless on a presentment or indictment of a Grand Jury, except in cases arising in the land or naval forces, or in the Militia, when in actual service in time of War or public danger; nor shall any person be subject for the same offence to be twice put in jeopardy of life or limb; nor shall be compelled in any criminal case to be a witness against himself, nor be deprived of life, liberty, or property, without due process of law; nor shall private property be taken for public use, without just compensation.

[ARTICLE VI.]

In all criminal prosecutions, the accused shall enjoy the right to a speedy and public trial, by an impartial jury of the State and district wherein the crime shall have been committed, which district shall have been previously ascertained by law, and to be informed of the nature and cause of the accusation; to be confronted with the witnesses against him; to have compulsory process for obtaining witnesses in his favor, and to have the Assistance of Counsel for his defence.

[ARTICLE VII.]

In suits at common law, where the value in controversy shall exceed twenty dollars, the right of trial by jury shall be preserved, and no fact tried by a jury, shall be otherwise reexamined in any Court of the United States, than according to the rules of the common law.

[ARTICLE VIII.]

Excessive bail shall not be required, nor excessive fines imposed, nor cruel and unusual punishments inflicted.

[ARTICLE IX.]

The enumeration in the Constitution, of certain rights, shall not be construed to deny or disparage others retained by the people.

[ARTICLE X.]

The powers not delegated to the United States by the Constitution, nor prohibited by it to the States, are reserved to the States respectively, or to the people.

[Amendments I–X, in force 1791.]

[ARTICLE XI.] *

The Judicial power of the United States shall not be construed to extend to any suit in law or equity, commenced or prosecuted against one of the

* Adopted in 1798.

United States by Citizens of another State, or by Citizens or Subjects of any Foreign State.

[ARTICLE XII.] *

The Electors shall meet in their respective States and vote by ballot for President and Vice-President, one of whom, at least, shall not be an inhabitant of the same State with themselves; they shall name in their ballots the person voted for as President, and in distinct ballots the person voted for as Vice-President, and they shall make distinct lists of all persons voted for as President, and of all persons voted for as Vice-President, and of the number of votes for each, which lists they shall sign and certify, and transmit sealed to the seat of the government of the United States, directed to the President of the Senate;—The President of the Senate shall, in the presence of the Senate and House of Representatives, open all the certificates and the votes shall then be counted;—The person having the greatest number of votes for President, shall be the President, if such number be a majority of the whole number of Electors appointed; and if no person have such majority, then from the persons having the highest numbers not exceeding three on the list of those voted for as President, the House of Representatives shall choose immediately, by ballot, the President. But in choosing the President, the votes shall be taken by states, the representation from each state having one vote; a quorum for this purpose shall consist of a member or members from two-thirds of the states, and a majority of all the states shall be necessary to a choice. And if the House of Representatives shall not choose a President whenever the right of choice shall devolve upon them, before the fourth day of March next following, then the Vice-President shall act as President, as in the case of the death or other constitutional disability of the President.—The person having the greatest number of votes as Vice-President, shall be the Vice-President, if such number be a majority of the whole number of Electors appointed, and if no person have a majority, then from the two highest numbers on the list, the Senate shall choose the Vice-President; a quorum for the purpose shall consist of two-thirds of the whole number of Senators, and a majority of the whole number shall be necessary to a choice. But no person constitutionally ineligible to the office of President shall be eligible to that of Vice-President of the United States.

ARTICLE XIII.†

SECTION 1. Neither slavery nor involuntary servitude, except as a punishment for crime whereof the party shall have been duly convicted, shall exist within the United States, or any place subject to their jurisdiction.

SECTION 2. Congress shall have power to enforce this article by appropriate legislation.

ARTICLE XIV.‡

SECTION 1. All persons born or naturalized in the United States, and subject to the jurisdiction thereof, are citizens of the United States and of the

* Adopted in 1804.
† Adopted in 1865.
‡ Adopted in 1868, proclaimed July 28, 1868.

State wherein they reside. No State shall make or enforce any law which shall abridge the privileges or immunities of citizens of the United States; nor shall any State deprive any person of life, liberty, or property, without due process of law; nor deny to any person within its jurisdiction the equal protection of the laws.

SECTION 2. Representatives shall be apportioned among the several States according to their respective numbers, counting the whole number of persons in each State, excluding Indians not taxed. But when the right to vote at any election for the choice of electors for President and Vice-President of the United States, Representatives in Congress, the Executive and Judicial officers of a State, or the members of the Legislature thereof, is denied to any of the male inhabitants of such State, being twenty-one years of age, and citizens of the United States, or in any way abridged, except for participation in rebellion, or other crime, the basis of representation therein shall be reduced in the proportion which the number of such male citizens shall bear to the whole number of male citizens twenty-one years of age in such State.

SECTION 3. No person shall be a Senator or Representative in Congress, or elector of President and Vice-President, or hold any office, civil or military, under the United States, or under any State, who, having previously taken an oath, as a member of Congress, or as an officer of the United States, or as a member of any State legislature, or as an executive or judicial officer of any State, to support the Constitution of the United States, shall have engaged in insurrection or rebellion against the same, or given aid or comfort to the enemies thereof. But Congress may by a vote of two-thirds of each House, remove such disability.

SECTION 4. The validity of the public debt of the United States, authorized by law, including debts incurred for payment of pensions and bounties for services in suppressing insurrection or rebellion, shall not be questioned. But neither the United States nor any State shall assume or pay any debt or obligation incurred in aid of insurrection or rebellion against the United States, or any claim for the loss or emancipation of any slave; but all such debts, obligations, and claims shall be held illegal and void.

SECTION 5. The Congress shall have the power to enforce, by appropriate legislation, the provisions of this article.

ARTICLE XV.*

SECTION 1. The right of citizens of the United States to vote shall not be denied or abridged by the United States or by any State on account of race, color, or previous condition of servitude—

SECTION 2. The Congress shall have power to enforce this article by appropriate legislation.

ARTICLE XVI.†

The Congress shall have power to lay and collect taxes on incomes, from whatever source derived, without apportionment among the several States, and without regard to any census or enumeration.

* Proclaimed March 30, 1870.

† Passed July, 1909; proclaimed February 25, 1913.

ARTICLE XVII.*

The Senate of the United States shall be composed of two Senators from each State, elected by the people thereof, for six years; and each Senator shall have one vote. The electors in each State shall have the qualifications requisite for electors of the most numerous branch of the State legislatures.

When vacancies happen in the representation of any State in the Senate, the executive authority of such State shall issue writs of election to fill such vacancies: *Provided*, That the legislature of any State may empower the executive thereof to make temporary appointments until the people fill the vacancies by election as the legislature may direct.

This amendment shall not be so construed as to affect the election or term of any Senator chosen before it becomes valid as part of the Constitution.

ARTICLE XVIII.†

SECTION 1. After one year from the ratification of this article the manufacture, sale, or transportation of intoxicating liquors within, the importation thereof into, or the exportation thereof from the United States and all territory subject to the jurisdiction thereof for beverage purposes is hereby prohibited.

SECTION 2. The Congress and the several States shall have concurrent power to enforce this article by appropriate legislation.

SECTION 3. This article shall be inoperative unless it shall have been ratified as an amendment to the Constitution by the legislatures of the several States, as provided in the Constitution, within seven years from the date of the submission hereof to the States by the Congress.

ARTICLE XIX.‡

The right of citizens of the United States to vote shall not be denied or abridged by the United States or by any State on account of sex.

Congress shall have power to enforce this article by appropriate legislation.

ARTICLE XX.§

SECTION 1. The terms of the President and Vice-President shall end at noon on the 20th day of January, and the terms of Senators and Representatives at noon on the 3d day of January, of the years in which such terms would have ended if this article had not been ratified; and the terms of their successors shall then begin.

SECTION 2. The Congress shall assemble at least once in every year, and such meeting shall begin at noon on the 3d day of January, unless they shall by law appoint a different day.

SECTION 3. If, at the time fixed for the beginning of the term of the President, the President elect shall have died, the Vice-President elect shall become President. If a President shall not have been chosen before the time fixed for

* Passed May, 1912, in lieu of Article I, Section 3, clause I, of the Constitution and so much of clause 2 of the same Section as relates to the filling of vacancies; proclaimed May 31, 1913.

† Passed December 3, 1917; proclaimed January 29, 1919. Repealed by the 21st Amendment.

‡ Adopted in 1920.

§ Adopted in 1933.

the beginning of his term, or if the President elect shall have failed to qualify, then the Vice-President elect shall act as President until a President shall have qualified; and the Congress may by law provide for the case wherein neither a President elect nor a Vice-President elect shall have qualified, declaring who shall then act as President, or the manner in which one who is to act shall be selected, and such person shall act accordingly until a President or Vice-President shall have qualified.

SECTION 4. The Congress may by law provide for the case of the death of any of the persons from whom the House of Representatives may choose a President whenever the right of choice shall have devolved upon them, and for the case of the death of any of the persons from whom the Senate may choose a Vice-President whenever the right of choice shall have devolved upon them.

SECTION 5. Sections 1 and 2 shall take effect on the 15th day of October following the ratification of this article.

SECTION 6. This article shall be inoperative unless it shall have been ratified as an amendment to the Constitution by the legislatures of three-fourths of the several States within seven years from the date of its submission.

ARTICLE XXI.*

SECTION 1. The eighteenth article of amendment to the Constitution of the United States is hereby repealed.

SECTION 2. The transportation or importation into any State, Territory, or possession of the United States for delivery or use therein of intoxicating liquors, in violation of the laws thereof, is hereby prohibited.

SECTION 3. This article shall be inoperative unless it shall have been ratified as an amendment to the Constitution by conventions in the several States, as provided in the Constitution, within seven years from the date of the submission hereof to the States by the Congress.

ARTICLE XXII.†

No person shall be elected to the office of the President more than twice, and no person who has held the office of President, or acted as President, for more than two years of a term to which some other person was elected President shall be elected to the office of the President more than once.

But this Article shall not apply to any person holding the office of President when this Article was proposed by the Congress, and shall not prevent any person who may be holding the office of President, or acting as President, during the term within which this Article becomes operative from holding the office of President or acting as President during the remainder of such term.

* Adopted in 1933.
† Adopted in 1951.

II

ADMISSION OF STATES TO THE UNION

STATE	ENTERED UNION	STATE	ENTERED UNION
Alabama	1819	Nebraska	1867
Arizona	1912	Nevada	1864
Arkansas	1836	New Hampshire	1788
California	1850	New Jersey	1787
Colorado	1876	New Mexico	1912
Connecticut	1788	New York	1788
Delaware	1787	North Carolina	1789
Florida	1845	North Dakota	1889
Georgia	1788	Ohio	1803
Idaho	1890	Oklahoma	1907
Illinois	1818	Oregon	1859
Indiana	1816	Pennsylvania	1787
Iowa	1846	Rhode Island	1790
Kansas	1861	South Carolina	1788
Kentucky	1792	South Dakota	1889
Louisiana	1812	Tennessee	1796
Maine	1820	Texas	1845
Maryland	1788	Utah	1896
Massachusetts	1788	Vermont	1791
Michigan	1837	Virginia	1788
Minnesota	1858	Washington	1889
Mississippi	1817	West Virginia	1863
Missouri	1821	Wisconsin	1848
Montana	1889	Wyoming	1890

III

PRESIDENTIAL ELECTIONS, 1864–1948

YEAR	NUMBER OF STATES	PRESIDENTIAL CANDIDATE	POLITICAL PARTY	VOTE CAST ELECTORAL	VOTE CAST POPULAR
1864	36	ABRAHAM LINCOLN	Republican	212	2,213,665
		GEORGE B. MCCLELLAN	Democratic	21	1,805,237
		(Not voted)		81	
1868	37	ULYSSES S. GRANT	Republican	214	3,012,833
		HORATIO SEYMOUR	Democratic	80	2,703,249
		(Not voted)		23	
1872	37	ULYSSES S. GRANT	Republican	286	3,597,132
		HORACE GREELEY *(died before Electoral College met)*	Democratic; Liberal Republican.	80	2,834,125
		CHARLES O'CONOR	Straight Democratic.		29,489
		JAMES BLACK	Temperance		5,608
1876	38	RUTHERFORD B. HAYES	Republican	185	4,036,298
		SAMUEL J. TILDEN	Democratic	184	4,300,590
		PETER COOPER	Greenback		81,737
		GREEN CLAY SMITH	Prohibition		9,522
		JAMES B. WALKER	American		2,636
1880	38	JAMES A. GARFIELD	Republican	214	4,454,416
		WINFIELD S. HANCOCK	Democratic	155	4,444,952
		JAMES B. WEAVER	Greenback-Labor.		308,578
		NEAL DOW	Prohibition		10,305
		JOHN W. PHELPS	American		700
1884	38	GROVER CLEVELAND	Democratic	219	4,874,986
		JAMES G. BLAINE	Republican	182	4,851,981
		JOHN P. ST. JOHN	Prohibition		150,369
		BENJAMIN F. BUTLER	Greenback-Labor.		175,370
1888	38	BENJAMIN HARRISON	Republican	233	5,439,853
		GROVER CLEVELAND	Democratic	168	5,540,309
		CLINTON B. FISK	Prohibition		249,506
		ANSON J. STREETER	Union Labor		146,935
		ROBERT H. COWDREY	United Labor		2,818
		JAMES LANGDON CURTIS	American		1,600
1892	44	GROVER CLEVELAND	Democratic	277	5,556,918
		BENJAMIN HARRISON	Republican	145	5,176,108
		JAMES B. WEAVER	People's	22	1,041,028

YEAR	NUMBER OF STATES	PRESIDENTIAL CANDIDATE	POLITICAL PARTY	VOTE CAST ELECTORAL	VOTE CAST POPULAR
		JOHN BIDWELL	Prohibition		264,133
		SIMON WING	Socialist-Labor		21,164
1896	45	WILLIAM MCKINLEY	Republican	271	7,104,779
		WILLIAM J. BRYAN	Democratic; People's.	176	6,502,925
		JOHN M. PALMER	Nationalist Democratic.		133,148
		JOSHUA LEVERING	Prohibition		132,007
		CHAS. H. MATCHETT	Socialist-Labor		36,274
		CHAS. E. BENTLEY	Nationalist		13,969
1900	45	WILLIAM MCKINLEY	Republican	292	7,207,923
		WILLIAM J. BRYAN	Democratic; Populist.	155	6,358,133
		JOHN C. WOOLLEY	Prohibition		208,914
		EUGENE V. DEBS	Socialist Democrat.		87,814
		WHARTON BARKER	People's		50,373
		JOS. F. MALLONEY	Socialist-Labor		39,739
		SETH H. ELLIS	Union Reform		5,698
		JONAH F. R. LEONARD	United Christian		5,500
1904	45	THEODORE ROOSEVELT	Republican	336	7,623,486
		ALTON B. PARKER	Democratic	140	5,077,911
		EUGENE V. DEBS	Socialist		402,283
		SILAS C. SWALLOW	Prohibition		258,536
		THOMAS E. WATSON	People's		117,183
		CHARLES H. CORREGAN	Socialist-Labor		31,249
		AUSTIN HOLCOMB	Continental		1,000
1908	46	WILLIAM H. TAFT	Republican	321	7,678,908
		WILLIAM J. BRYAN	Democratic	162	6,409,104
		EUGENE V. DEBS	Socialist		420,793
		EUGENE W. CHAFIN	Prohibition		253,840
		THOMAS L. HISGEN	Independence		82,872
		THOMAS E. WATSON	People's		29,100
		AUGUST GILLHAUS	Socialist-Labor		14,021
		DANIEL B. TURNEY	United Christian		500
1912	48	WOODROW WILSON	Democratic	435	6,293,454
		WILLIAM H. TAFT	Republican	8	3,484,980
		THEODORE ROOSEVELT	Progressive	88	4,119,538
		EUGENE V. DEBS	Socialist		900,672
		EUGENE W. CHAFIN	Prohibition		206,275
		ARTHUR E. REIMER	Socialist-Labor		28,750
1916	48	WOODROW WILSON	Democratic	277	9,129,606
		CHAS. E. HUGHES	Republican	254	8,538,221
		A. L. BENSON	Socialist		585,113
		J. FRANK HANLY	Prohibition		220,506
		ARTHUR E. REIMER	Socialist-Labor		13,403
		(Various candidates)	Progressive		41,894
1920	48	WARREN G. HARDING	Republican	404	16,152,200
		JAMES M. COX	Democratic	127	9,147,353
		EUGENE V. DEBS	Socialist		919,799
		P. P. CHRISTENSEN	Farmer-Labor		265,411
		AARON S. WATKINS	Prohibition		189,408
		W. W. COX	Socialist-Labor		31,715
		ROBERT C. MACAULEY	Single Tax		5,837
		JAMES E. FERGUSON	American		48,000

YEAR	NUMBER OF STATES	PRESIDENTIAL CANDIDATE	POLITICAL PARTY	VOTE CAST ELECTORAL	VOTE CAST POPULAR
1924	48	Calvin Coolidge	Republican	382	15,725,016
		John W. Davis	Democratic	136	8,386,503
		Robert LaFollette	Progressive	13	4,822,856
		Herman P. Faris	Prohibition		57,520
		Frank T. Johns	Socialist-Labor		36,428
		William Z. Foster	Workers		36,386
		Gilbert O. Nations	American		23,967
		William J. Wallace	Commonwealth Land.		1,532
1928	48	Herbert Hoover	Republican	444	21,391,381
		Alfred E. Smith	Democratic	87	15,016,443
		Norman Thomas	Socialist		267,835
		William Z. Foster	Workers		21,181
		Verne L. Reynolds	Socialist-Labor		21,603
		William F. Varney	Prohibition		20,106
		Frank E. Webb	Farmer-Labor		6,390
1932	48	Franklin D. Roosevelt.	Democratic	472	22,821,857
		Herbert Hoover	Republican	59	15,761,841
		Norman Thomas	Socialist		881,951
		William Z. Foster	Communist		102,785
		Verne L. Reynolds	Socialist-Labor		33,276
		William D. Upshaw	Prohibition		81,869
		William H. Harvey	Liberty		53,425
		Jacob S. Coxey, Sr.	Farmer-Labor		7,309
1936	48	Franklin D. Roosevelt.	Democratic; Amer. Labor.	523	27,751,597
		Alfred M. Landon	Republican	8	16,679,583
		William Lemke	Union, Royal Oak; Nat'l Union for Social Justice, 3d Party; Independent.		882,479
		Norman Thomas	Socialist		187,720
		Earl Browder	Communist		80,159
		D. Leigh Colvin	Prohibition; Com'nwealth		37,847
		John W. Aiken	Socialist-Labor; Indst'l Labor.		12,777
1940	48	Franklin D. Roosevelt.	Democratic; Amer. Labor.	449	27,244,160
		Wendell L. Willkie	Republican	82	22,305,198
		Norman Thomas	Socialist; Progressive.		99,557
		Roger Q. Babson	Prohibition; National Prohibition.		57,812
		Earl Browder	Communist		46,251
1944	48	Franklin D. Roosevelt.	Democratic; Amer. Labor; Liberal.	432	25,602,504
		Thomas E. Dewey	Republican	99	22,006,285
		Norman Thomas	Socialist		80,518
		Claude A. Watson	Prohibition		74,758

YEAR	NUMBER OF STATES	PRESIDENTIAL CANDIDATE	POLITICAL PARTY	VOTE CAST ELECTORAL	POPULAR
		Edward A. Teichert	Socialist-Labor; Industrial Government.		45,336
		(Unpledged)	Texas Regulars		135,439
1948	48	Harry S. Truman	Democratic; Liberal.	303	24,105,695
		Thomas E. Dewey	Republican	189	21,969,170
		J. Strom Thurmond	States' Rights Democrat.	39	1,169,021
		Henry A. Wallace	Progressive; American Labor.		1,156,103
		Norman Thomas	Socialist		139,009
		Claude A. Watson	Prohibition		103,216
		Edward A. Teichert	Socialist-Labor; Industrial Government.		29,061
		Farrel Dobbs	Socialist Workers; Militant Workers.		13,613

IV

PRESIDENTS AND CABINETS 1865–1950

ANDREW JOHNSON 1865–9	
Secretary of State	WILLIAM H. SEWARD, 1865–9
Secretary of Treasury	HUGH McCULLOCH, 1865–9
Secretary of War	EDWIN M. STANTON, 1865–7
	ULYSSES S. GRANT, 1867–8
	LORENZO THOMAS, 1868
	JOHN M. SCHOFIELD, 1868–9
Secretary of Navy	GIDEON WELLES, 1865–9
Secretary of Interior	JOHN P. USHER, 1865
	JAMES HARLAN, 1865–6
	ORVILLE H. BROWNING, 1866–9
Postmaster General	WILLIAM DENNISON, 1865–6
	ALEXANDER RANDALL, 1866–9
Attorney General	JAMES SPEED, 1865–6
	HENRY STANBERY, 1866–8
	WILLIAM M. EVARTS, 1868–9
ULYSSES S. GRANT 1869–77	
SCHUYLER COLFAX 1869–73	
HENRY WILSON 1873–7	
Secretary of State	ELIHU B. WASHBURNE, 1869
	HAMILTON FISH, 1869–77
Secretary of Treasury	GEORGE S. BOUTWELL, 1869–73
	WILLIAM A. RICHARDSON, 1873–4
	BENJAMIN H. BRISTOW, 1874–6
	LOT M. MORRILL, 1876–7
Secretary of War	JOHN A. RAWLINS, 1869
	WILLIAM T. SHERMAN, 1869
	WILLIAM W. BELKNAP, 1869–76
	ALPHONSO TAFT, 1876
	JAMES D. CAMERON, 1876–7
Secretary of Navy	ADOLPH E. BORIE, 1869
	GEORGE M. ROBESON, 1869–77

Secretary of Interior	JACOB D. COX, 1869–70
	COLUMBUS DELANO, 1870–5
	ZACHARY CHANDLER, 1875–7
Postmaster General	JOHN A. J. CRESWELL, 1869–74
	JAMES W. MARSHALL, 1874
	MARSHALL JEWELL, 1874–6
	JAMES N. TYNER, 1876–7
Attorney General	EBENEZER R. HOAR, 1869–70
	AMOS T. AKERMAN, 1870–1
	GEORGE H. WILLIAMS, 1871–5
	EDWARD PIERREPONT, 1875–6
	ALPHONSO TAFT, 1876–7

RUTHERFORD B. HAYES 1877–81
WILLIAM A. WHEELER

Secretary of State	WILLIAM M. EVARTS, 1877–81
Secretary of Treasury	JOHN SHERMAN, 1877–81
Secretary of War	GEORGE W. MCCRARY, 1877–9
	ALEXANDER RAMSEY, 1879–81
Secretary of Navy	RICHARD W. THOMPSON, 1877–81
	NATHAN GOFF, JR., 1881
Secretary of Interior	CARL SCHURZ, 1877–81
Postmaster General	DAVID M. KEY, 1877–80
	HORACE MAYNARD, 1880–1
Attorney General	CHARLES DEVENS, 1877–81

JAMES A. GARFIELD 1881
CHESTER A. ARTHUR

Secretary of State	JAMES G. BLAINE, 1881
Secretary of Treasury	WILLIAM WINDOM, 1881
Secretary of War	ROBERT T. LINCOLN, 1881
Secretary of Navy	WILLIAM H. HUNT, 1881
Secretary of Interior	SAMUEL J. KIRKWOOD, 1881
Postmaster General	THOMAS L. JAMES, 1881
Attorney General	WAYNE MACVEAGH, 1881

CHESTER A. ARTHUR 1881–5

Secretary of State	FREDERICK T. FRELINGHUYSEN, 1881–5
Secretary of Treasury	CHARLES J. FOLGER, 1881–4
	WALTER Q. GRESHAM, 1884
	HUGH MCCULLOCH, 1884–5
Secretary of War	ROBERT T. LINCOLN, 1881–5
Secretary of Navy	WILLIAM E. CHANDLER, 1881–5
Secretary of Interior	HENRY M. TELLER, 1881–5
Postmaster General	TIMOTHY O. HOWE, 1881–3
	WALTER Q. GRESHAM, 1883–4
	FRANK HATTON, 1884–5

Attorney General	BENJAMIN H. BREWSTER, 1881–5
GROVER CLEVELAND 1885–9	
T. A. HENDRICKS	
Secretary of State	THOMAS F. BAYARD, 1885–9
Secretary of Treasury	DANIEL MANNING, 1885–7
	CHARLES S. FAIRCHILD, 1887–9
Secretary of War	WILLIAM C. ENDICOTT, 1885–9
Secretary of Navy	WILLIAM C. WHITNEY, 1885–9
Secretary of Interior	LUCIUS Q. C. LAMAR, 1885–8
	WILLIAM F. VILAS, 1888–9
Secretary of Agriculture	NORMAN J. COLMAN, 1889
Postmaster General	WILLIAM F. VILAR, 1885–8
	DON M. DICKINSON, 1888–9
Attorney General	AUGUSTUS H. GARLAND, 1885–9
BENJAMIN HARRISON 1889–93	
LEVI P. MORTON	
Secretary of State	JAMES G. BLAINE, 1889–92
	JOHN W. FOSTER, 1892–3
Secretary of Treasury	WILLIAM WINDOM, 1889–91
	CHARLES FOSTER, 1891–3
Secretary of War	REDFIELD PROCTER, 1889–91
	STEPHEN B. ELKINS, 1881–3
Secretary of Navy	BENJAMIN F. TRACY, 1889–93
Secretary of Interior	JOHN W. NOBLE, 1889–93
Secretary of Agriculture	JEREMIAH M. RUSK, 1889–93
Postmaster General	JOHN WANAMAKER, 1889–93
Attorney General	WILLIAM H. H. MILLER, 1889–93
GROVER CLEVELAND 1893–7	
ADLAI E. STEVENSON	
Secretary of State	WALTER Q. GRESHAM, 1893–5
	RICHARD OLNEY, 1895–7
Secretary of Treasury	JOHN G. CARLISLE, 1893–7
Secretary of War	DANIEL S. LAMONT, 1893–7
Secretary of Navy	HILARY A. HERBERT, 1893–7
Secretary of Interior	HOKE SMITH, 1893–6
	DAVID R. FRANCIS, 1896–7
Secretary of Agriculture	J. STERLING MORTON, 1893–7
Postmaster General	WILSON S. BISSEL, 1893–5
	WILLIAM L. WILSON, 1895–7
Attorney General	RICHARD OLNEY, 1893–5
	JUDSON HARMON, 1895–7
WILLIAM MCKINLEY 1897–1901	
GARRET A. HOBART 1897–1901	
THEODORE ROOSEVELT 1901	

Secretary of State — JOHN SHERMAN, 1897–8
WILLIAM R. DAY, 1898
JOHN HAY, 1898–1901
Secretary of Treasury — LYMAN J. GAGE, 1897–1901
Secretary of War — RUSSELL A. ALGER, 1897–9
ELIHU ROOT, 1899–1901
Secretary of Navy — JOHN D. LONG, 1897–1901
Secretary of Interior — CORNELIUS N. BLISS, 1897–9
ETHAN A. HITCHCOCK, 1899–1901
Secretary of Agriculture — JAMES WILSON, 1897–1901
Postmaster General — JAMES A. GARY, 1897–8
CHARLES E. SMITH, 1898–1901
Attorney General — JOSEPH MCKENNA, 1897
JOHN W. GRIGGS, 1897–1901
PHILANDER C. KNOX, 1901

THEODORE ROOSEVELT 1901–09
CHARLES FAIRBANKS 1905–09

Secretary of State — JOHN HAY, 1901–05
ELIHU ROOT, 1905–09
ROBERT BACON, 1909
Secretary of Treasury — LYMAN J. GAGE, 1901–02
LESLIE M. SHAW, 1902–07
GEORGE B. CORTELYOU, 1907–09
Secretary of War — ELIHU ROOT, 1901–04
WILLIAM H. TAFT, 1904–08
LUKE E. WRIGHT, 1908–09
Secretary of Navy — JOHN D. LONG, 1901–02
WILLIAM H. MOODY, 1902–04
PAUL MORTON, 1904–05
CHARLES J. BONAPARTE, 1905–07
VICTOR H. METCALF, 1907–08
TRUMAN H. NEWBERRY, 1908–09
Secretary of Interior — ETHAN A. HITCHCOCK, 1901–07
JAMES R. GARFIELD, 1907–09
Secretary of Agriculture — JAMES WILSON, 1901–09
Secretary of Commerce and Labor — GEORGE B. CORTELYOU, 1903–04
VICTOR H. METCALF, 1904–06
OSCAR S. STRAUS, 1907–09
Postmaster General — CHARLES E. SMITH, 1901–02
HENRY C. PAYNE, 1902–04
ROBERT J. WYNNE, 1904–05
GEORGE B. CORTELYOU, 1905–07
GEORGE VON L. MEYER, 1907–09
Attorney General — PHILANDER C. KNOX, 1901–04
WILLIAM H. MOODY, 1904–06
CHARLES J. BONAPARTE, 1906–09

WILLIAM H. TAFT 1909–13
JAMES S. SHERMAN

Secretary of State	PHILANDER C. KNOX, 1909–13
Secretary of Treasury	FRANKLIN MACVEAGH, 1909–13
Secretary of War	JACOB M. DICKINSON, 1909–11
	HENRY L. STIMSON, 1911–13
Secretary of Navy	GEORGE VON L. MEYER, 1909–13
Secretary of Interior	RICHARD A. BALLINGER, 1909–11
	WALTER L. FISHER, 1911–13
Secretary of Agriculture	JAMES WILSON, 1909–13
Secretary of Commerce and Labor	CHARLES NAGEL, 1909–13
Postmaster General	FRANK H. HITCHCOCK, 1909–13
Attorney General	GEORGE W. WICKERSHAM, 1909–13

WOODROW WILSON 1913–21
THOMAS R. MARSHALL

Secretary of State	WILLIAM J. BRYAN, 1913–15
	ROBERT LANSING, 1915–20
	BAINBRIDGE COLBY, 1920–1
Secretary of Treasury	WILLIAM G. MCADOO, 1913–19
	CARTER GLASS, 1919–20
	DAVID F. HOUSTON, 1920–1
Secretary of War	LINDLEY M. GARRISON, 1913–16
	NEWTON D. BAKER, 1916–21
Secretary of Navy	JOSEPHUS DANIELS, 1913–21
Secretary of Interior	FRANKLIN K. LANE, 1913–20
	JOHN B. PAYNE, 1920–1
Secretary of Agriculture	DAVID F. HOUSTON, 1913–20
	EDWARD T. MEREDITH, 1920–1
Secretary of Commerce	WILLIAM C. REDFIELD, 1913–19
	JOSHUA W. ALEXANDER, 1919–21
Secretary of Labor	WILLIAM B. WILSON, 1913–21
Postmaster General	ALBERT S. BURLESON, 1913–21
Attorney General	JAMES C. MCREYNOLDS, 1913–14
	THOMAS W. GREGORY, 1914–19
	A. MITCHELL PALMER, 1919–21

WARREN G. HARDING 1921–3
CALVIN COOLIDGE

Secretary of State	CHARLES E. HUGHES, 1921–3
Secretary of Treasury	ANDREW W. MELLON, 1921–3
Secretary of War	JOHN W. WEEKS, 1921–3
Secretary of Navy	EDWIN DENBY, 1921–3
Secretary of Interior	ALBERT B. FALL, 1921–3
	HUBERT WORK, 1923

Secretary of Agriculture	Henry C. Wallace, 1921–3
Secretary of Commerce	Herbert C. Hoover, 1921–3
Secretary of Labor	James J. Davis, 1921–3
Postmaster General	Will H. Hays, 1921–2
	Hubert Work, 1922–3
	Harry S. New, 1923
Attorney General	Harry M. Daugherty, 1921–3

Calvin Coolidge 1923–9
Charles G. Dawes 1925–9

Secretary of State	Charles E. Hughes, 1923–5
	Frank B. Kellogg, 1925–9
Secretary of Treasury	Andrew W. Mellon, 1923–9
Secretary of War	John W. Weeks, 1923–5
	Dwight F. Davis, 1925–9
Secretary of Navy	Edwin Denby, 1923–4
	Curtis D. Wilbur, 1924–9
Secretary of Interior	Hubert Work, 1923–8
	Roy O. West, 1928–9
Secretary of Agriculture	Henry C. Wallace, 1923–4
	Howard M. Gore, 1924–5
	William M. Jardine, 1925–9
Secretary of Commerce	Herbert C. Hoover, 1923–5
	William F. Whiting, 1925–9
Secretary of Labor	James J. Davis, 1923–9
Postmaster General	Harry S. New, 1923–9
Attorney General	Harry M. Daugherty, 1923–4
	Harlan F. Stone, 1924–5
	John D. Sargent, 1925–9

Herbert C. Hoover 1929–33
Charles Curtis

Secretary of State	Henry L. Stimson, 1929–33
Secretary of Treasury	Andrew W. Mellon, 1929–32
	Ogden L. Mills, 1932–3
Secretary of War	James W. Good, 1929
	Patrick J. Hurley, 1929–33
Secretary of Navy	Charles F. Adams, 1929–33
Secretary of Interior	Ray L. Wilbur, 1929–33
Secretary of Agriculture	Arthur M. Hyde, 1929–33
Secretary of Commerce	Robert P. Lamont, 1929–32
	Roy D. Chapin, 1932–3
Secretary of Labor	William N. Doak, 1930–3
Postmaster General	Walter F. Brown, 1929–33
Attorney General	William D. Mitchell, 1929–33

FRANKLIN DELANO ROOSEVELT 1933–45
JOHN NANCE GARNER 1933–41
HENRY A. WALLACE 1941–5
HARRY S. TRUMAN 1945

Secretary of State	CORDELL HULL, 1933–44
	EDWARD R. STETTINIUS, JR., 1944–5
Secretary of Treasury	WILLIAM H. WOODIN, 1933–4
	HENRY MORGENTHAU, JR., 1934–45
Secretary of War	GEORGE H. DERN, 1933–6
	HARRY H. WOODRING, 1936–40
	HENRY L. STIMSON, 1940–5
Secretary of Navy	CLAUDE A. SWANSON, 1933–40
	CHARLES EDISON, 1940
	FRANK KNOX, 1940–4
	JAMES V. FORRESTAL, 1944–5
Secretary of Interior	HAROLD L. ICKES, 1933–45
Secretary of Agriculture	HENRY A. WALLACE, 1933–40
	CLAUDE R. WICKARD, 1940–5
Secretary of Commerce	DANIEL C. ROPER, 1933–9
	HARRY L. HOPKINS, 1939–40
	JESSE JONES, 1940–5
	HENRY A. WALLACE, 1945
Secretary of Labor	FRANCIS PERKINS, 1933–45
Postmaster General	JAMES A. FARLEY, 1933–40
	FRANK C. WALKER, 1940–5
Attorney General	HOMER S. CUMMINGS, 1933–9
	FRANK MURPHY, 1939–40
	ROBERT JACKSON, 1940–1
	FRANCIS BIDDLE, 1941–5

HARRY S. TRUMAN 1945–
ALBEN W. BARKLEY 1949–

Secretary of State	JAMES F. BYRNES, 1945–7
	GEORGE C. MARSHALL, 1947–9
	DEAN G. ACHESON, 1949–
Secretary of Treasury	FRED M. VINSON, 1945–6
	JOHN W. SNYDER, 1946–
Secretary of War	ROBERT H. PATTERSON, 1945–7
	KENNETH C. ROYALL, 1947
Secretary of Navy	JAMES V. FORRESTAL, 1945–7
Secretary of Defense	JAMES V. FORRESTAL, 1947–9
	LOUIS A. JOHNSON, 1949–50
	GEORGE C. MARSHALL, 1950–1
Secretary of Interior	HAROLD L. ICKES, 1945–6
	JULIUS A. KRUG, 1946–9
	OSCAR L. CHAPMAN, 1949–
Secretary of Agriculture	CLINTON P. ANDERSON, 1945–8
	CHARLES F. BRANNAN, 1948–

Secretary of Commerce	HENRY C. WALLACE, 1945
	W. AVERELL HARRIMAN, 1946–8
	CHARLES W. SAWYER, 1948–
Secretary of Labor	LEWIS B. SCHWELLENBACH, 1945–8
	MAURICE J. TOBIN, 1948–
Postmaster General	ROBERT E. HANNEGAN, 1945–7
	JESSE L. DONALDSON, 1947–
Attorney General	TOM C. CLARK, 1945–9
	J. HOWARD McGRATH, 1949–

V

JUSTICES OF THE UNITED STATES SUPREME COURT, 1860–1950

NAME	SERVICE	
Chief Justices in Italics	TERM	YEARS
John McLean, Ohio	1829–61	32
James M. Wayne, Ga.	1835–67	32
Roger B. Taney, Md.	1836–64	28
John Catron, Tenn.	1837–65	28
Peter V. Daniel, Va.	1841–60	19
Samuel Nelson, N. Y.	1845–72	27
Robert C. Grier, Pa.	1846–70	24
John A. Campbell, Ala.	1853–61	8
Nathan Clifford, Me.	1858–81	23
Noah H. Swayne, Ohio	1862–81	20
Samuel F. Miller, Iowa	1862–90	28
David Davis, Ill.	1862–77	15
Stephen J. Field, Cal.	1863–97	34
Salmon P. Chase, Ohio	1864–73	9
William Strong, Pa.	1870–80	10
Joseph P. Bradley, N. J.	1870–92	22
Ward Hunt, N. Y.	1872–82	10
Morrison R. Waite, Ohio	1874–88	14
John M. Harlan, Ky.	1877–1911	34
William B. Woods, Ga.	1880–7	7
Stanley Matthews, Ohio	1881–9	8
Horace Gray, Mass.	1881–1902	21
Samuel Blatchford, N. Y.	1882–93	11
Lucius Q. C. Lamar, Miss.	1888–93	5
Melville W. Fuller, Ill.	1888–1910	22
David J. Brewer, Kan.	1889–1910	21
Henry B. Brown, Mich.	1890–1906	16
George Shiras, Jr., Pa.	1892–1903	11
Howell E. Jackson, Tenn.	1893–1895	2

NAME *Chief Justices in Italics*	SERVICE TERM	 YEARS
Edward D. White, La.	1894–1910	16
Rufus W. Peckham, N. Y.	1895–1910	14
Joseph McKenna, Cal.	1898–1925	27
Oliver W. Holmes, Mass.	1902–32	29
William R. Day, Ohio	1903–22	19
William H. Moody, Mass.	1906–10	4
Horace H. Lurton, Tenn.	1910–14	5
Charles E. Hughes, N. Y.	1910–16	6
Willis Van Devanter, Wyo.	1911–37	26
Joseph R. Lamar, Ga.	1911–16	6
Edward D. White, La.	1910–21	11
Mahlon Pitney, N. J.	1912–22	12
Jas. C. McReynolds, Tenn.	1914–41	27
Louis D. Brandeis, Mass.	1916–39	23
John H. Clark, Ohio	1916–22	6
William H. Taft, Conn.	1921–30	9
George Sutherland, Utah	1922–38	16
Pierce Butler, Minn.	1922–39	17
Edward T. Sanford, Tenn.	1923–30	7
Harlan F. Stone, N. Y.	1925–41	16
Charles E. Hughes, N. Y.	1930–41	11
Owen J. Roberts, Pa.	1930–45	15
Benjamin N. Cardozo, N. Y.	1932–8	6
Hugo Black, Ala.	1937–	
Stanley Reed, Ky.	1938–	
Felix Frankfurter, Mass.	1939–	
William O. Douglas, Conn.	1939–	
Frank Murphy, Mich.	1940–9	9
Harlan F. Stone, N. Y.	1941–6	5
James F. Byrnes, S. C.	1941–2	2
Robert H. Jackson, N. Y.	1941–	
Wiley B. Rutledge, Iowa	1943–9	6
Harold H. Burton, Ohio	1945–	
Fred M. Vinson, Ky.	1946–	
Thomas C. Clark, Texas	1949–	
Sherman Minton, Ind.	1949–	

VI

STATISTICAL TABLES

UNITED STATES POPULATION, 1860–1950

DIVISION AND STATE	1860	1870	1880	1890	1900	1910	1920	1930	1940	1950
United States	**31,443,321**	**39,818,449**	**50,155,783**	**62,947,714**	**75,994,575**	**91,972,266**	**105,710,620**	**122,775,046**	**131,669,275**	**150,697,361**
New England	**3,135,283**	**3,487,924**	**4,010,529**	**4,700,749**	**5,592,017**	**6,552,681**	**7,400,909**	**8,166,341**	**8,437,290**	**9,314,453**
Maine	628,279	626,915	648,936	661,086	694,466	742,371	768,014	797,423	847,226	913,774
New Hampshire	326,073	318,300	346,991	376,530	411,588	430,572	443,083	465,293	491,524	533,242
Vermont	315,098	330,551	332,286	332,422	343,641	355,956	352,428	359,611	359,231	377,747
Massachusetts	1,231,066	1,457,351	1,783,085	2,238,947	2,805,346	3,366,416	3,852,356	4,249,614	4,316,721	4,690,514
Rhode Island	174,620	217,353	276,531	345,506	428,556	542,610	604,397	687,497	713,346	791,896
Connecticut	460,147	537,454	622,700	746,258	908,420	1,114,756	1,380,631	1,606,903	1,709,242	2,007,280
Middle Atlantic	**7,458,985**	**8,810,806**	**10,496,878**	**12,706,220**	**15,454,678**	**19,315,892**	**22,261,144**	**26,260,750**	**27,539,487**	**30,163,533**
New York	3,880,735	4,382,759	5,082,871	6,003,174	7,268,894	9,113,614	10,385,227	12,588,066	13,479,142	14,830,192
New Jersey	672,035	906,096	1,131,116	1,444,933	1,883,669	2,537,167	3,155,900	4,041,334	4,160,165	4,835,329
Pennsylvania	2,906,215	3,521,951	4,282,891	5,258,113	6,302,115	7,665,111	8,720,017	9,631,350	9,900,180	10,498,012
East North Central	**6,926,884**	**9,124,517**	**11,206,668**	**13,478,305**	**15,985,581**	**18,250,621**	**21,475,543**	**25,297,185**	**26,626,342**	**30,399,368**
Ohio	2,339,511	2,665,260	3,198,062	3,672,329	4,157,545	4,767,121	5,759,394	6,646,697	6,907,612	7,946,627
Indiana	1,350,428	1,680,637	1,978,301	2,192,404	2,516,462	2,700,876	2,930,390	3,238,503	3,427,796	3,934,224
Illinois	1,711,951	2,539,891	3,077,871	3,826,352	4,821,550	5,638,591	6,485,280	7,630,654	7,897,241	8,712,176
Michigan	749,113	1,184,059	1,636,937	2,093,890	2,420,982	2,810,173	3,668,412	4,842,325	5,256,106	6,371,766
Wisconsin	775,881	1,054,670	1,315,497	1,693,330	2,069,042	2,333,860	2,632,067	2,939,006	3,137,587	3,434,576
West North Central	**2,169,832**	**3,856,594**	**6,157,443**	**8,932,112**	**10,347,423**	**11,637,921**	**12,544,249**	**13,296,915**	**13,516,990**	**14,061,394**
Minnesota	172,023	439,706	780,773	1,310,283	1,751,394	2,075,708	2,387,125	2,563,953	2,792,300	2,982,483
Iowa	674,913	1,194,020	1,624,615	1,912,297	2,231,853	2,224,771	2,404,021	2,470,939	2,538,268	2,621,073
Missouri	1,182,012	1,721,295	2,168,380	2,679,185	3,106,665	3,293,335	3,404,055	3,629,367	3,784,664	3,954,653
North Dakota		2,405	36,909	190,983	319,146	577,056	646,872	680,845	641,935	619,636
South Dakota	4,837	11,776	98,268	348,600	401,570	583,888	636,547	692,849	642,961	652,740
Nebraska	28,841	122,993	452,402	1,062,656	1,066,300	1,192,214	1,296,372	1,377,963	1,315,834	1,325,510
Kansas	107,206	364,399	996,096	1,428,108	1,470,495	1,690,949	1,769,257	1,880,999	1,801,028	1,905,299

South Atlantic	**5,364,703**	**5,853,610**	**7,597,197**	**8,857,922**	**10,443,480**	**12,194,895**	**13,990,272**	**15,793,589**	**17,823,151**	**21,182,335**
Delaware	112,216	125,015	146,608	168,493	184,735	202,322	223,003	238,380	266,505	318,085
Maryland	687,049	780,894	934,943	1,042,390	1,188,044	1,295,346	1,449,661	1,631,526	1,821,244	2,343,001
Dist. of Columbia	75,080	131,700	177,624	230,392	278,718	331,069	437,571	486,869	663,091	802,178
Virginia	1,596,318	1,225,163	1,512,565	1,655,980	1,854,184	2,061,612	2,309,187	2,421,851	2,677,773	3,318,680
West Virginia		442,014	618,457	762,794	958,800	1,221,119	1,463,701	1,729,205	1,901,974	2,005,552
North Carolina	992,622	1,071,361	1,399,750	1,617,949	1,893,810	2,206,287	2,559,123	3,170,276	3,571,623	4,061,929
South Carolina	703,708	705,606	995,577	1,151,149	1,340,316	1,515,400	1,683,724	1,738,765	1,899,804	2,117,027
Georgia	1,057,286	1,184,109	1,542,180	1,837,353	2,216,331	2,609,121	2,895,832	2,908,506	3,123,723	3,444,578
Florida	140,424	187,748	269,493	391,422	528,542	752,619	968,470	1,468,211	1,897,414	2,771,305
East South Central	**4,020,991**	**4,404,445**	**5,585,151**	**6,429,154**	**7,547,757**	**8,409,901**	**8,893,307**	**9,887,214**	**10,778,225**	**11,477,181**
Kentucky	1,155,684	1,321,011	1,648,690	1,858,635	2,147,174	2,289,905	2,416,630	2,614,589	2,845,627	2,944,806
Tennessee	1,109,801	1,258,520	1,542,359	1,767,518	2,020,616	2,184,789	2,337,885	2,616,556	2,915,841	3,291,718
Alabama	964,201	996,992	1,262,505	1,513,401	1,828,697	2,138,093	2,348,174	2,646,248	2,832,961	3,061,743
Mississippi	791,305	827,922	1,131,597	1,289,600	1,551,270	1,797,114	1,790,618	2,009,821	2,183,796	2,178,914
West South Central	**1,747,667**	**2,029,965**	**3,334,220**	**4,740,983**	**6,532,290**	**8,784,534**	**10,242,224**	**12,176,830**	**13,064,525**	**14,537,572**
Arkansas	435,450	484,471	802,525	1,128,211	1,311,564	1,574,449	1,752,204	1,854,482	1,949,387	1,909,511
Louisiana	708,002	726,915	939,946	1,118,588	1,381,625	1,656,388	1,798,509	2,101,593	2,363,880	2,683,516
Oklahoma				258,657	790,391	1,657,155	2,028,283	2,396,040	2,336,434	2,233,351
Texas	604,215	818,579	1,591,749	2,235,527	3,048,710	3,896,542	4,663,228	5,824,715	6,414,824	7,711,194
Mountain	**174,923**	**315,385**	**653,119**	**1,213,935**	**1,674,657**	**2,633,517**	**3,336,101**	**3,701,789**	**4,150,003**	**5,074,998**
Montana		20,595	39,159	142,924	243,329	376,053	548,889	537,606	559,456	591,024
Idaho		14,999	32,610	88,548	161,772	325,594	431,866	445,032	524,873	588,637
Wyoming		9,118	20,789	62,555	92,531	145,965	194,402	225,565	250,742	290,529
Colorado	34,277	39,864	194,327	413,249	539,700	799,024	939,629	1,035,791	1,123,296	1,325,089
New Mexico	93,516	91,874	119,565	160,282	195,310	327,301	360,350	423,317	531,818	681,187
Arizona		9,658	40,440	88,243	122,931	204,354	334,162	435,573	499,261	749,587
Utah	40,273	86,786	143,963	210,779	276,749	373,351	449,396	507,847	550,310	688,862
Nevada	6,857	42,491	62,266	47,355	42,335	81,875	77,407	91,058	110,247	160,083
Pacific	**444,053**	**675,125**	**1,114,578**	**1,888,334**	**2,416,692**	**4,192,304**	**5,566,871**	**8,194,433**	**9,733,262**	**14,486,527**
Washington	11,594	23,955	75,116	357,232	518,103	1,141,990	1,356,621	1,563,396	1,736,191	2,378,963
Oregon	52,465	90,923	174,768	317,704	413,536	672,765	783,389	953,786	1,089,684	1,521,341
California	379,994	560,247	864,694	1,213,398	1,485,053	2,377,549	3,426,861	5,677,251	6,907,387	10,586,223

IMMIGRATION, BY COUNTRY OF ORIGIN, BY DECADES: 1851 TO 1950

COUNTRY	1851–1860	1861–1870	1871–1880	1881–1890	1891–1900	1901–1910	1911–1920	1921–1930	1931–1940	1941–1950
All countries, total	**2,598,214**	**2,314,824**	**2,812,191**	**5,246,613**	**3,687,564**	**8,795,386**	**5,735,811**	**4,107,209**	**528,431**	**1,035,039**
Europe, total	**2,452,660**	**2,065,270**	**2,272,262**	**4,737,046**	**3,558,978**	**8,136,016**	**4,376,564**	**2,477,853**	**348,289**	**621,704**
Belgium	4,738	6,734	7,221	20,177	18,167	41,635	33,746	15,846	4,817	12,189
Bulgaria					160	39,280	22,533	2,945	938	375
Czechoslovakia							3,426	102,194	14,393	8,347
Denmark	3,749	17,094	31,771	88,132	50,231	65,285	41,983	32,430	2,559	5,393
Eire	914,119	435,778	436,871	655,482	388,416	339,065	146,181	220,591	10,973	27,503
Northern Ireland									2,194	.....
Finland							756	16,691	2,146	2,503
France	76,358	35,986	72,206	50,464	30,770	73,379	61,897	49,610	12,623	38,809
Germany	951,667	787,468	718,182	1,452,970	505,152	341,498	143,945	412,202	117,621	226,578
Austria						2,145,266	453,649	32,868		24,860
Hungary		7,800	72,969	353,719	592,707		442,693	30,680	7,861	3,469
Great Britain:										
England	247,125	222,277	437,706	644,680	216,726	388,017	249,944	157,420	21,756	112,252
Scotland	38,331	38,769	87,564	149,869	44,188	120,469	78,357	159,781	6,887	16,131
Wales	6,319	4,313	6,631	12,640	10,557	17,464	13,107	13,012	735	3,209
United Kingdom not specified	132,199	341,537	16,142	168	67					
Greece	31	72	210	2,308	15,979	167,519	184,201	51,084	9,119	8,973
Italy	9,231	11,725	55,759	307,309	651,893	2,045,877	1,109,524	455,315	68,028	57,661
Netherlands	10,789	9,102	16,541	53,701	26,758	48,262	43,718	26,948	7,150	14,860
Norway	20,931	71,631	95,323	176,586	95,015	190,505	66,395	68,531	4,740	10,100
Sweden		37,667	115,922	391,776	226,266	249,534	95,074	97,249	3,960	10,665
Poland	1,164	2,027	12,970	51,806	96,720		4,813	227,734	17,026	7,571
Portugal	1,055	2,658	14,082	16,978	27,508	69,149	89,732	29,994	3,329	7,423
Rumania			11	6,348	12,750	53,008	13,311	67,646	3,871	1,076
Soviet Union (Russia)	457	2,512	39,284	213,282	505,290	1,597,306	921,201	61,742	1,356	548

Spain	9,298	6,697	5,266	4,419	8,731	27,935	68,611	28,958	3,258	2,898
Switzerland	25,011	23,286	28,293	81,988	31,179	34,922	23,091	29,676	5,512	10,547
Turkey in Europe	83	129	337	1,562	3,626	79,976	54,677	14,659	737	580
Yugoslavia							1,888	49,064	5,835	1,576
Other Europe	5	8	1,001	682	122	665	8,111	22,983	8,865	5,608
Asia, total	**41,455**	**64,630**	**123,823**	**68,380**	**71,236**	**243,567**	**192,559**	**97,400**	**15,344**	**31,780**
China	41,397	64,301	123,201	61,711	14,799	20,605	21,278	29,907	4,928	16,709
Japan		186	149	2,270	25,942	129,797	83,837	33,462	1,948	1,555
Turkey in Asia		2	67	2,220	26,799	77,393	79,389	19,165	328	218
Other Asia	58	141	406	2,179	3,696	15,772	8,055	14,866	8,140	13,298
America, total	**74,720**	**166,607**	**404,044**	**426,967**	**38,972**	**361,888**	**1,143,671**	**1,516,716**	**160,037**	**354,804**
Canada and Newfoundland	59,309	153,878	383,640	393,304	3,311	179,226	742,185	924,515	108,527	171,698
Mexico	3,078	2,191	5,162	1,913	971	49,642	219,004	459,287	22,319	60,589
Central America	449	95	157	404	549	8,192	17,159	15,769	5,861	21,601
South America	1,224	1,397	1,128	2,304	1,075	17,280	41,899	42,215	7,803	21,831
West Indies	10,660	9,046	13,957	29,042	33,066	107,548	123,424	74,899	15,502	49,745
Other America								31	25	29,340
Africa	210	312	358	857	350	7,368	8,443	6,286	1,750	7,367
Australia, Tasmania, and New Zealand		36	9,886	7,017	2,740	11,975	12,348	8,299	2,231	13,805
Pacific Islands (not specified)			1,028	5,557	1,225	1,049	1,079	427	780	5,437
All other countries	29,169	17,969	790	789	14,063	33,523	1,147	228		142

EXPENDITURES AND GROSS DEBT OF THE FEDERAL GOVERNMENT, 1861–1948

YEARLY AVERAGE OF YEAR ENDING JUNE 30	EXPENDITURES (THOUSANDS OF DOLLARS)							GROSS DEBT	
	TOTAL	ARMY DEPT. (FORMERLY WAR DEPT.)	NAVY DEPT.	INDIANS	VETERANS' PENSIONS	INTEREST ON THE PUBLIC DEBT	ALL OTHER	AMOUNT (MILLIONS OF DOLLARS)	PER CAPITA (DOLLARS)
1861–5	683,785	547,753	65,330	3,203	4,858	34,601	28,040	2,678	75.01
1866–70	377,642	127,816	28,383	4,488	23,428	135,441	58,087	2,436	61.06
1871–5	287,460	40,186	23,327	7,504	30,166	111,580	74,696	2,156	47.84
1876–80	255,598	37,170	15,990	5,405	35,051	100,191	61,791	2,091	41.60
1881–5	257,691	43,010	15,863	7,328	57,790	63,742	69,958	1,579	27.86
1886–90	279,134	40,085	17,872	6,429	82,657	44,027	88,064	1,122	17.80
1891–5	363,599	50,326	29,185	10,651	140,186	29,402	103,849	1,097	15.76
1896–1900	457,451	111,278	48,086	11,832	141,642	38,164	106,450	1,263	16.60
1901–05	535,559	133,362	86,287	11,711	140,114	27,849	136,236	1,132	13.51
1906–10	639,178	169,050	112,872	15,338	151,329	22,673	167,916	1,147	12.41
1911–15	720,253	198,792	134,062	20,744	164,897	22,519	179,239	1,191	11.85
1916–20	8,065,333	3,212,420	882,132	30,833	187,143	375,371	3,377,434	24,299	228.23
1921–5	3,578,989	540,176	427,748	42,125	244,784	973,696	1,350,460	20,516	177.12
1926–30	3,182,807	404,999	340,343	37,676	223,507	737,680	1,438,602	16,185	131.51
1931–5	5,214,874	457,185	358,831	25,384	279,008	695,549	3,398,916	28,701	225.55
1936–40	8,275,309	698,674	649,179	36,795	408,758	904,707	5,577,196	42,968	325.59
1941–5	64,242,521	32,143,689	17,673,156	30,207	514,797	2,080,921	11,799,750	258,682	1,853.21
1932	4,659,203	476,305	357,518	26,125	232,521	599,277	2,967,457	19,487	156.10
1933	4,622,865	434,621	349,373	22,722	234,990	689,365	2,891,794	22,539	179.48

1934	6,693,900	408,587	296,927	23,373	319,322	756,617	4,889,073	27,053	214.07
1935	6,520,966	487,995	436,266	27,919	373,805	820,926	4,374,055	28,701	225.55
1936	8,493,486	618,587	528,882	28,876	399,066	749,397	6,168,678	33,779	263.79
1937	7,756,021	628,104	556,674	36,933	396,047	866,384	5,271,879	36,425	282.75
1938	6,978,802	644,264	596,130	33,378	402,779	926,281	4,375,971	37,165	286.27
1939	8,965,555	695,256	672,722	46,964	416,721	940,540	6,193,351	40,440	308.98
1940	9,182,682	907,160	891,485	37,821	429,178	1,040,936	5,876,103	42,968	325.59
1941	13,386,554	3,938,943	2,313,058	33,588	433,148	1,110,693	5,557,124	48,961	367.57
1942	34,186,529	14,325,508	8,579,589	31,839	431,294	1,260,085	9,558,213	72,422	537.80
1943	79,621,932	42,525,563	20,888,349	24,665	442,394	1,808,160	13,932,801	136,696	1,001.46
1944	95,315,065	49,438,330	26,537,634	31,266	494,959	2,608,980	16,203,896	201,003	1,455.67
1945	98,702,525	50,490,102	30,047,152	29,680	772,190	3,616,686	13,746,715	258,682	1,853.21
1946	60,703,060	27,986,769	15,160,754	35,495	1,261,415	4,721,958	11,536,669	269,422	1,907.62
1947	39,288,819	9,172,139	5,597,203	37,369	1,929,226	4,957,922	17,594,959	258,286	1,793.23
1948	33,791,301	7,698,556	4,284,619	41,147	2,080,130	5,211,102	14,475,746	252,292	1,721.30

RECEIPTS AND SURPLUS OR DEFICIT OF THE FEDERAL GOVERNMENT, 1861–1948

(In thousands of dollars)

YEARLY AVERAGE OF YEAR ENDING JUNE 30	RECEIPTS							SURPLUS (+) OR DEFICIT (−), RECEIPTS COMPARED WITH EXPENDITURES
				INTERNAL REVENUE				
	NET	TOTAL	CUSTOMS	INCOME AND PROFITS TAXES	OTHER	SALES OF PUBLIC LANDS	OTHER RECEIPTS	
1861–5	160,907	160,907	68,989	28,005	54,566	555	19,994	−522,878
1866–70	447,301	447,301	178,903	50,604	171,316	2,110	44,368	+69,659
1871–5	336,830	336,830	186,200	7,760	112,217	2,223	28,429	+49,370
1876–80	288,124	288,124	146,594		116,697	1,025	23,808	+32,526
1881–5	366,961	366,961	201,963	29	132,102	6,086	26,799	+109,270
1886–90	375,448	375,448	216,557		126,683	8,097	24,111	+96,314
1891–5	352,891	352,891	176,861	77	150,228	2,650	23,136	−10,708
1896–1900	434,877	434,877	185,089		206,623	1,526	41,639	−22,574
1901–05	559,481	559,481	260,117		255,374	5,670	38,321	+23,922
1906–10	628,508	628,508	310,599	20,952	257,145	7,310	49,265	−10,670
1911–15	710,227	710,227	289,363	49,738	307,116	3,755	60,256	−10,025
1916–20	3,483,653	3,483,653	225,301	1,952,471	893,212	1,813	410,855	−4,581,680
1921–5	4,306,673	4,306,673	464,027	2,111,093	1,052,604	846	678,104	+727,684
1926–30	4,069,138	4,069,138	588,636	2,224,537	671,331	494	584,140	+886,331
1931–5	2,770,973	2,838,216	322,729	1,116,203	1,186,498	138	212,648	−2,443,900
1936–40	5,043,557	5,442,480	379,957	2,108,871	2,740,862	121	212,669	−3,231,753
1941–5	26,155,670	27,653,194	378,227	19,470,335	6,146,815	136	1,657,680	−38,086,851

1932	1,923,913	2,005,725	327,755	1,057,336	503,670	170	116,794	−2,735,290
1933	2,021,213	2,079,697	250,750	746,206	858,218	103	224,420	−2,601,652
1934	3,064,268	3,115,554	313,434	817,961	1,822,642	99	161,417	−3,629,632
1935	3,729,914	3,800,467	343,353	1,099,119	2,178,571	87	179,337	−2,791,052
1936	4,068,937	4,115,957	386,812	1,426,575	2,086,276	74	216,219	−4,424,549
1937	4,978,601	5,293,590	486,357	2,163,414	2,433,726	71	210,022	−2,777,421
1938	5,802,186	6,241,661	359,187	2,640,285	3,034,034	96	208,060	−1,176,617
1939	5,103,397	5,667,824	318,837	2,188,757	2,972,464	248	187,517	−3,862,158
1940	5,264,663	5,893,368	348,591	2,125,325	3,177,809	117	241,526	−3,918,019
1941	7,227,281	7,995,612	391,870	3,469,638	3,892,037	178	241,888	−6,159,272
1942	12,696,286	13,676,680	388,948	7,960,465	5,032,653	90	294,525	−21,490,243
1943	22,201,502	23,402,322	324,291	16,093,669	6,050,300	129	933,933	−57,420,430
1944	43,891,673	45,441,049	431,252	34,654,852	7,030,135	99	3,324,711	−51,423,393
1945	44,761,609	47,750,306	354,776	35,173,051	8,728,951	184	3,493,345	−53,940,916
1946	40,026,889	44,238,135	435,475	30,884,796	9,425,537	127	3,492,200	−20,676,171
1947	40,042,606	44,508,189	494,078	29,305,568	10,073,840	143	4,634,559	+753,788
1948	42,210,770	46,098,807	421,723	31,170,968	10,682,517	214	3,823,385	+8,419,470

EMPLOYMENT AND PAY ROLLS OF THE FEDERAL GOVERNMENT, 1929–1948

YEAR OR MONTH	EMPLOYMENT: AVERAGE FOR YEAR OR AS OF FIRST OF MONTH				PAY ROLLS (THOUSANDS OF DOLLARS): TOTAL FOR YEAR OR FOR MONTH			
	TOTAL	EXECUTIVE	LEGISLATIVE	JUDICIAL	TOTAL	EXECUTIVE	LEGISLATIVE	JUDICIAL
1929	596,250	590,562	4,092	1,596	1,079,794	1,063,056	11,303	5,435
1930	610,931	604,948	4,231	1,752	1,117,830	1,100,273	11,686	5,871
1931	624,366	618,240	4,310	1,816	1,128,630	1,110,677	11,904	6,049
1932	621,580	615,432	4,366	1,782	1,059,138	1,041,792	11,552	5,794
1933	630,054	623,887	4,407	1,760	972,126	956,562	10,555	5,009
1934	718,765	712,209	4,731	1,825	1,169,370	1,151,547	12,521	5,302
1935	819,575	812,779	4,910	1,886	1,417,991	1,398,383	13,906	5,702
1936	893,590	886,431	5,124	2,035	1,604,860	1,584,485	14,429	5,946
1937	902,055	894,742	5,203	2,110	1,613,699	1,593,227	14,455	6,017
1938	900,410	893,033	5,233	2,144	1,626,622	1,605,741	14,511	6,370
1939	968,596	960,963	5,373	2,260	1,757,292	1,735,834	14,767	6,691
1940	1,077,691	1,069,371	5,879	2,441	1,978,152	1,955,068	15,640	7,444
1941	1,432,724	1,424,099	6,081	2,544	2,524,903	2,501,105	16,032	7,766
1942	2,233,280	2,224,246	6,401	2,633	4,431,091	4,406,373	16,625	8,093
1943	3,165,337	3,156,530	6,171	2,636	7,858,131	7,831,305	17,785	9,041
1944	3,337,318	3,328,469	6,189	2,660	8,301,111	8,273,709	18,127	9,275
1945	3,569,092	3,559,963	6,376	2,753	8,153,686	8,122,973	20,537	10,176
1946	2,703,814	2,694,120	6,636	3,058	6,754,625	6,717,837	23,929	12,859
1947	2,153,170	2,142,825	7,127	3,218	5,966,107	5,922,339	29,074	14,694
1948	2,066,545	2,055,790	7,273	3,482	6,223,486	6,176,414	30,891	16,181

PUBLIC ELEMENTARY AND SECONDARY SCHOOLS—SUMMARY, 1870–1947

ITEM	1870	1880	1890	1900	1910
Total population	38,558,371	50,155,783	62,622,250	75,602,515	91,972,266
Population 5–17 years, inclusive	12,055,443	15,065,767	18,543,201	21,404,322	24,239,948
Percent of total population	31.3	30.0	29.6	28.3	26.4
Pupils enrolled in public schools	6,871,522	9,867,395	12,722,631	15,503,110	17,813,852
Percent of total population	17.82	19.67	20.32	20.51	19.37
Percent of population 5–17, inclusive	57.00	65.50	68.61	72.43	73.49
Average daily attendance	4,077,347	6,144,143	8,153,635	10,632,772	12,827,307
Percent of pupils enrolled	59.3	62.3	64.1	68.6	72.0
Average number of days schools in session	132.2	130.3	134.7	144.3	157.5
Average number of days attended per enrolled pupil	78.4	81.1	86.3	99.0	113.0
Number of teachers	200,515	286,593	363,922	423,062	523,210
Male	77,529	122,795	125,525	126,588	110,481
Female	122,986	163,798	238,397	296,474	412,729
Percent male teachers	38.7	42.8	34.5	29.9	21.1
Salaries: Teachers, supervisors, and principals (thousands of dollars)	37,833	55,943	91,836	137,688	253,915
Average annual salary per teacher	$189	$195	$252	$325	$485
Total expenditure for education (thousands of dollars)	63,397	78,095	140,507	214,965	426,250
Per capita of total population	$1.64	$1.56	$2.24	$2.84	$4.63
Per capita of population 5–17, inclusive	$5.26	$5.18	$7.58	$10.04	$17.58
Per pupil enrolled	$9.23	$7.91	$11.04	$13.87	$23.93
Per pupil in average attendance	$15.55	$12.71	$17.23	$20.22	$33.23

ITEM	1920	1930	1940	1944	1946	1947
Total population	105,710,620	122,775,046	131,669,275	138,083,449	139,893,406	143,405,000
Population 5–17 years, inclusive	27,728,788	31,571,322	29,745,246	28,930,000	28,944,000	29,317,000
Percent of total population	26.2	25.7	22.6	21.0	20.7	20.4
Pupils enrolled in public schools	21,578,316	25,678,015	25,433,542	23,266,616	23,299,941	23,659,158
Percent of total population	20.4	20.9	19.3	16.9	16.7	16.5
Percent of population 5–17, inclusive	77.8	81.3	85.5	80.4	80.5	80.7
Average daily attendance	16,150,035	21,264,886	22,042,151	19,602,772	19,848,507	20,448,656
Percent of pupils enrolled	74.8	82.8	86.7	84.3	85.2	86.4
Average number of days schools in session	161.9	172.7	175.0	175.5	176.8	176.2
Average number of days attended per enrolled pupil	121.2	143.0	151.7	147.9	150.6	152.3
Number of teachers	679,533	854,263	875,477	827,990	831,026	833,512
Male	95,666	141,771	194,725	126,672	138,209	153,297
Female	583,867	712,492	680,752	701,318	692,817	680,215
Percent male teachers	14.1	16.6	22.2	15.3	16.6	18.4
Salaries: Teachers, supervisors, and principals (thousands of dollars)	590,120	1,250,427	1,314,342	1,494,507	1,730,563	1,979,657
Average annual salary per teacher	$871	$1,420	$1,441	$1,728	$1,995	$2,254
Total expenditure for education (thousands of dollars)	1,036,151	2,316,790	2,344,049	2,452,581	2,906,886	3,419,994
Per capita of total population	$9.80	$18.87	$17.77	$17.76	$20.78	$23.85
Per capita of population 5–17, inclusive	$37.37	$73.38	$78.65	$84.78	$100.43	$116.66
Per pupil enrolled	$48.02	$89.84	$91.64	$105.04	$124.27	$143.77
Per pupil in average attendance	$64.16	$108.49	$105.74	$124.68	$145.88	$166.34

WHOLESALE PRICES—INDEXES, BY MAJOR COMMODITY GROUPS, 1890–1948

(1926 = 100)

PERIOD	ALL COMMODITIES	FARM PRODUCTS	FOODS	HIDES AND LEATHER PRODUCTS	TEXTILE PRODUCTS	FUEL AND LIGHTING	METALS AND METAL PRODUCTS	BUILDING MATERIALS	CHEMICALS AND ALLIED PRODUCTS	HOUSE FURNISHING GOODS	MISCELLANEOUS
1890	56.2	50.4	55.5	47.5	57.8	38.1	105.3	46.5	73.2	49.9	97.9
1895	48.8	43.9	47.3	49.4	44.3	40.3	70.4	38.8	64.7	43.5	88.9
1900	56.1	50.5	50.8	49.4	53.3	46.3	98.0	46.2	82.1	48.9	102.0
1905	60.1	56.4	55.1	53.9	54.1	49.6	89.1	48.1	82.3	49.7	117.4
1910	70.4	74.3	64.9	60.2	58.4	47.6	85.2	55.3	82.0	54.0	152.7
1915	69.5	71.5	65.4	75.5	54.1	51.8	86.3	53.5	112.0	56.0	86.9
1920	154.4	150.7	137.4	171.3	164.8	163.7	149.4	150.1	164.7	141.8	167.5
1925	103.5	109.8	100.2	105.3	108.3	96.5	103.2	101.7	101.8	103.1	109.0
1929	95.3	104.9	99.9	109.1	90.4	83.0	100.5	95.4	94.0	94.3	82.6
1932	64.8	48.2	61.0	72.9	54.9	70.3	80.2	71.4	73.9	75.1	64.4
1935	80.0	78.8	83.7	89.6	70.9	73.5	86.4	85.3	79.0	80.6	68.3
1939	77.1	65.3	70.4	95.6	69.7	73.1	94.4	90.5	76.0	86.3	74.8
1940	78.6	67.7	71.3	100.8	73.8	71.7	95.8	94.8	77.0	88.5	77.3
1941	87.3	82.4	82.7	108.3	84.8	76.2	99.4	103.2	84.4	94.3	82.0
1942	98.8	105.9	99.6	117.7	96.9	78.5	103.8	110.2	95.5	102.4	89.7
1943	103.1	122.6	106.6	117.5	97.4	80.8	103.8	111.4	94.9	102.7	92.2
1944	104.0	123.3	104.9	116.7	98.4	83.0	103.8	115.5	95.2	104.3	93.6
1945	105.8	128.2	106.2	118.1	100.1	84.0	104.7	117.8	95.2	104.5	94.7
1946	121.1	148.9	130.7	137.2	116.3	90.1	115.5	132.6	101.4	111.6	100.3
1947	152.1	181.2	168.7	182.4	141.7	108.7	145.0	179.7	127.3	131.1	115.5
1948	165.1	188.3	179.1	188.8	149.8	134.2	163.6	199.1	135.7	144.5	120.5

EXPORTS OF UNITED STATES MERCHANDISE, AND IMPORTS, 1861–1949

(In thousands of dollars)

YEARLY AVERAGE OR YEAR	TOTAL	CRUDE MATERIALS	CRUDE FOODSTUFFS	MANUFACTURED FOODSTUFFS	SEMI-MANUFACTURES	FINISHED MANUFACTURES
EXPORTS OF UNITED STATES MERCHANDISE						
1861–70	238,947	105,643	32,764	50,446	12,047	38,048
1871–80	574,889	216,219	117,030	128,599	26,428	86,614
1881–90	750,146	269,174	135,711	189,489	38,534	117,239
1891–1900	1,006,183	295,876	182,812	255,670	82,422	189,404
1901–10	1,589,000	493,391	164,900	316,800	205,170	408,740
1911–15	2,331,648	716,637	205,939	333,971	359,239	715,861
1915–20	6,416,513	1,168,995	587,588	1,133,226	987,185	2,539,520
1921–5	4,310,221	1,187,056	420,002	600,710	536,793	1,565,660
1926–30	4,687,788	1,143,762	299,794	455,814	662,688	2,125,730
1931–5	1,988,914	601,344	76,528	175,686	288,622	846,734
1936–40	3,166,518	603,209	119,282	174,998	610,984	1,658,045
1941–5	9,922,152	573,224	165,301	1,154,443	931,461	7,098,070
1940	3,934,181	463,678	74,018	166,871	900,022	2,329,590
1941	5,019,877	361,741	83,578	418,457	771,442	3,384,659
1942	8,003,113	418,013	67,838	924,699	920,275	5,672,288
1943	12,841,542	661,782	109,067	1,550,738	1,089,400	9,430,557
1944	14,161,544	553,962	133,826	1,632,605	1,096,674	10,744,477
1945	9,584,684	870,623	432,147	1,245,727	779,515	6,256,672
1946	9,500,184	1,415,808	648,103	1,522,400	895,125	5,018,748
1947	14,252,285	1,578,541	848,887	1,483,157	1,734,329	8,607,371
1948	12,532,093	1,488,449	1,265,820	1,313,704	1,370,393	7,093,726
1949	11,885,196	1,780,303	1,340,527	885,771	1,354,073	6,524,521
IMPORTS						
1861–70	331,867	41,939	45,261	62,997	45,688	135,982
1871–80	535,222	92,268	85,532	110,913	69,839	176,671
1881–90	692,187	147,852	106,253	122,978	102,335	212,769
1891–1900	763,328	201,870	129,177	129,425	105,919	196,938
1901–10	1,158,500	394,659	136,675	139,438	200,693	287,036
1911–15	1,712,319	597,701	219,035	215,144	297,476	382,963
1915–20	3,358,354	1,347,667	408,152	544,549	574,421	483,566
1921–5	3,450,103	1,290,375	382,539	448,089	609,225	719,875
1926–30	4,033,469	1,484,123	506,616	398,310	762,034	882,385
1931–5	1,704,267	492,638	265,985	233,963	319,123	392,558
1936–40	2,440,042	807,235	319,603	345,523	510,950	456,731
1941–5	3,475,593	1,147,159	568,713	400,069	735,153	624,499
1940	2,540,656	1,010,841	285,066	277,444	558,606	408,699
1941	3,221,954	1,376,440	376,179	322,058	724,226	423,051
1942	2,780,317	1,060,713	348,576	274,507	639,506	457,015
1943	3,390,101	1,037,386	584,227	421,157	677,505	669,826
1944	3,887,490	1,078,173	841,348	520,979	706,235	740,755
1945	4,098,101	1,183,081	693,235	461,644	928,291	831,850
1946	4,824,902	1,729,074	814,403	503,946	930,600	846,879
1947	5,666,321	1,766,160	1,016,775	655,698	1,244,908	982,781
1948	7,092,032	2,147,007	1,271,611	731,173	1,633,140	1,309,101
1949	6,598,058	1,855,145	1,333,201	741,633	1,421,974	1,246,105

AGRICULTURAL COMMODITIES—PRODUCTION, BY CHIEF KINDS, 1860–1948

YEAR	CORN	WHEAT	RICE (IN TERMS OF CLEANED)	SUGAR: BEET (CHIEFLY REFINED)	SUGAR: CANE (CHIEFLY RAW)	COTTON: RUNNING BALES	COTTON: 500-POUND BALES	TOBACCO
	1,000 bushels	*1,000 bushels*	*1,000 pounds*	*1,000 pounds*	*1,000 pounds*	*Thousands*	*Thousands*	*1,000 pounds*
1860	838,793	173,105	106,279		274,725	3,849	3,841	434,209
1870	1,124,775	254,429	54,889	896	178,304	4,352	4,025	345,045
1880	1,706,673	502,257	111,869	1,120	285,302	6,606	6,357	469,395
1885	2,057,807	399,931	150,195	1,344	302,754	6,576	6,369	610,500
1890	1,650,446	449,042	136,800	7,748	497,170	8,653	8,562	647,535
1895	2,534,762	542,119	206,250	65,452	543,636	7,161	7,146	745,000
1900	2,661,978	599,315	272,028	172,164	623,772	10,102	10,124	851,980
1904	2,686,624	555,571	533,778	484,226	829,990	13,451	13,438	856,595
1905	2,954,148	706,026	445,500	625,842	781,204	10,495	10,576	938,865
1906	3,032,910	740,509	493,750	967,224	544,320	12,983	13,274	972,510
1907	2,613,797	628,764	576,417	927,256	788,480	11,058	11,106	885,620
1908	2,566,742	642,818	622,139	851,768	828,800	13,086	13,241	835,645
1909	2,611,157	683,927	655,167	1,024,000	676,000	10,073	10,005	1,053,818
1910	2,852,794	625,476	686,972	1,020,000	724,000	11,568	11,609	1,142,320
1911	2,474,635	618,166	629,500	1,200,000	736,000	15,553	15,694	940,935
1912	2,947,842	730,011	658,333	1,386,000	332,000	13,489	13,703	1,117,415
1913	2,272,540	751,101	672,500	1,466,000	614,000	13,983	14,153	991,605
1914	2,523,750	897,487	652,167	1,444,000	504,000	15,906	16,112	1,036,745
1915	2,829,044	1,008,637	725,194	1,748,000	282,000	11,068	11,172	1,157,425
1916	2,425,206	634,572	1,098,444	1,642,000	634,000	11,364	11,448	1,206,785
1917	2,908,242	619,790	964,278	1,530,000	502,000	11,248	11,284	1,325,530
1918	2,441,249	904,130	1,111,056	1,522,000	580,000	11,906	12,018	1,444,505
1919	2,678,541	952,097	1,191,972	1,452,000	250,000	11,326	11,411	1,444,206
1920	3,070,604	843,277	1,434,667	2,178,000	360,000	13,271	13,429	1,509,212

1921	2,928,442	818,964	1,090,944	2,040,000	668,000	7,978	7,945	1,004,928
1922	2,707,306	846,649	1,157,306	1,350,000	604,000	9,729	9,755	1,254,304
1923	2,875,292	759,482	923,278	1,762,000	336,000	10,171	10,140	1,517,583
1924	2,223,123	841,617	906,750	2,180,000	180,000	13,639	13,630	1,244,928
1925	2,798,367	668,700	917,667	1,826,000	284,000	16,123	16,105	1,376,008
1926	2,546,972	832,213	1,167,361	1,794,000	96,000	17,755	17,978	1,289,272
1927	2,616,120	875,059	1,236,028	2,186,000	144,000	12,783	12,956	1,211,311
1928	2,665,516	914,373	1,217,611	2,122,000	272,000	14,297	14,477	1,373,214
1929	2,515,937	824,183	1,098,167	2,036,000	436,000	14,548	14,825	1,532,676
1930	2,080,130	886,522	1,248,028	2,416,000	430,000	13,756	13,932	1,648,037
1931	2,575,927	941,540	1,239,250	2,312,000	368,000	16,629	17,097	1,565,088
1932	2,930,352	756,307	1,156,083	2,714,000	530,000	12,710	13,003	1,018,011
1933	2,397,593	552,215	1,045,861	3,284,000	500,000	12,664	13,047	1,371,965
1934	1,448,920	526,052	1,084,639	2,320,000	534,000	9,472	9,636	1,084,589
1935	2,299,363	628,227	1,095,889	2,370,000	766,000	10,420	10,638	1,302,041
1936	1,505,689	629,880	1,383,889	2,608,000	874,000	12,141	12,399	1,162,838
1937	2,642,978	873,914	1,483,944	2,566,000	924,000	18,252	18,946	1,569,023
1938	2,548,753	919,913	1,458,500	3,352,000	1,166,000	11,623	11,943	1,385,573
1939	2,580,985	741,210	1,501,722	3,388,000	1,008,000	11,481	11,817	1,880,629
1940	2,457,146	814,646	1,512,028	3,512,000	664,000	12,298	12,566	1,460,441
1941	2,651,889	941,970	1,425,639	2,982,000	838,000	10,495	10,744	1,261,839
1942	3,068,562	969,381	1,889,678	3,238,000	920,000	12,438	12,817	1,408,394
1943	2,965,980	843,813	1,901,491	1,870,000	996,000	11,129	11,427	1,406,190
1944	3,088,110	1,060,111	2,012,573	1,958,000	874,000	11,839	12,230	1,954,699
1945	2,880,933	1,108,224	1,992,690	2,366,000	950,000	8,813	9,015	1,994,262
1946	3,249,950	1,153,046	2,111,578	2,846,000	850,000	8,517	8,640	2,321,596
1947	2,383,970	1,367,186	2,288,274	3,430,000	752,000	11,557	11,857	2,110,131
1948	3,681,793	1,313,534	2,362,667	2,558,000	954,000	14,580	14,877	1,980,325

MINERAL PRODUCTS OF THE UNITED STATES, 1881–1948

(All figures in millions of dollars)

YEARLY AVERAGE OR YEAR	TOTAL	METALLIC	NONMETALLIC			YEAR	TOTAL	METALLIC	NONMETALLIC		
			TOTAL	FUELS	OTHER				TOTAL	FUELS	OTHER
1881–5	426	194	232	171	61	1930	4,765	986	3,779	2,765	1,015
1886–90	541	249	292	215	78	1931	3,167	570	2,597	1,892	704
1891–5	592	245	347	248	99	1932	2,462	286	2,176	1,743	432
1896–1900	828	366	462	307	154	1933	2,555	417	2,138	1,683	455
1901–05	1,392	578	814	546	267	1934	3,325	549	2,776	2,233	543
1906–10	1,887	769	1,118	746	372	1935	3,650	733	2,917	2,330	587
1911–15	2,220	821	1,400	967	433	1936	4,557	1,082	3,475	2,759	716
1916–20	5,129	1,798	3,331	2,602	729	1937	5,413	1,468	3,945	3,201	745
1921–5	5,151	1,154	3,997	2,943	1,054	1938	4,363	893	3,471	2,820	650
1926–30	5,556	1,276	4,280	3,088	1,192	1939	4,914	1,292	3,623	2,834	788
1931–5	3,032	511	2,521	1,977	544	1940	5,614	1,679	3,935	3,117	819
1936–40	4,972	1,283	3,690	2,946	744	1941	6,878	2,132	4,746	3,708	1,038
1941–5	7,817	2,260	5,557	4,562	995	1942	7,576	2,364	5,212	4,103	1,109
1924	5,306	1,233	4,072	2,899	1,174	1943	8,072	2,488	5,584	4,608	976
1925	5,678	1,382	4,295	3,059	1,237	1944	8,417	2,340	6,077	5,178	899
1926	6,214	1,405	4,808	3,542	1,266	1945	8,141	1,975	6,166	5,212	954
1927	5,530	1,221	4,309	3,060	1,249	1946	8,896	1,825	7,071	5,760	1,311
1928	5,385	1,288	4,097	2,885	1,212	1947	12,484	2,909	9,575	7,941	1,634
1929	5,888	1,480	4,407	3,191	1,217	1948	15,670	3,510	12,160	10,266	1,894

MANUFACTURES—SUMMARY, 1849–1947

(Figures for 1849 to 1919 include establishments whose products were valued at $500 or more; for 1921 to 1939, establishments whose products were valued at $5,000 or more; for 1947, figures cover all establishments employing 1 or more persons at any time during year)

CENSUS YEAR	NUMBER OF ESTABLISHMENTS	NUMBER OF PROPRIETORS AND FIRM MEMBERS	ALL EMPLOYEES: NUMBER (AVERAGE FOR YEAR)	ALL EMPLOYEES: SALARIES AND WAGES ($1,000)	PRODUCTION WORKERS: NUMBER (AVERAGE FOR YEAR)	PRODUCTION WORKERS: WAGES ($1,000)	VALUE ADDED ($1,000)
Factories and hand and neighborhood industries:							
1849	123,025	*	*	*	957,059	236,755	463,983
1859	140,433	*	*	*	1,311,246	378,879	854,257
1869	252,148	*	*	*	2,053,996	620,467	1,395,119
1879	253,852	*	*	*	2,732,595	947,954	1,972,756
1889	353,864	*	4,586,494	2,209,058	4,129,355	1,820,854	4,102,301
1899	509,490	*	5,478,301	2,595,566	5,097,562	2,206,547	5,474,892
Factories, excluding hand and neighborhood industries:							
1899	204,750	*	4,850,019	2,258,654	4,501,919	1,892,574	4,646,981
1904	213,444	225,115	5,674,957	2,990,937	5,181,660	2,440,851	6,019,171
1909	264,810	272,421	7,012,066	4,105,470	6,261,736	3,205,213	8,160,075
1914	268,436	258,560	7,514,186	5,015,977	6,602,287	3,782,322	9,385,622
1919	270,231	249,865	9,836,801	12,426,902	8,464,916	9,664,009	23,841,624
1921	192,059	172,291	7,557,364	9,870,199	6,475,474	7,451,299	17,252,775
1923	192,096	147,958	9,474,658	12,996,460	8,194,170	10,148,624	24,569,487
1925	183,877	132,971	9,142,417	12,957,707	7,871,409	9,979,649	25,667,624
1927	187,629	132,151	9,072,052	13,123,135	7,848,070	10,099,465	26,325,394
1929	206,663	132,686	9,659,742	14,284,282	8,369,705	10,884,919	30,591,435
1931	171,450	*	*	*	6,163,144	6,688,541	18,600,532
1933	139,325	72,267	6,557,925	6,237,800	5,787,611	4,940,146	14,007,540
1935	167,916	81,521	8,262,295	9,564,754	7,203,794	7,311,329	18,552,553
1937	166,794	99,268	9,786,402	12,829,749	8,569,231	10,112,883	25,173,539
1939	173,802	123,655	9,527,306	12,706,102	7,808,205	8,997,515	24,487,304
1947	240,881	188,948	14,294,304	39,689,527	11,916,188	30,242,343	74,425,825

* Not available.

RAILROAD MILEAGE, 1860–1948

REGIONS	1860	1870	1880	1890	1900	1910	1920	1930	1940	1948
UNITED STATES	30,626	52,922	93,267	163,597	193,346	240,439	252,845	249,052	233,670	225,149
NEW ENGLAND	3,660	4,494	5,982	6,718	7,521	7,921	7,942	7,596	6,677	6,397
MIDDLE ATLANTIC	5,840	9,709	13,832	18,161	20,709	21,980	22,293	21,752	20,175	19,291
SOUTH ATLANTIC	5,976	7,349	9,789	18,270	23,362	29,795	32,380	31,644	29,475	28,205
EAST NORTH CENTRAL	9,583	14,701	25,109	36,924	41,007	44,928	44,904	43,770	41,281	39,946
WEST NORTH CENTRAL	1,472	8,046	19,094	38,354	42,988	49,730	52,180	51,400	48,293	47,379
EAST SOUTH CENTRAL	3,392	4,656	6,343	11,144	13,343	17,074	17,754	17,452	16,179	15,602
WEST SOUTH CENTRAL	680	1,417	5,044	13,782	18,221	31,122	32,972	33,227	31,497	30,084
MOUNTAIN		1,466	5,082	12,676	15,808	22,956	25,170	24,973	23,518	22,286
PACIFIC	23	1,084	2,992	7,567	10,389	14,932	17,248	17,238	16,575	15,959
ALASKA TERRITORY					22	390	246	790	536	567
HAWAII TERRITORY						175	243	232	192	25

MOTOR VEHICLES—FACTORY SALES AND REGISTRATIONS, 1900–48

YEAR	FACTORY SALES: NUMBER (IN THOUSANDS) TOTAL	PASSENGER CARS	MOTOR TRUCKS	WHOLESALE VALUE (THOUSANDS OF DOLLARS) TOTAL	PASSENGER CARS	MOTOR TRUCKS	REGISTRATIONS (IN THOUSANDS): TOTAL (EXCL. PUBLICLY OWNED)	PASSENGER CARS, AND TAXIS	MOTOR TRUCKS AND BUSSES
1900	4	4		4,899	4,899		8	8	
1905	25	24	1	40,000	38,670	1,330	79	77	1
1910	187	181	6	225,000	215,340	9,660	469	458	10
1915	970	896	74	701,778	575,978	125,800	2,491	2,332	159
1920	2,227	1,906	322	2,232,420	1,809,171	423,249	9,239	8,132	1,108
1922	2,544	2,274	270	1,720,564	1,494,514	226,050	12,274	10,704	1,570
1923	4,034	3,625	409	2,504,810	2,196,272	308,538	15,102	13,253	1,849
1924	3,603	3,186	417	2,288,677	1,970,097	318,581	17,613	15,436	2,177
1925	4,266	3,735	531	2,916,770	2,458,370	458,400	19,941	17,440	2,501
1926	4,301	3,784	517	3,092,188	2,640,065	452,123	22,053	19,221	2,832
1927	3,401	2,937	465	2,584,802	2,164,671	420,131	23,140	20,142	2,997
1928	4,359	3,815	543	3,013,622	2,576,490	437,132	24,512	21,308	3,204
1929	5,358	4,587	771	3,413,148	2,847,119	566,030	26,503	23,060	3,442
1930	3,356	2,785	571	2,034,835	1,645,399	389,437	26,532	22,973	3,559
1931	2,390	1,973	417	1,373,691	1,111,274	262,418	25,862	22,330	3,532
1932	1,371	1,135	235	754,485	618,291	136,193	24,133	20,832	3,300
1933	1,920	1,574	347	948,806	762,737	186,069	23,877	20,586	3,290
1934	2,753	2,178	575	1,467,260	1,147,116	320,144	24,954	21,472	3,482
1935	3,947	3,252	695	2,088,834	1,709,426	379,408	26,230	22,495	3,735
1936	4,454	3,670	785	2,478,467	2,015,646	462,820	28,172	24,108	4,064
1937	4,809	3,916	893	2,778,227	2,243,732	534,495	29,706	25,391	4,315
1938	2,489	2,001	488	1,570,950	1,236,802	334,148	29,443	25,167	4,276
1939	3,577	2,867	710	2,260,018	1,765,189	494,829	30,615	26,140	4,476
1940	4,472	3,717	755	2,938,474	2,370,654	567,820	32,035	27,372	4,663
1941	4,841	3,780	1,061	3,637,006	2,567,206	1,069,800	34,472	29,524	4,948
1942	1,042	223	819	1,591,270	163,814	1,427,457	32,579	27,869	4,710
1943	700		700	1,451,896	102	1,451,794	30,500	25,913	4,587
1944	738	1	738	1,701,376	447	1,700,929	30,086	25,466	4,620
1945	725	70	656	1,239,210	57,255	1,181,956	30,638	25,691	4,947
1946	3,090	2,149	941	3,023,028	1,979,781	1,043,247	33,946	28,100	5,846
1947	4,798	3,558	1,240	5,673,739	3,963,896	1,709,843	37,360	30,719	6,642
1948	5,285	3,909	1,376	6,711,612	4,853,402	1,858,210	40,622	33,261	7,361

MERCHANT MARINE OF THE WORLD AND OF THE UNITED STATES, 1895–1949

(Vessels of 100 tons and over)

YEAR	WORLD TOTAL	UNITED STATES
	1,000 tons	*1,000 tons*
1895	25,086	2,165
1900	28,957	2,750
1905	35,998	3,996
1910	41,915	5,059
1915	49,262	5,893
1920	57,314	16,049
1925	64,641	15,377
1930	69,608	14,046
1935	64,886	12,852
1937	66,286	12,429
1938	67,847	12,050
1939	69,440	12,003
1947	84,356	32,891
1948	81,074	29,602
1949	83,346	28,224

THE LABOR FORCE, 1860–1940

		ALL PERSONS 10 YEARS OLD AND OVER				WOMEN IN LABOR FORCE OR GAINFULLY OCCUPIED, 15 YEARS OLD AND OVER		
		NUMBER OF PERSONS ENGAGED IN—						
		ALL OCCUPATIONS				TOTAL	MARRIED	
YEAR	POPULATION 10 YEARS OLD AND OVER	NUMBER	PERCENT OF POPULATION 10 AND OVER	NONAGRICULTURAL PURSUITS	AGRICULTURAL PURSUITS	NUMBER	NUMBER	PERCENT
1860	22,429,625	10,532,750	47.0	4,325,116	6,207,634			
1870	29,123,683	12,924,951	44.4	6,075,179	6,849,772			
1880	36,761,607	17,392,099	47.3	8,807,289	8,584,810			
1890	47,413,559	23,318,183	49.2	13,379,810	9,938,373	3,712,144	515,260	13.9
1900	57,949,824	29,073,233	50.2	18,161,235	10,911,998	4,997,415	769,477	15.4
1910	71,580,270	37,370,794	52.2	25,779,027	11,591,767	7,639,828	1,890,661	24.7
1920	82,739,315	42,433,535	51.3	30,984,765	11,448,770	8,346,796	1,920,281	23.0
1930	98,723,047	48,829,920	49.5	38,357,922	10,471,998	10,632,227	3,071,302	28.9
1940	110,443,129	52,148,251	47.2	42,985,704	9,162,547	13,840,000	5,040,000	36.4
1950	120,185,361	61,457,262	51.3	53,950,623	7,506,639	17,670,000		

WORK STOPPAGES, 1929–48

YEAR	WORK STOPPAGES BEGINNING IN YEAR		WORKERS INVOLVED		MAN-DAYS IDLE			INDEXES (1935–39 = 100)		
	NUMBER	AVERAGE DURATION (CALENDAR DAYS)	NUMBER (THOUSANDS)	PERCENT OF TOTAL EMPLOYED	NUMBER (THOUSANDS)	PERCENT OF ESTIMATED WORKING TIME	PER WORKER INVOLVED	WORK STOPPAGES	WORKERS INVOLVED	MAN-DAYS IDLE
1929	921	22.6	289	1.2	5,350	.07	18.5	32	26	32
1930	637	22.3	183	.8	3,320	.05	18.1	22	16	20
1931	810	18.8	342	1.6	6,890	.11	20.2	28	30	41
1932	841	19.6	324	1.8	10,500	.23	32.4	29	29	62
1933	1,695	16.9	1,170	6.3	16,900	.36	14.4	59	104	100
1934	1,856	19.5	1,470	7.2	19,600	.38	13.4	65	130	116
1935	2,014	23.8	1,120	5.2	15,500	.29	13.8	70	99	91
1936	2,172	23.3	789	3.1	13,900	.21	17.6	76	70	82
1937	4,740	20.3	1,860	7.2	28,400	.43	15.3	166	165	168
1938	2,772	23.6	688	2.8	9,150	.15	13.3	97	61	54
1939	2,613	23.4	1,170	4.7	17,800	.28	15.2	91	104	105
1940	2,508	20.9	577	2.3	6,700	.10	11.6	88	51	40
1941	4,288	18.3	2,360	8.4	23,000	.32	9.8	150	210	136
1942	2,968	11.7	840	2.8	4,180	.05	5.0	104	75	25
1943	3,752	5.0	1,980	6.9	13,500	.15	6.8	131	176	80
1944	4,956	5.6	2,120	7.0	8,720	.09	4.1	173	188	51
1945	4,750	9.9	3,470	12.2	38,000	.47	11.0	166	308	224
1946	4,985	24.2	4,600	14.5	116,000	1.43	25.2	174	408	684
1947	3,693	25.6	2,170	6.5	34,600	.41	15.9	129	193	204
1948	3,419	21.8	1,960	5.5	34,100	.37	17.4	119	174	201

LABOR UNION MEMBERSHIP, 1931–49

YEAR	ALL UNIONS, TOTAL MEMBERSHIP (1,000)	AMERICAN FEDERATION OF LABOR		CONGRESS OF INDUSTRIAL ORGANIZATIONS		INDEPENDENT OR UNAFFILIATED UNIONS, TOTAL MEMBERSHIP (1,000)
		NUMBER OF AFFILIATED UNIONS	TOTAL MEMBERSHIP (1,000)	NUMBER OF AFFILIATED UNIONS	TOTAL MEMBERSHIP (1,000)	
1931	3,526	105	2,890			636
1932	3,226	106	2,532			694
1933	2,857	108	2,127			730
1934	3,249	109	2,608			641
1935	3,728	109	3,045			683
1936	4,164	111	3,422			742
1937	7,218	100	2,861	32	3,718	639
1938	8,265	102	3,623	42	4,038	604
1939	8,980	104	4,006	45	4,000	974
1940	8,944	105	4,247	42	3,625	1,072
1941	10,489	106	4,569	41	5,000	920
1942	10,762	102	5,483	39	4,195	1,084
1943	13,642	99	6,564	40	5,285	1,793
1944	14,621	100	6,807	41	5,935	1,879
1945	14,796	102	6,931	40	6,000	1,865
1946	14,974	102	7,152	40	6,000	1,822
1947	15,414	105	7,578	41	6,000	1,836
1948	14,000–16,000	105	7,221	40	*	1,800–2,500
1949	14,000–16,000	107	7,241	39	*	1,800–2,500

* Not available.

BIBLIOGRAPHY

THE literature of American History is voluminous and constantly growing. This bibliography makes no pretense of being exhaustive and all-inclusive; only the most important and useful titles are cited. Two reading lists have been prepared. The first includes titles that we believe will be most helpful as supplementary reading. The second and longer list is intended for the convenience of advanced students and others who desire wider knowledge of the topics discussed in the several chapters and sections of this book. Consequently, both lists follow the book's organization. To assist the reader further the lists are preceded by citations of general works.

1. BIBLIOGRAPHICAL GUIDES

One of the most recent and valuable aids is H. P. Beers, *Bibliographies in American History: Guide to Materials for Research* (1942). Useful also are the annual volumes of bibliography sponsored by the American Historical Association and prepared by Grace G. Griffin and others under the title *Writings on American History* (1906–1938). W. H. Allison and others, *Guide to Historical Literature* (1931) is a general bibliography. Of the older bibliographies the following are still authoritative: Edward Channing, A. B. Hart, and F. J. Turner, *Guide to the Study and Reading of American History* (1912) contains classified lists of books including general and special histories, geography, travel, biography, state and local history, literature, education, music, fine arts, and special topics relating to constitutional, diplomatic, economic, social and religious history. J. N. Larned (ed.), *Literature of American History* (1902) has signed evaluations or reviews of over four thousand important books. A. P. C. Griffin, *Bibliography of American Historical Societies, The United States and the Dominion of Canada* (2nd ed., 1907) has tables of contents of all important historical societies in the United States from their foundation; it also has a subject index. It appeared as Volume II of the Annual Report of the American Historical Association in 1905. The most complete guide to American agricultural history is E. E. Edwards, *A Bibliography of the History of Agriculture in the United States.* (1930)

The use of Federal public documents published before 1881 is made laborious by the inadequacies of indexes. B. P. Poore, *A Descriptive Catalogue of the Government Publications of the United States, September 5, 1774–March 4, 1881* (1885) was published as Senate Miscellaneous Document No. 67, 48th Cong., 2 sess. Unfortunately it is without subject entries. This difficulty was partially overcome when in 1902 there was published *Tables of and Annotated Index to Congressional Series of United States Public Documents.* J. G. Ames, *Comprehensive Index to the Publications of the United States Government, 1881–1893* (2 vols., 1905) appeared as *House Document* No. 754, 58 Cong. 2 sess. Since 1893 a separate index for each

Congress has been published. For those interested in economic history the most comprehensive guide to state documents is A. R. Hasse, *Index to Economic Material in Documents of the States of the United States* (13 vols., 1907–22). Also see Poole's *Index to Periodicals* (1893) and *Reader's Guide to Periodical Literature* (1901–)

2. DICTIONARIES AND ENCYCLOPEDIAS

Appleton's Cyclopedia of American Biography (1886–1922), though largely superseded by more recent works, is still useful. Allen Johnson and Dumas Malone (eds.), *Dictionary of American Biography* (20 vols., 1928–36), modeled after the *British Dictionary of National Biography,* contains 14,000 biographies of Americans with a bibliography at end of each biography and maintains high levels of scholarship and literary style. E. R. A. Seligman (ed.), *Encyclopaedia of the Social Sciences* (15 vols., 1930–5) should also be consulted by those interested in social and economic history. James T. Adams and R. V. Coleman (eds.), *Dictionary of American History* (6 vols., 1940) is a useful reference to anyone in search of specific facts, events, trends or policies relating to American history.

3. PERIODICALS

The American Historical Review (1895–) is the organ of the American Historical Association founded in 1884. It reviews all new historical literature and in each of its quarterly issues prints important articles and documents. The following periodicals also include valuable book reviews as well as lists of current books and articles: *Annals* of the American Academy of Political and Social Science (1890–), *Political Science Quarterly* (1886–), *American Economic Review* (1911–), *Journal of Economic History* (1941–), and *Agricultural History* (1927–). Of the many state, regional, or subject periodicals the best are the *Mississippi Valley Historical Review* (1915–), *The New England Quarterly* (1928–), *New York History* (1919–), *The William and Mary Quarterly,* (1892–), the *Pennsylvania Magazine of History and Biography* (1877–), *Journal of Negro History* (1916–), the *Proceedings and Collections of the Massachusetts Historical Society* (1791–), the *Proceedings of the American Antiquarian Society* (1812–), *Journal of Southern History* (1935–), *Catholic Historical Review* (1915–).

4. GEOGRAPHICAL BACKGROUND

R. H. Brown, *Historical Geography of the United States* (1948), E. C. Semple, *American History and Its Geographic Conditions* (revd. 1933) and A. P. Brigham, *Geographic Influences in American History* (1903) are pioneer works still standard. Isaiah Bowman, *Forest Physiography* (1911) and J. R. Smith, *North America* (1942) are the best descriptive accounts of the geography of the United States. Isaiah Bowman, *The New World* (1928) and N. S. Shaler (ed.), *The United States of America* (2 vols., 1894) stress the relation of geography to economics and history. A. B. Hulbert, *Soil* (1930) traces its influence on American history; his *Historic Highways of America* (16 vols., 1902–05) is a monographic collection on the great rivers and highways of the United States. Constance L. Skinner (ed.), *The Rivers of America* (1937–) interprets parts of our history against a geographical background. The three most usable historical atlases are D. R. Fox, *Harpers Atlas of American History* (1920). C. O. Paullin, *Atlas of the Historical Geography of the United States* (1932) and C. L. and E. H. Lord, *Historical Atlas of the United States* (1944). Those interested in maps should also consult E. M. Avery, *A History of the United States* (7 vols., 1904–10).

5. COMPREHENSIVE HISTORIES OF THE UNITED STATES

No individual work of a comprehensive nature covers the history of the United States from its beginning to the present; only co-operative undertakings have succeeded in this enterprise. The outstanding effort by an individual is Edward Channing *A History of the United States* (6 vols., 1905–25), which carries the story to 1865. Based on source materials and singularly free from inaccuracies, this work is most dependable. During the twentieth century co-operative histories of the United States have increased in number. The first important series to appear was A. B. Hart (ed.), *The American Nation: A History* (28 vols., 1904–18). Volumes uneven in content, but each contains excellent maps and bibliography; a new series of this work is now being prepared under the editorship of H. S. Commager. Another co-operative enterprise in historical writing is Allen Johnson and Allan Nevins (eds.), *Chronicles of America* (56 vols., 1918–51). These volumes though short and popular in literary style are, with some exceptions, scholarly and cover all phases of American history through the administration of Franklin D. Roosevelt; this series is uneven in merit. A. M. Schlesinger and D. R. Fox (eds.), *A History of American Life* (13 vols., 1927–48) with its emphasis upon social and intellectual rather than political history is unquestionably the most important work of its kind to date; it is especially valuable for bibliography. Henry David and others (eds.), *The Economic History of the United States* (9 vols. 1945–), now in progress, will be extremely useful for the history of the economic development of the United States. R. E. Spiller and others, *Literary History of the United States* (3 vols., 1948) is a major co-operative effort with a comprehensive bibliography constituting the third volume. R. H. Gabriel (ed.), *The Pageant of America* (15 vols., 1925–9) is a successful co-operative attempt to present the story of the United States through pictures and other graphic material. It should be supplemented by J. T. Adams (ed.), *Album of American History* (4 vols., 1944–8), Stefan Lorant, *The Presidency: A Pictorial History of Presidential Executives from Washington to Truman* (1951); and Marshall Davidson, *Life in America* (2 vols., 1951). The outstanding comprehensive interpretative work covering the entire period is C. A. and M. R. Beard, *The Rise of American Civilization: I, The Agricultural Era* (rev., 1933); *II, The Industrial Era* (rev., 1933); *III, America in Midpassage* (1939); *IV, The American Spirit* (1942). More factual but also interpretative is Joseph Dorfman, *The Economic Mind in American Civilization* (3 vols., 1946–9), which has detailed bibliography. In the field of biography, *The American Statesman* series (40 vols., 1898–1917), edited by John T. Morse, Jr., is comprehensive, but uneven; a new edition of this work is now being prepared under the editorship of Oscar Handlin.

Important for the colonial period are: H. L. Osgood, *The American Colonies in the Seventeenth Century* (3 vols., 1904–07) and *The American Colonies in the Eighteenth Century* (4 vols., 1924–5), C. M. Andrews, *The Colonial Period of American History* (4 vols., 1934–8), George Bancroft, *History of the United States* (10 vols., 1834–75). Bancroft catches the buoyant spirit of America, but his treatment is somewhat partisan and provincial. J. A. Doyle, *English Colonies in America* (5 vols., 1882–1907) best represents the English viewpoint. Osgood is excellent on the development of colonial political institutions. Another comprehensive work of great value is L. H. Gipson, *The British Empire before the American Revolution* (1936–). To date seven volumes have been published.

Of the general histories of the United States during the period from the Revolution to 1865 the following should be consulted: James Schouler, *History of the United States of America, Under the Constitution* (7 vols., 1880–1913). Though biased and somewhat antiquated and peculiar in style, it contains much that is extremely valuable on political and constitutional matters. John B. McMaster, *A History of the People of the United States, from the Revolution to the Civil War* (8 vols., 1883–1913), which covers the years 1784–1861 is rich in social and economic facts and records obtained largely from newspapers and other contemporary sources; it is badly organized, however, and is difficult to read consecutively. It is supplemented by a ninth volume, *A History of the People of the United States during Lincoln's Administration* (1927). E. P. Oberholtzer, *A History of the United States Since the Civil War* (5 vols., 1917–37) continues the work of McMaster and brings the story to 1901. Henry Adams's *History of the United States of America During the Administrations of Jefferson and Madison* (9 vols., 1889–91) covers the administrations of Jefferson and Madison. The first volume contains a valuable account of the state of society in 1800. Herbert Agar (ed.), *The Formative Years* (2 vols., 1947) is a convenient condensation of this famous work. See also Richard Hildreth, *The History of the United States of America* (6 vols., 1856–60), and Hermann von Holst, *Constitutional and Political History of the United States* (new ed., 8 vols., 1899). The first five volumes of J. R. Rhodes, *History of the United States from the Compromise of 1850* (9 vols., 1893–1919) give a detailed account of the causes and events of the Civil War. The same period is now being re-examined by Allan Nevins. To date four volumes have been published: *Ordeal of the Union* (2 vols., 1947); *The Emergence of Lincoln* (2 vols., 1950). Admirable in almost every respect, these four volumes cover the years 1847 through 1861.

6. SOURCE MATERIALS

There is no lack of collections of source materials. The following are commended: H. S. Commager (ed.), *Documents of American History* (5th ed., 1949) excellent for political and constitutional sources; so also is William McDonald, *Documentary Source Book of American History, 1606–1926* (3rd ed., 1926). L. M. Hacker and H. S. Zahler, *The Shaping of the American Tradition* (2 vols., 1947) contains a voluminous amount of social, economic, and cultural material that is most illuminating; H. S. Commager and Allan Nevins (eds.), *The Heritage of America* (rev. ed., 1949) contains good materials on American social development; extremely useful are A. B. Hart (ed.), *American History Told by Contemporaries* (5 vols., 1897–1929) and Willard Thorp, M. E. Curti, and Carlos Baker (eds.), *American Issues* (2 vols., 1941). The principal source books on economic history are G. S. Callender, *Selections from the Economic History of the United States, 1765–1860* (1909) which has excellent introductory essays, E. L. Bogart and C. M. Thompson, *Readings in the Economic History of the United States* (1916), and F. Flügel and H. U. Faulkner, *Readings in the Economic and Social History of the United States* (1929). Those wishing source material on other special subjects should consult R. J. Bartlett, *The Record of American Diplomacy* (1947), I. F. Woestemeyer and J. M. Gambrill, *The Westward Movement* (1939), and L. B. Schmidt and E. D. Ross, *Readings in the Economic History of American Agriculture* (1925).

7. SPECIAL PHASES OF AMERICAN DEVELOPMENT

Useful on certain phases of American history are the following books:

1. *Economic History:* E. C. Kirkland, *A History of American Economic Life* (rev. ed., 1939); H. U. Faulkner, *American Economic History* (6th ed., 1949); E. L. Bogart and D. L. Kemmerer, *Economic History of the American People* (rev. ed., 1947); B. and L. M. Mitchell, *American Economic History* (1947); F. A. Shannon, *America's Economic Growth* (3rd ed., 1951) and C. W. Wright, *Economic History of the United States* (rev. ed., 1949) are the best of the one-volume economic histories. Several aspects of American economic history are treated in the volumes published by the Carnegie Institute of Washington. Though inadequate and uneven in merit, they are still very useful: E. R. Johnson et al., *History of Domestic and Foreign Commerce of the United States* (2 vols., 1915); B. H. Meyer et al., *History of Transportation in the United States Before 1860* (1917); F. W. Taussig, *The Tariff History of the United States* (8th ed., 1931); V. S. Clark, *History of Manufactures in the United States,* (new ed., 3 vols., 1929); P. W. Bidwell and J. A. Falconer, *History of Agriculture in the Northern United States, 1620–1860* (1925) and L. C. Gray, *History of Agriculture in the Southern United States to 1860* (2 vols., 1933). All of these works have extensive bibliographies.

2. *Financial History.* D. R. Dewey, *Financial History of the United States,* (12th ed., 1936) is the standard authority. It should be supplemented by W. J. Schultz and M. R. Caine, *Financial Development of the United States* (1937).

3. *Agriculture and Land Policies:* The definitive history of American agriculture is yet to be written. Joseph Schafer, *The Social History of American Agriculture*

(1936) is a brief outline. An older work is A. H. Sanford, *The Story of Agriculture in the United States* (1916). Far more satisfactory is E. E. Edwards, "American Agriculture—The First 300 Years," United States Department of Agriculture, *Yearbook* (1940). The newest treatise on public lands is R. M. Robbins, *Our Landed Heritage: The Public Domain, 1776–1936* (1942). An older work is B. H. Hibbard, *A History of the Public Land Policies* (1924). For a mass of undigested factual information, consult Thomas Donaldson, *The Public Domain* (1884).

4. *Immigration:* The best accounts are M. L. Hansen, *The Immigrant in American History* (1940) and *The Atlantic Migration, 1607–1860* (1940); J. R. Commons, *Races and Immigrants in America* (new ed., 1920); and G. M. Stephenson, *A History of American Immigration, 1820–1924* (1926). M. R. Davie, *World Immigration* (1936) gives valuable comparative material, a helpful list of immigrant biographies, and considerable literary material treating immigrants and immigration; Edith Abbott, *Historical Aspects of the Immigration Problem: Select Documents* (1926) also contains valuable source material. See also Carl Wittke, *We Who Built America* (1948) and Oscar Handlin's excellent *The Uprooted: The Epic Story of the Great Migrations that Made the American People* (1951).

5. *Constitutional History:* Consult A. C. McLaughlin, *A Constitutional History of the United States* (1935); C. B. Swisher, *American Constitutional Development* (1943); H. C. Hockett, *The Constitutional History of the United States, 1776–1876* (2 vols., 1939); B. F. Wright, *The Growth of American Constitutional Law* (1942); A. H. Kelly and W. A. Harbison, *The American Constitution, Its Origins and Development* (1948) and R. L. Schuyler, *The Constitution of the United States* (1923).

6. *Foreign Relations:* T. A. Bailey, *A Diplomatic History of the American People* (4th ed., 1950) and S. F. Bemis, *The Diplomatic History of the United States* (rev. ed., 1948) are standard one-volume surveys. There is a wealth of material in S. F. Bemis (ed.), *The American Secretaries of State and Their Diplomacy* (10 vols., 1927–9). For our relations with Canada, see J. T. Shotwell (ed.), *The Relation of Canada with the United States* (14 vols., 1939). The best collection of treaties in convenient form is W. M. Malloy, *Treaties, Conventions, International Acts, Protocols, and Agreements between the United States and Other Powers 1776–1937* (4 vols., 1910–37). The documentary history of foreign relations is available in the following government compilations: *Diplomatic Correspondence of the United States, 1783–1789* (7 vols., 1833–4); American State Papers, *Foreign Relations 1789–1828* (6 vols., 1832–61) and since 1870, *Papers Relating to the Foreign Relations of the United States,* in one or more annual volumes. Between 1828 and 1860 the papers on foreign relations of the United States have not been collected and are to be found only in congressional documents. From 1860 to 1870 they were published annually under various titles. Students for foreign relations will find rich material in J. B. Moore, *History and Digest of the International Arbitrations to which the United States has been a Party* (6 vols., 1898), and *A Digest of International Law* (8 vols., 1906).

7. *Military and Naval History.* Few comprehensive accounts of these aspects of American history have as yet been written. Consult O. L. Spaulding, *The United States Army in War and Peace* (1937); H. and M. Sprout, *The Rise of American Naval Power, 1776–1918* (1939); C. S. Alden and A. Westcott, *The United States Navy* (1943); D. W. Knox, *A History of the United States Navy* (1948); and C. H. Metcalf, *A History of the United States Marine Corps* (1939). Among the many works dealing with wars to which the United States has been a party the following may be cited: On the War of Independence: C. F. Adams, *Studies Military and Diplomatic, 1775–1865* (1911); G. W. Allen, *A Naval History of the American Revolution* (2 vols., 1913); W. M. Wallace, *Appeal to Arms* (1951). *The War of 1812.* A. T. Mahan, *Sea Power in Its Relations to the War of 1812* (2 vols., 1905); C. P. Lucas, *The Canadian War of 1812* (1906). Mexican War: R. S. Henry, *The Story of the Mexican War* (1950); J. H. Smith, *The War with Mexico* (2 vols., 1919). Civil War: J. C. Ropes and W. R. Livermore, *The Story of the Civil War* (4 vols., 1894–1913); J. G. Randall, *Civil War and Reconstruction* (1937); F. A. Shannon, *The Organization and Administration of the Union Army* (2 vols., 1928); R. S. Henry,

Story of the Confederacy (1931); D. S. Freeman, *R. E. Lee, A Biography* (4 vols., 1934–7) and by the same author, *Lee's Lieutenants* (3 vols., 1942–4) and *Lee's Dispatches to Davis* (1915); J. T. Scharf, *History of the Confederate States Navy* (1886); D. D. Porter, *The Naval History of the Civil War* (1887); J. P. Baxter, III, *The Introduction of the Ironclad Warship* (1933); H. S. Commager, *The Blue and the Gray* (2 vols., 1950).

8. *Travel and Travelers' Descriptions:* The best anthologies of travelers' accounts are H. S. Commager, *America in Perspective* (1947) and Oscar Handlin, *This Was America* (1949). Also consult J. L. Mesick, *The English Traveler in America, 1785–1835* (1922); Allan Nevins, *America Through British Eyes* (1948); H. T. Tuckerman, *America and Her Commentators* (1864); Frank Monaghan, *French Travelers in the United States, 1765–1832* (1933); R. G. Thwaites (ed.), *Early Western Travels* (32 vols., 1904–7) and S. J. Buck, *Travel and Description, 1765–1865* (1914). On conditions of travel, consult Seymour Dunbar, *A History of Travel in America* (4 vols., 1915).

9. *Education:* An older text is E. P. Cubberly, *Public Education in the United States* (1919). It should be supplemented by Paul Monroe (ed.), *A Cyclopedia of Education* (5 vols., 1911–13). Useful also are M. E. Curti, *The Social Ideas of American Educators* (1935); E. W. Knight, *Education in the United States* (rev. ed., 1941); E. G. Dexter, *A History of Education in the United States* (1922); C. F. Thwing, *A History of Higher Education in America* (1906); T. A. Woody, *A History of Women's Education in the United States* (2 vols., 1929); and C. G. Woodson, *The Education of the Negro Prior to 1861* (1915).

10. *The Fine Arts and Music.* For architecture, consult Sahdkichi Hartmann, *A History of American Art* (2 vols., 1902); C. H. Caffin, *The Story of American Painting* (1907); Eugen Neuhaus, *The History and Ideals of American Art* (1931); Alan Burroughs, *Limners and Likenesses: Three Centuries of American Painting* (1936); J. T. Flexner, *America's Old Masters* (1939); Samuel Isham and Royal Cortissoz, *The History of American Painting* (new ed., 1936); Jerome Mellquist, *The Emergence of an American Art* (1942); Homer St. Gaudens, *The American Artist and His Times* (1941), and Oliver W. Larkin, *Art and Life in America* (1949). The beginnings of American sculpture are appraised in Lorado Taft, *The History of American Sculpture* (rev. ed., 1924) and W. H. Downes, *The Life and Works of Winslow Homer* (1911). The most useful surveys of American music are L. C. Elson, *The History of American Music* (rev. ed., 1925) and J. T. Howard, *Our American Music* (1931). They may be supplemented by H. C. Lahee, *Annals of Music in America* (1922); T. F. Hamlin, *The American Spirit in Architecture* (1926); Lewis Mumford, *Sticks and Stones: A Study of American Architecture and Civilization* (1924); and H. B. Major, *The Domestic Architecture of the Early American Republic* (1926). The graphic arts are best covered by Frank Weitenkampf, *American Graphic Art* (1912) and the drama by A. H. Quinn, *A History of the American Drama from the Beginning to the Civil War* (1923).

11. *Science, Religion, and Philosophy.* On science Max Meisel (comp.), *A Bibliography of American Natural History: The Pioneer Century 1769–1865* (3 vols., 1924–9) is for those who desire acquaintance with scientific progress in America before and during the Civil War. See also the excellent survey, W. M. and M. S. C. Smallwood, *Natural History and the American Mind* (1941). The following are also helpful: E. W. Bryn, *The Progress of Invention in the Nineteenth Century* (1900); Waldemar Kaempffert, *A Popular History of American Inventions* (2 vols., 1924); L. L. Woodruff (ed.), *The Development of the Sciences* (1923); John Fiske, *A Century of Science,* (1899); E. S. Dana and others, *A Century of Science in America* (1918); D. J. Struik, *Yankee Science in the Making* (1948); Bernard Jaffe, *Men of Science in America* (1944) and F. R. Packard, *History of Medicine in the United States* (2 vols., 1931). The most usable books on religion are H. K. Rowe, *The History of Religion in the United States* (1924); W. W. Sweet, *The Story of Religions in America* (1930) and T. C. Hall, *Religious Background of American Culture* (1930). For more detailed accounts of leading denominations, consult Philip Schaff and others, *The American Church History Series* (13 vols., 1893–1901);

J. G. Shea, *A History of the Catholic Church in the United States* (4 vols., 1886–92); H. E. Luccock and P. Hutchinson, *The Story of Methodism* (1926); W. S. Perry, *History of the American Episcopal Church* (2 vols., 1885); and Williston Walker, *A History of the Congregational Churches in the United States* (1894). E. B. Greene, *Religion and the State* (1941) examines a recurring theme in history of America. Two older works on the history of American philosophy are still useful: Woodbridge Riley, *American Thought from Puritanism to Pragmatism and Beyond* (new ed., 1922) and H. G. Townsend, *Philosophical Ideas in the United States* (1934). More recent treatises are H. W. Schneider, *A History of American Philosophy* (1946) and W. H. Werkmeister, *A History of Philosophical Ideas in America* (1949).

12. *Intellectual History.* Among the major works are Harvey Wish, *Society and Thought in Early America* (1950); Alexis de Tocqueville, *Democracy in America* (new ed., 2 vols., 1945); V. L. Parrington, *Main Currents in American Thought* (3 vols., 1927–30); M. E. Curti, *The Growth of American Thought* (1951); R. H. Gabriel, *The Course of American Democratic Thought* (1940).

8. HISTORIOGRAPHY

For those desiring a critical estimate of American historiography the following will be useful: W. T. Hutchinson (ed.), *The Marcus W. Jernegan Essays in American Historiography* (1937); Michael Kraus, *A History of American History* (1937); H. E. Barnes, *A History of Historical Writing* (1937); Allan Nevins, *The Gateway to History* (1938); and Herman Ausubel, *Historians and Their Craft; a Study of the Presidential Addresses of the American Historical Association* (1950).

A SELECTED BIBLIOGRAPHY FOR CLASS ASSIGNMENTS

1. LEGACY OF CIVIL WAR

The best brief discussion of this period is to be found in L. M. Hacker and B. B. Kendrick, *The United States Since 1865* (4th ed., 1949), Chaps. 1–3 and J. G. Randall, *The Civil War and Reconstruction* (1937), especially chaps. 30–5. On constitutional problems read W. A. Dunning, *Reconstruction, Political and Economic, 1865–1877* (1907), and C. B. Swisher, *American Constitutional Development* (1943), chap. 15. The election of 1868 is handled adequately by C. H. Coleman, *The Election of 1868* (1933) and that of 1876, by P. L. Haworth, *The Hayes-Tilden Election* (rev. ed., 1927). H. K. Beale, *The Critical Year: A Study of Andrew Johnson and Reconstruction* (1930) covers the early part of Johnson's administration. Useful on the Ku-Klux Klan is S. F. Horn, *Invisible Empire: The Story of the Ku Klux Klan, 1866–71* (1939). On the Grant scandals, see D. C. Seitz, *The Dreadful Decade, 1869–79* (1926) and Allan Nevins, *Hamilton Fish: The Inner History of the Grant Administration* (1936). E. D. Ross, *The Liberal Republican Movement* (1919) traces this political movement from its beginning. The social aspects of period are discussed by Allan Nevins, *The Emergence of Modern America, 1865–1878* (1928).

For source material consult, H. S. Commager, *Documents of American History* (5 ed., 1949), nos. 229, 234–9, 244, 248–56, 258, 267, 269–74, 276–86, 288–93, 296–7.

2. THE LAST FRONTIER

F. L. Paxson, *History of the American Frontier* (1924) is a systematic but not too lively discussion; see especially chaps. 50–9. By far the best works for this chapter are W. P. Webb, *The Great Plains* (1931) and F. A. Shannon, *The Farmer's Last Frontier: Agriculture, 1860–1897* (1945), chaps. 2, 3, 7–10. On mining, consult W. J. Trimble, *The Mining Advance into the Inland Empire* (1914). E. S. Osgood, *The Day of the Cattleman* (1929) is excellent on the cattle kingdom. There is abundant material on the Indians in John Collier, *The Indians of the Americas* (1947).

For source materials, see F. Flügel and H. U. Faulkner, *Readings in the Economic and Social History of the United States* (1929) pp. 473–6, 750–64; H. S. Commager, *Documents of American History*, nos. 302, 304, 315.

3. THE DEVELOPMENT OF A NATIONAL RAIL SYSTEM

For a general introductory account see John Moody, *The Railroad Builders* (1919), especially chaps. 6–12. E. R. Johnson and T. W. Van Metre, *Principles of Railroad Transportation* (1921), chaps. 2–9, 14–31. The history of the Western railroads is told in lively fashion in R. E. Riegel, *The Story of the Western Railroads* (1926). See also J. B. Hedges, *Henry Villard and the Railways of the Northwest* (1930). For different types of railroad builders and promoters, read H. G. Pearson, *An American Railroad builder, John Murray Forbes* (1911) and Oscar Lewis, *The Big Four: the Story of Huntington, Stanford, Hopkins, and Crocker, and of the Building of the Central Pacific* (1938). The best accounts of railroad finance are W. Z. Ripley, *Railroads: Finance and Organization* (1915) and F. A. Cleveland and F. W. Powell, *Railroad Promotion and Capitalization in the United States* (1909). Congressional aid to railroads is handled adequately by L. H. Haney in his *Congressional History of Railways 1850–1887* (1910). For railroad regulation consult I. F. Sharfman, *The Interstate Commerce Commission* (4 vols., 1931–7).

For source material, see F. Flügel and H. U. Faulkner, *Readings in the Economic and Social History of the United States,* already cited, chap. 15; and H. S. Commager, *Documents of American History,* nos. 215, 294, 314, 318, 319.

4. INDUSTRIAL EVOLUTION AND REVOLUTION

E. C. Kirkland, *A History of American Economic Life* (rev. ed., 1950), chap. 11 and H. U. Faulkner, *American Economic History* (6th ed., 1949), chap. 20 are brief surveys. For a more detailed account, see V. S. Clark, *History of Manufactures in the United States* (rev. ed., 1929), Vol. II, chaps. 1, 6, 13, 14, 44; Vol. III, chaps. 1, 22. B. J. Hendrick, *The Age of Big Business* (1919) is a useful summary. National Industrial Conference Board, *A Graphic Analysis of the Census of Manufactures, 1849 to 1919* (1923) is excellent. A highly intelligent interpretation of the last decades of the nineteenth century can be found in I. M. Tarbell, *The Nationalizing of Business, 1878–1898* (1936) especially chaps. 4, 5, 11. On the tariff the standard authority is F. W. Taussig, *The Tariff History of the United States* (rev. ed., 1931). Carter Goodrich and others, *Migration and Economic Opportunity* (1936) is indispensable for industrial regionalism. On competition and concentration, see H. R. Seager and C. A. Gulick, Jr., *Trust and Corporation Problems* (1929) and M. W. Watkins, *Industrial Combinations and Public Policy* (1927). Lewis Corey, *The House of Morgan* (1930) gives an admirable picture of finance capitalism at work. See also John Moody, *The Masters of Capital* (1919). On the transformation of the South, see C. Vann Woodward, *Origins of the New South, 1877–1913* (1951).

For source material, see F. Flügel and H. U. Faulkner, *Readings in the Economic and Social History of the United States,* pp. 793–835; H. S. Commager, *Documents of American History,* nos. 215, 231, 320, 339.

5. THE INDUSTRIAL WORKER

Excellent brief accounts are E. C. Kirkland, *A History of American Economic Life* (rev. ed., 1950), chap. 13 and H. U. Faulkner, *American Economic History* (6th ed., 1949), chap. 22. More detailed accounts are E. Stein and others, *Labor Problems in America* (1940); J. R. Commons and others, *History of Labor in the United States* (1918–35), Vol. III, on labor legislation and Vol. IV, on labor movements; C. R. Daugherty, *Labor Problems in American Industry* (1936), chaps. 16–18; and N. J. Ware, *The Labor Movement in the United States, 1860–1895* (1929). Herbert Harris, *American Labor* (1939) is excellent on growth of unions. Henry David, *The History of the Haymarket Affair: A Study in the American Social-Revolutionary and Labor Movements* (1936) is unsurpassed. It may be supplemented with Samuel Yellen, *American Labor Struggles* (1936). On Negro labor C. H. Wesley, *Negro Labor in the United States, 1850–1925* (1927) is best. For radical unionism, see P. F. Brissenden, *The I. W. W., A Study of American Syndicalism* (1919). On trade unionism, consult Selig Perlman, *History of Trade Unionism in the United States* (1922) and Leo Wolman, *The Growth of American Trade Unions, 1880–1923* (1924). For the effect of immigration on American labor, see Carl Wittke, *We Who Built America: The Saga of the Immigrant* (1939) and I. A. Hourwich, *Immigration and Labor* (rev. ed., 1922). L. L. Lorwin, *The American Federation of Labor* (1933) is most useful on this topic. On labor and the law, see E. E. Witte, *The Government in Labor Disputes* (1932).

For source material, see F. Flügel and H. U. Faulkner, *Readings in the Economic and Social History of the United States,* chap. 18; H. S. Commager, *Documents of American History,* nos. 233, 295, 298, 301, 310, 326, 334–46, 364–6, 368, 403, 413–15, 421, 430, 434, 444, 451, 473, 474.

6. THE COMMERCIAL FARMER

For an excellent brief survey, read E. C. Kirkland, *A History of American Economic Life* (rev. ed., 1950), chap. 12. The best detailed account is F. A. Shannon,

The Farmer's Last Frontier, Agriculture, 1860–1897 (1945), especially chaps. 4–14. On mechanization an older work H. W. Quaintance, *The Influence of Farm Machinery on Production and Labor* (1904) is still useful. The best account on farm tenancy is E. A. Goldenweiser and L. E. Truesdell, *Farm Tenancy in the United States,* Census Monographs no. 4, 1920 census (1924). On farm credit, see E. S. Sparks, *History and Theory of Agricultural Credit in the United States* (1932). For agrarian discontent, see S. J. Buck, *The Agrarian Crusade* (1920) and *The Granger Movement* (1913) chaps. 1–3, 8–9; J. D. Hicks, *The Populist Revolt: A History of the Farmers' Alliance and People's Party* (1931); and P. R. Fossum, *The Agrarian Movement in North Dakota* (1925), which is very good on the Non-Partisan League.

For source material, consult F. Flügel and H. U. Faulkner, *Readings in the Economic and Social History of the United States,* chap. 17; L. B. Schmidt and E. E. Ross, *Readings in the Economic History of American Agriculture* (1925); and H. S. Commager, *Documents of American History,* nos. 214, 216, 287, 294, 316, 323–5.

7. NEW AND OLD CULTURAL PATTERNS

General accounts are given in M. E. Curti, *The Growth of American Thought* (rev. 1951) chaps. 20–22 and V. L. Parrington, *Main Currents in American Thought* (1927–30), Vol. III. Equally valuable are Allan Nevins, *The Emergence of Modern America, 1865–1878* (1928), chaps. 8–10, 12, and A. M. Schlesinger, *The Rise of the City, 1878–1898* (1933), chaps. 4–11. On education, consult E. P. Cubberley, *Public Education in the United States* (1919) and C. F. Thwing, *A History of Higher Education in America* (1906). On religion, W. W. Sweet, *The Story of Religions in America* (1930) is a general study. On newspapers and the development of the magazine, see F. L. Mott, *American Journalism* (1941) and *A History of American Magazines* (1930–8), Vol. III. The best treatment of literature is Parrington, cited above; Oscar Cargill, *Intellectual America: Ideas on the March* (1941); and R. E. Spiller and others (eds.), *Literary History of the United States* (1948), Vol. II. On art and architecture, see Suzanne La Follette, *Art in America* (1929). J. T. Howard, *Our American Music* (1931) is the standard work on this subject.

For source material, see L. M. Hacker and H. S. Zahler. *The Shaping of the American Tradition* (1947), pp. 703–24.

8. THE POLITICS OF CONFORMITY AND REVOLT

C. A. and M. R. Beard, *The Rise of American Civilization* (1927–42), Vol. II, chaps. 23–4 give a brief summary of the leading events and their meaning. For a more detailed account, see J. F. Rhodes, *History of the United States from the Compromise of 1850* (1900–28), Vol. 8, especially chaps. 7–9, 14–17. For the Hayes administration, see H. J. Eckenrode, *Rutherford B. Hayes, Statesman of Reunion* (1930), chaps. 10–11. Garfield's campaign and administration is handled adequately by R. G. Caldwell, *James A. Garfield, Party Chieftain* (1931), chaps. 14–15. Allan Nevins, *Grover Cleveland: A Study in Courage* (1932), chaps. 11–31, is the best account of Cleveland's campaigns and administration. His chapter 36 in the same volume and C. S. Olcott, *William McKinley* (1917), Vol. II, pp. 293–326, and Paxton Hibben, *The Peerless Leader, William Jennings Bryan* (1929) chaps. 15–17 together give a several-sided description of the campaign of 1896. C. R. Fish, *The Civil Service and the Patronage* (1905) is the standard work on the subject. On the currency issue, see A. B. Hepburn, *A History of Currency in the United States* (rev. ed., 1924).

For source material, see H. S. Commager, *Documents of American History,* nos. 297–300, 303, 308, 312, 317.

9. OVERSEAS EXPANSION

An excellent brief survey covering this topic will be found in Chapter 15 of E. C. Kirkland, *A History of American Economic Life,* cited previously. It should be followed by C. A. Beard, *The Idea of National Interest* (1934). On the Venezuelan dispute, consult Allan Nevins, *Grover Cleveland,* cited previously, chap. 34 and Dexter Perkins, *The Monroe Doctrine, 1867–1907* (1937). Samoa is treated fully in G. H. Ryden, *The Foreign Policy of the United States in Relation to Samoa* (1933). On Hawaii, see S. F. Bemis, *A Diplomatic History of the United States* (rev. ed., 1950), chap. 25 and J. W. Pratt, *Expansionists of 1898* (1936), chap. 2–4. On the martial spirit and the war with Spain, see Walter Millis, *The Martial Spirit: A Study of Our War with Spain* (1931).

For source material, see H. S. Commager, *Documents of American History,* nos. 268, 281, 305, 329–31, 340, 345–52.

10. THE AMERICAN EMPIRE

On colonial holdings and administration, read W. H. Haas, *The American Empire* (1940). For the Far East, see S. F. Bemis, *A Diplomatic History of the United States,* cited previously, chaps. 13–36, 40, and A. W. Griswold, *The Far Eastern Policy of the United States* (1938), chaps. 2–7. On Panama and the canal, consult J. F. Rippy, *The Capitalists and Colombia* (1931), chaps. 2–5 and T. A. Bailey, *A Diplomatic History of the American People* (4th ed., 1950), chap. 32. On Santo Domingo, see M. M. Knight, *The Americans in Santo Domingo* (1928), chaps. 1–9. Central America is treated by G. H. Stuart, *Latin America and the United States* (4th ed., 1943), chaps. 13–14. On Mexico, see C. W. Hackett, *The Mexican Revolution and the United States, 1910–1926* (1926). For criticism of American imperialistic expansion, read Scott Nearing and Joseph Freeman, *Dollar Diplomacy* (1925) and A. K. Weinberg, *Manifest Destiny: A Study of Nationalist Expansion in American History* (1935).

For source material, see H. S. Commager, *Documents of American History,* nos. 360, 360–3, 367, 369–72, 375, 385, 386, 412, 446; and R. J. Bartlett, *Record of American Diplomacy,* pp. 391–425, 534–46.

11. THE PROGRESSIVE MOVEMENT

Consult B. P. DeWitt, *The Progressive Movement* (1915) and Herbert Croly, *The Promise of American Life* (1909). Even more important are H. U. Faulkner, *The Quest for Social Justice, 1898–1914,* chaps. 1, 5, 7–13; Louis Filler, *Crusaders for American Liberalism* (1939); and John Chamberlain, *Farewell to Reform.* On agitation for reform, see C. C. Regier, *The Era of the Muckrakers* (1932) and Lincoln Steffens, *Autobiography* (2 vols., 1931). M. E. Curti, *The Growth of American Thought,* chaps. 24–5, is also valuable.

For source material, see H. S. Commager, *Documents of American History,* nos. 301, 313, 371, 376, 384, 406, 407, 432, 433.

12. T. R., TAFT, AND WILSON

On T. R., read H. F. Pringle, *Theodore Roosevelt* (1931), especially chaps. 11–14, and G. E. Mowry, *Theodore Roosevelt and the Progressive Movement* (1946). On Business consolidation, see H. R. Seager and C. A. Gulick Jr., *Trust and Corporation Problems,* chap. 5 and John Moody, *Masters of Capital.* On safeguarding the peoples interests, consult C. R. Van Hise and L. Havemeyer, *Conservation of Our Natural Resources* (1930). The best account of Taft's administration is to be found in H. F. Pringle, *The Life and Times of William Howard Taft* (2 vols., 1939), chaps. 22–8, and K. W. Hechler, *Insurgency: Personalities and Policies of the Taft Era* (1940). On Wilson and the New Freedom, see James Kerney, *Political Education of Woodrow Wilson* (1926); A. S. Link, *Wilson, The Road to the White House* (1947), which describe his early career and the election of 1912; and Woodrow Wilson, *The New Freedom* (1913). F. L. Paxson, *The Prewar Years* (1936) skillfully summarizes Wilson's first administration.

For source material, see H. S. Commager, *Documents of American History,* nos. 355, 356, 360–3, 367, 369–87, 389–98, 402, 404, 410–12.

13. WORLD WAR I

For the European background, consult S. B. Fay, *Origins of the World War* (2 vols., 1928) and H. E. Barnes, *The Genesis of the World War* (rev. ed., 1929). On the causes for American participation, see C. H. Grattan, *Why We Fought* (1929), especially chaps. 2, 3; Walter Millis, *The Road to War* (1935), chaps. 9–12; C. C. Tansill, *America Goes to War* (1938), chaps. 2–4; and J. D. Squires, *British Propaganda at Home and in the United States from 1914 to 1917* (1935), especially chaps. 3–4. For the war years, consult F. L. Paxson, *America at War, 1917–1918* (1939). On mobilization of American resources, see A. D. Noyes, *The War Period of American Finance, 1908–1925* (1926), chaps. 2–5; G. B. Clarkson, *Industrial America in the World War* (1923), chaps. 12–30. On military history, see C. J. H. Hayes, *A Brief History of the Great War* (1920). The diplomatic events of the war are covered by S. F. Bemis, *A Diplomatic History of the United States*, chap. 32 and by T. A. Bailey, *A Diplomatic History of the American People*, chaps. 37–40. On the Versailles treaty consult Paul Birdsall, *Versailles Twenty Years After* (1941) and T. A. Bailey, *Woodrow Wilson and the Lost Peace* (1944).

For source material, see H. S. Commager, *Documents of American History*, nos. 400, 405, 408, 409, 416–18, 423–9, 435, 436, 442.

14. THE GOLDEN AGE OF AMERICAN BUSINESS

H. U. Faulkner, *From Versailles to the New Deal* (1950), a recent addition to the Chronicles of America series, is the best brief account. With it should be read George Soule, *Prosperity Decade: From War to Depression: 1917–1929* (1947) and F. L. Allen, *Only Yesterday* (1931). On business consolidation, see H. W. Laidler, *Concentration of Control in American Industry* (1931), chap. 23, and A. A. Berle, Jr. and G. C. Means, *The Modern Corporation and Private Property* (1932), chaps. 2–5. On the export of American capital, read Cleona Lewis, *America's Stake in International Investments* (1938) or J. T. Madden, Marcus Nadler, and H. C. Sauvain, *America's Experience as a Creditor Nation* (1937). On foreign trade for the twenties, see W. C. Redfield, *Dependent America* (1926) and the National Industrial Conference Board, *Trends in the Foreign Trade of the United States* (1930).

For source material, see H. S. Commager, *Documents of American History*, nos. 424, 430–3, 437–41, 450–6, 458, 459, 468, 470, 472.

15. FROM NORMALCY TO DEPRESSION

The references listed for Chapter 14 apply to this chapter also. In addition, read D. L. Dumond, *America in Our Time, 1896–1946* (1947). On agriculture, see J. D. Black, *Agricultural Reform in the United States* (1929), part I. The decline of organized labor is discussed by L. L. Lorwin, *The American Federation of Labor* (1933), chaps. 8–11. On the relation of government and business, see D. M. Keezer and Stacy May, *The Public Control of Business* (1930). On prohibition, read Peter Odegard, *Pressure Politics, The Story of the Anti-Saloon League* (1928) and Charles Merz, *The Dry Decade* (1931). On curtailing immigration, see R. L. Garis, *Immigration Restriction* (1927).

For source material, see H. S. Commager, *Documents of American History*, nos. 432–4, 438, 450, 461–2, 465–71.

16. THE NEW DEAL AND AMERICAN CAPITALISM

The best book on this subject is Basil Rauch, *The History of the New Deal, 1933–1938* (1944). With it should be read Broadus Mitchell, *Depression Decade: From New Era through New Deal, 1929–1941* (1947). For the N.R.A., consult L. S. Lyons and others, *The National Recovery Administration* (1935) chaps. 1–10, and Donald Richberg, *The Rainbow* (1936), chaps. 9–12. On the A.A.A., see E. G. Nourse, *Three Years of the A.A.A.* (1937). On labor, see Herbert Harris, *American Labor* (1939) and *Labor's Civil War* (1940). The early years of the C.I.O. are described by J. R. Walsh, *C.I.O.: Industrial Unionism in Action* (1937). On other

New Deal activity, consult C. A. and M. R. Beard, *America in Midpassage* (1939).
For source material, see H. S. Commager, *Documents of American History*, nos. 475–87, 493–505, 507–12, 515–20, 525, 529, 531.

17. RELIEF AND REHABILITATION UNDER THE NEW DEAL

See the references listed for Chapter 16 and, in addition, Harold Barger and H. H. Landsberg, *American Agriculture, 1899–1939* (1942), the last five chapters, and A. D. Gayer, *Public Works in Prosperity and Depression* (1935). See also D. E. Brogan, *The Era of Franklin D. Roosevelt: A Chronicle of the New Deal and Global War* (1951), in the Chronicles of America series.

18. AMERICAN CULTURE IN THE MACHINE AGE

General accounts are P. W. Slosson, *The Great Crusade and After, 1914–1928* (1930) and Dixon Wecter, *The Age of the Great Depression, 1929–1941* (1948). In addition to these the student will gain insight and understanding by reading H. E. Stearns (ed.), *Civilization in the United States* (1922); M. E. Curti, *The Growth of American Thought*, chap. 27; F. L. Allen, *Only Yesterday*, and *Since Yesterday* (1940); and R. S. and H. M. Lynd, *Middletown* (1929).
For source material, see H. S. Commager, *Documents of American History*, nos, 455–6, 463–5, 471, 487, 499, 511, 513, 528, 532, 533, 544, 559, 570.

19. FROM ISOLATION TO INTERVENTION

On the European background, consult C. G. Haines and R. J. S. Hoffman, *The Origins and Background of the Second World War* (2nd ed., 1947), especially chaps. 5–13. On neutrality, read E. M. Earle, *Against this Torrent* (1941). Our relations with Latin America are treated by S. F. Bemis, *The Latin American Policy of the United States* (1943), chaps. 21–2 and with the Far East, in T. A. Bisson, *American Policy in the Far East, 1931–1940* (1940) chaps. 5–15. The contest between isolation and intervention and the move for lend-lease is discussed by Walter Johnson, *The Battle Against Isolation* (1944). For the diplomatic background of the war released by the Department of State, read *Peace and War, United States Foreign Policy, 1931–1941* (1943).
For source materials, see H. S. Commager, *Documents of American History*, nos. 488–92, 506, 514, 521–7, 529–35, 538, 540, 551, 558.

20. WORLD WAR II AND ITS AFTERMATH

On the military history of the war, read H. S. Commager, *The Story of the Second World War* (1945) or R. W. Shugg and H. A. DeWeerd, *World War II, A Concise History* (1946). The naval history of the war is skillfully detailed by S. E. Morison, *History of the United States Naval Operations in World War II* (7 vols., 1947–51). Volume II covers the operations in North African waters for 1942–3. Walter Karig, Earl Buton, and S. L. Freeland, *Battle Report: The Atlantic War* (1947) was written by navy officers. C. Vann Woodward, *The Battle for Leyte Gulf* (1947) is highly interesting. On American war production, consult D. M. Nelson, *Arsenal of Democracy* (1946). The problems of making the peace are discussed by V. M. Dean, *The Four Cornerstones of Peace* (1946) and J. F. Byrnes, *Speaking Frankly* (1947). On matters of postwar foreign policy, read Sumner Welles, *Where are We Heading?* (1946) and Walter Lippmann, *The Cold War* (1947). On the domestic scene, read the lively but judicious account by John Gunther, *Inside U. S. A.* (rev. ed., 1951). On the United Nations, see L. M. Goodrich and Edvard Hambro, *Charter of the United Nations: Commentary and Documents* (1946).
For source material, see H. S. Commager, *Documents of American History*, nos. 536, 541, 542, 550, 552–4, 556, 560, 565, 566.

GENERAL BIBLIOGRAPHY

Chapter I
Legacy of Civil War

General Works. The best single work covering the topics discussed in this chapter is the admirable volume by J. G. Randall, *The Civil War and Reconstruction* (1937), which contains a carefully selected bibliography. An even briefer and highly interpretative account is Volume II, Chapter I of C. A. and M. R. Beard, *The Rise of American Civilization* (4 vols., 1927–42). W. A. Dunning's older work, *Reconstruction, Political and Economic, 1865–1877* (1907), in the American Nation series, is still valuable as is his *Essays on the Civil War and Reconstruction* (1904). J. F. Rhodes, *History of the United States from the Compromise of 1850* (9 vols., 1900–1928), Volumes V–VII, is very useful for political (but neglects economic) history. It should be supplemented by Volumes I–III of E. P. Oberholtzer, *A History of the United States Since the Civil War* (5 vols., 1917–37); W. L. Fleming, *The Sequel of Appomattox* (1919), in the Chronicles of America series; Allan Nevins, *The Emergence of Modern America, 1865–1878* (1928), in the History of American Life series; and E. M. Coulter, *The South During Reconstruction, 1865–1877* (1947), in A History of the South series. C. G. Bowers, *The Tragic Era: The Revolution after Lincoln* (1929) is a well written but untrustworthy account. P. H. Buck, *The Road to Reunion, 1865–1900* (1937) is an excellent account of the efforts toward reconciliation of the North and South.

The Victorious North. The psychological atmosphere of the North after 1865 is evident in E. D. Fite's *Social and Industrial Conditions in the North during the Civil War* (1910). A contemporary account by S. M. Peto, *The Resources and Prospects of America, Ascertained During a Visit . . . in 1865* (1866) is also useful for the same purpose. For social, economic and political changes in particular Northern states, see A. C. Cole, *The Era of the Civil War, 1848–1870* (1919); A. C. Flick (ed.), *History of the State of New York* (1933–7), Vol. III; C. M. Knapp, *New Jersey Politics during . . . the Civil War and Reconstruction* (1924); and Frederick Merk, *Economic History of Wisconsin During the Civil War Decade* (1916).

The Defeated South. On the general aspects see Volume I of E. P. Oberholtzer, *The United States since the Civil War,* previously cited. Also consult F. B. Simkins, *The South, Old and New, 1820–1947* (1947); and W. B. Hesseltine, *The South In American History* (1943). Accounts of travelers to the South are very valuable. See especially, Robert Somers, *The Southern States since the War, 1870–1* (1871), good on the state of agriculture and industry; Sidney Andrews, *The South Since the War* (1866), observations of a newspaper correspondent; Whitelaw Reid, *After the War: A Southern Tour* (1866) observations by a future editor of the New York Tribune; and J. T. Trowbridge, *The South* (1866). Though biased and therefore not always completely reliable, reminiscences of Southerners afford insight into the psychology of the people of the defeated area. See Joseph LeConte, *The Autobiography of Joseph LeConte* (1903); M. B. Chesnut, *A Diary from Dixie* (1905); F. B. Leigh, *Ten Years on a Georgia Plantation since the War* (1883); Mrs. M. L. Avary, *Dixie after the War* (1906); G. C. Eggleston, *A Rebel's Recollections* (1875), Mrs. Roger Pryor, *Reminiscences of Peace and War* (1904), and E. W. Pringle, *Chronicles of Chicora Wood* (1922). For those who wish a more detailed, Northern account of Southern conditions, see the report of Carl Schurz to President Johnson in the autumn of 1865, *Senate Executive Documents,* 39 Cong., 1 Sess., No. 2 and the report of B. D. Gruman, April, 1866 in *Senate Executive Documents,* 39 Cong., 1 Sess., No. 43.

Lincoln and Johnson and the Radicals. The old work by J. W. Burgess, *Reconstruction and the Constitution, 1866–1876* (1902) is colored by the author's nationalistic bias. Much more readable and reliable are the accounts in W. A. Dunning, *Essays on the Civil War and Reconstruction* and J. G. Randall, *The Civil War and Reconstruction,* already cited. See also H. K. Beale's illuminating articles "Reconstruction" in Volume XIII, *Encyclopaedia of the Social Sciences* (1934), edited by E. R. A. Seligman and Alvin Johnson, and "On Rewriting Reconstruction History," *American Historical Review,* Vol. XLV, pp. 807–827 (July, 1940). R. S. Henry, *The Story of Reconstruction* (1938) is valuable, but very detailed. On Lincoln's Reconstruction policy, see C. H. McCarthy, *Lincoln's Plan of Reconstruction* (1901) and J. G. Randall, *Constitutional Problems under Lincoln* (1926). T. H. Williams, *Lincoln and the Radicals* (1941) is excellent. On President Johnson and the Radicals the best treatment is H. K. Beale, *The Critical Year: A Study of Andrew Johnson and Reconstruction* (1930). See also C. E. Chadsey, *The Struggle Between President Johnson and Congress over Reconstruction* (1896); G. F. Milton, *The Age of Hate: Andrew Johnson and the Radicals* (1930), a scholarly account and superior to Chadsey; Edward Stanwood, *A History of the Presidency* (2 vols., 1916), standard treatment; L. P. Stryker, *Andrew Johnson, A Study in Courage* (1929), prejudiced and at times dull; R. W. Winston, *Andrew Johnson, Plebian and Patriot* (1928), which reads fairly well; and E. M. McPherson, *The Political History of the United States During Reconstruction* (1871), which contains source material. On the Fourteenth Amendment, see B. B. Kendrick, *The Journal of the Joint Committee of Fifteen on Reconstruction* (1914); C. A. Beard, *The Supreme Court and the Constitution* (1912); W. D. Guthrie, *Lectures on the Fourteenth Amendment* (1898); Jacobus Ten Broek, *The Antislavery Origins of the Fourteenth Amendment* (1951); and H. E. Flack, *The Adoption of the Fourteenth Amendment* (1908). On the Fifteenth Amendment, see J. M. Mathews, *Legislative and Judicial History of the Fifteenth Amendment* (1909). On the impeachment proceedings against President Johnson, consult D. M. DeWitt, *The Impeachment and Trial of Andrew Johnson* (1903), a skilful analysis, and the account on this topic in W. A. Dunning's *Essays on Civil War and Reconstruction,* cited earlier. There is rich material on the various aspects of Reconstruction and the conflict between the Administration and the Radical element in Congress in the biographical studies of the more outstanding personages of the period. Among the more important are J. A. Woodburn, *The Life of Thaddeus Stevens* (1913); A. B. Miller, *Thaddeus Stevens* (1939); R. N. Current, *Old Thad Stevens, A Story of Ambition* (1942), which is largely political; T. F. Woodley, *Great Leveler: The Life of Thaddeus Stevens* (1937), which presents new facts; J. T. Morse, Jr. (ed.), *The Diary of Gideon Welles* (3 vols., 1911) and H. K. Beale, "Is the Printed Diary of Gideon Welles Reliable?" *American Historical Review,* Vol. XXX, pp. 547–52 (1925); T. C. Pease and J. G. Randall (eds.), *The Diary of Orville Hickman Browning* (2 vols. 1925–33); W. C. Harris, *Public Life of Zachariah Chandler, 1851–1875* (1917); D. V. Smith, *Chase and Civil War Politics* (1931); D. B. Chidsey, *The Gentleman from New York: A Life of Roscoe Conkling* (1935); B. C. Steiner, *Life of Henry Winter Davis* (1916); R. P. Ludlum, "Joshua Giddings, Radical," *Mississippi Valley Historical Review,* Vol. XXIII, pp. 49–60 (1936); G. F. Hoar, *Autobiography of Seventy Years* (2 vols., 1903); G. W. Julian, *Political Recollections, 1840 to 1872* (1884); C. M. Fuess, *Carl Schurz, Reformer (1829–1906)* (1932); Frederic Bancroft, *The Life of William H. Seward* (2 vols., 1900); Moorfield Storey, *Charles Sumner* (1900); Horace White, *The Life of Lyman Trumbull* (1913); J. G. Blaine, *Twenty Years of Congress: From Lincoln to Garfield* (2 vols., 1884–6); C. R. Williams (ed.), *The Diary and Letters of Rutherford B. Hayes* (5 vols., 1922–6); W. D. Foulke, *Life of Oliver P. Morton, Including His Important Speeches* (2 vols., 1899); G. C. Gorham, *Life and Public Services of Edwin M. Stanton* (2 vols., 1899), which is not too satisfactory; C. L. Barrows, *William M. Evarts* (1941); Margaret Clapp, *Forgotten First Citizen: John Bigelow* (1947); Glyndon Van Deusen, *Thurlow Weed* (1947); Henry Adams, *The Education of Henry Adams: An Autobiography* (1918); Horace Greeley, *Recollections of a Busy Life*

(1868); and C. F. Adams, Jr., *Charles Francis Adams* (1900). For the biographies of other political leaders, consult the *Dictionary of American Biography*, already cited.

Radical Rule in the South. The literature on this topic is considerable. In addition to the volumes cited in the above paragraphs, consult the monographs on each of the seceded states: W. L. Fleming, *Civil War and Reconstruction in Alabama* (1905); J. W. Garner, *Reconstruction in Mississippi* (1901); J. G. De R. Hamilton, *Reconstruction in North Carolina* (1914); Ella Lonn, *Reconstruction in Louisiana after 1868* (1918); W. M. Caskey, *Secession and Restoration of Louisiana* (1938); Garnie McGinty, *Louisiana Redeemed, The Overthrow of Carpet-Bag Rule, 1876–1880* (1941); J. R. Ficklen, *History of Reconstruction in Louisiana* (1910); J. P. Hollis, *The Early Reconstruction Period in South Carolina* (1905); J. S. Reynolds, *Reconstruction in South Carolina, 1865–77* (1905); F. B. Simkins and R. H. Woody, *South Carolina During Reconstruction* (1932); C. W. Ramsdell, *Reconstruction in Texas* (1910); E. M. Coulter, *The Civil War and Readjustment in Kentucky* (1926); H. J. Eckenrode, *The Political History of Virginia During the Reconstruction* (1904); W. W. Davis, *The Civil War and Reconstruction in Florida* (1913); J. W. Fertig, *The Secession and Reconstruction of Tennessee* (1898); J. W. Patton, *Unionism and Reconstruction in Tennessee, 1860–1869* (1934); T. S. Staples, *Reconstruction in Arkansas, 1862–1874* (1923); D. Y. Thomas, *Arkansas in War and Reconstruction 1861–1874* (1926); John Wallace, *Carpetbag Rule in Florida* (1888); J. C. McGregor, *The Disruption of Virginia* (1922); E. C. Woolley, *The Reconstruction of Georgia* (1901); and C. M. Thompson, *Reconstruction in Georgia, Economic, Social, Political, 1865–1872* (1915). Treating the entire South during the decade after the Civil War are E. M. Coulter, *The South During Reconstruction, 1865–1877* (1947), W. E. B. DuBois, *Black Reconstruction* (1935), a detailed and challenging interpretation; W. A. Sinclair, *The Aftermath of Slavery* (1905); and W. L. Fleming's authoritative work, *Documentary History of Reconstruction* (2 vols., 1906–07). See also the essays dealing with Reconstruction in *Studies in Southern History* inscribed to W. A. Dunning. The following biographies contain valuable material on Reconstruction: E. M. Coulter, *W. G. Brownlow* (1937); C. H. Ambler, *Francis H. Pierpont* (1937); H. J. Pearce, Jr., *Benjamin H. Hill, Secession and Reconstruction* (1928); W. A. Cate, *Lucius Q. C. Lamar* (1935) and N. M. Blake, *William Mahone* (1935). On the freedmen during Reconstruction, consult W. E. B. DuBois, *Black Reconstruction,* cited above, and P. A. Bruce, *The Plantation Negro as a Freedman* (1889). G. T. Stephenson, *Race Distinctions in American Law* (1910) covers Black Codes and other legislation affecting freedmen. Paul Lewinson, *Race, Class, and Party* (1932) is also valuable. See also P. S. Peirce, *The Freedmen's Bureau* (1904); L. J. Webster, *The Operation of the Freedmen's Bureau in South Carolina* (1916), in the Smith College studies in history; V. L. Wharton, *The Negro in Mississippi, 1865–1890* (1948); A. A. Taylor, *The Negro in South Carolina During the Reconstruction* (1924) and *The Negro in the Reconstruction of Virginia* (1926). Important too in connection with the freedmen is H. L. Swint, *The Northern Teacher in the South, 1862–1870* (1941). On Negro government and the restoration of white rule in the South, see the lively but unreliable volume by J. S. Pike, *The Prostrate State: South Carolina Under Negro Government* (1874); Charles Nordhoff, *The Cotton States in 1875* (1876); and R. F. Dibble, *Albion W. Tourgée* (1921). A satisfactory history of the Ku-Klux Klan is yet to be written. J. C. Lester and D. L. Wilson, *Ku Klux Klan, Its Origin, Growth, and Disbandment* (new ed., 1905) and S. L. Davis, *Authentic History, Ku Klux Klan, 1865–1877* (1924) are both inferior to S. F. Horn, *Invisible Empire: The Story of the Ku Klux Klan, 1866–1871* (1939). The best brief account is to be found in W. G. Brown, *The Lower South in American History* (1902). On the restoration of white rule, see also Walter Allen, *Governor Chamberlain's Administration in South Carolina* (1888) and E. L. Wells, *Hampton and Reconstruction* (1907). Those who wish to view Reconstruction from the angle of race relations should consult B. G. Brawley, *A Social History of the American Negro* (1921); C. R. Johnson, *The Negro in American Civilization* (1930); G. W. Williams, *History of the Negro Race in*

America, 1619–1880 (2 vols., 1883); J. H. Franklin, *From Slavery to Freedom: A History of American Negroes* (1947); and most important of all, the brilliant study by Gunnar Myrdal, *An American Dilemma: The Negro Problem and Modern Democracy* (2 vols., 1944).

Grantism. For an understanding of Grant in public life, consult the following: Lloyd Lewis, *Captain Sam Grant* (1950), for his early life; Helen Todd, *A Man Named Grant* (1940), interesting, but not entirely reliable; L. A. Coolidge, *Ulysses S. Grant* (1917); W. B. Hesseltine, *Ulysses S. Grant, Politician* (1935), an excellent study; H. S. Garland, *Ulysses S. Grant: His Life and Character* (1898); Matthew Josephson, *The Politicos, 1865–1896* (1938), which is popular; and W. E. Woodward, *Meet General Grant* (1928), which is somewhat superficial. For Grant's elevation to the presidency, see C. H. Coleman, *The Election of 1868* (1933). The best single volume on Grant's administration is Allan Nevins, *Hamilton Fish; The Inner History of the Grant Administration* (1936). It may be supplemented with profit by the biographical accounts listed above and Carl Schurz, *Reminiscences* (3 vols., 1907–08); Hugh McCulloch, *Men and Measures of Half a Century* (1888); John Sherman, *Recollections of Forty Years* (2 vols., 1895); and A. D. White, *Autobiography of Andrew Dickson White* (2 vols., 1905). On financial questions and other domestic political matters, see W. C. Mitchell, *A History of the Greenbacks* (1903); D. C. Barrett, *The Greenback and Resumption of Specie Payments, 1862–1879* (1931); A. D. Noyes, *Forty Years of American Finance* (1909); A. B. Hepburn, *A History of Currency in the United States* (rev. ed., 1924); A. S. Bolles, *The Financial History of the United States* (3 vols., 1896), Vol. III; and D. R. Dewey, *Financial History of the United States* (new ed., 1936). For the Legal Tender cases, consult R. E. Cushman, *Leading Constitutional Decisions* (9th ed., 1950), Charles Warren, *The Supreme Court in United States History* (rev. ed., 2 vols., 1937); E. J. James, *Some Considerations on the Legal Tender Decisions* (1887); G. F. Hoar, *The Charge against President Grant of Packing the Supreme Court* (1896); and Sidney Ratner, "Was the Supreme Court Packed by President Grant?" *Political Science Quarterly*, Vol. L (1935). For Civil Service, see C. R. Fish, *The Civil Service and the Patronage* (1905). On the tariff, consult the standard works: F. W. Taussig, *The Tariff History of the United States* (8th ed., 1931) and Edward Stanwood, *American Tariff Controversies in the Nineteenth Century* (2 vols., 1903). Valuable for the subject covered is M. S. Wildman, *Money Inflation in the United States* (1905). The Panic of 1873 is treated adequately by E. R. McCartney, *The Crisis of 1873* (1935). Other helpful works are C. A. Collman, *Our Mysterious Panics, 1830–1930: A Story of Events and the Men Involved* (1931); H. M. Larson, *Jay Cooke, Private Banker* (1936); O. C. Lightner, *The History of Business Depressions* (1922); E. P. Oberholtzer, *Jay Cooke, Financier of the Civil War* (2 vols., 1907); W. C. Mitchell, *Business Cycles* (1913); and O. M. W. Sprague, *History of Crises Under the National Banking System* (1910), *Senate Document*, 61st Cong., 2nd Sess., No. 538. The literature on the corruption of the Grant Administrations is voluminous. The accounts in Rhodes and Oberholtzer may be supplemented by the following: S. P. Orth, *The Boss and the Machine* (1919), in the Chronicles of America series; C. F. Adams and Henry Adams, *Chapters of Erie, and Other Essays* (1871); J. B. Crawford, *The Credit Mobilier of America* (1880); D. C. Seitz, *The Dreadful Decade, 1869–1879* (1926), which is lively and exaggerated; R. H. Fuller, *Jubilee Jim: The Life of Colonel James Fisk, Jr.*, (1928), which is highly journalistic; D. T. Lynch, *"Boss" Tweed: The Story of a Grim Generation* (1927), the story of Tammany Hall at its worst, and *The Wild Seventies* (1941); R. I. Warshow, *Jay Gould* (1928); K. G. Crawford, *The Pressure Boys* (1939); M. R. Werner, *Tammany Hall* (1928), scholarly; Bouck White, *The Book of Daniel Drew* (1910); A. D. H. Smith, *Commodore Vanderbilt* (1927); A. B. Paine, *Thomas Nast, His Period and His Pictures* (1904); and F. C. Sharp and P. G. Fox, *Business Ethics, Studies in Fair Competition* (1937). E. D. Ross, *The Liberal Republican Movement* (1919) is definitive. Other works on this topic are T. S. Barclay, *The Liberal Republican Movement in Missouri, 1865–1871* (1926); Joseph Schafer, *Carl Schurz, Militant Liberal* (1930); and D. C. Seitz,

Horace Greeley, Founder of the New York Tribune (1926). On foreign affairs see S. F. Bemis (ed.), *The American Secretaries of State and Their Diplomacy* (10 vols., 1927–9), Vol. VII. On the Alaska purchase, consult J. M. Callahan, *The Alaska Purchase and Americo-Canadian Relations* (1908); J. P. Nichols, *Alaska* (1924) and S. R. Tompkins, *Alaska, Promyshlennik and Sourdough* (1945). B. P. Thomas, *Russo-America Relations, 1815–1867* (1930) gives the necessary background for the Alaska negotiations. F. E. Chadwick treats the *Virginius* affair in his *Relations of the United States and Spain, Diplomacy* (1909). H. M. Hyde, *Mexican Empire, The History of Maximilian and Carlota of Mexico* (1946) is a scholarly presentation. A companion account is Ralph Roeder, *Juarez and His Mexico* (2 vols., 1947). The Alabama claims and the Geneva arbitration are covered by J. B. Moore's *History and Digest of the International Arbitrations* (1898), Vol. I, chap. 14; J. C. B. Davis, *Mr. Fish and the Alabama Claims* (1893), and Volume III of *The Cambridge History of British Foreign Policy* (3 vols., 1922–3). On the Fenian raids, see J. M. Callahan, *American Foreign Policy in Canadian Relations* (1937); H. Keenleyside, *Canada and the United States* (1929); L. B. Shippee, *Canadian-American Relations, 1849–1874* (1939); and Goldwin Smith, *The Treaty of Washington, 1871: A Study in Imperial History* (1941). C. C. Tansill's *The Purchase of the Danish West Indies* (1932) and his *The United States and Santo Domingo, 1798–1873* (1938) are definitive. J. M. Callahan, *Cuba and International Relations* (1899) and C. L. Jones, *Caribbean Interests of the United States* (1916) are masterly accounts.

The Compromise of 1877. P. L. Haworth, *The Hayes-Tilden Election* (rev. ed., 1927) is the standard work on this event. See also W. W. Davis, *The Civil War and Reconstruction in Florida* (1913); Ella Lonn, *Reconstruction in Louisiana after 1868* (1918); F. B. Simkins and R. H. Woody, *South Carolina During Reconstruction* (1932). The following biographies are indispensable: A. C. Flick, *Samuel Jones Tilden* (1939); L. B. Richardson, *William E. Chandler, Republican* (1940), a biography of the chairman of the Republican National Committee in 1876; Allan Nevins, *Abram S. Hewitt: with Some Account of Peter Cooper* (1935); H. J. Eckenrode, *Rutherford B. Hayes, Statesman of Reunion* (1930); and C. R. Williams, *The Life of Rutherford B. Hayes*, (2 vols., 1914). C. Vann Woodward, *Reunion and Reaction* (1951) sheds much new light on the election.

Chapter II

The Last Frontier

The literature concerning the disappearance of frontier America is extensive. On this see F. J. Turner and Frederick Merk, *List of References on the History of the West* (rev. ed., 1922). R. A. Billington, *Westward Expansion* (1949) is an admirable text and contains a carefully selected bibliography covering all phases of the westward movement. But most important of all is W. P. Webb's excellent volume, *The Great Plains* (1931), which is indispensable for understanding the history of the Trans-Mississippi West. The last chapters of F. L. Paxson, *History of the American Frontier, 1763–1893* (1924) and his *The Last American Frontier* (1910) are helpful summaries. E. D. Branch, *Westward: The Romance of the American Frontier* (1930); D. E. Clark, *The West in American History* (1937); R. E. Riegel, *America Moves West* (rev. ed., 1947); Cardinal Goodwin, *The Trans-Mississippi West* (1922) and Emerson Hough, *The Passing of the Frontier* (1918), in the Chronicles of America series, are general accounts. E. P. Oberholtzer, *A History of the United States Since the Civil War* (5 vols., 1917–37) and Allan Nevins, *The Emergence of Modern America, 1865–1878* (1927), in the History of American Life series, are rich in material. The history of the several Western states by H. H. Bancroft, *Works* (34 vols., 1882–90) are storehouses of valuable material; so are the regional histories, notably, H. E. Briggs, *Frontiers of the Northwest: A History of the Upper Missouri Valley* (1940); Everett Dick, *The Sod-House Frontier, 1854–1890* (1937) which is excellent on frontier life; S. L. Clemens (Mark Twain), *Roughing It* (2 vols., 1872); G. W. Fuller, *The Inland Empire of the Pacific Northwest* (3 vols., 1928); Oscar Winther, *The Great Northwest* (2nd ed., 1950); C. C. Rister, *The Southwestern Frontier—1865–1881* (1928); R. N. Richardson and C. C. Rister, *The Greater Southwest* (1934); J. C. Caughey, *History of The Pacific Coast* (1933); and C. C. Rister, *Land Hunger: David L. Payne and the Oklahoma Boomers* (1942). On the administration of Western territories, see E. S. Pomeroy, *The Territories and the United States, 1861–1890* (1947). The best accounts of Western land speculation are to be found in A. M. Sakolski, *The Great American Land Bubble* (1932) and A. N. Chandler, *Land Title Origins, A Tale of Force and Fraud* (1945).

The Last Stand of the First Americans. Much of the literature on the Indians consists of highly romanticized accounts. Among the historically trustworthy works that merit consideration are G. B. Grinnell, *The Story of the Indian* (1895); F. E. Leupp, *The Indian and his Problem* (1910); W. C. Macleod, *The American Indian Frontier* (1928); John Collier, *Indians of the Americas* (1947); Paul Radin, *The Story of the American Indian* (1934); Angie Debo, *And Still the Waters Run* (1940); G. D. Harmon, *Sixty Years of Indian Affairs* (1941); F. W. Seymour, *The Story of the Red Man* (1929), a well-written popular account; and P. E. Byrne, *Soldiers of the Plain* (1926), which is highly sympathetic to the Indian. For particular tribes, see E. E. Dale, *Cherokee Cavaliers: Forty Years of Cherokee History* (1939) and his *The Indians of the Southwest: A Century of Development Under the United States* (1949); G. B. Grinnell, *The Fighting Cheyennes* (1915); F. C. Lockwood, *The Apache Indians* (1938); R. N. Richardson, *The Comanche Barrier to South Plains Settlement* (1933); Grant Foreman, *The Five Civilized Tribes* (1934); Angie Debo, *The Rise and Fall of the Choctaw Republic* (1934); and Woodworth Clum, *Apache Agent* (1936). On Indian warfare, consult Robert Gessner, *Massacre* (1931); P. I. Wellman, *Death on the Prairie* (1934) and *Death in the Desert* (1935); Stanley Vestal, *Sitting Bull* (1932) and *Warpath: The True Story of the Fighting Sioux* (1934); W. P. Webb, *The Texas Rangers* (1935); J. P. Dunn, *Massacres of the Mountains: A History of the Indian Wars of the Far West* (1886); C. T. Brady, *Northwest Fights and Fighters* (1907); and C. A. Fee, *Chief Joseph* (1936). The best accounts of the conflict between Indians and whites are Philip Sheridan, *Personal Memoirs* (2 vols., 1888); Marguerite Merington (ed.), *The Custer Story* (1950); Frederic Van de Water, *Glory Hunter: A Life of General Custer* (1934); N. A. Miles, *Serving the Republic* (1911); and F. C. Carrington, *My Army Life and the Fort Phil. Kearney Massacre* (1910). For Indian policy and the crusade for more humane treatment of the Indian, see Lewis Meriam and others, *The Problem of Indian Administration* (1928); G. D. Harmon, *Sixty Years of Indian Affairs* (1941); L. B. Priest, *Uncle Sam's Stepchildren, The Reformation of the United States Indian Policy, 1865–1887* (1942); and L. F. Schmeckebier, *The Office of Indian Affairs* (1927). See also H. H. Jackson, *A Century of Dishonor* (1887), a passionate plea for reform; G. W. Manypenny, *Our Indian Wards* (1880); Ethelbert Talbot, *My People of the Plains* (1906); James McLaughlin, *My Friend the Indian* (1910); and M. A. DeW. Howe, *Portrait of An Independent, Moorfield Storey, 1845–1929* (1932). J. P. Kinney's *A Continent Lost—A Civilization Won: Indian Land Tenure in America* (1937) and E. D. Branch, *The Hunting of the Buffalo* (1929) deal with special topics.

The Mining Frontier. The best introduction to the history of the mining kingdom is T. A. Rickard, *A History of American Mining* (1932). It may be profitably supplemented with his more detailed account, *Man and Metals* (2 vols., 1932). H. H. Bancroft's *Histories of the Western States,* already cited, are rich sources of valuable material on this topic. See also G. C. Quiett, *Pay Dirt: A Panorama of American Gold Rushes* (1936), a popular account, as are C. B. Glasscock, *Gold in Them Hills* (1932) and *The War of the Copper Kings* (1935). Glasscock's, *Big Bonanza* (1931); C. H. Shinn, *The Story of the Mine* (1901); G. D. Lyman's *The Saga of the Comstock Lode* (1934) and E. Lord, *Comstock Mining and Miners* (monograph United States Geological Survey, no. 9, 1883) are concerned principally with the Comstock Lode. Oscar Lewis, *Silver Kings* (1947) is for popular consumption. S. E. White, *The Forty Niners* (1918), in the Chronicles of America series and R. G. Cleland, *A History of California: The American Period* (1922) are lively accounts of the gold rush and its aftermath. W. J. Trimble, *The Mining Advance into the Inland Empire* (1914) is a scholarly presentation of an important development. Though not descriptive of the last frontier W. B. Gates, Jr., *Michigan Copper and Boston Dollars: An Economic History of the Michigan Copper Mining Industry* (1951) sheds light on the mining industry of the period.

The Cattle Kingdom. W. P. Webb's *The Great Plains,* previously cited, is unexcelled. Other excellent works are E. S. Osgood, *The Day of the Cattleman* (1929); E. E. Dale, *The Range Cattle Industry* (1930); Louis Pelzer, *The Cattlemen's Frontier* (1936); O. B. Peake, *The Colorado Range Cattle Industry* (1937); J. Evetts Haley, *The XIT Ranch of Texas* (1929), story of the X.I.T. ranch; and M. G. Burlingame, *The Montana Frontier* (1942), the last three being studies of special areas. Two other vivid portrayals of cattle areas are Struthers Burt, *Powder River* (1938) and Charles Lindsay, *The Big Horn Basin* (1932). The character and activities of the cowboy are best seen in Emerson Hough, *The Story of the Cowboy* (1897), P. A. Rollins, *The Cowboy* (rev. ed., 1936); E. D. Branch, *The Cowboy and His Interpreters* (1926); P. I. Wellman, *The Trampling Herd* (1939); R. M. Wright, *Dodge City, The Cowboy Capital* (1913); W. M. Raine and W. C. Barnes, *Cattle* (1930); Will James, *American Cowboy* (1942); Andy Adams, *The Log of a Cowboy* (1931) and Reed Anthony, *Cowman* (1907). For interesting contemporary accounts, see J. G. McCoy, *Historic Sketches of the Cattle Trade of the West and Southwest* (1940) written in 1874 and Stuart Henry, *Conquering Our Great American Plains* (1930). For an account of the trails, the cow towns, and the long drive see, in addition to Webb's *The Great Plains,* G. R. Hebard and E. A. Brininstool, *The Bozeman Trail* (2 vols., 1922). The sheep frontier is treated in E. N. Wentworth's *America's Sheep Trails* (1948) and R. G. Cleland's *The Cattle on a Thousand Hills* (1941). On range balladry, consult J. A. Lomax, *Cowboy Songs* (1910) and *Songs of the Cattle Trail and Cow Camp* (1919), Badger Clark, *Sun and Saddle Leather* (1915), and E. F. Piper, *Barbed Wire and other Poems* (1917).

The Farmer's Frontier. The outstanding authority is F. A. Shannon, *The Farmer's Last Frontier, 1860–1897* (1945), in the Economic History of the United States series. On the public lands, consult G. I. Dubois and G. S. Matthews, *Galusha A. Grow, Father of the Homestead Act* (1917), R. M. Robbins, *Our Landed Heritage: The Public Domain, 1776–1936* (1942); B. H. Hibbard, *A History of the Public Land Policies* (1924); and Thomas Donaldson, *The Public Domain* (1884), which contains a mass of valuable undigested information. Also see P. W. Gates, "The Homestead Act in an Incongruous Land System," *American Historical Review,* Vol. XLI, no. 4 (July, 1946), pp. 652–81, and F. A. Shannon, "The Homestead Act and the Labor Surplus," *American Historical Review,* Vol. XLI, no. 4 (July, 1936), pp. 637–51. Willis Drummond, *Brief Description of the Public Lands of the United States of America, Prepared by the Commissioner of the General Land-Office for the Information of Foreigners Seeking a Home in the United States* (1873); H. N. Copp, *The American Settler's Guide: A Brief Exposition of the Public Land System of the United States of America* (2nd ed., 1882); and Henry George, *Our Land and Land Policy* (1902). On the settlement of the Trans-Mississippi West, see W. S. Thompson and P. K. Whelpton, *Population Trends in the United States* (1933); C. W. Thornthwaite and H. I. Slentz, *Internal Migration in the United States* (1934), excellent for maps; and C. L. Goodrich and Others, *Migration and Economic Opportunity* (1936). The farmer's difficulties with the cattlemen are set forth in a number of Federal government publications. Consult especially the 1880 *Report* of the Public Lands Commission; *Senate Executive Document* no. 127, 48th Cong., 1st Sess. (1883); *House Report,* no. 1809, 47th Cong. 1st Sess. (1881); and *House Miscellaneous Document* no. 45, 47th Cong., 2nd Sess. (1882), Vols. I–III. A number of works dealing with various vicissitudes of the frontier farmer should also be mentioned. For his troubles with the sheep rancher, see E. A. Carman, H. A.

Heath, and John Minto, *The History and Present Condition of the Sheep Industry in the United States* (United States Dept. of Agr., Bureau of Animal Husbandry, Special Report, 1892); on adjustment to a new physical environment, J. C. Malin, "The Adaptation of the Agricultural System to Sub-Humid Environment" *Agricultural History,* Vol. X (July, 1936), pp. 118–42; and for water supply and fencing, W. P. Webb, *The Great Plains,* already cited, which is unequaled. On fencing the last may be supplemented by E. W. Hayter, "Barbed Wire Fencing—a Prairie Invention," *Agricultural History,* Vol. XIII, (Oct., 1939), pp. 180–207 and "The Fencing of Western Railroads," *ibid.,* Vol. XIX, pp. 163–7. Information concerning the everyday life of the frontier farmer is dealt with by Everett Dick, *The Sod-House Frontier, 1854–1890* (1937) and *Vanguards of the Frontier* (1941); R. R. Wilson, *Out of the West* (1936); John Ise, *Sod and Stubble: The Story of A Kansas Homestead* (1936); A. F. Bentley, "The Condition of the Western Farmer as Illustrated by the Economic History of a Nebraska Township," Johns Hopkins University *Studies in Historical and Political Science,* Vol. XI (1893) pp. 285–370; H. E. Briggs, *Frontiers of the Northwest: A History of the Upper Missouri Valley* (1940); Ole Rolvaäg, *Giants in the Earth* (1929); Willa Cather, *O Pioneers!* (1913); E. J. Dies, *Titans of the Soil: Great Builders of Agriculture* (1949); Hamlin Garland, *Boy Life on the Prairie* (1899); Seth Humphrey, *Following the Prairie Frontier* (1931); and Joseph Schafer, *The Social History of American Agriculture* (1936).

Chapter III

The Development of a National Rail System

Although the story of the development of a number of our railroads has been competently traced, a first class history of American railroads is yet to be written. Two volumes in the Chronicles of America series can be highly recommended as an introduction to the subject. These are John Moody, *The Railroad Builders* (1919) and *The Masters of Capital* (1919). These should be followed by S. H. Holbrook, *The Story of American Railroads* (1947); A. C. Laut, *The Romance of the Rails* (2 vols., 1929); E. R. Johnson and T. W. Van Metre, *Principles of Railroad Transportation* (rev. ed., 1932). Other brief résumés are E. R. Johnson, *American Railway Transportation* (rev. ed., 1908); C. F. Adams, Jr., *Railroads: Their Origin and Problems* (rev. ed., 1887); A. T. Hadley, *Railroad Transportation* (1885); F. L. McVey, *Railroad Transportation* (1921); I. L. Sharfman, *The American Railroad Problem* (1921); Eliot Jones, *Principles of Railway Transportation* (1924); Slason Thompson, *A Short History of American Railways* (1925); M. D. Stevers, *Steel Trails* (1933); and Lebert St. Clair, *Transportation* (1933). The last two are popular presentations. For contemporary information, consult the *American Railroad Journal* (1832–71); H. V. Poore, *Poore's Manual of the Railroads of the United States* (1868–1925); the *Commercial and Financial Chronicle* (1865–1925); *The Final Report of the Industrial Commission* (1902); and the *Annual Reports* of the Interstate Commerce Commission. The government documents of the utmost importance to anyone concerned with the history of American railroads are the famous Windom Report, entitled *Report of the Select Committee on Transportation-Routes to the Seaboard,* 43rd Cong., 1st Sess., Senate Report no. 307, parts 1–2 (1874); the Cullom Report, *Report of the Senate Select Committee on Interstate Commerce,* 49th Cong., 1st Sess., Senate Report no. 46, parts 1–2 (1886); and the Hepburn Committee, *Proceedings of the Select Committee on Railroads, New York Assembly* (5 vols., 1879). There is a wealth of biographic material that covers practically every part of the history of American railroads. See especially the account of Daniel C. Drew, Jay Gould, and Cornelius Vanderbilt in the *Dictionary of American Biography* and J. G. Pyle, *The Life of James J. Hill* (2 vols., 1917) and George Kennan, *E. H. Harriman* (2 vols., 1922). Both of these are typically "authorized" treatments, and therefore sympathetic. H. J. Eckenrode and P. W. Edmunds, *E. H. Harriman: The Little Giant of Wall Street* (1933) is unfortunately not objective. A. D. H. Smith, *Commodore Vanderbilt* (1927) suffers likewise. Lewis Corey, *The House of Morgan* (1930) is authoritative and excellent on the part played by J. P. Morgan in railroad consolidation. J. B. Hedges, *Henry Villard and the Railways of the Northwest* (1930) is scholarly. Oscar Lewis, *The Big Four: The Story of Huntington, Stanford, Hopkins, and Crocker, and of the Building of the Central Pacific* (1938) is lively. G. T. Clark, *Leland Stanford* (1931) is an earlier work. E. P. Oberholtzer, *Jay Cooke, Financier of the Civil War* (2 vols., 1907) is first rate, as is H. G. Larson, *Jay Cooke, Private Banker* (1936). H. G. Pearson, *An American Railroad Builder, John Murray Forbes* (1911) is excellent. Not to be overlooked is H. G. Prout, *A Life of George Westinghouse* (1921). A. D. Turnbull, *John Stevens, An American Record* (1928) is an interesting account of a pioneer in railroad building and equipment. M. W. Schlegel, *Franklin B. Gowan: Ruler of the Reading* (1948) sheds light on this anthracite carrier. N. C. Wilson and F. J. Taylor, *Southern Pacific: The Roaring Story of a Fighting Railroad* (1951) is a popular account but of interest to serious students.

The Growth and Consolidation of American Railroads in the East and Middle West. Most of the material on this topic is to be found in the following: L. H. Haney, *A Congressional History of Railways in the United States to 1850* (1908); C. R. Fish, *The Restoration of the Southern Railroads* (1919); W. F. Gephart, *Transportation and Industrial Development in the Middle West* (1909); E. H. Mott, *Between the Ocean and the Lakes: The Story of Erie* (1899); C. F. Adams, *Chapters of Erie* (1871); H. D. Dozier, *A History of the Atlantic Coast Line Railroad* (1920); J. I. Bogen, *The Anthracite Railroads* (1927); S. M. Derrick, *Centennial History of South Carolina Railroad* (1930); Edward Hungerford, *The Story of the Baltimore and Ohio Railroad, 1827–1927* (2 vols., 1928) and *Men and Iron; the History of the New York Central* (1938); F. W. Stevens, *The Beginnings of the New York Central Railroad* (1926); T. F. Joyce, *The Boston and Maine Railroad* (1925); H. W. Schotter, *The Growth and Development of the Pennsylvania Railroad Company* (1927); Paul Gates, *The Illinois Central Railroad and Its Colonization Work* (1934); and *A Century of Progress: History of the Delaware and Hudson Company* (1925).

Railroad Growth and Consolidation in the Trans Mississippi. The literature on the railroads of the West is extensive. The more important material is to be found in L. H. Haney, *A Congressional History of Railways in the United States, 1850–1887* (1910); R. E. Riegel, *The Story of the Western Railroads* (1926), the best single volume; J. P. Davis, *The Union Pacific Railway* (1896); G. M. Dodge, *How We Built the Union Pacific Railway* (1910); Stuart Daggett, *Chapters on the History of the Southern Pacific* (1922); G. D. Bradley, *The Story of the Santa Fe* (1920); A. M. Borak, "The Chicago, Milwaukee and St. Paul Railroad," *Journal of Economic and Business History*, Vol. III (November, 1930), pp. 81–117; H. G. Brownson, *History of the Illinois Central Railroad to 1870* (1915); J. B. Hedges, *Henry Villard and the Railways of the North West* (1930); Oscar Lewis, *The Big Four: The Story of Huntington, Stanford, Hopkins, and Crocker, and of the Building of the Central Pacific* (1938); R. C. Overton, *Burlington West: A Colonization History of the Burlington Railroad* (1941), a lively account; E. L. Sabin, *Building the Pacific Railway* (1919); W. H. Stennett, *Yesterday and Today: A History of the Chicago and Northwestern Railway System* (1910); Montgomery Schuyler, *Westward the Course of Empire* (1906); and H. K. White, *History of the Union Pacific Railway* (1895).

Financing the Railroads. On this topic, consult W. Z. Ripley, *Railroads: Finance and Organization* (1915); F. A. Cleveland and F. W. Powell, *Railroad Promotion and Capitalization in the United States* (1909), which contains excellent biography. See also G. W. Julian, "Railway Influence in the Land Office," *North American Review*, Vol. CXXXVI, pp. 237 ff., which is invaluable; J. B. Sanborn, *Congressional Grants of Land in Aid of Railways* (1899); and J. W. Million, *State Aid to Railways in Missouri* (1896).

Exploiting the Railroads. Of the voluminous literature on this subject the following are most useful: The *Report* of the United States Pacific Railway Commission of 1887 (5 vols., 50th Cong. 1st Sess: *Senate Executive Document* no. 51); and, in addition, for the scandals in connection with the building of the Union Pacific, the Central Pacific and other roads, J. B. Crawford, *The Credit Mobilier* (1880), and Oscar Lewis, *The Big Four,* previously cited. Excellent studies of railroad financial malpractice are Max Lowenthal, *The Investor Pays* (1933) and E. G. Campbell, *The Reorganization of the American Railroad System, 1893–1900* (1938). Valuable for the earlier period is F. C. Hicks (ed.), *High Finance in the Sixties* (1929). More journalistic and muckraking in quality are C. E. Russell, *Stories of the Great Railroads* (1912); Gustavus Myers, *History of the Great American Fortunes* (3 vols., 1910); and Matthew Josephson, *The Robber Barons: The Great American Capitalists, 1861–1901* (1934). On the electric railroad, see the *Proceedings of the Federal Electric Railway Commission* (3 vols., 1920) and the much more usable treatment of this material by D. F. Wilcox, *Analysis of the Electric Railway Problem: Report to the Federal Electric Railways Commission* (1921).

State and Federal Regulation. In addition to the above, the conditions paving the way for government regulation are discussed in S. J. Buck, *The Granger Movement* (1913); C. S. Langstroth, *Railway Cooperation . . . in the United States* (1899), a story of early railroad pools; W. Larrabee, *The Railroad Question* (1893); and W. Z. Ripley, *Railroads, Rates and Regulations* (1912); A. T. Hadley, *Railroad Transportation, Its History and Its Laws* (1885); W. J. Cunningham, *American Railroads: Government Control and Reconstruction Policies* (1922); B. H. Meyer, *Railroad Legislation in the United States* (1903). R. E. Cushman, *The Independent Regulatory Commissions* (1941) and Walter Thompson, *Federal Centralization: a Study and Criticism of the Expanding Scope of Congressional Legislation* (1923) cover the history of government regulation. The constitutional aspects are reviewed in E. S. Corwin, *The Commerce Power versus States Rights* (1936) and Felix Frankfurter, *The Commerce Clause under Marshall, Taney and Waite* (1937). For court decisions, see A. R. Ellingwood and W. Coombs (eds.), *The Government and Railroad Transportation* (1930). I. L. Sharfman, *The Interstate Commerce Commission* (4 vols., 1931–7).

Chapter IV

Industrial Evolution and Revolution

The history of this many-sided subject remains to be written. The factual material for such a history is available in the voluminous *Reports* of the Census Bureau and the comprehensive *Report of the Industrial Commission* (19 vols., 1902). Helpful also to the author of a history of industrial America would be *A Graphic Analysis of the Census of Manufactures of the United States, 1849–1919* (1923) prepared by the National Industrial Conference Board. V. S. Clark's *History of Manufactures in the United States 1860–1914* (1928) is highly factual and woefully lacking in interpretation. C. D. Wright, *The Industrial Evolution of the United States* (1897) is still useful but, like Clark, leans to the factual side. As a kind of antidote to these two volumes the student should read L. M. Hacker, *The Triumph of American Capitalism* (1940); T. C. Cochran and William Miller, *The Age of Enterprise* (1942); Lewis Mumford, *Technics and Civilization* (1934); and Jerome Davis, *Capitalism and Its Culture* (1936). The several volumes of the History of American Life series covering the years since 1865, and especially Allan Nevins, *The Emergence of Modern America, 1865–1878* (1927), I. M. Tarbell, *The Nationalizing of Business, 1878–1898* (1936), and H. U. Faulkner, *The Quest for Social Justice, 1898–1914* (1931), contain both valuable material and bibliographical references on the several topics included in this chapter. B. J. Hendrick, *The Age of Big Business* (1921), in the Chronicles of America series is a popular survey; and Malcolm Keir, *Manufacturing Industries in America* (1920) is a scholarly account. All of the several texts on American economic history have chapters on the revolutionary changes that have transformed America economically, and culturally as well. See especially, Chapter 11 in E. C. Kirkland, *A History of American Economic Life* (rev. ed., 1947); H. U. Faulkner, *American Economic History* (rev. ed., 1937); F. A. Shannon, *America's Economic Growth* (1940); and Chester Wright, *Economic History of the United States* (2nd ed., 1949). There are also quantities of valuable material in Herbert Hoover and others, *Recent Economic Changes in the United States* (2 vols., 1929) evidencing the results of industrial transformation.

Government Aid to Industry. This aid has been both direct and indirect. Most important, perhaps, as far as industry is concerned, has been the protection of the home market. On the tariff, see P. Ashley, *Modern Tariff History* (3rd ed., 1920); Edward Stanwood, *American Tariff Controversies in the Nineteenth Century* (1903); F. W. Taussig, *Some Aspects of the Tariff Question* (3rd ed., 1931) and *Tariff History of the United States* (8th ed., 1931); W. S. Culbertson, "The Making of Tariffs," *Yale Review* (January, 1923), and "Tariff Problems of the United States" *Annals of the American Academy of Political and Social Science,* Vol. CXLI (January, 1929). There are rich storehouses of material on the tariff in Robert McElroy, *Grover Cleveland* (1923); Allan Nevins, *Grover Cleveland* (1932); J. A. Barnes, *John J. Carlisle* (1931); and C. S. Olcott, *The Life of William McKinley* (2 vols., 1916). Other government aids to industry include marketing facilities, improved roads, and other means of communications. On the postal system, see D. C. Roper, *The United States Post Office* (1917). On waterways, consult *Inland Water Transportation in the United States,* Department of Commerce, Bureau of Foreign and Domestic Commerce, Miscellaneous Series no. 119 (1923).

Growth of Basic American Industries. The history of many industries is yet to be written. On the textile industry, consult T. M. Young, *The American Cotton Industry* (1902); P. H. Nystrom, *Textiles* (1916); B. F. Lemert, *The Cotton Textile Industry of the Southern Appalachian Piedmont* (1933); J. H. Burgy, *The New England Cotton Textile Industry: A Study in Industrial Geography* (1932); A. H. Cole, *The American Wool Manufacture* (2 vols., 1926) M. T. Copeland, *The Cotton Manufacturing Industry of the United States* (1912); and P. T. Cherington, *The Wool Industry* (1916). For the oil industry the reader may profitably consult P. H. Giddens, *The Birth of the Oil Industry* (1938); G. W. Stocking, *The Oil Industry and the Competitive System* (1925); John Ise, *The United States Oil Policy* (1926); I. M. Tarbell, *The History of the Standard Oil Company* (2 vols., 1904); not entirely satisfactory; and C. C. Rister, *Oil: Titan of the Southwest* (1949), which is excellent. Allan Nevins, *John D. Rockefeller: The Heroic Age of American Enterprise* (2 vols., 1940) is a comprehensive study that opens many doors to the oil industry. Less favorable to Rockefeller is J. T. Flynn, *God's Gold: The Story of Rockefeller and His Times* (1932). *The Report of the Commissioner of Corporations on the Petroleum Industry,* parts 1 and 2 (1907) and *Report of the Federal Trade Commission on the Petroleum Industry: Prices, Profits and Competition* (1928) are of major importance. On lumbering, see John Ise, *The United States Forest Policy* (1920); S. H. Holbrook, *Holy Old Mackinaw: A Natural History of the American Lumberjack* (1938); and the *Report on the Lumber Industry by the Bureau of Corporations,* Department of Commerce and Labor (1913). Several works on the coal industry are worth while: W. H. Hamilton and H. R. Wright, *The Case of Bituminous Coal* (1925); *Report of the United States Coal Commission* (5 vols., 1925) and *What the Coal Commission Found* (1925) by the staff of the commission; and Eliot Jones, *The Anthracite Coal Combination* (1914). The story of iron and steel is incomplete, but the following are important: J. D. Swank, *History of the Manufacture of Iron and Steel in All Ages* (2nd ed., 1892); J. R. Smith, *The Story of Iron and Steel* (1908); O. A. Backert (ed.), *The A. B. C. of Iron and Steel* (5th ed., 1925); Abraham Berglund, *The United States Steel Corporation* (1907); J. H. Bridge, *The Inside History of the Carnegie Steel Company* (1903), an exposé; Arundel Cotter, *The Authentic History of the United States Steel Corporation* (1916) and *United States Steel: A Corporation with a Soul* (1921), an apology to soften and, if possible, fend off an impending government investigation and labor trouble; H. B. Vanderblue and W. L. Crum, *The Iron Industry in Prosperity and Depression* (1927); B. J. Hendrick, *The Life of Andrew Carnegie* (2 vols., 1932), "official" and noncritical; Allan Nevins, *Abram S. Hewitt: With Some Account of Peter Cooper* (1935); I. M. Tarbell, *The Life of Elbert H. Gary: The Story of Steel* (1925), an apology; Andrew Carnegie, *The Autobiography of Andrew Carnegie* (1920, best foot always forward!; George Harvey, *Henry Clay Frick, The Man* (1928), one man's portrayal; J. K. Winkler, *Incredible Carnegie: The Life of Andrew Carnegie (1835–1919)* (1931), an eulogistic account; F. P. Wirth, *The Discovery and Exploitation of the Minnesota Iron Lands* (1937); Paul de Kruif, *Seven Iron Men* (1929), interesting but unreliable; and S. H. Holbrook, *Iron Brew: A Century of American Ore and Steel* (1939), written for popular consumption. On the automobile the best works to date are R. C. Epstein, *The Automobile Industry: Its Economic and Commercial Development* (1928); L. H. Seltzer, *A Financial History of the American Automobile Industry* (1928); Arthur Pound, *The Turning Wheel* (1934), the story of General Motors; Henry Ford, *My Life and Work* (1922) an autobiography; and E. P. Norwood, *Ford Men and Methods* (1931). The history of the electrical industry must yet be written. On Edison, see F. L. Dyer and T. C. Martin, *Edison, His Life and Inventions* (2 vols., 1929) and G. S. Bryan, *Edison, the Man and His Work* (1926). Studies of the meat industry are C. B. Kuhlmann, *The Development of the Flour-Milling Industry in the United States* (1929), excellent; R. A. Clemen, *The American Livestock and Meat Industry* (1923), which should be examined in connection with *Report of the Commissioner of Corporations on the Beef Industry* (1905) and the *Report of the Federal Trade Commission on the Meat Packing Industry,* parts 1–3 (1918–20); L. F. Swift, *The Yankee of the Yards: The Biography of Gustavus Franklin Swift* (1927), another eulogistic biography. On the leather industry, see F. J. Allen, *The Shoe Industry* (1916); B. E. Hazard, *The Organization of the Boot and Shoe Industry in Massachusetts Before 1875* (1921). See also R. G. Blakey, *The United States Beet-Sugar Industry and the Tariff* (1912) and Alfred Lief, *Harvey Firestone: Free Man of Enterprise* (1952), a laudatory treatment.

Industrial Development in the West and South. The Twelfth Census of the United States, Vol. VII, on manufacturing, is indispensable for this topic. Also see C. Goodrich and others, *Migration and Economic Opportunity* (1936); F. B. Garver, F. M. Boddy, and A. J. Nixon, *The Location of Manufactures in the United States 1899–1929* (1933); G. E. McLaughlin, *Growth of American Manufacturing Areas: A Comparative Analysis with Special Emphasis on Trends in the Pittsburgh District* (1938); H. W. Odum, *Southern Regions of the United States* (1936); R. B. Vance, *Human Geography of the South* (1932); Broadus Mitchell and G. S. Mitchell, *The Industrial Revolution in the South* (1930); B. F. Lemert, *The Cotton Textile Industry of the Southern Appalachian Piedmont,* already cited; and M. H. Ross, *Machine Age in the Hills* (1933). Twentieth-century tendencies are discussed in Jonathan Daniels, *A Southerner Discovers the South* (1938).

The Concentration of Industry. John Moody, *The Masters of Capital* (1919) and B. J. Hendrick, *The Age of Big Business* (1919), both in the Chronicles of America series, are introductory surveys. They should be followed by two older but still useful volumes: John Moody, *The Truth About the Trusts* (1904) and R. T. Ely, *Monopolies and Trusts* (1900). The best general texts on the trust problem are Eliot Jones, *The Trust Problem in the United States* (1921). H. R. Seager and C. A. Gulick, Jr., *Trust and Corporation Problems* (1929); J. W. Jenks and W. E. Clark, *The Trust Problem* (4th ed., 1917); and L. H. Haney, *Business Organization and Combination* (rev. ed., 1914). W. Z. Ripley, *Trusts, Pools and Corporations* (rev. ed., 1916) is useful for source materials. On Concentration Itself, see C. R. Van Hise, *Concentration and Control* (rev. ed., 1914) and H. W. Laidler, *Concentration of Control in American Industry* (1931). Important, too, are J. R. Commons, *Legal Foundations of American Capitalism* (1924), and O. F. Boucke, *Laissez Faire and After* (1932). Agitation against the ills of big business is best seen in Henry George, *Progress and Poverty,* already cited; Edward Bellamy, *Looking Backward, 2000–1887* (1888); H. D. Lloyd, *Wealth Against Commonwealth* (1894); and C. Lloyd,

Henry Demarest Lloyd (2 vols., 1912). Henry George's beliefs are summarized in L. F. Post, *The Prophet of San Francisco* (1930) and G. R. Geiger, *The Philosophy of Henry George* (1933). C. C. Regier, *The Era of the Muckrakers* (1932), C. E. Russell, *Bare Hands and Stone Walls* (1933); Lincoln Steffens, *The Autobiography of Lincoln Steffens* (2 vols., 1931) and H. U. Faulkner, *The Quest for Social Justice, 1898–1914,* previously cited, are indispensable for those interested in the literature of protest. Evidence that George, Bellamy Lloyd and the others had cause to agitate for reform is to be found not only in the Windom, Cullom, and Hepburn *Reports,* cited in the previous chapter, but also in the *Preliminary Report of the Industrial Commission on Trusts and Industrial Combinations* (1900), in the Commission's Report, and the *Report of the Committee Pursuant to House Resolutions 429 and 504 to Investigate the Concentration of the Control of Money and Credit* (Pujo Committee) 62nd Cong. 3rd Sess., *House of Representatives Report,* no. 1593 (1913). Other valuable sources of information are H. R. Mussey, *Combination in the Mining Industry: A Study of Concentration in Lake Superior Iron Ore Production* (1905); and J. W. Stenman, *The Financial History of the American Telephone and Telegraph Industry* (1925).

From Industrial to Finance Capitalism. On this topic, consult Lewis Corey, *The House of Morgan,* already cited; Harvey O'Connor, *Mellon's Millions* (1933); J. W. Jenkins, *James B. Duke, Master Builder* (1927); Cyrus Adler, *Jacob H. Schiff: His Life and Letters* (2 vols., 1928); Robert McElroy, *Levi Parsons Morton* (1930); Henry Clews, *Fifty Years in Wall Street* (1908); T. W. Lawson, *Frenzied Finance* (1905), an overstated exposé; Arthur Pound and S. T. Moore (eds.), *They Told Barron* (1930); L. D. Brandeis, *Other People's Money, and How the Bankers Use It* (1914); W. Z. Ripley, *Main Street and Wall Street* (1927); M. G. Myers, *The New York Money Market* (1931) and F. C. James, *The Growth of Chicago Banks* (1938).

The Government and Industrial Concentration. The history of government regulation is treated in M. W. Watkins, *Industrial Combinations and Public Policy* (1927); D. M. Keezer and Stacy May, *The Public Control of Business* (1930); J. D. Clark, *The Federal Trust Policy* (1931); A. H. Walker, *History of the Sherman Law of the United States of America* (1910), which is highly interpretative; O. W. Knauth, *The Policy of the United States Towards Industrial Monopoly* (1914), which is badly organized, but contains much on the Sherman Anti-Trust Act. For the legislative background of the law, see *Bills and Debates in Congress Relating to Trusts,* 57th Cong., 2nd Sess., *Senate Document* no. 147 (1903). For legal aspects of the law, consult W. H. Taft, *The Anti-Trust Act and the Supreme Court* (1914). On the early history of the Federal Trade Commission, consult G. C. Henderson, *The Federal Trade Commission* (1924). Woodrow Wilson's attitude towards government regulation of business is summarized in his *The New Freedom* (1913). The question of business ethics is discussed at length by the following: Werner Sombart, *The Quintessence of Capitalism* (1915); R. H. Tawney, *Religion and the Rise of Capitalism: A Historical Study* (1926); Chamber of Commerce of the United States, *Principles of Business Conduct* (1924); E. L. Herrmance, *The Ethics of Business* (1926); and C. F. Taeusch, *Professional and Business Ethics* (1926).

CHAPTER V

The Industrial Worker

The standard authority on the labor movement is J. R. Commons and others, *History of Labour in the United States* (4 vols., 1918–35). Unfortunately his monumental *A Documentary History of American Industrial Society* (11 vols., 1910–11) stops at 1880. Since 1890, this gap has been partially filled by the *Bulletin of the Bureau of Labor,* which subsequently became the *Bulletin of the United States Bureau of Labor Statistics,* a veritable encyclopedia of information on wages, hours, prices, union standards and industrial accidents. *The Monthly Labor Review*, also a government publication, is useful. Very helpful, too, is the *Report of the Industrial Commission*, previously cited; Volumes VII, XII, XIV, and XVIII are especially important on labor. The biennial *Census on Manufactures* and *The Report of the Commission on Industrial Relations*, 64th Cong., 1st Sess., *Senate Document* no. 415 (11 vols., 1916) contain valuable material. P. H. Douglas, C. N. Hitchcock, and W. E. Atkins, *The Worker in Modern Economic Society* (1923) is a collection of readings. A very brief but suggestive treatise covering the entire period is Mary Beard, *A Short History of the American Labor Movement* (1920). Other one volume summaries are: G. C. Groat, *An Introduction to the Study of Organized Labor in America* (1919); F. T. Carlton, *The History and Problems of Organized Labor* (rev. ed., 1920); G. S. Watkins, *An Introduction to the Study of Labor Problems* (1922); R. T. Ely, *The Labor Movement in the United States* (1905); and N. J. Ware, *The Labor Movement in America, 1860–1895* (1929). A more recent survey by C. R. Daugherty, *Labor Problems in American Industry* (1933), is excellent.

The Labor Supply. Our principal sources of labor supply have been from increase of native-born population and from immigration. On the former the reports of the United States Bureau of the Census are indispensable. See especially *A Century of Population Growth from the First Census of the United States to the Twelfth, 1790–1900* (1909) and *Negro Population 1790–1915* (1918). There is also valuable material in W. S. Thompson, *Population Problems* (1930); W. S. Rossiter, *Increase of Population in the United States, 1910–1920* (1922), Census Monograph I; Frank Lorimer and Frederick Osborn, *Dynamics of Population: Social and Biological Significance of Changing Birth Rates in the United States* (1934); and Committee on Recent Economic Changes, *Recent Economic Changes in the United States* (1929). The principal source of information about immigration is the *Report of the Immigration Commission* (42 vols., 1911) and the two-volume abstract thereof, 61st Cong., 3rd Sess., *Senate Document* no. 747 (1911); J. W. Jenks and W. J. Lanck, *The Immigration Problem* (4th ed., rev. 1917) is a one-volume synopsis of this report. Other worthwhile volumes are J. R. Commons, *Races and Immigrants in America* (1907); I. A. Hourwich, *Immigration and Labor* (rev. ed., 1923); M. L. Hansen, *The Immigrant in American History* (1940); Maurice Davie, *World Immigration* (1936); A. B. Faust, *The German Element in the United States* (2 vols., 1909); H. J. Ford, *The Scotch-Irish in America* (1915); Theodore Blegen, *Norwegian Migration to America* (2 vols., 1931–40); F. E. Janson, *The Background of Swedish Immigration, 1840–1930* (1931); J. S. Lindberg, *The Background of Swedish Emigration to the United States* (1930); K. C. Babcock, *The Scandinavian Element in the United States* (1914); E. G. Balch, *Our Slavic Fellow Citizens* (1910); C. S. Bernheimer, *The Russian Jew in the United States* (1905); H. P. Fairchild, *Greek Immigration to the United States* (1911); Thomas Capek, *The Czechs in America* (1920); R. F. Foerster, *The Italian Emigration of Our Times* (1919); Samuel Joseph, *Jewish Immigration to the United States from 1881 to 1910* (1914); Jerome Davis, *The Russian Immigrant* (1922); William I. Thomas and Florian Znaniecki, *The Polish Peasant in Europe and America* (1927); M. Gamio, *Mexican Immigration to the United States* (1930); Harry Jerome, *Migration and Business Cycles* (1926); M. R. Coolidge, *Chinese Immigration* (1909); G. F. Seward, *Chinese Immigration, in Its Social and Economical Aspects* (1881); S. L. Gulick, *The American Japanese Problem* (1914); E. G. Mears, *Resident Orientals on the American Pacific Coast* (1927); E. S. Brunner, *Immigrant Farmers and Their Children* (1929); Grace Abbott, *The Immigrant and the Community* (1917); Herman Feldman, *Racial Factors in American Industry* (1931); Edith Abbott, *Historical Aspects of the Immigration Problem* (1926) and *Immigration: Select Documents and Case Records* (1924); E. L. Anderson, *We Americans* (1937); and Carl Wittke, *We Who Built America: The Saga of the Immigrant* (1939). Students will also profit from O. E. Rölvaag, *Giants in the Earth: A Saga of the Prairie* (1927) and *Peder Victorious* (1929); Edna Ferber, *American Beauty* (1931) and Gladys H. Carroll, *As the Earth Turns* (1933), both tales of immigrant life in rural New England; and Abraham Cahan, *The Rise of David Levinsky* (1917), a stirring account of a New York

Jewish immigrant. On Negro labor, consult C. H. Wesley, *Negro Labor in the United States, 1850–1925* (1927); S. D. Spero and A. L. Harris, *The Black Worker* (1931), C. G. Woodson, *A Century of Negro Migration* (1918); and C. Goodrich and others, *Migration and Economic Opportunity, the Report of the Study of Population Redistribution* (1936). For the women and children workers, see the *Report on the Conditions of Women and Child Wage Earners in the United States*, 61st Cong., 2nd Sess., *Senate Report* no. 645 (19 vols., 1910–12) and the subsequent reports issued by the Women's Bureau and Children's of the Department of Labor. Certain volumes in the 1911 *Report* are most valuable; E. L. Otey, *The Beginnings of Child Labor Legislation in Certain States: A Comparative Study* (Vol. VI); H. L. Sumner, *History of Women in Industry in the United States* (Vol. IX); and J. B. Andrews and W. D. P. Bliss, *History of Women in Trade Unions* (Vol. X). Also consult A. M. Anderson, *Women in the Factory* (1922) and John Spargo, *The Bitter Cry of the Children* (1906), old but still useful; and J. A. Hill, *Women in Gainful Occupations, 1870 to 1920* (1929), Census monograph no. 9.

The Growth of the Labor Movement. The literature on this topic is abundant, but the following are adequate: Herbert Harris, *American Labor* (1939); Selig Perlman, *A History of Trade Unionism in the United States* (1922); R. F. Hoxie, *Trade Unionism in the United States* (1917); S. P. Orth, *The Armies of Labor* (1919), in the Chronicles of America series; N. J. Ware, *The Labor Movement in the United States, 1860–1895* (1929); Leo Wolman, *The Growth of Trade Unions, 1880–1923* (1924); L. L. Lorwin, *The American Federation of Labor; History, Policies, and Prospects* (1933); T. S. Adams and H. L. Sumner, *Labor Problems* (1905); W. B. Catlin, *The Labor Problem in the United States and Great Britain* (rev. ed., 1935); M. C. Cahill, *Shorter Hours: A Study of the Movement since the Civil War* (1932); and D. D. Lescohier, *The Knights of St. Crispin, 1867–1874* (1910). On labor in particular industries, see L. L. Lorwin, *The Women's Garment Workers* (1924); Herbert Lahne, *The Cotton Mill Worker* (1944); A. E. Galster, *The Labor Movement in the Shoe Industry* (1924); Andrew Roy, *A History of the Coal Miners of the United States* (1907); A. E. Suffern, *The Coal Miner's Struggle for Industrial Status* (1926); Anna Rochester, *Labor and Coal* (1931), written from a left-wing point of view; H. L. Herring, *Welfare Work in Mill Villages: The Story of Extra-Mill Activities in North Carolina* (1929); J. A. Fitch, *The Steel Workers* (1910); C. A. Gulick, Jr., *Labor Policy of the United States Steel Corporation* (1924); R. W. Dunn, *Labor and Automobiles* (1929); Grace Hutchins, *Labor and Silk* (1929); and Charlotte Todes, *Labor and Lumber* (1931). There is a wealth of valuable material on the history of the labor movement in biographical sources: Samuel Gompers, *Seventy Years of Life and Labor* (2 vols., 1925); L. S. Reed, *The Labor Philosophy of Samuel Gompers* (1930); R. H. Harvey, *Samuel Gompers, Champion of the Toiling Masses* (1935); J. R. Buchanan, *The Story of a Labor Agitator* (1903); and T. V. Powderly, *Thirty Years of Labor, 1859 to 1889* (1889); H. J. Carman, Henry David, and Paul Guthrie (eds.), *The Path I Trod: The Autobiography of Terrence V. Powderly* (1940); Elsie Glück, *John Mitchell, Miner* (1929); W. D. Haywood, *Bill Haywood's Book* (1929); Ray Ginger, *The Bending Cross* (1949), the story of Eugene V. Debs; Brand Whitlock, *Forty Years of It* (1914); and J. R. Commons, *Trade Unionism and Labor Problems* (1905).

The Theory and Practice of Class Consciousness. P. W. Brissenden's *The I. W. W., A Study of American Syndicalism* (1919) is the standard authority but should be supplemented by J. S. Gambs, *The Decline of the I. W. W.* (1932). Also see J. G. Brooks, *American Syndicalism: The I. W. W.* (1913) and John Spargo, *Syndicalism, Industrial Unionism and Socialism* (1913). For other radical labor movements, consult C. H. Parker, *The Casual Laborer, and Other Essays* (1920); George Soule, *The New Unionism in the Clothing Industry* (1920); D. J. Saposs, *Left Wing Unionism* (1926); James O'Neal, *American Communism* (1927); Anthony Bimba, *The History of the American Working Class* (1927); Nathan Fine, *Labor and Farmer Parties in the United States, 1828–1928* (1928); J. A. Fitch, *The Causes of Industrial Unrest* (1924); Louis Adamic, *Dynamite, the Story of Class Violence in America* (rev. ed., 1934); Samuel Yellen, *American Labor Struggles* (1936); Henry David,

The History of the Haymarket Affair: A Study in the American Social-Revolutionary and Labor Movements (1936), an admirable volume in every respect; Bureau of Labor, *Report on Strike of Textile Workers in Lawrence, Mass., in 1912*, 62nd Cong., 2nd Sess., *Senate Document* no. 870 (1912); J. W. Coleman, *The Molly Maguire Riots: Industrial Conflict in the Pennsylvania Coal Region* (1936); United States Strike Commission, *Report on the Chicago Strike of June–July, 1894* (1895); Carter Goodrich, *The Miner's Freedom* (1925); Winthorp Lane, *Civil War in West Virginia* (1921); A. F. Hinrichs, *The United Mine Workers of America, and the Non-Union Coal Fields* (1923); C. E. Bonnett, *Employers' Associations in the United States* (1922); Edward Levinson, *I Break Strikes! The Technique of Pearl L. Bergoff* (1935); Leo Huberman, *The Labor Spy Racket* (1937); United States Strike Commission, *Report on the Chicago Strike of June–July, 1894* (1895); Clinch Calkins, *Spy Overhead, the Story of Industrial Espionage* (1937); A. G. Taylor, *Labor Policies of the National Association of Manufacturers* (1928); Benjamin Rastall, *The Labor History of the Cripple Creek District* (1908); Almont Lindsey, *The Pullman Strike* (1942); Harry Barnard, *Eagle Forgotten* (1938); Tom Tippett, *When Southern Labor Stirs* (1931); and G. S. Mitchell, *Textile Unionism in the South* (1931).

State and Federal Labor Legislation. This topic may be prefaced by John Lombardi, *Labor's Voice in the Cabinet: A History of the Department of Labor from Its Origin to 1921* (1942); E. E. Witte, *The Government in Labor Disputes* (1932); A. T. Mason, *Organized Labor and the Law* (1925); Edward Berman, *Labor and the Sherman Act* (1930): On state labor legislation, consult A. M. Edwards, *The Labor Legislation of Connecticut* (1907); F. R. Fairchild, *The Factory Legislation of the State of New York* (1905); A. S. Field, *The Child Labor Policy of New Jersey* (1909); J. L. Barnard, *Factory Legislation in Pennsylvania* (1907); J. K. Towles, *Factory Legislation of Rhode Island* (1908); C. E. Persons et al., *Labor Laws and Their Enforcement, with Special Reference to Massachusetts* (1911); E. F. Baker, *Protective Labor Legislation, with Special Reference to Women in the State of New York* (1925); C. E. Beyer, *History of Labor Legislation for Women in Three States*, Department of Labor, Women's Bureau, Bulletin no. 66 (1929); and E. R. Beckner, *A History of Labor Legislation in Illinois* (1929). Also see J. R. Commons and J. B. Andrews, *Principles of Labor Legislation* (new ed., 1936); and H. L. Sumner, *The Working Children of Boston* (1922).

Organized Labor and the Courts. G. G. Groat, *Attitude of American Courts in Labor Cases* (1911) is excellent; so is Felix Frankfurter and Nathan Greene, *The Labor Injunction* (1930). These should be supplemented by *The Dissenting Opinions of Mr. Justice Holmes* (1929) and *The Social and Economic Views of Mr. Justice Brandeis* (1930), both edited by Alfred Lief. M. R. Carroll, *Labor and Politics: The Attitude of the American Federation of Labor Toward Legislation and Politics* (1923) and Edward Berman, *Labor Disputes and the President of the United States* (1924) are valuable. A. R. Ellingwood and W. Coombs, *The Government and Labor* (1926) and Carl Raushenbush and Emmanuel Stein, *Labor Cases and Materials* (1941) furnish collections of source materials and court decisions.

Chapter VI

The Commercial Farmer

Unfortunately there is no history of American agriculture for the period after 1860 comparable to L. C. Gray, *History of Agriculture in the Southern United States to 1860* (2 vols., 1933) and P. W. Bidwell and J. I. Falconer, *History of Agriculture in the Northern United States, 1620–1860* (1925). Nevertheless, there is a great mass of monographic literature and an almost inexhaustible supply of official publications and other documentary material. The best bibliographies of this material are E. E. Edwards, *A Bibliography of the History of Agriculture in the United States,* Department of Agriculture, Miscellaneous Publication No. 84 (1930) and L. B. Schmidt, *Topical Studies and References on the History of American Agriculture* (4th ed., 1940). Exceedingly important, too, are the *Bulletins of the Department of Agriculture,* the *Bulletins of the Office of Experiment Stations,* the *Annual Reports of the Secretary of Agriculture,* and the *Yearbooks of the Department of Agriculture.* Certain of the *Yearbooks* are especially valuable. That for 1899, for example, devoted nearly 700 of its 880 pages to the history of different phases of agriculture; those for 1921–25 contain monographic material on farm crops and farm life; the *Yearbooks* for 1936 and 1937 are excellent handbooks on agricultural genetics; that for 1938 is one of the best accounts ever written on agricultural soils; the *Yearbook for 1940* is unsurpassed for its wealth of monographic material, including the admirable summary by E. E. Edwards, *American Agriculture —The First 300 Years* (1940). Volumes X and XI on agriculture of the *Report of the Industrial Commission,* already cited, are disappointing. The *Statistical Abstract* (1879–), the various decenial censuses, the *Yearbooks,* and the special *United States Census of Agriculture* (3 vols., 1925) are indispensable for statistical data. For maps, charts, and other graphic material, consult O. E. Baker (ed.), *Atlas of American Agriculture* (8 vols., 1917–35), published by United States Department of Agriculture. For the geographical basis, see J. R. Smith, *North Amèrica* (1925).

The Growth of American Agriculture. The best single volume carrying the period from 1860 to the end of the century is F. A. Shannon, *The Farmer's Last Frontier: Agriculture, 1860–1897* (1945), in the Economic History of the United States series. Brief accounts are A. H. Sanford, *The Story of Agriculture in the United States* (1916); E. L. Bogart, *Economic History of American Agriculture* (1923); and Joseph Schafer, *The Social History of American Agriculture* (1936). These volumes may be profitably supplemented by L. B. Schmidt and E. D. Ross (eds.), *Readings in the Economic History of American Agriculture* (1925). L. H. Bailey, *Cyclopedia of American Agriculture* (4 vols., 1907–09), especially Volume IV, contains much material that indicates the agricultural expansion of the nation. On irrigation and reclamation, see Elwood Mead, *Irrigation Institutions* (1903), an old work but still useful; R. P. Teele, *The Economics of Land Reclamation in the United States* (1927), first rate; *The U. S. Reclamation Service: Its History, Activities and Organization,* Service Monograph of the United States Government, No. 2 (1919); and J. W. Haw and F. E. Schmidt, *Report on Federal Reclamation to the Secretary of the Interior* (1935), an excellent summary. On agricultural settlement, see bibliography, Chapter II above and R. T. Hill, *The Public Domain and Democracy* (1910); E. Van D. Robinson, *Early Economic Conditions and the Development of Agriculture in Minnesota* (1915); Rupert Vance, *Human Geography of the South* (1932); H. W. Odum, *Southern Regions of the United States* (1936); Joseph Schafer, *A History of Agriculture in Wisconsin* (1922); B. H. Hibbard, *The History of Agriculture in Dane County* (1904); J. G. Thompson, *The Rise and Decline of the Wheat Growing Industry in Wisconsin* (1909); U. P. Hedrick, *A History of Agriculture in the State of New York* (1933); H. F. Wilson, *The Hill Country of Northern New England, 1790–1930* (1936); and E. J. Wickson, *Rural California* (1923).

Improved Machines and Techniques. The best treatises on agricultural machinery are R. L. Ardrey, *American Agricultural Implements; A Review of Invention and Development in the Agricultural Implement Industry of the United States* (1894); E. H. Knight, *Agricultural Implements,* a report to the Commissioners of Agriculture on the Paris Exposition of 1878, 46th Cong., 3rd Sess., *House Executive Document* 42, part 5; E. W. Byrn, *The Progress of Invention in the Nineteenth Century* (1900); Waldemar Kaempffert (ed.), *A Popular History of American Invention* (2 vols., 1924), section of Volume II, pp. 1246–1309; R. M. La Follette (ed.) *The Making of America* (10 vols., 1905), especially Vol. V, pp. 332–42; H. N. Casson, *The Romance of the Reaper* (1908); W. MacDonald, *Makers of Modern Agriculture* (1913); and L. W. Ellis and E. A. Rumeley, *Power and the Plow* (1911). The second volume of W. T. Hutchinson's *Cyrus Hall McCormick* (2 vols., 1935) contains an exhaustive account of the development of post-Civil War harvesting machinery. Leo Rogin, *The Introduction of Farm Machinery in Its Relation to the Productivity of Labor in the Agriculture of the United States During the Nineteenth Century* (1931) deals primarily with the plow and with wheat production. For the influence of machinery since 1900, see O. E. Baker, "Changes in Production and Consumption of Our Farm Products and the Trend of Population," *Annals of the American Academy of Political and Social Science,* (March, 1929). The rôle played by the Federal government in furthering agricultural expansion is described by W. L. Wanlass, *The United States Department of Agriculture, A Study in Administration* (1920), A. C. True and V. A. Clark, *The Agricultural Experiment Stations in the United States* (1900). The Bureaus of the Department of Agriculture are elaborated by Milton Conover, *The Office of Experiment Stations* (1924); F. W. Powell, *The Bureau of Animal Industry* (1927); G. A. Weber, *The Bureau of Chemistry and Soils* (1928); Janks Cameron, *The Bureau of Dairy Industry* (1929); and G. A. Weber, *The Plant Quarantine and Control Administration* (1930). On agricultural education the best work is A. C. True, *A History of Agricultural Extension Work in the United States, 1785–1923,* Department of Agriculture, Miscellaneous Publication No. 15 (1928) and *A History of Agricultural Education in the United States, 1785–1925,* Department of Agriculture, Miscellaneous Publication No. 36 (1929). See, too, J. C. Bailey, *Seaman A. Knapp, Schoolmaster of American Agriculture* (1945). E. D. Ross *Democracy's College; The Land-Grant Movement in the Formative Stage* (1942); W. H. Shepardson, *Agricultural Education in the United States* (1929); and Eugene Davenport, *Education for Efficiency* (1909). On scientific agriculture, consult O. M. Kile, *The New Agriculture* (1932); A. C. True, *A History of Agricultural Experimentation and Research in the United States 1607–1925* (1937); Paul de Kruif, *Hunger Fighters* (1928); L. O. Howard, *A History of Applied Entomology,* Smithsonian Miscellaneous Collections, Vol. 84 (1930) and his *Fighting the Insects* (1933); D. G. Fairchild, *The World Was My Garden; Travels of a Plant Explorer* (1938); D. S. Jordan and V. Kellogg, *The Scientific Aspects of Luther Burbank's Work* (1909); H. S. Williams, *Luther Burbank, His Life and Work* (1915); and W. E. Smythe, *The Conquest of Arid America* (rev. ed., 1905). There are also many valuable articles on agricultural science in *Agricultural History.* Among the more important of these are: B. T. Galloway, "Plant Pathology; A Review of the Development of the Science in the United States," Vol. II, pp. 49–60; A. G. McCall, "The Development of Soil Science," Vol. V, pp. 43–56; K. A. Ryerson, "History and Significance of the Foreign Plant Introduction Work of the United States Development of Agriculture," Vol. VII, pp. 110–28; C. R. Ball, "The History of American Wheat Improvement," Vol. IV, pp. 48–71; and G. F. Johnson, "The Early History of Copper Fungicides," Vol. IX, pp. 67–9.

Agricultural Specialization. On this topic the reader should consult F. I. Anderson, *The Farmer of Tomorrow* (1913); T. B. Gold, *Handbook of Connecticut Agriculture* (1901); C. H. Eckles, *Dairy Cattle and Milk Production* (rev. ed., 1939).

The Farmer's Market. There is much valuable material on this topic in three older works: "American Produce Exchange Markets," *Annals of the American Academy of Political and Social Science,* Vol. XXXVIII, No. 2 (1911); Volume VI of the *Report of the Industrial Commission,* already cited, on the "Distribution of Farm Products"; and H. C. Emery, *Speculation on the Stock and Produce Exchanges of the United States* (1896). More recent publications are H. M. Larson, *The Wheat Market and the Farmer in Minnesota, 1858–1900* (1926); C. H. Taylor, *History of the Board of Trade of the City of Chicago* (3 vols., 1917); *Report of the Federal Trade Commission on the Grain Trade* (7 vols., 1920–6), especially Vols. I–III; *Report of Federal Trade Commission on Methods and Operations of Grain Exporters* (2 vols., 1922–3); and W. H. Hubbard, *Cotton and the Cotton Market* (1923), which is very good.

The Farmer as Businessman and Worker. The subject of farm co-operatives is best discussed by A. H. Hirsch, "Efforts of the Grange in the Middle West to Control the Price of Farm Machinery, 1870–1880," *Mississippi Valley Historical Review,* Vol. XV, pp. 473–96. O. N. Refsell, "The Farmer's Elevator Movement," *Journal of Political Economy,* Vol. XXII, pp. 872–95, 969–91; W. Gee and E. A. Terry,

The Cotton Coöperatives in the Southeast (1933); and E. G. Nourse, *Fifty Years of Farmers' Elevators in Iowa,* Bulletin of Agriculture and Mechanic Arts No. 211 (1923). For later developments see O. M. Kile, *The Farm Bureau Movement* (1921); R. H. Elsworth, *Agricultural Cooperative Associations, Marketing and Purchasing, 1925,* Department of Agriculture Technical Bulletin No. 40 (1928); and E. A. Stokdyk and C. H. West, *The Farm Board* (1930). On the marketing of livestock, see E. G. Nourse and J. G. Knapp, *The Cooperative Marketing of Livestock* (1931). The problems of the Pacific coast fruit-shippers are discussed by R. M. MacCurdy, *The History of the California Fruit Growers Exchange* (1925).

Patterns of Agrarian Discontent. The best brief volume on this topic is S. J. Buck, *The Agrarian Crusade* (1920), in the Chronicles of America series. The same author's *The Granger Movement* (1913) is the standard authority on this subject. Equally authoritative is J. D. Hicks' *The Populist Revolt* (1931). Unsympathetic is F. L. Mcvey, *The Populist Movement* (1896). Also see F. B. Simkins, *The Tillman Movement in South Carolina* (1926), and his *Pitchfork Ben Tillman, South Carolinian* (1944); C. Vann Woodward, *Tom Watson; Agrarian Rebel* (1938), and his *Origins of the New South* (1951), which contains an understanding account of Southern Populism in addition to much new material on the South between the years, 1876–1913; A. M. Arnett, *The Populist Movement in Georgia* (1922); W. D. Sheldon, *Populism in the Old Dominion; Virginia Farm Politics, 1885–1900* (1935); W. J. Bryan, *The First Battle* (1896); Elmer Ellis, *Henry Moore Teller, Defender of the West* (1941); F. E. Haynes, *James Baird Weaver* (1919) and *Third Party Movements Since the Civil War, with Special Reference to Iowa; A Study in Social Politics* (1916); Nathan Fine, *Labor and Farmer Parties in the United States, 1828–1928* (1928); and the following articles: J. D. Hicks, "The Political Career of Ignatius Donnelly," *Mississippi Valley Historical Review,* Vol. VIII, pp. 80–132; H. C. Nixon, "The Economic Basis of the Populist Movement in Iowa," *Iowa Journal of History and Politics,* Vol. XXI, pp. 373–96 and "The Populist Movement in Iowa," ibid., Vol. XXIV, pp. 3–107; L. W. Fuller, "Colorado's Revolt Against Capitalism, "*Mississippi Valley Historical Review,* Vol. XXI, pp. 343–60; D. M. Robinson, "Tennessee Politics and the Agrarian Revolt," ibid., Vol. XX, pp. 365–80; C. M. Destler, "Consummation of a Labor-Populist Alliance in Illinois," ibid., Vol. XXVII, pp. 589–602; Sidney Glazer, "Patrons of Industry in Michigan," ibid., Vol. XXIV, pp. 185–94; and Harvey Wish, "John P. Altgeld and the Backbone of the Campaign of 1896," ibid., Vol. XXIV, pp. 503–18. For a vicious attack on the Populist movement read F. B. Tracy, "Rise and Doom of the Populist Party," *The Forum,* Vol. XVI, pp. 241–50. The principal grievances of the farmer, in addition to prices and marketing, were centered on credit and tenancy. On the former, see E. S. Sparks, *History and Theory of Agricultural Credit in the United States* (1932); J. B. Norman, *Farm Credits in the United States and Canada* (1924); and Clara Eliot, *The Farmers' Campaign for Credit* (1927). On tenancy, consult the 1923 *Agricultural Yearbook;* L. C. Gray "The Trend in Farm Ownership," *Annals of the American Academy of Political and Social Science* (March, 1929); *Farm Tenancy, Report of the President's Committee, Prepared Under the Auspices of the National Resources Committee* (1937); E. A. Goldenweiser and L. E. Truesdell, *Farm Tenancy in the United States,* Census Monographs No. 4, 1920 Census (1924); and J. D. Black and R. H. Allen, "The Growth of Farm Tenancy in the United States," *Quarterly Journal of Economics,* Vol. LI, pp. 393–425. Farm discontent is also reflected in such volumes as C. E. Russell, *Bare Hands and Stone Walls* (1933); J. W. Witham, *Fifty Years on the Firing Line* (1924); Herbert Quick, *One Man's Life* (1925), *Vandemark's Folly* (1922), and *The Hawkeye* (1923); Mari Sandoz, *Old Jules* (1935); Hamlin Garland, *A Son of the Middle Border* (1917); Willa Cather, *O Pioneers!* (1913) and *My Antonia* (1918); Ole Rolvaäg, *Giants in the Earth* (1927); Frank Norris, *The Octopus* (1901); W. A. White, *A Certain Rich Man* (1909); G. H. Carroll, *As The Earth Turns* (1933); Ellen Glasgow, *Barren Ground* (1925); Edward Howe, *The Story of a Country Town* (1884); Louis Bromfield, *The Farm* (1933); Ruth Suckow, *Iowa Interiors* (1926) and *The Folks* (1934); and Josephine Johnson, *Now in November* (1934).

Chapter VII

New and Old Cultural Patterns

Though he did not live to complete it, V. L. Parrington's *Beginnings of Critical Realism in America, 1860–1920* (1930), the third volume of his provocative and pioneering *Main Currents in American Thought,* previously cited, contains some rewarding ideas on the various cultural patterns that developed in post-Civil War America. More recent works include H. S. Commager, *The American Mind* (1950); R. H. Gabriel, *The Course of American Democratic Thought* (1940); Elmer Ellis, *Mr. Dooley's America* (1941); Walter Johnson, *William Allen White's America* (1947); Joseph Dorfman, *Thorstein Veblen and His America* (1934); M. E. Curti, *Growth of American Thought* (1943); and Chapter 25 of Volume II of C. A. and M. R. Beard, *The Rise of American Civilization* (4 vols., 1927–42). The biographic and autobiographic material of leading spokesmen of the period constitutes an indispensable source of information. See Worthington C. Ford (ed.) *The Letters of Henry Adams* (2 vols., 1930–8); Henry James (ed.), *The Letters of William James* (2 vols., 1920); M. A. De Wolfe Howe, *John Jay Chapman and His Letters* (1937); N. S. Shaler, *Autobiography* (1909); Raphael Pumpelly, *My Reminiscences* (1918); W. D. Howells, *Literary Friends and Acquaintances* (1900); E. Bisland, *Life and Letters of Lafcadio Hearn* (2 vols., 1906); Rollo Ogden (ed.), *Life and Letters of E. L. Godkin* (2 vols., 1907); Van Wyck Brooks, *The Times of Melville and Whitman* (1947); Bernard DeVoto, *Mark Twain's America* (1932); J. S. Clark, *The Life and Letters of John Fiske,* (2 vols., 1917); Henry Holt, *Garrulities of an Octogenarian Editor* (1923); Mildred Howells, *Life and Letters of William Dean Howells* (2 vols., 1928); Hamlin Garland, *A Son of the Middle Border* (1917); and *The Autobiography of William Allen White* (1946). The novels of Mark Twain, Edith Wharton, Henry James, W. D. Howells, Ellen Glasgow, and Booth Tarkington portray the character of the period.

The Expansion of Educational Opportunities. For details, Paul Monroe (ed.), *Cyclopedia of American Education* (5 vols., 1911–13) is the standard work. Three widely used texts are E. P. Cubberly, *Public Education in the United States* (rev. ed., 1934); E. G. Dexter, *A History of Education in the United States* (1904); and R. G. Boone, *Education in the United States* (1909). Useful also are N. M. Butler (ed.), *Education in the United States* (2 vols., 1900); C. D. Aborn and others (eds.), *Pioneers of the Kindergarten in America* (1924); S. E. Parker, *History of Modern Elementary Education* (1912), a standard treatise for period covered; E. E. Brown, *The Making of Our Middle Schools* (1903); E. W. Knight, *Influence of Reconstruction on Education in the South* (1913) and *Public Education in the South* (1922); C. W. Dabney, *Universal Education in the South* (2 vols., 1936); J. A. Burns, *The Growth and Development of the Catholic School System in the United States* (1912); B. T. Washington, *Up From Slavery* (new ed., 1937) and *The Story of My Life and Work* (1900); J. L. M. Curry, *Education of the Negroes since 1860* (1894); W. E. B. DuBois, *The Negro Common School* (1901); E. E. Slosson, *The American Spirit in Education* (1921), in the Chronicles of America series. Three works of prime significance are M. E. Curti, *The Social Ideas of American Educators* (1935); H. K. Beale, *Are American Teachers Free?* (1936); and J. L. M. Curry, *A Brief Sketch of George Peabody, and a History of the Peabody Education Fund through Thirty Years* (1898). Another work of special importance is Thomas Woody, *A History of Women's Education in the United States* (2 vols., 1929), which is scholarly and definitive. For later trends, see I. L. Kandel (ed.), *Twenty-Five Years of American Education* (1924); John Dewey, *The School and Society* (1899) and his *Democracy and Education* (1916); John and Evelyn Dewey, *Schools of Tomorrow* (1915); and Irving King, *Education for Social Efficiency* (1913). On country schools, see J. D. Eggleston and R. W. Bruére, *The Work of the Rural School* (1913). Mabel Newcomer's *Financial Statistics of Public Education in the United States, 1910–1920* (1924) is excellent. On education for adults, see R. L. Lurie, *The Challenge of the Forum* (1930); J. L. Hurlbut, *The Story of Chautauqua* (1921); H. A. Orchard, *Fifty Years of Chautauqua* (1923); V. and R. O. Case, *We Called It Culture; The Story of Chautauqua* (1948); and A. E. Bestor, *Chautauqua Publications* (1934). The history of the public library is best told by the following: S. H. Ditzion, *Arsenals of a Democratic Culture* (1947); S. S. Green, *The Public Library Movement in the United States 1853–1893* (1913); A. E. Bostwick, *The American Public Library* (4th rev., 1929); R. D. Leigh, *The Public Library in the United States* (1950); and W. I. Fletcher, *Public Libraries in America* (1894).

Universities and the Higher Learning. On higher education the standard authority is C. F. Thwing, *The American College in American Life* (1897); *College Administration* (1900); *A History of Higher Education in America* (1906); *A History of Education in the United States Since the Civil War* (1910), which emphasizes university education; and *The American and the German University* (1928). College histories are appearing at an increasing tempo. Already the following have appeared: D. C. Gilman, *The Launching of a University* (1906) and Fabian Franklin, *The Life of Daniel Coit Gilman* (1910) tell the story of Johns Hopkins; S. E. Morison, *The Founding of Harvard College* (1935), his *Three Centuries of Harvard, 1636–1936* (1936), and Henry James, III, *Charles W. Eliot* (2 vols., 1930) give the story of Harvard; G. S. Hall, *Life and Confessions of a Psychologist* (1923), recounts the story of the founding of Clark University; A. D. White, *Autobiography* (2 vols., 1905) and C. L. Becker, *Cornell University: Founders and Founding* (1943) tells the history of Cornell University. See Jonas Viles, *The University of Missouri* (1939); Walter Dyson, *Howard University* (1941); Thomas LeDuc, *Piety and Intellect at Amherst College, 1865–1912* (1946); Robert Fletcher, *A History of Oberlin College . . . Through the Civil War* (2 vols., 1943); Edwin Mims, *History of Vanderbilt University* (1946); and M. E. Curti and Vernon Carstensen, *The University of Wisconsin* (1949). E. E. Slosson, *Great American Universities* (1910) is a popular account, while Abraham Flexner, *The American College* (1908) is detailed and scholarly. Another careful study is that by L. V. Koos, *The Junior College* (1924). The question of academic freedom is handled brilliantly by Thorstein Veblen, *The Higher Learning in America* (1918). Upton Sinclair, *The Goose-Step* (1923) supplements Veblen by pointing out many infractions. Two works on the education of adults at the university level are L. E. Reber, *University Extension in the United States* (1914) and A. J. L. Klein, *Correspondence Study in Universities and Colleges* (1920), both being bulletins of the United States Bureau of Education. Two volumes of some historical significance are H. D. Sheldon, *Student Life and Customs* (1901) and W. T. Field, *Eight O'Clock Chapel* (1927).

The Church in Rural and Urban America. During the decades between the Civil War and the end of the nineteenth century, religion both in spirit and practice was challenged by the rise and spread of new scientific and philosophical ideas. For these ideas, consult H. W. Schneider, *A History of American Philosophy* (1946), the best single volume survey; George Santayana, *Winds of Doctrine* (1913); Philip Wiener, *Evolution and the Founders of Pragmatism* (1949); Richard Hofstadter, *Social Darwinism in American Thought, 1860–1915* (1944), which is excellent; W. H. Werkmeister, *A History of Philosophical Ideas in America* (1949), a very helpful introduction to American philosophical spokesmen; G. P. Adams and W. P. Montague (eds.), *Contemporary American Philosophy* (2 vols., 1930); John Dewey, *The Influence of Darwin on Philosophy* (1910); S. Chugerman, *Lester F. Ward, the American Aristotle* (1939); H. S. Commager, *The American Mind,* previously cited, especially the chapters on William James and Lester Ward; R. B. Perry, *The Thought and Character of William James* (1948); and William James, *The Will to Believe* (1897), *The Varieties of Religious Experience* (1902), and *Pragmatism* (1907). For the impact of these ideas on religion, consult Willard Sperry, *Religion in America* (1946); W. E. Garrison, *The March of Faith* (1933); J. W. Draper, *History of the Conflict Between Religion and Science* (1875); John Fiske, *A Century of Science* (1899); J. Y. Simpson, *Landmarks in the Struggle Between Science and Religion* (1925); A. D. White, *History of the Warfare of*

Science with Theology in Christendom (2 vols., 1896); B. J. Loewenbery, "Darwinism Comes to America, 1859–1900," *Mississippi Valley Historical Review*, Vol. XXVIII, pp. 309–65 (1941); A. P. Stokes, *Church and State in the United States* (3 vols., 1950); C. H. Hopkins, *The Rise of the Social Gospel in American Protestantism, 1865–1915* (1940); H. F. May, *Protestant Churches and Industrial America* (1949); and George Harris, *A Century's Change in Religion* (1914). A. V. G. Allen, *Life and Letters of Phillips Brooks* (3 vols., 1901) is the story of a forceful and influential churchman who outwardly, at least, remained indifferent, though not antagonistic, to the forces that were remaking religion. On Christian socialism the reader should consult Francis Peabody, *Jesus Christ and the Social Question* (1915); Walter Rauschenbusch, *Christianity and the Social Crisis* (1907) and *Christianizing the Social Order* (1912); W. J. Tucker, *My Generation* (1919); J. F. Clarke, *Autobiography, Diary and Correspondence* (1891); J. Dombrowski, *The Early Days of Christian Socialism in America* (1936); Lyman Abbott, *Christianity and Social Problems* (1896) and *Reminiscences* (1915); Washington Gladden, *Recollections* (1909); William Lawrence, *Memories of a Happy Life* (1926); Josiah Strong, *Religious Movements for Social Betterment* (1900); M. E. Chase, *A Goodly Heritage* (1932); G. B. Smith (ed.), *Religious Thought in the Last Quarter Century* (1927); and W. M. Tippy, *The Church a Community Force* (1914), which describes activities of a sociological church. The urban impact on religion is seen in A. I. Abell, *The Urban Impact on American Protestantism, 1865–1900* (1943). On this problem, also consult Theodore Maynard, *The Story of American Catholicism* (1941); Gerald Shaughnessy, *Has the Immigrant Kept the Faith?* (1925); and Joseph Leiser, *American Judaism* (1925). Of greatest importance for the student of Catholicism are A. S. Will, *Life of Cardinal Gibbons* (2 vols., 1922) and F. J. Zwierlein, *The Life and Letters of Bishop McQuaid* (3 vols., 1925–7). The best treatment of anti-Catholic sentiment is H. J. Desmond, *The A.P.A. Movement* (1912). On revivalism, see F. G. Beardsley, *A History of American Revivals* (rev. ed., 1912); Gamaliel Bradford, *D. L. Moody* (1927); H. D. Farish, *The Circuit Rider Dismounts: A Social History of Southern Methodism, 1865–1900* (1938); and W. W. Sweet, *Revivalism in America, Its Origin, Growth and Decline* (1944). An interesting volume is S. G. Cole, *The History of Fundamentalism* (1931). For a sophisticated account of tendencies on the eve of the 1929 depression, see Gilbert Seldes, *The Stammering Century* (1928). On foreign missions, see J. S. Dennis, *Centennial Survey of Christian Missions* (1902). The Salvation Army, largely an urban organization, is described by three of its leaders: Maud Ballington Booth, *Beneath Two Flags* (1889); Ballington Booth, *From Ocean to Ocean* (1891); and F. de L. Booth-Tucker, *The Social Relief Work of the Salvation Army in the United States* (1900). No satisfactory historical account of Christian Science has yet appeared. The literature on its founder is contradictory. The official biography by Sibyl Wilbur, *The Life of Mary Baker Eddy* (rev. ed., 1913) has the approval of the Church, whereas Georgine Milmine, *The Life of Mary Baker G. Eddy and the History of Christian Science* (1909) and E. F. Dakin, *Mrs. Eddy, the Biography of a Virginal Mind* (1929) are both unacceptable to it. On the American Sunday School, see E. W. Rice, *The Sunday School Movement, 1780–1917* (1917). On the trend toward church consolidation, consult E. R. Hooker, *United Churches* (1926).

Newspapers for the Masses. The number and volume of newspapers published increased in almost geometric progression after 1870. Almost none was indexed, and with the exception of the metropolitan papers—and not all of them—their history is yet to be written. The best general accounts are F. L. Mott, *American Journalism: A History of Newspapers in the United States through 260 Years, 1690 to 1950* (rev. ed., 1950) and W. G. Bleyer, *Main Currents in the History of American Journalism* (1927). Particular newspapers have had their history written: Elmer Davis, *History of the New York Times, 1851–1921* (1921); E. Francis Brown, *Raymond of the Times* (1951); Gerald Johnson, *An Honorable Titan, a Biographical Study of Adolph S. Ochs* (1946); Allan Nevins, *The Evening Post: A Century of Journalism* (1922); G. S. Merriam, *The Life and Times of Samuel Bowles* (2 vols., 1885), editor of the *Springfield* (Mass.) *Republican;* Richard Hooker, *The Story of an Independent Newspaper* (1924), the story of the *Springfield Republican;* J. E. Chamberlain, *The Boston Transcript* (1930); Horace Greeley, *Recollections of a Busy Life* (1868); D. C. Seitz, *Joseph Pulitzer, His Life and Letters* (1924) and *The James Gordon Bennetts* (1928); J. K. Winkler, *W. R. Hearst* (1928); E. S. Bates and O. Carlson, *Hearst, Lord of San Simeon* (1936); F. M. O'Brien, *The Story of the Sun* (1928); Harry Baehr, *The New York Tribune Since the War* (1936); and Gerald Johnson and others, *The Sunpapers of Baltimore* (1937). O. G. Villard, *Some Newspapers and Newspaper-Men* (rev. ed., 1926) contains brilliant pen portraits. Victor Rosewater, *History of Coöperative News-Gathering in the United States* (1930) traces the progress of co-operative journalism. See, too, Oliver Gramling, *AP; the Story of News* (1940), and Meyer Berger, *The Story of the New York Times* (1951).

The Development of the Popular Magazine. For the historian, magazines are a real source of material on many aspects of life. Winifred Gregory (comp.), *Union List of Serials in Libraries of the United States and Canada* (rev. ed., 1943) contains the most complete list of magazines with date and place of issue. *Poole's Index to Periodical Literature* provides a subject guide to the contents of the more important magazines. F. L. Mott, *A History of American Magazines* (3 vols., 1938) is thorough; Volume III covers the period since 1865. Algernon Tassin, *The Magazine in America* (1916) is readable but highly opinionated. Few magazine histories have been published. See, however, M. A. DeW. Howe, *The Atlantic Monthly and Its Makers* (1919) and the following biographic references: L. F. Tooker, *The Joys and Tribulations of an Editor* (1924), R. U. Johnson, *Remembered Yesterdays* (1923); George Britt, *Forty Years—Forty Millions: The Career of Frank A. Munsey* (1935); Rollo Ogden, *Life and Letters of Edwin Lawrence Godkin* (2 vols., 1907); S. S. McClure, *My Autobiography* (1914); and Edward Bok, *The Americanization of Edward Bok* (1920), the editor's story of how the *Ladies' Home Journal* gained pre-eminence.

Regional and National Trends in Literature. As indicated elsewhere in this volume the two indispensable works on American literature are the *Cambridge History of American Literature,* edited by W. P. Trent and others, and R. E. Spiller and others (eds.), *Literary History of the United States.* Rich also in bibliographic material is W. F. Taylor, *The History of American Letters* (1930). Other useful works are V. L. Parrington, *Main Currents in American Thought,* Vol. III; and F. L. Pattee, *A History of American Literature Since 1870* (1915) and his *The New American Literature 1890–1930* (1930); Constance Rourke's *American Humor* (1931), which is unmatched; Bliss Perry, *The American Spirit in Literature* (1918), in the Chronicles of America series; and S. T. Williams, *The American Spirit in Letters* (1926), in The Pageant of America series. National in interest too are Alfred Kazin, *On Native Grounds* (1942) and W. F. Taylor, *The Economic Novel in America* (1942). Ludwig Lewisohn, *Expression in America* (1932) approaches American literature from a Freudian angle and is taken to task by H. S. Commager in *The American Mind,* previously cited. A regional study of prime importance in literary criticism is Van Wyck Brooks, *New England: Indian Summer, 1865–1915* (1940). See also his splendid survey *The Times of Melville and Whitman* (1947). Lucy Hazard, *The Frontier in American Literature* (1927) and D. A. Dondore, *The Prairie and the Making of Middle America* (1926) are first class volumes. Other excellent studies of regional figures are A. H. Starke, *Sidney Lanier* (1933) and J. F. Harris, *The Life and Letters of Joel Chandler Harris* (1918). On Mark Twain and Walt Whitman the reader has a considerable field from which to pick. For the former see Parrington's admirable essay in Volume III of *Main Currents in American Thought;* cited; A. B. Paine, *Mark Twain: A Biography* (3 vols., rev. ed., 1935) and *A Short Life of Mark Twain* (1920); W. D. Howells, *My Mark Twain* (1910); Van Wyck Brooks, *The Ordeal of Mark Twain* (1920), a frustrated-man theory with which Bernard DeVoto quarrels in his *Mark Twain's America* (1932). On Whitman the best of the many biographies are Newton Arvin, *Whitman* (1938); Emory Holloway, *Whitman* (1926); and H. S. Canby, *Walt Whitman, an American* (1943). Similarly, the literature on William Dean Howells is voluminous, but the better accounts are those by Parrington in Volume III of his *Main Currents in American Thought;* D. G. Cooke, *William Dean Howells* (1922); and O. W. Firkins, *William Dean Howells* (1924). Best of all are Howells own writings, for he gives us a picture of American middle-class life and thought that even his biographers fail to fathom completely. Probably the best of the many studies on Henry James is F. O. Matthiessen, *The James Family* (1947) and *Henry James: The Major Phase* (1944). Interesting also are Rebecca West, *Henry James* (1916) and Van Wyck Brooks, *The Pilgrimage of Henry James* (1925). F. O. Matthiessen's *Sarah Orne Jewett* (1929) is a masterpiece. Less charming but very competent is Genevieve Taggard's *Life and Mind of Emily Dickinson* (1930). David Henry, *William Vaughn Moody* (1934) and John Manly (ed.), *The Poems and Plays of William Vaughn Moody* (2 vols., 1912) do justice to this poet. C. H. Dennis, *Eugene Field's Creative Years* (1924); Thomas Beer, *Stephen Crane* (1926); John Berryman, *Stephen Crane* (1950); Ferris Greenslet, *The Life of Thomas Bailey Aldrich* (1908); G. M. Gould, *Life and Letters of Edmund Clarence Stedman* (2 vols., 1910); A. R. Burr, *Weir Mitchell* (1929); and Franklin Walker, *Frank Norris* (1932) are satisfactory portrayals. H. R. Mayes, *Alger: A Biography Without A Hero* (1928) and M. A. Roe, *E. P. Roe* (1899) are biographies of influential if not great literary personages. Edmund Pearson's *Dime Novels* (1929) describes juvenile thrillers. See also Richard Chase, *Emily Dickinson* (1951) in the American Men of Letters series.

The Arts in a Business Age. Perhaps the best over-all brief surveys are H. Cahill and A. Barr, *Art in America: A Complete Survey* (1935) and O. W. Larkin, *Art and Life in America* (1949). Other works of varying quality but all worthy of examination are C. H. Caffin, *The Story of American Painting* (1907); Alan Burroughs *Limners and Likenesses: Three Centuries of American Painting* (1936); Samuel Isham, *The History of American Painting* (rev. ed., 1927); J. C. Van Dyke, *American Painting and Its Tradition* (1919); Homer St. Gaudens, *The American Artist and His Times* (1941), beautifully illustrated; Cecilia Beaux, *Background with Figures* (1930), an autobiography; A. Young, *Art Young, His Life and Times* (1939), the autobiography of a great American cartoonist; George Biddle, *An American Artist's Story* (1939); T. H. Benton, *An Artist in America* (1937); E. H. Blashfield, *Mural Painting in America* (1913); Frank Weitenkampf, *American Graphic Art* (rev. ed., 1924); William Murrell, *A History of American Graphic Humor* (2 vols., 1933–8); and A. B. Maurice and F. T. Cooper, *The History of the Nineteenth Century in Caricature* (1904). Of the numerous biographies the following are recommended: Kenyon Cox, *Winslow Homer* (1914); Lloyd Goodrich, *Winslow Homer* (1944); W. H. Downes, *The Life and Works of Winslow Homer* (1911); George Inness, Jr., *Life, Art, and Letters of George Inness* (1917); Elizabeth McCausland, *George Inness* (1946); F. J. Mather, *Homer Martin* (1912); Henry C. White, *Life and Art of Dwight William Tryon* (1930); Royal Cortissoz, *John LaFarge* (1911); W. H. Downes, *John Sargent, His Life and Work* (1925); E. R. and J. Pennell, *The Life of James McNeill Whistler* (rev. ed., 1911); E. L. Cary, *The Works of James McNeill Whistler* (1907); C. D. Abbott, *Howard Pyle* (1925); J. W. McSpadden, *Famous Painters of America* (rev. ed., 1916); and Royal Cortissoz, *American Artists* (1923). Wolfgang Born, *American Landscape Painting* (1948); Eugene Neuhaus, *The History and Ideals of American Art* (1931); and Fairfax Downey, *Portrait of an Era as Drawn by C. P. Gibson* (1936).

For sculpture, consult Lorado Taft, *The History of American Sculpture* (rev. ed., 1924); Adeline Adams, *The Spirit of American Sculpture* (rev. ed., 1929); and Joseph Hudnut, *Modern Sculpture* (1929). J. W. McSpadden, *Famous Sculptors of America* (1924) and Royal Cortissoz, *Augustus St. Gaudens* (1907) are highly instructive; on St. Gaudens consult also Homer St. Gaudens (ed.), *The Reminiscences of Augustus Saint Gaudens* (2 vols., 1913).

Four comprehensive surveys on American music have been published on this period: L. C. Elson, *The History of American Music* (rev. ed., 1925); W. L. Hubbard (ed.), *The American History and Encyclopedia of Music* (12 vols., 1910); Arthur Farwell and W. D. Darby (eds.), *Music in America,* Vol. IV of *The Art of Music* (14 vols., 1915–17), edited by D. G. Mason; and J. T. Howard, *Our Ameri-*

can Music (1941), the best. For orchestral music, see C. E. Russell, *The American Orchestra and Theodore Thomas* (1927); M. A. DeW. Howe, *The Boston Symphony Orchestra* (rev. ed., 1931); F. A. Wister, *Twenty-Five Years of the Philadelphia Orchestra, 1900–1925* (1925). For grand opera, consult H. C. Lahee, *Grand Opera in America* (1902); E. E. Hipsher, *American Opera and Its Composers* (1934); and H. E. Krehbiel, *More Chapters of Opera* (1919). On Negro music the best authorities are Dorothy Scarborough, *On the Trail of Negro Folk Songs* (1925); H. E. Krehbiel, *Afro-American Folksongs* (1914); J. W. Johnson, *Book of American Negro Spirituals* (1925); and R. H. Dett, *Religious Folk Songs of the Negro as Sung at Hampton Institute* (1927). For popular songs, see C. K. Harris, *After the Ball, Forty Years of Melody* (1926) and Sigmund Spaeth, *Read 'Em and Weep* (1926) and his *Weep Some More, My Lady* (1927). Julius Mattfeld (comp.), *The Folk Music of the Western Hemisphere* (1925) contains much material on the folk music of Negroes, cowboys, lumberjacks, mountaineers, sailors, miners, and so on.

Form and Function in American Architecture. The standard works are T. E. Tallmadge, *The Story of Architecture in America* (1927); S. Fiske Kimball, *American Architecture* (1928); and G. H. Edgell, *The American Architecture of Today* (1928). T. F. Hamlin, *The American Spirit in Architecture* (1926), in the Pageant of America series, contains valuable illustrative material. Lewis Mumford, *Sticks and Stones* (1924) is a brilliant interpretative account; see also his *The Brown Decades* (1931). W. A. Starrett, *Skyscrapers and the Men Who Build Them* (1928) traces the origin of this distinctly American architectural form. The following biographies are most valuable: M. G. Van Rensselaer, *Henry Hobson Richardson, and His Works* (1888); Harriet Monroe, *John Wellborn Root* (1896); Charles Moore, *Daniel H. Burnham, Architect, Planner of Cities* (2 vols., 1921) and *The Life and Times of Charles Follen McKim* (1929); Louis Sullivan, *Autobiography of An Idea* (1924); Frederick Gutheim (ed.), *Frank Lloyd Wright on Architecture* (1941); C. C. Baldwin, *Stanford White* (1931); and F. L. Wright, *An Autobiography* (1943).

CHAPTER VIII

The Politics of Conformity and Revolt

A first class political history covering the last two decades of the nineteenth century is yet to be written. Neither of the two general histories, J. F. Rhodes, *History of the United States from the Compromise of 1850* (9 vols., 1900–28) and E. P. Oberholtzer, *A History of the United States Since the Civil War* (5 vols., 1917–37) are satisfactory. E. E. Sparks, *National Development, 1877–1885* (1907) and D. R. Dewey, *National Problems, 1885–1897* (1907), in the American Nation series, need the benefit of more recent scholarship. Volume II of C. A. and M. R. Beard, *The Rise of American Civilization* (4 vols., rev. and enl., 1933) is excellent but suffers from brevity. H. T. Peck, *Twenty Years of the Republic, 1885–1905* (1906) is a popular, well-written account. On parties and politics, consult Edward Stanwood, *A History of the Presidency* (2 vols., 1928); E. E. Robinson, *The Evolution of American Political Parties* (1924); W. E. Binkley, *American Political Parties* (1943); C. E. Merriam, *The American Party System* (4th ed., 1949); M. Ostrogorski, *Democracy and the Organization of Political Parties* (2 vols., 1902); H. J. Ford, *The Rise and Growth of American Politics* (1898); and Nathan Fine, *Labor and Farmer Parties in the United States, 1828–1928* (1928). For institutional history James Bryce, *The American Commonwealth* (new ed., 2 vols., rev. 1931–3) and Herbert Agar, *The Price of Union* (1950) are unsurpassed. Fortunately, the student delving into the political history of the years after Reconstruction has at his disposal a wealth of material in the form of memoirs, biographies, and autobiographies. For brief accounts of those who played a part on the political scene there is the *Dictionary of American Biography*. See also Matthew Josephson, *The Politicos, 1865–*

1896 (1938); W. A. White, *Masks in a Pageant* (1928); and A. W. Dunn, *From Harrison to Harding* (2 vols., 1922). Also consult N. W. Stephenson, *Nelson W. Aldrich: A Leader in American Politics* (1930), which is very partisan; Harry Barnard, *Eagle Forgotten, The Life of John P. Altgeld* (1938); G. F. Howe, *Chester A. Arthur* (1934); S. H. Acheson, *Joe Bailey, The Last of the Democrats* (1932); Margaret Clapp, *Forgotten First Citizen: John Bigelow* (1947); D. S. Muzzey, *James G. Blaine, A Political Idol of Other Days* (1934), which is excellent; C. E. Russell, *Blaine of Maine: His Life and Times* (1931); Lew Wallace, *The Life of Gen. Ben Harrison* (1888), a campaign biography; J. G. Blaine, *Twenty Years in Congress* (2 vols., 1884–6); W. V. Byars, *An American Commoner: The Life and Times of Richard Parks Bland* (1900), the only full length biography of "Silver Dick"; L. W. Busbey, *Uncle Joe Cannon* (1927), which is overly sympathetic; J. A. Barnes, *John G. Carlisle, Financial Statesman* (1931), which is excellent, especially on money questions; L. B. Richardson, *William E. Chandler, Republican* (1940); Robert McElroy, *Grover Cleveland* (2 vols., 1923), which is too eulogistic; Allan Nevins, *Grover Cleveland: A Study in Courage* (1932), which is well balanced and may be supplemented by *Letters of Grover Cleveland, 1850–1908* (1933), edited by the same author; S. M. Cullom, *Fifty Years of Public Service* (1911); D. B. Chidsey, *The Gentleman from New York: A Life of Roscoe Conkling* (1935); A. R. Conkling, *Life and Letters of Roscoe Conkling* (1889); D. L. Alexander, *Four Famous New Yorkers: The Political Careers of Cleveland, Platt, Hill and Roosevelt* (1923); Ray Ginger, *The Bending Cross: Eugene V. Debs* (1949); T. C. Smith, *Life and Letters of James Abram Garfield* (2 vols., 1925); R. G. Caldwell, *James A. Garfield, Party Chieftain* (1931); Herbert Croly, *Marcus Alonzo Hanna* (1912); Thomas Beer, *Hanna* (1929); Paxton Hibben, *The Peerless Leader: William Jennings Bryan* (1929) and M. R. Werner, *Bryan* (1929), both satirical; J. C. Long, *Bryan, the Great Commoner* (1928); W. J. Bryan, *The First Battle: A Story of the Campaign of 1896* (1896); Tyler Dennett, *John Hay: From Poetry to Politics* (1933), which is excellent; W. R. Thayer, *John Hay* (2 vols., 1910); C. R. Williams, *The Life of Rutherford B. Hayes* (2 vols., 1914), an able presentation; H. J. Eckenrode, *Rutherford B. Hayes, Statesman of Reunion* (1930), a good study; C. R. Williams, *The Diary and Letters of Rutherford Birchard Hayes* (5 vols., 1922–6); Allan Nevins, *Abram S. Hewitt: With Some Account of Peter Cooper* (1935); F. H. Gillett, *George Frisbie Hoar* (1934); G. F. Hoar, *Autobiography of Seventy Years* (2 vols., 1903); G. G. Clarke, *George W. Julian* (1923); W. A. Cate, *Lucius Q. C. Lamar, Secession and Reunion* (1935), which is first rate; Robert McElroy, *Levi P. Morton: Banker, Diplomat, Statesman* (1930); R. D. Bowden, *Boise Penrose* (1937); H. F. Gosnell, *Boss Platt and His New York Machine* (1924); T. C. Platt, *Autobiography of Thomas Collier Platt* (1910); Rollo Ogden, *The Life and Letters of Edwin Lawrence Godkin* (2 vols., 1907); Edward Cary, *George William Curtis* (1894); W. A. Robinson, *Thomas B. Reed, Parliamentarian* (1930); S. W. McCall, *The Life of Thomas Brackett Reed* (1911), eulogistic; C. M. Fuess, *Carl Schurz, Reformer* (1932); Joseph Schafter, *Carl Schurz, Militant Liberal* (1930); Carl Schurz, *Reminiscences* (3 vols., 1907–08); John Sherman, *John Sherman's Recollections of Forty Years in the House, Senate and Cabinet* (2 vols., 1895), dull, as is T. E. Burton, *John Sherman* (1906); Matilda Gresham, *Life of Walter Quinton Gresham, 1832–95* (2 vols., 1919); Royal Cortissoz, *The Life of Whitelaw Reid* (2 vols., 1921); Elmer Ellis, *Henry Moore Teller, Defender of the West* (1941); A. C. Flick, *Samuel Jones Tilden: A Study in Political Sagacity* (1939), which is definitive and displaces John Bigelow, *The Life of Samuel J. Tilden* (2 vols., 1895); F. E. Haynes, *James Baird Weaver* (1919), excellent; M. A. Hirsch, *William C. Whitney* (1948); Walter Johnson, *William Allen White's America* (1947); and C. S. Olcott, *The Life of William McKinley* (2 vols., 1916), which is somewhat uncritical.

Hayes, Garfield and Arthur. On Hayes's administration, see J. W. Burgess, *Administration of President Hayes* (1916), scholarly; F. E. Haynes, *Third Party Movements Since the Civil War, with Special Reference to Iowa,* previously cited, which discusses the Greenback movement; A. D. Noyes, *Forty Years of American Finance*

(1898); W. C. Mitchell, *A History of the Greenbacks* (1903); J. L. Laughlin, *History of Bimetallism in the United States* (4th ed., 1897); E. B. Usher, *The Greenback Movement of 1875–1884 and Wisconsin's Part in It* (1911). For Garfield and Arthur, see Henry Adams, *The Education of Henry Adams* (1927); K. H. Porter, *National Party Platforms* (1924); C. R. Fish, *The Civil Service and the Patronage* (1905); A. B. Sageser, *The First Two Decades of the Pendelton Act* (1935), a thorough study; and F. M. Stewart, *The National Civil Service Reform League* (1929).

Cleveland and Harrison. H. C. Thomas, *The Return of the Democratic Party to Power in 1884* (1919) is the standard authority; see also H. J. Ford, *The Cleveland Era* (1919), in the Chronicles of America series. On pensions, see W. H. Glasson, *Federal Military Pensions in the United States* (1918) and J. W. Oliver, *History of the Civil War Military Pensions* (1917). On the tariff controversy, consult P. W. C. Ashley, *Modern Tariff History* (1904); Edward Stanwood, *American Tariff Controversies in the Nineteenth Century* (2 vols., 1903); F. W. Taussig, *The Tariff History of the United States* (rev. ed., 1931); Hugh McCulloch, *Men and Measures of Half a Century* (1888); W. D. Orcutt, *Burrows of Michigan and the Republican Party* (2 vols., 1917), which gives arguments for high protection; and I. M. Tarbell, *The Tariff in Our Times* (1911), an unbiased account. For Cleveland's second election the best account is G. H. Knoles, *The Presidential Campaign and Election of 1892* (1942).

The Currency Issue and the Gold Standard. On monetary standards, see references cited under Hayes, Garfield and Arthur above and D. R. Dewey, *Financial History of the United States* (12th ed., 1936); A. B. Hepburn, *A History of Coinage and Currency in the United States and the Perennial Contest for Sound Money* (1905); M. S. Wildman, *Money Inflation in the United States* (1905); Horace White, *Money and Banking* (rev. ed., 1914); W. H. Harvey, *Coin's Financial School* (1894), propaganda for cheap money; and Grover Cleveland, *Presidential Problems* (1904). On the Panic of 1893 the standard book is W. J. Lauck, *The Causes of the Panic of 1893* (1907), which emphasizes the monetary situation as principal cause; not definitive, but better is F. B. Weberg, *The Background of the Panic of 1893* (1929). On unemployment and industrial unrest, consult D. L. McMurry, *Coxeys Army* (1929). The Pullman and its aftermath are discussed in Harry Barnard, *Eagle Forgotten, the Life of John Peter Altgeld,* cited earlier, which gives Altgeld's position in the Cleveland-Altgeld controversy; Edward Berman, *Labor Disputes and the President of the United States* (1924); Grover Cleveland, *The Government in the Chicago Strike of 1894* (1913); Henry James, *Richard Olney and His Public Service* (1923); Coleman McAlister, *Eugene V. Debs: A Man Unafraid* (1930), which discusses Debs' relation with Pullman strike; Almont Lindsey, *The Pullman Strike* (1942); and *United States Strike Commission, Report,* 53rd Cong., 3rd Sess., Senate Executive Document no. 7. For the Homestead strike, see George Harvey, *Henry Clay Frick,* cited earlier. On the income-tax decision, consult Sidney Ratner, *American Taxation* (1941); Charles Warren, *The Supreme Court in United States History* (3 vols., final rev., 1937) Vol. III; and L. Boudin, *Government by Judiciary* (1932). For relations with the Morgan interests on the bond issue, consult Lewis Corey, *The House of Morgan* (1930) and F. L. Allen, *The Great Pierpont Morgan* (1949).

The Agrarian Protest. See the references under "Patterns of Agrarian Protest," Chapter 6, and B. B. Kendrick, "Agrarian Discontent in the South, 1880–1890," *American Historical Association Report* (1920), pp. 267–72 (1925); Hallie Farmer, "Economic Background of Frontier Populism," *Mississippi Valley Historical Review,* Vol. X, pp. 406–27 (March, 1924); C. R. Miller, "Background of Populism in Kansas," ibid., Vol. XI (March, 1925), pp. 469–89; C. McA. Destler, *American Radicalism, 1865–1901, Essays and Documents* (1946); and his "Western Radicalism 1865–1901," *Mississippi Valley Historical Review,* Vol. XXXI (December, 1944), pp. 335–68; and P. R. Fossum, *The Agrarian Movement in North Dakota* (1925).

The Campaign of 1896 and Its Aftermath. In addition to the biographic material listed at the beginning of this chapter and especially that dealing with Bryan and

McKinley, consult H. T. Peck, *Twenty Years of the Republic, 1885–1905,* already cited; C. Vann Woodward, *Tom Watson, Agrarian Rebel* (1938); Walter Johnson, *William Allen White's America,* cited previously; and Harvey Wish, "John Peter Altgeld and the Background of the Campaign of 1896," *Mississippi Valley Historical Review,* Vol. XXIV, pp. 503–18 (March, 1938). For the gold Democrats and the split in the Democratic party, see Mark Hirsch, *William C. Whitney,* cited above, and J. C. Olson, *J. Sterling Morton* (1942). For source material, see W. J. Bryan, *The First Battle,* cited above, and H. S. Commager, *Documents of American History* (5th ed., 1950).

Chapter IX

Overseas Expansion

S. F. Bemis and G. G. Griffin, *Guide to the Diplomatic History of the United States* (1935) is indispensable for bibliography. See also S. F. Bemis (ed.), *The American Secretaries of State and Their Diplomacy* (10 vols., 1927–9); Vols. VI and VIII cover this chapter. The two most satisfactory texts are T. A. Bailey, *A Diplomatic History of the American People* (4th ed., 1950) and S. F. Bemis, *A Diplomatic History of the United States* (3rd ed., 1950). Other texts are R. G. Adams, *A History of the Foreign Policy of the United States* (1924); J. H. Latané and D. W. Wainhouse, *A History of American Foreign Policy* (rev. ed., 1940); L. M. Sears, *A History of American Foreign Relations* (rev. 3rd ed., 1936); and W. F. Johnson, *American Foreign Relations* (2 vols., 1916). On the psychology of imperialism, consult J. A. Hobson, *Imperialism* (rev. 3rd ed., 1938); P. T. Moon, *Imperialism and World Politics* (1926); and A. K. Weinberg, *Manifest Destiny: A Study of Nationalist Expansion in American History* (1935). A. L. P. Dennis, *Adventures in American Diplomacy, 1896–1906* (1928) is valuable for the period covered. B. H. Williams, *Economic Foreign Policy of the United States* (1929) and Dexter Perkins, *Hands Off: A History of the Monroe Doctrine* (1941) are excellent.

Imperialist Without a Mandate. F. E. Chadwick, *The Relations of the United States and Spain, Diplomacy* (1909), discusses the *Virginius* affair. See also R. W. Logan, *The Diplomatic Relations of the United States with Haiti, 1776–1891* (1941). C. C. Tansill, *The Purchase of the Danish West Indies* (1932) treats Seward's designs; and his *The United States and Santo Domingo, 1789–1873* (1938) is excellent. Allan Nevins, *Hamilton Fish,* already cited, is indispensable on the diplomacy of the Grant Administration. Nor should A. F. Tyler's *The Foreign Policy of James G. Blaine* (1927) be overlooked. Sumner Welles, *Naboth's Vineyard* (1928) covers American imperialistic ambitions in the island of Santo Domingo.

The Will to Expand. The Alabama Claims, Venezuelan crisis, and other matters are covered by W. A. Dunning, *The British Empire and the United States* (1914); R. W. Mowat, *The Diplomatic Relations of Great Britain and the United States* (1925); G. R. Dulebohn, *Principles of Foreign Policy Under the Cleveland Administration* (1941); Dexter Perkins, *The Monroe Doctrine, 1867–1907* (1937) and C. C. Tansill, *The Foreign Policy of Thomas F. Bayard, 1885–1897* (1940); valuable also in this connection are Henry James, *Richard Olney and His Public Service* (1923) and Allan Nevins, *Hamilton Fish* (1936). For Canadian-American relations, see the excellent volume by J. B. Brebner, *The North Atlantic Triangle: The Interplay of Canada, the United States, and Great Britain* (1945); L. B. Shippee, *Canadian American Relations, 1849–1874* (1939); Goldwin Smith, *The Treaty of Washington, 1871: A Study in Imperial History* (1941); P. E. Corbett, *The Settlement of Canadian-American Disputes* (1937); and Brainerd Dyer, *The Public Career of William M. Evarts* (1933). On the acquisition of Alaska, consult J. M. Callahan, *The Alaska Purchase and Americo-Canadian Relations* (1908); J. P. Nichols, *Alaska. . . . Under the Rule of the United States* (1924), a first-rate account; V. J. Farrar, *The Annexation of Russian America to the United States*

(1937), containing new material; T. A. Bailey, "Why The United States Purchased Alaska," *Pacific Historical Review,* Vol. III, pp. 39–49 (1934); B. P. Thomas, *Russo-American Relations, 1815–1867* (1930) and S. R. Tompkins, *Alaska, Promyshlennik and Sourdough* (1945), which summarizes the Alaska purchase.

Intervention in Samoa. The best accounts are R. L. Stevenson, *A Footnote to History: Eight Years of Trouble in Samoa* (1892); J. W. Foster, *American Diplomacy in the Orient* (1903); J. M. Callahan, *American Relations in the Pacific and in the Far East, 1784–1900* (1901); and G. H. Ryden, *The Foreign Policy of the United States in Relation of Samoa* (1933), which is excellent.

The Annexation of Hawaii. The accounts in Rhodes and Oberholtzer are somewhat superficial. See S. K. Stevens, *American Expansion in Hawaii, 1842–1898* (1945); Charles Nordhoff, *Northern California, Oregon and the Sandwich Islands* (1874), which sheds light on American penetration; C. Whitney, *Hawaiian America* (1899); Katherine Coman, *The History of Contract Labor in the Hawaiian Islands* (1903); S. B. Dole, *Memoirs of the Hawaiian Revolution* (1936); J. E. Carpenter, *America in Hawaii* (1899); and Tyler Dennett, *Americans in Eastern Asia* (1922). G. F. Hoar, *Autobiography,* already cited, and R. F. Pettigrew, *The Course of Empire* (1920) are the reactions of anti-imperialist senators. J. W. Pratt, *Expansionists of 1898* (1936), presents new materials and fresh interpretation. See also H. W. Bradley, *The American Frontier in Hawaii: The Pioneers, 1789–1843* (1942) and his "Hawaii and the American Penetration of the Northeastern Pacific, 1801–1845," *Pacific Historical Review,* Vol. XII, pp. 277–86 (1943). For the period of pre-American penetration, see R. S. Kuykendall, *The Hawaiian Kingdom, 1778–1854* (1938).

The Martial Spirit. On this topic, see C. A. Beard, *The Idea of National Interest* (1934); B. H. Williams, *Economic Foreign Policy of the United States,* previously cited; Scott Nearing and Joseph Freeman, *Dollar Diplomacy* (1925); J. F. Rhodes, *The McKinley and Roosevelt Administrations, 1897–1902* (1922); Joseph Wisan, *The Cuban Crisis as Reflected in the New York Press, (1895–1898)* (1934); Marcus Wilkerson, *Public Opinion and the Spanish-American War* (1932); and G. W. Auxier, "The Propaganda Activities of the Cuban *Junta* in Precipitating the Spanish-American War, 1895–1898," *Hispanic American Historical Review,* Vol. XIX (1939), pp. 286–305. J. W. Pratt, *Expansionists of 1898,* previously cited, is indispensable for the emotional and psychological background of imperialism. Illuminating, too, are J. B. Moore, *Four Phases of American Development: Federalism-Democracy-Imperialism-Expansion* (1912); A. T. Mahan, *From Sail to Steam: Recollections on Naval Life* (1907); and C. C. Taylor, *The Life of Admiral Mahan* (1920); W. D. Puleston, *Mahan* (1939). R. S. West, *Admirals of American Empire* (1948) tells the story of Dewey, Simpson, and other Great White Fleet Admirals. H. F. Pringle, *Theodore Roosevelt* (1931); and C. G. Bowers, *Beveridge and the Progressive Era* (1932) are accounts of two leading imperialists.

Liquidating the Spanish Empire. The leading authorities are F. E. Chadwick, *The Relations of the United States and Spain* (2 vols., 1909–11); Walter Millis, *The Martial Spirit: A Study of Our War with Spain* (1931); E. J. Benton, *International Law and Diplomacy of the Spanish-American War* (1908); Orestes Ferrara, *The Last Spanish War* (1937), which sheds new light on the basis of material from the Spanish archives; J. D. Long, *The New American Navy, 1897–1902* (1913), which argues for a bigger navy; A. T. Mahan, *Lessons of the War with Spain* (1899); R. A. Alger, *The Spanish American War* (1901), by the Secretary of War; T. R. Roosevelt, *The Rough Riders* (1899); George Dewey, *Autobiography* (1913); N. A. Miles, *Serving the Republic* (1911); J. W. Pratt, *Expansionists of 1898,* already cited; C. D. Sigsbee, *The "Maine": An Account of Her Destruction in Havana Harbor* (1899); H. H. Sargent, *The Campaign of Santiago de Cuba* (3 vols., 1907), which discusses the principal naval and military campaigns in Cuba; W. S. Schley, *Forty-Five Years Under the Flag* (1904); Joseph Wheeler, *The Santiago Campaign* (1898); John Bigelow, *Reminiscences of the Santiago Campaign* (1899); and Frederick Funston, *Memories of Two Wars* (1911). On foreign relations during the war, see R. A. Reuter, *Anglo-American Relations During the Spanish-American War*

(1924); L. B. Shipee, "Germany and the Spanish-American War," *American Historical Review*, Vol. XX (July, 1925), pp. 754–77; and R. H. Heindel, *The American Impact on Britain, 1898–1914* (1940). Important, too, are Tyler Dennett, *John Hay: From Poetry to Politics*, already cited; P. C. Jessup, *Elihu Root* (2 vols., 1938); and Royal Cortissoz, *The Life of Whitelaw Reid* (2 vols., 1921). For the Treaty of Paris, see the volumes by Chadwick and Benton above and *Papers on the Treaty of Paris*, 55th Cong., 3rd Sess., Senate Document no. 62. The hue and cry against imperialistic expansion by the United States was loudly expressed in the writings of the anti-imperialists. See especially M. E. Curti, *Bryan and World Peace* (1931); Moorfield Storey and M. P. Lichauco, *The Conquest of the Philippines by the United States, 1898–1925* (1926); A. S. Pier, *American Apostles to the Philippines* (1950); M. A. DeW. Howe, *Portrait of an Independent, Moorfield Storey* (1932); G. F. Hoar, *Autobiography of Seventy Years*, cited earlier, and the *Autobiography of Andrew Carnegie* (1920); F. H. Harrington, "The Anti-Imperialist Movement in the United States, 1898–1900," *Mississippi Valley Historical Review*, Vol. XXII (September, 1935), pp. 211–23; and T. A. Bailey, "Was the Presidential Election of 1900 a Mandate on Imperialism?," ibid., Vol. XXIV (June, 1937), pp. 43–52.

Chapter X

The American Empire

The acquisition of a colonial empire brought to the United States many vexing problems. By all odds the most valuable single volume is J. W. Pratt's admirable *America's Colonial Experiment: How the United States Gained, Governed, and in Part Gave Away a Colonial Empire* (1950). On the constitutional status of these acquisitions, see W. F. Willoughby, *Territories and Dependencies of the United States* (1905); C. F. Randolph, *The Law and Policy of Annexation* (1901); and C. E. Magoon, *Report on the Legal Status of the Territory. . . . Acquired by the United States During the War with Spain* (1900).

Problems of Administration. The best single volume is probably W. H. Haas, *The American Empire* (1940). W. D. Boyce, *United States Colonies and Dependencies* (1914); A. L. P. Dennis, *Adventures in American Diplomacy, 1896–1906*, previously cited; J. H. Latané, *America as a World Power, 1897–1907* (1907), in the American Nations series; J. F. Rippy, *Latin America in World Politics* (rev. ed., 1931); G. H. Stuart, *Latin America and the United States* (4th ed., 1943). J. E. Thomson, *Our Atlantic Possessions* (1928) and *Our Pacific Possessions* (1931), are both very readable. On Cuba, consult L. H. Jenks, *Our Cuban Colony, A Study in Sugar* (1928); Carleton Beals, *The Crime of Cuba* (1934), far from objective; H. F. Guggenheim, *The United States and Cuba* (1934), a defense of United States domination of the island; D. A. Lockmiller, *Magoon in Cuba: A History of the Second Intervention, 1906–1909* (1938), a defense of Magoon's regime; and C. L. Jones, *Caribbean Interests of the United States* (1916). See also A. G. Robinson, *Cuba and the Intervention* (1905); G. H. Stuart, *Cuba and Its International Relations* (1923); and C. E. Chapman, *A History of the Cuban Republic* (1927). Three works cover the essential material on Puerto Rico: B. W. and J. W. Diffie, *Porto Rico: A Broken Pledge* (1931), which is extremely critical of American occupation. Knowlton Mixer, *Porto Rico* (1926), which traces the history of American occupation, and V. S. Clark and others, *Porto Rico and Its Problems* (1930), an objective survey. On the Philippines the literature is large. See D. C. Worcester, *The Philippines Past and Present* (2 vols., 1914), which discusses the administration of the islands to 1913; C. B. Elliot, *The Philippines* (1917); W. C. Forbes, *The Philippine Islands* (2 vols., 1928), a careful evaluation by an admirer of American achievement; J. H. Blount, *The American Occupation of the Philippines, 1898–1912,* (1912); J. A. Le Roy, *The Americans in the Philippines* (2 vols., 1914); D. P. Barrows, *A History of the Philippines* (rev. ed., 1924); F. B. Harrison, *The Cornerstone of Philippine Inde-*

pendence (1922), an account by an anti-imperialistic Governor General; Nicholas Roosevelt, *The Philippines, A Treasure and a Problem* (1926); J. S. Reyes, *Legislative History of America's Economic Policy Toward the Philippines* (1923); J. R. Hayden, *The Philippines, A Study in National Development* (1942), an able study; Grayson Kirk, *Philippine Independence* (1936), an able survey; and H. Hagedorn, *Leonard Wood* (2 vols., 1931), which defends an unpopular Governor.

Power Politics in the Far East. On this subject there is also abundant literature. See J. M. Callahan, *American Relations in the Pacific and in the Far East,* previously cited; Tyler Dennett, *Americans in Eastern Asia* (1922); T. F. Millard, *America and the Far Eastern Question* (1909); F. R. Dulles, *China and America. . . . since 1784* (1946); J. W. Foster, *American Diplomacy in the Orient* (1903); A. W. Griswold, *The Far Eastern Policy of the United States* (1938); W. W. Willoughby, *Foreign Rights and Interests in China* (2 vols., rev., 1927), which covers the relations of the great powers to China; H. K. Norton, *China and the Powers* (1927); J. G. Reid, *The Manchu Abdication and the Powers, 1908–1912* (1935), which is excellent; J. V. A. MacMurray, *Treaties and Agreements With and Concerning China, 1894–1919* (2 vols., 1921); P. S. Rensch, *An American Diplomat in China* (1922); P. H. Clyde, *A History of the Modern and Contemporary Far East* (1937); G. H. Blakeslee, *Conflicts of Policy in the Far East* (1934) M. Pao, *The Open Door Doctrine in Relation to China* (1923); P. H. Clements, *The Boxer Rebellion* (1915), scholarly; H. Chung, *The Oriental Policy of the United States* (1919); P. J. Treat, *Japan and the United States, 1853–1921,* (2nd ed., 1928), *The Diplomatic Relations Between the United States and Japan, 1853–1895* (1932), and the companion volume, *Diplomatic Relations Between the United States and Japan, 1895–1905* (1938); F. R. Dulles, *Forty Years of American-Japanese Relations* (1937); and J. A. Barnes (ed.), *Empire in the East* (1934), which is highly critical of American policy.

The Struggle for the Panama Canal. For historical background, see H. G. Miller, *The Isthmian Highway* (rev. ed., 1932); J. B. Bishop, *The Panama Gateway* (1913); and W. J. Abbott, *Panama and the Canal* (1914). For the creation of the Republic of Panama, consult Philippe Bunau-Varilla, *Panama, The Creation, Destruction, and Resurrection* (1914), by the leading conspirator; W. D. McCain, *The United States and the Republic of Panama* (1937); and H. F. Pringle, *Theodore Roosevelt* (1931), which is highly critical of Roosevelt's part in creating the new republic. On the actual selection and building of the canal, see D. C. Miner, *The Fight for the Panama Route* (1940), excellent; M. P. DuVal, *Cadiz to Cathay* (1940) and his *And the Mountains Will Move; the Story of the Building of the Panama Canal* (1947); Gerstle Mack, *The Land Divided* (1944); J. B. and F. Bishop, *Goethals, Genius of the Panama Canal* (1930); C. I. Judson, *Soldier Doctor* (1942), the life of Gorgas; and B. J. Hendrick, *W. C. Gorgas, His Life and Work* (1924). Other works of value are: H. C. Hill, *Roosevelt and the Caribbean* (1927); E. R. Johnson, *The Panama Canal and Commerce* (1916); W. H. Callcott, *The Caribbean Policy of the United States, 1890–1920* (1942); J. F. Rippy, *The Capitalists and Colombia* (1931), which describes Panama's revolution; M. W. Williams, *Anglo-American Isthmian Diplomacy, 1815–1915* (1916), an able study; Scott Nearing and Joseph Freeman, *Dollar Diplomacy,* cited earlier, which is biased; J. B. Bishop, *Theodore Roosevelt and His Times* (2 vols., 1920); and the congressional investigations: *Diplomatic History of Panama,* 63rd Cong., 2nd Sess., Senate Document no. 474, and *Senate Committee on Interoceanic Canals,* 59th Cong., 2nd Sess., Senate Document no. 401.

Business and Imperialism. The best bibliographic sources are P. T. Moon, *Syllabus on International Relations* (1925); and the quarterly lists of books in *Foreign Affairs* (1922–). There is both textual and bibliographic material in R. L. Buell, *International Relations* (rev. ed., 1932); W. S. Culbertson, *International Economic Policies* (1925); P. T. Moon, *Imperialism and World Politics,* cited previously; and Achille Viallate, *Economic Imperialism and International Relations During the Last Fifty Years* (1923). For trade between continental United States and its colonial overseas empire, see E. R. Johnson and others, *History of Domestic and Foreign*

Commerce of the United States (2 vols., 1915) and National Industrial Conference Board, *Trends in the Foreign Trade of the United States* (1930). On economic relations of the United States with various parts of its colonial empire, consult H. W. Clarke, *History of Alaska* and J. P. Nichols, *Alaska. . . . Under the Rule of the United States,* both cited earlier; C. Whitney, *Hawaiian America,* cited above; A. D. Gayer, E. K. James and others, *The Sugar Economy of Porto Rico* (1938); B. W. and J. W. Diffie, *Porto Rico: A Broken Pledge,* cited above; R. S. Tucker, "A Balance Sheet of the Philippines," *Harvard Business Review,* Vol. VIII, pp. 10–23; and C. A. Thompson, *Conditions in the Philippine Islands,* 69th Cong., 2nd Sess., Senate Document no. 180 (1926). "Philippine Independence," *Foreign Policy Association Information Service,* Vol. VI, nos. 3-4 contains admirable summaries of economic developments. For American trade relations in the Orient, see Tyler Dennett, *Americans in Eastern Asia,* cited above; Chong Su See, *The Foreign Trade of China* (1919); C. F. Remer, *The Foreign Trade of China* (1926); Shü-lun Pan, *The Trade of the United States with China* (1924). On trade with the Caribbean islands, consult C. L. Jones, *Caribbean Backgrounds and Prospects* (1931); M. M. Knight, *The Americans in Santo Domingo* (1928) and C. C. Tansill, *The United States and Santo Domingo, 1798–1873,* previously cited; A. C. Millspaugh, *Haiti Under American Control, 1915–1930* (1931); and L. H. Jenks, *Our Cuban Colony,* cited above.

Chapter XI

The Progressive Movement

Though a mass of material on the subject has appeared, an adequate history of the Progressive movement is yet to be written. The best over-all interpretation to date is John Chamberlain, *Farewell to Reform* (1932). It may be supplemented with the *Autobiography of Lincoln Steffens* (2 vols., 1931); B. P. DeWitt, *The Progressive Movement* (1915); H. U. Faulkner, *The Quest for Social Justice, 1898–1914* (1931), in the History of American Life series, and C. M. Destler, *The Influence of Edward Kellogg upon American Radicalism, 1865–1901* (1932). In Volumes II and III Mark Sullivan, *Our Times: The United States, 1900–1925* (6 vols., 1926–35) presents in lively style the essential social background. For the philosophical basis, see Herbert Croly, *The Promise of American Life* (1909) and *Progressive Democracy* (1914); Walter Weyl, *The New Democracy* (rev. ed., 1920); Walter Lippmann, *Preface to Politics* (1913) and *Drift and Mastery* (1914); and T. N. Carver, *Essays in Social Justice* (1915). Extremely valuable in the same respect are Joseph Dorfman's *Thorstein Veblen and His America* (1934) and *The Economic Mind in American Civilization* (4 vols., 1946–50), Vol. III. For the political philosophy of the movement, consult C. E. Merriam, *American Political Ideas, 1865–1917* (1920); E. R. Lewis, *A History of American Political Thought from the Civil War to the World War* (1937); and V. L. Parrington, *Main Currents in American Thought,* Vol. III (*Beginning of Critical Realism in America*). For the influence of big business on the movement, see E. A. Ross, *Sin and Society* (1907); Matthew Josephson, *The Robber Barons* (1934); Gustavus Myers, *History of Great American Fortunes* (3 vols., 1910); C. B. Spahr, *An Essay on the Present Distribution of Wealth in the United States* (1896); J. A. Ryan, *A Living Wage* (1906); Robert Hunter, *Poverty* (1904); and F. L. Allen, *The Lords of Creation* (1935). Out of a voluminous biographic and autobiographic literature the following are highly recommended: G. R. Geiger, *The Philosophy of Henry George* (1931); A. E. Morgan, *The Philosophy of Edward Bellamy* (1945) and *Edward Bellamy* (1944); *La Follette's Autobiography* (1913); C. E. Russell, *Bare Hands and Stone Walls* (1933); F. C. Howe, *Confessions of a Reformer* (1925); Morris Hillquit, *Loose Leaves from a Busy Life* (1934); Ida Tarbell, *All in the Day's Work* (1939); W. A. White, *The Autobiography of William Allen White* (1946); Walter Johnson, *William*

Allen White's America (1947) and *Selected Letters of William Allen White* (1947); S. S. McClure, *My Autobiography* (1914); Brand Whitlock, *Forty Years of It* (1913) and Allan Nevins (ed.), *The Letters of Brand Whitlock* (1936); R. G. Baker, *American Chronicle* (1945); Oscar Ameringer, *If You Don't Weaken* (1940); Mary Vorse, *A Footnote to Folly* (1935); Caroline Lloyd, *Life of Henry Demarest Lloyd* (2 vols., 1912); M. A. DeW. Howe, *Portrait of an Independent, Moorfield Storey* (1932); Tom Johnson, *My Story* (1911); Claude Bowers, *Beveridge and the Progressive Era* (1932); and H. F. Williamson, *Edward Atkinson* (1934).

The Progressive Spirit. In addition to the references already listed above, see Louis Filler, *Crusaders for American Liberalism* (1939), an admirable portrayal; Harold Howland, *Theodore Roosevelt and His Times* (1921), in the Chronicles of America series; C. C. McCarthy, *The Wisconsin Idea* (1912), the movement explained by a supporter of La Follette; F. E. Haynes, *Social Politics in the United States* (1924); Edward Fitzpatrick, *McCarthy of Wisconsin* (1944), a biography of the author of *The Wisconsin Idea,* cited above, and not of the later, accusing Senator McCarthy from the same state; F. C. Howe, *Wisconsin, an Experiment in Democracy* (1912); and E. N. Doan, *The La Follettes and the Wisconsin Idea* (1947).

The Muckrakers. On this topic, consult C. C. Regier, *The Era of the Muckrakers* (1932). This volume should be supplemented by the above and Lincoln Steffens, *The Shame of the Cities* (1904) and *Upbuilders* (1909); D. G. Phillips, "The Treason of the Senate" in *Cosmopolitan* (1906); Thomas Lawson, *Frenzied Finance* (1905); Franklin Hichborn, *"The System" as Uncovered by the San Francisco Graft Prosecution* (1915); Fremont Older, *My Own Story* (1919); F. C. Howe, *The City, The Hope of Democracy* (1905); R. C. Brooks, *Corruption in American Politics and Life* (1910). Writers of contemporary literature also contributed to the cause of reform. In fact some were labeled Muckrakers. Consult F. M. Crawford, *An American Politician* (1885); Brand Whitlock, *The Thirteenth District* (1902) and *The Turn of the Balance* (1924); Theodore Dreiser, *The Titan* (1914) and *The Financier* (1912); Winston Churchill, *Coniston* (1906) and *Mr. Crewe's Career* (1908); Booth Tarkington, *The Turmoil* (1915) and *The Midlanders* (1923); J. W. De Forest, *Honest John Vane* (1875) and *Playing the Mischief* (1875); D. G. Phillips, *The Plum Tree* (1905); and W. A. White, *In the Heart of a Fool* (1919) and *A Certain Rich Man* (1909).

The Struggle Against Boss Rule. Consult the above and A. O. Barton, *La Follette's Winning of Wisconsin, 1894–1904* (1922); K. W. Hechler, *Insurgency: Personalities and Policies of the Taft Era* (1940), which describes the revolt of the Progressives in Congress; F. E. Haynes, *Third Party Movements Since the Civil War* (1916); Carter Harrison, *Stormy Years* (1935); W. D. Foulke, *Fighting the Spoilsmen* (1919); C. W. Patton, *The Battle for Municipal Reform* (1940); A. H. Eaton, *The Oregon System* (1912); W. B. Munro, *The Initiative, Referendum and Recall* (1912) and J. A. Riis, *A Ten Years War* (1900); J. D. Barnett, *The Operation of the Initiative, Referendum and Recall in Oregon* (1915); C. A. Beard and B. E. Schultz, *Documents on the Statewide Initiative, Referendum and Recall* (1912); F. A. Ogg, *National Progress, 1907–1917* (1918), in the American Nation series; G. E. Mowry, *Theodore Roosevelt and the Progressive Movement* (1946), excellent; Tso-Shuen Chang, *History and Analysis of the Commission and City-Manager Plans of Municipal Government in the United States* (1918); C. D. Thompson, *Public Ownership* (1925); F. H. MacGregor, *City Government by Commission* (1911); and J. J. Hamilton, *The Dethronement of the City Boss* (1910).

Aid for the Underprivileged. In addition to Walter Rauschenbush's *Christianity and the Social Crisis* (1907) and *Christianizing the Social Order* (1912), see, on housing, R. W. DeForest and Laurence Veiller, *The Tenement House Problem* (2 vols., 1903), which contains report of New York State Tenement House Commission of 1900. These volumes should be supplemented by E. E. Wood, *The Housing of the Unskilled Wage Earner* (1919). Edith Abbott, *The Tenements of Chicago 1908–1935* (1936) is a very scholarly study. But the classic work against overcrowded tenements as breeding places for vice, crime, and epidemics was Jacob

Riis, *How the Other Half Lives* (1890). The history of social settlements to the date of its publication is summarized by R. A. Woods and A. J. Kennedy, *The Settlement Horizon* (1922). It should be supplemented by Jane Addams, *Forty Years at Hull House* (1935) and Lillian D. Wald, *The House on Henry Street* (1915) and *Windows on Henry Street* (1934). See, too, J. W. Linn, *Jane Addams* (1935) and W. E. Wise, *Jane Addams of Hull House* (1935). On safeguarding children, see G. B. Margold, *Problems of Child Welfare* (1914); Jacob Riis, *The Battle with the Slums* (1902); Homer Folks, *The Care of Destitute, Neglected and Delinquent Children* (1902); H. H. Hart, *Selective Migration as a Factor in Child Welfare in the United States* (1915); John Spargo, *The Bitter Cry of the Children* (1906), which pictures child labor conditions; and H. L. Sumner and E. A. Merritt, *Child Labor Legislation in the United States* (1915), United States Department of Labor, Children's Bureau, Industrial Series no. 1. H. H. Lou, *Juvenile Courts in the United States* (1927) is a first-rate study. For improvement in the status of women, see C. C. Catt and N. R. Shuler, *Woman Suffrage and Politics* (1926); E. C. Stanton and others, *History of Woman Suffrage* (6 vols., 1881–1922), a detailed account; I. H. Irwin, *Angels and Amazons* (1933); J. L. Wilson, *The Legal and Political Status of Women in the United States* (1912); R. L. Dorr, *What Eight Million Women Want* (1910), the objectives of the "new woman"; T. S. McMahon, *Women and Economic Evolution* (1912); and Jessie Taft, *The Woman Movement from the Point of View of Social Consciousness* (1915). On civil rights for women consult A. E. Hecker, *A Short History of Women's Rights from the Days of Augustus to the Present Time* (2nd ed., 1914). On living standards, consult C. B. Spahr, *The Present Distribution of Wealth in the United States* (1896); Robert Hunter, *Poverty* (1904); J. A. Ryan, *A Living Wage* (1906), cited above; P. H. Douglas, *Real Wages in the United States, 1890–1926* (1930), which is authoritative; Alice Henry, *The Trade Union Woman* (1915); and L. H. Gulick and L. P. Ayres, *Medical Inspection of Schools* (1908); F. H. Streightoff, *The Standard of Living among the Industrial People of America* (1911); and Whitney Coombs, *The Wages of Unskilled Labor in Manufacturing Industries in the United States 1890–1920* (1926). The need for better facilities for recreation during the period considered can be obtained from C. E. Rainwater, *The Play Movement in the United States* (1921) and H. S. Curtis, *The Play Movement and Its Significance* (1917). For charities the best volumes are F. D. Watson, *The Charity Organization Movement in the United States* (1922) and A. G. Warner, *American Charities* (rev. ed., 1908). The problem of crime, especially as it relates to the underprivileged, is discussed by Sheldon Glueck, *Crime and Justice* (1936) and C. R. Henderson (ed.), *Correction and Prevention* (4 vols., 1910). The race question is ably handled by Booker T. Washington, *Up from Slavery* (1901); A. F. Raper, *The Tragedy of Lynching* (1933); R. S. Baker, *Following the Color Line* (1908); and Walter White, *Rope and Faggot* (1929). For Indian reform, consult Oliver Lafarge (ed.), *The Changing Indian* (1942) and M. A. DeW. Howe, *The Portrait of an Independent, Moorfield Storey* (1922). Associated with the underprivileged is the temperance movement. On this, see Mary Earhart, *Frances Willard: From Prayers to Politics* (1944); Ray Strachey, *Frances Willard: Her Life and Work* (1912); and F. E. Willard, *Glimpses of Fifty Years* (1889), reminiscences. See also P. H. Odegard, *Pressure Politics* (1928); and Justin Steuart, *Wayne Wheeler, Dry Boss* (1928).

Chapter XII

T. R., Taft, and Wilson

J. F. Rhodes, *The McKinley and Roosevelt Administrations* (1922) is disappointing principally for its failure to deal adequately with the underlying economic forces. F. A. Ogg, *National Progress, 1907–1917* (1918), in the American Nation series, is old and somewhat superficial. Mark Sullivan, *Our Times; the United States,*

1900–1925, cited previously, has much useful material presented in lively style. D. L. Dumond, *Roosevelt to Roosevelt* (1937) is a useful survey. A. W. Dunn, *From Harrison to Harding* (2 vols., 1922) is a journalistic survey by a Washington newspaper correspondent. Harold Howland, *Theodore Roosevelt and His Times* (1921), in the Chronicles of America series, is also thin. Matthew Josephson, *The President Makers* (1940) is straight political narrative. H. H. Kohlsaat, *From McKinley to Harding* (1923) is little more than reminiscences.

The Strenuous Life. The two best volumes on Roosevelt are *Theodore Roosevelt; an Autobiography* (1913) and H. F. Pringle, *Theodore Roosevelt* (1931). J. B. Bishop, *Theodore Roosevelt and His Time Shown in His Own Letters* (2 vols., 1920) is an authorized version and, as so frequently happens in such cases, is disappointing. W. R. Thayer, *Theodore Roosevelt, An Intimate Biography* (1919), written by a friend and admirer, is far from objective. The most recent edition of Roosevelt's works, edited by E. E. Morison, as well as older editions, leave no doubt about either Roosevelt's dynamic qualities or his strenuous life. T. R. Roosevelt and H. C. Lodge, *Selections from the Correspondence of Theodore Roosevelt and Henry Cabot Lodge, 1884–1918* (2 vols., 1925) does little to enhance the reputation of either man. W. F. McCaleb, *Theodore Roosevelt* (1931) and Lewis Einstein, *Roosevelt, His Mind in Action* (1930) are both first rate; so is G. E. Mowry's *Theodore Roosevelt and the Progressive Movement* (1946). No one should overlook Albert Shaw, *A Cartoon History of Roosevelt's Career* (1910). Also valuable in understanding Roosevelt and his administration are N. W. Stephenson, *Nelson W. Aldrich: A Leader in American Politics* (1930); Champ Clark, *My Quarter Century of American Politics* (1920); *The Autobiography of Lincoln Steffens,* cited earlier; Tyler Dennett, *John Hay: From Poetry to Politics,* previously cited; and P. C. Jessup, *Elihu Root,* cited above.

Theodore Roosevelt and the Trusts. See the references listed in the preceding sections of this chapter and H. R. Seager and C. A. Gulick, Jr., *Trust and Corporation Problems* (1929); Eliot Jones, *The Trust Problem in the United States* (1921); J. W. Jenks and W. E. Clark, *The Trust Problem* (rev. 5th ed., 1929); B. H. Meyer, *A History of the Northern Securities Case* (1906); J. G. Pyle, *The Life of James J. Hill* (2 vols., 1917), good for account of struggle between government and the railroads; W. Z. Ripley, *Railroads: Rates and Regulations* (1912) and *Railroads: Finance and Organization* (1915), useful on this topic; I. M. Tarbell, *The Life of Elbert H. Gary: The Story of Steel* (1925); A. H. Walker, *History of the Sherman Law of the United States of America* (1910); W. H. Taft, *The Anti-Trust Act and the Supreme Court* (1914); D. M. Keezer and Stacy May, *The Public Control of Business* (1930); F. B. Clark, *Constitutional Doctrines of Justice Harlan* (1915); and Lewis Corey, *The House of Morgan* (1930).

Safeguarding the People's Interests. For the early beginnings of the conservation movement, see Gifford Pinchot, *Breaking New Ground* (1947). Roosevelt's part in conservation is admirably told in G. E. Mowry, *Theodore Roosevelt and the Progressive Movement,* cited above; Roosevelt's *Autobiography,* previously cited; and Gifford Pinchot, *The Fight for Conservation* (1910). Two general works of differing character are H. W. Fairbanks, *Conservation Reader* (1920), and C. R. Van Hise and L. Havemeyer, *Conservation of Natural Resources in the United States* (1930). On land reclamation and irrigation, see B. H. Hibbard, *A History of Public Land Policies* (1924); A. B. Darling (ed.), *The Public Papers of Francis G. Newlands* (2 vols., 1932); F. H. Newell, *Irrigation in the United States* (rev. ed., 1906); and W. E. Smythe, *The Conquest of Arid America* (1900). W. G. Van Name, *Vanishing Forest Reserves* (1929) takes the United States Forestry Service to task for its laxity and want of vision. Also see John Ise, *The United States Forest Policy* (1920). On pure food and drug legislation there is a good account in Mark Sullivan, *Our Times, The United States, 1900–1925,* Volumes I and II. See also C. G. Bowers, *Beveridge and the Progressive Era,* cited earlier; and H. W. Wiley, *An Autobiography* (1930).

The Taft Administration. The best treatment of Taft's administration is H. F. Pringle, *The Life and Times of William Howard Taft* (1939). Other works of lesser importance are A. W. Butt, *Taft and Roosevelt: The Intimate Letters of Archie Butt* (2 vols., 1930), impressions of a White House aide; C. E. Barker, *With President Taft in the White House: Memories of William Howard Taft* (1947), reminiscences; Mrs. W. H. Taft, *Recollections of Full Years* (1914), Taft's earlier activities; O. S. Straus, *Under Four Administrations: From Cleveland to Taft* (1922), by Roosevelt's Secretary of Commerce; M. A. DeW. Howe, *George von Lengerke Meyer, His Life and Public Service* (1920), a biographical account of Taft's Secretary of the Navy; L. W. Busbey, *Uncle Joe Cannon* (1927), a second-rate biography of a second-rate man; and Blair Bolles, *Tyrant from Illinois* (1951). On the tariff controversies R. M. La Follette, *La Follette's Autobiography*, cited earlier, is excellent. See also F. W. Taussig, *The Tariff History of the United States* (rev. ed., 1931); N. W. Stephenson, *Nelson W. Aldrich*, already cited; U. S. Tariff Commission, *Reciprocity with Canada* (1920); and L. E. Ellis, *Reciprocity; 1911: A Study on Canadian-American Relations* (1939). On the Ballinger-Pinchot controversy, Pinchot presents his case in *The Fight for Conservation* (1910). But this should be supplemented by R. M. Stahl, *The Ballinger-Pinchot Controversy* (1926) and A. T. Mason, *Bureaucracy Convicts Itself: The Ballinger-Pinchot Controversy* (1941). K. W. Hechler, *Insurgency: Personalities and Policies of the Taft Era*, cited earlier, is an admirable study that sheds much light on this controversy.

The Scholar in Politics. Anyone who desires to understand the political career of Taft's successor to the presidency should start with Arthur Link's splendid volume, *Wilson: The Road to the White House* (1947) which deals with Wilson's development to 1912. It may be followed with profit by James Kerney, *The Political Education of Woodrow Wilson* (1926), an excellent study of Wilson's connection with New Jersey politics. The best single volume account is H. C. F. Bell, *Woodrow Wilson and the People* (1945). For a psychological interpretation, consult W. A. White, *Woodrow Wilson: The Man, His Times and His Task* (1924). J. P. Tumulty, *Woodrow Wilson as I Knew Him* (1921), by his private secretary; John M. Blum, *Joe Tumulty and the Wilson Era* (1951); W. E. Dodd, *Woodrow Wilson and His Work* (rev., 1932); Ruth Cranston, *The Story of Woodrow Wilson, Twenty-Eighth President of the United States, Pioneer of World Democracy* (1945); and Josephus Daniels, *The Wilson Era: Years of Peace, 1910–1917* (1944), by a member of Wilson's cabinet, are all sympathetic accounts. Eleanor W. McAdoo, *The Woodrow Wilsons* (1937), by a daughter, and Edith B. Wilson, *My Memoir* (1939), by his widow, are also laudatory but revealing. Those who desire a more comprehensive and detailed narrative should consult R. S. Baker, *Woodrow Wilson: Life and Letters* (8 vols., 1927–39), the authorized biography, and R. S. Baker and W. E. Dodd (eds.), *The Public Papers of Woodrow Wilson* (6 vols., 1925–7). The election of 1912 is best described by W. J. Bryan, *A Tale of Two Conventions* (1912); D. P. DeWitt, *The Progressive Movement;* G. E. Mowry, *Theodore Roosevelt and the Progressive Movement;* K. W. Hechler, *Insurgency: Personalities and Policies of the Taft Era,* and H. F. Pringle, *Theodore Roosevelt* and *The Life and Times of William Howard Taft,* all of which, with the exception of the Bryan volume, have been previously cited. Volume III of Mark Sullivan's *Our Times: The United States, 1900–1925* recaptures much of the color and excitement of the campaign. Other works, somewhat less reliable, that deal with the election are Victor Rosewater, *Back Stage in 1912* (1932), which defends the Republican National Committee; O. K. Davis, *Released for Publication: Some Inside Political History of Theodore Roosevelt and His Times* (1925); W. F. McCombs, *Making Woodrow Wilson President* (1921), which provides background; Champ Clark, *My Quarter Century of American Politics,* cited earlier; Donald Richberg, *Tents of the Mighty* (1930); and Wayne Williams, *William Jennings Bryan* (1936). The attitude of Wilson's opponent in the presidential campaign of 1916 is described admirably in M. J. Pusey, *Charles Evans Hughes* (2 vols., 1951).

The New Freedom. Wilson's speeches delivered during the campaign of 1912 and brought together in book form, *The New Freedom* (1913) not only revealed his philosophy but pointed in the direction that he was to follow in matters of domestic policy. The best accounts, giving the reader opportunity to judge the degree to which Wilson was successful in putting his theories into practice, are F. L. Paxson, *American Democracy and the World War* (3 vols., 1936–48), Vol. I, *The Pre-War Years, 1913–1917;* R. S. Baker, *Woodrow Wilson, Life and Letters,* cited above, Vols. III, IV; and William Diamond, *Economic Thought of Woodrow Wilson* (1943). These may be supplemented by Charles Seymour (ed.), *The Intimate Papers of Colonel House* (4 vols., 1926–8) and G. S. Viereck, *The Strangest Friendship in History* (1932), on the relations between Wilson and House; W. J. and M. B. Bryan, *The Memoirs of William Jennings Bryan* (1925); D. F. Houston, *Eight Years with Wilson's Cabinet, 1913–1920* (2 vols., 1926); W. C. Redfield, *With Congress and Cabinet* (1924); A. W. Lane and L. H. Wall, *The Letters of Franklin K. Lane, Personal and Political* (1922); W. G. McAdoo, *Crowded Years* (1931); T. R. Marshall, *Recollections* (1925); and B. J. Hendrick, *Life and Letters of Walter H. Page* (3 vols., 1922–5). On particular domestic policies the following are recommended: On taxation reforms, Sidney Ratner, *American Taxation* (1942); on the tariff, F. W. Taussig, *Tariff History of the United States* (rev. ed., 1931) and *Some Aspects of the Tariff Question* (rev. ed., 1931); and H. P. Willis, "The Tariff of 1913," *Journal of Political Economy,* Vol. XXII, pp. 1–40. For the Federal Reserve system, consult E. W. Kemmerer, *The A.B.C. of the Federal Reserve System* (11th ed., 1938); H. P. Willis, *The Federal Reserve System* (1923); P. M. Warburg, *The Federal Reserve System* (2 vols., 1930), on its beginnings, with a criticism; W. P. G. Harding, *Formative Period of the Federal Reserve System* (1925); S. E. Harris, *Twenty Years of the Federal Reserve Policy, Including an Extended Discussion of the Monetary Crisis 1927–1933* (2 vols., 1933), an exhaustive treatment; J. L. Laughlin, *The Federal Reserve Act, Its Origin and Problems* (1933), an excellent history of the act; and A. D. Noyes, *War Period of American Finance, 1908–1925* (1926). On financial concentration, see the *Report* of the Pujo committee, 62nd Cong., 3rd Sess., House Report no. 1593, cited earlier, which is summarized in understandable language by L. D. Brandeis, *Other People's Money, and How the Bankers Use It,* also previously cited. The *Report* of the Industrial Commission of 1915, 64th Cong., 1st Sess., Senate Document no. 415, already cited, is digested in A. A. Berle, Jr. and G. C. Means, *The Modern Corporation and Private Property* (1932). On this topic there is also valuable material in Lewis Corey, *The House of Morgan,* cited earlier; T. W. Lamont, *Henry P. Davison* (1933); and Cyrus Adler, *Jacob Henry Schiff, His Life and Letters* (2 vols., 1921). On trusts and business regulation, see Edward Berman, *Labor and the Sherman Act* (1930); G. C. Henderson, *The Federal Trade Commission* (1924); T. C. Blaisdell, *The Federal Trade Commission: An Experiment in the Control of Business* (1932); O. W. Knauth, *The Policy of the United States Toward Industrial Monopoly* (1913); F. A. Fetter, *The Masquerade of Monopoly* (1931), critical of trust legislation: M. W. Watkins, *Industrial Combinations and Public Policy* (1927); and J. D. Clark, *The Federal Trust Policy* (1931). On labor and the farmer, see E. C. Robbins, "The Trainmen's Eight Hour Day," *Political Science Quarterly,* Vol. XXXI (Dec., 1916), pp. 541–57, and Vol. XXXII (September, 1917), pp. 412–28; R. Fuller, *Child Labor and the Constitution* (1923); W. S. Holt, *The Federal Farm Loan Bureau* (1924); and O. R. Agresti, *David Lubin* (1922).

CHAPTER XIII

World War I

The literature on America's part in World War I is already very extensive. That part of it concerned with the reasons for the participation of the United States is mostly controversial. Indispensable for bibliographic and reference purposes is W. G. Leland and N. D. Mereness, *Introduction to the American Official Sources for the Economic and Social History of the World War* (1926). Prepared primarily for the studies in the economic and social history of the war, edited by J. T. Shotwell, it is especially useful to the student who wishes to understand the relations of the various branches of the Federal government to the individual citizen—for example, the Food Administration and the Council of National Defense. It also includes a great mass of statistical material gathered in many offices of the government. These compilations bear upon all phases of economic life and activity.

The United States, England, and Germany, 1870–1914. The best book on the European background is H. E. Barnes, *World Politics in Modern Civilization* (1930). Two other general accounts should also be read: F. L. Paxson, *American Democracy and the World War* (1936) cited earlier, especially Vol. I, and C. C. Tansill, *America Goes to War* (1938), anti-Wilson in spirit. H. E. Barnes, *Genesis of the World War* (rev. ed., 1929) is a forthright revisionist's point of view. S. B. Fay, *The Origins of the World War* (2 vols., rev. ed., 1930) and B. E. Schmitt, *The Coming of the War* (2 vols., 1930), though differing markedly in emphasis and interpretation, are indispensable for background. These secondary works may be supplemented by important documentary materials: the annual *Foreign Relations of the United States;* R. S. Baker and W. E. Dodd (eds.), *The Public Papers of Woodrow Wilson,* cited earlier; J. B. Scott (ed.), *A Survey of International Relations between the United States and Germany, August 1, 1914—April 6, 1917* (1917); J. B. Scott, *Diplomatic Correspondence between the United States and Germany, August, 1914—April, 1917* (1917); and Carleton Savage (ed.), *Policy of the United States toward Maritime Commerce in War* (1934); David Lloyd George, *War Memoirs* (6 vols., 1933–7); Charles Seymour, *The Intimate Papers of Colonel House,* already cited; H. H. Asquith, *Moments of Memory* (1937); Stephen Gwynn, *Letters and Friendships of Sir Cecil Spring Rice* (1929) and C. E. Schieber, *The Transformation of American Sentiment toward Germany 1870–1914* (1921).

The War of Words. See H. C. Peterson, *Propaganda for War: The Campaign against American Neutrality 1914–1917* (1939); T. A. Bailey, *The Man in the Street: Impact of American Public Opinion on Foreign Policy* (1948); H. D. Lasswell, *Propaganda Technique in the World War* (1927); C. H. Grattan, *Why We Fought* (1929); J. D. Squires, *British Propaganda at Home and in the United States 1914–1917* (1935); H. Lavine and J. Wachsler, *War Propaganda and the United States* (1940); Walter Millis, *Road to War* (1935), a popular account; J. Heinrich von Bernstorff, *My Three Years in America* (1920) and *Memoirs* (1936); C. J. Child, *The German-Americans in Politics 1914–1917* (1939), first rate; J. P. Jones and P. M. Hollister, *German Secret Service in America* (1918); G. S. Viereck, *Spreading Seeds of Hate* (1930); A. Ponsonby, *Falsehood in War Time* (1928); R. H. Heindel, *The American Impact on Britain, 1898–1914* (1940); and L. M. Gelber, *The Rise of Anglo-American Friendship* (1938).

War Trade and Loans. On this topic, consult Herbert Feis, *Europe, The World's Banker, 1870–1914* (1930); C. K. Hobson, *The Export of Capital* (1914); C. A. Beard, *The Idea of National Interest* (1934); R. W. Dunn, *American Foreign Investments* (1926); A. D. Noyes, *War Period of American Finance, 1908–1925* (1926). Also consult J. S. Bassett, *Our War with Germany* (1919) and J. B. McMaster, *The United States in the World War* (2 vols., 1918–20).

The Diplomacy of Neutrality. In addition to the books already cited in this chapter, see the official state papers published in the United States Department of State, *Papers Relating to the Foreign Relations of the United States: 1914, 1915, 1916, 1917 War Supplements* (1928–31). Also consult M. E. Curti, *Bryan and World Peace* (1931); J. Kenworthy Strabolgi and G. Young, *Freedom of the Seas* (1928), good on British blockade; A. M. McDiarmid, *The American Defense of Neutral Rights, 1914–1917* (1939), excellent; Edwin Borchard and W. P. Lage, *Neutrality for the United States* (1937), which questions whether the United States was entirely neutral; T. A. Bailey, *The Policy of the United States Toward Neutrals* (1942); Edgar Turlington, *Neutrality* (4 vols., 1935–6), especially Volume III; A. M. Arnett, *Claude Kitchin and the Wilson War Policies* (1937), which is critical of Wilson; Charles Seymour, *American Diplomacy During the World War* (1934), excellent in content and presentation; J. W. Garner, *International Law and the World War* (1937), a legalistic approach; N. D. Baker, "Why We Went to

War," *Foreign Affairs,* Vol. XV, pp. 1–86; T. A. Bailey "The Sinking of the Lusitania," *American Historical Review,* Vol. XLI, pp. 54–73; Harley Notter, *The Origins of the Foreign Policy of Woodrow Wilson* (1937), an able study; and H. C. Syrett, "The Business Press and American Neutrality, 1914–1917," *Mississippi Valley Historical Review,* Vol. XXXII, pp. 215–30 (September, 1945), which exonerates the business press from war mongering prior to 1917.

The End of Neutrality. With the declaration of war, neutrality quickly gave way to preparedness. One of the best works on this aspect of the Wilson Administration is Benedict Crowell and R. F. Wilson, *How America Went to War* (6 vols., 1921). On military organization and build-up, consult W. F. Willoughby, *Government Organization in War Time and After* (1919); Arthur Bullard, *Mobilizing America* (1917); B. M. Baruch, *American Industry in the War: A Report of the War Industries Board* (1921); W. G. McAdoo, *Crowded Years,* already cited; W. D. Hines, *War History of American Railroads* (1928); and E. N. Hurley, *The New Merchant Marine* (1920).

The War Front. The best statistical summary of America's military and naval contribution to World War I was prepared by L. P. Ayres in *The War with Germany* (2nd ed., 1919) at the direction of the War Department. On the military campaigns, see J. J. Pershing, *Final Report* (1919) and *My Experiences in the World War* (2 vols., 1931), a good account; and the unfinished 17 volume documentary history now being prepared by the Historical Branch of the United States Army under the title *The United States Army in the World War, 1917–1919.* T. G. Frothingham, *American Reinforcement in the World War* (1927) is well organized. There are also a number of interesting and informative volumes by commanding officers and others. Among these are Thomas Shipley, *The History of the A.E.F.* (1920); W. J. Wilgus, *Transporting the A.E.F. in Western Europe, 1917–1919* (1931), a description of the transport service; R. L. Bullard, *Personalities and Reminiscences of the War* (1925); J. G. Harbord, *The American Army in France, 1917–1918* (1936); H. Liggett, *Commanding an American Army* (1925); Johnson Hagood, *The Services of Supply: A Memoir of the Great War* (1927); E. N. Hurley, *The Bridge to France* (1927); A. W. Page, *Our 110 Day's Fighting* (1920); F. V. Greene, *Our First Year in the Great War* (1918); Edouard Réquin, *America's Race to Victory* (1919); Frederick Palmer, *America in France* (1918) and *Our Greatest Battle* (1919); R. J. Beamish and F. A. March, *America's Part in the World War* (1919); Dale Van Every, *The A.E.F. in Battle* (1928); and J. C. Wise, *The Turn of the Tide* (1920). On the naval history of the war, consult T. G. Frothingham, *The Naval History of the World War* (3 vols., 1924–6); Josephus Daniels, *Our Navy at War* (1922), by the Secretary of the Navy; Louis Guichard, *The Naval Blockade, 1914–1918* (1930); H. J. James, *German Subs in Yankee Waters* (1940); W. S. Sims and B. J. Hendrick, *The Victory at Sea* (1920); Albert Gleaves, *A History of the Transport Service* (1921); E. E. Morison, *Admiral Sims and the Modern American Navy* (1942); and R. H. Gibson and M. Prendergast, *The German Submarine War, 1914–1918* (1931). Excellent brief histories of the entire struggle are B. H. L. Hart, *The Real War, 1914–1918* (1930) and C. J. H. Hayes, *Brief History of the Great War* (1920).

The Home Front. The most informative and most readable volumes are E. A. Powell, *The Army Behind the Army* (1919); Frederick Palmer, *Newton D. Baker: America at War* (2 vols., 1931); E. H. Crowder, *The Spirit of Selective Service* (1920); G. B. Clarkson, *Industrial America in the World War* (1923); Norman Thomas, *The Conscientious Objector in America* (1923) and C. M. Case, *Non Violent Coercion* (1923); Zechariah Chafee, Jr., *Freedom of Speech* (1920); George Creel, *How We Advertised America* (1920); J. R. Mock and Cedric Larson, *Words that Won the War: The Story of the Committee on Public Information, 1917–1919* (1939); Samuel Gompers, *American Labor and the War* (1919); Alexander Bing, *War-Time Strikes and Their Adjustment* (1921); H. S. Hanna, and W. J. Lauck, *Wages and the War* (1918); G. S. Watkins, *Labor Problems and Labor Administration in the United States during the World War* (1920); E. L. Bogart, *Direct and Indirect Costs of the Great World War* (rev. ed., 1920); J. M. Clark,

The Costs of the World War to the American People (1931); J. A. Emery and N. B. Williams, *Governmental War Agencies Affecting Business* (1918); W. S. Culbertson, *Commercial Policy in War Time and After* (1919); F. H. Dixon, *Railroads and Government: Their Relations in the United States, 1910–1921* (1922); C. R. Van Hise, *Conservation and Regulation in the United States during the World War* (1917); F. M. Surface, *The Grain Trade during the World War* (1928); "Mobilizing America's Resources for the War," *Annals of the American Academy of Political and Social Science,* Vol. LXXVIII (1918); H. P. Davison, *The American Red Cross in the Great War* (1919); P. R. Kolbe, *The Colleges in War Times and After* (1919); I. C. Clarke, *American Women and the World War* (1918); J. A. B. Scherer, *The Nation at War* (1918), which describes state councils of defense and the varying local enthusiasm, indifference, or undercover hostility to the war. P. W. Slosson, *The Great Crusade and After, 1914–1928* (1930), in the History of American Life series, is excellent for its description of American social life in wartime. Valuable, too, for the same reason, is Mark Sullivan's *Our Times: The United States, 1900–1925,* Vol. V. J. B. McMaster, *The United States in the World War* and J. S. Bassett, *Our War with Germany,* both cited earlier, though not easy reading, contain a mass of valuable detail.

The Fight for a Just Peace. For termination of actual warfare, see H. R. Rudin, *Armistice, 1918* (1944), a scholarly study buttressed by documents. The standard authority on the peace conference is H. W. V. Temperley and others, *A History of the Peace Conference of Paris* (6 vols., 1920–4). This lengthy work may well be preceded by R. C. Binkley, "Ten Years of Peace Conference History," *Journal of Modern History,* Vol. I, pp. 607–30 and the same author's "New Light on the Paris Peace Conference," *Political Science Quarterly,* Vol. XLVI, pp. 335–61; 509–47. It may well be followed by a good brief summary to be found in either F. L. Benns, *Europe Since 1914* (rev. ed., 1935) or W. C. Langsam, *The World Since 1914* (rev. ed., 1933). Wilson's rôle at the Paris conference is the subject of dispute. Laudatory of him and his work are R. S. Baker, *Woodrow Wilson and World Settlement* (3 vols., 1922) and *What Wilson Did at Paris* (1919); E. M. House and Charles Seymour (ed.), *What Really Happened at Paris* (1921); D. H. Miller, *The Drafting of the Covenant* (2 vols., 1928), by one of the participants; Paul Birdsall, *Versailles Twenty Years After* (1941); and J. T. Shotwell, *At the Paris Peace Conference* (1937), the observations of a trained and highly objective historian. Critical of Wilson is T. A. Bailey, *Woodrow Wilson and the Lost Peace* (1944), and *Woodrow Wilson and the Great Betrayal* (1945). Critical of both Wilson and the peace treaty itself is J. M. Keynes, *Economic Consequences of the Peace* (1920). By some the Keynes volume is regarded as "brilliant," by others as "superficial and misleading," especially as far as Wilson is concerned. The truth lies between these extremes. Other valuable works on the Paris conference are Robert Lansing, *Peace Negotiations, A Personal Narrative* (1921) and *The Big Four and others of the Peace Conference* (1921). Allan Nevins, *Henry White: Thirty Years of American Diplomacy* (1930) and Frederick Palmer, *Bliss, Peacemaker: The Life and Letters of General Tasker Howard Bliss* (1934) are biographies of two of the peacemakers. Harold Nicolson, *Peace Making, 1919* (1939) and Stephen Bonsal, *Unfinished Business* (1944) are careful studies. B. M. Baruch, *The Making of the Reparation and Economic Sections of the Treaty* (1920) sheds light on that vexing subject. C. H. Haskins and R. H. Lord, *Some Problems of the Peace Conference* (1920) is illuminating. A. Tardieu, *The Truth About the Treaty* (1921) presents the case for France, while K. F. Nowak, *Versailles* (1928) presents a German interpretation extremely critical of Wilson. For source materials other than those already cited, see J. B. Scott (ed.), *Official Statements of War Aims and Peace Proposals* (1921).

The Lost Peace. On this topic, too, some of the literature is controversial. On the League of Nations and American rejection of the treaty, see J. S. Bassett, *The League of Nations* (1928); J. H. Latané, *Development of the League of Nations Idea: Documents and Correspondence of Theodore Marburg* (2 vols., 1932); D. F. Fleming, *The United States and the League of Nations, 1918–1920* (1932) and *The United States and World Organization, 1920–1933* (1938); W. S. Holt, *Treaties*

Defeated by the Senate (1933), which includes the Treaty of Versailles; and H. C. Lodge, *The Senate and the League of Nations* (1925), a defense of the Senate's action in refusing to approve the treaty. Allan Cranston, *The Killing of the Peace* (1945) is an excellent analysis of the causes for the wrecking of this particular effort to achieve world peace. Other volumes of value are Kenneth Colegrove, *The American Senate and World Peace* (1944); J. T. Shotwell, *The Origins of International Labor Organization* (2 vols., 1934); D. H. Miller, *The Peace Pact of Paris* (1928), which deals with Kellogg Pact; M. O. Hudson, *The Permanent Court of International Justice, and the Question of American Participation* (1925); D. F. Fleming, *The United States and the World Court* (1945); and Frank Simonds, *How Europe Made Peace Without America* (1927) and *Can America Stay at Home?* (1932).

CHAPTER XIV

The Golden Age of American Business

For the decade of the nineteen twenties the following works can be recommended: D. L. Dumond, *Roosevelt to Roosevelt: The United States in the Twentieth Century* (1937) and *America in Our Time, 1896–1946* (1947); C. A. and M. R. Beard, *The Rise of American Civilization,* Vols. II (*The Industrial Era*) and III (*America in Midpassage*); Harvey Wish, *Contemporary America* (1945); H. B. Parkes, *Recent America* (1941); and F. R. Dulles, *Twentieth Century America* (1945). For the political history of the period, see J. C. Malin, *The United States After the World War* (1930). On social economic development there is rich material in Mark Sullivan, *Our Times: The United States, 1900–1925,* Vol. VI; P. W. Slosson, *The Great Crusade and After, 1914–1928,* already cited; and H. U. Faulkner, *From Versailles to the New Deal* (1950), in the Chronicles of America series. S. H. Adams, *Incredible Era: The Life and Times of Warren Gamaliel Harding* (1939) covers the campaign of 1920 and gives much information about Harding. It should be supplemented by the article on Harding in the *Dictionary of American Biography* by Allan Nevins. J. T. Adams, *Our Business Civilization: Some Aspects of American Culture* (1929) is a suggestive interpretation and F. L. Allen, *Only Yesterday* (1931) gives journalistic color and atmosphere. By far the best analysis of a cross-section of American culture in the twenties is R. S. and H. M. Lynd, *Middletown* (1929), a brilliant study of a small Midwestern city (Muncie, Indiana). The real factual backbone for this chapter, however, is to be found, not in texts or journalistic accounts, but in government documents and reports and in books built upon or around such materials. Three of these works are indispensable to anyone who would understand the Golden Age of American business: The President's Conference on Unemployment, *Recent Economic Changes in the United States* (2 vols., 1929); F. C. Mills, *Economic Tendencies in the United States* (1932) and the President's Research Committee on Social Trends, *Recent Social Trends in the United States* (2 vols., 1933). To these may be added E. G. Nourse and associates, *America's Capacity to Produce* (1934) and the Report of the Subcommittee on Technology to the National Resources Committee, *Technological Trends and National Policy* (1937). Lewis Mumford's *Technics and Civilization* (1934) is highly stimulating.

From Depression to Prosperity. As in all immediate postwar periods, demobilization and a downward turn of the business cycle followed World War I. On demobilization, see Volume VI of B. Crowell and R. F. Wilson, *How America Went to War,* cited previously; Roger Burlingame, *Peace Veterans* (1932); H. U. Faulkner, *From Versailles to the New Deal,* already cited; Dixon Wecter, *When Johnny Comes Marching Home* (1944); Rogers MacVeagh, *The Transportation Act, 1920: Its Sources, History and Text* (1923), the story of return of railroads to private control; Katherine Mayo, *Soldiers What Next!* (1934), on the problems of the veteran; National Industrial Conference Board, *The World War Veterans and the Federal*

Treasury (1932), which discusses the veterans bonus, and *The American Merchant Marine Problem* (1929); and P. W. Slosson, *The Great Crusade and After, 1914–1928,* cited above. On the brief depression, see P. L. Haworth, *The United States in Our Own Times, 1865–1935* (1935); E. A. Filene, *The Way Out: A Forecast of Coming Changes in American Business and Industry* (1924); E. R. A. Seligman, *The Economics of Farm Relief* (1929); and George Soule, *Prosperity Decade; From War to Depression: 1917–1929* (1947).

American Industry During the Boom. At the head of the list stands *Recent Economic Changes in the United States,* cited above, with its numerous special articles and statistical estimates. It may be supplemented by the monthly *Bulletins* of the Federal Department of Labor; the *Report* of the Federal Trade Commission on *National Wealth and Income* (1926), 69th Cong. 1st Sess., Senate Document no. 126; the *Report* of the Census Bureau on *Wealth, Debt, and Taxation, 1922* (1924); the report of the National Industrial Conference Board on *Wages in the United States 1914–1929* (1930); and the report of the National Bureau of Economic Research, *Income in the United States* (2 vols., 1921–3). Several general treatments should be noted: R. G. Tugwell, *Industry's Coming of Age* (1927); T. N. Carver, *Present Economic Revolution in the United States* (1925); L. M. Hacker, *The Triumph of American Capitalism* (1940); T. C. Cochran and William Miller, *The Age of Enterprise* (1942); H. T. Warshow, *Representative Industries in the United States* (1938); and Garet Garrett, *The American Omen* (1928). Other valuable works are W. I. King, *Wealth and Income of the People of the United States* (1915); H. G. Moulton, *Income and Economic Progress* (1935); A. L. Bernheim (ed.), *Big Business, Its Growth and Its Place* (1939); Carter Goodrich and others, *Migration and Economic Opportunity* (1936); F. B. Garver, F. M. Boddy, and A. J. Nixon, *The Location of Manufacturers in the United States, 1899–1929* (1933); G. E. McLaughlin, *Growth of American Manufacturing Areas: A Comparative Analysis with Special Emphasis on Trends in the Pittsburgh District* (1938); B. F. Lemert, *The Cotton Textile Industry of the Southern Appalachian Piedmont,* cited previously; J. W. Jenkins, *James B. Duke, Master Builder* (1927) on the tobacco industry; Anton Mohr, *The Oil War* (1926); E. H. Davenport and S. R. Cooke, *The Oil Trusts and Anglo-American Relations* (1924); Ludwell Denny, *We Fight for Oil* (1928); Harry Jerome, *Mechanization in Industry* (1934); W. N. Polakov, *The Power Age: Its Quest and Challenge* (1933); Alexander Findlay, *Chemistry in the Service of Man* (5th ed., 1939); C. L. Mantell, *Sparks from the Electrode* (1933); William Haynes, *Men, Money and Molecules* (1936), Paul Schubert, *The Electric Word: The Rise of Radio* (1928); and A. E. Krows, *The Talkies* (1930); A. F. Harlow, *Old Wires and New Waves* (1936). On Business organization, see A. R. Burns, *The Decline of Competition: A Study of the Evolution of American Industry* (1936) and A. A. Berle and G. C. Means, *The Modern Corporation and Private Property,* already cited. Of the other books on this subject, Stuart Chase, *Men and Machines* (1929), criticizes existing economic arrangements; and his *Prosperity: Fact or Myth* (1929) is also critical. Stuart Chase and F. J. Schlink, *Your Money's Worth* (1927) is an attack on high-pressure advertising. On mass production, consult the Taylor Society, *Scientific Management in American Industry* (1929); Stuart Chase, *The Tragedy of Waste* (1928); C. A. Beard (ed.), *Whither Mankind?* (1928); and E. L. Bogart and C. E. Landon, *Modern Industry* (1927). Valuable also are P. M. Mazur, *American Prosperity* (1928), F. W. Wile (ed.), *A Century of Industrial Progress* (1928); Herbert Hoover, *American Individualism* (1922), a statement of Republican party creed; and his *The New Day* (1928), more of the same; W. Z. Ripley, *Main Street and Wall Street* (1927), on methods of high finance; and Lewis Corey, *Decline of American Capitalism* (1934), a Marxist interpretation. Opinions of foreign students about American prosperity are J. E. Barker, *America's Secret: The Causes of Her Economic Success* (1927); George Peel, *The Economic Impact of America* (1928); G. K. Simonds and J. G. Thompson, *The American Way to Prosperity* (1928); Albert Demangeon, *America and the Race for World Dominion* (1921), a French view; and Julius Hirsch, *Das Amerikanische Wirtschaftwunder* (1926). That American prosperity and continued economic well-being depends on the welfare of other parts of the world is the thesis of W. C. Redfield, *Dependent America* (1926).

Control of Business. Though business enjoyed a comparatively free rein during the Golden Age, government control was not entirely absent. As an introduction to this topic, see D. M. Keezer and Stacy May, *The Public Control of Business* (1930). On transportation, see Rogers Macveagh, *The Transportation Act of 1920: Its Sources, History and Text,* cited above; D. P. Locklin, *Railroad Regulation since 1920* (1928); H. G. Moulton and associates, *The American Transportation Problem* (1933); The Interstate Commerce Commission, *Regulation of Transportation Agencies: Report of Federal Coordination of Transportation on the Regulation of Transportation Agencies other than Railroads and on Proposed Changes in Railroad Regulation* (1934), 73rd Cong., 2nd Sess., Senate Document no. 152; and A. R. Ellington and W. Coombs, *The Government and Railroad Transportation,* cited earlier. Water power and utilities concentration is best discussed by J. C. Bonbright and G. C. Means, *The Holding Company, Its Public Significance and Its Regulation* (1932); J. H. Stehman, *The Financial History of the American Telephone and Telegraph Company* (1925); Federal Trade Commission, *Electric-Power Industry* (2 vols., 1927–8); J. G. Kerwin, *Federal Water Power Legislation* (1926); H. S. Raushenbush, *The Power Fight* (1932); and C. O. Hardy, *Recent Growth of the Electric Light and Power Industry* (1929). On the public debt and taxation, consult Sidney Ratner, *American Taxation,* already cited; C. L. King, *Public Finance* (1935); and Twentieth Century Fund, *Facing the Tax Problem* (1937).

On trusts and mergers in general, see, in addition to the references listed above, H. W. Laidler, *Concentration of Control in American Industry* (1931); W. J. A. Donald, *Trade Associations* (1933); F. A. Fetter, *Masquerade of Monopoly* (1931); National Industrial Conference Board, *Mergers and the Law* (1929); J. T. Flynn, *Security Speculation* (1934); H. G. Moulton, *The Financial Organization of Socity* (1920), and his *Financial Organization and the Economic System* (1938); Anna Rochester, *Rulers of America* (1936), a left-of-center interpretation; Ferdinand Lundberg, *America's Sixty Families* (1937); and Twentieth Century Fund, *Big Business, Its Growth and Its Place* (1937) and *How Profitable is Big Business?* (1937). For concentration in particular industries, consult Reavis Cox, *Competition in the American Tobacco Industry, 1911–1932* (1933) and J. W. Jenkins, *James B. Duke, Master Builder,* previously cited; D. H. Wallace, *Market Control in the Aluminum Industry* (1937); M. W. Watkins, *Oil: Stabilization or Conservation* (1937). The chain-store development is another excellent example of business concentration. See "A and P and the Hartfords," *Fortune* (March, 1933); "Case History of a Chain Store," *Fortune* (November, 1934), the story of W. T. Grant; and "Woolworth's $250,000,000 Trick," *Fortune* (November, 1933). See also the account of the DuPonts in *Fortune* (November, 1934) and (December, 1934). For America's participation in the cartel movement, consult Robert Liefmann, *International Cartels, Combines and Trusts* (1927); Alfred Plummer, *International Combines in Modern Industry* (1934); and W. F. Notz, *Representative International Cartels, Combines and Trusts* (1929).

Exporting American Capital. For background, see C. K. Hobson, *The Export of Capital* (1914) and Herbert Feis, *Europe, The World's Banker, 1870–1914* (1930). The activity of America in overseas investment is described by R. W. Dunn, *American Foreign Investments* (1926); P. M. Mazur, *America Looks Abroad* (1930); Hiram Motherwell, *Imperial Dollar* (1929); B. H. Williams, *Economic Foreign Policy of the United States* (1929); C. A. Beard, *The Idea of National Interest* (1934) and *The Open Door at Home* (1934), Scott Nearing and Joseph Freeman, *Dollar Diplomacy* (1925); Scott Nearing, *The Twilight of Empire* (1930); Nicholas Roosevelt, *America and England?* (1930); C. Lewis and K. T. Schlotterbeck, *America's Stake in International Investments* (1938). America's postwar investments in Germany are discussed by R. R. Kuczynski, *American Loans to Germany* (1927); Max Winkler, *Foreign Bonds, An Autopsy* (1933); J. T. Madden, Marcus Nadler and H. C. Sauvain, *America's Experience as a Creditor Nation* (1937); and R. A. Young, *Handbook on American Underwriting of Foreign*

Securities (1930) and *The International Financial Position of the United States* (1929). On particular countries or regions, see, for the Far East, C. F. Remer, *American Investments in China* (1929), a good description of American penetration to that date; P. H. Clyde, *International Rivalries in Manchuria, 1689–1922* (rev., 1928), a pro-Japanese point of view; Herbert Croly, *Willard Straight* (1924), which describes, among other things, the efforts of a member of the House of Morgan to increase American investments in China and especially in Manchuria, F. V. Field, *American Participation in the China Consortiums* (1931); G. Odate, *Japan's Financial Relations with the United States* (1922). On Latin America, consult F. M. Halsey, *Investments in Latin America* (1925); M. A. Marsh, *The Bankers in Bolivia* (1928); J. F. Rippy, *The Capitalists and Colombia* (1931); D. M. Phelps, *Migration of Industry to South America* (1936); A. D. Gayer, P. T. Homan, and E. K. James, *The Sugar Economy of Porto Rico* (1938); C. L. Jones, *Mexico and Its Reconstruction* (1921), F. W. Powell, *The Railroads of Mexico* (1921); C. W. Hackett, *The Mexican Revolution and the United States, 1910–1926* (1926); Edgar Turlington, *Mexico and Her Foreign Creditors* (1930); F. S. Dunn, *The Diplomatic Protection of Americans in Mexico* (1933). There is also valuable material on American investments in Mexico. The two best books on the United States and Mexico are: Ernest H. Gruening, *Mexico and Its Heritage* (1928) and J. F. Rippy, *The United States and Mexico* (1926) and in the two volumes of the *Investigation of Mexican Affairs by the Committee on Foreign Relations of the United States* (1920), 66th Cong. 2nd Sess. *Sen. Doc.* No. 285. For Canada see the admirable volume by H. L. Keenleyside, *Canada and the United States* (1929). It may be supplemented by two special volumes which are part of a larger detailed study on the relationship of Canada and the United States sponsored by the Carnegie Endowment for International Peace. These are W. J. Wilgus, *The Railway Interrelations of the United States and Canada* (1937) and H. Marshall, F. A. Southard Jr. and K. W. Taylor, *Canadian-American Industry; A Study in International Investment* (1936).

Exporting American Goods. In addition to the references listed above and especially in the last paragraph see *The Commerce Year Book* which with the exception of 1927 was published annually between 1922 and 1932 by the Federal Department of Commerce. Other publications by the Department of great value to the student of foreign trade are *Special Agents Series, Miscellaneous Series, Special Consular Reports, Trade Information Bulletin* and *Trade Promotion Series.* The Department's annual *Foreign Commerce and Navigation of the United States* is likewise valuable. For a detailed description of each of these publications see L. F. Schmeckebier and G. A. Weber, *The Bureau of Foreign and Domestic Commerce; Its History, Activities, and Organization* (1924). Useful also for the period covered by this chapter is National Industrial Conference Board, *Trends in the Foreign Trade of the United States* (1930). The best discussion of imports is to be found in B. B. Wallace and L. R. Edminster, *International Control of Raw Materials* (1930) and W. C. Redfield, *Dependent America,* already cited. For particular commodities, countries, or regions, see E. G. Nourse, *American Agriculture and the European Market* (1924). For trade with the Far East, consult "The New Pacific," *Survey of American Foreign Relations for 1930;* A. W. Griswold, *The Far Eastern Policy of the United States* (1938); C. F. Remer, *The Foreign Trade of China* (1926); Carl Crow, *Four Hundred Million Customers* (1937); Shü-Lun Pan, *The Trade of the United States with China,* already cited; S. Uyehara, *The Industry and Trade of Japan* (rev. ed., 1936). On Latin America there is much material on foreign trade in C. L. Jones, *Caribbean Backgrounds and Prospects* (1931); "The Caribbean," *Survey of American Foreign Relations for 1929;* C. D. Kepner and J. H. Soothill, *The Banana Empire: A Case Study of Economic Imperialism* (1935) and C. D. Kepner, *Social Aspects of the Banana Industry* (1936). On the merchant marine, see W. P. Elderton, *Shipping Problems, 1916–1921* (1927); J. C. Malin, *The United States After the World War,* previously cited; Brookings Institution, *United States Shipping Board* (1931); and L. W. Maxwell, *Discriminating Duties and the American Merchant Marine* (1926). The influence of tariffs on foreign trade may be seen in F. W. Taussig, *Tariff History of the United States* and *Some Aspects of the Tariff Question,* both cited earlier. See also Abraham Berglund and P. G. Wright, *The Tariff on Iron and Steel* (1929); L. R. Edminster, *The Cattle Industry and the Tariff* (1926); M. A. Smith *The Tariff on Wool* (1926); P. G. Wright, *Sugar in Relation to the Tariff* (1924) and *The Tariff on Animal and Vegetable Oils* (1928); and B. B. Wallace and L. R. Edminster, *International Control of Raw Materials,* already cited.

The Cult of Business. That business was in the saddle and riding hard during the decade following World War I is evident when one looks at the state of both the commercial farmer and organized labor and realizes the rôle played by the business man in American life. On this, consult J. T. Adams, *Our Business Civilization: Some Aspects of American Culture,* and *Recent Social Trends,* both cited above. The business ethics of the Golden Age of the twenties also came under scrutiny. For background, read Werner Sombart, *The Quintessence of Capitalism* (1915) and R. H. Tawney, *Religion and the Rise of Capitalism: A Historical Study* (1926). These should be followed by the Chamber of Commerce of the United States, *Principles of Business Conduct* (1924); E. L. Heermance, *The Ethics of Business, A Study of Current Standards* (1926); and C. F. Taeusch, *Professional and Business Ethics* (1926).

CHAPTER XV

From Normalcy to Depression

The general works cited for the preceding chapter will serve as background for this chapter too. In addition, consult Nathan Fine, *Labor and Farmer Parties in the United States,* cited earlier; W. A. White, *Masks in a Pageant,* also cited before, and his *A Puritan in Babylon, The Story of Calvin Coolidge* (1938), excellent; Calvin Coolidge, *The Autobiography of Calvin Coolidge* (1929); C. M. Fuess, *Calvin Coolidge, The Man from Vermont* (1940), inferior to White's volume; Alfred Lief, *Democracy's Norris* (1939); G. W. Norris, *Fighting Liberal* (1945); C. O. Johnson, *Borah of Idaho* (1936); J. M. Cox, *Through My Years* (1946); H. F. Pringle, *Alfred E. Smith: A Critical Study* (1927); A. E. Smith, *Up To Now: An Autobiography* (1929); W. H. Allen, *Al Smith, Tammany Hall* (1928), a critical account; Harvey O'Connor, *Mellon's Millions* (1933), sharply critical; Will Irwin, *Herbert Hoover, A Reminiscent Biography* (1928); Herbert Hoover, *Memoirs of Herbert Hoover: Years of Adventure, 1874–1920* (1951), an autobiography, and his *American Individualism* (1922), *The Challenge to Liberty* (1934), and *The New Day* (1928), the last containing campaign speeches and his political creed; K. C. McKay, *The Progressive Movement of 1924* (1947), a full-length study of election campaign of that year; R. V. Peel and T. C. Donnelly, *The Campaign of 1928* (1931), a good analysis; W. S. Myers and W. H. Newton, *The Hoover Administration* (1936); R. L. Wilbur and A. M. Hyde, *The Hoover Policies* (1937); W. S. Myers, *The Foreign Policies of Herbert Hoover, 1929–1933* (1940)—the last three are highly partisan—and R. S. Allen, *Washington Merry-Go-Round* (1931).

The Advent of Normalcy. Three items stand out in connection with the defeat of Wilson and the return of the Republicans to power: political and economic reaction; spiritual and intellectual repression; and betrayals of public trust. On repression and intolerance the best works are Zechariah Chafee, Jr., *Freedom of Speech* (1920) and *Free Speech in the United States* (1941); J. M. Mecklin, *The Ku Klux Klan: a Study of the American Mind* (1924); E. S. Bates, *This Land of Liberty* (1930); Walter Lippmann, *American Inquisitors* (1928); B. L. Pierce, *Public Opinion and the Teaching of History in the United States* (1926); A. G. Hays, *Let Freedom Ring* (rev. ed., 1937), an account of the activities of the American Civil Liberties Union, and *Trial by Prejudice* (1933); Will Irwin, *How Red Is America?* (1927); H. K. Beale, *Are American Teachers Free?* (1936); W. E. Garrison, *Intolerance* (1934); M. L. Ernst, *The First Freedom* (1946); Francis Biddle,

The Fear of Freedom (1951), which discusses historically the effect of anxiety and fear upon national security and free institutions; O. K. Fraenkel, *Our Civil Liberties* (1944); George Seldes, *Freedom of the Press* (1935); E. M. Borchard, *Convicting the Innocent* (1932); and Maynard Shipley, *The War on Modern Science* (1927). On intolerance toward the Negro, see Gunnar Myrdal, *An American Dilemma* (1944); R. B. Vance, *All These People* (1946); R. R. Moton, *What the Negro Thinks* (1929); and B. H. Nelson, *The Fourteenth Amendment and the Negro since 1920* (1946). On the Mooney-Billings and Sacco-Vanzetti cases, consult, for the first, the report of the Wickersham Committee, 71st Cong., 2nd sess., House Document no. 252 and H. T. Hunt, *The Case of Thomas J. Mooney and Warren K. Billings* (1929); for the second, Jeannette Marks, *Thirteen Days,* (1929), the story of the efforts to stay the execution; Felix Frankfurter, *The Case of Sacco and Vanzetti* (1927), a legal analysis by an outstanding authority; O. K. Fraenkel (ed.), *The Sacco-Vanzetti Case* (1931), extremely valuable for source material; and Louis Joughin and Edmund Morgan, *The Legacy of Sacco and Vanzetti* (1948). For the hysteria about undesirable aliens, consult Jane Clark, *Deportation of Aliens from the United States to Europe* (1931) and F. C. Howe, *The Confessions of a Reformer,* cited earlier. For the student interested in repression and intolerance there is much of value in O. G. Villard, *Fighting Years* (1939), the autobiography of a distinguished editor of the *Nation;* André Siegfried, *America Comes of Age,* previously cited; and Harvey Wish, *Contemporary America* (1945). For the betrayal of public trust, consult C. A. Beard, *The Rise of American Civilization,* Vol. III (*America in Midpassage*); M. R. Werner, *Privileged Characters* (1935); M. E. Ravage, *The Story of Teapot Dome* (1924); W. B. and J. B. Northrop, *The Insolvence of Office* (1932); Norman Thomas and Paul Blanchard, *What's the Matter with New York* (1932); Lloyd Lewis and H. J. Smith, *Chicago, The History of Its Reputation* (1929); and C. E. Merriam, *Chicago* (1929).

Coolidge and Hoover. See the works listed above for this chapter and in addition the following on special topics that were of concern during the decade of the twenties: On immigration and Americanization, see J. W. Jenks and W. J. Lauck, *The Immigration Problem* (6th ed., 1926); G. M. Stephenson, *A History of American Immigration, 1820–1924* (1926); R. L. Garis, *Immigration Restriction* (1927); R. E. Park, *The Immigrant Press and Its Control* (1922); E. deS. Brunner, *Immigrant Farmers and Their Children* (1929); E. A. Steiner, *The Making of a Great Race: Racial and Religious Cross-Currents in the United States* (1929); T. L. Stoddard, *Re-forging America* (1927) and William MacDougall, *Is America Safe for Democracy?* (1921), which are anti-alien; M. R. Davie, *World Immigration, With Special Reference to the United States* (1936); Manuel Gamio, *Mexican Immigration to the United States* (1930); and R. W. Paul, *The Abrogation of the Gentlemen's Agreement* (1936), which discusses the Immigration Act of 1924. On prohibition the most satisfactory works are E. H. Cherrington, *The Evolution of Prohibition in the United States of America* (1920), good for background; Peter Odegard, *Pressure Politics, The Story of the Anti-Saloon League* (1928); Justin Steuart, *Wayne Wheeler, Dry Boss* (1928); D. L. Colvin, *Prohibition in the United States* (1926); Charles Merz, *Dry Decade* (1931); M. B. Bruère, *Does Prohibition Work?* (1927); Mary Earhart, *Frances Willard: From Prayers to Politics* (1945); Herman Feldman, *Prohibition: Its Economic and Industrial Aspects* (1927); H. Asbury, *The Great Illusion* (1950); V. Dabney, *Dry Messiah: The Life of Bishop Cannon* (1949), which is excellent; National Commission on Law Enforcement, *Report on the Enforcement of the Prohibition Laws of the United States* (1931), 71st Cong., 3rd Sess., House Document no. 722; and L. V. Harrison and Elizabeth Laine, *After Repeal* (1936). On the peace movement, see J. S. Bassett, *The League of Nations* (1928), factual but dull; David Bryn-Jones, *Frank B. Kellogg* (1937); D. F. Fleming, *The United States and the World Court* (1945) and *The United States and World Organization, 1920–33* (1938); D. H. Miller, *The Peace Pact of Paris* (1928), which treats the Kellogg Pact; J. T. Shotwell, *War as an Instrument of National Policy* (1929); W. E. Rappard, *The Quest for Peace Since the World War* (1940); and M. O. Hudson, *The World Court, 1921–*

1938 (5th ed., 1938). The subject of inter-Allied debts and reparation payments is handled adequately by C. Bergmann, *The History of Reparations* (1927); C. G. Dawes, *A Journal of Reparations* (1939), the story of the Dawes Plan; National Industrial Conference Board, *The Inter-Ally Debts and the United States* (1925); H. G. Moulton and Leo Pasvolsky, *World War Debt Settlements* (1926) and *War Debts and World Prosperity* (1932); and Allan Nevins, *The United States in a Chaotic World* (1950), in the Chronicles of America series, which is good on war debts. On naval limitation, see the general treatments by S. F. Bemis, *Diplomatic History of the United States* (rev. ed., 1950); C. P. Howland (ed.), *Survey of American Foreign Relations 1928–1931* (4 vols., 1928–31); and W. S. Myers, *The Foreign Policies of Herbert Hoover, 1929–33* (1940). More particularly, consult R. L. Buell, *The Washington Conference* (1922); C. G. Dawes, *Journal as Ambassador to Great Britain,* cited above, for material on the abortive London Naval Conference; Yomato Ichihashi, *The Washington Conference and After* (1928); Harold and Margaret Sprout, *Toward a New Order of Sea Power* (1940); B. H. Williams, *The United States and Disarmament* (1931); Mark Sullivan, *The Great Adventure at Washington* (1922), a journalistic account; and C. L. Hoag, *Preface to Preparedness* (1941), an excellent study of public opinion on Washington Conference. On the United States and Latin America there is abundant material in J. F. Rippy, *Latin America in World Politics* (3rd ed., 1938); Carleton Beals, *Mexican Maze* (1931); Ernest Gruening, *Mexico and Its Heritage,* cited earlier; M. M. Knight, *The Americans in Santo Domingo,* cited above; A. C. Millspaugh, *Haiti Under American Control, 1915–30,* cited previously; L. L. Montague, *Haiti and the United States, 1719–1938* (1940); Harold Nicolson, *Dwight Morrow* (1935); H. L. Stimson, *American Policy in Nicaragua* (1927); and A. Alvarez, *The Monroe Doctrine* (1924). On relations with Russia, consult W. S. Graves, *America's Siberian Adventure, 1918–1920* (1931) and F. L. Schuman, *American Policy Toward Russia since 1917* (1928).

The Government and Business Enterprise. See the references listed under "Control of Business" in Chapter 14 and the following on the courts, business enterprise, and property: J. R. Commons, *Legal Foundations of Capitalism* (1924); Louis Boudin, *Government by Judiciary* (2 vols., 1932); Charles Warren, *The Supreme Court in United States History,* Vol. III, already cited; E. S. Corwin, *Twilight of the Supreme Court* (1934); Felix Frankfurter (ed.), *Mr. Justice Holmes and the Constitution* (1927); Max Lerner, *The Mind and Faith of Justice Holmes* (1943); J. P. Pollard, *Mr. Justice Cardozo* (1935); M. R. Cohen, *Law and the Social Order* (1933); S. J. Konefsky, *Chief Justice Stone and the Supreme Court* (1945); and A. T. Mason, *Brandeis A Free Man's Life* (1946).

The Government and the Farmer. On this topic, see B. H. Hibbard, *Effects of the Great War Upon Agriculture in the United States and Great Britain* (1919); W. Gee, *The Place of Agriculture in American Life* (1930); U. S. Chamber of Commerce, *Large Scale Farming* (1929); J. D. Black, *Agricultural Reform in the United States* (1929); Bernhard Ostrolenk, *The Surplus Farmer* (1932); L. M. Hacker, "The Farmer is Doomed," John Day Pamphlets (1933); Clara Eliot, *The Farmer's Campaign for Credit,* cited earlier; J. E. Boyle, *Farm Relief: A Brief on the McNary-Haugen Plan* (1928); A. A. Bruce, *Non-Partisan League* (1921), adversely critical; H. E. Gaston, *The Nonpartisan League* (1920) friendly; B. H. Hibbard, *Marketing Agricultural Products* (1921), which sheds light on the postwar situation; E. G. Nourse, *American Agriculture and the European Market* (1924); Arthur Capper, *The Agricultural Bloc* (1922), which explains the reasons for its existence; and Edward Wiest, *Agricultural Organization in the United States* (1923), a study of the Farm Bureau. On farm co-operatives, see H. H. Bakken and M. A. Schaars, *The Economics of Cooperative Marketing* (1937); F. E. Clark and L. D. H. Weld, *Marketing Agricultural Products in the United States* (1932), a text; R. H. Elsworth, *Agricultural Cooperative Associations, Marketing and Purchasing, 1925* (1928), Department of Agriculture Technical Bulletin no. 40 and his *Cooperative Marketing and Purchasing, 1920–1930* (1930), Department of Agriculture Circular no. 121; C. L. Christensen, *Farmer's Cooperative Associations in the United States* (1929), Department of Agriculture Circular no. 94; and Federal Trade Commission, *Cooperative Marketing* (1928), 70th Cong., 1st Sess., Senate Document no. 93 an exhaustive study. E. H. Wiecking, *The Farm Real Estate Situation* (1927), Department of Agriculture Circular no. 377; Macy Campbell, *Rural Life at the Crossroads* (1927); R. C. Engberg, *Industrial Prosperity and the Farmer* (1927); a symposium "The Agricultural Situation in the United States," *Annals of the American Academy of Political and Social Science,* Vols. CXVII (1925) and CXLIX (1929); and E. R. Eastman, *These Changing Times* (1927). On technical changes, consult the Agriculture Yearbooks for 1936 and 1937 for plant and animal breeding, and that for 1938 for soil conservation. See also H. S. Person, *Little Waters: A Study of Headwater Streams and Other Little Waters, Their Use and Relations to the Land* (1936); Russell Lord, *To Hold This Soil* (1938), Department of Agriculture, Miscellaneous Publication no. 321; and Stuart Chase, *Rich Land, Poor Land* (1936), an excellent popularization. On farm tenancy, consult E. A. Goldenweise and L. E. Truesdell, *Farm Tenancy in the United States,* cited previously.

The Decline of Organized Labor. A good introduction to this topic is Herbert Harris, *American Labor* (1939 and V. W. Lanfear, *Business Fluctuations and the American Labor Movement, 1915–1922* (1924). Equally good is Selig Perlman, *A History of Trade Unionism in the United States* (rev. ed., 1950); and Leo Wolman, *Ebb and Flow in American Trade Unionism* (1936) is indispensable for this period. See also C. R. Daugherty, *Labor Problems in American Industry* (rev. ed., 1938); L. L. Lorwin, *The American Federation of Labor: History, Policies and Prospects* (1933); Herman Feldman, *Racial Factors in American Industry,* cited previously; and R. W. Dunn, *The Americanization of Labor* (1927). On the steel strike of 1919, consult Abraham Epstein, *The Challenge of the Aged* (1928). Interchurch World Movement, *Report on the Steel Strike of 1919* (1920) is sympathetic to strikers and based on insufficient evidence; Marshall Olds, *Analysis of the Interchurch World Movement Report on the Steel Strike* (1922) suffers from same deficiencies as the document he analyzes; W. Z. Foster, *The Great Steel Strike and Its Lessons* (1920) justifies the strikers. More objective is C. A. Gulick, Jr., *Labor Policy of the United States Steel Corporation* (1924) and C. R. Daugherty, M. G. De Chazeau, and S. S. Stratton, *The Economics of the Iron and Steel Industry* (2 vols., 1937). See also H. B. Davis, *Labor and Steel* (1933) and Harvey O'Connor, *Steel-Dictator* (1935). On textile unrest, which also characterized the decade of the twenties, see G. S. Mitchell, *Textile Unionism in the South* (1931); Samuel Yellen, *American Labor Struggles* (1936) and A. Berglund, G. T. Starnes and F. T. De Vyver, *Labor in the Industrial South* (1930). For radical unionism, see J. S. Gambs, *The Decline of the I. W. W.* (1932). L. V. Kennedy, *The Negro Peasant Turns Cityward* (1930) outlines reasons. On the influx of women into industry, consult Grace Hutchins, *Women Who Work* (1934); S. P. Breckenridge, *Women in the Twentieth Century, A Study of Their Political, Social and Economic Activities* (1933); and N. E. Pidgeon, *Women in the Economy of the United States* (1937), Department of Labor, Women's Bureau Bulletin no. 155, an excellent summary. On child labor, see K. D. Lumpkin and D. S. Douglas, *Child Workers in America* (1937). The offensive against labor is treated by Savel Zimand, *The Open Shop Drive* (1921); J. I. Seidman, *The Yellow Dog Contract* (1932); and Leo Huberman, *The Labor Spy Racket* (1937). On welfare capitalism, see B. M. Selekman and Mary Van Kleeck, *Employes' Representation in Coal Mines* (1924), which describes the Colorado Fuel and Iron industrial representation plan; B. M. Selekman, *Employes' Representation in Steel Works* (1924); R. F. Foerster and E. H. Dietel, *Employee Stock Ownership in the United States* (1926); National Industrial Conference Board, *Employee Stock Purchase Plans in the United States* (1928); and M. W. Latimer, *Industrial Pension Systems in the United States and Canada* (2 vols., 1932). The attitude of the government in labor disputes during the Golden Age is obtainable in E. E. Witte, *The Government in Labor Disputes* (1932). It may be supplemented with Felix Frankfurter and Nathan Greene, *The Labor Injunction* (1930).

From Boom to Bust. The Brookings Institution, *The Recovery Problem in the United States* (1936) analyzes the causes of the depression. It should be supplemented by E. L. Dulles, *Depression and Reconstruction: A Study of Causes and Controls* (1936); A. M. Bernheim and M. G. Schneider (eds.), *Security Markets* (1935); F. W. Hirst, *Wall Street and Lombard Street* (1931); Maurice Levin and others, *America's Capacity to Consume* (1934); Lionel Robbins, *The Great Depression* (1934); Lewis Corey, *The Crises of the Middle Class* (1935); Irving Fisher, *The Stock Market Crash and After* (1930); W. B. Donham, *Business Adrift* (1931) and J. M. Clark, *Strategic Factors in Business Cycles* (1934). Other important works on this topic are F. C. Mills, *Economic Tendencies in the United States,* previously cited; National Industrial Conference Board, *Major Forces in World Business Depression* (1931); Broadus Mitchell, *Depression Decade* (1947); W. C. Schluter, *Economic Cycles and Crises* (1933); E. M. Patterson, *The World's Economic Dilemma* (1930); F. T. Pecora, *Wall Street Under Oath* (1939), the revelations by the attorney for the Senate Committee on Banking about activities of Wall Street during the twenties; G. V. Seldes, *The Years of the Locust* (*America, 1929–1932*) (1933); Norman Thomas, *The Plight of the Sharecropper* (1934); C. S. Johnson and others, *The Collapse of Cotton Tenancy* (1935), a statistical summary; Max Winkler, *Foreign Bonds, an Autopsy* (1933); and Dixon Wecter, *The Age of the Great Depression, 1929–1941* (1948), in the History of American Life series, first chapter of which is entitled "From Riches to Rags."

The Government and the Depression. Mr. Hoover's methods of dealing with the depression are discussed at length by W. S. Myers and W. H. Newton, *The Hoover Administration: A Documented Narrative* and R. L. Wilbur and A. M. Hyde, *The Hoover Policies,* both previously cited. These may be supplemented by W. S. Myers, (ed.), *The State Papers and Other Public Writings of Herbert Hoover,* cited earlier. Also consult T. G. Joslin, *Hoover Off the Record* (1934), by a former secretary; R. G. Tugwell, *Mr. Hoover's Economic Policy* (1932), critical and valuable; and W. W. Waters, *B. E. F.: The Whole Story of the Bonus Army* (1933), the story of veterans' bonus demands. On the campaign of 1932 and Hoover's defeat, the best account is R. V. Peel and T. C. Donnelly, *The 1932 Campaign,* cited above. F. D. Roosevelt, *Looking Forward* (1933) includes Roosevelt's more important campaign speeches. For election statistics, see E. E. Robinson, *The Presidential Vote, 1896–1932* (1934).

CHAPTER XVI

The New Deal and American Capitalism

The literature on the New Deal is already immense and with each passing year becomes larger. Perhaps the best introductory survey is D. W. Brogan, *The Era of Franklin D. Roosevelt: A Chronicle of the New Deal and Global War* (1950), in the Chronicles of America series. D. L. Dumond, :*From Roosevelt to Roosevelt,* cited earlier, is extremely good on the shift from Hoover to Roosevelt. Basil Rauch, *History of the New Deal 1933–38* (1944) is a first-rate appraisal. Other valuable works are C. A. Beard and G. H. E. Smith, *The Old Deal and the New* (1940); C. A. Beard, *The Future Comes: A Study of the New Deal* (1933); E. K. Lindley, *Half Way With Roosevelt* (rev. ed., 1937) and *The Roosevelt Revolution, First Phase* (1933); L. M. Hacker, *A Short History of the New Deal* (1934), which covers first year only, and his *Shaping of the American Tradition* (1947), sec. XI; Columbia University Commission, *Economic Reconstruction: Report of the Columbia University Commission* (1934); Broadus Mitchell, *Depression Decade: From New Era Through New Deal, 1929–1941* (1947); Leo Gurko, *The Angry Decade* (1947); F. D. Roosevelt, *On Our Way,* cited above; S. C. Wallace, *The New Deal in Action* (1934); C. A. and M. R. Beard, *America in Midpassage* (1939), Volume III of *The Rise of American Civilization;* B. L. Landis, *The Third American Revolution:*

An Interpretation (1933); A. M. Schlesinger, *The New Deal in Action, 1933–1939* (1940); Stuart Chase, *A New Deal* (1932); George Soule, *A Planned Society* (1934) and *The Coming American Revolution* (1934), and *The Future of Liberty* (1936); and L. P. Ayres, *Economics of Recovery* (1934), which discusses the early stages of New Deal. On Roosevelt and his Administrations *The Public Papers and Addresses of Franklin D. Roosevelt* (9 vols., 1938–41), edited by Roosevelt himself and S. I. Rosenman, are basic. Roosevelt's early speeches and comments appear in *Looking Forward* and *On Our Way,* cited above; later ones can be found in *Rendezvous with History* (1944) and *Nothing to Fear* (1946). Useful in understanding the New Deal and its chief protagonist are the following personal accounts, biographies, and memoirs: Eleanor Roosevelt, *This Is My Story* (1939), which is autobiographical; E. K. Lindley, *Franklin D. Roosevelt: A Career in Progressive Democracy* (1931), a campaign biography; Emil Ludwig, *Roosevelt: A Study in Fortune and Power* (1938); Gerald Johnson, *Roosevelt: Dictator or Democrat?* (1941); R. E. Sherwood, *Roosevelt and Hopkins: An Intimate History* (1948); Frances Perkins, *The Roosevelt I Knew* (1946), full of approbation; H. L. Ickes, *Back to Work: The Story of P. W. A.* (1935) and *The Autobiography of a Curmudgeon* (1943), which is pungent; D. C. Roper, *Fifty Years of Public Life* (1941), colorless; J. A. Farley, *Jim Farley's Story: The Roosevelt Years* (1948); Raymond Moley, *After Seven Years* (1939), which reflects disenchantment; Cordell Hull, *Memoirs* (2 vols., 1948); I. H. Hoover, *Forty-Two Years in the White House,* cited earlier; E. W. Starling and Thomas Sugrue, *Starling of the White House* (1946); R. T. McIntire, *White House Physician* (1946); Huey Long, *Every Man a King* (1933); F. E. Townshend, *New Horizons* (1943); H. L. Stimson, *On Active Service in Peace and War* (1948); and J. F. Byrnes, *Speaking Frankly* (1947); Karl Schriftgiesser, *The Amazing Roosevelt Family, 1613–1942* (1942); and John Gunther, *Roosevelt in Retrospect* (1950), an excellent character analysis. Very critical are J. P. Warburg, *Hell Bent for Election* (1936); J. T. Flynn, *Country Squire in the White House* (1940); and William MacDonald, *The Menace of Recovery* (1934); Norman Thomas, *After the New Deal What?* (1936); Herbert Hoover, *The Challenge to Liberty,* cited above, and *Addresses upon the American Road, 1933–1938* (1938); Benjamin Stolberg and W. J. Vinton, *The Economic Consequences of the New Deal* (1935); D. R. Richberg, *Rainbow* (1936), a study in disillusionment; Eli Ginzberg, *Illusion of Economic Stability* (1939); F. A. Von Hayek, *Collectivist Economic Planning* (1935); M. A. Hallgren, *The Gay Reformer* (1935) and Lewis Corey, *The Decline of American Capitalism* (1934).

The Nature of the New Deal. In addition to the above works the following will be found helpful: Mordecai Ezekiel, *$2500 a Year: From Scarcity to Abundance* (1936); H. A. Wallace, *America Must Choose* (1934) and *New Frontiers* (1934); R. G. Tugwell, *The Industrial Discipline and the Governmental Arts* (1933) and *The Battle for Democracy* (1935); H. W. Laidler, *A Program for Modern America* (1936); Walter Lippmann, *The Method of Freedom* (1934), critical; A. B. Adams, *National Economic Security* (1936); Brookings Institution, *Recovery Problem in the United States* (1937); and "The New Deal: An Analysis and An Appraisal," *London Economist,* October 5, 1936, a balanced viewpoint from an English source.

The Politics of the New Deal. See the works already listed for this chapter, especially the personal material; and J. T. Salter (ed.), *American Politician* (1938); A. M. Landon, *America at the Crossroads,* cited previously, which gives the views of the Republican candidate in the presidential campaign of 1936; Wendell Willkie, *This is Wendell Willkie* (1940), a collection of campaign speeches; J. McG. Burns, *Congress on Trial* (1949), which analyzes the work of World War II and postwar Congresses; W. B. Hesseltine, *The Rise and Fall of Third Parties from Anti-Masonry to Wallace* (1948); and C. A. M. Ewing's *Presidential Elections from Abraham Lincoln to Franklin D. Roosevelt* (1940) and *Congressional Elections, 1896–1944* (1947), both of which are highly statistical, as is E. E. Robinson, *They Voted for Roosevelt: The Presidential Vote, 1932–44* (1947). On third and fourth terms, consult C. W. Stein, *The Third Term Tradition* (1943). J. A. Farley, *Behind the Ballots: The Personal History of a Politician* (1938) is informing on the election of 1936. On expansion of government, see G. C. S. Benson, *The New Centralization* (1941); K. G. Crawford, *The Pressure Boys* (1939); E. P. Herring, *Public Administration and the Public Interest* (1936); A. N. Holcombe, *The New Party Politics* (1933); F. R. Kent, *Without Grease* (1936); J. L. McCamy, *Government Publicity: Its Practice in Federal Administration* (1939); John McDiarmid, *Government Corporations and Federal Funds* (1939); M. N. McGreary, *Development of Congressional Investigative Power* (1940); Stuart Chase, *Government in Business* (1935); A. C. Millspaugh, *Democracy, Efficiency, Stability: An Appraisal of American Government* (1942); and Thorsten Sellen and Donald Young, "Pressure Groups and Propaganda," *Annals of the American Academy of Political and Social Science,* Vol. CLXXIX (May, 1935). On governmental reorganization, see Lewis Meriam and L. F. Schmeckebier, *Reorganization of the National Government,* cited earlier. On expanding government costs, see Twentieth Century Fund, *Facing the Tax Problem* (1937) and Lucius Wilmerding, *The Spending Power* (1943). On the Supreme Court fight, consult E. S. Corwin, *Court Over Constitution* (1938), *The Twilight of the Supreme Court* (4th ed., 1935) and *Constitutional Revolution* (1941); E. M. Eriksson, *The Supreme Court and the New Deal* (1941), which has a good bibliography; R. H. Jackson, *The Struggle for Judicial Supremacy: A Study of a Crisis of American Power Politics* (1941); and Joseph Alsop and Turner Catledge, *The 168 Days* (1938), a popular treatment. See also M. L. Ernst, *The Ultimate Power* (1937); Irving Brant, *Storm over the Constitution* (1936); C. P. Curtis, *Lions under the Throne* (1947); B. H. Levy, *Our Constitution: Tool or Testament?* (1941); and Wesley McCune, *The Nine Young Men* (1947). C. H. Pritchett, *The Roosevelt Court* (1948) deals with cases and decisions during the Roosevelt period.

Banking and Currency Legislation. A good summary of the crisis is to be found in J. I. Bogen and Marcus Nadler, *The Banking Crisis* (1933). Also consult C. C. Chapman, *The Development of American Business and Banking Thought, 1913–1936* (rev. ed., 1936); E. D. Kennedy, *Dividends to Pay* (1939); B. H. Beckhart, *The New York Money Market* (4 vols., 1932); W. R. Burgess, *The Reserve Banks and the Money Market* (1936); N. H. Jacoby and R. J. Saulnier, *Business, Finance and Banking* (1948); H. G. Moulton, *The Financial Organization of Society* (1931); F. T. Pecora, *Wall Street Under Oath,* cited before; Emanuel Stein, *Government and the Investor* (1941); R. L. Weissman, *The New Federal Reserve System* (1936) and *The New Wall Street* (1939); and E. R. Taus, *Central Banking Functions of the United States Treasury, 1789–1941* (1943). For government and the banking business, see Reconstruction Finance Corporation, *Seven Year Report to the President and the Congress of the United States* (1939) and Jesse H. Jones with Edward Angly, *Fifty Billion Dollars: My Thirteen Years with the RFC (1932–1945)* (1951). Also consult H. J. Bittermann, *State and Federal Grants-in-Aid* (1938). Critical of the practices of the stock exchanges are J. T. Flynn, *Security Speculation, Its Economic Effects* (1934) and B. J. Reis, *False Security, The Betrayal of the American Investor* (1937). On guaranty of bank deposits, see Guy Emerson, "Guaranty of Deposits under the Banking Act of 1933," *Quarterly Journal of Economics,* Vol. XLVIII, pp. 229–44; A. D. Gayer, "The Banking Act of 1935," *Journal of Political Economy,* Vol. XLIII, pp. 743–62.

Money and Its Control. Consult *National Industrial Conference Board, The New Monetary System of the United States* (1934); Leo Pasvolsky, *Current Monetary Issues* (1933); Twentieth Century Fund, *Debts and Recovery, 1929–1937* (1938); A. W. Crawford, *Monetary Management Under the New Deal* (1940); and J. D. Paris, *Monetary Policies of the United States, 1932–1938* (1938), a detailed but very hostile treatment. A. Nussbaum, *Money in the Law, National and International* (1950) and G. G. Johnson, *The Treasury and Monetary Policy, 1933–1938* (1939) are useful for monetary policy and the history of fiscal developments. On special features, see R. B. Westerfield, *Our Silver Debacle* (1936); G. F. Warren and F. A. Pearson, *Prices* (1933); R. Cassady, Jr. and A. R. Lipgren, "International Trade and Devaluation of the Dollar, 1932–1934," *Quarterly Journal of Economics,* Vol. L, pp. 415–35; A. R. Lipgren, "Devaluation of the Dollar in Relation to Exports and Imports," *Journal of Political Economy,* Vol. XLIV, pp. 70–83; A. E. Harris, "British and American Exchange Policies: The American Experience," *Quarterly Journal of Economics,* Vol. XLVIII, pp. 686–726; and N. L. Silverstein, "Effects of the American Devaluation on Prices and Export Trade," *American Economic Review,* Vol. XXVII, pp. 279–93.

Curbing Competition and Monopoly. A. R. Burns, *The Decline of Competition* already cited, is useful on this topic. See also J. M. Clark, *The Social Control of Business,* cited earlier; L. S. Lyon and Victor Abramson, *Government and Economic Life* (2 vols., 1939–40); Merle Fainsod and Lincoln Gordon, *Government and the American Economy* (1941); L. S. Lyon and others, *The National Recovery Administration* (1935); M. F. Gallagher, *Government Rules Industry* (1934); C. F. Roos, *NRA Economic Planning* (1937); G. B. Galloway, *Industrial Planning under Codes* (1935); President's Committee of Industrial Analysis, *National Recovery Administration* (1937), a critical appraisal; E. T. Grether, *Price Control under Fair Trade Legislation* (1939); and H. S. Johnson, *The Blue Eagle from Egg to Earth* (1935), an account of the N.R.A. by its administrator. For the reaction of private enterprise to regulation, see S. H. Walker and Paul Sklar, *The Regulations of Collective Bargaining under the National Industrial Recovery Act.*

Labor Legislation. The best material on this subject is to be found in Emanuel Stein and others, *Labor and the New Deal* (1934) and C. R. Daugherty, *Labor under the NRA* (1934). Also see R. R. R. Brooks, *Unions of Their Own Choosing* (1939), which gives the background of Wagner Act; L. L. Lorwin and Arthur Wubnig, *Labor Relations Boards* (1935); S. H. Walker and Paul Sklar, *Business Finds Its Voice* (1938); Joseph Rosenfarb, *The National Labor Policy and How It Works* (1940); and Twentieth Century Fund, *Labor and the Government, An Investigation of the Rôle of the Government in Labor Relations* (1935) and, in briefer compass, *Governmental Protection of Labor's Right to Organize.* Trade practices under the N.R.A. and in other forms since its invalidation by the Supreme Court are best discussed in B. A. Zorn and C. J. Feldman, *Business under the New Price Laws* (1937); B. Werne (ed.), *Business and the Robinson-Patman Law* (1938); and Wright Patman, *The Robinson-Patman Act* (1938).

The Growth of Industrial Unionism. This topic is covered adequately by Herbert Harris, *American Labor* (1939) and *Labor's Civil War* (1940); M. R. Clark and S. F. Simon, *The Labor Movement in America* (1938); J. R. Walsh, *C.I.O.: Industrial Unionism in Action* (1937); Edward Levinson, *Labor on the March* (1938), violently anti-A.F. of L.; Benjamin Stolberg, *The Story of the CIO* (1938), which reaches conclusions based on incomplete evidence; Mary Vorse, *Labor's New Millions* (1938); H. R. Cayton and G. S. Mitchell, *Black Workers and the New Unions* (1939); Sterling Spero and A. H. Harris, *The Black Worker* (1931); Twentieth Century Fund, *Trends in Collective Bargaining* (1945); and H. R. Northrup, *Organized Labor and the Negro* (1944). Harold Seidman, *Labor Czars* (1938), discusses racketeering; Clinch Calkins, *Spy Overhead* (1937), describes industrial espionage. C. R. Walker, *American City, A Rank-and-File History* (1937) is a case history. The growth of unionism in an unorganized industry is traced by H. J. Lahne, *The Cotton Mill Worker* (1944). For the rising demands of military production, see Twentieth Century Fund, *Labor and National Defense* (1941).

Chapter XVII

Relief and Rehabilitation Under the New Deal

The general references listed at the beginning of Chapter 16 apply here as well.

Subsidizing the Commercial Farmer. See references under "The Government and the Farmer" in Chapter 15. To these should be added E. G. Nourse and others, *Three Years of the Agricultural Adjustment Administration* (1937); U. S. Department of Agriculture, *Yearbook of Agriculture, 1940* (1940), which gives briefly the background of New Deal legislation; H. I. Richards, *Cotton and the A.A.A.* (1936); J. S. Davis, *Wheat and the A.A.A.* (1935); H. B. Rowe, *Tobacco Under the A.A.A.* (1935); Harold Barger and H. H. Landsberg, *American Agriculture, 1899–1939* (1942); H. A. Wallace, *New Frontiers* (1934); C. T. Schmidt, *American Farmers in the World Crisis* (1941); E. G. Nourse, *Marketing Agreements Under the A.A.A.* (1935); Jules Backman, *Government Price Fixing* (1938); and O. E. Baker, Ralph Borsodi and M. L. Wilson, *Agriculture in Modern Life* (1939).

Aiding the Marginal Farmer. For the "little" farmer, consult E. deS. Brunner and J. H. Kolb, *Rural Social Trends* (1933); E. deS. Brunner and Irving Lorge, *Rural Trends in Depression Years . . . 1930–36* (1937); E. D. Sanderson, *Research Memorandum on Rural Life in the Depression* (1937); C. E. Lively and Conrad Taeuber, *Rural Migration in the United States* (1939); Stuart Chase, *Rich Land, Poor Land* (1936); F. M. Vreeland and E. J. Fitzgerald, *Farm-City Migration and Industry's Labor Reserve* (1939); J. N. Webb, *The Migratory-Casual Worker* (1937); U. S. Department of Labor, *Migration of Workers* (2 vols., 1938); Carey McWilliams, *Factories in the Field* (1939) and *Ill Fares the Land* (1942); C. C. Taylor, H. W. Wheeler and E. L. Kirkpatrick, *Disadvantaged Classes in American Agriculture* (1938); C. C. Zimmerman and N. L. Whetten, *Rural Families on Relief* (1938), C. S. Johnson, W. W. Alexander, and E. R. Embree, *The Collapse of Cotton Tenancy* (1935); A. F. Raper, *Preface to Peasantry* (1936); I. deA. Reid, *Share-croppers All* (1941); T. J. Woofter, Jr. and Ellen Winston, *Seven Lean Years* (1939); Waller Wynne, Jr., *Five Years of Rural Relief* (1938); Jonathan Daniels, *A Southerner Discovers the South* (1938); and R. G. Tugwell, *Stricken Land* (1947). John Steinbeck's *Grapes of Wrath* also sheds light on the problem of the rural migratory worker.

Relief Grants and Jobs for the Unemployed. Dixon Wecter, *The Age of the Great Depression, 1929–1941,* cited earlier, gives the over-all picture. It may be supplemented by A. D. Gayer, *Public Works in Prosperity and Depression* (1935); H. L. Hopkins, *Spending to Save, The Complete Story of Relief* (1936); H. L. Ickes, *Back to Work: The Story of P.W.A.* (1935); L. V. Armstrong, *We Too, Are the People* (1938), the story of relief in a Michigan village; Eli Ginzberg and associates, *Unemployed* (1943); J. N. Leonard, *Three Years Down* (1939); J. C. Brown, *Public Relief, 1929–1939* (1940); A. E. Burns and E. A. Williams, *A Survey of Relief and Security Programs* (1938) and *Federal Work, Security and Relief Programs* (1941); National Resources Planning Board, *Security, Work, and Relief Policies* (1942) and *Development of Resources and Stabilization of Employment in the United States* (1942); A. W. Macmahon, J. D. Millett, and Gladys Ogden, *The Administration of Federal Work Relief* (1941); J. F. Isakoff, *The Public Works Administration* (1938); F. S. Chapin and S. A. Queen, *Social Work in the Depression* (1937) and R. C. and M. K. White, *Research Memorandum on Social Aspects of Relief Policies in the Depression* (1937); Jacob Baker, *Concerning Government Benefits* (1936); George Biddle, *American Artist's Story* (1939); Willson Whitman, *Bread and Circuses* (1937), on the W.P.A. theater project; Grace Overmyer, *Government and the Arts* (1939); Hallie Flanagan, *Arena* (1940); Kenneth Holland and T. E. Hill, *Youth in the CCC Camps* (1942); L. L. Lorwin, *Youth Work Programs* (1941); D. G. Howard, *WPA and Federal Relief Policy* (1943), excellent; and D. S. Campbell, F. H. Bair, and O. L. Harvey, *Educational Activities of the Works Progress Administration* (1939). For the human side, see E. W. Bakke, *The Unemployed Worker* (1940) and *Citizens Without Work* (1940); J. M. Williams, *Human Aspects of Unemployment and Relief* (1933); and M. D. Lane and Francis Steegmuller, *America on Relief* (1938). On the subject of the usefulness of relief and pump-priming, consult H. L. Ickes, *Back to Work: The Story of P.W.A.* (1936) and J. K. Galbraith and C. G. Johnson, Jr., *Economic Effects of the Federal Public Works Expenditures, 1933–1938* (1940).

Social Security and Housing Program. The basic problem of social security is discussed by Abraham Epstein, *Insecurity, A Challenge to America* (rev. ed., 1938). See also Social Security Board, *Security in America* (1937); P. H. Douglas, *Social Security in the United States* (rev. ed., 1939); I. G. Carter (ed.), "Appraising the

Social Security Program," *Annals of the American Academy of Political and Social Science,* Vol. CCII, (1939); I. M. Rubinow, *The Quest for Security* (1934); E. M. Burns, *Toward Social Security* (1936); Lewis Meriam, *Relief and Social Security* (1946); James Parker, *Social Security Reserves* (1942); and Marietta Stevenson and Ralph Spear, *The Social Security Program* (1936). For valuable material on social security given for the most part by experts at congressional hearings, see *Social Security in America, the Factual Background of the Social Security Act, as Summarized from Staff Reports to the Committee on Economic Security* (1937). Pressure for old-age assistance is described in Twentieth Century Fund, *The Townsend Crusade* (1936).

Housing, as far as the New Deal was concerned, was part of the larger concept of planning, which in turn was thought of in terms of city and region. Although a definitive work on cities has yet to be written, see E. C. Ridley and O. F. Nolting (eds.), *What the Depression Has Done to Cities* (1935), which discusses, among other items, municipal finance, health, housing, hospitals, schools, and public libraries; National Resources Committee, *Status of City and County Planning in the United States* (1937) and *Our Cities* (1937); W. F. Ogburn, *Social Characteristics of Cities* (1937); G. R. Leighton, *Five Cities* (1939); and Lewis Mumford, *The Culture of Cities* (1938), which presents a brilliant case for planning.

The best works on housing are M. W. Straus and Talbot Wegg, *Housing Comes of Age* (1938), mainly about P.W.A. construction; E. E. Wood, *Recent Trends in American Housing* (1931) and *Slums and Blighted Areas in the United States* (1935), both illuminating; Harold Aronovici, *Housing the Masses* (1939), which has good bibliography; James Ford and others, *Slums and Housing, With Special Reference to New York City* (2 vols., 1936), which is detailed and good for historical perspective; James and K. M. Ford, *The Modern House in America* (1940), which discusses mostly new trends; L. W. Post, *The Challenge of Housing* (1938); T. R. Carskadon, *Houses for Tomorrow* (rev. ed., 1945); Nathan Straus, *The Seven Myths of Housing* (1944); and L. H. Pink, *The New Day in Housing* (1928). For an account of restrictions in the building trades, see the report of The Temporary National Economic Committee, *Toward More Housing* (1940).

On the region, see National Resources Committee, *Regional Factors in National Planning and Development* (1935). Other official agencies have also sponsored important reports. In the period between 1936 and 1943, for example, the National Resources Planning Board was responsible for thirteen *Regional Planning Reports,* beginning with the Pacific Northwest and closing with Puerto Rico. From the same source came in 1937, no less than twenty-two *Drainage Basin Reports.* Of nonofficial publications H. W. Odum and H. E. Moore, *American Regionalism: A Cultural Historical Approach to National Integration* (1938) is the most important. The principal experiment in regional planning is, to date, the T.V.A. On this, consult the authoritative volume by David Lilienthal, *TVA: Democracy on the March* (1945), which has a complete bibliography. Valuable also are C. L. Hodge, *The Tennessee Valley Authority* (1938), a scholarly presentation; Willson Whitman, *God's Valley* (1939), which stresses human angle; C. H. Pritchett, *TVA: A Study in Public Administration* (1943); R. L. Duffus and others, *The Valley and Its People* (1944); Russell R. Lord, *Behold Our Land* (1938); J. F. Carter, *The Future is Ours* (1939); Philip Selznick, *TVA and the Grass Roots* (1949), a sociological study; and Julian Huxley, *TVA: Adventure in Planning* (1943), an English view. R. L. Neuberger and S. B. Kahn, *Integrity: The Life of George W. Norris* (1937) is a second-rate biography of the person who perhaps more than anyone else was responsible for T.V.A. On T.V.A. and the power utilities, see J. C. Bonbright, *Public Utilities and the National Power Policies* (1940) and Twentieth Century Fund, *The Power Industry and the Public Interest,* already cited. On conservation, see Carter Goodrich and others, *Migration and Economic Opportunity,* previously cited, which stresses depressed and overpopulated areas; Resettlement Administration, *The Resettlement Administration* (1935); H. H. Bennett, *Conservation Farming Practices and Flood Control* (1936); Stuart Chase, *Rich Land, Poor Land,* cited above, and P. B. Sears, *Deserts on the March* (1935), both popular treatments; and A. E. Parkins and J. R. Whitaker (eds.), *Our National Resources and Their Conservation* (1936).

That the movement for conservation as well as other features of the New Deal was slowing down even before the coming World War II was evident to many. On this, see Harold Barger, *Outlay and Income in the United States, 1921–38* (1942); R. C. Epstein, *Industrial Profits in the United States* (1934); Solomon Fabricant, *Employment in Manufacturing, 1899–1939* (1942) and *Labor Savings in American Industry, 1899–1939* (1945); Simon Kuznets, *Commodity Flow and Capital Formation* (1938) and *National Income and Its Composition, 1919–1938* (2 vols., 1941); F. C. Mills, *Prices in Recession and Recovery, A Survey of Recent Changes* (1936); National Resources Committee, *Technological Trends and National Policy* (1937); and A. H. Hansen, *Full Recovery or Stagnation?* (1938), on the recession of 1937–8.

CHAPTER XVIII

American Culture in the Machine Age

During the last quarter of a century several attempts have been made to take inventory of American culture in the machine age. As a consequence there is a considerable body of literature that merits serious consideration. For background, see Crane Brinton, *Ideas and Men: The Story of Western Thought* (1950). Works of greatest significance and value are Van Wyck Brooks, *The Confident Years: 1885–1915* (1952), which recreates a generation of vigor, vitality, and variety; H. S. Commager, *The American Mind* (1950), which is concerned with American character and deals with such items as literature, journalism, philosophy, religion, sociology, economics, history, politics, law and architecture; Denis Brogan, *The American Character* (1944), a penetrating analysis of American life and institutions by an Englishman; H. J. Laski, *The American Democracy* (1948), by an Englishman well acquainted with America, who condemns its materialism and intolerance; Lloyd Morris, *Postscript to Yesterday; America: The Last Fifty Years* (1947), excellent on society, literature, and philosophy of the last half-century, and his *Not So Long Ago* (1949), which describes social changes with emphasis on the rôle of automobile, radio, and movies; and John Gunther, *Inside U. S. A.* (rev., 1951), a detailed, journalistic account that emphasizes the war years. For a social anthropologist's ideas of what is fundamentally American, see Margaret Mead, *Male and Female* (1949) and *And Keep Your Power Dry* (1943). Other works are C. A. and M. R. Beard, *America in Midpassage*, cited earlier; Mark Sullivan, *Our Times: The United States, 1900–1925*, Vol. VI; P. W. Slosson, *The Great Crusade and After, 1914–1928*, and Dixon Wecter, *The Age of the Great Depression, 1929–1941*, volumes in The History of American Life series, previously cited; H. B. Parkes, *The American Experience: An Interpretation of the History and Civilization of the American People* (1947), scholarly; D. L. Cohn, *Combustion on Wheels, An Informal History of the Automobile Age* (1944), for popular consumption; J. W. Chase (ed.), *Years of the Modern: An American Appraisal* (1949), a symposium contrasting the security of average American of the midtwentieth century with that of average American of 1900.

The Standardization of American Life. Much of the material bearing on this topic is to be found in the works listed above. Others that will be of outstanding value are R. S. and H. M. Lynd, *Middletown* (1929) and *Middletown in Transition* (1937); E. H. Gruening (ed.), *These United States* (2 vols., 1923–4); H. E. Stearns (ed.), *Civilization in the United States, An Inquiry by Thirty Americans* (1922); J. T. Adams, *Our Business Civilization*, cited earlier; Walter Johnson, *William Allen White's America* (1947); C. B. Davis, *The Age of Indiscretion* (1950); Laurence Greene, *The Era of Wonderful Nonsense* (1939); President's Research Committee on Social Trends, *Recent Social Trends in the United States*, cited previously; J. C.

Ransom, F. L. Owsley and others, *I'll Take My Stand* (1930); Caroline Ware, *Greenwich Village, 1920–30* (1935); F. L. Allen, *Only Yesterday*, cited before; Anna de Koven, *Women in Cycles of Culture* (1941), Alfred Bingham, *Insurgent America* (1935); Franz Alexander, *Our Age of Unreason* (rev. ed., 1951); T. H. Greer, *American Social Reform Movements: Their Patterns Since 1865* (1949); Ernie Pyle, *Home Country* (1947); and a series of articles "Recent Social Trends," *American Journal of Sociology*, Vol. LXVII (May, 1942). As contributions to the standardization of American life the automobile, airplane, movie, radio and television are important. On the automobile, see R. C. Epstein, *The Automobile Industry* (1928); E. D. Kennedy, *The Automobile Industry: The Coming of Age of Capitalism's Favorite Child* (1941), which is very good; C. B. Glasscock, *The Gasoline Age, the Story of the Men Who Made It* (1937); H. L. Barber, *Story of the Automobile* (1917); and C. L. Dearing, *American Highway Policy* (1941). On aviation, see "Fleet Birds of a Feather," *Fortune* (May, 1933) pp. 23 ff.; Henry A. Bruno, *Wings over America* (1942); W. F. Ogburn, *Social Effects of Aviation* (1946). There is also some material in J. H. Frederick, *Commercial Air Transportation* (rev. ed., 51). On communications, consult Paul Schubert, *The Electric Word: The Rise of Radio* (1928); A. E. Krows, *The Talkies* (1930); A. F. Harlow, *Old Wires and New Waves* (1936); Hadley Cantril and G. W. Allport, *The Psychology of Radio* (1935); H. S. Hettinger, "New Horizons in Radio," *Annals of the American Academy of Political and Social Science*, Vol. CCXIII (1941); Llewellyn White, *The American Radio* (1947); A. N. Goldsmith and H. A. Lescarboura, *This Thing Called Broadcasting* (1930); K. S. Tyler, *Modern Radio* (1944); and Hadley Cantril, *The Invasion from Mars* (1940), which deals with radio-generated mass hysteria. On the movies the best works are M. D. Haettig, *Economic Control of the Motion Picture Industry* (1944); Deems Taylor, M. Peterson, and B. Hale, *A Pictorial History of the Movies* (1943); Margaret Thorp, *America at the Movies* (1939); P. F. Lazarsfeld, *Radio and the Printed Page* (1940); W. M. Seabury, *The Public and the Motion Picture Industry* (1926); L. C. Rosten, *Hollywood: The Movie Colony, The Movie Makers* (1941) amusing; Lewis Jacobs, *The Rise of the American Film* (1939); Gilbert Seldes, *The Seven Lively Arts* (1924); R. A. Inglis, *Freedom of the Movies* (1947); and Edgar Dale, *The Content of Motion Pictures* (1935). For movie censorship, see R. G. Moley, *The Hays Office* (1945). Another valuable work on standardization of American life is Roger Burlinghame, *Engines of Democracy: Inventions and Society in Mature America* (1940). Newspapers, periodicals, and books are another medium of standardization. See Commission on Freedom of the Press, *A Free and Responsible Press: A General Report on Mass Communication: Newspapers, Radio, Motion Pictures, Magazines, and Books* (1947); R. W. Jones, *Journalism in the United States* (1947), which stresses the social-economic background of press; and F. L. Mott, *American Journalism: A History of Newspapers in the United States through 260 years: 1690 to 1950* (rev. ed., 1950), a good survey. Mott is also the authority on magazine literature; see his *A History of American Magazines*, Vol. III. It may be supplemented by Coulton Waugh, *The Comics* (1947). On books, see R. L. Duffus, *Our Starving Libraries* (1933), which discusses the impact of hard times; O. H. Cheney, *Economic Survey of the Book Industry, 1930–1931* (1931); Jacob Loft, *The Printing Trades* (1944), which emphasizes labor; Douglas Waples and R. W. Tyler, *What People Want to Read About* (1931); and A. P. Hackett, *Fifty Years of Best Sellers, 1895–1945* (1945).

Writers of the Lost Generation. Those interested in this topic and the one that follows would profit by consulting R. E. Spiller and others (eds.), *Literary History of the United States* and H. S. Commager, *The American Mind*, cited earlier; both have excellent bibliographies. Interpretive accounts are given in V. L. Parrington's *Main Currents in American Thought* (1930); M. Cowley, *Exile's Return* (rev. 1951); Alfred Kazin's *On Native Grounds* (1942); Oscar Cargill, *Intellectual America* (1941); J. W. Krutch, *The Modern Temper* (1929); and Harry Hartwick, *The Foreground of American Literature* (1934). See also P. H. Boynton, *Some Contemporary Americans* (1924), *More Contemporary Americans* (1927), and *America in Contemporary Fiction* (1940); S. P. Sherman, *On Contemporary Literature* (rev. ed., 1931) and *Points of View* (1924); H. L. Mencken, *A Book of Prefaces* (1917); Carl and Mark Van Doren, *American and British Literature since 1890* (rev. ed., 1939). A. H. Quinn, *American Fiction* (1936) and F. L. Pattee, *The New American Literature, 1890–1930* (1930) are lightweight in content and interpretation. For biographical and critical studies, see Norman Foerster (ed.), *The Reinterpretation of American Literature* (1928); Burton Rascoe, *Theodore Dreiser* (1925); J. L. Jessup, *The Faith of our Feminists* (1950); F. O. Matthiessen, *Theodore Dreiser* (1951); Dorothy Dudley, *Forgotten Frontiers: Dreiser and the Land of the Free* (1932); B. R. Redman, *Edwin Arlington Robinson* (1926) Herman Hagedorn, *Edwin Arlington Robinson* (1938); Emory Neff, *Edward Arlington Robinson* (1948); F. O. Matthiessen, *The Achievement of T. S. Eliot* (1935); D. D. Paige (ed.), *The Letters of Ezra Pound, 1907–1941* (1950); R. M. Lovett, *Edith Wharton* (1925); and Percy Lubbock, *A Portrait of Edith Wharton* (1947); W. Manchester, *Disturber of the Peace* (1950); A. Mizener, *The Far Side of Paradise* (1951). The best authorities on poetry are Alfred Kreymborg, *A History of American Poetry* (1934); Conrad Aiken, *Scepticisms* (1919); Louis Untermeyer, *The New Era in American Poetry* (1919); Amy Lowell, *Tendencies in Modern American Poetry* (1917); Harriet Monroe, *Poets and Their Art* (1926); and Babette Deutsch, *This Modern Poetry* (1935). Two works do justice to the drama: A. H. Quinn, *A History of the American Drama from the Civil War to the Present* (rev. ed., 1936) and J. W. Krutch, *The American Drama Since 1918* (1939).

Literature of Protest and Affirmation. In addition to the references listed for this chapter the following are most important: H. E. Luccock, *American Mirror: Social, Ethical and Religious Aspects of American Literature, 1930–1940* (1940); Granville Hicks, *The Great Tradition* (rev. ed., 1935); Maxwell Geismar, *Writers in Crisis* (1942) and *The Last of the Provincials* (1947); J. W. Beach, *American Fiction, 1920–1940* (1941); Leo Gurko, *The Angry Decade*, cited earlier; and W. M. Frohock, *The Novel of Violence in America, 1920–1950* (1950). The character of the literature of protest and affirmation can perhaps be best understood by reading it, rather than reading about it. Recommended in this respect are writings of Sinclair Lewis, particularly his *Main Street* (1920) and other novels satirizing self-satisfied middle-class America; Brand Whitlock, *J. Hardin & Son* (1923); Edgar Lee Masters, *The Spoon River Anthology* (1915); Sherwood Anderson, *Winesburg, Ohio* (1919); F. S. Fitzgerald, *This Side of Paradise* (1921), *The Beautiful and Damned* (1922), *Tender is the Night* (1934) *The Great Gatsby* (1925) and *The Last Tycoon* (1941). Even more outspoken were the writers of the thirties: Theodore Dreiser, *An American Tragedy* (1925) and *Tragic America* (1931); James Farrell, *Studs Lonigan* (1935); John Dos Passos, *U. S. A.* (1937); Thomas Wolfe, *Of Time and the River* (1935) and *The Web and the Rock* (1939); John Steinbeck, *The Grapes of Wrath* (1939); and Erskine Caldwell, *Tobacco Road* (1932). See also J. W. Aldridge, *After the Lost Generation.*

The Arts. O. W. Larkin, *Art and Life in America* (1949) has an excellent bibliography. Good for background is F. P. Keppel and R. L. Duffus, *The Arts in American Life* (1933). Jacob Baker, *Government Aid During the Depression to Professional, Technical and Other Service Workers* (1936) and Grace Overmyer, *Government and the Arts* (1939) are informative. See also Martha Cheney, *Modern Art in America* (1939); H. Cahill and A. H. Barr (eds.), *Art in America in Modern Times* (1935); and Augustus St. Gaudens, *The American Artist and His Times* (1941). On painting and sculpture, see Sheldon Cheney, *The Story of Modern Art* (1941); Peyton Boswell, Jr., *Modern American Painting* (1940), an excellent text; C. B. Ely, *The Modern Tendency in American Painting* (1925); Frederick Wight, *Milestones of American Painting in our Century* (1949); Samuel Kootz, *Modern American Painters* (1930); Robert Henri, *The Art Spirit* (1923); The Museum of Modern Art Catalogue, *New Horizons in American Art* (1936), which shows the best work done under the W.P.A.; Lorado Taft, *The History of American Sculpture* (rev. ed., 1924); A. V. Adams, *The Spirit of American Sculpture* (1923); and most important of all Joseph Hudnut, *Modern Sculpture* (1929). There is much valuable material in George Biddle, *An American Artist's Story* (1939), autobiography of the father of Federal art program; T. H. Benton, *An Artist in America* (1937); Rockwell Kent, *This Is My Own* (1940); H. A. Read, *Robert Henri* (1931); Elisabeth Cary, *George Luks* (1931); G. P. DuBois, *William J. Glackens* (1931); Royal Cortissoz, *Guy Pène DuBois* (1931); and Constance Rourke, *Charles Sheeler* (1938). On music, see C. Reis, *Composers in America* (1938); J. T. Howard's detailed and authoritative *Our American Music* (3rd ed., 1946); Aaron Copland, *Our New Music* (1941); Isaac Goldberg, *Tin Pan Alley* (1930); Herbert Graf, *The Opera and Its Future in America* (1941); Lazare Saminsky, *Music of Our Day* (rev. ed., 1939); and D. G. Mason, *The Dilemma of American Music* (1928). For popular music, consult S. W. Finkelstein, *Jazz: A People's Music* (1948); H. O. Osgood, *So This is Jazz* (1926); W. Sargeant, *Jazz Hot and Hybrid* (1939); and Gilbert Seldes, *The Seven Lively Arts,* cited above. For biographic material, see J. T. Howard, *Our Contemporary Composers* (1941). On architecture, see John McAndrew, *Guide to Modern Architecture, Northeast States* (1940) and Elizabeth Mock (ed.), *Built in U. S. A., 1932–1944* (1944); Talbot Hamlin, *Architecture, An Art for All Men* (1947); F. L. Wright, *Modern Architecture* (1931); T. E. Tallmadge, *The Story of Architecture in America* (1927); S. Fiske Kimball, *American Architecture* (1928); G. H. Edgell, *The American Architecture of Today* (1928); and W. A. Starrett, *Skyscrapers and the Men Who Build Them* (1928). Extremely useful also are R. A. Cram, *My Life in Architecture* (1936), by an exponent of Gothic; F. L. Wright, *An Autobiography* (1932), by a champion of the modern; and L. H. Sullivan, *The Autobiography of An Idea* (1924), which emphasizes the relation of architecture to society.

Science, Religion and Education. For general introductions to physical science in the machine age, read S. M. and L. F. Rosen, *Technology and Society* (1941) and Lewis Mumford, *Technics and Civilization* (1934). These may well be followed by Bernard Jaffe's useful study, *Men of Science in America: the Role of Science in the Growth of Our Country* (1944); James Stokley, *Science Remakes Our World* (1946); Harold Ward (ed.), *New Worlds in Science* (1941); J. E. Thornton, *Science and Social Change* (1939); National Resources Committee, *Technological Trends and National Policy* (1937) and *Energy Resources and National Policy* (1939); and Bernard Jaffe, *Outposts of Science* (1935). On particular subjects, see R. T. Young, *Biology in America* (1922); G. W. Gray, *New World Pictures* (1936), an introduction to physics and astronomy; E. P. Hubble, *The Observational Approach to Cosmology* (1937); H. B. Lemon, *From Galileo to Cosmic Rays* (1934); G. R. Harrison, *Atoms in Action* (1939); A. K. Solomon, *Why Smash Atoms?* (1940); R. A. Millikan, *Electrons (+ and −), Protons, Photons, Neutrons, Mesotrons and Cosmic Rays* (rev. ed., 1947), somewhat technical, and his *Autobiography* (1950); Richard Goldschmidt, *Ascaris* (1937), a summary of basic knowledge in biology; T. H. Morgan, *The Scientific Basis of Evolution* (2nd. ed., 1935); W. B. Cannon, *The Wisdom of the Body* (rev. ed., 1939), physiologic advances; E. E. Freudenthal, *Flight into History: The Wright Brothers and the Air Age* (1949); Henry Borsook, *Vitamins* (1940); William S. Haynes, *Men, Money and Molecules* (1936); Wheeler McMillen, *New Riches from the Soil* (1946); and L. I. Dublin, "Science in Modern Industry," *Annals of the American Academy of Political and Social Science,* Vol. CXIX (1925). For the advances in medicine, see Paul de Kruif, *The Fight for Life* (1938), which is somewhat emotional; Harold Ward (ed.), *New Worlds in Medicine* (1946); B. J. Stern, *Society and Medical Progress* (1941) and *American Medical Practice in the Perspectives of a Century* (1945), both concerned with social implications; M. M. Davis, *America Organizes Medicine* (1941); H. E. Sigerest, *Medicine and Human Welfare* (1941); G. W. Gray, *The Advancing Front of Medicine* (1941); R. H. Shryock, *The Development of Modern Medicine* (1947); and James Rorty, *American Medicine Mobilizes* (1939), which describes clash between American Medical Association and sponsors of the Wagner health bill of 1938. Biographic material of importance is to be found in Helen Clapesattle, *The Doctors Mayo* (1941) and S. R. and F. T. Flexner, *William Henry Welch and the Heroic Age of American Medicine* (1941). On medical care, see Hugh Cabot, *The Doctor's Bill* (1935).

The social sciences await a comprehensive study. H. S. Commager's *The American Mind,* already cited, will prove most helpful. See also H. E. Barnes, *The New History and the Social Studies* (1925) and, M. G. White, *Social Thought in America* (1949). For economic thought, consult P. T. Homan, *Contemporary Economic Thought* (1928); Joseph Dorfman, *The Economic Mind in American Civilization,* Vol. III, cited previously; H. W. Odum (ed.), *American Masters of Social Science* (1927); W. T. Hutchinson (ed.), *Essays in American Historiography* (1937); G. A. Lundberg and others, *Trends in American Sociology* (1929); H. E. Barnes and Howard Becker, *Social Thought from Lore to Science* (1938); C. H. Page, *Class and American Sociology* (1940); and F. N. House, *The Development of Sociology* (1936). Three autobiographic accounts will also prove helpful: E. A. Ross, *Seventy Years of It* (1936); R. T. Ely, *Ground Under Our Feet* (1938); and J. R. Commons, *Myself* (1934). The religious situation in the machine age is discussed by H. S. Commager, *The American Mind,* cited earlier. See also H. K. Rowe, *The History of Religion in the United States* (1924), the concluding chapter; T. C. Hall, *The Religious Background of American Culture* (1930); A. B. Bass, *Protestantism in the United States* (1929), an inventory; W. A. Brown, *The Church in America; A Study of the Present Condition and Future Prospects of American Protestantism* (1922); H. P. Douglass, *The Church in the Changing City* (1927); H. P. Douglass and E. deS. Brunner, *The Protestant Church as a Social Institution* (1935); J. A. Ryan, *Seven Troubled Years, 1930–1936* (1937), the situation as seen by a liberal Catholic; and Marcus Bach, *They Have Found a Faith* (1946), which describes the cultists. Some of the religious spokesmen as well as others expressed concern about the weakening of family ties and the changing mores of youth. On this topic there is helpful material in E. R. Groves and W. F. Ogburn, *American Marriage and Family Relationships* (1928); A. G. Spencer, *The Family and Its Members* (1923), Elizabeth Benson, *The Younger Generation* (1927); Miriam Van Waters, *Parents on Probation* (1927) and *Our Changing Morality* (1928); and B. B. Lindsey, *The Revolt of Modern Youth* (1925). Of the extensive literature on education the following can be recommended: I. L. Kandel (ed.), *Twenty-Five Years of American Education* (1924) and E. W. Knight, *Education in the United States* (rev. ed., 1941); and A. E. Meyer, *The Development of Education in the Twentieth Century* (1939). Sanford Winston, *Illiteracy in the United States* (1930) is illuminating. It may be supplemented with John Dewey, *Democracy and Education* (1916); M. E. Curti, *The Social Ideas of American Educators* (1935); R. B. Raup, *Education and Organized Interests* (1936); W. S. Deffenbaugh, *Recent Movements in City School Systems* (1927); T. H. Briggs, *The Junior High School* (1920); H. B. Bruner, *The Junior High School at Work* (1925); and National Educational Association, *Education and Economic Well-being in American Democracy* (1940). On higher education, consult D. A. Robertson and E. R. Holme (eds.), *American Universities and Colleges* (1928). Thorstein Veblen, *The Higher Learning in America* (1918); R. M. Hutchins, *The Higher Learning in America* (1936); and J. E. Kirkpatrick, *The American College and Its Rulers* (1926) are all highly critical. Specific reforms in curricula may be reviewed in R. F. Butts, *The College Charts Its Course* (1939); Alexander Meiklejohn, *Freedom and the College* (1923) R. C. Brooks, *Reading for Honors at Swarthmore* (1927); Frank Aydelotte, *Honors Courses in American Colleges and Universities* (1924); Jacques Barzun and H. R. Steeves (eds.), *A College Program in Action* (1944), a description of educational programs in Columbia College; *Education in a Free Society* (1945) the famous Harvard Report; C. H. Faust (ed.), *The College at Chicago* (1949); and the Report of the President's Commission. Upton Sinclair, *The Goose Step* (1923) deals with academic freedom. See also R. H. Edwards, J. M. Artman, and G. M. Fisher, *Undergraduates: A Study of Morale in Twenty-three American Colleges and Universities* (1928); F. P. Keppel, *The Undergraduate and His College* (1917), sound advice by a great dean of an undergraduate college; Percy Marks, *Which Way Parnassus* (1926); J. A. Benn, *Columbus Undergraduate* (1928); R. L. Duffus, *Democracy Enters College* (1936); J. A. Hawes, *Twenty Years Among the Twenty Year Olds* (1929); R. S. Lynd, *Knowledge for What? The Place of the*

Social Science in American Culture (1939); J. U. Nef, *The United States and Civilization* (1942); and E. V. Hollis, *Philanthropic Foundations and Higher Education* (1938) discuss important items. On education for adults there is valuable material in L. E. Reber, *University Extension in the United States* (1914); Dorothy Rowden, *Two Handbooks on Adult Education* (1934, 1936); M. A. Cartwright, *Ten Years of Adult Education* (1935); and R. A. Beals and Leon Brody (comp.), *The Literature of Adult Education* (1941). There is a useful, brief account of education in the three volumes of the History of American Life series that spans the greater part of the first half of the twentieth century: H. U. Faulkner, *The Quest for Social Justice, 1898–1914;* P. W. Slosson, *The Great Crusade and After, 1914–1928* and Dixon Wecter, *The Age of the Great Depression, 1929–1941,* all previously cited.

Leisure and Recreation. The best historical treatment is F. R. Dulles, *America Learns to Play; A History of Popular Recreation, 1607–1940* (1940). Valuable also are J. F. Steiner, *Americans at Play* (1933), Gove Hambidge, *Time to Live* (1933), on the use of leisure time; R. B. Weaver, *Amusements and Sports in American Life* (1939); M. M. Willey and S. A. Rice, *Communication Agencies and Social Life* (1933), on touring, pleasure travel, and related matters; R. Cummings (ed.), *Dictionary of Sports* (1949); D. Houlgate, *The Football Thesaurus* (1946); R. M. Smith, *Baseball: A Historical Narrative* (1947); E. A. Rice, *A Brief History of Physical Education* (1926); A. M. Weyand, *American Football* (1926), historical L. F. Harmer, *Public Recreation: A Study of Parks, Playgrounds and Other Outdoor Recreation Facilities* (1928); L. H. Weir (ed.), *Parks, A Manual of Municipal and County Parks* (2 vols., 1928); and National Recreation Association, *Park Recreation Areas in the United States: 1940* (1940).

Chapter XIX

From Isolation to Intervention

For background, read Allan Nevins, *The New Deal and World Affairs* (1950), in the Chronicles of America series; C. G. Haines and R. J. S. Hoffman, *The Origins and Background of the Second World War* (2nd ed., 1947); J. W. Gantenbein, *Documentary Background of World War II, 1931–1941* (1943); Kenneth Ingram, *Years of Crisis, 1919–1945* (1947); D. E. Lee, *Ten Years: The World on the Way to War, 1930–1940* (1942); F. L. Schuman, *Design for Power* (1942); S. H. Roberts, *The House that Hitler Built* (1937); J. W. Wheeler-Bennett, *Pipe Dream of Peace: The Story of the Collapse of Disarmament* (1935); and J. T. Shotwell, *On the Rim of the Abyss* (1936). Other useful works are J. H. Borgese, *Goliath: The March of Fascism* (1937); V. M. Dean, *Europe in Retreat* (1941); Merze Tate, *The Disarmament Illusion* (1942); Gaetano Salvenini, *Under the Axe of Fascism* (1936) and *The Fascist Dictatorship in Italy* (1927); C. T. Schmidt, *The Corporate State in Action: Italy under Fascism* (1939); R. A. Brady, *The Spirit and Structure of German Fascism* (1937); F. L. Neumann, *Behemoth, The Structure and Practice of National Socialism* (1944); Gustav Stolper, *German Economy, 1870–1940* (1940); Herman Rauschning, *The Revolution of Nihilism: Warning to the West* (1939), and *Voice of Destruction* (1940); Otto Tolischus, *They Wanted War* (1940); W. L. Shirer, *Berlin Diary* (1934–1941) (1941); and G. E. R. Gedye, *Betrayal in Central Europe; Austria and Czechoslovakia: The Fallen Bastions* (1939). The best account of what official England was observing and thinking about the European scene is set forth in W. S. Churchill's war history, *The Gathering Storm* (1948). For Russia, consult F. L. Schuman, *Soviet Politics at Home and Abroad* (1946); Rudolph Schlesinger, *The Spirit of Post-War Russia: Soviet Ideology, 1917–1946* (1947); Julian Towster, *Political Power in the USSR, 1917–1947* (1948); and Isaac Deutscher, *Stalin: A Political Biography* (1949).

Peace at Bargain Rates. C. A. Beard, *American Foreign Policy in the Making, 1932–1940* (1946) is severely critical of Roosevelt policies. See N. J. Spykman,

America's Strategy in World Politics (1942); F. H. Simonds, *American Foreign Policy in the Post-War Years* (1935); P. C. Jessup, *International Security: The American Rôle in Collective Action for Peace* (1935); Dexter Perkins, *America and Two World Wars* (1944); Cordell Hull, *Memoirs of Cordell Hull* (1948); and J. F. Rippy, *America and the Strife of Europe* (1938).

Marine Diplomacy. Consult the references in the preceding paragraph and, in addition, Volume X of S. F. Bemis (ed.), *The American Secretaries of State,* cited previously; Allan Nevins, *The United States in a Chaotic World* (1950), in the Chronicles of America series; W. A. Myers, *The Foreign Policies of Herbert Hoover, 1929–1933;* R. L. Buell, *The Washington Conference* and Ichihashi Yamato, *The Washington Conference and After,* all previously cited; and Allan Nevins, *America in World Affairs* (1941).

The Good Neighbor Policy. The most authoritative accounts are S. F. Bemis, *The Latin American Policy of the United States* (1943); J. F. Rippy, *Latin America in World Politics* (rev. ed., 1938) and *The Caribbean Danger Zone* (1940); H. C. Herring, *Good Neighbors* (1941); Carnegie Endowment for International Peace, *The International Conferences of American States* (2 vols., 1931–40); C. L. Jones, *The Caribbean Since 1900* (1936); C. A. Beard, *The Open Door at Home* (1934); Sumner Welles, *The Time for Decision* (1944); A. P. Whitaker, *Americas to the South* (1939); and *The United States and South America, The Northern Republics* (1948); L. D. Baldwin, *The Story of the Americas* (1943); Lawrence Duggan, *The Americas: The Search for Hemispheric Security* (1949); Dexter Perkins, *Hands Off: A History of the Monroe Doctrine* (1941); M. W. Williams, *The Peoples and Politics of Latin America* (rev. ed., 1945); Duncan Aikman, *The All-American Front* (1940); Virginia Prewett, *The Americas and Tomorrow* (1944); Charles Wertenbaker, *A New Doctrine for the Americas* (1941); Frank Tannenbaum, *Mexico* (1950); Carleton Beals, *The Coming Struggle for Latin America* (1938); W. A. M. Burden, *The Struggle for Airways in Latin America* (1943); C. G. Fenwick, *The Inter-American Regional System* (1949); Ray Josephs, *Latin America: Continent in Crisis* (1948); G. H. Stuart, *Latin America and the United States* (4th ed., 1943); and T. R. Ybarra, *America Faces South* (1939). The *Survey of American Foreign Relations,* issued annually by the Council on Foreign Relations, and the Foreign Policy Reports for the decade of the thirties are especially valuable.

Retreat in the Far East. The best works on this topic are T. A. Bisson, *America's Far Eastern Policy* (1945); J. C. Grew, *Ten Years in Japan* (1944); W. W. Willoughby, *Japan's Case Examined* (1940); W. C. Johnstone, *The United States and Japan's New Order* (1941); Hugo Byas, *Government by Assassination* (1942); Otto Tolischus, *Tokyo Record* (1943); S. K. Hornbeck, *The United States and the Far East* (1942); H. S. Quigley, *Far Eastern War, 1937–1941* (1942); H. S. Quigley and G. H. Blakeslee, *The Far East: An International Survey* (1938); J. K. Fairbank, *The United States and China* (1948); F. R. Dulles, *China and America . . . since 1784* (1946) and *Forty Years of American-Japanese Relations* (1937); A. W. Griswold, *The Far Eastern Policy of the United States* (1938); J. C. Grew, *Ten Years in Japan* (1944); E. A. Falk, *From Perry to Pearl Harbor* (1943); S. E. Morison, *The Rising Sun in the Pacific, 1931–1942* (1948); Owen Lattimore, *Manchuria, Cradle of Conflict* (1932); Nathaniel Peffer, *Prerequisites to Peace in the Far East* (1940); H. L. Stimson, *The Far Eastern Crisis* (1936).

The Quest for Neutrality. See the general works listed at the beginning of this chapter and C. G. Fenwick, *American Neutrality, Trial and Failure* (1940); W. E. Rappard, *The Quest for Peace Since the World War* (1940); Herbert Feis, *The Road to Pearl Harbor* (1950); United States, Department of State, *Peace and War, United States Foreign Policy, 1931–1941* (1943); J. R. Carlson, *Undercover* (1943); E. M. Earle, *Against This Torrent* (1941); R. L. Buell, *Isolated America* (1940); H. F. Armstrong, *When There Is No Peace* (1939); Edwin Borchard and W. P. Page, *Neutrality for the United States* (rev. ed., 1940); Joseph Alsop and Robert Kintuer, *American White Paper: The Story of American Diplomacy and the Second World War* (1940); and A. W. Dulles and H. F. Armstrong, *Can America Stay Neutral?* (1939).

Isolationists and Interventionists. See the works listed above and C. A. Beard, *A Foreign Policy for America* (1940); H. W. Baldwin and Sheppard Stone (eds.), *We Saw It Happen* (1938); W. E. Dodd, Jr. and Martha Dodd (eds.), *Ambassador Dodd's Diary, 1933–1938* (1941); Meno Lovenstein, *American Opinion of Soviet Russia* (1941), based on current literature from 1917 to 1939; E. Tupper and G. E. McReynolds, *Japan in American Public Opinion* (1937); Walter Johnson, *The Battle Against Isolation* (1944); T. A. Bailey, *The Man in the Street* (1948); W. W. Willoughby, *Japan's Case Examined* (1940); Sumner Welles, *The Time for Decision* (1944); and W. H. Shephardson, *The Interests of the United States as a World Power* (1942); W. O. Scroggs, *The United States in World Affairs, 1939* (1940); Lewis Mumford, *Men Must Act* (1939); Harold Lavine and J. A. Wechsler, *War Propaganda and the United States* (1940); and Michael Sayers and A. E. Kahn, *Sabotage: The Secret War Against America* (1942). Also see W. L. Langer and S. E. Gleason, *The Challenge to Isolation, 1937–1940* (1952).

Pearl Harbor: America Goes to War. The best accounts to date on this topic are Forest Davis and E. K. Lindley, *How War Came* (1942); Basil Rauch, *Roosevelt, From Munich to Pearl Harbor* (1950); Winston Churchill, *The Second World War: Their Finest Hour* (1949); H. S. Commager, *The Story of the Second World War* (1945); Walter Millis, *This Is Pearl Harbor! The United States and Japan—1941* (1947); G. Morgenstern, *Pearl Harbor; The Story of the Secret War* (1947); and M. Grodzins, *Americans Betrayed, Politics and the Japanese Evacuation* (1949).

Chapter XX

World War II and Its Aftermath

The best introductory accounts are C. G. Haines and R. J. S. Hoffman, *Origins and Background of the Second World War,* cited earlier; W. S. Churchill, *The Second World War: The Gathering Storm, 1919–1939* (1948); Allan Nevins and L. M. Hacker, *The United States and Its Place in World Affairs, 1918–1943* (1943); R. W. Shugg and H. A. DeWeerd, *World War II, A Concise History* (1946); H. S. Commager, *The Story of the Second World War* (1945); and R. C. K. Ensor, *A Miniature History of the War* (2nd ed., 1946), an English view; Fletcher Pratt, *War for the World* (1950), in the Chronicles of America series; Floyd Cave and others, *Origins and Consequences of World War II* (1948); F. T. Miller, *History of World War II* (1946); W. P. Hall, *Iron out of Cavalry* (1946); Cyril Falls, *The Second World War* (1948), excellent; and J. F. C. Fuller, *The Second World War* (1939–45), far from objective. For longer accounts, see Edgar McInnis, *The War* (6 vols., 1940–6) and Sir Ronald Storrs and Philip Graves (eds.) *A Record of the War* (1940–47). This may be supplemented profitably by Winston Churchill's *The Second World War* (1948–50), five volumes of which have appeared, and his six volumes of wartime speeches: *While England Slept* (1938); *Blood, Sweat, and Tears* (1941); *The Unrelenting Struggle* (1942); *The End of the Beginning* (1943); *Onward to Victory* (1944); and *The Dawn of Liberation* (1945). *The Public Papers and Addresses of Franklin D. Roosevelt,* cited previously, will also prove to be helpful in adding light to these several-volume histories of the war. See also Walter Millis (ed.), *The Forrestal Diaries* (1951). Waverley Root, *The Secret History of the War* (3 vols., 1945–6) is rich in details, but anti-Department of State. American preparation for war in terms of man power and other resources is best described by H. J. Tobin and P. W. Bidwell, *Mobilizing Civilian America* (1940); United States Office of Facts and Figures, *The American Preparation for War* (1942); Pendleton Herring, *The Impact of War* (1941); W. F. Ogburn and others, *American Society in Wartime* (1943); L. B. Hershey, *Selective Service in Peacetime* (1941) and *Selective Service in Wartime* (1942, 1944, 1945); S. Menefee, *Assignment: U. S. A.* (1943); M. Rosebery, *This Day's Madness* (1944); D. M. Nelson, *Arsenal of Democracy, The Story of American War Production* (1946); S. E. Harris, *The Economics of America at War* (1943) and *Price and Related Controls in the United States* (1945); Emanuel Stein, J. D. Magee, and W. J. Ronan, *Our War Economy: Government, Production, Finance* (1943); S. H. Slichter, *The American Economy* (1948); Emanuel Stein and Jules Backman, *War Economics* (1942); G. H. Moore, *Production of Industrial Materials in World War I and II* (1944); War Production Board, *War Production in 1945* (1946); F. A. Howard, *Buna Rubber: The Birth of an Industry* (1947); Smaller War Plants Corporation, *Economic Concentration and World War II* (1946); E. Stettinius, *Lend Lease, Weapon for Victory* (1944); Eliot Janeway, *The Struggle for Survival: A Chronicle of Economic Mobilization in World War II* (1951), Chronicles of America series.

Global War. Of the enormous literature dealing with the military and naval aspects of World War II, one must of necessity be selective. For the careful student, official sources are indispensable. The history of army operations is now being officially prepared under the title *The United States Army in World War II.* When completed, this set will probably run to a hundred volumes; eight have already been published under the competent editorship of K. R. Greenfield. The activities of the Air Force will be described in a series entitled *Army Air Forces in World War II.* Four volumes have appeared under the editorship of W. F. Craven and J. L. Cate. This work should be supplemented with the official *United States Strategic Bombing Survey.* A semiofficial *History of United States Naval Operations in World War II* is being published under the guidance of S. E. Morison. Seven volumes have already appeared. For maps, see the American Forces in Action series prepared by the War Department Historical Division. Useful in this respect is Francis Brown (ed.), *The War in Maps* (1944), based on maps that appeared in the *New York Times.* See Fletcher Pratt, *War for the World: A Chronicle of Our Fighting Forces in World War II* (1951), Chronicles of America series.

On sea power and the fight for control of the Atlantic, consult Bernard Brodie, *Sea Power in the Machine Age* (1941) and *A Guide to Naval Strategy* (1944); Fletcher Pratt, *The Navy's War,* (1944); W. D. Puleston, *The Influence of Sea Power in World War II* (1948); and Gilbert Cant, *America's Navy in World War II* (1943). For the battle of the Atlantic the authoritative work is S. E. Morison, *The Battle for the Atlantic, 1939–1943* (1947), Vol. I of the History of the United States Naval Operations series. Other works of importance are Gilbert Cant, *The War at Sea* (1942); D. S. Ballantine, *U. S. Naval Logistics in the Second World War* (1947); and Robert Carse, *There Go the Ships* (1942), the story of naval convoys to the Arctic, and his *Lifeline* (1943), which describes the work of the merchant marine.

For the war in the Pacific, see, in addition to the volumes of S. E. Morison's History of United States Naval Operations series, Gilbert Cant, *The Great Pacific Victory from the Solomons to Tokyo* (1946); W. F. Halsey and J. Bryan, *Admiral Halsey's Story* (1947); Clive Howard and Joe Whitley, *One Damned Island After Another* (1946), an account of Seventh Air Force; Frazier Hunt, *MacArthur and the War Against Japan* (1944); Foster Hailey, *Pacific Battle Line* (1944), which terminates with end of 1943; Walter Karig and Wellbourne Kelley, *Battle Report* (5 vols., 1944–9); L. H. Brereton, *The Brereton Diaries* (1946); John Hersey, *Men on Bataan* (1942) and *Into the Valley* (1943); C. P. Romulo, *I Saw the Fall of the Philippines* (1942); E. B. Miller, *Bataan Uncensored* (1949); Allison Ind, *Bataan, The Judgment Seat* (1944); and Richard Tregaskis, *Guadalcanal Diary* (1943). The fight for New Guinea is described by Pat Robinson, *The Fight for New Guinea* (1943) and G. H. Johnston, *The Toughest Fighting in the World* (1943). On Leyte Gulf, see J. A. Field, *The Japanese at Leyte Gulf: The Shō Operation* (1947); and C. Vann Woodward, *The Battle for Leyte Gulf* (1947). Roy Appleman and others, *Okinawa: The Last Battle* (1948) is informative. For China, consult Robert Hotz, *With General Chennault* (1943); C. L. Chennault, *Way of a Fighter* (1949); T. H. White (ed.), *The Stilwell Papers* (1948); and Jack Belden, *Retreat with Stilwell* (1944). On Burma, see C. J. Rolo, *Wingate's Raiders* (1944). For the atom bomb and Hiroshima, see H. D. Smyth, *Atomic Energy for Military Purposes* (1945); Bernard Brodie (ed.), *The Absolute Weapon:*

Atomic Power and World Order (1946); John Hersey, *Hiroshima* (1946); Cyril Falls, *The Nature of Modern Warfare* (1941); and Oliver Jensen, *Carrier War* (1945), important. The Pacific war from the angle of a Japanese can be obtained in Masuo Kato, *The Lost War* (1946).

On the war in the Mediterranean, see Philip Guedalla, *The Middle East, 1940–1942* (1944). W. L. Langer, *Our Vichy Gamble* (1947) is a first-rate summary. On the relation of Spain to the war, see C. J. H. Hayes, *Wartime Mission in Spain, 1942–45,* (1946); and T. J. Hamilton, *Appeasement's Child* (1943). On the African campaign the best accounts are A. C. Clifford, *The Conquest of North Africa, 1940–43,* (1943); Alan Moorehead, *The Mediterranean Front* (1942), and *Montgomery, a Biography* (1946). The official account by Sir B. L. Montgomery, *El Alamein to the River Sangro* (1948) should be read in connection with Strategicus, *From Dunkirk to Benghazi* (1941), by an anonymous British military critic, and Sir Frances de Guingand, *Operation Victory* (1947). The Italian campaign is handled adequately by Christopher Buckley, *The Road to Rome* (1945) and Alan Moorehead, *Eclipse* (1945). See also the four volumes prepared by the Historical Division of the War Department as part of its American Forces in Action series: *Anzio Beachhead* (1948), *Salerno* (1944), *From the Volturno to the Winter Line* (1944), and *The Winter Line* (1945). The best description of the fighting from the soldiers' point of view can be found in Ernie Pyle's *Brave Men* (1945). Other valuable accounts are R. M. Ingersoll, *The Battle is the Pay-Off* (1943); Wesley Gallagher, *Back Door to Berlin* (1943) and Richard Tregaskis, *Invasion Diary* (1944). The story of the landing of troops and supplies is told by S. E. Morison, *Operations in North African Waters* (1947–8); D. D. Eisenhower, *Crusade in Europe* (1948); and H. C. Butcher, *Three Years with Eisenhower* (1946).

For the war in the main European theater, see on planning the invasion D. D. Eisenhower, *Crusade in Europe,* cited above; Sir B. L. Montgomery, *Normandy to the Baltic* (1948); Sir Francis de Guingand, *Operation Victory,* cited above; Sir Gifford Martel, *Our Armoured Forces* (1945); Alan Melville, *First Tide* (1945); and Sir Frederick Morgan, *Overture to Overlord* (1950). The invasion itself is described by John Gunther, *D Day* (1944); C. C. Wertenbaker, *Invasion* (1944); J. M. Brown, *Many a Watchful Night* (1944); W. W. Chaplin, *The Fifty-two days* (1944); Everett Holles, *Unconditional Surrender* (1945); and Ralph Ingersoll, *Top Secret* (1946). Battles and campaigns are described by those in command in official reports and in personal accounts. Of the latter, see in addition to those of Eisenhower, Montgomery, Halsey, Stilwell and Chennault, already mentioned, the following: B. G. Wallace, *Patton and His Third Army* (1946); H. H. Arnold, *Global Mission* (1949); W. D. Leahy, *I Was There* (1950); Oliver LaFarge, *The Eagle in the Egg* (1949), the story of the Air Force Command; Stewart Alsop and Thomas Braden, *Sub Rosa* (1946), the history of the O.S.S.; G. S. Patton, *War As I Knew It* (1947); Robert Payne, *The Marshall Story: A Biography of General George C. Marshall* (1951); and Omar N. Bradley, *A Soldier's Story* (1951).

On the Battle of the Bulge, see R. E. Merriam, *Dark December* (1947) and S. L. A. Marshall, *Rendezvous with Destiny; Bastogne* (1948). For the Russian part in the struggle, see J. R. Deane, *The Strange Alliance* (1947); J. E. Davies, *Mission to Moscow* (1941) and W. E. D. Allen and Paul Misatoff, *The Russian Campaign of 1941–43* (1948) and *The Russian Campaigns of 1944–45* (1949). Germany's defeat is admirably described by B. H. L. Hart, *The German Generals Talk* (1948); Milton Shulman, *Defeat in the West* (1947); and H. R. Trevor-Roper, *The Last Days of Hitler* (1947).

The Civilian and the War. W. F. Ogburn (ed.), *American Society in Wartime* (1943); John Dos Passos, *State of the Nation* (1944); Carey McWilliams, *Prejudice; Japanese Americans: Symbol of Racial Intolerance* (1944); H. L. Childs and J. Whitton, *Propaganda by Shortwave* (1943); M. E. Curti, "The American Mind in Three Wars," *Journal of the History of Ideas,* Vol. III (June 1942); C. C. Pratt, *Psychology: The Third Dimension of War* (1942); G. B. Watson (ed.), *Civilian Morale* (1942); J. Goodman (ed.), *While You Were Gone: A Report on Wartime*

Life in the United States (1946). On wartime government and administration, consult W. H. Nichols and J. A. Vieg, *Wartime Government in Operation* (1943); W. J. Wilson and others, *The Beginnings of OPA* (1947); H. C. Mansfield and others, *A Short History of OPA* (1948); L. D. White (ed.), *Civil Service in Wartime* (1945); Luther Gulick, *Administrative Reflections from World War II* (1948); and Pendleton Herring, *Impact of War* (1941). On mobilizing science, see E. C. Andrus, D. W. Brouk, and others, *Advances in Military Medicine* (2 vols., 1948); J. P. Baxter, *Scientists Against Time* (1946); and H. D. Smyth, *Atomic Energy for Military Purposes* (1945).

On the economics of the war, see, in addition the works listed above, K. C. Stokes, *Regional Shifts in Population, Production and Markets, 1939–43* (1943); C. O. Hardy, *Wartime Control of Prices* (1941); Meyer Jacobstein and H. G. Moulton, *Effects of the Defense Program on Prices, Wages and Profits* (1941); F. C. Mills, *Prices in a War Economy* (1942); *National Product: War and Prewar* (1944) and *National Product in Wartime* (1945); W. L. Crum, J. H. Fennelly, and L. H. Seltzer, *Fiscal Planning for Total War* (1942). On economic warfare, consult Antonin Basch, *The New Economic Warfare* (1941); R. W. B. Clarke, *Britain's Blockade* (1940); Paul Emzig, *Economic Warfare, 1939–40* (1940); D. L. Gordon and Royden Dangerfield, *Hidden Weapon* (1947); C. L. Leith, J. W. Furness, and Cleona Lewis, *World Minerals and World Peace* (1943); and T. Reveille, *Spoil of Europe: The Nazi Technique in Political and Economic Conquest* (1941). On American labor and agriculture in wartime the best works are Aaron Levenstein, *Labor Today and Tomorrow* (1945); S. T. Willmans and Herbert Harris, *Trends in Collective Bargaining* (1945); W. W. Wilcox, *The Farmer in the Second World War* (1947).

Postwar Domestic Problems. Instead of solving our domestic problems, World War II aggravated them. On labor, see Aleine Austin, *The Labor Story, A Popular History of American Labor, 1786–1949* (1949), thin; Henry Millis and E. C. Brown, *From the Wagner Act to Taft-Hartley: A Study of National Labor Policy and Labor Relations* (1950); C. O. Gregory, *Labor and the Law* (rev. ed., 1949); C. E. Warne, K. W. Lumpkin and others, *Labor in Post-War America* (1949); Harold Metz, *Labor Policy of the Federal Government* (1945); F. H. Harrison and R. Dubin, *Patterns of Union Management Relations* (1947); L. Howe and A. Widick, *The U.A.W. and Walter Reuther* (1949); D. I. Ash and George Rifkin, *The Taft-Hartley Law* (1947); and C. A. Madison, *American Labor Leaders: The Personalities and Forces in the Labor Movement* (1950), pen portraits of sixteen labor leaders. On the veteran, consult C. G. Botte, *The New Veteran* (1946); R. S. Martin, *The Best Is None Too Good* (1948); J. H. Miller and J. S. Allen, *Veterans Challenge the Colleges* (1947); G. K. Pratt, *Soldier to Civilian* (1944); and H. A. Wallace, *Sixty Million Jobs* (1945). On civil rights, read *To Secure These Rights: Report of the President's Committee on Civil Rights* (1949); Ellis Arnall, *The Shore Dimly Seen* (1946); Hodding Carter, *Southern Legacy* (1950); Milton Konvitz, *The Constitution and Civil Rights* (1947). On debt and inflation there is a constantly growing literature. Much of the writing on these problems is to be found in the files of the *New York Times*, the *Nation*, *Fortune*, *Harpers*, and the *Atlantic*. See also Freda Utley, *The High Cost of Vengeance: How Our German Policy Is Leading Us to Bankruptcy and War* (1949); B. M. Anderson, *Economics and the Public Welfare: Financial and Economic History of the United States, 1914–1946* (1949); Seymour Harris (ed.), *Economic Reconstruction* (1945); C. C. Abbott, *Financing Business During......the Transition* (1946); B. M. Baruch and J. M. Hancock, *Report on War and Post War Adjustment Policies;* Board of Governors of Federal Reserve System, *Public Finance and Full Employment* (1945); J. M. Clark, *Demobilization of Wartime Economic Controls* (1944); M. G. de Chazeau, A. G. Hart, G. C. Means, and others, *Jobs and Markets* (1946); H. M. Groves, *Postwar Taxation and Economic Progress* (1946); C. B. Hoover, *International Trade and Domestic Employment* (1945); C. O. Hardy, *Prices, Wages, and Unemployment* (1946); A. D. H. Kaplan, *Liquidation of War Production* (1945); H. G. Moulton and K. T. Schlotterbeck, *Collapse or Boom at the End of the War* (1942); T. W. Schultz, *Agriculture in an Unstable Economy* (1945); J. H. Williams, *Postwar Monetary Plans and Other Essays* (1945); Twentieth Century Fund, *America's Needs and Resources* (1947); B. M. Anderson, J. M. Clark, and others, *Financing American Prosperity* (1946); Simon Kuznets, *National Income* (1946); and H. C. Murphy, *The National Debt in War and Transition* (1950). On Communism, see N. Weyl, *The Story of Disloyalty and Betrayal in American History* (1950); G. Marion, *The Communist Trials* (1949).

The United States and the United Nations. For a brief survey, read Arne Sigrid, *United Nations Primer* (1945). The case for world organization is ably presented by Crane Brinton, *From Many One: The Process of Political Integration and the Problem of World Government* (1948). F. A. Cave and others, *The Origins and Consequences of World War II* (1948) is rich in material on the United Nations. For background, see W. L. Willkie, *One World* (1943); H. A. Wallace, *The Century of the Common Man* (1943); J. C. Campbell and others, *The United States in World Affairs, 1945–1947* (1947); K. W. Colgrove, *The American Senate and World Peace* (1944); Emery Reves, *Anatomy of Peace* (1946); United States Department of State, Publications no. 2353, *The Charter of the United Nations* (1945) and no. 2774, *The Making of the Peace Treaties* (1947); E. S. Corwin, *The Constitution and World Organization* (1944); Norman Cousins, *Modern Man Is Obsolete* (1945); R. J. S. Hoffman, *Durable Peace: A Study in American National Policy* (1944); and J B. Whitton (ed.), *The Second Chance: America and the Peace* (1944). There is also valuable material in Cordell Hull, *The Memoirs of Cordell Hull,* cited earlier. On the structure and operation of the United Nations, consult L. M. Goodrich, and Edvard Hambro, *Charter of the United Nations, Commentary and Documents* (1946); Tom Galt, *How the United Nations Works* (1947); Louis Dolevit, *The United Nations, A Handbook of the New World Organization* (1946); *The United Nations at Work; Basic Documents* (1947); Julian Huxley, *UNESCO: Its Purpose and Philosophy* (1948); Herman Finer, *The United Nations Economic and Social Council* (1946); Clair Wilcox, *A Charter for World Trade* (1949); V. M. Dean, *The Four Cornerstones of Peace* (1946); and P. W. Bidwell, *The United States and the United Nations* (1943).

The United States and a Divided World. Dexter Perkins, *The Evolution of Domestic Foreign Policy* (1948) is an excellent survey. See also G. A. Almond, *The American People and Foreign Policy* (1950); J. C. Campbell and others, *The United States in World Affairs, 1945–1947* (1947) and *The United States in World Affairs, 1948–1949* (1949); E. A. Speiser, *The United States and the Near East* (1947); J. K. Fairbanks, *The United States and China* (1948); Crane Brinton, *The United States and Britain* (rev. ed., 1948); A. P. Whitaker, *The United States and South America, The Northern Republics* (1948); Carlos Davila, *We of the Americas* (1949); L. M. Goodrich and M. J. Carroll, *Documents on American Foreign Relations* (1945); K. S. Latourette, *The United States Moves Across the Pacific* (1946); H. J. Van Mook, *The Stakes of Democracy in Southeast Asia* (1950); William Reitzel, *The Mediterranean: Its Role in American Foreign Policy* (1948); W. B. Wilcox and R. B. Hall, *The United States in the Postwar World* (1947); H. J. Morgenthau, *Politics among Nations, the Struggle for Power and Peace* (1948); and Leland Stowe, *While Time Remains* (1946).

On the wartime trials and the occupation of Germany, consult R. H. Jackson, *The Case Against the Nazi War Criminals* (1946) and *The Nuremberg Case* (1947); Sheldon Glurek, *The Nuremberg Trials and Aggressive War* (1946); and Alexander Mitrokerich and Fred Miceke, *Doctors of Infamy, the Story of the Nazi Medical Crimes* (1949). On military occupation, see W. Friedmann, *The Allied Military Government of Germany* (1947); Harold Zink, *American Military Government in Germany* (1947); and C. J. Friedrich and others, *American Experiences in Military Government in World War II* (1948). The literature on atomic energy in a divided world grows larger. A few of the more important nontechnical works are D. V. Bradley, *No Place to Hide* (1948), on the Bikini experiments; P. W. S. Blackett, *Fear, War and the Bomb; Military and Political Consequences of Atomic Energy* (1949), a criticism of American policy by a British scientist; Sir Gerald

Dickens, *Bombing and Strategy: The Fallacy of Total War* (1947); Bernard Brodie (ed.), *The Absolute Weapon: Atomic Power and World Order* (1946); J. E. Johnsen, *The Atomic Bomb* (1946); Dexter Masters and Katherine Way (eds.), *One World or None* (1946); Norman Cousins, *Modern Man Is Obsolete* (1945); J. W. Campbell, *The Atomic Story* (1947); John Hersey, *Hiroshima* (1946); and W. L. Laurence, *Dawn Over Zero* (1946).

On Russia and the cold war, consult E. D. Carman, *Soviet Imperialism: Russia's Drive Toward World Dominion* (1950); Robert Stransz-Hupe and S. T. Possomy, *International Relations in the Age of Conflict between Democracy and Dictatorship* (1950); J. R. Deane, *The Strange Alliance* (1946); Barbara Ward, *The West at Bay* (1948); V. M. Dean, *The United States and Russia* (1947); W. H. Chamberlain, *The European Cockpit* (1947); J. F. Dulles, *War or Peace* (1950); Walter Lippmann, *The Cold War* (1947); Max Lerner, *World of the Great Powers* (1947); Lester Markel and others, *Public Opinion and Foreign Policy* (1948); E. A. Mourer, *The Nightmare of American Foreign Policy* (1948), highly critical; G. H. Stuart, *The Department of State* (1949), an able study; J. R. Deane and others, *Negotiating with the Russians* (1951); Felix Morley, *The Foreign Policy of the United States* (1951); G. F. Kennan, *American Diplomacy, 1900–1950* (1951); E. M. Zacharias, *Behind Closed Doors: The Secret History of the Cold War* (1950); W. B. Ziff, *Two Worlds* (1946); H. S. Commager (ed.), *America in Perspective: The United States through Foreign Eyes* (1947); Martin Ebon, *World Communism Today* (1948); and W. C. Bullitt, *The Great Globe Itself* (1946), very critical of Russia. For post-Yalta, see J. F. Byrnes, *Speaking Frankly* (1947), which contains information on both Yalta and Potsdam; W. B. Smith, *My Three Years in Moscow* (1949); and Lucius Clay, *Decision in Germany* (1950); Sumner Welles, *Where Are We Heading?* (1946) and B. G. Ivanyi and A. Bell, *Route to Potsdam* (1945) cover the Potsdam agreement. Marina Salvin, *The North Atlantic Pact* (1950) and H. L. Hoskins, *Atlantic Pact* (1949) describe briefly an agency of the expanding policy of containment.

Korea and the Domestic Scene. The best, general account of the country is McCune, *Korea Today* (1950) and an appraisal of the conflict without benefit of perspective is E. J. Kahn, Jr., *The Peculiar War* (1951). The recall of General MacArthur provoked a rash of books of which the best are John Gunther, *The Riddle of MacArthur* (1950) and R. H. Rovere and A. M. Schlesinger, Jr., *The General and the President* (1951).

A well-reasoned criticism of the methods employed by some officials in their attack on Communism is revealed in Francis Biddle, *The Fear of Freedom* (1951) and Owen Lattimore, *Ordeal by Slander* (1950). See also Allistair Cooke, *A Generation on Trial* (1950), an excellent study of the Chambers-Hiss affair by an Englishman. For estimates of the Truman administration see M. B. Schnapper (ed.), *The Truman Program* (1949), a collection of Truman's speeches; Jonathan Daniels, *The Man of Independence* (1950), the most perceptive of the biographies of Truman to date; R. S. Allen and W. V. Shannon, *The Truman Merry-Go-Round* (1950) and G. E. Allen, *Presidents Who Have Known Me* (1950), both of which emphasize the sensational; A. M. Smith, *Thank You, Mr. President* (1946), good on the early Truman. Two aspects of the 1948 election are treated in V. O. Key, Jr., *Southern Politics in State and Nation* (1949) and Lindsay Rogers, *The Pollsters* (1949).

INDEX

A NOTE ON THE TYPE

The text of this book is set in Caledonia, *a Linotype face which belongs to the family of printing types called "modern face" by printers—a term used to mark the change in style of type-letters that occurred about 1800. Caledonia borders on the general design of Scotch Modern, but is more freely drawn than that letter.*

The book was composed, printed, and bound by KINGSPORT PRESS, INC., *Kingsport, Tennessee.*

Designed by HARRY FORD.